D0142306

EFFECTIVE BEHAVIOR IN ORGANIZATIONS

The Irwin Series in Management and the Behavioral Sciences

EFFECTIVE BEHAVIOR IN ORGANIZATIONS

Learning from the Interplay of Cases, Concepts, and Student Experiences

Allan R. Cohen
Professor of Management
Babson College

Stephen L. Fink
Professor of Organizational Behavior
Whittemore School of Business and Economics
University of New Hampshire

Herman Gadon
Director of Executive Programs
University Extension
The University of California, San Diego

Robin D. Willits
Professor of Administration and Organization
Whittemore School of Business and Economics
University of New Hampshire

with the collaboration of
Natasha Josefowitz
Adjunct Professor
College of Health and Human Services
San Diego State University

Fourth Edition 1988

IRWIN

Homewood, Illinois 60430

Acquisitions editor: William R. Bayer
Developmental editor: Eleanore Snow
Project editor: Mary Lou Murphy
Production manager: Irene H. Sotiroff
Cover photo by Michel Tcherevkoff
Compositor: Bi-Comp, Incorporated
Typeface: 10/12 Caledonia
Printer: R. R. Donnelley & Sons Company

ISBN 0-256-05967-5

Library of Congress Catalog Card No. 87–82176

Printed in the United States of America

4 5 6 7 8 9 0 DO 5 4 3 2 1 0

PREFACE

This is an exciting time to be studying organizational behavior, and we have tried to make this edition of the book reflect that. Organizations and managers are struggling to find ways to gain the full cooperation and commitment of employees, trying to tap the talents of everyone in the organization. There is a new openness to leadership and organization techniques and a growing recognition of the need to manage well to maintain competitiveness. The relevance of organizational behavior has never been more salient; to capture that we have recast the opening chapter of the book. Many examples of current experiments and dilemmas are included to link the course to the current ferment in management.

The rest of the text has been similarly enriched with clarifying examples and concepts. Material has been added on the potency of generating commitment, ethical aspects of leadership, shared leadership among any interested or competent members, the use and abuse of power, understanding and managing stress, playing politics versus building mutually beneficial work relationships, the impact of gender on relationships, how individuals structure their worlds (including the Myers-Briggs approach), career planning and choices, rationalization, the impact of informal organization, and the way in which professional identity and values differentiate groups. In addition, discussion of the way in which key events can help shape group norms has been added to make it easier for students to trace the origin of norms that powerfully impact group performance.

Students appreciate the addition of boxes containing supplementary conceptual or skill tools; we have included new material on the Kolb learning styles model, the appropriateness of deviance under some circumstances, steps to increase effective communication, high-performing teams, alternatives for group decision making, and a simple questionnaire for tracking group process.

This edition of the book continues the unorthodox sequencing of the earlier editions, starting with a focus on groups, then the individual, two-person relationships, etc. We chose that sequencing to parallel unfolding classroom phenomena; we found that early in the course students worry about finding their place in a group. The text thus provides timely concepts that help the student understand what is being actively experienced in the classroom organization. Once secure in their group, students are readier to look at themselves and to explore together aspects of their personal systems. Consequently, we discuss individual behavior after the section on groups.

Over the years, some instructors have said that they would prefer to start with the individual as the basic building block and move from there to the larger systems. Thus we have edited the chapters to allow an instructor greater flexibility. This makes it easier to rearrange chapter sequence to focus on the individual, the pair, then the group. The chapters can readily be sequenced as follows: 1, 2, 7, 8, 9, 10, 3, 4, 5, 6, 11, 12, 13, 14, or in other ways that fit instructor preference.

With only a brief lecture on the Homans scheme preceding the assignment of Chapters 9 and 10, the instructor can follow alternate sequencing. As with any complex subject matter, all prior discussions enrich subsequent ones, so that a different chapter sequence merely alters which case discussions will have the benefit of constantly developing student sophistication. It would be wonderful if a method could be developed that would allow students to already know all later topics before studying early ones, but unfortunately no one has been able to devise a way to defeat this shortcoming of the human mind! All we can do is periodically revisit earlier topics with our newly acquired perspective—and learn to live with the perennial feeling that we could have been far more effective if only we had known "then" what we know now.

For their insightful suggestions on how to improve the book, we thank Sam Robinowitz, Rutgers, The State University, New Brunswick, New Jersey; Elliot Kushell, California State University, Fullerton; and Gregg Northcraft, University of Arizona, Tucson; Professor Ellen West, Portland State University; and our colleagues Lynne Rosansky and Rita Weathersby. Once again, Rich Sebastian helped with the exam questions. For coping with impossible handwriting and tiny marginal notes with grace and skill, we thank Mildred Prussing and Marjorie A. Kurtzman. Finally, we are very grateful to the Whittemore School (University of New Hampshire) Deans Dwight Ladd and Carole Aldrich, and Babson College Vice President for Academic Affairs Mel Copen, for their encouragement and support.

Allan R. Cohen
Stephen L. Fink
Herman Gadon
Robin D. Willits

PREFACE TO EARLIER EDITIONS

For the third edition of this book, we engaged in a fine-tuning process designed to make it even more useful for managerial students. We added more material on motivation, perception, interpersonal patterns, the dangers of heroic models of leadership, organizational structure, learning styles as a reflection of stage of ego development, stakeholder analysis, and managing change without formal power. The basic conceptual scheme now incorporates leadership style more explicitly, making clearer the interaction of organizational and job requirements with group members and the formal leader. Expectancy theory is more tightly woven into the material on motivating individuals. And the material on change focuses more directly on implementation and managing transitions.

Students using earlier editions enjoyed the boxed quotes; this time we included many excerpts from the popular press that show actual companies using ideas presented in the text to achieve better teamwork, greater commitment, and higher productivity. Illustrations from companies such as Hewlett-Packard, J. C. Penney, and Pillsbury increase the credibility and practicality of the concepts derived from research and theory. With all the current attention to the need for different ways of managing and organizing work—in order to compete with the Japanese, manage the new work force, cope with high interest rates, and raise quality or excellence—there should be little question that organizational behavior is relevant and useful to managers. We worked to make that apparent.

As usual, there are many people to thank for their help. Dorothy Hai of St. Bonaventure, James Cashman of the University of Alabama, Elizabeth M. Coote of Loyola University at New Orleans, and Erik Larson of Oregon State all made useful comments in their reviews. Larry Cummings and Kirby Warren again provided constructive support. Richard J. Sebastian of St. Cloud University created exam questions. And excellent typing aid was provided by Pamela Dyson, Beri Ellis, Mildred Prussing, and Darlene Thorn. To all of the above, and to our students for their suggestions and reinforcement, we are grateful.

When we wrote the first edition of this book, we had considerable data from our own classes indicating that it and the course designed for it actually worked and that students enjoyed it. We have been gratified to find that hundreds of teachers in widely differing settings have had similarly successful results. While we have utilized (and in this edition referenced) recent research, the book works because it is written to be useful for students who want to manage, rather than as a research document.

The book is designed for a basic introductory course in managing human behavior in organizations. The topics covered include individual behavior, interpersonal relationships, small groups, intergroup relations, leadership, and change. All are dealt with in the context of diverse formal organizations (industrial, educational, governmental, health care, and so on). While previous courses in the social and/or behavioral sciences can be helpful, the book is written to be understood by the student with no prior exposure to the field.

Organizational behavior courses usually have at least several goals, including the mastery of a body of theory and research findings; improvements in analytical ability and decision-making capacity; clarification of student values; increased interpersonal and group skills; and development of leadership ability. While individual instructors may emphasize some goals more than others, ultimately all the goals converge toward educating for *action,* for enhanced student ability to be effective in an organization.

Thus we have based this book on the assumption that students best learn effective organizational behavior by practicing it on realistic problems or dilemmas, and then reflecting upon their efforts, utilizing concepts, theories, reasoning, and guidance. By playing back and forth between action and analysis, students develop the ability to conceptualize and learn from their experience. In our efforts over the past 20 years to implement our premises in the classroom, we dealt with the following general issues:

1. How can students be persuaded to solve problems using behavioral science theory as a way of going beyond common sense, even while recognizing that theory is not sufficient to insure correct or usable answers?
2. How do we help students prepare for the ambiguity and uncertainty of organizational life without overwhelming them with complexity?
3. How can students be taught to increase both their analytical abilities and their interactive skills?
4. Similarly, how can the gap be bridged between teaching cognitive content, such as theory and research findings, and teaching affective skills, usually through experience?
5. How do classroom teachers convey to inexperienced students the reality of the behavioral difficulties with which all members of organizations must cope? Students with little work experience tend to view organizational behavior as irrelevant or unnecessary

despite repeated surveys made several years after graduation, which indicate that, in retrospect, administration students highly value behavioral courses and wish they had taken more.
6. How can students be helped to live with the uncertainty that goes with a subject matter in which the "right answer" partly depends on the values of the particular manager?
7. In short, how can existing knowledge about organizations, groups, and individuals be used to teach those subjects in a way that does justice to their complexity and uncertainty, yet universality?

This book is the result of our struggles with these knotty dilemmas. We have tried to pull together and integrate the polar approaches to teaching organizational behavior represented by former books. Our approach is a balanced one in which concepts and cognitive material are applied to actual problems, utilizing classroom processes that reinforce and illuminate the conceptual material.

We think of the classroom as a real organization with genuine problems of leadership, structure, motivation, social pressure, interpersonal friction, and so forth, which parallel those in companies and elsewhere. Therefore, we integrate the textual material with the students' ongoing classroom experiences in analyzing cases, participating in simulations and exercises, working in groups, taking directions from a "supervisor," and so on.

To foster the integration of concepts and experiences, we have written the text material in an informal, personal style, using examples and illustrations from the students' world of classrooms and campus organizations as well as from business and nonprofit organizations. Similarly, the cases have been chosen to represent a cross section of organizational life, especially those situations with which students can readily identify, whether in the university, industry, health field, government agency, or other educational institutions. Many cases have been written by students about their organizational experiences, furthering ease of identification. In addition, the cases were written with the book's central conceptual scheme in mind, so that there is sufficient data for practicing use of the analytical tools presented.

Because students sometimes have difficulty thinking of the printed word as representing particular individuals struggling to do their best, we have added to many cases artist's sketches of key characters, in order to aid student ability to treat the characters as actual people.

Sometimes it is difficult for students to grasp or retain theory in ways that permit easy application. Simply describing research findings or presenting a theory as developed by its author may leave students to their own inexperienced devices to find ways of translating the ideas into more useful forms. Thus we present as many concepts as possible in the form of situational *propositions* about behavior. We have found that propositional statements are more easily remembered and applied than unconnected strings of references, and that students readily adopt this format as a way of articulating their own insights and concepts. Rather than focus upon controversies in the research literature, or theory as received wisdom, we offer insights from research in a tentative form that is immediately testable by the student on a problem being faced. Most propositions, however, are referenced so that interested readers can pursue the ideas in depth. While trying to insure that no major concepts were omitted or oversimplified, we selected those we believe most useful in analysis of actual problems. We also worked to integrate propositions with a central conceptual scheme, relating all chapters and topics in the book to one another, so students see that the field is more than a series of disconnected topics.

In general, we have organized the book and course material so that a student can *experience* in the classroom a genuine organizational problem with real consequences while *analyzing* other people (through a case) in a similar dilemma using *concepts* or *research findings* about such problems. In this way, we hope to make the "medium" a reinforcing part of the conceptual "message."

Another way in which we have tried to demonstrate that the course material indeed is relevant to *any* managers, present or future, is by the inclusion of more than the usual amount of material on power, influence, and conflict in organizations. These often neglected areas generate strong student interest and maintain perspective when the book focuses on collaboration, listening, or cohesion. If we expect students to adopt contingency thinking, choosing behavior appropriate to the situation, we must acknowledge those unpleasant aspects of organizations calling for defensiveness or "political maneuvering," as well as the more congenial territories with which organizational behavior has usually been concerned. We have often had to fight down our own unintentional tendency to sound as if openness and trust were always appropriate managerial behavior; in doing so we believe that we have made the book more balanced and theoretically sound.

Working on the revision of this book has reinforced our awareness of the interdependencies necessary to complete such a complex task. In addition to those acknowledged for their contribution to the first edition, on which this one is based, we wish to thank some new colleagues who made useful suggestions for this revision. For these we thank Tom Chase, Steve Obert, Patricia Trow, and Rita Weathersby. Tom Law, Tom Maran, Stephanie E. New, and Paul Samuels were helpful research assistants, courtesy of the Whittemore School.

The comments of Curtis Cook, James C. Conant, and Gerald A. Gluck were extremely valuable in enhancing the book's teachability.

David Bradford's comments on our leadership material stimulated considerable rethinking, and we are really appreciative.

Once again Madeline Piper performed miracles of secretarial support. Her efficiency and cheerfulness continually amaze and delight us.

Among those who helped us develop the first edition, seven of our colleagues, most of them former students in earlier versions of the course for which the book was written, tested rough drafts in the classroom and gave us valuable feedback. For this help we thank Pat Canavan, Cotton Cleveland, Harry Noel, Richard Pastor, Randy Webb, Mary Anne Sharer, and Mike Williams.

More than 1,000 students used various drafts of the book, and for their responses, critical, constructive, and occasionally even positive, we are extremely grateful. They invariably let us know when our elegant designs and crackling prose confounded their best efforts to understand what we intended for them to learn; without them we would not have been able to attain whatever clarity finally emerged.

The editorial advice and encouragement we received from Larry Cummings and Kirby Warren deserve special mention. They were able to make helpful suggestions from within our point of view and raise issues from other perspectives in the field which proved extremely useful. Even when we disagreed with their comments, we felt that they understood what we were trying to do and wanted to aid us in doing it better. That kind of editorial relationship is rare, and we valued it highly.

We are also grateful to the organizers and participants of the Stanford-Berkeley Conference on Teaching Organizational Behavior. The stimulation received there was heady and came at just the right time. Many ideas and dilemmas expressed there found their way into our thinking and writing.

Several secretaries overcame the mysteries of our handwriting and marked-up drafts, including Marylou Chag, Linda Fitzgerald, and Jenifer McKinnon. But for uncomplainingly coping with manuscript crises and deadlines, far beyond the call of duty, we give special thanks to Madeline Piper and Susan Gilman. In addition, Patricia Trow, as our graduate assistant, cheerfully completed a number of assignments, which made our job easier.

We also thank Robert Bovenschulte and Michael Hartman for their unselfish sharing of ideas and advice.

Dean Jan Clee of the Whittemore School of Business and Economics and his administrative staff were also extremely supportive of our efforts, helping with logistics, teaching assignments, freedom to experiment, and all such things that academics sometimes only hope dean's offices will provide. Dean Charles Warden and Associate Dean Dwight Ladd have delightfully continued that tradition.

Finally, we want to mention our wives and families. They are a living part of this book, and their contributions to it and us could never be fully catalogued. In each of these small organizations, countless observations, propositions, complexities, and analyses unfold and develop. For letting us be ourselves even when that entailed long absences for writing and meetings, to Joyce, Elaine, Lydia, and our children, our thanks and love.

We have continued to learn from the devoted O.B. teachers who attend the O.B. Teaching Conferences and write for *Exchange.* We are proud to be in an academic field that still manages to value teaching and hope that our efforts in this book contribute to the tradition.

A. R. C.
S. L. F.
H. G.
R. D. W.

BRIEF CONTENTS

CONTENTS

14 THE MANAGER AS THE INITIATOR OF CHANGE IN THE ORGANIZATION 405

CASES 455

EFFECTIVE BEHAVIOR IN ORGANIZATIONS

1

INTRODUCTION

Managers interact with a great number of people. Precisely because they have been assigned to a managerial position, they automatically are expected to form relationships in many directions.

In many of our huge corporations we treat people like commodities. And people cannot be managed. Inventories can be managed, but people must be led. And when people are reacting to being treated improperly, they are not doing their best work. And when they're not doing their best work, our international competitors can beat us. That is the core of our problem. It's not robots, it's not technology, it's how we treat our people. (Newsweek)[1]

"May you live in exciting times!" In China, this statement is hurled as a curse; centuries of upheaval, revolutions, and counterrevolutions have created a longing for stability and predictability in daily life. Whether excitement is a curse or a stimulant, you are studying management in exciting times. Dramatic changes in global competition, government regulations, work force composition, and employee expectations have led to an explosion of experimentation with leadership and organizational methods. Some of the forces altering traditional assumptions include:

- Tough competition from Japanese companies, some of whom are successfully operating plants in the United States, and increasing competition from companies in South Korea, Taiwan, and Singapore with even lower wage rates.
- Crumbling boundaries between industries, as new technologies, loosening government regulations, unprecedented mergers, acquisitions, and spin-offs create opportunities. For example, banks and insurance companies are increasingly in competition to provide financial services, while Sears has entered the credit card business.
- Women entering the work force in increasing numbers, occupying (or deserving) jobs that formerly were held only by men. Over half of all married women with children now work full time, and increasing numbers of women have aspirations to rise in management rather than just provide supplementary income.

[1] Ross Perot, Founder of EDS, interviewed after having his shares purchased for $700 million by GM because he was "irritating" to top management and the board. From "Perot to Smith: GM Must Change," *Newsweek*, December 15, 1986.

- Members of minority groups, some of whom do not speak English, making important contributions to the work force and becoming increasingly ambitious. They bring their various subcultures' attitudes and behavior to their organizations—or are assumed to, by unknowledgeable or biased whites.
- Employees becoming more educated, bringing with them expectations that their jobs should be challenging and meaningful. A sense of entitlement to important, fulfilling work and to a voice in decision making is a frequent by-product of higher education. From blue-collar workers to specialized-knowledge workers, these beliefs are now widespread, and unresponsive organizations can no longer count on automatic company loyalty to hold employees who are frustrated at blocked opportunities to contribute. (*The Wall Street Journal*)[2]
- A stubborn economy that manages to combine high inflation with low growth (stagflation), or reduced inflation, large federal budgets, and still low growth, making it increasingly difficult to rack up profits and growth by doing the tried and true thing.

What have companies been doing about these changes? Even a casual reading of the business press reveals a great ferment in American industry.

Experiments in factory organization are proliferating, spurred by Japanese success in producing high-quality products at lower costs:

> The success of Japanese plants in the United States has been attributed, in part, to management's approach to dealing with employees in ways that build trust and foster loyalty. "Workers given responsibility for running the production line will care about and catch mistakes, but only if they trust management. . . . Japanese managers elicit cooperation by presenting themselves as equals. At Nissan USA, Honda, and NUMMI (a Toyota–GM joint venture) there are no privileged parking lots for executives. Honda's top executives eat in the employee cafeteria—there are no private dining rooms for big shots. Everybody there wears white overalls with his or her first name sewn on them. Employees are called associates. Honda President Irimajiri has no office. He sits in the same room with a hundred other white-collar workers." (*Business Week*)[3]

> Of its modern, highly automated plant in College Station, Texas, "The key," says Westinghouse, "is not the robots but the people. Employees work in teams of 8 to 12. Members devise their own solutions to problems. Teams measure daily how each person's performance compares with that of other members and how the team's performance compares

[2] "Loyalty Ebbs at Many Companies as Employees Grow Disillusioned." *The Wall Street Journal*, July 11, 1986.

[3] "The Difference Japanese Management Makes," *Business Week*, July 14, 1986.

with the plant's." The changes have forced the company to seek a new kind of employee. Applicants must submit to interviews and tests that measure initiative, ability to take advice, creativity, and skills. Only about 5 percent are hired. (*Business Week*)[4]

At General Motors' Saturn plants, the basic work groups consist of teams who decide which member does what, maintain their equipment, order supplies, etc. "Like experimental teams already working in a few GM facilities, the Saturn units all will be responsible for controlling variable costs and doing quality inspections. But they will have far more authority than that. If a team comes up with a better idea for a new piece of equipment, Saturn's finance and purchasing departments must respond. The experts can't shrug off suggestions, as they tended to before. They must reach a consensus with the team. Power, in a word, will rest with the workers." (*Business Week*)[5]

"Preemployment programs . . . are gaining the attention of automakers seeking to cut turnover and to assemble motivated work forces that can handle increasingly complex jobs and maintain ever higher product-quality standards." (*The Wall Street Journal*)[6]

"At Enfield (a Digital Equipment plant) . . . each circuitboard is put together from start to finish by one of several teams. The 18 people on each team divide the work among themselves and assemble the modules from the moment the raw materials are delivered to the plant to the time the finished product is shipped out the door. . . . Workers set their own hours, plan their own schedules, check their own work, and take team responsibility for each board. There are no time clocks, no security guards, no quality control officers, and every employee has a key to the building." (*Boston Globe*)[7]

Also, experiments in pay are going on at many levels. In addition to new "pay-for-knowledge" rather than "pay-for-job-grade" systems being introduced at factories, there is renewed attention to profit sharing,[8] incentive-pay systems,[9] and bonuses.

- "Everyone is looking at team bonus plans," says an AT&T spokesman. Aetna Life & Casualty Co. studied several approaches; it recently began a "star performance program" to give modest bonuses for creative and cost-saving ideas. Xerox Corp. started a small-scale award program for work teams in its upstate New York operations.

[4] "The Plant of Tomorrow Is in Texas Today," *Business Week*, July 28, 1986.

[5] "How Power Will Be Balanced on Saturn's Shop Floor," *Business Week*, August 5, 1985.

[6] "Job Tryouts Without Pay Get More Testing in U.S. Auto Plants." *The Wall Street Journal*, January 10, 1985.

[7] "Trying the Bossless System," *Boston Globe*, October 14, 1984.

[8] "The Promise in Profit Sharing," *New York Times*, February 9, 1986.

[9] "Ohio Firm Relies on Incentive-Pay System to Motivate Workers and Maintain Profits." *The Wall Street Journal*, March 12, 1983.

- "Incentive pay is being pushed down within the corporate organization," says AT&T. A survey of 601 corporations by Hay Group, a Philadelphia consultant, says 18 percent have extended their bonus plans to lower levels of management. (*The Wall Street Journal*)[10]

A great deal of attention is being placed on finding ways of blending different cultures or changing a firm's culture, as firms merge, make acquisitions, enter joint ventures, or face new competition.[11]

Injecting new energy, creativity, and initiative has also become a preoccupation of many large companies that have become bureaucratized and rigid. Gifford Pinchot (author of *Intrapreneurship*), Rosabeth Kanter (author of *The Change Masters*), and other consultants are making speeches and advising companies on how to become more innovative, receptive to new ways, or willing to take risk. In a similar vein, several books on creating excellence in organizations have become best-sellers as managers grasp for ways to improve their performance and that of their organizations.[12]

In turn, organizations are struggling with ways to raise individual and collective performance, through management training (companies spent over $50 *billion* on all forms of training in 1986!), new policies, and procedures.[13]

All of this activity and experimentation can be highly unsettling, knocking cherished assumptions and beliefs askew, but it can also provide a tremendously stimulating challenge. Although this book (indeed, any book) cannot provide you with all the answers to the behavioral dilemmas facing managers today, it will provide you with a way to understand and address the issues and to practice some of the key skills needed. We urge you to plunge into this course. More than

[10] "Bonus Awards Spread as Employers Try to Reward Effort but Limit Pay Costs." *The Wall Street Journal*, December 31, 1985.

[11] See "Corporate Odd Couples: Joint Ventures Are All the Rage, but the Matches Often Don't Work Out," *Business Week*, July 21, 1986; "Growing Pains: A Spate of Acquisitions Puts American Express in a Management Bind," *The Wall Street Journal*, August 15, 1984; "Cultural Change: Pressed by Its Rivals, Procter & Gamble Is Altering Its Ways," *The Wall Street Journal*, May 20, 1985; and "How Ross Perot's Shock Troops (from Electronic Data Systems) Ran into Flak at GM," *Business Week*, February 11, 1985.

[12] See T. Peters and S. Waterman, *In Search of Excellence: Lessons from America's Best-Managed Corporations* (New York: Harper & Row, 1982); T. Peters and N. Austin, *Passion for Excellence* (New York: Random House, 1985); D. Bradford and A. Cohen, *Managing for Excellence* (New York: Wiley-Interscience, 1984); and C. Hickman and M. Silva, *Creating Excellence* (New York: New American Library, 1984).

[13] See "The Not-So-Fast Track: Firms Try Promoting Hotshots More Slowly," *The Wall Street Journal*, March 24, 1986; "Keeping in Touch: More Corporate Chiefs Seek Direct Contact with Staff, Customers," *The Wall Street Journal*, February 24, 1985; "Businesses Crack down on Workers Who Cheat to Help the Company," *The Wall Street Journal*, June 13, 1986; and "Demanding Pepsi Co. Is Attempting to Make Work Nicer for Managers," *The Wall Street Journal*, October 23, 1984.

ever before, your career success will depend upon you being able to effectively manage the behavior of others—and of yourself.

BASIC PREMISE: LEARNING TO LEARN ABOUT ORGANIZATIONS, EVERYWHERE

Even if you have not yet worked in a company like those mentioned above, you have a considerable amount of relevant experience on which to draw. Much of what you can learn about organizational behavior is quite accessible; it goes on around you all the time. You are a member of a family; may live with other people; belong to some clubs, teams, or committees; have a job involving others; eat and shop where people work; and so on. The university itself is a large organization containing many smaller organizations: the fraternity or sorority, academic departments, business and other administrative offices. Even the classroom is an organization. You are in a position to see many of the main ingredients of organizational life in your everyday contacts. All these groupings have implicit, if not explicit, goals, structures, and policies. These in turn seek to direct behavior in certain ways. They shape people's interactions with each other, and they are potentially a major source of an individual's productivity, satisfactions, and personal learning or development. In short, you have immediately at hand ready-made opportunities to study organizational behavior. This book will help you learn to look at and understand more of your living and working experiences, as well as prepare you for your career.

Throughout this book you will be asked to analyze your own behavior—at work, in the classroom, and in your interactions with others. Analogies will be drawn with other organizational settings, through either student experience or the use of case studies. Theories and concepts will be introduced as tools for helping you make sense out of your observations and experiences. The objectives of this book and the course for which it is designed are aimed at enhancing your ability to learn from experience, to test what you learn against new experience, and to extract new learning in a continuing fashion. In that way the organizational challenges of the 1990s and on into the 21st century will be approachable.

> *Experience is a school where a man learns what a big fool he has been.*
>
> Josh Billings
> 1818–1885

CENTRAL THEME: LEARNING THROUGH DOING AND REFLECTING: THE MANAGER AS INVOLVED ACTOR

A central theme throughout the book is the idea of "learning through doing and reflecting." In order to learn how to *behave* effectively, rather than just *understand* behavior, it is necessary to be active and engaged as well as reflective and thoughtful. This calls for a different educational model from what you may be used to. Most college classrooms are not organized to give practice in action and conceptualizing skills, but rather to enhance acquisition and understanding of material that may not have immediate direct application. In such classes the professor does most of the talking and grading; students listen, individually write notes and papers, take exams, answer some questions, and address most of their comments to the professor. But just as in a biology lab, where you have to *practice* dissecting a frog in order to learn the relevant skills, in a course designed to improve your organizational *effectiveness* a more active student role is necessary.

This means that you still need to master ideas, theories, and concepts, but then you practice using them in complex, unique situations, step back and observe how well you achieved your intentions, think about how to modify your ideas and/or your behavior, then try again in new situations. Therefore, in a course in organizational behavior the classroom needs to become a kind of learning laboratory in which you, the student, have the opportunity to test out, practice, try, experiment with, and utilize the variety of concepts and ideas that are the subject matter of the book. It means that as you proceed you look for connections between what you are learning and your own behavior, as well as the behavior of individuals around you. Differences in class size and duration may limit the opportunity for such experiential learning during regular class hours. Nonetheless, when taking part in any organized activity, you can make observations and apply your conclusions to those relationships important to you in the classroom and outside (e.g., in the dormitory, on part-time jobs, and in campus organizations).

Part of what makes this course exciting—and occasionally frustrating—is that students, like managers, are highly *involved actors*, an integral component of the situations they are trying to understand and manage or change. It is like trying to run and tie your shoe at the same time. Managers cannot call time-out or say "pay no attention to me while I watch and decide what is going on"; their presence and the way people feel about bosses means that even no action or no decision has a powerful impact.

Suppose, for example, that two students in a class begin to argue over a point. No matter what the instructor says, including saying nothing, there will be an effect on the class members. The class members' reactions will depend in part on whether they perceive the instructor as approving or disapproving the open conflict between students, on which side they think the instructor believes is correct, on how well the instructor appears to handle the disagreement, and so forth. In organizations the same kinds of issues affect managers. They have nowhere to hide, and indeed they are quite often part of any problem. A manager's behavior is an inherent part of the problem, no matter how "innocent" the manager feels!

> *It is an inherent property of intelligence that it can jump out of the task which it is performing, and survey what it has done; it is always looking for, and often finding, patterns.*
>
> Douglas R. Hofstadter, *Gödel, Escher, Bach: An Eternal Golden Braid*

In this course your actions, your classmates' actions, and the instructor's actions are all likely to be factors in any problem that may arise.

One dilemma you will certainly face is the struggle to remain appropriately detached or objective while you are personally involved in the learning experience. In sociology this role is called "participant-observer"; it poses a dilemma because of the natural tendency of people to become *less* detached or objective as they become more involved in a given situation. The fine line is difficult to maintain: *Too much detachment can minimize one's appreciation and understanding of another person or a set of interactions, but too much involvement can bias (even distort) one's perspective.*

The learning process you will use—alternating between experience and conceptualization—will also provide plenty of practice in struggling with this dilemma. You will have to maintain openness to learning and a scientific attitude toward situations, some of which you are part of. What we mean by a *scientific attitude* in this respect is the process of *(a)* sorting out what is going on in one's relationships, *(b)* increasing the ability to predict likely outcomes of one's own and others' behaviors, and *(c)* thereby making more informed choices, which can *(d)* be checked for results against expectations. *It is the act of comparing the intent of any one of our actions with the effect of that action, and then learning from it.* Such an attitude requires that you constantly question, examine, and evaluate the consequences of your actions so that you learn from both your failures and your successes.

A word of caution is in order. Although careful and rigorous analysis is important for managers, reasoning is not a substitute for intuition. Recent research on how even scientists work has revealed the important part hunches, guesses, and wild leaps of intuition play in

A MODEL OF THE LEARNING PROCESS

D. Kolb has developed a model of the learning process. He conceptualizes how you and I learn as a four-stage cycle: (1) direct experience, (2) observation with reflection, (3) formulation of abstract concepts and generalizations, and (4) testing of hypotheses developed from stage 3. This cycle, as diagrammed below, requires that one be able to:

1. Plunge right in and start doing (Concrete Experience).
2. Observe and reflect on that experience, looking for patterns and significances (Reflective Observation).
3. Develop concepts and generalizations to bring order to what one has observed and make further sense of it. In Kolb's words, "create concepts that integrate observations into sound theories" (Abstract Conceptualization).
4. Set up hypotheses and carry out experiments to test the theories and concepts developed in stage 3 (Active Experimentation).

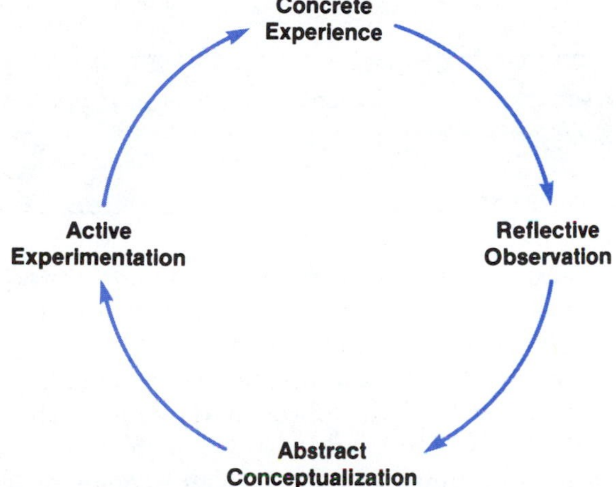

The four stages build on one another, yet each requires different types of skills. For example, it may require courage and fast thinking to just jump in and learn as you go, but require a different ability to state what one has learned in abstract terms that can communicate that insight to others as guidance for other circumstances. As you might guess, most of us are more skillful and more comfortable with one stage than another. The individual who can develop capabilities for all four stages can be more rounded than others; and barring that, the individual who is aware of his/her strengths and limits can more easily avoid overusing or misusing one approach to learning.

Source: David Kolb, *The Learning Style Inventory: Technical Manual* (Boston: McBer, 1976).

forming theory. Managers also require the use of this less-analytical capacity. Because all problems do not come in neat, orderly pieces, managers need to be tuned to what their instincts signal them as much as to formal deductive reasoning. Overdoing it in either direction, however, can lead to disaster. Seat-of-the-pants decisions can be brilliant—or merely a reflection of the manager's prejudices and blind spots. Rigorous analysis can prevent stupid mistakes or freeze the manager into analysis paralysis. In their study of America's most successful companies, Peters and Waterman (1982) found repeated examples of managers and companies that analyzed things to death and thereby missed opportunities to quickly try things out and learn from experience. Mintzberg (1976) summarized research on the human brain and argued that some managerial functions, such as planning, required use of the left half of the brain (which controls logical, abstract reasoning) while the more people-oriented parts of managing require the more wholistic, intuitive right brain. In general, as a manager you will have to use all of your capacities to sort out what is going on and to formulate sensible action plans.

> *There is absolutely no inevitability as long as there is a willingness to contemplate what is happening.*
>
> Marshall McLuhan

The complexities involved can be demonstrated by an example. Suppose you were asked to make recommendations about a strange new sport, the rules for which you did not know. Can you imagine, for example, what the first tennis match you ever saw might be like? Some people dressed in abbreviated white costumes dash around hacking at a fuzzy sphere with a lollipop-shaped stick, shouting about "love!" Yet sometimes when the sphere comes near them, they step aside and do not wave their sticks but appear to stare intently at some white lines on the ground. The participants stop and start quite suddenly, changing positions, throwing the sphere in the air and batting at it, crouching carefully, or running rapidly toward the long, webbed object hanging between the participants. Before you could ever offer sensible advice, you would have to *watch* carefully for any *patterns* to the game, *deduce the rules* (How long would it take you to figure out the scoring rules, that "love" meant no points, a certain number of points make a "set," and so forth?), *test your assumptions* about how the game works *by predicting what will happen next* ("The first hitter aims for the opposite forecourt, so if I am correct about service rules, the second try must hit in that area or a point will be lost."), and slowly begin to *see the order in the apparent chaos*.

As you become increasingly sophisticated you could begin to draw conclusions about the internal workings and strategy of the game, making connections between when to rush the net, when to lob over

BRITISH ON NFL

The Minnesota Vikings and St. Louis Cardinals played the first NFL football game on British soil last night. . . .

All eyes were on the British contingent in the crowd to see if they liked the game. . . .

"All those people out there with big shoulders just running into each other and hiding the ball under them while they run," said Bernard Lockhurst, traffic coordinator at the game. "The clock stops, they huddle, shout out numbers, clap hands, and then they start hitting each other all over again. I mean, is that all football is about?"

United Press International
Boston Globe
August 7, 1983

an opponent's head, and so forth. Whether you systematically dissected the components of each stroke and its relation to the opponent's weaknesses or just observed until you had some hunches about what was likely to be effective, you would have to operate as a kind of scientist or detective—gathering data, asking questions of it, forming tentative conclusions based on apparent patterns, testing those by more observation, and so on. In that way you would establish an order to the buzzing confusion you first experienced.

I'm not smart. I try to observe. Millions saw the apple fall, but Newton was the one who asked why.

Bernard Baruch

Trying to make sense out of an organization can be equally confusing and even more challenging, since you are at the same time a part of what you are observing, affecting it and effected by it. People at work don't often hold still for examination by impartial, detached observers, and they seldom behave by such explicit, preagreed rules as tennis players do.

CHARGE TO GRADUATING SENIORS, 1983

The real world is not arranged for my convenience or yours. It is rarely arranged for my knowledge or yours. It is indeed rarely arranged.

G. Armour Craig
Acting President
Amherst College

Whatever may be the context of your role in an organization now or in the future, you will need the skills of searching for patterns and connections, making predictions, testing out the consequences of an action or decision that you make, collecting information as to success, and modifying your actions accordingly. You will need to adopt and maintain an attitude of tentativeness; that is, a readiness to change your mind, to modify your views, to change your theory, to acknowledge your mistakes, and to take corrective action. Have you ever had or seen a boss who is so concerned about being right and so closed to feedback that he/she makes inappropriate decisions, saying in effect, "Don't confuse me with the facts"? Such a person is not open enough to be a good manager.

> *No man can reveal to you aught but that which already lies half asleep in the dawning of your knowledge. . . . If he is indeed wise he does not bid you enter the house of his wisdom, but rather leads you to the threshold of your own mind.*
>
> Kahlil Gibran
> *The Prophet*

Propositions

As you progress through the book, examining and learning from your observations and experiences, you can build your own managerial model in the form of hypotheses and concepts—what we call *propositions*—that will help to guide your actions. An example of a **proposition** is the authors' belief that: **experiencing and analyzing behavior is likely to produce more learning of organizational skills than merely reading or hearing about it.** A proposition can be tested and modified if necessary, then applied to other situations. The process of making propositions will aid in your development as a more effective manager and as a more competent individual. You have a chance to develop a way of looking at people in organizations that goes beyond any specific information you acquire; managers who have internalized a way of learning from experience should be able to continue learning in the changing situations facing them at work.

Throughout the book, we have used the propositional format as a way of highlighting major concepts. These propositions serve to integrate various findings from the research and experience of organizational experts. Wherever possible and useful we have identified at the end of a proposition some source in the literature keyed to selected readings at the end of each chapter, where an interested reader might find more information related to the area covered by the proposition.

In many instances the propositions were derived by the authors from their own experience and knowledge in the field. Specific sources for the propositions could not be provided in such instances, but we did include references to closely related literature for students interested in pursuing a given topic.

In summary then, this book is concerned with the preparation of students who plan to become either managers of people or effective organizational members and who will leave a course that uses it possessing skills in the following areas: (1) identifying problems, (2) understanding their origins, (3) predicting their consequences, (4) considering gains and losses of those consequences for the short and long run, (5) possessing the willingness and capacity to choose well from among alternatives, and (6) extracting useful learning from experiences in which they are also part of the action and have an investment in the outcome. In short, this book seeks to cultivate the rare qualities of insight, analysis, and judgment. Its emphasis is on knowledge utilization, the marriage of theory to practice, and the development of managerial skills, and not just on the acquisition of knowledge for its own sake.

WHAT DOES A MANAGER DO?

We have been looking at the way in which this book tries to reflect some of the complexities inherent in the manager's job. But just what do managers do? How do they spend their time? What makes the job so difficult?[14]

Building Relationships

Although some students think of managing as primarily involved with financial calculations, the thing to note is that managers interact with a great number of people. Because they have been assigned a managerial position, they automatically are expected to form relationships in many directions: with those who work directly for them (subordinates), with their boss or bosses (superiors), with others in comparable positions in the organization (peers), and with a variety of outsiders such as customers, board members, and attendees at industry or professional meetings. Every manager is in a boundary position between the unit he or she supervises and other parts of the organization or the organization's environment. In that position the manager is a symbol

[14] Much of this section is based on the research of Henry Mintzberg, reported in *The Nature of Managerial Work* and in "The Manager's Job: Folklore and Fact" in the *Harvard Business Review*. (See Suggested Readings at the end of this chapter for complete references.)

of the unit as well as the one ultimately responsible for inspiring or leading the unit's members to high performance. Thus, managers are forced into relationships with many people whose goodwill they need in order to be successful.

> *Outplacement counselors claim most of their assignments involve competent executives who lost their jobs because of personal incompatibility, political infighting, or corporate reorganizations. Of all the major reasons for terminating a competent manager, problems resulting from interpersonal relationships is by far number one on the list.*
>
> Carl W. Menk, President
> Boyden Associates, Inc.

Giving and Receiving Information

Relationships with others are needed in order for the manager to acquire information for sensible action. The manager must know what is going on inside and outside the organization—who is performing well, who is having troubles, what competitors are doing, what projects are proceeding well, what opportunities are available, and the like. While some of this information may be available from written material or reports, most managers find that the best sources of current, useful information are individuals seen face-to-face or on the phone. This kind of information requires careful interpretation since others may be reluctant (or unable) to say exactly what they mean. Thus, the relationships which managers automatically form as a result of their position need to be open and mutually satisfying for acquiring timely information and for passing that information on to others who need it.

Decisions

The information is needed, in turn, in order for the manager to make appropriate decisions. Managers have to decide how available resources—money, people, materials, and time—will be distributed throughout the unit being managed. Even more important, the manger must be a source of, and support to, new ideas, projects, methods, and opportunities. The effective manager cannot wait for innovation but must take the lead in insuring it.

Another important set of decision-making activities arises from problems that others in the organization can't solve. Whether the problem is deciding what to do about a large canceled order or settling a dispute between two other managers who disagree about the potential for producing a new product, managers are frequently called on to handle disturbances or deviations from the usual routine.

Finally, managers must often serve as negotiators on behalf of their organization. If they are managers of a unit, they must try to persuade higher management to approve their budget request so they may acquire what they believe to be sufficient resources. They may have to negotiate salaries or working conditions with individuals or groups of employees, contracts with important customers, priorities with other units, and the like.

The activities of the manager can be summarized in the following box:[15]

MINTZBERG'S CATEGORIES OF MANAGERIAL FUNCTIONS

Interpersonal (Relationship) Functions

Symbolic figurehead (represents organization to the world).
Liaison (contacts with others outside the unit).
Supervisor (hiring, training, motivating subordinates).

Informational Functions

Monitor (collecting data within and outside the unit).
Disseminator (circulating information to unit employees).
Spokesman (circulating information outside the unit).

Decision Functions

Innovator (initiating and designing changes).
Disturbance handler (dealing with nonroutine problems).
Resource allocator (parceling out time, money, materials).
Negotiator (seeking favorable conditions from others).

As you can see, managerial work is demanding. The manager must be good at building relationships, gathering information, and making decisions—all of which affect future relationships, access to information, and future decisions! As noted earlier, the manager acts on but is also a part of the organization, and people in organizations have feelings that affect how they respond. They are more likely to provide accurate information or carry out organizational tasks well when they trust their manager.

[15] These activities or roles are described in more detail in Chapter 12.

NEEDED MANAGERIAL SKILLS

We can identify crucial managerial skills by looking at the activities described above and spelling out what it would take to do the manager's job well.

Think about the kinds of skills necessary to do these activities. In order to carry out the interpersonal activities, for example, a manager would need public speaking skills, a sense of how to dress appropriately relative to the expectations of others, the ability to talk easily with others and to build trusting relationships so that many people will be open with him/her, the willingness to exert power when cooperation is lacking, a sincere interest in others and in listening to them, the ability to inspire others to work for organizational goals, good judgment of others' personalities and capacities, a knack for sizing up new situations, and so on.

To perform the informational functions well, the manager needs to be able to extract information from conversation, observations, and reading; must be able to judge who has the needed information and to whom it should be circulated; and again, be articulate about organizational goals. These in turn require that the manager be able to ask good questions, be observant and attentive to what is happening around him/her, and be skillful at reading between the lines as well as realizing what is not being said or discussed.

The decisional roles call for imagination, openness to ideas, will-

WHERE THE ACTION IS: EXECUTIVES IN STAFF JOBS SEEK LINE POSITIONS

In some cases, ex-consultants and staffpeople have trouble adjusting to the pace of line management, the need to set priorities and make decisions quickly. Dan Carroll, a former Booz, Allen consultant who was president of Gould, Inc., in the late 1970s, frustrated underlings and created minor gridlock in the executive suite when he got too preoccupied with overanalyzing some relatively small investment. "I made a couple of mountains out of molehills," Mr. Carroll concedes.

He later went back to consulting, and now runs his own firm. But most of the ex-consultants and staff experts who have tasted line management have gotten hooked on the action. Says Mr. Sponholz of Chemical, "It's like a boxing match. The bell rings at 8:30 and you just keep punching till 6."

Consulting seems drab by comparison. "I was bored," Geoffrey Dunbar says of his days as a consultant. "After you've done your 10th management study, they all begin to look the same. And the glamour of rubbing shoulders with very senior people wears thin; instead of just being with them, you'd like to be one of them."

Source: Jeff Bailey. Reprinted by permission of *The Wall Street Journal*,

ingness to take risks, courage under fire, analytical ability, logic, bargaining skills (including the ability to bluff, sense others' positions and boundaries), and a sense of timing.

The list of required skills can be easily expanded; it is undoubtedly easier to name needed skills than acquire them! Yet at the heart of these skills are very human qualities that involve making relationships with many different people. Without good relationships the manager cannot carry out many of the other functions that constitute managerial work.

At this point it might be useful for you to assess some of your own managerial skills, using the various abilities noted above as the criteria. You could take each item (e.g., public speaking, knack for sizing up new situations) and rate yourself in terms of both ability and confidence (or comfort) in that skill. You might even repeat the process from time to time to measure your development in those skills relevant to this course. Finally, you could check out your own observations with those of others to provide more objectivity.

Managing Time: A Key Skill

Forming friendships is not enough, just as merely being technically competent is not enough. The person who wishes to advance in an organization needs to be aware of the implications for action inherent in the job of the manager.

For example, one of the fundamental issues for managers is where to spend time. The research on managerial jobs reveals that there is almost always an abundance of work, especially since so much time must be spent interacting with others. Managers seem to prefer to gather their data firsthand by talking directly with others, which means that there are constant short conversations going on. The manager has to decide with whom to talk, for how long, whether to pursue particular individuals or wait for interactions to happen, and so on. At any given time there are likely to be many possible activities for a manager. Furthermore, managerial work is fragmented and variable, with many interruptions. The phone rings; subordinates want answers, attention, and approval; the boss wants the same; colleagues need help. Research on managerial work shows that managers average less than nine minutes on half of all the things they do in a day.

Should the pressing deskwork be completed, or would a walk through the plant reveal something important about operations? Or perhaps a meeting with a friend who works at a bank would uncover some useful information about future interest rates. Or a chat with an unhappy employee might save a valuable person who will be difficult to replace. And the phone keeps ringing with "urgent" calls.

Somehow the effective manager has to learn to manage time rather than be managed by it. Self-discipline and conscious attention are necessary, as is a definition of "work" that includes a lot of relationship building with a variety of people.

16 TIME-SAVING MANAGERIAL PRACTICES
(Can You Apply These to Student Life?)

Clarify Goals

1. Develop and use clear, long-range goals.
2. Clearly establish what to accomplish each month, week, day, and by each task.

Plan Ahead

3. Use a Daily "To-Do" List to plan and prioritize each day's activities.
4. Before meetings, review agenda, clarify your objectives, get information, anticipate events, and plan actions.
5. Set deadlines for major tasks.

Manage Daily Activities

6. Do important tasks first. Avoid trap of "getting small items out of way." Do tough jobs at your best times.
7. For big projects, divide task into manageable parts and sequence.
8. Handle each piece of paper only once, or note next step.
9. Stick to your agenda. Include restricted moments of relaxation and socializing.
10. Bring work to use during unavoidable idle time while waiting or traveling.
11. Limit interruptions. Close office door, reschedule drop-in visitors, ask secretary to hold phone calls, schedule "thinking time" and honor it.

Organize Your Workplace

12. Clear desk of clutter and other distractions.
13. Develop usable filing system and tickler file.

Spend Time Efficiently

14. Use 80/20 rule: 80 percent of the results are determined by 20 percent of the decisions. Concentrate on those.
15. Review actions to learn from past mistakes, but don't pick at imperfections and waste time on regrets.

Sources: Alan Lakein, *How to Get Control of Your Time and Your Life* (New York: David McKay, 1973); R. Alec MacKenzie, *The Time Trap* (New York: McGraw-Hill, 1975).

Many managers, especially new ones, think of their work as only the technical decision-making part of the day. They see all the people contacts as intrusions getting in the way of real work. But as we have tried to show by carefully examining what managers do, connecting with other people is an essential part of the job, and not necessarily the first thing to eliminate in order to "save time."

> *For many new employees . . . reality shock consisted of the discovery . . . that other people in the organization were a roadblock to what they wanted to get done. Others in the organization did not seem as smart as they should be, seemed illogical . . . irrational . . . lazy, unproductive, or unmotivated. . . . [New managers] did not want to have to learn to deal with other people; they simply wanted them to go away. . . . Those who resisted this reality . . . at an emotional level used up their energy in denial and complaint rather than in problem solving.*
>
> (Based on interviews with Sloan School Alumni during the first year after graduation)
>
> Source: Edgar H. Schein, *Career Dynamics: Matching Individual and Organizational Needs* (Reading, Mass.: Addison-Wesley Publishing, 1978).

Therefore, effective managers learn how to make activities fold in on one another and serve double purposes. For example, they use lunch time and short coffee breaks to chat informally with people they might not otherwise easily see, yet who have useful tidbits about the company, the market, projects, and the like.

Organizational Politics and Getting Ahead

Similarly, when asked to serve on committees or task forces, alert managers look at the assignment as an opportunity rather than a burden. Serving on a committee brings them into contact with people from other parts of the organization, and they use the contact to establish relationships and gather data (often during the "holes" in a meeting—when people are just arriving or leaving, or when a few go to the bathroom during a break, and so on).

Furthermore, managers who want to get ahead realize that committee work allows them the opportunity to "show their stuff," to demonstrate to people who might be their direct boss or subordinate in the future that they are competent, reliable, hardworking, and easy to work with.

Thus, as simple an activity as going prepared to a committee meeting serves several purposes—relationship building, data collection, visibility creation, and the formation of a good reputation, which might lead to future promotions (Cohen & Stein, 1980).

Another way in which managers, especially those new to a particular organization, can create alliances is by observing what social activities, interests, style of dress, and the like are valued by high-level

WHAT'S NEW IN OFFICE POLITICS

"We're all equal in this family," said the company president as he welcomed Wiloughby Sharp, then a management trainee, to the employee fold. The two men, along with a beaming personnel manager, rode the elevator down from the president's penthouse. The president was going to the lobby, Mr. Sharp to the second floor.

"As I pushed the second-floor button, I saw the personnel manager's face go red," recalled Mr. Sharp, now head of his own company, Machine Language, which is based in New York City. "Evidently we weren't all equal in this family—I was supposed to ride with the president to the first floor and then back up to the second."

The experience so thoroughly turned Mr. Sharp off to the politics of corporate life that he left the company six months later and has been self-employed ever since. But not all people have the psychological makeup or the financial cushion needed to walk away from corporate America. For them, a realization that corporate futures can be made or broken by the rules of office politics is essential.

Such seemingly mundane matters as choosing luncheon companions, deciding when to send memos and to whom, recognizing who is in ill favor and to be avoided, and learning to deal with the idiosyncracies of the top brass can be as important to success as on-the-job performance.

Indeed, corporate politics are growing ever more intense. Corporations are cutting back on management staffing, leaving lower-level employees competing for fewer promotions. "Corporations are going to keep people in positions longer, and the frustration level will be higher," warned Bill Gould, president of the Association of Executive Search Consultants. The likely result: more maneuvering, buck passing, and backstabbing.

Source: *New York Times*, Sunday, October 14, 1984. © by the New York Times Company. Reproduced with permission.

ON THE VIRTUES OF LEARNING GIN RUMMY

"I picked up the game . . . with Procter & Gamble. P&G had acquired Folger Coffee and sent me . . . to study the financial structure. The Folger people saw me as an outsider; they gave me the cold shoulder.

"I soon noticed that everybody played gin rummy at lunch and, although that didn't seem very businesslike to me, I decided I should play to see what the attraction was.

"Well, it was fun. Besides that, I got to know the people in a way you don't get to in a pure business relationship. Once I began playing gin, I was accepted by everyone."

Sam Phillips
Chairman of the Board, *Acton Corporation*
Quoted in *Inc. Magazine*, January 1981

managers in the organization. They can then adapt to those things that do not violate their sense of themselves. Those who do what others in the organization value are likely to more easily form relationships around shared interests and to seem more trustworthy. Was it a coincidence that everyone on President Kennedy's staff "just happened" to play touch football, while those on President Carter's staff seemed to prefer softball? If you worked for President Reagan would you find horseback riding more interesting?

> *The true test of somebody who's really good at power is that nothing interests him or her more than other people's problems, because it's an opportunity to be decisive and to exert authority over another person.*
>
> Michael Korda

Of course, all of these things do not make up for lack of ability, but their absence can make those who have the power to help advance one's career uncomfortable. Furthermore, there is no law which demands that you try to get ahead. Many people, including those who study administration, do not place high value on career advancement. But should you want to get ahead, it helps to know how to do so intelligently.

Problems of Women and Minorities

It is worth noting here that women or members of various minority groups are often at an automatic disadvantage in organizations traditionally run by white males because their visible physical "difference" from the majority makes some majority members uncomfortable or less trusting. The fewer the minority members in the organization at managerial levels, the greater the difficulty they are likely to have in being perceived as trustworthy, that is, as similar enough to be "one of us" where there are sensitive issues. As unfair as this is to those who are seen as "different" in whatever way, it is useful to understand that in organizations social judgments of individuals are made as well as technical judgments, and these evaluations are often based on such things as dress, sex, color, "style," and the like. It is not accidental that as more women decided to attempt to move upward in organizations, articles and books began to appear for them on such subjects as "How to Dress for Success," "Office Politics," and "How to Avoid Threatening Your Boss." Even if it is not true that only women who wear tailored blue suits can get ahead in business organizations (as one advisor claims), women, just like any others who choose to try to get ahead, need to be aware of what they can do to inspire comfort and confidence in them by the organization's decision makers. Trusting relationships are not a nicety of organizational life—they are fundamental to managerial work.

Gamesmanship

> *At board of directors meetings, "the one unmatched asset is the ability to yawn with your mouth closed."*
>
> Robert K. Mueller
> *Behind the Boardroom Door*

In many ways the above may sound to you as if we were seeing managers (both men and women) as having to "play politics" constantly or play a phony game. It certainly can, and sometimes does, become insincere and manipulative. But it can also be a matter of doing that which will avoid surprises, reduce misunderstanding, increase trust, and encourage cooperation, that is, facilitating good decision making and making it easier for people to work together. The line between effectiveness and "gamesmanship" is vague, and every manager at times must make some concession to playing the game. You alone will need to decide where to draw the line, but we want to emphasize that it is not necessarily all phony and can be both functional and genuine. In fact, since most people can spot insincere and artificial behavior quite easily, getting ahead through relationships usually requires that you be genuinely interested in others. Otherwise, they will be cautious toward you, which is exactly the opposite of what is necessary.

> *We get rid of anyone who starts in with office politics, plotting, or backstabbing. If you have to keep looking over your shoulder, you can't play the game well!*
>
> Senior Vice President
> Fortune 500 Company

NOTHING IS AS SIMPLE AS IT SEEMS

As should be clear by now, if you long for a job in which people never get in the way, all problems are easily defined with their causes clear and known, decisions are simple, future events are quite predictable, and you can almost immediately find out whether you made the correct decision, you probably ought to think again about a managerial career. Organizational life is much too complex for a handful of rules, theories, or slogans to be automatically applied to every problem. While the behavioral science theories and concepts in this book should be helpful to you in figuring out what is going on, or even in guiding an action, they are by no means sufficient for all problems you will encounter, nor easy to apply. They are more helpful than common sense alone, but they do not come with 10-year money-back guarantees.

> *For every problem there is a solution which is simple, direct, and wrong.*
>
> H. L. Mencken

Multiple Causality

For one thing, most behavior of any significance has multiple causes and multiple consequences. For example, how can you explain why extremely intelligent, caring managers at NASA decided to proceed with the Challenger shuttle launch on a cold January 28, 1986, when, as tragically proved true, the rubber rocket seals would not hold in temperatures below 50 degrees? Although it is an all-too-human trait to want to find a single villain—a simple cause that explains everything—a combination of many factors allowed NASA to send astronauts to their deaths while millions watched on TV.

Key NASA officials were warned the night before the launch by Morton Thiokol managers and engineers but discounted the data. They thought the evidence was not conclusive. The many delays in this and previous launches had created a sense of urgency about pushing ahead. National media had begun to belittle NASA delays. The string of successful missions may have engendered overconfidence that somehow things would work out as they always had; NASA culture reinforced managers for a "can do" attitude and for cool unflappability. As in other large organizations, mid-level personnel were used to withholding "bad news" from higher-ups, and communications often became distorted as they passed up and down the organization. Internal politics and rivalries probably helped shape what managers and engineers told one another.

At Thiokol, the contractor for the rocket boosters, similar pressures impacted key players. Furthermore, the company was competing vigorously with several other corporations to get future shuttle contracts. It is difficult to continue to say "no launch" to a customer who says, "I am appalled" as NASA official George Hardy did, or to another official, Lawrence Malloy, who reacted to Thiokol's reservations by saying, "My God, Thiokol, when do you want me to launch, next April?" Thiokol's engineers, who fought the decision but were overruled by their managers, backed off out of doubt about how certain they could be, natural fears of continuing to argue with their bosses, and even personal distaste for conflict.

Undoubtedly there are other reasons for the foolhardy decision; the ones listed are just some of those made public after the disaster. If you had been asked right after the explosion to "solve the problem once and for all," think about how easily you could have missed the complexities and focused on "firing the incompetent guy who said to launch" or "replacing the lousy contractor." Though either or both of those actions might ultimately be part of a solution, if that's all you did, the other complex forces would undoubtedly cause similar problems to occur in the future. *Oversimplifying your diagnosis of the cause(s) of problems almost always leads to incorrect or insufficient remedial action.* This kind of leap to hasty, oversimplified conclusions happens all the time in organizations; dramatic events like the Challenger explosion are just rare public glimpses of what happens when diagnosis misfires.

> *Seek simplicity; then distrust it.*
>
> Alfred North Whitehead

Here's another dramatic example: one of the world's largest consulting firms was approached by a manufacturer of tubing made from a rare metal. The manufacturer said that its problem was the *measurement of faulty tubing;* the tubing came out of the extruding machines so fast that, by the time they could examine it, too much product would be wasted if the diameter and tensile strength were off. Could a gauge be devised that would constantly monitor quality as the tubing was extruded? The consulting firm took on the project with delight, since its quality control division could utilize very advanced technology to devise an entirely new kind of measuring gauge. One year and several hundred thousand dollars later, a new gauge was perfected, to everyone's delight. The new gauge was installed but, unfortunately, within another year the manufacturing company went broke because such an extremely high proportion of the tubing produced had to be scrapped. Although with the new gauge they were immediately aware of quality problems, the *real* problem was that the extruding machines were inadequately designed. The scrap problem was not primarily one of measurement but one of *faulty production* in the first place due to poor equipment design! An improper problem definition led to an elegant but not very relevant decision.

As a manager you will have to learn to see many, often interconnected, causes for behavior. Let's say you encounter a work group that is not performing well. How will you decide ways to improve its performance? More important than the "perfect latest and greatest technique," which may not fit the particular problem, will be to trace backward from the problem to find its overlapping and reinforcing causes (see Figure 1–1). Behind any important problem is a tangled web of forces that together form a fabric of causes. In the case of the poorly performing work group, some of the causes might be a combination of (*a*) poor leadership, (*b*) inadequate training and knowledge, (*c*) a change in quality of materials, (*d*) improper procedures, (*e*) members who are bored by their work or overwhelmed by it, (*f*) pay that doesn't seem fair to members, or (*g*) lack of penalties for poor performance and/or lack of rewards for excellent performance.

Though the problem may stand out clearly, its components will require careful analysis. If all the causes aren't identified, it will be easy to overfocus on one cause, make the same kind of mistake as the consulting firm, and "go down the tubes." *In analyzing cases in this course or in actual organizational problems, beware of the temptation to oversimplify your explanations.*

Uncertainty

Another problem facing managers is that they must make decisions under uncertain conditions, often before all the desired data are in. Quite often there is insufficient time for thorough study, or the roots of the problem are not accessible to the person who must decide. For example, employees are often afraid to tell *any* boss all they know, especially if what they say might include criticism of the boss. And even if they were to be completely open, they might not fully know their own motivations or other necessary information. Finally, the conditions at the time of the decision can change by the time it is implemented, so that what looks sensible at one time may seem foolish later. When energy planners decided to create a large underground oil reserve for the United States in the Utah salt domes, they had no reason to expect it would be needed before 1980. Therefore they delayed installation of pumps to get the oil out in order to save taxpayers' money. They could not foresee that in early 1979 the Shah of Iran would be forced to leave Iran, Iranian production would stop completely for several months, and that they would look foolish with millions of barrels of oil stored underground and no way to pump it on short notice. Because it takes over three years to design, build, and

FIGURE 1–1
Many Possible Causes for Any Given Problem

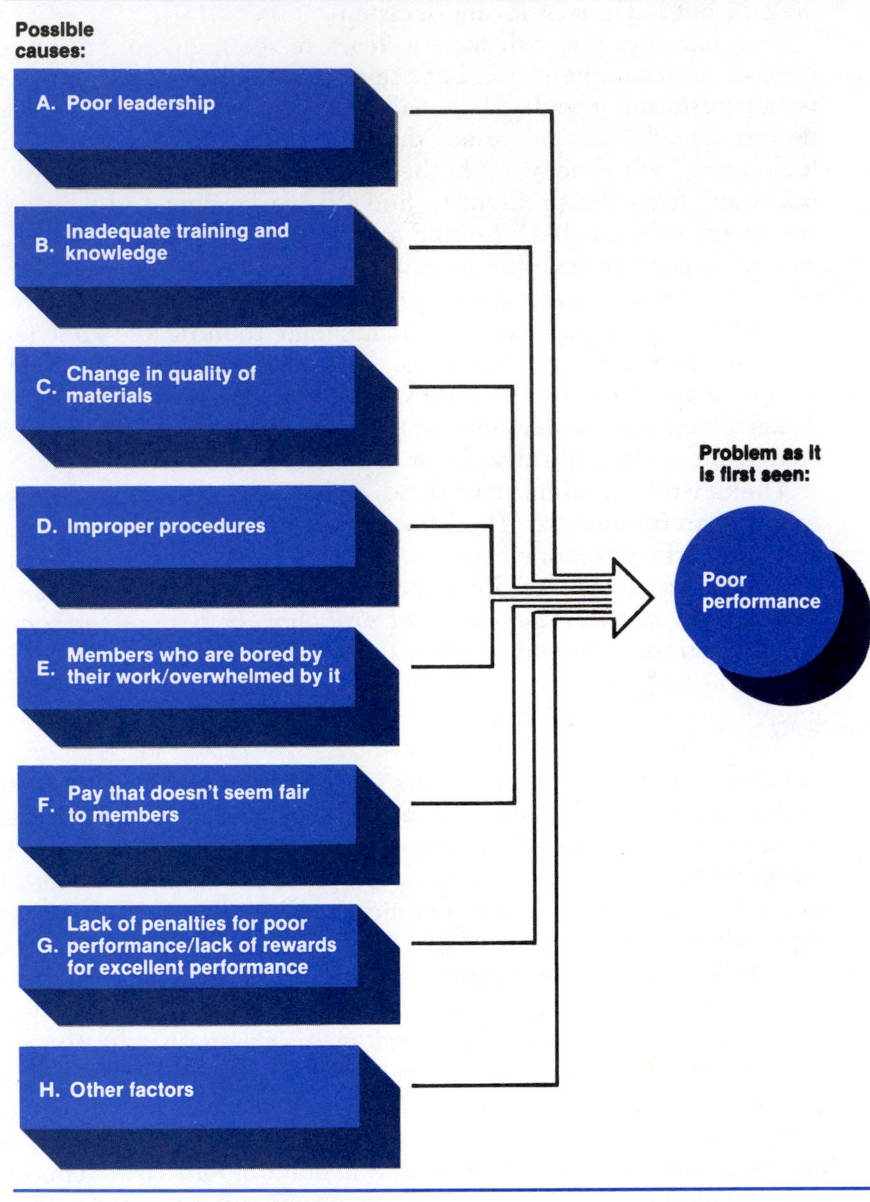

Possible causes:
A. Poor leadership
B. Inadequate training and knowledge
C. Change in quality of materials
D. Improper procedures
E. Members who are bored by their work/overwhelmed by it
F. Pay that doesn't seem fair to members
G. Lack of penalties for poor performance/lack of rewards for excellent performance
H. Other factors
Problem as it is first seen:
Poor performance

market a new car, numerous automobile manufacturers have built gas-guzzlers when consumers wanted economy, or produced compact cars when family-size was preferred.

> *I can live with doubt and uncertainty. I think it's much more interesting to live not knowing than to have answers which might be wrong.*
>
> Professor Richard Feynmann
> *The Economist*
> December 26, 1981

Living with Consequences of Decisions

Managers must also live with the consequences of their decisions. They do not have the luxury of leisurely tinkering with something inside a sealed vacuum flask and being able to put aside the experiment when it is not going well. As suggested earlier, even deciding to do nothing is a decision that can affect a manager deeply, since that will not stop a chain of consequences from following, including changed perceptions of him/her by subordinates, colleagues, and boss.

Because the manager lives in a complex world of multiple causes and effects, makes decisions under time pressure and uncertainty, and must live with the consequences of decisions made under imperfect conditions, a specific ability is needed. It is the knack of thinking in terms of probable outcomes rather than certain ones, of figuring and playing the odds. Anything managers can do to predict likely outcomes more accurately, to increase the possibility of correct action, even when they cannot be *sure* about what will happen, is a great asset. If even "no decision" is a decision, the ability to take risks when outcomes are not certain becomes an important managerial attribute.

The pressures of managerial work lead to a relatively high degree of stress for managers as they struggle to cope with all the demands placed upon them. For some, the stress leads to physical or psychological problems. Yet successful managers are apparently people who thrive on the challenges inherent in their work; they consistently report in polls a greater degree of job satisfaction than, for example, hourly workers, who have less responsibility and challenge in their work. In studying organizational behavior, you will have the chance to practice being a managerial decision maker and also to see whether you enjoy being in the hot seat that managers sit in.

You may be placed in a position of having to act and live through the consequences of each action or decision. For example, you may be asked to participate in group projects; if you decide not to say anything to the members of your group who shirk their responsibilities for fear of hurting their feelings, you will be one of those who will live with the outcome. And conversely, should you decide to confront them you would have another set of consequences to cope with. Which way you choose to handle such a dilemma and which consequences you are willing to accept depend upon your *own* personal values; no one else can tell you what is worth living with. Even in a class discussion or case analysis, you must decide whether or not to express your views and must live with the consequences (both good and bad) of the choice you make: for learning, clarifying your ideas, gaining credit for contributing to class discussion, or for your relationships and reputation with other students.

When you analyze cases, try to think of the people in them as being, like you, real individuals struggling to do the best they can in accordance with their values. The more you can project yourself into their positions, imagine yourself to be in their shoes, the better you will understand why things are happening—and the more interesting the cases will be.

Through this continual process of being placed in organizational situations where you must make decisions about how to behave and then see what happens, your skills and organizational effectiveness should be improved. Most often you will find that there is no *one* correct answer to the dilemmas or situations you face. Since one person's meat can be another's poison, the correct solution will be quite different depending upon the values of the decider.

Almost any course of action, as a manager or in daily life, will entail costs as well as benefits. In assessing alternative courses of action, the effective manager does not expect to find a choice with no costs, but seeks the choice that on balance involves the least net cost or the maximum net benefit. By identifying in advance all the likely costs, the effective decision maker can also identify steps to minimize the costs that become a reality.

A MODEL FOR MAKING DECISIONS

The need to be clear about the desires of the person making a decision will be apparent throughout the book. The decision maker must find a way to assess what *demands the situation places* upon those involved, what solutions (and their consequences) would be *personally desirable* to him/her, and what *possible alternatives* can accommodate both the situation and the decision maker (see Figure 1–2).

Sometimes the particular task, the people involved in doing it, or the organizational context calls for or demands certain decisions and

FIGURE 1–2
Interplay between the Decision Maker and the Problem Situation

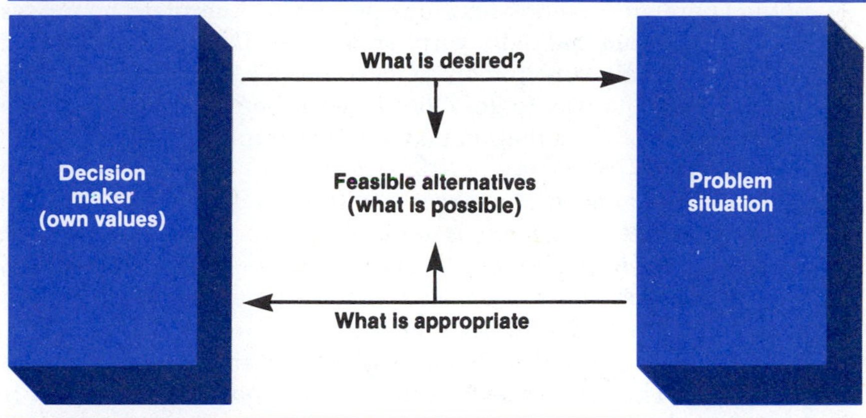

results. The head of the organizational unit may want a specified increase in productivity, or the task may call for a particular level of informational flow, or the employees may need some minimum amount of direction. *The situation itself is a powerful determinant of what is appropriate as a decision.*

On the other hand, the manager, being a part of the situation and affected by it, cannot ignore his or her personal values in making the decision. As indicated earlier, what one manager might be happy to contend with another might find extremely unpleasant and vice versa.

In the classroom organization, for example, every teacher has to make some decisions about an evaluation system, just as do managers of any organizational unit. In most universities there are some overall limits to the grading system imposed upon everyone, including the form in which they will be reported, the requirement that there be grades, sometimes the rough distribution among them, and so forth. *These are part of the demands of the situation.* Furthermore, the general pressures on students to perform, the requirements for work in other courses, and student attitudes about grading are also part of the situation setting limits as to what the faculty member can do.

Nevertheless, the inclinations of the individual instructor are also an important factor in determining a grading system. Does he/she want grades to *entice* students or to *threaten* them into learning? Does he/she worry more about the student who might "beat the system" or the one who responds best to being trusted? How important does the instructor think it is to use grades for developmental feedback so that students may improve performance, versus using grades to make final evaluations of what was learned? The teacher's own values cannot help but shape what decision is right for him/her.

Furthermore, between the demands of the situation and the values of the instructor there are many alternative ways of accommodating both. There are several variations between a complete honor system with self-grading and daily surprise quizzes. Often there is in organizations a certain amount of "wiggle room" in which the decision maker can find a way to get close to what he/she wants even though the demands of the situation may not be completely favorable or "co-operative."

As a student and as a manager it will be useful for you to be able to distinguish between *what is appropriate to the situation, what is personally desired,* and *what alternatives are thus feasible.* **There is no one best way to manage. What is best depends upon the situation and the values of the decision maker.**

The rest of the course should give you ample opportunities for practicing. The text, cases, exercises, and your instructor will try to help you clarify your own values and make better estimates of how well they will be served by what you do in a variety of human situations. While we would hardly claim that practice makes perfect, it should increase the probabilities of your being able to make sensible decisions that get you what you want and enhance your ability to learn from experience.

LEARNING STYLES

A course that demands active participation and application of concepts to actual complex situations can create some difficulties. We have already noted our assumptions about the interplay of experience and conceptualization, moving back and forth among doing, formulating conclusions, and testing them on new situations. We believe that such a process most closely replicates the process that managers (and other organizational members) go through at work.

Some individuals are not accustomed to learning in such active experimenting and conceptualizing modes. They are more used to passive learning in which they are most distant from the phenomena being studied. While that mode of learning is valid for mastering some subject matter, it is less appropriate for studying organizational behavior, especially where there is an emphasis on developing managerial skills.

Furthermore, since the work of managers is so fundamentally intertwined with other people, it is desirable to add some collaborative modes of learning to the individual competitive modes more common in other kinds of courses. Learning from and with others is an important part of mastering skills needed for working effectively in organizations. One need not abandon the desire to do well in comparison to others in order to practice mutual teaching and learning. Your classmates will have sufficient diversity of experiences, skill, opinions, attitudes, and values to insure that someone in the course or task groups will have a different way of seeing the issues raised by the cases and concepts. Indeed, you may be shocked to find that no matter how well you prepare a case and how certain you are of your views, class discussion will reveal many angles you never thought of, along with viewpoints with which you profoundly disagree—held by students equally prepared and certain of their correctness! Learning to bend and reconsider when there is something new, yet be convincing and persuasive when you can help others gain perspective, is difficult to master.

What complicates issues of differences in learning style is the fact that individuals are at different stages in terms of their basic views of the world. Researchers have identified stages of development that individuals pass through or get stuck at, depending on their capacity to learn from making choices and experiencing new circumstances. The stage at which an individual is makes a great deal of difference in how that person approaches education and new learning (Weathersby, 1981) as well as how he/she thinks about other organizational issues such as power, authority, work, goals, and interpersonal relationships. People at different stages tend to respond somewhat differently to leadership opportunities, and they often make different decisions about priorities based on how they understand the world (see Figure 1–3). Sometimes communication problems are the result of people genuinely trying to talk to each other from different stages. You may find it helpful to locate yourself and others you know on the chart in Figure 1–3 and also to use it to set some goals for your own learning and development.

Try to keep in mind that there is nothing inherently good or bad in any of these stages; they simply identify important issues with which we all struggle as we learn and grow. Furthermore, the issues represented at any given stage may actually be lifelong, that is, they never really disappear and in some way may always influence your perception of a given situation.

As you approach and move through this course it could be valuable for you to examine your own learning style; how the stage you are at (as best as you can assess it) affects your perceptions of the course, the instructor, and other students (especially those who are at a different stage); and, most important, your way of learning the material presented. Remember, your future skills as a manager might depend in part on your ability to understand and appreciate the differences among your employees and how these will affect their perceptions of you and how you manage.

All of this means that some students may find the book and course for which it is intended rather disconcerting at first. However, we do hold to the belief that as potential managers it is ultimately necessary

FIGURE 1–3
Educational Attitudes and Life Stages (Development over time)

Life Stage	*Educational Attitudes*
Opportunistic Self-protective; competitive with, and ready to blame others; likely to think in only vague general terms or either/or concepts; breaks rules for personal gain; modest self-understanding.	College is a thing you do after high school; it's a drag but important. Professors are the people in charge of a course who show you what to do and keep you on track. Grades are what count; you work for the grade more than for "learning."
Socially oriented Concerned with belonging and acceptance; typically friendly and nice toward others (except outsiders); often relies on stereotypes and clichés; concerned about rules and with what one "should" do.	College is where you get the education that helps you get a better job and prepares you for the future. Professors are the experts who provide the facts and the answers. They tell you whether or not you understand the material. Grades are important as a means to a good job and are the reward for hard work and ability.
Goal oriented Achievement oriented, has long-term goals; focused toward mutual responsibilities in relationships; increased conceptual complexity; has self-evaluated standards; greater understanding of self and others.	The point of college is for you to grow as a person, developing your potentials, skills, and awareness for a more meaningful life. Professors' knowledge, competence, and standards of excellence give them authority. They can help one learn by exchanging ideas and modeling their way of studying issues. Grades are important to show if one has mastered the standards in a course. They don't always represent the amount one learns. In some courses I gain a lot even though I don't get a good grade.
Self-defining and relativistic Concerned with individuality and self-fulfillment, yet also justice and humanity; desires autonomy in relationships yet is tolerant of others; thinks complexly, seeing issues from multiple points of view; lives with conflicts in personal obligations, needs, and roles while striving to resolve them.	College is a major step in a process of emotional and intellectual development that will continue throughout life. Professors are an important resource that students can draw on as makes sense. In the end, though, I'm the one who is really responsible for my learning. Grades are a measure of performance in the classroom. Their primary importance lies in giving information about how one is doing in the professor's eyes, which is only part of the story.

Table developed by Rita P. Weathersby, adapted from the work of Jane Loevinger and Rita Weathersby.

> *We are apt to think that our ideas are the creation of our own wisdom, but the truth is that they are the result of experiences through outside contact.*
>
> *Without studying or being taught by others, we cannot formulate even a single idea. Therefore it can be said that a person who can create ideas worthy of note is a person who learned much from others.*
>
> *If we are willing to learn, everything in this world can be our teacher.*
>
> *With sincerity we hope to absorb wisdom from all people and all things. It is from this attitude that fresh and brilliant ideas are created. The sincere willingness to learn is the first step toward "Prosperity."*
>
> Konosuke Matsushita

to be able to use all modes of learning—active, passive, collaborative, competitive, concrete, and abstract—and that the modes inherent in using cases and treating the classroom as an organization often need reinforcement. Therefore, practicing them in and out of class even when they feel awkward is a worthwhile way of expanding your ability to learn in situations that call for active participation.

In other words, the process we are suggesting that you use in this course is not just for the course itself; it is a process that can serve you throughout life. The cases and exercises are all designed to put you in the position of a manager or organizational member who has to decide what is going on, what the situation calls for, what alternatives exist for resolving the problem(s) or dilemma(s) faced, and ultimately what consequences your values will permit you to accept. In the book, as in life, we do not expect easy solutions to present themselves very often; the chance to practice sorting out complexities and making informed choices can nevertheless be enjoyable if you plunge wholeheartedly into doing it.

> *The mind is a fire to be kindled, not a vessel to be filled.*
>
> Plutarch

KEY CONCEPTS FROM CHAPTER 1

1. We live in a constantly changing world.
2. Basic premise: Much of what you can learn about organizational behavior goes on around you all the time.
3. Central theme:
   a. Learning through doing and reflecting.
   b. The manager as involved actor.

4. The scientific attitude is the act of comparing the intent of actions with their effects and then learning from the process.
5. The manager, by virtue of position, has relationships that are necessary to acquire information in order to make decisions.
6. Managing requires:
   a. Awareness of multiple causality.
   b. Decisions under uncertainty.
   c. Living with consequences of decisions.
7. Decision making requires consideration of:
   a. What is appropriate to the situation (task, people, organizational context).
   b. What is possible.
   c. What is desired by the individual(s) (values, goals, limits of tolerance).
8. Learning styles: The desirability of active collaborative learning.

SUGGESTED READINGS

Adler, N. J. "Women Do Not Want International Careers, and Other Myths about International Management." *Organizational Dynamics,* Autumn 1984, pp. 66–79.

Bennis, W. G. "Goals and Metagoals of Laboratory Training." *Human Relations Training News,* Fall 1962, National Training Laboratories, Washington, D.C., pp. 1–4.

Berelson, B., and G. Steiner. *Human Behavior: An Inventory of Scientific Findings.* New York: Harcourt Brace Jovanovich, 1964.

Cohen, A. R. "Beyond Simulation: The Classroom as Organization." *The Teaching of Organization Behavior Journal,* Spring and Summer 1976.

Cohen, A. R., and B. A. Stein. "Task Forces in Management: A Key Development Tool." *The NABW Journal,* November–December 1980.

Cooper, E. A., and G. V. Barrett. "Equal Pay and Gender: Implications of Court Cases for Personnel Practices." *Academy of Management Review,* January 1984, pp. 84–93.

DeFrank, R. S.; M. T. Matteson; D. M. Schweiger; and J. M. Ivancevich. "The Impact of Culture on the Management Practices of American and Japanese CEOs." *Organizational Dynamics,* Spring 1985, pp. 62–76.

Ferris, G. R., and J. A. Wagner III. "Quality Circles in the United States: A Conceptual Reevaluation." *Journal of Applied Behavioral Science* 21, no. 2 (1985), pp. 155–68.

Finkelstein, J., and D. A. H. Newman. "The Third Industrial Revolution: A Special Challenge to Managers." *Organizational Dynamics* 12 (1984), pp. 53–65.

French, J. L., and A. R. Rosenstein. "Employee Ownership, Work Attitudes, and Power Relationships." *Academy of Management Journal* 27 (1984), pp. 861–69.

Gilligan, C. *In a Different Voice: Psychological Theory and Women's Development.* Cambridge, Mass.: Harvard University Press, 1982.

Goldstein, S. G. "Organizational Dualism and Quality Circles." *Academy of Management Review,* July 1985, pp. 504–17.

Gorman, A. H. *Teachers and Learners: The Interactive Process of Education.* Boston: Allyn & Bacon, 1969.

Grasha, A. F. "Observations on Relating Teaching Goals to Student Response Styles and Classroom Methods." *American Psychologist* 27 (1972), pp. 144–47.

Greenhaus, J. H., and N. J. Beutell. "Sources of Conflict between Work and Family Roles." *Academy of Management Review* 10 (1985), pp. 76–88.

Jamieson, D. W., and K. W. Thomas. "Power and Conflict in the Student-Teacher Relationship." *Journal of Applied Behavioral Science* 10 (1974), pp. 321–36.

Kohlberg, L. "Stage and Sequence: The Cognitive Developmental Approach to Socialization." In *Handbook of Socialization Theory and Research,* ed. D. Goslin. Skokie, Ill.: Rand McNally, 1969.

Kolb, D. "Toward a Typology of Learning Styles and Learning Environments: An Investigation of the Impact of Learning Styles and Discipline Demands on the Academic Performance, Social Adaption, and Career Choices of M.I.T. Seniors," a Working Paper, No. 688-73. Cambridge: Massachusetts Institute of Technology, Sloan School of Management, 1973.

________. *The Learning Style Inventory: Technical Manual.* Boston: McBer, 1976.

Loevinger, J. *Ego Development: Conceptions and Theories.* San Francisco: Jossey-Bass, 1976.

Louis, M. R. "Surprise and Sense Making: What Newcomers Experience in Entering Unfamiliar Organization Settings." *Administrative Science Quarterly* 25 (1980), pp. 226–51.

Meyer, G. W., and R. G. Stott. "Quality Circles: Panacea or Pandora's Box?" *Organizational Dynamics,* Spring 1985, pp. 34–50.

Mintzberg, H. *The Nature of Managerial Work.* New York: Harper & Row, 1973.

________. "The Manager's Job: Folklore and Fact." *Harvard Business Review,* July–August 1975.

________. "Planning on the Left Side and Managing on the Right." *Harvard Business Review,* July–August 1976.

McGregor, D. *The Professional Manager.* New York: McGraw-Hill, 1967.

Munchus, G., III. "Employer–Employee-Based Quality Circles in Japan: Human Resource Policy Implications for American Firms." *Academy of Management Review,* April 1983, pp. 225–61.

Nonaka, I., and J. K. Johansson. "Japanese Management: What about the 'Hard' Skills?" *Academy of Management Review,* April 1985, pp. 181–91.

Perry, W. G., Jr. "Cognitive and Ethical Growth: The Making of Meaning." In *The Modern American College,* ed. A. W. Chickering. San Francisco: Jossey-Bass, 1981.

Peters, T., and S. Waterman. *In Search of Excellence: Lessons from America's Best-Managed Corporations.* New York: Harper & Row, 1982.

Rogers, C. R. *Freedom to Learn.* Columbus, Ohio: Charles E. Merrill Publishing, 1969.

Shamir, B., and I. Salomon. "Work-At-Home and the Quality of Working Life." *Academy of Management Review,* July 1985, pp. 455–64.

Simon, H. A. *Administrative Behavior.* 2nd ed. New York: Macmillan, 1957.

________. *The New Science of Management Decision.* New York: Harper & Row, 1960.

Torrence, W. D. "Blending East and West: With Difficulties along the Way." *Organizational Dynamics,* Autumn 1984, pp. 23–34.

Ueno, I.; R. R. Blake; and J. S. Mouton. "The Productivity Battle: A Behavioral Science Analysis of Japan and the United States." *Journal of Applied Behavioral Science* 20, no. 1 (1984), pp. 49–58.

Weathersby, R. P. "Ego Development." In *The Modern American College,* ed. A. W. Chickering. San Francisco: Jossey-Bass, 1981.

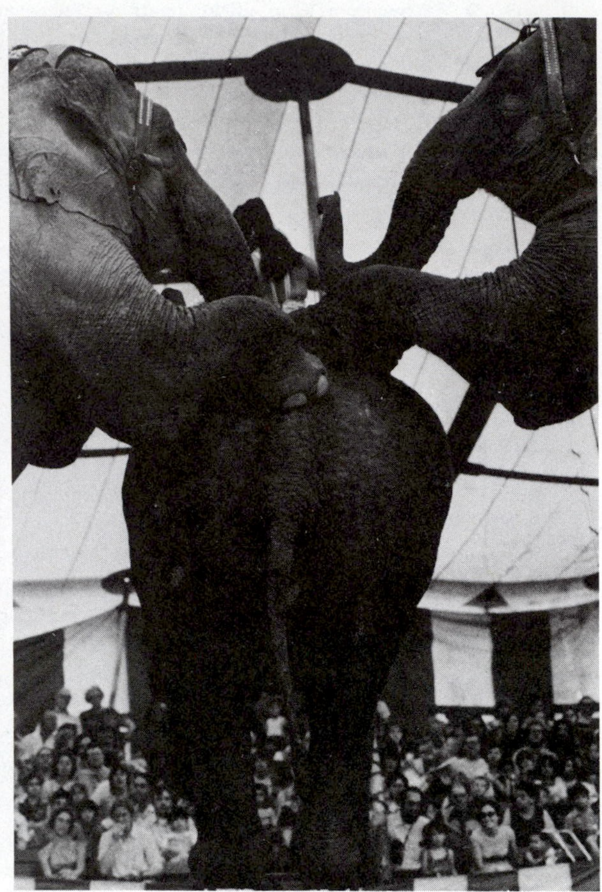

2

THE TOTAL ORGANIZATION AND THE CONCEPT OF SYSTEMS

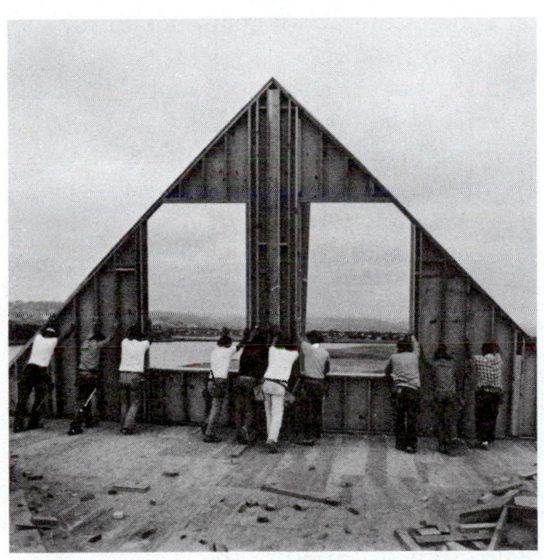

Modern organizations have introduced variations on the original pyramid model, because the world does not always arrange itself to fit its neat but oversimplified set of assumptions.

Organizations evolved as a consequence of people attempting to solve complex problems. When a problem requires the efforts of more than one person, some kind of organization is necessary in order to get the work done. Whether the problem requires a few or many to work together—a pair of lumberjacks sawing logs or several hundred thousand employees providing national telephone service—the existence of an organization raises a series of fundamental questions or dilemmas, which must be resolved in order to accomplish the organization's goals. Imagine what it takes to get any complex job done:

1. Goals must be determined, agreed upon, and disseminated (goal setting).
2. Some way of making decisions about goals and all subsequent tasks must be found (decision making).
3. The various tasks necessary to achieve the goals must be divided and allocated (division of labor).
4. People who are willing to and capable of doing the tasks must be found, employed, trained, and assigned to the tasks (recruiting).
5. Somehow timely information must be conveyed to those who need it to do their tasks (communications).
6. A way must be found to get organizational members to do the necessary work (motivation).
7. A way must be found to insure adequate performance of the tasks (control).
8. A way must be found to insure coordination of the tasks (coordination).
9. A way must be found to measure and modify all of the above when the conditions leading to the original goals change (environmental scanning and organizational mission).

The problems of trying to decide what an organization should do, who should do it, and how they should divide work, coordinate efforts, and so forth, have provided challenges for thousands of years. Imagine the organization required to build the pyramids in Egypt or the aqueducts in the Roman Empire. Even the first primitive hunting band had to decide who would do what, where it would hunt, what would happen to the hunter who was disabled, less skilled, or uncooperative. Much of this book is devoted to exploring aspects of the broad issues listed above primarily as they affect the small work group. The goals of each work group in an organization should reflect and contribute to the goals of that organization. The group's membership will be determined by the organization's recruiting policies, and the behavior of individual group members will be influenced by the organization's controls and rewards.

THE TRADITIONAL ORGANIZATION

Over the centuries many ways of organizing people have been imagined. Early organizations were often quite simple, with a boss or owner-manager and employees with more-or-less specific jobs. As the organizations grew, the need grew for subunits with supervisors. Until these organizations became fairly large, they could remain quite loose. As long as the entrepreneur was around and could personally know and supervise everyone, relationships, job assignments, and communications could be informal. Even today young, recently formed companies that are growing rapidly and managed by an entrepreneur who founded the organization are often only loosely structured. There is so much to do that little time is spent worrying about spelling out boundaries, roles, and rules.

Nevertheless, as size increases, something more systematic is needed. In large organizations the most frequent form is the bureaucratic hierarchy, usually represented by boxes and lines in a formal organization chart. The traditional organization chart often looks like a pyramid, with many people at the bottom of the chart and increasingly fewer at the top. See Figure 2–1, which pictorially represents certain guidelines for how the traditional large organization goes about its work:

1. Decisions are made by specified people in a hierarchy, which gives increasingly broader powers to those who are higher in the organization.
2. There are a set of explicit rules governing the rights and duties of employees.
3. Labor is divided into carefully prescribed jobs by specialty.
4. A set of procedures governs how to deal with problems as they arise from the work.
5. Relationships are impersonal, objective, and fair.
6. Selection and promotion are based on technical competence.
7. Coordination of the work is done through the chain of command (hierarchy).

FIGURE 2–1
Pyramidal Organization Chart

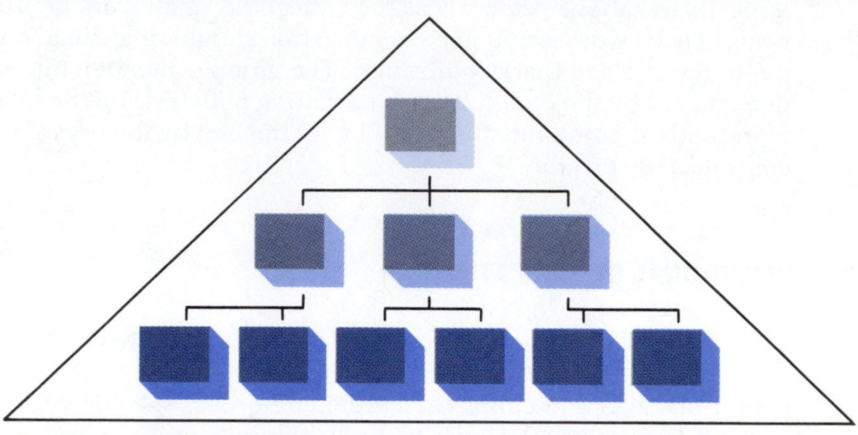

8. Disagreements between units at the same level are referred up the chain for resolution.
9. Rewards tend to be formalized and uniform.

Such a chart implies who has direct powers over the work activities of others, who is responsible for certain activities, and therefore who should talk to whom and about what. The pyramidal model assumes that most problems can be foreseen in advance and logically dealt with by rules and regulations and that positions higher in the chart indicate greater knowledge and competence as well as greater rights and powers.

Along with such formalized relationships among people, most organizations develop explicit methods of rewarding people's behavior. By means of wages or salaries, fringe benefits, opportunities for advancement, and so forth, organizations seek to attract and hold employees, get high levels of performance out of them, and stimulate initiative and commitment to organizational goals. Similarly, through the use of planning, budgetary constraints, production schedules, and the like, organizations attempt to exercise control over employee behavior to insure the efficient attainment of their goals.

In traditional (sometimes called "classical") organizations, it is generally assumed that carefully spelled out duties, hierarchical structures, procedures, rules, rewards, and controls will create in advance a system that can handle most, if not all, the important decisions and problems inherent in their operations. The idea is to "preprogram" the organization's response to any contingency—usually by predetermined procedures and action choices; otherwise by referring the matter to a designated authority, typically higher up the hierarchy, for action on the (presumably few) exceptions. This works well in stable, unchanging conditions.

The world, however, has not always arranged itself to fit this neat but oversimplified set of assumptions. Problems are not always predictable; greater expertise about particular issues does not always reside in the person with the highest position in the organization. Necessary information may be possessed by those not directly connected on the chart, and yet they must interact directly or action will be unreasonably delayed. This often causes a bending of the rules as people make informal, direct contact with one another and base decisions on personal relationships as well as on those laid out by the organization chart.

Thus, one of the early departures from the traditional model of an organization was the emergence of informal coordination and the settlement of disagreements among departments through direct unofficial contacts, often without any involvement of people higher in the chain of command. Sometimes, as the value of such direct contact became more and more evident over time, this form of working relationship was legitimized and even formalized in job descriptions and in the creation of special roles such as expeditor or liaison person. But, every organization has both a formal and an informal organization. While the formal organization is intended to define the boundaries and proper roles for members of the organization, the actual work that is done usually depends upon people's abilities to take actions when a situation calls for them. These cannot always be prescribed in advance by the formal organization, thus requiring the informal organization to pick up the slack, to compensate for what has not been anticipated. As long as the two systems complement each other, the total organization can be effective; when informal activities begin to disrupt or block the formal objectives, managers get concerned and need to correct something in either the formal or the informal organization.

THE BASES OF DEPARTMENTALIZATION

In setting up a traditional organization one must grapple with a fundamental issue, namely *how* to cluster activities into departments—by function? by product? by customer or service? by geographic area? Although very small companies or agencies may not have to make such sharp differentiations, most large ones do. The complexities of a large system make it imperative to create manageable units. Normally these units and their respective subunits are logically derived from the expressed goals of the organization and are modified by the requirements of the technology needed to produce the service or product.

A hospital needs various types of professional personnel (physicians, nurses, aides, lab technicians) and offers various services (convalescent wards, emergency rooms, operating rooms, administrative departments, and so on). Do you organize around the particular services provided—which would require a mixture of professional personnel in a given unit? Many hospitals do just that. But what about utilizing occupational groupings—a nursing department, a housekeeping department, a physical therapy department, and the like? Don't these also make sense, so that people with common goals, skills, languages, and interests will talk with, guide, and stimulate one another? Indeed, we do find such departments in most institutions.

Similarly, in a manufacturing firm we might find functional subdivisions, such as sales, production, research and development, and personnel, or find units established around a particular product or product line. The latter would involve a mixture of the personnel identified in the functional setup. Which makes the most sense? Is one better than the other? For what purposes? Can they be combined somehow?

There are no simple answers to these questions; there are costs and benefits associated with any given way of organizing. For example, an organization that has a sales function and a production department will almost certainly be faced with some inherent conflicts. Salespeople inevitably want to serve the customer quickly, to be able to respond to changing market demands, and to build a high level of credibility with their clientele. From the point of view of sales any product should be produced whenever the customer wants it. Production people, however, want to standardize as much as possible, reduce costs, and make operations as predictable as possible. They would like to produce only one product for long times so as to reduce setup and errors. The former think in terms of change and flexibility, the latter in terms of stability and long-range continuity. Disagreements and even conflicts are inevitable, although not necessarily to the detriment of the company. Can you imagine if either sales or production had exclusive control over decisions and commitments? The company would either be way out on a limb all the time or totally unresponsive to a normally turbulent world. It is the *balance* that actually leads to the best decisions for the company.

There are times when an organization can operate best through its functional units, times when it needs the product, the region, or the service as its structural format. There are also situations where no single basis seems appropriate. Instead, a combination of bases seems to serve system goals better.

THINKING SMALL—LARGE COMPUTER FIRMS SPROUT LITTLE DIVISIONS FOR GOOD, FAST WORK

Companies say that small groups, given great freedom, can react better and more quickly to the abrupt changes in electronics technology that constantly buffet the valley. Unlike industries where change is more gradual, computer makers must regularly come up with new products or enhancements of the old, and for ever-lower costs. An electric-toaster model might sell for years, but a computer, particularly at the lower-priced end of the market, might have a life span of only 18 months before technology passes it by.

Apple Computer Inc. turned to a small group to help develop its Lisa, a $10,000 easy-to-use machine for businesspeople. Timex Corp. did likewise to get into the computer business quickly with its Timex Sinclair 1000. Daniel Ross, the vice president and chief operating officer of the Timex Computer unit, says one virtue of the small group approach is that responsibility gets pushed to lower-level employees. Also, he says, small groups can better focus their energies on a single goal. "Creativity is fostered in this kind of organization," he says.

Even giant International Business Machines Corp. has recognized the need for small working groups, especially in producing new products. It has formed 14 "independent business units" to capture the entrepreneurial spirit in work on such product lines as factory robotic systems. "The centralized organization just prevented innovation," says Peter Wright, a longtime IBM watcher and the director of research for the Gartner Group, a research concern. "They had problems because good ideas weren't getting out to the marketplace."

Source: Erik Larson and Carrie Dolan. Reprinted by permission of *The Wall Street Journal*,

VARIATIONS FROM THE TRADITIONAL ORGANIZATION

The Linking-Pin Model

Over the past 40–50 years, modern organizations have introduced variations on the original pyramidal model in order to accommodate the infinite variety of, and often unpredictable, interconnections that are required for any complex system to cope with its problems. While it is not the subject of this book to discuss the broader questions of organization theory and management (sometimes referred to as a *macro*perspective), it would be useful to note some ways in which large organizations have attempted to create structures that are more adaptable to today's problems.

Rensis Likert (1961), for example, proposed that organizations be viewed as a set of interrelated *groupings* of people, arranged in a hierarchy with managers serving as link-pins connecting the groups. A given manager, according to this conception, is both a member of a peer group of managers with comparable responsibilities and a leader-member of his or her own department or group. This role typically involves leading subordinates in *group discussions and decision making*, and then *representing* the group's needs and views in meetings of the higher (peer manager) group—which is also oriented to reach decisions through group discussion and consensus. Figure 2–2 depicts the manager's multiple group membership and link-pin position between groups.

Thus, managers link the various subparts of the organization in ways that serve to keep important information flowing through the system, maintain a sense of total organization, and minimize the kinds of problems and errors often associated with the strictly bureaucratic way of operating. While not a major departure from the traditional model, Likert's approach contains profound implications for the managerial roles and functions described in Chapter 1.

The Matrix Model

One of the most recent organizational forms, designed to obtain the advantages of two bases simultaneously, is called the matrix model. In this model an individual or a work group is structurally subject to the direction of two bosses, one typically representing a functional concern (e.g., manufacturing) and the other a product, customer, or service concern (e.g., the project office) as depicted in Figure 2–3.

A matrix organization attempts to build into its formal structure a great variety of legitimate connections, vertically, horizontally, and diagonally. Many of the relationships that might, out of necessity, occur informally in a classical organization are depicted in a matrix as legitimate aspects of the formal organization. The philosophy behind this is to facilitate in the most efficient way possible the flow of needed information and expertise to places where it is needed. It is presumably a way of minimizing so-called red tape and the danger of important decisions being hung up in the limited channels of a pyramid. Furthermore, the matrix model is flexible enough to accommodate the introduction of temporary groups (task forces, committees, and the like), is effectively able to move resources to the scenes of action where they are needed, and, in general, introduces changes without running into the kinds of long-standing vested interests so often found in more fixed forms of organization. It is most needed when external conditions are rapidly changing.

Finally, the matrix organization provides the kinds of structure that can include functional units and product/service units under the same hierarchical roof—thereby building on the strengths of each way of organizing without having to choose one way to the exclusion of an-

FIGURE 2–2
Organization Chart with Linking-Pin Model

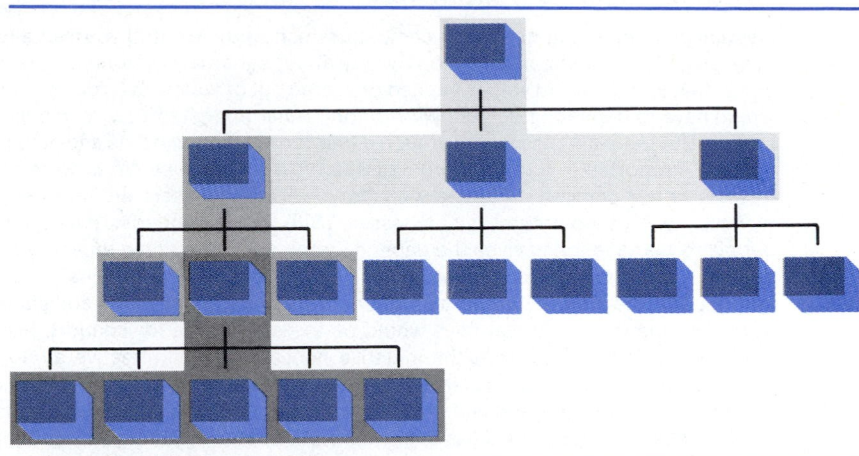

other, and striking a balance between functional needs and product/service needs. But as you can imagine, a matrix structure is not a panacea; it is a structural form that is not easy to operate successfully. People have to be interpersonally competent, good at dealing with conflict, and able to tolerate the ambiguity of a two-boss system.

FIGURE 2–3
Matrix Organization

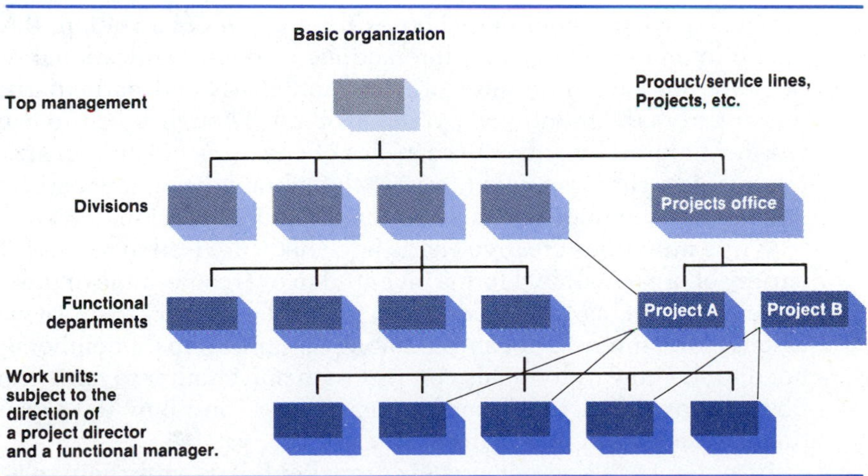

HOW ABOUT NO STRUCTURE AT ALL?

Imagine yourself being hired by a company which said, "Go find yourself a job someplace in the company and don't worry about a job description or a title or any of that stuff." Would you be excited or scared out of your wits? You certainly would have to depend upon your wits (among other things) to survive in such a system. But there are places where such a free-form structure exists and actually works. As reported in the August 1982 issue of *INC. Magazine,* W. L. Gore and Associates is a company where you create your own job; there are no existing niches, "no titles, no orders, and no bosses." Bill Gore, the founder, encourages people to manage themselves; he depends upon voluntary commitment. It has worked successfully for this manufacturer; would it work for everyone?

For some the lack of written rules, the reliance on emergent roles and status, as well as the lack of formal titles would be too ambiguous for comfort. Many would find it difficult to exert the initiative necessary to be effective at Gore. Others would find the opportunity to "try their wings" without the constraint of written job descriptions and within a system where everyone is invited to speak up and take initiative regardless of formal rank appealing and exciting. What would be best for you? Under what system, more of a traditional structure or more of a Gore structure, would you be most satisfied and likely to grow and develop? This is a question worth considering. Research shows that young graduates do better in the long run if they are neither underchallenged nor overchallenged in their first jobs. Gore would be too challenging for some; a bureaucratic organization not enough for others. The more you can know yourself and so pick an organization and position that will challenge you but not overburden you, the more likely you are to learn and develop.

THE NEED FOR A COMMON LANGUAGE OF RELATIONSHIPS

No matter what model one chooses for a given organization, the dynamic interconnections and interactions among organizational members are not shown on most organization charts and particularly are missing from the traditional pyramidal chart. Though a picture may be worth a thousand words, the snapshot of one aspect of an organization frozen into a chart can never capture the vibrant movement and groupings among members in an actual ongoing organization.

While numerous creative charts have been devised to represent the variety of organizational forms invented to overcome some of the coordination problems described above, it is still necessary to find a way to discuss the interrelationships among organizational members. We need to see how individuals connect with one another to form groups, how groups interact to form the organization, and how the organization interacts with its environment.

In order to talk about organizational subparts and their relationships, we will need a special language enabling us to see the parallels between the workings of groups and organizations of various sizes, purposes, and membership. We will want to talk about commonalities (and differences) among a group of 12 assemblers in a factory, an entire insurance company, a team of teachers working out a curriculum, or a group of seven tax adjusters in a government revenue office. Though we do not want to throw out the everyday words like *group*, *company*, and *organization*, we need a language that can incorporate all of these when necessary and not be limited to the images associated with particular words. For example, the word *company* may imply private ownership, profits, and either money-grubbing capitalists or efficient management, depending on one's orientation. Yet even government-owned companies, such as municipal transit systems or those operating under public regulation (for example, the phone companies), or a commune making candles as a means of support must still deal with the same kinds of organizational issues outlined above.

Therefore we shall utilize the language of social system analysis, which allows us to interchange the most general word *system* with *group* or *organization* when we wish to emphasize the similarities in diverse groupings. Furthermore, the word *system* emphasizes *interdependencies among subparts*, an advantage we will explain more fully below.

THE ELEMENTS AND BOUNDARIES OF A SYSTEM

A *system* is *any set of mutually interdependent elements*. Mutual interdependence means that a change in any one element causes some corresponding change in the others. In turn, those changes will have an impact back on the original changed element. An example of a simple physical system is the heating system in a house. It consists of a source of heat, a thermostat, and a means of delivering heat to various parts of the house. Drops in temperature below a preset level cause the thermostat to send a signal to start the furnace, which delivers heat until the temperature rises in the house; this registers on the thermostat, which then turns off the furnace until the temperature drops again, and so on in a repetitive (and these days, increasingly expensive!) cycle. The constant interplay among these elements, mu-

> *The organism always works as a whole. We have not a liver or a heart. We are liver and heart and brain and so on. We are not a summation of parts, but a coordination . . . all these different bits that go into the making of an organism.*
>
> F. S. Perls
> *Gestalt Therapy Verbatim*

tually adjusting to maintain a roughly constant temperature in the house, demonstrates a system achieving *equilibrium,* in which the system parts are constantly tending toward a particular steady state.

In order to achieve equilibrium, the system depends upon various *feedback* mechanisms. The thermostat cannot make the "decision" to turn the furnace on or off without "information" from the surrounding air (note Figure 2–4). Imagine, for example, if a member of the household hung a warm coat over the thermostat in a cold and drafty room. The feedback cycle would be disrupted; the thermostat would receive inaccurate information ("the room is very warm") and would signal the furnace to shut off irrespective of the actual temperature of the air (now blocked off by the coat) in the room. *The control mechanisms that maintain equilibrium in any system are dependent upon accurate feedback from various parts of the system and its surrounding environment.*

It is usually easy to identify the *boundaries* of a physical system in relation to the environment in which it exists. The heating system's three components are affected by external factors, such as weather, quality of insulation in the house, temperature desired by the inhabitants, and cost of fuel, yet can be easily identified as separate from these other factors. Nevertheless, the heating system can also be seen, depending on one's interests, as a subpart of other, larger systems that include these external factors: the lighting-heating-plumbing (support) system of the house, the house relative to other houses, a contributor to human pollution systems, and so forth. Thus how broadly or narrowly we bound a system is a strategic decision based on what will work for the problem(s) needing solution.

These issues (equilibrium, boundaries, and subsystems) are even more complex when looking at *human* social organizations.

FIGURE 2–4
Heating System in a Home

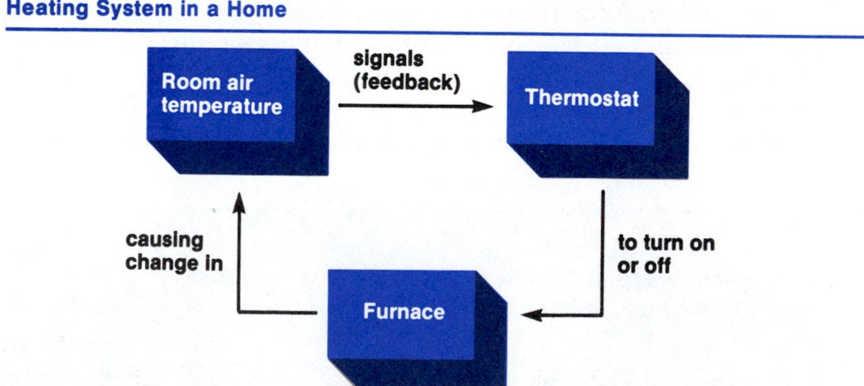

A social system can also be seen as consisting of a set of mutually interdependent elements which, when viewed together as an organized whole, can be given a boundary separating the interrelated elements from their environment. For social systems the elements are *behavior* and *attitudes.* An interrelated set of behaviors (interactions and activities) and attitudes (perceptions, feelings, and values) comprise a social system.[1] Since interactions, or exchanges between people, are assumed to be connected with all other elements (by definition) and are observable and countable, they can be used to help draw boundaries around social systems. *Boundaries can* thus *be* operationally *defined by the relative number of interactions among any set of people.* For particular analytical purposes *a social system is any number of people who have relatively more interactions with one another than with others.*

Implicit in this definition is the notion that virtually any system is a subsystem in some larger system(s), since the system is delimited by *relative* numbers of interactions. Just as the house heating system can for some purposes be seen as the total system (say, if checking out the accuracy of the thermostat) but for other purposes is a subsystem in a larger system, any group of people can be viewed from several perspectives. All the vice presidents in a bank are a social system in that they interact more with one another than with the tellers; but vice presidents and tellers together form another system, since all employees interact with one another more frequently than with, for example, the employees of other banks in the same city.

And like the physical system, which tends toward equilibrium, social systems tend to develop self-adjusting behaviors, which stabilize relationships, make the behavior of those in the system more predictable to members than it would be to others, and perpetuate the system's goals.

As you might guess, the larger the system in question, the more tenuous are the interdependencies. If we speak of the American people as a social system it may well be true that the way you relate to classmates is affected by and affects the way parents treat children 2,000 miles away, but the connections are not readily traceable and may be unprovable anyway. For our purposes in this book, we will focus on social systems with clearer boundaries and with more easily observable interconnections.

An example that is probably familiar to you is the class scheduling system in a university. Each decision involves and affects numerous people—students, professors, the registrar's office, advisors, building custodians, secretaries, and so on. A professor decides to limit enroll-

[1] These terms are our adaptations of the conceptual scheme of George Homans, elaborated more fully for small groups in Chapter 3.

ment in a course that normally draws large numbers of students; one result is that students find their options limited and are forced to select other courses, which increases demand for space in the other course, which may require a change of room to accommodate more students, which bumps another class out of a room, and so on and so on. What seemed to the professor like a simple change causes headaches for many and may well result in pressure on the professor from the dean to accept more students in the course! You can probably think of numerous examples in this same context where attempts to change something at one place in the system results in all kinds of reverberations, good and bad, in other parts of the system. What helps some people may generate problems for other people in the same system.

> *The entire ocean is affected by a pebble.*
>
> Blaise Pascal

FUNCTIONAL AND DYSFUNCTIONAL ASPECTS OF A SYSTEM

As you can see, a given action or decision can be functional for some members of a system and dysfunctional for others. The real challenge of managing an organization lies in finding ways to maximize the functional consequences of decisions, minimize dysfunctional effects, and work creatively with situations that inevitably (and often usefully) involve both.

Similarly, because most people are members of more than one social system, it is important to recognize the ways in which the same behavior may be functional in one system and not in another. For example, in most organizations those who reach executive ranks do so not only because of technical skill or knowledge but also because their behavior "fits," that is, makes other executives comfortable to be with them. Knowing how to behave at the country club, on the golf course, or in the executive dining room is often an important consideration in attaining promotion. Selecting executives by how they fit socially into the higher echelon's particular pastimes can in the short run be highly functional for maintaining harmony. Especially where the potentials for conflict and disagreement are great, as they always are at the top of a large organization, it is much more comfortable to limit fights to those who are "one of our kind," whatever that kind happens to be.

- *The executive should take all the steps he can to insure that he is personally compatible with superiors.*
- *The executive should take exceptional care to find subordinates who combine technical competence with reliability, dependability, and loyalty.*

Source: Robert McMurray, "Power and the Ambitious Executive," *Harvard Business Review*, November–December 1973.

Yet the consequences of using such criteria as part of the selection process can be, and have been, extremely dysfunctional for many groups shut out of the top ranks by color, sex, ethnicity, or background. There are surely many more talented leaders among blacks, women, Hispanics, Jews, and non-Ivy League graduates than appear, for example, among the top ranks of most banks and insurance companies. Not only is the organization ultimately deprived of vast pools of talent and different points of view, but each of the groups is disproportionately kept from advancing, obtaining higher salaries, and power.

Thus what is, at least for awhile, quite functional in one system can be dysfunctional in others because they have different objectives or purposes. And, as is hinted at in the executive example, *the same behavior can be both functional (promoting harmony) and dysfunctional (reducing talent and diversity available) within a system.* For example, one university sent all secretaries home one excruciatingly hot, humid summer afternoon out of a sense of concern for people's feelings and comfort. Unfortunately, this action, which presumably contributed to morale and overall employee relations, backfired in other parts of the system. The university administration sent the secretaries home but not the ground crews working out in the hot sun or the maintenance workers in the various shops across campus. These groups felt discriminated against and unfairly treated. Their morale and attitude toward management were hardly improved. What was functional for one part of the system was dysfunctional for another.

Any act can be analyzed in terms of how well it serves to sustain over time, in relation to surrounding environments, the system(s) in which it occurs. The value one places on whether an act is dysfunctional or not depends on one's point of view. A functional behavior in a system one disagrees with can be considered "bad" (for example, teaching more effective motivational techniques to recruiters for the Ku Klux Klan), and a dysfunctional act in a system one disagrees with can be considered "good" (for example, a new assembly worker refusing to go along with cheating in her work group, and reporting it to management).

THE SUPERVISOR. The supervisor provides an illustration of the difficulty of being functional in all systems. The supervisor is often called the person in the middle. This means that on the one hand management expects him/her to "get the work out from the workers" and push for higher production, while on the other hand the workers (some of whom the supervisor has probably worked with as an equal) expect him/her to be "one of the gang" and understand their problems in attaining, or reasons for not wanting to attain, higher production. Using the language of social systems, the supervisor has membership in two different systems with conflicting goals and finds this a difficult position. Often it can only be solved by withdrawal from the workers—in effect, by giving up membership in their system. Or the supervisor may become extremely permissive with and protective of the workers—in effect, conspiring with them to keep undesirable information from flowing upward. In this case, he/she has forfeited membership in the management system or has at least tried to. Management may not be quite so willing to lose the supervisor and may, in fact, put on even more pressure to increase production. Their efforts feed back on him/her and perpetuate the problem.

AMHERST HAS YOUNG COACH IN ITS ARENA

Last year Arena played hockey for Amherst. . . . This year Arena is the head coach at Amherst and his club is off to a six-game winning streak in Division 3. And, at 23, he's also the youngest hockey coach in the country.

Arena had to change his philosophy. He couldn't pal around with players he had been so friendly with for three seasons.

"I don't hang around with the players as I did in the past," said Arena. "You just can't do it. I'd have a hard time correcting players if I were too friendly with them.

"So, what we did was to agree on a feeling that we're all in this program together and we all want to do the job well. I really like the guys, but most of the time I just see them at practices and games. The players really understand, and we got off to a great start.

"So, instead of being friendly friendly, we're thinking more team friendly, and it has been working."

Source: Bob Monahan, *Boston Globe*, January 1, 1984. Reprinted courtesy of the *Boston Globe*.

But beside the two group systems, management and workers, and the larger system—management, supervisor, workers—the supervisor's personality system is also involved. The supervisor has some views of personal integrity, goals, and ambitions. One kind of person would be concerned about getting ahead in the organization and would respond to the pressure from management by transmitting the pressure to the workers. Leaving aside for a moment the possible negative consequences this pressure might have on his/her ability to secure cooperation from the workers, we can say that the action "pressure on workers" would be functional both for the management system, insofar as it maintains it, and for the supervisor's personality system. By conforming to management's desires, the supervisor can also satisfy his own.

However, the supervisor who values highly the friendship of those worked with may reject management's pressure completely and behave as if his/her position were no different from the people below. In this case the pressure, which is functional for management because it maintains management's beliefs about "the nature of workers" and "management's right to manage," is dysfunctional for the supervisor. To behave that way would not be consistent with his/her own values. Thus, the same act might be functional for one system, yet dysfunctional for another.

Here, however, as elsewhere, the situation may be complicated even more by *unintended and unanticipated consequences,* which can follow from any particular act. In the example above, management's pressure may be functional to the maintenance of what it believes about good managing but may also be in part a *cause* for the need for pressure. Pressure applied repeatedly may cause workers to feel mistrusted, therefore resentful, therefore less cooperative, therefore "requiring" more pressure. The pressure becomes part of a larger system of interdependent relationships, in which management behavior toward workers is both cause and effect of worker behavior and vice versa. Though the pressure may reinforce management solidarity by "confirming" its beliefs about workers, in the larger system presumably designed to make profits for the enterprise as a whole, the pressure may not be as useful as it appears to management (see Figure 2–5).

In short, there may be functional and dysfunctional effects of the same behavior; whether or not the behavior is functional depends on the system in which one judges the behavior. Consequences unintended by the person often occur because too few or wrong systems are considered when anticipating results. One of the manager's key tasks is to insure that behavior which is functional for particular subsystems, but dysfunctional for the organization as a whole, is somehow modified so that the total organization does not suffer. This is easier said than done, and much of this course will be aimed at giving you practice in making changes that do not backfire.

> *We create the city and the city creates us.*
>
> Winston Churchill

FIGURE 2–5
Example of Self-Reinforcing System with Functional and Dysfunctional Behavior

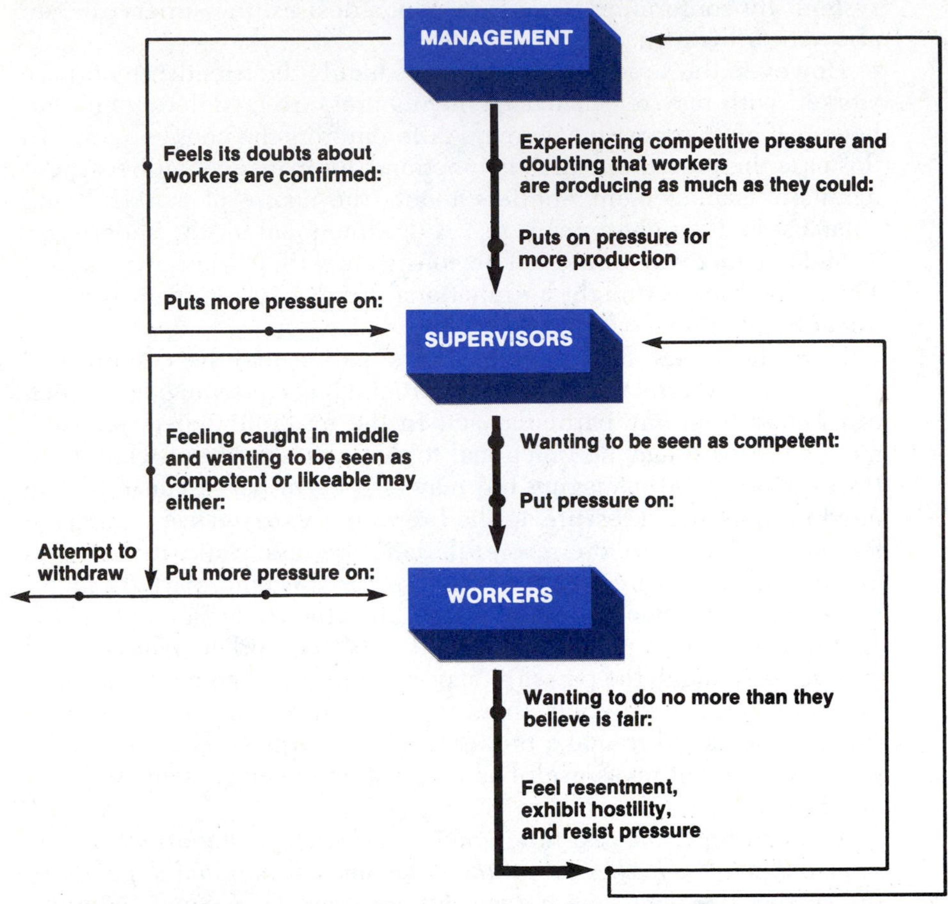

OPENNESS OF SYSTEMS AND TRANSFORMATION PROCESSES

Throughout this discussion of social systems we have only referred in passing to the environment of the system. In effect we have talked as if the various systems used as examples were sealed off from their environments, more or less *closed* to outside influences. That was necessary to simplify discussion of a complex subject, but now that you have completely mastered the systems concept(!), we can go on to complicate matters a bit.

Ultimately all organizations are open systems—that is, engaged in constant transactions with their environments, which usually consist of a number of other systems. An organization receives *inputs* from its surroundings in the form of finances, raw materials, people, ideas, equipment, and so forth. It then does something to the inputs in a *transformation process,* such as machining pieces, assembling parts, processing information, calculating numbers, building facilities, or treating patients. After these *internal operations* it sends some kind of finished *output* back into the environment, ranging from tangible products like automobiles and refrigerators, to changed people like recovered patients or educated students, to idea products like reports, analyses, or announcements. The outputs, in turn, become inputs to other systems (see Figure 2–6).

Since organizations are so interrelated with their environments, to remain in equilibrium they must make constant adjustments in the way they operate in order to take into account and cope with changes in inputs and demand for outputs. For example, when wool shortages send prices soaring in the carpet industry, substitutes such as Acrilan must be found and developed in order to not exceed the price range of most consumers. A marketing research firm might collect new data on attitudes from carefully defined groupings and even redefine its sampling group as income levels and population movements shift. A government agency responsible for promoting foreign trade might stay in touch with changes in congressional laws, presidential policy, and foreign government attitudes in order to provide useful guidelines. On the output side, organizational systems need to stay aware of changes in demand, whether for low-mileage cars, liberal arts graduates, or rented warehouse space. Drastic decreases in demand can easily threaten an organization's survival.

All of these environmental changes can and do affect the internal transformation process. *Any system will make adjustments in policies, rules, regulations, and other operating behavior in order to attempt to survive and maintain itself in relation to its environment.*

Though organizations often make mistakes, either in interpreting environmental changes or in attempting to compensate for them, the

FIGURE 2–6
An Open System

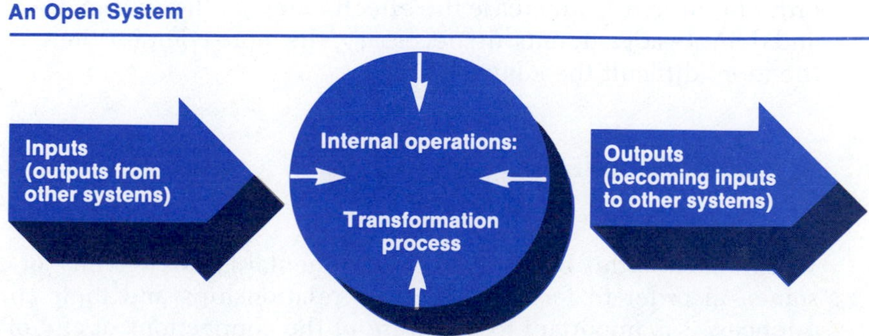

> *A hen is only an egg's way of making another egg.*
>
> Samuel Butler
> *Life and Habit*

organization will attempt to do what is functional for its survival. One classic example was the March of Dimes organization shifting to other childhood diseases when polio, its original reason for existing, was conquered. Similarly, open *social* systems in organizations are very much affected by the environment around them. The attitudes members bring with them from the wider culture, the particular people who are available to join the system, and economic conditions and their effects on member alternatives for employment are all factors that affect behavior within the system. For example, when (1) jobs are readily available, (2) young college graduates are the main groups of employees, and (3) there is widespread disillusionment with institutions in general, the ability of administrators to successfully give direct arbitrary orders without explanation is likely to be considerably diminished. Conversely, when jobs are scarce, employees tend to put up with many forms of treatment they would actively resist in better times.

Further, the demands and standards of whoever receives the social system's output will also affect internal operations. If the system is a total organization, the customers or clients will have considerable influence over the end products, and their response will often force internal adjustments fostering greater chances of survival. If the system is a subsystem of an organization, like a work team on the shop floor or a group of nursing administrators, its "clients" will be other parts of the organization, including management, and pressures for the appropriate quality and quantity of output will include everything from general disapproval and loss of privileges to reduced pay and threats of firing.

In general then, any system must make at least minimal alterations in its internal operations, based on feedback from its environment, in order to survive. To increase the effectiveness of the system, frequent and delicate adjustments are necessary; the more complex the system, the more difficult the adjustments.

THE INTERCONNECTEDNESS OF SUBSYSTEMS AND LEVELS

While much of this book treats environmental facts as givens, or constants, in order to focus on internal relationships and their consequences, it is important to be aware of the connections of any of the systems we look at (small groups, individual, interpersonal, leadership, and intergroup) to the systems and subsystems surrounding them. *The power in systems thinking lies in remembering to trace through what is connectable to what; to check to see if (1) a behavior that does not at first make sense can be seen as functional to* some *systems(s) and (2) a change in one aspect of a system will lead to other changes that are in the desired direction.* Many a manager's greatest difficulties occur when he/she starts to solve a problem in one subsystem without seeing its connections and roots in a wider setting. Managers who forget to use the observation powers of scientists to test if they are addressing the right problem are like Americans traveling in a foreign country who speak English to a non-English-speaking resident and, when not understood, repeat the same phrase over again, s-l-o-w-l-y and LOUDER.

For example, we have seen managers, excited by a management development tool like stress management, try to solve problems of unclear or overloaded job responsibilities by sending all their subordinates off to learn meditation and relaxation techniques. After the executives have learned to relax in the off-the-job training session (often conducted at a plush resort hotel), they return to work and soon find themselves more upset than ever, because higher-level management fears delegating authority, demands high performance, and has still not clarified what is expected of the subordinates. Not only do the original problems remain unsolved, but a potentially useful training tool for some situations gets a bad name.

It is important therefore to shift focus periodically from problem relationships within a subsystem to the links of that subsystem with others. For example, sometimes a fish is the last one to discover water, exactly because water is "always" there. The fish can spend its time worrying about its food and digestion as long as it is in the water and breathing automatically. Only when it is yanked out of the water does it notice its absence. With people, as with fish, it often takes a catastrophe (or an outside observer) to make visible the fundamental interconnections between the system and its environment. It is helpful, then, occasionally to take a detached view of puzzling behavior and ask *what function it is serving for whom,* rather than too quickly judge it harshly as irrelevant, wasteful, immoral, or foolish. Systems thinking encourages *understanding and acceptance of others' behavior,* at least as a first step in viewing organizations.

EQUILIBRIUM VERSUS CHANGE IN SYSTEMS

As indicated earlier, every system has a tendency to maintain a state of balance, or *equilibrium.* When the flow of raw materials into a manufacturing firm is balanced by the flow of products out of the company, that system can be described as maintaining a state of equilibrium. Should machinery break down, workers go on strike, poor planning occur, and so forth (all transformation processes), the system is thrown out of balance; management then devotes its attention to the reestablishment of equilibrium (repair the machinery, settle the strike, revise schedules). The process is similar to the way the human body works when it experiences stress from disease or accident. One or another subsystem (such as circulatory, autonomic, and respiratory) or a combination of them mobilizes to reestablish the balance of survival-related processes.

While the integrity of a system depends upon its ability to maintain a basic state of equilibrium, its *development* and long-run survival often depend upon the abilty to realign aspects of its subsystems and modify its transformation processes; this makes disequilibrium at times inevitable and desirable. If a system for too long resists fundamental environmental changes; it will eventually decay; if it is too responsive it may lose its ability to sustain its coherence and identity. A company, for example, can get into trouble if it does not adjust to consumer interests, but it can also lose money if it tries to cater to every whim. **In short, every system works toward an internal state of equilibrium by maintaining its existing balance of forces (the status quo); at the same time, every system struggles to respond to the pressures for change as the surrounding environment demands it.**

> *In any organization, large or small, there must be a certain clarity and orderliness; if things fall into disorder nothing can be accomplished. Yet orderliness, as such, is static and lifeless, so there must be plenty of elbow room and people for breaking through the established order.*
>
> *Therefore, any organization has to strive continuously for the orderliness of order and the disorderliness of creative* freedom. *And the specific danger inherent in large-scale organization is that its natural bias and tendency favor order at the expense of creative freedom.*
>
> E. Schumacher
> *Small is Beautiful*, p. 229.

While you need not accept the status quo just because you understand its functions better, we suggest that you maintain a healthy respect for the resistance of systems to change as well as for the ability of system members to reestablish equilibrium when new inputs are attempted by managers. If every system changed continually, life would be just too confusing and unpredictable to act. One confirmation of this emerged from Freud's work; it was the realization that even neurotic behavior causing great pain to an individual will be clung to as long as it is providing more satisfaction to the person than the uncertain rewards of giving it up. In systems terms, if one of the interdependent elements gives at least partial satisfaction to the personality system, it may persist despite its partially dysfunctional consequences for the total system. In fact, the individual system may be sustaining or integrating itself by the very tension that exists between the functional and dysfunctional consequences of various elements.

Larger social systems, like individual systems, can persist for long periods of time with some dysfunctional elements; remember the managing system that was partly causing worker resistance as well as trying to overcome it? Groups, as well as individuals, may persist in behavior that is less than fully functional for the maintenance of the total system if partial satisfaction of some needs is being derived from the behavior. Present partial satisfactions are often preferred over uncertain future ones because the costs involved in attaining new satisfactions may not seem worth the risk involved.

Understand the many functions of any behavior you observe before judging it as right or wrong, good or bad. And when you do act, watch for the connected reactions you didn't expect, so that you can adjust your plans.

KEY CONCEPTS FROM CHAPTER 2

1. Fundamental issues for any organization to accomplish its work:
   a. Goals.
   b. Decision making.
   c. Division of labor.
   d. Recruiting.
   e. Communications.
   f. Motivation.
   g. Control.
   h. Coordination.
   i. Environmental scanning and organizational mission.
   j. Rewards.
2. The form of an organization can vary widely.
   a. Departmentalization, by product, by customer or service, by function, by geographic area, or by some combination of each.
   b. The traditional pyramidal structure.
   c. The linking-pin model.
   d. The matrix model.
3. A system is any set of mutually interdependent elements. Every system is composed of subsystems and is itself a subsystem of a larger system. Changes in one part of a system are likely to lead to changes in other parts.
4. The boundaries of a social system are defined by the relative number of interactions among any set of people.

5. Any action can be functional for one (or more) system(s), but dysfunctional for another.
6. Any act can be both functional and dysfunctional for the same system.
7. All organizations are open systems, and:
   a. Take in inputs, transform them into outputs, and exchange those outputs with their environment for new inputs.
   b. Seek to maintain equilibrium by resisting changes in their environment.
   c. Adjust to environmental changes or decay.

SUGGESTED READINGS

Ashforth, B. E. "Climate Formation: Issues and Extensions." *Academy of Management Review,* October 1985, pp. 837–47.

Beckett, J. A. *Management Dynamics: The New Synthesis.* New York: McGraw-Hill, 1971.

Benedetto, R. F. *Matrix Management.* Dubuque, Iowa: Kendall/Hunt, 1985.

Bertalanffy, L. von. *General Systems Theory: Foundations, Development, Applications.* New York: George Braziller, 1968.

Churchman, C. West. *The Systems Approach.* New York: Dell Publishing, 1968.

Davis, S., and P. Lawrence. *Matrix.* Reading, Mass.: Addison-Wesley Publishing, 1977.

Drucker, P. F. *Technology, Management, and Society.* New York: Harper & Row, 1970.

Fink, S.; R. S. Jenks; and R. Willits. *Designing and Managing Organizations.* Homewood, Ill.: Richard D. Irwin, 1983.

Galbraith, J. *Organization Design.* Reading, Mass.: Addison-Wesley Publishing, 1977.

Hall, R. H. *Organizations, Structure and Process.* Englewood Cliffs, N.J.: Prentice-Hall, 1972.

Katz, D., and R. L. Kahn. *The Social Psychology of Organizations.* New York: John Wiley & Sons, 1966.

Keidel, R. *Game Plans: Sports Strategies for Business.* New York: E. P. Dutton, 1985.

Lawrence, P. R., and J. W. Lorsch. "Differentiation and Integration in Complex Organizations." *Administrative Science Quarterly* 12 (1967), p. 2.

________. *Organization and Environment.* Boston: Division of Research, Graduate School of Business, Harvard University, 1967.

Likert, R. *New Patterns of Management.* New York: McGraw-Hill, 1961.

Miles, R. E. *Theories of Management: Implications for Organizational Behavior and Development.* New York: McGraw-Hill, 1975.

Schein, E. H. *Organizational Psychology.* 2nd ed. Englewood Cliffs, N.J.: Prentice-Hall, 1970.

Seiler, J. A. *Systems Analysis in Organizational Behavior.* Homewood, Ill.: Richard D. Irwin and the Dorsey Press, 1967.

Weick, K. E. *The Social Psychology of Organizing.* Reading, Mass.: Addison-Wesley Publishing, 1979.

Woodward, J. *Industrial Organization: Theory and Practice.* New York: Oxford University Press, 1965.

3

THE WORK GROUP

Technology sets limits on what social interactions and emergent behavior are possible and causes interactions to occur. Even noise level affects the likelihood of social discourse.

One of the most important subsystems in any organization is the work group. Though many students and managers think of organizations as consisting of a collection of individuals, each doing a separate and distinct job, much of the world's work is actually done in some kind of group. Even when the individual employee is not formally assigned to a clearly defined group of people, much of his/her work will likely be carried out in conjunction with a particular set of other people, and feelings of "being part of a group" will emerge. Even executives who often like to think of themselves as rugged individualists seldom work alone or in isolation; they are members of a top management team, committees, task forces, study groups, and so forth, which directly affect their success or failure in the organization.

Yet it is not easy to work effectively in a group. Anyone who has ever had to coordinate activities and come to decisions in conjunction with other people will remember at times having felt something like, "If only I could get rid of the others, I could do this job much better myself and save a lot of time, too!" Working together, at least in most Western individualistic cultures, is not easily or automatically accomplished.

WHY GROUPS?

Why then is group work so recurrent? Perhaps the most important reason is that few jobs can be done alone. Only when it is clear that one person has much greater expertise than the combined efforts of others could yield, or when solo work will be good training, is work best done by lone individuals. It takes more than one person's energy, knowledge, skills, and time to get most complicated jobs done. That is increasingly the case as organizations become more technologically complex and require ever greater numbers of experts. Furthermore, when tasks are even the least bit complex, a division of labor makes it possible to use individual efforts more systematically and to take advantage of different talents and skills. A committee studying ways to cut fuel consumption in a company, for example, could have all members engage in the same research and discussion activities, but the complexities of the task make it desirable to divide up the work. One member might review technical literature, another survey the existing heating/cooling system, a third investigate what other companies have done, another check costs of conversion to alternate fuels, and so forth.

Yet in such a committee, as in other group activities where participants have different assignments from one another, activities must somehow be coordinated in order to not duplicate efforts, leave something undone, or work at cross purposes. Thus, a group must find a way to allocate work, coordinate activities, define and agree upon goals, and then gain the commitment of members to carry out the group's work in a manner consistent with its objectives.

TEAMWORK PAYS OFF AT PENNEY'S
As Committees Tackle Management Problems, Company Profits Soar

In a year when most retailers are taking their lumps, J. C. Penney Company shines. . . . If Penney executives are asked, they are likely to credit the company's recent success to a new management style keyed to group decision making and implementation. . . . It [the team approach] allows dissenting views to be ironed out before final plans are made. That, in turn, lets the company implement plans far more smoothly than if it were handing down edicts.

Source: *Business Week,* April 12, 1982, pp. 107–8.

Groups also exist for another, more personal, set of reasons. Even where a task does not call for coordinated effort, people working near one another often form relationships to fill social needs for conversation, companionship, or friendship. Human beings are social animals and seem to need human association as much as they need food and drink. So groups often form for reasons above and beyond needs for task coordination. Indeed, for many members of work groups individual needs for social relationship may be even more powerful in affecting behavior than organizational objectives.

Long before getting jobs, everyone has developed considerable experience with groups; they are the primary units of all social systems. Most people are born into a group—the family—and spend the greater part of their lives living, working, and playing in a wide variety of groups. When young, they belong to gangs or clubs. As they grow up, they tend to move into social settings where group belonging gives support and provides avenues to do things they could not do by themselves. Thus, it is not surprising that, in the work world, people continue to find groups to be a principal vehicle for carrying out tasks, not solely to seek superior organization goals through collective effort, but to meet individual needs as well.

What is more surprising is how difficult it is for groups in organizations to be effective and satisfying to their members. Occasionally this is caused by groups being utilized to do what could better be executed by one individual, as implied in the old joke: "A camel is a horse designed by a committee." More often, however, groups are just not run effectively; members do not know how to help the group take fullest advantage of its potential. We will address this issue in depth in Chapter 6 because we believe that the ability to help make a group function effectively can be learned and is worth learning. Thus we aim to help you improve both your *understanding* of how task groups work and your *skills* at getting what you want from the work groups of which you become a member.

Though many of the concepts we will introduce apply equally well to nonorganizational groups, we will focus on those that are task oriented, because at least half of an adult's waking life is spent at work and most education does not give emphasis to this important area of concern. Nonwork applications of what is learned can be a personal bonus for mastering the course materials.

Since you have probably had some experience in groups, we can call upon your past experiences to bring to life the several concepts we need to build on. For example, you probably remember groups in which you played a dominant part and others in which you were more on the sidelines, times when you were part of the "in group" and times when you were on the "outs." Perhaps you can think about some of the groups of which you currently are or have recently been a member. How are they organized? What is your place in them? Who controls them? Is there equality among members or a "pecking order"? These are the kinds of questions we will be addressing throughout the next few chapters.

The answers to these questions, among others, will help to give you a better understanding of how groups function and what determines the effectiveness of a group in meeting its goals. As we go along, we encourage you to use your own immediate and past experiences to validate the theories and concepts that will be introduced. Most of these concepts will also be directly applicable to the classroom setting and will help you to understand various aspects of your own experiences as the course unfolds. You should come out with a better sense of the consequences of your own membership in various groups, how your sense of individuality is affected, and how you can strike a balance among (1) your needs, (2) those of other individual members, and (3) the needs of the group as an entity.

HOW DO YOU KNOW WHEN A GROUP IS?

What exactly do we mean by a "group"? Is it any collection of individuals, like strangers at a bus stop, or is it something more? As explained in Chapter 2, any social system is defined by the relative number of interactions among its components. Though the boundary can be drawn anywhere, depending on one's purpose, work groups often are clearly identifiable to others and to their own members. From now on we will use the word *group* to mean small face-to-face groups, consisting of more than 2 people and usually no more than 12 or 15. Such a group has an existence over an extended period of time, tends to see itself as separate and distinguishable from others around it, and has members who are mutually aware of their membership. As noted in the beginning of this chapter, some organizational groups are not formally defined as such but function nevertheless as distinguishable units.

If a group appears to its members as a useful vehicle for meeting individual needs, then keeping relationships going among members of any group becomes an end in itself. This is why the size of the group is an important factor. If a group becomes too large, it is difficult for the members to maintain direct personal relations, and there is an increasing chance of fragmentation into subgroups.

In summary then, we can determine the existence of a group by noting its *size*, its *degree of differentiation from other groups*, the *existence of personal relations that have some duration, identification of the members with the group*, and often some *common goals*.

Thus a small collection of people waiting at a bus stop would not be a group by the definition we use in this book. While every individual presumably has the same goal, namely to catch a bus, it is not a common goal in the sense of being a goal that will result from joint effort. While a few individuals might be friends, most would be strangers or, at best, "nodding acquaintances" from the same neighborhood. Furthermore, individually they would not think of themselves as an identifiable group.

By defining groups as stated above we include the following types:

1. Groups that are permanent parts of an ongoing organization, like departments or work teams.
2. Temporary task groups, like a committee or special problem-solving group whose life is compressed into a defined span of time. (Note the differences from ongoing groups in the box on page 71.)
3. Groups that are voluntarily formed purely for friendship or other social needs as noted earlier; these will not be our focus but must

be considered since they exist within and across types (1) and (2) above and directly influence these formal system groups.

You might like to note the characteristics of any groups of which you are a member and to share these with other students both within and outside of the groups in question. This process should give you a clearer sense of the existence of each group. It might also provide you with some perspective on the degree to which your memberships in a number of different groups at one time influence the pattern of your own life.

THE NEED FOR SOME CONCEPTS

Students have often asked us why it is necessary to have a fancy conceptual scheme for analyzing groups. Isn't common sense enough? Unfortunately, common sense can carry you just so far—and usually not far enough. Social science has given us some valuable organizing principles that fortunately help to sort out what otherwise might be an undifferentiated mass. Everything that one sees can appear equally important—and there are many things one is not likely to notice without some kind of guideposts. The ultimate object of analysis is action: doing something to solve problems or to sustain good results. But action is too risky without good analysis of *why* things are as they are. We all need ways of figuring out just what factors have led to the particular behaviors we find in groups of which we're a part or which we somehow have to manage.

Though in actuality no social system sits while you hold different parts constant, for analytical purposes we will take the liberty of talking as if various components of a work group can be separately examined. Only then can you begin to improve your ability to understand and affect the behavior of the groups of which you are a member.

We will start by introducing a basic social system conceptual scheme, which will help you to organize the pieces and put together the puzzle that explains why a group has developed in its particular way and what might be done to alter its development.

The scheme we have chosen identifies four essential factors: (1) everything that people and the organization bring to a group, (2) what the job itself requires, (3) what behavior and feelings result from (1) and (2), and (4) the consequences of what is actually happening. The scheme is a systematic way of identifying what is going on, why it is going on, and what difference it makes.

DIFFERENCES BETWEEN ONGOING WORK GROUPS AND TEMPORARY GROUPS

Ongoing Groups	*Temporary Groups*
Conduct most organization work that is predictable, ongoing, regular.	Used for unusual projects or problems when diversity of opinion, talent, or expertise needed. Task forces, committees, project teams.
Job surrounded with a sense of permanence; a presumption that, with satisfactory performance and the absence of unforeseen catastrophe, the group will continue indefinitely.	Job is temporary, to be worked on until done; then members are expected to disperse to some other task(s) with some other group(s).
Existence of a common identity (as a member of this department or work group) and the sense of a common purpose. Can result in too little diversity of opinion and/or in forced conformity.	Member primary loyalty is elsewhere to ongoing "home" group; often act as "representatives," not independent problem solvers. Difficult to achieve common purpose. Can result in maneuvering for advantage, defensiveness about home group, hidden agendas to settle old scores. Members less committed to temporary group, may withhold their time, energy, expertise.
History of working together often results in considerable knowledge about one another and patterned role relationships; makes working together comfortable. Danger of freezing others into existing behavior roles.	Sense of working with "strangers"; need to develop skills of building effective relationships rapidly and being effective in dealing with emergent process problems promptly.
A recognized boss: focal point for resolving issues and making decisions when all else fails. Also a recognized source of organizational rewards.	Likely to be self-governing or led by a chairperson with less clearly defined authority and less power; rewards for effort unclear, while home-group work piles up; individual members may see opportunity of contact with people from other parts of the organization (sometimes in higher positions) as way to make good impression. Can lead to "grandstanding": focus on audience, not problems.

A CLOSER LOOK AT SOCIAL SYSTEM CONCEPTS

In Chapter 2 you were introduced to the concept of a social system consisting of two mutually interdependent elements: *behavior* and *attitudes.*[1] We will now look at groups in depth, expanding on the concepts to heighten their analytical usefulness.

Behavior

The most directly observable aspect of a social system is the *behavior* of its members, that is, their *interactions* and *activities. Interactions—exchanges of words or objects among two or more members—* are particularly crucial types of behavior, since their frequency helps determine system boundaries, friendships, and other feelings. Other types of behavior can be categorized as *activities—that which members do while they are in the group except for their interactions with other people*—such as operating a machine, writing on paper, and issuing a license. In addition to these kinds of work-related activities, there are likely to be a variety of nonwork activities such as drinking coffee, listening to music, or tapping a pipe on the table.

Attitudes

Attitudes constitute the other category used for sorting out the parts of a social system. These can include neutral *perceptions* ("Whenever I help Charley, he smiles."), *feelings* ("I like my job."), or *values* ("Nothing is more important than being honest in my dealings with the people I work with."). When all three are combined, the result is reflected in the unique way in which each individual perceives a given situation or reacts to others. We will look at such issues in depth in Chapters 8 and 10 when we discuss the importance of the self-concept and the complexities for interpersonal communication. For now, keep in mind that these are important elements of any social system.

Norms

Perhaps the most important type of attitudes is that which members of any group inevitably develop about how members in good standing *ought* to behave in that group. These attitudes we call *norms;* they are the cement that holds a group together, because they tell members

[1] The balance of this chapter is our adaptation of the work of George C. Homans in *The Human Group* (New York: Harcourt Brace Jovanovich, 1950) and in *Social Behavior: Its Elementary Forms* (New York: Harcourt Brace Jovanovich, 1961).

exactly what behavior is believed desirable to foster the group's goals and maintain its existence. *Norms are unwritten rules, shared beliefs of most group members about what behavior is appropriate and attainable to be a member in good standing.* Behind every norm is the implicit statement: "Follow this norm because if you don't the group will be harmed somehow." For example, some common norms in student groups are: "Don't act as if you're trying to impress the person with authority" (as in, "Don't brownnose the teacher."), "Don't act like a big deal," "Participate at least a little, but don't dominate the conversation," "Try not to say anything that will hurt other members' feelings." Can you see what members of a student group might perceive as the dangers if these norms were not followed? Here are a few norms of an executive group at the head office of a national company: "Executives do not bring their lunches," "Eat or take coffee only with your own group, unless you have specific business with others," "Always wear your suit jacket when going in or out of the building, no matter how hot it is," "Carry only a thin zipper briefcase, not the three- or five-inch one the company gives out."

Norms such as these are not always explicit; often they are understood implicitly (or assumed to be understood). Frequently the only way a norm is observable is by inadvertently breaking it and seeing others' reactions. If a norm has been broken, members will usually react in some kind of negative way—with a dirty look, a sarcastic comment, a "joke" that has a cutting edge, even a physical punishment such as a "friendly" punch on the arm, or some other negative response. Those who consistently violate norms and cannot be pushed into going along will usually be given the worst punishment of all: They will be ignored and considered inferior. Norms are not written on all members' foreheads; they can only be inferred from watching actual behavior since they are not the behavior itself but the *beliefs* in most members' minds about what behavior should be.[2] While behavior common to all members of a group usually indicates existence of a norm, it may also just be coincidental or customary. Some checking out of what members believe, or observing whether a nonconformer is punished, may be necessary to establish a norm's existence.

Since norms are not universal—in some executive groups, for example, it may be considered phony *not* to try to impress the boss or weak *not* to dominate conversations—each group develops its own norms, which give the group its particular character. And very often groups feel not only that their norms are useful ways of guiding members' behavior but are inevitable, correct, and better than any possible

[2] Individual ideas about how members ought to behave, which are not widely held by the group, are not called norms; rather they are individual beliefs.

alternatives. Thus violation of the norms by current members or even members of other groups is judged quite harshly even though an outside observer might be puzzled at the intensity of the group members' beliefs in its own ways.

> *The longer I was in the world of managers, the more I missed my union buddies, their ribald spirit, our singing together, their sensuousness, their sexuality. By comparison, managers were a deadhead lot who had traded humor and sensuality for the role-playing Kabuki world of the corporate headquarters. I have met more people having fun as clowns on one plant floor than in all of the many corporate headquarters I have gone in and out of.*
>
> [From an interview of a manager, Bob Schrank]
> Bob Sales
> *Boston Globe*

Have you ever entered a new group and found, quite accidentally, that you have violated members' notions of "proper" behavior? Here is an example of a new employee discovering a powerful norm:

> A young business student got a summer job working at a bank as a credit trainee. He arrived on a hot Monday morning in a suit and tie and reported for work on the 16th floor. As the air conditioning had been off during the weekend, the open office where all trainees sat was quite warm. Noticing that others had removed their jackets and hung them over the backs of their chairs, the new employee did the same. At 10 A.M., everyone got up for coffee break at a wagon brought to the floor. Afterward, the eager newcomer returned to his desk and resumed studying the material he had been given. Soon his neighbor was motioning to him to put on his jacket. "Thanks, but I'm comfortable this way," he replied. A few minutes later the neighbor cleared his throat and said in a whisper, "It's time to put on your jacket." Enjoying being in his shirtsleeves, the newcomer smiled but continued as he was. A few minutes later the neighbor, now looking irritated, said, "Really, we all put our jackets on now; you should too!" Genuinely bewildered at this apparently irrational ignoring of the temperature but not wanting to create problems with strangers, the puzzled student put on his jacket and resisted no more. But his initial enthusiasm for banking diminished. It wasn't until many years later that he realized that putting on jackets after 10 A.M. was probably a reflection of public opening hours at the bank and that the trainees did what the loan officers were doing down on the first floor.

Norms can be useful in helping facilitate the group's work or they can hinder it. And they can be highly conscious and explicit or unconscious and automatic. Occasionally, norms can even take on the quality of *magic*, as in the bank example. That is, behavior that may once have been productive continues to be enforced even when there is no longer any use for it (except to bind members together). But whatever their degree of helpfulness and consciousness, when norms are agreed to by most members and strongly held they have a powerful impact on behavior.

> *At the* New York Times *the cub reporters sit in the last row of desks . . . ; as they prove themselves they move up row by row. Beginning reporters who unknowingly sit at a vacant desk a row or two up from the back are politely but firmly told where they belong.*
>
> Kim Foltz
> *Harper's*, July 1974

Norms tend to develop around particular subjects of interest to group members. Among other areas, most groups have norms about how much effort and output is expected of members, how to dress (as at the bank described above), the use and meaning of time, the degree to which expressions of feeling are allowed, how to handle conflict, and so forth. The longer groups work together, the more likely they are to develop elaborate sets of norms to guide behavior. One of the difficulties faced by temporary groups is the need to establish shared norms among members who may have quite different ideas about appropriate behavior, based on the norms of their various home groups. Can you generate a list of norms from any group(s) of which you are a member? Which norms are task-related? Which serve personal interests of members? Which are counterproductive? Answering these questions can give you valuable insights into the group and your behavior in it. It can also be the first step in changing norms that are not useful or desirable.

Sources of Norms

Where do these powerful guidelines for behavior come from? Some are derived from the general culture of the country or region in which the group exists. Most Americans, for example, are raised with great consciousness about the value of time, and a high percentage of adults wear watches. Thus, these general attitudes about time often carry over into organizational groups, which emphasize being on time, getting right to work, and so on. In many Asian and Latin American cultures, time is not seen as a continuous line that is running out, and its value is different, so that being on time for meetings is less likely to emerge as a group norm.

Some norms originate in the culture of the particular organization (that is, in the general practices and attitudes of the wider organization) and then are carried into particular groups. For example, IBM for years stressed that male executive employees should wear white shirts and dark suits. There was general acceptance by IBM employees that this mode of dress was proper, so that in most IBM executive groups formal dress readily became the norm. Even at offsite training programs held in resort hotels, IBM salesmen were likely to be wearing dark suits and white shirts even when groups from other companies using the facilities dressed in casual clothes.

The new president of a conservative company that did not especially welcome him used his understanding of norms to test how well he was doing in winning other executives over to his side. Noting that all executives wore a tie and jacket in the office, he began to take off his jacket as soon as he got to the office and would walk around all day in shirtsleeves. By observing which executives started to take off their jackets at work, he had a quick and visible indicator of "converts" and could tell at a glance whether he was making progress in gaining allies.

Other norms may be carried into a group by members with a common background and common interests—ethnic, educational, or religious. For example, work groups with a majority of southern Europeans are likely to expect members to be readily expressive of feelings, while a group of northern Europeans may expect restraint and understatement from members. Similarly, groups composed of minority members or women are more likely to value expressiveness than groups of white males, reflecting the socialization of the wider society. Student groups in a classroom are likely to reflect the norms of the school itself. A large-city business school may encourage one to be aggressive and competitive, while a small rural liberal arts college may be more likely to encourage one to be polite and avoid conflict.

Finally, some norms arise from critical incidents or events in a group's life, which cause the group to learn "the way things ought to be." Perhaps an angry fight between two members over the correctness of a work procedure led to a reprimand from a supervisor for fighting—and from that experience the group developed a strong norm that insists "no one should air his troubles or disagree with a fellow member in front of anyone from management." Sometimes norms come from overreactions or overgeneralizations from one or two experiences—and then remain untested because "everyone knows" that dire consequences will follow if the norm is violated.

Values

Another important type of attitudes is *values.* While *norms are shared ideas of "correct" behavior in the group, values are more fundamental notions of ideal behavior, usually unattainable but to be striven for.* Values are seldom explicit but very much shape how members interpret events and form expectations about behavior.

For example, in some groups members believe that it is "right" that individuals should always put group needs ahead of their own personal interests. Individuals are expected to subordinate their desires for the betterment of the total group. An extreme version of this value is found in the traditional families in India, where even marriage and career choice are made by elders with overall family benefit in mind. The extreme opposite of such values might be found in a contemporary American family where each child is taught from an early age to listen to his/her conscience and make choices accordingly.

In a work setting, such group values as work before pleasure, friendship and loyalty above all, the customer is always right, or everyone should look out for his own interests strongly determine how members behave, even though they are not always attainable.

Quite often, however, conflicting values may be held by various members of a group or even by one member, and this can cause serious tension at crucial times. For example, telling the truth is a commonly held value but so is avoiding hurting others. These two values are not always compatible. In groups there are often value differences underlying questions of how important it is to talk through strong disagreements: "majority rules" (so outvoted members should accept defeat gracefully) versus "everyone gets his day in court" (so dissatisfied members must somehow be placated).

In general, it is important to look and listen for underlying values even though groups do not always make their values explicit.

THE BASIC SOCIAL SYSTEM CONCEPTUAL SCHEME

With a more developed picture of the elements of any social system, we are now ready to present the basic conceptual scheme of this book. The material that follows is designed to help you sort out the *causes* of behavior from the *symptoms* you can observe. It is hard enough to observe accurately what is going on since people do not hold still for leisurely study, do not always say why they are behaving as they are (or do not know), or change their behavior when an outsider is watching. But even seeing clearly may not explain why a group is acting as it is—holding down production, sabotaging quality, voluntarily working extra hours without complaint, protecting one another, fighting about everything—in short, behaving in ways that are functional and should be preserved or dysfunctional and should be changed. The difficulty is in being able to analyze all the factors that together account for or cause the behavior. Since most behavior is caused by many interwoven forces, it is important to identify more than just one or two. This will ultimately allow for sensible action.

REQUIRED VERSUS EMERGENT BEHAVIOR

A helpful conceptual distinction in tracing the source of behavior and attitudes is to separate out that part of a group's behavior and attitudes which is *required* or *given* by the larger system (organization) of which it is a part and that which emerges from the interactions of the group (see Figure 3–1). *The required system is what the organization requires of group members as part of their jobs.* The required component (which we shall call the *required system*) usually centers on the tasks assigned to the group: assemble so many parts per hour, sell so many machines per month, visit so many welfare clients per week, and so forth. Most organizations, however, also require certain other behavior and attitudes, which are assumed to relate to effective conduct of the task. Usually, there are (1) some *required activities* like the task-related ones above, (2) some *required interactions:* "Get the forms from Clerk A, inquire if there are any more, and after checking them over give Agent C an assignment," and (3) some *required attitudes* such as "Don't be insolent when receiving instructions," or "Be loyal to our products," or "Don't make fun of the clients." These requirements are developed by the organization and are frequently called the "formal system." They are usually contained in job descriptions and organizational rulebooks and in directions from superiors, though sometimes they are just seen as "part of the job" and are not spelled out. Written procedures, regulations, and rules—about what to do, with whom to talk, and how to feel—are a formal framework intended to guide the behavior of employees.

FIGURE 3–1
Separating the Required from the Emergent System

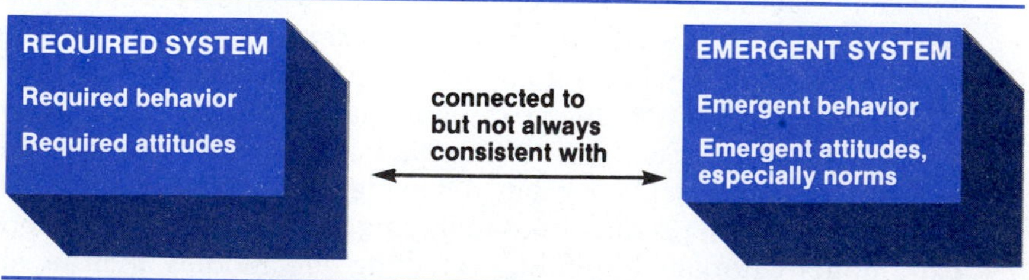

SUPERVISORY REQUIREMENTS AND STYLE

Sometimes job requirements are not written down but are conveyed by the supervisor or other supervisors as demands or rules about what is supposed to happen. The supervisor's style, based on assumptions about how to lead or manage, will create required activities, interactions, and attitudes. A boss, for example, who thinks that subordinates will try to get away with murder will require many written reports, frequent meetings to check up on progress, considerable deference, and pledges of loyalty. While none of these requirements may be written down, they are nevertheless part of the required system for members of that task group.

Furthermore, a boss, as a member of management, tends to behave in keeping with the norms of his/her own reference group (other managers at the same level). These norms may then be translated into job requirements for his/her subordinates. One fairly high executive in a pharmaceutical company started out allowing his managers the freedom to govern their own working hours (within reason). Later, when he discovered that this practice was not consistent with what his peers did (even though there was no company rule about managerial hours), he made it a formal requirement that his managers all come to work at 7:30 A.M. Interestingly enough, the source of this 7:30 custom was the founder of the company, who happened to enjoy starting work early!

For analytical purposes we will treat the group's supervisor, creating and passing on requirements for job performance to group members, as outside of the group, even though, from some points of view, the boss could be considered a group member.

The boss's style in passing on demands also has an impact on the group's responses and must be taken into account. Although leadership style and its impact on performance will be examined in greater detail in Chapters 11 and 12, for now it is sufficient to call attention to possible variations in the major elements of style—how controlling, task-oriented, person-concerned, explicit, and cautious the boss is—and to suggest that you include a look at it in tracing behavior that emerges from the group.

EMERGENT BEHAVIOR

Inevitably, because people are social beings with needs greater and more complex than those of machines, a variety of behavior and attitudes will begin to *emerge* and over time take on relatively stable patterns. Making frequent appointments through a secretary leads to small talk and slowly to some kind of relationship in which a greater amount of information, ideas, and feelings are exchanged than a few informational questions about the boss's availability. The worker at the opposite bench with whom coordination is necessary ventures opinions and complaints, suggests having a coffee break together, slowly becomes a friend, and perhaps visits you when you're sick. In these kinds of ways a social system elaborates itself, leading to *emergent* and lasting behavior and attitudes that go way beyond what was originally required just to do the job. Some of what emerges will be elaboration on how to do the task, how much to produce, and so on, while the remainder will be related to purely social relationships, such as who has coffee with whom and who likes whom. *In both cases, it is this emergent (informal) system which gives a group its particular identity,* its view of who should do what, who should have influence, and how close members should feel.

Even the actual leadership of a group may emerge as different than the designated leader. It isn't always the formally named supervisor of a group who has the most influence over decisions and group activities; members with special expertise or skill may well become the most respected or influential persons. The member(s) who emerge with leadership influence may support or oppose, supplement or undermine, the formal supervisor. Group members may or may not be explicit about who provides the real leadership of the group, but they will usually recognize the informal leader(s) in some way—by being extra respectful, deferring slightly, or just by addressing questions or requests for help to them.

It is not surprising that the emergent system often influences the performance of a group as much as or more than the required system. It is important to understand the significance and potency of emergent systems since they can outweigh even formal orders issued from above. Emergent social systems acquire their own life, which is connected to but goes beyond what is required by the formal organization.

It is important to note that a well-developed emergent system with strong norms for behavior can feel to any member as if the group-approved behavior is "required" of him/her. For example, if there is a strongly enforced emergent norm that "each member must produce at least 80 parts per hour," this may feel like a "requirement" to the new group member, even though management may not formally require any particular hourly output. For our purposes behavior "demanded" by a group of its members is still called *emergent* provided that it is a result of group ideas rather than forced organizational requirements imposed from outside the group.

When examining a required system and trying to predict likely emergent behavior, some of the questions you might ask are:

1. What tasks are required? What is it people have to do when they are working? How are they likely to feel about the tasks?

2. Who is required to interact with whom, and what relationships are likely to result?
3. What attitudes are required, and are these attitudes likely to cause resentment or enthusiasm?

BACKGROUND FACTORS

But how can we connect what emerges to what is required? Don't personalities and personal preferences make more difference than the requirements of the job? That indeed is a question worth exploring.

Personal Systems

People do bring something of their history with them when they enter a group. The values and feelings they have about what kind of behavior is proper, desirable, or possible are carried with them and influence how they react to what happens in the group, as well as whether or not they will choose to accept what happens. While we will explore in the chapters on individual behavior more about how individuals influence, and are influenced by, the world around them, at this stage of analysis we take personality characteristics as *givens* in each group. That is, the person arrives at the group with some set of attitudes which, when mixed with those of others, help create whatever emerges.

For our purposes, the individual in the group is also the "carrier" of the wider culture insofar as he/she brings along norms, values, and perceptions that are introduced into the group through the members. For example, there are widespread beliefs in the United States about the desirability of democratic procedures, especially among peers. If several members of a student study group carry these widely held beliefs, someone is likely to suggest that the group work without a formal leader or make decisions only by informal consensus. Since many members share such beliefs, it is easy for the attitude from the wider culture to be accepted and adopted as a norm in the study group. What individuals have learned from the broader culture and their experiences in it becomes a (background) factor in determining the social system that will emerge in the group.

As suggested earlier, of special significance are the values, feelings, and attitudes of formally designated leaders, as these aspects of personality determine their leadership style. Remember that the style of a leader can have important consequences for what emerges.

The set of attitudes a person brings to the group, the way the person sees him/herself and sees what is proper behavior, we call the "personal system." The sum of all the individual members' personal systems, plus that of any supervisor or designated leader, is an impor-

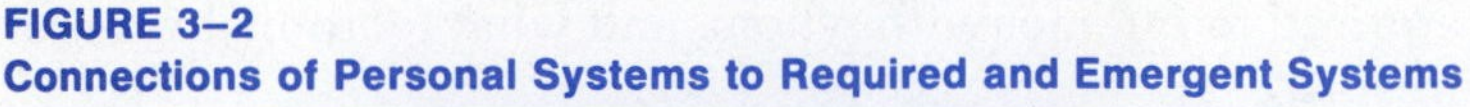
FIGURE 3–2
Connections of Personal Systems to Required and Emergent Systems

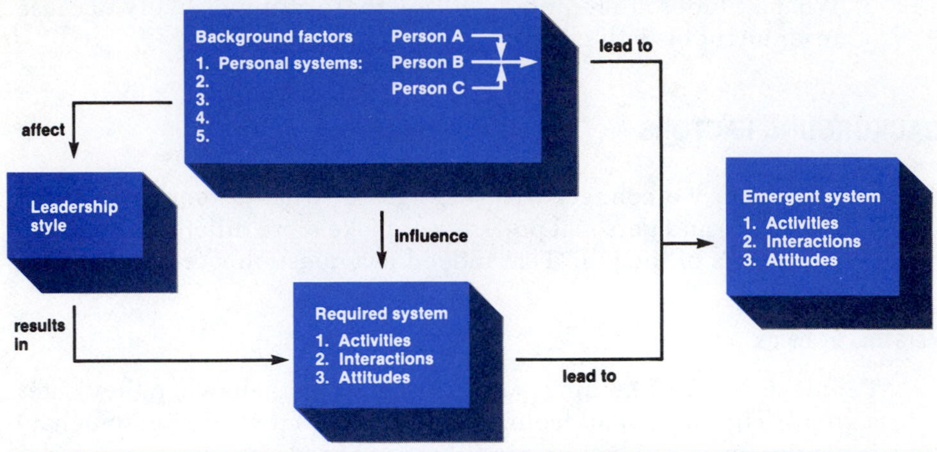

tant background factor needed to understand what emerges in a group. All these personal systems combine with the job requirements to affect the emergent system (see Figure 3–2).

Nevertheless, job requirements and/or the group's emergent system often can be so powerful and overwhelming that even people with quite different personal systems will behave similarly when placed in a job. There is a tendency in organizations to overcredit individual personality defects for problems and to underestimate the impact of job requirements and the surrounding situation.

When trying to trace the source of a group's particular emergent system, some questions you might ask about the personal systems of members are:

1. How do individual members see themselves? How do these views combine to help explain the choices the group has made about how to make decisions, produce, relate to one another, and so forth?
2. Why have members accepted or rejected the group's norms? What makes individual members receptive or resistant to the group's accepted way of doing things?
3. Why do some members respond differently to the same set of requirements and leadership style?
4. Do the backgrounds of various members help explain why they initiated key or prominent events?
5. What is the fit between the required system and the members' personal systems? Are the requirements likely to be accepted as proper by the people who happen to be group members?

External Status

Another aspect of people (outside of their personalities), which tends to be overlooked as an influence on what emerges in a group, is the person's position or status in other settings—home, community, social groups, organizations. People's external (to the group) status influences how they see themselves and how others in the group see them.

For example, if a student task group is formed in a course and one member is president of student government and widely respected on campus, other members are likely to turn to that person for leadership. In turn, the person is likely to begin to take on leadership functions even if he/she is not the most suited to be leader for the given task. Similarly, in an organizational task force or committee the member who has the highest position or title in the organization is likely to become chairperson of the group. While this does not always happen, for reasons you might like to think about, position outside a group initially tends to affect position within it. In general, **the higher a person's status outside a group, the higher a position or rank he/she will be accorded in a new group, at least at the beginning (Homans, 1950).** Does this fit with your experience?

In tracing the sources of the emergent system, you might ask:

1. How does a member's external status relate to his/her position within the group at different times? (The next chapter will look in greater detail at member positions in the group.)
2. Is a valuable contributor being ignored because of low external status relative to other members?
3. Are some people getting more influence than their actual contribution merits because of high external status?

Organizational Culture

Culture is a catchall word summarizing the way things are generally done, the prevailing atmosphere or climate, general notions (sometimes explicit but often just understood and taken for granted) about how members of the organization are supposed to act and feel, what is rewarded, and so on. The term *organization culture* here refers to the culture of the wider organization (system) of which the group (subsystem) being analyzed is a part. One way to think of organizational culture is in terms of the social context or environment in which the work group is located. Another way of thinking about organizational culture is that just as small groups develop norms for behavior, larger organizations tend to develop general norms that apply to every member, regardless of position (Steele & Jenks, 1977).

For example, in one insurance company in New England, many employees have noted that the norms within the company included such things as: "Don't make waves," "Avoid conflicts by joking or shutting up," "Be informal and on a first-name basis with everyone," "Work long hours and don't be a clock watcher." Whether an organization's climate is friendly or hostile, whether organization members in general are trusted and assumed to be motivated or suspected and considered irresponsible, whether disagreements are buried or encouraged, whether individuality is suppressed or fostered, and so forth, all make a difference to what people bring to the group. The organization's usual ways of handling such issues affect the beliefs and feelings with which members will approach a group. Every organization has general norms of some kind, and every group in the organization is subject to those norms and is likely to reflect them in some way.

However, the reflection may not always be a clear one since every group tends to develop its own unique character—partly a reflection of its particular membership. Consequently, a group's norms will be an *elaboration* of, a *distortion* of, and a direct *reflection* of the culture (customs) of the larger organization.

THE CONCEPT OF CORPORATE CULTURE

In a recent best-selling book*, Terrence Deal and Allan Kennedy describe the ways in which corporations develop complex and powerful cultures (like any society) and how these cultures influence the behavior patterns of employees at all levels. Deal and Kennedy identify five elements of culture:

1. *Business environment*—a company's place in the business world as defined by its products, competitors, customers, technology, etc.
2. *Values*—the basic concepts and beliefs of an organization, as well as its standards for achievement.
3. *Heroes*—the people who personify the cultural values and serve as role models for employees.
4. *Rites and rituals*—the systematic and programmed routines of day-to-day life in the company (including ceremonies).
5. *The cultural network*—the "carrier" of the corporate values and heroic mythology. It includes "storytellers, spies, priests, cabals, and whispers."

* *Corporate Cultures* (Reading, Mass.: Addison-Wesley Publishing, 1982).

In tracing the sources of the emergent system, you might ask:

1. What is the organization's culture as reflected in generally held beliefs about the way things ought to be?
2. Do any of the group's norms reflect the wider organization's culture and how the influence was transmitted?
3. Are the group's norms and procedures consistent with or in opposition to the wider culture?

LIFE AT IBM

When Thomas J. Watson, Sr., died in 1956, some might have thought the IBM spirit of the stiff white collar was destined to die with him. But indications are that the founder's legacy of decorum to International Business Machines Corp. still burns bright. . . .

Besides its great success with computers, IBM has a reputation in the corporate world for another standout trait: an almost proprietary concern with its employees' behavior, appearance, and attitudes.

What this means to employees is a lot of rules. And these rules, from broad, unwritten ones calling for "tasteful" dress to specific ones setting salesmen's quotas, draw their force at IBM from another legacy of the founder: the value placed on loyalty. Mr. Watson believed that joining IBM was an act calling for absolute fidelity to the company in matters big and small. . . .

What it all amounts to is a kind of IBM culture, a set of attitudes and approaches shared to a greater or lesser degree by IBMers everywhere. This culture, as gleaned from talks with former as well as current employees, is so pervasive that, as one nine-year (former) employee puts it, leaving the company "was like emigrating."

Source: Susan Chase. Reprinted by permission of *The Wall Street Journal*, © Dow Jones & Company, Inc., April 8, 1982. All rights reserved.

Technology and Layout

Technology refers to the means by which work is done. It can include the machines, tools, and materials used; the sequence or flow of operations; the way in which work arrives and is processed (continuously or in batches); the pace and timing of work as controlled by machine speed; deadlines and interdependencies with other parts of the organization; noise level; and procedures, processes, and forms used in doing work. It can also include the level and kind of expertise or technical skill needed to do the work.

In a group at a manufacturing job, the technology will usually include some machines that have to be operated by group members. In a group working in service jobs, the technology may not utilize machines but may involve meetings, discussion, and deskwork and require a few tools such as pens, pencils, paper, forms, telephones, and a place to sit. As you can see, the technology of a service group, *when it calls primarily for talking with others,* is almost identical with the required system, that is, in describing the technology it will be necessary to include a description of many of the required activities and interactions. But this overlap should serve as an indicator of how important the technology is for explaining eventual emergent behavior.

In addition, the way in which space is used and equipment is laid out can be considered part of technology. Where machinery is located;

the height of walls, desks, cabinets, or machines; the placing of seats, work stations, or offices; and general size of the spaces utilized can all affect behavior.

Both technology and layout are important background factors because they determine many things for people in the organization: amount of individual attention, involvement and judgment needed; degree of interaction, communication, and cooperation necessary to complete work; numbers of people who must be present; and the like. In turn, these constraints affect who is likely to, must, or cannot interact with whom, and when. Thus technology and layout both set limits on what social interactions and emergent behavior are possible, and both cause various interactions to occur. They also affect what behavior can be required.

For example, it is difficult to form a relationship with someone who must constantly tend a machine on the other side of a thunderously noisy nine-foot-high stamping machine; on the other hand a quiet, open office with desks placed side by side makes conversation with neighbors easy. Three people sitting next to one another and feeding cashed checks into a microfilm machine so that the bank will have a record of transactions can easily talk with one another while working. The machines are quiet, do not require close attention, and are located physically near one another. Contrast this with boiler loaders standing in front of roaring furnaces, shoveling coal in as needed, working intensively for half-hour bursts, then resting in a cooler area for 15 minutes. At the least, if there is conversation it will come in short snatches and have to be shouted to one another over the roar of the furnaces. It's not hard to see that different norms and ways of working together are likely to emerge.

DUNBARTON WON'T DUMP ITS DUMP

DUNBARTON (AP)—Dunbarton voters have decided not to dump their dump, saying it is a social institution.

"The dump is a meeting place. It's a spot where we get a chance to see other people," said resident Walter Smith. . . .

Town selectmen recommended house-to-house garbage pickup, fearing injuries and possible lawsuits from the dump. But they faced about an hour of opposition from residents who attended the Tuesday night town meeting.

Selectmen said the dump was becoming dangerous with some residents falling in with their garbage.

Foster's Daily Democrat
Dover, New Hampshire
March 15, 1979

Similarly, the timing of when shift members report and leave can be an important factor in communications and therefore important in the emergent system. Organizations that need around-the-clock coverage and high sharing of information (like hospitals) schedule differently than organizations that only work a second shift when there is great demand, and when the second shift's work is self-explanatory.

All of these factors, loosely grouped under technology, shape what is and can be required and are usually fixed or determined in advance or outside of the group's existence. In turn, this will affect the emergent system.

When trying to trace what emerges to technology, you might ask questions like:

1. What is the effect of the technology on what activities and interactions are required?
2. What is the nature of the group's technology in terms of numbers of people needed, when they must be in certain places, how much latitude they have in physical movement, variations of work methods used, judgment? How does all this affect how members feel?
3. What kinds of interactions and activities are made easy or not possible because of the layout, noise level, flow of work, and so forth?
4. What kind of expertise is required by the technology, and how does that affect who group members are, how they see one another, how they will be supervised, and so on?

Reward System

One of the best ways to predict behavior in any work group is to look at what behavior is actually rewarded. Most people tend to do what will get them rewarded. This can be a bit tricky because organizations (or managers, or parents) don't always actually reward what they say they will; subordinates do not always correctly interpret what is going to be rewarded; and groups of people sometimes refuse to value the organization's rewards because the benefits of acceptance by peers outweigh those of management.

Nevertheless, it is very useful to identify the formal and informal reward systems in an organization when trying to understand group behavior. Just as technology is often determined apart from the particular members of the group, the organization's formal reward system (pay, recognition, praise, opportunities for advancement, responsibility, and the like) is usually established before the group exists. Informal reward systems, on the other hand, are often not so explicit. The particular leader, supervisor, or manager of a group may have his/her own ideas about what behavior should be rewarded. The leader's assumptions about what motivates people in general, what kind of people are in the group being led, what kinds of behavior demonstrate hard work, competence, promise, and/or loyalty, all can affect what rewards are available to a group.

The combination of formal and informal organizational rewards is a background factor that affects what is required and what emerges, as well as whether or not employees fully respond to offered rewards and punishments. It is important to remember that sometimes a group's emergent system will be in opposition to the organization's reward system or at least not fully consistent with it. Workers, for example, can become quite skeptical about incentive schemes, believing fervently that if they increase output they will soon be required to produce the new higher amount regularly and that the incentive pay or bonus will somehow be taken away or altered so that they end up worse off than when they started. Some groups will decide that to "protect" themselves they should perform only to minimum expectations rather than respond with full effort to the organization's rewards. And occasionally individuals or groups will produce much more—and try much harder—than the organization is able or willing to reward. Thus, it is necessary to probe carefully when analyzing the impact of the organization's reward system on emergent behavior.

In tracing emergent behavior to the reward system, you might ask how pay is determined and what effect that has on behavior, whether

FIGURE 3–3
The Connection between Background Factors and the Required and Emergent Systems

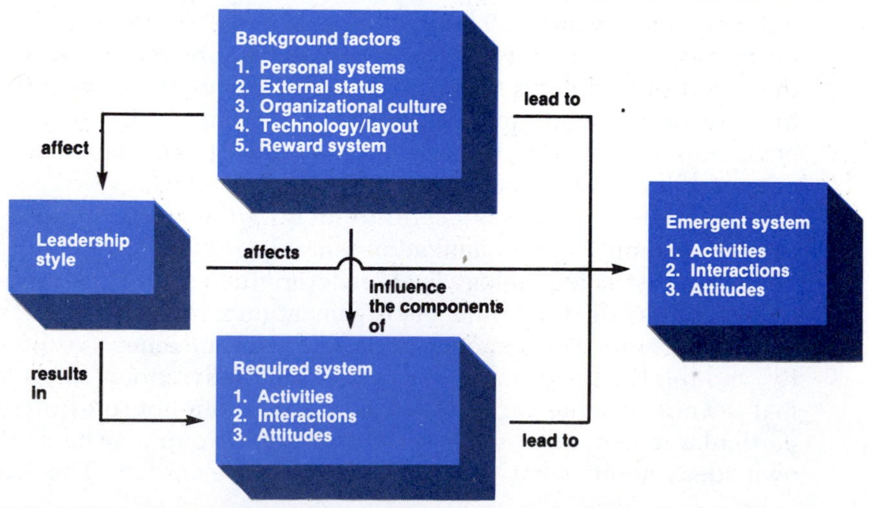

the pay system encourages competition or cooperation among members, what the available rewards are besides pay, whether good performance can be easily measured and rewarded or bad performance measured and punished, and how that will affect emergent behavior.

All of the above factors—personal system, external status, organizational culture, technology, layout, and reward system—can be thought of as background factors, preconditions to the group's existence that help determine what will be required of members and also what emerges in their behavior (see Figure 3–3). Note that these factors may also affect one another; it is by their particular combination that behavior will be determined.

KEY EVENTS AND THE EMERGENT SYSTEM

Key events that occur during the life of a group also influence the emergent system. The background factors and the required system set the direction in which the emergent system is likely to develop, but that process of development is dynamic and interactive. Events may reinforce, modify, or undercut that ongoing direction. As we discussed earlier, norms are often created by a group's reaction to some dramatic event such as a quarrel among members, a scolding by management, or a breakthrough on a tough issue yielding a sense of accomplishment and a norm to henceforth confront issues early. Other events may make it clearer to members that either a certain norm exists or it is really fairly unimportant and not likely to be strongly enforced. Still other events, such as one member doing a bang-up job, may determine who ends up in particular roles or who has more influence than one might have predicted from knowing the background factors alone. The emergent system is constantly evolving as time and *events* occur.

THE CONSEQUENCES OF EMERGENT SYSTEMS

All of what has been discussed so far in this chapter must be seen from the perspective of final results. The connections among background factors and required and emergent systems are important primarily in terms of the functionality or dysfunctionality of the consequences for the organization and its members. We can assess the consequences of whatever emergent system develops along several dimensions.

Productivity

Any work organization will be interested in *productivity:* how well the group does its required tasks, cost per unit of output, ability to meet deadlines, quality of output, and so on. Though many managers, particularly in small private companies, maintain that productivity and, in turn, profits are all the consequences they care to know about, in fact few people with managerial responsibility actually operate only on this dimension.

Satisfaction

For a variety of reasons managers also are interested in the satisfaction of members of their organization. While there is *no* necessary connection between satisfaction and productivity (a subject we will explore later), the actual satisfaction people derive from their work and membership in a particular group is important enough in its effects on the people involved as well as on their productivity to merit close examination in each situation we study. In fact, in some work groups, achieving satisfaction (close friendship, comfortable relations) may be the only dimension *members* are interested in. If you are in a class task group, you might like to check whether this proves to be true!

Development

A third dimension to which we will also pay attention is that of individual and group development/growth/learning. **A group may be reasonably productive and satisfied but preventing its members from developing, from learning anything that will increase (*a*) their individual skills or abilities, (*b*) the range of resources available to the group, or (*c*) their ability to function effectively as a group in changed circumstances.** For example, a student task group may be dividing up the work in a way that produces good reports or papers but teaches members no new skills. An expert report writer may be doing most of the work, using already developed abilities but leaving other members underutilized and unstretched.

Not only would this diminish individual member learning, but it would also mean that the group is giving itself less opportunity to learn to function effectively as a whole. This can easily happen to a classroom group that does well on its first project, then becomes fixated on that successful approach and never tries alternative ways of functioning.

Just as production is not necessarily correlated with satisfaction, group development can be independent of either. Conversely, development or learning can be occurring even when productivity and satisfaction are low. For example, even dissatisfied misfits in a job may be developing valuable skills; disgruntled employees often leave to start their own ventures, fueled by discontent and what they have learned from the job and from others. The dimension of development and learning is important to assess along with the other two dimensions of productivity and satisfaction. Administrators who are concerned about the long-run enhancement of their organization's human resources will also value this dimension. However, some managers, feeling under pressure for immediate results, may push productivity at the expense of satisfaction or development.

It is important to note again what was stated in Chapter 2, that it may not be possible in any given situation to achieve high performance on all three dimensions. An individual or group may make or have to make trade-offs among these dimensions. What to sacrifice for which benefits is determined by the values of the person(s) choosing. Our concern is to make any action's likely consequences along all three dimensions more explicit in advance, so that choices can be more informed. But we will offer no magical or easy solutions guaranteeing wealth, happiness, and growth to everyone.

We can complete Figure 3–3 by adding what we have just described. Whatever the emergent behavior and attitudes of a group, their functionality should be assessed along at least three dimensions: productivity, satisfaction, and development (see Figure 3–4).

These consequences will then be judged by those members of an organization who feel responsible for performance; as you might guess, should they judge the consequences negatively they are likely to make some changes in the required system. If productivity, for example, is seen as too low, changes might be made in the type of equipment used, the pay system, the closeness of supervision, the personnel, or whatever those responsible assume to make a difference. Can you see that changes in the required system might in turn affect the emergent system with new consequences for productivity, learning, or satisfaction? Adjustments in one area will lead to responses in other areas until a new equilibrium is reached in the balance among the various components of the group.

All too often, unfortunately, the consequences of change are not those anticipated by the changer; tightening up on supervision might lead to sabotage rather than more productivity, for example. But that is worth closer attention and will be looked at again in the book's final chapter. For now we suggest you begin to get in the habit of sorting, as best you can, what you see in groups into the five categories we have suggested: background factors, required system, leadership style, emergent system, and the consequences for productivity, satisfaction, and development. Then try to trace the connections among them: What causes what; what seems to be associated with what; what seems unexplainable and needs more investigation?

FIGURE 3–4
The Complete Basic Social System Conceptual Scheme

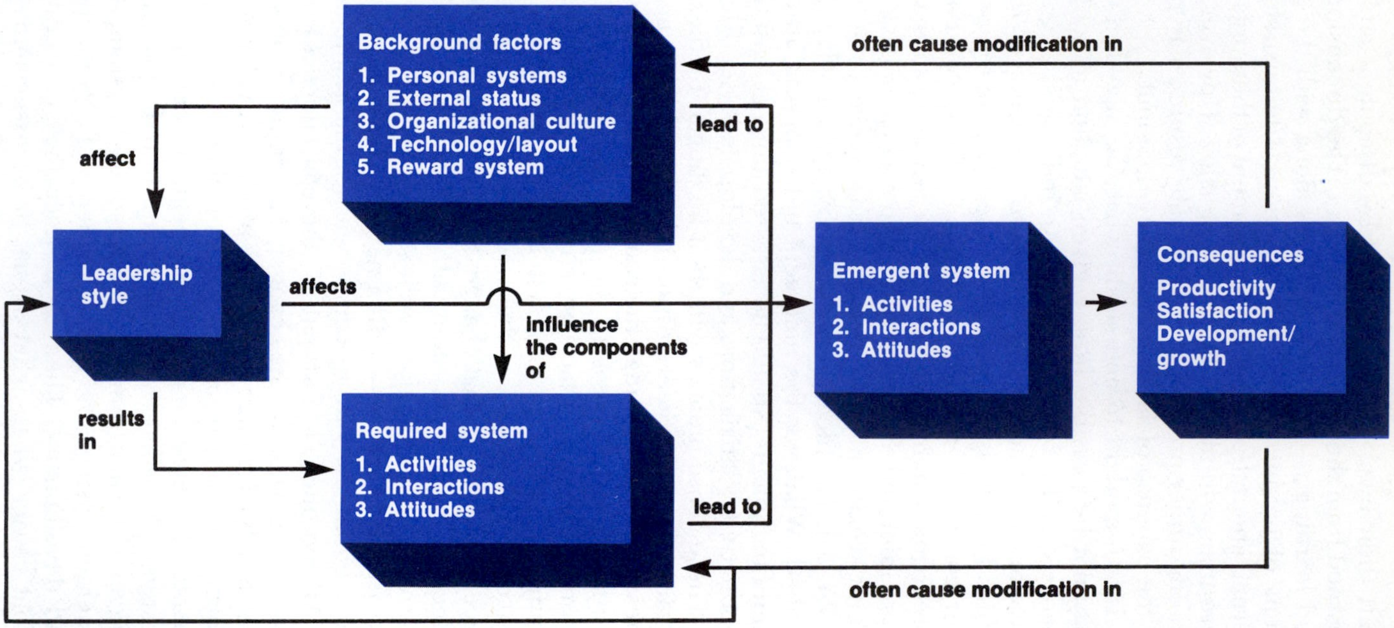

Background factors
1. Personal systems
2. External status
3. Organizational culture
4. Technology/layout
5. Reward system

affect

Leadership style

affects

influence the components of

results in

Required system
1. Activities
2. Interactions
3. Attitudes

lead to

lead to

Emergent system
1. Activities
2. Interactions
3. Attitudes

Consequences
Productivity
Satisfaction
Development/growth

often cause modification in

often cause modification in

THE RELATIONSHIPS BETWEEN REQUIRED AND EMERGENT SYSTEMS

It is important to note again that what emerges in groups will not necessarily be supportive of the required system; in fact, emergent behavior and attitudes may well be in conflict with the required tasks imposed from above or by the situation. Sometimes work groups elaborate on ways to improve their performance, inventing improved methods, informally helping one another, and so forth. They even may develop an emergent system that compensates for deficiencies in the required system, as when norms develop in a paper mill that the nearest person to a paper break, regardless of formal position, immediately will start to rethread the paper in order to minimize waste. At other times, however, groups develop norms of limiting production, holding back effort, or even sabotaging the product. Anyone who has ever had an unfixable rattle in a car knows that auto workers may have said "nuts to you" when feeling negative and done things like toss some bolts into a panel as it was about to be permanently sealed.

A key challenge for you will be to attempt to develop a series of propositions (hypotheses, generalizations) to predict when emergent systems are likely to be in conflict with the required system and when not. Can you trace what the relationships are between leadership style, technology, task requirements, member backgrounds, and so on, and the kind of system that emerges? The more useful the generalizations you can formulate, the more effective you can be in making informed managerial choices. And of course you need to be ready to modify your propositions when you come across contradictory evidence.

We are suggesting that it is often possible to predict likely emergent behavior if what is "given" by the situation—the background factors, leadership style, and required system—are known in advance. Surprisingly to many students, the particular individuals in a situation may make less difference to what happens than the situation and its requirements. The demands of the task, technology, or management style often can pull behavior from a group regardless of who the particular members are. This is often referred to as the "office making the person," elevating its occupant and forcing growth in whomever fills the leadership role. Recent history with respect to the presidency of the United States has proven, however, in a painfully glaring way that occupying even the highest political office in no way *guarantees* particularly elevated behavior. The pulls are there, however, just as in any organizational situation, and often have induced more noble and strong behavior from presidents than they had exhibited earlier in their careers.

As you move through the course, try to notice if you are increas-

AN EXAMPLE OF A WORK GROUP ON A COLLEGE CAMPUS

If several college students were hired by a college to be a grounds crew for the summer, the kind of work group they become can be explained and even predicted by references to the interplay of who they are (personal systems), other background factors, their boss's style, and the behavior required of them by the college. Let us assume the following:

- The students have similar interests, are all individuals with a strong sense of responsibility, need the job, and view outdoor work as a desirable summer job.
- The crew boss is an older, full-time college employee who takes pride in keeping the college grounds looking nice, has led summer crews before, and relates well with college-age people.
- The college is a prestigious institution with a tradition of maintaining a lovely campus and has a reputation for being a good place to work.
- The grounds crew is paid by the hour worked at a reasonable rate. The results of what it does or does not do are highly visible to the general public as well as to the crew boss.
- The work required of the crew includes cutting grass, raking up clippings, picking up trash, spreading loam and wood chips, planting and watering flowers, etc. A certain amount of coordination and cooperation among the crew members is necessary for efficiency. Some care is required to not damage the shrubbery or the equipment. Since the campus is in use throughout the summer, the crew is expected to exhibit courtesy toward any pedestrians who may be passing and not spray them with water, etc. Finally, the college expects the crew to work steadily and give a full day of work, but it does not demand an unreasonable work pace.

Given these background factors and requirements, it would not be surprising if the crew developed into a hardworking and satisfied group. It's likely to develop a norm of getting the job done even if it means working a little bit beyond the normal break time. Talking while working and even some occasional horseplay would probably go on, although not in a manner that slowed efficiency or endangered equipment. Overall, the consequences probably would include satisfactory productivity in the eyes of the college, general job satisfaction for the crew, but only a modest amount of learning of new skills by the crew members. These results are particularly likely if the interplay of background factors and requirements are reinforced by a few key events early in the life of the crew, such as the president of the college happening upon the crew just as it is finishing planting flowers under the flagpole and warmly expressing justified appreciation for a job well done.

Change a few of the factors described above and the emergent behaviors and consequences could be quite different. What if the job were a last-resort job for the students, and the college had a reputation as a low-paying, insensitive employer? What if the college's budget led to the hiring of a crew so small that the workload far exceeded what it could reasonably be expected to produce? What if the president saw only one flower out of alignment and criticized the crew for that while ignoring their overall good work? While one change in the overall array of background factors, requirements, and key events might not make a big difference in what emerged, it would not take much change in the situation from that outlined to yield quite different norms and results.

ingly able to anticipate the kinds of behavior, norms, productivity, satisfaction, and so forth, to which a given set of requirements and background factors lead. We will try to help you improve your predictive abilities by what follows.

As an aid in helping you get started—to analyze cases, your own classroom group, the group you work in—the next chapters contain a series of propositions (tentative hypotheses) based on research, empirical observation, and experience. We have tried to build them up in a logical sequence and have also attempted to show how you can connect various pieces of what is observable. That type of analysis goes beyond just using the concepts as fancy labels for behavior; it is a way of trying to *explain* what happens by referring to other connected happenings. In that way possible choice points where your decision as a manager can make a difference to outcomes should become visible.

KEY CONCEPTS FROM CHAPTER 3

1. A group can be defined by its:
   a. Size.
   b. Degree of autonomy.
   c. Differentiation from other groups.
   d. Interrelationships of some duration.
   e. Identification of members with the group.
   f. Common goals and symbols.
2. Behavior in group.
   a. Interactions.
   b. Activities.
3. Attitudes in group.
   a. Perceptions.
   b. Feelings.
   c. Norms.
   d. Values.
4. The basic social system conceptual scheme.
   a. Background factors.
      (1) Personal systems.
      (2) External status.
      (3) Organizational culture.
      (4) Technology/layout.
      (5) Reward system.
   b. Required system.
   c. Leadership style.
   d. Key events.
   e. Emergent system.
   f. Consequences: productivity, satisfaction, and development.

SUGGESTED READINGS

Bradford, L. P., and D. Mial. "When Is a Group?" *Educational Leadership* 21 (1963). pp. 147–51.

Cartwright, D., and A. Zander. *Group Dynamics: Research and Theory.* New York: Harper & Row, 1953.

Hare, A. P. *Handbook of Small Group Research.* New York: Free Press, 1962.

________. *Handbook of Small Group Research.* 2nd ed. New York: Free Press, 1976.

Homans, G. C. *The Human Group.* New York: Harcourt Brace Jovanovich, 1950.

________. "Social Behavior as Exchange." *American Journal of Sociology,* May 1958, pp. 597–606.

________. *Social Behavior: Its Elementary Forms.* New York: Harcourt Brace Jovanovich, 1961.

Jones, G. R. "Task Visibility, Free Riding, and Shirking: Explaining the Effect of Structure and Technology on Employee Behavior." *Academy of Management Review,* October 1984, pp. 684–95.

Lincoln, J. R., and J. Miller. "Work and Friendship Ties in Organizations: A Comparative Analysis of Relational Networks." *Administrative Science Quarterly,* June 1979, pp. 181–99.

Luft, J. "Living Systems: The Group." *Behavioral Science* 16 (1971), pp. 302–98.

Napier, R. W., and M. K. Gershenfeld. *Groups: Theory and Experience.* Boston: Houghton Mifflin, 1973.

Orth, C. D., III. *Social Structure and Learning Climate; The First Year at the Harvard Business School.* Boston: Division of Research, Graduate School of Business, Harvard University, 1963.

Pettigrew, A. M. "On Studying Organizational Cultures." *Administrative Science Quarterly,* December 1979, pp. 570–81.

Shaw, M. E. *Group Dynamics: The Psychology of Small Group Behavior.* New York: McGraw-Hill, 1971.

Smith, P. B. *Groups within Organizations.* New York: Harper & Row, 1973.

Steele, F., and R. S. Jenks. *The Feel of the Work Place.* Reading, Mass.: Addison-Wesley Publishing, 1977.

Thibaut, J. W., and H. Kelley. *The Social Psychology of Groups.* New York: John Wiley & Sons, 1969.

Trice, H. M., and J. M. Beyer. "Studying Organizational Cultures through Rites and Ceremonials." *Academy of Management Review,* October 1984, pp. 653–69.

Wholey, D. R., and J. W. Brittain. "Organizational Ecology: Findings and Implications." *Academy of Management Review,* July 1986, pp. 513–33.

Zander, A. *Groups at Work.* San Francisco: Jossey-Bass, 1977.

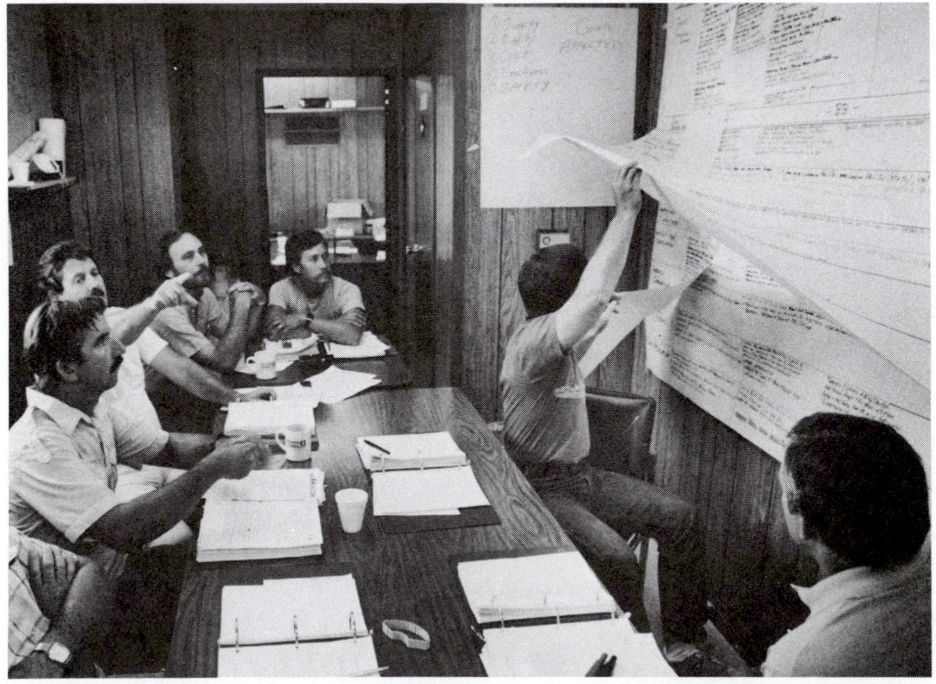

4

COHESIVENESS IN GROUPS

Integration

Group cohesion will be increased by acceptance of a superordinate goal subscribed to by most members.

A crucial emergent factor in any work group is the degree to which members turn out to like each other and the group as a whole. A group that is close and unified will behave differently, for better or worse, than one that is distant and fragmented. In this chapter we will look at *what* makes a group stick together. The consequence of sticking together for productivity, satisfaction, and development is ultimately a more important issue, but let us first try to understand what pulls a group together. With a better understanding of the factors that lead to closeness, a manager is more likely to succeed in efforts to increase or decrease this important emergent characteristic of groups.

In an effort to spell out the propositions about closeness, we begin with some elementary "building blocks" of relationships. While the first proposition looks obvious, it is often overlooked and is important to those that come later. Remember from Chapter 3 that technology, work layout, required interactions, and the arrangement of space affect the chances of people talking with one another; we can restate that idea more formally:

The greater the opportunity/requirements for interactions, the greater the likelihood of interaction occurring (Homans, 1950, 1961).

That leads directly to the next proposition, which is fundamental to all human relationships:

The more frequent the interaction among people, the greater the likelihood of their developing positive feelings for one another (Homans, 1950, 1961).

And in turn:

The greater the positive feelings among people, the more frequently they will interact (Homans, 1950, 1961).

In other words, if you like someone, you will probably choose to spend more time with him/her than with someone you do not like.

People tend to approach other people they see as attractive and to avoid those they see as unattractive. Though most people have gen-

> *It is easier for a man to be loyal to his club than to his planet; the bylaws are shorter and he is personally acquainted with the other members.*
>
> E. B. White
> *One Man's Meat*

eral ideas about what kind of people they do not like, these general feelings are often easily overcome when they actually interact with and get to know a particular person or group of people. While knowing someone does not guarantee liking, it is rather difficult to like someone you do not know. In fact, people are often surprised to find how likeable others are once they've had the opportunity to interact with them.

> *I know I don't like it because I've never tried it.*
>
> Ad for Guinness Stout

These propositions must be modified or at least qualified under certain conditions. For example, when there are strong prior negative feelings on the part of one or more interactor or when there are extreme status differences between those interacting, interaction may only increase prior feelings of dislike or distance and may lead to avoidance or superficial contact. When interaction reveals strong value differences, individuals may decide to avoid one another for fear of getting into heated arguments. Furthermore, even positive interactions cannot increase indefinitely; at some point they will level off and reach a kind of equilibrium where both parties are either interacting enough to satisfy their needs or are prevented by task requirements from interacting further.

While there are exceptions, these propositions are surprisingly applicable to many different situations and have potent implications for managers. Consider different ways in which you might use them to design an organization: To resolve conflicts? To help make work more interesting? These simple propositions, when combined with others that follow (and which you develop yourself on the basis of your observations) can help explain the variety of emergent systems you will encounter.

FACTORS THAT INCREASE COHESION

Required Interactions

Let us extend these propositions, utilizing the research that has been done on small groups, to show some of the connections that can be made among the components of the scheme we have outlined. The previous propositions suggest that once there is a work reason for people to interact they will begin to do it more often and will develop some liking for one another beyond the original task reason for their interaction. Thus: **The more frequent the interactions required by the job, the more likely that *social* relationships and behavior will develop along with task relationships and behavior (Homans, 1950, 1961).** This is another way of describing the relationship between required and emergent interactions discussed in Chapter 3.

When members of a group begin to like one another and like being in the group, then the group will have attraction for the members, and acceptance from the group will be seen as desirable by them. In other words: **The more attractive the group, the more *cohesive* it will be (Festinger, Schacter, & Back, 1950).** As the emerging social relationships form, the group will develop norms—ideas about what behavior is expected of group members. **The more cohesive the group, the more eager individuals will be for membership, and thus the more likely they will be to conform to the group's norms.** Another way of saying this is: **The more cohesive the group, the more influence it has on its members. The less certain and clear a group's norms and standards are, the less control it will have over its members (Festinger et al., 1950; Homans, 1961).**

From the point of view of a total group, finding ways of getting members to feel attracted to and willing to be influenced by the group is extremely desirable; a group can best reach its goals when it has everyone's allegiance and willingness to sacrifice personal desires on behalf of the group. From the individual's point of view, however, cohesion may be a mixed blessing in that there are personal costs in return for whatever may be the satisfaction of being an accepted member. The individual may have to forgo preferred ways of relating to others, put out greater effort than is desired, or give more time and concern than is comfortable. In Chapter 7 we will explore more of the dilemma faced by the individual trying to decide how much to give up for the closeness offered by the group; we want to note for now, however, that while membership has a price for the individual, insofar as the participation of all members is necessary or valuable for achieving the *group's* goals, the creation of group cohesiveness is important.

Common Attitudes and Values

Since cohesion has such a strong impact upon behavior in a group, it is useful to understand some of the ways in which it can be increased or decreased. We have already shown how cohesion is increased by frequent interaction, but a number of other factors can affect it. For example, if members of a group come to it with similar attitudes and values, cohesion is much more likely to occur rapidly. **The greater the similarity in member attitudes and values brought to the group, the greater the likelihood of cohesion in a group (Homans, 1961).**

> **A MOST "PROPER" MANAGER**
>
> *A manager was offered a job at an investment banking firm in Boston. The firm's executives were all "proper Bostonians," educated at Ivy League schools. The manager was subsequently told he had been hired because the firm had decided to broaden the types of people employed, and during interviews he had learned how different he was (despite his technical competence):*
>
> 1. *He owned a power boat (and did not sail).*
> 2. *His MBA degree was from the University of Massachusetts, not Dartmouth or Harvard.*
> 3. *He wanted to leave early one afternoon each week to coach Little League (not play squash).*

Superordinate Goal

Along the same lines, when there are differences among group members, if there is some kind of overarching goal to which group members subscribe, cohesion is likely to increase. For example, a product invention group at a large consumer goods firm consisted of members with very different backgrounds: a chemist, a marketing expert, a production engineer, and a nutritionist. Whenever they met, they argued about how to proceed, feasibility of ideas, desirability of particular products to consumers, the capacity of the company to produce certain items—even what technical language to use when discussing ideas. But all members knew that their reputations and ultimately the company's future depended upon their success in coming up with profitable new products. This commitment to the shared overall goal of new product creation pulled them past their frequent disagreements and made them fiercely loyal to their team. They prided themselves on their creativity and their collective practicality. Thus: **Group cohesion will be increased by the existence of a superordinate goal(s) subscribed to by the members (Sherif, 1967).**

A Common Enemy

Similarly, you probably have had experience with another kind of superordinate goal: dislike for a common enemy. If people have the same enemy, they are likely to feel a kinship; this general notion has long been used effectively by politicians in a number of countries to try to create a sense of national cohesion that overrides the variety of self-interests among different groups. And in a smaller group as well: **Group cohesion will be increased by the perceived existence of a common enemy (Blake & Mouton, 1961).**

The common enemy may not necessarily be a hated enemy. Even friendly competition among groups usually has the effect of pushing group members to feel closer to one another. If by the time you read this you have already done a class exercise in groups, you may have noticed how the presence of other groups working on the same tasks seemed to cause people in your group to like one another more and perhaps even to begin to make joking comments about how much better your group was than the others. In Chapter 13 we will look more closely at relationships across groups, but for now it is important to note that the presence of competing or even potentially competing groups often makes members within groups feel closer to one another. In some situations, especially in our competitively oriented Western society, this phenomenon is so powerful that even when a multigroup activity is conducted in which groups are *not* being compared to one another, group members still act as if it were a competitive situation and seem to feel cohesive just by being near other groups visibly working on a similar activity.

Success in Achieving Goals

Another factor that can lead to greater feeling of liking among group members is for the group to be successful in achieving its goals. If a group seems to be successful at getting what it wants, that makes the group more attractive to members and seems to carry over in the way that members feel about one another. Thus: **Group cohesion will be increased by success in achieving the group's goals (Sherif & Sherif, 1953).**

A connected factor affecting group cohesion has to do with the relative position of the group in relation to other groups in the same overall organization. As you might expect, the higher the status of a particular group in relation to other groups, the more attractive it will seem to members. This is apparently true for everyone but Groucho Marx, who once said, "I wouldn't want to belong to any club which would have me as a member." But for others of us less witty or perceptive: **Group cohesion is increased in proportion to the status of the**

group relative to other groups in the system (Cartwright & Zander, 1968).

Low External Interactions

A related issue from a somewhat opposite point of view has to do with the amount of time that group members are required to spend away from the group. If group members by the nature of their job have to relate to many outsiders (including others in the same organization but not in the group), they are less likely to feel strong allegiance to their own group. This is very often true of certain kinds of professional employees who spend a good portion of their time dealing with the problems of nonspecialists in their organization and who also spend time at professional meetings with people from other organizations in order to keep up to date in their specialty, whether it is engineering, medicine, law, or whatever. Similarly, an organization's purchasing agent will often have to spend more time dealing with outsiders than fellow organization members, leading to reduced loyalty to his/her own department and organization. Thus: **Group cohesion will be increased when there is a low frequency of required external interactions (Homans, 1950).**

Resolution of Differences

Every group will at times have differences of opinions; how they are resolved affects cohesion. If a group has repeated problems with resolving differences among members because of strong differences of opinion, values, or working style, the members' liking for one another will tend to decrease even when the group manages to be successful. Thus: **The more easily and frequently member differences are settled in a way satisfactory to all members, the greater will be group cohesion (Deutsch, 1968).** Nevertheless success, even if arrived at by a cantankerous process, can soothe many bad feelings. A winning group usually overlooks its differences; a losing group often finds fault with its members.

Availability of Resources

Finally, the way members feel about each other is frequently affected by the availability of resources to the whole group. When resources such as money, supplies, prestige, or recognition are scarce, group members are likely to feel competitive with one another. Conversely, when there is an abundance of whatever resources the group needs, members are likely to see each other more charitably and therefore like each other more. **Group cohesion will increase under conditions**

of abundant resources. For example, when the staff of an innovative health center saw government grants rolling in, they felt close to the other "pioneers" on the staff. When government money dried up and even weekly paychecks were in jeopardy, dissension and anger toward one another broke out.

The preceding propositions all relate to group integration. The cohesiveness or attractiveness of a group and the power of its norms to regulate behavior are major aspects of emergent systems and are important factors for diagnosing and predicting group behavior. As explained, cohesiveness is influenced by background factors, such as similarity in member attitudes, and by attributes of the required system, such as the necessity for interaction. By carefully tracing what is brought to the work group and what is required of it, it is possible to make sense of the degree of closeness that emerges. But keep in mind that "nothing is as simple as it seems" (see Chapter 1). Cohesiveness is the result of many factors; a careful analysis requires that you think in terms of multiple causality.

While all of the above propositions have been phrased in terms of what positively increases cohesion, they are also intended to be reversible in terms of what decreases cohesion. As a manager you may wish at any given time to increase or decrease cohesion among a particular group and may be able to affect differing aspects of the conditions cited by the propositions. Deciding in which direction cohesion should be pushed and then how to do it requires a careful assessment of existing conditions.

> The manager of a large department store was faced with customer complaints about waiting time for service. Upon investigation, he found that many of the full-time salespeople congregated near the fitting rooms for conversation. They enjoyed one another's company so much that they found it difficult to interrupt the gossip and joking to go wait on customers. The manager had to find a way to decrease the group's cohesion without creating major resentment that would interfere with selling enthusiasm. How might such a problem be approached? Would it be wise to crack down and prohibit all social talk? What would be the effect of physically rearranging the work area?

CONSEQUENCES OF COHESION FOR PRODUCTIVITY, SATISFACTION, AND DEVELOPMENT

Productivity

Since a cohesive group is one in which members adhere to the norms, it should not be surprising that in such a group norms are likely to develop not only in regard to general behavior, but also about member productivity. The group will usually arrive at a strong sense of how much each member should produce and how much variation from that level will be tolerated, and then encourage the members to produce at or near that level. Whether production is measured in widgets/hour as in a manufacturing group or in "sufficient hours spent preparing an analysis" as in a student task group: **The more cohesive the group, the more similar will be the output of individual members (Homans, 1950).**

Another way of looking at the effect of cohesiveness on productivity is in terms of how much effort members will make to see that the productivity norms, high or low, are followed. As you might expect: **The more cohesive the group, the more it will try to enforce compliance with its norms about productivity.** Cohesive groups will work hard to get members to increase output if it is lower than the group thinks appropriate and also will supply pressure to hold down the output of members who embarrass the group by producing "too much."

You may remember from Chapter 3 that a group's idea of what is the proper amount to produce may be only vaguely related to higher management's or the rest of the organization's ideas of the proper amount. In general, if the group feels in sympathy with or supported by "higher management" (or those who define good performance), it will have a tendency to enforce a fairly high level of productivity on its members and vice versa. Since a cohesive group will bring member productivity into line: **The greater the cohesion of the group, the higher productivity will be if the group supports the organization's goals, and the lower productivity will be if the group resists the organization's goals (Zaleznik, Christensen, & Roethlisberger, 1958).**

A cohesive group that wants to produce more will pull even its weaker members along quite effectively. But the group that sticks together can thus be irritatingly resistant to efforts to increase its productivity when, for whatever reason, it does not wish to raise output. What does this suggest to you, as a future manager, about your relationships to task groups reporting to you and about the conditions under which their cohesiveness might be desirable?

Group cohesiveness can also either enhance or stifle productivity, depending upon the members' willingness to be open with one another. On the one hand, in a cohesive group members feel close enough to one another to be able to discuss issues and problems frankly. Closeness should make explorations of issues easier, since all members can presumably be trusted with information and with members' feelings.

On the other hand, when people feel attracted to a group, they may see the risk of offending someone they like as greater than if the others didn't matter. Holding back opinions, feelings, or ideas because the

QUALITY CIRCLES

The Quality Circles approach—voluntary groups of about 10 workers who meet with a supervisor to make suggestions about how to solve shop floor quality problems—provides an excellent example of how groups of workers can become highly productive as a result of having common goals, achieving success, and having frequent required interactions. While this technology was developed for the purpose of improving product quality on the production floor, extra benefits—increased worker commitment, higher morale, lower turnover, etc.—are predictable from the propositions about cohesion. All of these outcomes benefit productivity. Indeed, companies like Toyota, where almost all employees participate in QC programs, report greater numbers of useful suggestions per worker than companies without formal programs. Many companies have found that equivalent "problem-solving teams" among white-collar workers (technicians, administrators, sales support, etc.) can yield similar benefits.

QUALITY CIRCLES AT A JAPANESE COMPANY'S AMERICAN PLANT

On a recent day, one of Sharp's "Quality Circles" is meeting. Led by a trained leader, Sharp's Quality Circles "brainstorm" ideas, select a problem to be solved, and then collect data on the problem. Later, the problem and possibly a solution are presented to Mr. Hagusa [President, Sharp Manufacturing, USA] *and other members of management.*

Two Innovations

At one table, five microwave assembly workers are discussing one worker's innovation: a metal dowel that fits into the center hole of a five-hole microwave oven bracket. "I saw that people were having trouble lining up the holes," says Randy Howle, "but if someone before them had put in the center screw, the person didn't have a problem." So Mr. Howle developed the metal dowel, which, when slipped into the middle hole, aligns the bracket while the other four holes are screwed down.

At another table, a group of employees are discussing a second innovation: a plastic tabletop with countersunk holes in which to stand screws. The device makes the screws simple to pick up and keeps them from rolling off the table and onto the floor. As a result, productivity has improved by seven units a day, the circle leader says.

However, Sharp doesn't expect a dollar payback from the circles, which meet on company time. Instead, a manager explains, the circles are a "human relations program."

Source: Reprinted by permission of *The Wall Street Journal*, © Dow Jones & Company, Inc., April 29, 1983. All rights reserved.

approval of others is so important that it can't be tested can lead to unproductive decisions.

When cohesiveness is a result of great similarity in member attitudes, values, and external status, it can lead to decreased productivity over time (Gillespie & Birnbaum, 1980). The similarities apparently act as a filter against disconfirming information and events, so that the ease of working together is overwhelmed by the problems of collective resistance to disconfirming inputs. While managers often fear that heterogeneity in a task group will lead to conflict among members and to low group productivity, it is important for them to realize that too much homogeneity can eventually result in mediocre group performance.

TIME TO TRUST THE GOVERNMENT AGAIN, RIGHT?

The most awkward moments I can remember from my brief stint in government came at staff meetings when someone at the table would suddenly clear his or her throat and launch into a carefully considered exposition on how and why a particular policy was all wrong or wasn't working. What makes those moments stand out is that they were so infrequent. They were almost invariably followed by an embarrassed silence, a sudden flurry of paper-shuffling around the table, stares into the middle distance and a quick change of subject. Afterwards, one or two participants might go up privately to the dissenter to voice their support.

Source: Hodding Carter III. Reprinted by permission of *The Wall Street Journal*,

Very cohesive groups run the risk of falling victim to "groupthink" (Janis, 1972). Groupthink is a mode of thought and behavior that occurs "when the members' strivings for unanimity override their motivation to realistically appraise alternative courses of action." As a result, the group easily overestimates its own capabilities, cuts itself off from new information, and becomes smug about its own views and judgments. (See the box that discusses groupthink for more detail on its symptoms and some steps that can be taken to guard against it.) Thus overcohesiveness can be stifling to a group's effectiveness because members hesitate to risk offending someone—or the group has fallen into groupthink.

Satisfaction

A cohesive group will by definition have a high overall level of satisfaction; presumably a group attractive to its members is satisfying. Individual members, however, may very much feel that the norms of the group call for behavior that is not easily given. Belonging to a close cohesive group can be a warm supportive experience, but for some the embrace of the group may feel a bit suffocating. Should that happen to many members of the group, its cohesiveness may well begin to suffer as members struggle to assert their own individuality.

GROUPTHINK

Where groups become very cohesive, there is danger that they become victims of their own closeness.

Symptoms

1. Illusions of the group as invulnerable.
2. Rationalizing away data that disconfirm assumptions and beliefs.
3. Unquestioned belief in group's inherent morality.
4. Stereotyping competitors as weak, evil, stupid, and so on.
5. Direct pressure on deviants to conform.
6. Self-censorship by members.
7. Illusion of unanimity (silence equals consent).
8. Self-appointed "mind guards"—protecting group from disconfirming data.

Prevention Steps

A_1. Leader encourage open expression of doubt.
A_2. Leader accept criticism of his/her opinions.
B. Higher-status members offer opinions last.
C. Get recommendations from a duplicate group.
D. Periodically divide into subgroups.
E. Members get reaction of trusted outsiders.
F. Invite trusted outsiders to join discussion periodically.
G. Assign someone the role of devil's advocate.
H. Develop scenarios of rivals' possible actions.

Source: Adapted from Irving Janis, *Victims of Groupthink* (Boston: Houghton Mifflin, 1972).

But the positive feelings from being a member of a cohesive group can be sufficient for some people to overcome even low pay, unpleasant physical conditions, harsh bosses, and so forth.

Development and Learning

A cohesive group can provide excellent opportunities for members to help and learn from one another. In fact, that can be part of what attracts members. The sharing of knowledge, skills, and experiences can be very rewarding and growth promoting. Some groups, however, achieve cohesion only at the expense of individual growth. The group becomes so anxious to maintain a certain kind of harmony that it suppresses individual knowledge and differences for fear of making some members feel unequal or inadequate.

Cohesion achieved in this way may not hinder the group from producing adequately and may be reasonably satisfying to members who want the security of minimal competition and differences among peers, but it can serve to "freeze" growth at a particular point. A student task group can, for example, see to it that everyone does his/her share of assignments, warmly socialize in and out of class, and support all members with liking and warmth, yet still prevent maximum individual learning. A quieter member who would learn valuable debating skills from being prodded to defend his/her ideas may be allowed to make contributions behind the scenes and thus never be forced to practice new skills. Or an argumentative member with a unique point of view might be cajoled into "not pushing so hard, for the good of the group," and thus never really be faced with the consequences of such a style nor have a chance to think through and persuade others about his/her views.

On the other hand, if a group lacks cohesiveness individual and group learning may be inhibited. It often takes at least a minimally supportive environment for members to take any risks in expressing ideas, defending unpopular views, and so forth. Also, if a group lacks cohesiveness it will probably have difficulty looking at its own process or confronting conflicts and thereby be less able to "learn" as a group or develop its capacity to function effectively. Therefore the degree of cohesiveness in a group can have either positive or negative consequences for development; it takes careful analysis of the particular situation to assess the effects.

The next chapter explores further the connections between group cohesion and effectiveness by looking at the other side of cohesiveness, those forces that separate and differentiate group members. Even the most cohesive groups have differences among members that must be dealt with and that impact the group's productivity, satisfaction, and development.

KEY CONCEPTS FROM CHAPTER 4

1. Propositions on group cohesiveness:
   a. The more interactions, the more positive feelings.
   b. The more positive feelings, the more interactions.
   c. The more attractive the group, the more cohesiveness.
   d. The more cohesive the group, the more eagerness for membership.
   e. The more eagerness for membership, the more conformity to group's norms. Therefore:
   f. The more cohesive the group, the more influence it has on its members.
   g. The less clear the group's norms, the less control it has over its members.
2. Group cohesiveness is increased by:
   a. Similarity in attitudes, values, and goals.
   b. Existence of a common enemy.
   c. Acceptance of superordinate goals.
   d. Success in achieving goals.
   e. High status relative to other groups.
   f. Low number of required external interactions.
   g. Differences settled in satisfactory way to all members.
   h. Conditions of abundant resources.

3. High cohesiveness correlates with productivity, satisfaction, and development:
   a. Members' productivity similar in a cohesive group.
   b. Group productivity high if the group values productiveness.
   c. Member satisfaction high, by definition.
   d. Member development may be high or low.

SUGGESTED READINGS

Blake, R., and J. Mouton. "Reactions to Intergroup Competition under Win-Lose Competition." *Management Science,* July 1961, pp. 420–25.

Cartwright, D., and Z. Zander. *Group Dynamics: Research and Theory.* New York: Harper & Row, 1968.

Deutsch, M. "The Effects of Cooperation and Competition upon Group Process." In *Group Dynamics: Research and Theory,* ed. D. Cartwright and A. Zander. New York: Harper & Row, 1968.

Feldman, D. C. "The Development and Enforcement of Group Norms." *Academy of Management Review,* January 1984, pp. 47–53.

Festinger, L.; S. Schacter; and K. Back. *Social Pressures in Informal Groups: A Study of a Housing Project.* New York: Harper & Row, 1950.

Gillespie, D. F., and P. H. Birnbaum. "Status Concordance, Coordination, and Success in Interdisciplinary Research Teams." *Human Relations* 33, no. 1 (1980), pp. 41–56.

Harvey, J. B., and C. R. Boettger. "Improving Communication within a Managerial Work Group." *Journal of Applied Behavioral Science,* March–April 1971, pp. 154–79.

Homans, G. C. *The Human Group.* New York: Harcourt Brace Jovanovich, 1950.

________. *Social Behavior: Its Elementary Forms.* New York: Harcourt Brace Jovanovich, 1961.

Homestead, M. S. *The Small Group.* New York: Random House, 1969.

Janis, I. *Victims of Groupthink.* Boston: Houghton Mifflin, 1972.

Napier, R. W., and M. K. Gershenfeld. *Groups: Theory and Experience.* Boston: Houghton Mifflin, 1973.

Schachter, S. *The Psychology of Affiliation.* Stanford, Calif.: Stanford University Press, 1959.

Seashore, S. E. *Group Cohesiveness in the Industrial Work Group.* Ann Arbor, Mich.: Survey Research Center, Institute for Social Research, 1964.

Sherif, M. *Group Conflict and Cooperation: Their Social Psychology.* Boston: Routledge & Kegan Paul, 1967.

Sherif, M., and C. Sherif. *Groups in Harmony and Tension.* New York: Harper & Row, 1953.

Skinner, B. F. *Walden II.* New York: Macmillan, 1948.

Smith, P. B. *Groups within Organizations.* New York: Harper & Row, 1973.

Steele, F. I. "Physical Settings and Social Interaction." In *Physical Settings and Organization Development.* Reading, Mass.: Addison-Wesley Publishing, 1973.

Zaleznik, A.; C. R. Christensen; and F. J. Roethlisberger. *The Motivation, Productivity, and Satisfaction of Workers.* Boston: Harvard Business School, 1958.

5

DIFFERENTIATION IN GROUPS

Building Internal Structure as a Basis for Productivity

The more an individual group member fails to conform to the group's norm, the more frequently negative sentiments will be expressed toward that person.

After looking at integration—what it is that makes a group stick together and be attractive to members—it is important to examine the way groups differentiate their members in terms of value to the group. Few groups have total equality among all members; some individuals obtain more respect and influence, some more liking, others less of one or the other. Over time a group will develop relative positions or "ranks" for its members; that is, members acquire different status from one another. In this chapter we will look at three key factors that determine the relative positions of group members: (1) status brought to the group from outside, (2) individual adherence to group norms, and (3) group-related roles assumed by members. These factors contribute to individual member influences, which ultimately influence group productivity, satisfaction, and development.

[Janet Axelrod, vice president of Lotus Development Corporation, discussing her company's aversion to executive perks on the PBS program "Adam Smith's Money World"]:

None of us had any kind of interest in being people who lived in ivory towers and traveled around in limousines. It's not just that it wasn't in our lifestyle, it wasn't what we wanted to be. And we didn't see any reason for it. It seemed like an awful money sink, and artificial separations among people. Status-related differences between people are an unnecessary division, and none of us wanted to be divided in that way. A lot of big, heavy industry in this country was born out of this kind of robber-baron mentality, and we're not in that anymore; it's just not the way we do business.

Source: "Notable & Quotable." Reprinted by permission of *The Wall Street Journal*, © Dow Jones & Company, Inc., November 5, 1985. All rights reserved.

The notion of status differences as something to observe and discuss often makes Americans uncomfortable because of their widespread professed beliefs about everyone being created equal and the equally widespread general belief that differences among people working together should be minimized or ignored. The United States is one of a handful of countries where such beliefs are widely espoused. In most parts of the world the ideas that some people are more worthy and esteemed than others, and that everyone has a rank or status that can be precisely identified relative to all others, are accepted as obviously true.

A VICE PRESIDENT BY ANY OTHER NAME STILL MIGHT LEAVE SOME PEOPLE CONFUSED

Bank titles bewilder most outsiders, who assume that anybody at the bank not wielding a mop is an assistant vice president.

Now the titles are changing. But outsiders may wind up no less confused. How does "group executive," for example, improve on "executive vice president"? And how do you reply when somebody introduces himself as "vice president, branch manager, individual banking, Memphis"? . . .

The original purpose of bank titles was to give officers the authority to make loans and approve other transactions. Over the years, however, the titles proliferated since they were increasingly used to confer status. Banks relied on the vice presidential title particularly, "to make customers feel they were dealing with an important person," says George Parker, who lectures on management at Stanford Business School. "And pretty soon, a vice president wasn't such a big deal."

Source: Helen Cogan. Reprinted by permission of *The Wall Street Journal*, © Dow Jones & Company, Inc., June 11, 1985. All rights reserved.

While Americans acknowledge broad differences in status—doctor (professional) higher than garbage collector (blue-collar), professor higher than student (sometimes?)—the idea is resisted in groups of peers or those who see themselves as "about the same." The sameness usually refers to broad categories such as students, middle managers, or board members, and there is often resistance to the possibility that, in fact, even in a group of peers differences in status emerge, are identifiable, and have important consequences for the group and individuals in it.

For example, one of the most common norms students bring to task groups is "we are all equal," which means that no one student member is supposed to be able to dominate others, tell them what to do, or give orders. Yet it is clear that it would be extremely unlikely to have all members possessing equal skills in generating ideas, organizing, analyzing, writing, or interacting socially. As a result, once the group takes on some tasks, various members emerge with different status in the group.

No two men can be half an hour together but one shall acquire an evident superiority over the other.

Samuel Johnson
Boswell's *Life of Samuel Johnson*

Just which attributes of members will result in high ranking depends upon the norms and standards of the particular group; in some groups status goes to those who help most with the tasks, while in others status goes to those who make members feel most comfortable and at ease. But inevitably groups do develop some informal ranking of members even if they do not discuss it directly. Though each group must be separately studied to determine the basis for status in that group, in general: **Members who contribute most to task accomplishment are accorded the most *respect* in the group, while members who contribute most to social accomplishment (development of relationships) are accorded the most *liking* in the group (Bales, 1958).** One's position on these two dimensions (respect and liking) determines a person's overall status in the group, with the weights attached to each determined by the group's emergent norms and values.

BASES OF DIFFERENTIATION

Initial Ranking: External Status and Status Congruence

While over the long run each member's status in a group will be based on the member's contribution to whatever the group values, early status in a group is usually related to the status of each group member outside the group. In a company task force set up to investigate ways of awarding bonuses to outstanding performers in the group, for example, a senior vice president will usually be given more respect at first than a personnel department assistant despite the possibility that the personnel assistant may indeed know more about alternative bonus systems and their consequences. **The higher the background factor of external status, the higher the initial internal status of a group member (Homans, 1950).**

But it is not always obvious what attributes group members will use to rank status in the world outside the group. What some people consider high-status attributes might not be seen that way at all by others, particularly if an attribute is not judged to be relevant to the group's purposes. For example, in the bonus system task force just mentioned, being a senior vice president would probably yield a higher rank than being a personnel assistant. But within a group of workers trying to decide how to request a change in working hours, the personnel assistant's knowledge of rules and procedures, plus his/her membership on the bonus task force, is likely to result in high status there. Similarly, a high-status judge might be given little respect in a group that has crashed in the desert if his/her survival skills are comparatively low. A mechanic might be given higher status in this situation even though he/she would be seen as lower status in other circumstances.

Furthermore, many other factors may go into setting a person's status. We have been talking about profession and, by implication, income as two important factors, but there are others that often make a difference: age, sex, education (where and how long), ethnicity, marital status, and even the region born in. In student task groups, class standing, major subject, and work experience are often important determinants too, since careers are not yet established. Some of these factors, such as education and profession, are achievable by work and ability, while others, such as age, sex, and ethnicity, the person is born with or gets by just existing. Though the rankings may in no way be "fair" or just, especially to those who are low status, some kind of ranking exists everywhere. In many cultures higher status goes to those who are older, male, married, highly educated, have high incomes, and are members of the dominant ethnic group. In any particular group, however, some of these factors might be reversed, as in these examples you may recognize: "never trust anyone over 30," "ivory-tower pointy-headed intellectuals," "fat cats," "male chauvinist pigs," and "honkies."

In general: **The higher a person is on all of these external dimensions (or other valued ones), the higher his/her emergent status within a group, and vice versa.** To any particular group, however, one factor may be seen as overriding all others; in certain organizations, for example, if you aren't a WASP (or whatever the dominant ethnic background), being high status on all the other factors will not make up for lack of status on that dimension.

Not only can we look at how high a person is on several status factors in order to estimate likely internal status, but we can also make some predictions about emergent behavior based on how consistent a person's status ranking is *across* factors. For example, some people are high or low in status on all factors; we call that *status congruency.*

If the senior vice president in our example were a 60-year-old male, married, had an MBA, and was descended from someone who came over on the Mayflower, he would be congruently high status on all factors. Conversely, in New Hampshire at least, if the personnel assistant were female, 20 years old, French-Canadian, unmarried, new to the company, and had not gone beyond high school, she would be congruently low status on all factors. But suppose the senior vice president was a 28-year-old black women who was completing a part-time MBA program. Or suppose the personnel assistant was a 40-year-old former philosophy professor who had changed careers and was showing great promise and potential. Can you see in these examples how the status factors of each would then be inconsistent with one another, "out of line," or *incongruent?* (See Figure 5–1.) Can you imagine how difficult it might then be for the bonus system task force members to "place" or rank each one? What might be their reaction?

FIGURE 5–1
Illustration of How Different People Can Be Ranked along Several Status Dimensions

Person	*Age*	*Sex*	*Education*	*Ethnicity*	*Profession*	*Income*	
A	High	High	High	High	High	High	= High status, congruent
B	Low	Low	Low	Low	Low	Low	= Low status, congruent
C	Low	Low	High	High	High	High	= High status, incongruent
D	…	…	…	…	…	…	= and so forth

Conformity to Norms as a Determinant of Emergent Status

We have previously looked at the way norms emerge and how cohesiveness increases conformity to group norms. But no matter how attractive a group is and no matter how much members wish to belong, it is almost never possible for every member to go along with all of a group's norms. Sometimes norms call for behavior beyond the capacity of individuals in the group, as, for example, "Everyone should make creative contributions to the group's efforts." Some people have more of the skills needed by a group than do others, and when the norms call for those particular skills they are at a natural advantage. If a student task group desires high grades and must produce excellent written analyses to get them, the individual member who is good at performing such analysis and at writing clear conclusions will naturally be better able to conform to norms about contributing to the group's goals. Another member might be an excellent amateur carpenter but not be valued as highly in the group since such manual skills are not necessary for achieving high performance.

Other norms ask individuals to do what goes too strongly "against the grain," irritating the person's fundamental values and personality. For example, some groups ask that all members act humbly even to the point of denying any needs for individual recognition. To a person raised with strong emphasis on individual competition and a belief in sinking or swimming on one's own best efforts, being modest about successes may be either impossible or seem too "wrong" to be tolerated, let alone tried.

For such a person conformity to a norm of "humility" is a virtual impossibility even if other aspects of the group make membership attractive. In a more gentle, unjudging world, the inability or unwillingness to conform to what are, after all, only one group's particular idiosyncratic norms would go unpunished. The desirability, for example, of false humility has not been proclaimed from on high as the one true way; in fact, just around the corner (perhaps in our competitive individual's family) sits a group with equal conviction about the rightness of savoring glory when it is earned!

It is important to state explicitly that we are not talking about conformists and nonconformists as absolute personality types; all people have some group or groups to whose norms and values they conform, even when they are physically present elsewhere. The question is only whether a person will (or can) conform to a *particular* group's norms while a member. Nonconformity in that context is usually a sign of subscription and conformity to some other group's standards. If when in Rome a person does not "do as the Romans do," it is usually because he/she thinks that "doing as Americans/English/Germans (select your own category) do" is better, nicer, or more comfortable than going along with the present company.

Yet despite the fact that particular norms about productivity and other kinds of behavior can vary sharply from group to group, each group's ideas about proper behavior often become enshrined or "sacred," as if there were no other possible way to behave and still be a good person. Once a group has clear ideas about proper levels of productivity, for example, it will expend considerable energy trying to bring members who deviate from them (hereafter referred to as *"deviants"*) into line. Thus: **The more an individual group member fails to conform to the group's norms, the more frequently negative sentiments will be expressed toward him/her (Homans, 1961).**

DEVIANCY CAN BE APPROPRIATE

While the idea of being a deviant in a group seems to have a negative connotation, there often are times when the behavior of a group violates the personal values of a member and may force that member to make a choice between conformity to group pressure for the sake of harmony and standing up for one's convictions. Making the former choice is usually easier and is likely to be supported by the other group members. The price that is paid is paid primarily by the one member. The choice to deviate by being true to personal values is the tougher decision but at least helps the individual to retain a sense of integrity. It may, in the long run, even help the group by establishing a norm that supports individual integrity. Therefore, when you use the term *deviant,* be careful not to prejudge it negatively; it is a relative matter that can only be judged in context, that is, by what the person is deviating from.

The particular form of expression for negative sentiments can vary, depending on the general style of group members and the particular norm being enforced. Some groups may use sarcasm, irony, and indirect hints to let a member know he/she is not conforming properly, while other groups may use nods, winks, facial mugging, or "gentle love-taps" to admonish deviating members. In the classic Hawthorne experiments (Roethlisberger & Dickson, 1939) where the relationship between social relations and productivity was first explored, one work group was observed in which deviants who produced "too much" were hit on the upper arm with the fist, a process called "binging." This was a crude but effective way to see to it that no one person produced so much that management would start to ask why all workers could not do the same each day.

Whatever the particular medium of expression, every group will have ways of "punishing" its deviant members, and most will have at least some members who cannot or will not conform to its norms, leading to differences in rank. When the group expresses dislike for a member who isn't conforming, it often produces defensiveness or aggression in that member, which in turn can lead to greater punishment by the group and to new attempts to bring the member into line. After awhile, however, the group will begin to ignore the deviant as if to punish him/her by withholding what the group sees as desirable relationships. **The less a member conforms to a group's norms, the greater will be the interaction directed at him/her for some time. Should the interaction fail to bring the member into conformity with the norms, interaction will sharply decrease (Homans, 1961).**

Conversely, the more closely a person conforms to the group's norms and carries out the group's ideas of proper behavior, the better the person will be liked by other group members and become a *regular* member of the group. **The greater a member's conformity to the group's important norms, the greater the group's liking for the member (Homans, 1961).**

The people who are best able to conform to the group's norms—because of skills, attributes, resources possessed by them, earned or otherwise—are likely to emerge as informal leaders in the group and be the most respected by other members. Just *what* the group does value varies from group to group and may not be fairly distributed among members. In one classic study, the most important attribute a member could have was being Irish, an attribute not easily acquired by non-Irish aspirants but possessed by enough group members to make it crucial.[1] **The member(s) who conform most closely to a group's norms have the highest probability of emerging as informal leader(s) of the group (Homans, 1961).**

Interestingly, the informal leaders of a group can end up also having the most license to break the group's norms occasionally without punishment. It is as if a person builds up credits in the "liking and conformity-to-norms account" and thus can be the most free to

[1] A. Zaleznik, R. Christensen, and F. Roethlisberger, *The Motivation, Productivity, and Satisfaction of Workers* (Boston: Division of Research, Graduate School of Business, Harvard University, 1958).

"spend" the accumulated credit when he or she desires to. Thus, we have to add the counterproposition: **Informal group leaders may occasionally violate norms without punishment, provided that they have earned their leadership by general conformity to the group's norms (Homans, 1961).**

Many task groups, however, also have some members who refuse to follow the group's norms. Students, for example, who violate student norms by preparing for every class, reading all the suggested readings as well as the required readings in the course, challenging the teacher, and filling up class time with questions and arguments will often not be swayed by any punishments their classmates can generate. What normally happens after the other members give up all efforts to bring the deviant around is that he/she ends up being isolated from the group. In Chapters 7 and 8 we will examine individual motives in a way that might help explain why a person would resist peer pressure. However, you can see that those who choose, for whatever reasons, to resist the pressure of group norms often start out as deviants and end up as isolates.

External Status: How It Relates to Acceptance of Group Norms

Insofar as having a certain ethnic background, age, educational attainment, and so forth, makes it likely that a person will share particular attitudes with others of the same background, external status allows group members to quickly "place" new group members. Of course, not *all* middle-aged male second-generation Lithuanian-Americans, for example, are the same in all of their beliefs, values, and behaviors, nor are *all* sophomore women at, say, Radcliffe College the same. But within each category of people, common experiences and background can and often do lead to common tendencies, especially as compared to other groups. Most Radcliffe sophomores are probably more like one another than they are like the Lithuanian-born males. Even when there are genuine differences among people within any one category, many outsiders *assume* commonalities—often by stereotypes. But apart from stereotypes, most people's values are based on how they were raised and their experiences thereafter, and various status factors do give shorthand hints at what a person's beliefs are *likely* to be. Thus, though external status may not *accurately* reflect a person's beliefs and may even sometimes be misleading, groups in their early phases seem to rely on it to place members.

When a group's norms are strongly held, it is often extremely difficult for anyone who was raised from childhood with different beliefs to go along. A Maine native, taught Yankee independence from birth, is likely to be upset and uncomfortable in a work group of immigrant

Italians who believe in helping one another on and off the job, freely borrowing and lending money, tools, and even food, and frequently stopping work to laugh and joke loudly together. The worker from Maine will probably not want or be able to go along with the others' norms, and thus will be isolated, while the member of the Italian subgroup who is most spontaneous and generous will probably be most respected. In some other group the exact opposite could be true, and the independent Downeaster would be most respected.

Elizabeth Kovacs was until recently employed by the firm of Q Peanuts as a peanut packer. She was in the habit of arriving at work up to 90 minutes before her 8 A.M. job. She used the time to sit in the canteen with newspapers and coffee and "get myself into the mood for a day's hard work."

Miss Kovacs' fellow workers, though, did not like this one bit. They prevailed on management to issue a warning to her about the insidious practice. When the warning produced no change in the lady's habits, she was fired.

Source: *The Wall Street Journal.*

Whatever attributes a particular group treats as high status, external status and status congruence appear to have the following consequences for internal membership rank (Zaleznik, Christensen & Roethlisberger, 1958):

1. **High external status congruent members tend to become regular members.** It is as if a group coalesces around those whose status is uniformly high when they come to the group. Perhaps the people who come with lower external status look to those with greater status to see how things are supposed to develop, thereby helping the high status congruent members become central.
2. **Relatively high status but incongruent members tend to end up as isolates.** Those who do not "fit" easily into one category create some confusion in others, causing neither respect nor liking. The ultimate result is often isolation, perhaps because the basically high-status person will not as strongly "need" that particular group's approval.
3. **Low external status members, regardless of congruence, tend to become deviants.** Those whose overall status is low when they enter a group seem to find difficulty in breaking free from the group but cannot fully follow norms to become regulars. They are thus likely to perpetuate within the group the low status they arrive with. Some low-status people who don't care about the group for one reason or another may become isolates, perhaps because they perceive little to lose from ignoring the group.

Roles as Differentiators of Group Members

Can you imagine what life would be like if there were no predictability to anyone's behavior? How would you behave, for example, if you could never be sure of your father's reactions? Suppose you never knew which friends you could count on for cheering up, or blowing off steam, or talking through serious problems, or playing your favorite sport? Wouldn't life be chaotic if you had to make anew every single choice of behavior every time you saw another person? It would be similar to entering a foreign culture every day of your life. While the spontaneity of it all could be exciting, it might paralyze many of us and wear out the rest.

As people interact, however, individuals slowly arrive at patterned behavior, where each party begins to learn the other's likes and dislikes, needs, sensitive areas, and so forth, and can begin to accommodate to one another. A person comes to expect certain behavior and attitudes from others, and they come to expect particular behavior and attitudes from him/her. When you know the types of behavior or pattern expected of you in a particular situation, you have learned a role and automatically know what to do when in that situation. The way you then behave is not necessarily how you are in all situations, but it is likely to be repeated by you whenever you are with that particular group of people or in that situation. This kind of "specialized" behavior is another way of differentiating members, resulting in a consistent place in the group for all who take on a patterned role. Here is an example of the role behavior of a young faculty member in a business school:

> At faculty meetings I find myself frequently raising challenging, possibly unanswerable questions about curriculum and educational philosophy, making my colleagues uncomfortable but sometimes forcing them to deal with issues on a more fundamental level. They now more-or-less expect this of me, that I'll take the role of the "resident radical" who tries to pull the rug out from under their assumptions, and thus they relate to me with a kind of stubbornness, which "pulls" even more questioning from me. Every group which discusses complex issues needs to have the status quo challenged; something about my personality lets me step in to fill that role, and the challenging function is thus taken care of.
>
> But at another meeting I attend, where I am on the board of directors of a community social agency, my behavior is quite different. Because there are many people on the board with low educational levels and little knowledge about organizations, there is great need for expert information on how to set organizational goals and how to make decisions. Because I have some knowledge of these matters and am seen by other board members as a "business professor," at board meetings I tend to be much more in the role of "expert advice-giver" and "problem solver,"

so I probably act more responsibly and less mischievously than at faculty meetings.

In each case the group has a good sense of what to expect from me and vice versa, which is convenient and saves considerable time and confusion about who will do what. Particular types of behavior are almost automatically called forth.

At the same time, having well-established roles also acts as a constraint on the choices made by me and the others. At faculty meetings it is hard for me to get in on proposing realistic solutions to curriculum problems, because others assume that if I am proposing something it's probably too "far out." Conversely, by my questioning role I probably prevent others from being as critical and assumption-examining as they might like to be.

Similarly, there are times when I'd prefer to miss agency board meetings and relax with my family, or times when I would like to just joke around or toss out wild ideas, and many instances when I wish others would speak up more; but the responsibility of the role I'm in keeps me behaving in a helpful, problem-solving way. And, conversely, it is possible that some of the low-participating community members might feel freer to make constructive suggestions if I didn't preempt that role.

As with other kinds of deviance, behaving in ways not expected by others will cause discomfort in group members and lead to attempts to force the person back into the role. This can be uncomfortable for the individual trying to expand the role as well as for group members affected by the changes.

Thus, while our various roles are convenient they restrict our possible behaviors insofar as we choose to continue in them. Role behavior makes life more predictable and constrained by differentiating people according to particular behaviors expected of them and then reinforcing each role occupant for consistently taking that role. We expand on this in Chapter 10.

Though the patterns may vary to a greater or lesser degree, work group members inevitably acquire roles bringing their own styles and preferences to the group's requirements. Members respond to the needs of the group with their own personal styles and fairly rapidly begin to develop repetitive patterns of behavior. As group members notice one another's emerging patterns, they acquire expectations of how each person will behave, which reinforce whatever behavioral tendencies were exhibited, and soon a whole network of expectations is created, which helps make each person's participation predictable.

Few people have either so limited a repertoire of possible behaviors within them or so clear a notion of what they will not do that they can completely resist responding to others' expectations of them. Whether the behavioral pattern originates from within or from the strong expectations of others, when a person is treated as if he/she were *supposed* to act in a certain way, frequently that person will begin to do so, that is, produce the expected pattern.

Conformity to expectations by others is not inevitable, of course, and sometimes people resist being drafted into roles that do not fit. In our classes, for example, we often see athletes, treated at first as if they are only "jocks" uninterested in learning, struggle to not accept such a demeaning role and to become contributing group members. Roles assigned on the basis of external characteristics like sex, age, or appearance are probably less difficult to resist than those based on actual behavior, but they are by no means easy to escape. It takes a very determined person to continue to refuse to be what others expect, and such determination is rare. We will explore this question more closely in Chapters 8 and 10, especially in relation to conditions under which refusal is most likely. At present we can say that for most people concerned with readily finding a comfortable place in a group, acceptance of particular roles is likely if the roles are not too incongruent with how they view themselves.

For example, early in the life of a new group there will often be some uncomfortable silences, since members do not know one another and feel cautious about risking opinions without being sure of reactions. Inevitably some member will become uncomfortable enough with the silence to think up something to say just to ease the tension. It only takes a few such events to initiate expectations of the silence breaker. In some groups that member will then usually be expected to be an idea initiator and be appreciated for that. In another group with different needs, the silence breaker might be seen as bidding for leadership and be "assigned" (often implicitly) the role of "aspiring leader." Of course, the style and particular words used by silence breakers also make a difference as to how they will be perceived. If it is done with some humor, for example, that member may come to be seen as a great tension releaser and be appreciatingly expected to take that role, to fulfill that function whenever the atmosphere in the group becomes tense. On the other hand, the person who breaks silence by nervous chattering may not be so appreciated even when members notice and expect it.

In general, *roles in groups can be categorized by whether they serve to (1) help accomplish the group task (task-oriented), (2) help maintain good relationships among members (socially oriented), or (3) express individual needs or goals unrelated to the group's purposes (self-oriented).*

Any role behavior reflects the person's personality and needs, but from the group point of view the behavior will be seen as more valuable if it also fulfills a need of the group for getting the job done or for sustaining satisfying relationships.

Furthermore, it is important to remember that one person might take on several of these roles or that at different times several members might perform in the same role. How widely distributed and firmly established roles are is an interesting indicator of the degree of crystallization or fluidity of a group's structure. Sometimes particular individuals acquire a "monopoly" on a role, and no one else can take it even though for the task at hand the other(s) would be best suited. **A group will be less effective if some or many capable members are prevented from taking needed roles.**

The following roles have been found useful and common in successful task groups:

Roles related to accomplishing the group's tasks[2]

1. Idea initiator: Proposes tasks or goals, defines problems, suggests procedures or ideas for solving problems.
2. Information seeker: Requests facts, seeks information about a group concern, asks for expression of feelings, requests statements or estimates, solicits expressions of value, seeks suggestions and ideas.
3. Information provider: Offers facts, provides information about a group concern, states beliefs about matters before the group, gives suggestions and ideas.
4. Problem clarifier: Interprets ideas or suggestions, clears up confusion, defines terms, indicates alternatives and issues, gets group back on track.
5. Summarizer: Pulls together related ideas, restates suggestions after the group has discussed them, offers a decision or conclusion for the group to weigh.
6. Consensus tester: Asks to see if group is nearing decision, sends up "trial balloons" to test a possible conclusion.

Roles related to the group's social relationships

1. Harmonizer (joker or soother): Attempts to reconcile disagreements, reduces tension, gets members to explore differences.
2. Gatekeeper: Helps keep communication channels open, facilitates everyone's participation, suggests procedures that permit sharing of what members have to say.
3. Supporter: Exudes friendliness, warmth, and responsiveness to others; encourages, supports, acknowledges, and accepts others' contributions.
4. Compromiser: When own idea or status is involved in a conflict, offers compromise, yielding of status, admitting error or modifying position in interest of maintaining group cohesion.

[2] Adapted from K. Benne and P. Sheats, "Functional Roles of Group Members," *Journal of Social Issues* 4, no. 2 (1948), pp. 41–49.

5. Standards monitor: Tests whether group is satisfied with way it is proceeding, points out explicit or implicit operating norms to see if they are desired.

The variety of self-oriented roles is endless. Some (like "group clown") may be tolerated or neglected, while others (like "wet blanket," "playboy," "dominator," "self-confessor," or "bragger") may prove to be extremely annoying to other members and hinder group functioning. **In an effective task group, there will be a relatively low amount of self-oriented role behavior and a balance between task- and social-related roles as necessary.**

Sometimes such self-oriented behavior may be quite functional for a group, serving to release tension or smooth over differences. Reactions of group members to the self-oriented behavior of a "fight picker" or a "show-off" will depend on the frequency of the behavior and its timing. For example, a good wisecrack in the presence of a disliked authority figure may be gratefully appreciated, but constant joking when others want to work can become quite irritating.

SOME DYSFUNCTIONAL GROUP ROLES

Most people have had experience with group members whose behavior seems to serve mainly as an obstacle to getting anything done. In moderation their role behavior may be, and often is, helpful to the group; in excess it blocks progress. Below are listed a few of these roles (you can probably add to the list yourself):

- *Nitpicker:* Argues endlessly about the meanings of words and seems to dwell on nonessentials.
- *Endless talker:* Seems unable to let go of a topic and move on, going over the same points repeatedly.
- *Group humorist:* Uses every opportunity to make a joke, fool around, and distract group from its task.
- *Organizer:* Spends more time talking about what the group should be working on than working on it.
- *Topic jumper:* Cannot seem to stick to the point, goes off on tangents, jumps ahead, or goes back to a point already adequately discussed.

The various roles that members take on become part of how they are ranked by the group. In some groups idea initiators are most valued. As pointed out previously, high task contributors are usually respected, while high social contributors are usually liked; but each group will weigh the value of these patterns by its own standards and goals. **In general, the more a member fills both the task and social roles, the higher will be his/her status in the group. Members who only take either task or social roles tend to become overspecialized;**

their emergent status then depends on how highly the group values their "specialty."

At times you may find yourself playing multiple roles in a group, some of which may even conflict. For example, if you happen to be the best-informed member of a group working on a specific task, you are likely to be both an idea initiator and an information provider with little difficulty, but you could find it hard to also be a gatekeeper. The first two roles supplement one another, but the third one requires a different orientation toward the other members of the group. However, if you *can* learn to master such a combination of roles, it can certainly enhance your status as a group leader as well as a contributing member.

BEHAVIOR AS A RESULT OF STATUS DIFFERENTIATION

The status or rank of a group member may not be explicit or directly discussed by group members, but it is usually inferred from observing member behavior. In general: **Lower-status members defer to higher-status members, allowing higher-status members to *(a)* initiate interactions, *(b)* make statements without being challenged, and *(c)* administer informal rewards or punishments. Higher-status members will usually talk more, talk "for the group" in public situations, make more contacts with outsiders, and usually have the widest number of connections within the group (Whyte, 1955).** Even body posture and seating arrangements can reflect status differences: Higher-status members sit at or near the head of the conference table (or where they sit becomes the head); if the group is talking informally they will be at the physical center of the grouping; they are looked at when others are speaking; they tend to sit more erectly or confidently. They can even interrupt others or change the subject.

In general, at least in the United States, there are strong expectations about how high- and low-status people are supposed to behave. In a given situation people who are clearly higher status are expected to be "nice" and not lord it over others. It is a form of noblesse oblige, with expressions of the person's higher status being subtle and designed to not make others feel bad even though they are lower status. In turn, lower-status people are expected to "know their place" and not presume on the privileges of those with higher status; those who do not properly defer are considered "uppity." Because of the democratic ideals in the United States, little of this is talked about directly; but if you have trouble believing it, try testing it in a social or work situation.

> *A principle of organization [necessary for] advanced social life . . . in higher vertebrates is the so-called ranking order. Under this rule every individual in the society knows which one is stronger and which weaker than itself, so that everyone can retreat from the stronger and expect submission from the weaker.*
>
> Konrad Lorenz
> *On Aggression*

Influence

No matter how egalitarian the ideals of a work group, it is unlikely that all members can contribute equally along those dimensions—task or social—that the group values. Even where external status is roughly equal, as the group interacts some members will have better ideas, warmer personalities, or whatever is seen as desirable. As others perceive these differential talents, their possessors will be allowed more say about what the group should do, directions it should take, how decisions should be made, and so forth. *This ability to affect the behavior of others in particular directions* we define as *influence.*

Whether it is explicitly acknowledged or not, as a result of external status, adherence to norms, and roles taken, every member will have some differential degree of influence on others in the group. Some members will be more listened to or taken into account than others, and in most groups after awhile everyone knows reasonably accurately the relative standing of members in terms of influence. In student and other peer groups these differences are often denied, or at least talking about them is seen as taboo for fear of hurting feelings. Nevertheless, differences inevitably exist and can be documented by an observer. Since internal influence in a group correlates with internal status, it can be noted by the same kinds of behavior: deference, assertion, physical spacing, and so on. Just as the thoughtful manager will want to know about status differentials in groups, so will he/she want to be a careful observer of influence differentials and of how influence is acquired within a group.

In general we can predict that: **When members have congruently high external status, conform to the group's norms, and fulfill task and social roles, they will be accorded high emergent status and therefore have high influence within the group.** (See Figure 5–2.) If some of these factors are different, an altered proposition would be necessary to predict amount of influence within the group. Can you assess the relative influence of members of task groups to which you belong and then trace the influence to the factors discussed in this chapter?

The process of sorting out member influence and status is so impor-

FIGURE 5–2
Determinants of Group Status and Influence

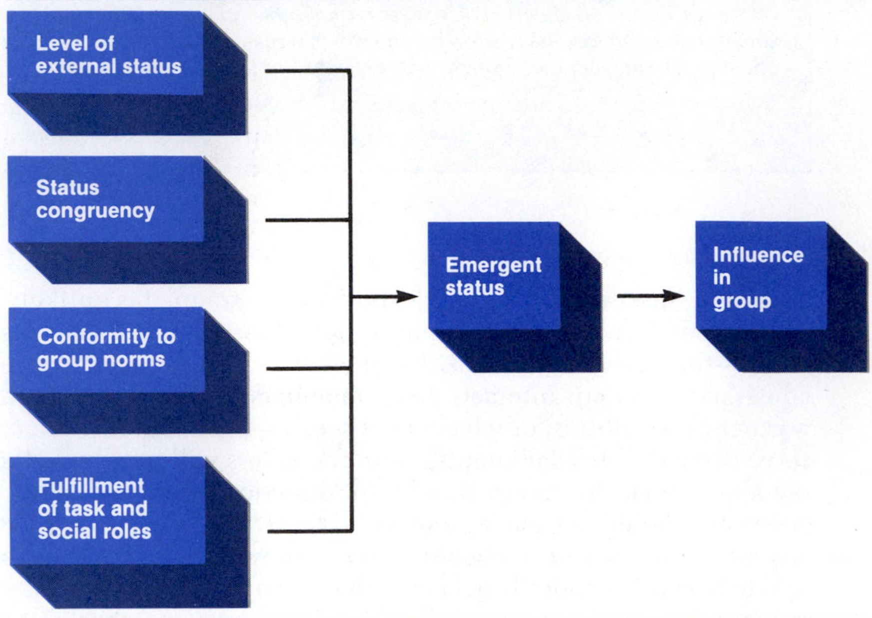

tant to a group's development that everything can be viewed from this perspective.[3] A group can be visualized as beginning with members sizing one another up and jockeying to find a satisfactory position in the group. The work of the group will become the means for jostling or infighting until each member has a relative position or rank with which he/she is satisfied. Though not everyone can be simultaneously at the top in terms of influence, stability can be achieved when all members accept the rank allotted them. If anyone is unhappy with his/her emergent position, new struggles will break out. The efforts to alter status then surface through attempts to conform more closely to norms, to change them, or to shift roles.

When you join a new group, you have some choice about the nature and degree of status you achieve. While you cannot change your external status, if you are willing to go along with group norms, take on task and social roles, and avoid self-serving behavior, you are likely to gain status and influence. Furthermore, while at first it may seem difficult to take initiative and speak up, a failure to do so will certainly limit your influence. On the other hand, talking too much can shut people

[3] The following formulation was originally suggested by one of our students, Nfor Susungi.

off, and while it makes you visible for the moment, it may hurt you in the long run.

A group will not reach a stable equilibrium where all its energies can be focused on its task until its internal rankings are essentially accepted by all. Then a kind of cohesion can be reached. In this view, a group cannot be fully productive until it has arrived at a somewhat "crystallized" or accepted structure. Until differences of opinion about "proper" ranking are settled by the members of a group, it is less likely to be fully productive since so much energy and attention must go into coping with individual restlessness.

On the other hand: **A structure that is too crystallized, where everyone "knows his place" only too well, can also have difficulties in producing, especially when tasks are changing and quick responsiveness is needed.** You might find comfort and security in knowing your niche in a group, but you might also find it somewhat limiting when it comes to challenge and new learning.

When a member tries to change rank, his/her influence is tested; a successful alteration of position indicates that the person had more influence than he/she was being credited with, while an unsuccessful attempt confirms or lowers the person's position. However, it can often be worth the risk of testing your influence; you lose little and you might discover that it is greater than you thought.

Subgroup

If group members are differentiated by how closely they adhere to group norms, there is a good possibility that they will form subgroups based on their degree of conformity to the norms. In addition other kinds of subgroupings often emerge on the basis of mutual personality attractions, previous friendships, common interests outside the group, shared positions on crucial issues, and so on. In a classroom task group, for example, subgroups may develop among those who are serious scholars, those who are fraternity/sorority members, the athletes, the campus activists, and others.

As soon as more than two people are in a group, the possibility exists of some of them joining up and then taking sides. **The greater the numbers of people in a group, the more likely is subgroup division.** It is rare that a group does not develop some cliques.

> *The worst cliques are those which consist of one man.*
>
> George Bernard Shaw

For the manager the important issue is not whether subgroups exist but the basis for their formation and the consequences for group functioning. If the subgroups exist because of differing but complementary task abilities, they may be quite functional for accomplishing group goals. Even if based primarily on social considerations, they may or may not hinder communications among members, foster cooperation or conflict, prevent or facilitate accomplishment of tasks, increase or decrease satisfaction, and so forth. Though it is certainly easier to assess the consequences of subgroup formation than do anything about it, it is an important factor in determining member standing and resultant productivity, satisfaction, and development.

One of the most serious subgroup problems rises when the smallest subgroup has only one member who is made to be a "subgroup" because he or she is visibly different than the others. The lone woman in an all-male group or the lone black in an all-white group—whom we can refer to as the token when the person is treated as a symbol rather than as an individual—often has special problems exactly because he or she has no (or very few) other subgroup members who are obviously alike and therefore appears to be even more different than the others than may actually be the case. While members of the dominant subgroup sometimes may actually have more in common with one another than with the token, often it may only be an untested assumption that the token is significantly different. In either case their attitude can make it difficult for the token to know how to behave. When a joke is made about Speedy Gonzales, does the only Puerto Rican laugh, become angry, or pretend he hasn't heard it? None of these responses is very satisfactory, so that even if the token has many other things in common with the others, he/she often has a hard time establishing the common bonds (Kanter, 1977). This can lead to communication and cooperation barriers, which affect the group's ability to coordinate its work.

It could be important and useful for you to test some of the above notions in groups of which you are a member. Often such problems exist just below the surface and need to be brought into the open.

CONSEQUENCES OF MEMBER DIFFERENTIATION FOR PRODUCTIVITY, SATISFACTION, AND DEVELOPMENT

In Chapter 4 we looked at how cohesiveness is connected to a group's production, pulling individual member output toward what the group's norms define as appropriate. Even noncohesive work groups, however, develop at least rough ideas about what is too much work and what is too little. Different groups have particular nicknames, richer than *deviants* or *isolates,* for people who don't carry their own load or for those who are so gifted or willing to work so hard that they make others look bad by their output. Those members who produce "too much" are often seen as "rate busters" or, as they are known in student circles, "curve breakers." Conversely, "slackers" or "goof-offs" are those who just cannot or will not produce at a pace satisfactory to the particular group's members. In general, then, a person's standing in a group is partly determined by how closely he/she conforms to the group's norms and is particularly affected by adherence to norms about individual output. Conversely, once a person's rank is established a particular level of output is likely to follow. Of course, the degree of required task interdependence will affect individual freedom to vary production, with jobs that can be done alone more easily subject to individual variation.

An interesting irony of the above observations is that: **In a high-producing group the isolates and/or deviants are likely to be low producers, while in a group that holds down productivity the isolates are likely to be high producers!** A person may choose not to conform so as not to work so hard or so little, or may be pushed into isolation out of inability to produce at about the group's desired rate. Similarly, a person who desires to be an accepted member will adjust productivity upward or downward to meet the group's norms. Whatever the cause, there is no doubt that rank within the group is connected to productivity.

A dramatic example of just how powerful a force is exerted upon members to produce according to group norms was reported in *Street Corner Society,* a detailed account of a group of young underemployed men who "hung around" together (Whyte, 1955). One of the valued skills in the group turned out to be bowling ability. But other qualities such as social skills, intelligence, and power of self-expression were dominant in giving members status; as you might expect, bowling expertise is not perfectly correlated with ability to argue well or talk to many people. One of the lower-status members of the gang was the "best" bowler when measured by scores attained when bowling casually; but whenever the gang bowled competitively his scores would inevitably fall below those of the gang's leaders!

The low-status expert bowler may not have been fully aware of why he didn't do as well when with the others, but the pressure and razzing from the gang to have his "productivity" fall into line affected him enough temporarily to alter his ability to produce. In general, under competitive stress the gang's bowling scores almost always perfectly reflected their relative status, even though some lower-ranking members had more ability than they could deliver when being "kept in their places" by the others.

In a work group some of the differentiation of members will follow from the task requirements. If various members are required to do different tasks some group valuation of the respective worth of each task will probably emerge. Those who do jobs that the group sees as crucial to its success will probably be given higher status than others.[4] When the group ranks members by the difficulty of the task each performs, the group is likely to be relatively high in output. Thus: **The more that member differentiation is based on task requirements, the more productive the group is likely to be.**

On the other hand, if member rank is largely based on external status the group is only likely to be high producing if by coincidence the factors that determine external status are also those that would determine genuine contributions to the group's tasks. **The more that member differentiation is based on external status, the less productive the group is likely to be (unless external status happens to coincide with needed group skills).**

Summary Productivity Proposition

Differentiation, of course, need not be inconsistent with group cohesion. Though cohesive groups sometimes cling together and enforce false equality even when differentiation would be appropriate, as in the case of groupthink, a group can be both differentiated and attractive to members. A highly differentiated group can be quite cohesive if all members believe that their positions accurately reflect their contributions, satisfy their needs, and lead to effective performance. In fact, if the group's tasks can best be done by each member *first* working on different aspects of the tasks and *then* coordinating individual efforts, the more differentiated *and* the more cohesive the group needs to be in order to produce at a high rate. Furthermore, if the group supports the organization's goals it will pull the highest possible productivity from its members. **The greater the differentiation *and* cohesion of a group with norms supporting the organization's goals, the greater its productivity is likely to be (Lawrence & Lorsch, 1967).**

Satisfaction and Development

As suggested earlier a group that is highly differentiated but in which each member accepts his/her status can be highly satisfied. Where differentiation, however, is a result of factors that some members do not accept as appropriate, considerable dissatisfaction can result. For example, if a work group automatically assigns low status to its female members, forcing them to do all the menial tasks and ignoring their contributions to the important jobs, there can only be general satisfac-

[4] This has its parallel in organizations, where individuals associated with important priorities (e.g., sales, engineering, etc.) tend to be highly influential.

HIGH-PERFORMING TEAMS

As reflected in some of the trends noted in Chapter 1, the concept of a high-performing team has emerged as an important part of an effective organization. In fact, some companies, usually in the high-tech area, try to conceive of their total organization as a high-performing team. Obviously, for most of us the idea brings to mind a small group of people performing a task rapidly and cooperatively, like a basketball team in a fast break. In fact, that metaphor is often used to describe the way a team of workers on a shop floor can operate when given the opportunity to take charge of their own operations and output.

High-performing teams can be developed in many different kinds of organizations and at almost any level of operation. Think of a medical team dealing with an emergency situation, a research and development group pressing to stay at the forefront of competitive technology, or a group of high-level managers making decisions on competitive prices in a rapidly changing, turbulent world market. All these situations demand a strong commitment of team members to the task and to working as a team. Exchange of information must be free and open, and there needs to be a willingness to keep the group's goals ahead of any personal goals or issues. The different talents and knowledge of all members need to be tapped. Leadership may be constantly shifting as the task demands, and any formal team leader is more likely to be playing an integrative role than a directing role, paying as much attention to group process as to group task.

tion if the women accept their lower ranking. If, as increasingly is the case, however, they want to be accorded whatever status they earn by merit rather than automatically being given low (or high) status merely because of sex, the group will have dissension and low satisfaction.

When group members take on roles and ranks that restrict them to merely doing what they know well, growth will naturally be limited. A group highly differentiated on the basis of adherence to norms that support maximum productivity can be very efficient but can limit chances for members to learn new jobs, try new skills, or be creative about work processes. **If the group's tasks are routine a rigid structure may be most productive but least growth promoting. Tasks calling for creativity and responsiveness, however, are not likely to be performed well by a rigidly differentiated group.** Furthermore, as we indicated with respect to a crystallized group, rigid differentiation is likely to be quite frustrating to members who want to learn and grow. For example, a group trying to think up a new commercial product like a labor-saving small appliance would have difficulty being imaginative if only the marketing person could give input on what customers might like, only the production manager could comment on how items can be built, and so forth. A free flow of ideas is called for regardless of the members' status and position in order for the group to be creative.

On the other hand, an insufficiently differentiated group may be highly productive at creative tasks, stimulate great learning by members, but be anxiety provoking at the same time. The lack of clear positioning can cause considerable uncertainty and nervousness for some members even while allowing them maximum opportunities for growth.

Finally, as you might expect by now, an underdifferentiated group will probably be quite ineffective at performing routine tasks, thereby dragging down morale when results are poor, and probably leading to little growth except for those few members who can take advantage of the looseness to pursue their own ends.

The degree of differentiation and cohesion in a group then are important emergent outcomes of the way the group works together. They greatly affect a group's performance, satisfaction, and learning. While we have tried to show how cohesion and differentiation come about, a more detailed look at how groups function as they go about their business can be useful in assessing their effectiveness. In the next chapter we examine more closely the working processes of groups to help you more readily judge what is effective group behavior as it is occurring in the emergent system.

KEY CONCEPTS FROM CHAPTER 5

1. Overall status in group determined by:
   a. Respect: accorded to high task accomplishment.
   b. Liking: accorded to high social accomplishment.
2. Initial ranking.
   a. The higher the background of external status, the higher the initial internal status of a group member.
3. Status affects behavior.
   a. The higher a person is on dimensions valued by the group and the more norms are conformed to, the higher his/her status within the group and vice versa. Members who conform are regulars; the greatest conformers become informal leaders and may violate group norms. Consistency of relative positions on dimensions determines degree of status congruence.
   b. Deviant: member who does not conform to group's norms; most negative attitudes expressed to that member.
   c. Isolate: conforms even less to group's norms; interactions with isolate very infrequent.
4. Roles determine status and group effectiveness.
   a. Task-oriented.
   b. Socially oriented.
   c. Self-oriented and other dysfunctional group roles.
   d. The pressure of balancing multiple roles.
5. The greater the number of people in a group, the more likely is subgroup formation.
6. Influence.
   a. The ability to affect the behavior of others in particular directions.
   b. Affected by rank.

7. Differentiation and cohesion are related to productivity, satisfaction, and development.
   a. Relation to task requirements.
   b. Relation to external status.
   c. Relation to support of organization's goals.

SUGGESTED READINGS

Bales, R. F. "Task Roles and Social Roles in Problem-Solving Groups." In *Readings in Social Psychology.* 3rd ed., ed. E. Maccoby, T. M. Newcomb, and E. L. Hartley. New York: Holt, Rinehart & Winston, 1958.

Bales, R. F., and F. L. Strodtbeck. "Phases in Group Problem Solving." *Journal of Abnormal and Social Psychology* 46 (1951), p. 485.

Benne, K., and P. Sheats. "Functional Roles of Group Members." *Journal of Social Issues* 4, no. 2 (1948), pp. 41–49.

Grinnell, S. B. "The Informal Action Group: One Way to Collaborate in a University." *Journal of Applied Behavioral Science* 5 (1969), pp. 75–103.

Hollander, E. P. *Leaders, Groups, and Influence.* New York: Oxford University Press, 1964.

Hopkins, T. H. *The Exercise of Influence in Small Groups.* Totowa, N.J.: Bedminster Press, 1964.

Homans, G. *The Human Group.* New York: Harcourt Brace Jovanovich, 1950.

________. *Social Behavior: Its Elementary Forms.* New York: Harcourt Brace Jovanovich, 1961.

Jacobs, T. O. *Leadership and Exchange in Formal Organization.* Springfield, Va.: National Technical Information Service, U.S. Department of Commerce, 1970.

Kahn, R. L.; D. M. Wolfe; R. P. Quinn; and J. D. Snoek. *Organizational Stress: Studies in Role Conflict and Ambiguity.* New York: John Wiley & Sons, 1964.

Kanter, R. M. *Men and Women of the Corporation.* New York: Basic Books, 1977.

Lawrence, P. R., and J. Lorsch. *Organization and Environment.* Homewood, Ill.: Richard D. Irwin, 1967.

Maier, N. R. F. "Assets and Liabilities in Problem Solving: The Need for an Integrated Function." *Psychological Review* 74 (1967), p. 244.

________. "Male versus Female Discussion Leaders." *Personnel Psychology* 23 (1970), pp. 455–61.

Roethlisberger, F., and W. Dickson. *Management and the Worker.* Cambridge, Mass.: Harvard University Press, 1939.

Thompson, V. A. *Modern Organization.* New York: Alfred A. Knopf, 1961.

Whyte, W. F. *Street Corner Society.* Rev. ed. Chicago: University of Chicago Press, 1955.

Zaleznik, A.; R. Christensen; and F. Roethlisberger. *The Motivation, Productivity, and Satisfaction of Workers.* Boston: Division of Research, Graduate School of Business, Harvard University, 1958.

6

DEVELOPING GROUP EFFECTIVENESS

Emergent Processes

The greater the time pressure, the more appropriate it will be for a group to make decisions by a vote or even by the unilateral decision of its leader.

Do you think you could tell from observing a group how well it is working? What criteria would you use? We have suggested that you judge by the outcomes—productivity, member satisfaction, and development. While these are the ultimate criteria of group effectiveness, it would be hard for a group to improve its operations as it went along if this were the only way to make judgments. To wait for the final outcomes to occur can be too late. Nor is progress toward those final outcomes necessarily an adequate basis for corrective action, since progress may become visible only when it is too late to take such action. Therefore it is important for a group to have some basis for evaluating its emergent processes as it carries out a given task. The group needs to raise such questions as: "Are we working in the right way?" "Does everyone adequately understand his or her job?" "Are we avoiding important issues?" and "How do people feel about the objectives of the work?" To the extent that a group has available some set of criteria by which to assess its processes, it is in a stronger position to improve the way it goes about a task.

The effectiveness of any group depends upon several factors. Appropriate human and technological resources are background factors that establish both the possibilities and the limits for productive outcomes. Further, the policies and directives that make up the required system have direct influence over the effectiveness of a working group. Accordingly, most managers pay a great deal of attention to both background and required aspects of a work setting; they take great pains to select the right people for a job and to spell out job requirements and specifications. Yet the emergent processes of a work group, which are equally important, are often overlooked except when they overtly disrupt the work. Even when managers recognize the importance of dealing with emergent processes, they often lack a useful set of criteria by which to judge.

> For example, the top planning group of an aerospace firm was having a great deal of trouble producing useful plans. Their meetings often wandered from their stated agenda to rambling discussions of new books about youth in America, psychological interpretations of current events, and so on. In the meantime corporate profits were steadily declining. Though the vice president for planning was not happy with the way the

group worked, he would not risk pushing the group to examine its own processes, partly because he did not know how to judge them himself. Meetings got worse and worse, frustration grew, and finally individual members began to quit for other jobs.

While Chapters 4 and 5 examined the emergent *properties* of a group (its structure or state of integration/differentiation at any point in time), this chapter will focus upon the emergent *processes* (the dynamics) of a group as it functions. In short, the chapter will use a kind of social-psychological "microscope" to examine *how* a group operates.

As a starting point, we will look at issues faced by every working group, how these issues determine the criteria by which to evaluate the appropriateness of a given group's process, and how these evaluations need to take into account the particular situation of the group (for example, its purpose, size, composition, surrounding circumstances, and so forth). While it will not be possible to cover all the varieties of situations and show how the criteria apply in every case, we will give you a general sense of how to fit the two together. The bulk of the chapter uses two contrasting case examples to demonstrate how to consider situational factors when evaluating a group's process.

ISSUES FACING EVERY WORK GROUP

Every work group has to deal with the same general issues regardless of whether it is a group of machinists on a shop floor, surgeons and nurses in an operating room, executives at a strategy meeting, or students on a task force. It is the *way* in which a group goes about dealing with each of these issues and resolving the accompanying dilemmas that constitutes the group's emergent system and thus its effectiveness. While the dilemmas are similar for all groups, there are many possible ways of resolving them; and while groups vary in what the members consider desirable or preferable, different circumstances call for different approaches.

Figure 6–1 shows 11 issues facing every work group.[1] Corresponding to each issue, we have listed sets of questions with which a group must cope. We suggest that you study the chart carefully, see how it applies to any group of which you are a member, and evaluate how well that group has gone about dealing with the issues. Even before

[1] A number of years ago, Douglas McGregor, a leading organizational theorist, described 11 criteria of an effective working group. While his studies were specific to certain kinds of groups (mainly executives), the issues inherent in McGregor's criteria serve as a useful framework for this chapter. See D. McGregor, *The Human Side of Enterprise* (New York: McGraw-Hill, 1960).

FIGURE 6–1
Issues Facing Any Work Group

Issue	*Questions*
1. Atmosphere and relationships.	What kinds of relationships should there be among members? How close and friendly, formal or informal?
2. Member participation.	How much participation should be required of members? Some more than others? All equally? Are some members more needed than others?
3. Goal understanding and acceptance.	How much do members need to *understand* group goals? How much do they need to *accept* to be *committed* to the goals? Everyone equally? Some more than others?
4. Listening and information sharing.	How is information to be shared? Who needs to know what? Who should listen most to whom?
5. Handling disagreements and conflict.	How should disagreements or conflicts be handled? To what extent should they be resolved? Brushed aside? Handled by dictate?
6. Decision making.	How should decisions be made? Consensus? Voting? One-person rule? Secret ballot?
7. Evaluation of member performance.	How is evaluation to be managed? Everyone appraises everyone else? A few take the responsibility? Is it to be avoided?
8. Expressing feelings.	How should feelings be expressed? Only about the task? Openly and directly?
9. Division of labor.	How are task assignments to be made? Voluntarily? By discussion? By leaders?
10. Leadership.	Who should lead? How should leadership *functions* be exercised? Shared? Elected? Appointed from outside?
11. Attention to process.	How should the group monitor and improve its own process? Ongoing feedback from members? Formal procedures? Avoiding direct discussion?

we go into detail on these 11 criteria of an effective group, you can probably discover some useful ways to apply them for yourself.

Every one of these issues can be related to some key aspect of a group's activities, interactions, attitudes, and norms. In examining group process, you might be looking at who is doing what, how he/she is doing it, who is interacting with whom, what seem to be the prevailing feelings, what kind of norm(s) has emerged in relation to a given issue, and so forth. Which of these questions demands attention depends entirely upon the particular situation, its complexity, and its history. For the sake of convenience throughout this chapter we will use the word *process* as a general term referring to any one or more of these emergent aspects of a group. It will be your job to determine *which* aspect of group "process" needs evaluation in any given set of circumstances. However, it is important to pay particular attention to group *norms,* since these govern the internal workings of a group. Because norms are difficult to change, their functionality needs to be examined as they emerge and before they become set in concrete. In fact, the 11 issues can be thought of as a classification system for group norms and therefore serve as a systematic guide to their evaluation.

WHAT THE WORK SITUATION REQUIRES

Many factors can be used to determine differences in what kind of group process is appropriate to the job. We will focus on *five* that tend to have direct and important consequences. These are:

Size of the work group.

Distribution of resources (expertise) in the group.

Complexity and/or diversity of the task.

Time pressure on the group to produce.

Degree of task interdependence required.

As we discuss each of these factors, we will generate propositions that describe the effects that each factor has on a work group. After we have discussed the factors, we will look at two examples that represent sharp contrasts in relation to all five of them. Then, using the examples as a point of reference, we will discuss each of the 11 criteria (Figure 6–1) and see how they describe effective working groups of very different kinds.

Size of the Work Group

From your experience in groups of varying sizes, have you noticed how small groups have a different "feel" than large groups? The small group allows closer relationships, a deeper knowledge of the members, and a better sense of the whole picture at any given time. These are seen as advantages by many people, and consequently they prefer working in a small group. Others are happier in a less intimate atmo-

sphere, prefer the greater anonymity of the larger group, and like the security of knowing there are more people to do the work and carry necessary group maintenance tasks.

Obviously, there has to be a trade-off in the various advantages of large versus small groups, many of which are primarily a matter of personal preference and many a matter of the inherent constraints posed by size. For example, it takes greater effort and more formal procedures to make sure that everyone in a large group is fully informed in matters concerning them. It also takes more time and effort to coordinate the work of more people. While these issues influence the ease of conducting the group's operations, they may or may not detract from its ultimate effectiveness. Remember, our primary concern here has to do with the utilization of resources in carrying out a task. In this regard we can say that in most instances: **The smaller the group, the fewer total resources there are available for work; however, it is easier to obtain full participation and coordination of individual effort (Bales & Borgatta, 1955; Seta, Paulus, & Schkade, 1976).** There may be rare exceptions to this proposition. John F. Kennedy once joked at a dinner of outstanding contributors to American life, "Never before have so many brains and talents been present in the same room at one time with the possible exception of the day when Thomas Jefferson dined alone!" Normally, however, fewer people mean fewer work resources, with the result that each carries a greater burden.

Distribution of Resources (Expertise) in the Group

Suppose an instructor assigned you to a group of students to work on a problem involving the use of quantitative analysis. It's likely that you would depend upon the group member(s) who knew such methods best to take the most active part in the task. If the relevant abilities were evenly distributed among the members, the load would not fall upon any one or two individuals but could be shared by all. The proposition in this regard follows very directly from the example. **The more evenly distributed are the resources (levels of expertise) of a group among its members, the more appropriate is total member participation.** This does not rule out the option of assigning specific jobs to only one or two members; it indicates only that the degree to which the assignments can appropriately be spread around depends upon the distribution of resources. It can be as wasteful to give specific work to members who are unable to do that particular task as it is to ignore the most expert member. It also can be appropriate at times to have someone other than the most expert member carry out a task, in order to increase the individual's skills and thus enhance the group's development.

Complexity and/or Diversity of the Work

Suppose the task assigned in the example above were simply to determine the probability of occurrence of an event using some clearly specified information. While it would certainly take some ability to complete the assignment, it is likely that any one person who had studied probability could do it. If the assignment were much more complicated (like determining various production costs for a given product based upon information on personnel turnover, salary levels, overhead rates, market demand, and fluctuations in availability and costs of raw materials), the task might better be handled by the combined talents of several people. The proposition that follows from this is: **The greater the task complexity/diversity, the more appropriate it is to utilize the resources of a number of people (Heise & Miller, 1951).** It allows for the handling of a greater *amount* and *diversity* of information and in more complicated forms. Simple tasks call for simple information and fewer resources for completion.

In developing a plan of action for completing a complex task, groups are sometimes unable to work out every specific step ahead of time and to anticipate every contingency that might arise. Under such circumstances it becomes important for those who are implementing different aspects of the plan to "make the plan work" by adjusting and adapting to the contingencies encountered and coordinating their alterations with those responsible for other parts of the plan. Yet this kind of creative and responsible behavior is likely to be impossible if the individual lacks knowledge about the rationale behind the plan, nor is that person likely to be attentive to "making the plan work" if lacking in commitment to the plan. Thus another important proposition is: **The more likely it is that unexpected contingencies demanding immediate adaptation will occur in carrying out a task, the greater the need for members to have full information about the work plan's rationale and be committed to the objectives of the plan (Steers, 1977).** Since the commitment to a course of action often rests on involvement in the development of the planned action and a consequent sense of ownership of the plan, a corollary proposition follows from the above: **The greater the need for individual members to make adjustments to a plan of action, the greater the need for them to share in the original planning and decision making.**

Time Pressure on the Group to Produce

This factor poses a paradox. When the time pressure is greatest, very often decisions are most critical. When decisions are most critical, the multiple resources of a group are most needed, and thus the working process of that group is of greatest import. Yet the pressure to produce often makes it impossible to take the time to examine group process even if it is operating poorly. Failure to take the time to look at process perpetuates that dysfunctional process; stopping to work on process eats up valuable time and can increase the stress with respect to the task. While either option is costly, the easiest time to work on group process issues is when there is adequate opportunity to deal with them fully; under pressure this is not likely to occur. Therefore the proposition we suggest in this instance is that: **The greater the time pressure, the less appropriate it is for the group to work on process issues (Isenberg, 1979).** One implication of this statement is that when time demands are at their lowest levels, the group should examine its ways of working to prepare itself to deal more effectively with the periods of high pressure. When there are impending deadlines, a group needs to function well reflexively, though it is often only under pressure that group members realize what they have not settled! Thus it seems most useful to work on group processes early and on low-risk tasks where time is not crucial, then build on this base for key tasks and/or time constraints.

Time can also affect decision making and leadership. When time pressure is great, there is often insufficient opportunity for the whole group to talk things through thoroughly to a consensus. A quicker means of reaching a decision may be needed. The proposition that follows is: **The greater the time pressure, the more appropriate it will be for a group to make decisions by vote or even by the unilateral action of its designated leader rather than by consensus.** (We will have more to say about the impact of time on leader behavior in Chapter 12.)

Degree of Task Interdependence Required

A group of auto workers assembling a new car probably has its individual tasks pretty well routinized. They may talk a lot to each other, but it is not required in order to do the work. Their interactions depend more on personal preferences, mutual attractions, interests outside the task, and so forth—what we have called emergent factors. There is some degree of interdependence among the tasks each is performing because some jobs cannot proceed until others have been completed. However, the bases of the interdependence are clear-cut and require relatively little exchange of information in an ongoing manner. By way of contrast, a group of friends playing touch football constantly needs to exchange information on strategy, weak spots in the other team, mistakes in their own play, and so on. These exchanges are demanded by the nature of their task almost from moment to moment. The player throwing a pass needs to be able to anticipate where the receiver will be and who will be blocking the onrushing opponents. Whether or not the auto workers ever develop any degree of friendship, mutual understanding seems only peripherally related to task accomplishment. In the case of the touch football team, it is extremely useful for the members to know a great deal about each other's abilities as well as to develop a sense of confidence in and support for each other. The degree of required interdependence leads to what we might call a *team,* which goes a step beyond what we call a group.

The proposition that applies in this instance is: **The greater the degree of task interdependence required, the more important it is for group members to maintain continuing exchanges with and have knowledge of each other as persons.** The proposition refers primarily to task-related information. Whether or not personal friendships as opposed to working colleagueships develop in the course of the interactions is again a matter of member preferences and opportunities. It is not critical to the group's success, though likely when there is high interdependence. Think, for example, of fire fighters, whose very lives depend on one another's skill, knowledge, and performance. It is not surprising that while they work together their families become close, spend time together, and form relationships beyond what is directly required by work.

When You Put All the Factors Together

It is not easy to manage a group well. (For some ideas on how to manage a single meeting, see accompanying box.) Each of the five factors can vary and can yield a tremendous variety of possible combinations. You find small groups with an imbalanced distribution of resources, working on simple tasks under high pressure (as in a group monitoring an automated chemical process) or large groups with high task interdependence working on complex tasks under little pressure (as in a corporate research lab). There are obviously too many possible combinations to explore each one. It might be useful and fun for you to generate different combinations and to see if you can think of groups that fit; or you might take a look at some groups you know and see if you can describe them in terms of these five factors. Later, as we discuss the kinds of group processes that are appropriate to a given set of circumstances, you can determine how those processes apply to your own examples. For illustration we will utilize two case examples of a highly contrasting nature. In this way we can highlight the importance of considering the situation when you determine what kind of group processes are appropriate.

THE CASE OF THE FACULTY GROUP

Suppose you were observing a group of seven faculty members working on the development of a new interdisciplinary graduate program in the social sciences. Their individual backgrounds are varied, they are each highly knowledgeable in one or another area of social science, and they are all considered to be competent teachers and scholars. The task before them involves many different specialties that need to be integrated, a lot of uncertainty about the outcomes of this type of educational venture, and a tremendous amount of material that needs to be prepared and reviewed in order to put together a proposal that can be accepted by colleagues and administrators. There is very little outside pressure to complete the proposal, so the group can take whatever time it wishes for the task. Since the entire concept of the program involves careful integration of all their ideas and expertise, every aspect of the work demands highly interdependent working relationships.

GUIDELINES FOR RUNNING A MEETING

Most people resent poor meetings that waste time. Careful advanced planning and preparation can help, especially when time pressures mean that attention to process during a meeting will be inappropriate. Some tips on improving meetings:

I. Plan for the meeting (chairperson).
   1. Define objectives.
   2. Think through who should attend: diverse viewpoints, knowledge, degrees of commitment.
   3. Develop agenda and estimate time for each major agenda item (all necessary resources, no unnecessary resources).
   4. Make clear what is expected from the group on each item: information sharing, advice, exploration, or decision.
   5. Schedule unimportant items last.
   6. Avoid regular meetings lasting more than 1½ hours.

II. Facilitate attendee preparation.
   1. Provide sufficient notice and directions about time and place.
   2. Circulate agenda.
   3. Circulate, as appropriate, background materials (handouts).
   4. Contact selected attendees beforehand to cultivate preparedness, interest, and so on. On major issues, it is useful to talk to everyone ahead of time, to anticipate clashes, avoid hopeless battles, and the like.

III. Provide suitable physical facilities.
   1. Adequate space and furniture.
   2. Necessary equipment (flip charts, markers, projectors with extra bulbs, blackboard).
   3. Appropriate location ("neutral" territory, away from telephone, freedom from interruption, near data files, and so on).
   4. Refreshments, if appropriate.

(continued)

IV. Conducting the meeting (chairperson).
  1. Start on time.
  2. Set stage: review purpose, introduce new members, and the like.
  3. Exercise control.
    a. Follow agenda.
    b. Prevent one or two from hogging "air time."
    c. Manage time (seek decision when appropriate, move on to next item, and so on).
    d. Cut off side conversations.
    e. Appoint someone to take notes.
    f. Define issues.
    g. Ask many questions.
  4. Manage process.
    a. "Gate keep"—insure everyone gets a chance to speak.
    b. Stop interruptions.
    c. Initiate a "stretch," open windows, and the like.
    d. Clarify misunderstandings.
    e. Don't take silence as agreement; do not force early consensus.
    f. Stop to find out why discussion is not going well when that occurs.
    g. Summarize.
  5. Speak more to group than to individuals.
  6. Finish on time!

V. Participating in meeting (members).
  1. Prepare self for meeting (read handouts, and so on).
  2. If can't attend, inform chairperson.
  3. Be on time.
  4. Exercise self-discipline (stick to topic, do not interrupt).
  5. Practice "active listening."
  6. Contribute to managing the meeting's process.
  7. Carry out, subsequently, responsibilities assigned.

VI. Concluding the meeting.
  1. Summarize decisions reached.
  2. Review responsibility assignments and clarify next steps (who, to do what).
  3. Take time to asses the meeting's process, if necessary.
  4. Schedule next meeting (if appropriate).

VII. Follow-up.
  1. Prepare and distribute notes.
  2. Follow up on carrying out of assignments.

THE CASE OF THE RESTAURANT STAFF

Let's look at another group that differs from the first. It consists of 25 members of the staff of a high-class restaurant. The group includes various levels of expertise from the head chef and maître d' on down to the dishwashers and busboys, as well as wide variations in experience in a food service industry. The tasks themselves are not very complex except for the chef's; each person has a clearly defined job with a very limited range of diversity. The restaurant has an excellent reputation to maintain, and every member of the staff is under pressure to be on his or her toes at all times, paying attention to the quality of the food, the service, the cleanliness of the tables and floor, and so forth. While the job that any one person performs, especially at such levels as chef or maître d', can affect the whole operation, each person's work is sharply enough differentiated so that much of it can be performed independently of the other employees. However, key points where coordination is needed are such matters as preparing orders in time, picking up food as it is ready to be served, getting tables cleared off fast enough to prepare for the next customer, and so on. But once a system has been devised these are routine matters and do not require elaborate or intensive discussion and analysis by the staff at the time of execution.

HOW THE CRITERIA APPLY TO EACH GROUP

THE FACULTY GROUP. The group of faculty members working on a graduate program proposal can be described as:

A. A small group with
B. Evenly distributed resources,
C. Dealing with a complex and diverse task,
D. Under little external time pressure,
E. But requiring a high level of interdependence.

Under these circumstances the appropriate group processes would tend to be as follows:

1. Informal atmosphere with close, friendly relationships.
2. Full participation of all members equally.
3. High level of goal understanding and acceptance on the part of every group member.
4. Complete sharing of all information, with every member listening to every other member.
5. Disagreements discussed and resolved, not set aside.
6. Decisions made by group consensus.
7. Criticism of performance open and direct among all group members.
8. Feelings about task expressed openly and directly.
9. Task assignments made and accepted through discussion and negotiation; as voluntary as possible.
10. Leadership shared freely and changed along with corresponding changes in situational demands.
11. Group devotes significant blocks of time to the discussion of its own process.

THE RESTAURANT STAFF. The staff of the high-class restaurant can be described as:

A. A large group with
B. Highly differentiated resources,
C. Dealing with simple and narrow tasks, except for a few highly skilled jobs like chef,
D. Under a high level of time pressure,
E. With a relatively low level of task interdependence except at a few key points.

Under these circumstances the appropriate group processes would tend to be:

1. Formal atmosphere with task-relevant relationships.
2. Participation in discussions based upon expertise.
3. Understanding and acceptance of goals related to level and scope of job responsibilities.
4. Members obtain information from and listen to those other members possessing greater relevant knowledge.
5. Only those disagreements directly interfering with task are dealt with; final resolution determined by those members with greatest expertise.
6. Decisions made by those with relevant level of knowledge and expertise.
7. Criticism of work made by those members with the requisite knowledge and experience.
8. Feelings expressed through prescribed procedures.
9. Assignments made by those members with greatest level of knowledge and expertise.
10. Leadership on any given aspect of task determined by the relevant knowledge and experience.
11. Very little time devoted to examining group process; procedures are devised by higher-level members and carried out in a formal manner.

As you compare the two pictures just drawn, you might have some personal reactions to them. The first one portrays a kind of setting that many but not all people prefer, while the second has the ring of a small bureaucracy and may not be quite as attractive to you, though there are people who do prefer working in more structured, defined settings. Again we wish to remind you that what actually happens in any given situation is not just a matter of what the nature of the situation requires or calls for; it is also a matter of what other options are possible and what the members of any group might consider most desirable for them. The staff of the restaurant might very well *choose* to operate in a manner similar to that of the faculty group, but it would be fighting an uphill battle in the face of what the task situation demands. For example, try to imagine 25 people struggling to resolve all the disagreements that can occur in such a large group. How feasible would it be for such a group to arrive at a consensus on all issues? What would be the costs of ignoring the many years of experience and the levels of expertise that some individuals possess, in order to widen and maximize member participation? And what would happen

A PROCESS THERMOMETER
Group Self-Assessment Questionnaire

Instructions: First, individually check the one space that most closely expresses how you would describe the group on each characteristic. Then, tally the combined perceptions and jointly discuss their implications.

	1	2	3	4	5	
1. Atmosphere and relationships						
Supportive	____	____	____	____	____	Competitive (each for his/herself)
Personal (warm and close)	____	____	____	____	____	Impersonal (cool and distant)
Energetic	____	____	____	____	____	Lethargic
Cohesive	____	____	____	____	____	Fragmented
2. Member participation						
All equally	____	____	____	____	____	Primarily just a few
Easy to get "air time"	____	____	____	____	____	Hard to get "air time"
3. Goal understanding and acceptance						
Clear (understood)	____	____	____	____	____	Unclear (vague)
Supported by all	____	____	____	____	____	Unsupported by many
4. Listening and sharing of information						
Members listen carefully	____	____	____	____	____	Members don't really listen
Members usually understand one another	____	____	____	____	____	Members often misinterpret what others say
Everyone knows what's going on	____	____	____	____	____	Only a few are "in the know"
5. Handling disagreements and conflict						
Alternate views explored	____	____	____	____	____	Alternate views brushed aside
Tensions confronted and dealt with	____	____	____	____	____	Tensions avoided
6. Decision making						
Influence is widely shared	____	____	____	____	____	A few exert a lot of influence

(*continued*)

if everyone criticized everyone else and freely expressed all their feelings about every aspect of their work? Though such a set of choices might be made to work, it would consume extraordinary energy, and in the long run it would be unlikely to get the work done effectively.

What both situations have in common is that they are maximizing the use of group member resources. They appropriately differ from

	1	2	3	4	5	
Reflective of a full discussion	____	____	____	____	____	Quickly by majority rules
7. Evaluation of member performance						
Feedback given openly and constructively	____	____	____	____	____	Feedback avoided
8. Expressing feelings						
Expressed openly	____	____	____	____	____	Kept bottled up
Personal concerns accepted	____	____	____	____	____	Only task concerns shared
9. Division of labor						
Roles clearly defined and stable	____	____	____	____	____	Roles vary depending on individual interests
10. Leadership						
A clear leader(s) exists	____	____	____	____	____	Leadership functions (acts) are done by all
Member differentiation appropriate and accepted	____	____	____	____	____	Jockeying for position is occurring
11. Attention to process						
Process often discussed in the whole group	____	____	____	____	____	Process seldom discussed in the whole group
Has beneficial norms	____	____	____	____	____	Has restrictive norms
12. Consequences: The group—						
Is very productive	____	____	____	____	____	Is very unproductive
Gives me satisfaction	____	____	____	____	____	Gives me little satisfaction
Facilitates my learning and development	____	____	____	____	____	Restricts my learning and development

each other in *how* they use their resources, but they can be equally high in the outcomes of productivity, worker satisfaction, and development.

PROCESS CAN BE CHANGED

Are we saying that a group is "stuck" with a set of processes dictated by circumstances? No. We are saying that a given group needs to consider the nature of its circumstances in judging the effectiveness of its own processes. A large group applying small group standards will create difficulties for itself. And this same reasoning applies to each of the five conditions discussed earlier.

However, a group can *change* its circumstances. A large group can subdivide into smaller groups, each of which can utilize effective small group process criteria. Further, if the subdivisions equalize the levels of expertise in each subgrouping, then other criteria begin to change in their applications. At the restaurant, for example, it may be that waiters in each area can usefully meet to discuss possible areas of cooperation; or chef, maître d', and key waiters might periodically examine the way orders are transmitted. Factors like task complexity and required interdependence may be less subject to change, but even these allow the possibility of exploring various forms of innovation and work variation. For example, individuals normally assigned to one kind of task can exchange jobs with others in order to learn a wider range of tasks.

We do consider it critical, however, for a work group to remember to utilize its full range of resources in order to be effective. **If the task calls for differentiated levels of expertise in a group, then the effectiveness of that group's process will depend upon the degree to which it gives influence to appropriate members.** By way of contrast: **If the task calls for evenly distributed resources among the members of a group, then the effectiveness of the group's process will depend upon the degree to which influence is equally shared among the members.**

Task Group Effectiveness Develops over Time

In taking steps to diagnose the appropriateness of a group's process and to change that process, one must not only consider the work situation as discussed above but also one other aspect of the group: its phase of development as a task group.

No group can expect to be instantly effective. Groups are known to go through developmental phases or periods during which certain of the 11 issues are central and require resolution before the group can move on to deal with other issues and eventually establish its best working process. You as an individual can probably remember some stages you went through during your life when certain issues were dominant. For example, before you became an independent adult you may have had to work through a period of counterdependence in which you were struggling to prove yourself. Similarly, groups typically have to resolve membership issues before they can focus on issues of confrontation and reach full working expectations. The time it takes for a group to work through the phases will vary with the backgrounds of its members. If the members have had little experience working in groups, the process is liable to be slow and even cumbersome. While groups composed of members who have had experience can usually proceed more rapidly, if the range of experience is great and some become impatient with the needs of others, the process may also be slow.

Furthermore, just as counterdependent feelings can be rekindled in individuals from time to time throughout life by the actions of teachers, bosses, and others, so too groups do not necessarily leave a given phase of development permanently. From time to time they must recycle to rework old issues that were not fully resolved or to modify their resolutions in the face of new events or new members.

Consequently, a manager who assigns people to a committee or task force needs to understand that it may take some time for that group to reach its full effectiveness. Similarly, as you seek to diagnose the groups of which you are a member, try to consider what phase they are in and what steps you can take to facilitate their appropriate movement to the next phase. Also do not be surprised if at times you and the group need to recycle and work some more on an issue that was previously resolved.

In the next section we discuss five phases of group development:

Membership.

Subgrouping.

Confrontation.

Individual differentiation.

Collaboration.

As you consider these concepts, remember that they are very general and, while descriptive of many groups, they should not be taken as inevitable for any given group. As with individuals, every group has its unique character and manner of development.

FIVE PHASES OF GROUP DEVELOPMENT

Phase 1—Membership

When a group is newly formed, the members typically wonder about whether they will have a place in the group and will find acceptance in it. They wonder whether others perceive the goals of the group as they do and whether the goals of the group that emerge (are clarified) will be ones to which they can give commitment. Will the price of membership in terms of expected behavior (norms) and the benefits of membership (support, acceptance, goal accomplishment) warrant their psychological joining of the group? In short, members tend to be concerned with their own safety and place in the group rather than with collective efforts toward the task. Issues of participation and membership, goals, and (in a covert way) evaluation are important.

The atmosphere is likely to be strained, leading to superficial and polite interaction conducted with caution. While some individuals may respond to the ambiguity of the situation with an extra amount of activity and talk (in an attempt to establish some definition), others will tend to be hesitant and reserved.

Members are likely to feel quite dependent on the designated leader if there is one (as usually is the case in businesses), or look to the wider organization for clarification if there is not. Members often approach tasks with high energy but little coordination.

Any attempt to diagnose who ultimately will exert leadership is prone to great error, although early "activists" sometimes may be propelled into leadership positions that they ultimately cannot sustain. Listening may be quite intense as people have their antennas out to discover the rules of the road; but distortion is likely (hearing what one wants to hear for safety), and there is little sharing and testing of understanding and interpretation.

Members need to get acquainted and begin to share expectations about goals and objectives. Efforts to rush this process by demanding that people reveal intimate facts about themselves can be disastrous, but full attention to the task with no effort to get acquainted and no sharing of self can also be inhibitive. The need is to become acquainted with one another and begin the process of goal clarification.

Similar attempts to establish norms about handling conflict openly or allowing full expression of feelings, while given lip service, are generally premature and therefore ineffective during this phase. Those issues will come up later.

Phase 2—Subgrouping

As members begin to get acquainted and identify others who share some of their expectations, pairing and other subgroupings occur. The issue of relationships begins to come to center stage as individuals focus on similarities and dissimilarities and seek out others for friendship, acceptance, and support (allies on task issues).

Relationships may tend to be clinging, as members hang on to those who seem similar among potentially dangerous others. Members begin to express some feeling of warmth within the subgroupings, and the overall atmosphere can become more relaxed even though information flow will still be somewhat guarded.

A person in the authority position is likely to be resisted regardless of what he or she says, and if there is not a designated leader, then there will be resistance to anyone who tries to take charge. Group members complain to one another about the impossible task that the organization has given them or about other aspects of the wider organization. Energy for working on the task tends to sag, and while members begin to cooperate (at least with their new-found allies), there is little planning of task activities.

Sometimes groups in this phase develop a sense of unanimity of purpose and cohesiveness that may, in fact, be phony, based on a tendency to avoid conflict and withhold evaluations.

One danger is that pairings and subgroups form so quickly after people gain some knowledge of one another in Phase 1 that there is a lack of linkages across subgroups. Knowledge of and some linkage with all group members can be most important for pooling resources and resolving the nearly inevitable disagreements and conflicts that typically emerge in Phase 3.

Another danger during Phase 2 is that the subgroups develop spokespersons so that total group discussions are conducted by only a few members, and a pattern of narrow participation is established irrespective of the requirements of the work situation. This too can inhibit conflict resolution in Phase 3.

Phase 3—Confrontation

During this stage, relationships between subgroupings come to the fore along with leadership and the handling of disagreement as members seek to influence the direction and operating practices of the group. Struggles for individual power and influence are common. Questions of member roles and division of labor often emerge along with issues of relative contribution and member evaluation.

Listening is often likely to reach a low ebb, with heated exchanges revealing feelings that may have previously been avoided, suppressed, or denied.

One danger is the temptation to avoid conflict by patching things over prematurely before the issues are fully explored and by establishing norms against rocking the boat or raising controversial subjects. When this happens the disagreements and any associated bad feelings among members go underground, ready to affect future business in often indirect and insidious ways.

A second danger is that disagreement and conflict are dealt with strictly through power, so that one individual or one subgroup "wins" and others "lose"; the issue remains unresolved. Someone emerges as a loser, often resulting in either withdrawal or warfare. Withdrawal reduces the group's resources and is hardly a source of satisfaction and growth for the individuals involved. Warfare, which is typically carried over to the next task facing the group, is a sure way to guarantee lowered productivity and energies devoted to attack and self-defense rather than growth. A third danger is merely a continuation of the struggle and a lack of energy for any new projects.

There is also great opportunity in this phase. When groups are able to resolve differences (whether interpersonal or task oriented) successfully, the payoff can be immense as the group moves on to Phase 4. Resolution can be accomplished through finding a new, integrative solution, an open discussion of differences leading to clarification of misunderstandings, or the assistance of an outsider in helping the group listen better and improve its process. Success in dealing with disagreement and conflict can build group cohesiveness, members' skills, and confidence in the group's ability to deal with future issues.

Phase 4—Individual Differentiation

During this phase the issues of division of labor and member evaluation are likely to be dominant. Members begin to become more accepting of differences among themselves, and there emerges a deeper and genuine concern for one another. Task assignments are based on skills, interests, and desires to grow. Roles and status become differentiated, but members respect one another's contributions. Such a division of labor often rests upon a more open, yet supportive, level of member evaluation than existed during the earlier stages. As time progresses and differentiation occurs, this stage may be marked by a kind of euphoria as group members realize that it will be possible to belong to this group without having to fight to the death or totally give in to majority wishes.

The atmosphere during this period is likely to involve cohesion, satisfaction, and trust as a result of having successfully overcome the conflicts of Phase 3 (yet include some underlying tension over the process of member evaluation and differentiation); there is an overall feeling of confidence and progress.

Leadership may have evolved with one or two individuals having dominant roles, yet without a sense of imposed domination. Instead members see the pattern as functional. In addition there is likely to be effective listening so that even the least influential member has the potential to exert influence and thereby share leadership.

Phase 5—Collaboration

Too few groups reach this stage. In it members focus on ways to complement one another's strengths and weaknesses and find that they can honestly level with one another without its leading to disruption. Members support one another when they genuinely agree, and they argue with one another when they genuinely disagree. Responsibility is distributed among members on the basis of individual competence, and leadership passes around the group on the basis of competence to do particular activities. The entire group achieves a cooperative and interdependent relationship with the rest of the organization, providing input to the organization as needed and taking the organization's needs into account when doing work and making decisions. The group learns how to balance individual and group efforts on tasks, allowing individual members to do tasks alone when they have highly differential expertise and doing tasks cooperatively when many opinions and points of view are needed. Learning activities are geared to optimize individual contributions so that each individual can work toward his or her higher potential.

The issue of process is central as the group seeks to maintain the effectiveness developed as a result of its successful progress through the preceding stages. There is always potential need for a group to reexamine its process as it faces new task problems and as members individually grow and develop. Furthermore, as working conditions change, aspects of issues bypassed on the way through the five stages may become important. Consequently, a typical group recycles through aspects of these five phases again and again.

Figure 6–2 outlines typical ways in which the 11 issues facing a group manifest themselves as operating characteristics during the five phases of group development.

HELPING GROUP MOVEMENT TOWARD GREATER EFFECTIVENESS

We started this chapter by asking how you can tell how well a group is working without waiting for the ultimate outcomes to occur. Implicitly we also were asking what a group could do to improve its way of working. We suggest that you begin by observing the group's emergent system, noting how it has resolved the 11 issues that any group faces, and then evaluating whether that process has been appropriate given the group's situation (size, resources, task and time pressure). Such a diagnosis sets the stage for taking corrective action if and where it is needed.

In general, the way to move the group along is to pay careful attention to the underlying concerns of group members and then either

FIGURE 6–2
Common Operating Characteristics during Stages of Group Development

	STAGES	
Issues	*I Membership*	*II Subgrouping*
Atmosphere and relationships.	Cautiousness.	Greater closeness within subgroups.
Participation.	Superficial and polite.	In subgroups by subgroup leaders.
Goal understanding and acceptance.	Unclear.	Some greater clarity, but misperceptions likely.
Listening and information sharing.	Intense but high distortion and low sharing.	Within subgroups, similarities overperceived.
Disagreement and conflict.	Not likely to emerge; if it does, will be angry and chaotic.	False unanimity.
Decision making.	Dominated by more active members.	Fragmented, deadlocks.
Evaluation of performance.	Done by all, but not shared.	Across subgroups.
Expression of feelings.	Avoided, suppressed.	Positive only within subgroups, mild "digs" across groupings.
Division of labor.	Little, if any.	Struggles over jobs.
Leadership.	Disjointed.	Resisted.
Attention to process.	Ignored.	Noticed but avoided.

Source: Adapted from Steven L. Obert, "The Development of Organizational Task Groups" (Ph.D. dissertation, Case-Western Reserve University, 1979).

discuss these directly to allay fears or take actions that will deal with the concerns indirectly. For example, say that a group you are in is having difficulties coming to decisions because each of three subgroups insists on its own point of view. One approach is to comment on the deadlock, ask if others agree that the struggle is between subgroups each wanting its way, and then talk about how to reach a decision that would not make one or two subgroups feel defeated.

The less direct approach might include such suggestions as asking members to restate other's arguments before making their own; proposing that the group divide in half, with each half composed of members from each of the subgroups so that freer discussion might take

STAGES		
III Confrontation	IV Individual Differentiation	V Collaboration
Close within subgroups, hostility between subgroups.	Confidence and satisfaction.	Supportive and open.
Heated exchanges.	Individuals come in and out based on expertise.	Fluid, people speak freely.
Fought over.	Agreed upon.	Commitment.
Poor.	Fairly good.	Good.
Frequent.	Based on honest differences.	Resolved as it occurs.
Based on power.	Based on individual expertise.	Collective when all resources needed, individual when one expert.
Highly judgmental.	Done as basis for differentiation but with respect.	Open, shared, developmental.
Coming out, anger.	Increasingly open.	Expressed openly.
Differentiation resisted.	High differentiation based on expertise.	Differentiation and integration, as appropriate.
Power struggles common.	Structured or shared.	Shared.
Used as weapon.	Attended to compulsively or too uncritically.	Attended to as appropriate.

place; proposing that the group stop trying so hard to decide among the existing alternatives and begin to brainstorm new solutions that might integrate the opposing viewpoints; or arranging a break from task activities, with lots of informal interaction.

All of these steps are designed to allow a group to improve on its emergent processes and to get past a development phase in which it may have become blocked. One caution, however: A group should not try to rush too rapidly through Phases 1 to 4 in the hopes of avoiding all difficulties. Groups need time to develop, and any suggestions you make will be accepted most readily when others feel stuck and want help in moving. Also remember that circumstances change. A periodic

SEVERAL WAYS GROUPS MAKE DECISIONS

1. By the unilateral action of one dominating member or designated chairperson (autocratic).
2. By the unilateral action of a dominant subgroup acting as a power block by imposing its will.
3. By assumption, with silence taken as agreement, a ploy often used by a subgroup to exert dominance.
4. By default (inaction). Inaction is a decision to either stay with the status quo or allow "fate" to decide.
5. By democratic vote (dominance of the majority).
6. By unanimous agreement, perhaps resulting from a thoughtful, open discussion and exchange of ideas.
7. By consensus. Note, consensus is not the same as unanimity in that some members will still not be in agreement even after prolonged discussion, but they will be willing to go along and allow the group to act as most members see appropriate. Such willingness to go along with the majority under true consensus is an outgrowth of those in the minority feeling that their views have been heard, understood, and actively considered, and that the common goals of the group can be served best by action rather than further discussion.

reassessment can provide a group with the data by which to insure that its processes continue to serve its goals and objectives.

It is important to note that groups sometimes evolve without direct action by the manager, or in a way not anticipated by the manager, as a result of key events. A crisis forces the group to work long hours and deal with its problems; a higher-level executive comments publicly on the group's performance; a member lets the group down by not delivering what was promised—such critical events, as mentioned previously, can propel a group backward or forward in its development.

By the time you have read this you may have had sufficient experience in a classroom task group to be able to apply the various criteria to your own experience. Can you correlate how well your group has done on group assignments with the way you have been operating? What should you change? What seems to have worked well? Why?

The performance of your group depends on your ability to analyze the task demands, determine the appropriate set of processes, discuss how they vary from what you have been doing, and make whatever changes are necessary (consistent with your desires). As awkward as it may feel to discuss openly the way you have been making decisions, talking and listening to one another, handling disagreements, and so forth, it is in your collective interest to do so if you haven't already. The ability to find ways to correct a group's (or organization's, or individual's) process is a crucial one that can serve you well throughout your organizational career.

THE CITICORP TEAM

On the accomplishment at Citibank that he [Walter B. Wriston, Chairman of Citicorp] *is proudest of: "We've got a management team, a group of people around the world who work together as a team. I didn't do it, but I had a part in it. At the end of a day, that's what makes a difference."*

Source: John Brooks, *New Yorker,* January 5, 1981.

KEY CONCEPTS FROM CHAPTER 6

1. Group effectiveness related to emergent processes.
2. Process issues faced by every work group:
   a. Atmosphere and relationships.
   b. Member participation.
   c. Goal understanding and acceptance.
   d. Listening and information sharing.
   e. Handling disagreements and conflicts.
   f. Decision making.
   g. Evaluation of member performance.
   h. Expressing feelings.
   i. Work assignments.
   j. Leadership.
   k. Process evaluation.
3. Factors affecting appropriateness of group process:
   a. Size.
   b. Distribution of resources.
   c. Task complexity/diversity.
   d. Time pressure.
   e. Degree of interdependence.
4. The smaller the group, the fewer total resources and the more appropriate is participation by all.
5. The more evenly distributed the resources (expertise), the more appropriate is total member participation.
6. The greater the complexity/diversity, the more resources needed.
7. The greater the time pressure, the less time for process.
8. The greater the task interdependence, the greater the need for continuous exchanges and knowledge of each other on the part of group members.
9. The greater the member participation, the greater the level of commitment to goals.
10. Evaluation of group process needs to be made relative to the group's phase of development. Five phases described:

a. Membership.
b. Subgrouping.
c. Confrontation.
d. Individual differentiation.
e. Collaboration.

SUGGESTED READINGS

Albanese, R., and D. D. Van Fleet. "Rational Behavior in Groups: The Free-Riding Tendency." *Academy of Management Review,* April 1985, pp. 244–55.

Argyris, C. "T-Groups for Organizational Effectiveness." *Harvard Business Review* 42 (1964), pp. 60–68.

Bales, R. F. *Interaction Process Analysis.* Reading, Mass.: Addison-Wesley Publishing, 1950.

Bales, R. F., and E. F. Borgatta. "Size of Group as a Factor in the Interaction Profile." In *Small Groups,* ed. A. P. Hare et al. New York: Alfred A. Knopf, 1955.

Bennis, W., and H. Shepard. "A Theory of Group Development." *Human Relations* 9 (1956), pp. 415–37.

Brown, K. A. "Explaining Group Poor Performance: An Attributional Analysis." *Academy of Management Review,* January 1984, pp. 54–63.

Campbell, J., and M. Dunnette. "Effectiveness of T-Group Experiences in Managerial Training Development." *Psychological Bulletin* 70 (1968), pp. 73–103.

Davis, J. H. *Group Performance.* Reading, Mass.: Addison-Wesley Publishing, 1969.

Hackman, J. R., and C. G. Morris. "Improving Groups' Performance Effectiveness." In *Perspectives on Behavior in Organizations,* ed. J. R. Hackman, E. E. Lawler, and L. W. Porter. New York: McGraw-Hill, 1977.

Hart, S.; M. Boroush; G. Enk; and W. Hornick. "Managing Complexity through Consensus Mapping: Technology for the Structuring of Group Decisions." *Academy of Management Review,* July 1985, pp. 587–600.

Heise, G. A., and G. A. Miller. "Problem Solving by Groups Using Various Communication Nets." *Journal of Abnormal Psychology* 46 (1951), pp. 327–35.

Isenberg, D. J. "Some Effects of Time Pressure on Leadership and Decision-Making Accuracy in Small Groups." Unpublished paper, Harvard University, 1979.

Jewell, L. N., and H. J. Reitz. *Group Effectiveness in Organizations.* Glenview, Ill.: Scott, Foresman, 1981.

Krantz, J. "Group Process under Conditions of Organizational Decline." *Journal of Applied Behavioral Science* 21, no. 1 (1985), pp. 1–18.

Luft, J. *Group Processes.* 3rd ed. Palo Alto, Calif.: Mayfield, 1984.

McGregor, D. *The Human Side of Enterprise.* New York: McGraw-Hill, 1960.

Miles, M. B. *Learning to Work in Groups: A Program Guide for Educational Leaders.* New York: Teachers College Press, Teachers College, Columbia University, 1959.

Patton, B. R., and K. Giffin. *Problem-Solving Group Interaction.* New York: Harper & Row, 1973.

Rice, A. K. *Productivity and Social Organization: The Ahmedabad Experiment.* London: Tavistock, 1958.

Rubin, I. M., and R. Beckhard. "Factors Affecting the Effectiveness of Health Teams." *Milbank Quarterly,* July 1972.

Schein, E. *Process Consultation.* Reading, Mass.: Addison-Wesley Publishing, 1969.

Seeger, J. A. "No Innate Phases in Group Problem Solving." *Academy of Management Review,* October 1983, pp. 683–89.

Seta, J. J.; P. B. Paulus; and J. K. Schkade. "Effects of Group Size and Proximity under Cooperative and Competitive Conditions." *Journal of Personality and Social Psychology* 98, no. 2 (1976), pp. 47–53.

Shaw, M. E. *Group Dynamics: The Psychology of Small Group Behavior.* New York: McGraw-Hill, 1981.

Steers, R. J. "Antecedents and Outcomes of Organizational Commitment." *Administrative Science Quarterly* 22 (1977), pp. 46–56.

Tuckman, B. W. "Developmental Sequence in Small Groups." *Psychological Bulletin* 63 (1965), pp. 384–99.

Wanous, J. P.; A. E. Reichers; and S. D. Malik. "Organizational Socialization and Group Development: Toward an Integrative Perspective." *Academy of Management Review,* October 1984, pp. 670–83.

Watson, G. "Resistance to Change." In *The Planning of Change,* ed. Bennis, Benne, and Chin. 2nd ed. New York: Holt, Rinehart & Winston, 1969.

Zander, A. *Making Groups Effective.* San Francisco: Jossey-Bass, 1982.

Service Manager

7

BASIC HUMAN NEEDS AND REWARDS

The intrinsic pleasure of conquering a complex task can be a powerful motivator quite apart from pay or praise received.

One member of a student task group attends all meetings but inevitably sits silently through the discussions. Though his grade depends partly on the contribution he makes to solving problems in the group and he has clearly done the necessary reading, he cannot be enticed or bullied into talking. He responds to all questions aimed at drawing him out with brief yes or no answers. When pressed for an opinion, he mutters something like, "I agree with Ellen." How would you explain and deal with his behavior?

Joe Wexler is a 40-year-old machinist who keeps getting fired from jobs.[1] *In his current job he is once again heading for trouble. He keeps posting notices on the shop bulletin board, criticizing the company and its management practices, quoting poems, and citing chess problems in order to "broaden horizons" among fellow workers. As chess champion of the city, he is clearly intelligent and able to see that his actions are provoking his boss; why does he continue to defy the requests to keep his notices down?*

Throughout your life you have seen examples of people behaving in ways that do not make sense to you, that seem wrong, foolish, self-defeating, or totally incomprehensible. Sometimes you can shrug your shoulders and walk away; but as an organizational member, particularly one with managerial responsibilities, you cannot avoid dealing with difficult people. Furthermore, you can undoubtedly remember times when you were behaving in a way that seemed perfectly clear and logical to you but was totally baffling to, or misunderstood by, your parents, boss, or friends. How to understand what is happening inside yourself or in another person is one of the most challenging yet important abilities you can acquire.

In this chapter we focus our attention on what is desired by individuals themselves, quite apart from what is called for by the total organization or immediate work group. One of our core premises is that *for individuals much of organizational life requires balancing their own needs and desires with those of the organization.* Sometimes it is possible to satisfy the person and the organization with the same

[1] "Howard Atkins and Joseph Wexler" case, copyright by President and Fellows, Harvard College.

action; occasionally it is totally impossible to meet the needs of both. More often people at work must find ways to somehow be true to themselves while still meeting organizational or group demands.

A person joining a work group goes through a series of possible choices about what joining will mean, including the following:

1. How friendly do I want to be? How close? Will others allow that? (Atmosphere and relationship)[2]
2. How much do I want to participate? Can I be as quiet/active as I'd like? (Member participation)
3. Are the group's goals compatible with mine? If I have different goals, will there be a place for me? Should I seek a more compatible group or try to change my goals? Can I shape the group's goals? (Goal understanding and acceptance)
4. Will I be able to get the information I need to do my work? To whom do I have to listen? Can I get others to listen to me? (Listening and information sharing)
5. How freely can I disagree? Will others disagree with me? Can I fight for what I believe in? (Handling disagreements and conflict)
6. Will I have a say in important decisions? (Decision making)
7. Will I be able to tell others how they are doing? Who will tell me? (Criticism of member performance)
8. How open can I be about my feelings? (Expressing feelings)
9. Who will decide what I do? How much say can I have over that? Will I get to do the tasks that I'm good at? That I like? That I want to learn? (Division of labor)
10. Will I be able to exert influence on the group? What happens if I try? (Leadership)
11. If I don't like the way we are doing things, can I say so? (Attention to process)

In each case, there is the possibility of (*a*) accepting the group's way of doing things, (*b*) trying to change it, or (*c*) refusing to go along with the particular behavior.

The answers to these questions depend partly on the group's norms and operating procedures and partly on the consequences one is willing to live with. As we have pointed out earlier, the behavior approved in one situation may be frowned upon in another; what we are interested in now is what makes an individual respond in his or her particular way, given the external system's norms and values.

How does a person choose whether to go along with the group or organization or even with another person? What motivates one person to accept willingly some group members doing almost nothing to con-

[2] In parenthesis we show the parallel issue that the group itself must resolve, such as how to make decisions, what atmosphere to create, etc.

tribute to solving group tasks, while another responds to the same problem with confrontation of the slackers, and still another fumes privately but only smiles in the group? How can we understand individual differences and similarities? With which of the following two quotes do you agree?

> What is most personal is most general. (Rogers, 1961, p. 536)
>
> Behavior is determined . . . by a personal, individual way of perceiving which is not identical to that of any other individual. (Combs & Snygg, 1959, p. 19)

We will proceed on the assumption that *both* of the above contradictory statements are true. In some ways we are all the same, and we can understand particular behaviors through universal feelings and motives. In other ways each of us represents a unique combination of elements, which adds variety to life but makes prediction of behavior much more complicated.

For the manager as involved actor, the problem is one of finding some useful concepts to guide generalizations about people, other concepts to help understand the uniqueness of each person, and some guidelines to help know when to use which. That is not an easy task. There are a variety of theories about motivation and many schemes for categorizing behavior. Some are catchy but shallow; others are sophisticated but so complicated that they confuse rather than illuminate.

CHAPTERS 7 AND 8: FROM THE GENERAL TO THE PARTICULAR

In this chapter we will introduce you to some theories about human needs in general. Psychologists have may ways of categorizing human needs; we will use those most useful for understanding individual behavior at work. However, such theories tend to be quite broad and include wide variations in behavior. For example, we will refer to the "need for recognition" as a concept for understanding some aspects of behavior; while that notion might provide a possible insight into someone like Joe Wexler, the chess champ, it will fail to capture the particular *individual's* way of meeting that need. To understand the latter requires other frames of reference that tap into the individual's own world. Chapter 8 will be devoted to a concept we have found useful for understanding an individual's behavior: the *personal system.* It will be suggested as the stepping stone into the world of another person, the key mechanism that modifies needs and produces particular behavior (see Figure 7–1). Through it we can come to understand and appreciate more fully the actions and attitudes of those around us.

FIGURE 7–1
The Personal System in Relation to Needs and Behavior

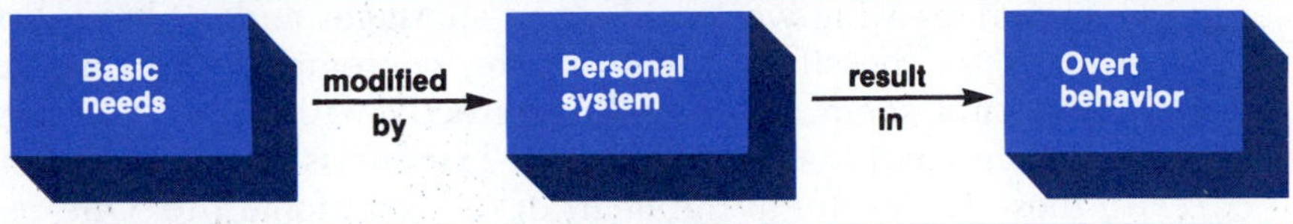

FUNDAMENTAL HUMAN NEEDS[3]

Survival Needs

The most uncomplicated behavior is found in infants. When they are hungry, thirsty, or uncomfortable, they cry; when they are happy, they smile or giggle; and when they are sleepy, they sleep. How simple a set of rules for predicting behavior! Through observing and studying infants, psychologists have learned a great deal about the universal forces governing behavior; the infant's life is much less complicated than the adult's. Not many adults cry when hungry or thirsty; whether or not they cry when in pain depends upon what was learned as children. But at least people still smile and laugh when they are happy, and some people even go to sleep when they are sleepy. Although people tend to complicate the ways of meeting basic human needs, the needs must still be met; *survival* depends on it.

In order to survive, one must have enough air, water, food, protection from physical dangers, and so forth. The infant obviously is dependent upon others to have survival needs met; the best it can do is give some signals of hunger, thirst, or discomfort. Fortunately, as mentioned above, the range of adult responses to the infant's signals requires little thought as to the uniqueness of the individual infant. Survival needs can be met in fairly universal ways. Even as they grow and mature, people develop fairly similar methods of meeting these needs. Tastes and preferences develop, but the basic ingredients for survival are more or less universal.

Another characteristic of survival needs is that they demand relatively immediate gratification. Any parent will attest to that. The human organism will not tolerate deprivation of basic needs for very long without experiencing some level of threat. While you personally may not have had to endure prolonged periods of hunger or thirst or

[3] Much of this section is based upon the concepts of A. H. Maslow, F. Herzberg, R. White, and D. McClelland. For references to the work of these authors, see Suggested Readings at the end of this chapter.

physical discomfort, can you see that even the fear of deprivation, let alone the experience of it, can act as a strong motivator?

Though increasing worldwide food shortages and ecological problems make the possibility less remote, contemporary organizations usually do not seem to be dealing directly with thirsty, hungry, or physically uncomfortable employees. The fact is, however, that *indirectly* those issues are at the heart of organizational life. One reason why people work, and probably the most universal reason, is to survive—that is, to provide themselves with all the means necessary to guarantee adequate nourishment and protection from harm. And knowing this, it is possible for managers of organizations to expect people to exchange work effort for contribution to survival. While human motivation to work is certainly not governed solely by survival needs, it does seem to be based strongly enough upon them to account for the success of wage incentives, fringe benefits, pension plans, health benefits, and the whole myriad of programs typical of modern industry.

Those of you who have had to work can undoubtedly remember how important your paycheck was to you. People who are threatened about their survival will put up with almost any work conditions in order to earn the money necessary for food and shelter. Can you imagine yourself, however, spending your entire life in a job that satisfied only your basic needs? Most people seek something more from their work. What are some of the other sources of motivation?

Social Needs

Again we look to the developing infant for some clues. So far the little person has survived; he or she is adequately fed, clothed, and protected. Not enough. We have already spoken of the human being as a social being; infants deprived of some basic minimal level of human contact do not grow in healthy ways. Normally the family provides the primary context for meeting the social needs of the infant, the needs for human contact and affection. This important ingredient is a kind of support base that provides a sense of belonging and the beginnings of feelings of personal worth. While the individual might survive the absence of such a support base, it is not likely to be a very healthy existence and can set the stage for a lifetime of desperately seeking a state of social belonging or of apathetic withdrawal from human contact.

Like the survival needs, the social needs do not just disappear from the scene once provided for. They continue to exert important influences on individuals' behavior throughout their entire lives. Also like the survival needs, when threatened they tend to prompt people into some kind of definite action. Think about those times when you have felt alone, isolated, deprived of the kinds of warmth and support that

> *One thing all child psychologists agree on in child rearing, teaching, or coaching . . . is that a person who is loved learns to love. They disagree on everything else, whether to be strict or lax or whatever, but they do agree that great results come when human beings know they are loved and accepted, not tolerated. Nobody wants to be just tolerated.*
>
> Source: Bill Curry [former pro football player, currently coach at Georgia Institute of Technology], *Christian Science Monitor*, September 26, 1968.

human contact alone can offer. You seek out your friends or your family or even casual acquaintances. When it gets really bad, you may hang around a public place just to be in the presence of others, or you may even approach a total stranger to strike up a conversation.

> *No more fiendish punishment could be devised, were such a thing physically possible, than that one should be turned loose in society and remain absolutely unnoticed by all the members thereof.*
>
> William James
> *The Principles of Psychology XII*

Unlike the survival needs, the social needs do not seem to demand immediate gratification, at least among most adults. When necessary a person can await the return of a valued friend, although a letter or even just thinking about the other can provide some degree of comfort. Also, the social needs are expressed and satisfied in a greater number of ways than are the more basic survival needs. Look at the variety of social systems people live in, the differences in family relationships, and the varying patterns of friendship and social groupings. In short, the social needs of people seem to have some relation to survival but not quite the critical character of the needs for air, water, food, safety, and so forth. And while they exert powerful influence on all our behavior, they are subject to wide variations in style.

For many years organizational managers paid little attention to the social needs of people. It was assumed that the economic reward of "a fair day's pay" would elicit a fair day's work and that worker needs required no more attention. That assumption is only valid under certain limited conditions. Most people simply need more than just the pay for work, especially if they feel reasonably sure that they can get their needs for survival met elsewhere if necessary. In situations where there are no other options for employment, however, human beings can be forced to work without any social interaction for very long stretches. Such a situation was observed by one of the authors at a very productive tile factory in India, which employed unskilled migrants from a poor region with a severe chronic drought. Though workers in this factory stood face-to-face in groups of four, they were not allowed to speak to one another all day. The supervisor rigidly enforced the "no talking" rule, yet no one quit. The factory was twice as productive with half as many workers as the company from which the production process was licensed. The factory owner realized that he could get highly dependent workers who were so grateful to have a job and, therefore, food that they could be intimidated into working extremely hard without any interaction. Since there were many such dependent persons around, workers who talked or did anything wrong were fired on the spot. In this instance, workers' social needs were not activated because survival needs were so great.

Nevertheless, over the years it has been discovered that workers' productivity is usually governed to a great extent by their social relationships, a point we have already discussed in detail in earlier chapters. What we wish to bring out here are the motivating forces behind those social interaction patterns. When permitted and/or encouraged and when the physical setting does not constrain it, the social needs will make themselves visible. It is a process as inevitable as eating when you are hungry. When managers attempt to constrain social behavior beyond certain limits, the need does not disappear; it only becomes coupled with frustration and seeks alternative outlets. For example, one factory erected a barricade between women employees seated opposite one another so as to discourage "distracting" conversation. This resulted in a significant increase in the number of trips the women made to the washroom! The thoughtful manager is careful to look at the ways in which social behaviors may be functional or dysfunctional to the work effort. That distinction makes it possible to provide ways to encourage the former and eliminate the latter.

Many of the cases you are studying in this book address problems of worker behavior involving a mix of work-related and social-related activities. It is often tempting to treat all social behavior as dysfunctional and consequently to recommend a hard-line approach to eliminate it. We have already raised this issue with respect to the notions of a group's required and emergent systems, the latter generally involving social behavior of one sort or another. Here we are reemphasizing the same issue but focusing on human motivation. Arbitrarily curtailing all social behavior of workers not only overlooks the significance of emergent behavior but goes counter to the very foundations of human needs.

So far we have talked about two fundamental sets of needs, those that affect survival and those that are of a social nature. Now we will go on to areas of motivation that appear a little later in the individual's developmental years. These areas are of major significance for the learning and growth of the individual.

Higher-Level Needs

Most people are motivated by a range of needs that go well beyond survival and social belonging. They begin at a very early age to seek the approval and recognition of others and to seek a sense of personal respect that tells them that they are achieving something in this world, that they are leaving their mark on it in some way. For some people the route to self-esteem is through being productive, for some it lies in achieving higher and higher levels of prominence and recognition, and for others it comes through achieving power, authority, and responsibility. It is through the satisfaction of these needs, particularly through work, that people feel adequate and can grow and develop into fuller human beings.

Even beyond needs for achievement, recognition, responsibility, and so forth, there seems to be something more human beings each strive for, something that in some way reflects the inner potential inherent in each person. Such terms as *self-realization* or *self-actualization* have been used to identify this level of needs. Whatever one calls it, the reward for fulfilling any need at this level seems to be in the process itself and not necessarily in the responses of others. It is the doing, the engaging in the act itself that carries its own reward.

Another way of thinking about these kinds of accomplishments has been called the need for competence or mastery. Even very young children may spend hours attempting to master skills, aptitudes, and abilities that are not directly connected to any safety or social rewards. Have you ever seen a baby repeatedly practice pulling itself upright? As adults we still have the need to master new areas, whether work related or not. The intrinsic pleasure of conquering a complex task can be a powerful motivator quite apart from the pay or praise received. Hobbies can give pleasure just from engaging in them. Some people have jobs that involve high levels of creativity, imagination, and problem-solving ability—jobs that drive them to work very long hours without them even seeming to notice the effort. They can acknowledge the importance of the rewards that satisfy other needs such as security of income, recognition by their organization, and so forth; but many insist that the overriding satisfaction is in the creative process itself. Can you think of activities, work or otherwise, that tend to absorb your time and energy for no other reason than the joy of engaging in them?

Other ways in which people meet needs for self-realization include learning and expanding knowledge, developing a philosophy of life, pursuing religious interests, and similar activities yielding a sense of self-expansion and growth. In recent years many people have "gone back to the soil," that is, they have discovered the sense of personal satisfaction and joy that lies in the process of raising plants, flowers, and crops of various sorts. It may be that the development of a total sense of appreciation for life and all its potential is the ultimate in self-realization.

If you examine the kinds of learning experiences you have had that have been the most personally rewarding, they are likely to be the ones that tap into the widest range of your needs, especially higher-level ones. For some the most satisfying learning (when they feel most engaged and alive) happens during a course or school experience. For others it is in their jobs. The satisfaction related to that kind of experience may be self-realization, a sense that you are realizing some inner potential for learning and growth.

As you pursue a career, it may be important for you to consider the full range of your own needs that can be met through work. Furthermore, if you ever become a manager who can influence the overall work environment, you may then need to remain aware of the great variety of human needs that may be fulfilled in that environment. In the next section we will look at the variations in needs as they pertain to different people, different circumstances, and combinations of both. Though the connection between any concrete item of behavior and the needs leading to it may be obscure, almost anything a person does can be traced to the desire to satisfy some survival, social, or higher-order need.

Individual Variations in Human Needs

While all of the needs discussed—survival, social, self-esteem, mastery, or self-actualization—appear to be universally operating for everyone some of the time, each person has different intensities of each need, and these intensities change in different situations. Some people, for example, are so preoccupied with gaining social acceptance that they hardly acknowledge or act on their other needs; it is as if they are "frozen" at one level of need and cannot unthaw enough to use the full range of human responses in them. Could that, for example, be a clue to understanding the silent group member, who perhaps so fears rejection that it becomes almost impossible to say anything that might be ridiculed? The need for social acceptance might be driving out needs for learning, mastery, or recognition.

There is controversy among psychologists about whether the needs discussed above all exist simultaneously in people or are indeed arranged in a hierarchy of importance.[4]

[4] This controversy seems to reflect the principal difference between the points of view of Maslow and Herzberg—the former proposing the hierarchy model, the latter insisting that survival needs ("hygiene factors") and growth needs ("motivators") exist along independent dimensions. (See Suggested Readings for references.)

On the one hand, there is considerable evidence that a hierarchy does exist and that the lower-level needs (that is, those that are more survival oriented) must be satisfied before the individual is able to devote energy to higher-level needs. A frequently cited example is the starving man who is not likely to be concerned about his self-esteem until his belly is filled, as in the Indian company cited earlier. There is also evidence from the area of child development that supports this concern. Children who are deprived of basic satisfactions during the early years are often found to be limited in their degree of total psychological growth; they tend to remain insecure and survival oriented even as adults.

On the other side of the issue are the many exceptions; examples of people who pay little attention to their basic needs, devoting their energies to intellectual or creative pursuits. There is also evidence from studies in organizations indicating that higher-level needs may exist separately and alongside of survival needs. It has been shown that workers who are very unhappy with pay, working conditions, fringe benefits, and so forth, can still respond positively to improved opportunities for responsibility and advancement, as well as to a broadening of the work tasks themselves. Some researchers argue that the notion of a hierarchy is not especially relevant to the manager; the important thing to recognize is the significance of higher-level human needs as critical motivators for work. They stress that an organization is seeing only a limited picture of human needs when it pays attention solely to such items as pay and working conditions (survival issues) to the exclusion of worker esteem, achievement, and opportunities for self-realization.

We can look at this issue in still another way. Whether or not *all* employees could potentially respond to work that is more challenging, complex, and engaging, there are many who are prepared for whatever reasons to settle for low responsibility and autonomy if pay is adequate and working conditions decent. Managers can choose, therefore, to seek out such people for routine work, see that they are well paid, and ignore any unmet needs at work. Conversely, they can find those who are most concerned with self-realization to do the more inventive complex tasks and then give them scope for creativity. This kind of thinking fits the notion of appropriateness to the situation, at least in terms of short-term productivity.

But there are problems inherent in this approach. Even if sufficient people of each type could be found (and that is becoming increasingly difficult as younger people come to expect more fulfillment from work), there is still the question of long-term development of the human resources of the organization. Is it possible that the managerial assumption of low worker motivation, leading to jobs that are purposely kept routine, forces workers to set their sights only on pay and other survival rewards? Is that reaction likely to be seen by managers as confirmation of low motivation, which then locks in the very behavior that causes the problem? To what extent is this a self-fulfilling prophecy? Is it important for employees to learn new skills and aptitudes or just to perform routinely what they already know? Is it desirable, ethically and pragmatically, to keep satisfaction at the lowest acceptable level, ignoring social and higher needs, which may be less visible? Will that gain the desired level of commitment, imagination, loyalty? Is it healthy for an organization to have most of its employees just going through the motions, leaving all responsibility and decisions to a few "higher ups"? Do not an increasing number of organizations have tasks that demand employees to be dedicated and willing to go beyond the minimum requirements?

If you want more than a short-term adequate fit, then there are many ways to explore the design of work to meet a greater range of human needs. Jobs requiring only robot-like, repetitive activities can be automated or redesigned to be more challenging. Parts of various jobs can be combined to enrich the work of any one employee. Jobs can be rotated to provide variety and change of pace. Workers can be given more responsibility and autonomy through more delegation of decision making and through opportunities to set their own working hours, work pace, and work methods. (See Chapter 14 for more detail about possible changes.)

All of these methods have costs associated with them and are partly dependent on the availability of employees who want to engage themselves in work rather than just put in time to get the money to satisfy needs elsewhere. Some jobs do not lend themselves to redesign or would be too expensive to change. Cost considerations will surely play a part in deciding whether to try to find security-oriented employees to fit existing routine work or to change the nature of the work itself. But money (or short-term profits in profit-making organizations) is not the only consideration when looking at the fit between motivation and work. The satisfaction and learning of organizational members have important consequences, too.

One final point worth mentioning is the fact that human beings have an incredible ability to accommodate themselves (perhaps even resign themselves) to unpleasant or adverse conditions. Coal miners, boiler tenders in the hold of a ship, and the like, somehow seem to accept the unhappy conditions as a normal part of their existence. Perhaps much of the sense of discomfort—even outrage—to which social scientists allude in describing these work environments may not exist all that strongly in the minds of the workers in the situations. Therefore one should think twice before automatically assuming that what appears to be a repetitive, unstimulating job is in fact so to a person in such a job. Enrichment might best be defined by the potentially enriched.

Summary Propositions

Regardless of whether or not we assume a strict hierarchy of needs, we can state that: **There are a wide variety of human needs operating at work.** In order to motivate organizational members, some diagnosis must be made of which particular needs are most important and then a system of rewards (pay, responsibility, and so forth) developed to fit. **(1) The closer the fit between member needs and organization rewards, the higher productivity will be. (2) The higher the level of needs, the more varied the rewards necessary to achieve productivity, satisfaction, and individual development. Conversely, the lower the level of needs, the less varied need be the rewards (Lawler, 1971; Guzzo, 1979; Pinder, 1977; Myers, 1964).**

THE MANAGER AND THE REWARD SYSTEM

How can managers learn to use rewards to accomplish their objectives? A social system maintains its existence by virtue of its ability to meet the needs of its members. The behavior of the members that contributes to the system must be reinforced, that is, rewarded, encouraged, and supported. In an organization the manager exercises principal control over the reward system; yet many managers fail to appreciate how their own behavior and decisions may reinforce or discourage desired behavior on the part of employees.

SOME CONCEPTS OF MOTIVATION

Theorist	*Principal Concepts*
Maslow	Viewed human motivation in hierarchy beginning with basic needs related to *survival* and developing into higher-level needs related to growth. Specific need hierarchy included: *a.* Physiological. *b.* Safety (physical and psychological). *c.* Love. *d.* Esteem (by self and by others). *e.* Self-actualization. Although not developed from research in work environments, concept valuable in understanding behavior at work.

(continued)

Herzberg	Identified higher- and lower-level needs; former labeled *motivators,* latter *hygiene factors.* Two-factor theory developed from research in industry; discovered that attempts to reduce dissatisfactions among workers by increasing pay, adding benefits, improving working conditions, and so on, failed to sustain motivation to work. Found that long-term satisfactions in work stemmed more from achievement, opportunities, recognition, and the like: things built into work, not just added on. Job enlargement and enrichment came from Herzberg's work; are ways of strengthening motivators.
McClelland	McClelland's early work concerned *need for achievement* and *need for affiliation,* both considered important sources of motivation in work environment. Research on need for achievement provided important insights into growth of industrial societies and showed a link between need for achievement and entrepreneurial behavior. More recent work pertained to *need for power.* Provided insights into behavior of leaders and their impact on society. Distinction between *personalized power* and *socialized power* may be critical step in removing negative connotation of power.
White	Suggested that desire for *competency* is a powerful force behind much of human behavior.
Festinger	Experience of *dissonance,* being psychologically uncomfortable, viewed as source of motivation. Person acts to reduce dissonance either by avoiding dissonant situations or by acting to change source of dissonance. If source is discrepancy between internal idea and external situation, person will either modify idea or attempt to change situation.
Horney	Saw behavior in terms of three interpersonal response traits: *a.* Moving *toward* people. *b.* Moving *against* people. *c.* Moving *away from* people. Helped to understand difficulties in interpersonal relations. Better interpersonal relations seen as dependent upon awareness and control of dominant response trait.

BEHAVIOR IS GOVERNED BY OUTCOMES

It seems fairly obvious that: **People tend to repeat behavior that is rewarded, avoid behavior that is punished, and drop or forget behavior that produces neither (Skinner, 1969).** In other words the outcomes of one's actions play a major role in determining one's future actions. If one knows that putting in extra hours leads to more money, one is likely to put in the extra time if more money is a current goal. If one knows that his/her pay will be docked for being late to work, the alarm clock is likely to be set with time to spare. If extra hard work goes unrewarded, it will probably soon fade from a person's repertoire in that situation.

As a manager one is in a position to reward, punish, or ignore many different kinds of behavior. The manager's choices will have important effects upon worker productivity, satisfaction, development, and ultimately upon the overall climate of the work environment. Given all the complexities of human behavior, some guidelines would be useful for improving your skills in managing behavior. While by no means exhaustive, the following represent seven key principles:

1. Rewards usually work better than punishments.
2. Intrinsic rewards usually are more effective than extrinsic rewards.
3. The timing of rewards is important to their effectiveness.
4. Conflicting sources: Behavior that results in both reward and punishment produces conflict.
5. Avoidance of negative outcomes and their associated feelings and perceptions are important determinants of behavior.
6. Feelings and perceptions become associated with outcomes.
7. Rewards are perceived in comparison to others'.

Reward versus Punishment

Although managers may give lip service to "the power of positive thinking," they often become more concerned about controlling than rewarding employees. For example, can you think of instructors who always seem to worry about students getting away with something? They are likely to offer more punishments for doing something wrong than rewards for doing something right. Such a pattern may or may not be very effective in bringing about productive behavior in either workers or students; it normally is not very satisfying or conducive to development.

While behavior that is ignored tends to disappear, behavior that is punished—either directly or by withholding anticipated rewards—is more likely to go underground, particularly if it is related to some important need. Imagine working at a routine, monotonous job and being punished for even talking to your co-workers. Does it eliminate your social needs? When the "punisher" is not present, the behavior is likely to appear and may then be rewarded by the response of others, by the satisfaction of meeting the social need, and even by the joy of "getting back at the boss."

For example, in a state prison where the prisoners make automobile license plates it has been the usual practice for the guards to impose very tight control over the behavior of the prisoners and to punish infractions of the rules severely. Despite (or perhaps because of?) this punitive control, the prisoners managed to outwit their guards by printing letters upside down, putting foul language on plates, and even making ashtrays out of the metal.

You can see how a manager can become trapped by building a control system based on punishment instead of a reward system based on positive incentives connected to basic needs. The fact is you may be able to reduce the frequency or strength of some behavior through punitive measures, but you are not likely to eliminate the chances that it will occur again.

Often you can get people to do what you want by using the threat of punishment for not doing it. It may only work, however, as long as you have a "captive" group of employees, that is, workers whose options are limited. If the shoe is on the other foot and you are forced to compete for good workers, rewards may be the only basis by which you will be able to retain your employees, much less get high productivity from them.

In short then, the use of punishment to manage behavior *can* produce desired outcomes under certain conditions and may even be appropriate (for example, when the behavior poses an immediate threat to the system). However: **Most behavior is more effectively managed by the use of rewards and positive incentives than by the use of punishment (Skinner, 1969).**

Intrinsic or Extrinsic Rewards

Rewards that occur apart from the work process are called *extrinsic*. Pay, benefits, bonuses, special privileges, and so forth, are examples of extrinsic rewards. *Intrinsic* rewards are those that are built into the work itself, including such factors as a sense of accomplishment, a chance to be creative, or the challenge of the work. Extrinsic rewards require constant attention and revision on the part of management, while intrinsic rewards are more immediate outcomes of an individual's efforts. If you are taking a course in something you enjoy, one reward lies in the learning process itself. If the course is required and irrelevant to you, the only reward may be the grade, which is clearly extrinsic.

In most cases: **Intrinsic rewards are more effective and long lasting than extrinsic ones (Guzzo, 1979; Pinder, 1977).** Job enrichment and enlargement seem to be methods of increasing the intrinsic rewards of work. The basic survival needs are appropriately met by extrinsic rewards, but the social and higher-level needs are best met through intrinsic rewards. Look at the difference between a situation in which social interaction is a legitimate part of the work process (as in the assembly teams at Cummins Engine) and that in which it is treated as a "fringe benefit" of getting the work done (for example, a coffee break or company social event). The former tends to be more effective in terms of making multiple rewards intrinsic to the work; the later forces a separation between the task rewards and the social rewards, consequently reducing the payoff directly associated with the work.

> *One of the responsibilities of a senior executive is to be sure that people in the organization have the opportunity to enjoy life, not endure it. Bureaucratic hierarchies are very frequently endured, not enjoyed.*
>
> Fletcher Byron, Chairman of the Board and
> Chief Executive Officer of Koppers, Inc.
> *Organizational Dynamics*
> Summer 1978

Obviously, extrinsic rewards are part of any organization's performance incentives, and under certain conditions (monotonous work, nonchanging technology and work patterns, and so forth) management needs to depend upon extrinsic factors to motivate employees. In general, when an extrinsic reward system is necessary, it is most likely to be effective under the following conditions (Lawler, 1971).

1. Rewards that are important in the eyes of the employees can be tied to performance.
2. Information pertaining to *how* rewards are given is open and public.
3. Management is willing to explain the system to employees.
4. There is adequate variation in the rewards to match varying needs and performance.
5. Performance can be measured.
6. Meaningful performance appraisal occurs.
7. A high level of trust exists between management and employees.

The absence of these conditions tends to breed lack of interest and suspicion about "the name of the game."

One final point needs to be made here. Since many jobs have both intrinsic and extrinsic rewards, it is important to consider what happens when you combine them. Logic tells us that it is a simple additive relationship: the more rewards present, both intrinsic and extrinsic, the stronger will be the person's work effort. However, some research findings (Deci, 1972), suggest that this logic is not necessarily valid. There is evidence that in some instances extrinsic and intrinsic rewards are negatively related, that is, can work against one another. More specifically, in a situation that is already intrinsically rewarding, the addition of extrinsic rewards may actually reduce the effectiveness of the intrinsic rewards. The explanation for this is in terms of the *perception* of the person receiving the rewards. We will say more in Chapter 8 about individual variations in responses to common rewards, but for now it should be noted that a person perceiving an activity as rewarding in itself might, if overpaid (in some form) for engaging in that activity, tend to devaluate the intrinsic worth of the activity. A competent musician, for example, might tend to perceive less intrinsic reward in performing as the payment for performing increases. That's why "going commercial" is feared. Obviously other factors may affect the person's perception, but it is important to be aware of a not-so-simple connection between types of rewards on a job and what will be seen as rewarding.

On the other side of the argument is evidence that supports an additive relationship between intrinsic and extrinsic rewards. For example, entrepreneurs, who are high in the need for achievement, tend to find success rewarding in itself and money, while a less important reward in its own right, serving as a symbol of that success. Thus the two kinds of rewards reinforce each other (McClelland, 1961). Consistent with this is support for the notion that the two kinds of rewards tend to be additive when they occur close in time and when both are clearly contingent upon performance.[5]

Consider this issue in a familiar context, course grading. On the one hand, if you are interested in the subject matter and find it intrinsically rewarding to work hard in a course, the grade you receive may not be the most important reward, but you would certainly hope to receive a grade commensurate with your effort and performance. However, if the instructor and the other students overemphasize the importance of the grade, it might very well reduce some of your own enthusiasm for the course content.

The Timing of Rewards

While intrinsic rewards are built into the work itself, extrinsic rewards normally occur some time after the task has been accomplished. *How much time* lapses between effort and reward and *how regular* the time intervals are can have important effects on behavior. As a student you must have experienced wide variations in the time intervals between exams and grades. Most students seem to prefer the shortest possible intervals. Can you see how your study habits may also be related to the timing of exams? As long as you know in advance when tests will occur, and assuming that a good grade is a relevant reward, you can plan to do most of your studying just prior to the exams and put in the least effort just after them. But suppose the instructor uses surprise

[5] For a more complete discussion of the issue, see W. C. Hamner and D. Organ, *Organizational Behavior* (Plano, Tex.: Business Publications, 1978), chap. 3.

quizzes throughout the semester and you cannot predict when you will be tested? Chances are you will maintain a moderately high level of effort all the time, in part to maximize the odds of receiving a decent grade but also to avoid the chance of being punished by failure.

Different organizations have different patterns of dispensing their rewards. While promotions, raises, bonuses, and the like, tend to occur at regular long-term intervals in most places, some organizations make these more or less directly contingent upon job performance: the rewards are timed to reinforce their connection to performance. Where the connection is vague, which can occur when the rewards are poorly timed, employees can easily begin to wonder about the payoff for hard work.

Wages and salaries in most cases are governed by many more factors than just individual work output. However, where a person's income *is* a direct consequence of work produced (products sold, services provided, and so forth), then the timing of the income can have strong effects upon the work output. Regular predictable return encourages a high level of productivity; delays and uncertainties about payments can easily result in reduced performance. A salesperson working on a commission basis usually counts on receiving that commission within a short time of having earned it. Can you see how important it can be for a company that depends upon high sales (and uses a commission system for its salespeople) to minimize the lapsed time between a sale and a commission?

While there are many ways to schedule rewards both in the classroom and in a work environment and while there are considerable variations among people and circumstances, you may find the following guidelines useful (Lawler, 1971, 1973; Guzzo, 1979):

1. **Predictable frequent rewards that are directly connected to work behavior tend to result in a high overall level of performance.**
2. **Predictable but infrequent rewards that are directly connected to work behavior tend to result in peaks and valleys of performance; the peaks occur as the reward time is approached, and the valleys occur just after the reward is received.**
3. **Unpredictable rewards that are directly connected to work behavior tend to result in moderately high overall levels of performance but also in some dysfunctional anxiety.**

The first principle seems to be especially important when people are concerned about survival, as might be the case during economic hard times. **Regular frequent wages or salaries tend to be most functional for survival needs.** A business that is struggling to meet its payroll or forced to owe its employees back pay is faced with an uncertain reward system. Depending upon the loyalty of the employees, the history of the company, and the potential threats to its survival, management will need to pay special attention to alternative rewards in order to maintain productivity.

CONFLICTING SOURCES OF REWARDS

Think how easy it would be to manage people if all you had to worry about were simple connections between behavior and rewards. However, as you well know from all the previous chapters, not all the rewards and punishments are in the hands of the manager. Peer relationships and a variety of personal factors also come into play. For example, a worker may be rewarded by the boss for being productive and punished by co-workers for being a "rate buster." What happens then is that he/she is caught between conflicting outcomes, which definitely complicates choices. The two sources of reward seem to be mutually exclusive and contradictory. The worker's final choice will depend upon the relative strengths of the rewards and punishments related to each choice and the relative strengths of the needs involved.

A manager who is aware of potential conflicts of this kind has many options for dealing with them. In most respects his/her choice must consider the given situation. However, we can say in general that: **It is better to add attractiveness to desired outcomes than it is to add threat to undesired alternatives.**

It seldom takes more than one burn to teach a child not to touch a hot stove. Even the sight of the stove can conjure up a strong enough fear to make the child avoid a second contact. In many ways, adults behave like burned children; a bad experience with some behavior leads to avoidance of that behavior and any circumstance associated with it. Of course, one person's bad experience may be another's pleasure; some few people (called masochists) learn to consider particular types of pain as rewarding. Regardless of what causes discomfort, however, if there is no way to avoid an unrewarding situation, then the person is forced to live with his/her anxieties. If, for example, your past performances on exams have not been rewarding, you probably would like to avoid future ones. Just the thought of another exam can raise your anxiety to an uncomfortable level.

One of the interesting aspects is the fact that: **Avoidance behavior is itself rewarding; it reduces one's tensions and makes one feel better—at least for the moment.** Did you ever put off studying until the last moment, preferring to take your chances with how you might feel later? What about the shy man who is afraid to ask the boss for a raise? He goes as far as the boss's door and then, with a sigh of relief, returns to his desk.

The price you pay for avoidance behavior is that you often lose out on something else that you want. The employee mentioned above may never get that raise until he/she has pushed open the boss's door and asked for the raise. Remember Snoopy's pal, Charlie Brown? He anguished over the little red-headed girl but could never move himself beyond the fantasy of talking to her. He approached to a point, then turned back, only to experience the "reward" of reducing his tension. Can you think of different people or experiences that attracted you but generated such anxiety that in the final analysis you gave in to avoidance? What price did you pay? What effect did your behavior have on your feelings about yourself?

You probably know people who tend to make others anxious. Sometimes, a manager is a source of fear for employees simply because of the power he/she possesses. If the manager's behavior tends to be punitive, then he/she is likely to generate avoidance behavior in employees. Many executives have been known to say, "My door is always open to my employees," only to wonder why few pass through that door or, worse yet, only to assume that the employees have no problems.

As a manager you will often be in a position to affect your employees' tensions and fears in conscious ways; how you choose to do so can be a very important matter. You can maintain a high level of control through the use of punitive and withholding behavior. You may get people to do what you want but at a price for you and for them. Avoidance behavior tends to develop consequences leading to a climate of mistrust and secrecy, which is not very conducive to the development of human resources.

Feelings about Outcomes

When you are rewarded for your behavior, it usually makes you feel good (except when you have done something you are ashamed of just to curry favor; then rewards may bring guilt). Generally, however, rewarded behavior itself becomes associated with good feelings. These feelings can be secondary rewards for the behavior and increase the chances of its occurrence. **The more positive the feelings one associates with a given kind of behavior, the more firmly entrenched that behavior becomes (Lawler, 1971).** If you do something that gets you respect, liking, money, and advancement (multiple payoffs), you are likely to place a high value on that behavior; it becomes associated not only with the positive outcomes but also with a range of good feelings about yourself. Your feelings about various aspects of a situation (including people, surroundings, and so forth) with rewarding outcomes tend to become associated with the rewards. You tend to view the setting as a good place to work, the boss as a nice guy, and your co-workers as good people to work with. Out of these feelings grows your judgment about the climate of the organization. Can you think of ways in which getting a good grade on a paper can generalize by association to other aspects of a course, including the instructor, the text, other students, and even the attractiveness of the classroom?

Rewards in Comparison to Others

It is also true that our feelings about a given reward are affected by what others receive. You might feel relieved to receive a B on a paper after worrying about getting a lower grade; but then, after learning that a classmate received an A on a paper you thought was no better than yours, your relief may change to resentment. We all tend to view things comparatively and make our judgments on the basis of relative fairness. It is a matter of *equity* (Adams, 1963), that is, the relative worth of what we receive when compared with what others receive for the same (or similar) work.

A blatant example of a current uncorrected inequity is the difference in salary levels of women versus men in the same occupations. Feeling underpaid is not an absolute judgment, it is a *relative* matter. Even if women's salaries were raised substantially, the sense of inequity would not change until the *differential* was eliminated. You can probably think of examples when your perceptions and feelings about a given reward (pay, promotion, special benefits, etc.) were affected by what others received. Anyone's general attitude toward a place of employment (or school, for that matter) is strongly affected by perceptions about fairness.

Circumstances can also affect one's feelings about an inequity.

PITTING WORKERS AGAINST EACH OTHER OFTEN BACKFIRES, FIRMS ARE FINDING

To prod branch managers to perform better, a European bank encouraged them to compete against each other to produce the most improved results.

The winner was promised a bonus. But the outcome was disappointing. The bank discovered that a greedy officer had steered a customer to a rival bank rather than help another branch manager win the bonus.

Companies often pit manager against manager in the hope that the race will bring out the best in both. When monitored properly, internal competition can boost employees' egos and help them feel they control their own destiny. "It's healthy," says organizational psychologist Raf Haddock. "There's a human drive to compete and to strive." But the competition can get out of hand when the stakes are too high or supervisors get careless.

Sales Contests

Sales contests, a widespread form of competition, have also produced some awkward situations for the companies that sponsor them. Data General Corp., a

(continued)

Westboro, Massachusetts, computer maker, caught its salesman for the Texas area poaching on Oklahoma's turf. An office copier salesman for another company asked a Lawrence, Kansas, customer to sign up for a copier even though the customer wasn't going to go through with the purchase. The salesman "just wanted to win his trip to Hawaii," says the customer, who refused to help him out.

What Works

Just posting performance rankings hurt the efficiency of a Los Angeles-based workman's compensation insurance company. It ranked offices according to how frequently they distributed disability payments on time. But a former employee recalls that when one office got a claim that was meant for another, workers frequently used the mail rather than the telephone to reroute the information in an attempt to lower the rankings of competitors.

Some companies embarrass workers to goad them on, but humiliation can backfire. Data General used to award a statue of a horse's rear end to the region with the worst quarterly record of meeting its goals. The company thought the award worked fine. "It became a real rallying point," says William D. Jobe, a former vice president who created the award. "Nobody wanted to take that home with them." . . . .

Some Drawbacks

Management consultant Reed Whittle sees significant drawbacks in automatically pushing promising employees to compete. "The idea is to put them all in a dark room with a knife, and the guy who comes out is the best guy," he says. But "while they're in their slicing each other up, the competition is out there slicing you up." . . . .

To head off problems from competition, consultants recommend issuing formal performance evaluations regularly and rewarding all producing employees in some way. Thomas Peters, a management professor at Stanford University, cites the reward and evaluation system of Tupperware International, a subsidiary of Dart & Kraft Inc. The sales agents who host Tupperware parties, where the company's household containers are marketed, meet to compare results every week. Mr. Peters says that "unless you're sick, lame, lazy, or drunk on the job, you get a ribbon or a prize." The system, he says, "works like a charm; Tupperware is coining the bucks." In 1981, Tupperware earnings accounted for 28 percent of the parent's pretax profit of $862.8 million.

Long Term versus Short Term

In many cases, instinct alone will lead to competition. Some time ago, Hewlett-Packard Co. told its managers to stress inventory control and posted rankings of how each division was doing. Pretty soon executives vied for the best ideas. "We used to stand around in the halls and say, 'Hey, I've got an idea,'" recalls Douglas C. Spreng, a manager whose division sliced its inventory in half.

For their efforts Mr. Spreng and several other manufacturing managers were named general managers, posts previously dominated by marketing executives. "Those promotions haven't been lost on other people," says Mr. Spreng. "The manufacturing manager who came up underneath me picked up the ball and carried it on."

Source: Heywood Klein. Reprinted by permission of *The Wall Street Journal*, © Dow Jones & Company, Inc., July 15, 1982.

When Chrysler Corporation was close to bankruptcy, the workers were willing to accept lower wages relative to their counterparts at GM and Ford; the company's survival and consequently the workers' very livelihoods were at stake. Then, when Chrysler began to show profits again, the workers became more and more conscious of the $2-per-hour difference between their wages and those at the other companies. Whatever the reasons—self-esteem, sense of fairness, need to be repaid for earlier sacrifices—the differential was no longer acceptable, and it became a powerful determinant of the workers' behavior and attitudes.

Complicating the issue of equity even further is the possibility of making comparisons with many different kinds of groups. Does a machinist working for a medium-size manufacturing firm in semirural Ohio compare her wages to assemblers and supervisors or secretaries and managers, to other female employees in her firm or in town, to machinists in nearby firms, to machinists in comparable firms in Cleveland and Cincinnati, or to her husband, who is a high school teacher in Akron? Many managers have run into serious difficulties because the comparisons they made about rewards to employees were different from the groups used by their employees as a reference point. And, of course, not all employees, and not all employees in a given category, may agree on the standard of comparison. Two of the authors of this book argued for years about whether faculty salaries at the University of New Hampshire were high (as they were in comparison to other state employees) or low (as they were in comparison to other universities). Although you will need to investigate carefully before you just assume to whom any individual or group compares itself, people generally compare first to those closest to home—within their own job category and with others in the firm who work nearby. You neglect easily visible comparisons at your peril.

INDIVIDUAL VARIATIONS

While the principles discussed so far tend to have general applicability, their relative importance may vary with people and circumstances, and there may also be exceptions to one or more of them. Some people, for example, seem to have a high tolerance for uncertainty and are not bothered by unpredictable rewards; and some people show little concern about pay differences (equity).

How would you assess yourself? Do you see yourself as someone who functions best in a system of frequent regular rewards? Or do you operate best when you can anticipate the possibility of some "big payoff" despite the uncertainty of when that will occur? Do you respond best to intrinsically rewarding work, or do you need external rewards to get you going? Do you spend time comparing your rewards with those of others or pay little attention to how they're doing? Your answers may suggest something about the kind of career or lifestyle you choose. Also, as a future manager you will need to understand a variety of other people's preferences in order to make sure that your reward system leads to the highest levels of productivity, satisfaction, and development. Even such a simple matter as the timing of rewards can make a critical difference in your success.

The Importance of Individual Expectancies

You can see that managing rewards in an organization is no easy task. It may be that in general some people respond mostly to intrinsic rewards (perhaps people with higher-level needs) and some more to extrinsic rewards. But in the final analysis it is very likely that the individual's own assessment of a situation and expectancies about his/her behavior in relation to valued rewards will be the most relevant way to understand behavior (Lawler, 1973).

How much effort would you put forth in order to obtain a given reward? Obviously, your answer to that would depend upon how *attractive* the reward is to you and the extent to which you really *expected* to receive that reward for a given effort. How often have you heard students say things like, "Getting an A is not that important to me; it just isn't worth the effort in that course," or "You can break your back for an A in his course, but the chances are you won't get it anyway"?

It is just these kinds of individual *expectancies* that make it difficult for a manager to predict how strongly motivated a worker will be, even with an excellent reward system. Each of us places a slightly (or not so slightly) different premium on the different rewards; each of us decides how hard we want to work for a given reward; each of us has his/her own assessment of how likely it is that we are able to do what is necessary for the desired reward; and each of us has a different level of confidence that the organization will actually come through with promised incentives (raises, bonuses, promotions, etc.). Thus, even before we move on to the concept of the personal system, you can readily appreciate how important it is for a manager to be cautious in using very general concepts of human motivation to design and manage a reward system. Understanding people in general is usually not enough to manage effectively.

In the final analysis, you cannot really understand the effects of the rewards and punishments you dispense unless you understand how these are *perceived* by their recipients. After downing an enormous meal, one witty Irishman proclaimed, "Thanks be for that little snack; some folks might have called it a meal!" To understand which is which and for whom, you will need to look within individuals, into each personal system.

KEY CONCEPTS FROM CHAPTER 7

1. Group processes and individual dilemmas:
   a. Accepting the group's way of doing things.
   b. Trying to change it.
   c. Refusing to go along with particular behavior.
2. *a.* Basic needs (survival, social, higher-level needs)
      modified by
   b. Personal system
      result in
   c. Overt behavior.
3. The hierarchy of needs is individual; however, there are tendencies which exist universally.
4. The closer the fit between member needs and organization rewards, the higher the productivity.
5. The higher the level of needs, the more varied can be the rewards to achieve productivity, satisfaction, and development.
6. Behavior is governed by outcomes:
   a. Rewards better than punishments.
   b. Intrinsic rewards more effective than extrinsic.
   c. Importance of the timing of rewards.
   d. Conflict is produced by behavior that results in both reward and punishment. This sometimes leads to avoidance behavior.
   e. Feelings and perceptions associated with outcomes.
   f. Avoidance of outcomes is important determinant of behavior.
   g. Comparison to rewards received by others.
7. Individual variations and the importance of expectancies.

SUGGESTED READINGS

Adams, J. S. "Towards an Understanding of Inequity." *Journal of Abnormal and Social Psychology* 67 (1963), pp. 422–36.

Aldag, R., and A. Brief. *Task Design and Employee Motivation.* Glenview, Ill.: Scott, Foresman, 1979.

Argyris, C. *Integrating the Individual and the Organization.* New York: John Wiley & Sons, 1964.

Bennis, W. G.; D. E. Berlew; E. H. Schein; and F. I. Steele. "Some Interpersonal Aspects of Self-Confirmation." In *Interpersonal Dynamics,* ed. Bennis, Berlew, Schein, and Steele. 3rd ed. Homewood, Ill.: Dorsey Press, 1973, pp. 127–42.

Broedling, L. "The Uses of the Intrinsic-Extrinsic Distinction in Explaining Motivation and Organizational Behavior." *Academy of Management Review,* April 1977, pp. 267–76.

Bullock, R. J., and E. E. Lawler. "Gainsharing: A Few Questions and Fewer Answers." *Human Resource Management* 23 (1984), pp. 23–40.

Combs, A. W., and D. Snygg. *Individual Behavior.* New York: Harper & Row, 1959, p. 19.

Cummings, L. L. "Compensation, Culture, and Motivation: A Systems Perspective." *Organizational Dynamics* 12 (1984), pp. 33–44.

Deci, E. L. "The Effects of Contingent and Noncontingent Rewards and Controls on Intrinsic Motivation." *Organizational Behavior and Human Performance* 8 (1972), pp. 217–29.

Dunnette, M. D. *Work and Nonwork in the Year 2001.* Monterey, Calif.: Brooks/Cole Publishing, 1973.

Eden, D. "Self-Fulfilling Prophecy as a Management Tool: Harnessing Pygmalion." *Academy of Management Review,* January 1984, pp. 64–73.

Festinger, L. *A Theory of Cognitive Dissonance.* Stanford, Calif.: Stanford University Press, 1957.

Gellerman, S. W. *Motivation and Productivity.* New York: American Management Association, 1963.

Guest, R. H. "Quality of Worklife—Learning from Tarrytown." *Harvard Business Review,* July–August 1979, pp. 76–87.

Guzzo, R. A. "Types of Rewards, Cognitions, and Work Motivation." *Academy of Management Review,* January 1979, pp. 75–86.

Hackman, J. R.; E. E. Lawlor III; and L. W. Porter. *Perspectives on Behavior in Organizations.* New York: McGraw-Hill, 1977. In particular, see the following therein:

Dowling, W. F. "Job Redesign on the Assembly Lines: Farewell to Blue-Collar Blues?" pp. 227–42.

Hackman, J. R. "Designing Work for Individuals and for Groups," pp. 242–56.

Hamner, W. C. "How to Ruin Motivation with Pay," pp. 287–97.

Nadler, D. A., and E. L. Lawler. "Motivation: A Diagnostic Approach," pp. 26–38.

Wanous, J. P. "Who Wants Job Enrichment?" pp. 257–63.

Hamner, W. C., and D. Organ. *Organizational Behavior.* Plano, Tex.: Business Publications, 1978.

Herzberg, F. *Work and the Nature of Man.* Cleveland, Ohio: World Publishing, 1966.

________. "One More Time: How Do You Motivate Employees?" *Harvard Business Review* 46 (1968), pp. 53–62.

Herzberg, F.; B. Mausner; and B. Snyderman. *The Motivation to Work.* New York: John Wiley & Sons, 1959.

Horney, K. *Our Inner Conflicts.* New York: W. W. Norton, 1945.

Kiggundu, M. N. "Task Interdependence and the Theory of Job Design." *Academy of Management Review,* July 1981, pp. 499–508.

Lawler, E. L. *Pay and Organizational Effectiveness: Psychological View.* New York: McGraw-Hill, 1971.

________. *Motivation in Work Organizations.* Monterey, Calif: Brooks/Cole Publishing, 1973.

Levinson, H.; C. R. Price; K. J. Munden; H. J. Mandl; and C. M. Solley. *Men, Management, and Mental Health.* Cambridge, Mass.: Harvard University Press, 1963.

Londom, M. and G. R. Oldham. "A Comparison of Group and Individual Incentive Plans." *Academy of Management Journal,* March 1977, pp. 34–41.

Machungwa, P. D., and N. Schmitt. "Work Motivation in a Developing Country." *Journal of Applied Psychology* 68 (1983), pp. 31–42.

Major, B., and E. Konar. "An Investigation of Sex Differences in Pay Expectations and Their Possible Causes." *Academy of Management Journal* 27 (1984), pp. 777–92.

Maslow, A. *Motivation and Personality.* 2nd ed. New York: Harper & Row, 1970.

McClelland, D. C. *The Achieving Society.* New York: Van Nostrand Reinhold, 1961.

________. *Power: The Inner Experience.* New York: Irvington Publishers, 1975.

Mitchell, T. R. "Motivation: New Directions for Theory, Research, and Practice." *Academy of Management Review,* January 1982, pp. 80–88.

Mount, M. K., and P. M. Muchinsky. "Person-Environment Congruence and Employee Job Satisfaction: A Test of Holland's Theory." *Journal of Vocational Behavior* 13 (1978), pp. 84–100.

Myers, M. S. "Who Are Your Motivated Workers?" *Harvard Business Review* 42 (1964), pp. 73–88.

________. "Overcoming Union Opposition to Job Enrichment." *Harvard Business Review* 49 (1971), pp. 37–49.

Nadler, D. A., and E. E. Lawler III. "Quality of Work Life: Perspectives and Directions." *Organizational Dynamics,* Winter 1983, pp. 20–30.

Pate, L. E. "Cognitive versus Reinforcement Views of Intrinsic Motivation." *Academy of Management Review,* July 1978, pp. 505–14.

Pinder, C. C. "Concerning the Application of Human Motivation Theories in Organizational Settings." *Academy of Management Review* 2 (1977), pp. 384–97.

Roberts, K. H., and W. Glick. "The Job Characteristics Approach to Task Design: A Critical Review." *Journal of Applied Psychology* 66 (1981), pp. 193–217.

Roethlisberger, F. J., and W. Dickson. *Management and the Worker,* science ed. New York: John Wiley & Sons, 1964.

Rogers, C. *On Becoming a Person.* Boston: Houghton Mifflin, 1961.

Sayles, L. "Job Enrichment: Little That's New—And Right for the Wrong Reasons." Proceedings of the Industrial Relations Research Association, Madison, Wisconsin, 1973.

Shostak, A. B. *Blue-Collar Stress.* Reading, Mass.: Addison-Wesley Publishing, 1980.

Skinner, B. F. *Contingencies of Reinforcement.* New York: Appleton-Century-Crofts, 1969.

Steers, R. M., and R. T. Mowday. "The Motivational Properties of Tasks." *Academy of Management Review,* October 1977, pp. 645–58.

Stonich, P. J. "The Performance Measurement and Reward System: Critical to Strategic Management." *Organizational Dynamics,* Winter 1984, pp. 45–57.

Tosi, H., and L. Tosi. "What Managers Need to Know about Knowledge-Based Pay." *Organizational Dynamics,* Winter 1986, pp. 52–64.

Vroom, V. *Work and Motivation.* New York: John Wiley & Sons, 1964.

Weiner, N. *The Human Use of Human Beings.* New York: Doubleday Publishing, 1964.

White, R. W. "Motivation Reconsidered: The Concept of Competence." *Psychological Review* 66 (1959), pp. 297–333.

Wofford, J. C. "A Goal-Energy-Effort Requirement Model of Work Behavior." *Academy of Management Review* 4 (1979), pp. 193–201.

SCOTT

▸ ▸ ▸ 8

THE PERSONAL SYSTEM

People engage in behavior that is consistent with their goals, competencies, beliefs, and values—as they see them.

If, as a potential manager, you wish to understand the behavior of another individual, you will have to go beyond concepts that simply apply to "most people" and to needs in general. It is necessary to develop some insights into the unique ways in which each person operates from his or her own frame of reference. To understand someone whose behavior is puzzling, surprising, or contrary to your expectations requires a way of getting inside that person, seeing the world as he/she does. **From within, an individual's behavior makes sense, is understandable and reasonable, even when not clear from outside (Combs & Snygg, 1959).** We will discuss the various components of a personal system that seem to be most useful in understanding a person's behavior.

Many psychologists—following Skinner—argue that we should stick to observables and leave alone the "black box," that is, what goes on inside the person. To them inference is, at best, crude speculation far removed from real measurable data. They claim that it does the human being an injustice to fill up the black box with vague concepts, insisting that it is enough to study overt behavior and to make our predictions from that.

There is a great deal of validity to the position of such behaviorists, and managers cannot afford to overlook it. The best predictor of future behavior *is* previous behavior. When you hire somebody for a job, the key questions you ask pertain to *prior performance.* When you decide to promote someone, you are usually making a prediction that his/her future behavior is likely to be consistent with past behavior. It is possible for managers to hire, fire, promote, and make job changes quite effectively using only performance data (observable behavior) as their criteria. Whether or not they ever *understand* the behavior—that, is, can explain *why* it occurs—is another matter entirely, one which requires developing some ways of explaining what goes on inside that so-called black box.

We do not expect to turn you into a psychologist, nor do we think that a manager must be an expert on all the intricacies of human behavior. Individuals are so complex anyway, perhaps even more than the social systems they create, that even experts seldom lay claim to all "the answers." What we do hope to provide for you is a way to appreciate some of the inner workings of a person (including yourself) and some tools for organizing your picture of an individual so that you can understand and explain and more effectively predict behavior, not just classify it. While it is not easy to make useful inferences about things that cannot be directly observed, people tend to do it anyway. It is not hard to interpret the motives of, or label, people in categories based upon quick observations; motives are *attributed* to others based on their behavior. Using some of the following concepts, you will improve your ability to make such judgments or, perhaps more important, slow down the process of coming to conclusions that tend to filter future inputs and lock in false definitions.

It is not easy to see how the world looks to someone else; few of us have been very well trained in such empathic skills. Fortunately, there are some ways of getting clues about how people see themselves and how that affects their behavior.

In the pages that follow we will take a careful look at the personal system as an important modifier of human needs. We begin by providing an overall scheme showing where the personal system fits into the total sequence of events that determine the behavior of an individual. We have already covered the topic of basic human needs and have pointed out that the connection between needs and actions is a very complicated one involving all the variations of individual personality. Without going into detail just yet, we can say that the general sequence is that shown in Figure 8–1. While the personal system is only one factor in this sequence, it is the most complex one and carries the key to understanding individual behavior. It is that critical link to understanding a person's expectancies regarding his/her actions in a given situation; the expectancies are then the immediate preludes to actions.

FIGURE 8–1
The Connection between Needs and Actions

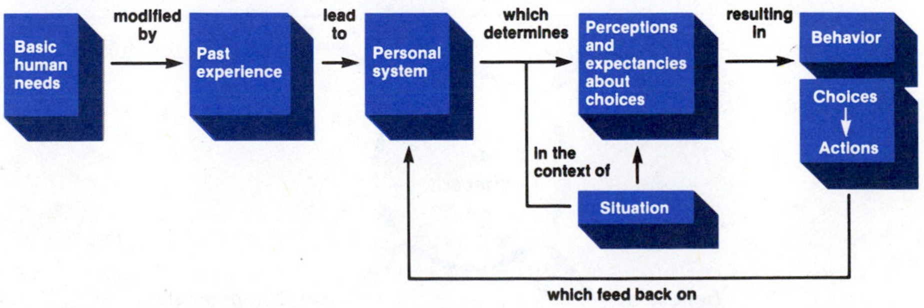

STRUCTURE OF THE PERSONAL SYSTEM

The personal system is structured around four basic subsystems plus a derived subsystem that exerts a unifying force on the others. The basic subsystems are:

Personal goals.
Competencies.
Beliefs.
Values.

The unifying force is the *self-concept.*

It is important to keep in mind that we are still thinking in systems terms; that is, we recognize that the various aspects of an individual are all interrelated. Growth and change in any one component of the personal system always affect the others. Let's examine each of these components (see Figure 8–2).

Personal Goals

Goals are those objects or events in the future that we strive for in order to meet our basic needs. A given goal (for example, a high income) may be related to several needs (such as security, prestige, and achievement). Also, several goals (for example, success as a manager, generating new ideas, and studying art) may all be related to one basic need (perhaps to actualize creative potential). Can you identify some of your goals as a student and relate them to basic needs? Is it likely, for example, that one of your primary goals in this course is to get a good grade? For some students the high grade means security in school, for others it means achievement, and still others see the grade as only one of many goals related to learning and self-actualization. In

FIGURE 8–2
The Personal System

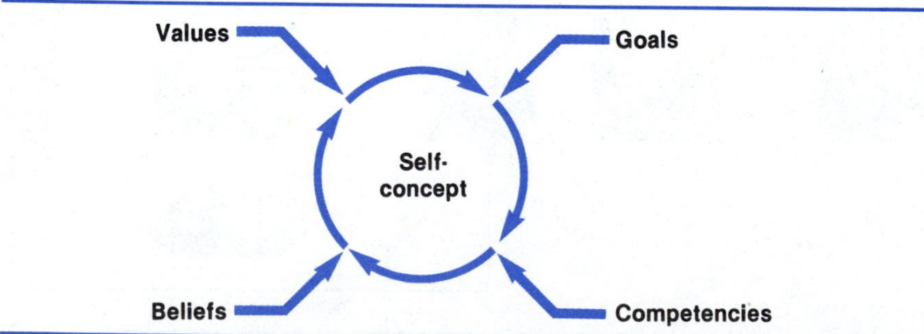

a work situation such things as promotions, salary increases, or the chance to work on challenging new projects serve as goals for employees. While these goals clearly tap into one or another basic need, the connections vary from one personal system to another. The task of a manager involves maintaining compatibility among the goals of individuals, those of subparts of the organization, and those of the total system.

If you were to list your various goals, you could probably arrange them in some rough order of importance. Like the hierarchy of universal needs, a person tends to have a hierarchy of personal goals. Having a hierarchy helps one to set priorities and to resolve internal conflicts between goals. An example of an internal conflict might be the person whose goals include both rapid advancement in a career and also having a close family. Both require high levels of commitment but frequently pull a person in opposite directions. Currently, women are increasingly faced with this particular dilemma, and for some, priorities are changing dramatically. Many men experience the same pulls.

If you knew only a person's goals, you could probably explain significant aspects of that person's behavior. From the other side, it's often fairly easy to infer a person's goal(s) by observing the person's behavior (although it's not a bad idea to ask!). As a manager you will almost always be concerned about the individual goals of those you work with, in particular as they pertain to your own goals and to those of the larger system.

One of the paradoxes of life is that people sometimes don't know what their goals are until they've reached them. Have you ever had the experience of realizing how much you wanted something only *after* you got it—or failed to get it? One's concept of oneself often makes it difficult to recognize certain aspects of one's own personal system. Later in this chapter we will examine just how the self-concept can both include and block out parts of a person's total personal system.

How well people can meet their goals depends in part upon the *competencies* they have developed, which we will discuss next.

Competencies

Competencies are the areas of knowledge, ability, and skill that increase an individual's effectiveness in dealing with the world. People are not born with competencies; they must *learn* them, though each person has varied natural capacities in different areas. Since the learning process is time and energy consuming, people tend to have a great investment in their competencies. While one may at times be willing and able to modify one's goals in a given situation, it is more difficult to alter competencies; new learning and change take time. Each person tends to be good at particular activities and strives constantly to reinforce these by engaging in behaviors that utilize them. When circumstances either block one from doing what one is good at or require one to do things one is not well qualified to do, then a person experiences some degree of threat.

A person does not always see his/her own competencies as others do. Managers often "surprise" their employees by telling them what a fine or poor job they are doing. While it is possible to predict performance from an external assessment of a person's competence, to *understand* behavior usually requires knowing that person's *own* view of the competencies.

Take the perpetually silent group member, for example. Though there can be many reasons for a person staying silent, one such student explained that he saw himself as hardworking but not very intelligent, and he greatly feared making a fool of himself in front of the group. At the beginning he thought he would play it safe for awhile and then slowly get in; but once the group noticed his silence, he felt the possibility of "screwing up" was even greater, since anything he said would stand out more and be carefully evaluated. As someone who "couldn't stand being laughed at," it was better to have the group confused about his silence than "sure he wasn't smart enough." And even when he had something useful to say, which was often, since he believed himself to be conscientious and thus always prepared well, the words would freeze in his throat. When someone was "nice" to him, he felt all the more embarrassed for not contributing, and when he was confronted about it, he was sure he had been correct about the danger of being ridiculed. In effect he became boxed into the role of "noncontributing member" by both his own fears and the emergent expectations of the group members. While the box was mostly of his own making, it appeared quite different when seen from inside than when examined from without. Not knowing his internal concerns, his group members viewed him as a lazy goof-off.

In general, we can say that competencies form an important part of the personal system. To the extent that an individual can find ways to translate competencies into effective behavior, the individual experiences reinforcement of them. **The wider the range of one's competencies, the more likely one is to find avenues for their fulfillment. The narrower the range, the more limited one feels in coping with the world, and the more limited one is in the possible range of goals one can attain in life.**

Beliefs

Beliefs are ideas people have about the world and how it operates. Everyone has beliefs about people, human nature, what life is all about, what the business world is like, what professors are like, and so on. A person brings beliefs into every situation and seeks to confirm those that fit the situation. Sometimes events do not support one's beliefs, and one is surprised (pleasantly at times, unhappily at others). If the disconfirmation is very strong, one becomes defensive, disparaging, resistant, and so forth. People like to have events support their beliefs; it makes them feel "right" and helps them to maintain a stable "fix" on the world. Can you think of some beliefs that you brought into this course? Did you believe, for example, that organizational behavior is all common sense? Was that confirmed or disconfirmed? Did you have some preconceived ideas about how groups function? What happened to these ideas?

One of the dilemmas posed by a person's beliefs is the fact that they often become *self-fulfilling prophecies:* Somehow people have a way of making things happen (even bad things) that they believe "always happen." Have you ever failed in a task mainly because you expected to fail? When you're sure you can't do something, you normally lose the very drive it takes to succeed in a difficult task. Of course, there is the satisfaction of knowing that you were right in the first place, which is a small but concrete consolation.

Managers can trap themselves into a set of beliefs that are dysfunctional but self-confirming. Some years ago Douglas McGregor (whom you already know from Chapter 6) described two distinctly different sets of managerial beliefs. One set (1960, chap. 3), which he labeled "Theory X," includes assumptions such as:

1. The average human being has an inherent dislike of work and will avoid it if he can.
2. Most people need to be coerced, controlled, directed, threatened with punishment to get them to put forth adequate effort toward the achievement of organizational objectives.
3. The average human being prefers to be directed, wishes to avoid responsibility, has relatively little ambition, wants security above all.

Think about how a manager with such beliefs might react if he/she noticed two employees lingering past the normal lunch hour. Would the manager bother to find out if they were discussing something work-related? Many managers would be prone to assume otherwise and would reprimand the employees, who in turn just might "prove" the manager to be correct by reacting negatively and by figuring that they might just as well be what the boss thinks they are anyway. The other set of assumptions (1960, chap. 4), which McGregor labeled "Theory Y," includes the following:

1. The expenditure of physical and mental effort in work is as natural as play or rest.

2. People will exercise self-direction and self-control in the service of objectives to which they are committed.
3. Commitment to objectives is a function of the rewards associated with their achievement.
4. The average human being learns under proper conditions not only to accept but to seek responsibility.

How do your beliefs compare with those in Theory X and Theory Y? Can you apply them directly to the classroom scene? Which beliefs do you think your instructor holds? What about other instructors? Can you infer which set of beliefs are held from the behavior you see? Can you, for example, see how believing Theory X would lead to being tough and demanding in almost every situation, whereas Theory Y can lead to toughness and high expectations in one situation but gentle prodding in another? Managers very often confirm their assumptions by treating people in ways that bring out the very behavior they expect, thus confirming what they believed in the first place. Have you ever had your parents treat you "like a child" and then find yourself behaving like a child? What about the teacher who believes that students will cheat if they are not watched carefully? That often leads to extensive controls, which students resent. Thus, the minute the teacher stops "watchdogging," cheating will occur. On the other hand, the manager who is willing to delegate more responsibility often discovers, lo and behold, that people are capable of taking it. Obviously this is not always the case; there will always be people (workers, students, and others) who do seem to operate best under Theory X assumptions and others who do best in a Theory Y setting. *No one set of beliefs is valid for all situations.* Competent, flexible managers are open to all possibilities, all kinds of people, and all kinds of situations. Their beliefs remain tentative, always subject to testing and revision.

One way of looking at the concept of "theory" is to view it as a set of beliefs, but ones that have been developed from systematic observation and research. Just as any beliefs tend to guide a person's behavior, managers use theory to guide their behavior in relation to members of an organization. And just as the validity of many beliefs depends upon the circumstances, the theories of a manager are most useful when they are open to the *contingencies* of the situation.

In the next section we will discuss the core of people's beliefs, namely *values.*

Values

Values tend to form the foundation of a person's character. While some of one's values may change over the course of a lifetime, they do tend to remain fairly deeply entrenched in one's personality. A person develops a sense of right or wrong, good or bad, beginning quite early in life. Many of one's ideas change through the teenage years, but as mature adults, we tend to hold on to and defend some basic core within us, which tells one *what is really important in life and basic to one as an individual*. Examples of values would be such ideas as:

a. Always being honest with others.
b. Always standing on your own two feet and not burdening others with your problem.
c. Always facing up to life's difficulties and not running away.
d. Never deliberately hurting another's feelings.
e. Never letting anyone feel you have not lived up to your responsibilities.
f. Always doing your best at any activity you try.
g. Never going "overboard" about interests.
h. Never allowing anyone to get ahead of you.
i. Never putting your faith in individuals, only institutions.

These are the kinds of attitudes that a person normally refuses to violate; they determine people's integrity as individuals. Following one's values enhances the basic sense of personal worth; failing to follow them causes guilt, shame, and self-doubt.

Values also tend to exist in a hierarchy of importance. Some are likely to be more central than others. When people experience value conflict, this hierarchical arrangement often helps them to make a decision. For example, an accountant needs help solving an audit; she believes in standing on her own two feet, so she does not want to seek help. But she also believes that it is even *more* important to be fair to the client, so she goes beyond her independence values and consults with an expert colleague.

Internal value conflicts are often very hard to resolve. For example, imagine yourself in a position where you must fire an employee for being absent too much due to alcoholism. One of your values is to always be honest and another is to always be kind. How would you balance these values against one another? Can you find a way to honor them both? For some people, being honest with the person might be felt as an unkind act or being kind to the person as a dishonest act. Perhaps you can think of examples in your own life where you found yourself in a values conflict. In situations like that the way one sees oneself not only guides behavior but is also *forged,* making future choices more consistent with one's most deeply held values.

It is not unusual to find yourself in circumstances where your values conflict with your needs or goals. Suppose, for example, in order to be successful, advance, and be recognized by your superiors in an organization, you had to engage in behavior that you considered unacceptable (e.g., political backbiting, concealing information about a defective product, using the rumor mill to make a rival look bad). Your goal of advancement—perhaps even your need to survive in an uncertain job market—could push you to behave in ways that conflict with your values, at least your *intended* values. What you end up doing

MORALITY AND INTEGRITY AREN'T YUPPIE TRAITS

*Regarding "Why Wasn't $1 Million a Year Enough?" (*Legal Affairs, *August 25), in the course of our firm's work in selecting and training management and professional job candidates for our clients, we have found that—despite their financial competence and expertise—many of the so-called yuppies are seriously lacking in basic business ethics and morality and often in personal integrity. Interviews and psychological tests have revealed that many of these obviously bright and talented young men are simply amoral and exceedingly hedonistic. They want the best of everything now—not tomorrow—and they are perfectly willing to cut corners to achieve what they want in the fastest manner possible. They believe that the end justifies the means. Only recently have our business schools started to offer courses in ethics. Hopefully, these courses will do some good. And, I hope they have not come too late in the education of our MBAs.*

Source: Erwin S. Stanton. President, E.S. Stanton & Associates, New York. Reprinted from the September 15, 1986 issue of *Business Week* by special permission.

BUSINESSES CRACK DOWN ON WORKERS WHO CHEAT TO HELP THE COMPANY

Alan J. Russ considers what he did cheating for his boss.

As manager of a division accounting department at TRW, Inc., the 45-year-old Mr. Russ would inflate the number of hours spent making fan blades for military planes, thus raising the price of the blades. Mr. Russ maintains that such "ballooning" was condoned by his immediate supervisor. "It wasn't cloak-and-dagger," he says. "It was standard operating procedure."

So it came as a jolt to the 18-year TRW veteran when, 18 months ago, he was ushered into an office at quitting time and fired for what he had been doing. The Cleveland-based electronics and automotive parts company subsequently dismissed or disciplined 29 other employees for "irregularities and unethical behavior." TRW denies that cheating was an accepted part of anyone's job.

In many ways, Mr. Russ's experience reflects the increasing attention being focused on workers cheating for their companies. While it's unclear whether such cheating is actually on the rise, it has become more visible as both the government and businesses crack down on practices like ballooning, particularly among defense contractors. Those found cheating—even at their boss's request—are now more likely to be fired than merely reprimanded. Some of them, like Mr. Russ, are in turn taking their bosses to court.

Source: Gregory Stricharchuk. Reprinted by permission of *The Wall Street Journal*,

might then reflect your *adopted* values. Can you think of current or recent situations in your life that illustrate this dilemma? You might explore the issue of student cheating in these terms, looking at the pressures to survive, compete, be honest, get high grades, all as potential sources of conflicts between students' goals and values.

In short, we can say that the area of personal values serves as the principal governing body of the personal system. **The individual is enhanced by behavior that reinforces values, less affected by behavior that is not value laden, and violated by behavior that is not consistent with deeply held values. The value component of the personal system can limit the range of goals, competencies, and beliefs allowable, and it tends to evoke the strongest defensive behavior when under threat or challenge (Combs & Snygg, 1959).**

Rationalizing: An Easy Escape

By and large, most people try to act in ways that move them toward their goals and also conform to their personal values and sense of right and wrong. Thus, most individuals will work hard to gain a desired promotion yet not engage in deceit and underhanded actions to gain that goal. Nonetheless, humans are all too skilled at justifying their behavior even when, from an outside perspective, it looks like a clear violation of their values. We say, "How on earth could you have done such a thing?" and they say, "I had no choice," or "It wasn't my responsibility; I was just following orders," and so forth. Most reasons that people invent to justify their behavior sound reasonable and help reduce some of the "dissonance" they feel. (See Chapter 7 reference to Festinger in box on motivation.) But the rationalization process only serves as a defense against the potential pain from violating one's own values. Remember the Challenger explosion and the comments made by NASA officials mentioned in Chapter 1?

The Nuremberg trials confronted many people with gross violations of human values and established, at least implicitly, a precedent for holding individuals responsible for their own choices. However, living by one's principles can sometimes be very difficult. The B. F. Goodrich experience is an excellent example of how an essentially honest person, when faced with a threat to basic security (e.g., keeping a job and providing for family), may end up violating a fundamental value (in this case, honesty).[1] An engineer in the company was ordered to report inaccurate information on tests of brake linings for an air force plane. He did so and then justified his action as a way of protecting the financial security of his family. Is this an acceptable

[1] K. Vandivier, "Why Should My Conscience Bother Me?" in *In the Name of Profit*, ed. R. Heilbroner (Garden City, N.Y.: Doubleday, 1972), pp. 3–26, 28–31.

course of action or not? Does understanding and compassion justify the violation of "what is right"? Would that such choices were simple and clear!

In our discussion of leadership in a later chapter, we will return to this issue in the context of ethics in business decisions. In the meantime, it is important for you to be conscious of the values and ethics that affect your personal choices; these will establish the foundation for the kinds of decisions you may make in the future as a manager or leader.

THE SELF-CONCEPT

The general consistency of the personal system is organized by the individual's *self-concept—the way the person sees him/herself.* The self-concept reflects the person's own unique way of organizing goals, competencies, beliefs, and values. Competencies are normally developed in order to meet goals, which in turn must fit with beliefs and values. For example, a man who decides to become an accountant is likely to be someone who sees himself as methodical, believes in the fallibility of people, and is dedicated to the values of being orderly and cautious. His manner of behavior is likely to be quiet and sober, his dress fairly inconspicuous, and his car somewhat conservative. In short: **A person's self-concept generally has enough internal consistency so that it is possible to infer various aspects of the person from other known aspects.**

People strive to maintain their concepts of themselves by engaging in behavior that is consistent with their goals, competencies, beliefs, and values as they see them (Rogers, 1961), even to the point of pain or failure to achieve stated goals. Insofar as people succeed in confirming their self-concepts, they experience a basic sense of adequacy and worth. Sometimes people become so highly invested in protecting their self-concepts that they begin to have difficulty in seeing themselves as others do. This can lead to defensive behavior and to interpersonal conflicts, issues which we will go into later in this chapter and again in Chapters 9 and 10.

People also strive to enhance their self-concepts by learning and by developing themselves toward some "ideal self" (Rogers, 1961). This tendency can often pose a dilemma for the individual. To enhance one's self-concept may mean change in some aspects of it; and to change one's self-concept runs counter to the tendency to maintain and/or protect it. It is a struggle between the security of knowing what one is and the risk in becoming something more. However, while a person may often feel comfortable with the idea of simply "being what he/she is," most people do strive to live up to their ideal selves

WHO AM I REALLY?

Compulsive

Disorder disturbs me, no question.
I don't like unwashed dishes in the sink
And am ashamed of such silliness.
I arrive earlier and earlier for planes
And don't admit it to all of my colleagues
Because it looks a bit wimpy.
I seek and respect flexibility in others, but I know in my heart
That my own flexibility is slipping away, and I fight to keep it.

Naive

Naive has served me well.
I really believe that one comes out ahead by trusting people.
They sometimes let one down but not often.
Failure to trust people spreads waves of caution and fear, and I find that is bad.
Sometimes I get fooled, and sometimes I feel like a fool,
But, overall, being naive has served me well.
It may bring me down one day.

Sense of Humor

Somehow, a sense of humor has always been central to me.
It has served me well
To divert conflict, ease situations, and make life better.
Sometimes whimsy gets the better of me,
But irony, word play, and punning all come naturally
And have made up a lot of my life.

Integrity

It sounds corny, but to me it is central.
It is what we come into the world with, and that's about all.
I really believe it cannot be fully replaced if compromised.
To me, integrity and honesty are core issues.
I hate it when businessmen are nailed for being corrupt,
And I do not think it is necessary.
Maybe this is pompous, and
Maybe I have not been "put to the test,"
But I like to believe that I will go out as I came in—
With my integrity intact.

To Summarize

For me, life seems to consist of finding out what one will not be (not a great athlete, an opera singer, or a scientist)
And what one might be (a successful businessman, a father, and a husband).
One can keep learning (and that is fun and rewarding),
Continue to broaden one's horizons (and that is good),
Create one's own future (and that is a privilege).
One can be a decent human being,
And that's what it's all about.

By Robert Saldich, Senior Vice President of Raychem Corporation in Menlo Park, California. Written for the 25th reunion yearbook of his 1961 MBA class at Harvard Business School.

as much as possible. To the extent that the ideal self is not too discrepant from the perceived self, it serves as an incentive to learn and grow. When the discrepancy is too great, the person is likely to suffer from a lack of self-acceptance, which in turn leads to self-doubt and then to behavior that, sadly enough, tends to confirm the low self-concept.

Sometimes, as we've stated earlier, people engage in behavior that from an outside perspective seems puzzling and even self-defeating. Perhaps you have known students who are capable of doing outstanding work in their courses but settle for Bs by exerting minimal effort. From your own perspective you might wonder what is gained by that behavior. You know that the students see themselves as bright; how could "settling for a B" confirm that? From inside, such a student's reasoning might go as follows: "I don't need to get As to prove I'm smart; look how easily I can get Bs with hardly any effort." It seems that: **Behavior that appears illogical or self-defeating from an outside perspective usually makes sense when viewed from inside; people generally make choices that are consistent with their self-concepts (Rogers, 1961).**

SELF-CONCEPT AND PERCEPTION

One of the major issues in understanding others lies in the nature of all human perception. Organizational reality—what others and the organization expect, reward, or demand—can only be known by any individual through his/her *own* perceptions. Although it makes many people uncomfortable to acknowledge this, what a person sees and hears tends to be selective and to involve a degree of distortion shaped by the person's self-concept; *one perceives what one needs or expects to perceive.* For example, a good accountant can glance at a page full of figures and almost see mistakes "jump out." The correct numbers are barely seen; those that don't fit are noticed. Remember the story about the tailor who finally met his idol, President Kennedy? When asked what the president was like, he replied, "Oh, I'd say a 42 long with a slight slope to the right shoulder." An organization having difficulty will be seen differently by the production, marketing, and accounting managers; each is likely to perceive the area he/she is most familiar with as needing the most resources but doing the best job.

This selective process can be functional; it saves time, allows people to concentrate on what's really important, and can help them perceive the meaning in incomplete messages, words, and so forth. On the other hand, distortion and selection can be dysfunctional; expecting the boss to be aloof and distant, for example, can make his nervousness or shyness seem cold and "confirm" what is expected. When natural perceptual processes keep people from seeing what would be useful to see, they can create real difficulties.

In addition, since any mental concept is an abstraction and therefore a simplification of reality, distortion is an inevitable part of committing experience to memory. Humans fit experience into preexisting conceptions, discarding details and lumping things together. This can be functional (just as is selective perception); it allows the creation of a degree of order from chaos. By equating new experiences with old ones, previous experiences can be utilized. But this efficient sorting method also has potential dangers: The new can be overly distorted to fit preexisting concepts, ignoring important details, failing to discriminate differences, and resulting in stereotyping rather than accuracy.

In short, a person's self-concept—the way in which his/her goals, beliefs, competencies and values come together—alters how everything is seen. What one person would perceive as a rotten break, another sees as a golden opportunity. Comments that one person sees as unbearable pressure from others to conform to the group's norms about preparing well for meetings, another dismisses as just joking around. What one student sees as a smile on the professor's face, another sees as a smirk.

The extent to which people perceive events as threatening will depend upon their past history with similar events. Since each of our histories has been uniquely different, it becomes difficult to anticipate just how someone else will react to a situation. In general: **The more emotionally loaded an event is (for whatever reasons) for an individual, the greater will be the tendency for perceptual distortion to occur.**

Fortunately, much of what occurs on a day-to-day basis in most organizations can be viewed by many without strong feelings and therefore with relatively low distortion or disagreement. But most of the important challenges for managers involve emotionally loaded situations—such as confronting resistant subordinates or peers, trying to please or move the boss, or struggling to pull a meeting together to reach a decision to which all will commit—and arouse just the kinds of reactions that strongly affect perceptions.

Defensive Behavior

In many cases the maintenance of the self-concept depends upon the retention of certain beliefs, even when these are no longer valid by external standards. The following case illustrates vividly the way in which a strongly held set of beliefs about self can prevent disconfirming data from being accepted:

> The chief executive of a small manufacturing company in England had been the one to build the organization from its beginnings, when there were only a few dozen employees. He believed that it was important for

a manager to be close to his employees, to be seen down on the shop floor lending support and interest to the work effort. He made daily trips through the small plant, talking to the men and offering help wherever it was needed. He was competent in his style of managing, the men knew him well, and he really enjoyed working in this way. Over the years, the company grew rapidly to nearly 600 employees. The chief executive continued to make his appearances on the shop floor, but these were more sporadic and less personal, since there was more territory to cover and many new people. Most of the new employees did not know him personally, did not understand why he showed up, and could not predict when he would appear. Consequently, they became fearful of this behavior. Unfortunately, the executive was not aware of these fears; he continued to assume that he was generating the same welcome response he received in the early days. It was obvious that he had a great investment in continuing this behavior, since it was intimately connected with his concept of himself as a friendly, informal, personally concerned executive.

At a meeting of the top management team one day, a subordinate who wanted to be helpful informed the executive that his travels around the plant were generating a great deal of fear and mistrust. The executive dismissed the idea as nonsense, insisting that the men in the plant really enjoyed the visits from the boss. After a few persistent attempts by the manager to convince the executive otherwise, the latter finally reacted with a violent outburst, stating that people who were afraid of him were simply stupid and did not understand his intent. The subordinate gave up, puzzled about why his helpful information was so badly received.

This example illustrates how data that appears to another as pertaining only to someone's expectancies may, in fact, cut very deeply into the core of that person's self-concept. The information not only challenged the executive's goals, it also implied to him that he was violating his own beliefs and values as well as behaving incompetently as a manager. The example also illustrates the capacity of individuals to block out disconfirming data that is too threatening to the self-concept.

When people encounter data that does not gibe with their self-concept, defensive behavior is likely. The data may be denied, projected onto someone else, twisted to have a more acceptable meaning, or attacked as not valid. A person's defenses protect him/her from being too uncomfortable, from having to change too rapidly, from too easily letting go of the self-view the person has built up. Yet insofar as defenses prevent new data from being incorporated, evaluated, and responded to, they keep a person from learning and growing. The problem for you as a manager is how to recognize defensiveness in yourself and others and how to respond to it in a way that increases the likelihood of learning and decreases the rejection of new information and ideas.

In summary, we can offer the following propositions:

1. **The greater the threat of information or events to a person's self-concept, the greater the likelihood of a defensive response and vice versa.**
2. **The more defensive a person's response, the less the likelihood of learning and growth.**
3. **Refusal to consider disconfirming data, regardless of the form the refusal takes, is an indicator of defensive reactions.**
4. **Attempts to tear down the defenses of another are likely to increase defensiveness; learning and openness to new experience are more likely when the defensive person feels safe and can lower his/her own defenses (Harrison, 1962).**

This last proposition circles back to the first; responses that do not threaten another's self-concept are most likely to reduce defensiveness. If you can sense what other persons value, what is important to how they define themselves, you can back off from whatever is threatening the self-concept and allow them more elbowroom.

The comfort of behavior that is known makes it hard to allow in the new data necessary for learning. There is inevitably tension between the desire to expand one's knowledge and repertoire of behavior and the desire to stick with the familiar. Where do you come out in this human dilemma? Do you see yourself as someone who usually prefers new experiences or as a person who likes the familiar, tried, and true? Can you formulate a proposition or two that describe how you personally deal with the contradictory desires for growth and security?

In what follows, as we look at the connections between self-concept and norms, roles and rewards, keep in mind that each person's unique self-concept (and level of defensiveness) shapes the way that external phenomena are interpreted. For much of the book, events are described as if any objective observer would see the same thing, but that is really just a convenient way to convey concepts. In action, it is necessary to take time to understand the way key actors interpret what is going on; the more you can understand about each person's self-concept, the easier it will be to formulate actions that meet your objectives.

THE SELF-CONCEPT AND BEHAVIOR

In the remainder of the chapter, we will discuss how the personal system as organized around the self-concept determines the behavior of the individual. We will first examine the ways in which the norms and role obligations of a given situation can combine with an individual's self-concept to exert powerful influences over behavior. Then we will discuss the effects upon actual behavior of a person's expectancies (positive and negative) regarding the probable consequences of his/her choices. Finally we will discuss some of the broad implications of an individual's choices with respect to careers, lifestyle, and the development of a basic sense of one's own adequacy and worth in this world. Our intent is to help you to gain some insights and perspectives on yourself, as well as to facilitate your knowledge of others, whether as a future manager or as a member of any social system.

The basic proposition that underlies this section is that: **All other things being equal, the behavior most likely to occur in a given situation is that which the individual expects to best maintain and/or enhance his/her self-concept.**

Norms and the Self-Concept

One reason a group may become cohesive is because it confirms the members' self-concepts; its *norms* (unwritten rules governing member behavior) are congruent with the members' values and beliefs, provide for the exercising of their competencies, and support the achievement of personal goals. Obviously, one of the reasons why a group's norms are what they are is because of its members' self-concepts, which were brought to the group in the first place. However, because of variations in member needs and self-concepts, it is very unusual to find a group in which *all* the norms support *all* self-concepts at *all* times. Also, since people tend to be members of many different groups during their lives, they experience wide variations in the degree to which their self-concepts are supported by the norms that are present in a given situation. While a person may seek out settings that are likely to be self-confirming, it is very difficult to completely avoid situations in which there is pressure to conform to norms that conflict with some aspect of the person's self-concept.

You have undoubtedly experienced times when those around you seem to be pressuring you into behaving in a way that runs counter to some aspect of your self-concept. For example, in task groups it is not uncommon for some kind of norm to develop in relation to having a beer after work. Your goal may be to stick to soft drinks, but if you have no basic value opposed to drinking alcohol, the chances are fairly good that you will give in to the pressure of the norm. If, on the other hand, your feelings run deeper, then your resistance to the pressure will obviously be greater.

> *What a dependency if you want everybody to love you!*
>
> F. S. Perls
> *Gestalt Theory Verbatim*, p. 36

The dilemma with respect to resisting norms is likely to be greatest when your livelihood is at stake. It may be important to your survival to remain a "member in good standing" of a work group. What normally happens, then, is that: **Norm pressures that go only against goals tend to result in conformity, while pressures that go against competencies, beliefs, and/or values are likely to result in deviance or isolation.** The norms and values of a group are equivalent to the values of the individual; they are the respective "oughts" of their system. As such they are resistant to change. **Conflicts between group and individual at the values level tend to be irreconcilable, at least without major sacrifice on the part of either the individual or the group (Scott, 1965; Simon, Howe, & Kirschenbaum, 1972; Whyte, 1957).**

In one classroom work group a norm had developed to do the least work possible yet still get a "decent" grade. All of the students in the group liked the idea and supported the norm except one. Her goal in the class was to learn as much as possible, and she believed it important and right to give an all-out effort on every project. The rest of the group members were afraid that she would have enough influence (since she was the most knowledgeable member) to change the developing norm. They put more pressure on her, only to get back more resistance. She went from group deviant to group isolate, eventually not attending meetings of the group and doing most of the coursework on her own. Her concept of herself as a "good student" was so basic that she could not bring herself to violate it even though the situation called for her to attempt exerting influence on the group.

Therefore: **The willingness to conform to group norms is a product of the closeness of the norms to one's self-concept (Rogers, 1961).** The costs and benefits of conforming must be weighed against the costs and benefits of deviating. Sometimes the choice will be obviously toward conforming; sometimes it will involve a hard struggle; and sometimes individuals reach a point beyond which they cannot comply. Can you think of instances in which each of these was true? How did you manage your own cost/benefit equation?

You should not, however, overlook the importance of the fact that it is partly through membership in groups that you can acquire and practice new competencies, enhance your goals by collaborating with others, and test the validity of many of your beliefs. Either quick compliance to norms or quick rejection of them can offer very little opportunity to learn and grow. It may be that those instances in which you are forced to *struggle* with the choice are the ones that benefit you the most.

Roles and the Self-Concept

A role is made up of a particular set of behaviors and attitudes that accompany a given position in a social system. Roles are shaped by the expectations others have about the person occupying the role. Roles serve to confirm or disconfirm the self-concepts of those who occupy them, as well as provide ways for individuals to broaden their self-concepts. For example, in most task groups in which leadership is allowed to emerge freely as the group develops, it is those individuals who see themselves as leaders among their peers who most readily take on the leadership roles. Insofar as the group supports this, the individual is able to reaffirm his/her self-concept via the behaviors associated with the role. The role is likely to be consistent with the person's goals ("I want to be a leader"), beliefs ("A group needs leadership"), competencies ("I know how to pull a group together"), and values ("It is of the utmost importance to get the work out; I know how to do it so I should take the initiative"). In other cases individuals who might wish to be leaders but doubt their competencies can—with some help and a little push—try out leadership roles until they have broadened their self-concepts to include that kind of role, at least in some situations.

MAN'S WORK IS NEVER DONE

Travelers on airplanes flying the eastern seaboard began complaining that the aircraft were filthy. Management consultants hastened to Miami, where the planes were cleaned, only to find that virility rather than carelessness was at issue. . . . The Cuban-American men on the maintenance crews insisted on using brooms instead of vacuum cleaners, [which] *were "the tools of women."*

[The consultants] *made the pastel-colored machines bulkier, had them painted gray and labeled "industrial vacuum cleaner." They issued a technical manual. And they organized military-style competitions among the workers to see who was quickest at taking apart, cleaning, and reassembling his vacuum cleaner. The plan was successful: The brooms were discarded; the customers satisfied.*

No matter how a particular role is defined by a boss, peers, tradition, and so forth: **The individual's own unique perception of the role obligations determines his/her reaction to the prospect of adopting the role. To the extent that a role is perceived to be congruent with the self-concept, the individual is inclined to adopt it; to the extent that a role is perceived to be incongruent with any aspect of the self-concept, the individual is inclined to reject it (Goffman, 1959).**

An example with important implications for society relates to women and the roles they choose. As more and more women reject the self-concept of constant "supporters of men," they increasingly resist the kinds of roles that accompany such a position in society. The issue goes well beyond a matter of goals; it clearly pertains to the competencies of women as compared with men in almost all fields of work, and it is without doubt a basic matter of beliefs and values, especially in a society that espouses equality.

This issue has appeared more frequently in the classroom as more women students enter courses in management and administration. Tradition tended to draw the female students into various secondary roles in task groups. They often fell right into the "secretarial role" and into other roles of a supportive and maintenance nature, including, sometimes, making sure that the group was well nurtured. Somehow it was never a male student who determined that the group needed homemade brownies at its meetings. Recently many women students have overtly rejected the secretarial role, some with more vigor than others. Even though the fulfillment of such a role is highly functional for the group, it may be equally dysfunctional for the person asked to fill it. Obviously, this issue is not clear cut, especially for many women who have built major aspects of their self-concepts upon role behaviors that, while not fostering their own growth, have been important sources of self-confirmation. It is not easy for anyone to give up behaviors that are comfortable, even if limiting.

Because roles are important vehicles for giving order and consistency to a person's behavior in a social system, they often serve as a source of support for a person's basic sense of adequacy. People derive their sense of adequacy by doing the things at which they are competent and by learning to be competent at the things they value. Every time people are faced with a situation that goes beyond their competence, they feel a blow to the self-concept, to a sense of personal adequacy; every time individuals experience success in some activity, they enhance their sense of adequacy and confirm their concept of themselves as competent.

To the extent that individuals can build their lives around roles that enhance competencies, they will develop a basic sense of adequacy. To the extent that individuals find themselves cast into roles that conflict with or fail to utilize competencies, they will tend to develop a sense of inadequacy. Obviously, very few people can structure their lives so that their various roles are all congruent with their self-concepts; everyone has to do the drudgery jobs at one time or another. There is little self-confirmation in doing dishes, taking out garbage, balancing the checkbook, straightening up the workplace, and so forth. But these things have to be done, and most people at least have the competence to do them. The problems occur when people feel pressured to do things that do not fit with their competencies, at least as seen from inside, or when they feel constrained by circumstances from exercising the competencies they possess. Imagine yourself in a job in which all your previous training has little use. You see others in the organization doing things that you know you could do as well or better, but the role you are cast into in the system does not allow you to engage in any of those activities. That can be more than frustrating; it could even be degrading. People in dead-end or low-ceiling jobs often feel this way. Then again, imagine what it might be like to be assigned to a job long before you are ready for it, only to perform at a mediocre level. This is hardly conducive to developing a sense of personal adequacy. Employees in rapidly growing firms sometimes find themselves in this position, swept upward in a series of promotions until they reach a point where they lack the requisite knowledge to perform adequately. Then they spend a great deal of time worrying about being "found out."

OLD SELF-CONCEPTS NEVER DIE

One of the authors interviewed a 50-year-old man who had once been president of his own company but was now one of a number of executives in a small manufacturing firm. He still had a concept of himself as "top man" and frequently made decisions that were later countermanded by the chief executive of the company. Making his own decisions reinforced the concept he held of himself in the old role as president but created problems in his present situation. Regardless of the quality of the decision, being overruled served to reinforce the former president's subordinate role in the firm. He had a great deal of difficulty accepting that role, since the behavior that went with it failed to reinforce his own sense of competency as a manager, resulting in a loss of his sense of personal adequacy. This once high-level executive spent a great deal of his time telling stories about the good old days when he found himself making really tough decisions.

Sometimes a role conflict can go very deep and hit on matters of personal worth. This happens when a role calls for a kind of behavior that the person believes is wrong. Since most positions in an organization entail multiple roles, especially as one moves up the hierarchy of the system, most people at one time or another are called upon to adopt a role that goes against their personal values. For example, at some time an executive may be assigned to be the "hatchet man" in a situation needing strong action. On the one hand, while his/her values as related to the total system might support such a decision, a concern for employee security might not support it. Though learning to live with that kind of problem may be a useful aid to executive success, the price that is paid for violating one's own values may appear later as insomnia, ulcers, nervous conditions, and so forth. Or it may lead to a shift in the violated values. It depends on how deep they and the beliefs that support them are. In either case, tension between values and role obligations is a major source of stress. The important thing for you to look at now is the relationship between your values and the ways in which various roles may call upon you to behave inconsistently with your self-concept. **To the extent that individuals adopt roles that support their values, they experience themselves as worthwhile; to the extent that individuals violate these values, they doubt their personal worth (Goffman, 1959).**

Rewards and the Self-Concept

Just as roles can call for behavior that violates an individual's values, so can the organization's formal or informal reward system. In Chapter 7 we referred briefly to the idea that different individuals might perceive the same reward differently. Having added the construct of the self-concept, we can now expand on the relation between rewards and individual responses to them.

Rewards will be viewed by each individual in terms of:

1. How valuable the reward is, given the person's goals and values. To the individual who wants group acceptance above all, for example, cash incentives for extraordinary performance may not be perceived as particularly valuable. Any rewards requiring getting ahead of peers would be undervalued by such individuals.

2. How compatible the activity required to gain the reward is with the person's goals, values, beliefs, and competencies. A chance to receive a bonus and have one's picture in the company newsletter may be seen as quite valuable, but if to get it the introverted financial analyst would have to start selling new accounts, the reward may not induce the requisite behavior.

3. How the rewards offered compare to those available to relevant others, and who is seen as relevant, will also be influenced by the person's goals, beliefs, and values. Individuals who are ambitious will tend to compare their rewards to those higher in the organization and to those in highly successful organizations. Individuals who desire acceptance will compare themselves to their immediate peers. Individuals who are competitive will also compare themselves to peers and will struggle for even very small relative advantage. In one group of up-and-coming managers there was intense interest in what the boss did about pay raise differentials that meted less than a $3 per week spread against base salaries of $40,000–$50,000 per year! Clearly, symbolic differences were at stake.

Expectancies and the Self-Concept

The influence of the situational factors discussed above (norms, roles, and rewards) and of other factors on individual behavior is ultimately mediated by the individual's expectancies. This was mentioned in

Chapter 7, but it warrants emphasis now that we've developed a more complete picture of the personal system.

Before you make a choice you usually appraise the situation and decide which alternatives are likely to result in self-enhancement. Few people like to waste their efforts, and even fewer wish to engage in behavior that goes against their goals, beliefs, and so forth. To deal with the matter of choosing the best course of action in a situation, your appraisal takes the form of a kind of prediction: "The chances are that if I do thus and so, I will achieve what I want." You make a statement (implicit or explicit) of your expectancy regarding the probable outcome. It's like being your own personal scientist, making hypotheses, testing them out, revising them when they prove wrong, and holding on to the ones that prove accurate. As discussed in the previous chapter, outcomes that are rewarding tend to create and reinforce the expectancies that are positive. By the same token, outcomes that are nonrewarding or punishing lead to expectancies that are neutral or negative.

> *One's attitude toward oneself is the single most important factor in healing or staying well.*
>
> Bernie S. Siegel, M.D.
> In *Love, Medicine & Miracles*

In essence, the behavior most likely to occur is that which the person *expects* to most enhance self-concept. When the expectancy and the self-concept fit together in relation to some behavior, no dilemma is experienced. But what happens when an anticipated outcome involves some risk to self, yet no alternatives exist to meet goals? For example, say you have a concept of yourself as bright and as capable of putting your ideas into words very clearly. Your goal is to be outspoken in a classroom so that you can have some reaction to your ideas from the instructor. You now find yourself in a class in which the instructor refuses to entertain questions until he completes his lectures; but you always find that there is no time left for discussion at the end of the class. You can choose to keep your mouth shut, expecting a negative reaction should you speak up, or you can say something anyway in order to move toward your goal. For anyone to predict what you are likely to do would require that they know: (*a*) the strength of your goal to speak out; (*b*) your expectancy regarding the negative consequences of speaking out; and (*c*) your expectancy regarding the positive and negative consequences for your self-concept in not speaking out. Obviously, predicting an individual's behavior is not a simple matter, but we can offer a few guidelines for making predictions. These guidelines will also be useful to you when you attempt to formulate sets of personal propositions.

Guideline Propositions for Predicting Individual Behavior

1. **The greater the strength of expectancy that a particular behavior will have a positive outcome, the more likely it is that the behavior will occur, and vice versa.**
2. **To the extent that a particular behavior is perceived to be positively related to the maintenance and enhancement of the self-concept, the behavior is likely to become an ongoing part of the individual's repertoire (Nadler & Lawler, 1977).**
3. **The more limited an individual's range of competencies, the more likely is an existing competency to be used regardless of situational appropriateness.**

Figure 8–3 shows the ways in which behavior and self-concept are linked; it also summarizes the concepts we have discussed in this chapter.

FIGURE 8–3
How Behavior Results from Perceptions and Expectancies as Influenced by the Self-Concept

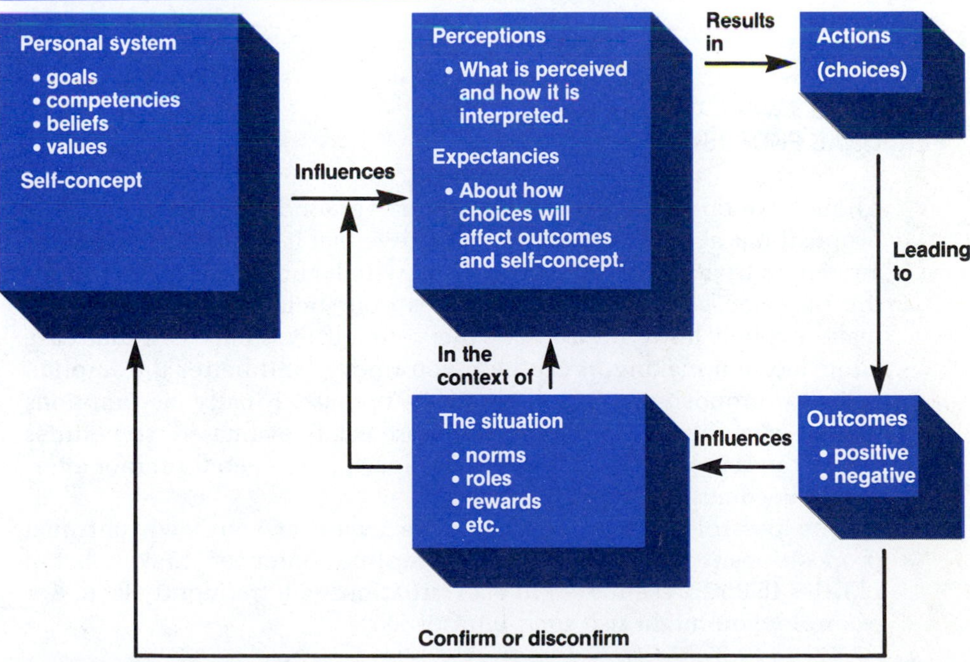

SITUATIONAL DETERMINANTS OF THE SELF-CONCEPT

Have you ever seen a person you had experienced as knowledgeable, decisive, and confident unexpectedly become hesitant, unsure of him/herself, and almost shy? One young woman who was poised, confident, and often an initiator (leader) in student activities worked in a retail store for three years after graduation and then joined the Peace Corps. While overseas she appeared tentative, diffident, and was slow to deal with problems. How might one explain this contrast in behavior?

She felt that her usual pattern of behavior would elicit negative outcomes and reactions that would disconfirm her self-concept. In addition, we can also infer that she saw herself somewhat differently in the new situation. Instead of seeing herself as knowledgeable, competent, and legitimate to exert leadership, she saw herself as a neophyte, lacking knowledge about the situation, and as such obligated to act more as a "guest" than a "member of the family." She also lacked the support systems she had at home. In a sense, her self-concept was different in the two situations.

Thus, in seeking to explain or predict someone's behavior, we need to remember that while an individual's self-concept develops slowly and is relatively stable, it is also partly situationally dependent. We vary our behavior in each situation to maintain and enhance our self-concept, and each situation can influence how we see and feel about ourselves.

BECOMING AWARE OF YOUR OWN PERSONAL PROPOSITIONS

Though we do not propose that you carry around an ever-ready list of propositions about yourself, we do believe that it is worth the effort for anyone to try to clarify the bases upon which choices are made. Since the way you see yourself determines your behavior, it is useful to make explicit how you are viewing yourself. Not only can that ease your decision making, it can help you understand better the implicit personal propositions by which others operate. Finally, assumptions that are specifically spelled out are more easily evaluated; sometimes when you see your own assumptions clearly, the need for minor alterations becomes apparent.

One possible way to become more aware of your own personal propositions is to use a series of incomplete sentences. Make a list of phrases that represent the kinds of situations you frequently face. For example, you might use such phrases as:

Whenever I have a job to do that I don't like, I tend to. . . .

When I am in competition with others, I tend to. . . .

When I want someone to like me, I tend to. . . .

When I am afraid of failing, I tend to. . . .

If I try my hardest, I tend to. . . .

If I am true to my own values in a group, I will. . . .

If you just let your thoughts fill in the incomplete sentences without any censoring, you can get to some of the ways in which your self-concept is determining your expectations and, thus, your behavior in both positive and negative directions.

Another way of approaching clarity about your working propositions is to try to state the underlying assumption behind each of your most frequent concerns as a person. For example, if you avoid much interaction with group members because you worry about being hurt in relationships, the underlying premise might be: "If I am vulnerable and let others get too close, they will hurt me."

If you always act warm and friendly to everyone, whether or not you mean it, the premise might be: "If I don't make people feel I like them, they may attack me."

Another kind of premise, related to feelings of competence, could be stated, "If I ever let myself be caught unprepared, I will be extremely embarrassed." The opposite might go: "If I try my hardest and then don't do well, I will be more disappointed than if I do just enough to get by."

Underlying most of your behavior will be propositions of the sort just mentioned. Can you list those that most frequently seem to control your behavior? Once stated, it can be useful then to assess under what conditions each statement is likely to be true and under what conditions it may be inaccurate.

The way in which we formulate our personal propositions is also influenced by how we make sense, cognitively, of what we observe happening in the world around us. This is discussed in the next section.

STRUCTURING THE WORLD AROUND US

When you study, do you focus on details or look at the larger picture? When you take a trip, do you get sidetracked and pay attention to all the points along the way or focus on "getting there"? When you shop, are you quick to make a decision, or do you feel compelled to check out every possibility so that you *know* you've made the right decision?

Among the things that make us different from each other, one of the most interesting is the way in which each of us organizes or structures his/her world. And this is often a source of puzzlement. Jane wonders how Jack can get anything done with such a disorganized approach to tasks and a desk that looks like a tornado hit it. Jack wonders how Jane can enjoy her work since she is so compulsive, makes a list of activities for the day, and arranges the papers on her desk in neat piles. Jane goes crazy trying to keep Jack focused on an issue or problem; Jack loves to explore all the implications or related issues as they pop into his head. Jane tries to control Jack; Jack tries to loosen Jane up. Sound familiar?

Psychologists have long studied differences in the ways people structure their worlds, that is, the *thinking* processes that people use in managing their lives. How people organize their thinking affects what they are likely to *perceive* in a given situation, what they are likely to remember most readily and how they plan and organize work for themselves and for others.

In the example above, Jack was a *divergent* thinker and Jane was a *convergent* thinker. Although that is not the only difference between them, it is clearly an important one that can either be a source of conflict or a basis for building a *complementary* work relationship, one that capitalizes on the differences as *strengths*. Most decisions by managers are complex enough to require some ability to look at implications and consequences (a divergent thought process) as well as move things to some conclusion and action (a convergent thought process). Some people can do both, but usually because they have consciously developed the side of themselves that was not a natural tendency in the first place. Some successful managers have been smart enough to surround themselves with people who *collectively* are both divergent and convergent thinkers.

In recent years, a conceptual framework for understanding individual differences has become very popular among organizational behavior teachers, students, consultants, and managers. It is rooted in the personality theory of Carl Jung but has been translated into a set of concepts and tools that have very practical applications. The principal proponent of this work has been Isabel Briggs Myers, who published a widely used instrument and series of supporting texts designed to help people understand themselves and others better. Although we will not describe this approach in detail, we will provide a summary of the basic theory and its applications in a way that should give you some insights into people, including yourself. If you are interested in studying the approach in greater depth, a useful place to begin is with the book *Gifts Differing* by Isabel Briggs Myers.

THE MYERS-BRIGGS MODEL

The model describes people in terms of four dimensions:

1. Introversion—Extraversion.
2. Sensing—Intuition.
3. Thinking—Feeling.
4. Judging—Perceiving.

Let's look first at each dimension separately and then discuss what kinds of pictures emerge as they combine. Keep in mind as you consider this approach that these dimensions do not represent fixed traits in people, but rather they identify *processes* that everyone is capable of using, even though each individual has a propensity for operating at one or another end of each dimension. Furthermore, keep in mind that people change as they grow, developing skills that broaden their abilities to engage in behavior that may not have been "natural" or preferred in earlier stages of life. Also, circumstances often pull out of us capacities heretofore untapped.

1. Introversion—Extraversion

Where do you get your cues for making decisions or taking action? From inside yourself or from other people? If your tendency is to be a kind of "loner," mostly responding to your inner world, you are probably an *introvert*. If you tend to be highly social and responsive to other people in your world, you are probably an *extravert*. Again, although we are guilty of using the terms as labels, they are not intended to reflect lifetime boxes; you may tend to be more introverted than extraverted, or vice versa, or you may even be somewhere in the middle. As a manager it will pay you to be sensitive to cues both outside and inside yourself, sometimes responding more to one than the other but always looking for an appropriate balance. The research engineer whose style is highly introverted may find the demands of others to be a source of tension when promoted to a managerial role. Sometimes the dilemma results in poor management; hopefully, it can be an opportunity for the individual to broaden his/her way of structuring the world.

2. Sensing—Intuition

Jack says, "Let's go with it; I have a hunch we're on the right track." Jane says, "I need more information; it all seems too ambiguous for me to go ahead." Who's right? Either? Neither? Both? Probably all of the above. Since most management decisions have some inherent uncertainty, each of us approaches the situation in his/her own style. Jack trusts his past experience and the intuitive sense that he has built from it; Jane trusts real data, what she can *see,* or *hear,* or *touch,* etc., as the correct means of making decisions. Again, maybe some combination, some balance of the two approaches, produces effective decisions. Furthermore, some situations demand a thorough search of facts, while others are better suited to hunches that are not easily explained.

Sherlock Holmes usually approached a case by building pieces of information into a careful, logically deduced conclusion. Hercule Poirot was not so "logical," depending more on his ability to make leaps in thought, to fit pieces into a whole in a sudden flash of insight. Are you Holmes or Poirot? You may need to become a little of each. In fact, even Sherlock Holmes at times acted on pure intuition, and Poirot was always careful to pay attention to details. The world of a manager demands a combination of intuitive and sensing abilities.

3. Thinking—Feeling

A good manager uses both mind and heart. Did you ever hear the conjugation "I am firm, you are stubborn, he is pig-headed!"? You tend to view yourself as a rational, thinking person; somehow that's considered a "good" way to be. Other people—especially those who don't see things the way you do—are less rational, more emotional; and that's not so good. We're beginning to recognize that *all* of us are a combination of rational and nonrational, or, as defined in the present context, *thinkers* and *feelers.* At one time the business world had a norm that said, "Keep your feelings out of your decisions." That is much less the case nowadays. It is recognized that how you feel about a decision can determine the success of its implementation just as much as the logic of that decision. The realities of organizational life often evoke emotions that play a dominant role in a manager's behavior. Fear of failure, fear of the boss, excitement about a new product, compassion for an employee, anger at another person, etc., are but a few examples of emotional forces that appear in the day-to-day life of a firm.

Even though you may tend or prefer to use thinking as your way of dealing with the world, you would be unrealistic to believe that your feelings don't enter the process. Or, if you trust your feelings more than your logic, you may find that your actions lack consistency and coherence. Thinkers (forgive the label) see feelers as soft-headed do-gooders; feelers see thinkers as cold hard-asses. These stereotypes generate conflict; the differences could be useful complements to one another if understood and appreciated. The implications for male–

female work relationships should be obvious, especially with the history of stereotyping in that arena.

4. Judging—Perceiving

The distinction here is similar to the one made earlier regarding convergent and divergent thinking. A tendency toward *judging* means a preference for getting things finished and settled, not leaving loose ends, using a structured plan to do work, and a low tolerance for ambiguity. This is a different use of the term; it does not refer to passing judgment on something or someone, in the usual sense of "judging." A tendency toward *perceiving* means a preference for exploring many routes, leaving things open, seeking change, starting a variety of activities (which often remain unfinished), and a high tolerance for ambiguity. Do you see yourself at the extreme of either judging or perceiving? To be effective as a manager, over the long run you'll need to operate at times in a perceiving mode—for example, when you are trying to understand a problem—and at times in a judging mode—for example, when you are trying to move people to act on the solution to a problem. The tensions that develop between "perceivers" and "judgers" can, as in the previous dimensions, be sources of irreconcilable conflict or effective problem solving.

Combining the Dimensions

There is a well-researched instrument designed to help you understand your "type." It measures your preferences or tendencies along the four dimensions and generates a picture that combines the dimensions into 16 possible categories. If you are interested, your instructor may be able to help you obtain access to the instrument, but its use is carefully controlled through professionally trained people who can administer, score, and interpret the data. In the absence of this, you can at least explore for yourself, possibly with the help of people who know you best, how the four dimensions fit together for you. Figure 8–4 shows brief descriptions of the 16 possibilities. It could be interesting and fun to locate yourself and discuss your reactions with others.

An awareness of these differences in ways of dealing with the world and an awareness that each process can contribute to solving a concrete problem can help you to:

1. View someone else's approach simply as "different," not bad or inferior, with its own potential to contribute, however frustrating it may seem.

FIGURE 8–4
Characteristics Frequently Associated with Each Type

		Sensing Types — *With Thinking*	*Sensing Types* — *With Feeling*
Introverts	*Judging*	*ISTJ* Serious, quiet, earn success by concentration and thoroughness. Practical, orderly, matter-of-fact, logical, realistic, and dependable. See to it that everything is well organized. Take responsibility. Make up their own minds as to what should be accomplished and work toward it steadily, regardless of protests or distractions. Live their outer life more with thinking, inner more with sensing.	*ISFJ* Quiet, friendly, responsible, and conscientious. Work devotedly to meet their obligations. Lend stability to any project or group. Thorough, painstaking, accurate. May need time to master technical subjects, as their interests are not often technical. Patient with detail and routine. Loyal, considerate, concerned with how other people feel. Live their outer life more with feeling, inner more with sensing.
Introverts	*Perceptive*	*ISTP* Cool onlookers, quiet, reserved, observing and analyzing life with detached curiosity and unexpected flashes of original humor. Usually interested in impersonal principles, cause and effect, or how and why mechanical things work. Exert themselves no more than they think necessary, because any waste of energy would be inefficient. Live their outer life more with sensing, inner more with thinking.	*ISFP* Retiring, quietly friendly, sensitive, modest about their abilities. Shun disagreements, do not force their opinions or values on others. Usually do not care to lead but are often loyal followers. May be rather relaxed about assignments or getting things done, because they enjoy the present moment and do not want to spoil it by undue haste or exertion. Live their outer life more with sensing, inner more with feeling.
Extraverts	*Perceptive*	*ESTP* Matter-of-fact, do not worry or hurry, enjoy whatever comes along. Tend to like mechanical things and sports, with friends on the side. May be a bit blunt or insensitive. Adaptable, tolerant, generally conservative in values. Dislike long explanations. Are best with real things that can be worked, handled, taken apart, or put back together. Live their outer life more with sensing, inner more with thinking.	*ESFP* Outgoing, easygoing, accepting, friendly, fond of a good time. Like sports and making things. Know what's going on and join in eagerly. Find remembering facts easier than mastering theories. Are best in situations that need sound common sense and practical ability with people as well as with things. Live their outer life more with sensing, inner more with feeling.
Extraverts	*Judging*	*ESTJ* Practical realists, matter-of-fact, with a natural head for business or mechanics. Not interested in subjects they see no use for, but can apply themselves when necessary. Like to organize and run activities. Tend to run things well, especially if they remember to consider other people's feelings and points of view when making their decisions. Live their outer life more with thinking, inner more with sensing.	*ESFJ* Warm-hearted, talkative, popular, conscientious, born cooperators, active committee members. Always doing something nice for someone. Work best with plenty of encouragement and praise. Little interest in abstract thinking or technical subjects. Main interest is in things that directly and visibly affect people's lives. Live their outer life more with feeling, inner more with sensing.

Note: A questionnaire to assess these 16 types, called the Myers-Briggs Type Indicator, is available for purchase from Consulting Psychologists Press, Inc.

* I = Introverted; E = Extraverted; S = Sensing; N = Intuition; F = Feeling; T = Thinking; P = Perceiving; J = Judging.

Intuitives		
With Feeling	*With Thinking*	
INFJ Succeed by perseverance, originality, and desire to do whatever is needed or wanted. Put their best efforts into their work. Quietly forceful, conscientious, concerned for others. Respected for their firm principles. Likely to be honored and followed for their clear convictions as to how best to serve the common good. Live their outer life more with feeling, inner more with intuition.	*INTJ* Have original minds and great drive, which they use only for their own purposes. In fields that appeal to them, they have a fine power to organize a job and carry it through with or without help. Skeptical, critical, independent, determined, often stubborn. Must learn to yield less important points in order to win the most important. Live their outer life more with thinking, inner more with intuition.	*Judging* *Introverts*
INFP Full of enthusiasms and loyalties, but seldom talk of these until they know you well. Care about learning, ideas, language, and independent projects of their own. Apt to be on yearbook staff, perhaps as editor. Tend to undertake too much, then somehow get it done. Friendly, but often too absorbed in what they are doing to be sociable or notice much. Live their outer life more with intuition, inner more with feeling.	*INTP* Quiet, reserved, impersonal. Especially enjoy theoretical or scientific subjects. Logical to the point of hair-splitting. Interested mainly in ideas, with little liking for parties or small talk. Tend to have very sharply defined interests. Need to choose careers where some strong interest of theirs can be used and useful. Live their outer life more with intuition, inner more with thinking.	*Introverts* *Perceptive*
ENFP Warmly enthusiastic, high-spirited, ingenious, imaginative. Able to do almost anything that interests them. Quick with a solution for any difficulty and ready to help anyone with a problem. Often rely on their ability to improvise instead of preparing in advance. Can always find compelling reasons for whatever they want. Live their outer life with more intuition, inner more with feeling.	*ENTP* Quick, ingenious, good at many things. Stimulating company, alert and outspoken, argue for fun on either side of a question. Resourceful in solving new and challenging problems, but may neglect routine assignments. Turn to one new interest after another. Can always find logical reasons for whatever they want. Live their outer life more with intuition, inner more with thinking.	*Perceptive* *Extraverts*
ENFJ Responsive and responsible. Feel real concern for what others think and want, and try to handle things with due regard for other people's feelings. Can present a proposal or lead a group discussion with ease and tact. Sociable, popular, sympathetic. Responsive to praise and criticism. Live their outer life more with feeling, inner more with intuition.	*ENTJ* Hearty, frank, decisive, leaders in activities. Usually good in anything that requires reasoning and intelligent talk, such as public speaking. Are well informed and keep adding to their fund of knowledge. May sometimes be more positive and confident than their experience in an area warrants. Live their outer life more with thinking, inner more with intuition.	*Extraverts* *Judging*

Source: Reproduced by special permission of the publisher, Consulting Psychologists Press, Inc., Palo Alto, Calif. 94306, from *Introduction to Type* by Isabel Briggs Myers. Copyright © 1960. Further reproduction is prohibited without the publisher's consent.

2. Consider trying a different "tack" if you find yourself stuck in dealing with some situation.
3. Recognize the need to supplement your own natural pattern by consulting with others and seeking to broaden your own repertoire of approaches.

LIFE CHOICES

The ice cream lovers among the readers of this book will recognize that, in some respects, life is like a trip to an ice cream parlor. There are so many flavors from which to choose that any choice can seem incredibly difficult, especially given the limits of one's stomach and purse. Some people enter the parlor with their minds made up and their eyes closed to all the alternative flavors. "If vanilla was good before, it will be good enough now." Others decide to include several flavors so as to avoid too narrow a choice, eating more than they need to maximize the opportunities available. And still others gaze longingly at all the flavors, feeling overwhelmed and possibly hoping that someone else might make the choice for them. Perhaps the saddest outcome is when a person finally makes a choice and, while eating the ice cream, continues to think about the other flavors that *might* have been chosen. Is there a better way to kill the enjoyment?

Can you see how many aspects of life are like the imaginary ice cream parlor? Choices about careers, schools, courses, professors, what movie to go to, whether or not to join a fraternity or sorority, and if so, which one involve similar struggles. At least with ice cream you can always go back the next day and choose another flavor. Such areas as careers, marriage, and so forth, are not easy to change the next day; they generally involve more long-term commitments. If people are uncertain about such choices, they often try to avoid making them.

> *When choosing between two evils, I always like to take the one I've never tried before.*
>
> Mae West
> In *Klondike Annie*

The fact is, every choice is usually a decision to rule out other alternatives. Although some people manage to "have their cake and eat it too," most people are forced to leave many unopened doors behind. You can try to keep all your options open at all times, but you will pay a price. Like a child eating chocolate who wonders if strawberry would taste better, the joy of the chosen experience is diminished.

If you think about the lives of the people you most admire, you can probably identify some theme running through each, a theme that reflects a chosen *direction* to life. Psychoanalyst Victor Frankl discovered as a result of painful years in a Nazi concentration camp that the survival and growth of individuals depend in part upon their ability to identify *meaning* in every experience. He was in fact one of the few survivors of the Nazi tortures, and he attributes this to his absolute *commitment to meaning in every moment* of his own existence (Frankl, 1959).

To avoid choice altogether is to avoid commitment to anything or anyone. Perhaps a child can afford to permit all choices to be made by others as long as the world is a trustworthy place. You may even know adults whose roles in life seem to involve being passive and helpless, remaining relatively uncommitted to anything or anyone. The payoff for them, of course, is that they can never be held responsible in the long run, since they never made any choices or commitments in the first place.

I'm giving you a definite maybe.

Samuel Goldwyn

To make a choice is to make a commitment. How one does or does not live up to one's commitments is another matter. But it does seem to follow from what is known about human growth and development that *active choice* resulting in active commitment tends to foster maturation of the self-concept. This is not to suggest that commitment to a decision never means reexamining that decision. That would be foolhardy. You can never know all the possible outcomes of any given choice. Even trying a new flavor of ice cream involves *some* uncertainty as to whether or not you will like it.

CHOOSING

Ah, God, it were an easy matter to choose a Calling, had one all time to live in! I should be 50 years a Barrister, 50 a Physician, 50 a Clergyman, 50 a Soldier! Aye, and 50 a Thief, and 50 a Judge. All Roads are fine Roads, none more than another. . . . to choose ten were no trouble; to choose one, impossible! All Trades, all Crafts, all Professions are wondrous, but none is finer than the rest together. I cannot choose.

John Barth
The Sot-Weed Factor, 1960

Important choices always involve some measure of risk to the self. Fear of taking risk can lead to fear of making important choices. And making a commitment usually involves some degree of risk regarding one's ability to live up to that commitment. Therefore, fear of disappointing others can lead to avoidance of commitment.

Can you apply some of these ideas to yourself? Are there central themes running through your personal propositions that reflect your basic attitudes toward making important choices, making commitments, and taking risks? Such themes are basic to managerial behavior, where you are always required to make choices, make commitments, and often take risks.

Life Phases and Life Choices

The kinds of choices you make and the commitments involved are very often a reflection of the period of life in which you find yourself. Unique as you might see yourself, there is no doubt that many of the things you have and will experience are also experienced by others. In fact, there are some fairly predictable phases of life that most people go through. This is fortunate, since it can help you to understand yourself and others better. And each of these phases seems to contain some new needs, struggles, and choices along with some old familiar ones that somehow were never completely "put to rest."

Figure 8–5 shows examples of life phases in terms of key events and typical issues that characterize them. Study the chart and see where you fit in. Also see if it gives you some insights into people you know—parents, friends, co-workers, your boss, and so on. Can you see how the things that motivate them are a result of both their unique personality and the place or places they are in their lives? These insights can help you as a manager to understand your employees and help them to plan career paths consistent with their life phases. Keep in mind that these phases are very general, can vary a great deal from person to person, may even occur in a different sequence for some, and, in rare instances, might not even apply to a person whose key life events have been extraordinary.

One phase deserving some special attention is the 40s—the period that is often referred to as the midlife (or midcareer) crisis. In the same way that people at age 22 might be carefully considering the kinds of career and life choices they are making, many people find themselves reexamining those choices against the backdrop of experience after 20 or 30 years in a career. This often leads to a major change of direction—an upheaval of sorts. It feels like a crisis in that it can mean letting go of a very familiar, secure state of existence and entering a very unknown state often full of risks and anxiety. At times a fear of disappointing oneself and others prevents a risky choice, but a will-

FIGURE 8–5
Adult Life Phases

Age	*Key Events*	*Characteristic Tensions*
Late teens	Leave home, new roles, and more autonomous living arrangements; college, travel, army, job. Initial decisions about what to study, career, love relationships.	A balance between "being in" and "moving out" of the family. For women, career versus marriage. Search for identity. Testing limits. Struggle with authority.
Early to mid-20s	Provisional commitment to occupation and first stages of a career; being hired; first job; adjusting to work world. Marriage, decision to have a child.	"Doing what one should." Living and building for the future. Dreams versus reality. Struggle for opportunity. For women, struggle to find place in male work world versus security of socially accepted woman's role.
Late 20s to early 30s	Change occupation or direction within an occupation. Go back to school. Marriage, parenthood, part-time job (for married women).	"What is life all about now that I'm doing what I should? What do I want out of life?" For women, awareness of unfulfilled needs either as wife/mother or as career woman desire to start career or desire to have children ("last chance").
Mid- to late 30s	Pursue family activities. Children old enough for mother to return to school. Important promotion in work. Plateau reached in career.	Concern to establish order and stability in life and with "making it," with setting long-range goals and meeting them. Awareness of passing youth. Fear of "settling in," having missed something. For women, struggle to enter or reenter career or go back to school. Self-doubts versus self-confidence.
The 40s	Change in activities from realization that life ambitions might not develop. Change of career; empty nest; a second career for women whose first career was in the home. Death of parents.	Awareness of bodily decline, aging, own mortality; emergence of feminine aspects of self for men, masculine aspects for women. Feeling of stagnation. Need for renewal, to prove self, to reaffirm youth. For women, recognizing the tougher side, fear of being a "beginner" in a career, feeling of being out of place in a youth-oriented culture, and discomfort with own success in career. Fear of lacking an identity.
The 50s	Last chance for women to have a career or vigorously pursue a deferred life goal or interests. Reaching highest level of status in career *or* settling for less.	An imperative to change so that deferred goals can be accomplished—"It is perhaps late, but there are things I would like to do in the last half of my life." A mellowing of feelings and relationships; spouse is increasingly important. Greater comfort with self, or fear of never living up to own aspirations. Renewed sense of purpose, self-acceptance, and vigor *or* Feelings of doubt and self-pity. For women, achieving sense of wholeness through integration of both sides of self; for those who entered career late, a struggle similar to that of man in the 40s.
The 60s (and beyond)	Retirement of self and spouse; aging; health problems. Loss of stamina.	Review of accomplishments. Eagerness to share everyday human joys and sorrows; family is important; death is a new presence. Concern about having made one's mark on the world. Desire to grow old gracefully. Renewed need to belong, but fear of being dependent.

Source: Based on Rita Weathersby, *Developmental Perspective on Adults' Uses of Formal Education* (doctoral dissertation, Harvard University, 1977); and G. Sheehy, *Passages: Predictable Crises of Adult Life* (New York: E. P. Dutton, 1976).

ingness to push past that fear can be the very thing needed to generate renewed commitment to life, to work, to oneself, and to others. The feared disappointment very often reveals itself as a myth. Unfortunately, the struggles you currently face do not magically disappear after age 21 or 25 or 30. They usually reappear in new (and sometimes old) forms, only to challenge you again.

UNDERSTANDING AND MANAGING STRESS

At any stage of life, stress can be a factor affecting performance. Those who experience too little stress may not call into play their best attention and energy; those who experience too much stress may become immobilized, repeat useless behavior, or scatter their efforts. Moderate amounts of experienced stress generate focus and mobilize a person's resources. Performance is actually enhanced under moderate amounts of stress. Some of the recent attention to stress reduction ignores the utility of stress for accomplishment.

COMBATTING STRESS—WITH THE HELP OF HIGH TECH

For some time, researchers have related stress to a variety of physical ailments, including high blood pressure, heart disease, colitis, ulcers, migraine headaches, insomnia, back injuries, and eczema. The American Heart Association estimates that recruiting replacements for executives who die of heart disease costs American industry $700 million annually. Some researchers place the total cost of stress-related illness as high as $750 per worker per year. . . . "Many executives would rather pay [for stress management training] *out of their own pocket than admit to a 'weakness.'" But the need for ways to channel pressure is still there. "You can be as competitive as you need to be. We don't attempt to change anyone's life or personality. We teach people constructive ways to deal with that stress."*

Source: Marilyn J. Cohodas, *Boston Business Journal*, March 24, 1986.

Compounding the problem is the fact that individuals vary enormously in their tolerance for externally caused stress. The same situation can be perceived as excruciatingly overbearing or as wonderfully challenging by individuals with different self-concepts. Thus there is no way to create universally appropriate levels of stress. It is sometimes possible, however, to identify signals that individuals are experiencing so much stress that their performance is impeded. It is important to know how to "read" them in yourself and in others, especially when you are responsible for the performance of others.

Signs of Stress

How do you tell when someone is feeling a high level of stress and may need some relief from it? Fortunately, some symptoms are fairly overt and readily recognized. Unfortunately, the person feeling the stress is often the first to *deny* it! In other words, *you* may be the one to recognize another person's need for help before that person does. Or vice versa! You may notice that the other is irritable, not concentrating on work, missing deadlines, not socializing, and so on. If these things are pointed out, the response may be "I'm fine, thank you, just need more sleep" or "I don't know what you're talking about!"

Some signs of stress are *covert* or have very subtle overt aspects. Feeling anxious may or may not be very visible to others; upset stomach, headache, exhaustion, and many other physical symptoms are likely to be known only to the person experiencing them. Even feeling distracted and unable to stay focused on a task may remain hidden from others for a long time.

Given the many indicators that can signal stress, is anyone ever *free* of it? As a manager, it is difficult to judge when a situation is serious enough to warrant some action. After all, anyone can show some of these symptoms at almost any time in a given day.

Here are some guidelines for knowing when to pay special attention to someone (including yourself) who is showing signs of stress:

1. If the signs persist for a prolonged period of time (weeks or months), then they should be judged serious and potentially damaging to the health and welfare of the person.
2. If *many* signs of stress are occurring at the same time, it is probable that the *level* of stress is unduly high and is not likely to subside quickly.
3. If the *behavior* of the person is out of character, that is, represents a departure from what is *normal for that person,* and *it persists,* then the level of stress is likely to be unhealthily high. A person's behavior in this context should not be judged against a "most people" standard, nor should it be compared to your *own* behavior. Everyone is different, and those differences need to be appreciated. An exuberant, socially active salesperson who has become consistently quiet and withdrawn is probably in trouble. By contrast, a laboratory researcher who normally works best alone may be showing signs of stress by becoming loud and boisterous at social events.

No simple magic formula exists for making these judgments, especially since they are so personal in nature. There is a fine line where personal and managerial concern crosses the other's right to privacy.

However, part of managerial responsibility is to develop people, not just supervise task completion, so a delicate balancing act is required. People develop as total individuals, not just as performers of tasks.

Some Organizational Sources of Stress and Ways to Cope

People move through many different contexts: work, family, school, social activities, etc. Each has its own stresses and strains. It isn't always possible to keep the stress from one area of life totally separate from the other areas. A conflict at home can easily be displaced on an employee at work—and vice versa. Therefore, whatever the source of stress, its effects are often played out in other contexts.

Nevertheless, as a manager, you won't be in a position or have the responsibility to deal with an employee's home life, even if problems there sometimes spill over into the workplace. But you can help your employees organize and carry out their jobs in ways that minimize unnecessary stress.

Here are four major sources of job-related stress:

1. Uncertainty or ambiguity.
2. Unfinished tasks and intrusions.
3. Role expectations.
4. Growth and development.

UNCERTAINTY OR AMBIGUITY. The greater your confidence, the better you perform; the more certainty you have in a task, the greater confidence you feel; the more information you have about a task, the more certainty you have and the greater confidence you feel. Think about the jobs that have made you feel best. They probably involved these elements. By contrast, situations in which you lacked the information you needed created uncertainty, and, therefore, you felt less confident about your performance.

The failure of a manager to provide employees with the information they need to carry out a task creates a gap of uncertainty, which inevitably produces stress. If a manager is consistently amiss in providing available and needed information, high uncertainty and, consequently, high stress are likely to be created. The world is inherently uncertain, and there are a great many sources of uncertainty over which managers have no control. However, a conscious attempt to reduce the uncertainty as much as possible can at least minimize the level of stress and help maintain performance. Conversely, cautious individuals, especially those overstressed by uncertainty, may not make every effort to gather information, ask questions of their boss and peers, or fill in the gaps as much as possible before and during the execution of a job. Guesswork can then compound the uncertainty with bad decisions. If you are in a situation where you are unsure about how to proceed, take the initiative to inquire. That doesn't always produce the desired answers, but forging ahead blindly doesn't either.

Since some people have a greater tolerance for ambiguity than others, relatively turbulent work environments can be stimulating and challenging, rather than a source of stress. But those who prefer a more structured, less ambiguous setting ought to pursue work—or be helped to find jobs—in a relatively stable and controllable arena.

UNFINISHED TASKS AND INTRUSIONS. Do you recognize this scenario? No matter how hard you try, it seems as though you can never fit all your tasks into the time available. Some things take longer than expected, you keep getting interrupted, a critical piece of information isn't there when you need it, something else comes up that takes precedence, and so on and so on and so on. The net result is that you carry around a lot of unfinished business. The cycle that begins with awareness of a need for action and ends with completion of that action often gets interrupted midstream. That plays on your mind and intrudes in other activities. You can't sleep, are distracted at home, and unable to focus your energies on immediate tasks at work.

An accumulation of unfinished business can easily become a major source of anxiety and produce enough stress to immobilize even the most competent person. It can become so overwhelming that the person begins to feel helpless and hopeless, unsure where to begin or even if it's worthwhile to *try* to begin.

(If you belong to the International Society of Procrastinators, you recognize this all too well. Of course, you probably never got around to sending in your dues, so you're no longer a member of that esteemed group!)

What can be done about all this accumulated unfinished business? First, start somewhere: set *priorities*. One option is to start with the quick and easy tasks, creating a sense of making progress. Some people have to start with the most important and pressing jobs—big or small, difficult or easy—and, once the jobs are completed, feel a great burden removed. Wherever the start—and it may not make a lot of difference—the tension release will be its own reward.

Part of setting priorities is deciding whether or not some tasks can be ignored or done poorly. David Bradford's law number 8 is "Any job worth doing may be worth doing mediocrely." It is remarkable how releasing it can be to deliberately *decide* to slide by on low-consequence tasks. Deliberate choice is necessary, however, because some tasks poorly done can come back to haunt you and make things worse.

Some people create unfinished business and, consequently, a great deal of stress for themselves by not knowing what to let go of. A need to be involved in everything can be an awful burden. For any given task, or part of a task, ask yourself, "Do *I* have to be the one to do this? Do *I* even have to be involved at all?" It may be difficult for many people to let go of control, but doing so can certainly help to reduce stress.

Some find that distancing themselves from their work setting for even a short time can help them get a better perspective on what seems overwhelming. Being *in* the setting that's generating the stress only serves to heighten the stress and to impede clear, constructive thinking. A "breather" reduces the immediate tension and helps to mobilize personal resources more effectively.

It is worth mentioning that there is general agreement about the value of proper diet and exercise in preparing people for dealing with stress, whatever its source. Many people under pressure fail to take care of themselves, generating a cycle that results in poor sleep, fatigue, and low tolerance for doing the tasks that would relieve the feelings of stress. This physical aspect of coping with stress is easily attended to, once recognized.

ROLE EXPECTATIONS. At times the expectations associated with fulfilling a role can produce major stress. There is not enough time to finish an assigned project; unexpected changes occur that require some rethinking about a task; several tasks are being demanded, and are all called "top priority"; the list is endless. Many people push on and try to fulfill the expectations by working harder or putting in more time, sometimes only to end up with a situation that is totally out of control. While embarrassment may be a barrier to going to your boss and asking for more time or for help, it clearly makes sense to do so. It makes sense to *renegotiate* the role expectations before disaster occurs.

An effective manager will learn how to spot the signs of stress that signal "overload" and will initiate a process of renegotiation, sometimes even before the employee does. Mutual expectations will be established that will encourage subordinates to initiate such contacts when the occasion calls for it. This can be a useful way to prevent burnout, avoid losing some good people who simply leave in order to get away from the stress, and, in general, promote productivity in employees.

As a student, there have undoubtedly been many times when you needed that extra time or help and couldn't bring yourself to "renegotiate" with your instructor. Some instructors, like some managers, are not very open to such a process and may simply tell you to meet your commitments as assigned. Sometimes, external realities make renegotiation impossible. But the situation is worth testing; and you may be pleasantly surprised by the willingness of most people to be flexible.

Finally, when *you* become a manager, you may want to keep all this in mind; the employee facing you is like *you* facing an instructor or a boss at an earlier time.

GROWTH AND DEVELOPMENT. Most people are attracted both to growth and to preserving things as they are. There's a side of everyone that likes the security and comfort of the status quo. You know what you're good at and where your support comes from. It's a kind of comfort zone that gives a solid base in life. However, living only in that comfort zone can eventually become boring and even lead to restlessness for something different. Therefore, people decide (or are pushed by circumstances) to venture forth into a new arena, stretching in new ways. This leads to inevitable uncertainty, getting into skill areas never before attempted. It also means living with the stress that accompanies such steps. There's always the chance of failure or of making a fool of oneself. While in the learning process, it isn't always great consolation to know that you will eventually feel stronger for having taken the risk, whatever the outcomes, or that disaster fantasies often exceed the eventual realities. While it may not always be true that there is "no gain without pain," growth is seldom completely comfortable.

A fulfilling life, then, necessarily involves stress of one kind or another. But as today's new venture becomes part of tomorrow's comfort zone, you learn to seek change and growth, and you build an increasing tolerance for the stress that goes along with it. You may even become addicted to growth and development, and that's not a bad addiction to have.

How to Deal with Stress

As already mentioned, there are steps one can take to manage the stress that tends to creep into any job:

1. Cultivate self-awareness so as to recognize stress symptoms.
2. Assess your tolerance for ambiguity, and seek to move into a situation that doesn't chronically exceed your limits.
3. Monitor your diet and exercise schedule, and practice good health activities to enhance your physical capacity to handle stress.
4. When faced with too many tasks, try to get started and focus on them one at a time.
5. Set priorities for each day's work.
6. Delegate by asking yourself if a particular task really requires your involvement.
7. Check on whether you are doing a task unnecessarily well; try to avoid being a perfectionist when "perfect" isn't necessary.

8. Don't overconcentrate. Take a break occasionally, or even "sleep on a problem."
9. Renegotiate role expectations.

KEY CONCEPTS FROM CHAPTER 8

1. *a.* Basic human needs,
   modified by
   b. Past experience,
   lead to
   c. Personal system (in the context or a situation),
   which determines
   d. Perceptions and defensiveness.
   e. Expectancies regarding choices
   result in
   f. Behavior—choices—actions,
   which feed back on the personal system.
2. The structure of the personal system:
   a. Personal goals,
   b. Competencies,
   c. Beliefs,
   d. Values,
3. All organized around the self-concept.
4. Rationalizing: An escape from the pain of violating one's values.
5. Perceptions: Everything interpreted through individual filters.
6. Defensive behavior:
   a. The greater the threat to a person's self-concept, the greater the defensive response.
   b. The greater the threat to a person's self-concept, the less learning and growth.
   c. Important to attempt to find a nonthreatening alternative.
7. Self-concept and norms:
   a. The willingness to conform to group norms is a product of the closeness of the norms to one's self-concept.
   b. Costs and benefits of conforming weighed against costs and benefits of deviating.
8. Self-concept and roles:
   a. To the extent that a role is perceived as congruent with the self-concept, inclination is to adopt it.
   b. To the extent it is seen as incongruent with any aspect of the self-concept, inclination is to reject it.
   c. To the extent roles are adopted that support values, one experiences self as worthwhile.
   d. To the extent that one violates these values, one doubts personal worth.
9. Self-concept and rewards:
   a. Worth of rewards determined by goals and values.
   b. Activity acquired to gain reward must be compatible with goals, competencies, beliefs, and values.
   c. Reaction to rewards influenced by what relevant others receive.

10. To predict behavior, one would have to know:
    a. Strength of the goals directing the particular behavior.
    b. Expectancies regarding the positive and the negative consequences from the environment.
    c. Expectancies regarding the positive and negative consequences to the self-concept.
11. *a.* Expectancies—regarding choices (positive versus negative outcomes)—result in
    b. Behavior—choices (actions, learning defenses), which confirm or disconfirm the self-concept.
12. Personal propositions serve as guides to decisions in life.
13. The ways in which people organize and structure their worlds provide important clues to understanding individual differences.
    a. The Myers-Briggs Model.
    b. Sixteen personality types.
14. Life choices are influenced by life phases.
15. Understanding and managing stress:
    a. How serious depends on number and persistence of symptoms in context of what is normal for person.
    b. Sources of stress related to: ambiguity, unfinished tasks, role expectations, and personal growth.
    c. When managing stress, attend to physical, psychological, and social factors.

SUGGESTED READINGS

Adams, J. D., ed. *Understanding and Managing Stress.* San Diego: University Associates, 1980.

Allport, G.; P. Vernon; and G. Lindzey. *Study of Values.* 3rd ed. Boston: Houghton Mifflin, 1970.

Axley, S. R. "Managerial and Organizational Communication in Terms of the Conduit Metaphor." *Academy of Management Review,* July 1984, pp. 428–37.

Beehr, T. A., and J. E. Newman. "Job Stress, Employee Health, and Organizational Effectiveness: A Facet Analysis, Model, and Literature Review." *Personnel Psychology* 30 (1978), pp. 665–99.

Bhagat, R. S. "Effects of Stressful Life Events on Individual Performance Effectiveness and Work Adjustment Processes within Organizational Settings: A Research Model." *Academy of Management Review,* October 1983, pp. 660–71.

Brief, A. P., and R. J. Aldag. "The Self in Work Organizations: A Conceptual Review." *Academy of Management Review,* January 1980, pp. 75–88.

Brief, A. P., and S. J. Motowidlo. "Prosocial Organizational Behaviors." *Academy of Management Review,* October 1986, pp. 710–25.

Brown, M. "Values—A Necessary but Neglected Ingredient of Motivation on the Job." *Academy of Management Review,* October 1976, pp. 15–23.

Brunson, B. I., and K. A. Matthews. "The Type A Coronary-Prone Behavior Pattern and Reactions to Uncontrollable Stress: An Analysis of Performance Strategies, Affect, and Attributions during Failures." *Journal of Personality and Social Psychology* 40 (1981), pp. 906–18.

Carroll, S. J., and D. J. Gillen. "The Classical Management Functions: Are They Really Outdated?" *Proceedings, Academy of Management,* 1984, pp. 512–14.

Charles, A. W. "The Self-Concept in Management." *Advanced Management Journal,* April 1971, pp. 32–38.

Cohen, S. "After-Effects of Stress on Human Performance and Social Behavior." *Psychological Bulletin* 88 (1980), pp. 82–108.

Combs, A., and D. Snygg. *Individual Behavior.* New York: Harper & Row, 1959.

Cooper, C. L., and J. Marshall. "Occupational Sources of Stress: A Review of the Literature Relating to Coronary Heart Disease and Mental Ill Health." *Journal of Occupational Psychology* 49 (1976), pp. 11–28.

Diamond, M. A., and S. Allcorn. "Psychological Barriers to Personal Responsibility." *Organizational Dynamics,* Spring 1984, pp. 66–77.

Dozier, J. B., and M. P. Miceli. "Potential Predictors of Whistle-Blowing: A Prosocial Behavior Perspective." *Academy of Management Review,* October 1985, pp. 823–46.

Dyer, W. G., and J. H. Dyer. "The M*A*S*H Generation: Implications for Future Organization Values." *Organizational Dynamics* 12 (1984), pp. 66–79.

Felson, R. B. "Ambiguity and Bias in the Self-Concept." *Social Psychology Quarterly* 44 (1981), pp. 64–69.

Frankl, V. *From Death Camp to Existentialism.* Boston: Beacon Press, 1959.

Gioia, D. A., and P. P. Poole. "Scripts in Organizational Behavior." *Academy of Management Review,* July 1984, pp. 449–59.

Goffman, E. *The Presentation of Self in Everyday Life.* Garden City, N.Y.: Doubleday Publishing, 1959.

Greer, C. R., and M. A. D. Castro. "The Relationship between Perceived Unit Effectiveness and Occupational Stress: The Case of Purchasing Agents." *Journal of Applied Behavioral Science* 22, no. 2 (1986), pp. 159–76.

Guth, W. T., and R. Tagiuri. "Personal Values and Corporate Strategies." *Harvard Business Review* 45 (1965), pp. 123–32.

Hall, D. T. *Careers in Organizations.* Santa Monica, Calif.: Goodyear Publishing, 1976.

Haney, W. V. "A Comparative Study of Unilateral and Bilateral Communication." *Academy of Management Journal* 7 (1964), pp. 128–36.

Harrison, R. "Defenses and the Need to Know." *Human Relations Training News* 6 (1962).

Jansen, E. and M. A. Von Glinow. "Ethical Ambivalence and Organizational Reward Systems." *Academy of Management Review,* October 1985, pp. 814–22.

Jick, T. D., and L. F. Mitz. "Sex Differences in Work Stress." *Academy of Management Review,* July 1985, pp. 408–20.

Jourard, S. *The Transparent Self.* Rev. ed. New York: Van Nostrand Reinhold, 1971.

Kahn, R. L.; D. M. Wolfe; R. P. Quinn; J. D. Snoek; and R. A. Rosenthal. *Organizational Stress: Studies in Role Conflict and Ambiguity.* New York: John Wiley & Sons, 1964.

Karasek, R. A. "Job Demands, Job Decision Latitude, and Mental Strain." *Administrative Science Quarterly* 24 (1979), pp. 285–308.

Leiter, M. P., and K. A. Meechan. "Role Structure and Burnout in the Field of Human Services." *Journal of Applied Behavioral Science* 22, no. 1 (1986), pp. 47–52.

Levinson, D. *The Seasons of a Man's Life.* New York: Alfred A. Knopf, 1978.

London, M. "Toward a Theory of Career Motivation." *Academy of Management Review,* October 1983, pp. 620–30.

Manz, C. C. "Self-Leadership: Toward an Expanded Theory of Self-Influence Processes in Organizations." *Academy of Management Review,* July 1986, pp. 585–600.

Matteson, M. T., and J. M. Ivancevich. "The Coronary-Prone Behavior Pattern: A Review and Appraisal." *Social Science and Medicine* 14 (1980), pp. 337–51.

McGregor, D. *The Human Side of Enterprise.* New York: McGraw-Hill, 1960.

Mihal, W. L.; P. A. Sorce; and T. E. Comte. "A Process Model of Individual Career Decision Making." *Academy of Management Review,* January 1984, pp. 95–103.

Morse, J. J., and J. W. Lorsch. "Beyond Theory Y." *Harvard Business Review,* May–June 1970, pp. 61–68.

Nadler, D., and E. Lawler. "Motivation: A Diagnostic Approach." In *Perspectives on Behavior in Organizations,* ed. J. R. Hackman, E. E. Lawler, and L. W. Porter. New York: McGraw-Hill, 1977, chap. 3.

Nelson, D. L., and J. C. Quick. "Professional Women: Are Distress and Disease Inevitable?" *Academy of Management Review,* April 1985, pp. 206–18.

Pittner, M. S., and B. Houston. "Response to Stress, Cognitive Coping Strategies, and the Type A Behavior Pattern." *Journal of Personality and Social Psychology* 39 (1980), pp. 147–57.

Rhodes, S. R., and M. Doering. "An Integrated Model of Career Motivation." *Academy of Management Review,* October 1983, pp. 631–39.

Rogers, C. *On Becoming a Person.* Boston: Houghton Mifflin, 1961.

Ross, J., and K. Ferris. "Interpersonal Attraction and Organizational Outcomes: A Field Examination." *Administrative Science Quarterly,* December 1981, pp. 617–32.

Schuler, R. S. "Definition and Conceptualization of Stress in Organizations." *Organizational Behavior and Human Performance* 2 (1980), pp. 184–215.

Scott, W. A. *Values and Organizations.* Skokie, Ill.: Rand McNally, 1965.

Sheehy, G. *Passages: Predictable Crises of Adult Life.* New York: E. P. Dutton, 1976.

Simon, S. B.; L. W. Howe; and H. Kirschenbaum. *Values and Clarification.* New York: Hart Publishing, 1972.

Stead, B. A. *Women in Management.* 2nd ed. Englewood Cliffs, N.J.: Prentice-Hall, 1985.

Terkel, S. *Working.* New York: Pantheon Books, 1974.

Tharenou, P., and P. Harker. "Moderating Influence of Self-Esteem on Relationships between Job Complexity, Performance, and Satisfaction." *Journal of Applied Psychology* 69 (1984), pp. 623–32.

Vaillant, G. *Adaptation to Life.* Boston: Little, Brown, 1977.

Weathersby, R. *Developmental Perspective on Adults' Uses of Formal Education.* Doctoral dissertation, Harvard University, 1977.

Werther, W. B., Jr.; W. Ruch; and L. McClure. *Productivity through People.* St. Paul, Minn.: West Publishing, 1986.

Whetten, D. A. "Coping with Incompatible Expectations: An Integrated View of Role Conflict." *Administrative Science Quarterly,* June 1978, pp. 254–71.

White, R. W. "The Process of Natural Growth." In *Organizational Behavior and Administration,* ed. P. R. Lawrence and J. A. Seiler. Homewood, Ill.: Richard D. Irwin, 1965.

Whyte, W. H., Jr. *The Organization Man.* New York: Doubleday Publishing, 1957.

9

THE TWO-PERSON WORK RELATIONSHIP

Job Requirements and Background Factors

To what extent and in what ways does the job require that two people interact in order to do their work?

> *If it weren't for the people around here we could get some work done.*
>
> Manager's lament

Wherever two people get together to do a job, the outcome depends on *how they get along*. If they bicker, backbite, build grudges, or avoid one another, they are less likely to be productive, satisfied, or growing than if they enjoy being together and are mutually supportive and appreciative of one another's abilities. In a work setting where you may be *required* to work with somebody not of your own choosing, you may have added difficulties with which to cope.

However, you can learn to understand and improve your work relationships, even with people not of your own choosing. It goes without saying that interpersonal relations occur at all levels in an organization; in fact, an organization can be thought of as consisting of a *network* of interconnected relationships.

While some jobs are carried out in relative isolation and remain little affected by interpersonal factors, most work either requires or encourages interaction among individuals. **The more a job requires two people to work together, the more important is the kind of working relationship that develops.** Even where the interaction is only peripheral to the task, the relationship can still become a source of satisfaction or frustration and thus affect the total work effort in important ways. Think about some of the jobs you have held. What do you remember about them? Often the most important aspects will be the people you worked with, either because they were a source of help and enjoyment on the job or because they got in your way and made life miserable for you. These issues are often just as critical in an organization as the nature of the work itself. Good interpersonal relations support the work effort; bad ones can kill it.

In this context the usually bitter observation, "It isn't what you know, but whom you know (and who knows you) that counts," is accurate. Being interpersonally competent, able to make effective relationships, *is* indeed a skill that an organization member should have. In a network of relationships, the person who cannot meet others and build working relationships carries a heavy handicap. In contemporary organizations more and more jobs require the ability to work effectively with diverse individuals.

MANAGING INTERPERSONAL RELATIONSHIPS

If you are a manager, the interpersonal relationships among your employees can have a major effect on your ability to achieve goals. You try your utmost to get a job done, and two of your key people can't seem to work together. Why? What do you do? Is it some kind of personality conflict? Is there something about the job that's creating the problem? Did you as a manager fail to do something?

Similarly, as an organizational member, you may find that there is someone you are supposed to work with who bothers you. Ed jokes when you are serious, is never on time when you pride yourself on punctuality, and uses 50 words where 3 would do fine. From his point of view, of course, you're too sober, can't relax, and never seem to enjoy exploring all the interesting byways of problems. As a consequence, both of you avoid one another whenever possible, and when you have to talk to one another both of you walk away dissatisfied. Is it Ed's fault? Does he have a personality defect? Are your joint assignments impossible? Could you do anything to improve the relationship if you wanted to?

Trying to sort out all the possible reasons why people do or don't work well together can be frustrating. There are some concepts that can help you to do the sorting out, can provide some semblance of orderly thinking, and can even offer some clues to managing these kinds of problems.

In many ways the two-person relationship is simply the smallest form of a group. Both involve communication processes, role relationships, status differences, expectations for behavior, degrees of liking and respect, and, ultimately, consequences for productivity, satisfaction, and development. In examining two-person relationships, therefore, we will focus on the fit between personal systems and job requirements, since these two aspects most strongly affect interpersonal relationships.

Job Requirements

A job's required activities, interactions, and attitudes will have an important effect on relationships because they so directly determine what a person does, with whom it is done, and what feelings will be brought along. There are several questions we can ask to get at the impact of job requirements on relationships. First, to what extent and in what ways does the job require that two people *interact* in order to do their work? Second, are the required *activities* spelled out in such a way as to make it easy or difficult for the two people to cooperate? And third, are the *attitudes* required of each such that they will be able to work toward a common goal, resolve disagreements, share information, and so on?

Many interpersonal difficulties arise less from personality differences than from the demands of the job. This is especially so when the two people work for different parts of the organization. With different bosses, different jobs, and therefore different demands on them, what looks like personality clashes may just be responses to quite incompatible job requirements. Even within one unit, incompatible job demands can lead to difficulties.

For example, Harry and Betty are product managers, each reporting to Ben. Each is expected to increase sales every year while holding down expenses. In many geographic areas they use the same salespeople because sales of neither of their products are large enough to occupy the full time of a salesperson. Ben asks them to make their best case at budget time for why each should get a larger share of the department's budget. He posts their monthly sales and profit figures on a big chart over his desk. Each can only increase sales by getting salespeople to spend more time on his or her product. The products at times require calling on different customers. In such a situation it will not be terribly surprising to find that Harry and Betty are very competitive with one another, say nasty things about the "selfishness" of the other, and firmly believe that the personality of the other is unpleasant if not downright sickening. Yet, with a more compatible set of job requirements, they might both find that they enjoy each other's drive and scrappiness and even admire one another.

The fundamental issue is how psychologically close or distant two people are required to be in order to carry out a given task. Imagine yourself at a soft drink bottling plant. John is inspecting racks of empty bottles, checking for chips or cracks. When a defective bottle is spotted, his job is to remove it from the rack before it goes past. If the bottles are knocked over in the process, then John is supposed to throw a switch that stops the movement of the bottles so that he can stand them all up again. It is a simple task to perform, it does not change over time, and there are no risk factors involved, merely the simple judgment: defective/not defective. It does not call for any interaction with the person nearby, and the outcome of the work is obvious and certain. In short, the job requires no relationship between any two people who may be performing it. The only exception might be when a new worker comes on; then it would seem to be appropriate for one of the other workers to familiarize the new person with the task and to serve as a temporary helper.

Contrast the above situation with that of the director of education at a private residential treatment center for disturbed children. Marie is concerned with assessing the needs of 38 children; designing individualized educational programs that will also be therapeutic; finding, selecting, and supervising staff to carry out the programs; and so forth. There are new issues emerging constantly and new territory to be entered in almost every case. She is dealing with the whole gamut of human factors and is constantly faced with her own impact on the children and staff. Marie needs to have frequent contact with teachers in order to maintain consistency in ways of handling children as well as to guarantee proper individual attention. Finally, there is uncertainty in each situation; outcomes are not easily predicted and involve a great deal of risk and guesswork. Clearly this kind of work situation requires a broad range of possible interpersonal relationships. John's job and Marie's job can be contrasted along several dimensions, including:

1. How simple or complex the task is.
2. The degree to which the people involved in the task possess differential expertise.
3. The extent to which human factors (feelings, attitudes, behaviors of people) are involved in the work, as opposed to technical factors alone.
4. The frequency of human interaction or contact fostered by the task situation.
5. The degree of certainty with which the outcomes of actions can be predicted.

Normally, a work situation that is simple, is equally familiar to both workers, is low in human factors, demands little interaction, and has high certainty of outcomes calls for a *minimal task relationship*. In contrast, a work situation that is complex, is unfamiliar to one of the workers, is high in human factors, demands a great deal of interaction, and has a high degree of uncertainty with respect to outcomes calls for a much broader type of interpersonal relationship, something closer to a *colleagueship*. Obviously, there is a range of situations between the two extremes and therefore a range of relationships that might fit the different situations.

A Range of Required Work Relationships[1]

In the *minimal task relationship* each person's behavior and the exchange of information are determined by the specific demands of the

[1] Based on concepts presented in W. G. Bennis, D. E. Berlew, E. H. Schein, and F. I. Steele, *Interpersonal Dynamics*, 3rd ed. (Chicago: Dorsey Press, 1973), pp. 495–518.

task and its accompanying roles. An example is the operating room nurse and the surgeon. Normally, the only required exchange between them pertains to the surgeon's need for instruments and the sharing of information pertaining to the welfare of the patient. No more complex a relationship is called for in order to complete the work effectively.

Although minimal task may characterize a great many required work relationships, in an age of complex technology we find that most work relationships demand interactions beyond just minimal task. For example, consider two workers on a paper-making machine; the feeder at one end needs to know how the paper is coming out at the other end so that appropriate adjustments can be made. Various hand signals or brief phone conversations (the machine is long and noisy) are exchanged to get the proper thickness and tensile strength of paper. An important element of the task is *reality testing,* an exchange of information in which each individual checks out with the other his/her perceptions or interpretations of *(a)* the nature of the overall task (i.e., the realities of the situation) and *(b)* the effects of his/her own actions on the task (i.e., how effective or competent he/she is being). An example at a higher level in an organization occurs when two managers are comparing assessments of their employees. Each is checking his or her perceptions (of reality) against the other's.

Perhaps one of the most familiar kinds of work relationships is the superior/subordinate relationship, which usually occurs when one person possesses greater knowledge, experience, or authority than the other. Consequently, some element of control or influence is being exerted over one person by the other. Some common examples of *controlling/influencing relationships* include teacher–student, parent–child, and therapist–patient. In the work setting, a frequently occurring relationship of this type would be one in which one worker is training another (perhaps a newcomer); another example would be a supervisory relationship in which one person possesses greater expertise than the other.

With the element of control present we often find some of the more difficult management problems, primarily because different people have different needs for control or to be controlled.

You can see that each element we have added beyond the simple minimal task level makes the relationship more complex, demands more frequent interactions between the parties, and increases the degree of task interdependence involved. As already indicated, the ultimate in a complex work relationship seems to be the *colleagueship,* in which two individuals have developed a liking and a concern for each other's welfare. It often occurs above and beyond the strict requirements of the task but is appropriate for peers who are collaborating on a complex task. Ideas bubble back and forth; work goes on during some social occasions; and social talk sometimes occurs during work.

Some managers insist that one can never mix business with friendship; others take the opposite view that one cannot work successfully with another person unless close, friendly relations are maintained. As you might suspect, both points of view contain some grain of truth, but neither is valid for all situations. In fact, it is safe to say that no one level of interpersonal relationship is appropriate to every work situation, even though the minimal task aspect of relationships will almost always be one component. Figure 9–1 summarizes the connection between job requirements and the type of task relationships that may be required.

Each aspect of work relationships leads to different outcomes. The result of a good *minimal task* relationship is competent performance, which is normally a principal objective of the organization. A poor relationship of this type leads to very visible output problems that demand direct attention. The outcome of good *reality testing* is confirmation of the individuals' interpretations of the situation. Failures in this aspect of a relationship tend to produce lowered self-esteem and distorted pictures of the overall task. The outcome of an effective *controlling/influencing* relationship is *improved performance* on the part of the person being influenced and *satisfaction* on the part of the controller. An ineffective relationship in this area tends to result in less than adequate competence on the part of the worker (subordinate) and increasing dependency of that person on the controller (superior). With respect to *colleague relationships*, effectiveness leads to all the above outcomes as well as to *solidarity*, which can serve as an important support base for both people. If the colleague relationship fails to develop well, the outcome often includes alienation, hostility, and/or ambivalence on the part of one or both persons.

FIGURE 9–1
Summary of Connection between Job Requirements and Kinds of Task Relationships

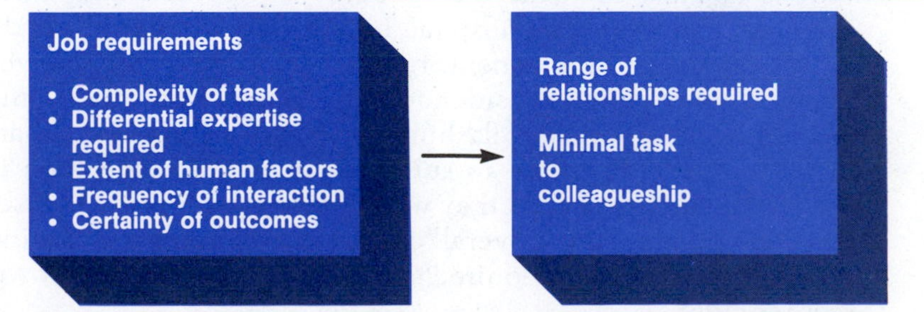

Background Factors

While job requirements are important determinants of interpersonal relationships, we cannot leave out the powerful influences of certain background factors, including the organization's culture, its technology, its reward system, the external status of the individuals in the relationship, and (perhaps most important of all) the personal systems of those individuals.

Organizational Culture

Just as the general climate and ways of doing things affect work group behavior, they also affect interpersonal relationships. In some organizations, a lot of attitudes discourage anything more than distant impersonal relationships. People say or believe things like "familiarity breeds contempt," "let's keep personalities out of business," and so forth. Other organizations have cultures where closeness is encouraged, as reflected in attitudes like "I can't work with somebody I don't know," "we're like family here," "you can't treat people like machines," and so on.

The culture of a particular organization is often a reflection of the wider culture from which its members come. The general culture may emphasize not revealing feelings or weaknesses, keeping problems to oneself, avoiding crying when upset (if male); or it might encourage openness and expressiveness, close relationships, and the like.

The more open the usual interpersonal style in the organization, the greater the likelihood of any two members being open when interacting; the greater the general politicking, competitiveness, aggressiveness, and hostility in an organization, the greater the likelihood of any two members being cautious with one another; and the more sociable and personal the climate, the greater the likelihood of two persons sharing nonwork information and feelings along with the minimum necessary task exchanges (Steele & Jenks, 1977). People take their cues from what is going on around them and usually respond, at least in part, to what they perceive are general expectations.

It is not just in Rome that people "do as the Romans do." For example, in one big-city hospital, backstabbing, yelling, and dramatic power plays were the general rule. Individual executives who were warm, charming, and considerate outside of the hospital would regularly interact with knives flashing when at work. "That's what I have to do in that crazy place to survive," they'd say, and then go after fellow executives in ways they would never think of doing elsewhere. Thus the organization's overall culture can have a powerful influence on relationships (both required and emergent) as they occur within its environment.

Technology and Layout

The primary interpersonal effect of technology and layout comes from the way in which machine or desk placement, work sequence, and physical barriers create the *need* and *opportunity to interact*. A fundamental proposition of this book is that greater interaction tends to lead to greater liking, and this is true for pairs of people just as it is for groups. People who, for whatever quirk of layout, share a confined space, or have to talk to one another to coordinate something, or even find themselves consistently waiting in line next to one another to pick up materials, are likely to begin talking. Once talking, they tend to speak of more than task issues and from there start a positive relationship.

If, however, the technology or layout consistently forces one person to be dependent on the other, greater potential for trouble exists. Dependence often leads to dominance in one and resentment in the other. Forced interaction can thus lead to negative feelings.

On the other hand, it will be difficult for any relationship to form between people who are physically separated, have no need to interact, are given their breaks at different times, and can barely hear one another because of noisy equipment. Occasionally, however, when individuals share a particularly unpleasant job in unpleasant surroundings, they band together to commiserate, and positive feelings result.

In these ways, technology and layout can affect the emergence of positive and negative relationships, even *require* a minimal task relationship, or prevent a relationship from developing at all.

Reward System

Reward systems can affect relationships by two mechanisms: (1) emphasis on individual competitiveness versus emphasis on collaborative effort and (2) public versus private payoffs. Reward systems that pay (in any currency, including money, recognition, or promotion) only for individual effort do not encourage positive relationships between potential competitors, especially where the system allocates a relatively fixed amount of reward. Since it would be hard to be friends with someone whom you have just beaten out of a larger share of the pie, individuals in such situations tend to keep their distance from one another.

Conversely, some reward systems encourage working together toward common goals and thus induce relatively positive mutual feelings as long as the other is trying hard and carrying his or her load.

The effects of public knowledge on individual rewards is harder to assess. Where everyone's salary is different and known, potentials for mutual jealousy abound. On the other hand, guessing at how others are doing may also lead to suspicions and jealousy, although some people might prefer not having to think about differences. In general, rewards openly given, except when they are group rewards, probably decrease potential intimacy between individuals and reinforce some distance, even if a polite distance.

External Status

When any two people have to work together, they are likely to be influenced by the external status of each other. If from different parts of the same organization, the person with the higher organizational position is likely to expect to take the initiative, be deferred to, speak for the pair when talking to others about their work, and have the last word. If their external status is roughly equal, each will probably expect both of them to act more like colleagues—speaking frankly, able to argue and interrupt one another, sharing responsibility and visibility if there is any, alternating the lead in a spontaneous way, and not trying to score points at the other's expense.

The same rough expectations are likely to hold for two people from different organizations. If a person of lower back-home rank does not "properly defer" to one of a higher back-home rank, the lower-status person is likely to be seen as "uppity" and pushy. Between roughly equal rank people, if one starts to dominate, that person will be seen as "too big for his/her britches" or as "putting on airs." And in turn, higher-status people who are especially open and friendly may be seen as gracious but run the risk of coming across as weak. In short, when analyzing two-person relationships, external status should be examined for its effect on attitudes and, in turn, on the relationships.

Of course, all of the background factors discussed are only general pressures or influences on relationships. Any one individual with a unique personal system may override these background tendencies.

Personal Systems

We have already devoted considerable attention to the importance of personal systems as background factors in group behavior. In Chapter 8 we discussed in detail the various components of a personal system, in particular the self-concept. In the present chapter *the respective personal systems of two people are viewed as major determinants of their emergent relationship,* particularly in the context of the required system. The "fit" between their respective goals, competencies, beliefs, values, and self-concepts is an important basis for explaining the quality of interactions between any two individuals.

It should not be surprising that, when given the opportunity, people tend to build relationships with those who have similar values, beliefs, abilities, and goals. Birds of a feather do flock together; the chances of speaking "the same language" make communication easier and more comfortable. In some circumstances, however, opposites attract. This is especially true when the opposite qualities are complementary to one another—when one person's skills fill vital gaps in the other's repertoire of skills, or when the values of one are attractive because they somehow suggest a way past the other's flat sides.

The most desirable kind of relationship permits the exercise of choices, generates feelings of competence, and produces confirmation of cherished values. Anyone would prefer relationships that reinforce all aspects of the self, although each aspect usually has a different priority. Goals are open to compromise; it is usually possible to accept alternative ways of doing things in a relationship, providing that they don't seriously threaten either the sense of competence or fundamental beliefs or values. Competencies are less open to compromise, but they are learnable—again provided that they are consistent with values. Values and beliefs normally are not negotiable; they go very deep and pertain to the integrity of the individual.

Which relationships in your own life would you classify as the most and least satisfying? In all probability, the most rewarding ones gave you self-confirmation, while the least rewarding ones had the opposite effect. In any current relationship in which you are experiencing problems, it might be useful for you to diagnose the levels at which the problems exist. Are they primarily goal conflicts? If so, the chances are fairly good that you can work them out. However, if they reflect more basic differences in beliefs or values, the problem is likely to be harder to settle. Resolution of conflict in any work relationship depends upon the level of the personal system the conflict taps into.

The required task relationship can be another source of difficulty. An individual having a limited concept of his/her abilities, for example, may find any relationship beyond minimal task somewhat threatening. Or someone who is used to seeing him/herself exclusively in the role of "boss" may have problems with a colleague type of relationship, preferring to be the superior member of a controlling/influencing relationship. Therefore it is important for you as a manager to pay attention to the kinds of working relationships you demand of your employees and how your requirements fit with their personal systems. While you cannot constantly redefine work relationships just to suit workers' preferences, some awareness of these contingencies may save you a great deal of aggravation in the long run.

Sex Differences: The Male–Female Relationship at Work

Gender and our expectations because of gender are another aspect of the personal system that shapes relationships. This factor is becoming increasingly important for relationships in the work setting.

In our society, females and males tend to have been brought up differently, steered toward different social roles and careers, and encouraged to develop different aspects of their personal systems. For example, with which gender do you associate each of the following roles: secretary, engineer, homemaker, manager, physician, elementary school teacher, community volunteer worker, and truck driver? Is one gender predominant in some roles? Similarly, with which gender would you associate each of the following personality traits: forceful/assertive, competitive, nurturant, unemotional, rational/logical, and intuitive? Whatever differences you see are partly the result of how we are socialized, and research has shown that this differential socialization starts at birth. Parents and adults treat baby boys and baby girls differently (dress, toys, gentleness in handling, emphasis on appearance, etc.). Consequently, while there is great variety among women and men—so that some women are more forceful than some men, and some men more intuitive than some women, etc.—many have been channeled toward different roles and personal traits.

This has meant that certain jobs and professions have been populated predominantly by men and others by women. It has also meant that women tended to take on the supportive roles in life, such as secretary or nurse, which meant that women were often in the less powerful positions in the work world. Even in elementary school teaching, where women predominate, the principals have typically been men. This also meant that each gender has often been criticized for not exhibiting the attributes that are stereotypic for that gender. Thus, women who are forceful and assertive are often criticized as being aggressive and unfeminine, and men who exhibit sensitivity and perceptiveness to the feelings of others are frequently seen as weak.

But this pattern has been changing as more women work and pursue careers, as members of both genders insist on a wider choice of lifestyles beyond that dictated by societal stereotypes, and as people have begun to value growth as a whole person capable of a wider range of personal traits than suggested by the gender stereotype. Women are moving into jobs as managers in what has been a male world; men are opting to be less workaholic; and many couples are dealing with the pressure of balancing dual careers and raising children. As a result of these changes, men need to learn to work with women as peers and bosses, while women need to learn to work with men as peers and subordinates. Both need to learn to work with the other as work colleagues, not just as dates, lovers, neighbors, and spouses of business acquaintances. In other words, everyone can deal with others more as unique individual human beings and less as sex role stereotypes.

Specifically, this means that many men must learn to be comfortable and nondefensive in dealing with women who are assertive, who are no more supportive than male colleagues, and who respond as equals. Men may also need to learn how to bargain and even "fight" with women as well as to take orders from a woman. Above all, many men must learn to treat women as fellow professionals regardless of their sexual attractiveness, and to give up behaviors that many women are increasingly finding demeaning (e.g., being called "honey") or sexually harassing (comments with sexual innuendo, overly familiar touching, etc.). Similarly, women must learn to utilize and exert power, develop personal support systems, and deal with men (who have a lot yet to learn about dealing with women as professionals) in ways that are firm and educate yet don't create resentment unnecessarily. Both are likely to need to develop their own personal systems toward being comfortable and competent in a wider range of behaviors.

Finally, more often today women and men must find ways to build marriage relationships as dual-career couples, where sharing housework, balancing career demands, and mutual supportiveness, along with careful time management, are essential.

Throughout this discussion we have said women and men will "tend" to need to learn so as to emphasize that there is great variety among individuals. Many women do exert initiative and act decisively; many men have good intuition and can act supportively. Nonetheless, many need to learn new patterns. Some will find adaptation to a multigender work world more difficult than others; some may choose to move into careers where more of the older patterns apply; but all can benefit from being aware of the changes that are occurring in our society, and all must consider the implications for work relationships, applying the concepts of the next chapter to build and maintain good work relationships with both genders.

Other Differences: Demographic Diversity

When you are in college you usually are dealing with people of similar age and even of similar socioeconomic backgrounds. Most older people with whom you will be in contact are likely to be instructors and administrators rather than peers (fellow students). This is not likely to be true in the work world where diversity is common. As employees and as managers, relationships must be built with a wide variety of people of diverse backgrounds: age, race, religion, socioeconomic class, education, and occupational orientation. You will need to continue to develop your ability to relate to many different individuals.

Interpersonal Styles

Yet another aspect of personal systems that shapes relationships is *interpersonal style,* the general way in which each person tends to interact with others.

> I've been working for Mr. Whiting for more than five years, and he still is stiff and formal with me. It takes getting used to—I think I'm getting there, but I confess that I wish he'd loosen up once in awhile. I've never seen him express any anger, at least not openly. I can usually tell when he is mad about something. He doesn't show much joy either, though I really believe he likes his job. And I think he likes and respects me—I hope so, anyway. Sometimes, when we're working on a report together, he really gets into exploring ideas. But that's the most I get. As for me, I prefer to get in there and mix it up with someone. I think I pick my own people so I can do more of that. It's not as quiet in my area as it is in Mr. W's office, but you know you're doing something.

This statement came from a manager who was interviewed in regard to his methods of management; he was contrasting his interpersonal work style with that of his boss. He eventually changed jobs, and he attributed that decision to his frustration in dealing with his boss. He liked and respected the man, but he could not interact with him satisfactorily.

What this kind of situation illustrates is the importance of *interpersonal style*—that is, *how* you interact with those around you. In the example, the effect was especially significant, since it involved a high-level executive whose behavior carried a great deal of weight in the organization. The man's limited ways of interacting with others were not suited to the demands of the job, that is, dealing effectively with a variety of people.

Only in recent years has the issue of interpersonal style been given much attention in organizational literature. But now it is viewed as a matter of *competency* and therefore is being treated as a vital aspect of managerial effectiveness. (See Chapters 1 and 11 on managerial roles.) It is important for managers in their various interpersonal roles to be aware of *how* they interact with others and the effects of their style on others' performance.

Some Styles of Interaction

Almost no one behaves in exactly the same way in every situation; some settings and people call forth different behavior than do others.

Only a very brave or disturbed person would treat his boss, mother, and lover with the same kinds and style of interactions. But almost everyone does have a preferred or dominant interaction style of some sort, a style that fits his/her self-concept, a style with which he/she feels most comfortable. When given the opportunity, that style will be used for interaction with other organizational members. For example, a woman principal of a school saw herself as ambitious, confident, extremely capable, and honest. When at school board or other community meetings, she related to others in an open, challenging way. She did this even when others were more cautious and guarded in their styles and responded to her with fear.

POLITICAL ENEMIES, PERSONAL FRIENDS

[During a TV interview, House Speaker Thomas P. O'Neill, Jr., tells David Hartman, host of "Good Morning America":] *"I never expected to be in politics. I guess I got Potomac fever, and that's why I'm still here." O'Neill also says that, while he disagrees with President Ronald Reagan, it only happens during the daytime, and after 6 P.M. they are friends. O'Neill adds: "There's no hatred in my heart because someone disagrees with me."*

Source: Sam Heilner, "Tuesday's People," *Boston Globe*, February 2, 1982.

While it is difficult to describe interaction styles, we will use a few general categories to make discussion manageable.[2] As you consider each of the styles we describe, you might try to picture yourself in various settings that seem to pull that particular way of interacting from you. Some people are very different at home, at work, with friends, on a date, and so forth. Others show only slight variations from their "usual" style. See where you fit in.

One style involves *conventional-polite* forms of exchange, those that are governed mainly by social convention and what is normally considered "acceptable and polite" behavior. When any two people meet for the first time they are likely to start in this style; some people, however, prefer to keep as many relationships as possible that way. Their conversation tends to remain at an impersonal and cordial level, and its content stays within the bounds of what is easiest to talk about.

A second style of interaction is *speculative-tentative*. The person who prefers this kind of interaction examines, questions, and evaluates everything and everyone in a careful manner, usually with the intent of trying to learn and understand. Conclusions tend to be tentative and open to modification, with fixed positions seldom taken. What

[2] Based on concept developed by W. F. Hill, *Hill Interaction Matrix* (Los Angeles: Youth Study Center, University of Southern California, 1965).

is discussed this way may be anything from the task at hand to the relationship itself. The main quality of the interaction process generated by this style is an open flow of exchanges that are seldom emotionally loaded or threatening. In many ways this style of interaction has some of the low-key quality of the conventional-polite type of interaction. It is what you would expect in a discussion about future careers, for example, where exploration of a great deal of data, thoughtfulness, generation of alternatives, and their consequences are all appropriate.

A third style of interaction is *aggressive-argumentative*. It is when a person vigorously takes fixed positions on issues and pushes his/her own arguments. The person's feelings tend to be strong, while listening tends to be poor. This style often results in dominance. Interactions with such a person can be stimulating or frustrating, depending on the other's preferences; either way, the interactions are seldom dull and require high-energy responses.

PARTING OF THE WAYS
Law-Firm Breakup Is Tale of Dashed Hopes and Bitter Feelings

As the summer rolled by, frictions in the firm became intense. Mr. Califano's temper became so fierce that he couldn't keep most secretaries for more than a short time, sources say. (By one count, he went through eight secretaries while at the firm.) He also became the bane of younger lawyers at the firm, "nearly destroying some" with sharp criticism. Often the young lawyers would then go to Mr. Ross for help, causing another problem. "Ross was getting tired of putting the pieces back together—he was beginning to feel like the office therapist." . . .

Differences between Mr. Califano and the other partners over expansion also came to a head. In a series of heated arguments during the summer—even during Mr. Califano's August vacation on Cape Cod—the partners made a final effort to talk Mr. Califano into bringing more talent into the firm. To no avail.

"They didn't think they'd get 100 percent of what they wanted, they'd have settled for 60 percent, but Joe wouldn't give at all," says a friend of one of the other partners.

Source: Reprinted by permission of *The Wall Street Journal*, © Dow Jones & Company, Inc., June 8, 1983. All rights reserved.

A fourth style of interaction is *expressive-confrontive*. It is one in which the person using it expresses openly and directly thoughts and feelings about situations and people. People who relate in this way often develop very close working relationships and intimate friendships. The range of feelings expressed is very wide and varies from anger to tenderness—whatever is actually being felt. People who find expressive-confronting interactions personally rewarding vary considerably regarding how often and with whom they consider such interactions desirable, but they usually try to get there in a relationship as rapidly as possible.

Obviously, these four categories do not exhaust the possible ways of viewing interaction styles, but they can be useful in understanding some of the sources of friction in two-person relationships.

Apart from what is called for by the job itself, people who prefer one style may fit compatibly with some styles but generate friction when with others. For example, the person who naturally prefers conventional-polite forms of interactions will probably be made exceedingly uncomfortable by the person who loves an expressive-confronting style, but may feel quite at ease with a speculative-tentative person. The confident female principal, for example, often intimidated teachers who preferred that interaction with women remain "proper" and "polite."

An important thing to keep in mind is that you interact with many other individuals whose styles may be similar to or different than your own preferred style, and therefore your sense of interpersonal competence can be very strongly affected by the *range* of interaction styles of which you are capable. It could be useful for you to assess your competence in this area by looking at your ability to deal with a variety of people and situations that require you to interact in different ways, sometimes not in the manner you prefer.

While almost anyone will respond partly to the situation (as when two strangers meet and both use a conventional-polite style), when there is *ambiguity* in the situation, people see and define it largely from their own respective frames of references. Thus, to a proper New Englander the fifth year of knowing someone may be too early for open warmth and expressiveness, while to a Southern Californian five minutes of polite but friendly conversation may be seen as enough to begin some self-revelation.

Similarly, the same desires and feelings may be expressed quite differently, depending on the preferred styles of those involved. Two "expressives" might show genuine liking by grand and sweeping statements, strong pledges of caring, and lots of hugging or backslapping, while two "conventionals" might never use the actual words, "I like you," but show it through thoughtful gestures like remembering to send a birthday card, inquiring after a sick relative, and so forth.

Nevertheless, much behavior is affected by the situation and its requirements as well as by the desires or preferences of those in it. To better understand what interpersonal behavior is appropriate under which work conditions, we turn now to task requirements and their impact on relationships.

When Interaction Styles Meet Job Requirements

What happens when you take a job in which you are required to interact with others in a manner that does not match your preference? How can you know in advance whether or not the job requirements are likely to fit your style? From a manager's point of view, is there a way to match interaction styles with required work relationships?

We cannot offer any specific guidelines without risking an arbitrary classification of people. There are no pure types; most people show a blend and a variation of styles that fit different situations. However, as in the example of the executive discussed earlier, some people seem to be more limited than others, at least in regard to their preferences or comfort. Therefore the thing to keep in mind, as you look at your own interpersonal competence and its development, is the issue of *range* of styles. When you want to, can you adjust your style to fit task requirements and the desires and styles of others?

EASON TAKES CHARGE FOR PATRIOTS

This game is all about communication, both people knowing what's expected of each other. The best time to get things straight is right then. The more you understand people, the better you can communicate, although there are still times people can't believe I say the things I say. . . .

People are different [Eason said], *You treat them all differently. I can get up two inches from Craig's face and rant and rave like a nut and he knows it's nothing personal. There are other guys you don't do that to.*

Knowing who's who comes after being with them for awhile. You have to have open communication where sensitivity isn't involved and ego isn't involved.

Source: Tony Eason, New England Patriot quarterback. *Boston Globe,* September 10, 1985. Reprinted courtesy of the *Boston Globe.*

In general: **The more complex a required work relationship tends to be, the wider the range of interaction styles needed by the individuals in that relationship (Argyris, 1962; Moment & Zaleznik, 1963).**

This point represents a critical issue for many managers who aspire to higher and higher positions in an organization. So often a person trained to do a specific kind of work (for example, accounting), which may require little interaction with others beyond a minimal task level, is promoted to a managerial position, only to be confronted with his/her limited range of interaction styles. A high-pressured negotiating session, for example, may require aggressive-argumentative behavior, and the person simply cannot do it. He/she may attempt to handle things in the accustomed polite or speculative manner more characteristic of "the old job."

EX-CHIEF OF RECOVERING AM INTERNATIONAL APPEARS TO BE A VICTIM OF HIS OWN SUCCESS

The resignation of Mr. Freeman [chairman, CEO, and president], *46 years old, was apparently forced by the board. . . .*

"It's tragic that someone who has turned a company around like Joe can't stay and run it," says William Givens, president of ECRM, an AM unit sold to its management last September. . . .

While directors credit him with an excellent job of reviving AM, they believe that the rejuvenated company needs a different kind of manager as it comes out of Chapter 11. Mr. Freeman served both at AM and elsewhere as chief financial officer and is highly regarded for his financial ability and integrity. But even Mr. Freeman's admirers say he is better with numbers than with people, shy in public, and not a good speaker. . . .

Mr. Banta [who will become chairman] *. . . says the new period requires "greater emphasis on strategic planning, marketing, and market research, and therefore a more unique range of talents and management skills. Also, we need to more closely address all of the 'people' aspects of our business." . . .*

Mr. Freeman displayed "a lack of sensitivity to people issues and people opinions. The term I've heard people use is interpersonal skills, and Joe isn't as strong in those skills as some CEOs." A high-level company insider is more blunt. "Joe was a loner," he says. "He didn't generate staff loyalty. People didn't work to do it for him." On the other hand, he says, "Banta has the presence to win people over by talking to them."

Source: Meg Cox. Reprinted by permission of *The Wall Street Journal*,

Of course, the opposite extreme is also possible. Have you known people who seem to be expressive and confronting no matter what the circumstances? It's as though they have an overdeveloped need to *relate!* Even the most routine impersonal tasks are converted into rituals of personal intimacy.

It should be obvious that no one style of interaction is suitable for all work relationships. Having a wide repertoire of styles can help you to adapt effectively to the demands of a complex work environment. However, even with a wide repertoire, you are likely to prefer to relate to others in certain ways more than in other ways. Note this experience of a young man working for a summer as a plumber's helper:

> I was assigned to an older, very experienced man who was used to working alone. The boss assigned the man to teach me whatever skills were needed on the job. I was eager to learn; he did not know how to teach or help me and preferred not to try. I tried to be friends with the

FIGURE 9–2
Job Requirements and Background Factors' Effects on Interpersonal Relationships

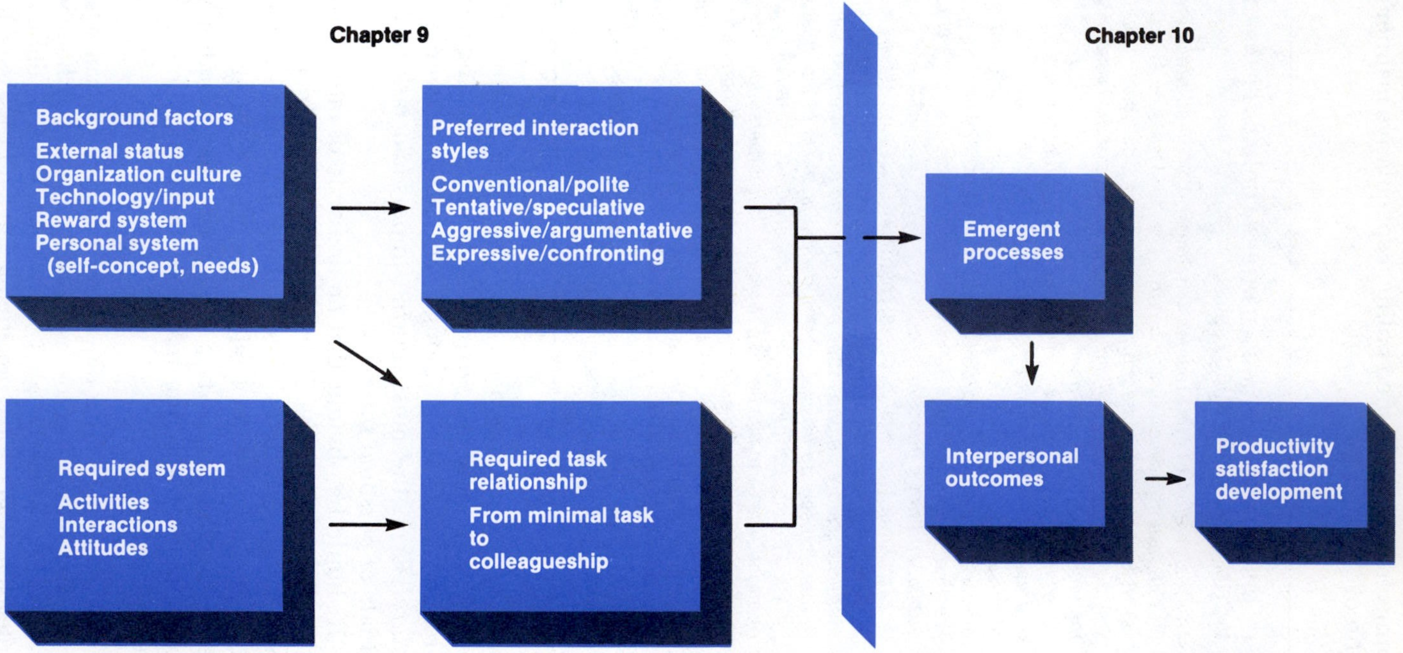

Chapter 9

Background factors
External status
Organization culture
Technology/input
Reward system
Personal system
(self-concept, needs)

Preferred interaction styles
Conventional/polite
Tentative/speculative
Aggressive/argumentative
Expressive/confronting

Required system
Activities
Interactions
Attitudes

Required task relationship
From minimal task to colleagueship

Chapter 10

Emergent processes

Interpersonal outcomes

Productivity satisfaction development

> man; he felt that friendships had no place in a work setting. At times when I thought he had overlooked something on the job, I pointed this out. It only made him angry; he thought I was questioning his ability to do the job. I finally settled for doing simple jobs that I could figure out for myself. I initiated very little conversation with him, except at lunch or over coffee when it was "all right." He was satisfied; I was not.

The relationship illustrates an incompatibility between the job requirements and the preferred interaction styles of the two people involved. We can also see how different levels of the self-concept were affected. The rejection of friendship or colleagueship at work by the older man was a matter of beliefs or values and probably was unchangeable. The assistant's desire for colleagueship was probably less a matter of values than a goal; thus, he was able to adapt. The plumber's lack of competence to teach and be helpful was a matter that could not have made him feel good about himself. Similarly, the assistant must have felt inadequate, wanting to be shown what to do so that he could gradually undertake more interesting assignments and not be totally dependent.

The issue of respective goals was something for the two individuals to negotiate. It is possible that if the older man had had the competence to teach the assistant, then he might have been more open to the latter's observations and "trouble shooting." While the younger man was not specifically assigned to that role, it was one that might have been both helpful and desirable in the relationship, though not strictly necessary.

In summary, we can offer the following propositions:

1. **To the extent that a required work relationship is compatible with the preferred interaction styles of both persons assigned to it, the relationship will be accepted.**
2. **To the extent that a required work relationship is incompatible with the preferred interaction styles of either or both persons assigned to it, the relationship will be resisted; the degree of resistance will depend upon the level of the personal system or self-concept affected in either or both individuals.**

In either event, the actual relationship that emerges is likely to vary from that required, either elaborating on it toward the colleagueship or pulling back toward a less involving type.

In Chapter 10 we will examine what actually happens in a relationship once the two people begin to interact. Before proceeding, however, we suggest that you examine Figure 9–2 as a way of reviewing what we have covered so far. The left-hand side of the figure is filled in with the concepts of Chapter 9; the right-hand side will be completed in Chapter 10.

KEY CONCEPTS FROM CHAPTER 9

1. An organization is a network of interpersonal relationships.
2. Social system schema applied to interpersonal relations.
   a. Required system.
      (1) Ways in which two people are required to work together.
      (2) How close or distant they need to be to carry out the task.
      (3) Nature of task.
         (*i*) Simple or complex.
         (*ii*) Differential expertise.
         (*iii*) Human factors involved.
         (*iv*) Frequency of required interactions.
         (*v*) Degree of certainty in outcomes.
      (4) Range of required work relationships.
         (*i*) Minimal task to colleagueship.
         (*ii*) Relevance of reality testing and control in relationship.
   b. Background factors.
      (1) Organizational culture.
         (*i*) Supportive, open climate fosters close trusting relationships; climate of suspicion fosters distance and mistrust.
      (2) Technology and layout.
         (*i*) Opportunities versus barriers to interaction.
      (3) Reward system.
         (*i*) Importance of rewards for collaboration versus rewards for competition.
      (4) External status.
         (*i*) Differential status creates barriers to colleagueship.
      (5) Personal systems.
         (*i*) Compatibility versus incompatibility in goals, competencies, beliefs, and values.
         (*ii*) Gender differences: The male-female relationship at work.
         (*iii*) Role of interpersonal styles:
            Conventional-polite.
            Speculative-tentative.
            Aggressive-argumentative.
            Expressive-confrontive.
         (*iv*) The more complex a required work relationship, the wider the range of interpersonal styles needed.
         (*v*) Importance of compatibilities among required work relationship and the preferred interaction styles of both parties.

SUGGESTED READINGS

Athos, A., and J. Gabarro. *Interpersonal Behavior.* Englewood Cliffs, N.J.: Prentice-Hall, 1978.

Argyris, C. *Interpersonal Competence and Organizational Effectiveness.* Homewood, Ill.: Richard D. Irwin and Dorsey Press, 1962.

Bowers, D. G. "What Would Make 11,500 People Quit Their Jobs?" *Organizational Dynamics,* Winter 1983, pp. 5–19.

Cowill, N. L. *The New Partnership: Women & Men in Organizations.* Palo Alto, Calif.: Mayfield, 1982.

Crary, M. "Managing Attraction and Intimacy at Work." In *Organizational Dynamics,* Spring 1987, pp. 26–41.

Fisher, R., and W. Ury. *Getting to Yes.* New York: Penguin Books, 1983.

Goffman, E. *The Presentation of Self in Everyday Life.* New York: Doubleday Publishing, 1959.

Hill, W. F. *Hill Interaction Matrix.* Los Angeles: Youth Study Center, University of Southern California, 1965.

Hocker, J. L., and W. W. Wilmot. *Interpersonal Conflict.* 2nd ed. Dubuque, Iowa: Wm. C. Brown, 1985.

Homans, G. *The Human Group.* New York: Harcourt Brace Jovanovich, 1950.

________. *Social Behavior: Its Elementary Forms.* New York: Harcourt Brace Jovanovich, 1961.

Johnson, P. B. "Women and Interpersonal Power." In *Women and Sex Roles,* ed. I. H. Frieze, J. E. Parsons, P. B. Johnson, D. N. Ruble, and G. L. Zelman. New York: W. W. Norton, 1978.

Kahn, R. L.; D. M. Wolfe; R. P. Quinn; and J. Diedrich Snoek. *Organizational Stress: Studies in Role Conflict and Ambiguity.* New York: John Wiley & Sons, 1964.

Leader, G. C. "Interpersonally Skillful Bank Officers View Their Behavior." *Journal of Applied Behavioral Science* 9 (1973), pp. 484–97.

Levinson, H. "The Abrasive Personality." *Harvard Business Review,* May–June 1978, pp. 86–94.

Mainiero, L. A. "A Review and Analysis of Power Dynamics in Organizational Romances." *Academy of Management Review,* October 1986, pp. 750–62.

Miramontes, D. J. *How to Deal with Sexual Harassment.* San Diego: Network Communications, 1984.

Moment, D., and A. Zaleznik. *Role Development and Interpersonal Competence.* Cambridge, Mass.: Harvard University Press, 1963.

Quinn, R. E., and P. L. Les. "Attraction and Harassment: Dynamics of Sexual Politics in the Workplace." *Organizational Dynamics* 12 (1984), pp. 35–46.

Schutz, W. C. *FIRO: A Three-Dimensional Theory of Interpersonal Behavior.* New York: Holt, Rinehart & Winston, 1958.

________. "Interpersonal Underworld." *Harvard Business Review* 36 (1958), pp. 123–35.

Steckler, N. A., and R. Rosenthal. "Sex Differences in Nonverbal and Verbal Communication with Bosses, Peers, and Subordinates." *Journal of Applied Psychology* 70 (1985), pp. 157–63.

Steele, F., and S. Jenks. *The Feel of the Work Place.* Reading, Mass.: Addison-Wesley Publishing, 1977.

10

THE TWO-PERSON WORK RELATIONSHIP

Processes and Outcomes

A positive relationship leads to good outcomes for both task accomplishment and member satisfaction.

"I've got to find a way to get Endrunn off my back," complained Mark Buckley, six months after becoming president of Vitacorp. "I'll be damned if I'll let him interfere in this company as he does in the others he's responsible for. If I give him any encouragement at all he's ready to bolt into all kinds of operating areas. And he's dangerous with any information, because then he thinks he can be a hero. He impulsively leaps to conclusions and starts making promises or giving orders to my people. He alternates between being too political or too quick on the trigger, so I give him absolutely no information he doesn't have to know!"

Buckley was adamant about Oliver Endrunn, group vice president for the conglomerate that owned Vitacorp. He was convinced that the best way to keep an aggressive, self-confident person like Endrunn safely at bay was to avoid supplying him with "ammunition."

For his part, Endrunn was equally frustrated with Buckley. "Mark's very clever, but too political. I don't want to interfere with his operations, since he knows his business better than I do, but I can't be uninformed when my boss wants to know what's going on. And until I get to know Mark well enough to be sure that he's going to keep doing things right, I've got to stay on top of the action. After all, my tail is on the line. So I've had to cultivate my own sources of information in his organization; I just chat with people to get an idea of what's going on. I almost never want to take action on what I find out, but he can't expect me to fly blind. If he were more open, things would be a lot easier."

In Chapter 9 we looked at the background and required factors that affect interpersonal relationships. Now we turn to an examination of what emerges from the interplay of these factors. Any two individuals are likely to have appreciable latitude to establish a type of relationship that is to their liking, and to adopt an interpersonal style that fits their preferences. Nevertheless, much can happen in a relationship that can lead to misunderstanding, disagreement, and friction. Mark Buckley and Oliver Endrunn are intelligent, high-level executives who have to work together, yet they irritate each other. Thus what emerges takes "working at," both to develop it in a positive direction and to maintain it once it has been developed.

In discussing steps individuals can take to build and maintain positive relationships, we need to look at several *interpersonal processes* that are crucial for any relationship, namely:

- Adaptation to what is required and to one another.
- Communication.
- Reciprocity.
- Trust and other feelings.
- Dealing with blind spots (need for feedback).

In the pages that follow we shall discuss each of these processes in some detail and indicate steps the individuals can take to foster a positive relationship.

As we do this, keep in mind what we mean by a positive relationship. A positive work relationship is, first, one in which the required task gets done properly and with reasonable efficiency. Second, the relationship must at the same time be reasonably satisfying to both parties and foster, or at least not hinder, individual growth and development. What constitutes satisfaction will depend on what is desired and also on what is expected given the situation. For example, you may be quite satisfied with a polite but distant relationship with the elevator operator in your building, but quite dissatisfied with such a conventional interpersonal style with your direct supervisor. Satisfaction will also depend on the relationship enhancing, or at least not disconfirming, each member's self-concept. Finally, a relationship will hardly remain positive unless the two parties are able to deal with the frictions that almost inevitably arise in any sustained relationship. A positive relationship leads to outcomes good for both task accomplishment and member satisfaction, on an ongoing basis.

ADAPTATION TO WHAT IS REQUIRED AND TO ONE ANOTHER

When individuals first enter into a work relationship there may be some discrepancy between what is required and what is expected or desired by one or both individuals. For example, Buckley wants autonomy and control, while Endrunn wants information and reassurance. To the extent that each party can diagnose the situation accurately and adapt to what is required and to what the other expects and desires, relationships will develop in a positive direction. In some cases, this may mean that one party must make all of the adaptation, as in the case of the plumber's helper discussed in Chapter 9. In most cases, both must adapt, such as when two engineers of equal experience are working on a joint design project. To blindly ignore the issue or refuse to adapt is to insure the emergence of a less than positive relationship. To adapt within the range of what is at least tolerable is the way to move in a positive direction. If, however, the degree of adaptation is so great as to violate either person's self-concept, then the participants will need to openly confront the issue and find a resolution or else try to leave the situation. Finally, throughout the life of a relationship there may be times when either individual will need to adapt his/her interpersonal style to fit a particular event. Thus adaptation is usually required early in a relationship, to build in a positive direction, and also to a lesser degree throughout its existence.

One factor that can make it difficult for individuals to adapt to one another is differences in how each structures the world around them. Consider the possible difficulties individuals at different places on the four dimensions o. the Myers-Briggs model discussed in Chapter 8 might have:

INTROVERSION—EXTRAVERSION. An individual at the extraversion end of the scale, who might instinctively make it a point to touch base with many others before acting, might be seen by someone at the introversion end of the scale as indecisive, overly political, or wasting time socializing. Conversely, the former might view the latter's tendency to go it alone and avoid opportunities to interact with others as a sign of aloofness and even snobbishness.

SENSING—INTUITION. Similarly, the individual who always seeks facts before acting (sensing) may easily view someone who acts more on intuitive insight as "impulsive" and as acting on mere whim without "doing their homework." The latter, in turn, might view the former's care in getting all the facts before deciding as a case of worrying excessively about details and even as decision avoidance.

THINKING—FEELING. Thinkers are likely to see themselves as capable of making the hard decisions based on a logical analysis of a situation, and they see Feelers as tenderhearted, given to irrational judgments, and too easily swayed by emotions and compassion. By contrast, Feeling types will see themselves as sensitive, considerate and responsive to people's needs, and will see Thinking types as hardnosed, distant, and insensitive.

JUDGING—PERCEIVING. The differences here are especially interesting since they bear directly upon the problem-solving aspect of a manager's job. Perceivers see themselves as good at seeing all the diverse implications of a problem, and they enjoy exploring these. They see Judgers as pushing too rapidly toward solutions and unwilling to spend the necessary amount of time really digging into a problem.

The Judgers tend to get impatient with the Perceivers, seeing them as never able to arrive at a solution, always going off on tangents, or getting sidetracked. Judgers see themselves as decisive and capable of getting quickly to the heart of the matter and on with the business at hand.

IMPLICATIONS FOR WORKING RELATIONSHIPS. Awareness of the differences described above can be very helpful in understanding two-person work relationships. For one thing, the two people can learn to understand and even appreciate their differences. For another, it provides a way to look at *complementarity* in work relationships. Most situations call for a variety of managerial approaches, including the ability to use thoughts, feelings, intuition, judgment, and perceptions. Mutual adaptation can facilitate drawing on one another as sources of information.

COMMUNICATIONS

In any relationship, people must communicate; and such communication is always subject to distortion and misunderstanding. Even what may be a fairly simple and straightforward exchange of factual information in a minimal task relationship is subject to miscommunication. The likelihood of miscommunication becomes greater when the information being exchanged is more complex and emotionally charged. Misunderstanding can block the development of a relationship and create tension in an otherwise positive relationship. Unless the parties involved have the skill and the inclination to minimize miscommunication and to correct misunderstanding as it occurs, a positive relationship is not likely to develop or be maintained. So we turn now to an extended discussion of the nature of human communication.

What happens when one person talks to another? The process is so complicated that it is a wonder that anyone ever understands and is understood. This section will include a description of the communication process and the factors that ease or hinder understanding.

Communication between people involves a exchange of *(a)* the content of what is being discussed, *(b)* feelings about the subject matter at hand, *(c)* feelings about the other person, and *(d)* feelings about self (see Figure 10–1).

The same exchange can be seen another way: what Speaker A says is modified by B's self-concept (which includes how B interprets A's self-concept). For example, A is B's boss. B has had many troubles in the past with people in authority—parents, teachers, bosses. He sees himself as having been misunderstood and unappreciated by them. A is in a hurry, doesn't know B's background, so calls over his shoulder

FIGURE 10–1
Four Levels of Exchange between Speaker and Listener

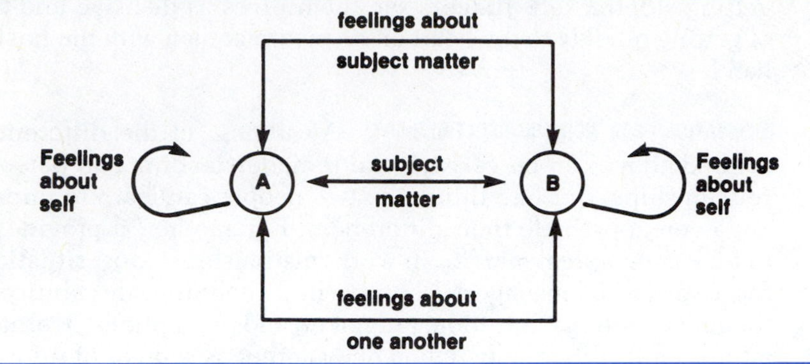

on the way by, "Hey, lend a hand, will you?" B hears this as a criticism, reddens, and mutters to himself at the "attack" (see Figure 10–2).

This gets even more complicated as the self-concept of each alters the way messages are sent as compared to the actual feelings of the speaker. That is, A is feeling angry at B's apparent uncooperativeness and wants to reprimand B; but A sees himself as a kind person, so he tries to soften the blow through indirection. Instead of saying what he feels—"You infuriate me when you sit there doodling while I work hard"—he says, "Isn't it amazing how some people just can't cooperate with others?" B—who sees himself as an intelligent person, eager to be helpful when he gets an original idea, but sees A as typically

FIGURE 10–2
Other's Statements Are Modified by Receiver's Self-Concept

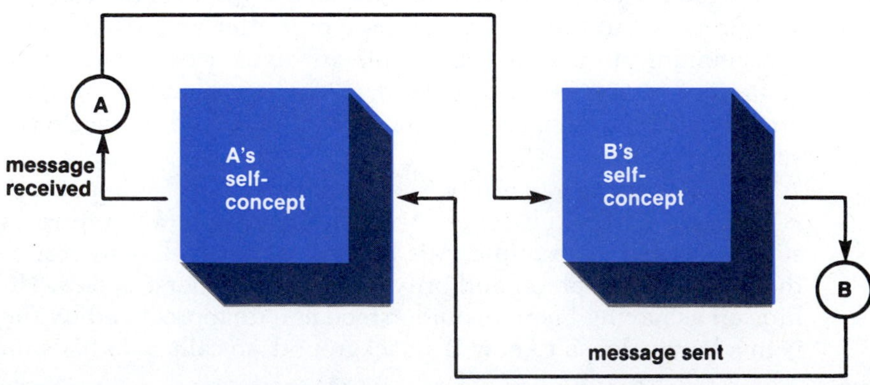

aggressive and impatient—feels puzzled about where A's remarks concerning cooperation come from, misses the feeling, and replies to the content, "Well, it depends on the people involved, but I don't think cooperation is so difficult." A starts to steam; B senses it but doesn't know why. The relationship begins to deteriorate (see Figure 10–3).

The potentials for difficulties are great. Let's take a closer look at the barriers to communication, above and beyond the perceptual ones already discussed in Chapter 7.

Barriers to Communication

CHARACTERISTICS OF LANGUAGE. The very nature of language constitutes a barrier to communication. Many words are imprecise. The meaning of "level" to a carpenter is quite different than to a landscape contractor who is putting in a new lawn. How many is "a few?" Does "right away" mean drop the bucket with molten metal, or first pour it and then start the next job? In the sentence, "Where do I begin?", is "where" a location or a procedure?

Many words have multiple meanings; miscommunication occurs when the two parties apply different interpretations. The purchasing agent who orders track spikes to repair the railroad siding may be surprised to receive a pair of running shoes. "Write," "right (correct)," "right (not left)," and "Wright" all sound the same, right? Sometimes words have different meanings to different subcultures of the country. Have you ever ordered a "milk shake" in Boston? To get ice cream, as in other parts of the country, you must order a "frappe." And don't ask for a "Boston cooler"; you have to call it a "root beer float." Similarly, a machinist's caliper measures diameter, whereas a nurseryman's caliper measures circumference! And what kind of "nursery" do you mean, anyway?

FIGURE 10–3
Self-Concepts and Perceptions of Other Filter Messages In and Out

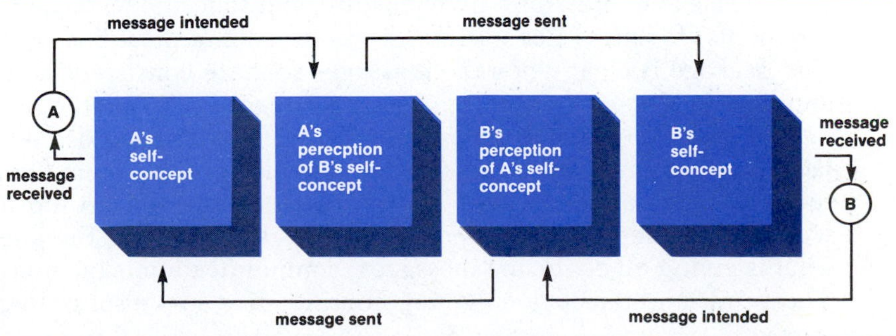

The fact that words are imprecise and have multiple meanings has become an ever greater threat to communication as society has become more interconnected and mobile. The possibility has increased of contact with someone with a different background and, hence, a different way of using words. The fact that words are imprecise and have several meanings is also one reason why jargon develops. Jargon at its best is designed to avoid ambiguity, and, when used for this purpose, it can be helpful. On the other hand, "P. req." for purchase requisition, "M.I." for myocardial infarction (heart attack), or "social systems" for groups and organizations can be unintelligible to the outsider, even when efficient for the insider.

> *I'm willing to discuss it; I just don't want to talk about it.*
>
> Mr. Fairly Bear
> A Shari Lewis Puppet

Finally, words have an emotional coloring that influences the communication process because they trigger mental associations and emotional responses. Consider the following: "I want a large slab of slaughtered cow" versus "I would like the king-size cut of prime roast beef"; "let us hear the egghead's comments" versus "let us be informed by the expert intellectual." The words *slaughtered cow* conjure up many distasteful images that do not enhance people's appetites even though they may, in fact, be more precise than the term *prime roast beef*. Often the emotional color is communicated rather than the intended meaning. The first time you hear an intern call an elderly patient for whom no treatment is possible a "crock," it is not likely to be easy to respond neutrally.

MULTIPLE CHANNELS. Messages are transmitted by more than words; content and especially feelings are transmitted by gestures, voice intonations, facial expressions, body posture, and so forth. All these media (elements) for messages go into the same communications package. The package is clear when the messages sent are consistent with one another. This occurs when everything fits together; when the nonverbal enriches the verbal, when the "music" fits the words. When a facial expression or a gesture or a tone of voice doesn't seem to match the words, "static" is created. Have you seen someone get red in the face, pound the table, and declare, "What do you mean I'm angry?" That is giving off confusing messages; communication is incongruent. The words and music don't go together; it's like a love song sung to a

SOME STEPS TO INSURE EFFECTIVE COMMUNICATION

If you want to communicate effectively, try some or all of the following:

Choosing Your Words

1. Talk in words that are likely to have meaning and clarity to the other person (e.g., "speak in the language of the listener").
2. Anticipate different ways your message could be interpreted, try to speak unambiguously, be alert to evidence that what you meant isn't what it meant to the other.
3. Allow yourself to be spontaneous and open. Express your feelings. Speak your mind, but consider talking *about* what you are feeling, instead of emoting, if the other person is likely to be put on the defensive by your expressiveness or is basically uncomfortable when faced with strong emotion.

Attending to Nonverbal Messages

1. Pay attention to tone of voice, facial expressions, body posture, hesitations, etc. What do they communicate in addition to the message in the words? (Listen to the music as well as the words.)
2. Pay attention to your own manner. Are you congruent? Does your tone, etc., fit your words and reflect your inner feeling?
3. If you sense something is bothering the other person besides what is being said directly, consider raising that to the surface by some such statement as: "Is ________ also at work here?" "Are you also concerned about ________ ?" "Is there something else beneath the surface here?"

Timing and Situation

1. Don't raise "heavy" issues when the other person is preoccupied or there isn't time to deal with them properly.
2. Consider the setting when you raise a topic for discussion. Is it too public? Will it be distracting? Will it cause misinterpretation (e.g., be seen as really unimportant or said for public consumption only)?
3. Ignore small points you may differ with and focus on the main theme. Don't digress to argue over minor errors or points of disagreement.
4. Deal with issues and tensions early. Try to handle problems while they are still small.

Testing for Understanding

1. Invite the other person to restate what you've said in his/her own words and test whether you've been clear.
2. Restate what the other said in your own words and thereby test that you have fully understood.

Preserving the Relationship

1. Don't hog the air time—give the other person an opportunity to be heard.
2. Be careful you aren't so busy preparing your response that you don't really pay full attention.
3. Don't interrupt.
4. Acknowledge that which is of worth in what someone is saying, even if you disagree with the basic message.
5. If the other person makes an especially good point, say so. Give positive feedback when you can do so sincerely.

march tempo. Since nonverbal messages tend to be ambiguous in meaning, thereby leaving room for interpretation by the other person, misunderstanding is possible. An embarrassed smile can easily be seen as implying agreement when it really means "I'm too embarrassed to say how ridiculous I think your idea is." Frowns of concentration may be seen as disapproval, and so forth.

THE STATE OF MIND OF THE TWO PEOPLE. When a person is feeling any strong emotions (anger, fear, defensiveness, and so forth), it is very difficult to *listen* to another person. Here is where *both* parties are subject to perceptual distortions. What usually happens is that A's emotion triggers a similar emotion in B; then both have trouble listening to each other. For example, an aggressive-argumentative exchange often contains emotionally charged, defensive kinds of messages. Effective communication becomes blocked, the tensions increase, and the whole cycle escalates. Is this kind of pattern familiar to you? It is likely that everyone has faced similar problems and could benefit from learning how to change the quality of a communication process when it is blocked, defensive, and nonsupportive of the participants.

When possible differences in mental set, emotional state, channels used, words chosen, and so forth are added together, it becomes apparent how difficult it would be for the message sent to be the same as the message received. How many times have you argued about what was "really" said in a conversation? Each person "*knows* what *I* said" and each "*knows* what *I* heard," even though both are sure the other is wrong. Some degree of distortion seems inevitable in communication.

Some Common Problems of Communication

The following are some examples of the kinds of interpersonal communication problems that frequently occur:

AMBIGUOUS COMMUNICATIONS: THE MIXED MESSAGE. This kind of problem occurs when several channels are in operation at the same time and they are not completely in tune with each other. One channel may be sending a message that is different from or contradictory to another, making the message difficult to understand. For example, the words are polite or even friendly, but the tone of voice is angry or hostile (as might be the case with sarcasm). Another example is when the words are a question, but the manner of expression is an assertion. Have you heard someone say, "Wouldn't it be a good idea to . . . ?" when he/she really means, "You'd be a fool not to . . ."? Such ambiguous communication is likely to occur when a manager is trying to behave in a participative manner with subordinates but really wants to maintain absolute control over outcomes.

INCOMPLETE COMMUNICATION: THE THROWAWAY LINE. This kind of communication occurs when enough of a message is sent to indicate the presence of an issue, but not enough to make clear what the issue really is or how serious it is. For example, in the middle of discussing one issue a reference is made to another problem, but it is offhand and passed over very quickly. It can be a very disruptive kind of behavior. Note the following example:

> An executive had the habit of referring offhandedly to extraneous issues during important meetings, when the issues could not be discussed appropriately. On one occasion when discussing union relations, he said to one of his managers, "Though I was pleased with the way you handled the shop steward when he said the company is antiunion, I didn't like your interrupting me in the middle of my sentence in front of him; but never mind that now."

The target of the throwaway line (as it is sometimes called in the theater) was taken off guard by the comment and found it difficult to concentrate on the issue at hand; he worried about the implication of having displeased his boss.

This kind of communication tends to raise anxiety and leave the recipient in the unfortunate position of having to fill in the rest of the message with his/her own fantasies, which are often worse than the actual situation.

NONVERBAL SIGNALS: THE PERSON'S EMOTIONAL STATE. Watch a busy executive going about his or her business; note the speed of movement, facial expression, posture, and so forth. It doesn't take much to interpret rapid pace, furrowed brow, and thrust-out chin as, "I am harassed and under pressure; don't bother me with trivial matters." Most people communicate something of this sort when feeling overworked. At times, however, such nonverbal behavior can become a part of a person's everyday style to the point of constantly appearing harassed even when not. If one is unaware of the unintended message, it is a blind spot that can leave one puzzled by the reactions of others to it. In the example just given, the person may wonder why people don't come around to talk over problems even when they would be welcome. Are you aware of the kinds of signals expressed in your nonverbal behavior? Does your characteristic body posture say "I like myself" or "I feel insignificant"? Does your facial expression usually suggest anger, fear, curiosity, or what? Do you sit in a way that says "don't approach me" or "I am receptive to new relationships and ideas?" This may be an area worth exploring with your fellow students or co-workers. Though you can sometimes guess at how you are seen by observing the way others react to you, asking for feedback is probably the best way to find out, though not always the most comfortable.

> *So don't listen to the words; just listen to what the voice tells you, what the movements tell you, what the posture tells you, what the image tells you.*
>
> F. S. Perls
> *Gestalt Theory Verbatim*, p. 57

NONVERBAL SIGNALS: THE SECRET SOCIETY. While nonverbal communication goes on all the time, often two people develop "special" signals to each other, such as a knowing look, nod, or smile, a warning of threat, a smile of support, and many other signs and gestures. These forms of communication can be very handy or convenient, and they also tend to confirm the solidarity of the relationship. However, they also may convey a sense of a "secret society" with its own special language; this is likely to wall off others and be dysfunctional to outside relationships. In some situations this type of communication is very important. For example, in negotiation sessions it is important to know how others on your side feel about things as they happen without openly conferring. But even in these situations, it heightens feelings of exclusion and can have negative consequences, too.

With these aspects and difficulties of communication in mind, we can summarize with the following working proposition: **The greater the *(a)* complexity of a subject, *(b)* importance of a subject to the parties involved, and *(c)* feelings aroused by the subject, the greater the possibilities for distortion, and therefore the greater the need for each to check with the other on what has been heard and said (Giffin & Patton, 1974).**

You can probably understand by now why so many managers tend to classify human relations difficulties as "communication problems." While the phrase is often just a catchall to reduce things to their simplest possible form and can cover up the problem more than illuminate it, the observation is not too far off the mark. It is hard for people to understand one another. And while accurate understanding in no way guarantees agreement, there is little advantage in trying to sort out relationships through the additional static of unclear messages. It is worth the effort to practice listening to feelings as well as words and to check out meanings when clarity is not certain. Effective communication is a basic step in building relationships.

It Takes Both People for Communication to Work

One person alone cannot establish effective communication; he/she has no means of checking out whether or not the intended message was the received one. Because of the probability that some distortion will take place, good communication requires an exchange of messages, a two-way process. For A to disclose something to B without knowing how it was received is only half the process. And the more important the disclosure is to A, the more vital it is for A to check out its reception.

Think about the relationship between Buckley and Endrunn, which was presented at the beginning of the chapter. If Buckley decided to tell Endrunn that he didn't want him to talk to Buckley's subordinates, what would Endrunn hear? Given his view of Buckley as political and closed, he might interpret it as a power grab rather than a concern for the position in which this could put the subordinate. That could lead to a downward spiral in the relationship. Many exchanges, especially around work routines and the like, require a minimum amount of checking out; they are least subject to distortion. But even these communications can, if badly managed, lead to misunderstandings that may become more significant and require a great deal of clarifying. *An accumulation of little miscommunications often builds into a major source of conflict between two people.*

> *I only wish I could find an institute that teaches people how to listen. After all, a good manager needs to listen at least as much as he needs to talk . . . real communication goes in both directions.*
>
> Lee Iacocca
> *Iacocca: An Autobiography*

This is not to suggest that every message you send to another person requires a response or acknowledgment from that person, and vice versa. Very often a simple nod of the head or observing the subsequent behavior of the other person is enough to complete the process. But: **As a task becomes more complex, as a relationship requires more avenues and frequency of communication, it calls for more attention to whatever processes insure accuracy of communication.** This principle becomes doubly important when there is some degree of tension in the situation. **The key to more effective listening is the willingness to listen and respond appropriately to the feelings being expressed as well as to the content (Rogers & Farson, 1976).** An acceptance of the existence of feelings and the legitimacy of the other person having them, even when you don't agree, usually eases the tension created when a person feels misunderstood or put down by the listener and also allows a focus on whatever is generating the original feelings.

GUIDELINES FOR ACTIVE LISTENING

Objectives: To help others gain clear understanding of their situations, so they can take responsible action. To demonstrate your appreciation of meaning and feelings behind other's statements, of worth of other person, and of your willingness to listen without passing judgment.

Do:	*Don't:*
1. Create supportive atmosphere.	1. Try to change other's views.
2. Listen for feelings as well as words.	2. Solve problem for other.
3. Note cues—gestures, tone of voice, body positions, eye movements, breathing, and the like.	3. Give advice (no matter how obvious the solution is for you). 4. Pass judgment.
4. Occasionally test for understanding: "Is this what you meant?"	5. Explain or interpret other's behavior. 6. Give false reassurances.
5. Demonstrate acceptance and understanding, verbally and nonverbally.	7. Attack back if the other is hostile to you—understand the source of the anger.
6. Ask exploratory, open-ended questions.	8. Ask questions about "why" the feelings.

Source: Based on Carl Rogers and Richard Farson, "Active Listening," in *Effective Behavior in Organizations,* ed. Cohen et al. (Homewood, Ill.: Richard D. Irwin, 1976).

RECIPROCITY

Throughout this chapter we have implicitly and explicitly raised questions about the connection between what one person wants and how that affects, and is affected by, what another person wants. For a relationship to continue, there needs to be some kind of mutual accommodation of each to the other, some *reciprocity* between what each gives and gets.

Just as roles develop among group members to fulfill particular group functions and are selected by individuals in line with their self-concepts, people often develop interpersonal role relationships at work.

The norm that it is obligatory to "pay back" roughly what one has "received" is almost universal and operates between individuals, groups, organizations, or even societies. Though disputes can arise about whether what one party offers is sufficient to repay the other's original "gift" (How many "thank you's" does it take to satisfy your friend of the opposite sex that you really liked the sweater?), virtually everyone accepts that everything should somehow be repaid. Gratefulness for help, dinner invitation for dinner invitation, warmth for kindnesses; whatever the currency, mutual satisfaction of debts over time is necessary to sustain an equal relationship. And failure to repay leads either to breaking off the relationship or to continued obligations and status differentials.

"Noblesse oblige," or taking care of those who are less fortunate, is a way of dealing with unequal abilities to repay, though even in that type of relationship deference, loyalty, and gratitude are expected in return for more durable goods.

This universal *norm of reciprocity* serves to stabilize relationships, to bring them into a steady state, which allows predictability and continuity. You may remember that the taking of *roles* serves much the same function. When behavior becomes patterned, meeting the expectations of others in a particular social system, everyone has a clear idea of what to expect and how to treat others. Each person develops a set pattern of behavior that provides something for the other; as long as what is provided is desired, the relationship is easy to maintain. A member of an organization by virtue of accepting a position in it will find that others have expectations about the type of relationships deemed appropriate for someone in that role. Just as the plumber had some ideas about what kind of interpersonal behavior a plumber's assistant should exhibit and Buckley and Endrunn had ideas about how a president and group vice president should relate, organizational members develop expectations that the role occupant cannot easily ignore despite personal preferences that might be different. It takes a while for each party to alter expectations and preferences to fit the other.

> *Friendship is seldom lasting but between equals. . . . Benefits which cannot be repaid and obligations which cannot be discharged are not commonly found to increase affection; they excite gratitude indeed and heighten veneration but commonly take away that easy freedom and familiarity of intercourse without which . . . there cannot be friendship.*
>
> Samuel Johnson
> *The Rambler No. 64*

To build and maintain a relationship, one needs to fulfill the norm of reciprocity; yet the currency of "exchange" is often rather subtle. (It is not always as easy as, "You bought lunch yesterday; today I will buy.") For example, if you and another manager had occasion to assemble your teams for joint meetings sometimes in her conference room and sometimes in yours, and it had become customary for whichever one of you was on home turf to sit at the head of the conference table, it could violate expectations of reciprocity if you were to quickly move into that seat in her conference room. If the seating has come to mean a recognition of one another's status, breaking the pattern could easily be seen as an attempt to dominate and a failure to properly reciprocate her usual recognition of your status. It may not be possible to fully avoid failures of reciprocity, but you need to be alert to what is expected of you in return for what others have done for you, and to choose consciously whether or not to honor the expectations. Conversely, if you eventually want something from another person, you can utilize reciprocity by doing something useful—helping the other to meet his/her personal or organizational goals—and asking for a "return on your investment" when necessary. This need not be done in a harsh, demanding way; since most people recognize when they "owe you one," they will naturally want to pay you back.

In any ongoing relationship there are usually mutual expectations; as long as they are honored the relationship remains stable. Often, however, the expectations are unclear or unrealistic, or one of the parties finds it difficult to live up to them. One who is wise in such a situation will discuss the issue with the other and attempt to modify the expectations in line with reality. All too often people are prone to let a situation build, perhaps because of embarrassment or a feeling that "one must always honor a commitment," until things have gotten out of control. Then, unfortunately, the relationship might end or require a major effort to rectify. If there is a lesson in this, it is that *every relationship needs nurturing, and continuing attention to mutual expectations is essential to the maintenance of reciprocity.*

In short, as needs and/or circumstances change, people may need to renegotiate their expectations of each other, a process that takes time and effort but pays off in mutual growth.

TRUST AND OTHER FEELINGS

How you handle reciprocity and other aspects of the relationship will generate a range of feelings within you and the other party, and these feelings in turn affect the relationship. Fundamentally, the feelings tie back to the impact of the relationship on each of your self-concepts.

Every relationship has the potential for confirming or disconfirming the participants' self-concepts. Whatever is sought in the relationship—whether it is liking, respect, or influence—a satisfying relationship confirms people's view of themselves and makes them feel good about who they believe they are. When two people agree in their goals, it makes them both feel supported; when they affirm each other's competencies, they feel a sense of adequacy; and when they reinforce each other's beliefs and values, they each feel worthy. **A relationship that makes each person feel supported, adequate, and**

worthy will generally lead to mutual feelings of closeness, warmth, and trust. By way of contrast, a relationship that makes each person feel unsupported, inadequate, and unworthy will generally lead to mutual feelings of distance, coldness, and suspicion (Rogers, 1961).

The terms *closeness* (versus distance), *warmth* (versus coldness, and *trust* (versus suspicion) take on different meanings in different kinds of relationships. Closeness and warmth are mainly a matter of degree. For example, a minimal task relationship would certainly not draw two people as close or generate as many warm feelings as would a colleagueship; the stakes are different in each case. But even a minimal task relationship in which each person experiences self-confirmation can lead to some degree of closeness and warmth.

Trust

With respect to trust, the situation is more complex; trust is a central issue in all human relationships both within and outside of organizations. Trust can refer to several aspects of a relationship: (1) how much confidence you have in the other's competence and ability to do whatever needs doing, (2) how sound you believe the other's judgment to be, (3) your belief in the extent to which the other is willing to be helpful to you, and (4) how certain you are that the other has genuine concern for your welfare rather than any desire to harm you.

Since trust can refer to any or all of these areas, it is useful to be clear about which area you mean when you use the concept and helpful to check what others mean by it. "I don't trust you" is a very different statement when it means "Your lack of carpentry skills make me doubt whether you can build that chest" than it is when it means "I think you would drop it on my toes at the first opportunity." Remember Theory X and Theory Y from Chapter 8? They are sets of beliefs that express greater or lesser trust in the motives of others.

Trust is the lubrication that makes it possible for organizations to work. It's hard to imagine an organization without some semblance of trust operating somehow, somewhere.

Source: W. Bennis and B. Nanus, *Leaders* (New York: Harper & Row, 1985).

While deep and all-encompassing trust may not be called for in a work situation, when it does emerge it can make work easier. It does this by forming the basis for greater *openness* in the relationship on all fronts. For example, two close friends probably will feel greater freedom to be open and honest in task-related areas than would two relative strangers. The two friends are more likely to be willing to take *risks* with one another, that is, to say things that may be critical or revealing in the belief that the other person will hear it accurately and not use it in a destructive way. While the level of trust in a relationship can develop gradually over time, through the course of interactions, very often it takes some kind of risky behavior in relation to the other person to build trust at the deepest levels. To deepen a relationship requires that someone take initiative in trusting the other—say, to do a really tough part of a joint task—before he/she can be certain of the consequences. If neither will take the risk of trusting at least a little, the relationship remains at the same level of caution and suspicion. Note the way Buckley and Endrunn cannot improve their relationship unless one or the other is willing to take the initiative and be more open.

On the other hand, when someone violates trust (especially when it has involved some personal risk) the relationship is usually damaged. The effect may be temporary or permanent, depending upon how deeply the violation affected the self-concept. It is easier to forgive a co-worker who goofed up some piece of the job or whose interpretation of a task was grossly in error than it is to forgive a friend or close colleague for taking an action that puts one in a bad light with others.

In general, then: **The greater the trust one has in another's competence, judgment, helpfulness, or concern, the more open one will be about matters relating to that aspect(s) of the relationship. In turn, the more one feels trusted, the easier it is to be open (Walton, 1969; Rogers, 1961; Egan, 1973).**

But how can we go about building and maintaining trust? As just implied, in part one must act with integrity and not violate whatever trust exists. This requires meeting commitments made to the other person and maintaining such confidences as may occur. Even where you have information that was not given you "in confidence," you need to use common sense about raising issues in public that put the other person on the spot unnecessarily or unexpectedly. If the organization's culture is one where everything is open and above board, there may be very little that can't be brought up at any time, but in most cultures there are some constraints. In general, people do not like to be caught by surprise, especially high-level managers in front of their bosses or even peers. Consequently, common sense usually suggests raising issues in private or at least alerting an individual ahead of time. A person who exhibits such common sense will be seen as more trustworthy than someone who shows no sensitivity to another's feelings about not being caught off guard or embarrassed in public.

Still another way to build trust, apart from doing your own job well, is by being open about your own actions and intentions. It is not easy to trust someone who is secretive and who "plays the cards close to the vest." Keeping others informed not only avoids surprises but reduces the threat that the unknown entails. In part this means being sensitive to others' needs to know what is going on, and in part it means making yourself more vulnerable.

DEALING WITH BLIND SPOTS: THE NEED FOR FEEDBACK

The development of a relationship involves the behavior of both parties; to make it easier to look at the interconnection, see Figure 10–4. It shows the relationship from the perspective of each person and also what the combinations of their separate perspectives produce. From each person's vantage point there are aspects of the relationship that are *known* (that each is aware of) and aspects that are *not known*. What both persons are aware of (upper left box) are those things that have been shared openly; what neither person is aware of (lower right box) are those things that have not made their appearance in the relationship, the future unknowns that may or may not emerge. The other two boxes determine the direction in which the relationship is to develop, if it develops at all. They include those aspects of the relationship that one person or the other is aware of, but not both. What person A alone is aware of (has not shared with person B) in the

FIGURE 10–4
Model of a Two Person Relationship

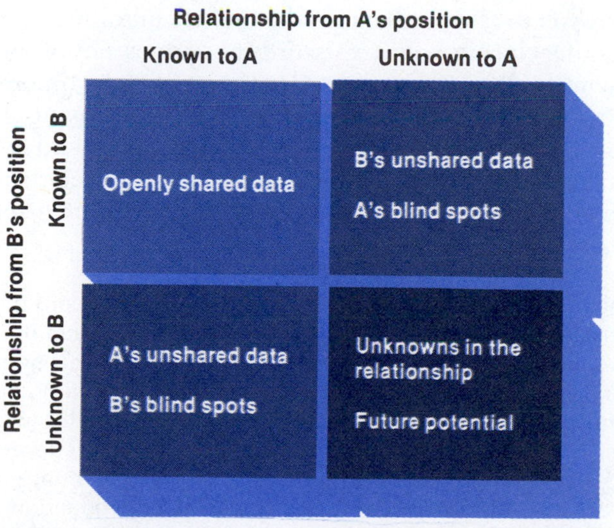

Note: This model is a modification of the "Johari Window," a concept presented in J. Luft, *Group Processes* (Palo Alto, Calif.: National Press Books, 1970).

relationship, we call B's "blind spots" (and vice versa). The blind spots can be positive or negative in nature, but as long as they remain hidden from one person or the other, they tend to serve as obstacles to the development of a mutually enhancing relationship. **The fewer the number of blind spots one has, the greater the understanding of one's impact on others, and the greater the opportunity to choose alternative behaviors (Jourard, 1971; Luft, 1970).** It is discouraging and a handicap to be misunderstood or misjudged on the basis of some behavior or mannerism of which one is not aware; you can't change what you do not know about.

In order for anyone to improve performance, please another, or change self-defeating behavior, it is necessary to be aware of the impact one is having on the other(s). Since we can best alter mistakes or unintentional consequences *with* information on the impact of our behavior, rather than without it, telling me how I am coming across is a kind of gift. It is the feedback of data, which cannot be acquired nearly so effectively, if at all, in any other way. The feedback process in which information is given on the consequences of certain actions is central to any human relationship in which learning is desired or necessary. For example, if a group member's constant jokes bother you, making it even hard to take his/her valuable contributions seriously, you prevent that person from learning how to be more effective if you do not tell him/her.

But there is a dilemma in all of this. If trust is required for openness and feedback is a form of openness that can be risky (since the receiver may not welcome it as intended), how can you get others to give you the feedback you need? How can you build sufficient trust toward you to allow others to take the risk of telling you how you come across? Declaring your trustworthiness does not often work; the person who feels a risk will not easily accept testimonials! Usually it requires that you go first, taking the risk of disclosing something about yourself—your perceptions, feelings, concerns, and so forth. Self-disclosure builds trust. But self-disclosure can also be risky; it may not be received as intended, or it may be used against the discloser. Consider the following example:

> The production manager and sales manager of a record player manufacturer must write a joint report to their boss on whether or not to produce new compact disc sets. The sales manager's job will be made easier if the model is added to the line; her salespeople want to be able to meet competition with up-to-date models even though sales will not at first be too high. The production manager's job will be made more difficult if the newly designed machine is put into production, since there are already problems with the existing level of production. If the wrong decision is made, it will be costly to both of them. Do they work together to examine all aspects of the problem, or does each hold back

information unfavorable to their respective positions? If the sales manager admits that she has doubts about the market potential of compact disc sets and suspects the sales staff is only using the lack of them as an excuse for poor efforts, will the production manager pounce on that and force a negative decision? Conversely, if he tells her that a special assembly line could be set up to minimize disruption to present production, will she take advantage of that to force a positive decision? Would either use the other's revelation to look good to the boss? Can they build sufficient trust to be able to share *all* the needed inputs and come to a sensible decision in which each does what is best for the company regardless of personal inconvenience? The degree of trust, openness, and closeness between them will have crucial ramifications for the company—and for their relationship in the future.

In general, we can say that:

1. **The greater the extent of openness in self-disclosure and feedback, the greater will be the resulting level of trust.**
2. **The greater the level of openness that is required, the greater the level of risk experienced.**
3. **The greater the level of risk required, the greater the level of trust that is needed for openness.**

WHAT TO DO WHEN AN EMPLOYEE IS TALENTED—AND A PAIN IN THE NECK

Psychologists call them "compensators"; human resource professionals call them "abrasive." Co-workers and bosses call them a pain in the neck.

Look around your office and there's probably one lurking: the employee whose personality manages to irritate, disrupt, demoralize, or alienate.

He also may be doing his job well, thereby causing one of the more perplexing workplace issues for managers: How to cope with or change an employee's frustrating, and often ingrained, behavior. And when a star performer is the culprit, "it's as difficult a decision as any for a manager to make," says John Lenkey, a Richmond, Virginia, consultant.

Too often, consultants say, the decision is to do nothing or to fire. But neither choice is desirable: It isn't easy to justify holding onto a disruptive employee, particularly at a time of budget cuts. And firing a talented employee for personality reasons may invite a lawsuit. Moreover, firing or doing nothing often means wasting a potentially valuable employee.

Uncomfortable, but Necessary

So, more companies are urging managers to deal with troublesome employees head on, as uncomfortable as that may be. They also are teaching employees to more effectively deal with problem co-workers; as participatory management spreads, with workers more involved in management decisions, it's increasingly important that employees learn how to confront bothersome peers without damaging egos or provoking fisticuffs.

Source: Larry Reibstein. Reprinted by permission of *The Wall Street Journal*, © Dow Jones & Company, Inc., August 8, 1986. All rights reserved.

4. The closer that self-disclosure and/or feedback come to the core of the self-concept, the greater the level of risk that is experienced and the higher the level of trust necessary for openness (Rogers, 1961; Egan, 1973).

You need trust in order to take the risk of being open. But it is hard to develop sufficient trust until you do take the risk of being open. If

GUIDELINES FOR GIVING FEEDBACK

Giving feedback should be analogous to holding up a mirror where individuals can see themselves as others see them and learn how their actions have been affecting others. It is *not* telling others what is wrong with them nor telling them how they *should* change. It is offering your perceptions and describing your feelings in a nonjudgmental manner as data that recipients can use as they find appropriate.

1. Examine your own motives.
   Be sure your intention is to be helpful, not to show how perceptive and superior you are, or to hurt the other.
2. Consider the *receiver's readiness* to hear your feedback.
   In general, feedback is most useful when it is sought, rather than when it is volunteered. When possible, wait for signs of other wanting it; nevertheless,
3. Give feedback promptly.
   Feedback given soon after the event, except when the individual is upset or otherwise not ready to listen, is better than that given when details are no longer clear in anyone's mind.
4. *Be descriptive* rather than evaluative.
   Describe what the person did and any feelings it aroused in you, but do not label or evaluate it. ("You interrupted me and that frustrates me because I lose track" is descriptive; "You were rude" is evaluative.)
5. *Deal in specifics,* not generalities.
   Describe concrete events. ("You interrupted me when I was reviewing . . ." versus "You try to hog all the air time.")
6. *Offer* feedback; do not try to impose it.
   Give information as something the receiver can consider and explore, not as a command that he/she change.
7. Offer feedback in a *spirit of tentativeness.*
   Offer feedback as one person's perceptions, not as "the truth." Being dogmatic usually puts people on the defensive.
8. *Be open to receiving feedback yourself.*
   Your actions may be contributing to the other's behavior; not everyone may feel the same as you do about the other, which reflects on your perceptions as well as on the other's behavior.
9. *Avoid overload.*
   Focus only on what is most important and changeable.
10. Watch for behavior of other while receiving feedback, which confirms or disconfirms the feedback.

the risk is positively responded to, the first critical step in building trust is established; if not, then you are left only with the satisfaction of knowing that you had the courage to take the risk. Risking mistakenly can be disastrous; risking too cautiously can be isolating.

Furthermore, it is occasionally necessary to work with someone whom you do not trust; finding a way to get the job done without either making yourself vulnerable or offending the other person is a valuable skill to acquire. While open, trusting relationships are freeing and satisfying, plunging into acting as if the person will respond in kind just because you would prefer it is like diving into a new swimming place without checking for rocks beneath the surface. Conversely, assuming that *all* water is loaded with sharks can rob you of a great deal of pleasure.

Unfortunately, it is almost impossible to develop guidelines for judging when it is worth risking openness and trust. As in other human situations, you have to decide whether the expected gains are sufficiently greater than the potential losses to be worth the possibility of a failure. Keep in mind that trust is usually built a little at a time. Pushing too hard and/or too fast can scare off the other person and also may be too risky for you; not pushing at all, however, is not likely to produce any change. Normally, though, your own willingness to *begin* being open will result in a reciprocal response.

Mark Buckley, for example, needs to gently initiate discussions with Oliver Endrunn about ways of effectively striking a balance between being informed and being unnecessarily interfering; blasting Endrunn for bypassing him would only make Endrunn defensive and angry. From his side, Endrunn can talk with Buckley about what information would help him relax so that he wouldn't have to seek it all the time; attacking Buckley for being too closed and political would simply lead to further guardedness.

A Recap

To recap our discussion to this point, individuals involved in a relationship can steer it in a positive direction by being adaptable to the requirements of the job and the desires of the other person, by developing and practicing good communication skills so as to minimize and deal with misunderstanding, by honoring and utilizing the norm of reciprocity to maintain a balanced exchange, by acting with integrity in a manner that keeps the other informed about actions, intentions, and expectations, and by seeking to reduce mutual blind spots through self-disclosure and feedback. These practices will also be useful in doing the maintenance work to keep a positive relationship from falling into decline. If careful attention is given to these interpersonal processes, the result should be a good relationship leading to productivity, satisfaction, and even individual development. We close this chapter with a look at some other outcomes of a relationship that are related to productivity, satisfaction, and development.

OUTCOMES OF INTERPERSONAL RELATIONSHIPS

Liking and Respect

It's possible for two people to work together, even productively, without developing much liking or respect for one another. In a minimal task relationship this probably poses little problem, at least for getting the work done. However, as discussed in Chapter 7, most people have more needs than those that pertain only to the task; therefore, few people would find very desirable, for long, a work relationship that lacks liking and respect.

Liking is normally related to the personal and social aspects of a relationship. If the quality of communication between two people is such that feelings of closeness, warmth, and trust develop, the outcome will obviously be liking. Even if the task does not require such interpersonal communication, if the individuals themselves desire it, if their backgrounds are compatible, and if the opportunities for interaction are present, then the chances are good that their relationship will result in liking. Any one of these factors, however, can affect the outcome. For example, in one company two members of a management team had very similar styles of interacting—both were aggressive and argumentative. Their interpersonal process was terrible; neither could listen to or understand the other. Consequently, they maintained a kind of distance, coolness, and mistrust, which resulted in mutual dislike. While they did, in fact, respect each other's abilities in the job, their dislike made work unpleasant for the entire team.

> *It is not necessary to understand things in order to argue about them.*
>
> Beaumarchais

In a work relationship mutual respect normally occurs as a result of the recognition of one another's competencies. Can you think of people you hold in esteem because of their abilities? Are they all people you also like? As discussed in Chapter 5, feelings of respect may not be consistent with liking. The example above illustrates this point. Furthermore, co-workers may develop a high level of task-related trust but never feel close or warm on a more personal level. And while their processes of communication may be poor when feelings are involved, the two people may be perfectly capable of exchanging needed information about the work as the situation requires it.

In short, we can say that:

1. **In a minimal task relationship, liking and respect need only be minimal in order to get the task done.**
2. **The degree of liking needed in a task relationship depends upon the preferences of the individuals but also tends to be more appropriate to relationships that extend beyond the minimal task level.**
3. **The degree of respect needed in a task relationship increases as task interdependence increases and as the differentiated abilities of each person are required for satisfactory completion of the job.**
4. **To the extent that personal closeness, warmth, and trust emerge, liking will result.**
5. **To the extent that task-related trust emerges, respect will result (Bennis, Berlew, Schein, & Steele, 1973).**

While it may at times seem difficult to be both liked and respected, the two outcomes are not mutually exclusive. The assumption that they are can, in fact, result in the unfortunate situation in which a manager says, "I'd rather be respected than liked; at least I'll get the job done." Have you ever heard this or a similar expression? What is unfortunate is that such a manager limits the range of his own interpersonal competence and consequently may remain unresponsive to the needs of many employees. Insofar as a job requires more than a minimal task relationship, the development of *both* liking and respect can have important consequences for productivity, satisfaction, and development. Let's examine these consequences in the form of some propositions.

PROPOSITIONS LINKING LIKING AND RESPECT TO PRODUCTIVITY, SATISFACTION, AND DEVELOPMENT. While the connections are neither simple nor direct, since many other variables need to be considered, there does (except for minimal task) seem to be some very general relationship between liking and respect on the one hand and productivity, satisfaction, and development on the other. We will list the propositions without elaboration; you ought to be able to apply them to your own experience and to examples you may study.

1. **When liking and respect are both high, productivity, satisfaction, and development tend to be enhanced.**
2. **When liking and respect are both low, productivity, satisfaction, and development tend to be reduced.**
3. **When liking is high and respect is low, productivity tends to be reduced, satisfaction tends to be enhanced, and development may be affected either way.**

4. When liking is low and respect is high, productivity tends to be enhanced, satisfaction tends to be reduced, and development may be affected either way.

Keep in mind that these statements represent very general tendencies; that is, when all other things are equal, then the factors of liking and respect can provide predictive guidelines to productivity, satisfaction, and development. A deeper understanding of the connections, especially in regard to development in a relationship, can be obtained by examining the quality of the patterned role relationships that emerge between two people. We will look at these next.

PATTERNED ROLE RELATIONSHIPS

In order for a work relationship to be sustained at anything more than the absolute minimum required by the task or for a nonrequired relationship to continue, a mutually satisfactory role relationship will have to emerge.

The role relationships people establish with others become important sources of stability in their lives; they count on them to help maintain personal identity, a basic sense of adequacy, and a sense of worth. Yet, once established, role relationships become very difficult to break out of even when they are no longer fully desired or are preventing needed growth and change. For example, think about the kinds of role relationships you have with members of that familiar organization, your family. How much have these changed as you have grown older? Do you find yourself being drawn into some of your "old behavior" every time you visit your parents? Well-developed role patterns are very hard to break. They tend to determine and shape a great deal of our behavior, and when they are outmoded, they serve to constrain a great many more satisfying possibilities in the relationships. Here is a 36-year-old professional person describing his relationship with his 27-year-old brother:

> When I get together with my youngest brother, I automatically fall into "older brother" behavior, giving advice (that he may or may not want), looking after him, paying the check when we eat out, and so on. Even though I try to treat him like the full-fledged adult he is, old habits are hard to break, and I slide into my most familiar and well-practiced role with him. He in turn falls into playing "kid brother," asking advice, appearing a bit unsure of himself, letting me initiate, and so forth. We have a well-established role relationship, which is convenient because it lets each of us know in advance a lot about how the other is likely to behave and react, and it saves considerable time and confusion each time we see each other.

At the same time, by definition, it also restricts each of our possible choices. Unless we are willing to make the other uncomfortable and challenge mutual expectations, he cannot really be assertive with me and I cannot easily be helpless, confused, or needy with him. So at the same time that our roles are convenient, they also constrain our behavior as long as we choose to continue them.

We tend to take for granted those to whom we are the closest. Often we get so accustomed to seeing them and hearing from them that we lose the ability to listen to what they are really saying or to appreciate the quality—good or bad—of what they are doing.

Source: W. Bennis and B. Nanus, *Leaders* (New York: Harper & Row, 1985).

Another example was observed at a large urban hospital:

The director of nursing, an attractive woman, had allowed the male administrators to treat her as a "dumb blonde," pleasant but not very smart. Their discomfort at the possibility that she might be beautiful *and* competent led them to treat her that way; her discomfort at upsetting their expectations and possibly being seen as an "aggressive bitch" led her to play along.

At a training session with her female assistant director, she was confronted about this behavior and began to practice using her considerable analytical abilities. Shortly after, she was at a meeting of her peers, male directors of other departments. Someone made a snide comment about something in her jurisdiction; she came back with a fast, concise, and powerful rebuttal. When all the dropped jaws were restored to the astonished faces, one of the men said, "I'm glad to see that your nice legs haven't been affected by your brains," a not very subtle attempt to get her back in role. She had to struggle hard to continue making contributions; eventually she left the hospital for a similar job where she could start fresh.

Have you ever experienced a similar dilemma? It is a problem that frequently occurs, exactly *because* the relationship is reciprocal, when you attempt to change your behavior toward another person. You can decide, "From now on I'm going to be different with so-and-so." Then when you try it, "so-and-so" either resists the change, thinks you're crazy, or simply overlooks your new behavior as a temporary phenomenon. Psychotherapists struggle with this issue when they seek to bring about change in a client's behavior and other key people in the client's life continue to cast him or her into the old roles. As a gag song put it, "I Can't Get Adjusted to the You that Got Adjusted to Me." Sometimes, even when a person changes in ways that you find desirable, it can be difficult to begin treating that person in new ways! It means building whole new role relationships, which also means changing some of your own behavior to match the other person's. In short, to establish a new role requires stepping out of the old one. That isn't easy.

Can you see the implications of this problem for individuals who want to move upward in an organization? Every promotion or job change calls for new role relationships or altered ones with former colleagues and superiors. It can create great problems to become the supervisor of someone who formerly trained or managed you; how does one change from "promising young trainee" to "responsible executive"? Not everyone can easily let go of established patterns.

Self-Sealing Reciprocal Relationships

Even more difficult than changing one person's role in a relationship is addressing the problem of mutually reinforcing limiting patterns. When two people have trouble working together, it is often because each produces in the other the very behavior that most irritates the counterpart, reinforcing the original behavior and keeping the pattern going. For example, Buckley wants autonomy and resents Endrunn's interference, so he withholds information, which induces Endrunn to poke around for information, reinforcing Buckley's conviction that he must give less information, which reinforces Endrunn's conviction that Buckley is closed and therefore won't voluntarily give information, etc. (See diagram of the self-sealing loop.)

Self-Sealing Loop

Buckley	*Endrunn*
Wants autonomy	Wants information
↓	↓
Withholds information	Talks to Buckley's subordinates

This kind of endless loop can be called a *self-sealing reciprocal relationship*. The more each tries to deal with the other in the usual way, the worse the problem gets. This is often the source of continuing interpersonal struggles. Here's another example:

> Max is the cigar-smoking, aggressive vice president of manufacturing in a consumer goods company. The order entry department, where sales of the thousands of pieces sold by the sales force are recorded and transmitted to the factory, reports to manufacturing. Max is proud of his operation though he knows it isn't perfect. Shawn is the ambitious sales vice president. He can't make his bonus if manufacturing doesn't deliver. Lately there have been problems with the order entry department. Shawn raises it at an executive committee meeting. He attacks by say-

ing, "Order entry should report to sales. Their performance stinks." Max counters, "Nothing's wrong with them, and they'd be worse if they reported to sales." Shawn can't stand being put off, so he attacks again. This gets Max to fight harder. The more Shawn makes it a battle over turf, who "owns" order entry, the more Max insists that performance is fine. Shawn's grabbing for turf makes Max defensive; Max's denials of problems make Shawn more determined to get control. And so it goes, through many rounds.

In all of this, the actual problem with order entry is forgotten; Shawn and Max are in a self-sealing loop that makes anything but "attack and defend" impossible to discuss.

It is very difficult for one party in such a closed relationship to bring it to a halt; once inside a self-sealing loop, it is hard to see the pattern and to see how you are contributing to the problem. It's always crystal clear to each party what the other is doing wrong. A fellow worker, however, can often see the pattern. Once someone points it out, the involved parties can much more easily see how to break it. Max could first say, "OK, Shawn, let's actually look at the problems you're having and see how to fix them." Or Shawn could first say, "Maybe the issue isn't to whom order entry should report, but how we can get faster turnaround and more accuracy. Let's go after that, Max." Similarly, Mark Buckley could decide to supply Endrunn with much *more* information, and point out that he's willing to continue if Endrunn will stop jumping in with instructions to Buckley's subordinates. Or, Endrunn could say to Mark, "In order to be comfortable I need to feel informed. If I interfere as a result, let me know. I want you to be able to be effective."

One party's admission of what he or she is doing to perpetuate the problem is often enough to break the sealed reciprocal pattern and lead to problem solving. In general, when you're having trouble with someone else, it's useful to look for what you might be doing that contributes to the problem. Poor relationships are seldom caused completely by one side. And since reciprocity is likely to be the tie that links related roles together, *changing your own behavior may indeed be likely to induce changes in the behavior of another.* If you start treating your parents as if they were serious adult friends and as if you were also a mature adult, they will have to accommodate somehow to the alterations in your behavior. If the co-worker who avoids responsibility is treated responsibly and expected to come through when needed, he/she may in fact be less likely to let you down than otherwise.

Insofar as a relationship exists in which both parties feel connected to one another, there is potential leverage for affecting the other's behavior by altering your own. Though the pulls are likely to be great to get back into the old roles, it is worth exploring whether a role relationship that is giving you trouble can be redefined into a new set of reciprocal roles through your own initiative. When that works, it can be very freeing and can lead to greater influence over the work environment you are in.

In short, the patterned role relationships that emerge in a work environment have important consequences for productivity, satisfaction, and development. While certain kinds of fixed patterns can enhance both productivity and satisfaction, as when the various aspects of two people's jobs are reciprocal, the developmental aspects of a relationship normally pertain to learning and change. When two people learn from one another, when they are able to create new role patterns as tasks and needs demand them, then the relationship will enhance all three outcomes, especially development. While work relationships of this kind may be rare and difficult to build, they are indeed worth the effort in the long run. We hope that the concepts and examples offered in this and the previous chapter will aid you in your own quest for growth-promoting work relationships.

SUMMARY

Figure 10–5 illustrates the total picture we have covered in Chapters 9 and 10. It should be obvious by now just how complicated a two-person relationship can be; we hope to have provided a coherent picture by following the sequence of factors shown in the chart. For your own practice, you might attempt to trace some relationships with which you are familiar through the sequence; you can go in either direction. For example, you might begin with the outcomes and try to analyze how they came about. By working your way back through processes, looking at the required relationship (if it's a work context), and considering the backgrounds and circumstances, you might be able to explain the relationship in some depth. Were the outcomes predictable from any of the factors identified in the scheme? Possibly you can use this approach in a forward direction, that is, to predict the probable outcomes of some current interpersonal relationships as you see them emerging.

By developing your diagnostic skills in this fashion, you can identify ways to alter the interpersonal processes to improve the relationship. If you can develop such interpersonal skill, you can't help but become a better manager of your own relationships and, if it's ever required of you, a better manager of other people's work relationships.

As stated earlier in this chapter, interpersonal competence is a basic ingredient of effective management; it makes a critical difference in how much *influence* you may exercise in relation to peers, superiors, and subordinates. In the next chapter, we will show just how the

FIGURE 10–5
Schema for Analyzing Two-Person Work Relationship

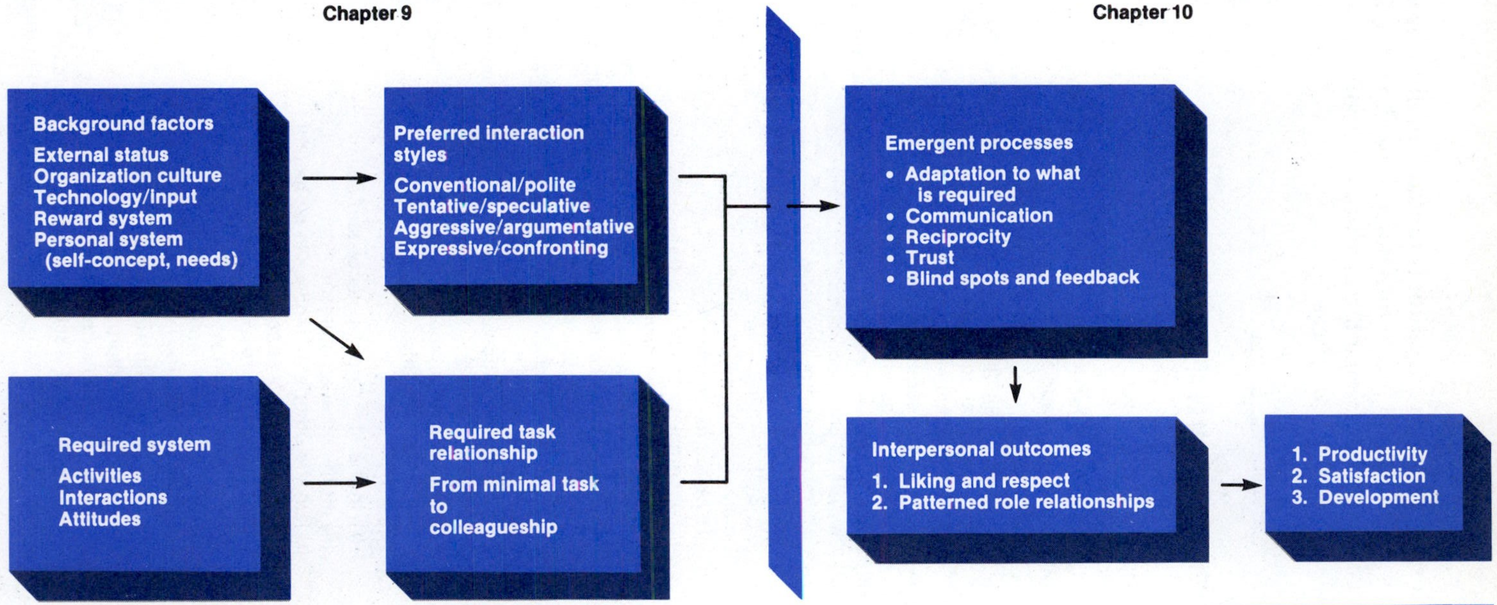

Chapter 9

Background factors
External status
Organization culture
Technology/input
Reward system
Personal system
(self-concept, needs)

Preferred interaction styles
Conventional/polite
Tentative/speculative
Aggressive/argumentative
Expressive/confronting

Required system
Activities
Interactions
Attitudes

Required task relationship
From minimal task to colleagueship

Chapter 10

Emergent processes
• Adaptation to what is required
• Communication
• Reciprocity
• Trust
• Blind spots and feedback

Interpersonal outcomes
1. Liking and respect
2. Patterned role relationships

1. Productivity
2. Satisfaction
3. Development

leadership in an organization is fundamentally a process of influence. You will be able to judge for yourself just how the interpersonal factors covered in this chapter constitute important background factors for leadership effectiveness.

KEY CONCEPTS FROM CHAPTER 10

1. Interpersonal processes.
   a. Adaptation to:
      (1) What is required.
      (2) The other person's expectations and desires.
   b. Communication.
      (1) Levels of exchange between speaker and listener:
         (*i*) Feelings about subject matter.
         (*ii*) Subject matter.
         (*iii*) Feelings about one another.
         (*iv*) Feelings about self.
      (2) Self-concepts and perceptions of other filter messages in and out.
      (3) Barriers to communication.
         (*i*) Imprecision of language.
         (*ii*) Multiple channels (verbal and nonverbal).
         (*iii*) State of mind.
      (4) Common problems of communication.
         (*i*) Mixed messages.
         (*ii*) Incomplete communication.
         (*iii*) Unconscious nonverbal signals.
         (*iv*) Conscious nonverbal signals.
         (*v*) The greater the emotional involvement with a subject, the greater the likelihood of distortion.
      (5) It takes both people for communication to work.
   c. Reciprocity.
      (1) To maintain a relationship, one must fulfill the norm of reciprocity.
   d. Trust and other feelings.
      (1) Feeling supported, adequate, and worthy leads to closeness, warmth, and trust in a relationship.
      (2) Trust.
         (*i*) In the other's competence and ability.
         (*ii*) In the other's judgment.
         (*iii*) In the other's willingness to be helpful.
         (*iv*) In the other's concern for your welfare.
      (3) Trust is easily destroyed, unless you:
         (*i*) Act with integrity.
         (*ii*) Maintain confidentialities.
         (*iii*) Do your job effectively.
         (*iv*) Avoid inappropriate secrecy.
         (*v*) Keep others informed.
   e. Dealing with blind spots (the need for feedback).
      (1) Openness and self-disclosure reduce blind spots.
      (2) Openness often means taking a risk, but can build trust.

   f. Attention to interpersonal processes is necessary to:
      (1) Build a positive relationship.
      (2) Maintain a positive relationship.

2. Outcomes of interpersonal relationships.
   a. Liking and respect.
      (1) To the extent that personal closeness, warmth, and trust emerge, liking will result.
      (2) To the extent that task-related trust emerges, respect will result.
      (3) Correlations of liking and respect with productivity, satisfaction, and development.
   b. Patterned role relationships.
      (1) A source of stability in people's lives.
      (2) Can become self-sealing.
         (*i*) To break the pattern requires both to change.
3. A positive relationship is one in which:
   a. The required task gets done properly and with reasonable efficiency (productivity).
   b. The parties involved are reasonably satisfied (satisfaction).
   c. The growth of both is fostered, or at least not hindered (development).

SUGGESTED READINGS

Athos, A., and J. Gabarro. *Interpersonal Behavior.* Englewood Cliffs, N.J.: Prentice-Hall, 1978.

Beier, E. G. "Nonverbal Communication: How We Send Emotional Messages." *Psychology Today* 8 (1974), pp. 53–56.

Bennis, W.; D. Berlew; E. Schein; and F. I. Steele. *Interpersonal Dynamics.* 3rd ed. Chicago: Dorsey Press, 1973.

Collins, E. G. C., and T. B. Blodgett. "Sexual Harassment . . . Some See It . . . Some Won't." *Harvard Business Review,* March–April 1981, pp. 76–95.

Davis, K. "Grapevine Communication among Lower and Middle Managers." *Personnel Journal,* April 1969, pp. 269–72.

Egan, G. *Face to Face.* Monterey, Calif.: Brooks/Cole Publishing, 1973.

Fidler, L. A., and J. D. Johnson. "Communication and Innovation Implementation." *Academy of Management Review* 9 (1984), pp. 704–11.

Giffin, K., and B. R. Patton. *Personal Communication in Human Relations.* Columbus, Ohio: Charles E. Merrill Publishing, 1974.

Hall, E. T. *The Silent Language.* Greenwich, Conn.: Fawcett Publications, 1959.

Halperin, K.; C. R. Snyer; R. J. Shenkkel; and B. K. Houston. "Effects of Source Status and Message Favorability on Acceptance of Personality Feedback." *Journal of Applied Psychology* 61 (1976), pp. 85–88.

Haney, W. V. *Communication: Pattern and Incidence.* Homewood, Ill.: Richard D. Irwin, 1960.

Harris, T. A. *I'm OK, You're OK.* New York: Harper & Row, 1967.

Hayes, M. A. "Nonverbal Communication: Expression without Words." In *Readings in Interpersonal and Organizational Communication,* ed. R. C. Huseman, C. M. Logue, and D. L. Freshley. Boston: Holbrook Press, 1973.

Jacoby, J.; D. Mazursky; T. Troutman; and A. Kuss. "When Feedback Is Ignored: Disutility of Outcome Feedback." *Journal of Applied Psychology* 69 (1984), pp. 531–45.

Jongeward, D. *Everybody Wins: Transactional Analysis Applied to Organizations.* Reading, Mass.: Addison-Wesley Publishing, 1973.

Jourard, S. M. *The Transparent Self.* Rev. ed. New York: Van Nostrand Reinhold, 1971.

Luft, J. *Group Processes.* Palo Alto, Calif.: National Press Books, 1970.

Mangham, I. L. *Interactions and Interventions in Organizations.* New York: John Wiley & Sons, 1978.

Maslow, A. H. *Eupsychian Management.* Homewood, Ill.: Richard D. Irwin and Dorsey Press, 1965.

Rogers, C. "The Characteristics of a Helping Relationship." *On Becoming a Person.* Boston: Houghton Mifflin, 1961, pp. 39–58.

Rogers, C., and R. E. Farson. "Active Listening." In *Effective Behavior in Organizations.* 1st ed. Ed. Cohen et al. Homewood, Ill.: Richard D. Irwin, 1976.

Walton, R. E. "Interpersonal Confrontation and Basic Third-Party Functions: A Case Study." *Journal of Applied Behavioral Science* 4 (1968), pp. 327–44.

________. *Interpersonal Peacemaking: Confrontations and Third-Party Consultation.* Reading, Mass.: Addison-Wesley Publishing, 1969.

Zaleznik, A., and D. Moment. *The Dynamics of Interpersonal Behavior.* New York: John Wiley & Sons, 1964.

C.JONES
11
ERVING
CHEEKS
10

11

LEADERSHIP

Exerting Influence and Power

The core problem for leaders involves getting others to do what is necessary to accomplish the organization's goals.

The topic of leadership has fascinated people through the ages. After much discussion and research, the pursuit of a universal definition of effective leadership is still intriguing but elusive. The world awaits definitive answers to such questions as: What makes a good leader? Who can be a leader? Can anyone be a leader? Can leadership skills be taught? What makes followers follow? What are the limits to leadership?

Social science researchers for years pursued the notion that there must be some common qualities shared by all leaders. Many long lists of sterling qualities (aggressiveness, wisdom, charisma, courage, and so forth) have been generated but have not been found to apply to all leaders in all situations. To be effective a leader's qualities must relate somehow to the situation he/she is in and to the nature of the followers. This view is consistent with the situational approach taken throughout this book, yet is just barely beginning to be widely accepted. The belief does not easily fade away that General Patton, Mahatma Gandhi, Vince Lombardi, Golda Meir, and Martin Luther King—or the presidents of GM, AT&T, IBM, and John Hancock—must have had exactly the same qualities.

As you might expect, however, insofar as there are common components to the manager's or leader's job, a few traits appear to be consistent requirements. In Chapter 1 we induced from Mintzberg's analysis of a manager's job some of the skills required by a manager. You will recall that a manager needs interpersonal skills to acquire information needed for decision making. For example, leaders need to have the ability to influence other people's behavior, a readiness to absorb interpersonal stress, the capacity to structure social interaction systems to task needs, some self-confidence, and the drive to exercise initiative in social situations, all of which are directly related to the nature of managerial work.

Effective leaders also have a strong drive for responsibility and task completion, energy and persistence for accomplishing goals, a willingness to tolerate frustration and delay (since working with and through others does not always result in immediate action!), some willingness to take risks and be original in solving problems, and, perhaps most important, a willingness to accept the consequences of making decisions and taking action (Stogdill, 1974).

In general, you can see that these traits are closely related to the kinds of situations in which virtually all leaders find themselves, having to make relationships in order to accomplish tasks and having to take responsibility for their system's performance.

The *particular* requirements for effective leadership in each situation, however, may well outweigh all of these traits or make only certain ones critical in importance. As we will show in Chapter 12, different kinds of tasks, different kinds of subordinates, and differing leader characteristics all affect what leader behavior will be effective. Thus, possession of the qualities listed does *not* guarantee that one will become a leader, nor does the absence of any one of them rule out the possibility of becoming an effective leader. We must therefore emphasize that the potential for leadership may be assumed to be widely distributed among the general population, and a wide variety of leader behaviors may be effective in particular situations (McGregor, 1960).

What, then, must be taken into account by leaders who wish to be effective in their particular organization? What behavior works best under what conditions? That is what we shall explore in this and the next chapter. We will begin in this chapter with an analysis of leadership in general as the exercise of power and influence, then continue in Chapter 12 with the roles of formally appointed managers and their leadership choices.

LEADERSHIP AS INFLUENCE

The core problem for leaders in organizations involves getting others to do what is necessary to accomplish the organization's goals. This is a complex process, since the goals as well as the means for accomplishing them are often unclear, subject to discussion or negotiation, and can change over time. A leader's boss (or bosses), peers, and subordinates all will have ideas about what should be done and how to do it, and they are likely to try to get their ideas heard. Furthermore, leaders are only human and unlikely to know everything, so they need to be able to alter their views when others make good points.

Nevertheless, once goals are determined, leaders or managers must find a way to create the conditions that will cause (or allow) subordinates to work hard and to direct that work toward organizational ends. This may call for many different kinds of influence behavior aimed in many directions: negotiating a larger budget; getting other departments to deliver accurate and timely information; providing vision, direction, or training to subordinates; simplifying or complicating work; obtaining a deserved salary increase for someone, and so forth. All these activities—up, sideways, and down—ultimately are aimed at getting others, especially subordinates, to do what is necessary to accomplish successfully the work of the system being led.

> *Leadership is the ability to get men to do what they don't want to do and like it.*
>
> Harry Truman

As countless leaders have discovered countless times, this is all much easier said than done. Subordinates don't always know how to work well, don't always work as hard as is necessary, and don't automatically care about the unit's or organization's success. The fact is, leaders are interdependent with many others, especially their followers. They have impact on, and in turn are affected by, those with whom they must work. The key element is the *influence* the leader has on others and the *influence* they have in return. For this reason we can think of leadership as a *process* in which the involved parties *influence* one another in particular ways. *Influence is any act or potential act that affects the behavior of another person(s).* Let's look at the implications of using the concept.

First of all, influence cannot happen in isolation from others; it takes at least two to "tangle," just as with interpersonal relationships. The person who wants to influence must find someone to influence. Second, if you think about it carefully, you will see that only in the most extreme situations could *one* person in an influence transaction have *all* the influence, that is, affect the other's behavior without being affected in turn by the other's reaction. The machinist who leaps to attention when his boss gives an order, the secretary who bursts into tears when feeling that a request to work late is unreasonable, the student who challenges an assignment due the day after vacation, all exert influence on the person trying to influence them.

Cooperating humbly, for example, affects the person who is asking for cooperation and "pulls" more of the same from him/her. As Gandhi showed so well in India, humble, passive noncooperation can have a profound influence on those giving orders. Even the person who follows directions he/she knows are wrong out of fear of being fired or punished has influence on the behavior of the tyrant, allowing further exploitation and mistakes, since the directions were not resisted.

We must be careful, then, to remember that influence only succeeds in moving others in desired directions when the *net* influence, the amount of A's influence on B compared with B's influence on A, is greater. In the classroom or on the job, students and workers can be less *or* more influential than teachers and supervisors. *Leadership is net influence in a direction desired by the person possessing it.*

To understand this process better, we need to look at various types of influence. One important aspect of influence is whether or not it is formal or informal, part of a job's definition or acquired in some other way. *Formal influence is influence prescribed for the holder of an "office" or position in a particular social system.* It is influence *assigned* to a position. The coach of a team has formal influence in initiating practice sessions, selecting starting players and substitutes, and so forth. *Informal influence is influence not prescribed for the office holder but nevertheless affecting other members of the social system.* On the same team, for example, there may be several players whose advice other players and even the coach seek on such matters as techniques and strategy against opponents. Though by position the players have no special influence allotted or assigned to them, their knowledge and/or personal attractiveness and magnetism give them influence anyway. Influence based on special knowledge is *expert* influence, while influence based on personal charm is called *charisma.*

In addition to the distinction between formal and informal influence (i.e., assigned or unassigned), we need to add the concepts of legitimacy and illegitimacy. Legitimate influence is exerted by a person who is seen as having the right to do so by those influenced. In other words, legitimate influence is *accepted as proper* by the person being influenced. Conversely, illegitimate influence is exerted by a person not seen as having the right to do so by those being influenced. Illegitimate influence is *not accepted as proper* by the person being influenced. The basis for considering an influencer as legitimate may be (1) a positive assessment of his/her personal qualities, such as competence, experience, and age and/or (2) the acceptance of the process (such as election, appointment, or automatic succession) by which the person acquired a role calling for the exercise of influence. Legitimacy will usually be limited to areas within the scope of the system and its goals. For example, most people will believe that the boss may legitimately give orders about how to sell a machine but not about where to go on vacation. But within the scope of the organization, orders, requests, and directions will be seen as proper when they come from someone who has acquired an office by an approved process or has personal qualities considered appropriate.

> *To despise legitimate authority, no matter in whom it is invested, is unlawful; it is rebellion against God's will.*
>
> Leo XIII
> *Immortale Dei*
> November 1, 1885

On the other hand, even in the army—where soldiers are taught to "salute the uniform, not the man," suggesting that mere appointment to rank guarantees legitimacy—a soldier may refuse to follow direct orders under a variety of circumstances. For example, if the commanding officer has disruptive personality characteristics or has acquired his office in objectionable ways, such as perceived favoritism, there may be rebellion. Furthermore, when influence is not seen as acquired legitimately, soldiers and other subordinates have many ways of subverting any orders from a person whose influence they do not accept, such as dragging their heels by following literally all rules in the books. Going passive is a common way of resisting what is seen as illegitimate influence.

Since having formal influence does not insure legitimacy nor does having informal influence insure illegitimacy, it is useful to combine the two categories into the four possible combinations, as shown in Figure 11–1.

By looking at the combinations we can see the ways in which influence is exercised. *Formal-legitimate influence* is what is usually meant when people say "the boss has the authority" to enforce particular behaviors. It *is the influence both prescribed for the holder of an office in a social system and seen as his/her right to exert by the other members of it.* Many leadership activities in organizations involve formal-legitimate influence by someone who has been assigned a role with supervisory responsibilities and who can use organizational means to reward or punish subordinates. The right to hire, fire, promote, and adjust pay reinforces this kind of influence.

Since most people who accept jobs in an organization are reasona-

FIGURE 11–1
Examples of Types of Influence

	Formal (assigned)	*Informal (not assigned)*
Legitimate (accepted as proper).	Boss gives work-related orders to subordinate: "Stop making widgets and begin making frammisses." Teacher assigns an analytical paper, based on concepts in the text.	Respected colleague helps you solve a problem by showing you the proper order to make calculations. Basketball benchwarmer notices flaw in opponent's defense, convinces coach to alter offense.
Illegitimate (not accepted as proper).	Boss makes strong hints about subordinate's family life: "Send your son to a private school." Instructor puts a student in charge of class discussion.	Co-worker threatens to beat you up if you continue to produce so much. Fellow students ridicule you for asking questions in class, despite instructor's request for questions.

bly willing to accept directions from their "boss" on job-related matters, legitimacy is often taken for granted and assumed to go with any formal role. During such times as the student strikes in the late 1960s and early 1970s or the rebellions of workers in France, it becomes evident that the legitimacy of those with formal organizational positions is precarious and rests upon the attitudes of the "followers." Students challenged the rights of professors to determine subject matter, give exams and grades, hire and fire colleagues; and they exerted influence on other activities that had traditionally been seen as part of faculty prerogatives. Pressure from workers in several European countries has led to change in what were traditionally considered management's prerogatives. In several countries, workers must even be consulted for such decisions as plant location and new investments in equipment. Thus the boundaries of legitimacy for decisions is changing. Furthermore, legitimacy, even for someone in a formal position, must be earned and may occasionally need renewal. At different times a formal leader may find legitimacy slipping away because of questions about competence or about the way in which the person is leading. Similarly, some subordinates may see the boss as legitimate while others don't. It is often the case that an appointed leader is perceived as legitimate by those with similar backgrounds and as illegitimate by those with backgrounds different than the leader's. A scientist might not, for example, accept the influence of an engineer as a project leader as readily as would another engineer. Since legitimacy is an attitude about a person by other persons, it can change just as do other attitudes. Nevertheless, much of the work of organizations is done because there is a considerable amount of legitimacy granted to those in formal positions; but that is by no means the only kind of leadership exerted.

A great deal of influence is based upon knowledge, expertise (whether perceived or real), or personal charm rather than position (French & Raven, 1960). *This informal-legitimate influence by a member of a social system stands apart from the prescribed influence of his/her office but is accepted as within one's rights by the others in the system.* It is not predictable from organization charts but is essential to organizational functioning. Some people know things or behave in charismatic ways that others value, regardless of position, and are given influence accordingly. The most expert tax assessor in an Internal Revenue Service office may be consulted by other assessors and listened to even though he/she has no formal assignment to help others. The rewards and punishments available to this kind of influencer are more personal; that is, he/she can give or withhold important information and/or support in return for gratitude and respect.

Leadership in classroom groups is often of the "expert" kind, with the most knowledgeable member(s) of the group gradually becoming respected and listened to even when there is no formal leader. In fact, among many student groups, only a person with recognized expertise can take or be given leadership and then only for particular matters. There is a widespread student norm that no peer should give orders or directions to another student, so that even those students put in leadership roles by a class exercise often hold back from initiating the giving of directions.

> *And these considerations . . . hamstrung LaGuardia in his dealings with* [Robert] *Moses: Moses' popularity; Moses' immense influence with a governor and a legislature from whom the mayor constantly needed favors; Moses' ability to ram through the great public works that the mayor desperately wanted . . . scandal-free and in time for the next election. With good reason, he doubted whether anyone else could. The powers that the mayor possessed over Moses' authorities in theory he did not possess in practice. Political realities gave him no choice but to allow Moses to remain at their head. And the mayor knew it.*
>
> *Moses knew it too. After reading the bond agreements and contracts, LaGuardia dropped all further discussion of the authorities' powers. Moses never raised the matter again. But thereafter he treated LaGuardia not as his superior but as an equal. In the areas in which he was interested—transportation and recreation—Robert Moses, who had never been elected by the people of the city to any office, was thence forward to have at least as much voice in determining the city's future as any official the people* had *elected—including the mayor.*
>
> Source: Robert A. Caro, *The Power Broker* (New York: Alfred A. Knopf, 1974).

Conversely, a fellow student making a "grab for power" will usually be resisted by other students. Sometimes such a person has quickly volunteered for a leadership role before others dare to, and is allowed to take it despite feelings that "it isn't right"; in that case the student has *formal-illegitimate influence,* which may not last long, unless he/she is seen as helping the group reach its goals. Similarly, in organizations where members are accustomed to having considerable say in matters affecting them, the boss's decision to create a new position located between him/her and the others ("because the work load is too heavy for me") can result in resentment toward *whomever* is put in that new job and lead to only grudging cooperation. If that person, however, has the formal authorization to administer some organizational rewards and punishments, he/she may end up with considerable influence anyway.

Finally, *the person who acquires influence over others by personal access to some valued rewards or feared punishments is using informal-illegitimate influence.* Physical threats by a fellow worker can coerce compliance that would otherwise be refused, as can special relationships with higher-ups. In one school system, for example, by maintaining a close relationship with several powerful school board

> *Sir Brian is well aware that the time has come for the Cavendish* [Laboratory] *to rethink its priorities again, but he favours devolving responsibility for this. He is telling the people in his own group to think the priorities out for themselves. A dictator, he says, would cause enormous anger.*
>
> *A dictator is one thing. A strong leader might be welcome in the laboratory. In 1979, Sir Brian handed over to Professor Alan Cook as head of the Cavendish. . . . Left keeping Professor Cook's job warm* [while he's on sabbatical] *is Sir Sam Edwards. . . . Unlike Sir Brian, he thinks the head of the Cavendish still is powerful. He reckons that Cambridge's committee structure puts power into the hands of somebody who really wants to wield it. However, as only acting head of the Cavendish, Sir Sam reckons he cannot take strategic decisions.*
>
> *The lab does have an able manager, Mr. John Deakin, its secretary. . . . He takes on most of the administrative load that normally falls to heads of departments, leaving professors free to get on with teaching and research. It is an excellent arrangement. But there are some decisions only a department head can take.*
>
> Source: *The Economist*, February 27, 1982, p. 83.

members, the music director forced principals to release students for weeklong band trips and to arrange schedules to suit his convenience. He thus obtained more influence over principals than was called for by his position or was seen as his right by them. Though he obtained compliance, he also created considerable resentment and was constantly criticized behind his back by the principals.

Taking Initiative as an Act of Leadership

Have you ever found yourself in a class that was hot and stuffy to the point that you and other students were having trouble concentrating on the lecture or discussion? What do you do? Wait and hope the instructor will recognize the problem and call a break; or raise your hand, point out the difficulty, and suggest opening some windows and taking a break? Raising your hand could be an act of leadership. To wait for the designated leader (instructor) to act can mean missing an opportunity to make it a better class. Taking initiative might have the payoff of enhancing your influence (or status) but also involves the risk of being "shot down" by the formal leader of the class.

In the next chapter we examine the obligations and choices of those who have been formally appointed to managerial positions, that is, who are in a formal role. In this chapter we have been discussing the exercise of influence by anyone and have defined *leadership as influence*. We might also define leadership as those *actions that move a group toward its goals* (such as opening a window when the room is stuffy). The distinction between formal and informal leadership is a useful reminder that as group members and as subordinates anyone can exert influence (leadership)—and often should. In small work groups it is important for all members to take initiative. Similarly, it can be important that a subordinate exert initiative in a staff meeting or a committee meeting and not just wait for all leadership to come from the designated manager or chairperson.

How People Are Influenced

There are three processes (not mutually exclusive) by which people are influenced—*compliance, identification,* and *internalization* (Kelman, 1961). The very same behavior (namely, doing what you are told to do by another person) can stem from any one or a combination of these processes.

Compliance amounts to doing something because of the costs of not doing it. You go along with the "order" on the outside, but inside you may feel resentment or resignation. Any leader's influence can rest on compliance, particularly where there is fear of punishment or a desire to gain some reward; this may be the only way in which an informal-illegitimate leader can exert influence. Where compliance is operating, leaders will be successful only as long as they have control over whatever it is followers need or want.

Identification occurs when you are influenced by someone because of the attractiveness of that person, because the person either is likable and has charisma or represents something to which you aspire (e.g., an important position). Formal, designated leaders or managers often exert influence because subordinates identify with them. They may also be legitimized by their subordinates through the same process.

Identification with a charismatic leader can dramatically affect behavior for people who want to believe in lofty goals that will somehow be ennobling. When such people see a leader as having a grand vision of what is possible and offering specific means for achieving their dreams, they identify with the leader and dedicate themselves to the cause. This can lead to extraordinary efforts by followers on behalf of the leader and thus unusually high organizational performance. That is why effective high-level executives spend so much time creating a vision or "story" about where they see their organization (or unit) going and then telling and retelling it to colleagues, subordinates, and outsiders (Peters, 1978).

Ironically, it has been claimed that charismatic leaders only succeed because they make followers feel weak and dependent. But recent research has demonstrated that some charismatic leaders can make followers feel *more* powerful, *more* confident, and *more* capable, not less (McClelland, 1975). Followers come to see themselves as achieving their *own* goals through the leader, not as having the lead-

> *A statesman who too far outruns the experience of his people will fail in achieving a domestic consensus, however wise his policies.* [On the other hand], *a statesman who limits his policies to the experience of his people is doomed to sterility.*
>
> Henry Kissinger
> *Time*, November 8, 1976

er's goals forced on them. When this happens, influence through identification with the leader can spread to another mode, internalization.

Internalization, the third kind of influence, happens when leaders have the necessary expertise and values to be credible to their followers; they come to believe that what the leader suggests is in fact the best course of action for them. The leader's opinions are seen as valid and trustworthy. The effect is that followers internalize the leader's opinions, thus giving full legitimization to the leader—formally designated or not.

> *. . . the ultimate paradox of social leadership and social power. To be an effective leader, one must turn all of his so-called followers into leaders.*
>
> David C. McClelland
> *Power: The Inner Experience*

Over the long run, the most successful managers are those whose influence is based on credibility—that is, where the followers are convinced by the logic of the leader's ideas and requests, and internalize the influence.

You can see how a combination of these factors can have different effects. Compliance may be necessary under certain conditions (e.g., an emergency or when the task is minor and implementation easily enforced) but is difficult for a manager to sustain. Some people will do what you want strictly out of compliance and some because they identify with you or your position. To maximize your effectiveness as a leader, however, it is best to build credibility and reach people through internalization, so that they will do what is necessary because they want to.

POWER

The capacity to exert influence is power. (Often "power" and "influence" are used interchangeably.) People who have the ability to exert one or more of the four types of influence have power, which can be used toward the organization's ends or toward subgroup or individual goals, including those in direct opposition to organizational goals. As suggested earlier, no one is completely without influence, but some people have more net influence than others and hence more power.

Power is often perceived to be a bit "dirty," at least in the United States, though in the past few years the idea of acquiring power has begun to become more respectable. A few best-selling books on power[1] have helped bring power tactics out of the closet (or at least out of the corporation suite) and made power discussable. But power is more than a set of sneaky tactics for grinding others into the dirt; *power in organizations is the ability to make things happen* (Kanter, 1977). Organizational work cannot be done without that ability, and managers need to understand it in order to bring together the people and resources to accomplish what must be done.

> *Nobody minds being subjected to the power of somebody who's genuinely interested in getting the job out and making more money and exacting maximum performance. But nobody wants to be told that they have to have their pencils sharpened and the erasers all facing in the same direction before they leave the office at night.*
>
> Michael Korda
> "Psychodynamics of Power"
> *Mainliner,* March 1977

Sources of Power in Organizations

How, then, is power obtained by individuals in organizations? In general: **The more legitimate one is perceived to be, the greater the likelihood of acceptance of one's attempts to influence, and the less resentment at going along (Simon, 1957).** Power goes to those who are seen as having a right to it. Conversely, the less legitimate forms of influence breed resistance and resentment, though they will probably enhance the power of someone who already possesses other kinds of legitimate influence.

Additionally, informal influence is often necessary for those with formal influence if they want more than grudging cooperation; when a formally designated leader does not have some knowledge seen as helpful by subordinates, it will be difficult to secure more than token compliance. As organizations become more complex and technically demanding, more people in leadership positions do *not* have the tech-

[1] Examples: *Power: How to Get It and How to Use It,* by Michael Korda; *Winning through Intimidation,* by Robert Ringer; *The Power Broker,* by Robert Caro.

nical expertise necessary to gain influence beyond that of their own job description, making it hard for them to get full cooperation from those who know more than they do about some other aspects of the job. They must then find ways of gaining informal influence through their own personal attractiveness and their ability to make friendly relationships—or they must settle for a low-power position relative to their subordinates.

Perhaps the primary source of power is the ability to enhance the organization positively in relation to its "environment" or key problems (Pfeffer, 1977; Pfeffer & Salancik, 1977). Those who can help the organization achieve its goals by overcoming the most difficult, pressing, and dangerous problems are likely to acquire power. A marketing expert in a company that can sell everything it can make but cannot solve its production problems is less likely to gain power than the production engineer who can eliminate the bottlenecks. So it helps either to acquire skills that are (and will be) critical to the organization or to seek employment where the skills one has are most likely to be needed.

Furthermore, it helps to do things that are not routine, that are unusual or extraordinary in the organization. **A person who performs critical tasks in a way that is already established and routinized will receive less power than a person who develops new methods or procedures, starts a new unit or task, creates a new project or product (Kanter, 1977).** That is why those who are organizationally ambitious do not like to be the second or third person in a job; they would prefer to be the first to do a job, so that they can most easily leave their mark. And in any job they move into, they often seek early changes in something, even office layout or decor, to show that they intend to do things differently.

That suggests a third important aspect of power acquisition: It is not enough to be doing extraordinary, critical activities; one's efforts must be visible and recognized. **Power goes not just to those who do well, but to those who are also *seen* to do well (Kanter, 1977).** (In fact, some cynics claim that appearance is all, though it is hard to sustain power when one does not actually produce.) Those who want power must find ways to achieve recognition. Among other things, it is a political process.

This can happen in many ways. A well-written and well-timed report can help promote visibility, as can a well-presented oral report at a meeting. The opportunity to make a presentation to higher-ups creates a natural chance for "showing one's stuff" and for demonstrating the importance and relevance of the work done. Similarly, serving on committees, often seen as a nuisance, is a chance to show others besides one's boss what one can do. "Doing one's homework" before meetings often helps both to make a good impression and to lead to more responsibility and thus power within the committee. Those who want power look for responsibility, for chances to demonstrate ability to get things done.

REP. BOLLING TAKES HIS LEAVE OF POWER

It took me 32 years to realize that it's sometimes more important to have the trappings of power than power itself. If you've got a good-looking room with a nice chandelier, your colleagues may think you've got power. Actually, all you've got is a chandelier and room. Washington is full of illusions like that.

Source: Dennis Farney. *The Wall Street Journal*, January 1, 1982.

Through committee work or social contacts, power seekers make connections with one or more people higher in the organization. A higher-up who thinks a person shows promise might become a kind of "sponsor" who will look after the aspirant's career, help create opportunities, and build reputation. Also, when people are perceived as "having a friend or friends in high places," then others may defer to them or seek them out even without direct intervention on the powerful person's part.

Since power is a social process of influencing others to act, it comes in part from being able to do things for others that obligate them to be helpful in return by fulfilling the norm of reciprocity (Gouldner, 1960; Kotter, 1979). Thus the person seeking power needs to find ways to be helpful to others in the organization. Volunteering to handle unpleasant tasks, finding ways to make others' jobs easier, and doing favors whenever possible are all ways of creating obligations, which can be collected on when needed. That is exactly how politicians, who have to be interested in power, build it.

Another way of looking at this is in terms of control of key rewards and punishments in the organization. Power reflects the ability to give rewards or punishments in order to get others to do what one believes needs to be done (Kotter, 1979). **The more a person has access to controlling rewards and punishments, the greater his/her power (French & Raven, 1960).** Thus a person who can give the formal rewards or use the formula punishments of an organization—hiring, firing, promoting, adjusting salary, allocating choice assignments or space, giving recommendations, and so forth—*and* give informal rewards or punishments, such as help, information, and liking, will have the most power. Just what the rewards and punishments are depends on the organization and the perceptions of those in it; but whatever it is that people value or fear, those who control it will have power to influence behavior. Attention to what the rewards are to those in the organization, who manages them, and which departments or units currently get them in greatest proportion, can aid in determining how to get control of them. At the very least, power seekers figure out what rewards they already control so that they can more wisely use them to create obligations or induce cooperation when needed. One common accessible reward (even at lower levels of the organization) is finishing, on time, work that someone else needs and is waiting for. That builds gratitude—or, as it is called in some organizations, "chits"—which can be "cashed in" when needed.

LABOR LETTER

Firing Rights are eroded by courts, forcing employers to revise methods.

The long-held right to fire employees "at will" has been limited by state court decisions. As a result, "you can still fire people," says a New York apparel concern executive, but if companies aren't careful, "you can have some very expensive consequences" if employees sue. Corporate personnel manuals "are getting very detailed" as protection against legal action, says Columbia University professor David Lewin.

Source: *The Wall Street Journal*, October 1, 1985.

One interesting aspect of the kind of power that is associated with rewards is the power obtained by helping to relieve people's anxieties (reduce their tensions). "Got a problem? Go see Joe. He'll help you work it out." In fact, when this kind of power is carried to an extreme, unusually high expectations can be imposed on the holder and may even put a strain on that person's ability to retain that power.

Pfeffer (1977) points out the power one obtains by being seen as someone who can reduce uncertainty in an otherwise chaotic situation. Given the nature of organizations today, this source of power is undoubtedly on the increase. Most people have a limited tolerance for uncertainty (or ambiguity); the person who can help to reduce that uncertainty is likely to attract a following. It is not unlike the following of any person who is viewed as "having the answers."

None of the methods described provide for easy access to power; in fact, sheer willingness to work hard is almost always a requisite for acquiring power. As should be clear by now, hard work alone may not be sufficient—it is necessary to work at critical unusual tasks with or for people who recognize what you are doing—but without hard work it is extremely difficult to acquire power. Furthermore, **a desire for power with little genuine concern for the well-being of the organization and for other members can be very destructive to the organization—and even to the power seeker.**

Consequences of Possessing Power

Regardless of the source of power, its possession tends to lead toward certain consequences. These can be stated in the following propositions (Berelson & Steiner, 1964),

1. **The more power attributed to a person, the more he/she is the recipient of:**
   a. **Communication.**
   b. **Solicitous behavior.**
   c. **Deference by others seeking power.**

This proposition suggests that those with power will be deferred to and that when those with less power are in the presence of powerful persons, they will address comments to them more than to one another. Large discrepancies in power between individuals, however, can interfere with successful work. If subordinates do not have sufficient power, they often will not be able to get their work done because they can't get the resources or responses they need. This in turn reduces the leader's power. Furthermore, large power gaps often lead to avoidance of the high-power person by the low-power person and to distorted communications—telling the powerful person what one thinks that person wants to hear. Any powerful person will have to be keenly aware of this problem and work hard to find ways to make less powerful people feel comfortable enough to tell the truth. Without accurate communications (and probably multiple sources), a powerful person will lose touch with actual feelings and is likely to make mistakes.

2. **The more a person is treated as though he/she has power, the greater will be his/her self-esteem.**

"THAT REPORT IS ON MY COFFEE TABLE"

Many of your readers . . . have aspirations of becoming wealthy and powerful. If they succeed, however, I hope their egos will not require offices with private saunas and push-button controls. If one is important and powerful, the right people know it. If not, hand-painted china will not change it.

With the economy in a depression, dividends being omitted, and millions unemployed, it is embarrassing to read about the conspicuous consumption and crystalline egos of America's top executives. What we need is offices that look like offices, not living rooms.

Source: From a letter to the editor of *The Wall Street Journal* by Sam Bosch, January 28, 1982.

Feeling deferred to, powerful people have a tendency to begin to view themselves as important, which enhances how they feel about

WANT OFFICE STATUS? REMOVE ALL PAPERS FROM TOP OF DESK AND THEN REMOVE THE DESK; VERY-TOP BOSSES FAVOR LIVING ROOM ATMOSPHERE

The next time you're in an executive's office, ask yourself the following questions:

- *Is the desk big and imposing with lots of drawers?*
- *Is there an expensive desktop pen-and-pencil set in evidence?*
- *Are important-looking documents stacked about?*

To keen observers of the corporate scene, an affirmative answer to any of those questions has but one indication: Almost as surely as if he wore a short-sleeved shirt and a clip-on bow tie, the occupant of the office can be stamped as lower echelon. At the very top, "Everybody wants an office that doesn't look like an office," explains Rita St. Clair, the president of her own Baltimore, Maryland, design firm—which is to say no one wants unsightly evidence of paperwork or desks that look like desks.

According to Mrs. St. Clair and other cognoscenti of office decor, the offices of today's really powerful executives show few if any signs that any work is performed there. Those at the top, says Mrs. St. Clair, want a "relaxed, living room–library feeling." Says Sydney Kastner, the president of a West Coast design firm: "Today the idea is to be accessible. Executives don't want offices anymore that give the feeling you're entering the Vatican."

Edward E. Elson, the president of a privately owned Atlanta news distribution agency, achieves the "home, sweet home" look with an 18th-century Chinese rug, six club chairs, a pony-skin lounge chair, and no desk at all. Whenever he needs to write, he settles down with a lap pad.

"Visitors are disarmed," Mr. Elson says. "My office gives the impression that there is more to this guy than just business."

Working Fireplaces

Elsewhere the living room–library atmosphere is imparted by a working fireplace. PepsiCo Inc.'s chairman, Donald Kendall, had one installed in his office on the top floor of a three-story building at company headquarters in Purchase, New York. And Sanford Weill, the chairman of Shearson/American Express Inc., had one installed in his office in Manhattan's World Trade Center. (In Mr. Weill's case, the touch of warmth wasn't attained without difficulty and, a company spokesman says, "a considerable amount" of money; the chairman's office is on the 106th floor of a 110-story building, and it was necessary to channel a chimney through four floors to reach the roof.)

This home away from home for the truly powerful is generally set off from the rest of the herd. (If the carpeting that runs through the hallways of the executive floor continues into an office, designers say, it's a dead giveaway that the occupant lacks status; for top people, Oriental rugs are de rigueur.) Often the big boss needn't leave his office even to entertain at lunch. "If it's really high-powered stuff," Mrs. St. Clair says, "you have a dining table set for four or six in your office and have lunch served by your own butler and cook."

And if you're really powerful, you have your own private dining room adjacent to your living room/library. That is a room distinct from the "executive dining room" used by the masses of lesser-titled folk. Guests of publisher Malcolm Forbes, for example, break bread with their host in the executive's personal dining room, where the table setting might include hand-painted Bavarian china and silver-gilt Faberge flatware.

Private Bathroom

Of course, home at the top of the heap isn't complete without a private bathroom—a convenience and a sanctuary that many corporate observers regard as the ultimate power symbol. True, sometimes the symbol is diluted; at Minnesota Mining & Manufacturing Co. in St. Paul, Minnesota, for example, one executive building houses no fewer than 37 private bathrooms. But the truly powerful at some companies go beyond mere bathrooms of the tile-and-porcelain, closet-sized variety; at Johnson Publishing Co. in Chicago, publisher John Johnson's bathroom has marble trimmings, an adjacent dressing area, and even a sauna. . . .

Source: Mary Bralove. Reprinted by permission of *The Wall Street Journal*, © *Dow Jones & Company, Inc., January 15, 1983. All rights reserved.*

themselves. Rosabeth Kanter (1977) points out the change in Gerald Ford's appearance after he—much to his own surprise—became president when Nixon resigned. Ford began to walk taller, speak more confidently, and in general demonstrate that having acquired power, even by default, made him feel better about himself.

Not surprisingly then, people who are powerful tend to seek one another out. Power breeds more power. Thus:

3. **The more power attributed to a person, the more that person will tend to identify with others who also have power.**
4. **Those with high-attributed power are attracted to and communicate more with others with high-attributed power than with those who have low-attributed power.**

Many political leaders have been known to shift their attention and allegiance from their constituencies to their fellow politicians. The same thing can happen in an organization, especially as people climb increasingly higher in the hierarchy. Are you familiar with instances in which an emergent social leader in a group was appointed formal leader by the system, thus enhancing his/her degree of influence? Very often the individual is then seen to "change"; he/she is seen as less friendly to "us mere workers" and as playing up to the powers that be. This frequently happens as people find themselves in new leadership roles, having influence over people in areas never before experienced.

In fact, one of the dangers of superiors having great power differentials over subordinates is that they begin to perceive any successes as due to their own skills and to discount the capacities of the subordinates. Great power differentials lead to overestimates by the powerful of their own contributions and to blindness to the contributions of others (Kipnis, 1976).

By examining these propositions, you can see why it is often said that power corrupts. The entire constellation of behavior and relationships that follow from the possession of influence generates a cycle in which people with high power tend to become more and more differentiated from those with low power, even though each is dependent upon the other. The person with power has it only because it is given by others; it ends the moment those who are doing the giving choose not to do so. A leader is a leader only so long as there are followers. It certainly raises the question of who really possesses the power, the one who leads or those being led.

> *There go my people. I must find out where they are going so I can lead them.*
>
> Anonymous

Another consequence of power for someone new to a position is the likelihood of being closely observed by subordinates as to where the leader's loyalties and priorities will be, how open they can be, how friendly and close the leader will allow them to be, and the like. Such early "testing" is often symbolic: The test is not direct, and the leader's reactions are carefully scrutinized for favorable and unfavorable signs of what is to come. A leader who is unaware that such testing is inevitable can make inadvertant mistakes that are hard to live down.

For example, one of five senior vice presidents of an insurance company was appointed president. Having been there a long time, he had many friends in the company. Two key events made problems for him. First, delighted and rather surprised at being named president, he decided to have a small party at his house to celebrate. Immediately, another senior vice president who had also wanted the job decided that the new president was "rubbing it in" and that the president was no longer going to be as easily influenced as he had been! A few days later, the president met with a group of middle managers. Two of his friends in that group (one a bright young woman whose career he had greatly helped), thinking that now that he was president some problems could at last be straightened out, raised questions about the way the problem was being handled. The president, feeling surprised at the questions and betrayed by his friends, snapped back an answer. Though he did not mean his answer to be more than an instant reaction to what was for him a sensitive issue, others at the meeting spread the word that the new president was going to be "very tough" and could not be disagreed with! The president had not been aware of the symbolic impact of his spontaneous and, to him, harmless reaction.

Consequences of Not Possessing Power

Although too much power can indeed be corrupting, so can too little. Since power is needed to make things happen in organizations—being without it means insufficient resources, information, and support—managers who lack it have difficulty being effective. The manager who does not know what is going on, can't get the needed budget, and is not backed by higher-ups will inevitably be resisted by subordinates. Why should they cooperate with someone who can't deliver?

THE BUREAUCRAT GETS THE LAST WORD

Ed Garvey was scheduled to make a business trip and needed a cash advance. He went to the controller's office to get the necessary signature on a form in order to receive the cash. Mr. Pomeroy, an administrative assistant, was the person whose signature Ed needed. But first Ed had to get past Mrs. Arnold, the secretary and receptionist in the controller's office. The conversation went like this:

Ed: *I'd like to see Mr. Pomeroy for just one minute. I need his signature for a cash advance.*

Mrs. Arnold: *Mr. Pomeroy is very busy, so you'll just have to wait. Please sit over there.*

Ed: *Mrs. Arnold, I really have to get back to my office. Could you ask Mr. Pomeroy if he could take a minute to sign this?*

Mrs. Arnold: *Well, I hate to interrupt him, but I'll see if he can take a moment. (Goes into Pomeroy's office and returns after about two minutes.) He'll see you, but you may have to leave the form here.*

Ed goes into Pomeroy's office and explains that this trip was a last-minute thing and he was under time pressure. The conversation went like this:

Pomeroy: *You know that at least 24 hours is required for approval of a cash advance.*

Ed: *I know, but I don't have 24 hours before I have to leave. I need the cash advance today.*

Pomeroy: *Well, I don't know if I can take it upon myself to sign this. If I break the rules for you I could end up with endless requests like this from others.*

Ed: *Look, this is an exceptional situation. The rules don't cover every situation.*

Pomeroy: *I know, but I do have a job to perform.*

Ed: *Would you get into trouble if you signed it?*

Pomeroy: *No, but I believe in following proper procedure, Mr. Garvey.*

Ed: *I do too, but sometimes other things are more important than rules. Is there someone over you I can go to?*

Pomeroy: *I don't think that will be necessary. I'll make the exception this time, Mr. Garvey, but please try to give me the proper notice in the future.*

Ed: *That's very nice of you, Mr. Pomeroy. Thank you.*

When Ed walked out, he had the signature, but he felt like he bought it with his soul.

As a result, managers who are in positions that yield too little power (or who fill their positions ineptly and lose what power they had) tend to:

1. **Overcontrol subordinates, trying to make them cooperate.**
2. **Become petty tyrants, taking out their frustration on anyone they can dominate.**
3. **Become turf-minded and rules-oriented, carving out a fiefdom where they can reign supreme (Kanter, 1977).**

In this way, powerlessness also corrupts, since managers who become so dominating are seldom effective. Their attempts to find someone on whom to exercise power only increase the resentment of their victims, causing even stronger attempts at domination, more resistance, and so on. Without the proper tools, few managers can be successful.

Liking versus Respect

It is not uncommon for those who have power to be not very well liked; as noted in the group chapters, the group members who contribute most to getting tasks accomplished are usually most respected but seldom most liked. Informal task leaders often have to trade liking for respect; while occasionally someone can get both, most often: **The more a leader strives for popularity, the less effective he/she becomes as task leader. Also, the more the leader strives to maintain task leadership, the more he/she will lose popularity (Slater, 1965).** Can you think of any conditions where these propositions would not be true? How important each factor is in comparison with the other depends upon the nature of the situation and the person involved in the leadership role. When a strong task leader brings a group through a very difficult situation, popularity may soar, at least for awhile.

All leaders have to struggle with the question of how close they can be with their followers. Can a leader also be a friend? If so, does this still allow him/her to push them into working harder? Or, if the leader remains distant, will the followers still feel the loyalty and commitment necessary to put forth sufficient effort?

For some situations and/or people, the task maintenance function must take priority over social maintenance; in other situations and/or for other individuals, the opposite might be true. The important thing to keep in mind is that there is more than one option and that there may be some trade-offs in each.

But *why* does this dilemma occur? Why is it so difficult to mix these functions? For one thing, not many people are really good at both; as a result, the task leader is likely to be someone who has the best skills or abilities related to the task (as it should be), and the social leader is

GUIDE TO MANAGING YOUR BOSS
Or Anyone Else You Don't Control

- Understand your boss and the forces surrounding him/her.
  - Boss's goals and objectives.
  - How boss is rewarded.
  - Pressures on boss:
    - From his/her boss.
    - From the organization.
    - From the environment.
  - Boss's power (capacity to mobilize resources).
  - Boss's strengths, weaknesses, blind spots, and hot buttons.
  - Boss's managerial style—preferred degree of:
    - Control.
    - Information received and shared.
    - Formality.
    - Openness.
- Work to make your boss's life easier.
  - Aid in accomplishing boss's goals.
  - Increase boss's visibility and reputation.
  - Pick up tasks boss doesn't like or isn't good at.
- Tie your requests/preferences to boss's/organization's goals; show how giving you what you want will help achieve the goals.
- Ask boss for evaluation of how you can perform better.
  - If boss is uncomfortable, offer self-appraisal to ease discussion.
- Keep boss informed.
  - With frequency preferred by boss.
  - With level of detail preferred by boss.
  - In form preferred by boss:
    - Oral?
    - Brief reports?
    - Extensive reports?
    - Executive summary?
- Work to demonstrate dependability; keep your word.
- Reward boss whenever he/she manages in way you prefer.
  - Many bosses feel underappreciated.
  - Public praise increases boss's reputation, aiding obtaining of resources.

Source: Based on J. J. Gaberro and J. P. Kotter, "Managing Your Boss," *Harvard Business Review*, January–February 1980; and Allan R. Cohen, "How to Manage Your Boss," *Ms. Magazine*, February 1981.

often the most outgoing person in the group. If that's the case, then other group members tend to become dependent upon the task leader and may even see him/her as superior to the rest of the group. While this may generate respect for that individual, it also tends to breed resentment.

Furthermore, since people are social beings and usually have other interests in addition to interest in working well—or will retreat into socializing when tasks become unpleasant or might lead to conflict—

task leaders occasionally have to refocus attention back to getting the task done. As a result, when the task leader pressures others into working, they may feel grateful for the direction but also may feel resentful, annoyed, and resistant to the task (Zaleznik, 1963). This sequence of events is not inevitable and may be overcome when it leads to group success, but it occurs frequently enough to warrant particular attention. We have also found it to be characteristic of a great many work groups in our classes. Does it apply to your own experience?

There is yet another problem. With a few exceptions, most people have the greatest difficulty being totally honest or giving directions to

THE PENTAGON "CLUB" CLOSED RANKS TO SHUT OUT RESOR

Some defense officials sympathetic to Mr. Resor do feel, however, that he contributed to his own troubles by an unwillingness or inability to deal with the petty intrigues that are, after all, a cornerstone of any self-respecting bureaucracy.

"There was no major conspiracy to undermine Stan; it just happened, and he helped," said one. "You needed someone who could go to these little empires that have been built up and say, 'What are your priorities, what are the major issues, what are you doing?' Stan just waited for people to come to him, and very few did."

A top defense official said in exasperation: "This is a very tough place. There's a lot of power; a lot of money at stake. In comes Stanley Resor—a very decent gentleman, somewhat old-school, not a self-serving type in any way.

"He was entirely wrong for the job."

Source: Bernard Weinraub. *The New York Times,* Sunday, March 18, 1979, © 1977 by The New York Times Company. Reprinted by permission.

NO MORE NICE GUYS—SULLIVAN
Patriots Fire Erhardt

[Linebacker Steve Nelson]: *"Players at the professional level shouldn't need the discipline they get in high school and college . . . in the pros you should be more mature. The coach shouldn't have to scream at you to motivate you. First of all, you're being paid well. And you should play hard for your families. And for your pride. Apparently that wasn't enough for this squad. And now Ron Erhardt is the victim. . . . The thing that endeared Ron to a lot of us, including all the members of my family,"* added [owner] *Sullivan, "is the very thing that may have hurt him as a coach. I think he was just too nice a guy.*

"If you look around at the fellows who are consistently successful . . . they are all tough guys. Tom Landry is one of the great leaders in the Fellowship of Christian Athletes movement, but deep down he is a tough guy mentally. I know he doesn't tolerate anyone who he thinks isn't living by the rules.

"Chuck Noll is like a military leader. Don Shula is the same. So are Bud Grant and Johnny Madden."

Source: Ernie Roberts, *Boston Globe,* December 12, 1981. Reprinted courtesy of the *Boston Globe.*

those to whom they feel closest. When someone else is emotionally close, people feel the risk is great that the relationship will be harmed by saying negative things or giving directions. Thus they find themselves unable to ask much of close friends. A few people, however, find that when they build close, supportive relationships, they can be both demanding and caring—and be cared for and receive demands in return. This kind of openness allows closeness with subordinates without harming productivity, but it requires high skill and mutual commitment and probably only works where both boss and subordinate have roughly equal expertise.

THE USE AND ABUSE OF POWER

In general, it should be apparent by now that leadership can be an exciting opportunity to use power or influence for getting work done; but it can be abused. You have undoubtedly known or heard about people in power primarily to serve their own ends, and usually at the expense of others.

BERRY DEVOTED—TO DETAILS, PLAYERS
Raymond Berry Coached the New England Patriots into the Super Bowl

Here is a man without ambition or ego, following his instincts and insisting on pride, succeeding.

He is soft spoken, yet he is more firm in his discipline than Ron Meyer, the little disciplinarian who coached the Patriots to chaos previous to Berry. ("Meyer insisted on silly rules," says [General Manager, Patrick] *Sullivan, "while Raymond demands more important but fewer rules.") He will tell his players face to face their strengths and weaknesses, and they believe because he was one of the best of players himself.*

. . . "He's a wonderful man, and everybody loves him. . . and he has no ego problem and he'll never have one. He puts the club before himself always." . . . It is the identity of the team that Berry has most changed. Berry has little ego and the Patriots have few heroes; this is a team with Berry's personality.

"He is as tough as anybody you have ever seen," says Khayat, "tough in making decisions, and if he has to drop the hammer [on a discipline problem], *he does. It's family business, it's quiet, nobody knows about it, but he drops a hammer, I'll tell you. Fair, honest, true and through, and people appreciate that."*

During the off-season, Berry went across America to the homes of his players, eating, talking, and sleeping in their environments, "because I wanted to learn about them," says Berry, "and I came away learning from them. I'm a great believer in the individual styles of people, and this way I could learn about their children, their wives, their homes, and their situations. It probably did me more good than them."

Source: Michael Madden, *Boston Globe*, January 10, 1986. Reprinted courtesy of the *Boston Globe*.

David McClelland distinguishes between *personal* power and *socialized* power, the former referring to self-serving uses (or abuses) and the latter to uses that consider the effects (usually benefits) on others.[2] Sometimes it's difficult to make a clear distinction between the two, especially when a leader claims to be acting for the benefit of others yet engages in behavior that reflects anything but the best of motives. The actions of the Bagwan Rajneesh on "behalf" of his followers—who, incidentally, seemed to feel that 90 Rolls Royces were a deserved part of his benefits package—is a good case in point, as is the wealth, including an air-conditioned dog house, accumulated by Jim and Tammy Bakker.

An example closer to home is the manner in which some professors treat their students. Actions that intimidate or harass students represent a gross abuse of a faculty member's power. Whether intended or not, such behavior violates the ethical responsibilities of the role and certainly does little to enhance student learning. Have you ever heard an instructor say things like, "If you can't grasp this concept you probably don't belong in college!"? The intent *might* be to stimulate effort, but usually the effect is demoralizing.

Any act by a person in power that pressures another person to behave in ways that violate that person's sense of personal worth is a form of manipulation. At best, it's insensitive; at worst, it's a form of violence. Today's organizations are paying increasing attention to these kinds of issues, including the specific problem of sexual harassment in the workplace. Laws and policies are being developed, in part because of pressures from the courts, that are designed to protect individuals from sexual harassment in their jobs. What was once looked on as harmless teasing has come to be recognized as a humiliating abuse of power. Such behavior is now being seen as unacceptable and unprofessional as well as illegal. How long it will take to educate organizational leaders and managers, university professors, and the general public to understand such abuses and take action to prevent them remains to be seen. However, it is important for *you*—as a future manager and as someone who will possess power—to appreciate the ethical burdens of your job and the kinds of actions you might be required to take in living up to those ethics.

KEY CONCEPTS FROM CHAPTER 11

1. Leadership is mostly situational rather than determined by personality traits.
2. Leadership is an influence process with subordinates, peers, and colleagues. Even subordinates are not totally without influence; thus leadership is net influence.

[2] David C. McClelland, *Power: The Inner Experience* (New York: Irvington, 1975).

3. Influence is an act or potential act that affects the behavior of another person(s). Types of influence:
   a. Formal: prescribed by office or position.
   b. Informal: based on expertise or charisma.
   c. Legitimate: influencer seen by influenced as having the right to do so.
   d. Illegitimate: influencer seen by influenced as not having the right to do so.
   e. Types *a* and *b* can each combine with *c* or *d* when examining influence.
4. People can be influenced through:
   a. Compliance: fear of influencer.
   b. Identification: attraction to influencer.
   c. Internalization: belief in influencer's beliefs.
5. Power is the capacity to exert influence, to make things happen.
6. Power is based on:
   a. Greater legitimacy.
   b. Ability to enhance organization in relation to key problems.
   c. Doing new activities rather than routine.
   d. Visibility, recognition.
   e. Creating obligations through helpful acts.
   f. Controlling rewards and punishments.
   g. Reducing uncertainty.
7. The greater one's power, the more one receives:
   a. Communication.
   b. Solicitous behavior.
   c. Deference.
   d. Self-esteem.
   e. Close observation in new situations.
8. Powerlessness often leads to:
   a. Overcontrol.
   b. Petty tyranny.
   c. Rule orientation and turf-mindedness.
9. It is difficult for those with power to gain both respect and liking.
   a. Task orientation often breeds resentment.
   b. Closeness to followers may constrain task orientation.
10. The use and abuse of power.

SUGGESTED READINGS

Agor, W. H. "The Logic of Intuition: How Top Executives Make Important Decisions." *Organizational Dynamics,* Winter 1986, pp. 5–18.

Bass, B. M. "Leadership: Good, Better, Best." *Organizational Dynamics,* Winter 1985, pp. 26–40.

Berelson, B., and G. Steiner. *Human Behavior: An Inventory of Scientific Findings.* New York: Harcourt Brace Jovanovich, 1964.

Beyer, J. M. "Ideologies, Values, and Decision Making in Organizations." In *Handbook of Organizational Design,* vol. 2, ed. P. Nystrom and W. Starbuck. New York: Oxford University Press, 1981, pp. 166–97.

Caro, R. *The Power Broker.* New York: Alfred A. Knopf, 1974.

Cobb, A. T. "An Episodic Model of Power: Toward an Integration of Theory and Research." *Academy of Management Review,* July 1984, pp. 482–93.

Deaux, K. "Authority, Gender, Power, and Tokenism." *Journal of Applied Behavioral Science,* January–February–March 1978, pp. 22–26.

Dobbins, G. H., and S. J. Platz. "Sex Differences in Leadership: How Real Are They?" *Academy of Management Review,* January 1986, pp. 118–27.

French, J. R. P., Jr., and B. Raven. "The Bases of Social Power." In *Group Dynamics: Research and Theory,* ed. D. Cartwright and Z. Zander. New York: Harper & Row, 1960, pp. 607–23.

Gabarro, J. J., and J. P. Kotter. "Managing Your Boss." *Harvard Business Review,* January–February 1980, pp. 97–100.

Gouldner, A. "The Norm of Reciprocity: A Preliminary Statement." *American Sociological Review,* April 1960, pp. 161–78.

Heller, T. "Changing Authority Patterns: A Cultural Perspective." *Academy of Management Review,* July 1985, pp. 488–95.

Howell, J. P., and P. W. Dorfman. "Leadership and Substitutes for Leadership among Professional and Nonprofessional Workers." *Journal of Applied Behavioral Science* 22, no. 1 (1986), pp. 29–46.

Jay, A. *Management and Machiavelli.* New York: Holt, Rinehart & Winston, 1967.

Kanter, R. M. *Men and Women of the Corporation.* New York: Basic Books, 1977.

Kelman, H. C. "Processes of Opinion Change." *Public Opinion Quarterly,* Spring 1961, pp. 57–78.

King, D., and B. Bass. *Leadership, Power, and Influence.* Lafayette, Ind.: Herman C. Krannert Graduate School of Industrial Administration, Purdue University, 1970.

Kipnis, D. *The Powerholders.* Chicago: University of Chicago Press, 1976.

Korda, M. *Power: How to Get It and How to Use It.* New York: Simon & Schuster, 1977.

Kotter, J. P. *Power in Management.* New York: AMACOM, 1979.

________. *The General Managers.* New York: Free Press, 1982.

________. *Power and Influence.* New York: Free Press, 1985.

McClelland, D. C. *Power: The Inner Experience.* New York: Irvington, 1975.

McGregor, D. *The Human Side of Enterprise.* New York: McGraw-Hill, 1960.

________. *Leadership and Motivation.* Cambridge, Mass.: MIT Press, 1966.

________. *The Professional Manager.* New York: McGraw-Hill, 1967.

Peters, T. J. *"Symbols, Patterns, and Settings: An Optimistic Case for Getting Things Done." Organizational Dynamics,* Autumn 1978.

Pfeffer, J. "Power and Resource Allocation in Organizations." In *Psychological Foundations of Organizational Behavior,* ed. B. Staw. Santa Monica, Calif.: Goodyear Publishing, 1977.

________. *Power in Organizations.* Marshfield, Mass.: Pitman Publishing, 1981.

Pfeffer, J., and G. Salancik. "Who Gets Power and How They Hold on to It." *Organizational Dynamics,* Winter 1977.

Ringer, R. *Winning through Intimidation.* Los Angeles: Los Angeles Publishing, 1974.

Rosenbach, W. E., and R. L. Taylor, ed. *Contemporary Issues in Leadership.* Boulder: Westview, 1984.

Sayles, L. *Leadership: What Effective Managers Do and How They Do It.* New York: McGraw-Hill, 1979.

Schlesinger, L. A., and B. Oshry. "Quality of Work Life and the Manager: Muddle in the Middle." *Organizational Dynamics,* Summer 1984, pp. 4–19.

Simon, H. A. *Administrative Behavior.* New York: Free Press, 1957.

Slater, P. E. "Role Differentiation in Small Groups." *American Sociological Review* 20, 1965.

Stogdill, R. M. *Handbook of Leadership.* New York: Macmillan/Free Press, 1974.

Trevino, L. K. "Ethical Decision Making in Organizations: A Person-Situation Interactionist Model." *Academy of Management Review,* July 1986, pp. 601–17.

Zaleznik, A. "The Human Dilemmas of Leadership." *Harvard Business Review,* July–August 1963.

▸ ▸ ▸ 12

LEADERSHIP

Managerial Functions and Styles

The greater the differential knowledge of the leader, the more appropriate will be unilateral control.

MANAGERS AS FORMAL LEGITIMATE LEADERS: MANAGERIAL CHOICES

We looked in Chapter 11 at the ways in which power and influence can be used to get organizational work accomplished, regardless of organizational position. But the kinds of problems discussed there are especially applicable to those who have been assigned a managerial role with formal-legitimate influence.

While formally appointed managers, like peers who have acquired influence, need to balance relationships with work, they have a more complex set of choices that arise from holding a position organizationally defined as "above" the group. The responsibility and authority that goes with the position imposes its own set of considerations: What functions should the manager perform, with whom, and when; what style of leadership should be used; how are such decisions affected by the tasks to be accomplished, the manager's relative power and expertise, and the needs of subordinates? This chapter will address these crucial questions. Figure 12–1 shows the sequential relationship among the chapter's variables.

Managerial Functions

We begin by reviewing the set of functions that every manager must perform, which we introduced in Chapter 1. Here we will look more closely into these functions.

The manager's functions fall into three related groupings. One group, *interpersonal,* involves building and maintaining contacts and relationships with a variety of people located both inside and outside his/her organizational unit. A second group, *informational,* involves gathering and disseminating information inside the unit and to and from the external environment. The third group, *decision making,* involves making a range of decisions pertaining to internal operating practices and to exchanges with other units of the organization as well as the outside world.[1] (See Figure 12–2.)

[1] The managerial functions described here are an adaptation of managerial roles described by Henry Mintzberg, *The Nature of Managerial Work* (New York: Harper & Row, 1973).

FIGURE 12–1
Illustration of Managerial Choices Discussed in This Chapter

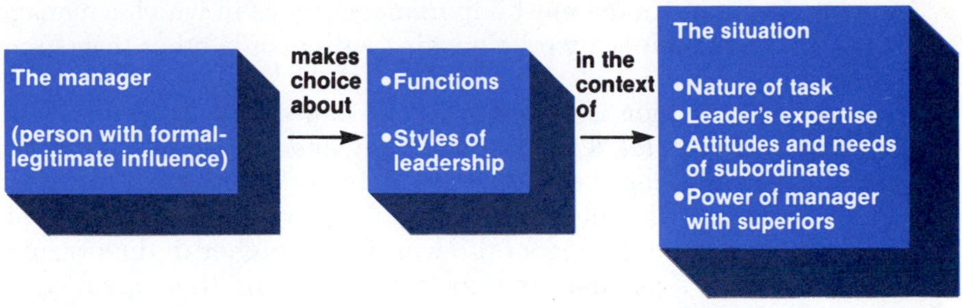

As may be evident from the above, these groupings are interrelated; in accomplishing one function, the manager often will make progress on another. For example, while building a relationship with the manager of another unit of the organization, the manager typically will be gathering and sharing information. Furthermore, the information a manager gains while carrying out an informational function may be crucial to his/her capability in carrying out the decision-making functions effectively. Let us now consider these interrelated functions in greater detail.

THE INTERPERSONAL FUNCTIONS. The manager relates to people both within and outside of his/her own subsystem. Students of leadership often

FIGURE 12–2
The Interrelationships among Managerial Functions

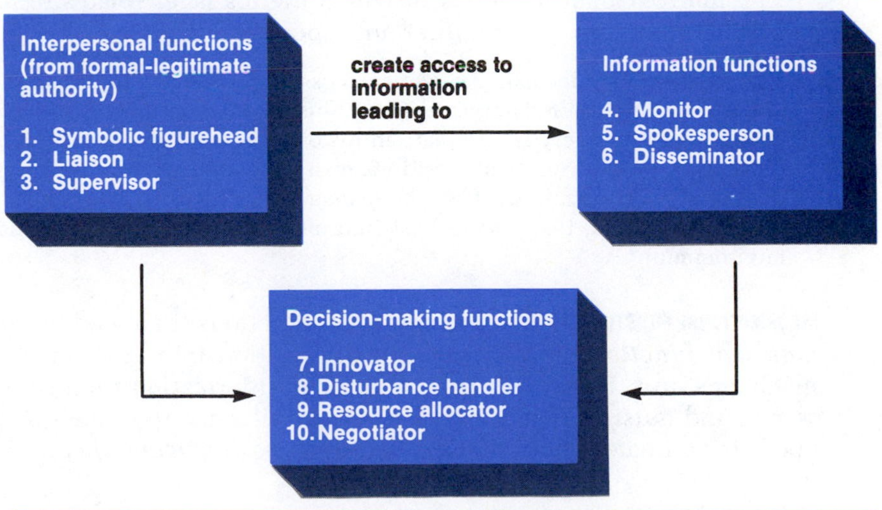

concentrate on the internal relationships of managers and think of their relationships with "outsiders" as nonessential or peripheral to the job. But some of the most important activities in which a manager engages involve building relationships with people other than subordinates.

One such function is that of *symbolic figurehead. It entails carrying out certain social, legal, inspirational, and ceremonial duties that simply go with being the head of an organizational system.* The manager's function is largely representational, serving to symbolize his/her organization to the rest of the world. The higher in the organization a manager's position, the greater will be the time spent in the symbolic figurehead function.

Closely related to this function is that of *liaison.* In carrying out the liaison function, the manager *gives and receives information and favors in order to learn what is going on elsewhere that can be useful within the unit.* Making contacts with people and then maintaining them are important activities, time-consuming but necessary if the manager is to stay informed on organizational politics, on new opportunities, on changes in demand for the organization's outputs, and so forth. Furthermore, the contacts make it possible to exchange other favors when necessary, facilitating internal operations.

The remaining interpersonal function is that of *supervisor,* a function one readily associates with managing. *It entails hiring, training, motivating, evaluating, and rewarding subordinates.* In carrying out this function the manager tries to find a way to blend individual needs and concerns with the organization's goals, so that the subordinates remain committed to doing what is necessary to meet the system's objectives.

The interpersonal functions in which the manager relates to relevant others serve to give him/her an important advantage:

> Through [them] the manager gains access to privileged information, and he emerges as the "nerve center" of his organization. He alone has formal access to every subordinate in his own organization, and he has unique access to a variety of outsiders, many of whom are nerve centers of their own organizations. Thus the manager is his organization's information generalist, that person best informed about its operations and environment.[2]

INFORMATIONAL FUNCTIONS. The interpersonal functions then lead to *informational functions,* which channel information into and out of the manager's unit. By serving as a *monitor* of information from sources within and outside of the unit, the manager keeps up to date on the operating climate. The activities include *designing ways of collecting*

[2] Mintzberg, *The Nature of Managerial Work.*

MORE CORPORATE CHIEFS SEEK DIRECT CONTACT WITH STAFF, CUSTOMERS

A small but growing number of corporate chiefs . . . are determined to know firsthand exactly what is happening at their companies and . . . are willing to go out of their way to find out. As a result, they are breaking with management practices in vogue since the 1950s that emphasized an aloof, rigid financial analysis rather than direct contact. . . .

"The number one managerial productivity problem in America is, quite simply, managers who are out of touch with their people and customers," asserts Thomas J. Peters, a management consultant and coauthor of In Search of Excellence. *"The alternative doesn't come from computer printouts," he says. "It comes from wandering around, directly sampling employees' environments."*

Source: Thomas F. O'Boyle. Reprinted by permission of *The Wall Street Journal,*

information (formally and informally), reading reports, questioning contacts and subordinates, observing others' activities, and so forth.

In turn, the manager has the function of *disseminator,* passing relevant information on to subordinates. Since the manager will often be the only one in a unit with access to some information, this job is important and requires good judgment in terms of what information to pass along and to whom. It requires such activities as *telling, announcing, memo writing, and telephoning.*

In addition to the internal dissemination function, there is an important *spokesman* function, which entails transmitting information outside the unit. This includes *informing, liaison contacts with others who influence the unit, lobbying, announcing, and so forth.*

[Theodore Brophy, chairman and CEO of GTE] *says he will resist any inclination to bark orders about GTE's overall strategy. "In a time as complex as the one we're living in . . . I surely don't have all the answers or all the information. I've got a lot of very talented people working here with me. Not to take advantage of that talent at this particular time would be the grossest of oversights."*

Source: Bernard Wysocki, Jr. "Executive Style: The Chief's Personality Can Have a Big Impact—For Better or Worse." *The Wall Street Journal,* September 11, 1984.

DECISION-MAKING FUNCTIONS. As a consequence of formal position and access to information, the manager performs several functions that involve making strategic decisions for the unit.

The *innovator* function calls for initiating and designing changes in the way the unit operates. In carrying out this task, the manager *diagnoses trends, envisions possibilities, plans improvements, invents programs and other solutions,* and in general *promotes innovation.*

A related decision-making function is that of *disturbance handler.* Here the manager takes charge and makes decisions when nonroutine disturbances or interpersonal conflicts call for responses that individual subordinates cannot devise. The manager functions as the generalist problem solver, putting out fires as they arise either as a result of subordinates' inability to anticipate and handle difficulties or as a consequence of innovations. **The lower the level of a manager in the organizational hierarchy, the greater will be the time spent on disturbance handling and other decision-making functions.** The need at lower levels of an organization is for maintaining the daily work flow, so these functions are predominant there.

Another decision-making function is that of *resource allocator.* The manager parcels out his/her unit's resources through a series of decisions on how members will spend time, materials, and funds as well as how they can utilize formal-legitimate influence. Resource allocation involves *deciding among proposals, controlling subordinate latitude, setting priorities, authorizing expenditures, and so forth.*

Finally, the manager serves as *negotiator* for important decisions involving other people inside and outside the organization. Negotiating involves *bargaining, trading, compromising, collaborating, avoiding, and other similar activities.*

Typically, the negotiating function builds upon several of the other managerial functions. In representing the unit, the manager serves as *symbolic figurehead* and *spokesman,* summarizing the organization's views. The negotiation will result in *resource allocation,* as something is given up or obtained from outside.

In brief, the 10 functions comprise the job of the formal-legitimate officeholder:

> The manager must design the work of his organization, monitor its internal and external environment, initiate change when desirable, and renew stability when faced with a disturbance. The manager must lead his subordinates to work effectively for the organization, and he must provide them with special information, some of which he gains through the network of contacts that he develops. In addition, the manager must perform a number of "housekeeping" duties, including informing outsiders, serving as figurehead, and leading major negotiations.[3]

Some of the 10 managerial functions differ on the basis of whether this focus is internal or external, as shown in Figure 12–3. This serves to emphasize the point that a manager "stands between his organizational unit and its environment,"[4] and his functions include looking outward to what is happening in other parts of the total organization and the environment as well as downward at what subordinates do.

[3] Ibid.
[4] Ibid.

FIGURE 12–3
Focus of Managerial Functions Relative to the System

	Internal	External
Interpersonal:		
1. Symbolic figurehead	X	X
2. Liaison		X
3. Supervisor	X	
Informational:		
4. Monitor	X	X
5. Disseminator	X	
6. Spokesperson		X
Decision-making:		
7. Innovator	X	X
8. Disturbance handler	X	X
9. Resource allocator	X	
10. Negotiator		X

While each of these functions is important, it is not always imperative that only the manager carry them out. Within an organization there may be individuals who can do some of the particular functions more effectively than the manager in charge. Subordinates can take responsibility in these areas as well as managers give it. If, for example, a manager is not very effective at public speaking when carrying out the spokesperson function, he/she may want to delegate some of the necessary activities to a good speaker on the staff. Similarly, it may be appropriate for a staff member to initiate delegation by offering his/her services and not merely waiting for the manager to give it.

Those activities, however, that require special current information to perform well may not be easily delegated unless others have high access to such special information. Nevertheless, most managers will be flooded with demands for their time and attention and must choose carefully which roles and functions to emphasize. There will seldom be enough time to stay in contact with all information sources, inspire and direct all subordinates, cope with all disturbances and needs for innovation, and so forth. The choice will constantly have to be made between another 15 minutes working on a problem in the office, a quick stroll through the plant to get a feel for morale, or an early arrival at a meeting with other executives in order to pick up some scraps of information about an upcoming crisis. The way in which the manager chooses to spend time determines his/her relative emphasis on the 10 roles, all of which are necessary and demanding. Success as a manager depends in part on the ability to choose correctly among roles and on the capacity to perform each of the roles well when necessary.

We have been looking at the nature of leadership as an influence process and at the various roles and functions a manager must fill. We turn now to a look at *how* a manager should do his job and under what conditions particular functions and styles are appropriate.

> *I had become the victim of an amorphous, unintentional conspiracy to prevent me from doing anything whatever to change the university's status quo. Even those of my associates who fully shared my goals were unconsciously doing the most to ensure that I would never find the time to begin. People play the old army game. They do not want to take responsibility for or bear the consequences of decisions that they should properly make.*
>
> Warren Bennis, former president, University of Cincinnati
> "Leadership: A Beleaguered Species"
> *Organizational Dynamics*

HOW LEADERSHIP IS EXERCISED; ALTERNATIVE STYLES

Situational Leadership

There are many ways to categorize leadership styles. One familiar classification distinguishes among autocratic, democratic, and laissez-faire approaches; another contrasts directive, supportive, participative, and achievement styles; yet another might compare "strictly business" with human relations approaches; the traditional paternalistic or charismatic has been contrasted with the routinized bureaucratic and the more fluid "organic-adaptive," and so on. Different writers have different schemes with differing labels for and theories about the effectiveness of each style. Since each of the schemes offers interesting shadings of description, there are overlaps among them; and since most leaders seldom use the same style in all situations, we have developed a way of describing leadership style without using any one set of labels. We believe that this allows greater flexibility in talking about style and greater accuracy in identifying its component parts. What we have chosen to do is spell out several underlying dimensions along which leaders can differ in carrying out their functions. Each leadership style is composed of a combination of positions along each of these dimensions. The particular labels for styles are less important than an understanding of the choices leaders can make in how they perform their roles.

As in the chapters on interpersonal relations, we assume that each person is likely to have a *preferred* leadership style, which he/she will opt for whenever possible, but that this should be tempered by what is *appropriate* to the organizational situation. We will be as explicit as possible about which leadership behavior is called for under which circumstances, though the possibilities are complex.

There are five dimensions we will use to describe how a leader might carry out his/her leadership functions.

1. Retaining control versus sharing control.
2. High task-concern versus low task-concern.
3. High person-concern versus low person-concern.
4. Explicit versus implicit expectations (degree of structure provided).
5. Cautious versus venturous.

Retaining versus Sharing Control

One of the most central dimensions of leadership style involves the degree of control exerted over the behavior of others. Control pervades organizational life. It can operate overtly or subtly; a manager can appear to be sharing control but actually retain it, as when opinions are asked but not accepted unless they fit a predetermined decision. Conversely, it can appear to be retained but actually shared, as when the manager insists on the final decision but gives great freedom to subordinates in choosing methods of analysis or implementation. You can ask some of the following questions in trying to analyze degree of control.

How much latitude is given to others to make their own decisions, to vary from standard procedures, rules, and regulations? How much discretion do they have before they have to consult with or get a decision from their manager? How many people are included and from what ranks? Does the manager use group meetings or one-to-one relationships? How much information is shared with them? How free are they to question advice or orders or to initiate ideas? Is work delegated to others or carried out by the manager? What kind of work is delegated, important or routine? How closely are they supervised; are they constantly watched, or is their performance only checked periodically? In short, are they encouraged to try to influence the way work is done? For any particular problem, the amount of control retained by the manager can vary considerably—from decisions made autonomously by the manager, to those where subordinates are consulted, to those made jointly *with* subordinates, and, finally, to those delegated completely to subordinates. Figure 12–4 shows the choices a manager can make about how much influence to share with subordinates.

> *According to underworld informants, one of the reasons that Carlo Gambino, who died a week ago Friday, was so effective as a Mafia leader, forging the biggest and richest crime family in the country, was that he shared decision making with others, a trusted group of his captains known in the family as "the administration," rather than ruling arbitrarily.*
>
> Source: Nicholas Gage. *New York Times*, October 24, 1976, © 1976 by The New York Times Company. Reprinted by permission.

FIGURE 12–4
Managerial Choices of How Much Influence to Share with Subordinates for Each Problem

Group Problems

1. You solve the problem or make the decision yourself, using information available to you at the time.
2. You obtain the necessary information from your subordinates, then decide the solution to the problem yourself. You may or may not tell your subordinates what the problem is, in getting the information from them. The role played by your subordinates in making the decision is clearly one of providing the necessary information to you, rather than generating or evaluating alternative solutions.
3. You share the problem with the relevant subordinates individually, getting their ideas and suggestions without bringing them together as a group. Then *you* make the decision, which may or may not reflect your subordinates' influence.
4. You share the problem with your subordinates as a group, obtaining their collective ideas and suggestions. Then you make the decision, which may or may not reflect your subordinates' influence.
5. You share the problem with your subordinates as a group. Together you generate and evaluate alternatives and attempt to reach agreement (consensus) on a solution. Your role is much like that of chairman. You do not try to influence the group to adopt "your" solution, and you are willing to accept and implement any solution that has the support of the entire group.

Individual Problems

1. You solve the problem or make the decision by yourself, using information available to you at the time.
2. You obtain the necessary information from your subordinate, then decide on the solution to the problem yourself. You may or may not tell the subordinate what the problem is, in getting the information from him. His role in making the decision is clearly one of providing the necessary information to you, rather than generating or evaluating alternative solutions.
3. You share the problem with your subordinate, getting his ideas and suggestions. Then you make a decision, which may or may not reflect his influence.
4. You share the problem with your subordinate, and together you analyze the problem and arrive at a mutually agreeable solution.
5. You delegate the problem to your subordinate, providing him with any relevant information that you possess, but giving him responsibility for solving the problem by himself. You may or may not request him to tell you what solution he has reached.

Adapted from V. Vroom and P. Yetton, *Leadership and Decision Making* (Pittsburgh: University of Pittsburgh Press, 1973).

High Task-Concern versus Low Task-Concern

While getting the work done is the essence of any leader's role, more or less attention can be paid to quantity of output, quality of work done, meeting deadlines, meeting output, expectations of other subsystems, or improving performance in general at any particular time. Managers can vary from constant preoccupation with output to negligible concern over it.

POINTS FOR EFFECTIVE DELEGATION

- Delegation is not abdication; you must manage it.
- Be clear about the assignment; check whether it is understood.
- Be clear about what results you expect, standards of performance.
- Be clear about known boundaries:
  How much authority is granted, over what issues.
  Budget allowed, if any.
  Territories to stay out of, political sensitivities.
- Establish mutually agreed checkpoints—frequency of contact, dates, indicators.
- Agree on how much and what kind of information you want.
- Agree about how much help you will give.

A manager can put production ahead of all other considerations—the feelings and safety of subordinates, their learning and development, the maintenance of equipment, and the reactions of customers or other members of the organization. At the other extreme, a manager can be relatively indifferent to task accomplishment, either out of negligence, oversecurity, or a belief in allowing subordinates to learn for themselves from their own mistakes. Some managers try to wring every last drop of production from employees, while others do not stress production unless it falls below acceptable minimum levels.

Focus on task is often contrasted with focus on the morale and welfare of people doing the task, though they need not be contradictory. For example, the supervisor of the credit department in a bank had to see to it that at least one employee stayed late each Friday to complete certain forms. At first he made a list on which he arbitrarily rotated the assignment. When the employees complained, he adopted a method that gave them more say over the decision and led to a more satisfactory solution that both provided coverage and allowed employee choice. It is often possible, therefore, to maintain a high level of task-concern without necessarily sacrificing the involvement and feelings of those affected.

High Concern for People versus Low Concern for People

As with concern for the task, the degree of a manager's concern for people may vary at any time.

What is the manager's consideration for others? How much attention does the leader pay to the personal feelings and attitudes of others? Do subordinates' preferences get considered when assigning work? Does the manager provide a warm, supportive working climate or an impersonal one? Are nontask-related concerns of others noted,

> *"Nice guys" in high corporate positions get the best results from subordinates.*
>
> *That's one conclusion from a study of 16,000 executives by Teleometrics International. The firm identified 13 percent of those surveyed as "high achievers"* [who] *tended to care about people as well as about profits. But the average achievers concentrated on production, while low achievers were obsessed with their own security.*
>
> *. . .* [L]*ow achievers displayed a basic distrust of subordinates' abilities; high achievers viewed them optimistically. High achievers sought advice from underlings; low achievers didn't. High achievers were listeners; moderate achievers listened only to superiors; and low achievers avoided communications, relying on policy manuals.*
>
> Source: *The Wall Street Journal,* August 22, 1978.

responded to, or sympathized with? How open is the leader about his/her human concerns, feelings, and so on? How close are others allowed to get? How much are others treated as people instead of as objects of production? Some managers focus all their attention on the effects of actions on the morale of those in their units, while others ignore it completely; clearly there are many options in between these extremes.

Explicit versus Implicit Expectations (Degree of Structure Provided)

How clear is the leader about what is expected of each individual? Are detailed methods of working spelled out? Are desired results made clear? Are rewards clearly related to job performance, generally related, or not apparently related? Do rewards relate to short-term or long-term performance, and is there agreement in advance on the criteria? How frequently and directly is feedback given to subordinates? Is the basis for feedback known in advance? How specified are the rules for advancement?

Leaders can be explicit about their expectations by using formal organizational procedures and rules or by personal communications with subordinates. The method chosen may make a difference to subordinates; some may prefer predetermined rules, regulations, and procedures, so that they can master them in advance or refer to the written word when they have questions. Others may prefer spontaneous case-by-case discussion of expectations, so that they can react to those expectations on the spot in a give-and-take discussion. Although formal procedures are usually intended to cover as many contingencies as possible, obviously no preestablished system can, in fact, anticipate them all.

A newly commissioned officer was assigned to a naval base. During his first week he heard constant complaints—about the authoritarian leadership style of the commanding officer, the facilities, the food, and the rules on the base. He spoke to the commanding officer about the low morale. The next day an order was circulated by the CO: "I understand morale here is low. I will not tolerate this. Effectively immediately, I order morale to improve."

An interesting paradox surrounding the issue of explicit versus implicit expectations lies in the fact that a leader can actually *enhance* some of his/her power by deliberately keeping things vague. The tension thus generated in subordinates becomes a leverage for control, since the leader can *choose* to relieve (or not) the tension at his/her own discretion. This is a very powerful technique (not without some possible serious costs) that some managers use. It also has the added "benefit" of giving the leader a way out of mistakes made by subordinates. "*I* never told you to do it that way! I can't help what you inferred!" Have you ever been on the receiving end of that kind of statement? It can be very powerful and frustrating, while it deteriorates the ultimate relationship.

Cautious versus Venturous

How venturesome are the leader's actions and decisions? How much risk is involved in decisions; how willing is the leader to make decisions that involve high risk? How often does the manager go beyond preexisting arrangements? How visible is the leader willing to be to other parts of the organization and its environments? In other words, how bold is the leader? As you will see, the degree of boldness demanded of a leader varies from one situation to another.

Can you use these five dimensions to think about leadership in your classroom task group, in jobs you hold, or in organizations to which you belong? What kinds of choices have you made along these dimensions when you had leadership responsibilities? Do you tend toward one "style," that is, a repeated cluster of similar choices? If your usual style has been "authoritarian," for example, you might have kept tight control over subordinates, been highly concerned with tasks, shown low people-concern, kept rules vague, and taken high risks in your decisions.

Whatever your usual style, were there occasions when you chose to lead in a quite different way because the situation seemed to call for it? And, most important, have you noticed any differential results of particular choices you or others have made on these dimensions? Has any one style seemed to work better than another? Did something work in one situation but not another? For example, when should a manager make a quick unilateral decision, and when should everyone be involved? We will deal with these latter kinds of questions next.

For example, how does the general manager of a drug company decide how to get his production, purchasing, and sales managers to cooperate in reducing inventories during a recession? Should he worry about their feelings, involve them in proposing solutions, develop some clear guidelines for them to cut inventories? Or how does the administrator of a hospital get the radiology department to cut down patient waiting-time for X rays? When patients sit waiting in the hallways for three hours while a technically interesting case is studied, how does the administrator deal with the stubborn but powerful chief radiologist? Can the administrator give a direct order to speed up? Can he offend the chief? What should he take into account in deciding? In order to deal with the endless series of dilemmas like these, it is necessary for a leader or manager to consider a number of situational factors.

CONTINGENCIES: FACTORS INVOLVED IN DETERMINING APPROPRIATE LEADERSHIP CHOICES

While it is probably easier to analyze what makes particular leadership styles effective than it is to actually *be* a good leader, there are a bewildering array of factors to keep in mind. We will isolate a number of situational aspects that should be taken into account in making appropriate leadership choices, but it is not possible to account for every contingency. Some of the important factors follow.

Nature of the Task Situation

Some jobs are very stable and predictable. Their processes are not subject to rapid technological change, the need for their output is established and constant, and rapid decisions are not necessary. All elements necessary for good performance are known and well defined. Each job is discrete and essentially repetitive. Under these conditions, it is not especially effective to give great autonomy to subordinates. **The more predictable the nature of the task situation, the more appropriate will be tight control, explicit expectations, formal standardized procedures, and cautiousness as leadership choices.** The converse is true for work that is less predictable in nature (Fiedler, 1967; and for an opposing view, House, 1971). **The less predictable the nature of the task situations, the more appropriate will be**

shared control, less explicit expectations, informal procedures, and risk-taking (Morse & Lorsch, 1970; Hersey & Blanchard, 1977).

Work that is inherently stressful or frustrating because of its difficulty calls for more consideration. **Under conditions of stressful work, high person-concern by the leader results in greater satisfaction (House, 1971).** Paying attention to needs of individuals may be done by providing greater structure or greater freedom; either can be a response to the person's needs.

> *Everyone will now be mobilized . . . and all boys old enough to carry a spear will be sent to Addis Ababa. Married men will take their wives to carry food and cook. Those without wives will take any woman without a husband. Women with small babies need not go. Those blind, those who cannot walk or for any reason cannot carry a spear are exempted. Anyone found at home after receipt of this order will be hanged.*
>
> Haile Selassie I
> Emperor of Ethiopia
> Upon invasion by Italy, 1935

Expertise of the Leader (as Compared to the Competence of the Subordinates)

A factor often related to the rate of change in the nature of the job is the amount of expert knowledge of the work possessed by the formal leader. When the leader clearly knows a great deal more about the work than any other members of the unit, whether through technical expertise or knowledge of the organization and its environment and their demands, it is costly to spend a lot of time asking for opinions, improvising methods, and sharing control. **The greater the differential knowledge of the leader, the more appropriate will be unilateral control (Fiedler, 1967).**

For example, small businessmen or leaders active in the entrepreneurial role often are so invested in what they are doing (emotionally even more than financially) and so immersed in their vision of what is possible that they literally can do any job in the organization better than anyone else. In those situations high task-concern and low sharing of influence is probably appropriate, if not inevitable.

Not only is unilateral control more effective when the boss knows more, but failure to exercise it can lead to employee frustration. People hate to be asked their opinion when the person asking already knows the answer, especially if the opinion is less expert and cannot change the asker's conclusions. A leader may occasionally wish to give an assignment to someone less skilled in order to help develop that person, but in that case the object is growth, not necessarily the best product. In general, a good rule of thumb is, "if you know the answer and what you plan to do, do not ask a subordinate's opinion." If you ask, you risk creating feelings of being manipulated, which decreases trust and, in turn, accuracy of communications upward. This does not rule out the potential value of allowing subordinates to ask questions in order to understand what is intended or to express their concerns about your planned action. Such airing of concerns can allay their doubts and build their belief in your decision in ways that will facilitate its implementation.

On the other hand, sharing control and soliciting opinions is appropriate for situations where the workers have knowledge equal to or greater than the leader, as is often the case for jobs requiring high technical input. In an information-oriented service economy, as is increasingly the case in the United States, there are more and more situations where each subordinate knows something that the boss does not. The director of a research lab, for example, may supervise Ph.D. specialists who know much more about some aspects of a problem than the director does; tight control and formal procedures would be self-defeating in that situation.

Attitudes and Needs of Subordinates

The amount of challenge or routine in a job often attracts people whose motivations match job requirements. When subordinates enjoy problem solving and difficult assignments, are dedicated to the work, and enjoy independence (i.e., are operating on higher-level needs), different leadership choices are called for than when they are passive, dependent, and threatened. **In general, the greater subordinates' needs for autonomy and independence, the less tight control by the leader is appropriate, and vice versa (Vroom, 1960; Strauss, 1963; Hersey & Blanchard, 1977).**

Less independent subordinates, however, call for greater control and explicitness of expectations. Subordinates who are more dependent, more extrinsically motivated, and/or have relatively low ability prefer high direction from their bosses. **Those who have high ability and/or are intrinsically motivated want to participate in decision making and do not like to be controlled (House, 1971).**

As suggested in Chapter 7 on individual motivation, while close supervision of those operating on lower-level needs may be productive in the short run, there are organizational and human consequences for satisfaction and learning, which also need to be taken into account. This connects to the issue of concern for people versus concern for task. Some researchers have claimed that high concern for both is always most effective, and, in general, either concern is ig-

DEMANDING PEPSICO IS ATTEMPTING TO MAKE WORK NICER FOR MANAGERS

Purchase, New York—Can PepsiCo, Inc., become a nicer place to work without losing the edge that has helped make it a highly profitable, $8 billion food and soft-drink company?

Its management thinks so. Although PepsiCo prizes the fast pace and demanding standards that make it so competitive, it worries about battle fatigue in the ranks. Says Andrall E. Pearson, the company's president: "We probably attract people who give ulcers, rather than those who get them."

Accordingly, PepsiCo has decided that a bit more backpatting and handholding are in order—but not so much, mind you, that standards slip. The time is ripe to focus on such "soft stuff," Mr. Pearson explains, because the company has recently rebounded from a financial slump. Wall Street is touting its stock, and earnings are headed for record levels.

But the principal motivation came last spring, when two surveys of PepsiCo's top 470 executives turned up some troubling job alienation. Many managers complained that they don't feel cared about as people, that they didn't know enough about what was happening in the company as a whole, and that they weren't told how they were doing in their jobs.

More Feedback

As a consequence, Mr. Pearson told executives at a big May meeting in the Bahamas that they need to give more feedback and demonstrate a "real interest" in subordinates.

Although the company doesn't claim to have made enormous strides in six months, it has started tinkering with a corporate environment that is often criticized for encouraging individualism at the expense of the collective effort. . . .

In addition, the company wants to emphasize the value of coaching and training, management traits that aren't rewarded now. In the future, promotions and pay will be based partly on how well an executive furthers the development of subordinates.

Source: Trish Hall. Reprinted by permission of *The Wall Street Journal*,

nored only at the leader's peril (Likert, 1961; Blake & Mouton, 1964). But in some situations, at least temporarily, one should probably take precedence over the other.

For those organizational members who have high needs for independence and love challenging tasks, high person-concern may be a bit superfluous. Leaving them alone to get on with the work, in a cordial way, can be very effective. At the other extreme, with subordinates who are operating on survival needs, warmth and support may not be necessary (though much appreciated if given).

Most organizational members, however, will be affected by a wider range of needs, including those for social approval, and will be quite responsive to a supportive climate. **Where the work itself is not espe-**

cially challenging or intrinsically fascinating but those doing it are not threatened about survival, high concern for people along with high concern for task is appropriate.

Leader's Upward Influence

For convenience we have been talking about "the leader" as if it were always one person with formal-legitimate influence and sufficient power to do whatever is needed. But the actual power of the leader or of those aspiring to perform leadership functions is a very important factor in determining appropriate leadership style. Even the supervisor or manager who is formally and legitimately in that position will have varying amounts of influence with subordinates, superiors, and peers. Leaders who have considerable influence with their superiors, for example, can take more risks in the decisions they make, vary more from formal procedures, and will receive greater support from subordinates than those who do not. **The greater the "upward" influence of a leader, the less it is necessary to share control with subordinates (Pelz, 1952).** Effective shared influence, however, is likely to increase the upward influence of a leader, since it can yield a solid support base when trying to persuade superiors. The leader who does not have clout with higher-ups or other outsiders must be cautious in changing formal procedures and spend time building support among subordinates in order to have a stronger base of influence; thus more sharing of control and concern for people will be appropriate. A common mistake for leaders of dissident groups is to become so caught up in fighting those with power that group members are ignored or not given much say; in a showdown the group members may not stand solidly behind the leader because they have not been "brought along."

Any leader with low legitimacy must worry about similar problems. It is not very effective to go around barking orders if those who are supposed to follow them do not accept your right to issue them. If legitimacy will not or cannot be conferred from an organizational superior, then it must be earned; involving others, giving warmth and support, and taking low risks are then most appropriate. A successful risky decision can break through to a new level of respect from subordinates; a failure can cause a bad case of terminal influence.

The power of the leader and his/her relationship with subordinates also affect the appropriateness of task concern. Leaders with high power and good relationships who are responsible for structured jobs are most effective when task oriented. Ironically, in the opposite conditions (low power, poor relationships, and low structure), task orientation is also appropriate. It is only when these conditions are moderate that predominant person-concern seems to work best. In sum: **Task-oriented leaders do best in situations that are highly favorable or highly unfavorable for exerting influence, while person-concerned leaders do best in moderately favorable conditions (Fiedler, 1967).**

In some settings an organization's traditions and culture will not legitimize influence when it is attempted in a style considered inappropriate. Faculty members in universities, for example, who are relatively independent, do unstructured work, and have relatively high power often only accept administrator influence when administrators do not behave in a controlling, cold way. Conversely, in some companies anything less than a gruff set of orders given as commands will be seen as weak and, therefore, unenforceable. In either type of organization, stylistic choices are limited by member willingness to give power only to those using particular influence modes. The organization's culture is another factor in determining appropriate style.

> *All authority belongs to the people.*
>
> Thomas Jefferson

With so many possible stylistic choices to make and so many situational factors to take into account, it is hard for an aspiring leader to sort out what to do when. For example, in general: **Less influence should be shared when subordinates are unconcerned about or unaffected by the decision and when they have less expertise than the manager. Greater sharing of influence should be used when subordinates' support and cooperation is needed, their knowledge is essential, or their commitment is necessary because they must carry out the decision (Vroom & Yetton, 1973).**

Still other factors need to be taken into account. **If time is short and a decision must be made, the leader should use the least participatory (most controlling) style suitable to solve the problem. If, however, the development of subordinates is very important, then the most participatory (least controlling) style that fits the problem should be used (Vroom & Yetton, 1973).**

Finally, the style exhibited by managers will be influenced by the managerial function (or role) they emphasize or concentrate their energies on. For example, managers whose situation requires them to concentrate on developing external relationships and monitoring what is happening in the environment are likely to have less time to supervise their subordinates and hence will be less controlling. However, they may also need to develop more explicit operating procedures so that their units present a consistent face to that outside world.

Making Choices

As you can see, there is a lot to take into account in deciding upon appropriate style. What is appropriate will vary not only in an overall way, but also from situation to situation, person to person, time to time. It is no wonder that some managers are tempted to just do what comes naturally, whether it fits or not, and let the chips fall where they may. In fact, one leading leadership theorist, Fred Fiedler (1967), has argued that managers cannot really change their styles through training (and implicitly, by choice) so that they should concentrate on getting into the situations that happen to fit their natural style. While it is clear that human beings are not infinitely malleable and cannot constantly and continually shift gears—and if they could, might badly confuse those around them—it seems overly pessimistic to conclude that no choice is possible. While there would never be time to examine *every* situation for the factors in it before having to decide how to lead, it is possible to step back from decisions periodically, go through the analysis we have explained, and roughly determine if (1) your usual leadership style generally fits the situations you are in, (2) there are particular variations in situations that call for a different style than your usual one, and you might more readily adjust when those situations arise, (3) you sometimes face situations calling for a leadership style you are not comfortable with, and therefore you need to practice acquiring the necessary skills or behavior, or (4) you want to get out of situations that demand behavior you cannot or do not want to learn. (See Figure 12–5.)

In Chapter 9 we talked about interpersonal competence as an important part of a manager's range of abilities, and we paid particular attention to the importance of developing a wide range of interpersonal styles in order to meet the demands of complex work situations. Successful leadership requires the same kind of mastery but with a

FIGURE 12–5
Making Choices (Leadership Style)

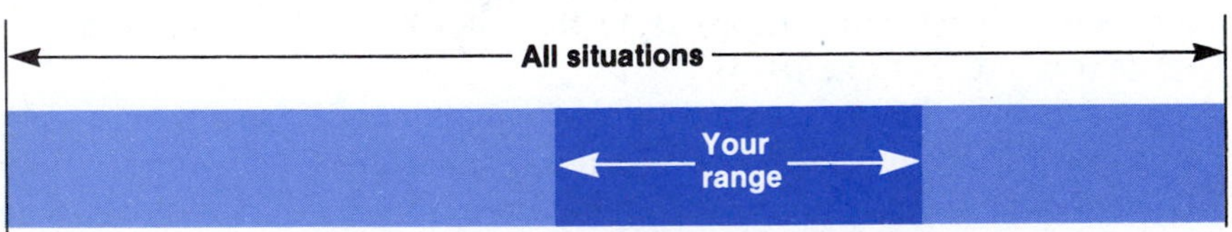

Adapt your style to fit the particular situation
or
Choose or move to a situation which your style fits or to which you can adapt directly, or with training.

special emphasis upon those interpersonal skills that enhance your influence and power in an organization. The wider the range of leadership styles available to you, the better able you are to exercise appropriate choices in a given situation.

As a way of trying to see how all the various contingencies might be used to make better leadership choices, we have included two extended examples.

EXAMPLE 1: THE PERSONNEL RECORD OFFICE

An experienced personnel officer is in charge of a group of six people whose job it is to go through the record of every new departing employee of the company and to transfer certain kinds of information onto index cards. They work in a large insurance company in which there is a high rate of employee turnover. Consequently, the workload is heavy and very steady. With a few exceptions, the people in this work group have been there for some years, and the work is fairly routine for them even when some special judgment is required. Some of the newer workers need occasional help but mostly to answer simple procedural questions. The records themselves vary in quality and ease with which they can be understood; there are variations from department to department and supervisor to supervisor. Certain departments and supervisors are preferred, and certain others are to be avoided. Therefore, one of the tasks is to divide the "plums" from the "prunes" in a way that is fair to everyone. The supervisor does that job.

The central leadership function in this case is one of maintenance and control over the flow of work. If it becomes bogged down, then there is an accumulation of records, which creates complaints from the vice president of personnel. Although he is a little more experienced than the others, the supervisor does not have any special expertise that others do not share. He normally answers the questions of the newer people, but in his absence several other employees can answer the questions just as well. He was appointed to his job because of seniority and demonstrated competence.

Because he has been there the longest, the supervisor of the records office carries sufficient influence among the workers to have the final say in any matter of controversy (of which there are few). Although he is not the most popular person there, his relations with the others are friendly, and he is given a fair amount of personal respect.

The supervisor's style of leadership is fairly formal; he has developed detailed established procedures and requires employees to follow them. Any departure from these could create a minor furor. He gives his main attention to the task at hand, does not concern himself very much with the feelings or attitudes of the other employees, except when there is an obvious problem, and he is able to rely upon the abilities of others to help keep the work moving. Finally, we can describe his style as cautious, since he is careful not to take upon himself any decisions that go outside the bounds of what is already prescribed.

The leadership conditions in this case are simple to describe. The main roles of the supervisor are as *monitor* and *resource allocator*, with most attention going to maintaining and controlling the work flow. The situation is *routine and clear*. From what we know about what kinds of leadership fit what kinds of circumstances, the match in this case seems to be an appropriate one. The supervisor has a *moderate amount of influence*, which is all that is needed to keep work moving in its normal, routine way. He has the influence because he is accepted as the *formal-legitimate* supervisor of the group and because his relations with the other employees are adequate given the relatively low level of personal commitment required by the task. His leadership style is also attuned to the situation. He shares a *little* of the *control* with the group members who possess the required expertise; he maintains a *high level of task-concern*, since the system demands accuracy and speed; he maintains only a *moderate level of person-concern*, enough just to keep tabs on serious problems, but not to the degree to which it might distract his attention from the task; he is *explicit* about what is expected and sticks to the *formal procedures*, which are adequate for completing the bulk of the workload; and he maintains *caution*, which keeps him and his department out of trouble.

A Change in Requirements

What might happen if some of the factors involved were changed? Suppose, for example, the insurance company's operations research group decided to introduce the use of computers into the personnel records office and wanted the workers to enter their information on computer terminals and learn how to read printout sheets. The supervisor is called in and trained in the use of the new system; then he is sent back to introduce it to his department members. We now have a very different situation from the previous one. It involves the *initiation* of a new *technology*, which makes the situation *nonroutine*. Since it is likely that the workers will feel some anxieties about their ability to learn the new methods and since they are for the moment dependent upon the supervisor's expertise, it calls for a different kind of leadership. Now he needs a high level of influence, which he may be able to get through his newly acquired expertise, provided that the others recognize it. With personal tensions running high, he now needs to maintain a high level of person-concern along with a very high level of task-concern. For the time being he may need to retain control, which makes sense in terms of his special knowledge and would also be functional in dealing with the anxieties of the clerks. The emphasis upon formal prescribed procedures continues to be appropriate for that portion of the work determined by the needs of the computer system, but now the situation requires a little more venturousness on the part of the supervisor with respect to helping the workers figure out how to make the new methods work.

The Effects of Changed Requirements on Leadership

Can you see how changing circumstances results in changing leadership requirements? If the supervisor in the case were not capable of or interested in learning the new technology or training others, the company would have been forced to consider changing the person in the leadership role. When technology changes rapidly, difficulties arise. Suppose, for example, the supervisor in the case just described were unable, even with full support, to handle the computer methods, but the company felt obliged to keep him in the supervisory role because of his seniority. Can you imagine how difficult it would have been for everyone concerned? His legitimacy would probably disappear and with it his influence as a leader. The increasing demand for management development programs springs from this kind of problem, namely, the need to maintain and upgrade knowledge and expertise in areas that require changing leadership.

EXECUTIVE STYLE: ROAD CAN BE BUMPY AS A NEW CHIEF TAKES OVER AND ATTEMPTS TO INVIGORATE THE COMPANY

Camden, New Jersey—When Harold Shaub was preparing to step down as president of Campbell Soup Company in 1982, he realized that Campbell was weak in marketing. "The company needed changes for the changing times," he says.

R. Gordon McGovern, the man he picked to succeed him, quickly shook the company up. He began reversing a 150-year-old habit of glorifying engineers over marketers. He prodded aides to turn out a slew of new products. He endorsed "the right to fail." Unlike his predecessor, he began wandering through the Campbell corridors every day and roaming through supermarkets. One manager says Mr. McGovern "put us on our toes."

The same sort of bumpy transition is taking place in any number of large corporations these days: A mild-mannered, uninspiring though competent chief gives way to an innovative, even iconoclastic, agent of change who can lead the troops into the business battles ahead.

To some students of management, it is a development long overdue. "One of the key problems facing organizations in American society is that they are underled and overmanaged," Warren Bennis, a business professor at the University of Southern California, wrote in a newsletter. As a result, he wrote, "They are not paying enough attention to doing the right thing, while paying too much attention to doing things right." . . .

[At Campbell] *the recent changes have been swift and sweeping. Mr. McGovern has reshuffled top management and divided the company into about 50 business units to encourage entrepreneurial spirit and creativity. It now doesn't matter who develops a product, so long as it gets developed. Thus, the Prego spaghetti sauce unit—not the frozen-food groups—initiated frozen Mexican dinners. And though it wasn't his job, Anthony J. Adams, director of market research, created "Today's Taste," a line of refrigerated entrees and side dishes soon to be test marketed.*

"It's like things are in constant motion," Mr. Adams says. "We are overloaded, but it's fun." . . .

After more than three years at the helm of Coca-Cola, Roberto Goizueta (pronounced goy-SWEH-tuh) says he wants to make sure "that I don't spend my time trying to keep things the same." It is a problem, consultants say, that afflicts every chief executive who is the instrument of rapid change. "It is human nature for a king to make changes after becoming king and then spend the rest of the time keeping things the same." Mr. Goizueta says.

Mr. Goizueta has awakened Coke, a profitable but heretofore sleepy giant. Its market share was slipping away to the more aggressive Pepsi-Cola and Philip Morris's 7Up. "There was a lot of hangdog thinking here," says Robert V. Waltemeyer, Coke's senior vice president, "as to how it would feel to be number two." Now Coke has strengthened its position as the number one soft-drink maker.

Employees also smarted under what they regarded as the "imperial chairmanship" of Mr. Goizueta's predecessor, J. Paul Austin, a shy man whom many underlings regarded as aloof or even autocratic. As a symbol, many latched onto his wife's penchant for decorating Coke's Atlanta headquarters, or her edict outlawing employee lunches in a nearby park so that pigeons wouldn't be attracted.

Strategy for the 80s

Mr. Goizueta is both shy and unassuming. (He lives in the same unpretentious house he bought 20 years ago as a Coke middle manager.) Nevertheless, he has firmly seized the reins of the company, making changes that he hopes will spawn further change. In a pamphlet he drafted on Coke's strategy for the 1980s, "intelligent individual risk-taking" was emphasized along with keeping Coke financially successful and number one in the soft-drink business.

At a meeting with executives in Palm Springs, Mr. Goizueta announced: "There are no sacred cows in this organization anymore." He slaughtered some of those cows by buying Columbia Pictures and rolling out Diet Coke to compete with other sugarless drinks, including the company's own Tab. (It had been regarded as heresy for Coke to venture outside the manufacturing business or to use the world's most recognizable trademark on anything but a sugared drink.) Both the Columbia and Diet Coke moves have been strong successes.

Under Mr. Goizueta, the Coke executive suite is acquiring a distinct international flavor. Six of the top 16 officers are foreign born, and Donald R. Keough, Coke's president and Mr. Goizueta's right-hand man, sometimes introduces himself at analyst meetings as the company's "token American."

Source: Danion Darlin. Reprinted by permission of *The Wall Street Journal*,

EXAMPLE 2: THE COMMUNITY ENVIRONMENTAL GROUP

A small group of citizens in a suburban area had become deeply concerned about the rapid growth of industry in their area. The pollution problems had grown to the point where many families were considering the possibility of moving away. The latest crisis centered around plans for expansion on the part of a plastics firm, one of the worst offenders in the region.

One evening a group of a dozen people meeting in one of their homes decided to create a citizens' organization in the hope of building total community opposition to the company's planned expansion. They realized that they faced a major undertaking with many constraints. As a voluntary organization they would have to depend upon the willingness of people to offer their time and efforts outside of their normal working hours. They needed to recruit more people, identify special resources in the area, raise money, get out publicity and information to the community, and on and on and on. Obviously, they needed leadership; the question was *who* could lead this kind of operation and what would be the best way to do it. No one seemed eager for the job. Finally, one of the women in the group (a pleasant, hardworking mother of four children) reluctantly offered to take on the leadership role. The rest of the group, with great relief, concurred with the idea. The new leader saw her job as gathering information, making phone calls, setting dates for meetings, asking for volunteers to help do important jobs like contacting community leaders who might support the effort, and so forth.

She wanted to make the organization as visible as possible as rapidly as possible but only in ways that would attract membership, not result in the group getting a reputation as a bunch of troublemakers. Therefore, she decided that it would be very important not to offend anyone; she had to build friendly relations wherever she went. With the help of a few other volunteers, she pushed ahead to build the organization. They began making the phone calls, contacting newspaper and television people to ask for coverage, writing pieces to be duplicated and circulated door to door, and so forth.

Their campaign met with only minimal success. People wanted to know *who* they were, what existing organization they represented, what they really knew about pollution to begin with, what facts they had about the actual expansion plans of the plastics company, and many more questions that they had difficulty answering. Somehow the organization was not developing as the group had hoped and as the leader had planned it. Before we examine why this was so, see if you can diagnose the problem yourself. See if you can spell out the leadership issues in the case and decide what was or was not appropriate for the circumstances.

In many respects this case illustrates one of the more difficult kinds of leadership problems. In fact, it probably goes beyond what any one person could normally handle as a leader. The situation calls for great skills in the roles of symbolic figurehead, innovator, coordinator/leader, liaison, spokesperson, negotiator; action must be taken on many fronts; and the situation is *turbulent* (or changing) and full of *uncertain outcomes*. Do you think *you* could handle it?

The appropriate leader for those circumstances would have to possess *a high degree of influence, a high level of expertise,* and possess (or be able to build) *good working relations* with the organization members. With respect to style of leadership, the person would have to *retain control* until the organization became solidly established, maintain a *very high level of task-concern* and *high level of person-concern*—the former for obvious reasons, the latter because of the unusually high level of commitment needed in voluntary organizations. The leader would have to improvise expectations, *not very explicitly,* and operate in a very *informal manner* since there are no established procedures. Finally, a *venturous approach* is needed, since there is no way to predict what might be behind all the doors that have to be opened.

As you can see, the person who had the leadership job in this case was not the best suited to the situation. One option she had was to draw in people who possessed the necessary expertise and abilities to compensate for what she lacked. Her own role might have been more focused on liaison work than some of the other needed roles and functions; that is also vital to an organization like the one just described. She might have been appropriate for that aspect of the leadership role, but clearly other resources were needed to meet the multitude of other demands.

As a way of summarizing what the two cases illustrate, let's see what kinds of propositions would apply. The proposition that would fit the personnel records case would go as follows:

In a work situation that calls for monitoring and resource allocation roles for a work process under routine conditions with employees who do not need high autonomy, the appropriate leader would be someone designated by the system, having moderate influence and minimally adequate leader-member relations; the appropriate style for that leader would be to share control moderately, maintain a high level of task-concern and a moderate level of person-concern, operate by explicit expectations using formal established procedures, and take little risk.

The proposition that would fit the community group case would go as follows:

In a work situation that calls for innovative and other initiating roles in relation to all aspects of the job under turbulent (nonroutine)

conditions with high subordinate independence, the appropriate leader would be someone with high influence, high expertise, and very good leader–member relations; the appropriate style would be to retain control but involve many others, maintain a high level of task-concern and a high level of person-concern, operate by low explicitness with informal improvised procedures, and take high risk.

CONDITIONS UNDER WHICH PARTICIPATIVE METHODS ARE APPROPRIATE

As you realize by now, each time one of the factors is changed, the proposition that applies also changes to some extent. Thus, you yourself will have to take on the task of generating propositions that fit the various combinations of factors you may encounter. If you understand the steps in doing that, then you have mastered a way of conceptualizing the leadership process, one that will be more useful to you than any simple fixed rules about what leaders should or should not do.

As the two cases indicate, however, there may be clusters of managerial behavior that are appropriate in changing or stable situations. Though no situation you encounter is likely to have all of these elements the same, they frequently go together.

As increasing numbers of employees have higher levels of education, a stronger belief in the appropriateness of having a say in the way things are run, and a desire for meaningful challenging work, managers are being pushed to use more participative styles. Pressure from below for more of a voice is a common phenomenon in many contemporary organizations. When it comes from subordinates who indeed have their own expertise to contribute, genuine participation is quite appropriate.

In general: **Leadership that fully involves those being led in decision making ("participative," "employee-centered") is most effective under the following conditions:**

a. **Decisions are nonroutine.**
b. **Nonstandardized information is flowing in or must be gathered through subordinates.**
c. **Actions are not being taken under severe time pressure.**
d. **Subordinates feel the need for independence, are intrinsically motivated, see participation as legitimate, are competent, have needed expertise and can work without close supervision, will take the organization's goals into account, can effect the implementation of decisions by acceptance or rejection of them, and therefore need to be committed to the decisions (Vroom & Yetton, 1973; Stogdill, 1974; Miles & Ritchie, 1971).**

Under these condtions, where it is not enough to merely have subordinates going through the motions, leaders must find a way to "capture subordinates' hearts," gain their full commitment to doing what is needed. This calls for an across-the-board effort by leaders, as outlined in the box below.

GAINING COMMITMENT FROM YOUR EMPLOYEES: SOME KEY POINTS

- For the *individual,* it depends upon:
  1. Involvement.
  2. Choice.
  3. Meeting positive expectations.
  4. Feeling supported and valued.
  5. Need fulfillment.
  6. Feedback that facilitates improvement.
  7. Intrinsic satisfactions.
  8. Challenge and opportunities to grow.
  9. Being treated fairly.
  10. Affirmation of self-concept.
- In *interpersonal relationships,* it depends upon:
  1. Mutual support, acceptance, and reinforcement of self.
  2. Openness where needed and appropriate.
  3. Trust and confidence (mutual).
  4. Compatible styles:
     a. Similar or
     b. Complementary.
  5. Acceptance and/or appreciation of differences.
  6. Opportunities to problem solve jointly.
  7. Willingness to manage conflicts.
- For a *group,* it depends upon:
  1. Norms that support organizational goals.
  2. Cohesiveness around those norms.
  3. Rewards at a group level.
  4. Group being valued by organization.
  5. Acceptance of individual differences in abilities, preferences, and values.
  6. Ability to match member resources to any given task.
- For the *total system,* it depends upon:
  1. The parts being aware of the whole.
  2. Groups being willing to accept each other's legitimacy and importance.
  3. Willingness of people to interact across group boundaries.
  4. Recognition of the importance of reciprocity.
  5. Appreciating the importance of diversity with respect to:
     a. Ideas and
     b. People.

Source: Stephen L. Fink, *Commitment: The Key to Performance,* draft.

Nevertheless, many managers struggle with the issue of how to balance an emphasis upon "getting the job done" with the importance of fully involving employees in the process of decision making. The question seems to be, "How much time can I afford to spend informing and discussing matters with my employees if it cuts into valuable work time?" Or the question might be phrased in sharper terms, like "Who's running the show, me or my workers?"

The Problem of Heroic Models

What causes these concerns, even when the conditions for greater participation are clearly present? One explanation is that American managers carry heroic images in their heads about leadership (Bradford & Cohen, 1984). Raised on such heroic models as the Lone Ranger riding to the rescue to leave the silver bullet in the nick of time, American managers assume that leadership requires knowing all the answers, taking on the whole department's burdens, and being responsible for everything going right. Although having all the answers was possible and likely in simpler times, thereby making overcontrolling styles appropriate, such conditions are increasingly rare. Yet managers cling to old models out of feelings of great responsibility and misguided notions about what leaders are supposed to do. Even managerial students carry these heroic assumptions around; as soon as a student is selected to be manager of a classroom task group, members expect the manager to be instantly enlightened, and the manager often starts acting as if special expertise was magically conferred, or worrying because "the answers" are no clearer to him or her than when just an ordinary group member!

MANAGER AS HERO

The showdown—in which everything depends on the hero's nerves of steel, complete command of the situation, quickness, and guts—dominates the fantasies of managers who grew up on cowboys and Indians, war movies, and male heroes. Even many women who have made it into middle management tend to think in these heroic terms although the specific image may be of Wonder Woman: beautiful, strong, surrounded by admirers but still the cleverest, toughest miracle worker around. It hardly matters that these images, largely based on the development of the Western frontier, may not be historically accurate. But even inaccurate myths can persist.

Although few managers consciously or deliberately imagine themselves to be exactly like these heroes, the models provided are powerful and pervasive. It is difficult to face the constant strains of managerial life without falling back on such organizing metaphors.

Source: Adapted from David L. Bradford and Allan R. Cohen, *Managing for Excellence; The Guide to Developing High Performance in Contemporary Organizations* (New York: John Wiley & Sons, 1984).

The heroic assumptions lead to two alternative models: the *manager-as-technician* and *manager-as-conductor*. Technicians try to have all the answers, just as they did when they were doing the work they are now managing. Their focus is on the technical content of the job; people problems are often seen as a nuisance, preventing "real work." Manager-conductors also feel overresponsible for their unit's success but try to maneuver their subordinates into arriving at the answer the conductor has already worked out. Conductors most often talk about being participative while carefully constraining participation. Too often "participation" is limited to allowing subordinate discussion without decision-making responsibility. Both conductors and technicians are preoccupied with control of subordinates, to see that "everything is done right," but it is exactly this overcontrol that tends to demotivate subordinates and reduce their commitment.

By working extraordinarily hard, outstanding heroic managers can be quite effective even when all the conditions are not appropriate for their styles, but they must run faster and faster to stay ahead of their subordinates.

Another model, more appropriate to the conditions fitting participative styles, has been called the *manager-as-developer*. Bradford and Cohen (1984) formulated this model as a result of working with managers who realized that the more traditional models were no longer fully effective. The manager-developer's basic orientation is to be concerned about seeing to it that problems get solved and work gets done in ways that develop subordinates' capacities for and commitment to sharing responsibility for the unit's success. To be effective, the manager-as-developer must accomplish the following three major tasks:

1. Work with direct subordinates as a team to collectively share responsibility for managing the unit.
2. Determine and gain commitment to a common, tangible vision of the department's goals and purposes; and
3. Work on the continuous development of individual subordinate skills, especially in the managerial/interpersonal areas needed to be an effective member of the shared responsibility team.

The manager-as-developer, then, seeks to develop in subordinates the willingness and ability to share the responsibility for departmental success. The manager must shape subordinates into a powerful, cooperative, hardworking, dedicated, and responsible team.

> The presence on a team of strong subordinates, even when they are held responsible for overall performance, does not automatically guarantee the kind of coordination necessary for excellence. The manager must determine and use a goal for the unit that helps members transcend their own interests. But merely putting people on a team with a unifying

> *Strong leaders articulate direction and save the organization from change via "drift." They create a vision of a possible future that allows themselves and others to see more clearly the focus to take.*
>
> Rosabeth Moss Kanter
> *The Change Masters*
>
> *Establishing an operative (tangible vision) requires two distinctly different tasks of the leader: to formulate an appropriate overarching goal and to gain its acceptance by the members. . . . Common to both . . . is an ability to think beyond the daily routine, to see a greater vision that ties day-to-day activities to a significant future goal.*
>
> David L. Bradford and Allan R. Cohen
> *Managing for Excellence*

goal and making them responsible is not enough. Subordinates may not have the skills they need to share responsibility effectively. Their technical knowledge may be too narrow, especially if they have been in highly specialized jobs. Even more likely, they may not have fully developed the necessary managerial or interpersonal skills; they may lack the ability to negotiate with and confront one another (and the boss), a full understanding of how all the parts of the organization fit together, or collective decision-making skills. The manager will need to pay continuous attention to the development of each direct subordinate's capacities.

The three elements of the manager-as-developer model are mutually reinforcing. By focusing on sharing responsibility for the overall departmental performance, a manager provides subordinates with the chance to have an impact. By emphasizing individual learning, he or she provides challenge. By teaching individuals the managerial and interpersonal skills needed to effectively share responsibility for the department, one rewards participation in running the unit with learning that both fosters further career opportunities and expands ability to reach excellence. Thus, subordinates are simultaneously made responsible, challenged, engaged, and stretched, which increases their motivation to perform well and expands their capacity to do so.

This style requires heroic effort, but not a heroic model. The developer does not drop the silver bullet and ride away into the sunset, but stays to build greater strength in the town and the townfolk.[5]

We are not suggesting that technical and conducting skills are not an important part of a manager's repertoire. Quite the contrary; these are often the very skills needed to establish credibility and to move the system. We *are* suggesting that in this day of knowledge-based

[5] D. L. Bradford and A. R. Cohen, *Managing for Excellence: The Guide to Developing High Performance in Contemporary Organizations* (New York: John Wiley & Sons, 1984).

work, managers must broaden their repertoire to include developer skills. They need to know such things as:

1. How to create the conditions and atmosphere that promote employee growth.
2. When *not* to manage an activity. (See box on delegation.)
3. How to provide support and guidance to subordinates without taking over the task.
4. How to help people learn from their mistakes. (Learning to give constructive feedback is essential.)
5. Biting their tongues while subordinates struggle to master new skills.
6. How to talk about departmental goals in a way that provides meaning and inspires extraordinary effort.

The role is not unlike that of an effective teacher. It is not a role easily come by, but the positive consequences of effective developer efforts tend to be long lasting and increase the quality of the work environment for all employees. Think about some of the best instructors you've had. Did they just present technical information? Did they manage the class in a highly controlled manner, carefully leading students to conclusions known to them in advance? Were they sensitive to students' needs for autonomy and for opportunities to learn from their own mistakes? Chances are the best teachers you had were the ones who had competencies in all three areas: they had the technical knowledge that commanded your respect; they knew how to sequence material and manage the learning process in ways that enhanced learning; and they knew when and how to give students room to learn in their own ways. Teachers who depend exclusively on one set of skills or one style tend to be limited in their effectiveness. Think about the impact on you of these different kinds of leadership in the classroom. The impact will be similar with respect to managers in the work setting.

Of course, even within highly changing organizations there are likely to be situations where the developer style is not appropriate. For example, time becomes an important factor when the environment demands rapid responses or when the leader feels rushed and pressured. Ironically, unless the need for decisions is extremely urgent, it may be most functional to talk through decisions thoroughly when they are most pressing and important; it requires great skill to prevent premature closure of discussion when the wolf, real or imagined, is at the door.

Subordinate readiness is also a crucial issue, only briefly mentioned earlier. Sometimes a subordinate is not as yet competent to handle certain matters. A leader who fails to consider the "state of readiness" of employees with respect to sharing leadership responsibilities can easily create more problems by pushing this approach than by exercising more unilateral control. Under conditions where employees prefer to have the legitimate leader give the orders and feel the need for close supervision, participative leadership is likely to be highly dysfunctional.

Thus: **When decisions are routine, actions are being taken under severe time pressure, information is standardized, and subordinates are dependent, more controlling forms of leadership are appropriate (Wilensky, 1957).** But to complicate the matter further, within any one organization the conditions surrounding each decision may vary. For example, subordinates may accept being controlled on some issues but not on others; some issues will need immediate decisions while others can be discussed at great length, and so forth. Effective leadership will fit not only the general situation but also the particular circumstances of each decision. That requires great flexibility and responsiveness as well as a genuinely "scientific" attitude on the part of the manager who is trying to decide how much participation by subordinates is appropriate and when.

It may not always be possible, however, to adjust your behavior to the demands of the situation. As yet there are no agreed-upon limits to human flexibility. Individuals vary in their ability to change behavior; it may well be that when you face a situation demanding a style that is not natural to your personality, the best option is to find another person to do it, change jobs, or work at restructuring the situation to fit your strengths. Your own capacity to learn new behavior is thus an additional factor to consider when choosing a leadership style.

FIRST CHICAGO'S DAVIS QUITS, LEAVING FIRM WITHOUT AN APPARENT SUCCESSOR AS CHIEF

George L. Davis, who had been seen as the man most likely to become First Chicago Corp's next chief executive officer, quit the big banking concern because of what sources said were differences over management style. . . . Mr. Davis found it difficult to adapt to the collegial style Mr. Sullivan sought for his banking "partnership," where coaxing was to replace bossing. Mr. Sullivan hoped that this approach would satisfy Mr. Davis's ambitions and, at the same time, keep the executives below him happy. "George struggled with that," a source said. "Bosses give orders." Some employees under Mr. Davis found him too overbearing.

Source: Jeff Bailey. *The Wall Street Journal*, October 20, 1986.

Similarly, the same factors that determine leadership *style* also can affect which managerial functions should be emphasized. When the environment demands rapid responses and considerable attention, the manager is likely to spend more time on external functions, such as spokesperson and negotiator, and less on the internal ones, such as supervisor. Conversely, when the manager's subordinates have less expertise than is needed to perform their tasks and only the manager can supply what is missing, greater emphasis may be placed internally on coaching and training. Again, however, individual capacity for flexibility serves to limit how easily a manager can *choose* what to do.

LEADERSHIP AND VALUES

Unfortunately, leadership is not just a matter of deciding what will work, and whether you can do it. The fundamental question has to do with how you personally feel about the exercise of power. Many people, including students who want to become managers, try to gain power through leadership roles at every opportunity and look down on anyone who is not interested in constantly enhancing power. For such power seekers, some time would be worthwhile spent thinking about their motives in wanting power and the uses to which they intend to put it when a fair measure has been acquired.

> *They who are in highest places and have the most power have the least liberty, because they are the most observed.*
>
> John Tillotson
> *Reflections*

On the other hand, many others, including even a few managerial students, fear leadership and its burdens and consequently refrain from exercising more than passive influence. Though some influence is inescapable since even silence has consequences on other system members, such "power avoiders" either define themselves as helpless and powerless or backpedal when responsibility hovers near. "It's good to have a leader because then I'll have someone to blame when things go wrong" is the widely held counterfoil to the belief that "no game is worth playing if I'm not the captain" (or at least struggling to become the captain's replacement). Those who shy away from leadership might profitably contemplate the costs of anyone holding back his/her full strength and what the world would be like if everyone played it so safe.

The values question arises in another way. Even if a controlling, task-centered, "authoritarian" leadership style works best in some situations with some people, do you want to (1) put yourself in such situations, (2) accept the conditions as fixed rather than trying to change them so that other styles become more appropriate, (3) focus on short-term results rather than long-term development of subordinates, or (4) live with the consequences of a society in which people who may currently work best under an authoritarian style are kept dependent, passive, and submissive? Are you willing to do what is necessary to maximize productivity regardless of the human costs?

Conversely, if a more influence-sharing, person-centered developer style is appropriate to get the work out, would you be willing to give up some control to get the best results? Could you respond to those you work with in a genuinely warm and supportive way even when you would prefer that they do what you want without questioning everything? Could you risk your own job by allowing others the optimal amount of influence?

Trying to follow a contingency model as a manager does not automatically make that leadership role easier; even when you can figure out *what* to do and whether you can do it, you still have to decide whether you *want* to do it. The garden of roses we never promised you is unfortunately strewn with thorns, and there is no simple way through it. There are hard choices at every turn.

IMPLICATIONS FOR CHOOSING JOBS AND CAREER PLANNING

As diagrammed in Figure 12–5, we believe that people are both malleable and limited in how much they can modify their competencies and values. This has implications for choosing a career, a particular organization, and a job. A professor has a great deal of autonomy and control over his or her activities and work schedule, needs to be constantly engaged in exploring new ideas and challenging old ones, and must be able to deal in abstract conceptualizations and communicate ideas effectively. Someone heading for an academic career needs to be comfortable in a system that places high value on ideas for their own sake and not just on immediate practicality. That individual also needs to be reasonably competent and interested in conducting research, teaching, and engaging in theoretical discourse. Given training, could your interests and values allow you to adapt to this role successfully and happily?

Similarly, many salespeople must interact with a wide range of customers, some politically liberal and some very conservative. This may mean that the salesperson must set aside, even deny, personal beliefs in the interest of maintaining a good relationship with the customer. Can you keep your mouth shut, or are you a person who must speak your mind on such value-laden topics as religion, politics, abortion, communism, etc.? The head of an advertising agency once said, "If you take a job with us, you must *believe* that the aspirin we advertise is the best, even though they all are made of essentially the same ingredients." Would such an organizational demand be one you could accept comfortably?

Sometimes, organizations get into trouble financially and operationally, and only drastic and unilateral action can save the day. Decisions must be made quickly, often on less than complete data. People may have their job assignments changed and even be fired. The decision maker in such a situation must live with being the one who "hurts" people, albeit to save the organization and other people, and the one who is often chastised, vilified, or hated. Not everyone can handle this role.

Earlier we talked about some of the ethical burdens of being a leader. If part of your ethical beliefs is the notion that it is wrong to hurt people, yet you have to take actions on behalf of the many that may hurt the few, you may find that you either have to live with that tension or get out of the role altogether. Have you ever heard the expression, "That person needs firing?" This is a handy way to avoid the responsibility for the act by translating it into a need of the employee. However, such a "need" (i.e., to be fired) doesn't appear in anyone's theory of motivation. In fact, there is no way to avoid your personal values when you exercise leadership.

As you consider your career and look for a job, consider the roles that you will find energizing because they challenge you yet do not exceed your range of adaptability in terms of competency and personal values.

KEY CONCEPTS FROM CHAPTER 12

1. Manager's interpersonal functions create access to information, which leads to informational functions, allowing for decision-making functions.
2. Preferred leadership style should be tempered by what is appropriate to the situation.
3. Dimensions of leadership style; degree of:
   a. Control retained.
   b. Task-concern.
   c. Person-concern.
   d. Explicitness of expectations.
   e. Caution.
4. Appropriate leadership style determined by:
   a. Nature of the task situation.
      (1) If routine, needs control, explicitness, and standardization.
      (2) Stressful tasks need high person-concern.
   b. Expertise of the leader.
      (1) The greater the expertise, the greater the appropriateness of control.

c. Attitudes and needs of subordinates.
   (1) The greater the subordinate need for independence and ability, the less appropriate is tight control.
   (2) If subordinates' survival is not threatened and work is not unusually challenging, high task- and people-concern appropriate.

d. Leader's upward influence.
   (1) The greater the leader's upward influence, the less the need to share control.

e. Leader's power with subordinates.
   (1) Person-concern best with moderate power and relationships.
   (2) Task-concern best with high or low power and relationships.

f. Organization's culture.

g. Need for subordinate commitment.
   (1) The greater the need, the more control should be shared.

h. Time pressure.
   (1) The greater the time pressure, the less appropriate is shared control.

i. Importance of subordinate development.
   (1) The greater the importance of subordinate development, the more control should be shared.

j. Managerial functions needed.

k. Leader's personal values and adaptability.

5. Participative leadership methods most appropriate when:
   a. Decisions nonroutine.
   b. Information nonstandardized.
   c. Low time pressure.
   d. Subordinates independent, intrinsically motivated, see participation as legitimate, are competent, will consider organizational goals, can affect the implementation.

6. General models of leadership:
   a. Heroic:
      (1) Manager-as-technician.
      (2) Manager-as-conductor.
   b. Manager-as-developer.

7. Implications for own choice of job and career.

SUGGESTED READINGS

Bass, B. M. *Leadership & Performance Beyond Expectations.* New York: Free Press, 1985.

Behling, O., and C. F. Rauch, Jr. "A Functional Perspective on Improving Leadership Effectiveness." *Organizational Dynamics,* Spring 1985, pp. 51–61.

Bennis, W. G., and B. Nanus. *Leaders.* New York: Harper & Row, 1985.

Blake, R. R. and J. S. Mouton. *The Managerial Grid.* Houston: Gulf Publishing, 1964.

________. "Interview." *Group and Organization Studies* 3, no. 4 (1978), pp. 401–26.

Bradford, D. L., and A. R. Cohen. *Managing for Excellence: The Guide to Developing High Performance in Contemporary Organizations.* New York: John Wiley & Sons, 1984.

Bragg, J. E., and I. R. Andrews. "Participative Decision Making: An Experimental Study in a Hospital." *Journal of Applied Behavioral Science* 9 (1973), pp. 727–35.

Dalton, M. *Men Who Manage.* New York: John Wiley & Sons, 1959.

Dienesch, R. M., and R. C. Liden. "Leader–Member Exchange Model of Leadership: A Critique and Further Development." *Academy of Management Review,* July 1986, pp. 618–34.

Dowling, W. F., Jr., and L. R. Sayles. *How Managers Motivate: The Imperatives of Supervision.* New York: McGraw-Hill, 1971.

Driscoll, J. W. "Trust and Participation in Organizational Decision Making as Predictors of Satisfaction." *Advanced Management Journal,* March 1978, pp. 44–56.

Fiedler, F. *A Theory of Leadership Effectiveness.* New York: McGraw-Hill, 1967.

________. "The Trouble with Leadership Training Is that It Doesn't Train Leaders." *Psychology Today* 6 (1973), p. 23.

Fiedler, F., and M. Chemers. *Leadership and Effective Management.* Glenview, Ill.: Scott, Foresman, 1974.

Field, R. H. G. "A Critique of the Vroom-Yetton Contingency Model of Leadership Behavior." *Academy of Management Review,* April 1979, pp. 249–57.

Graeff, C. L. "The Situational Leadership Theory: A Critical View." *Academy of Management Review,* April 1983, pp. 285–91.

Griffin, R. "Task Design Determinants of Effective Leader Behavior." *Academy of Management Review,* April 1979, pp. 215–24.

Hersey, P., and K. H. Blanchard. *Management of Organizational Behavior: Utilizing Human Resources.* 3rd ed. Englewood Cliffs, N.J.: Prentice-Hall, 1977.

Hinckley, S. R., Jr. "A Closer Look at Participation." *Organizational Dynamics,* Winter 1985, pp. 57–67.

House, R. "A Path-Goal Theory of Leader Effectiveness." *Administrative Science Quarterly,* September 1971, pp. 321–38.

Hunt, J., and L. Larson. *Contingency Approaches to Leadership.* Carbondale: Southern Illinois University Press, 1974.

Jacobs, T. O. *Leadership & Exchange in Formal Organization.* Springfield, Va.: National Technical Information Service, U.S. Department of Commerce, 1970.

Kanter, R. *Men and Women of the Corporation.* New York: Basic Books, 1977.

________. "Dilemmas of Managing Participation." *Organizational Dynamics,* Summer 1982, pp. 5–27.

Kaplan, R. E. "Trade Routes: The Manager's Network of Relationships." *Organizational Dynamics,* Spring 1984, pp. 37–52.

Katz, D., and R. L. Kahn. *The Social Psychology of Organizations.* New York: John Wiley & Sons, 1966.

Lawrence, P., and J. W. Lorsch. *Organization and Environment.* Boston: Harvard Business School, 1967.

Likert, R. *New Patterns of Management.* New York: McGraw-Hill, 1961.

Locke, E. A.; D. M. Schweiger; and G. P. Latham. "Participation in Decision Making: When Should It Be Used?" *Organizational Dynamics,* Winter 1986, pp. 65–79.

Luthans, F; S. A. Rosenkrantz; and H. W. Hennessey. "What Do Successful Managers Really Do? An Observation Study of Managerial Activities." *Journal of Applied Behavioral Science* 21, no. 3 (1985), pp. 255–70.

Maslow, A. *Eupsychian Management.* Homewood, Ill.: Richard D. Irwin and Dorsey Press, 1965.

McGregor, D. *The Human Side of Enterprise.* New York: McGraw-Hill, 1960.

________. *Leadership and Motivation.* Cambridge, Mass.: MIT Press, 1966.

________. *The Professional Manager.* New York: McGraw-Hill, 1967.

Miles, R., and J. B. Ritchie. "Participative Management: Quality versus Quantity." *California Management Review,* Summer 1971, pp. 48–56.

Milgrim, S. "Behavioral Study of Obedience." *Journal of Abnormal and Social Psychology* 67 (1963), pp. 371–78.

Mintzberg, H. *The Nature of Managerial Work.* New York: Harper & Row, 1973.

Mockler, R. J. "Situational Theory of Management." *Harvard Business Review,* May–June 1971, pp. 146–55.

Morse, J. J., and J. W. Lorsch. "Beyond Theory Y." *Harvard Business Review,* May–June 1970, pp. 61–68.

Pelz, D. C. "Influence: Key to Effective Leadership in the First-Line Supervisor." *Personnel* 29 (1952), pp. 209–17.

Sargent, A. *The Androgynous Manager.* New York: AMACOM, 1981.

Sashkin, M. "Participative Management Is an Ethical Imperative." *Organizational Dynamics,* Spring 1984, pp. 4–22.

Sayles, L. R. *Managerial Behavior.* New York: McGraw-Hill, 1964.

Sethi, S. P.; N. Namiki; and C. Swanson. *The False Promise of the Japanese Miracle.* New York: G. P. Putnam's Sons, 1984.

Steele, P. P., and R. L. Hubbard. "Management Styles, Perceptions of Substance Abuse, and Employee Assistance Programs in Organizations." *Journal of Applied Behavioral Science* 21, no. 3 (1985), pp. 271–86.

Stogdill, R. M. *Handbook of Leadership.* New York: MacMillan/Free Press, 1974.

Strauss, G. "Some Notes on Power Equalization." In *The Social Science of Organizations,* ed. H.J. Leavitt. Englewood Cliffs, N.J.: Prentice-Hall, 1963.

Tannenbaum, R., and W. Schmidt. "How to Choose a Leadership Style." *Harvard Business Review* 36 (1958), pp. 95–101.

Vroom, V. *Some Personality Determinants of the Effects of Participation.* Englewood Cliffs, N.J.: Prentice-Hall, 1960.

________. "Can Leaders Learn to Lead?" *Organizational Dynamics,* Winter 1976, pp. 17–28.

Vroom, V., and P. Yetton. *Leadership and Decision Making.* Pittsburgh: University of Pittsburgh Press, 1973.

Walton, R. E., and L. A. Schlesinger. "Do Supervisors Thrive in Participative Work Systems?" *Organizational Dynamics,* Winter 1979, pp. 25–38.

Wilensky, H. W. "Human Relations in the Work Place." *Research in Human Industrial Relations,* 12th ed. Ed. Conrad Arensberg. New York: Harper & Row, 1957.

‣ ‣ ‣ 13

RELATIONS AMONG GROUPS IN THE ORGANIZATION

The more differential the tasks necessary to accomplish the organization's work, the more appropriate it is to create separate subsystems for doing each task.

Since virtually every large organization requires some division of labor, it is usually necessary to have departments, branches, divisions, units, teams, and so forth, to accomplish the various tasks. Helping the individual subsystems do their parts and insuring that their work is integrated toward the goals of the organization as a whole is a key way in which a manager determines the system's overall effectiveness. When the organization has groups doing tasks that differ in terms of complexity, rate of change of the technology used, skills needed, length of time it takes to complete the task, and so forth, then the job of coordinating the subunits becomes a major managerial undertaking.

In general: **The more differentiated the tasks necessary to accomplish the organization's work, the more appropriate it is to create separate subsystems for doing each task.** And as you might expect: **Each subunit works best when organized in a way that fits the demands of its task (Lawrence & Lorsch, 1967).** The subunit's structure, personnel, operating style, reward system, and leadership should be matched to its particular tasks. In other words: **When the background factors and required system "fit" the unit's goals, it is most likely to be effective; when the emergent system also fits, it is even more likely to be effective.** Even when subunit organization is not perfectly matched to task, there is a tendency for the group to acquire an identity that is at least partly reflective of the type of work it does, the skills needed to do it, who the members are, the technology involved, the rate of change in the group's environment, and what behavior the organization rewards.

Think about a classroom task group in relation to other groups. You can sense a kind of group identity, which the members seek to maintain and enhance; it's like a group self-concept. The members have probably developed some distinct goals and preferences in working style, such as how to use their time, how task-oriented they wish to be, and how personal and close they permit members to become. They are likely to have some sense of the group's competencies, such as how well it discusses problems and how effectively it maintains participation. And the group surely has a set of beliefs and values reflected in its norms, ideals, and rules for what kinds of behaviors are acceptable or not. It is no different in any organization. **Work groups tend to develop a group concept, which they strive to maintain and enhance (Blake, Shepard, & Mouton, 1964).**

Part of the basis of the concept that develops is that people naturally gravitate into groups that reinforce their values. Most voluntary groups form on that basis, and their cohesiveness can be directly attributed to the fact that membership serves to reinforce basic personal values. While work groups in most organizations do not form on a voluntary basis, it is safe to say that the more differentiated a work group's task, the more likely will members be recruited who share *common background factors.* These may include education, professional identity, ethnic grouping, race, religion, common interests, and so forth. **The more similar are members' background factors, the clearer the group's emergent identity will tend to be.** Since in most organizations the division of labor is based upon specialized task and skill areas, work groups at all levels of the system will tend to be composed of people with similar backgrounds, at least in regard to a given skill area.

Rewards can have an especially potent effect on group identity. Different units responsible for different tasks are often rewarded for different behavior. For example, employees responsible for quality control are rewarded for making sure that products *do not deviate* from prescribed standards, whereas those in a research and development function are often rewarded for *experimenting* with *deviations* from previously established standards. Rewards that differentially reinforce behavior serve also to reinforce distinct group identities. Consequently, without strong organizational rewards for cooperation among such differentiated groups, it becomes difficult to achieve satisfactory integration of functions where needed.

> **INTERVIEWER:** *Did you have national anthems?*
> **2,000-YEAR-OLD MAN:** *It was very fragmented. It wasn't nations; it was caves. Each cave had a national anthem.*
> **INTERVIEWER:** *Do you remember the national anthem of your cave?*
> **2,000-YEAR-OLD MAN:** *I certainly do; I'll never forget it. You don't forget a national anthem in a minute.*
> **INTERVIEWER:** *Let me hear it, sir.*
> **2,000-YEAR-OLD MAN** [Singing]: *Let them all go to hell except cave 76.*
>
> *The 2000-Year-Old Man*
> Album by Carl Reiner & Mel Brooks

Furthermore: **The more cohesive the group, the clearer and more strongly felt the identity is likely to be to group members (Blake & Mouton, 1961).** As you may recall, in Chapter 4 we offered a number of propositions on the factors that increase a group's cohesiveness, including common values and goals, a common enemy, high required interactions, and low interactions required outside the group.

And we also postulated that the more cohesive the group, the more closely members would conform to the group's norms. Thus, when a group emergent system that is attractive to members develops out of what is required to get the work done, the group's way of doing things is likely to be seen by members not only as appropriate but also as extremely desirable and valuable. The *group's* "self-concept" becomes worth protecting.

VARIATIONS IN GROUP IDENTITY

What are some of the ways in which group identities may differ? How do differing emergent systems compare with one another? You will already have observed many groups in cases, in class, and at work, and have seen that they have different ways of doing things. In order to examine the reasons why groups sometimes have difficulty working together, we need to suggest a few important dimensions on which work groups often differ, to add to those discussed in Chapter 6 on group effectiveness.

Time Horizon

One important way group members in organizations may differ is in their view of time. Certain kinds of tasks tend to call for a relatively short-term time horizon, and others call for a long-term time horizon. These task "demands" transcend the fact that we all have different preferences for work pace. Basic research, for example, is not a process that can easily be hurried along, and it tends to require a rather distant time horizon. Competitive sales, on the other hand, normally calls for rapid decisions and a series of short-term checkpoints on the way to long-range objectives. **The time horizon tends to be shortest for those tasks that require immediate feedback and have outcomes that can provide such feedback; the time horizon tends to be longest for those tasks whose relevant outcomes and, consequently, sources of feedback are more delayed (Lawrence & Lorsch, 1967; Rice, 1969).** You can see how people in a marketing division of a company can measure their successes in terms of immediate sales and how inevitable it is that they would operate out of a relatively short time horizon. If, however, such sales commit other divisions of the system to delivery times that are incompatible with their own time horizons, some degree of conflict is bound to ensue. Research and development people, for example, may find such commitments impossible to meet and foreign to their concepts of how their work should be carried out. Each group is likely to deal with time issues in its own way and believe in the "correctness" of its procedures and assumptions. Since time is so much a part of everything in organizational life, it is often taken for granted. Groups with different time horizons frequently have difficulty understanding one another.

Are you a person who gets to meetings on time or even early? Or, perhaps, a person who is habitually late? Groups' and departments' attitudes toward time also differ in this respect, with some likely to start and stop meetings right on time while others are much more casual about how rigidly people are expected to stick to schedules. Since attitudes toward time often take on a connotation of good and bad, such differences can create tension. Imagine five researchers strolling into a meeting with production personnel, who all arrived at 3 minutes before 2:00, at 4, 6, and even 12 minutes after 2:00!

Perspective on the Task

Some units have jobs that keep members narrowly focused upon one aspect of the work. An extreme example would be on an assembly line, where the workers put the same kind of bolt in the same kind of hole all day long, never getting to see the end product or even some of the subassemblies. Contrast that task to one involving a quality check on the final product; the perspective of each is very different with respect to the scope of the task.

The broader the perspective on the task, the greater will be member awareness of task group interdependencies and the greater will be concern for the total effort (Blake et al., 1964). Normally, the higher a unit is in the hierarchy, the greater the likelihood of members seeing the "big picture," that is, the overall relation of subunits and their connections to organizational goals. Members of lower-level units often focus only on their particular set of tasks, with less sense of the context in which they are operating. But this difference in perspective is not limited to differences in hierarchical level. It can vary with the unit's required interactions with outside subsystems. **The greater the number of interactions required with other subsystems, the broader is a subsystem's task perspective likely to be (Lorsch & Lawrence, 1972).**

Because breadth of perspective can vary, different units can place different priorities on organizational goals. And subunit goals can seem more important than overall goals to a group with limited perspective. Thus there can be distinct differences among groups in perspective on tasks.

In order to broaden employees' perspectives, more and more companies are redesigning tasks in ways that expand worker responsibilities for carrying through several stages of a job. In addition, workers are being given increasing responsibility for managing and coordinating work activities individually and in groups. Some of these approaches are discussed in Chapter 14, but at this point we wanted to introduce you to the idea that many problems associated with a narrow task perspective are soluble through direct modification of the way in which the work is carried out.

Professional Identity

If you ever get the chance, talk to a quality control engineer about his/her priorities; do the same with people in sales, people in financial operations, and people in the human resources area of a company. Ask each group about their perceptions of the other groups. What you are likely to discover are some very fundamental differences in how each profession sees itself, its priorities, its importance to the total organization, and the qualities of the other groups. The very nature of the sales activity places a high premium on being able to make commitments to customers that the company can honor. This usually places heavy time pressures on the production end of the process. The very nature of the quality control function places a high premium on making sure that only the best gets delivered to the customer, even if it takes more time to get the product out. When these two sets of priorities collide, we have what is called an *inherent conflict,* that is, one that is a reflection of the background factors of the parties involved. Ironically, such conflicts are not all that undesirable, since the conflicting views are both usually legitimate. It is a manager's job to balance those views in ways that benefit the total organization and not to allow one side to dominate the other at the expense of the organization. In the example given, it is important to deliver a quality product to a customer, but also important to do so within a reasonable time. In a healthy organization, these differences are managed and do not become occasions for internally destructive consequences. But they do require attention and some skill on the part of a manager to keep things from deteriorating into win-lose or lose-lose battles. Unfortunately, the history of some interprofessional relations has been less than collaborative, union–management relations being a good example.

Attitudes toward Authority and Internal Structure

As you may recall from the chapters on leadership (11 and 12) and group effectiveness (6), the amount of control and participation in a group should be related to the group's needs in accomplishing its tasks. Groups where expertise is widely distributed and needed for the solution of complex, changing problems require a more participative, free-wheeling, noncontrolling style of operation than those where task requirements are clear and expertise strongly differentiated.

WHOSE TAKEOVER? SOME GM DATA PROCESSING PEOPLE FEEL THE AUTO FIRM, NOT EDS, WAS THE ONE ACQUIRED

Almost everyone agrees that the two companies have very different work environments. That of GM's white-collar work force, for example, reflects the omnipresent blue-collar unions, even though they represent fewer than 200 salaried workers. Strict job rules, restrictions, and guidelines make it difficult to reward strong performers in GM's lower ranks, managers say. White-collar workers ride the coattails of UAW members, usually getting any salary and benefit increases won in new union contracts. "Now we've got everything they've got, except one thing," a GM veteran says. "We don't have protection."

In contrast, successful EDS employees describe a brutally competitive atmosphere: low pay, strict personal discipline, and hard work. "EDS is very up-front about how to get on the fast track," a former EDS executive says. "Work hard, keep your nose clean, and keep that nose to the grindstone." H. Ross Perot (EDS's founder, currently its chairman, and also a GM director) is an Annapolis graduate who made a practice of hiring gung-ho types from the military. One result: Its employees are hard-charging, extremely loyal, and devoted to EDS and its leaders.

Upright personal conduct is demanded. The company outlaws drinking at lunch and frowns on extramarital affairs and abortions. But clothes are the most visible symbol of the difference between the two groups. EDS insists on a conservative dress code outlawing loud ties, short skirts, and even men's shoes with buckles or tassels.

"All the EDS people dress alike," a GM data processor says. "I swear they all have brown hair, medium build, and medium height." Because the issue is so sensitive, EDS modified its stand so that only GM employees working with EDS's outside customers must comply with the dress code. But one GM data processor notes that a co-worker who never used to dress up for work has begun wearing sport jackets every day.

Source: Reprinted by permission of *The Wall Street Journal*, © Dow Jones & Company, Inc., December 19, 1984. All rights reserved.

Furthermore, over time groups develop quite different notions about the proper style of leadership, the appropriate amount of latitude for individual decision making and involvement, and for allowable amounts of initiative. Can you see how groups that differ along these dimensions might view one another with less than full approval?

In many high-tech companies today there is a growing problem around the management of computer experts. Similar to research and development people, the computer engineers and scientists tend to be so heavily involved in their work that they often ignore the usual organizational rules about specific hours, reporting relationships, and general work habits. The dilemma for top management is how to allow these employees the freedom and latitude that suits them and fosters their productivity without incurring the resentment of other groups whose work style is more in line with traditional management practices. Is it possible to have two (or even more) different sets of rules for employees in the same organization? Here is where the emergent norms of a subpart of the total organization may be highly functional for that group's work, but be dysfunctional for total system harmony. As you will see a little further on, this problem can proliferate into intergroup stereotyping and rivalries, which are potentially damaging if they are not managed constructively.

Interpersonal Orientation

One further way in which group identities differ is in their orientation to interpersonal relations. Groups vary in terms of whether they value closeness or distance, openness or politeness, seriousness or kidding, and so forth. Members who have arrived at some agreement on how people should relate to one another often think that members of other groups with different orientations are strange or unlikable. Others are "too pushy and effusive" or "too cold," "too blunt" or "too indirect," "too pompous" or "too frivolous," depending on the group to which

THE STRANGER

The Stranger within my gate,
He may be true or kind,
But he does not talk my talk—
I cannot feel his mind.
I see the face and the eyes and the mouth,
But not the soul behind.

The men of my own stock,
They may do ill or well,
But they tell the lies I am wonted to,
They are used to the lies I tell;
And we do not need interpreters
When we go to buy and sell.

The men of my own stock,
Bitter bad they may be,
But, at least, they hear the things I hear,
And see the things I see;
And whatever I think of them and their likes
They think of the likes of me.

Rudyard Kipling

one belongs. Whatever the emergent orientation, "the way our group relates to people" comes to be seen as the best or only way for sensible people to deal with one another.

In one company a department made up of highly educated people with similar outside interests tended to socialize a great deal during nonworking hours and were demonstrably friendly even during working hours. Individuals who were not a part of that group developed a very distorted picture of the group, seeing it as a bunch of goof-offs who did not care about their work or the company. The fact that the department was one of the most productive in the company didn't seem to change the perception. Obviously, the perceivers were finding the behavior of this department to be a threat to some aspect of their self-concepts. Furthermore, it reflected a frequently observed tendency for members of one group to interpret the behavior of another group according to their own norms and values, which, unfortunately, leads to further misperceptions (Hall & Whyte, 1973).

Summary

Thus, in terms of *(a)* attitudes toward time, authority, and structure, *(b)* perspective on tasks, and *(c)* interpersonal orientation, organizational subsystems can and do differ. Each develops its own identity in coping with the tasks assigned to it. That identity is the group equivalent of individual self-concept; the more cohesive the group, the greater the members' commitment is to preserving and enhancing its identity and the more likely members are to see the group's way of doing things as correct, valuable, and superior to other groups' ways. Finally, insofar as group organization should follow from and be appropriate to the group's tasks: **The more differentiated a subsystem's tasks, the more effective it will be when its identity (or way of operating) is also differentiated from the identities of other subsystems.**

THE PRICE OF APPROPRIATE DIFFERENTIATION: PROBLEMS ARISING FROM STRONG GROUP IDENTITY

Unfortunately, however, as you by now may have anticipated: **The clearer and more distinct a subsystem's identity, the greater the difficulty in coordination with other subsystems when their tasks are interdependent (Blake & Mouton, 1961).** Insofar as differentiated groups carry on interdependent tasks, there is a need for coordination among them. And the greater the degree of interdependence, the more important is the coordination. In order for there to be effective intergroup coordination:

1. Each group must be aware of its own functions in relation to those of other groups.
2. Each group must be willing to maintain communication links with the other groups.
3. Each group must be willing to accept the legitimacy of the needs of the other groups.
4. Each group must be willing to meet its own needs within the framework of the total system.

But a group with a sharply differentiated identity is likely to resist any form of coordination that conflicts with its identity. **The extent of a group's resistance to coordination with other groups will be directly related to the degree to which the required interactions conflict with the group's basic norms, ideals, and values.**

Just as with individuals and relationships: **To the extent that a group perceives a relationship with another group as enhancing its own identity, it will strive to develop and maintain that relationship. To the extent that a group perceives a relationship with another group as in some way threatening its own identity, it will strive to resist or avoid that relationship.** In those instances in an organization where the nature of the task *requires* a working relationship between any two groups, these propositions become extremely important. **The more an intergroup relationship requires activities and interactions that are compatible with the identities of the groups involved, the more effective will that relationship be; the more it requires activities and interactions that are contradictory to the identities of either or both groups, the more that relationship will be a source of conflict.**

Once a group has developed a strong identity, there is a tendency to see any rival (or potential rival) group in predictably distorted ways. **Members of a differentiated cohesive group with a strong sense of its own identity will show the following tendencies (Blake & Mouton, 1961, 1964):**

1. **Perception of their own group as "better" than the other group.**
2. **An upgrading of their own ideas and a downgrading of the other group's ideas.**
3. **An overestimation of their own competence and an underestimation of the competence of the other group.**
4. **Overvaluation of their own leader(s) and undervaluation of the other group's leaders(s).**
5. **Avoidance or limiting of interactions and communications with the other group.**
6. **Distortion of information about the other group in ways that cast the other group in an unfavorable light.**
7. **Mistrust of the members of the other group.**

Perhaps you can recognize some or all of these tendencies from your own experience. Intergroup rivalries in school, competing gangs in the neighborhood, and organized team sports are all familiar examples. More troublesome, of course, are situations involving race relations, political and military conflicts, and the like. Prejudice feeds on limited and distorted information, strengthening the intensity with which the prejudiced beliefs are held and making the possibilities of misunderstanding and escalated conflict even greater.

Even when contradictory data are present, people tend to maintain stereotyped perceptions. The individual member of that group who behaves differently than what the stereotype suggests is always the "exception to the rule"; the individual who happens to behave according to the stereotype simply confirms its "validity." In our current era of social change, in which minorities and women are moving into more positions heretofore inaccessible to them, they face this kind of problem. Kanter (1977) calls this "double jeopardy" and finds that it places incredible stress on those who experience it. In short, the consequences of intergroup stereotyping include damaging effects on both group relations and individuals in the organization. We comment further on this issue later when we discuss the management of diversity.

Prejudice and war are more dramatic and dangerous manifestations of the tendency to misperceive other groups. But even within formal organizations these tendencies occur whenever two working units find themselves interdependent and in conflict. The conflict creates uncertainty and anxiety; often rumors develop about what one or another group is doing or plotting, which heightens the antagonism, causes "retaliation" in advance ("preemptive strikes" in military jargon), which in turn further angers the other group and "confirms" their worst suspicions. The more either or both groups see the conflict as a threat to group identity, the more evident these tendencies become and the more difficult it is to achieve resolution.

GROUP STATUS

We have been examining the sources of group identity as they follow from task differentiation and showing how the differentiation can lead to difficulties. But another aspect of a group's identity is important for understanding coordination problems.

It is inevitable that, in assigning jobs to various subsystems, an organization will confer differing amounts of legitimate influence to groups. Some subsystems will be expected to give orders to and initiate interaction with others; other subsystems will be expected to wait for initiatives from subsystems doing different jobs. This allocation of influence will usually be based on the flow of work, though it may not have a very explicit rationale. Whatever the reasoning behind the particular way power is allocated: **The more *legitimate power* a group has within the system, the more freedom it has to initiate actions and the more that other less powerful groups are dependent upon it to initiate actions (Seiler, 1963).** The marketing department in one firm might have the right to decide what products will be tested and sold, while the production department has to go along despite its reservations. In another organization, the financial group might be given the power to exert control over operating departments to insure adequate returns. But the formal-legitimate power of groups is not the only determinant of influence. The informal social system, as usual, has an important part to play.

Informal Group Status in the System

We have already pointed out in Chapter 11 about leadership, that influence in an organization is based upon both formal position and informal status, the latter being determined by a variety of factors including education, social status of a given profession or occupation, special abilities, "whom you know," how important the work is to the overall organization, and seniority. Just as some individuals in an organization seem to carry more informal influence than they have been formally assigned, because they have been around for a long time or do a very special kind of work, it is not unusual for a particular subsystem to possess informal influence and status that far exceed what is formally designated to it.

A common example of this is the case of technical staff in industry. While they do not normally possess the designated formal authority of line people who are responsible for the operations of the firm, their special expertise and advanced degrees often give them an informal status that carries a great deal of influence with top management. Or, it may lead them to *see* themselves as higher status and therefore as having more influence than they are formally assigned. It becomes an intergroup problem when line people and staff people compete for influence and control because legitimacy is in dispute. Take the case of efficiency experts coming into a department to study its operations and make recommendations for improving that department. It doesn't take much imagination to see how the outside experts can be seen as the "enemy," since they pose the threat of carrying more influence than the organizational chart indicates. Similarly, within a university, power is delegated from the board of trustees to the administration; but informal status is attributed to the faculty, who are seen as the backbone of the educational process. Who carries the most weight and with whom? Struggles around this kind of issue can generate great tension and serious questions about what outcomes are functional for the *total* system as opposed to any one of the competing subsystems.

Groups that possess expertise crucial to the success of an organization often have considerable power attributed to them by other groups whose status in the power hierarchy is lower. Consequently, one of the interesting paradoxes of organizational life is that groups with special power (especially when it is not related to the structural hierarchy) tend to be envied, resented, and yet paid extra deference by other, less powerful groups. It is typical of the tension between "haves" and "have nots" (Brown, 1978).

The more *informal status* a group has within the system, the more freedom it has to initiate actions and the more other lower-status groups are dependent upon it to initiate actions (Seiler, 1963). With the exception of the *source* (formal versus informal) of influence, this proposition is a repeat of the previous one. When a group has both legitimate power and informal status (for example, a medical staff running a hospital, engineers with advanced degrees managing a manufacturing company), one major source of intergroup conflict is eliminated. But most large organizations tend to promote people on the basis of demonstrated managerial competence, which may or may not have anything to do with technical expertise. High-status *professionals* often tend to view "mere administrators" as having less status and therefore as not legitimately able to control the professionals even though the organization chart assigns the administrators formal authority.

In short, the existence of the two important sources of influence frequently results in incongruencies in intergroup relations. These incongruencies exist when a group possesses higher legitimate power than other groups but lower informal status, or vice versa. **An incongruency between legitimate power and status tends to result in confusion about which group can exercise the greater freedom to take actions that affect the other and which group "has the right" to initiate interactions with the other (Seiler, 1963).** Can the university faculty decide to limit class sizes without considering the registration and facility problems that such an action poses? Can the administration decide to expand the university for financial reasons without obtaining faculty consent? Can the quality control expert stop production over the protests of the production manager? And when serious conflicts occur, how can one group initiate action without in some way affecting the identity of the other group?

Social Diversity and Intergroup Relations

The management of diverse professions and varied educational backgrounds of employees has long been known to practicing managers.

Similarly, most managers today are becoming increasingly conscious of the impact of employee social backgrounds on behavior and attitudes in the workplace. Differences in race, sex, age, and ethnicity are now becoming challenges for creative management, management that successfully *integrates* the work activities carried out by employees with such widely diverse backgrounds.

This diversity often gets played out in the relations among groups of employees in the same organization. The attitudes, perceptions, and problems that exist among groups in society are frequently carried into the work setting and create barriers to cooperation among groups that need to work together. Many nurses (mostly women) react to doctors (mostly men) in part from their perceptions as women reacting to men; young high-tech engineers often discount the opinions of older engineering managers because of the age difference; many white professional managers find it difficult to defer to the opinion of a black counterpart even when that person is obviously competent. These are all background attitudes that people bring into their organizations; they add to some of the already present intergroup problems. A competent manager needs to be sensitive to the *sources* of intergroup attitudes, especially when they are totally outside management's sphere of control.

PINPOINTING THE SOURCE OF AIR-TRAFFIC DISPUTES

Potential FAA supervisors are not screened for their ability to oversee subordinates, nor are they trained in employee relations. Moreover . . . superfluous layers of management tend to alienate regional FAA managers and leave top officials of the agency with little sense of the rigors of a controller's job. As a result, "although the dissatisfactions of controllers and managers arose for different reasons, the poor attitudes of each group reinforced each other."

[There is an] *age gap between supervisors and the well-educated, restless generation of controllers hired during the 1960s.*

Source: *Business Week,* April 5, 1982.

CHOOSING BETWEEN CONFLICT AND COOPERATION

For the manager, whether or not to attempt to do something about subsystems in conflict depends upon an assessment of the functionality of the dispute for the total organization. While conflict can be costly, as in the above example, in some cases it is a necessary part of achieving full consideration of legitimately differing viewpoints. Without conflict among subsystems, the total needs of the organization might be ignored in favor of the highest-status subsystem's needs or pushed aside by the more powerful subgroups. Allowing or even encouraging conflict by greater differentiation of group ways of working may be the only way to achieve some balance among subsystems, each of which would like to maximize its own effectiveness regardless of the consequences for the whole organization. Remember the rationale for the matrix organization in Chapter 2? Balanced decisions often require conflicts over issues.

For example, while the survival of a company might depend upon rapid sales pricing decisions, it may also be crucial for the company to maintain a reputation for quality products and service. If the quality control, engineering, and service departments all took the same short-term view as the sales department and exercised very little control over their individual employees in order to speed up decisions, they might get along better with sales but shortchange long-term quality. Only if the respective subgroups are properly differentiated, encouraged to fully express their respective points of view, and allowed to struggle with the trade-offs between keeping prices down and quality up will a proper balance be achieved.

Where intergroup problems surface as wasteful conflict, they need to be approached in terms of reducing conflict and building cooperation; where problems are created by disproportionate dominance of one subsystem, they need to be treated with measures to further differentiate subgroups and/or increase open conflict among the groups (Seiler, 1963; Blake et al., 1964; Kelly, 1970). In short, conflict can be a result of genuine differences in group values, which are reflected in disputes about desired system goals, in which case they may be functional and necessary for the total system. Without thorough discussion, the total system may be harmed. On the other hand, when conflict is a result of the group identification that often occurs with differentiated groups and goes beyond legitimate disagreements into stereotyping, sniping, and sabotaging, it can be very dysfunctional for the total system. Energy is used that could be better focused on the actual tasks.

Similarly, cooperation can be functional or dysfunctional for the total system, depending on whether it reflects genuine integration of efforts or covering up of disagreements that need to be aired in order to arrive at balanced decisions. And as noted in Chapter 2, there are times when it is not possible to produce functional consequences for all subsystems as well as for the total system. Imperfection is a price that must often be lived with in a complex organization.

TYPES OF INTERDEPENDENCE

The importance of intergroup cooperation versus conflict depends upon the degree and kind of interdependence of the work groups involved (Thompson, 1967). If, for example, the work of each subsystem contributes to the productivity or welfare of the total system but is not directly related to that of the other, there are very few, if any, coordination issues. This is sometimes called *"pooled interdependence."* The various subdivisions of a large department store (housewares, sporting goods, clothing, and so forth) might be a familiar example of pooled interdependence. Each can try to maximize its own sales effectiveness without hurting other units.

However, if the work is carried out in such a way that one group cannot begin its task until another has completed its work, then you can see the critical nature of interdependence. This type is called *"serial interdependence"*; it is typical of assembly line operations, construction companies, printing firms, and even health services where treatment at one point in the system depends upon diagnostic tests at an earlier point in the system.

The most complex kind of interdependence occurs when work groups need to exchange information on a continuing basis. This is called *"reciprocal interdependence."* In the development of plans for a new car model, for example, it is necessary for designers, engineers, market researchers, and production experts to exchange information and ideas over and over so that the final product is both innovative and sound.

You can probably see for yourself how the manager's job will vary with each of the three kinds of situations described above. In the case of pooled interdependence, a manager needs to make sure that each of the various groups maintains a satisfactory level of output but that no one group is in a position to hold up the work of any other. With serial interdependence and reciprocal interdependence, the task is more complex and difficult. In fact, very few modern-day work patterns have the simplicity of pooled interdependence alone; a great many have elements of all three types. Take, for example, a research and development firm in which scientists, engineers, designers, production specialists, and so forth all need to coordinate their efforts. The later stages of product manufacturing and testing are dependent upon the earlier stages of invention and development; the research chemists need to be aware of the manufacturing constraints, and the manufacturing people must understand the time it takes to develop new ideas. The overall process requires ongoing information exchange among the various groups, and it is all oriented toward the goals of the total system.

You can appreciate by now just how important it is for a manager to understand and develop competence in dealing with intergroup relations. Whether the fostering of conflict or cooperation is called for, it is important that the manager understand the need for differentiated subsystems, the likelihood of their developing diverse identities or cultures, and the need for methods to resolve wasteful conflict when greater coordination is needed to achieve serial or reciprocal interdependence. Similarly, managers should know some methods to achieve greater differentiation when too much harmony is creating imbalances.

> For example, one of the major international oil companies established foreign regional divisions, each of which was to attempt capture of a significant portion of a regional market. At the same time, the company headquarters insisted upon having final say on prices of products to new customers. Problems occurred when regional salespeople needed rapid decisions in order to make a sale and were delayed by the policy of checking back with headquarters. The regional people felt that they were in the best position to know the local scene and ought to be able to take action as that scene demanded; the headquarters people insisted that their perspective was more worldwide and that they were in a better position to evaluate the going price on the world market. Both groups were right, but neither could acknowledge the legitimacy of the other's viewpoint. The longer the conflict went on, the more it got complicated with stereotypes, sabotage, miscommunications, and the like.

We'll describe how the issue was resolved later in this chapter when we discuss approaches to intergroup problems. Do you think you could come up with some approaches of your own? It could be useful to then try to compare your approach with the one used in the actual situation.

FOUNDATIONS OF INTERGROUP COOPERATION

How, then, can cooperation be built when it is necessary? As you study the following propositions on the foundation of intergroup cooperation, see if you can recognize their parallel from the chapters on group behavior. In fact, the fundamental proposition is almost identical in both cases.

The more frequent the interaction between any two groups, the greater the tendency to cooperate with each other. However, as in the case of interactions among members of a group, it is important to qualify the above proposition. **To the extent that there is frequent and open information flow among groups in a system, common goals are more likely to develop (Gouldner, 1960).** And add to this proposition the following one: **The more that groups recognize and accept common goals, the more likely they are to cooperate (Walton & Dutton, 1969).**

These propositions are basic to the effective management of all intergroup relations in an organization. To the extent that managers use a "divide and rule" approach by preventing open exchanges of information among working units, they risk intergroup competition and conflict, possibly to the serious detriment of the total system. Where task interdependence necessitates cooperation, bringing key managers together frequently and encouraging constant flow of communications among various interdependent work units increase the likelihood of ongoing cooperation and goal achievement.

Since we also know that: **The more groups share a common source of threat, the more likely they are to cooperate,** it becomes crucial for manager to avoid becoming that "common source of threat." In competitive fields, the common source of threat obviously must be the outside competition. Here is where an effective manager can mobilize cooperative effort by making certain that any source of threat serving to bind groups together lies *outside* the system and does not have divisive effects inside the system.

There are three additional propositions that help to complete the foundation for intergroup cooperation:

1. **The more groups share common responsibility for problem solving and for decision making, the more likely they are to cooperate.**
2. **The more groups are able to establish joint memberships, the more likely they are to cooperate.**
3. **The more groups are willing to share and discuss their perceptions of each other, the more likely they are to cooperate (Blake et al., 1964).**

The Norm of Reciprocity

In order for the propositions stated above to be translated into effective strategies for managing intergroup operations, the various groups involved need to recognize the significance of their interrelationships. Each needs to recognize that its own identity can be enhanced by its contribution to another group, and each needs to recognize the obligations for a return contribution. This kind of "fair exchange" principal increases *mutual* functionality and is also functional to the system. This is part of the "norm of reciprocity" discussed in Chapter 10, and it is often considered to be a critical factor in maximizing interdependence (Gouldner, 1960).

An example of this norm in operation occurs in many business schools where several groupings of faculty, each from a different discipline, make decisions on curriculum content. With respect to each group's sense of its own importance it might be functional for it to dominate the decisions, but that would lead to an imbalanced program. The finance people would push for more finance courses, the marketing people for more marketing courses, the behavioral scientists for more organizational behavior courses, and so forth. If the faculty can establish a norm of reciprocity, then it is possible for each group to enhance the other, with the net result being a broad and balanced set of courses and a program that is functional for the school and the students.

On the other hand, if the groups are too understanding of the others, they may not demand the proper time for their own subject! Reciprocity can also become a form of "you scratch my back and I'll scratch yours," or "live and let live," which avoids tough priority decisions by giving everyone a bit of the goodies, deserved or not. It can be as dysfunctional to a total system to secure false peace as to fight endless battles.

METHODS FOR MAXIMIZING INTERGROUP COOPERATION

When greater cooperation is called for, several techniques can help foster it. Listed below are six basic strategies for maximizing intergroup cooperation. These approaches are both preventive and curative; that is, each may serve as a means of establishing intergroup cooperation from the start or as a means of resolving intergroup problems or conflicts that have already developed. Obviously, the more these strategies are in operation, the fewer problems are likely to develop; but few, if any, organizations are free from intergroup problems no matter how well they implement these approaches.

The six strategies are as follows:

1. Overlapping or multiple group membership.
2. Liaison or linkage people.
3. Joint task forces.
4. Joint group meetings.
5. Job exchanges across groups.
6. Physical proximity.

Let's examine each of these approaches and see the advantages and disadvantages of each. Keep in mind that different situations call for different strategies and also that combinations of two or more of the approaches are often appropriate. Each of the six strategies is directly or indirectly derivable from the propositions stated in the previous section.

Overlapping or Multiple Group Memberships

In most organizations, it is not unusual to be a member of more than one work group at any given time. A department manager, for example, is a member of both his/her own department and that group of people identifiable as department heads. (In a linking-pin organization, this is formalized in its structure.) Managers may also be assigned to a committee or task force to represent the interests of their own department on some matter of planning, policy, budget decisions, and so forth. This type of multiple group membership has the obvious advantages of keeping the several groups in contact with one another, helping the manager to coordinate efforts of the different groups, helping him/her to see various perspectives, time horizons, and styles of operating, as well as facilitating a total system perspective. In all these respects, such an approach is functional.

One of the problems, however, is the fact that multiple group membership can trap a person between the norms or goals of conflicting groups. For example, a committee or task force will tend to develop its own identity as it continues to meet. All members become subject to the emergent norms and pressures of the "new group" and may, at times, be faced with the dilemma of choosing between the interests of their "home group" and those of the "new group." To the extent that they maintain absolute loyalty to the interests of the home group ("We'll get every dollar we can for our department no matter how hard we have to fight"), they may hang up the new group; insofar as they succumb to the pressures and influence of the new group ("We have to cut our budget for the sake of the other departments"), the home group can accuse the manager of forsaking the department.

This dilemma may be further complicated by the fact that the more frequently the individual meets and interacts with the members of both groups, the more difficult the loyalty bind becomes. Remember, this often tends to occur in the absence of other sources of interaction between members of the two groups, in which case the individual (manager, in our example) is the principal link between the groups. As a manager becomes more aware, via committee membership, of the legitimacy of the views and needs of other groups and interacts more frequently with the members of the committee, greater mutual liking and respect will develop. The individual becomes most acutely aware of this loyalty bind when: *(a)* attempting to explain and defend each group's position to the other group and *(b)* each group increases pressure on the individual to hold firm and maintain loyalty.

In addition, the more the individual representing a group embodies the norms and values of that group, the greater will be the bind in the face of conflicting pressures. And the more *cohesive* that group is, the more pressure it will exert to take an unyielding position.

In short, the multiple group memberships generally experienced by managers in large organizations can serve important functions in maintaining intergroup interdependence, but they also have built into them some serious obstacles related to conflicting pressures from the different groups. Some of the difficulties, however, can be offset by implementing additional approaches for intergroup interactions, as you will see in the next few pages.

Liaison or Linkage People

Over the years as organizations have faced increasing complexities and uncertainties, it has become more important for them to be able to process information and make decisions rapidly. The classical chain of command has become obsolete in many areas of work. It simply cannot manage the demand for flexibility and responsiveness to change and uncertainty. It has become more imperative than ever for groups in a system to maintain a fairly constant and open flow of important information. As a result, heavy demands are made upon managers to serve as the critical information links for the various subunits of the system. But managers have their limits and in modern society can easily suffer from overload problems.

One important development that has occurred in response to this problem is the creation of liaison or linkage people for the groups in the organization. These individuals, or sometimes groups of individuals, are not normally identified with any one operational unit nor do they carry any specific task responsibilities. Their role is simply (and it may not be so simple) to coordinate the efforts of various work groups, to facilitate the necessary exchanges of information, and to help keep each unit apprised of the related activities of other units.

The advantages of utilizing liaisons who are not identified with existing work groups lie in their relative neutrality with respect to group pressures, their immunity from the sanctions of any single group, and their relative freedom to move back and forth in the system as the task demands it. One disadvantage, of course, lies in their lack of legitimate "clout" to make things happen. However, through demonstrated competence they can develop a great deal of informal influence.

Linking people and groups work best when their emergent norms and attitudes toward time, structure, authority, and so forth fall approximately halfway between those of the groups being linked. If either group sees the linking people as too similar to the other group, the rejected group members are likely to feel ganged up on or misunderstood.

Joint Task Forces

The creation of a joint task force composed of members of different work groups, even groups that have experienced some conflicts, tends to be a very powerful and effective way of breaking down sharp lines between groups (see Chapter 3 for notes on task forces). Each member of the task force enters the new group with the security and support of members of the old group, but it generally follows that the interactions among the members across old group lines tend to generate liking and respect that eventually supersedes old group differences. Certainly some loyalty binds will be experienced, and certainly the old group will never quite be the same. But the payoff in terms of greater productivity, mutual group enhancement, and a wider perspective for all individuals can more than compensate for the loss of "the way it used to be."

Joint Group Meetings

Meetings of total groups with one another go even further than joint task forces to break down barriers. Obviously, a small task force can get more work done, but there are times when it is appropriate for all the members of two or more work groups to meet together in a face-to-face situation. If there has been a history of conflicts between the groups, for example, it is likely that each has built up stereotypes of the other. Since stereotypes tend to be maintained in the absence of real data and direct contact, the logical step is to bring the groups together in a setting that will facilitate interaction. Under such circumstances, groups normally find it difficult to maintain the stereotypes and the related conflicts.

> Remember the oil company situation described earlier? The regional people had developed very negative stereotypes of the headquarters people, and vice versa. Since they were several thousand miles apart and had never even met each other, with the exception of a few top level managers, it was inevitable that their differences and their stereotypes would become fixed.
>
> The strategy that was employed as a first step to resolving the conflict was for each group to state explicitly its perceptions of the other and then to begin sharing these perceptions in a series of meetings designed to force a great deal of direct interaction. As you might guess, the stereotypes did not hold up for very long; the members of both groups began to perceive each other as individuals and to both like and respect one another. The joint meeting provided the necessary vehicle for the groups to recognize and accept their interdependence.
>
> Since meetings of all the members were too expensive and time-consuming to hold very often, they created several joint task forces whose purpose it was to stay on top of problems and decisions affecting both groups. They also agreed to have certain individuals serve as liaison persons whose job it was to maintain a constant and rapid flow of information from the region to headquarters and back.
>
> Whereas previously the managers were carrying the burden of all the problems and complaints and were consequently caught in the middle, the use of the above strategies for promoting intergroup cooperation ultimately removed a very dysfunctional load from the managers' backs.

Job Exchanges across Groups

It isn't very often that you find people from different departments exchanging jobs. You might even wonder how that makes sense. But it is difficult to appreciate another person's position until you've had a chance to walk in his/her shoes. Judgments about the behavior of other people are usually made from outside the situation. If that situation happens to involve the other person's membership in another group, judgment can be colored by previous perceptions of that group. Also, it may be difficult to understand how it feels to be a member of that other group. By exchanging members, chances are increased that members of each group can appreciate the needs and operations of the other. It has the same kind of benefits as a cultural exchange.

> In one large physical rehabilitation hospital, the chief of occupational therapy exchanged jobs with the chief of physical therapy for two weeks. This action established a pattern for cooperation between the two departments that had never before existed. Members of the two departments increased their contacts and began to learn many skills from each other. Whereas the relationship between the two departments had been built upon rivalry, with each trying to demonstrate its greater value to the patients, the outcome of the job exchange was each group's recognition of its own and the other's unique but interrelated contributions to the welfare of the patient.

Physical Proximity

Perhaps all too obvious but certainly not to be overlooked is the importance of physical distance in the relations between groups. If two work groups are in different buildings, the chances for interaction are minimal during the normal working hours. The best that can be hoped for is linkage people, joint task forces, occasional joint meetings, and the like. Given what we have already stated in regard to these strategies, we certainly do not underestimate their effect. But sometimes there is simply no substitute for frequent ongoing exchanges, both task related and of a social nature. None of the previous approaches allows much room for emergent social interactions among the members of the different groups. Each strategy is task related and normally has limited time boundaries. **To the extent that two working groups maintain a close physical proximity on a day-to-day basis, interactions are likely to develop that will enhance intergroup cooperation and minimize intergroup conflict.** Perhaps each of the other approaches is a poor approximation of this one, but necessary because of the great variety of organizational constraints that dictate physical separation (for example, job specialization, and the technology of the work). However, all too often managers overlook the obvious: the physical placement of people at work can have a major effect upon their performance. The physical proximity of working groups can be a significant factor in establishing their cooperation.

IMPLICATIONS FOR ORGANIZATIONAL CHANGE

As you will see in Chapter 14, groups can be important leverage points for bringing about change in an organization. The need for change is often related to the general issue of system interdependence and specifically to problems of intergroup cooperation. Any of the strategies for increasing cooperation represents a significant intervention into the system, whether utilized to resolve an existing conflict or as a means of minimizing the potential for future conflict. Even organizational change efforts that are not directly intended to affect the relationships among work groups more often than not do have some important impact on them. As you read through the chapter on organizational change, it would be useful to keep in mind the basic propositions related to intergroup cooperation and see how they relate to the basic concepts and strategies for change.

KEY CONCEPTS FROM CHAPTER 13

1. The more differentiated the tasks necessary to accomplish the work, the more appropriate it is to create subsystems.
2. Variations in group identity.
   a. Attitudes toward time, authority, and structure.
   b. Perspective on the task, including professional identity.
   c. Interpersonal orientation.
3. Intergroup coordination depends on:
   a. Awareness of own function in relation to others.
   b. Maintenance of communication links with others.
   c. Acceptance of legitimacy of the needs of others.
   d. Willingness to meet own needs within the framework of the total structure.
4. The degree of resistance to the above is related to resulting conflict with the group's basic norms, ideals, values.
5. Problems with strong group identity.
   a. Seeing one's group as better than other(s).
   b. Seeing one's ideas as better than other(s).
   c. Overestimation of own competence.
   d. Overvaluation of one's leader(s).
   e. Avoidance of interaction with other group.
   f. Distortion of information about other group.
   g. Mistrust of the members of the other group.
6. Groups may have formal or informal status.
7. Groups may have legitimate or illegitimate power.

8. Diversity of backgrounds contributes to intergroup conflict.
9. Cooperation and conflict may be either functional or dysfunctional to the total system.
10. Types of interdependence:
    a. Pooled.
    b. Serial.
    c. Reciprocal.
11. The foundation of intergroup cooperation.
    a. Frequent interactions.
    b. Frequent and open information flow.
    c. Development and acceptance of common goals.
    d. Sharing a common source of threat.
    e. Shared common responsibility.
    f. Ability to establish joint memberships.
    g. Willingness to share and discuss perceptions of each other.
12. The norm of reciprocity maximizes interdependence.
13. Methods for maximizing intergroup cooperation:
    a. Overlapping or multiple group membership.
    b. Liaison people.
    c. Joint task forces.
    d. Joint group meetings.
    e. Job exchanges.
    f. Physical proximity.

SUGGESTED READINGS

Alderfer, C. P. "Group and Intergroup Relations." In *Improving Life at Work,* ed. J. R. Hackman and J. L. Suttle. Santa Monica, Calif.: Goodyear Publishing, 1977.

Blake, R. R., and J. S. Mouton. "Reactions to Intergroup Competition under Win-Lose Competition." *Management Science,* July 1961, pp. 420–25.

________. "Overevaluation of Own Group's Product in Intergroup Competition." *Journal of Abnormal and Social Psychology* 64, no. 3 (1962), pp. 237–38.

Blake, R. R.; H. A. Shepard; and J. Mouton. *Managing Intergroup Conflict in Industry.* Houston: Gulf Publishing, 1964.

Brown, L. D. "Toward a Theory of Power and Intergroup Relations." In *Advances in Experiential Social Processes,* Vol. 1. Ed. C. L. Cooper and C. P. Alderfer. New York: John Wiley & Sons, 1978.

Dalton, D. R., and W. D. Todor. "Unanticipated Consequences of Union-Management Cooperation: An Interrupted Time Series Analysis." *Journal of Applied Behavioral Science* 20, no. 3 (1984), pp. 253–64.

Fisher, R., and W. Ury. *Getting to Yes: Negotiating Agreement without Giving In.* Boston: Houghton Mifflin, 1981.

Gouldner, A. "The Role of the Norm of Reciprocity in Social Stabilization." *American Sociological Review* 25 (1960), pp. 161–78.

Hall, E. T., and W. F. Whyte. "Intercultural Communication: A Guide to Men of Action." In *Readings in Managerial Psychology,* 2nd ed. Ed. H. J. Leavitt and L. R. Pondy. Chicago: University of Chicago Press, 1973.

Kanter, R. M. *Men and Women of the Corporation.* New York: Alfred A. Knopf, 1977.

Kelly, J. "Make Conflict Work for You." *Harvard Business Review,* July–August 1970, pp. 103–13.

Lawrence, P. R., and J. W. Lorsch. *Organization and Environment: Managing Differentiation and Integration.* Cambridge, Mass.: Division of Research, Graduate School of Business, Harvard University, 1967.

Leavitt, H. J., and J. Lipman-Blumen. "A Case for the Relational Managers." *Organizational Dynamics,* Summer 1980, pp. 27–41.

Lentz, S. S. "The Labor Model for Mediation and Its Application to the Resolution of Environmental Disputes." *Journal of Applied Behavioral Science* 22, no. 2 (1986), pp. 127–40.

Lewicki, R. J., and J. A. Litterer. *Negotiation.* Homewood, Ill.: Richard D. Irwin, 1985.

Lorsch, J. W., and P. R. Lawrence. *Managing Group and Intergroup Relations.* Homewood, Ill.: Richard D. Irwin and Dorsey Press, 1972, pp. 285–304.

McCann, J. E., and D. Ferry. "An Approach for Assessing and Managing Interunit Interdependence." *Academy of Management Review,* January 1979, pp. 113–20.

Rice, A. K. "Individual, Group, and Intergroup Behavior." *Human Relations* 22 (1969), pp. 565–84.

Schelling, T. C. *The Strategy of Conflict.* New York: Oxford University Press, 1960.

Seiler, J. A. "Diagnosing Interdepartmental Conflict." *Harvard Business Review,* September–October 1963.

Smith, K. K. "An Intergroup Perspective on Individual Behavior." In *Perspectives on Behavior in Organizations,* ed. J. R. Hackman, E. E. Lawler, and L. W. Porter. New York: McGraw-Hill, 1977.

Thomas, J. M., and W. G. Bennis, eds. *Management of Change and Conflict.* New York: Penguin Books, 1972.

Thompson, J. D. *Organizations in Action.* New York: McGraw-Hill, 1967.

Walton, R. E. "Third-Party Roles in Interdepartmental Conflict." *Industrial Relations* 7 (1967), pp. 24–43.

Walton, R. E., and J. M. Dutton. "The Management of Interdepartmental Conflict." *Administrative Science Quarterly* 14 (1969), pp. 73–84.

Von Laue, T. H. "Transubstantiation in the Study of African Reality." *African Affairs* 4, no. 10 (1975), pp. 401–19.

14

THE MANAGER AS THE INITIATOR OF CHANGE IN THE ORGANIZATION

People usually decide to make a change when things are not going the way they would prefer.

And my father . . . often told of an old parishioner of his who, in the course of a meeting, rose to his feet and declared, "Oh no, Mr. Reid. We've tried change, and we know it doesn't work."

Alastair Reid
"Reflections" (Scotland)
New Yorker, October 5, 1981

The potential exists for an American corporate renaissance, with its implied return to greatness. Because recent economic conditions have been so unfavorable for American business, leaders should be motivated to search for new solutions—and to engage their entire work force in the search. I argue that innovation is the key. Individuals can make a difference, but they need the tools and the opportunity to use them. They need to work in settings where they are valued and supported, their intelligence given a chance to blossom. They need to have the power to be able to take the initiative to innovate.

Rosabeth Moss Kanter
The Change Masters

This final chapter in the book is intended to serve two purposes. First, it deals with the general topic of organizational change, discussing the issues related to identifying the need for change, various approaches to the issues, and specific methods and techniques designed to implement change in an organization. In addition, the chapter also provides an overview of the entire book by referring to the various perspectives and concepts presented in the previous chapters as they prove to be relevant to the issue of change.

HOW DO YOU KNOW WHEN CHANGE IS NEEDED?

People usually decide to make a change when things are not going the way they would like. If your car engine runs poorly, you may change the spark plugs; if you find yourself short of money before the next paycheck, you may need to change your spending habits; if members of your family are constantly bickering, you may decide to change the patterns of interaction; and so forth. From the perspective of a manager, the need for change usually occurs when there is a problem related to *productivity, satisfaction,* and/or *development* in the system. It may be that the output of goods and services has fallen below expected levels, that an atmosphere of discouragement has emerged, that agency clients are protesting slow service, that people in the system are not learning and developing needed skills and abilities, or some combination of these. Even when the need for change is identified, it is possible for a manager to close his/her eyes and hope that the pressure for it will blow away; but such a stance more often than not will result in the manager becoming the passive victim of the change rather than its planner and initiator. We assume that as managers you will want to be as much in control as possible over what goes on around you.

This chapter will provide concepts and tools to help you assume a more activist stance. Even those who may never be faced with initiating a major organizational change still must deal with personnel coming and going, new forms of problems in daily work, unusual requests from outside a given work unit or from outside the system itself, and so forth. In that sense, an organization is like any living organism; it can decay or deteriorate over time without constant maintenance and rebuilding. Your ability (1) to anticipate the need for change as opposed to reacting after the fact, (2) to diagnose the nature of the change that is required rather than respond with the first thing that comes to mind, and (3) to make an intelligent choice of action steps rather than find the fastest way to escape the problem, can be the ultimate basis of your success.

Unfortunately, it is exceedingly difficult to manage change so as to produce desired results. Most people, groups, and organizations have remarkable resiliency and, like the child's bottom-weighted rubber punching clown, tend to return to the starting point as soon as the

> *We trained hard—but it seemed that every time we were beginning to form up into teams, we would be reorganized. I was to learn that later in life we tend to meet any new situation by reorganizing, and a wonderful method it can be for creating the illusion of progress while producing confusion, inefficiency, and demoralization.*
>
> Petronious Arbiter
> 66 A.D.

pressure is off. Furthermore, because of the interdependence of subsystems, a change in one place often pops up unexpectedly elsewhere, as shown in Chapter 2. It is not surprising that many people who have launched change projects give up in frustration and wonder why they did not "leave well enough alone."

As a member of an organization, it is not easy to change something in a desired direction without *(a)* eventual reversion to the previous state, *(b)* consequences somewhere in the organization that you did not anticipate, or *(c)* negative consequences cropping up that you did not intend (Bennis, Benne, & Chin, 1964).

Throughout the book, problems with change at different levels of the organization have been *implicit* in the analytical tools presented. For example, the social system conceptual scheme, indicating connections between consequences of the emergent system and alterations in the required system or background factors, points toward various focal points for change efforts.

We turn now to an *explicit* overview of the strategy for initiating and managing change. No single chapter, book, or course can make you an expert on managing change. We will be looking at how changes, even those aimed at technical processes, often create positive or negative consequences for the people in the organization. Insofar as it takes people to perform the internal transformation processes of the organization, their reactions to changes are of great interest to the manager. Further, we will offer some guidelines on changing behavior in ways that produce the least resistance and greatest chance of implementation and continuation. What we shall try to do is give you a sense of the various points at which a manager can intervene to accomplish goals, the variety of tools available for making desired changes, some sense of what tools might be appropriate for solving various kinds of problems, and at what point in the organization they should be applied.

WHERE TO START

One way to think about starting points for change is implicit in the organization of this book—by the numbers of people involved. Change may be aimed at the individual, pair, small group, two or more groups, the total organization, or at leaders themselves. The target for change efforts will depend upon a number of factors.

1. Where is the tension in the system?
2. How interconnected is the unit having the problem with other organizational units?

3. To what extent does the organization operate as a hierarchy?
4. Where in the system is there the most readiness for change?

Let's examine each of these questions in some detail.

Where Is the Tension?

It is often easier to get people to change when they are experiencing a moderate amount of discomfort. Those who are content with the way things are will resist changes that might increase tension; those who are suffering a great deal sometimes cling to the status quo because it is the only certainty they can identify. In classroom task groups, for example, you may have noticed that those individuals who are satisfied with the grades they are receiving resist efforts to change the way the group makes decisions, allocates work, and so on. At the other extreme, perhaps surprisingly, members who are very upset with their performance also may resist change. They often seem to freeze in unproductive patterns, repeating the same fruitless behavior even though it does not help. A poor performer may continue to miss many classes or prepare poorly for discussions, even though it is clear from outside that a change in these areas would be helpful. Have you ever seen someone who is worried about failing a math course continue to avoid doing practice problems? Great tension can create as much resistance to change as lack of it does. Thus, the system with the greatest need or the greatest pain is not always most receptive to change efforts. **In general, those who are experiencing moderate discomfort and tension are most amenable to change (Basil & Cook, 1974).** The tension can then serve as an impetus for change rather than as a signal for defensiveness.

How Interconnected Is the Problem Unit with Other Organizational Units?

Though ultimately all parts of an organization are interrelated, some units are relatively independent compared to others.

As you will remember from Chapter 13, units in an organization might have only pooled interdependence, where they are connected only by being part of the same organization; serial interdependence, where one unit's work is dependent upon receiving work from another; or reciprocal interdependence, where units need one another to do each one's work. The less "coupled" or linked units are to one another, as in pooled interdependence, the easier it will be to make changes without regard to consequences for other parts of the organization. For example, a research and development laboratory located miles away from the main offices and plant of a manufacturing com-

STAKEHOLDER ANALYSIS

A very useful tool for assessing interdependence and planning for the impact of a change on all affected subsystems is called *stakeholder analysis*. For any change attempt, there will be a number of parties (individuals, groups, or organizations) who have a stake in the outcome. Often the number of stakeholders is far greater than is at first apparent; the manager of a regional office in a federal agency was astounded when, using this tool, she identified 236 stakeholders on a key issue she was trying to resolve. As an aid to visualizing the concept, start by placing a brief label for the change in the center of a blank page, and draw a circle around it. Then, one at a time, add spokes linked to each possible stakeholder. (See example diagram using the Slade Company Case.)

Once all the possible stakeholders are identified, then go back and try to determine the following for each:

- What exactly are their stakes in the issue?
- What are their needs/desires in relation to the issue?
- What are their resources in relation to the issue? Information? Allies? Funds or supplies?
- Exactly how will they be affected by the change? Finances? Relationships with others? Status? Influence? Reputation?
- Is their cooperation/goodwill necessary, desirable, or unimportant?

Having done this kind of analysis for each stakeholder, do the same for yourself. What do you bring to the issue? Then prioritize those stakeholders most necessary for your success. Your attention should first be directed to figuring out what you can offer them from your resources that would fit with their needs or desires, in return for whatever you need from them. Before initiating action, however, try to trace through *all* the possible implications for all the stakeholders and plan accordingly. This can be tedious, but it saves a great deal of aggravation later. Too many good change ideas have been sunk because the well-intentioned manager did not anticipate who would be affected and how to deal with them.

While this kind of diagnosis does not tell you what to do, it helps to prevent glaring omissions and unanticipated consequences. There are enough unpleasant surprises in organizational life without those you create for yourself by poor diagnosis and planning!

pany can probably change rules on dress and working hours more easily and with fewer repercussions than could the assembly department at the plant. When an organizational unit is relatively independent because of location, power, structure, or task, changes are easier to implement. Thus: **The greater the autonomy of an organizational subsystem, the more readily can changes be implemented and the less will changes there cause problems for the rest of the organization (Cohen & Gadon, 1978b).**

Stakeholder Analysis Diagram for Slade Company Case

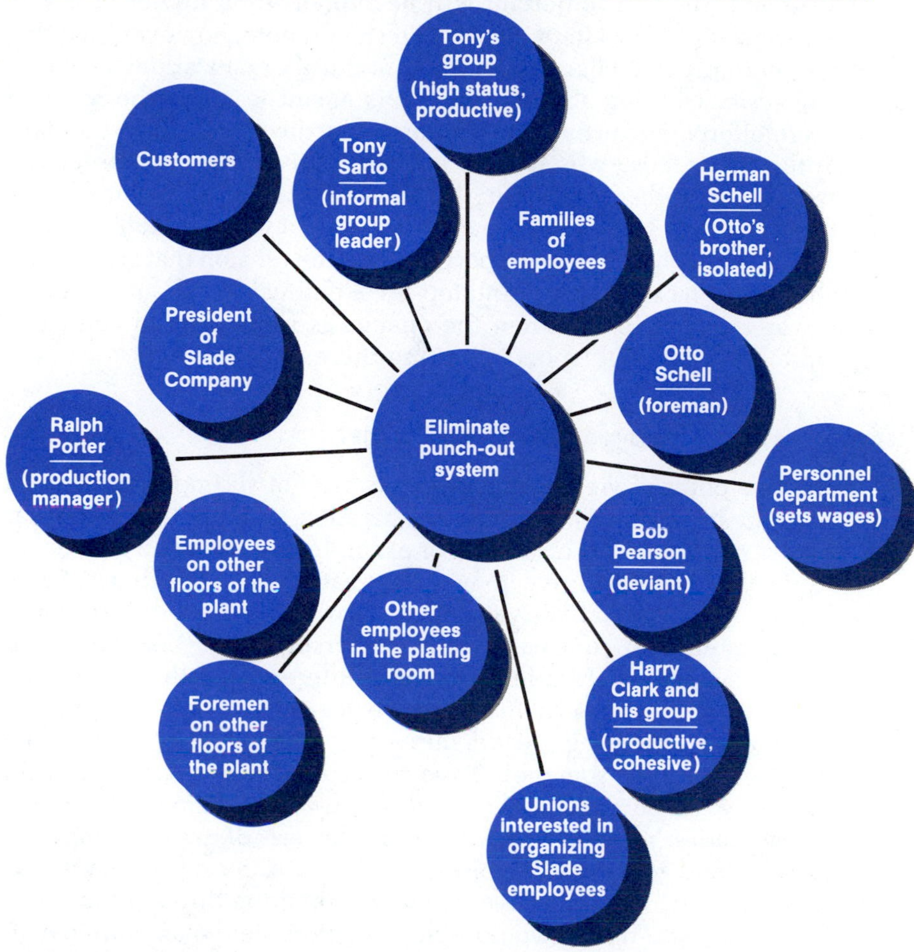

To What Extent Does the Organization Operate as a Hierarchy?

In strongly hierarchical organizations where control tends to be tight and top-down, changes that do not have the support of those at the head of the organization are likely to be short lived. While the tension may be felt at lower levels of the organization, insofar as changes below will have effects on higher levels, the support of those with the formal legitimate power must be acquired. It is disheartening and a waste of time to initiate change efforts that are squashed just as they begin to work because higher-ups are made uncomfortable by them. **The more hierarchical the organization, the higher the change efforts**

have to be aimed, or legitimized. In turn, the greater the autonomy of the subunit, the less important will be support from higher levels in the organization (Beckhard, 1967). We should note, however, that this does not imply that change in nonhierarchical organizations is necessarily *easier* to bring about; rather, it is meant to guide the focus of change efforts. Nevertheless, support from the top is almost always helpful. **When those who have to change receive clear, unambiguous messages from the top about the reasons for and inevitability of change, they are more likely to go along with it (Kanter, 1983; Peters & Waterman, 1982).** Clear support reduces the tension that arises from ambiguity or lack of clarity. And top-level enthusiasm about the exciting way things will be when the change is implemented can carry people past the rough spots in getting there.

Where Is the Most Readiness and Receptivity to Change?

From one point of view, starting points are not so important since a change in any one aspect of the organization is likely to affect other possible starting points anyway. For example, say you are trying to get Bill, who is noncooperative, to make a greater work contribution. The difficulties are caused by his attitude toward the individually oriented reward system and your controlling leadership style. You can begin trying to change his attitude by having conferences with him to show him the consequences of his negative feelings. But as soon as he begins to respond, your leadership style will be affected, and the reward system will somehow have to respond to his new behavior. Conversely, if you start by changing the reward system to encourage his cooperation more directly, his attitudes are likely to change accordingly, and you will be able to lead in a different, perhaps less controlling way. Nevertheless, it is worth thinking through the questions of *leverage:* Where would a change effort yield maximum payoff for the effort? As a manager it is useful to follow the principles of judo; rather than going against the resistance, go with it, so that a small amount of effort results in a proportionately large amount of movement.

Organizationally, this concept has two implications: **To initiate change, first try to determine where there is already inclination for movement in the desired direction and then start with the aspect of the problem that is least likely to be directly resisted (Lawrence, 1969; Bennis et al., 1964; Franklin, 1976).** In the above example it may well be easier to start with changing the reward system in a way that encourages and pays off for cooperation than to lecture at Bill, who already feels angry.

In analyzing the point of greatest leverage, it can be helpful to look at the functionality or dysfunctionality to the system of the behavior in

FIGURE 14–1
A Way of Diagnosing Where to Attempt Change

	Functional	Dysfunctional
Easily subject to change	A. Support	C. Concentrate
Not easily subject to change	B. Protect	D. Box off

Source: From a lecture presented by Steven J. Ruma, June 1971, Bethel, Me.

question and the degree to which it is subject to change. The possible combinations are represented in Figure 14–1.

RESISTANCE TO CHANGE

People do not necessarily resist change. We need only note how quickly people accepted television, which has changed social and recreational patterns a great deal, to realize that people in fact often embrace change. The issue is what people *perceive* to be the impact of change. People resist change when they perceive the consequences as negative. While individuals will differ in how ready they are to see negative consequences, and even though their reasons may appear illogical or even wrong to an outsider, people are not automatically resistant to change. People resist change for a *reason*, and a manager's task is to try to identify those reasons and, where possible, to plan the change so as to reduce or eliminate the negative effects and to correct misperceptions. Let us now examine some common reasons why people resist change and what a manager might do to reduce the negative consequences—and even enhance the positive consequences.

Change May Seem Threatening

Change usually means moving from the known to the unknown, from relative certainty to relative uncertainty, from the old familiar to the new unfamiliar. Obviously, if you like the status quo you will not feel any desire to leave it. But often, even when you are not all that happy with things as they are, you feel some resistance to giving them up, in part because of uncertainty that the change will be an improvement. Furthermore, if you had a hand in building or creating the present situation—which might include the physical setting in which you live or work, the relationships that have grown, the routines and procedures for work, etc.—you would be hard put to give it up easily. Even a long-awaited promotion means a change, which in turn means giving something up in order to move on. In short, *change means letting go of the past and present in order to move on into the future.*

> *A little insecurity is better than false overconfidence. The courage to recognize change and adapt to it is wiser than futile denial.*
>
> Source: Robert J. Samuelson, "Goodbye to the Age of Steel: The Industry Is Suffering the Fate of All Those Who Believe They're Impregnable," *Newsweek*, November 3, 1986.

It's all an odd paradox. People want to grow, but they often resist some of the very things that will enable them to grow, namely, making changes. Organizations must grow and develop, but they seem to fight continuous battles within themselves—often dragging their own employees kicking and screaming into the future, a future that is often an improvement over the past.

But is all that kicking and screaming necessary? Perhaps you can expect some resistance to change whenever it occurs, but there are ways to minimize the resistance. When you consider these you will see that a common denominator for all of them is the fact that they increase the degree to which people feel *control* over the events that affect them. And we know that to the extent that one has a sense of control over a situation, that situation will be perceived as less threatening.

One important point to keep in mind is the fact that a given proposed change may or may not be perceived by an individual as threatening. That perception is a unique product of that person's self-concept and the situation he/she faces. What looks like an exciting opportunity to me may look more like a loss of everything important to you. Many managers seem to overlook that simple idea and are puzzled by the fact that not all their employees instantly perceive the merits of a change they (the managers) have thought through for some time and in some detail. Trying something new may feel risky; one is more willing to take a risk when perceived threat is low. While change may always involve some degree of risk, a manager's attention to employees' fears of the unknown can reduce the degree of potential threat the employees may attribute to the change.

Finally, change is sometimes resisted just because the ideas are new and people haven't had a chance to get used to them or don't fully understand their implications. Often the person initiating change has been working on the issues for a long time and assumes that everyone else understands them equally well; the initiator's early struggles to accept the need for the changes and the time it took to become familiar with the issues may long be forgotten when a "plan" is presented to others for the first time. In such cases, information, education, and time alone can often take care of the resistance. That is why effective change managers "plant seeds" early, to allow ideas to germinate and become familiar (Kanter, 1983).

Change Can Mean Direct Loss

It is probably safe to assume that anyone will resist change who thinks that the changes will make him/her look bad or lose power, income, status, privileges, conveniences, friends, etc. For example, there is inevitable awkwardness in learning new skills, and employee resistance may just reflect anticipated embarrassment at having to go through learning something new. When change in such people is called for, it is important to provide the necessary training and emotional support for any awkwardness while learning.

Another example is those who perceive, correctly or not, that changes will cause them to become less central or influential. Except for those few people who may be feeling overburdened by power and responsibility, most people will not welcome changes that reduce their clout, even though the change might be good for the organization. It is hard to be selfless when one's own influence is at stake.

In these situations, negotiations with those affected may be necessary, with concessions made wherever possible. Face-saving devices may have to be invented for those whose status or clout cannot be preserved. Many organizations find it easier to preserve people's titles, salaries, or other symbols of status than to add insult to injury by removing all traces of former influence. Of course this sometimes gives the wrong message to others, who assume that nothing has changed, but with care it may be possible to preserve dignity while significantly altering degree of influence.

". . . I LOVE PROGRESS, BUT I HATE CHANGE!"

From a letter to the president of Amherst College from an alumnus, on whether to allow women to join fraternities.

Amherst Alumni Bulletin
June 1980

Change Can Disrupt the Social System

Managers attempting change sometimes forget that there are emergent *social* systems, which will also be affected by even "pure" technological changes or other alterations in the required system. A new set of machines for producing a product with less manual labor may force new social groupings, violating existing friendships and relationships. This can create resistance aimed at the machinery or at the management, apparently irrationally, since physical "working conditions" are improved. Those involved may be "unappreciative" when what is troubling them is their discomfort at altered relationships. Often those affected do not even consciously realize the source of their resistance or may feel embarrassed to state it directly.

Furthermore, even if a change is accepted by those directly affected, one must not overlook those who may be affected indirectly, those elsewhere in the system who are interdependent with the changed unit.

> A large corporation decided that it would have increasing problems if junior managers were not given more developmental training by their supervisors. The president of the company made an impassioned speech to all executives, explaining how important long-term development of subordinates was to the company. Even those executives, however, who were very positive about training subordinates soon found out that their annual bonuses depended only on the quarterly profitability of their units. Since developing subordinates took considerable time away from activities that could directly affect profits and had only long-term payoffs, all such activities were soon given mere lip service. Not until the executive bonus system was revised to reward developmental activities along with profits did serious developmental activities begin.
>
> Similarly, in the 1950s International Harvester developed an excellent human relations training program for supervisors; by the end of the program, supervisor attitudes were measurably different. When they got back on the jobs, however, many of their bosses ridiculed their learnings because the more considerate behavior taught in the program violated the organization's norms for leaders. Within six months not only had the new behavior disappeared, but supervisors were less satisfied and effective than before the training.

This lesson has had to be relearned more times than many managers would care to remember: **To produce lasting changes, related subsystems must also be altered to support the initial changes (Beckhard & Harris, 1977; Bennis, 1966, 1969).** Subsystems that will be most affected by changes and/or have the most power over the changing subsystem require attention also. Using stakeholder analysis can help identify related subsystems; others can be pinpointed by a review of background factors and the required system.

Although many situations do not allow for the involvement of the change targets in determining or shaping the change, it is well established that changes requiring the cooperation of those being changed are most likely to succeed when changees are allowed to participate in the change process.

In general: **The most effective way to insure that change is implemented with minimal resistance is to involve those affected by it in determining what it should be (Lawrence, 1969; Bennis 1966, 1969).** Even the collection of data is best done in collaboration with those who will be affected by the changes. If those affected are involved in diagnosis of the data and formulation of proposed solutions, successful implementation is more likely. Even the lowest-level worker may have important contributions to make to solve an organizational problem of which he/she is a part; an elegant solution imposed from above but not "owned" or accepted is not so elegant after all. The world's wastebaskets are filled with brilliant but unused recommendations.

There are many situations, however, where full participation is not possible or appropriate. If, for example, the problem is with employees who are incapable of improving their own performance even after training and they must inevitably be replaced, participation is probably not very appropriate even though it might be desirable from the employee's point of view. **When the necessary changes involve an opposing group(s) or individual(s) already committed to using illegitimate power to resist the changes, offers of involvement will probably be perceived as weakness and taken advantage of or as a trick and resented (Nadler, 1981).** As suggested in earlier chapters: **Participation and collaboration call for some basic level of trust in order to work; caution, distance, and legalistic negotiations are more appropriate when there is very low trust and/or high suspicion (Golembiewski, 1978).** Can you think of other situations where participation of those affected by the change would not be effective in achieving implementation?

Perhaps the first factor to remember in beginning change efforts is that: **Diagnosis should precede action (Argyris, 1970).** Stated directly, this point sounds obvious but is nonetheless important. Because those in managerial positions are often harassed and results oriented, they sometimes let impatience push them toward attempting solutions before the problem is clear. By now you have analyzed many problems where there were multiple, often hidden, causes for dysfunctional behavior. In organizations, as in life, there is seldom one simple, obvious cause for human problems. Some way is inevitably necessary of collecting data about the dimensions of the problem requiring change. Whether by interview, observation, questionnaire, or analysis of records, data on the social system aspects of the problem should be gathered and analyzed before solutions are determined.

Finally, one more related factor in beginning a change effort is: **Plans ought to be tentative and subject to alteration as feedback is received (Argyris, 1970).** Working out every detail of a change in advance, then plowing ahead regardless of responses along the way, is a fairly good recipe for creating unnecessary resistance. Most people do not like to feel powerless, overwhelmed, and ignored; if their legitimate objections and observations are belittled because they do not fit the master plan you have developed, they are unlikely to help make the changes successful. Again, this sounds obvious; but people with a vision, as you will be when you want to change something, often treat every negative reaction as a nuisance rather than as helpful data necessary for achieving a *workable* plan. In this sense you should *welcome* resisters because they are bringing important information you need to be effective. You might not want to assemble them all in the same room, since they might reinforce one another, but you certainly can benefit from their reactions as a way to reduce some of your blind spots and to make necessary modifications in your plans. The process itself also tends to help increase needed cooperation.

THE IMPORTANCE OF POWER FOR THE PERSON DESIRING CHANGE

To sustain lasting change it is seldom enough to be officially in charge of the person or group that is the target of change. Even a boss giving direct orders cannot guarantee that they will be obeyed, or obeyed in a wholehearted way that makes them work. Many managers have discovered too late that they did not have nearly as much ability to guarantee cooperation as their title and job description seemed to imply. Imagine how much more difficult it is, then, to achieve change when you are in a relatively low power position, either because those you want to change do not report to you directly or because, even if they do, you have few resources at your command to force compliance.

Since power is neither guaranteed by formal position (as you will recall from Chapter 11) nor prevented by lack of formal authority, it is useful to inventory the sources of power available to you. What information, resources, or support do you command that would be desirable to your change targets? What can you provide for them that would make the need for change more apparent or the problems associated with changing easier to bear? How hard will it be for you to gain access to whatever is needed? Will you be able to proceed with implementation whether or not the person or group resists?

> *To do his job well, any CEO must function and please those above him, such as his board, just as he must please those beneath him, or nothing will work. You've got to get consensus from both groups before you act. They're both watching you, and it's essential that you get their tacit approval, for the right reasons. Time spent making sure that what you're doing is well understood makes the chances for success much greater.*
>
> Source: Steve Weiner. *The Wall Street Journal, August 31, 1984.*

After making a careful diagnosis of the changer's power relative to the changee, a fundamental choice can be made. Initial attention can be focused on a vision of the future state desired, or on the problems with the way things are now. Although it is almost always useful to provide an image of the more desirable future, it is probably less necessary to start with that when you are relatively powerful. **The greater the change initiator's relative power, the more change can begin with a focus on current problems as opposed to a vision of the future.** When dealing with those who can easily refuse to cooperate, it becomes increasingly necessary to work on creating an attractive vision of what might be possible at a future date far enough away to reduce immediate threat (Beckhard & Harris, 1977). This is the social science version of "catching more flies with honey than with vinegar." Once the vision is created, it is possible to begin to work backward from it, identifying the steps that would be needed to get to that desirable future state and a timetable for implementing each one.

Relative power impacts tactics in another way. **The lower the power of the change initiator, the more it is necessary to look for allies, carefully building support among those who do control vital resources and those who will be needed to implement the change effectively (Mechanic, 1962; Kanter, 1983).** Changes that are directly under the control of the change initiator and within his or her job description require less extensive establishment of connections. Even there, however, if the cooperation of subordinates will be needed to make the change work well, efforts to sell them (or allow them enough say to sell themselves) will be necessary.

Inexperienced organizational members often underestimate the possibilities for accomplishing change when they cannot order it. They fail to identify the potential resources they can bring to bear on an issue: information, special services or priority services given to needed allies, recognition and praise, the chance to show others how they can look good to higher-ups by cooperating, potential new relationships, and so forth. You don't have to control others' salaries and promotions in order to gain cooperation; careful diagnosis of what you can offer and how that matches with what they need or desire will be necessary, however. Being in a lower-power position seldom means a total lack of potential power.

Similarly, it is also important to note that those in high-power positions are not obligated to use coercion every time they want change. Although sheer coercion or threats may be necessary in situations where there is great urgency and other tactics would not be practical, it is foolish to win a battle and lose the war. If the act of coercion causes anger and desire for retaliation, those who have been forced to change may well find ways to sabotage on the next issue or to undermine the changer. Greater power allows for pushing harder and more for explicit change efforts, but: **Change should always be initiated with the minimum amount of pressure necessary to accomplish the objectives (Kotter & Schlesinger, 1979; Harrison, 1970).** Since pressure usually breeds counterpressure, its use in excess of what is mandatory just invites problems.

THE ACTION–RESEARCH MODEL

The tentativeness and diagnostic activities called for above suggest that an action–research methodology is most appropriate for a planned change effort. Action–research begins with an identified problem. Data is then gathered so as to allow a diagnosis, which can produce a tentative solution, which is then implemented with the assumption that it is likely to cause new or unforeseen problems, which will, in turn, need to be evaluated, defined, diagnosed, and so forth. Thus, action-research methods assume a constantly evolving interplay between solutions, results, and new solutions. Figure 14–2 depicts the flow of steps in the model (Lippit, Watson, & Westley, 1958).

This model is a general one applicable to solving any kind of problem in an ongoing organization. It depends upon a sensible definition of the problem and the collection of relevant data, but to do that requires some preliminary way of thinking about diagnosis, which can help sort out the root causes and interconnections among the complex factors likely to underlie any interesting problem. To help you orga-

FIGURE 14–2
Action–Research Cycle

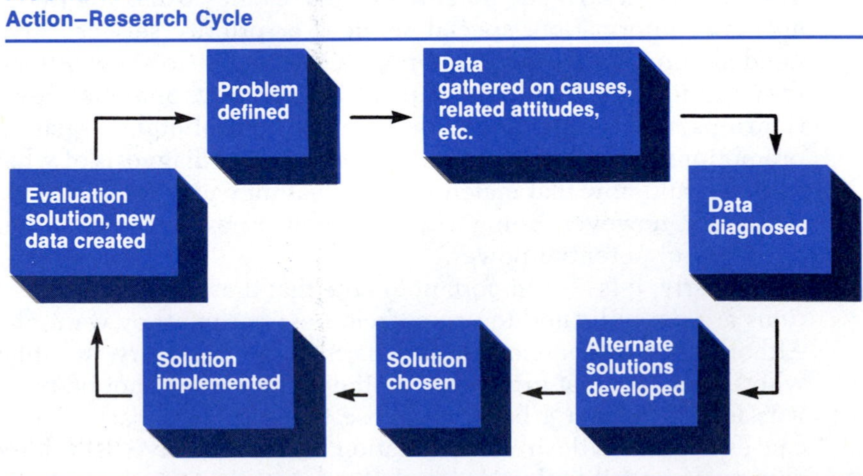

FIGURE 14–3
Change Problems Can Occur in Any Subsystem

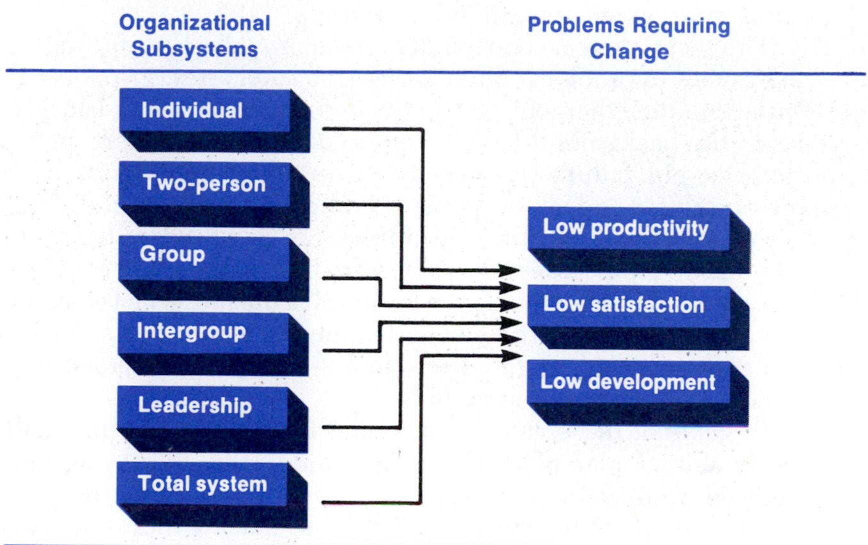

nize the way you think about change problems, we will show how the social system conceptual scheme used throughout the book can provide a useful diagnostic framework for organizational change. We have already noted that problems of productivity, satisfaction, or development can occur in any one or more subsystems of the total system (see Figure 14–3).

DIAGNOSTIC AIDS

Let's examine some procedures for tracing a problem back to its sources. Suppose, for example, a work group is having productivity problems because of insufficient resources. Efforts to improve its working *process* would probably be to no avail and, in fact, could complicate the problem even further. Suppose a manager is overloaded with work and cannot keep up with the pressure. It could easily be assumed that the wrong person has been chosen for the job when the problem is the way work is organized. You can probably think of many examples of how a misdiagnosis could lead to inappropriate and even destructive consequences. Remember, a symptom can have many possible causes; any physician will attest to the dangers of treating symptoms without knowing the underlying causes. It is the same thing for a manager who is attempting to make changes intended to eliminate a problem and/or to improve the system; treating the symptom without understanding the problem can easily lead to an amputation when an antibiotic would do.

The social system conceptual scheme provides a useful way of sorting causes of problems into manageable categories. Problems always surface in the emergent system (by definition), but their cause(s) may be in the background factors, required system, *or* emergent system. For example, failure of a work group to solve its problems effectively may be due to a lack of proper technical training for the job (background factor), unclear task requirements (required system), or decision-making processes that ignore valuable member contributions (emergent system). One way to approach a diagnosis of a change problem, then, is to sort the factors leading to it into the social system categories used throughout the book—background factors, required system, and emergent system.

In general, these categories should be examined sequentially for establishing a plan of attack. **Background factors tend to set limits on both the required and emergent systems.** Obviously it is useless to require people to behave in ways that are outside their range of competencies and then expect them to perform adequately. Nor is it sensible to establish output levels for the organization or one of its subunits that demand resources not present in the system and then expect adequate performance. For any organizational function, it is possible to list numerous background factors that place direct constraints upon both the required and emergent systems. What this line of reasoning suggests is that: **The first point of attack on any problem calling for change is a consideration of the background factors (Leavitt, 1978).**

If you have established that there are appropriate and adequate resources and that these are combined in ways suited to the organizational tasks, *then* you can move to examine the required and emergent systems with some degree of confidence that therein lies the cause(s) of the problem.

Since emergent behavior is governed by complex factors normally outside the direct control of a manager, strategies aimed at various aspects of the emergent systems tend to be complex, uncertain, and time consuming. Consequently, it makes sense to look next at the required system—at such matters as task definitions, work allocation, work patterns and routines, and who reports to whom. A manager is in a position to act directly upon these factors. **The required system tends to be the most directly and immediately within the control of management.**

Again we remind you of the possible importance of the involvement of those most directly affected by the change effort. Emergent systems can sabotage required systems; people who resent changes in their required work patterns can be very inventive about undermining the objectives of the change. Therefore, even though it is more direct and perhaps easier to change the required system, do not overlook consequences in areas of the emergent system.

Furthermore, a direct action at one point in the organization tends to reverberate at other points. For example, it may seem simple enough to redefine an individual's job if the diagnosis calls for that; however, that redefinition might affect a task relationship, thus calling for a realignment of roles. Again there seems to be no way to poke the system at point A without producing some reactions at points B and C.

If you as a manager can determine that you have the appropriate resources (background factors), task definitions (required system), and personal leadership style, then you can more confidently look for the sources of a problem in the emergent system (see Figure 14–4). It is similar to a physician ruling out several diagnoses before arriving at a final one. The importance of such a process of elimination is that strategies for change in the emergent system normally require in-depth data gathering and long-range procedures, and they often generate the greatest resistance. Thus interventions on the emergent system ought to be undertaken with caution when other options are not appropriate.

While it is impossible to offer definite diagnoses of the causes of emergent human problems out of their unique contexts, we have prepared Figure 14–5 with illustrative examples of causes of problems often associated with the various-size subsystems. It shows some possible causes of problems within each subsystem with variations for whether the cause is in the background factors, emergent, or required system. The examples of causes are meant to indicate possible diagnoses, not instant answers. More important is the process of examining

FIGURE 14–4
Steps in Problem Diagnosis

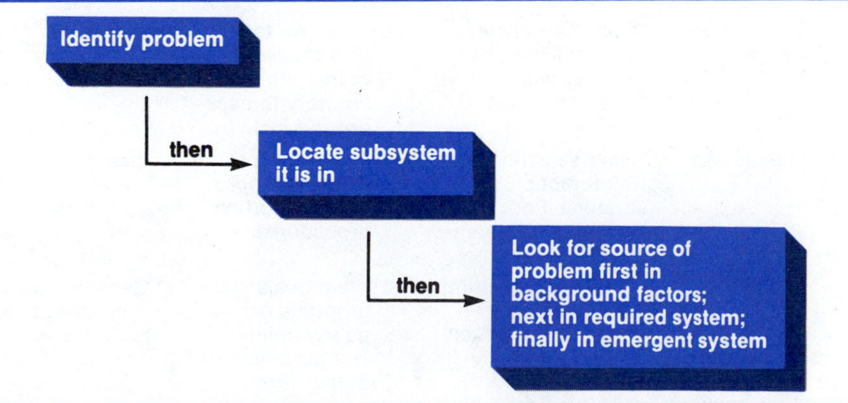

the underlying issues in a systematic way. Here is an example of how the chart might be used:

> A student group is having difficulty in producing high-quality case analyses despite seemingly endless hours of effort. Clearly some change is needed. Looking across Figure 14–5 in the row corresponding to the "group" subsystem, you can see that several possibilities exist: (1) the group may simply lack the intellectual resources to do the work (background factors); (2) the task requirements may not have been adequately

FIGURE 14–5
Possible Underlying Causes of Organizational Problems Requiring Change

(1) When the locus of the problem is:	and (2) the source of the problem is in the:		
	Background factors	Required system	Emergent system
	then (3) the causes might be:		
Individual	Poor match of individual with job; selection or promotion problem.	Task too easy or too difficult; poor job definition.	Job fails to fulfill range of needs; little chance for learning.
Two-person	Personality clash; conflict in basic styles, values, and so forth.	Poor role differentiation and/or integration in job description.	Misunderstandings, failure to deal with differences in preferences; unresolved feelings.
Group	Insufficient resources; poor group composition; bad physical setup; wrong behavior rewarded.	Task requirements poorly defined; role relationships unclear or inappropriate.	Poor working process in one or more of the 11 areas related to effectiveness.
Intergroup	Status and power conflicts of two professions; physical distance.	Conflict on task perspective; required interaction contrary to background factors.	Conflicting group styles; dysfunctional competition.
Leadership	Poor selection and promotion decisions. Poor training and preparation.	Overload of responsibility; inappropriate reporting procedures.	Individual not liked and/or respected; in conflict with other sources of power.
Total system	Geographic setting; limited labor market; physical conditions.	System goals inappropriate or poorly defined; inappropriate output levels.	General climate of malaise, suspicion, anxiety, pressure, and so forth.

explained to the members (required system); or (3) the group may have failed to develop the kinds of working processes that result in good analysis (emergent system). Obviously, all three of these factors may be operating, and each demands a different kind of remedy.

This rough guide to diagnosing the causes of organizational problems can help you focus on where action is needed. How to overcome each difficulty is not always obvious even after it is identified. We turn now to a brief survey of widely used change methods as a way of suggesting the range of approaches developed in the constant struggle by managers to maintain effective organizations.

METHODS OF ORGANIZATIONAL CHANGE

Since there is an endless variety of change methods available to managers and organizational experts, we can only discuss a limited number in this chapter. What we have chosen to do is to provide you with examples of strategies aimed at the background, required and emergent systems, and at the various-size groupings (individual, two-person, and so forth). Thus, we have organized the remainder of the chapter into three main sections: *(a)* change methods related to background factors, *(b)* those that focus upon the required system, and (c) those that address the emergent system most directly. Within each section we offer examples of methods that focus on each size subsystem. Also, to facilitate the presentation and organization of the material in each section, we provide a chart to serve as a map for our discussion.

Methods for Changing Background Factors

Figure 14–6 shows five general methods of change that deal directly with background factors; the focal point of each method is also identified. The focal point is not to be confused with the parts of the system that might be affected by the change; it simply refers to the place where the direct action is taken. The overall effects of any change action can spread to many subsystems of the organization.

PERSONNEL CHANGES. One of the crucial background factors in any work situation is the personal histories and resultant attitudes of the individuals concerned. Some change strategies are aimed at having an impact on what individuals bring to the situation and on which individuals are in the situation. The most direct way of affecting that is to replace individuals whose backgrounds cause difficulties with those who have appropriate skills, attitudes, and experiences.

FIGURE 14–6
Methods of Changing Background Factors

Method of Change	*Focal Point*
1. Personnel changes	Individual Two-person relationship Group Leadership
2. Training and education	Individual Leadership
3. Technology and layout	Any level
4. Incentive plans	Individual Group
5. Background culture	Total system

Though this method has been used at least since Adam and Eve were removed for failing to follow direct orders, it is not uncomplicated in practice. Firing or displacing people can cause difficulties in a variety of ways. The insecurity level of others may be raised, leading to greater defensiveness or decreased morale (though in some cases to improved performance); unions may form or react negatively; legal problems may develop; work may be fouled up until a suitable replacement is found, brought in, and prepared, and so forth. Furthermore, there is no automatic guarantee that the replacement will be more suitable than the predecessor. Nevertheless, at times the wrong person(s) is in a job that is otherwise well designed, and only replacement will solve the problem. If that is so, then the original selection procedures may need examination and attention to reduce the likelihood of the same problem arising again.

In some instances, the problem may be related more to a poor *combination* of people in a two-person relationship, in a group, or in a superior-subordinate relationship. The individuals involved may be perfectly competent for their work but, when put together, they produce dysfunctional behavior. Obviously, one option is to fire one or more individuals, but a more functional option in terms of organizational resources is to recombine the people into more compatible groupings or pairs. The diagnosis of "personality clash" fits this example; there can be basic values or style differences that are not likely to be resolved.

Another approach that many organizations have used is a system of executive assessment (often using elaborate psychological tests) to identify leadership potential. Assessment centers, where individuals go through a series of activities and organizational simulations while being closely observed, have spread rapidly as a way of trying to improve predictions about future managerial performance (Rice, 1978). It is not uncommon to find key decisions about promotion based upon these techniques. While their validity has been called into question by many organizational experts, these approaches have met with enough success to warrant their continued and apparently increased utilization.

TRAINING AND EDUCATION. Other ways have been developed to change individual perceptions, attitudes, or skills. A great deal of what goes on in organizational training programs is aimed at the individual, with the assumption that improved knowledge or attitudes will be translated into organizational payoff. Programs designed specifically to change individual behavior and interpersonal skills have been widely offered within organizations and by outside consultants, universities, and training firms. For example, training in achievement motivation has been developed by Harvard psychologist David McClelland. His research indicated high correlation of need for achievement with entrepreneurship, so he and his associates developed a training program that they claim can alter individual motivation. McClelland subsequently determined that effective managers, unlike entrepreneurs, require high needs for socialized power coupled with high inhibition of their purely personal interests. He has now developed ways of training to increase that kind of motivation (1975).

Many organizations pay particular attention to the training and development of their managers. They institute leadership training programs that focus upon learning managerial skills considered vital to effective leadership. Some of these programs operate on a year-round basis in the form of in-service education, and many occur in the form of intensive workshops designed to focus upon specific skills and methods. When successful, such programs can have a significant effect upon the competence that a manager brings to his or her job, with obvious implications for the emergent behavior of people under that manager.

Another kind of behavioral training, aimed at improving a person's interpersonal competence, is called sensitivity training or T- (for training) groups. In an unstructured group setting, participants learn about the basic dynamics of how groups work, receive feedback on their own behavior in the group and its impact on others, and have the opportunity to practice new behaviors in a controlled situation. Many variations of the original T-group have developed. Some have focused more on what goes on within each individual member so that self-concept and the personal system are clarified or altered. Others have concentrated on group process phenomena, attempting to improve the ability of individuals to understand, predict, evaluate, and change the way groups work. Still others have worked on particular aspects of behavior, like the use of power and influence, leadership skills, listening ability, and giving and receiving feedback (Bradford, Gibb, & Benne, 1964; Golembiewski & Blumberg, 1977).

Insofar as these kinds of training utilize experience-based methods, they often have strong emotional effects on the participants. But these individually oriented techniques suffer from some of the same difficulties of traditional training programs. First, even when measurable changes occur during training, they often fade out back on the job if not supported there. Second, new knowledge that for any reason cannot be utilized can be very frustrating, leading to anger, decreased morale, or even departure from the organization for anticipated greener pastures. Third, those who receive such intense training experiences and like them often become impatient with nonparticipants who do not sympathize with or cannot understand the participant's enthusiasm. Some rivalry can result between the "elite" few who are in the know and the "unenlightened masses." Thus an individual may bring to the work situation some new behaviors that are functional for a situation *outside* the work setting but dysfunctional to others on the job.

TECHNOLOGY AND WORK LAYOUT. Another background factor that can be changed to affect behavior is technology and/or work layout. Though all too often changes in technology ignore the consequences for social interaction, some sophisticated change efforts have consistently altered the existing technology to result in more satisfactory relationships and productivity. For example, both Saab and Volvo have experimented with the assembly line, reducing the monotony, isolation, and repetitiveness of work in an effort to allow group pride and interaction around whole tasks. These experiments are extremely expensive, involving huge capital expenditures, but have been undertaken because of labor force shortages and difficulties, which hampered production. In fact, the companies were facing staggeringly high rates of absenteeism—up to 20 percent daily—and employee turnover of 100 percent per year! The high education rates and generous unemployment benefits in Sweden had led to a widespread unwillingness to do boring, repetitive work. Thus, Saab and Volvo were virtually forced into being inventive at altering jobs and the assembly line to make work more satisfying. Similarly, American car manufacturers are acting on the need to make work more interesting.

Another series of experiments emanated from researchers at the Tavistock Institute in London. The method and organization of mining coal was changed to allow miners a more satisfying pattern of interaction and work, again allowing workers to gain the satisfaction of completing a whole task. Similar changes were made in weaving sheds in India. These large-scale changes in technology were made with explicit social system results in mind and have been quite successful.

A technological or work layout change need not be so elaborate in order to have substantial impacts on emergent behavior. Waitresses and cooks who were always fighting about unclear orders, differing priorities, and mistakes began to get along much better when a rotating spindle on which written orders could be clipped was introduced.

Orders had been called out by the waitresses, leading to frequent arguments about whether the waitress actually made the order, in what sequence the orders had come in, whether the cooks had forgotten what was said, and the like. Each side thought the other was stupid. The spindle allowed both automatic sequencing and easy visual grouping by the cooks, so that they could get all of an order together at the same time (Porter, 1962). Thus a problem that seemed to be wholly within the individuals involved was solved by a mechanical device that altered interaction patterns to fit existing attitudes and allowed differences to be easily checked and settled. Another simple change action can be the physical relocation of interdependent work groups to facilitate information flow, a method discussed in the previous chapter. Similarly, offices can be rearranged to facilitate interaction among those who need to work together more closely (Steele, 1976).

Technological changes can be very potent in yielding positive results but are often expensive, demand extensive revisions in the required system, and lead to unpredictable emergent behavior. As many organizations have discovered with dismay, a change that looks simple and could be helpful may produce an unanticipated series of negative reactions in many related subsystems. Few companies, for example, have easily made the transition from a manual accounting system to a computerized one, even though great benefits were anticipated. The people who had to make the new equipment work often reacted with less than enthusiasm. Current discussions about "the office of the future," featuring interlinked computer terminals and managers who enter data at the keyboard, often sound as naive about the human factors as did early discussions about computers for accounting purposes. The wise manager tries carefully to predict likely consequences of any change in technology or layout before beginning!

INCENTIVE PLANS. An organization's reward system is a background factor that can have a great impact on behavior when altered but requires considerable thought first. People in organizations tend to do what will be rewarded (in the currency they value, which usually includes, but is not limited to, pay) and tend not to bother doing what goes unrewarded, even though it may be appropriate to the organization's goals. Therefore, dramatic changes in behavior can often be accomplished through this indirect mechanism. Careful applications of the principles of behavior modification developed by B. F. Skinner have produced some dramatic results in a few organizations (Babb & Kopp, 1978; Feeney, 1973). It is not always easy, however, to be certain just what factors organizational members will consider to be rewarding, so what particular changes to make may not be obvious. And performance is not always easy to measure accurately enough to be able to accurately reward changes in it, as organization behavior modification requires. Numerous incentive schemes have faltered because they either did not fully anticipate the behaviors that would result from how productivity was calculated and rewarded or take into account the existing social patterns and their value to organizational members.

OHIO FIRM RELIES ON INCENTIVE-PAY SYSTEM TO MOTIVATE WORKERS AND MAINTAIN PROFITS

Lots of companies these days are huffing and puffing to find some good way to motivate workers. Lincoln Electric Company found the way it wanted in 1907 and says it has liked the results ever since.

The company relies on incentives. It pays most of its 2,500 employees on a piecework basis. In 1933, it added an annual bonus system. Based on performance, bonuses may exceed regular pay, and they apply far more extensively than in most companies. A secretary's mistakes, for example, can cut her bonus.

Some employees complain of pressure. But they stay around. Turnover is only 0.3 percent a month. The Cleveland company has no unions, and it avoids strikes. It says employees have averaged as much as $45,000 a year in good times. Sales and earnings have risen at a respectable pace.

Some employees says the system can generate unfriendly competition, too. A certain number of merit points are allotted to each department. An unusually high rating for one person usually means a lower rating for another. "There's a saying around here that you don't have a friend at Lincoln Electric," says a worker with nearly 20 years' service.

But management defends the system. "We don't feel hard work is harmful," Mr. Sabo says. It certainly hasn't hurt the company itself.

Source: Maryann Mrowca. Reprinted by permission of *The Wall Street Journal*,

An individual incentive plan that fosters competition among cohesive group members may well be sabotaged by resentful members. In our classes, for example, if we force students to rate each other's contributions to group products and insist that all members not be given the same grade, many groups devise clever ways of "beating the system" by rotating grades among members, using the minimum grade spread allowed, giving only one member a different grade on each project, and so forth. When the groups feel cohesive, an accurate grade reward for individual effort is worth less to them than the preservation of harmony. The same can be true when the pay is in dollars.

Furthermore, change in the reward system for any one subsystem will inevitably have consequences for those in other subsystems.

Therefore, even when localized changes produce desired results, the organizational ramifications may create difficulties. If one group, for example, responds to a new incentive-pay system by increasing production considerably, thereby earning pay perceived by others as "too high," the original change may end up being scuttled despite its effectiveness.

Also, only a few executives are likely to have sufficient power to avoid difficulty among subgroups by changing the reward system for the entire organization. When the power is available, it can lead to desired behavioral changes without any direct, personal change efforts and the resultant resistances.

SAYING ISN'T BELIEVING HERE

[Auerbach on one of the major reasons behind the Boston Celtics' continued success]: *We don't give bonus clauses in contracts. When we give a guy a contract, we give him everything he is worth in salary. We don't pay him for great statistics. We pay him for winning. That is why, when we have a big lead, our top guys don't mind coming out and letting the bench guys come in and play. On other teams, they have all of these incentive clauses, and their big guys don't want to come off the floor. They want to stay on for garbage time so they can build up their stats and make the incentive bonuses in the contract. It's a stupid way to do business. Our players never have to worry about that, and we don't get involved in petty arguments over playing time.*

Source: Will McDonough, *Boston Globe*, April 13, 1986. Reprinted courtesy of the *Boston Globe*.

BACKGROUND CULTURE. The final background factor we will discuss is the culture of the organization, that is, the customary way of doing things, attitudes and values that are "in the air" affecting everyone. (See box on corporate culture in Chapter 3.) Though ultimately any lasting systemwide behavioral change must affect the organization's culture, the overall culture is the most resistant aspect of any social system. The organization's attitudes about authority and how it should be used, interpersonal style, conflict, and so forth, will condition and affect all other changes—even what is seen as possible to change—and therefore require special attention. The approach to changing the organization's culture, however, may have to begin with changes in areas that are more directly manageable. But any change effort will benefit from being considered in terms of its effects on the overall culture of the organization and planned to either fit that total picture or change crucial aspects of it.

Roger Harrison, for example, found in his work in Europe that change efforts based on open expression of feelings were often resisted by executives from companies with cultures that strongly discourage such "emotionality." He developed new methods for altering behavior in conflict situations, utilizing negotiations about role obligations. These methods were more compatible with the organizational backgrounds from which the executives came (Harrison, 1972).

FORD'S IDEA MACHINE: A ONCE TROUBLED GIANT DISCOVERS A RECIPE FOR RECOVERY: CHANGE EVERYTHING

The test of Ford's cultural overhaul will come with the next recession. Many at Ford believe the changes will endure the next slump in car sales, but Kordick, head of Parts and Service Division, puts it most forcefully. "Would we try to make profit by getting rid of our people? I don't think people would stand for it. I've already said, if you tell me to put people on the street, I'd quit. I went through it once, and I'm not proud of it. I don't want to go through it again."

Source: Eric Gelman, *Newsweek*, November 24, 1986.

If, however, openness about feelings would have been functional for the organization, his methods would have had little impact on changing the culture that forbids that type of communication. Some other way of affecting the culture, rather than adapting to it, would be necessary—perhaps beginning with an intense group experience for the top executives, which might directly question existing beliefs and attitudes. But, as noted, direct attempts to change attitudes often increase resistance.

Ultimately, changing an organization's culture may require efforts along several fronts, utilizing a variety of approaches and supported from the top of the hierarchy. Since such efforts are expensive, require deep commitment from top executives who may not be fully comfortable with what behavior is required of them in a changed culture, and take several years to filter through the organization, you can see why such changes are difficult and rare.

I try to create a vision of where we want to go in the future, but I try to connect that vision to where we've been in the past. You have to start with where we are, so that the future is a natural extension of the past. In today's marketplace, innovation is very important.

What senior management needs to do is create an environment in which it's okay to innovate, to make mistakes, and to go forward. We need innovation, and I try to convey the idea that everyone in our organization counts in this regard. I'm trying to create an environment in which people can let go of the past without that being a scary process.

Gary Countryman, President
Liberty Mutual Insurance Company
Personal communication, 1984

Of course, one factor that determines the culture of any organization is its location or setting. A manufacturing plant located in South America may produce the same products as a similar plant in the United States, but the behavior of people in the respective settings will be very different because of obvious differences in the cultures of the two geographic areas. Even regional differences within the United States often determine differences in the culture of the same kinds of organizations in the different locations. For example, the rapid impersonal pace of a big-city environment tends to carry over into any system located there. Move that system to a rural area, where the pace is slower and the prevailing attitudes of people are different, and some very obvious differences within the organization itself may be observed.

Methods for Changing the Required System

Figure 14–7 summarizes the different approaches we will discuss.

REVISION OF JOB DESCRIPTION AND WORK RELATIONSHIPS. Job descriptions and organizational work relationships are two important determinants of behavior and interactions and often are a starting place for change efforts. Examining a job description to see if responsibilities are clear, sufficient information is available, boundaries are sufficiently well-defined, organizational authority is adequate, job activities needing interaction or coordination with others are spelled out, and then making appropriate changes, can result in markedly different behavior. A person who is not sure of what to do may perform so badly that he/she appears to be totally incompetent. With responsibilities clarified, the

FIGURE 14–7
Methods of Changing the Required System

Method of Change	*Focal Point*
1. Revision of job descriptions and work relationships: Reporting relationships. Task role assignments. Managerial responsibility.	Individual. Interpersonal. Intergroup. Leadership. Group.
2. Job modification: Job narrowing. Job enlargement. Job enrichment.	Individual. Two-person relation. Group.
3. Quality Circles; Problem-solving teams.	Group.
4. Alternative work schedules.	Individual. Group.
5. Reformulation of work objectives.	Total system.

same person may be able to do excellent work. On the other hand, tight, unambiguous job descriptions can inhibit innovation even while increasing predictability (Kanter, 1983). Similarly, changing who a person or group takes orders from can make a substantial difference in job performance. Changing the organizational level at which decisions are made, whether closer to the actual problem or closer to the top of the organization, can also have a significant impact on behavior.

These techniques of job analysis, centralization or decentralization of decision making, and similar restructuring have great appeal to managers because they appear to be rational and logical; there is no doubt that such structural changes can positively affect performance. But blueprints do not a bluebird make; human beings are remarkably inventive at getting around formal directions and plans. Organization charts and job descriptions, even when clear and relatively sophisticated, cannot take all contingencies and relationships into account. A certain amount of goodwill is necessary to effectively implement any structure. And, conversely, even a sloppy illogical structure can be made to work if those involved want it to. The attitudes people bring to the situation affect their response to any formal structure. Nevertheless, insofar as the structure determines interactions and these in turn lead to positive feelings, structural changes can affect attitudes as well as be affected by them. When lack of clarity or poor utilization of resources within the organization is at the heart of a behavioral problem, the methods described above can be extremely useful.

JOB MODIFICATION. Job requirements can also be the focus for change when the required activities, interactions, and attitudes are too difficult or too simple for the people in the system. Work that asks more of people than they are capable of giving may need to be broken into less complex or less demanding activities so that others can do part of what is needed, or rules and procedures may need to be established in order to simplify decision making.

> In recent years, for example, a number of ways have been developed to make physicians' jobs less demanding so that they can best utilize their expertise. The physician's assistant and nurse practitioner are new roles carved out of the total job of diagnosing and treating patients, to free the doctor from the more routine but time-consuming aspects of the job. The physician's assistant may be trained to treat certain common, non-serious problems like colds, coughs, and so forth, and to recognize more serious conditions that must be seen by the doctor.

In the same way, assembly lines and other routinized forms of doing work can be used to make a job simple enough for a relatively unskilled person to do. Carried to the extreme, some jobs can be broken down into such simple repetitive activities that machines can perform equally well. When trained personnel is scarce or very expensive and unemployment high so that few alternatives exist for employees, such methods can be effective.

On the other hand, overly mechanical, simple work can lead to boredom, lack of commitment, alienation, or sabotage, and the most elaborate change efforts have been geared to countering these effects. As mentioned in Chapter 7, a variety of ways have been invented to try to make work more interesting in the hopes of gaining improved performance and satisfaction. Job rotation, enlargement, and enrichment are all ways of making work more challenging. While the technology may remain the same, work is divided differently to provide more variety, challenge, and satisfaction, which hopefully lead to greater productivity.

QUALITY CIRCLES/PROBLEM-SOLVING TEAMS/EMPLOYEE INVOLVEMENT GROUPS

Spurred on by Japanese successes, many companies have tried variations of Quality Circles, allowing (or sometimes requiring) teams of employees to periodically discuss ways of improving quality, or productivity. Often the teams are taught formal problem-solving methods, statistical and logical, then asked to track and solve quality problems. In some variations, the teams pick the problems to work on, while in others they are assigned. Often the groups are natural work teams, though sometimes they are assigned or voluntarily form across areas and/or levels. This is a formalized method of tapping employee talent and, if properly managed, can produce startling results, reducing defects, need for rework, and unnecessary work procedures. Care has to be taken to include and support supervisors, to be clear about management expectations, and to insure management willingness to alter practices leading to quality problems; but it can be done (Schlesinger, 1982; Stein, 1983). Where there are unions, they must be included in the planning, usually through joint labor-management committees. Interestingly, many proponents of Quality Circles attribute their success to the use of statistical techniques and do not appreciate the motivational impact of bringing employees together and allowing them to influence the way work is done. In some organizations, excellent results have been obtained without using statistical methods; in others, Quality Circles using statistics have been abandoned because they were not properly managed.

In recent years a number of activities involving job modification and revision of work relationships have been described as efforts to improve *quality of working life*. Problems similar to those faced in Sweden—absenteeism, turnover, alienation, and boredom—have led a number of firms to experiment with reorganization of work to give more responsibility to employees, to build team cooperation in working on identifiable complete tasks or products, to eliminate conventional supervision (creating self-supervising, autonomous work groups), and in general to try to foster both greater satisfaction and productivity. Many different experiments have been lumped together under the "quality of work life" label, however, so the general category is hard to define. It does seem to indicate renewed attention to worker feelings about work, reflecting evidence that organizations ignore their employees at their own peril (Stein, 1983; Hackman & Suttle, 1977; Carlson, 1978).

ALTERNATIVE WORK SCHEDULES. For many years most people have worked on a fixed 5-day, 40-hour schedule. Considerable supervisory energy went into enforcing starting and stopping times, trying to prevent tardiness (which was considered to be undisciplined and a waste of valuable work time). But partly as a result of the organizational need to pay more attention to employee preferences and partly because organizations don't always need all employees at the traditional hours, there has been a rapid spread of innovative work schedules in the United States, Europe, and Japan.

More than 10 million people, for example, are now allowed to choose their own starting and stopping times within specified ranges, provided that they complete 8 hours a day or 40 hours a week. This option, called *flexible working hours,* allows individuals to balance personal needs with those of the organization. Organizational benefits include higher morale, decreased short-term absenteeism, virtual elimination of tardiness, and, in some cases, increases in productivity. Disadvantages are occasional difficulties in communications or getting people together for meetings as well as some discomfort on the part of traditional supervisors who do not know how to plan and evaluate work they are not always physically present to observe. The individual employee gains flexibility in terms of family needs, often major savings in daily travel time (by avoiding rush-hour traffic), and enhanced self-esteem from being trusted by the company to manage one's own time. Employees almost universally approve of flexible working hours when given the chance to try it.

The *compressed week* is a different schedule variation that does not usually permit flexibility but does allow for a full week's work to be completed in less than five days. Either the organization only remains open for four days or, more commonly, employees are scheduled for differing four- (or three-and-a-half-) day patterns such that there is greatest coverage on the busiest days. Compressed week arrangements can result in more efficient use of plant and equipment, availability of employees at odd hours (for example, it is easier to attract night-shift employees if they can have three consecutive days off), higher productivity, and greater satisfaction. The compressed week, however, is usually quite unattractive to women with school-age children (and, as child-rearing practices change, to men who want to spend time with their children) and to older employees who may tire more easily working longer hours.

Another schedule variation being used more frequently is permanent part-time work, sometimes combined with job sharing. Permanent part-time means that not only does the individual work part-time but does so at a job that is part of a career with proportional pay and benefits rather than low hourly wages. It is like other work, only for less than 40 hours a week, and may be divided up during the week at the mutual convenience of the individual and the employer. Job sharing is a variation of permanent part-time where two (or more) people share one full-time job, again by dividing working hours in a mutually convenient way.

Both of these variations can lead to greater productivity, availability of talented employees who would not otherwise be willing or able to work, and coverage at odd hours when full-time employees are not available. For example, one insurance company has "mother's hours," 10 A.M.–2 P.M., which attracts women with school-age children who would not be willing to work all day but are very capable and potential future full-time employees. Control Data Corporation has a plant that employs mostly black mothers and handicapped people at a variety of hours that fit organizational and individual needs. The plant is one of the most productive in the company.

All of these alternative arrangements when carefully planned can help companies improve morale and productivity at little cost. But they must be chosen in a way that fits the timing needs of the existing (or potential) work force and delivers employees at times when the company needs them. Otherwise, this kind of change in the required system can worsen morale problems and hinder productivity (Cohen & Gadon, 1978a).

REFORMULATION OF OBJECTIVES. Every individual and combination of people in an organization work toward certain objectives. Those objectives in turn fit into the broader framework of the total organization's objectives. Often the specific objectives at one level of the system may be out of phase or incongruent with those at another level and/or with those of the total system. This kind of problem calls for a reformulation of organizational objectives at one or another level in order to reestablish the necessary congruence for system interdependence. The focal point of such an approach may begin at any level, but it must also touch directly upon all others.

A specific approach called "management by objectives" has been developed in recent years. Its broad philosophy states in essence that worker and manager performance can best be evaluated in terms of their degree of success in meeting specifically defined organizational objectives. These objectives *(a)* pertain directly to and may be defined by each individual in the system, *(b)* demand coordination at a group and intergroup level, and *(c)* must be reflective of the overall organizational goals. When utilized effectively, management by objectives can be an important vehicle for encouraging individuals to take responsibility for their own performance and provides them with the measuring sticks to do that.

The method requires each employee to set objectives for some time period and then negotiate agreement on these with the employee's supervisor. Performance is then judged by how close to the objectives the individual comes within that time period, rather than on more intangible personal characteristics or global judgments about the person's worth. The process of defining and agreeing upon objectives represents an attempt both to plan effectively and to generate commitment on the part of the employee to reach the goals.

The principle of management by objectives is sensible and almost inevitably practiced in some form or other, even if not formally adopted; however, its practice can be difficult or abused. If performance is to be judged by agreed-upon objectives, then the objectives stated must somehow be measurable; this can eliminate some important but not easily defined variables. **The more specific are the objectives, the more easily is performance measured but the more likely it is that subtle factors will be ignored.** Furthermore, many managers use management by objectives without first securing the initiative and agreement of both those who are judging and those who are to be judged by the objectives. If the subordinates are not really committed to the objectives on which they will be judged, their performance is not likely to be as effective as it might otherwise be.

Methods for Changing the Emergent System

In one sense, all change is ultimately aimed at the emergent system. It is in emergent behavior that problems present themselves and require attention. However, some change strategies begin by directly attacking emergent behavior, even if ultimate solutions demand attention to background factors and/or the required system. Figure 14–8 refers to several different approaches to change in emergent factors.

COUNSELING. Many organizations provide individual help to employees who may be experiencing difficulties in handling work demands or who may be generally unhappy in their work. The physical and/or psychological pressures of a given type of work can often prove to be highly stressful; counseling is one tool to help an individual learn ways of handling tensions and, whenever possible, of minimizing their adverse consequences. When a problem is more directly related to interpersonal or social factors, the counseling is likely to focus upon

FIGURE 14–8
Methods of Changing Emergent Factors

Method of Change	*Focal Point*
1. Counseling.	Individual. Leadership.
2. Third-party consultation.	Two-person relation.
3. Task group training, team building.	Group.
4. Intergroup confrontation.	Intergroup relations.
5. Survey feedback.	Total system.
6. Executive planning and confrontation sessions.	Total system.

the individual's behavior, self-concept, and general attitude. Presumably, the use of counseling as a method of organizational change pertains to emergent behavior, that is, problems that the work situation brought out in the individual. Some organizations also offer help for problems that employees *bring* to the situation (for example, personality problems, alcoholism, and marital difficulties); more places advise such individuals about where they can get help from outside resources.

In a more positive way, individual counseling as a vehicle for leadership development can be a potent source of change. Many executives rely heavily upon the support and guidance of a trusted colleague, specialist, or consultant. Through such a process the individual manager can become more aware of his/her own goals, develop increased managerial competence, and learn how to maintain an integration of his/her personal beliefs and values with the goals of the organization.

THIRD-PARTY CONSULTATION. An extension of the counseling process occurs when two people encounter difficulties in working together and seek the help of a third party to resolve the issue(s). This technique has been in existence for a very long time; examples include friends helping friends, marriage counseling, and clergy offering advice to prospective marriage partners. (Of course, when the help is not requested, it might be called third-party interference.) In a work setting, the helper might be a peer, a supervisor, or some other objective person. The choice of third-party consultant should be dictated by the demands of the situation and the mutual preferences of the two people needing the help (Walton, 1969; Schein, 1969, 1987).

Even when there is no problem as such, there is usually room for improvement in any working relationship. In this regard, a manager always has the option, possibly even the obligation, and, hopefully, the skills to help subordinates to improve their productivity, satisfaction, and development by improving their work relationships. Such a proactive stance is more likely to facilitate a healthy work environment than would the more passive attitude of waiting until a problem occurs before taking action.

TASK GROUP TRAINING: PROCESS CONSULTATION AND TEAM BUILDING. Out of the experiences of T-groups (mentioned earlier) have developed several variations of task group training or team building. In most of these methods, people who work together on a day-to-day basis are directly taught to work together more effectively. A team-building effort might examine the ways in which the group members collaborate or compete, the way they make decisions, the way they set agenda items, the amount of openness with which members relate to one another, and so forth. The person introducing change might observe regular meetings and make observations about the group's process or might take the group away for a working retreat where processes are directly examined.

The most sophisticated versions of team building, however, do not assume that all the problems arise from the group's emergent behavior, but may be traced back to background factors such as the company's culture and reward system or to the required system and the way in which it determines influence and interactions. The advantage of team-building efforts is that once changes are accepted by the group, group members themselves can reinforce the new patterns of behavior, and individuals are not left isolated as they might be after T-group or other such forms of training. A team that has developed sufficient levels of trust will be able to work on whatever problems arise, in a self-correcting way that allows for changes in structure or technology as well as changes in member behavior (Cohen, Fink, & Gadon, 1978).

Even a successful team-building effort, however, can still create problems for members of adjoining subsystems or with those higher in the organizational hierarchy. The team that works well together may ignore outside interests and demands or see as inferior other groups that do not seem to be working so well. This can cause resentment or jealousy, creating problems in other parts of the system.

INTERGROUP CONFRONTATION. As you might expect, methods have also been developed for dealing with problems between groups. In Chapter 13 you were introduced to some of the kinds of issues that lead to conflict between groups; reemphasized here are those methods that work on finding ways to resolve conflicts between groups. Several mechanisms for structurally interweaving group members have been invented to allow diffusion of group boundaries, thereby lowering rivalry and commitment to each group's own preferred way of doing things. Direct exchanges of members, a new linking group made up of some members from each of the original groups, whether individually elected or selected by all groups together, and the utilization of independent judges or arbitrators are all ways of resolving difficulties between groups. Joint labor-management committees, created to foster and supervise quality of work life projects, are a widely publicized example of creating a new linking group to allow for cooperation. These committees usually have an equal number of union and management members.

As you will have seen during the intergroup section of the course, the inherent problem with these kinds of solutions is that those who form a new, supposedly independent group are likely to maintain allegiance to their own group and therefore have difficulties dealing with each other. Alternatively, they may link together into an independent system, which then has trouble getting support from the individual groups. A more direct way of trying to deal with feelings among group members has its roots in the T-group but is more structured and controlled. In the *intergroup confrontation laboratory,* groups exchange their collective opinion about how they see themselves and how they think the other group sees them and then work on the accuracy and stereotyping contained therein. Though risky and highly charged, this method can break through mutual hostilities, particularly when there are not fundamental value differences between the groups but only inaccurate perceptions (Blake, Mouton, & Sloma, 1965).

When direct confrontational methods work, whether between individuals or groups, it is because increased and more accurate communication is an appropriate solution to a problem involving some form of misperceptions. At other times, however, increased accuracy of communication can lead to further distancing among the involved parties, especially when it becomes clear that there are fundamental value differences that cannot be negotiated away. **In general, the more the problems among subsystems are based on value differences, the more appropriate are methods that involve arms-length, formal, and legalistic negotiations rather than greater openness and trust (Nadler, 1978; Walton & McKersie, 1965; Golembiewski, 1978).** When differing subsystems have high suspicions of each other and little trust, the most that can be hoped for is some kind of agreement to demarcate territories, live and let live within those boundaries, and then formulate specific rigid and observable contracts on a point-by-point basis as needed. It is naive to try to shortcut this process by methods that encourage openness, honesty, and vulnerability. Similarly, when problems can be resolved by better understanding and clarity, it is "paranoid" to be willing only to deal in legalistic and distinct contractual terms.

SUBSYSTEM CONFLICT RESOLUTION. The methodology for dealing with any two subsystems in conflict is worth spelling out in some detail:

1. The first phase of conflict resolution calls for a thorough understanding of each party's position. This can only be done if differences are brought out and made explicit, even at the risk of polarization, rather than minimized and papered over. The more clearly and dramatically differences are stated, the greater are the chances that individual members of each subsystem will begin to raise questions about the strength and clarity of their group's positions. Furthermore, unless subsystem members feel that they have had a chance to state their position clearly and be understood by conflicting subsystems, they will find it hard to acknowledge the possibility of not being 100 percent right.

2. Once differences are looked at in bold relief, then the opposing subsystems can begin to point out perceived inaccuracies in other group perceptions. As noted earlier, where differences are great and value-based, tough bargaining leading to contractual relationships is appropriate. It is vital to have a contract for each side to do specific activities under particular conditions, composed in a way that allows each to observe whether or not the terms of the contract are being honored. If, however, the differences are not fundamental and based on values, a more direct and trusting collaboration can be developed. Any attempt to minimize a genuine set of differences may lead very rapidly toward each side believing that the other is behaving suspiciously, and then the conflicts are quickly renewed (Walton, 1969).

SURVEY FEEDBACK. There's a paradox in all change efforts. On the one hand, those efforts aimed at changing subsystems suffer from the problems mentioned many times by now, namely, unintended consequences for other subsystems in the organization. On the other hand, efforts aimed at changing the *total* organization (particularly when it is a fairly large and complex one) often are so general and impersonal that they have very little impact on day-to-day behavior within a given subsystem. Ideally then, the total change effort has to deal somehow with that paradox. A method is needed that first collects data about total system problems at a given time, allows diagnosis by those at the head of the organization as to priorities in solving the problems, and then tackles problems in order of importance. One useful way of approaching such total system change is the survey-feedback method developed at the University of Michigan. A lengthy questionnaire on employee attitudes and perceptions of the organization is administered, tabulated, and the anonymous (with respect to individuals) results fed back by departments. When followed up with specific action plans in each department, utilizing some of the methods described earlier, this can be an effective way to begin a total system change effort (Bowers, 1973).

EXECUTIVE PLANNING AND CONFRONTATION SESSIONS. Another method, pioneered by Richard Beckhard (1967), is called the confrontation meeting. A large cross section of organizational executives is brought together for a concentrated period of time such as one day, assigned to small work groups, and asked to develop lists of organizational problems needing solution. When the groups have reported their lists, priorities are set for working on problems, various groups are given the responsibility to work on them, and deadlines are set for producing proposed solutions. Again, considerable follow-up is needed, utilizing some of the methods described earlier, such as team building, process consultation, or individual counseling; but this kind of "shock treatment" can be an excellent catalyst for generating energy to produce change. These methods and other comparable ones all follow the general action-research cycle described earlier on a somewhat more grand scale.

The underlying assumption of such change attempts is that the collection of data around problems or even the generation of lists of problems acts as a disconfirming and unfreezing process, which creates sufficient tension to motivate commitment toward change. However, if our earlier proposition about the greatest change following moderate amounts of tension is valid, then, in some organizations, methods that produce less tension may be called for. As suggested earlier, methods that utilize "vision building" can be used when data about current problems might prove so overwhelmingly threatening that it would paralyze action. It can also be used when there is insufficient tension in the present circumstances to arouse the desire to make needed long-term changes.

Another variation of this type of method is called *open system planning*. It involves top executives in thinking through the organization's relationships with its various environments and then developing a plan to maximize the effectiveness of each subsystem's transactions with its dominant environment(s) (Krone, 1975). Strategic planning systems also attempt to position the firm in relation to environmental opportunities and organizational strengths. The better schemes help top management work through the human, organizational, and procedural changes necessary to implement the strategy.

All such total organization methods run the danger of mobilizing considerable enthusiasm for change all at once and then creating frustration when the actual results take a long time, which inevitably they do. Aroused expectations that are unmet may be considerably more dysfunctional than never raising expectations in the first place. Whether or not one is willing to take that risk is very much a matter of

> *"Traditional" strategic planning is less relevant today than it seemed in the 70s, because everybody's planning horizon is shrinking rapidly.*
>
> *I herewith propose a new measure, "the Mean Time Between Surprises" (MTBS), and a set of propositions ("Surprise" is defined as any unpredicted event that materially affects the decision being made):*
>
> 1. *The MTBS has been dropping steadily.*
> 2. *The surprises are not simply* not *predicted but* unpredictable.
> 3. *The number of people or groups able to create a surprise has been growing steadily.*
>
> *These ideas take on greater urgency when we consider another measure: "the Mean Time to Make Decisions" (MTMD), which leads to several more propositions:*
>
> 1. *When MTBS is less than or equal to MTMD, an organization loses its ability to function effectively.*
> 2. *Proposition 1 describes the situation at most organizations most of the time.*
> 3. *The main determinant of MTMD is organizational design and structure, not intent, policy, or management style.*
>
> From "Surprise, Surprise" by Barry A. Stein, president, Goodmeasure, Inc., May 1983.

personal desires. Nevertheless, if organizations are to remain adaptive they must find ways of gaining commitment to whatever changes are necessary to keep the organization working toward its goals.

CHANGE MUST BE MANAGED

As is implied in all that has been said so far, change must be actively managed. It is not enough to see a problem and decide what the solution will be; the tough issue is how to get there from where you are. In addition to careful diagnosis and excellent selection of solutions, the process of moving to the desired state requires special attention, especially for changes of any complexity. **When large-scale change is involved, it is helpful to create a special structure for managing the transition—a high-level steering committee or advisory group that can link the changes to wider organizational goals, help overcome barriers or resistance, and anticipate connections to related subsystems (Beckhard & Harris, 1977; Kanter & Stein, 1980).** Even when the change desired is not so global, it is important to pay attention to what is and should be happening as you move from here to there. How will the change targets react? How are they feeling about the changes? Do they need extra support while they are learning new skills? Do the original plans make sense in light of new data? Is the pacing of the changes appropriate? How are others not directly involved being affected by the change? Do they have enough information about it to avoid rumors and negative fantasies?

PARADOXES OF ORGANIZATION LIFE

Change requires stability. Persistence requires flexibility.

Rosabeth Moss Kanter

Someone or some group needs to worry about and deal with these kinds of questions; your job as the manager of change is to do it or set up a mechanism for doing it. Many wonderful ideas have been killed off because no one managed the process of implementing them. Part of a good action plan is to think through these kinds of issues in advance insofar as possible, and then be ready to adapt and bend as you proceed. **Effective masters of change combine a steadfast vision of where they are going and a willingness to be flexible along the way (Kanter, 1983).** None of this happens by accident; change must be carefully managed.

AN OVERVIEW OF ORGANIZATIONAL CHANGE

We suspect that it might be a difficult task for you to develop an overall perspective on organizational change. The problems are many and complex, the procedures for diagnosis are loaded with uncertainties and pitfalls, and the methods of change are too complicated and varied to organize into a handy package. We hope that by our using the social systems conceptual scheme as a framework for the chapter, we helped you to appreciate the importance of asking many questions before arriving at a diagnosis of a problem and before selecting a change method that will be *appropriate* to the situation.

All too often when change is needed, the presence of tension or anxiety makes it difficult to go through a systematic, careful series of diagnostic steps. It seems easier, perhaps even desirable, to grab the first "treatment" that comes along. That is why in the history of organizational change there have been many sales pitches for one or another magic "elixir." Got a problem? Use Dr. Fixit's All-Purpose Employee Productivity Kit. While this may sound exaggerated, it is more the rule than the exception to find advocates of particularized methods touting claims of success no matter what the change problem. We caution you as prospective managers to maintain some degree of scientific skepticism; this is what can make the difference between an ordinary manager and an outstanding manager.

To a child with a hammer, everything looks like a nail.

ONE COMPANY'S QUEST FOR IMPROVED QUALITY

I'm sure most business managers believe that their companies already produce high-quality products. We have always stressed product quality at Hewlett-Packard Co., and we have always believed—until recently—that the "find it and fix it" method of ensuring good quality was adequate and cost effective.

But customers in recent years have come to expect much higher quality than ever before. Recognizing this, we decided several years ago to analyze in detail our methods and the costs of achieving good product quality. To our surprise, we calculated that as much as 25 percent of our manufacturing assets were actually tied up in reacting to quality problems. Using assets in this way, of course, drives up production costs and product prices, making us less competitive, in a relative sense, than we could be.

Were we, then, doing a good job of producing quality products at a fair price? And if we weren't, were other American businesses doing any better? Was it any wonder that U.S. industry was having its problems?

As we thought about this problem, it became apparent that we were facing an intriguing management challenge. With above-average quality standards already well established at Hewlett-Packard, it would be difficult to ask for better results. Yet it was apparent that major improvement was needed for us to retain a leadership position in the long run. Clearly, a bold approach was needed to convince people that a problem existed and to fully engage the entire organization in solving it.

The proper place to start, we concluded, was with a startling goal—one that would get attention. The goal we chose was a tenfold reduction in the failure rates of our products during the 1980s. We knew this represented a difficult challenge. But we also suspected that anything less dramatic wouldn't convey the importance we attached to this issue. By establishing a far-reaching goal and getting people to feel in their guts that the goal was reasonable, we felt some serious movement would begin to occur. We also knew the close linkage between higher quality, lower cost, and increased productivity would lead to other beneficial results for the company.

With the goal firmly established, the second step was to identify a nucleus of leading-edge people in our organization to champion the quality cause. But to do that we had to find ways of showing them what was possible in the quest for improved quality.

We decided to send a dozen first-line and second-line managers from manufacturing, product assurance, and related fields on a fact-finding tour of Japan to see what kinds of approaches worked well there—an interesting reversal from a few short years earlier.

Not surprisingly, our study team returned with tales of impressive quality achievements and low-cost manufacturing—always in combination. What's more, they described the Japanese quality-assurance technique in remarkably simple terms: "Doing it right the first time." More than any other experience, this visit confirmed our feelings that quality improvements weren't only possible but perhaps essential to driving down prices, increasing productivity, and maintaining our long-term competitiveness. And it triggered an almost crusade-like motivation among members of our study team to project this message companywide.

The next challenge was to find ways to spread the genuine enthusiasm and insight of these people throughout the organization. Several methods were available for this, and we used them all: training classes, newsletters, informal discussions, and so on. But the one that seemed to have the greatest impact was peer competition—one of the strongest motivational forces available to any organization.

It was interesting to watch this type

of competition take effect. People who long had thought they were doing a good job began to question long-accepted practices. Quality and productivity became the leading topics of many a coffee-break conversation, and in time more than 1,000 quality teams sprang up around the company.

When W. Edwards Deming and J. M. Juran, noted authorities on quality who helped rebuild Japanese industry following World War II, came to lecture at Hewlett-Packard, they drew packed audiences. Reports of even minor quality or productivity gains spread quickly throughout the company, inspiring others to emulate and perhaps exceed the original achievement. In time, the original nucleus of people had convinced just about everybody that much higher quality wasn't only attainable but would actually drive down costs because of productivity gains associated with doing things right the first time.

As we monitored the progress of this program, it became obvious to us that timely access to information is indispensable. Managers and supervisors who could easily call up on a computer terminal the latest parts-failure data, process schedules, rework information, and so on, could study cause-and-effect relationships much more clearly and make consistently better business decisions.

The logical fourth step, then, was to accelerate the spread of information-management tools throughout the company. Our intention, simply stated, was to insure that a broad range of people were given an opportunity to access needed information, experiment with it, and get instant feedback on their decisions. Perhaps more than any other factor, this process has greatly increased our knowledge of our business and made a major contribution to our overall approach to the quality/productivity issue.

What kinds of tangible results have we seen in the past few years? At one Hewlett-Packard product division, the cost of service and repair of desktop computers was reduced 35 percent through improved design and manufacturing techniques. At another division, production time for two of our most popular oscilloscopes dropped 30 percent, and product defects declined substantially, allowing us to cut prices 16 percent.

Vendors have been asked to become part of the total quality solution. As a result of workshops, performance evaluations, and clearly stated quality specifications, there have been major improvements in the quality of parts we purchase from outside suppliers. In one case, a supplier of logic chips for our HP 3000 business computer achieved a tenfold reduction in chip failure rates in just 15 months—to the point that we are no longer required to inspect every part that comes in.

In addition, the quality drive has helped us cut inventory companywide from 20.2 percent of sales at the end of fiscal 1979 to 15.5 percent at the end of 1982. Based on 1982 sales of $4.2 billion, that 4.7 percent decrease represents nearly $200 million we don't have tied up in inventory.

By our best estimates, we are perhaps a third of the way to our 10-year goal of a tenfold reduction in product failure rates. We haven't seen any flagging in the eagerness with which our people are addressing this issue, and they continue to find new areas ripe for improvement. It may take a few more years before we know that the goal is fully within grasp, but the results to date already have made the effort well worthwhile.

Mr. Young is president and chief executive officer of Hewlett-Packard Co. President Reagan recently named him chairman of the new Commission on Industrial Competitiveness.

Source: John A. Young, "Manager's Journal." Reprinted by permission of *The Wall Street Journal*,

Ultimately, however, no matter how astute you are as an observer of organizational culture, norms, and behavior or how shrewd at assessing organizational change techniques, you will be making choices that reflect your own values, your best assessment of what consequences you are willing to live with. We wish you valid predictions, good judgment, and informed choices in your managerial career.

KEY CONCEPTS FROM CHAPTER 14

1. Need for change when problems occur with respect to production, satisfaction, and/or development.
2. A manager can be the passive victim of change, or its initiator and planner.
3. Target for change depends on following factors:
   a. Tension in the system.
   b. Interconnection of the problem person or groups with other units.
   c. The organization's hierarchy.
   d. Place or point with most readiness for change.
4. Considerations in regard to target.
   a. Those experiencing moderate discomfort and tension are most amenable to change.
   b. The more autonomy in the subunit, the easier to implement change.
   c. The more hierarchical the organization, the higher the change effort will have to be aimed.
   d. The more autonomy in the subunit, the less important will be support from higher levels.
   e. Start where resistance is least likely.
   f. Diagnosis should precede action.
      (1) Is the behavior functional or dysfunctional?
      (2) Is it easily or not easily subject to change?
5. Resistance to change.
   a. People do not automatically resist change. They do so for a reason (however unclear and "illogical").
   b. People resist change when they perceive the consequences as negative, such as:
      (1) Perceived general threat from the unknown and from uncertainty.
      (2) Pain of letting go of the past with which one identifies.
      (3) Lack of control over what is happening (aggravated by not having time to get used to a new idea or plan).
      (4) Direct loss of:
         (*i*) "Face."
         (*ii*) Competency (relevant skills).
         (*iii*) Power and influence.
         (*iv*) Income, status, privileges, conveniences, friends, etc.
      (5) Disruption of the social system.
         (*i*) Technological changes often affect relationships.
         (*ii*) Pressure from other subsystems (interdependent).
   c. Resistance can be minimized by:
      (1) Providing accurate information and answers to questions.

(2) Ownership through participation in diagnosis and implementation planning.
(3) Reduction of direct negative impacts where possible and providing support, such as training, to help individuals to adapt.
(4) Allowing people time to get used to an idea.
(5) Utilizing the minimum amount of force possible.
(6) Being responsive to developments as the change is implemented (flexible and open to feedback).

6. The changer's relative power, an important consideration:
   a. Influences whether to emphasize current problems or to present a vision of the future.
   b. Influences need to look for allies.
   c. Influences the possibility of resorting to coercion in times of urgency.
   d. Should be used sparingly.
   e. Is not essential to gain cooperation, exert influence, and initiate change.
7. Action-research cycle.
   a. Constantly evolving interplay between solutions, results, and new solutions.
   b. Problem defined
      leads to
   c. Data gathered on causes, related attitudes, and the like
      leads to
   d. Diagnosis of data
      leads to
   e. Alternative solutions developed
      leads to
   f. Solution chosen
      leads to
   g. Solution implementation
      leads to
   h. Evaluation of solution; new data created
      leads to
   i. Redefinition of the problem(s).
8. Identification of problem.
   a. Locate subsystem it is in.
      (1) Look for source of problem:
         (*ii*) First in background factors.
         (*ii*) Next in required system.
         (*iii*) Finally in emergent system.
9. Methods of changing background factors:
   a. Personnel change.
   b. Training and education.
   c. Technology and layout.
   d. Incentive plans.
   e. Background culture.
10. Methods of changing the required system:
   a. Revision of job descriptions and work relationships.
   b. Job modification.
   c. Alternative work schedules.
   d. Reformulation of objectives.
11. Methods of changing the emergent system:
   a. Counseling.
   b. Third-party consultation.

c. Task group training: team building.
d. Intergroup confrontation: Dealing with two subsystems in conflict through understanding of each other's position; pointing out of perceived inaccuracies in other group's position.
e. Survey feedback.
f. Executive planning and confrontation sessions.

12. Change must be managed.

SUGGESTED READINGS

Argyris, C. *Intervention Theory and Method.* Reading, Mass.: Addison-Wesley Publishing, 1970.

Babb, H. W., and D. G. Kopp. "Applications of Behavior Modification in Organizations: A Review and Critique," *Academy of Management Review,* April 1978, pp. 281–92.

Basil, D. C., and C. W. Cook. *The Management of Change.* New York: McGraw-Hill, 1974.

Beckhard, R. "The Confrontation Meeting." *Harvard Business Review 45* (1967), pp. 149–55.

Beckhard, R., and R. T. Harris. *Organizational Transitions: Managing Complex Change.* Reading, Mass: Addison-Wesley Publishing, 1977.

Bennis, W. *Changing Organizations.* New York: John Wiley & Sons, 1966.

________. *Organizational Development: Its Nature, Origins, and Prospects.* Reading, Mass.: Addison-Wesley Publishing, 1969.

Bennis, W.; K. D. Benne; and R. Chin, eds. *The Planning of Change.* New York: Holt, Rinehart and Winston, 1964.

Blake, R. R.; J. S. Mouton; and R. L. Sloma. "The Union-Management Intergroup Laboratory: Strategy for Resolving Intergroup Conflict." *Journal of Applied Behavioral Science* 1, no. 1 (1965), pp. 25–57.

Bowers, D. G. "OD Techniques and Their Results in 23 Organizations." *Journal of Applied Behavioral Science* 9 (1973), pp. 21–43.

Bradford, L. P.; J. R. Gibb; and K. D. Benne, eds. *T-Group Theory and Laboratory Method.* New York: John Wiley & Sons, 1964.

Burke, W. W., ed. *The Cutting Edge: Current Theory and Practice in Organizational Development.* San Diego: University Associates, 1978.

Carlson, H. C. "GM's Quality-of-Work-Life Efforts . . . An Interview." *Personnel,* July–August 1978.

Coch, L., and J. R. French, Jr. "Overcoming Resistance to Change." *Human Relations Journal* 1 (1948), pp. 512–32.

Cohen, A. R. "Crisis Management: How to Turn Disasters into Advantages." *Management Review,* July–August 1982.

Cohen, A. R.; S. L. Fink; and H. Gadon. "Key Groups not T-Groups for Organizational Development." In *Consultants and Consulting Styles,* ed. D. Sinha. Delhi: Vision Books, 1978.

Cohen, A. R., and H. Gadon. *Alternative Work Schedules: Integrating Individual and Organizational Needs.* Reading, Mass.: Addison-Wesley Publishing, 1978. (a)

———. "Changing the Management Culture in a Public School System." *Journal of Applied Behavioral Science* 4, no. 2 (1978). (b)

Deal, T., and A. Kennedy. *Corporate Culture.* Reading, Mass.: Addison-Wesley Publishing, 1982.

Delbecq, A. L., and P. K. Mills. "Managerial Practices that Enhance Innovation." *Organizational Dynamics,* Summer 1985, pp. 24–34.

Dyer, W. G. *Strategies for Managing Change.* Reading, Mass.: Addison-Wesley Publishing, 1984.

Eden, D. "Team Development: A True Field Experiment at Three Levels of Rigor." *Journal of Applied Psychology* 70 (1985), pp. 94–100.

———. "OD and Self-Fulfilling Prophecy: Boosting Productivity by Raising Expectations." *Journal of Applied Behavioral Science* 22, no. 1 (1986), pp. 1–14.

Feeney, E. J. "At Emery Air Freight: Positive Reinforcement Boosts Performance." *Organizational Dynamics* 1 (1973), pp. 41–50.

Fiol, C. M., and M. A. Lyles. "Organizational Learning." *Academy of Management Review,* October 1985, pp. 803–13.

Franklin, J. L. "Characteristics of Successful and Unsuccessful Organization Development." *Journal of Applied Behavioral Science* 11, no. 4 (1976), pp. 471–92.

Gavin, J. F. "Observations from a Long-Term, Survey-Guided Consultation with a Mining Company." *Journal of Applied Behavioral Science* 21, no. 2 (1985), pp. 201–20.

Golembiewski, R. T. "Managing the Tension between OD Principles and Political Dynamics." In *The Cutting Edge: Current Theory and Practice in Organization Development,* ed. W. Burke. San Diego: University Associates, 1978.

Golembiewski, R. T., and A. Blumberg. *Sensitivity Training and the Laboratory Approach.* 3rd ed. Itasca, Ill.: F. E. Peacock Publishers, 1977.

Hackman, J. R., and J. L. Suttle. *Improving Life at Work.* Santa Monica, Calif.: Goodyear Publishing, 1977.

Harrison, R. "Choosing the Depth of Organizational Intervention." *Journal of Applied Behavioral Science* 6, no. 2 (1970), pp. 181–202.

———. "When Power Conflicts Trigger Team Spirit." *European Business,* Spring 1972.

Hawley, J. A. "Transforming Organizations through Vertical Linking." *Organizational Dynamics,* Winter 1984, pp. 68–80.

Huse, E. F., and T. G. Cummings. *Organizational Development and Change.* 3rd ed. St. Paul, Minn.: West Publishing, 1985.

Jenks, R. S. "An Action-Research Approach to Organizational Change." *Journal of Applied Behavioral Science* 6 (1970), pp. 131–50.

Kanter, R. M. *The Change Masters: Innovation for Productivity in the American Corporation.* New York: Simon & Schuster, 1983.

Kanter, R. M., and B. A. Stein. "Building the Parallel Organization: Creating Mechanisms for Permanent Quality of Work Life." *Journal of Applied Behavioral Science* 16, no. 3 (1980), pp. 371–88.

Kaplan, R. E.; M. M. Lombardo; and M. S. Mazique. "A Mirror for Managers: Using Simulation to Develop Management Teams." *Journal of Applied Behavioral Science* 21, no. 3 (1985), pp. 241–54.

Keidel, R. W. "Baseball, Football, and Basketball: Models for Business." *Organizational Dynamics,* Winter 1984, pp. 4–18.

Kimberly, J. R., and R. E. Quinn. *Managing Organizational Transitions.* Homewood, Ill.: Richard D. Irwin, 1984.

Kolodny, H. F., and B. Dresner. "Linking Arrangements and New Work Designs." *Organizational Dynamics,* Winter 1986, pp. 33–51.

Kotter, J., and L. Schlesinger. "Choosing Strategies for Change." *Harvard Business Review,* March–April 1979.

Krone, C. "Open Systems Redesign." In *New Technologies in Organizational Development: 2,* ed. J. D. Adams. San Diego: University Associates, 1975.

Lawrence, P. "How to Deal with Resistance to Change." *Harvard Business Review,* January–February 1969, p. 4.

Lawrence, P., and J. W. Lorsch. *Developing Organizations: Diagnoses and Action.* Reading, Mass.: Addison-Wesley Publishing, 1969.

Leavitt, H. J. *Managerial Psychology.* 4th ed. Chicago: University of Chicago Press, 1978.

Lipitt, R.: J. Watson; and B. Westley. *The Dynamics of Planned Change.* New York: Harcourt Brace Jovanovich, 1958.

Margulies, N., and A. Raia. *Conceptual Foundations of Organizational Development.* New York: McGraw-Hill, 1978.

Martin, P. Y.; D. Harrison; and D. DiNitto. "Advancement for Women in Hierarchical Organizations: A Multilevel Analysis of Problems and Prospects." *Journal of Applied Behavioral Science* 19, no. 1 (1983), pp. 19–34.

McClelland, D. C. *Power: The Inner Experience.* New York: Irvington, 1975.

Mechanic, D. "Sources of Power of Lower Participants in Complex Organizations." *Administrative Science Quarterly* 7, no. 3 (1962).

Michael, R. "Organizational Change Techniques: Their Present, Their Future." *Organizational Dynamics,* Summer 1982, pp. 67–80.

Mitchell, R. "Team Building by Disclosure of Internal Frames of Reference." *Journal of Applied Behavioral Science* 22, no. 1 (1986), pp. 15–28.

Nadler, D. A. "Consulting with Labor and Management: Some Learnings from Quality-of-Work-Life Projects." In *The Cutting Edge,* ed. W. W. Burke. San Diego: University Associates, 1978.

________. "Managing Organizational Change: An Integrative Perspective." *Journal of Applied Behavioral Science,* April–May–June 1981, pp. 191–211.

Nystrom, P. C., and W. H. Starbuck. "To Avoid Organizational Crises, Unlearn." *Organizational Dynamics,* Spring 1984, pp. 53–65.

Ouchi, W. G. *Theory Z.* Reading, Mass.: Addison-Wesley Publishing, 1981.

Pascale, R. T., and A. G. Athos. *The Art of Japanese Management.* New York: Simon & Schuster, 1981.

Peters, M., and V. Robinson. "The Origins and Status of Action Research." *Journal of Applied Behavioral Science* 20, no. 2 (1984), pp. 113–24.

Peters, T., and S. Waterman. *In Search of Excellence: Lessons from America's Best-Managed Corporations.* New York: Harper & Row, 1982.

Porter, E. H. "The Parable of the Spindle." *Harvard Business Review* 40, no. 3 (1962).

Reichers, A. E. "A Review and Reconceptualization of Organizational Commitment." *Academy of Management Review,* July 1985, pp. 465–76.

Rice, B. "Measuring Executive Muscle." *Psychology Today,* December 1978.

Schein, E. H. *Process Consultation: Its Role in Organization.* Reading, Mass.: Addison-Wesley Publishing, 1969.

________. *Process Consultation II.* Reading, Mass: Addison-Wesley Publishing, 1987.

Schlesinger, L. A. *Quality of Work Life and the Supervisor.* New York: Praeger Publishers, 1982.

Schwenk, C. R. "Information, Cognitive Biases, and Commitment to a Course of Action." *Academy of Management Review,* April 1986, pp. 298–310.

Steele, F. *Physical Settings and Organization Development.* Reading, Mass.: Addison-Wesley Publishing, 1976.

Stein, B. A. *Quality of Work Life in Action: Managing for Effectiveness.* New York: American Management Association, 1983.

Sutton, R. I.; K. M. Eisenhardt; and J. V. Jucker. "Managing Organizational Decline: Lessons from Atari." *Organizational Dynamics,* Spring 1986, pp. 17–29.

Walton, R. *Interpersonal Peacemaking: Confrontations and Third-Party Consultation.* Reading, Mass.: Addison-Wesley Publishing, 1969.

________. "A Vision-Led Approach to Management Restructuring." *Organizational Dynamics,* Spring 1986, pp. 4–16.

________, and R. B. McKersie. *A Behavioral Theory of Labor Negotiations: An Analysis of a Social Interaction System.* New York: McGraw-Hill, 1965.

White, L. P., and K. C. Wooten. "Ethical Dilemmas in Various Stages of Organizational Development." *Academy of Management Review,* October 1983, pp. 690–97.

CASES

Cases in this book not otherwise noted were prepared by, or with the help of, various individuals under the guidance of the authors. We are grateful to these individuals and organizations for their assistance. For reasons of preserving the anonymity of the organizations involved in the cases, we list the individuals' names below and gratefully acknowledge their contribution in this manner.

Andrea de Anguera	Gary Mongeon
M. M. Ashraff	*The New Hampshire*
Steven R. Bouchard	Andrew R. Nichols
Barbara A. Corriveau	Robert V. O'Brien
C. J. Crimmins	Judith Pearson
Mary Ellen D'Antonio	Barbara Ready
Stephen P. Day	Lauren Ready
Deborah Downs	Tetsuo Saitoh
Mary L. Hynes	Paul B. Samuels
Steve Lippman	Sandra Seiler
Judith H. Long	Jane C. Vogt
Robert P. Lopilado	Richard Weber
E. Thorn Mead	David Whall
Donna S. Miller	Charles E. Winn

▶ Anderson Manufacturing and Development Co.

"Ham" Wilson looked at the public relations man across his desk with irritation. Then, with his characteristic self-control in dealing with company colonels, he suppressed the quick words that were on his tongue.

It has been a rough morning—a morning of hard, disciplined argument over promotional copy for the new compacting machine. While Ham had become visibly upset and impatient to end the session, the PR man kept smiling, stubbornly fighting it out one point at a time. Ham disliked him intensely.

Although Anderson Manufacturing and Development had not had a PR man long, this guy was surely making up for lost time. Little by little he had taken under his wing everything that had anything to do with business development and promotion. He was young—somewhere in his early 30s, maybe four or five years older than Ham himself—and in spite of his smiling, driving assurance, technically ignorant. He didn't even understand what was basically new in the compactor, Ham thought with resentment.

Ham was proud of his compactor. He had directed its development from the beginning. The original concept had been tossed to him as a kind of challenge by his boss, the chief engineer, and Ham had given it long hours of exploratory thought and work on his own. And then he had become excited about it, sold it hard, and management had bought it. They had given him a tight budget and time schedule, and he had made it. He felt damn good about that machine.

"You keep approaching this copy in the wrong way, Ham," the PR man was saying.

"This is aimed at the guys who are holding the money bags, and you keep criticizing everything as though we were writing a technical report. I don't want to misrepresent your baby, believe me, but I'm trying to sell it. We've put a lot of money into its development, and we're going to put a lot more into its promotion. Now we've got to sell it. I need good copy. Everybody upstairs wants good copy."

Ham was tempted to tell him what everybody upstairs could do but checked himself again. He stared blankly at the copy, convinced that he was still right: it stunk. Worse, it seemed to border on dishonesty in some of its implications.

"What I would like to do," Ham finally said to PR, "is to have a

This case was prepared by Walter Milne under the direction of Professors A. H. Rubinstein and H. A. Shepard for courses in management of research and development conducted at the School of Industrial Management, Massachusetts Institute of Technology, Cambridge, Massachusetts, and is used with Dr. Shepard's permission.

chance to talk to the boss before we make a final decision on this. I don't want to let it go through as it stands on my own say-so."

"OK, Ham," said PR, "but remember that I have to get final copy to the printer by the end of the week. I think what we've got right now is all right," he added, "and I certainly wouldn't want to see it watered down any more."

PR left as he had come—smiling, self-sufficient, and with hearty good words.

What a joker, Ham thought to himself. He wondered how a guy like that could live with himself, how he could do Anderson Manufacturing any real good. Apparently he did—at any rate, he sat upstairs in a big room in executive row.

By way of contrast, Ham looked around his own little cubby. His battered desk and chair and one visitor's chair all but filled it. "The Conference Room," the boys called it. He laughed and then lost his laugh when a knock at the door reminded him that he had asked Holden to see him as soon as PR had left.

Bill Holden came in, easy and relaxed as always, and slouched into the chair at Ham's desk. He was a bright, young D.Sc. whom Ham himself had hired. But there were times when he wished he hadn't—and this was one of the times.

"Bill," Ham began, "I've just had a rough time with PR, and I'm not going to beat around the bush. When your test results weren't in last Friday, you promised me—quite literally promised me—that we'd have 'em first thing this morning. And we don't have 'em. We practically rescheduled the whole program so that you could do some additional work with the physics group, and now you haven't made the new schedule. What are we going to do about it?"

"I know I promised to have them today, Ham," said Holden, "and believe me, I was shooting for it. The physics group work just took more time than I had expected. We're on some pretty fundamental stuff, and Dr. Maul asked me to do some library work on it. The whole thing just ran beyond our original expectations."

"Bill," snapped Ham, "your attitude confuses me; honestly, it does. I don't doubt that the physics group is doing important work, but you knew damn well that you were assigned part time to my B project. And you knew that when I juggled the schedule I was doing it to give you a break—you, personally. I never should have done it, but you practically pleaded with me and promised that you would come through on schedule. What do you think we're doing here anyway?"

Ham was flushed and angry, but Holden let it roll off easily.

"I suppose we're doing a lot of different things," Holden said in a tone that seemed half apology, half challenge. "The Chief was talking to me just the other day about the importance of the physics group work and about what a vital part I could play in it. You know it's pretty fundamental stuff, and frankly, that's why it appealed to me. It's well related to my previous experience—some of my doctoral work. I thought that's why you rearranged the schedule."

"Bill," said Ham, "you're talking nonsense and you know it. If all my men felt the way you do about the job, about fitting their work into the pattern, why, the whole lab would fall apart."

"Well, the whole thing seemed reasonable to me," said Holden. "After all, we're working for the same boss, and good results in one place ought to be just as good as good results in another."

"Bill," said Ham in a rising voice, "you know damn well that's not so. Honestly, you're talking as though you were still a schoolboy, and it didn't matter what you did—as though you didn't have responsibility to anyone else."

"But I've done good work," said Holden.

"I know it, and everybody knows it," interrupted Ham. "You've been here what—two, three years? During that time you've had more good ideas than anybody else on the lot. You're a good man, and the Chief has given you a pretty free rein. That's why I can't understand this. You try to run your affairs like a one-man band, but this lab is not being run the way you think it is."

Holden just kept looking at Ham.

"Everybody seems to think I've been doing OK," Holden repeated defensively. "I've always tried to do my best."

"Sure you have," said Ham, "but you run around this place as though we were subsidized like the Royal Academy. You know we're not subsidized by anybody—we're organized to make money; and in order to make money we've got to push the stuff out the door. It matters a hell of a lot to me whether we do or not, because if we don't, it means my neck."

Ham looked at Holden and Holden looked at the floor, and there was a long silence.

Ham liked Holden, but he was also a little envious of him, for Holden had the *big* degree. He also had brains. In fact, he had been good for the lab, Ham had to admit, even though he never worried much about meeting a schedule.

But hell, he said to himself as Holden looked up, I have to worry about a schedule even if Bill would rather be doing other things. Sometimes, he thought, I'd rather be doing other things myself.

"Bill," said Ham, finally cutting into the long silence, "I'm sorry I lost my temper. I've never blown my stack like this before. I was wrong in doing it now."

"I'm sorry too, Ham," said Holden. "You make me feel as though I've let you down personally. You've been very decent with me, and I certainly didn't mean to let you down. If you want me to finish off the test runs. . . ."

"No, no need," interrupted Ham, a little wearily. "When I didn't have the final figures this morning, I took what you'd already done and passed it on to Porter. He's got one of his boys finishing it out. The Chief expected a report before this, but he hasn't been pressing me for it."

Ham doodled for a minute on his scratch pad and then went on: "This is no life-and-death matter, as you well know, Bill, and I'm sorry I acted as though it were. The point is not so much that you fouled up this schedule, but that you've fouled up for still another time. Anybody can understand missing once in a while, but it never seems to bother you that you have a reputation for never worrying about time. It would bother me. Every time I miss a schedule it bothers me."

Ham doodled again.

"You certainly know the things I've been saying are right, Bill," he said. "I think we should forget it for now, but let's understand that something's got to be done. I'll speak to the Chief as soon as I can, and we'll see what's to be done."

Holden backed out awkwardly, muttering apologies. As soon as he had left, Ham picked up the phone and called the Chief. The conversation was brief: Ham had a couple of problems he'd like to talk about; could he see the Chief sometime soon? "Sure" was the response—in about an hour, for lunch. Fine; done.

At lunch, the Chief characteristically opened right up with a hearty, "What's on your mind, Ham?" He asked it with a smile—a big, genuine, ready smile.

"Well, Chief, I had kind of a bad morning."

"I heard about it," said the Chief.

Ham didn't conceal his surprise. So PR had run to see the Chief, Ham thought. PR had tried to load the dice. That was a lousy trick.

"From PR?" Ham asked.

"No," said the Chief, looking hard at Ham, "from Bill Holden. He was in to see me after he left your office. He told me the whole story. And, as a matter of fact, Ham, there's a part of the story you don't know: Holden's being assigned to Doc Maul's group as part of a general reorganization that's been approved by the board."

Ham started, and he listened uneasily as the Chief began to explain. The reorganization was to involve the whole works. The lab was to be split into three groups. The Chief was to have overall charge, but the company was going to appoint an assistant chief engineer who would be responsible for some 40 engineers and as many nonprofessionals. Doc Maul was going to direct a smaller group on some of the more fundamental work. This was going to be a low-pressure group.

"Maul's group may not work out at all," the Chief went on, "but we're going to give it a try. It won't be much different from the way the physics group has operated anyway.

"This is where Holden fits in. He's to be a research associate—which, as you know, is a new title with us—Maul's right-hand man. Holden knows about this, and he's happy about it. I think one of the reasons he stopped into my office today was to check on whether you knew it, and, of course, you didn't.

"What happened was that Maul jumped the gun in telling Holden what his duties were to be, and Holden jumped the gun in acting like a research associate. He realizes that and he's sorry."

The Chief looked at Ham with an apologetic smile.

"I was going to tell you all this at the end of the week, Ham, after the executive committee had formally approved our plans. But let's forget Holden and get right down to brass tacks. Let's see what this is going to mean on our side of things."

Ham's uneasiness increased as the Chief went over things in more detail.

Maul was to become head scientist, he said. The Chief himself was to pick up two assistants. One of the two was to have the title of assistant chief engineer. He would work in parallel with the Chief and have charge of about a third of the groups. The other new appointment was to be assistant to the chief engineer—a kind of leg man for the Chief.

"Now, how do you fit into all this, Ham?" the Chief asked rhetorically. Ham took a big bite of pie and gestured his curiosity.

"We have discussed this whole thing pretty thoroughly," the Chief went on, "and we've looked at all the men we've got, and we've talked to some from outside in an exploratory way. After looking and talking, we're well decided we want you to be assistant chief engineer."

Ham grinned. This felt good. Here he'd been working his fanny off and up to now, he thought, there hadn't been any gold stars on his report card. This really felt good.

"Actually, Ham," the Chief was saying, "you've been doing a big part of this job already. You know our procedures, and you've proved you can keep on top of things. Whatever may have happened this morning, I'd read as just a bad day. The record shows you work well with the men and keep them happy and push the stuff out."

Ham thought to himself that this was right. He had been doing part of this job all along. It had started nearly two years ago when Maul was out sick and the Chief began to dump things in his lap. And when Maul came back, the lab started to grow and the Chief kept handing him things. There was no formal pattern—it was one of those things that had just developed.

Still, there had been plenty of time to participate in project work, too. Ham thought of the compactor. He had lived with that thing night and day. And that had been a good part of the setup as it was. Whenever something had come along that he had wanted to jump into, the Chief had always said to go ahead. And he had jumped into the compactor with both feet. That's the only way to do, Ham thought, when you really want to get something done.

The Chief was now talking specifics about the new job.

It would mean a substantial raise—about 15 percent. Better still, it would mean participation in the bonus plan. It would mean a big new office. And it would mean a lot of little things: a private secretary, a membership in the executives' club, office expenses for journals and magazines—a whole new potful of the niceties of life.

Ham had an impulse to jump up and shake the Chief's hand and to rush out and call his wife, who had taken the youngsters on a two-week trip to her mother's. But the impulse was only a quick flash. It passed and was replaced by something like fear. This wasn't something Ham wanted to jump into—not just like that anyway.

As the Chief went through the slow, deliberate ritual of filling and lighting his pipe, Ham expressed his thanks for being considered for the position. But while he said the right things fully and fluently, he thought of reasons for delaying his decision.

He thought of the reports, the judgments, the budgets, the people. He thought of sweating out one project while you were worrying about the next. And, strangely enough, he thought of PR.

He thought of PR because there was a guy he never wanted to be, a guy who was a kind of Mr. Management Merry-go-round in person. He wondered briefly if some day PR would wake up and realize he'd been running his whole life without ever catching up to anything. He wondered if some day after it was too late PR would wish he hadn't run so hard and so fast.

There was a pause, during which the Chief looked searchingly at Ham.

"You're thinking this is a pretty big decision, Ham?" the Chief asked.

Ham nodded. "A very big decision," he said with emphasis.

"I agree," said the Chief, "and naturally no one wants you to make a snap judgment about it. The vice president told me to tell you to take your time. Personally, I want you to take a good hard look at it.

"We both know," the Chief added, "that you did a whale of a fine job with the compactor, and it may be that that's the kind of thing you ought to stick with, that that's the kind of thing you really want. You've got to balance that equation for yourself, Ham. I emphasize this because if you do take the new appointment—and it's got a lot to offer—you ought to realize that you'll be completely away from the bench.

"When you sold me on the compactor," the Chief went on, "we arranged things so that you could see it through yourself. That wouldn't be likely to happen again. Of course, you'll sit on top of these things, and you'll take pride in these accomplishments, but in a different way—an entirely different way."

The Chief stopped talking and scratched a match to relight his pipe. Ham stirred his second cup of coffee.

"I understand what you're saying, all right," said Ham, "and believe me, I have very mixed feelings about it. I'm tempted by the new job—naturally—and I feel very flattered by the offer. But I do know that I like the purely technical side of things. And I know that if I took the new job I'd want to keep up in my field."

The Chief smiled at Ham as he waited for him to go on.

"I've enjoyed the courses I've been taking at the Institute," Ham continued, "and I'm satisfied that they've done me a lot of good. If I took this appointment, I'd keep working for my degree—just as I have been—one course at a time. And I'd probably sit in on some seminars. In fact, I'd try to keep up technically in every way I could."

The Chief smiled again and then spoke quickly and earnestly: "You can sell yourself on that line of argument pretty easily, Ham," said the Chief, "because it makes so much good sense on the face of it. But I'll give you long odds that it won't work that way. I don't want to be discouraging, but the older you get the harder it gets. It's hard to find the time—even harder to find the energy.

"Believe me," added the Chief with a wry smile, "I know. I went through it myself."

Ham thought about this. He thought of how little he really knew about the Chief. He did know he had been a top turbine man. And he knew the Chief had once won the Stalworthy medal "for outstanding contributions to turbine development." Not much of a medal, maybe, Ham thought, but still a medal—a symbol of achievement and recognition. Yet the Chief had traded this away for a stock-bonus deal with the Anderson company. Ham wondered if he had any regrets. He wished he knew.

"The fact is," Ham heard himself saying a little apologetically, "I'd rather thought that this year I might have a go at the degree on a half-time basis. You remember that we talked about this last year and you said then that the company would sponsor me."

"I did say that, Ham," replied the Chief, "and I'm sure that we can still do it if that's what you want."

"Well, I'm not sure at all," said Ham, "but I have a tentative program worked out and I've lined up a thesis."

"If this is what you want, Ham," returned the Chief, "I'd be the first to say Godspeed. My only advice would be to encourage you to pick a good thesis project. There are a lot of awfully facile theses written in that department, and I wouldn't want to see you fall into that kind of trap."

"As a matter of fact," Ham answered quickly, "I've got a pretty exciting project in prospect. Werner wants me to work with him, and you know his work. This could mean a lot for me professionally. There's no denying I would like that. I think anybody would."

"Ham," said the Chief quietly, "I understand your feelings perfectly, and I won't try to dissuade you if that's what you really want. You've got some good projects under your belt here, and a good job with Werner would never hurt you."

The Chief paused and brushed a few tobacco crumbs from the tablecloth to the floor.

"If I decide to finish up the degree on a half-time basis," Ham asked, "will I prejudice my chances here at the lab?"

"Ham, you know better than that, I hope," replied the Chief. "I'm with you either way. And as far as the people upstairs go, forget it. There's no problem there."

The Chief brushed at a last elusive crumb of tobacco.

"No, you won't prejudice your future, Ham," he added, "but it will be a different kind of future."

The Chief looked at Ham for a minute. Then he knocked his pipe on the ashtray and looked at his watch. The lunch was over.

When Ham returned to his desk, he sat down with the uneasy feeling that he hadn't been demonstrative enough in thanking the Chief for the opportunity he'd been offered. But he was interrupted by an unexpected call from Jack Masters, an old classmate and a fraternity brother of Ham's at the Institute. Jack was in town on business, and their brief hearty conversation quickly closed with arrangements for dinner at Ham's club.

As Ham cradled the phone, he let his mind savor past memories. He was glad Jack was in town, he decided. Jack was a real solid citizen. It would be good to see him.

During the next two hours, Ham tried to put some final changes into his annual report, which was due next week. It was not until long past midafternoon that he became aware that only his hands were busy with the papers in front of him. His mind was still churning with confusion over the decision that lay ahead. With a gesture of disgust, he pushed the papers to the back of his desk and left the office. Without real purpose, he walked the length of A wing until he stopped at the cell where George Porter was finishing up the tests that Holden should have done. Porter and one of his technicians were running things with a quiet, easy competency. Ham liked George—everybody did.

"How are things going?" Ham called. Porter grinned and held up a finger asking him to wait a minute. Ham waved an OK.

Ham never thought about George Porter much, but he thought about him now as he waited. He thought about him because he suddenly realized that Porter wasn't so very much different from him. Of course, he was 20 years older, but he had the same kind of background, the same kind of education. And Porter, Ham thought to himself, was a guy in a well-worn groove. For the first time, this realization worried him.

Back before the war, George Porter and one of the founders of the Anderson company had run a little one-horse shop. And there Porter had developed one of the basic patents that had brought Anderson Manufacturing into being. But Porter had never grown away from the first project. Not that he didn't keep improving it, for he did. Just last month, for instance, he had finished making changes that would let it be tied in with a computer-controlled line. A new series of Air Force contract orders had already come in on that development. That's the way Porter's baby was: high-quality and custom-built, and the military kept it well fed.

"Just about winding up, Ham," said Porter, coming out of the open cell. "It all went very easily, no troubles at all. The data look good."

Ham took the clipboard and scanned the data, plotting them mentally against the earlier runs. "They do look good," he said.

Porter, pleased, turned back to his technician. "They look good, Al," he shouted, and the technician grinned.

Ham thrust his hands into his pockets and leaned back against the wall as Porter and the technician kept feeding in the adjustments on the last run. Ham thought about Porter some more. He thought about how helpful Porter had been to him when he first joined the lab. Ham had been in Porter's group then, and they had been quite close for awhile.

Ham recalled his first visit to Porter's home. Porter lived in the country, and he farmed a little. It wasn't much of a farm, Ham supposed: a couple of hundred chickens, a cow, a small garden. He remembered how impressed he'd been that first night that everything they'd eaten—from the very tasty salad to the peach dessert—had been grown right there. Ham hadn't seen much of the Porters recently, for Ham's wife ran their social life and she didn't care for the Porters. He was sorry, for he rather liked George and his rawboned, easygoing wife.

Porter came out of the test cell and took the clipboard from Ham to record the data on the final run.

Funny, Porter's doing this job himself, Ham thought. After all, the tests were routine enough and a couple of technicians could have handled the job if company policy hadn't required that an engineer be present. But Porter could have covered this requisite by having one of his young engineers do the job. Yet he didn't, for that's the way Porter was—he never passed anything on to anybody else. He would worry, he once told Ham, that it wasn't being done right if he wasn't out there on the job. As Ham thought about this, he concluded that any worries Porter had were mighty little worries.

When the last run was completed, Ham took the clipboard again and looked at the final readings. They were right on the button.

"We'll all get the Anderson A of Approval for this one," Ham said, and Porter and the technician laughed at this reference to a standing company joke. Ham surprised himself by laughing, too.

"Flip you fellows for a Coke," he said. "Odd man pays." Porter laughed again.

"You know, Ham," he said, "that's probably the thousandth time you've tried to match me for a Coke, and I've never taken you up on it. Not today, either."

Ham smiled, threw back a friendly insult, and then added that the Cokes were on him. While Ham was getting them, Porter and the technician shut down the machine. Then they all lounged back on the bench beside the test cell, drank their Cokes, and talked. They talked trivia, and Ham didn't say much. But Porter and the technician talked easily, sharing a rough kind of camaraderie.

Ham finished his bottle first, exchanged pleasantries with the two men, and walked on down the wing. As he turned the corner to his office, he looked back to see Porter and the technician closing down for the day. Although he couldn't tell for sure, he thought Porter was whistling. Ham watched him for a minute and then, almost imperceptibly, shrugged his shoulders and walked slowly back to his office.

Ham met Jack Masters that evening in the lobby of the Engineer's Club. They exchanged quick greetings and went directly to the bar. It was a solid, comfortable bar, a good place to talk.

Over the first drink, Masters carried the conversation. He renewed old times, talked about new prospects. Masters was a good talker, and Ham enjoyed listening to him. He hadn't changed much, Ham thought, except that he was a little heavier, a little less volatile.

Masters was with National Company and had been in their New York office for nearly two years. He talked objectively and happily about his job. It seemed like a good deal, and Ham said so two or three times.

"Believe me, Ham," Masters kept saying in self-deprecation, "I'm nobody in the company."

Over the second drink, Ham edged the talk around to his own prospects. Masters was immediately interested. He asked the right questions and drew out the right details. He understood Ham's doubts quickly enough and as quickly dismissed them.

"Hell, Ham," he said as they went in to dinner, "you don't have a problem; you have an opportunity. You've been doing part of this job already, and you like it well enough—that ought to be all you need. I had to cut a lot of bait before I got this kind of bite."

"What do you mean, you 'had to cut bait'?" Ham asked. He was curious. And he was more than curious, for he was searching eagerly for any patterns of experience he might be able to match against his own.

Masters explained that after he'd been in National's Dallas operation for nearly three years he began to have an almost panicky fear that he was stagnating. His jobs had become routine and so had his raises. Masters had decided right then, as he put it, to fight his way out of the corner he was in. He did it by broadening himself technically. He did it by very deliberately avoiding getting stuck in the same kind of job too many times. He did it by smelling out every opportunity that was in the wind.

The break had come when his boss, an assistant to the chief engineer, went overseas to set up a new production facility in the Near East. This man's going left a kind of administrative vacuum, which the company decided not to fill. But Masters flew into it and picked up every responsibility he could. He made himself a kind of communications center. And when the assistant's leave was extended, Masters was appointed acting assistant in Dallas. Then before the first man returned, he was transferred to Jersey and then to New York.

"Well, your story's something like mine in some ways," said Ham, "only I didn't consciously try to bring anything off the way you did."

"That may be," said Masters, "but I think we all do this kind of thinking, whether it's conscious or not. Personally, I like to plan things out quite deliberately, for then you have more control over them. That just seems like a matter of good sense to me."

"What you're saying," said Ham with a laugh, "makes me feel a little like a country boy who's somehow getting along only because he's luckier than he ought to be. You're arguing that a guy has to be an opportunist to get ahead."

"Nothing opportunistic about it at all," Masters interrupted. "It's rather a question of creating opportunity and certainly a question of taking opportunity whenever it comes along. Take this new job of yours—if you don't take it, somebody else will. That's the way I look at things."

"Maybe I'm just quibbling," said Ham, "so let's say I'm ready to buy your argument. This is not what really bothers me anyway. What bothers me is how do you know you ought to get out of technical work; how do you convince yourself that you ought to throw it all away?"

Masters explained it very readily in terms of money and status. He told Ham that he had analyzed National Company as thoroughly as though he were going to invest a couple of million dollars in it. This was only good sense, he said, for there he was, investing his whole life in it. And his analysis showed that all the glory in National Company went to the guys in the management seats—all the glory, all the money, and all the status. He also discovered that more than half the top men in National had come up out of research and development in the first place, and so he decided that the odds were all in favor of his trying the same thing.

"Right now," Masters said, as though clinching the argument, "I'm making half again as much as the guys who came into the lab with me and stayed there. And I'm more flexible," he added. "I can do more things, and I'm worth more to the company."

Ham bristled a bit at this. The implication was that the man on the bench was some inferior kind of character, and he found himself resenting it. The argument was also clearly something of a personal challenge.

"All this may have been pretty clear-cut in your case, Jack," said Ham, "but I don't think it is in mine. You're with a big outfit—maybe that's where I should be, but I'm not—and I've got to look at my own situation. You fellows at National talk about millions the way we talk about thousands.

"Let's say I look at this thing pragmatically," Ham went on, "and I would agree with you that maybe this has been in my thinking all along. From a practical standpoint, I would say that you can afford to be secure and happy about your choice because your company is fat. If I were with National, I might feel the same way. You don't have to worry about finding your next job."

"You don't mean that," said Masters. "You know darn well that if I didn't do my job today, I'd be out on my can tomorrow. We're not running a philanthropy any more than you are."

"No, that's not what I mean," Ham rejoined. "What I mean is that you're insulated from all the wear and tear that affects a guy like me. You're not going to mess your job and you're not going out on your can. But I might."

Ham was wound up now.

"When the Chief talked to me today, Jack," he said, "he quoted a lot of figures about the progress of the company. But I'll be frank with you—we run on government contracts—we couldn't keep our shop open six months without the military."

Ham disclosed that one of his own projects had had a prospective government contract cut right out from under it, and some of the engineers had been let go. Ham worried that this might happen to the whole kit and caboodle. Then what would happen to the little guy low down on the management ladder, he asked?

"Would I go to you, to National Company, and say won't you please take me on? Would I say I'm a helluva good man even though I haven't any patents to prove it? Would I say I'm loyal and I need the work and if you take me on you'll never regret it?"

Ham was talking at Masters now rather than to him. He wasn't stopping for answers.

"The way I see it," he argued, "if I stick to the technical part of R&D, I've got money in the bank. I'm negotiable. I can go to anybody in the industry, and I can say here's what I've got and here's what I've done, and they can see it right away."

Ham stopped to sign the dinner checks and to order a second cup of coffee. He looked across at Masters again and apologized for his rush of words. He slowed himself down.

Maybe some of these arguments were pretty tenuous, he agreed, but there were other things. There was the plain and simple joy of accomplishment in good project work, for instance.

Ham had written Masters about the compactor, and now he was speaking feelingly about it. That was the kind of thing a guy had to immerse himself in and that was one of the joys he was talking about. If you went into administration full time, you kissed that sort of thing good-bye. And you lost something pretty substantial.

Ham let Masters chew over this point while they finished their coffee. Then they went out to the reading room, where they sat in a couple of comfortable chairs and flicked their cigarette ashes into the fireplace.

After a while Ham said: "Jack, I've been thinking pretty seriously about going back for my doctorate on a half-time basis. The company will sponsor me, and Professor Werner wants me to do my thesis under him."

"Well," said Masters, "I remember that you wrote me about a year ago to say that you were thinking about it. I wrote back and urged you to forget it, and I thought you had given it up."

Masters blew a few smoke rings and thoughtfully watched them flatten out and lose their shape.

"If you do go back on a half-time schedule, will you use your compactor for a thesis?" he asked Ham.

"No, I can't," said Ham, "the machine isn't really mine. I guess I didn't tell you that."

Ham explained that a friend of Bill Holden's—a local man—had come up with the basic concept. Holden had brought him around to see the Chief as a kind of personal favor.

"But believe me," Ham added quickly, "there was plenty wrong with that machine when we first saw it. The inventor didn't have a sound idea of the basic processes involved. In fact, the odds on this thing's paying off looked so slim that nobody really wanted to touch it. But then I came up with a process that made it look better, and we worked like hell on it, and now we've got something that's really good."

Masters took a last drag on his cigarette and flipped it into the fireplace.

"Suppose you do go back for this degree of yours on a half-time basis," he asked Ham, "what's going to become of it?"

"Why, just what I've been saying," said Ham. "In the first place, I think it's a good move, just from a practical point of view."

"I don't," Masters countered. "I think you're kidding yourself. Look at this guy Holden, for example. He's already *at* where you're only going to be. And all the time you're sweating out the earn-while-you-learn routine, he'll be jogging along piling up points. And then when you come back full time and give it the old college try to catch up, you'll find that all the heroes have already been made."

"Well, maybe you're right," laughed Ham, "but why couldn't I look around just the way you did, only from an R&D point of view? I might just look around for the spot where the R&D man is well off, and then I'd aim for that and try to hit it."

"You won't find it," said Masters with emphasis. "I laugh at this because I think of our annual report in which we say solemn things about basic R&D being the prime mover of everything that comes down the pike, and we publicly pat its little head and sing hymns of praise. And I'm telling you—off the record and as a friend—that all of this is hypocritical as hell. It's like a bad scenario with half the lines stolen from 'The Life of Louis Pasteur.' I don't know whom we think we're kidding—unless it's all the sweet old ladies who own most of our stock."

"That's pretty typical of some high-powered wheel in public relations," Ham laughed. And he laughed again recalling his morning meeting with PR over the promotional piece on the compactor.

"And maybe," Ham added with a smile, "this is a pretty good 'for instance' for my argument that by and large you'll find more honest substance in lab work than anywhere else on the lot."

"I won't argue that you won't find muttonheads in management," said Masters, "but you know darn well that you find them in the lab, too."

Ham nodded his agreement.

"You take the guys on the bench," Masters went on, "and you can pick among them qualitatively. And you know that on any team you've got a few with damn good brains. But you also know that you've got some other good brains seeing things through. It's not just the turn of the wheel that sends one group up and another group down. There are guys seeing things through all along the line. And some of them take plenty of risks."

Ham thought that this was right, too. He had bought a risk, he thought, when he had sold the Chief on the compactor. They had looked at him and said, "OK, it's your baby." It was a money-down, win-or-lose proposition; luckily he'd won.

In contrast, Ham thought of Holden and Holden's new appointment. This was a different kind of deal. The company would carry Holden as a kind of overhead. It was like a sweeps ticket; maybe they'd get their money back and maybe they wouldn't. The whole psychology of the thing was different.

Ham also thought of the pleasure he'd found in "seeing things through" for some of the men and some of the projects the Chief had assigned to him. There was a sense of accomplishment in this too, he thought.

"Jack," Ham finally said, "I haven't been trying to give you an argument to deny what you might call the joys of management. I've tasted some of them, and I've found that I liked them. It's just that I have very mixed feelings, and I've been trying to see it from all sides.

"And you know," he added after a pause, "I honestly feel that I'm almost ready to decide to take the job."

Masters looked at Ham and smiled broadly with sheer delight.

"Ham," he said, "that's the most sensible thing your befuddled old brain has produced tonight. Let's have a nightcap on it before you lose it."

As they had their nightcap, they talked about their families, and they made vague arrangements about getting together again "soon." When they had finished, Ham drove Masters back to his hotel. They were tired, and they rode most of the way in silence. It was not until Masters shook hands on leaving that he returned again to Ham's decision.

"Ham," he said, "maybe I've got more faith in your company than you have, but I think it's a comer. And I think in this new job you've got a helluva fine opportunity to grow with it. Frankly, I think you'd be a sucker to do anything else. Do yourself a favor and take the job."

"Jack, I'm almost ready to think I will," said Ham, as he waved good-bye. And maybe I will, he thought, as he drove the long 15 miles to Cooperstown. He was glad he had seen Jack, he decided as he turned into his drive. It had been good to talk with him.

The next morning at the plant Ham sat for a long time with his annual report again. And again he stared idly at the pages, thinking and worrying, especially worrying. He wished that he could avoid the decision altogether, that the Chief or somebody else would come up with some inevitabilities as to why it could go only one way or another.

As Ham sat worrying, his mail arrived. It provided something of a diversion, and he was grateful for its coming. He spotted among the usual run of internal mail a letter from the society. He read it with mounting disbelief, and then read it again to make sure. There was no mistaking what it said: his paper on the compactor had won the society's annual George Peabody Award for the best paper of the year by a young engineer. In stiff, formal phrases, the letter sent congratulations from the president of the society and outlined the awards night program at which the Peabody Medal would be presented.

Ham grinned, and the grin grew into a big bubble of elation. Quickly he tucked the letter in his pocket and hurried down the wing to see the Chief. The Chief was in, and he shared Ham's delight as he offered hearty congratulations. He also called the vice president with the news while Ham was still in the office. Ham could hear the vice president's voice gather enthusiasm and begin to dominate the conversation. He couldn't make out the words, but the sounds were friendly.

"He says that you're to make the society's schedule," said the Chief as he hung up, "and that your wife is to go with you if she can. And he wants you to take any extra time you may need on either side of the meeting—all at company expense, of course."

Ham felt good. It was nice to have these guys in your corner.

"You're not to let the new job make the slightest bit of difference in planning your schedule around this award," the Chief added.

Ham's bubble burst. There was no escaping the thing.

"He also says," the Chief went on, "that he would like to have an answer by the 27th, if possible. Now that they've made up their minds to move on this, they want to go ahead as quickly as possible."

Ham felt a sudden emptiness in his stomach. "Sure, Chief," he said, "by the 27th. I ought to have an answer all right, I've already given it a lot of thought."

"And Ham," said the Chief, smiling, "one last thing: be sure to get in touch with PR on this award so that we can exploit it as fully as possible for the company."

Ham nodded and said he would. He added a few words of personal thanks to the Chief and left. He wanted to get back to his office as quickly as possible. He wanted to come to grips with this thing. He wanted to get it settled.

As he hurried past the physics lab, he saw Holden—cup of coffee in hand—sitting at one of the tables, talking animatedly with Dr. Maul.

As Ham neared his own cubby, he saw Porter lounging near the door, waiting for him with the formal report on yesterday's run. And as Ham drew nearer, he could hear that Porter was whistling.

Anne Bogan

We're on the 32nd floor of a skyscraper, the office of a corporation president. She is his private secretary. The view of the river, railroad yards, bridges, and the city's skyline is astonishing.

"I've been an executive secretary for eight years. However, this is the first time I've been on the corporate end of things, working for the president. I found it a new experience. I love it, and I feel I'm learning a lot."

I become very impatient with dreamers. I respect the doers more than the dreamers. So many people, it seems to me, talk about all the things they want to do. They only talk, without accomplishing anything. The drifters are worse than the dreamers. Ones who really have no goals, no aspirations at all, just live from day to day. . . .

I enjoy one thing more than anything else on this job. That's the association I have with the other executives, not only my boss. There's a tremendous difference in the way they treat me than what I've known before. They treat me more as . . . on the executive level. They consult me on things, and I enjoy this. It stimulates me.

I know myself well enough to know that I've always enjoyed men more than women. Usually I can judge them very quickly when I meet a woman. I can't judge men that quickly. I seek out the few women I think I will enjoy. The others I get along with all right, but I feel no basic interest. I don't really enjoy having lunch with them and so on.

You can tell just from conversation what they talk about. It's quite easy. It's also very easy to tell which girls are going to last around the office and which ones aren't. Interest in their work. Many of them aren't, they just don't dig in. They're more interested in chatting in the washroom. I don't know if that's a change from other years. There's always been some who are really not especially career-minded, but they have to give a little bit and try a little harder. The others get by on as little as possible.

I feel like I'm sharing somewhat of the business life of the men. So I think I'm much happier as the secretary to an executive than I would be in some woman's field, where I could perhaps make more money. But it wouldn't be an extension of a successful executive. I'm perfectly happy in my status.

She came from a small town in Indiana and married at 18. She had graduated from high school and began working immediately for the town's large company. "My husband was a construction worker. We lived in a trailer, we moved around a lot. There's a lot of community living in that situation, and I grew pretty tired of it. You can get involved; you can become too friendly with people when you live too close. A lot of time can be wasted. It was years before I started doing this."

I have dinner with businessmen and enjoy this very much. I like the background music in some of these restaurants. It's soothing and it also adds a little warmth and doesn't disturb the conversation. I like the atmosphere and the caliber of people that usually you see and run into. People who have made it.

I think if I've been at all successful with men, it's because I'm a good listener and interested in their world. I enjoy it. I don't become bored with it. They tell me about their personal life too. Family problems, financial, and the problems of raising children. Most of the ones I'm referring to are divorced. In looking through the years they were married, I can see this is what probably happened. I know if I were the wife, I would be interested in their work. I feel the wife of an executive would be a better wife had she been a secretary first. As a secretary, you learn to adjust to the boss's moods. Many marriages would be happier if the wife would do that.

The Bagel Hockey Case

The Cafeteria for the Toronto Training Academy (TTA) was located on the first floor of the school's main residential hall. The cafeteria was open seven days a week. It consisted of a short-order grill, a salad and delicatessen bar, a soda fountain, and a hot-meals counter, although the latter was not operated on weekends. It was heavily utilized by the students and by others during the week for food and as a social center. On weekends its use was rather limited, since many TTA students were commuters and others left campus for the weekend. What business there was tended to come in spurts due in part to the use of the building for special workshops and other group activities.

During the weekend, the cafeteria employed a different crew of workers than during the week. All seven of the weekend employees were students except for the cashier, who was a housewife in her mid-30s. Two of the employees were attending high school; the senior student supervisor was from a two-year business college, and the remaining three workers were from TTA.

Ernie Slim, the senior student supervisor, had been employed at the cafeteria for four years, a long period of employment for the cafeteria, and had worked his way up from grill attendant to his supervisory position. He was a shy, friendly character who rarely worked directly with the public but spent most of his time in the back room making food preparations for take-out and banquet orders. Henry Delano, the junior student supervisor, was more personable with the customers, often standing and chatting with them. He spent most of his day walking around overseeing the other employees, sometimes helping them when they found themselves bogged down with orders, or working the grill and fountain positions by himself while others took breaks. Having had no previous experience before beginning the job, Henry was often forced to rely on employees below him to explain tasks.

Two male students usually worked the grill, and during slow hours of the day they were required to work in the dishroom. Two female students worked the fountain and deli bar and during slow hours bused cafeteria tables. The cashier's job only required her to attend the register and at the end of the day determine the total income. This position was always occupied (even during weekdays) by an older, more mature woman.

All worked under the general regulations of the cafeteria, which required that all employees be neatly and cleanly attired. Girls were to wear hairnets and blue smocks over skirts, while boys had to wear white work shirts and paper hats. Sideburns were not permitted to extend below the ear lobe, and beards were not allowed. Mustaches had to be neat and closely trimmed, not extending beyond the width of the upper lip. Good sanitary practices were expected of all employees, and the regulations included the statement: "Loud talking, singing, whistling, or horseplay will not be tolerated." A pay differential was established depending upon the individual's position, time employed, and whether or not the student had purchased a meal ticket. Weekend and weekday employees were on the same wage scale, and the pay range for grill and fountain employees was between the minimum wage and 30% higher, while the supervisors received double that of the employees. Except for the supervisors, the job was not considered a very desirable one; and, in fact, it had been a last-resort choice by every weekend employee.

Since the cafeteria was open from 12:30 to 7:00 on weekends, only one shift of workers was needed. All weekend employees worked on an eight-hour day and were allowed a half hour for dinner and given a 15-minute coffee break. These breaks were given at the discretion of the supervisors, but employees felt free to ask for them if they thought business was slow enough.

Scheduling, hiring, and firing were all done by the cafeteria manager, Mrs. Laraby, a middle-aged woman who had been manager for five years. She worked a 40-hour week, Monday through Friday, and rarely came into the cafeteria on weekends unless there was a special banquet to be set up. As manager she encouraged a relaxed working atmosphere but expected each employee to be responsible for his or her job and to strictly observe the regulations of the cafeteria. Although she was firm about what she expected of her workers, Mrs. Laraby was willing to listen to any problems encountered by the employees. As a result, they respected Mrs. Laraby and felt comfortable enough in her presence to joke with her, although they were careful not to whenever her boss was around.

Grill products were of the hamburger and hot dog variety; the fountain's main business was ice cream cones; the deli bar served salads, desserts, and cold sandwiches, most of which had been made during the week and were now in the "staling" process. All beverage machines were self-service. A customer passed down the food line and paid the cashier located at the end of the line.

During the weekends, no large quantity food preparation was done, leaving the large kitchen area desolate and open to all employees. This large back room was blocked from the customer's view by walls that separated it from the food service area. (See Exhibit 1.)

EXHIBIT 1

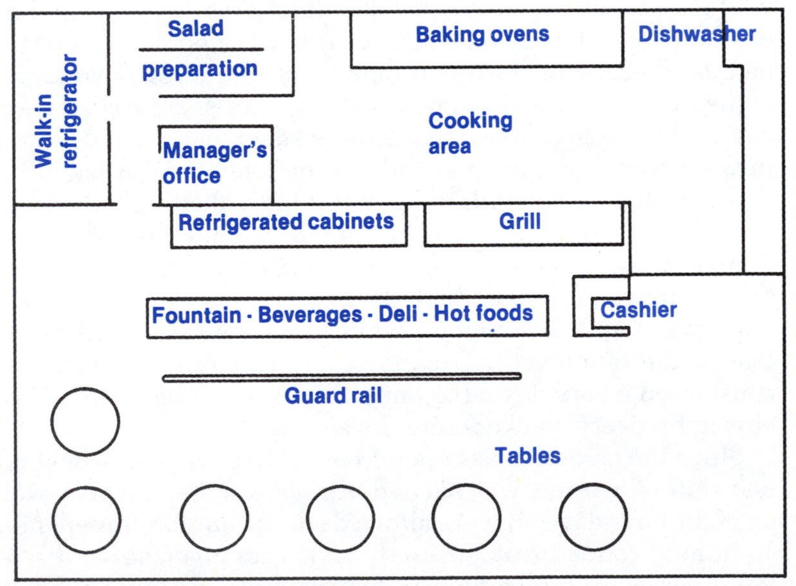

All employees performed the essential tasks that their jobs demanded of them, but without much enthusiasm. The working atmosphere was extremely relaxed and lenient, and since the work was menial, there was a flexible setup in which almost everyone could operate in another's position. Frequently the fountain person helped out the grill individual, and vice versa. However, a large portion of the working day passed with only a few customers trickling in. There was little opportunity to converse with friends coming through the food line, as was commonplace during the weekdays. This left the employees with much idle time.

The employees were close in age and shared common interests. Many friendships were formed. Supervisors were treated as equals, and joked and fooled around with the others. In the back room (kitchen) as time allowed, the male employees—including the supervisors—often engaged in a game of floor hockey, using brooms as sticks and a stale bagel as a puck. The crew also participated in other sports. One was "baseball" played with a spatula and a hard-boiled egg. Another was "king of the eggs." This game was particularly popular with the female employees. The idea was to find the "king egg" in a batch of hardboiled eggs destined to be used eventually in egg salad. The game required two players. Each chose an egg, then one party held her egg firmly in one hand while the other person used her egg to hit the immobile egg. The player whose egg withstood the impact without cracking was declared the winner and continued to challenge any other potential players. Of all the games, only baseball ruined any appreciable quantity of usable food.

There had never been any crackdown attempts on this behavior, which occurred only on weekends when the large kitchen was not in use and there were no older supervisors or managers present.

Participation in these events was left up to the individual, but the usual participants included the three male student workers and the supervisor. The fountain girls took part in games such as the egg cracking less frequently, while the cashier never participated in any events but read during long intervals between customers. The general attitude of all employees toward these tournaments was favorable except, as a fountain employee put it, "when you get stuck doing all the work while the others are out back having fun." On occasion, when employees were engaged in these tournaments, business picked up in the food service area. Then, the one or two individuals left attending the fountain or grill were swamped with orders, finding it impossible to leave their jobs and notify the others in the back room of the customer influx. It placed a lot of pressure on these workers, and if this happened it meant that customers waited a long period of time for their orders.

One Sunday, during a normal midday lull, the three men and the supervisor were deep into a game of bagel hockey in the back room. The participants were totally involved in their fun and did not notice that there was an influx of customers, that the other attendants were overwhelmed at both grill and fountain, and that the cashier was busy at her register. On this particular occasion, Mrs. Laraby, the cafeteria manager, decided to pick up a book she had left in her office. Entering through the cafeteria, she first came upon the swamped employees; then proceeding to enter the back room, she discovered an exuberant hockey game in progress!

Banana Time Case

This paper undertakes description and explanatory analysis of the social interaction which took place within a small work group of factory machine operatives during a two-month period of participant observation.

My fellow operatives and I spent our long days of simple, repetitive work in relative isolation from other employees of the factory. Our line of machines was sealed off from other work areas of the plant by the four walls of the clicking room. The one door of this room was usually closed. Even when it was kept open during periods of hot weather, the consequences were not social; it opened on an uninhabited storage room of the shipping department. Not even the sounds of work activity going on elsewhere in the factory carried to this isolated workplace. There were occasional contacts with outside employees, usually on matters connected with the work; but with the exception of the daily calls of one fellow who came to pick up finished materials for the next step in processing, such visits were sporadic and infrequent.

The clickers were of the genus punching machines; of mechanical construction similar to that of the better-known punch presses, their leading features were hammer and block. The hammer, or punching head, was approximately 8 inches by 12 inches at its flat striking surface. The descent upon the block was initially forced by the operator, who exerted pressure on a handle attached to the side of the hammer head. A few inches of travel downward established electrical connection for a sharp power-driven blow. The hammer also traveled by

Excerpted from Donald F. Roy, "'Banana Time,' Job Satisfaction, and Informal Interaction." Reproduced by permission of the Society for Applied Anthropology from *Human Organization* 18(4):151–168, Winter, 1959–60.

manual guidance in a horizontal plane to and from, and in an arc around, the central column of the machine. Thus the operator, up to the point of establishing electrical connections for the sudden and irrevocable downward thrust, had flexibility in maneuvering his instrument over the larger surface of the block. The latter, approximately 24 inches wide, 18 inches deep, and 10 inches thick, was made, like a butcher's block, of inlaid hardwood; it was set in the machine at a convenient waist height. On it the operator placed his materials, one sheet at a time if leather, stacks of sheets if plastic, to be cut with steel dies of assorted sizes and shapes. The particular die in use would be moved, by hand, from spot to spot over the materials each time a cut was made; less frequently, materials would be shifted on the block as the operator saw need for such adjustment.

Introduction to the new job, with its relatively simple machine skills and work routines, was accomplished with what proved to be, in my experience, an all-time minimum of job training. The clicking machine assigned to me was situated at one end of the row. Here the superintendent and one of the operators gave a few brief demonstrations, accompanied by bits of advice, which included a warning to keep hands clear of the descending hammer. After a short practice period, at the end of which the superintendent expressed satisfaction with progress and potentialities, I was left to develop my learning curve with no other supervision than that afforded by members of the work group. Further advice and assistance did come from time to time from my fellow operatives, sometimes upon request, sometimes unsolicited.

THE WORK GROUP

Absorbed at first in three related goals of improving my clicking skill, increasing my rate of output, and keeping my left hand unclicked, I paid little attention to my fellow operatives save to observe that they were friendly, middle-aged, foreign born, full of advice, and very talkative. Their names, according to the way they addressed each other, were George, Ike, and Sammy. George, a stocky fellow in his late 50s, operated the machine at the opposite end of the line; he, I later discovered, had emigrated in early youth from a country in southeastern Europe. Ike, stationed at George's left, was tall, slender, in his early 50s, and Jewish; he had come from eastern Europe in his youth. Sammy, number-three man in the line and my neighbor, was heavy set, in his late 50s, and Jewish; he had escaped from a country in eastern Europe just before Hitler's legions had moved in. All three men had been downwardly mobile as to occupation in recent years. George and Sammy had been proprietors of small businesses; the former had been "wiped out" when his uninsured establishment burned down; the latter had been entrepreneuring on a small scale before he left all behind him to flee the Germans. According to his account, Ike had left a highly skilled trade which he had practiced for years in Chicago.

THE WORK

It was evident to me before my first workday drew to a weary close that my clicking career was going to be a grim process of fighting the clock, the particular timepiece in this situation being an old-fashioned alarm clock which ticked away on a shelf near George's machine. I had struggled through many dreary rounds with the minutes and hours during the various phases of my industrial experience, but never had I been confronted with such a dismal combination of working conditions as the extra-long workday, the infinitesimal cerebral excitation, and the extreme limitation of physical movement. The contrast with a recent stint in the California oil fields was striking. This was no eight-hour day of racing hither and yon over desert and foothills with a rollicking crew of "roustabouts" on a variety of repair missions at oil wells, pipelines, and storage tanks. Here there were no afternoon dallyings to search the sands for horned toads, tarantulas, and rattlesnakes or to climb old wooden derricks for raven's nests with an eye out, of course, for the telltale streak of dust in the distance which gave ample warning of the approach of the boss. This was standing all day in one spot beside three old codgers in a dingy room looking out through barred windows at the bare walls of a brick warehouse, leg movements largely restricted to the shifting of body weight from one foot to the other, hand and arm movements confined, for the most part, to a simple repetitive sequence of place the die—punch the clicker—place the die—punch the clicker, and intellectual activity reduced to computing the hours to quitting time. It is true that from time to time a fresh stack of sheets would have to be substituted for the clicked-out old one; but the stack would have been prepared by someone else, and the exchange would be only a minute or two in the making. Now and then a box of finished work would have to be moved back out of the way, and an empty box brought up, but the moving back and the bringing up involved only a step or two. And there was the half hour for lunch and occasional trips to the lavatory or the drinking fountain to break up the day into digestible parts. But after each momentary respite, hammer and die were moving again: click—move die—click—move die.

I developed a game of work. The game developed was quite simple, so elementary, in fact, that its playing was reminiscent of rainy-day preoccupations in childhood when attention could be centered by the hour on colored bits of things of assorted sizes and shapes. But this adult activity was not mere pottering and piddling; what it lacked in the earlier imaginative content, it made up for in clean-cut structure. Fundamentally involved were: *(a)* variation in color of the materials cut, *(b)* variation in shapes of the dies used, and *(c)* a process called "scraping the block." The basic procedure which ordered the particular combination of components employed could be stated in the form: "As soon as I do so many of these, I'll click some brown ones." And with success in attaining the objective of working with brown materials, a new goal of "I'll get to do the white ones" might be set. Or the new goal might involve switching dies.

INFORMAL SOCIAL ACTIVITY OF THE WORK GROUP: TIMES AND THEMES

I began to take serious note of the social activity going on around me; my attentiveness to this activity came with growing involvement in it. What I heard at first, before I started to listen, was a stream of disconnected bits of communication which did not make much sense. Foreign accents were strong, and referents were not joined to coherent contexts of meaning. It was just "jabbering." What I saw at first, before I began to observe, was occasional flurries of horseplay that were so simple and unvarying in pattern and so childish in quality that they made no strong bid for attention. For example, Ike would regularly switch off the power at Sammy's machine whenever Sammy made a trip to the lavatory or the drinking fountain. Correlatively, Sammy invariably fell victim to the plot by making an attempt to operate his clicking hammer after returning to the shop. And as the simple pattern went, this blind stumbling into the trap was always followed by indignation and reproach from Sammy, smirking satisfaction from Ike, and mild paternal scolding from George. My interest in this procedure was at first confined to wondering when Ike would weary of his tedious joke or when Sammy would learn to check his power switch before trying the hammer.

Most of the breaks in the daily series were designated as "times" in the parlance of the clicker operators, and they featured the consumption of food or drink of one sort or another. There was coffee time, peach time, banana time, fish time, Coke time, and, of course, lunch time. Other interruptions which formed part of the series but were not verbally recognized as times were window time, pickup time, and the staggered quitting times of Sammy and Ike. These latter unnamed times did not involve the partaking of refreshments.

My attention was first drawn to this times business during my first week of employment when I was encouraged to join in the sharing of two peaches. It was Sammy who provided the peaches; he drew them from his lunch box after making the announcement, "Peach time!" On this first occasion I refused the proffered fruit but thereafter regularly consumed my half peach. Sammy continued to provide the peaches and to make the "Peach time!" announcement, although there were days when Ike would remind him that it was peach time, urging him to hurry up with the midmorning snack. Ike invariably complained about the quality of the fruit, and his complaints fed the fires of continued banter between peach donor and critical recipient. I did find the fruit a bit on the scrubby side but felt, before I achieved insight into the function of peach time, that Ike was showing poor manners by looking a gift horse in the mouth. I wondered why Sammy continued to share his peaches with such an ingrate.

Banana time followed peach time by approximately an hour. Sammy again provided the refreshments, namely, one banana. There was, however, no four-way sharing of Sammy's banana. Ike would gulp it down by himself after surreptitiously extracting it from Sammy's lunch box, kept on a shelf behind Sammy's work station. Each morning, after making the snatch, Ike would call out, "Banana time!" and proceed to down his prize while Sammy made futile protests and denunciations. George would join in with mild remonstrances, sometimes scolding Sammy for making so much fuss. The banana was one which Sammy brought for his own consumption at lunch time; he never did get to eat his banana but kept bringing one for his lunch. At first this daily theft startled and amazed me. Then I grew to look forward to the daily seizure and the verbal interaction which followed.

Window time came next. It followed banana time as a regular consequence of Ike's castigation by the indignant Sammy. After "taking" repeated references to himself as a person badly lacking in morality and character, Ike would "finally" retaliate by opening the window which faced Sammy's machine to let the "cold air" blow in on Sammy. The slandering which would, in its echolalic repetition, wear down Ike's patience and forbearance usually took the form of the invidious comparison: "George is a good daddy. Ike is a bad man! A very bad man!" Opening the window would take a little time to accomplish and would involve a great deal of verbal interplay between Ike and Sammy, both before and after the event. Ike would threaten, make feints toward the window, then finally open it. Sammy would protest, argue, and make claims that the air blowing in on him would give him a cold; he would eventually have to leave his machine to close the window. Sometimes the weather was slightly chilly, and the draft from the window unpleasant, but cool or hot, windy or still, window time arrived each day. (I assume that it was originally a cold-season development.) George's part in this interplay, in spite of the "good daddy" laudations, was to encourage Ike in his window work. He would stress the tonic values of fresh air and chide Sammy for his unappreciativeness.

THEMES

To put flesh, so to speak, on this interactional frame of times, my work group had developed various "themes" of verbal interplay, which had become standardized in their repetition. These topics of conversation ranged in quality from an extreme of nonsensical chatter to another extreme of serious discourse. Unlike the times, these themes flowed one into the other in no particular sequence of predictability. Serious conversation could suddenly melt into horseplay, and vice versa. In the middle of a serious discussion on the high cost of living, Ike might drop a weight behind the easily startled Sammy or hit him over the head with a dusty paper sack. Interaction would immediately drop to a low comedy exchange of slaps, threats, guffaws, and disapprobations, which would invariably include a 10-minute echolalia of "Ike is a bad man, a very bad man! George is a good daddy, a very fine man!" Or, on the other hand, a stream of such invidious comparisons as followed a surreptitious switching-off of Sammy's machine by the playful Ike might merge suddenly into a discussion of the pros and cons of saving for one's funeral.

"Kidding themes" were usually started by George or Ike, and Sammy was usually the butt of the joke. Sometimes Ike would have to "take it," seldom George. One favorite kidding theme involved Sammy's alleged receipt of $100 a month from his son. The points stressed were that Sammy did not have to work long hours or did not have to work at all, because he had a son to support him. George would always point out that he sent money to his daughter; she did not send money to him. Sammy received occasional calls from his wife, and his claim that these calls were requests to shop for groceries on the way home were greeted with feigned disbelief. Sammy was ribbed for being closely watched, bossed, and henpecked by his wife, and the expression, "Are you man or mouse?" became an echolalic utterance, used both in and out of the original context.

Serious themes included the relating of major misfortunes suffered in the past by group members. George referred again and again to the loss by fire of his business establishment. Ike's chief complaints centered around a chronically ill wife who had undergone various operations and periods of hospital care. Ike spoke with discouragement of the expenses attendant upon hiring a housekeeper for himself and his children; he referred with disappointment and disgust to a teenage son, an inept lad who "couldn't even fix his own lunch. He couldn't even make himself a sandwich!" Sammy's reminiscences centered on the loss of a flourishing business when he had to flee Europe ahead of the Nazi invasion.

There was one theme of especially solemn import, the "professor theme." This theme might also be termed "George's daughter's marriage theme," for the recent marriage of George's only child was inextricably bound up with George's connection with higher learning. The daughter had married the son of a professor who instructed in one of the local colleges. This professor theme was not in the strictest sense a conversation piece; when the subject came up George did all the talking. The two Jewish operatives remained silent as they listened with deep respect, if not actual awe, to George's accounts of the Big Wedding, which, including the wedding pictures, entailed an expense of $1,000. It was monologue, but there was listening, there was communication, the sacred communication of a temple, when George told of going for Sunday afternoon walks on the Midway with the professor or of joining the professor for a Sunday dinner. Whenever he spoke of the professor, his daughter, the wedding, or even of the new son-in-law, who remained for the most part in the background, a sort of incidental like the wedding cake, George was complete master of the interaction. His manner, in speaking to the rank-and-file of clicker operators, was indeed that of master deigning to notice his underlings. I came to the conclusion that it was the professor connection, not the straw-boss-ship or the extra nickel an hour, which provided the fount of George's superior status in the group.

▶ Barbara Herrick

She is 30; single. Her title is script supervisor/producer at a large advertising agency; working out of its Los Angeles office. She is also a vice president. Her accounts are primarily in food and cosmetics. "There's a myth: a woman is expected to be a food writer because she is assumed to know those things and a man doesn't. However, some of the best copy on razors and Volkswagens has been written by women."

She won several awards and considerable recognition for her com-

mercials. "You have to be absolutely on target, dramatic, and fast. You have to be aware of legal restrictions. The FTC gets tougher and tougher. You must understand budgetary matters: will it cost a million or can it be shot in a studio in one day?"

She came off a Kansas farm, one of four daughters. "During high school, I worked as a typist and was an extremely good one. I was compulsive about doing every tiny job very well." She graduated from the University of Missouri. According to Department of Labor statistics, she is in the upper 1 percent bracket of working women.

In her Beverly Hills apartment are paintings, sculpted works, recordings (classic, folk, jazz, and rock), and many books, most of them obviously well thumbed.

Men in my office doing similar work were being promoted, given raises and titles. Since I had done the bulk of the work, I made a stand and was promoted too. I needed the title, because clients figured that I'm just a face-man.

A face-man is a person who looks good, speaks well, and presents the work. I look well, I speak well, and I'm pleasant to have around after the business is over with—if they acknowledge me in business. We go to the lounge and have drinks. I can drink with the men but remain a lady. (Laughs.)

That's sort of my tacit business responsibility, although this has never been said to me directly. I know this is why I travel alone for the company a great deal. They don't anticipate any problems with my behavior. I equate it with being the good nigger.

On first meeting, I'm frequently taken for the secretary, you know, traveling with the boss. I'm here to keep somebody happy. Then I'm introduced as the writer. One said to me after the meeting was over and the drinking had started, "When I first saw you, I figured you were a—you know. I never knew you were the person *writing* this all the time." (Laughs.) Is it a married woman working for extra money? Is it a lesbian? Is it some higher-up's mistress?

I'm probably 1 of the 10 highest paid people in the agency. It would cause tremendous hard feelings if, say, I work with a man who's paid less. If a remark is made at a bar—"You make so much money, you could buy and sell me"—I toss it off, right? He's trying to find out. He can't equate me as a rival. They wonder where to put me, they wonder what my salary is.

Buy and sell me—yeah, there are a lot of phrases that show the reversal of roles. What comes to mind is swearing at a meeting. New clients are often very uptight. They feel they can't make any innuendos that might be suggestive. They don't know how to treat me. They don't know whether to acknowledge me as a woman or as another neuter person who's doing a job for them.

The first time, they don't look at me. At the first three meetings of this one client, if I would ask a direct question, they would answer and look at my boss or another man in the room. Even around the conference table, I don't attempt to be—the glasses, the bun, and totally asexual. That isn't the way I am. It's obvious that I'm a woman and enjoy being a woman. I'm not overly provocative either. It's the thin, good-nigger line that I have to toe.

I've developed a sixth sense about this. If a client will say, "Are you married?" I will often say yes, because that's the easiest way to deal with him if he needs that category for me. If it's more acceptable to him to have a young, attractive married woman in a business position comparable to his, terrific. It doesn't bother me. It makes me safer. He'll never be challenged. He can say. "She'd be sensational. I'd love to get her. I could show her what a real man is, but she's married." It's a way out for him.

Or there's the mistress thing: well, she's sleeping with the boss. That's acceptable to them. Or she's a frustrated, compulsive castrator. That's a category. Or lesbian. If I had short hair, wore suits, and talked in a gruff voice, that would be more acceptable than I am. It's when I transcend their labels, they don't quite know what to do. If someone wants a quick label and says, "I'll bet you're a big women's libber, aren't you?" I say, "Yeah, yeah." They have to place me.

I travel a lot. That's what gets very funny. We had a meeting in Montreal. It was one of those bride's magazines, honeymoon-type resorts, with heart-shaped beds and the heated pool. I was there for three days with nine men. All day long we were enclosed in this conference room. The agency account man went with me. I was to talk about the new products, using slides and movies. There were about 60 men in the conference room. I had to leave in such a hurry, I still had my gaucho pants and boots on.

The presentation went on for an hour and a half. There was tittering and giggling for about 40 minutes. Then you'd hear the shift in the audience. They got interested in what I was saying. Afterwards they had lunch sent up. Some of them never did talk to me. Others were interested in my life. They would say things like, "Have you read *The Sensuous Woman?*" (Laughs.) They didn't really want to know. If they were even more obvious, they probably would have said, "Say, did you hear the one about the farmer's daughter?" I'd have replied, "Of course, I'm one myself."

The night before, there was a rehearsal. Afterwards the account man suggested we go back to the hotel, have a nightcap, and get to bed early. It was a 9 A.M. meeting. We were sitting at the bar and he said, "Of course, you'll be staying in my room." I said, "What? I have a room." He said, "I just assumed. You're here and I'm here and we're both grown up." I said, "You assumed? You never even asked me whether I wanted to." My feelings obviously meant nothing to him. Apparently it was what you *did* if you're out of town and the woman is anything but a harelip and you're ready to go. His assumption was incredible.

We used to joke about him in the office. We'd call him Mr. Straight, because he was Mr. Straight. Very short hair, never grew sideburns, never wore wide ties, never, never swore, never would pick up an innuendo, super-super-conservative. No one would know, you see?

Mr. Straight is a man who'd never invite me to have a drink after work. He would never invite me to lunch alone. Would never, never make an overture to me. It was simply the fact that we were out of town and who would know? That poor son of a bitch had no notion what he was doing to my ego. I didn't want to destroy his. We had to work together the next day and continue to work together.

The excuse I gave is one I use many times. "Once when I was much younger and innocent, I slept with an account man. The guy turned out to be a bastard. I got a big reputation, and he made my life miserable because he had a loose mouth. And even though you're a terrifically nice guy and I'd like to sleep with you, I feel I can't. It's my policy. I'm older and wiser now. I don't do it. You have to understand that." It worked. I could never say to him, "You don't even understand how you insulted me."

It's the always-having-to-please conditioning. I don't want to make any enemies. Only of late, because I'm getting more secure and I'm valued by the agency, am I able to get mad at men and say, "F____ off!" But still I have to keep egos unruffled, smooth things over . . . I still work with him, and he never mentioned it again.

He'll occasionally touch my arm or catch my eye: We're really sympatico, aren't we baby? There may be 12 men and me sitting at a meeting and they can't call on one of the girls or the receptionist, he'd say, "Let's have some coffee, Barbara. Make mine black." I'm the waitress. I go do it because it's easier than to protest. If he'd known my salary is more than his I doubt that he'd have acted that way in Denver—or here.

Part of the resentment toward me and my salary is that I don't have a mortgage on a home in the Valley and three kids who have to go to private schools and a wife who spends at Saks, and you never know when you're going to lose your job in this business. Say, we're having a convivial drink among peers and we start grousing. I'm not allowed to grouse with the best of them. They say, "Oh, you? What do you need money for? You're a single woman. You've got the world by the balls." I hear that all the time.

If I'm being paid a lot of attention to, say by someone to whom I'm attracted, and we've done a job and we're in New York together for a week's stretch, we're in the same hotel, suppose I want to sleep with him? Why not? Here's my great double standard. You never hear it said about a man in my capacity—"He sleeps around." It would only be to his glory. It's expected, if he's there with a model, starlet, or secretary. In my case, I constantly worry about that. If I want to, I must be very careful. That's what I'm railing against.

This last shoot, it was an exasperating shot. It took hours. We were there all day. It was exhausting, frustrating. Between takes, the camera man, a darling man, would come back to where I was standing and put his arms around me. I didn't think anything of it. We're hardly f_______ on the set. It was his way of relaxing. I hear a comment later that night from the director: "You ought to watch your behavior on the set with the camera man." I said, "*Me* watch it? F___ that! Let *him* watch it." He was hired by me. I could fire him if I didn't like him. Why *me*, you see? *I* have to watch.

Clients. I get calls in my hotel room: "I want to discuss something about production today that didn't go right." I know what that means. I try to fend it off. I'm on this tightrope. I don't want to get into a drunken scene ever with a client and literally to shove him away. That's not going to do me any good. The only smart thing I can do is avoid that sort of scene. The way I avoid it is by suggesting an early morning breakfast meeting. I always have to make excuses: "I drank too much and my stomach is really upset, so I couldn't do it right now. We'll do it in the morning." Sometimes I'd like to say, "F___ off, I know what you want."

"I've had a secretary for the last three years. I hesitate to use her . . . . I won't ask her to do typing. It's hard for me to use her as I was used. She's bright and could be much more than a secretary. So I give her research assignments, things to look up, which might be fun for her. Rather than just say, 'Here, type this.'

"I'm an interesting figure to her. She says, 'When I think of Women's Lib I don't think of Germaine Greer or Kate Millett. I think of you.' She sees my life as a lot more glamorous than it really is. She admires the externals. She admires the apartment, the traveling. We shot two commercials just recently, one in Mexico, one in Nassau. Then I was in New York to edit them. That's three weeks. She takes care of all my travel details. She knows the company gave me an advance of well over a thousand dollars. I'm put up in fine hotels, travel first class. I can spend $90 at a dinner for two or three. I suppose it is something—little Barbara from a Kansas farm, and Christ! look where I am. But I don't think of it, which is a funny thing."

It used to be the token black at a big agency was very safe because he always had to be there. Now I'm definitely the token woman. In the current economic climate, I'm one of the few writers at my salary level getting job offers. Unemployment is high right now among people who do what I do. Yet I get calls: "Will you come and write on feminine hygiene products?" Another, involving a food account: "We need you, we'll pay you 30 grand and a contract. Be the answer for Such-and-Such Foods." I'm ideal because I'm young enough to have four or five solid years of experience behind me. I know how to handle myself or I wouldn't be where I am.

I'm very secure right now. But when someone says to me, "You don't have to worry," he's wrong. In a profession where I absolutely cannot age, I cannot be doing this at 38. For the next years, until I get too old, my future's secure in a very insecure business. It's like a race horse or a show horse. Although I'm holding the job on talent and responsibility, I got here partly because I'm attractive and it's a big kick for a client to know that for three days in Montreal there's going to be this young brunette, who's very good, mind you. I don't know how they talk about me, but I'd guess: "She's very good, but to look at her you'd never know it. She's a knockout."

I have a fear of hanging on past my usefulness. I've seen desperate women out of jobs who come around with their samples, which is the way all of us get jobs. A lot of women have been cut. Women who had soft jobs in an agency for years and are making maybe 15 thousand. In the current slump, this person is cut and some bright young kid from a college, who'll work for seven grand a year, comes in and works late every night.

Talk about gaps. In a room with a 22-year-old, there are areas in which I'm altogether lost. But not being a status-quo–type person, I've always thought ahead enough to keep pace with what's new. I certainly don't feel my usefulness as a writer is coming to an end. I'm talking strictly in terms of physical aging. (Laughs.) It's such a young business, not just the consumer part. It's young in terms of appearances. The client expects agency people, especially on the creative end, to dress a certain way, to be very fashionable. I haven't seen many women in any executive capacity age gracefully.

The bellbottoms, the beads, beards, and sideburns, that's the easy superficial way to feel part of the takeover culture. It's true also in terms of writing. What kind of music do you put behind the commercial? It's ridiculous to expect a sheltered 42-year-old to anticipate progressive rock. The danger of aging, beyond touch, out of reach with the younger market. . . .

The part I hate—it's funny. (Pause.) Most people in the business are delighted to present their work and get praise for it—and the credit and the laughter and everything in the commercial. I always hate that part. Deep down, I feel demeaned. Don't question the adjectives, don't argue, if it's a cologne or a shampoo. I know, 'cause I buy 'em myself. I'm the biggest sucker for buying an expensively packaged hoax thing. Face cream at eight dollars. And I sell and convince.

I used Erik Satie music for a cologne thing. The clients didn't know Satie from Roger Williams. I'm very good at what I do, dilettantism. I go into my act: we call it dog and pony time, showtime, tap dance. We laugh about it. He says, "Oh, that's beautiful, exactly right. How much will it cost us?" I say, "The music will cost you three grand. Those two commercials you want to do in Mexico and Nassau, that's 40 grand. There's no way I can bring it in for less." I'm this young woman, saying, "Give me $40,000 of your money and I will go away to Mexico and Nassau and bring you back a commercial, and you'll love it." It's blind faith.

Do I ever question what I'm selling? (A soft laugh.) All the time. I know a writer who quit a job equivalent to mine. She was making a lot of money, well thought of. She was working on a consumer finance account. It's blue-collar and black. She made this big stand. I said to her, in private, "I agree with you, but why is this your test case? You've been selling a cosmetic for years that is nothing but mineral oil and women are paying eight dollars for it. You've been selling a cake mix that you know is so full of preservatives that it would kill every rat in the lab. Why all of a sudden . . . ?"

If you're in the business, you're in the business, the f_____ business! You're a hustler. But because you're witty and glib . . . I've never pretended this is the best writing I can do. Every advertising writer has a novel in his drawer. Few of them ever do it.

I don't think what I do is necessary or that it performs a service. If it's a very fine product—and I've worked on some of those—I love it. It's when you get into that awful area of hope, cosmetics—you're just selling image and a hope. It's like the arthritis cure or cancer-quackery. You're saying to a lady, "Because this oil comes from the algae at the bottom of the sea, you're going to have a timeless face." It's a crock of s_____! I know it's part of my job. I do it. If I make the big stand my friend made, I'd lose my job. Can't do it. I'm expected to write whatever assignment I'm given. It's whorish. I haven't written enough to know what kind of writer I am. I suspect, rather than a writer, I'm a good reader. I think I'd make a good editor. I have read so many short stories that I bet I could turn out a better anthology than anybody's done yet, in certain categories. I remember, I appreciate, I have a feeling I could. . . .

POSTSCRIPT: *Shortly afterward she was battling an ulcer.*

Bennett Association (A)

In mid-October 1981, as Michael Silva reviewed his management plans for the Bennett Association, he wondered about all he needed to accomplish. Having been CEO for less than two weeks, he felt he needed to make some significant changes in the companies that formed the Bennett Association. He wanted to have a clear picture of his strategy before he began, because he would need to implement the changes as quickly as possible. Despite having worked with the company for six months as a consultant, Michael was unsure whether the actions he was considering would be sufficient to turn the company around. Developing suggestions as a consultant and implementing them as a CEO were two entirely different things!

Part of the problem, he believed, was the very nature of the company he now ran. A group of traditional, family-owned companies, the Bennett Association had developed a strong, conservative, even paternalistic culture, which could make it resist adapting to changing situations. Several members of the Bennett family still worked at the various Bennett companies, including three as presidents of the paint and glass business, the leasing company, and the car rental agency. Perhaps Michael's most important concern was Wallace F. Bennett, for 24 years the U.S. senator from Utah and current chairman of the Bennett board. Although the senator had pledged his support to Michael, clearly the senator's primary allegiance was to the company he had guided for 50 years, and to the 200 family members for whom it provided a source of income.

The association needed change, however. The banks had made that much evident when they demanded that an outside president be brought in to manage the association. For the last four years, the Bennett companies had lost money, and this trend was continuing in 1981. Michael's major concern was whether the tradition-bound Bennett family would accept the fundamental changes necessary to save the company.

Another consideration was how many of the changes he should implement before his six-week vacation began on December 1. A three-month delay might result in even larger losses. On the other hand, if he wasn't there to push for the changes, staff resistance could undermine implementation of his strategy.

HISTORY OF THE BENNETT ASSOCIATION

The Bennett Association was organized in 1917 as a Massachusetts trust, to function as a holding company responsible for the financial interests of the trust beneficiaries—the more than 200 descendants of John F. Bennett. The descendants received income from the trust according to the number of shares they held, which were similar to stock certificates. The decision-making authority rested with a board of trustees composed of family members. No nonfamily member could own shares.

Until 1983, Bennett Paint and Glass, originally a grain and feed store known as Sears and Liddle (which dated from 1882), was the primary source of the association's income. In 1884, John F. Bennett joined the company, and in 1900 he bought out the owners to save the store from bankruptcy and changed the name to Bennett's.

The company soon became profitable and began to manufacture paint in 1904. Profitability continued, and the physical plant doubled over the next 20 years. In 1920, John F.'s son Wallace, a graduate of the University of Utah, joined the growing company. In that year, Bennett's also entered the retail glass business.

Wallace was given increasing responsibility for the store's operations. By the mid-1920s, he was running the entire manufacturing and sales functions. His brother Harold, two years his junior, saw little opportunity for himself in the family business, and he began a career at ZCMI, a large department store chain in Utah. However, Harold retained a seat on the board of directors.

In 1932, a struggle for control of the company after the death of one of John F. Bennett's brothers ended with John F. narrowly retaining control. However, he became increasingly dependent upon his son Wallace to make day-to-day decisions. Although John F. Bennett remained president until his death in 1938, Wallace in effect ran the company.

During the next 10 years, under Wallace's guidance, the company not only survived the Depression but opened four new branches. During that period, Wallace developed a process that radically changed the paint industry. Until that time, all paint was tinted in the factory, with only 8–12 colors available to consumers. Dealers carried large inventories of the few colors in a variety of sizes. Although some experiments had been made with premeasured tubes of tint that could be added to basic white paint by the dealers to create varied colors, the process had met with limited acceptance.

Expanding on this idea, Wallace hired an interior decorator, who created 3,000 distinct colors of paint by mixing tints. In 1935, Wallace decided to distribute 1,320 colors, launching "Colorizer"—the nation's first controlled tinting system. With this new system, paint dealers could carry much lower inventories. Using white paint as a base, dealers could add specific amounts of pigment to create a previously unavailable spectrum of colors. In 1949, Bennett organized Colorizer Associates, a group of regional paint manufacturers, to promote the system nationally. These companies paid Bennett's royalties in exchange for tints and color cards. In 1981, Bennett's still owned and operated Colorizer Associates, although it represented a small stream of income.

In the late 1930s, Wallace expanded and diversified the association by acquiring a local Ford franchise—Bennett Motor Company—of which he became president.

In 1949, when he became president of the National Association of Manufacturers, headquartered in New York, Wallace turned the business over to his brother Richard (12 years younger than Wallace), who had worked in the company for some time. In 1950, after his stint as NAM president, Wallace returned to Utah to reassume control of Bennett's. Since Richard was reluctant to step down, Wallace, at the urging of several friends, chose to run for the U.S. Senate. He won and held the seat for four terms. (A more complete biography of Senator Bennett can be found in Exhibit 1.)

Under Richard's leadership, the Bennett Association continued to grow in profits and revenues. Although the Ford franchise was sold in 1967, the association retained two spin-off businesses: Bennett Leasing, which was involved in all types of automotive, truck, and equipment leasing, and a National Car Rental franchise at the Salt Lake City airport. In 1976, an advertising company, Admix, was created to meet the promotional requirements of the Bennett Association and other Salt Lake City businesses.

After Richard's unexpected death in 1976, operating control of the Bennett companies fell to Wallace (Wally) G. Bennett, the senator's oldest son. Although Richard had been formally president only of Bennett Paint and Glass, he had exercised strong, if informal, control over the other companies. When Wally assumed control, he focused all his attention on Bennett Paint and Glass, allowing the other company presidents freedom to manage their own operations. Although they still shared a common board of directors, the companies became increasingly independent, and each maintained control of its own finances. (See Exhibit 2 for a partial family tree.)

Serving with the senator on the board of directors in 1981 were his brother Harold, by then chairman of the board of ZCMI, nephews Richard K. Winters and Kenneth Smith, and nephew-in-law Donald Penny. Voting power was unequally distributed, with the Senator having three votes, Harold two, and the others one each.

EXHIBIT 1
Bennett, Wallace F(oster), November 13, 1898—manufacturer

The first of five children of John Foster and Rosetta (Wallace) Bennett, Wallace Foster Bennett was born November 13, 1898, in Salt Lake City, Utah. Both of his parents were of English ancestry and of the Mormon faith. At the time of Wallace's birth, his father, who had crossed the plains in a covered wagon at the age of three, was occupied in establishing the paint and glass concern, which his son now heads. Bennett has quoted with approval his father's dictum that "no transaction of any sort is good unless both sides profit from it."

Young Bennett attended the Salt Lake City public schools and the church high school known as the Latter-Day Saints University, where he took part in debating and choral singing (he says he has "an ordinary bass voice"). Graduated in 1916, he entered the University of Utah, where he majored in English and won a varsity letter in debating. A member of the university's ROTC, 19-year-old Wallace Bennett was commissioned a second lieutenant of infantry in September 1918, and he was assigned to Colorado College as an instructor. His own college education completed and the B.A. from Utah having been awarded to him in 1919, Bennett returned to Colorado as principal of a Mormon school, the San Luis State Academy at Manassa. "It was always my understanding," he has stated, "that I would come into the family business, in which I had spent most of my summers during high school and college. I returned to the business June 1, 1920, and have been with it ever since."

Beginning as an office clerk in the family's business, Bennett soon advanced to cashier, then production manager, then sales manager. He became secretary-treasurer by 1929, the year he also assumed the same post in the Jordan Valley Investment Company of Salt Lake City. Three years later, Wallace Bennett took over the general management of the Bennett Paint and Glass Company, with his father retaining the presidency. In that year, too, Bennett embarked on a one-hour daily broadcast series, called "The Observatory Hour," over station KSL.

During the depression of the 1930s, Bennett has recounted, none of his firm's employees was discharged, though this meant cutting wages. At his father's death in 1928, the eldest son became president and general manager, with one brother (Harold) serving as vice president and the other (Richard) as secretary-treasurer.

In 1939, he and several friends organized the Bennett Motor Company, a Ford dealership, with him as president. During the next eight years, Bennett Paint and Glass Company went through an expansion phase: in 1949, it had warehouses and seven retail stores to handle its stock of paints, enamels, polishes, cleansers, mirrors, and other "decorator and household specialties." What its president describes as the most modern paint manufacturing plant in the west was completed in 1948, two years after he shortened the firm name to "Bennett's." To illustrate his labor relations program to a NAM audience in 1948, Bennett told them, "The man who sweeps out our retail store calls me Wallace."

While retaining the presidency of the paint and glass company, in 1947 Bennett turned the management over to his brother Richard. Another business association of Bennett's is with Zion's Savings Bank and Trust Company, of which he is a director and executive committee member. The Utah manufacturer has, as well, served on the boards of the Utah Home Fire Insurance Company, the Utah Oil Refining Company, and the Bannock Hotel Corporation. He is a former president of the National Glass Distributors Association, a former vice president of the National Paint, Varnish, and Lacquer Association, and is a director and former chairman of the public relations committee of the Utah Manufacturers Association. These business interests were to result in his selection as a vice president and director of the National Association of Manufacturers.

In December 1948, Bennett addressed about 2,000 of them at a session on labor–management teamwork, declaring: "If we can give these people (employees) satisfaction as well as wages, we can overcome the philosophy of the class struggle. If we do not give them a feeling of partnership and achievement, then forces that would tear us apart will take over. Time is running out." Bennett was elected by the NAM board in December to succeed Morris Sayre as president. One statement Ben-

EXHIBIT 1 ***(Concluded)***

nett made was: "My selection is a recognition of the growing importance of western industry and of the importance of small business. This is the first time the presidency of the NAM has gone west of Chicago."

At his first press conference, the Utah businessman told reporters that he intended to spend his presidential year traveling throughout the United States, preaching "the partnership of the men who put up the money, and the men who do the work, and the men who tie the whole thing together," and the responsibility of management to convey this to the workers. He urged the NAM not to serve the interests of free industry alone, but of all freedom, because "if any part of freedom falls, the whole thing falls." Bennett has said that in his business he accepted the AFL glaziers' closed shop, despite his personal disapproval, because the closed shop was "traditional in the building trades." The new NAM president has also stated that his strongest competition came not from larger but from smaller firms, and he has recommended that the government deal with inflation by shifting its bonds from the hands of banks into those of private investors.

FINANCIAL SITUATION

Many internal and external factors contributed to the financial problems that the Bennett companies had faced since 1976. The Arab oil embargo and unprecedented levels of inflation had driven material costs higher and higher. However, to remain competitive, the paint company, for example, could not raise prices at a rate that would

EXHIBIT 2
Family Members in the Bennett Association

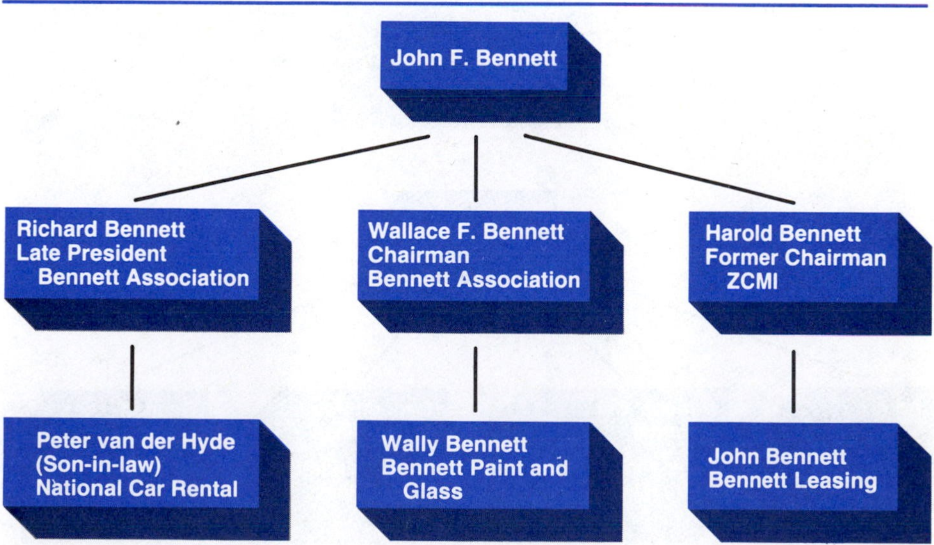

compensate for these increases. Compounding this problem was the lack of strong, central financial controls. Richard had been familiar with the financial needs of the various businesses and had relied on his experience to notice any expenses that appeared out of line. The weakness of this piecemeal control system and lack of centralized budget became painfully apparent, however, only when Wally assumed control. He was inexperienced with financial controls and could not convince his managers to institute a companywide budget.

As a result of these and other factors, in 1976 the Bennett Association suffered its first loss in over 100 years, and it continued to lose increasing amounts in successive years. In 1981, the anticipation of a $3.2 million loss on revenues of $28 million precipitated the bank's demand that an outside CEO be hired.

When Michael Silva became president, the Bennett Association included Bennett Leasing, Bennett Paint and Glass, National Car Rental, and Admix. The first three of these generated the majority of revenues and were headed by a member of the Bennett family. Each

EXHIBIT 3
Organization Chart of Bennett Association

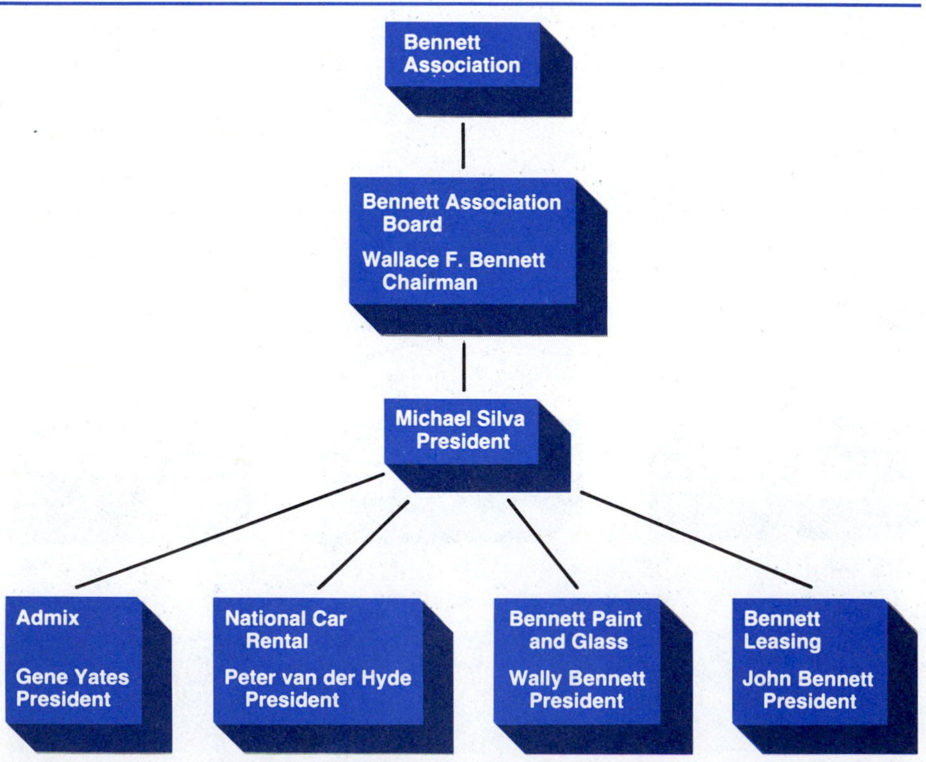

of the four was in a different market, however, and faced different challenges. (See Exhibit 3.)

Despite the five years of operating losses, the Bennett financial situation was not without its bright spots. The association owned more than $12 million in unencumbered assets, including eight acres of prime industrial land in Salt Lake City, various stocks and securities, buildings and manufacturing facilities, and stores in Utah, Nevada, and Idaho. In addition, the Bennett name was recognized and respected throughout the region.

THE BENNETT COMPANIES—INDUSTRY AND COMPANY BACKGROUND

Bennett Paint and Glass

In 1981, the paint and coatings industry was widely dispersed and included nearly 1,200 producers. Half of all the paints, varnishes, and lacquers sold covered buildings, predominantly houses. The second largest primary market was automobile and other original equipment manufacturers, which used a third of the coatings produced. The remaining share of the market went to special purpose coatings, which were high-performance coverings used to prolong equipment life in such industries as petroleum and chemicals. Forecasts over the next 10 years indicated that this segment would be the fastest growing in the coatings industry.

Building paint sales were seasonal, peaking in the spring and summer, and closely tied to the construction industry. Since 1979, the depressed housing and automobile markets had caused a slump in paint sales. (See Exhibit 4 regarding paint shipments.) In addition to the decline in new home construction, the recession had hurt sales in the large "repainting" market, since people could put off painting their homes. Recovery in the paint industry lagged that of the construction industry because coatings are applied toward the end of home building.

Employing a total of 345 people, Bennett Paint and Glass was the most well known of the Bennett companies and traditionally the most successful. Since the advent of the Colorizer concept in the 1930s, Bennett had dominated the paint business in Utah and Idaho. Bennett's original store on First South Street was well remembered by Salt Lake City residents, even though it had long since changed hands and now housed a dress shop. Although it was a well-established and prominent Salt Lake City business, Bennett's high visibility within the community nevertheless seemed disproportionate to its size.

As elsewhere, the paint and coatings market in Utah was frag-

EXHIBIT 4
Paint, Varnish, and Lacquer Trade Sales, 1971–1981 (millions of gallons)

Year	*Sales*
1971	431
1972	451.5
1973	424
1974	474.7
1975	451.5
1976	473.5
1977	486.2
1978	512.3
1979	571.3
1980	529.5
1981	504.9

Source: U.S. Department of Commerce, Bureau of the Census; *Kline Guide to the Paint Industry, 1981.*

mented and competitive. Neither Bennett nor any of its major competitors (Fuller-O'Brien, Howells, Pittsburgh Paint & Glass, and Sears) had much more than a 10 percent share of commercial and consumer sales. Estimates indicated that Bennett, with over $1 million in consumer sales, outsold Sears in this area.

The manufacturing, warehousing, distribution, and leasing operations of the paint and glass business were located on an eight-acre parcel of land on 23rd South in Salt Lake City. Topped by the Colorizer trademark, a bold spectrum of colors, Bennett's light-green, nine-story warehouse dwarfed all other buildings in the area and was easily visible from the nearby freeway. Under the same roof were the paint-manufacturing and the glass-tempering operations and one of Bennett's 14 retail outlets.

Representative of all the Bennett stores, the Salt Lake City outlet carried a complete line of Bennett paints along with painting supplies, bathroom and lighting fixtures, and a variety of sample windows. Windows were made to order for both walk-in customers and private contractors. Bennett also bid on window contracts offered by large, national construction companies, although it had recently had difficulty securing contracts.

BRANCH AND OUTLET SALES. Each Bennett retail outlet in Utah, Nevada, and Idaho employed between 10 and 20 people. Dealers reported to an area manager, who then reported to a sales vice president in Salt Lake City. In addition to the Bennett-owned branches, salespeople visited 200–300 independent hardware stores that stocked Bennett paint. Only about 20 percent of these stores generated the majority of all sales made through this channel. Salespeople were assigned to a specific geographical district, received a car and an expense account, and were paid on a commission basis.

Captive dealers purchased paint from Bennett at cost and then used a 50 percent markup to determine retail price. The dealers then either sold the paint to customers at full price or applied a variety of trade discounts. For example, depending upon the volume of business, contractors purchased supplies for as little as 10 percent above dealer cost. Each dealer's performance was evaluated by sales volume.

MANUFACTURING. Bennett manufactured a whole line of paints, including both latex and oil-based brands. The manufacturing facility included a research department (experimenting with different additives to improve product quality) and a maintenance staff of three full-time and two part-time people who kept the operation running smoothly. Productivity for the facility was 1969 gallons per worker per month in 1981, well below industry average. (See Exhibit 5.)

As president, Wally Bennett had added both the huge new warehouse and a modern tempering furnace, which gave Bennett state-of-the-art technology. The warehouse on 23rd South measured 80 feet × 80 feet × 80 feet, and merchandise was arranged along high corridors serviced by modern forklifts, which moved both vertically and horizontally. Thirty-nine employees working in three shifts staffed the warehouse. The morning shift filled the "will call" orders from the previous day, the afternoon shift stored the morning's paint production, and the night shift filled dealer orders.

Three unions represented workers in the plant: the Glaziers, the Allied Glass Workers, and the Steel Workers. In June 1981, the unions

EXHIBIT 5
Paint Industry Productivity, 1970–1980

Year	*Average Gallons Produced/Worker/Month*
1970	1,737
1971	1,931
1972	1,946
1973	1,959
1974	2,030
1975	2,154
1976	2,132
1977	2,184
1978	2,144
1979	2,371
1980	2,260

Source: *Kline Guide to the Paint Industry, 1981.*

called a strike for a wage increase. For several weeks management successfully ran the plant, and many felt that Bennett was on the verge of winning, but the unions compromised on a contract that provided a 5 percent wage increase each year for three years. Although some managers wanted to hold out, Wally Bennett decided to accept the compromise.

MANAGEMENT. Years of profitability had lulled most of Bennett's highly tenured employees into a strong sense of security. Both the managerial and production staffs seemed unresponsive to calls for financial improvement and appeared unaware of the toll the economy was taking on the company's income statement.

A particular problem had been the attitude of Jack Nielson, former executive vice president of Bennett. Jack Stevens, vice president of finance for the Bennett Association, commented on how Nielson's recent retirement had solved some of the problems:

> Jack was a vice president of production, and he had been something of a favored son of Richard. He was quite egotistical and difficult to work with at times. Anyone who opposed him created a lot of problems, since this guy would always lose his temper. Because of that and Wally's style, he seemed to exercise more dominance over Wally than any of the other people. Wally always appeared to be rather cautious with this guy and would listen to him more than anyone else. Unfortunately, this guy didn't always have the best business insights. He was an engineer by trade and had been running the production operation, but he was promoted to executive vice president and began to have a bigger say in the way the rest of the business was run. As a result, it was often very hard to get new ideas into motion.

Jack Stevens had also wanted to get the company to use some form of budgeting.

> I know that budgeting is an excellent tool for management, but to others at Bennett it is just an irritating accounting system. I provide each cost center with a history of their expenses for the current year, so all they have to do is put in a new number. The whole thing falls on deaf ears. When DeVon Johnson (currently vice president of marketing) came on board, he had an interest in it, but he can't implement it. Wally, in fact, came to me one day with a figure that represented the expenses that we would have for the coming year and asked me to calculate the amount of sales we would have to generate to cover those expenses. Jack O'Brien had said that we couldn't cut expenses without adversely affecting our sales function, so that number became our sales target for the year.

Bennett Leasing

The equipment-leasing industry dated from the 1950s, when tax credits and accelerated depreciation incentives for investment enhanced the popularity of equipment leasing. The industry experienced explosive growth in the 1960s, particularly in the transportation area (trucks, autos, airplanes, railroad cars), office and information-processing equipment, and industrial equipment and facilities. In 1981, leasing remained one of the fastest growing industries in the United States, with over 1,800 firms writing agreements for billions of dollars of equipment. Not only the number but the value of transactions had increased substantially, facilitated in part by the development of leveraged leasing. (Exhibit 6 describes leasing trends.) Inflation, risky business cycles, and high interest rates had forced firms of all sizes to turn to leasing.

Firms leased equipment for a variety of reasons, primarily to take advantage of tax credits and to have more flexible financing. Many small firms leased because they lacked sufficient capital to support debt financing of equipment purchases. Leasing companies could take advantage of certain tax benefits resulting from accelerated depreciation and investment tax credits and pass the benefits on, through reduced rates, to firms that couldn't. Differences in capital costs to a leasing company and an operating company encouraged leasing. Operating companies also gained more financial flexibility as leasing extended the length of financing, allowed constant-cost financing, and conserved working capital. Leases could be tailored to the needs of the lessee, such as those in seasonal businesses, and since few or no restrictive covenants were required, as with debt financing, firms could conserve existing lines of credit.

In addition to the numerous quantifiable benefits, leasing reduced the risk of equipment obsolescence, particularly in an era of rapid technological change, and often was simply more convenient than borrow-and-purchase options. The convenience factor was particularly influential in automobile leasing. While automobile purchases were down throughout the country in 1981, the leasing population remained stable and was expected to grow. Projections indicated that by 1985, over 40 percent of cars purchased would be lease financed, double the 1981 lease base.

EXHIBIT 6
Equipment-Leasing Growth

Year	*Equipment Cost Added (000s)*
1979	$ 8,039,000
1980	10,214,400
1981	13,374,700

Source: American Association of Equipment Lessors, *1982 Survey of Accounting and Business Practices; World Leasing Yearbook, 1982.*

With the growing acceptance of the equipment-leasing concept, there arose increasing demand for specialized leases and fast, low-cost maintenance plans. These trends, along with inflationary pressures, were forcing small leasing companies to tighten and streamline operations in order to compete in this highly competitive marketplace.

The Bennett Leasing Company was a holdover from the Bennett Association's expansion into the automobile industry in the 1930s. Senator Bennett retained his role as president of the franchise throughout his presidency of NAM and his Senate terms. He had turned over operating control to a resident manager, and, by 1967, when Ford announced that it didn't want absentee franchise owners, Bennett decided to sell. Although it could have resisted Ford's demands, the association sold the franchise, retaining the car and truck leasing and truck maintenance operations. These operations, headed by John Bennett, Harold's son, constituted the leasing company when Michael Silva arrived.

MANAGEMENT. Tall, laconic, and thoughtful, John Bennett bore a strong physical resemblance to other members of the family, especially his cousin Wally. John liked to thoroughly explore each business decision made by the company. His analytical style and careful consideration of each issue led many around him to observe that he might have been a good college professor. He enjoyed the people with whom he worked and felt that his organization was strong, stable, and customer oriented.

By 1981, Bennett Leasing had 35 employees and had had as many as 40 at one time. Although willing to lease nearly any type of equipment, automotive and truck leases to major fleet customers, small businesses, and individuals provided the bulk of the revenues. In 1981, 1,800 autos and light trucks were under lease.

Like many leasing companies using floating rate leases, Bennett Leasing lost money between 1979 and 1981 because of sustained high interest levels. Despite the increasing losses, neither the sales staff nor management appeared to be concerned. John Bennett commented:

> When Mike (Silva) took over the business, I realized that several changes needed to be made. I know that Michael is looking at the trucking business because it has lost money for us over the past several years, but I have some misgivings about that. I've been here since 1954, and I've noticed that the trucking business is the least interest-sensitive business that we have.

About half of the leasing company's employees worked in the trucking side of the business. The truck-leasing segment was growing along with the rest of the leasing industry, increasing the number of units in service by 31 percent and revenues by 22 percent in 10 years. At Bennett Leasing, many of the employees were experienced mechanics, involved in the maintenance operation. John added:

> Mike is wondering what to do with the people in our company. He just doesn't know them as well as I do. There are some of them who might be a bit mediocre, but they have some skills and experience that would be very hard to replace. Many of these people are good friends of mine, and some of them have been here longer than me. We probably need some change in the climate, but you also need stability, experience, and knowledge. We don't want to get rid of expertise.

National Car Rental

The car rental industry began in 1916, but the most rapid growth had occurred since 1960. Although 8 to 12 corporate systems could be considered the leading national firms in the business, as many as 5,000 independent firms and system licensees operated on a local or regional basis. By 1981, 40 million car rental transactions generated over $3 billion in revenues. The current 19 percent rate of growth was predicted to continue through 1981 because of the high cost of car ownership, the price of gasoline, and increasing reliance on "fly/drive" forms of business and vacation travel. (See Exhibit 7.)

The overwhelming majority of rental car service consumers were business travelers, and between 75 and 85 percent of rental car revenues were generated through rentals made at airports. More than 90 percent of car rental fleets were rented to commercial users.

The National Car Rental franchise at the Salt Lake City Airport became part of the Bennett Motor Company in 1959. The franchise had nearly 400 cars, and, in a good week, all were rented. Closely tied to tourism and business travel, the business was somewhat cyclical. In 1981, the winter snowfall in the Salt Lake City area had not been plentiful, and there was some concern throughout the area about the impact of this situation on the local economy. In addition, after Budget

EXHIBIT 7
Car Rental Growth—Selected Years

Year	*Units in Service*	*Revenues (millions of $)*
1970	319,000	$ 936
1972	341,000	1,048
1978	448,000	2,303
1980	512,000	3,349

Source: American Car Rental Association, 1983.

Rent-A-Car started a premium giveaway to increase business in October 1981, the other major rental companies, including National, became involved in a premium war. As a result, National Car Rental Corporation eventually lost $15 million, and the local Bennett-owned franchise dropped from third to fourth in its share of the Salt Lake area market.

On the other hand, Salt Lake City had been tabbed the second fastest growing city of the 1980s in the United States, and Western Airlines had plans to make Salt Lake City its new hub of operations, which would result in expansion of the airport. Many corporations were moving there, which increased the level of business travel. All these developments bode well for the local car rental franchise and the local economy and seemed like positive indicators for the Bennett franchise.

MANAGEMENT. Peter van der Heyde, president of the company, had run the franchise for many years. Born in Holland, he had married one of Richard Bennett's daughters and had then come to work for the Bennett Motor Company before it was sold. Peter worked closely with Richard until the latter's death, and many felt that if Richard had outlived his brothers, Peter might have been his successor. Tall and tanned, he still spoke with a slight Dutch accent.

> I try to run a tight ship here. I feel a moral obligation to the stockholders, and I think it's paid off. Our profit has gone up every year since I took over in 1976. In this business, it's very easy to lose customers and hard to get them back. I think you need three things to be successful here: good financing, good luck, and common sense.

Peter operated a lean, efficient business with no intermediate levels of supervision. Although concerned about the company as a whole, Peter was proudest of his own operation. Even when the other Bennett companies were losing money, the National franchise was always in the black. As one observer noted, "That company does nothing but generate cash. The nature of the work is relatively routine, so they can pay low wages, and all transactions are in cash or by credit cards."

Admix

Admix was the smallest of the Bennett companies, employing only five people. Most of its business was in developing commercials, and the operation stayed small by contracting out much of the work. Before coming to Admix, President Gene Yates had worked for several ad agencies managing large accounts, including Western Airlines and Rockwell International. Under his leadership, Admix had been profitable since its founding—unaffected by the depressed economy. It was not generally known that Bennett owned Admix; the company had deemphasized the relationship so as not to reduce the number of potential clients.

There was little interaction between Admix and the other companies owned by the Bennett Association. Michael Silva noted, "No one has paid much attention to Gene. He was making money before I came, and he seems to be doing OK now."

BENNETT ASSOCIATION: KEY MANAGEMENT PERSONNEL

Wally Bennett—Bennett Paint and Glass

The eldest son of the senator, Wally Bennett had spent his entire career with Bennett after serving in the military for three and one-half years. Like his father, he had attended the University of Utah and had then held a variety of positions at Bennett Paint and Glass (most recently as director of personnel) before taking control of the company in 1976. As were many family members, he was active in church and civic affairs.

Wally was tall, with greying hair, and had a patrician air about him. In his mid-50s, he was very popular around the Salt Lake area, and most people who met him found him very agreeable and enjoyed his company. Extremely sensitive to the needs and feelings of others in the business, he would often postpone decisions that might upset his

EXHIBIT 8
Key Management Personnel

	Position	*Years with Company*	*Approximate Age*
John Bennett	President, Bennett Leasing	20+	55
Wallace F. Bennett	Chairman, Bennett Association	50+	82
Wallace G. Bennett	President, Bennett Paint and Glass	25+	55
DeVon Johnson	Executive vice president, Bennett Paint and Glass	1	57
Michael Silva	CEO, Bennett Association	>1	30
Jack Stevens	Controller, Bennett Paint and Glass	5	52
Peter van der Hyde	President, National Car Rental	20+	53

staff until he could contact all the parties involved. He would gather his staff together to try to resolve many of the problems facing the company through consensus decision making. If the group could not arrive at a decision, he would often put the issue off until a later meeting, where it could be discussed more thoroughly.

He had inherited from his father a strong concern for the welfare of the company's employees, and he always tried to act in a way that reflected that concern. Although he maintained a high regard and respect for his father, Wally tended not to consult him on most business decisions. He relied mostly on his 25 years of experience in the company and on the expertise of his staff. While he could have exercised more control over the other Bennett companies, as did Richard before him, he chose to devote himself almost exclusively to the paint and glass business.

DeVon Johnson—Executive Vice President, Bennett Paint and Glass

DeVon Johnson was relatively new to the company. Immaculately and elegantly dressed, he tended to speak rapidly and directly, generating tremendous energy. Before coming to Bennett, he spent 35 years in the paint business with Fuller-O'Brien, where he rose from a stockboy to vice president of the company. Adhering to the management philosophy of "putting in a little more than you expect to get back," DeVon dramatically improved Fuller's sales and profits in each position he had held. He was the youngest branch manager in the history of the company. Eventually, because of the breadth of his sales and operations experience, Fuller began to depend on him to turn around problem areas.

DeVon resigned from Fuller-O'Brien for family reasons and contacted Bennett about a job shortly thereafter. He had been hired as vice president of marketing; by September 1981, he had replaced Jack Nielson, who retired, as executive vice president of the company.

DeVon had a full slate of objectives for the company. First, he felt it should become more customer oriented, particularly in responding to complaints more quickly. Second, he was concerned about plant productivity. Although fully staffed, plant output was below industry average. Third, DeVon wanted to increase Bennett's market share:

> I'd love to run a company 10 times this size. I don't like to sit still. I can't wait to get to work in the morning. I know that I'm impatient, but I've never been a flash in the pan. We're still learning here, and some of the people don't know what they can do yet. In the morning, I get here before 7:30, and I work through the day. I usually don't even leave the office for lunch, because I bring along a bag lunch that I can eat right here at my desk. I got used to that in other jobs, and I don't want to change now.

DeVon was concerned about the constraints he felt in meeting the challenges facing the company. Since it was a family-owned, traditional business led by the son of the chairman, implementing major changes would probably mean going back to the board repeatedly.

The lack of concern shown by others in the company about the growing losses also puzzled him. Despite all the problems, he didn't believe people were changing their approaches to the problems. Also, although he liked Wally and enjoyed working with him, he wasn't sure whether Wally's deliberate, consensus-oriented style was what Bennett needed to pull it out of this slide.

The Senator

Senator Wallace F. Bennett was an active board chairman. Known throughout the company and the family as "The Senator," he provided continuity to a company that had had three presidents in five years. His energy, creativity, and leadership skills served him well, not only in running the companies but also in his successful careers as president of NAM and as a U.S. senator. Throughout his terms in Congress, the senator had kept his post as chairman of the board and had kept abreast of company activities.

Eighty-two at the time Michael Silva became president, the senator remained physically and mentally active. His daily routine included long walks (up to six and a half miles) and a full schedule of activities at his office on the second story of the original Bennett building on First South. He was a prominent and respected figure in the city, involved in civic and church affairs.

The senator was ordinarily modest about his many accomplishments, but he exhibited a justifiable pride about Bennett's early years under his presidency:

> We were bold then. We dominated the paint business in Utah. When we developed the Colorizer concept, everyone told us it wouldn't work. But overnight, we revolutionized the paint business.
>
> I feel very close to Mike because we can give each other ideas. I think I have been able to suggest a few things that Mike has agreed with, and I know that he has come up with a lot of ideas on his own that I thought were great. I think we can be a good team.
>
> I wonder about the future of the Bennett Association. Within the company, there has been a real political struggle for power since Richard's death. I think we needed an outsider.

Michael Silva

Michael grew up in Hawaii and attended Brigham Young University, where he was active in school politics and competed successfully in several intercollegiate and national debate tournaments. Upon graduation, he enrolled in a master's program in organizational behavior at BYU, where his quick, analytical mind and remarkable verbal abilities soon distinguished him. Generally, Michael had gotten along well with the faculty and peers but at times appeared impatient and aloof. In an argument or discussion, Michael's debating prowess made him an intimidating opponent. Therefore, although he had completed 95 percent of the degree requirements and had grades well above the class average, several confrontations with faculty members caused him to leave the program shortly before graduation.

Michael was 30 years old when he took over as president of the Bennett Association but had a wealth of experience behind him. After leaving BYU, he had been through a series of remarkable job changes, each of which gave him more responsibility. He began as an assistant to the president of Skaggs Foods but, after a year, moved back to Hawaii to take a staff job as a corporate planner at State Savings and Loan, a large Hawaiian operation with assets of $500 million, 16 branches, and over 300 employees. At the S&L, he worked his way up to a position as assistant to the chairman of the board. After two years with State, he returned to the Intermountain West as manager of Peat, Marwick, Mitchell & Co.'s bank consulting unit. While Michael was in this position, Warren Pugh, owner of Cummins Intermountain Diesel Company, asked Michael to come straighten out his banking problems, which were costing the company tens of millions of dollars. He was able to put Cummins on a sound financial footing, but only by laying off 70 percent of the work force. Michael then moved to Arthur Young & Co. as manager of consulting services for the Salt Lake City office.

Michael began to work with the Bennett Association when it engaged the services of Arthur Young in late February 1981. In June 1981, the banks informed Bennett that, because of continued losses, they were going to call in their loans unless the company would agree to an outside CEO—a first in the history of the association. Bennett then also asked Arthur Young to help it find someone who could make the company profitable once again.

Several candidates with impressive credentials were interviewed by the senator and the board. Although each candidate had felt that he could improve Bennett's position, they all agreed a complete turnaround would take at least five years. The board (in particular, the senator) was not impressed with the applicants. He finally said, "Gentlemen, I don't think we need to go outside and look for people to help us. I think we have the man right here who is best suited for the job."

In August 1981, Michael was offered the job and, after some negotiation, signed a three-year contract as CEO of what would be called Bennett Enterprises, a central management company that would control the various companies owned by the Bennett Association. He would begin his duties as CEO in early October 1981.

MANAGEMENT STYLE. Michael's office, located in the Bennett Leasing Company building, was pleasantly, if sparsely, decorated. His office and his secretary's office were separated from the leasing operation by a heavy, black, swinging door, referred to as the "Iron Curtain." Relatively small by executive standards, the office had few of the trappings that one might associate with a CEO. He did have a small computer, one of two he owned. A small, framed quotation immediately caught the eye of any visitor:

> There is nothing more difficult to carry out, or more doubtful to success, nor more dangerous to handle, than to initiate a new order of things. For the reformer has enemies in all those who profit by the old order, and lukewarm supporters in all those who would support by the new order.

The existence of the Iron Curtain was significant. Michael was explicit about his non-open door policy. He was protective of his office time and went out of his way to make it difficult for people to find him. He believed that if people knew his time was valuable, and he was difficult to find, they were better prepared than otherwise when they did catch him. Besides, he felt his lack of availability often encouraged people to solve problems themselves.

He managed telephone calls with the same spirit. His secretary, Dixie Clark, screened all calls. Only those from his family or the senator were allowed to come through immediately. For all other calls, he was "out of the office" or "in a meeting." Periodically during the day, Michael would sort through the messages and return the calls that seemed important. By the end of the day, message slips littered his desk.

When he entered the building, he would greet everyone cheerfully, at times almost playfully. He seemed genuinely pleased with those in the company who would banter with him.

> That is something that I encourage. I like the atmosphere of mild sarcasm that we have created here. I encourage people to tease me because I get better information about how people are feeling. It's a type of informal communication.

SCHEDULE. Michael's daily routine as CEO followed one of two patterns. In the first, he arose early and arrived at the office at 5 or 6 A.M. He wrote, dictated correspondence, and planned until 8 or 9, when he began to see people and make calls. After lunch he went home to enjoy the rest of the day with his family. In the second pattern, Michael stayed home in the morning and helped prepare the children for school. He then arrived at the office around 10 A.M. and worked until lunch. After lunch he would remain at the office until around 3, when he went home to be with his family.

In the evenings, his schedule was less variable. He helped with dinner (he was an accomplished cook) and afterward put the children to bed. Often he worked (usually on his own writing) from 10 P.M. until 1 or 2 A.M. He seldom needed more than four or five hours of sleep.

> I have never worked one Saturday or one Sunday in my career. I don't think I have ever worked an eight-hour day. I made a decision when I started to work that my family was always going to come first in my life. This is the first job that has offered me real flexibility. I found that I could easily become too involved with my work, but I don't want to. I work hard at keeping my family number one. I don't want my work to become my life. I really like the freedom that this job could offer me now. I like both the freedom and the money, but I probably wouldn't give up the freedom for the money. I want time to be with my family. Time, in fact, probably drives everything I do. I'm something of a time fanatic. Everything is driven by my time resource. I won't take on anything that will require any more of my time than I already give.
>
> I don't think that it is any big deal to be a good manager. Most anyone could probably be a reasonable manager. The real question is whether you can do it differently. Can you do it in a way that doesn't eat up your life? Can you have an impact in your job, and still maintain a family life?
>
> I think that there are three roles that have to be mastered in management. You need to know strategy, the culture, and the numbers. The problem that you generally find is that few people who are sensitive to issues like culture enjoy working with numbers. You can usually find people who like to do two of those roles, but not all three.

SILVA DISCUSSES THE COMPANY. After assuming control of Bennett Enterprises on October 1, 1981, Michael felt that he had a good understanding of how the company operated, but he was unclear about which problems to attack first, which managers were reliable, and which approach he should take to making changes. He also knew that the six-week vacation he negotiated as a part of his contract was to begin soon, and he was unsure about initiating any major change only to have it sputter and die in his absence. Michael interviewed the key managers from each of the businesses and spent a considerable amount of time with the senator. He wanted to have as much input as possible before he began to implement a plan.

He talked at length about the situation he faced:

> When the company brought in all of the outside applicants for the job, they all took a strictly financial approach and said it would take at least five years to turn the company around. I don't think we have that much time, and I think we can do it in less than that. All of the other people they interviewed for this job said that it was a financial problem. I think the problem is as much cultural as it is financial.

Michael noted that employees at Bennett seemed to have an unwritten expectation that if they had a job with Bennett, they would never be laid off. Even during the Great Depression, no one at Bennett had been let go. Perhaps for this reason, even though the company was having severe financial troubles, there was a noticeable lack of concern among employees and managers about losing their jobs. They had made no special efforts to improve performance or productivity, or even to attract new customers. Some pressure had been put on the sales districts, but with limited response.

Commenting on his goals, Michael stated:

> We're going to have a difficult time turning this around. Our biggest businesses are tied directly to the housing and automobile markets, and so we are going to have a hard time if this recession gets any worse.
>
> We need to stress excellence—and making a profit in the long run. It's important to remember that all the variables that insure a profit in the long run are human resource variables. I want people to think they are the best. I will not stand for mediocrity. We should demand the absolute best from our people, but then pay them accordingly. Many companies try to pay their people the least amount possible and still keep them. I think that's crazy. I think you should pay them as much as possible to still make a profit. It makes a big difference in the way they think about themselves. More than anything, I think we should be strategy driven. We want to have revenues of $100 million by 1990.
>
> I want to be a leader here. The difference between a leader and a manager is that a manager manages systems and a leader manages values. We need to stress new values, those that emphasize performance. I need to have the confidence of the people here, because when an organization doesn't sense that their leader can get them through a crisis, they lose their incentive.

One factor Michael worried about particularly was the reaction of members of the Bennett family to any changes he might make:

> Part of my contract states that the board cannot counteract my decisions. They can cancel my contract at any time, but I don't have to get their approval for any of my decisions, and they can't counteract what I decide. I don't think I have time for an educational process each time I make a decision. Decisions will have to be made in a hurry, and I don't have the time to go back and forth with the board. I do stay in close contact with the senator, though. He has been very helpful so far. I probably see him two times a week, but I talk to him at least once a day.
>
> I like to define culture as the personality of a company, and so I think there are two ways to change that personality. The first is by long-term change, where you gradually work at some of the problem areas in the culture. The second is trauma, where you massively address the company problems.

Given its unique history, Michael was not sure which approach would be best for Bennett.

Bennett Association (B)

NOTE: *DO NOT READ* this case until instructed to do so by your instructor.

Convinced that the financial problems besetting the Bennett Association [see Bennett Association (A)] were actually symptoms of an unproductive culture, Michael Silva had instituted many changes over the last six months. Now, as the company was struggling to adjust to the radical changes he had made, he wondered what he could do to insure the success of his strategy. He knew the radical changes he made had caught the attention of the company and the Salt Lake business community, but he wasn't sure of the way the company and its employees would respond. (See Exhibit 1 for newspaper accounts of his new program.)

THE STRATEGY

Michael had begun to implement his strategy before leaving for Hawaii. He thought that since the company was already in considerable trouble with the banks, he needed to start making changes right away. Second, he believed that a gradual transition wouldn't work in this situation. Bennett's employees would have more time to resist a slow, long-term change, particularly if imposed by an "outsider." Quick action, he felt, was the key to return the company to profitability and satisfy the lenders.

Traditionally, management at the Bennett Association had rewarded tenure and loyalty, yet performance and productivity were needed to compete successfully in the marketplace. The work force at Bennett Paint and Glass and Bennett Leasing were not generating revenues commensurate with their size. Michael anticipated that the work force in these companies could be cut in half. He had also been skeptical about the quality of the management talent.

By December 1981, Silva had begun the first steps in a consolidated effort to change the Bennett Association. He had created Bennett Enterprises, the name of a new holding company to direct the affairs of all the operating companies. Prior to this, his position as CEO of the association was vaguely defined. Now, the presidents of each of the companies reported directly to him.

This material was prepared by Paul McKinnon, Assistant Professor of Business Administration, and Elizabeth Bartholomew.

EXHIBIT 1
Bennett's Undergoes Surgery, Emerges Healthy

A complete reorganization of the Bennett group of companies has been accomplished during the past two months, which trustees of the family-owned Utah business hope will guarantee its survival into the 21st century and beyond.

The restructuring of the three Bennett operating entities—Bennett Glass and Paint, Bennett Leasing Company, and the Salt Lake franchise for National Car Rental—has been accomplished through formation of a new parent company, Bennett Enterprises, and the hiring of a new chief executive to run it.

That man is Michael Silva, 30, a native of Hawaii and graduate of Brigham Young University, who has been given the mandate and the power as president and chief executive officer to expand Bennett into new businesses and triple current annual revenues of $32 million by the end of the decade.

"The family wants a $100 million conglomerate by 1990," declared Silva, adding that current revenues should be doubled in four years.

The move to bring in Silva marks the first time that operational control of the Bennett companies has been vested in someone not bearing the Bennett name since John F. Bennett rescued the failed Sears and Liddle Glass and Paint Company from bankruptcy at the turn of the century.

"In the last two or three years, we've come to realize there is too much family involvement," said former Utah Senator Wallace F. Bennett, John F. Bennett's eldest son and one of the five current trustees.

Bennett told the *Deseret News* that there are now more than 200 descendants of his father, all of whom benefit financially from the earnings of the three Bennett companies, of which the glass and paint operation goes back to the beginning days.

With the passage of time, ownership has become very spread out, he said, and the majority of the trustees determined it was time to find an outside executive to run things.

Arthur Young & Co. was brought in to make that search for them, but while it was going on the trustees realized that the executive assigned to them, Mike Silva, was the very man they wanted. On October 1 Silva took the helm.

Silva has been given the power both verbally and in his written contract to take any action he deems necessary—including the replacing of top executives—to implement the return of Bennett to profitability and growth in the years ahead.

As might be expected, that investiture of power in an outsider, and a young one at that, has not been met with total enthusiasm by some family members who have spent their entire careers with the company.

That's just a matter of time, though, believes Silva. Profitability and survival are the bottom line in family companies as they are in publicly held businesses, and if Silva can pull off the rescue plan, his last name won't matter much.

There have been rumors in the business community for some time that Bennett has been in trouble. Silva is not unaware of this fact, but while he does not deny that the company has had problems in light of business downturns that have hit the home-building industry, he insists the firm is sound.

In fact, he says, there are tremendous resources available to Bennett that simply haven't been utilized: significant holdings in real estate and securities and "hefty" retained earnings. "At market value, we're looking at in excess of $12 million" in unencumbered assets, said Silva.

The paint and glass business has become extremely competitive, and there are some who say Bennett hasn't kept up. Silva says he thinks the company hasn't really fallen behind but has spread itself into too many areas. He says Bennett Paint and Glass will restructure itself in its marketing position, specializing in a few areas where it can expect to be dominant.

Bennett also undertook a major expansion of its paint and glass facilities at 2100 S. 300 West two years ago—at just about the time the housing industry, along with construction and business in general, began to founder in a sea of tight money, inflation, and high interest rates. But those buildings and equipment are being paid

EXHIBIT 1 *(Concluded)*

off at an accelerated rate, said Silva, and he says the company, with those new facilities and a new glass furnace, will have a state-of-the-art plant.

In the meantime, everyone has the word that Silva wants a very tight, highly productive operation. "And that's for the employees' benefit," he notes.

For his part, Senator Bennett, now 83, says he is "optimistic and relieved" that the company founded by his father is no longer adrift and stagnant but is now moving aggressively toward a new chapter in its long and honorable history.

Bennett is set up as a Massachusetts business trust, the only company in Utah so organized. For tax purposes, it is treated as a corporation, and family members receive income from the trust according to shares they hold that are similar to stock certificates.

The man chosen to protect and expand those holdings, Mike Silva, was born and reared in Honolulu. He came to Utah to attend BYU and completed graduate work there in organizational behavior. He's married and is the father of four children.

Silva developed a management training program at Skaggs Corporation and was later assistant to the chairman of a savings and loan in Honolulu. He returned to Utah and became chief financial officer at Cummins Intermountain. He directed a bank consulting practice at Arthur Young & Co., and it was as a consultant to Bennett from Arthur Young that he came to the attention of the trustees.

By Max B. Knudson, business editor, *Deseret News,* Thursday, December 31, 1981. Reprinted by permission.

THE MEETINGS

Before leaving for Hawaii, Michael held a series of meetings with top managers from the various companies to explain his objectives. Michael made it clear that although some of the companies were in better shape than others, all would be required to improve their performance. Jack Stevens, controller and financial vice president of Bennett Paint and Glass, reported:

> In those first meetings, he gave us a very clear picture of how it was going to be from now on. We were going to emphasize performance and productivity, and we were going to work toward excellence. For the first time in this organization there were going to be consequences for not meeting goals. He said that for him, mediocrity would simply not be tolerated. There were people at that meeting who were not producing, and I'm sure they were uncomfortable. But the message was clear: Here is a guy who is looking for excellence in this company.

THE BUDGET

Michael had also requested the development of a budget for the Bennett companies, which finally gave Jack Stevens the authority to implement the system he had been working on for several years. Jack recounted the difficulty he had in implementing his budget:

> We had to redesign the general ledger system on the computer to fit the new budget. When we did it for the paint company, we designed in a lot of flexibility, which turned out to be a lifesaver, since we were in the middle of that job when Michael came to me and asked me to take on the financial responsibility for all the Bennett companies. I thought about it for a while, and, finally, the whole thing fell into place. We had the whole system working within two months.
>
> It was shortly after that point, which I guess was about five or six months after he began as president, that he told me I could relax. Up until that point, I wasn't sure if I was going to be fired or not. I figured I could find a job elsewhere, but I didn't know how I was doing here until then.

Michael lifted a thick book that contained the budget and performance-to-date information of the Bennett employees:

> I'm something of a fanatic about the budget. This is my primary method of control. It took about three months to prepare it in the first place, and we have already revised it several times. This is Jack's process. He developed it, he got the numbers, and he's done a great job. I like to think of him as a good manager who has been turned free.
>
> This budget is very detailed. It covers not only branches and departments but also individuals. It's very precise. I review it carefully every month, looking at our revenue, gross profit, expenses, but mostly the bottom line. I also look at their current expenses, their monthly expenses, performance versus budget, and current month versus the same month last year. I can see whether any one manager in the company is out of budget at any time, and this year, we are within 5 percent of our year-to-date budget. Everyone knows I expect them to manage by the budget system, and they know how important I think it is.

In conjunction with the budgeting system, Michael centralized common operating functions, such as purchasing. Also, he had combined all financial activities under Jack Stevens, as financial vice president of Bennett Enterprises. Under Michael's plan, executives of each company retained responsibility only for manufacturing and marketing. The results of this restructuring were a significant reduction in staff size and less duplication of effort.

WALLY BENNETT RETIRES

The radical changes in expectations and management (which will be outlined in the next sections) were difficult for everyone but particularly so for Wally Bennett. With a new CEO and new management systems in place, the very nature of the company he had managed seemed to be changing around him. In April 1982, at a meeting of the top management team of Bennett Enterprises, Michael announced that Wally had elected to take early retirement. Jack Stevens related:

> Mike had told me a day before the meeting what was going to happen. When we walked into the meeting, he said he would like to read us a letter. The letter was Wally's early retirement announcement, and it basically said that he had fought the good fight, and that he had managed the company for a lot of years and no longer felt the need to manage.

Mick Boyd, vice president of Bennett's glass division, observed, "Wally was probably the kindest, most decent person I had known, but he was not cut out for the business world." Another associate added, "Wally was a figurehead president, and people felt that."

BENNETT PAINT AND GLASS

Bennett Paint and Glass experienced the greatest repercussions from Michael's plan. When he assumed control, Bennett's retail and manufacturing operations employed nearly 350 people. His goal was to reduce the number to 212 by the end of 1982. Reductions were to come from both line and supervisory personnel and were based solely on individual performance. The process was neither easy nor pleasant; some managers with many years of service did not meet the standards set by Michael.

Commenting on the layoffs at Bennett, as well as those in other parts of the company, Michael admitted:

> This is the ugly part of this whole change effort. But to keep unproductive managers would send the wrong message to everyone else in the company. The old company fostered a system that created these managers and these attitudes. The managers we had couldn't quite do it, couldn't quite pull it together in our new system.
>
> It was a hard thing to do. There were letters to the editors and everything. (See Exhibit 2.) But I'm ruthless with executives. These guys are a commodity.

DeVon Johnson, previously executive vice president, was chosen to succeed Wally as president of Bennett Paint and Glass. He discussed that painful period:

> When we let people go, it was very hard. It was a most unpleasant thing to happen, but it had to be done. We had people who had been with the company for 30–35 years but were not productive at all. I would ask them what they did, or what their job was, and many couldn't provide good answers. This place was sinking out from under us.

DeVon had initiated several changes while he was Wally's executive vice president, and with Michael's support he introduced other plans designed to improve all facets of the paint and glass operations. To increase revenues, DeVon established a new pricing system for

EXHIBIT 2
Criticizes Paint Firm for Laying off Old-Timers

To the editor:

This letter is in response to your article on Bennett reorganization.

I'm glad 83-year-old Wallace Bennett and 30-year-old Mike Silva can now sleep well at night.

I can appreciate all businesses have to be reassessed and changed, but at the expense of some employees who have worked 30–40 years, and are 1–5 years away from retirement? *Ruthless* only describes the method used to terminate dedicated employees. *Selfish* is a more appropriate term for those who succeeded in doing a job that requires no business talent.

When you eliminate 41 percent of the positions, many at the top level, and happily say, "Bennett is now operating in the pink," you need to reevaluate your scruples. If I recall a "60 Minutes" documentary accurately, those employees close to retirement have a legal option to challenge their firing.

It was well known by the employees and the business community that, during his tenure as president, Wallace G. Bennett introduced several new things into the company to help prepare it for the future. This does not demonstrate lack of business skills, but rather business expertise.

It must be wonderful to sleep well, knowing 41 percent of your employees and their families no longer enjoy that luxury.

G. B. Johnson
Logan

Source: *Deseret News.*

paint. The factory began to sell paint to dealers at a 42 percent markup, so that Bennett's profit margin would no longer vary according to dealers' discount policies. Bennett suggested a range of retail prices; however, branch managers retained total discretion over their pricing policies. Bennett also sold the Colorizer System to Color Corporation of America. Not only did this generate more cash, but an arrangement with the purchaser allowed Bennett to continue to receive royalties.

Most of DeVon's actions, however, concerned cost reductions. He decreased the number of sales districts and assigned responsibility for sales to district and branch managers. He also reduced the plant work force substantially. He decreased the maintenance staff from 5 to 1, and reduced the warehouse operators to one shift, eliminating the need for 18 employees. In addition, he sold the store in Las Vegas, leaving the company with 12 branches. All of these moves, plus others, resulted in Bennett Paint and Glass meeting its goal of 212 employees by July 1982.

Product line changes were made to rationalize production and keep expenses within budget. Bennett offered fewer styles of windows to the general public than before and designed a new line to be marketed directly to architects.

DeVon also immediately reduced inventory and receivables by

$500,000 each and set up a plan to reduce inventory by at least that much in the future. As he succinctly explained, "You have to make cuts everywhere if you are going to turn something around."

Unable to find records of a capital budgeting process, DeVon introduced the AFE program—authority for expenditure. Expenditures over a specified amount had to be approved by the division head, the division vice president, and DeVon. Even if approved, an expenditure might be delayed if the budget required it.

DeVon created an evaluation and reward system to reinforce the objectives of reducing and controlling costs. Managers' bonuses depended on net profit, according to the following scale: 25 percent on

EXHIBIT 3

Memorandum

THE BENNETT ENTERPRISES

Date: April 14, 1982

To: Top management and middle management

From: Michael A. Silva

Subject: Personal and company image standards/costs

As you may expect, when new management is given responsibility for a company, changes will take place. The Bennett Association and its subsidiaries are no exception to this expectation. Positive attitudes and increased productivity are among those changes that must take place in order to move the companies into an acceptable financial position. Mediocrity will not be tolerated.

In addition, the image Company personnel project is critical. The management must represent the highest possible image of quality and excellence. Part of this image is one's personal appearance. The clothing and its maintenance are to indicate quality, pride, and excellence.

I know there are substantial costs incurred in projecting such an image. Therefore, you are to be allowed company expense to assist you in meeting and maintaining this image standard.

Top management may expense up to $1,000 of the annual cost of meeting the standard. Middle management may expense up to $500 of their costs.

The Bennett Association and its related companies will become well known for quality and excellence in our marketing areas, and you will have been an important part in building that image.

MAS

MAS/dc

the first $50,000; 15 percent on the second $50,000; and 10 percent on the next $50,000 of net profit.

The company also made a major effort to decertify the three unions. [See Bennett Association (A).] Dave Haran, Bennett's vice president of operations, summarized management's position:

> I'm not antiunion. I just don't feel we need them here. I want a fluid work force. I may wish to bring glass workers over to help with the paint area if need be. I want teamwork.

In addition to improving Bennett's financial situation, DeVon began a series of less tangible, but no less important, changes to enhance the company's image. He carpeted company headquarters, improved the fixtures and environment of the area, and encouraged employees to dress in a more traditional business style. This paralleled similar moves made by Silva for all top managers in Bennett Enterprises. (See Exhibit 3.)

BENNETT LEASING

Bennett Leasing also experienced immediate and dramatic changes. Although John Bennett, the president, agreed with many of the changes, he found implementation difficult, particularly the layoffs of senior, trusted employees. The fundamental changes made in the leasing operations were as follows:

1. Bennett sold the truck-leasing and maintenance operations, which had lost money for many years. Aside from reducing the number of people in the company by half, this one sale generated a cash inflow of $400,000.
2. The sales and managerial staff dropped from 35 to 10. Only three of the original staff remained, one of whom was John Bennett, the only manager Michael retained.
3. A new executive vice president, Leon Nason, came on board in May 1982. Michael and Leon were next-door neighbors, and Michael had been impressed enough by Leon to offer him a position in Bennett Leasing. Leon had previously worked for Beneficial Finance Company and Young Sign Company. Energetic, excitable, and aggressive, he had left Young Sign Company because it was too conservative. He hoped that, under Michael's leadership, he could help Bennett Leasing expand and improve profitability.

Relations between Leon and John Bennett were somewhat strained, however. John's deliberate and contemplative style caused Leon to become impatient and irritated. Leon's bold, aggressive, and sometimes brash style made John uneasy. Although there was no open acrimony between the two, meetings involving them were at times difficult. As John Bennett explained:

> Leon has made some major blunders, and I think he would be the first to tell you that he has. We are trying to tighten up some of our procedures now. Really, I'm the one who knows something about leasing. In this situation, I don't want to be a downer or any inhibiting factor in the changes we are making, but I've decided that I have to know a lot more about what is going on. Leon is very reasonable about telling you what he is doing when you ask him, but he doesn't usually get around to telling you unless you ask.

Leon expressed his view of the situation by saying:

> I run the company. After meeting John Bennett, you know why. I'm the guy who makes things click. John reviews the stuff we do and fiddles around with the inventory. It's frustrating for me from time to time. I'm more impulsive. I'll make a decision and that's it. John will have to think about it. I may be wrong, but I'm not going to fart around with it. If you're right 50 percent of the time, you're OK.

ADMIX AND NATIONAL CAR RENTAL

The sweeping changes set in motion by Michael had little effect on Admix or National Car Rental. Both companies had operated profitably for some time, so he chose to leave them alone. Since neither operation was in Bennett headquarters on 23rd South, these companies seemed less a part of the mainstream of activity than the paint and glass or the leasing companies.

MICHAEL'S REWARD SYSTEM

One of the more innovative of Michael's changes in the Bennett companies was his generous reward system for the top executives. This compensation plan applied to only six people: Michael, DeVon Johnson, John Bennett, Leon Nason, Jack Stevens, and Peter van der Heyde. Michael explained the reasoning behind the unique package:

> My job is very simple. I have to keep six people happy: the senator and these five managers. If you reward your managers, the results to the company are immediate. I want these people to be the best-paid managers at their level in the Salt Lake Valley.

In one of the few memos he issued, Michael laid out the philosophy behind the system and his expectations for it:

To meet the objectives of the trustees, we must develop and maintain one of the most effective executive groups in our respective industries and in our respective markets. As was stated in a previous management meeting, "Bennett Enterprises must develop the reputation for creating the ultimate in working environments; only then will quality executives be pleading to work with us."

In an effort to develop an effective team and subsequently maintain it, I have spent the last three months studying various compensation, benefits, and training systems. From my own training in organizational behavior and from my review of specific organizations, I suggest the following critical, though not original, observations:

A. Money ceases to motivate only when one has "enough." ("Enough" is a very personal objective.)
B. Once "enough" money is achieved, benefits and environment become important.
C. Effectiveness as an executive is a combination of physical, emotional, and mental health in addition to skills.
D. Support of family, particularly spouse, has significant impact on executive performance. With these observations in mind, I suggest the following compensation package to be implemented in gradual steps. The suggested plan certainly does not provide all of the benefits given by large corporations. However, I do feel it is an excellent program for our current corporate status and geography. (See Exhibit 4 for details of the benefits.)

In order to make this program work, two general conditions are required:

A. That the executive group produce outstanding results.
B. That the executive group be kept at a relatively small number of very high producers. We cannot create an executive bureaucracy.

I believe strongly that the organization must care for its executives or the good ones will ultimately go elsewhere. However, I also believe that the organization is under no obligation to maintain an executive who does not meet objectives. In short, "Unto whom much is given much is required."

Michael also noted that these executives were under no formal appraisal program; he preferred a continual evaluation process, which included frequent meetings. He explained, "We won't sit down at the end of the year and review their progress. They know how they're doing. If they aren't performing well, they know they will be asked to leave."

Predictably, bonuses in this executive compensation program would not be granted on a statistical evaluation of yearly performance. Concerned that too much emphasis on short-term performance might detract attention from long-term growth, Michael intended to grant bonuses based on his personal evaluation of executive performance.

EXHIBIT 4
The Executive Compensation Package

A. Salary	To be determined on annual basis.
B. Bonus	To be determined on annual basis.
C. Incentive travel with spouse	To be determined on annual basis.
D. Vacation	One month per year—noncumulative.
E. Sabbatical—educational or cultural	One month every three years.*
F. Medical insurance	Premiums fully paid.
G. Life insurance	To be determined.
H. Automobile	Class A type.
I. Family athletic club membership	Executive choice, with maximum.
J. Family recreation	One week/year at Sweetwater.†
K. Spouse travel	One business trip per year.
L. Business clothing allowance	$1,000 per year.
M. Retirement	45 percent of highest five-year average.
N. Company products	Purchased at established cost.
O. House accounts	No limit, cleared on annual basis.
P. Internal savings accounts	$1,000 deposits/withdrawals. Prime interest.

* The company would fund completely any activity chosen by the manager. This could include travel, educational programs, anything the manager chooses.

† Sweetwater is a resort community in St. George, Utah.

THE "NEW" BENNETT ASSOCIATION

Several key managers and the senator talked about the recent changes and about the future of Bennett Enterprises.

DeVon Johnson

"Many of the changes we made were either underway or under consideration before Mike came. He provided a lot of support, and I know that if Mike had not taken over, I would have left. I couldn't have taken it. I just didn't have time to argue with the board every time I wanted to make a change. Right now, I spend most of my time cleaning up the mistakes that others have made. But as a result of all the changes here at the warehouse, sales and marketing haven't gotten the attention they need.

"We are really looking for people to do more these days, rather than simply worrying over what is in it for them. The slowness of the turnaround here bothers me, but we *are* going to make money. We are going to move, but we are going to move intelligently.

"I don't see Mike that much on a day-to-day basis. I know that I have a budget that I must meet. When I make a large capital expenditure, I have to clear it with him. I have to regulate the salaries of my corporate people with him, but that is about all. I try to keep him informed, and I try not to blindside him with problems.

"Mike has developed a nice incentive system here. I believe that if people are productive, they shouldn't have to worry about finances. You should pay them well enough that they needn't be concerned about money. That is one thing Mike has done with us. We are already getting a better reputation as a place to work, and there are lots of people trying to get in. That's the type of situation you want to have."

Dave Haran

"Some of the cuts we make seem unfair and ruthless in people's eyes. We had to cut expenses. In a recession year, you can only sell so much.

"Other companies called us the "sleeping giant." DeVon woke us up."

Jack Stevens

"I'm pleased with the way things are going. I'm a big believer in following policy in business, and when people around here didn't follow policy, the axe never fell. I have a lot of respect for this new approach and the style of decision making. Decisions get made now much more quickly than before. We may make a few mistakes, but at least something is being done.

"This company now talks a lot about performance and productivity, and I know that if you perform, you will be rewarded well. I'm very pleased with the new compensation package. You know, Michael has some very big plans for the company. We want to be at $100 million by the end of the decade. If we support him well, then I think we can do that, and we will be compensated in accordance with that level of growth.

"Michael has done well in the time he has been here. He lets us know exactly what he expects of us, and we know that those who perform will be rewarded. We have reduced the staff, and we couldn't have done that without him. Wally was emotionally not capable of making the deep cuts that were necessary to save this company."

Leon Nason

"I think that people should be paid on performance and promoted on performance. If you're not performing, you need to step back and see why. My people know my rules: 'Be here, do the job, and do it right.' If they don't, I'll terminate them. If they do their job the way they are supposed to, they will get paid well for it.

"I have two major goals in this job. First, in five years, to make sure that what we did today is profitable. Second, turn this thing around so that it can run by itself, then go somewhere else in the company. I don't plan on being executive vice president of leasing for the rest of my life.

"I want continued profitability. My overall compensation is based on profitability. I'm not satisfied with my salary. I never will be. I couldn't care less what John Bennett makes, or DeVon Johnson. Screw those guys. We compete with each other. As far as I'm concerned, I want to maximize my money—make as much as I can for me.

"It's super working for Mike. First, he doesn't know anything about paint, glass, leasing, car rental, or advertising. But he hires people who do. As long as we are on plan and budget, he leaves us alone. His big term is *strategically professional*. We want to do things better than anyone else and do it professionally no matter what it is. And we will get paid better than anyone else in the industry."

John Bennett

"With the changes, I think we let some people go that we could have kept. There was a certain amount of expertise that we let go when we had this wholesale departure. Mike was worried that we didn't have the right people to turn it around, but we still had people who were effective. Mike formed his opinions about these people rather quickly, based on his own information. You couldn't find anything to criticize them about, but they weren't excellent. We did lose some valuable skills, though, and Leon can't replace those skills yet. He is a strong, colorful, forceful guy who is very different from me. That's fine.

"The worst thing that could happen in an organization would be to have a bunch of clones. He has tried a lot of new things, and he has made some blunders.

"I am a 100 percent admirer of Michael. He has great instincts, and he is a good leader. There are times when I think he's a genius. We don't always agree, but I think he's great. I don't think I have ever seen anyone who seems better prepared for a meeting. When he is asked questions that I know he couldn't have been expecting, he gives unruffled and persuasive answers. In the board meetings, he is always very calm, and I don't think I've ever seen him answer a question that he doesn't handle with total aplomb."

The Senator

"Mike and I really studied the business after he came onboard, and at the expense of sounding like I'm covering up for Wally, we have pretty well decided that the problems Wally encountered were already there when Richard died. We would have had trouble even if there hadn't been a change in management. Richard had already allowed a great deal of weakness to creep in. Wally hadn't been trained to do that type of job, since nobody expected Richard to die. No family member could have done what Mike did. No one could have made the deep cuts that were needed.

"Mike is the key to the transition, and I have complete confidence in his ability. We are a team, he and I. I don't interfere with him at all. He does his job. Ours is a relationship built on complete confidence.

"The biggest challenge for the company is how we are going to manage in the future. We simply have to regain our position in the marketplace. I think that Mike can do that for us."

Michael Silva

"If all these changes turn this company around, it would buy me some credibility, the sense that what I tell them will work. I hope it turns out well.

"The company needs to place a greater emphasis on strategy. Everything we do should be for the future. We should diversify in the future so we don't get caught in a recession like we did this time. We have determined that we *will* buy, and we have determined what we won't buy. What we haven't determined is *what* we will buy. We will probably follow a pattern of constrained diversity, looking for companies that do what we are already doing, or banks, or some computer service business. These are things that we could do right now without bringing on additional management expertise.

"The two biggest constraints we have are our human resources and cash. I won't buy a company unless I already have an outstanding manager to run it. I won't acquire anything that requires any more of my time to run it.

"I don't know, and honestly don't care, how each of the companies operates. Other than my top-management team, I don't know what people in the companies make a year, and I don't care. I probably should, but I don't think that's my job. My job is to keep six people happy. Beyond that, I don't have to do anything."

Blair, Inc.

The information for this case was obtained from Mr. Burton L. Davis, a recent employee of Blair, Inc.

Burton Davis started work last September as a mechanical engineer in the engine and motor division of the Blair Company, a large multiple-industry corporation. The division, with 400 employees, was the principal employer in Midland. Formed four years ago, the division designed and manufactured small gasoline combustion engines used in lawnmowers, motor scooters, snow throwers, portable saws, and power plants. Recently the division has begun to turn out small electric motors. Division sales were currently $6 million.

Davis, seven years out of Purdue, had previously worked as an automotive engineer for two major automobile manufacturers and had excellent references from both. His salary at Blair was $950 per month.

He found that the engineering offices were new, of modern design, and air-conditioned. Supporting personnel in drafting, machine shop, and laboratory were adequate, and excellent physical facilities were available. Fringe benefits were at or above the industry level. For instance, Davis was promised a two-week vacation before completing a full year of service. His moving expenses were paid in full, in addition to $500 for an earlier trip to locate suitable housing. His travel expenses had also been covered when he came to Midland to interview the division chief engineer, Charles Lyons, and the corporate executive personnel director.

Burton Davis was assigned to the design and development department (see Exhibit 1 for partial organization chart). Four of the six other engineers had no work experience with other employers (which was also true of the chief engineer) and had been with the company from 2 to 13 years.

Davis was assigned a numbered space in the main parking lot and was given a decal for his car window. Only the first three rows in this lot were reserved by number. Employment was high at the time, and the only space available was one vacated by a draftsman who had just resigned (see Exhibits 2 and 2A).

Davis soon noticed that more than half of those who parked in the two parking areas adjacent to the engineering offices were people he would not have expected to have more favorable parking locations than the engineers (see locations 6A and 6B, Exhibit 2A). Talking with

EXHIBIT 1

Partial Organization Chart: Engine and Motor Division

Chief Engineer Chas. Lyons (c)
Secretary
Supervisor Test Development G. Tully (c)
Electrical Engineer B. Swensen (c)
Product Stylist J. Schomer (c)
Chief Draftsman J. Barmeier
Supervisor Development Lab D. Graham
Supervisor Engine Shop V. Doran
Supervisor Machine Shop T. Michaels
Model Shop Technicians (4)
Janitor
Technicians (8) Mechanics (9)
Machinists (8)
Machinists (4)
Assistant Electrical Engineers N. Gray (c) P. Braun (c)
Stylists R. Randel (c) B. Roth (c)
Design Engineers B. Kashian (c) A. Jensen (c) H. McNichols (c) B. Davis (c)
Development Engineers M. Mason (c) F. Kelly (c) R. Cooper (c)
Designers M. Wynn (c) J. Stanley
Drafting Supervisor L. Stewart
Supervisor Records S. Bonura
Assistant Chief Draftsman W. Wright
Stenographer
Senior Draftsmen (15) Draftsmen (7)
Records Typist Clerks (3) Engineering Clerk
(c) = College degree

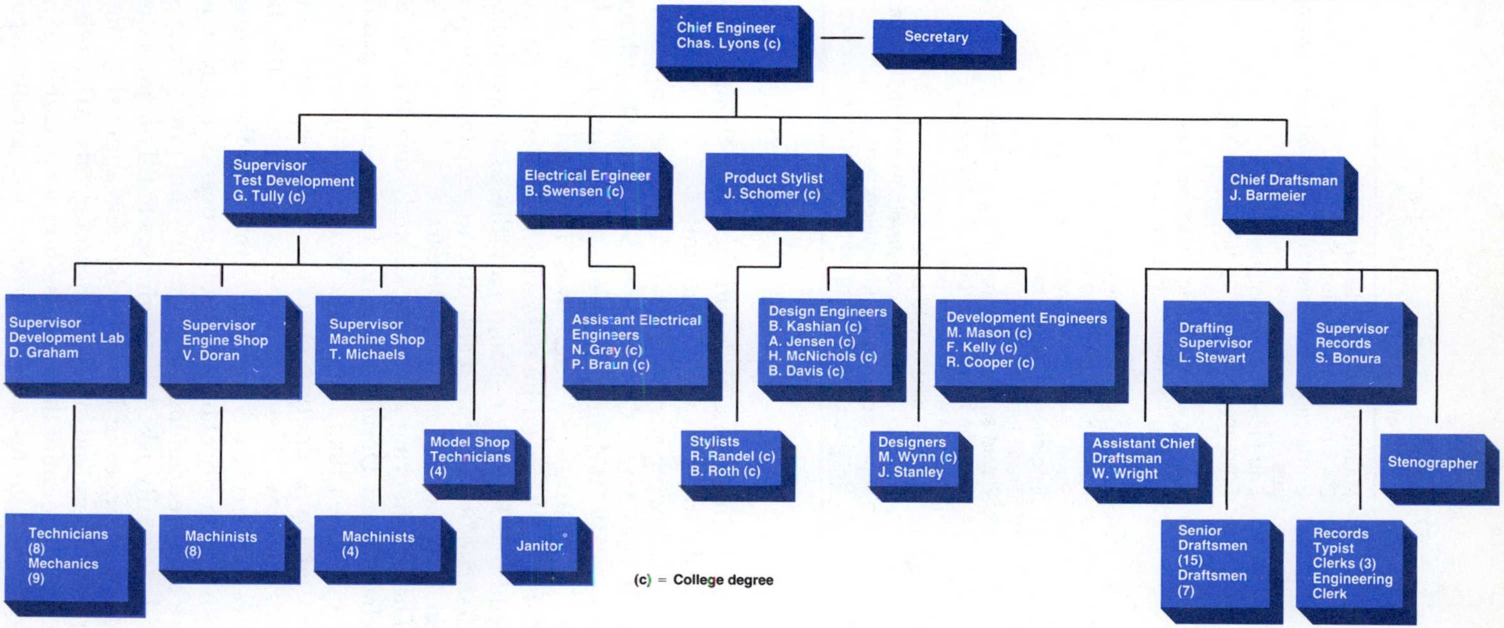

EXHIBIT 2
Index to Plant Layout in Exhibit 2A

1. Main office door—visitors only.
2. Division administration.
3. Entrance—all administrative and engineering employees.
4. Entrance—factory employees.
5. Entrance—engineering labs (not an employee entrance).
6. Parking—engineering personnel, reserved by name.
7. Parking—administrative personnel, reserved by number.
8. Parking—most of the engineers, reserved by number.
9. Parking—most of the draftsmen, reserved by number.
10. Parking—Burton Davis, reserved by number.
11. Engineering gate—open all day.
12. Truck loading dock.
13. Paved empty space (could park 8 cars).
14. Storage area (could park 10 cars).
15. Storage area (could park 5 cars).
16. Storage area (could park 10 cars).
17. Parking—supervisor of development lab, later, also, supervisor of test and development.
18. Parking—engineering station wagon and pickup truck.

his fellow engineers, he found they also thought it strange and had been irritated about it for some time.

The following personnel parked in these areas where space was reserved by name: C. Lyons, B. Swensen, T. Schomer, G. Tully, J. Barmeier, W. Wright, L. Stewart, S. Bonura, T. Michaels, V. Doran, and H. O'Brien. O'Brien was a disabled draftsman who used crutches—all agreed he deserved this location. Most engineers also agreed that Barmeier should park there; although his title was chief draftsman, he functioned almost as an assistant chief engineer and had been with the company for 20 years.

The engineering group felt strongly that Wright, Stewart, Bonura, Michaels, and Doran should not have parking privileges in a more desirable area than their own. Wright, assistant chief draftsman, supervised three drafting checkers and was seen constantly at Barmeier's elbow. The engineers called them "the Bobbsey twins." Stewart supervised some 20 draftsmen. In the engineers' view, his job consisted mainly of handing out timecards and paychecks. Draftsmen were allocated among the engineers and rarely changed assignments. Stewart usually asked the engineers to fill out job-rating sheets for the draftsmen since he had no basis for appraising their performance. Bonura supervised several office clericals. Michaels of the Machine Shop and Doran of the Engine Shop were called supervisors, but the engineering group felt that *foremen* was a more accurate term.

EXHIBIT 2A

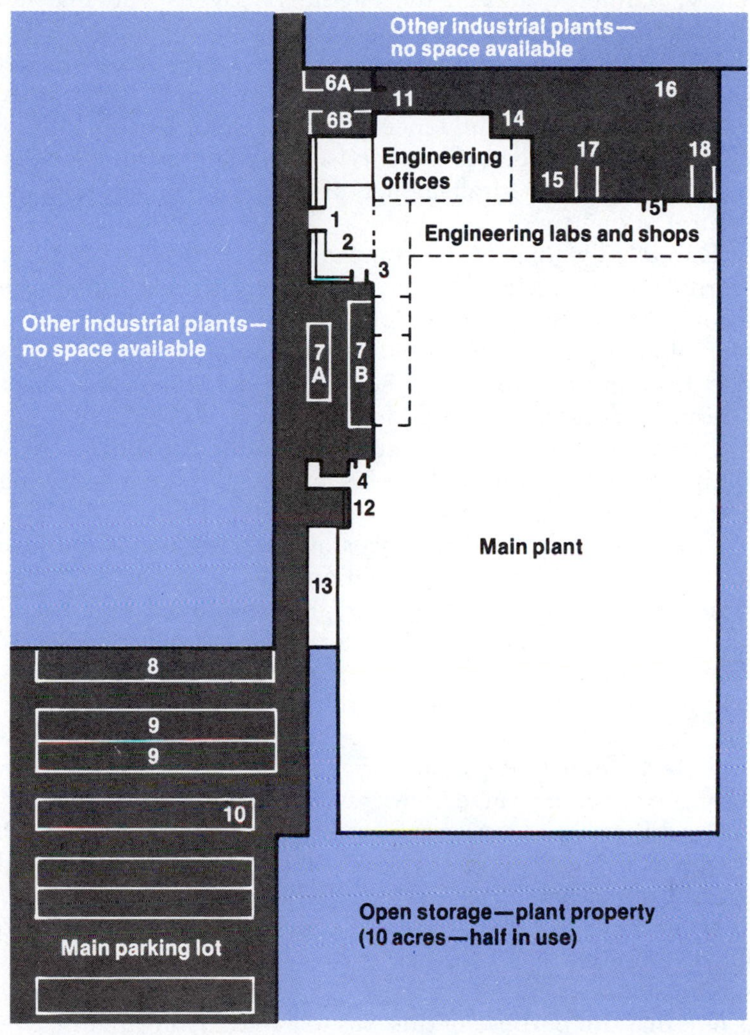

Arnold Jensen (eight years with the company) and Paul Cooper (two years with Blair and two with Ellington Electronics) told Davis they were glad to find someone else concerned about this situation. Other engineers agreed but were reluctant to make an issue of it. One of them told Davis he might be considered a "rabbler-rouser" if he talked too much about it.

From what Davis could determine, everyone had parked in the main lot until a few years back. Then two sections of grass were removed to make the small parking areas (6A and 6B in Exhibit 2A).

Since there wasn't room to include Lyons, Swensen, Schomer, Tully, Barmeier, and all the engineers, Lyons said that rather than draw a line among them he would not have any of the engineers park there. Instead, all "direct" supervisors were given reserved slots, which just filled the space in the new area. Some engineers felt that Barmeier may have influenced this decision. Technically, the engineers were not "direct" supervisors, although they might have as many as 10 people (draftsmen, typists, and so on) working under their control at one time.

Davis knew that every company had irritations with which one learned to live. However, as the weather grew worse, he walked through the unpaved gravel lot (which developed many holes in winter), plodded along the street (there was no sidewalk), and still halfway from the entrance, watched others drive in, park near the engineering offices, and enter before he reached the door.

Other things began to disturb him about his position. He found that Barmeier and Wright, without his approval, changed drawings he had released from engineering.

There were three blank boxes on each engineering drawing. The draftsman would initial the "drawn by" space; the checker, the "checked by"; and the engineer, the "approved by." Lyons usually also initialed the last box, which provided room for two sets of initials. A few months after Davis had started work, Wright started erasing the engineer's initials from the "approved" box, entered his own, and told the engineers to initial after the checker's in the middle box. Jensen and Davis immediately told Wright that he could put his own initials after the checker's since he was supposed to be the checker's supervisor and they were the engineers in charge of the project. Davis told Wright, "If you feel otherwise about it, let's go to Lyons right now." Wright immediately agreed to initial after the checker.

Sometime after this incident, a sign reading "Authorized Personnel Only" appeared on the door to the blueprint records storage room where Bonura and the clerks worked. Barmeier told the engineering group that the purpose of this was to avoid disturbing the overworked print girls and that the sign applied to all draftsmen and engineers. Although the engineers protested, Barmeier refused to change his stand. Lyons came by during the argument and moved the group into the conference room. The engineers explained that they often needed information from a tracing; a quick glance was enough before returning it to the file. Under the new system, they would have to order a print and wait to get the information. Lyons agreed with the engineers. Davis, Jensen, and Cooper were particularly pleased. Jensen said later, "At last *we* won something around here."

It gradually became apparent to Davis that Lyons planned most of the engineering for his engineers. When assigning a new project, he would suggest the handling of it in such detail that all chance of creative or original work was eliminated. He frequently went out in the drafting room and told layout draftsmen how he wanted things done. Sometimes he even failed to bring the responsible engineer in on the discussion.

No engineering meetings were held. The only regular meeting was a "production" meeting for which the division manager and his plant manager came to Lyons' office. Lyons was the only engineer in the meetings, although he often stepped out to get a drawing or to get a question answered from a design or developmental engineer whose project was under discussion at the time. On the rare occasions when an engineer *was* called into the meeting, it was without any advance warning, so that he was frequently unable to furnish the desired information on the spot. Barmeier, Wright, and Bonura sat in on all meetings. Since these were the only regular conferences, discussion inevitably went beyond production problems and dealt with new products and plans as well. The sales manager and the corporate director of engineering attended some of the meetings. To find out what was going on, the engineers relied on the grapevine or were forced to ask Barmeier, Wright, or Bonura. They rarely talked with Lyons except when he was giving them ideas on how he thought they should do their jobs.

Dissatisfaction grew among the engineers, although several still felt there was nothing to be gained by "stirring things up." Davis felt that if Lyons realized the extent of the developing morale problem, he would try to do something about it.

One evening he had an opportunity to talk to Lyons alone. He made it clear that he thought the situation was becoming critical. He told Lyons what he thought were the main points: the generally low status of the engineers and the feeling they had that they were not given enough responsibility. Davis pointed out that the parking situation was one of the main symbols of the engineers' status since it was a visible method of ranking. Lyons seemed uncomfortable throughout the discussion but said that he would think about it. Davis told Lyons that he was speaking only for himself but was sure his feelings were shared by most of the others. On leaving, Davis gave Lyons a reprint of an article on morale and suggested it might be of value.[1]

As months passed, no perceptible changes were made.[2] George Dunlop was hired to supervise the engineers with the title of "chief, design and development" and with the design and development engineers and the designers reporting to him. They had formerly reported

[1] A portion of the article is reproduced in Exhibit 3.

[2] During this period, Burton Davis typed a memo and circulated it informally among individuals in the division (see Exhibit 4).

EXHIBIT 3

Indicator Area	*High Morale Exists When—*	*Low Morale Exists When—*
1. The company	Lines of responsibility and authority are clear; coordination good; line staff teamwork generally productive; organization structure is flexible; managers can get to right official when necessary.	Authority overlaps; organizational structure is too complex; company has too many layers of review; communication breakdowns are frequent; reorganizations don't add up; committees interfere.
2. Company-division practices	Good rapport exists among managers; agreements are honored; men know where they stand and how they are doing; policies are clearly and quickly communicated; reward system is fair and current.	There's too much paperwork; managers have to beat the system; excessive rivalry exists among the departments; deadlines don't mean a thing; it is hard to get needed information; ideas die on vine.
3. Decisions	Decisions are tied in well to policies and plans; managers get chance to participate in decision making; delegation is adequate; bad decisions are withdrawn when necessary; accountability is clear.	Decisions are too slow, poorly timed; subordinate has little chance to participate in the making of decisions; delegation is meager, decisions unduly influenced by tradition; real issues are evaded.
4. Leadership	Staff meetings are well run and produce results; boss keeps subordinates informed of policies and plans affecting them; men know the scope of their responsibilities; boss shows dignity and fairness.	Assignments and orders of boss are unclear; men have to work without knowing policy limitations; boss sets unreasonable deadlines; too many attempts are made at regimentation; standards fall.
5. Group climate	Team takes pride in its performance; men will go to bat for each other; professional aims, standards are high; grievances of a member are heard; overall quality of group output is high grade.	Too many cliques exist; favoritism is shown some; work output is inadequate; one man dominates the group; bickering is common; there are recurrent rule violations; professional standards are low.
6. Job conditions	Managers find sufficient challenge in their jobs; abilities of men are utilized well; employees able to express their views; performance standards are realistic; workers get recognition when deserved.	It's difficult to get a job done; ideas put aside too often, too fast; men have to break rules to get action; boredom and restlessness are prevalent; pay scales lag behind the rates in other firms.
7. Status	Job privileges are modest but good; management is receptive to a man's views; talents are utilized; employees enjoy higher status in community because of their association with the company.	Favored few get recognition; opportunities for development are restricted; criticisms far exceed compliments; men must look out for themselves; firm has too many dead-end jobs.

EXHIBIT 4

Office Memo

ENGINE AND MOTOR ENGINEERING SECTION

To: "Supervisory" personnel

Subject: Fitness Program

Going along with the present Washington administration's emphasis on hiking as a means of improving the fitness of the American people, it is suggested that those Blair employees now parking near the building exchange parking places with the engine and motor section *engineers.* The engineers are in splendid shape from their long hikes and feel that it is only fair to share this conditioning. After a suitable "build-up" period, a rotation system will be worked out to insure the retention of all the fitness benefits.

The Personnel Department

directly to Lyons. (Dunlop parked in the engineering lot; Tully was moved to the rear with Graham, area 17 on Exhibit 2A—actually a more desirable spot, only 10 feet from a door.) Before Dunlop arrived, Lyons held a meeting with all salaried personnel to explain the decision to bring in a man from outside. He said that he thought the position could have been filled from within the company but that Edward King, the corporate director of engineering, thought that a man with considerable experience was needed. Davis considered it interesting that Lyons was only 34.

Dunlop was 48 years old and had worked as an executive engineer for National Motors, for Burling Aircraft, and for Duval Manufacturing. Lyons mentioned that people might wonder why a man with his background would come here. He explained that Dunlop liked small towns and enjoyed this type of work and that money was not that important to him. Davis commented later to Jensen that "executive engineer" at National Motors meant a big job and that Dunlop must have had a real setback somewhere along the way. The engineers considered it significant that Dunlop was placed in charge of seven engineers with the draftsmen and technicians still reporting to others. Moreover, Barmeier was still next to Lyons with no intermediary. They also noted that Dunlop had not been given the title of assistant chief engineer.

Several engineers with long experience with the firm believed they should have been candidates for the job. Other engineers thought Dunlop might become a useful go-between for them. They saw that Barmeier took care of *his* people and Tully took care of *his*. Perhaps the engineers now had someone to put in a few good words for them. Dunlop seemed, at first, to be a much better administrator than Lyons. At least, the engineers felt he "talked a good game." They began to tell him about things they felt needed improvement or correction. But after two months it became apparent that Dunlop had not recommended any changes to Lyons. It appeared to Davis and others that he was loathe to tell Lyons anything that might be disturbing. The engineers felt that he was "running scared."

Davis suggested to Jensen and Cooper that talking to Dunlop was not unlike a session with a psychiatrist. You talked about your problems and felt better even though nothing really changed. Whenever anyone returned from a talk with Dunlop, a colleague would ask, "Did you have a nice couch session?"

As the small group talked about their problems, the situation became almost unbearable to Davis. There was considerable talk of other jobs, and occasionally one of the men would have an interview with another firm. Finally, Davis, Jensen, and Cooper decided to approach Lyons in a group. They had decided that they would all leave anyway unless changes were made. This "group action" was distasteful to them, but they felt that it was the only way to get Lyons to realize he had a real problem to face. There seemed to be little to lose.

Following are some of the comments made by the engineers and Lyons as they talked in the chief engineer's office one evening after work:

Engineer: We feel a little silly talking about this, but since it does bother us and affects our morale, we feel you should know.

Engineer: The parking position ranks everyone, whether or not you believe it does.

Lyons: Where you park doesn't have anything to do with the way I rank you.

Engineer: We feel that as highly paid college graduates who actually do the creative work we should rank above "assistant chief draftsmen" and "foremen."

Engineer: Specifically, we feel that we should rank ahead of Wright, Stewart, Bonura, Doran, and Michaels.

Lyons: Do you feel you are better than those people?

Engineer: In terms of working for this company, yes. We would certainly be harder to replace. In any case, ranking is inevitable; we would like to think that you agree with us on where we rank.

Lyons: You know that you make much more money than those people, don't you?

Engineer: Yes, which is another reason for keeping the other symbols of rank in the same order.

Engineer: Salary is not a problem. We do not feel overpaid or underpaid in our present jobs.

Engineer: Whether or not *you* feel this is a problem, the fact that *we* feel it is a problem *makes* it a problem, by definition.
Engineer: The fact that parking ranks us in status actually affects our job efficiency as it relates to others. We have more trouble "getting things done" if we don't have the status to back it up.
Engineer: Saying that status symbols are unimportant doesn't make them go away. We live with status symbols all the time; unless they are distorted from the way most people expect to see them, they go unnoticed. Only when the symbol system gets out of line does it become a problem. This means that to have a smoothly functioning organization, an administrator has to consider status symbols and make every attempt to allocate them as his subordinates expect him to.
Engineer: Doran and Michaels are foremen, no matter what fancy names they are called. Stewart is the drafting supervisor and should rank under us, but Barmeier and Wright are doing engineer work. If you want to rank them above us that is your decision, but their titles should be changed. A chief draftsman and his assistant should never rank above any engineer. The situation is similar to the army, where a master sergeant may have many years of experience and be valuable, but he does not outrank the greenest second lieutenant.
Engineer: We note that you have the closest space to the door in the lots near engineering, and the division manager has the space closest to the door in the administration lot. Isn't it logical that the number two ranking people have the next spaces, and so on down the line? That's the way almost everyone looks at it.
Engineer: We don't care *where* we actually park. The question is *who* parks where. If everyone had the same long walk, there would be no problem.
Engineer: Locating our parking spaces more conveniently without changing the relative status of the spaces will be no solution at all.
Lyons: But where can I find more parking space?
Engineer: We think there are a number of areas that could be used, but some effort would be required. There is unused space in front of the plant (13 in Exhibit 2A), or space could be made available by moving some of the stored materials from the area east of engineering (14, 15, and 16 in Exhibit 2A). Even if you can't find space for improved parking for everyone, engineers should park in that lot. Not necessarily the three of us, but *engineers*.
Engineer: The fact that you don't or can't trust us with more responsibility affects our morale and job interest also.
Lyons: But I do give as much responsibility as possible.
Engineer: But you act as if you don't really trust us.
Lyons: It's not that I don't trust you; it's just that I want to see the job done right.

As the talk ended, Lyons appeared to be disturbed and concerned. He said that he would think about what had been said and would see if there was anything that he could do.

Nevertheless, the three engineers were sure that Lyons had not really understood them. In spite of their emphasis on "not where, but *who*," they sensed that the chief engineer believed that all they wanted was better, closer parking places. They felt he didn't understand their desire for more responsibility either; he seemed to think they had all the responsibility they had a right to expect. They agreed that his comment on "doing the job right" demonstrated how little effect they had had.

They predicted that any solution Lyons might devise would be unsatisfactory. They wondered if they should take any other steps or just wait and hope that Lyons had more understanding than they suspected. They realized that if the solution was unsatisfactory it was the end of the road. They could hardly start the process all over again.

Bob Knowlton

Bob Knowlton was sitting alone in the conference room of the laboratory. The rest of the group had gone. One of the secretaries had stopped and talked for awhile about her husband's coming induction into the army and had finally left. Bob, alone in the laboratory, slid a little further down in his chair, looking with satisfaction at the results of the first test run of the new photon unit.

He liked to stay after the others had gone. His appointment as project head was still new enough to give him a deep sense of pleasure. His eyes were on the graphs before him, but in his mind he could hear Dr. Jerrold, the project head, saying again, "There's one thing about this place that you can bank on. The sky is the limit for a man who can produce!" Knowlton felt again the tingle of happiness and embarrassment. Well, dammit, he said to himself, he had produced. He wasn't kidding anybody. He had come to the Simmons Laboratories two years ago. During a routine testing of some rejected Clanson components, he had stumbled on the idea of the photon correlator, and the rest just happened. Jerrold had been enthusiastic: A separate project had been set up for further research and development of the device, and he had gotten the job of running it. The whole sequence of events still seemed a little miraculous to Knowlton.

He shrugged out of the reverie and bent determinedly over the sheets when he heard someone come into the room behind him. He

This case was prepared by Professor Alex Bavelas for courses in management of research and development conducted at the School of Industrial Management, Massachusetts Institute of Technology, Cambridge, and is used with his permission.

looked up expectantly; Jerrold often stayed late himself and now and then dropped in for a chat. This always made the day's end especially pleasant for Bob. It wasn't Jerrold. The man who had come in was a stranger. He was tall, thin, and rather dark. He wore steel-rimmed glasses and had a very wide leather belt with a large brass buckle. Lucy remarked later that it was the kind of belt the Pilgrims must have worn.

The stranger smiled and introduced himself. "I'm Simon Fester. Are you Bob Knowlton?" Bob said yes, and they shook hands. "Doctor Jerrold said I might find you in. We were talking about your work, and I'm very much interested in what you are doing." Bob waved to a chair.

Fester didn't seem to belong in any of the standard categories of visitors: customer, visiting fireman, stockholder. Bob pointed to the sheets on the table. "There are the preliminary results of a test we're running. We've got a new gadget by the tail, and we're trying to understand it. It's not finished, but I can show you the section that we're testing."

He stood up, but Fester was deep in the graphs. After a moment, he looked up with an odd grin. "These look like plots of a Jennings surface. I've been playing around with some autocorrelation functions of surfaces—you know that stuff." Bob, who had no idea what he was referring to, grinned back and nodded, and immediately felt uncomfortable. "Let me show you the monster," he said, and led the way to the workroom.

After Fester left, Knowlton slowly put the graphs away, feeling vaguely annoyed. Then, as if he had made a decision, he quickly locked up and took the long way out so that he would pass Jerrold's office. But the office was locked. Knowlton wondered whether Jerrold and Fester had left together.

The next morning, Knowlton dropped into Jerrold's office, mentioned that he had talked with Fester, and asked who he was.

"Sit down for a minute," Jerrold said. "I want to talk to you about him. What do you think of him?" Knowlton replied truthfully that he thought Fester was very bright and probably very competent. Jerrold looked pleased.

"We're taking him on," he said. "He's had a very good background in a number of laboratories, and he seems to have ideas about the problems we're tackling here." Knowlton nodded in agreement, instantly wishing that Fester would not be placed with him.

"I don't know yet where he will finally land," Jerrold continued, "but he seems interested in what you are doing. I thought he might spend a little time with you by way of getting started." Knowlton nodded thoughtfully. "If his interest in your work continues, you can add him to your group."

"Well, he seemed to have some good ideas even without knowing exactly what we are doing." Knowlton answered. "I hope he stays; we'd be glad to have him."

Knowlton walked back to the lab with mixed feelings. He told himself that Fester would be good for the group. He was no dunce; he'd produce. Knowlton thought again of Jerrold's promise when he had promoted him—"the man who produces gets ahead in this outfit." The words seemed to carry the overtones of a threat now.

That day Fester didn't appear until midafternoon. He explained that he had had a long lunch with Jerrold, discussing his place in the lab. "Yes," said Knowlton, "I talked with Jerry this morning about it, and we both thought you might work with us for awhile."

Fester smiled in the same knowing way that he had smiled when he mentioned the Jennings surfaces. "I'd like to," he said.

Knowlton introduced Fester to the other members of the lab. Fester and Link, the mathematician of the group, hit it off well together and spent the rest of the afternoon discussing a method of analysis of patterns that Link had been worrying over the last month.

It was 6:30 when Knowlton finally left the lab that night. He had waited almost eagerly for the end of the day to come—when they would all be gone and he could sit in the quiet rooms, relax, and think it over. "Think what over?" he asked himself. He didn't know. Shortly after 5 P.M. they had all gone except Fester, and what followed was almost a duel. Knowlton was annoyed that he was being cheated out of his quiet period, and finally, resentfully determined that Fester should leave first.

Fester was sitting at the conference table reading, and Knowlton was sitting at his desk in the little glass-enclosed cubby that he used during the day when he needed to be undisturbed. Fester had gotten last year's progress reports out and was studying them carefully. The time dragged. Knowlton doodled on a pad, the tension growing inside him. What the hell did Fester think he was going to find in the reports?

Knowlton finally gave up, and they left the lab together. Fester took several of the reports with him to study in the evening. Knowlton asked him if he thought the reports gave a clear picture of the lab's activities.

"They're excellent," Fester answered with obvious sincerity. "They're not only good reports; what they report is damn good, too!" Knowlton was surprised at the relief he felt and grew almost jovial as he said good-night.

Driving home, Knowlton felt more optimistic about Fester's presence in the lab. He had never fully understood the analysis that Link was attempting. If there was anything wrong with Link's approach, Fester would probably spot it. "And if I'm any judge," he murmured, "he won't be especially diplomatic about it."

He described Fester to his wife, who was amused by the broad leather belt and brass buckle.

"It's the kind of belt that Pilgrims must have worn," she laughed. "I'm not worried about how he holds his pants up," he laughed with her. "I'm afraid that he's the kind that just has to make like a genius twice each day. And that can be pretty rough on the group."

Knowlton had been asleep for several hours when he was jerked awake by the telephone. He realized it had rung several times. He swung off the bed muttering about damn fools and telephones. It was Fester. Without any excuses, apparently oblivious of the time, he plunged into an excited recital of how Link's patterning problem could be solved.

Knowlton covered the mouthpiece to answer his wife's stage-whispered "Who is it?" "It's the genius," replied Knowlton.

Fester, completely ignoring the fact that it was 2:00 in the morning, proceeded in a very excited way to start in the middle of an explanation of a completely new approach to certain of the photon lab problems that he had stumbled on while analyzing past experiments. Knowlton managed to put some enthusiasm in his own voice and stood there, half-dazed and very uncomfortable, listening to Fester talk endlessly about what he had discovered. It was probably not only a new approach, but also an analysis that showed the inherent weakness of the previous experiment and how experimentation along that line would certainly have been inconclusive. The following day Knowlton spent the entire morning with Fester and Link, the mathematician, the customary morning meeting of Bob's group having been called off so that Fester's work of the previous night could be gone over intensively. Fester was very anxious that this be done, and Knowlton was not too unhappy to call the meeting off for reasons of his own.

For the next several days Fester sat in the back office that had been turned over to him and did nothing but read the progress reports of the work that had been done in the last six months. Knowlton caught himself feeling apprehensive about the reaction that Fester might have to some of his work. He was a little surprised at his own feelings. He had always been proud—although he had put on a convincingly modest face—of the way in which new ground in the study of photon measuring devices had been broken in his group. Now he wasn't sure, and it seemed to him that Fester might easily show that the line of research they had been following was unsound or even unimaginative.

The next morning (as was the custom) the members of the lab, including the girls, sat around a conference table. Bob always prided himself on the fact that the work of the lab was guided and evaluated by the group as a whole, and he was fond of repeating that it was not a waste of time to include secretaries in such meetings. Often, what started out as a boring recital of fundamental assumptions to a naive listener, uncovered new ways of regarding these assumptions that would not have occurred to the researcher who had long ago accepted them as a necessary basis for his work.

These group meetings also served Bob in another sense. He admitted to himself that he would have felt far less secure if he had had to direct the work out of his own mind, so to speak. With the group meeting as the principle of leadership, it was always possible to justify the exploration of blind alleys because of the general educative effect on the team. Fester was there; Lucy and Martha were there; Link was sitting next to Fester, their conversation concerning Link's mathematical study apparently continuing from yesterday. The other members, Bob Davenport, George Thurlow, and Arthur Oliver, were waiting quietly.

Knowlton, for reasons that he didn't quite understand, proposed for discussion this morning a problem that all of them had spent a great deal of time on previously with the conclusion that a solution was impossible, that there was no feasible way of treating it in an experimental fashion. When Knowlton proposed the problem, Davenport remarked that there was hardly any use of going over it again, that he was satisfied that there was no way of approaching the problem with the equipment and the physical capacities of the lab.

This statement had the effect of a shot of adrenalin on Fester. He said he would like to know what the problem was in detail and, walking to the blackboard, began setting down the "factors" as various members of the group began discussing the problem and simultaneously listing the reasons why it had been abandoned.

Very early in the description of the problem it was evident that Fester was going to disagree about the impossibility of attacking it. The group realized this, and finally the descriptive materials and their recounting of the reasoning that had led to its abandonment dwindled away. Fester began his statement, which, as it proceeded, might well have been prepared the previous night although Knowlton knew this was impossible. He couldn't help being impressed with the organized and logical way that Fester was presenting ideas that must have occurred to him only a few minutes before.

Fester had some things to say, however, which left Knowlton with a mixture of annoyance, irritation, and, at the same time, a rather smug feeling of superiority over Fester in at least one area. Fester was of the opinion that the way that the problem had been analyzed was really typical of group thinking, and with an air of sophistication which made it difficult for a listener to dissent, he proceeded to comment on the American emphasis on team ideas, satirically describing the ways in which they led to a "high level of mediocrity."

During this time Knowlton observed that Link stared studiously at the floor, and he was very conscious of George Thurlow's and Bob

Davenport's glances toward him at several points of Fester's little speech. Inwardly, Knowlton couldn't help feeling that this was one point at least in which Fester was off on the wrong foot. The whole lab, following Jerry's lead, talked—if not practiced—the theory of small research teams as the basic organization for effective research. Fester insisted that the problem could be approached and that he would like to study it for awhile himself.

Knowlton ended the morning session by remarking that the meetings would continue and that the very fact that a supposedly insoluble experimental problem was now going to get another chance was another indication of the value of such meetings. Fester immediately remarked that he was not at all averse to meetings for the purpose of informing the group of the progress of its members—that the point he wanted to make was that creative advances were seldom accomplished in such meetings, that they were made by the individual "living with" the problem closely and continuously, a sort of personal relationship to it.

Knowlton went on to say to Fester that he was very glad that Fester had raised these points and that he was sure the group would profit by reexamining the basis on which they had been operating. Knowlton agreed that individual effort was probably the basis for making the major advances but that he considered the group meetings useful primarily because of the effect they had on keeping the group together and on helping the weaker members of the group keep up with the ones who were able to advance more easily and quickly in the analysis of problems.

It was clear as days went by and meetings continued that Fester came to enjoy them because of the pattern which the meetings assumed. It became typical for Fester to hold forth, and it was unquestionably clear that he was more brilliant, better prepared on the various subjects which were germane to the problem being studied, and that he was more capable of going ahead than anyone there. Knowlton grew increasingly disturbed as he realized that his leadership of the group had been, in fact, taken over.

Whenever the subject of Fester was mentioned in occasional meetings with Dr. Jerrold, Knowlton would comment only on the ability and obvious capacity for work that Fester had. Somehow he never felt that he could mention his own discomforts, not only because they revealed a weakness on his own part, but also because it was quite clear that Jerrold himself was considerably impressed with Fester's work and with the contacts he had with him outside the photon laboratory.

Knowlton now began to feel that perhaps the intellectual advantages that Fester had brought to the group did not quite compensate for what he felt were evidences of a breakdown in the cooperative spirit he had seen in the group before Fester's coming. More and more of the morning meetings were skipped. Fester's opinion concerning the abilities of others of the group, with the exception of Link, was obviously low. At times during morning meetings or in smaller discussions he had been on the point of rudeness, refusing to pursue an argument when he claimed it was based on the other person's ignorance of the facts involved. His impatience of others led him to also make similar remarks to Dr. Jerrold. Knowlton inferred this from a conversation with Jerrold in which Jerrold asked whether Davenport and Oliver were going to be continued on; and his failure to mention Link, the mathematician, led Knowlton to feel that this was the result of private conversations between Fester and Jerrold.

It was not difficult for Knowlton to make a quite convincing case on whether the brilliance of Fester was sufficient recompense for the beginning of this breaking up of the group. He took the opportunity to speak privately with Davenport and with Oliver, and it was quite clear that both of them were uncomfortable because of Fester. Knowlton didn't press the discussion beyond the point of hearing them in one way or another say that they did feel awkward and that it was sometimes difficult for them to understand the arguments he advanced, but often embarrassing to ask him to fill in the background on which his arguments were based. Knowlton did not interview Link in this manner.

About six months after Fester's coming into the photon lab, a meeting was scheduled in which the sponsors of the research were coming in to get some idea of the work and its progress. It was customary at these meetings for project heads to present the research being conducted in their groups. The members of each group were invited to other meetings, which were held later in the day and open to all, but the special meetings were usually made up only of project heads, the head of the laboratory, and the sponsors.

As the time for the special meeting approached, it seemed to Knowlton that he must avoid the presentation at all cost. His reasons for this were that he could not trust himself to present the ideas and work that Fester had advanced, because of his apprehension as to whether he could present them in sufficient detail and answer such questions about them as might be asked. On the other hand, he did not feel he could ignore these newer lines of work and present only the material that he had done or that had been started before Fester's arrival. He felt also that it would not be beyond Fester at all, in his blunt and undiplomatic way—if he were present at the meeting, that is—to make comments on his [Knowlton's] presentation and reveal Knowlton's inadequacy. It also seemed quite clear that it would not be easy to keep Fester from attending the meeting, even though he was not on the administrative level of those invited.

Knowlton found an opportunity to speak to Jerrold and raised the question. He remarked to Jerrold that, with the meetings coming up and with the interest in the work and with the contributions that Fester had been making, he would probably like to come to these meetings, but there was a question of the feelings of the others in the group if Fester alone were invited. Jerrold passed this over very lightly by saying that he didn't think the group would fail to understand Fester's rather different position and that he thought that Fester by all means should be invited. Knowlton immediately said he had thought so, too; that Fester should present the work because much of it was work he had done; and, as Knowlton put it, that this would be a nice way to recognize Fester's contributions and to reward him, as he was eager to be recognized as a productive member of the lab. Jerrold agreed, and so the matter was decided.

Fester's presentation was very successful and in some ways dominated the meeting. He attracted the interest and attention of many of those who had come, and a long discussion followed his presentation. Later in the evening—with the entire laboratory staff present—in the cocktail period before the dinner, a little circle of people formed about Fester. One of them was Jerrold himself, and a lively discussion took place concerning the application of Fester's theory. All of this disturbed Knowlton, and his reaction and behavior were characteristic. He joined the circle, praised Fester to Jerrold and to others, and remarked on the brilliance of the work.

Knowlton, without consulting anyone, began at this time to take some interest in the possibility of a job elsewhere. After a few weeks he found that a new laboratory of considerable size was being organized in a nearby city, and that the kind of training he had would enable him to get a project-head job equivalent to the one he had at the lab with slightly more money.

He immediately accepted it and notified Jerrold by a letter, which he mailed on a Friday night to Jerrold's home. The letter was quite brief, and Jerrold was stunned. The letter merely said that he had found a better position; that there were personal reasons why he didn't want to appear at the lab any more; that he would be glad to come back at a later time from where he would be, some 40 miles away, to assist if there was any mixup at all in the past work; that he felt sure that Fester could, however, supply any leadership that was required for the group; and that his decision to leave so suddenly was based on some personal problems—he hinted at problems of health in his family, his mother and father. All of this was fictitious, of course. Jerrold took it at face value but still felt that this was very strange behavior and quite unaccountable, for he had always felt his relationship with Knowlton had been warm and that Knowlton was satisfied and, as a matter of fact, quite happy and productive.

Jerrold was considerably disturbed, because he had already decided to place Fester in charge of another project that was going to be set up very soon. He had been wondering how to explain this to Knowlton, in view of the obvious help Knowlton was getting from Fester and the high regard in which he held him. Jerrold had, as a matter of fact, considered the possibility that Knowlton could add to his staff another person with the kind of background and training that had been unique in Fester and had proved so valuable.

Jerrold did not make any attempt to meet Knowlton. In a way, he felt aggrieved about the whole thing. Fester, too, was suprised at the suddenness of Knowlton's departure and when Jerrold, in talking to him, asked him whether he had reasons to prefer to stay with the photon group instead of the project for the Air Force which was being organized, he chose the Air Force project and went on to that job the following week. The photon lab was hard hit. The leadership of the lab was given to Link with the understanding that this would be temporary until someone could come in to take over.

Boyd's Catering

Kirsten stopped cleaning the bakery case and looked to make sure that Emily wasn't watching her.

"Did you hear that Tracy quit yesterday?" she asked.

"Yeah, I couldn't believe it. Everyone thought she would be manager this summer. Tracy has worked here almost three years longer than any of us. She'll be a senior this year, so this will be her last summer working here. It was really a shock to her when Mrs. Boyd put Emily in charge."

"She always seemed to enjoy work until Emily came."

"Didn't we all?" I asked.

We both glanced at Emily. She was sitting up front, flipping through a magazine. Margot, Kirsten, and I were all getting ready to close the store. Closing was the worst part of the day, especially now that we had Emily as manager. She had never picked up a broom or washed a dish since she began working in May. I looked at my watch for what must have been the 100th time. Only 10 minutes left. I decided not to sweep the bakery. Emily probably wouldn't check. As I put the broom away, I realized that two months ago I never would have considered leaving without everything looking perfect for the next day.

While driving home, I tried to figure out why I hated work so much now. I had worked at Boyd's Catering for two years. Mrs. Boyd always had about five high school and college girls working over the summer. She was very selective about hiring people. She looked for those who would present a good image for the store. We were always very conscientious and took pride in the store and our work.

Mrs. Boyd and her partner, Mrs. Thompson, had opened Boyd's Catering four years ago. Mrs. Thompson had moved to Canada shortly after the opening and only visited a few times a year. The shop specialized in gourmet salads, sandwiches, and desserts. About 75 percent of the store's revenue came from catering. The rest was sales in the store. Business had been growing steadily and the shop had recently been reviewed by the *New York Times*. Everyone connected with Boyd's took pride in the high quality of its products and service. Mrs. Boyd managed the store full time during the winter. She was mainly responsible for the store's success. She had established a name for herself by catering out of her home for eight years. She now did little of the store's cooking, working instead as a general overseer. We all respected Mrs. Boyd's knowledge of food and ability to deal with even the most trying customers in a pleasant way. She was interested in every aspect of the business, including the help. She knew where each of us went to school and our special interests. Her concern for us was genuine, and we became equally interested in seeing her succeed in the catering business.

I considered myself lucky to have such a good job. There was always a lot of work to do, but most of the time no one complained. We all liked each other, and being busy helped the time go by quickly.

The problems began when Mrs. Boyd showed up one morning with her daughter Emily, who was home for the summer. Most of us had met Emily before. She was going to be a senior at Smith College and majored in archeology. Emily usually spent her vacations on archeology field trips. Mrs. Boyd loved to talk about Emily and always kept us up on where she was traveling and what she was studying. Emily had visited the store when she was home for breaks. Mrs. Boyd spent about an hour showing Emily how to work the cash register, close the store, and where everything was. She introduced Emily to the kitchen staff and everyone who worked on the floor. Mrs. Boyd informed us that Emily was going to be in charge. She told Emily to ask Tracy or me what to do if she had any questions. Emily was very pleasant and seemed enthused about the job. Mrs. Boyd then rushed off for an appointment.

We were all stunned. Emily went downstairs to look for something.

Margot, Kirsten, and I all looked at Tracy; we had been sure she would be made manager. Tracy looked as shocked as the rest of us.

"Well," she finally said, "we had better get back to those sandwiches, 'cause the lunch crowd will be here soon."

About 10 minutes later, Emily returned with a dusty old stool. She cleaned it up and sat down. Tracy and I looked at each other; no one ever sat down when they were working on the floor. There was always too much work to do: stock the bakery, make sandwiches, or put together special orders. How dare she sit down while we were working?

Emily tried to make conversation, but she only made things worse.

"I'm starving, what would you recommend for lunch?" Emily asked pleasantly. She was looking at Kirsten. Kirsten told Emily what her favorites were. Emily then went around the store and put together a lunch for herself. She sat down again and began to eat. Again we were shocked, but said nothing. No one ever ate in front of customers. We all took our lunches downstairs.

Emily tried again to make conversation. But we all began talking to each other in a conversation that excluded her. Why did she think she deserved so many special privileges? Did she expect us to be her friends when she wouldn't help with the work?

That evening Emily didn't help us close at all. She spent half an hour at the store next door talking with a friend of hers. She came back five minutes before we closed and asked if we were done. Tracy told her that the cases needed to be covered and the garbage taken out. Tracy thought Emily would volunteer to do it.

"Great," said Emily, "you should be out right on time." She then went downstairs to get her purse and punch out. No one could believe that she hadn't helped at all.

Things went downhill in the weeks to come. Emily did help wait on customers some, but we resented her more every day. She came to work wearing whatever she wanted instead of the white shirts the rest of us had to wear. Emily sat around most of the time and ate whenever she wanted. Mrs. Boyd only stopped in a few times a week, and she seemed to enjoy having some time off. This created more work for us and killed morale.

Once when Mrs. Boyd came in, Emily was next door visiting with her friend. Mrs. Boyd was mad at her but thought this was an isolated incident. No one wanted to be the one to tell her that it happened all the time.

To make things worse, there was a rumor that Emily was getting paid eight or nine dollars an hour. The rest of us made about half that and worked twice as hard. Gradually we began to slack off. We started to try to aggravate Emily. We moved slowly and stopped wearing the white shirts. There was no point to working hard, because no one seemed to notice when something was done especially well or not at all. We sat down all the time and began to eat whatever we wanted. We were allowed a half hour for lunch. Since lunch is the busiest time of the day, we had always just taken 10 or 15 minutes to sit downstairs. Now we took exactly half an hour. No one respected Emily at all because she knew so little about the store and had just gotten the job because of her mother. When she asked us to do things, we always took our time. The jobs we used to do without being told, we now had to be nagged to do. The store was not kept as clean as usual. There had been some mix-ups with special orders being sent off incomplete or with the wrong people. Worst of all, none of us cared. The days seemed to drag by. A number of customers had complained, but I doubt these complaints were making their way to Mrs. Boyd.

After about a month, friction began to build up between Tracy and Emily. We all did whatever Tracy asked and went to her when we had a question. Emily really resented this. When Tracy asked one of us to do something, Emily would give her a different job to do. Emily often went out of her way to be very polite when asking us to do things. Did she really think that a few *pleases* and *thank-yous* would make us move any faster? Why should we work when she wouldn't?

Yesterday, Tracy finally quit. She told Mrs. Boyd that she had been offered a job that paid more. Mrs. Boyd was very sorry to see Tracy leave. She had always been hard working and good natured. Mrs. Boyd seemed to have no idea of the problems in the store.

Margot, Kirsten, and I have all talked about quitting, especially now that Tracy is gone. But it's the middle of July, and we would have a hard time getting other jobs. At the same time, I don't know if I can take another month of this. No one is willing to confront Emily because she can tell her mother whatever she pleases about us. And, I have to admit, we have been slacking off. I would hate to lose Mrs. Boyd's respect. Mrs. Boyd only comes in once or twice a week and is always in a hurry. I would like to tell her about the problems we are having, but I don't know how she would react to criticism of her daughter. Maybe I should start to look for another job.

▶ The Brady Training Program

INTRODUCTION

"Well, I'm very happy you've accepted, Bill," said Dick Hubbard. "You are the type of person we believe will succeed here. You scored very well on the computer-aptitude test and seem to be very personable. Our next training class starts a week from Monday. I trust you can relocate by then; I've bumped another candidate in order to accept you."

Dick Hubbard shook hands with his new employee and directed him toward Brady Company's nursing office. Accepting the training position with the Information Systems Department was a big change for Bill Flynn, and he hoped he could meet the challenge. Flynn's only prior experience had been in computer sales. Because of this, Bill lacked technical expertise and felt as though he were flying by the seat of his pants. However, he seriously wanted to succeed in the computer field, so he decided to leave his sales position after only one year. Although he considered the technical aspects of computers to be quite uninteresting and difficult to learn, Bill was determined that they were a hurdle he would overcome. Flynn turned down two sales positions for the opportunity to gain some hands-on programming analysis, and hardware experience. His goal was to build a solid technical foundation from which to launch his career by investing at least two years on the technical side of the computer field.

INITIAL ORIENTATION

Things seemed to be happening very quickly. While speaking with the company nurse, Bill learned he could rent a room from her until he was able to find an apartment. In a matter of three hours he had changed jobs and arranged to relocate. He drove home that day somewhat pleased with himself while wondering what the near future held in store.

The first day on the job soon arrived. The new training group consisted of 11 people, 3 women and 8 men. Most of the members agreed that it would be a tough year, but well worth it by year's end. Each trainee had received a letter stating that they were to receive a salary

This case was prepared by William Duckett under the supervision of Professor Allan R. Cohen for classroom discussion.

of $11,000 for the first year. After 12 months and completion of all the required courses, the trainee was to receive a promotion and raise to $17,000 per year. Bill's letter named February 14, 1980, as the promotion date.

The orientation was administered by Al Gavin. He was one of three bosses the trainees were to report to and be reviewed by. Al was in charge of computer room operations, where the trainees were to work. The other two bosses were Dick Hubbard, the program coordinator, and Mark Toner, the department manager.

Al explained that the trainees would work eight-hour days and be rotated among the three shifts, spending approximately four months on each shift. The majority of the trainees were quite surprised, for until then, they had not heard any mention of night shift work. Al stated:

> Each trainee must complete all four training courses offered by the department. Each course will last for three months and be taught by department personnel. Two-and-a-half hour classes will be held Monday through Friday. Trainees are not to help one another. We are looking for people who can solve problems on their own. Besides, you are competing for the same positions; helping others could hurt your chances. All assistance is to be asked of the course instructor. All course assignments are to be handed in on time. A late or poorly completed assignment could mean termination. Each trainee will be reviewed after every project and judged eligible or ineligible to continue.

There were many surprised faces among the group. The trainees had not been aware of the competition for department positions. They were still not sure of the degree of competition when they left the orientation.

After the orientation the trainees seemed somewhat wary of one another, and for the most part they kept to themselves. All were attending the first course and engaged in very little discussion about the material. While working in computer operations, they constantly competed with one another. (See Exhibit 1 for an article on how one company increased productivity of software designers doing similar work.)

THE FIRST MONTH

Bill was able to make two friends that first month. The first was Harry Andrews, a family man with three young children. Harry was 30 years old and one of four former schoolteachers in the midst of a career change. Bill and Harry shared a similar sense of humor and enjoyed one another's company. It always broke the tension.

The second friend was Bob Hackey. Bob was a member of the last

EXHIBIT 1

Faced with Changing Work Force, TRW Pushes to Raise White-Collar Productivity

Redondo Beach, Calif.—When Dennis E. Hacker moved out of the crowded computer room where he and other TRW Inc. software designers hammered out computer code, two things happened. He felt isolated, and his productivity soared.

TRW put Mr. Hacker and 34 of his colleagues into private, windowless offices wired with state-of-the-art computer equipment: terminals that talk to the company computer network, electronic mail, teleconferencing facilities, and sophisticated programs that help write programs. The company expected the programmers to become more productive, but it didn't anticipate an increase of as much as 39 percent in the experiment's first year. "The results were so good we were reluctant to believe them," says Robert Williams, vice president of systems information and software development.

Particularly surprising were the reasons the programmers gave for their increased output. Predictably, they loved their electronic gadgets, but simple changes such as quiet, privacy, and comfortable chairs also helped a lot.

Mr. Hacker says he missed the friendly chaos of the bullpen during his first few days in solitary. "I didn't feel like part of the team anymore," he recalls. But he soon came to like his new surroundings. "I'd close the door and grind away at my work, and the next thing I knew I was getting hungry. I realized it was 6 P.M. and I'd worked right through the day."

The lesson for productivity, says Mr. Williams: "Don't overlook the simple things."

Changing Work Force

It is a lesson many U.S. companies could use as changes in the work force make old ideas about productivity less relevant. Generally, efforts to increase productivity have centered on blue-collar workers. They made up 31 percent of the country's total nonfarm work force in 1981, but by the year 2000 they'll be only 23 percent, says D. Quinn Mills, a labor expert at Harvard Business School.

At TRW, the change in the nature of the work force is outpacing the national rate. The company's products, ranging from car parts to satellite systems, increasingly require fewer manual workers and more white-collar or "knowledge" workers. While 40 percent of TRW's workers are now involved in manufacturing, that number will fall to 5 percent by the year 2000, says Henry P. Conn, TRW's former vice president for productivity and a consultant for the company.

In the past three years, TRW has moved to the forefront in white-collar productivity innovation, says Steve Leth, a specialist at the American Productivity Center in Houston.

The company decided to make productivity a priority because it knew it would be facing an upheaval in the nature of its work force. Ruben F. Mettler, TRW's chairman and chief executive officer, began the productivity effort in 1980. Despite a healthy increase each year in profits, he was also worried that TRW's decentralized, entrepreneurial management style meant some divisions were hoarding innovations and becoming complacent because of their good profit margins.

Improving white-collar productivity depends less on structural changes such as improving the efficiency of machines or layout, Mr. Conn says, than on analyzing how people use their time.

"There are high-priority activities and low-priority, time-wasting ones," says Mr. Conn, who works for a productivity concern in Atlanta owned by former

football star Fran Tarkenton. "You have to find activities where value is added, then eliminate everything else, either by automation or delegation."

For software writers, TRW wanted to eliminate time spent tracking down people on the telephone, filing, attending meetings, or staring out windows so as much time as possible could go to actually writing the lines of code that guide missiles or track satellites.

TRW decided to focus on code writers out of necessity. The company produces about 10 million lines of software code a year, making it the nation's second largest producer after International Business Machines Corp. "We wanted to participate in the growing market for software, but there is a shortage of qualified people to hire, so you have to get more than those you have," says Mr. Conn.

Results of the software pilot project are easily measurable by the number of lines of bug-free computer code produced. Other white-collar productivity projects—such as those involving company lawyers or managers—can't be measured as easily.

To find out how to raise productivity, TRW went to the producers. "Nobody knows what it takes to generate programs better than programmers," says Mr. Conn.

Out of the consultation came an office design that Mr. Hacker says he found "claustrophobic" at first but later learned to love: the beige, soundproof, windowless space designed with Spartan efficiency—a chair built to fit the human body, a white board, a bookshelf, a work table, and a computer terminal. Instead of working on code in their three-person or four-person offices and then running to the bullpen to feed a batch of work into the system, programmers stay in their offices, writing and testing work as they produce it.

To eliminate time-consuming filing and telephone calls, files are stored and messages are exchanged by computer. Again, the programmer doesn't have to move from his chair.

Matching Skill Levels

Before the productivity effort began in 1981, the software division posted productivity increases of 40 percent a decade—"not shabby," says Mr. Conn. Now, with the success of the pilot project, TRW expects 400 percent to 500 percent productivity growth in the next 10 years.

To achieve that, TRW is installing setups similar to Space Park's new facilities in Washington, D.C., Alabama, and Los Angeles, at an estimated cost of about $10,000 per programmer.

But psychologists warn about the long-term effects of such changes in the quality of people's work lives. Optimistic projections such as TRW's can be dashed in the long term if care isn't taken to measure human factors as well as product output, says Alexandra Saba, a Los Angeles industrial psychologist. Miss Saba worked on a study of similar workplace changes for Verbatim Corp., a supplier of magnetic storage media. She says the study found that depriving workers of face-to-face contact could be damaging.

"If you stick people into little cubicles they start suffering psychological effects and physiological effects of worker alienation," she says. "In the long term, productivity can actually go down."

Mr. Hacker says that isn't his experience. He had to leave the experimental offices when a code-writing project he was working on ended. Back in the old offices, surrounded by the press of humanity, he says he felt "an immediate decrease" in his productivity. He says he has learned to prefer a conference call on a computer screen to a casual chat in the corridor.

By Geraldine Brooks. Reprinted by permission of *The Wall Street Journal*,

training class and had just been promoted. He was 25, which was only two years older than Bill. Bill and Bob were very interested in sports and planned to go skiing together.

Bill was really struggling to complete the last assignment for the first course. It seemed to be about three weeks' worth of work but had to be completed in 10 days. Harry noticed the problem Bill was having and offered to help. They secretly met outside of work at Bill's new apartment. Harry's assistance got Bill on the right track, and he was able to complete the project on time. He vowed to help Harry in any way he could. The day after the assignment was due, there were two less members in the training class. Barbara Green, who always looked as though she were in a cold sweat from the daily pressure of the training program, had decided to quit. Another member, Glenn Reed, had submitted his assignment a day late. The following day he was asked to leave class by Mark Toner and was terminated from the training program.

A STUDY GROUP FORMS

Upon finding out about Glenn, Harry and Bill decided to meet at Bill's apartment on a biweekly basis to discuss problems and share ideas and discoveries. The very next week, Bob stopped over to see Bill while he and Harry were working on an assignment. They decided to break for a beer, and work crept into the conversation. Bob offered the following:

> You two had better stick together, but be very careful, don't let anyone know that you help each other. Share your ideas, but do separate work. The course instructors will look for too many similarities among trainee's projects. You can't trust any of these people. They want to see how much you can take. There are nine left in your class, and only three or four positions for you to fill. You are all very well qualified for the open positions. Each of you was selected from over 120 applicants. But being qualified is not enough. They will be very tough on you and apply extreme pressure to expose any possible weakness. They don't want to keep all of you, just the toughest three or four. Management maintains an extremely competitive environment among the department's systems analysts. They feel it improves quantity and quality of output. The competition can get very tiresome and rough, so they want to identify the tougher competitors as soon as possible.
>
> Yours is only the third training group. We are an experiment to see if they can produce almost perfectly homogeneous systems people who are superior to those they are able to hire from outside. It may cost their staff members valuable time, but they make it up by having trainees operate their computer on all shifts at a very low rate of pay. That's another reason for having a few extra trainees around.

Former trainees can be your worst enemies. They feel part of a select group that has made it through the program. The more that enter their ranks, the smaller a fish each one becomes. They will keep an eye on you and report any flaws that they think they notice. I don't mean to sound like such a malcontent. Fact is, I've located a very good position, and I plan to leave. My new employer was very excited to hire someone who had completed the Brady training program. The program has an extremely good reputation and deservedly so. Nowhere else can you learn so much, so fast. Many area businesses have heard of Brady's well-developed systems department. The computer vendor uses Brady as a model site. Some of the companies have even hired people that have either quit or washed out of the training program. They have had extremely good luck with them and find that they have had to spend very little time and expense on further training. These companies jump at the opportunity to hire someone who has completed the Brady training program. You'll see, soon you will be receiving daily calls from area placement firms.

THE STUDY GROUP EXPANDS

During the second course, Bill held a party for all the trainees at his apartment. He invited his two roommates and many of their friends. Bill was afraid that a party consisting of the training group alone might not be much fun. Cathy Moore, one of the two remaining women trainees, struck up a friendship with Bill's roommate, Rick, and they began to spend quite a lot of time with one another. As a result, Bill and Harry were having trouble concealing their meetings. Since Cathy was one of the sharpest trainees and she and Bill also were becoming quite good friends, Bill thought she should be part of the help sessions. Harry agreed, and they made the offer to Cathy, who was happy to join.

As the second course was drawing to a close, the pressure was mounting. Bill, Harry, and Cathy were all struggling. They were saddled with another large project to be completed in a very short amount of time.

Bill was working the third shift and arrived four hours early to spend some time on his project. His arrival surprised two of the other trainees; Chris Peck and Harold Breen were in the process of printing multiple computer files. Bill noticed that they were nervous and trying to hide something, so he checked the printouts. They were listings of the current project assignment as completed by several members of the previous class. Chris and Harold were upset and pleaded with Bill not to report them. Bill assured them that he had no intention of reporting anyone. He told them: "Listen, you guys, I'm relieved to find that I'm not the only one who is struggling here. We're all in trouble but refuse to admit it to one another. I don't have to tell you what a great help these printouts can be. Could you give me a copy of each of them?"

Chris and Harold got the copies for Bill. The next day he presented them to the study group, explaining that he could not divulge his source until the end of the training program. The members decided to split the completed projects among themselves and to study them for useful ideas, style, and problem-solving methods. They met two days later to share their discoveries. The three had found many good ideas along with quite a few poor ones. They were surprised to find that some of the former trainees who were very condescending to them were not as sharp as they were led to believe. Each member agreed to use the ideas only as reference, to keep the information in the strictest of confidence, and to complete their own individual work. They had learned more in those two days than in the previous three weeks.

The study group members submitted their projects on time but felt as though they were just keeping their heads above water. Two more people were let go the day after the project was due, but all the study group members had survived. Cathy was now the only woman remaining.

AN OPPORTUNITY

During the seventh month of the program, Bill and Harry were in their second month on the third shift. They would work from midnight to 8:00 A.M. and then have to attend a two-and-a-half-hour class during the day. They had three morning classes and two afternoon classes per week. Each trainee worked every other weekend. Almost all the trainees were present in the computer room every weekend, working on completing their project assignments.

On one particular third shift, about 3 A.M., Bill was delivering some computer printouts when he noticed that Mark Toner's office door was left ajar. The only people in the building were another trainee and a night watchman occasionally passing through. On impulse, Bill let himself into the office and closed the door. Mark's desk was not locked, and Bill decided to have a look through it. Quickly, he found the training program files. He couldn't believe the risk he was taking, but rationalized that not knowing what his reviewers thought of him could be a larger risk. He nervously opened the files. There was a long review form for each trainee, and Bill read all of them. Each form had four duplications of the same review criteria. As trainees progressed through the program, the form would follow them. They were judged on their ability to grasp and apply concepts, quality of work, attitude, compatibility, promptness, appearance, and competitive ranking among the other trainees. While reviewing an individual's performance, an instructor could read what the previous instructor had written about the trainee. Bill noticed that many of the first reviewer's comments had been duplicated by the second reviewer.

Bill's review was much better than he had anticipated. It did mention some doubt about his willingness to become part of the departmental organization. He wondered why this supposed weakness had not been pointed out to him. He felt uneasy and vulnerable.

The next day Bill told Harry and Cathy about his discovery. They couldn't believe he had done it. When asked why, Bill had trouble explaining; he had never done anything such as that before. Bill also told them about Victor Lawton's review. Victor was very well liked by all three of the study group members. He'd been married just over a year, and his wife was about to have their first child. It was written on Victor's review that he was a candidate for firing, so they decided to ask him to join them. Victor gladly accepted. The study group now consisted of four of the seven remaining trainees.

BUILDING GOODWILL

Bill had joined the company softball team, of which Al Gavin was the manager. They got to know one another outside of work and became fairly good friends. Bill really liked Al. He decided to build a better rapport with the other two bosses, although he was not very fond of either of them.

Mark Toner was an avid outdoorsman and had many fishing pictures on his office walls. Bill was originally from Vermont and still owned a cabin up in the mountains. He loved to fish and considered himself as somewhat of an expert. He slowly broke into conversations with Mark about fishing. Soon they were trading stories, and Bill showed Mark some pictures of one of his very successful fishing trips to the cabin. They made tentative plans for a trip to Bill's cabin for the following year. However, Bill had no intention of ever fishing with Mark.

Dick Hubbard's position called for occasional trips to Brady Company's Latin American operations. He was attempting to learn Spanish. Bill had spent a year in Colombia, South America, while in college. He spoke fluent Spanish and decided to use it to his advantage. He often conversed with Dick and acted more than happy to help Dick with the language. Dick was very interested in Bill's experiences in Colombia and, again, Bill acted more than happy to discuss them.

Some of the trainees expressed their displeasure with Bill's constant contact with the three bosses, but Bill only cared about the opinions of the study group members. He asked them what they thought. None of them seemed to mind; and Harry said, "Each one of us must do whatever we think it takes to complete the program." Bill gave them the following explanation:

> I have mixed emotions about my actions. At times I feel pretty underhanded, but I know the actions are justified. My back is against the wall; I can't afford not to complete this training program. I just quit my last job after only one year. I don't want to appear as though I can't stick with anything. Besides, I'm really interested and want to learn as much as I possibly can. By Brady's standards, I may be cheating a little bit, but I'm learning while I do it. I fully intend to finish in spite of these people. If anyone is going to win this game, I'm going to make sure it's me!

MAKING IT

The group agreed that each individual was playing a game of self-preservation. They felt that their chances of survival were greatly increased by the help they gave one another.

The final project for the third course was an extremely large assignment to be completed in 10 days. Everyone was working at a nerve-wracking pace. By now Bill was feeling more comfortable with his ability to complete the projects on time. He submitted the project a day early. Victor was the only one to be late handing in the project, because he had been very sick with the flu and had fallen behind. He submitted his project two days after it was due. The next day's class was interrupted by the department secretary, who notified Victor Lawton and Harold Breen that Mark Toner wanted to speak with them during the next break. They did not return after the break, and the instructor announced that they had been let go.

The remaining five employees were all of similar caliber. They wondered if more firing would take place and, if so, who would be next. No one dared to ask management. They knew that they were marketable by this point, but all were determined to prove they could finish the training program.

On February 14, 1980, shortly after the fourth and final course ended, five of the original trainees were still present. They were Bill, Harry, Cathy, Chris Peck, and Mike Sears. What seemed to be a very long year for Bill had ended in success. He had attained the tools he had set out to acquire.

After one week, the trainees began to wonder when they were going to receive their promotion and salary increase. Bill asked Mark Toner about the reviews. Mark replied, "Don't worry; we'll get to them, and they'll be retroactive."

WHAT NEXT?

Bill had been interviewing for about a month. He had made some very interesting contacts but had held off until the program was over. After hearing Mark's comment, he decided to pursue them more seriously. He had only taken two days of vacation time in the last year. He asked his bosses if he could take a week of vacation time he had saved. "I've pushed myself very hard all year and could use a rest before digging into a new assignment," he explained. He spent the entire week interviewing in Boston. Two positions were particularly interesting, and he met with each prospective employer twice. They expressed considerable interest in him and had much to offer. Both firms were large computer manufacturers, with a position open in their in-house systems departments. They both offered more than ample facilities and made Bill feel as though they really wanted him to be a part of their teams. Bill liked the idea of working for a computer manufacturer. He felt that almost all aspects of the industry would be available to him in one location. If he got his foot in the door and worked very hard, he should be able to select from many possible career paths.

Upon his return, Bill was notified that his review would take place on Thursday of the following week. By then, he had received written offers of employment from both of the companies that he was interested in. The salaries were higher than he expected to receive from Brady. That day Bill had lunch with all three bosses. As they finished their meal, Dick Hubbard said, "We're very impressed with your performance in the training program. By the manner in which you have progressed and improved throughout the year, we know that you can handle this business. We want you to be a part of our team. Welcome to the department!"

Bill turned to Dick and told him of the offers he had received and how interested he was. Dick exclaimed, "We'll better those offers; stay with us! How much are they for?" Bill gave them the figures, and they immediately made a counteroffer. To that, Bill replied, "I would like to go home and give it some serious thought. I'll let you know tomorrow."

▶ The Brewster-Seaview Landscaping Co.

NOTE: *DO NOT READ* this case until directed to do so by your instructor. It has been set up as a Prediction Case so that you can test your analysis by answering questions before reading the entire case.

PART I

During the summer of my freshman year in college, I worked for a small private landscaping company planting shrubs, seeding new lawns, cutting grass, and tending flower gardens. The company was located in my home town of Seaview, New Jersey, which is a rural community on the coast about 80 miles from Philadelphia. The company was owned and run by Joe Brewster, a 45-year-old man who had lived in Seaview all his life. He had started the company some years ago and not only handled the paperwork (payroll, bills, estimates, and so on) but also worked along with the crew six days a week.

The crew consisted of five guys ranging in age from 17 to 20 years. We all lived in towns around Seaview and had gone to the regional high school, which was physically located in Seaview. Only two of us were attending college, but all had been hired personally by Joe following a short, informal interview. I can't be completely certain about the others, but I think all of us and several others sought the job because we needed work, enjoyed the outdoors, and had heard that Joe paid well and was an OK guy to work for. Working hours were from 8 A.M. to 4:30 P.M. with an hour off for lunch, Monday through Saturday. Once in awhile we'd work overtime to help out some customer who had an urgent need. Each worker began at the same wage, with the understanding that hard workers would be rehired the next summer at a higher wage. Several of the crew I was part of had been rehired under this policy.

Most of the customers we serviced lived in Seaview, knew Joe personally, and seemed to respect him.

Joe owned one truck, which he used to transport all of us and necessary supplies and equipment from job to job. Each morning he would read off a list of houses that had to be completed that day. He would then leave it up to us to decide among ourselves who would do what task while at a particular house. We also were the ones who determined by our work pace how long we would spend at each house.

In doing the work itself, we were able to use our own ideas and methods. If we did a good job, Joe would always compliment us. If we lacked the necessary know-how or did a poor job, Joe was right there willing to help us.

At each house, Joe worked along with us doing basically the same work we did. He dressed the same as we did and was always very open and friendly toward us. He seldom "showed his authority," and he treated us as equals. Although our workday was scheduled to begin at 8, Joe never became upset nor penalized us if we were 10 or 15 minutes late. Our lunch hour was usually an hour long starting anytime between 11:30 and 12:30 depending on what time we, the crew, felt like eating. Each member brought his own lunch to work and any time during the day could take time off to go to the truck for a snack.

The crew itself became very well acquainted, and we were always free to talk and joke with each other at any time and did so. We enjoyed each other's company, although we did not socialize after hours.

We also became very friendly with the customers. They were always eager to talk to us as we worked, and Joe never objected. All in all, the job had a very relaxed, easygoing atmosphere. I, for one, felt little pressure to hurry and, like the others, respected and liked Joe very much.

Prediction Question

What will be the productivity in terms of quantity and quality of the work crew? Why?

PART II

The attitude we had toward the job was very high. We sometimes talked among ourselves about how we felt a sense of responsibility toward the job. While we talked and joked a lot while working, little horseplay occurred; and the talking and joking did not interfere with the work. We were always working steadily and efficiently, seeking to keep ahead of schedule. The days seemed to go fairly quickly, and a lot seemed to get done. I know Joe said that our output was 15 percent above that which other landscaping companies experienced with summer crews.

We also took a lot of pride in our work. Feeling responsible for the job we did, we were constantly checking and rechecking every job to be sure it was perfect. We were always willing to work overtime for Joe when he needed us to do so.

Discussion Question

What elements in the situation contributed to these positive results? Can you think of things that, if present, might have led to very different results? Explain how.

PART III

I returned the following summer to work for Joe because of the strong satisfaction I had with the job the summer before. So did the others. However, we were in for a surprise. Many things had changed. Joe had increased the number of workers to 10, bought another truck, and hired two young college graduates from Philadelphia as crew supervisors. His plan was to concentrate on the paperwork and on lining up new customers, leaving the direct guidance of the two work crews to the new supervisors.

Joe had hired the two supervisors during the early spring after interviewing a number of applicants. Both were young (23 and 24), from the city, and had degrees in agricultural management from Penn State, but had not known each other previously.

We "oldtimers" were assigned to one crew and five new workers were hired for the other crew. These new workers had little experience in landscaping. Except for the working hours, which were the same as during the previous summer, the two supervisors were told that they could run their crew in any manner they wished as long as they kept to the schedule prepared by Joe.

No one on the crew had known the supervisors before. Joe had found them through ads in the paper. The supervisors didn't dress quite as informally as Joe did, perhaps because they didn't do as much actual physical work, but they did dress casually in dungarees and shirts, the same as the crew. Though we called the supervisors by their first names, they did some nitpicky things. For example, Joe never cared who drove the truck or who did what job; sometimes a crew member would drive and Joe would talk with the rest of us. But the supervisors always drove the truck and decided when we would eat. Nor did the supervisors help us unload the tools as Joe had done. They stood around and watched us.

Both supervisors refused to tolerate tardiness in the morning and immediately set up a scheduled lunch hour, which would remain the same throughout the summer. We were no longer allowed to go to the truck for a snack during the day and were constantly being watched over by our supervisor. The supervisors assigned us to specific tasks to be done at each job and told us how "they" wanted them to be completed. They also told us how much time we were to spend doing each job. They refused to let us talk to each other or to the customers (except about business), saying that it "only wasted time and interfered with our work." It was a more structured, more formal atmosphere than the summer before.

Prediction Questions

1. What kind of issues or problems are likely to develop during the second summer? Why?
2. How will productivity compare with that of the previous summer in terms of quantity and quality? Why?
3. What would have been your advice to the two supervisors about how they could best approach their new role?

PART IV

I was disappointed at the new setup and a little bit surprised that Joe hadn't hired one of the more experienced members of the old crew as supervisor. But I figured it was necessary because of the increased volume of business, so I tried to make the best of it. However, very soon my attitude and that of the rest of the old crew fell significantly. We began to hate the new supervisors and soon developed a great disinterest in the work itself. While I'm a person who usually is very conscientious and responsible, I have to admit that before long I along with the others began to put little care or concern into my work. The supervisors soon found it very difficult to get anyone to work overtime.

The new employees didn't react as strongly as we did, but I could tell that they weren't working with much enthusiasm, either.

I thought about talking to the supervisors, but didn't because I'd only worked there the one year and figured that it was not my place to. The others were older than I and had worked there longer, so I figured that they should, but no one did. Instead, we talked among ourselves and individually griped to Joe.

Joe didn't seem to know how to deal with our complaints. He passed them off by saying "Oh . . . I'll talk to the supervisors and straighten it out with them." But nothing changed, and in fact they seemed to clamp down more and push even harder. This only made us madder. Our work rate continued to fall.

Incidentally, throughout this period we had little social interaction with the supervisors, but I noticed that they became more and more friendly with each other.

Meanwhile, the new crew's difficulties increased. Being new and inexperienced, they couldn't do the work as easily as we could. Also the supervisors didn't, or couldn't, give them any adequate training. Their productivity went lower and lower. The supervisors were very upset and yelled at them, pushing them to get out their quota. We felt sorry for them and tried to help them; but we concentrated on reluctantly meeting our own quota.

I don't think Joe realized that the supervisors were not teaching the new crewmen. He was very busy and not around much, and I think he assumed that they were training the new men. I think he began to put pressure on the supervisors as the work rate fell, because things continued to get worse. We couldn't talk to customers, which surprised them. We couldn't even accept drinks. Production lagged greatly as compared to the previous summer, and the two supervisors struggled to meet the schedule and deal with customer complaints about quality. By July 15th, the overall productivity of the company was 5 percent below "normal" and way below the previous summer.

As Joe became aware of this huge decrease in production, he became very concerned and wondered what to do about it.

Discussion Questions

1. What caused the poor production condition during the second summer?
2. How might this situation have been avoided from the beginning?
3. What should Joe do now?
4. Do you think the supervisors could have effectively adopted Joe's style of leadership? What kind of problems might they have had if they did? How should they have conducted themselves?

▸ The Captain's Table

NOTE: *DO NOT READ* this case until directed to do so by your instructor. It has been set up as a Prediction Case so that you can test your analysis by answering questions before reading the entire case.

PART I

The Captain's Table is located on a well-traveled highway near two small cities in the eastern part of the country. Employing a total of about 40 people as waitresses, cooks, kitchen help, bartenders, and hostesses, the Captain's Table caters to executives entertaining customers and "dress-up dining" by residents of the area. It also has rooms available for wedding parties and other social functions. Overall, it is considered to be one of the best restaurants in the area.

The owner of the Captain's Table, Mr. Rogers, had bought the restaurant in 1945 and, working closely with his manager, Bill Hayes, changed what was once a rather ordinary restaurant into a well-known and highly profitable enterprise. Over the years, the business relationship between Mr. Rogers and his manager had developed into a social relationship. Both men belonged to the same yacht club, where they frequently entertained one another for dinner, as well as to the same church. On the job Bill was given absolute authority to make decisions in Mr. Rogers' name.

Working closely with the manager was the head chef, Henry Plante, who often attended the informal meetings between Bill and Mr. Rogers where problems concerning the restaurant were discussed. With Mr. Rogers' approval, Bill and Henry had a business policy of allowing their employees the most freedom possible in the belief that this would produce a high degree of satisfaction and conscientiousness on the part of employees. As one of the waitresses exclaimed, "Working here is really a joy; everyone knows one another and gets along well."

In the kitchen, Henry exerted just enough authority to maintain discipline but allowed the frequent blow-offs that come from the long hours and hot working conditions. His only real rule was to "treat the customer to the meal you would like to eat." His success was demonstrated by the many compliments he received from the customers. His standard reply to such compliments was to thank the customer but explain that it was due to the contribution of his employees.

On several occasions when a well-known customer complimented him, Henry relayed the compliment to the rest of the kitchen help. This was well received and gave them great pride in their work. Said one employee about Henry, "I've worked in restaurants all my life, but here it's more than a job." It was the belief of many of the customers that it was Henry who made the restaurant a success.

In the dining room and lounge, Bill also allowed his employees considerable freedom and encouraged them to make immediate decisions on their own without prior consultations. Said Bill, "My people are good, intelligent people, and I have complete faith in them." Under this policy, the dining room personnel were allowed to fraternize with the kitchen help during the slow hours and even allowed to order drinks from the bar without fear of reprimand. When the monthly bar costs were tabulated, Bill never questioned any of the employees' signed slips. He had said many times that as long as they did a good job, he didn't care how much they drank. High morale and customer satisfaction attested to the job they did, and Bill saw no reason to change it. Interaction was high among all employees, and nearly everyone was on a first-name basis. Picnics and social events were arranged whenever possible to promote what was considered to be "one big, happy family."

On several occasions when the work was slow and the day tedious, the kitchen help would play a game called "Air Raid." This would always produce lots of banter and joking as the help would bang on pots and pans and hide under the preparation table, in anticipation of flying meatballs and other food left over from the day. It was not unusual to see Henry as bombardier leading the battle, and it usually ended by sending the waitresses to the bar with an order for beers for the "survivors." On Henry's day off, the dishwashers would help the cooks prepare the meals, and someone else was designated as "honorary bombardier" during the "Air Raid" game.

A few months ago Bill retired and left the restaurant to live in Florida. Before he left, Mr. Rogers ordered the restaurant closed for a day and gave a party for him with only employees and personal friends invited. Contributions of over $1,000 from the employees and a gold watch from Mr. Rogers with the inscription "To Bill, in appreciation for the many years of loyal service, 1945–1973" were given to him.

Discussion Questions

1. What kind of person should Mr. Rogers look for as a replacement for Bill? What criteria should he use in selecting a replacement? Why?
2. If you were Mr, Rogers, what are some of the questions you would ask applicants interviewing for the manager's job to help you judge their suitability?
3. What information would you be sure to give qualified applicants about the restaurant so that they too could make a judgment about whether they would fit in? Why?

PART II

Faced with the problem of replacing Bill, Mr. Rogers hired Robert Nielson. Nielson was a former maitre d' with extensive restaurant experience. He came highly recommended by the owner of another local restaurant. In an hour-long meeting with Henry and Mr. Rogers, Bob was told of the working relationship between employees and the former manager. In addition, the excellence of the restaurant was heavily emphasized and his new and expanded duties explained. As maitre d' he was in charge of front-of-the-house operations, but now he would be in charge of the entire restaurant. To this he replied, "I'm sure I can do a good job for you," and the meeting ended.

Although greeted with enthusiasm by everyone, only two weeks passed before Mr. Nielson began having problems with the help. As he constantly reminded people, "My name is Mr. Nielson, not Bill Hayes!"

As the new manager one of Bob's first actions was to keep a careful record of all bar expenditures. When his first monthly tabulation showed over $500 in free drinks, he was overheard to say, "This place is unbelievably sloppy. It may have made money, but there is enormous waste. Five hundred dollars for drinks per month is $6,000 per year directly off of profits, not to mention the inefficiency of people who are not completely sober." He brought the matter to Henry's attention and blamed the kitchen for excessive drinking. "How can anyone do his work when he's half drunk?" he fumed in a fit of anger. Henry's only reply was that no one was going to tell him and his help how much they could or could not drink and that he saw no reason to stop. The matter was dropped, but another problem arose on Henry's next day off.

As was the custom whenever Henry had a day off, several of the dishwashers pitched in to help prepare the meals in the kitchen. Due to an unpredicted noontime crowd, the kitchen ran short of clean dishes; and service slowed, although not considerably. "As a matter of fact," one waitress mentioned somewhat sarcastically to another, "no one but an old fussbudget like him would have ever noticed it." Bob, however, saw matters differently. Storming into the kitchen, he demanded to know what was going on. When he saw the dishwashers working on the preparations, he became quite angry and yelled at them to get back to their own jobs because they were not getting paid to do the cooking. "No-good, lazy cooks," he muttered as he left the kitchen. With the dishwashers no longer helping out, the cooks staged a mini-slowdown in protest. For the rest of the day, there was constant friction, with Bob barking orders like a marine drill sergeant and the cooks ignoring them. The end of the night saw Bob extend the dining room hours from 9 until 10 P.M., with the cooks and kitchen help vowing to throw him out bodily if he came back into the kitchen again.

The next day, Henry had just entered the restaurant when Bob accosted him. In an emotional tirade, Bob blamed the whole mess on Henry, exclaiming that his lack of responsible leadership would no longer be tolerated. Henry sat quietly until Bob left and then proceeded into the kitchen. When the dishwashers and cooks began talking all at once, Henry meekly threw up his hands and said, "I've had it with him," and was gone for the rest of the day. Although business was conducted as usual, morale was at an all-time low. When Henry failed to show up the following day, Bob became quite irritated and went in and out of the kitchen yelling at everyone in sight. Even the waitresses, to whom Bob had generally remained good natured, came under his verbal abuses. Finally, with everyone's patience wearing thin, the day came to an end.

During the next few months, the situation deteriorated even further. Henry was in and out of the kitchen, morale was low, the cooks were preparing sloppy meals, and no one any longer took much pride in his job. As one of the waitresses remarked, "I used to like working here, but now I'm looking for another job." Several of the other employees began to express similar feelings. Bob, blaming the deterioration of morale and the gradual loss of business on Henry and the rest of the kitchen help, hired a new cook to speed up and improve the quality of the meals. Henry, feeling that he was being replaced, went to Mr. Rogers and explained that although he had enjoyed working for him, he could no longer work under existing conditions and was going to quit. Solemnly, Mr. Rogers sat back and listened to Henry, wondering what he should do.

Discussion Questions

1. What factors led to the problems that have now developed?
2. What assumptions did Bill, Henry, Bob, and Mr. Rogers have *(a)* about human motivation and *(b)* about leadership?
3. What options did Henry have when Bob Nielson began to push him? Why did Henry respond as he did?
4. What problems, if any, would have occurred if Mr. Nielson had been "another Bill Hayes" in his manner of fulfilling his role?
5. What should Mr. Rogers do now? Why?

The Carpenter Case

Tom and Jane Carpenter are a young couple living comfortably in a New England town in the United States.

They have three children: Mary, 11; Jerry, 6; and Ann, 3.

Tom works in the headquarters of a manufacturing company as an executive in the engineering department. He has an excellent salary and up until now has been satisfied with his job. A quiet, handsome man of about 36 years, he is intelligent, sensitive, ambitious, and known as a "good family man." He has the respect of his colleagues and subordinates. The upper echelons of management regard him as a promising candidate for senior management in this company. Tom is

This case was prepared by Foulie Psalidas-Perlmutter, Ph.D., clinical psychologist, and is reproduced with her permission.

considered a practical man, able to take the changes in life with basic optimism and adaptability that appear to give him a maturity beyond his years. He likes the material wealth and comfort that his years of conscientious work have produced. He enjoys the status of his company which has an excellent name in its field, being considered one of the most progressive and future-minded of U.S. companies of this type.

If Tom is the practical member of the family, Jane is the "dreamer." She is a pretty, energetic woman of 30, a good wife and mother, and an active member of several committees and volunteer groups. She is strongly attached to both her family and her parents, who are in their early 60s and live in a nearby town. She is sincerely interested in many good causes and always finds the time and energy to devote to them. While she is not a very practical woman by nature, her enthusiasm for her projects is admired by her many friends.

Tom and Jane married early and struggled together for several years until they were able to achieve the comfortable life they have now. Their marital life has been happy and more or less undisturbed, and through the struggle of their earlier years they were able to develop between themselves a rewarding relationship. Although they have traveled to several parts of the United States with and without the children, neither Tom nor Jane had traveled abroad until two years ago. At that time Tom, together with three other executives, was sent to Latin America to explore the possibilities of setting up four new plants in different countries of Latin America.

Both Tom and Jane have been feeling more and more relaxed in the past years, since many of their dreams have been realized. They have a good family, financial security, and many friends. They are especially proud of their new home, recently finished. Jane has worked hard to find the furniture and the interior decorations they wanted, and now her dream house seems completed. They have both been so far generally satisfied with their children, who are well adjusted to their present environment. There have been certain problems with Mary, who is a very sensitive and shy girl, and with Jerry, who has had some difficulties adapting in school. But these were minor problems, and they have not seriously disturbed the otherwise happy family life.

Despite this very satisfactory picture of family life, there have recently been more and more occasions when Tom and Jane have felt (each one without admitting it to the other) that something is "missing."

More and more, Tom thinks that his life has become a comfortable routine. The new tasks he is given have less "challenge" and "adventure." For a long while he has been satisfied that his career had a steady development through the years. The time of anxiety and uncertainty has passed, but also with it the time of excitement and the inner feeling of searching and moving. He had begun to feel that he needs a change, and it was at that time that he was sent for two months to Latin America. Tom felt that this trip was one of the most interesting and rewarding events of his whole life. Being away for the first time from his family for such a long period, he missed them; and he was disappointed because the wives were not allowed to accompany their husbands on that trip. But the prospects of building up their company in Latin America have been very attractive, and he found that he liked to travel, to meet new people, to become acquainted with different ways of living, to be more a part of the "world" and of events outside of their hometown. The three other executives who took the trip with him had about the same feelings as he had. Each seemed to be a little weary of being "a little fish" at headquarters. The possibility of being a pioneer in the Latin American division to be created was an exciting prospect. Tom somehow felt reluctant to communicate to Jane all his satisfaction and his thoughts about that trip, as well as the fact that he was hoping to be chosen from among the executives to be responsible for setting up the plants in Latin America.

In a different way but with the same feelings of restlessness and discontent, there are times now that Jane feels that the pleasant well-organized life she has is lacking the excitement of unpredictability. She divides her time between many activities but finds herself at times dreaming about the world outside of her hometown. She wonders, like Tom, at times whether their life has not become too settled, an almost unaltered routine; but, unlike Tom, she checks herself by asking the simple question that, after all, isn't this what life really is?

When Tom came home with the news that Mr. Abbott, the president of the company, had offered him the key position in the Latin American operation, she was pleased to hear of the high esteem his superiors had for Tom. Actually, Jane too had been wondering for some time what could be the result of Tom's trip to Latin America. Although she would have liked to have been able to go with him at the time, the idea that she would have had to leave the children for such a long time forced her to exclude absolutely the possibility of her going, even if the wives of the executives had been allowed to go with them. After that, she used to wonder at times whether the company would choose him, if the decision was made. At that time the idea of having to move to a new environment was not an unpleasant one.

Now that the offer was a firm one with a high salary, cost-of-living expenses, and opportunity for travel throughout Latin America, she began to have some fears. As Tom talked excitedly about the challenging tasks he would have, her fears seemed to increase. She began to feel more and more that they had little to gain from this experience as regards their family and their life. It was a big step forward in Tom's career, to be sure, but Jane felt that Tom would be successful wherever he was. On the present job, Tom and she shared so much time together, while in the new job, as she understood it, Tom would have to travel a great deal. She was very unhappy and ashamed about her fears as opposed to Tom's enthusiasm and obvious willingness to venture ahead.

One evening she sat down by herself and tried to figure out why this new job was not so attractive to her. There was some urgency for Tom to make up his mind within a week, and she felt the need to understand what this decision to move abroad meant for her and for her family.

She tried to be honest with herself. She had fears, naturally, about moving to a new environment that was strange and where people spoke another language. She knew that the climate was very different, and she believed that the living conditions were likely to offer fewer comforts. She would be far from her friends and her elderly parents. Their furniture would have to be stored and their new house rented or sold, since it was not clear how many years Tom would need to get the four new plants going.

She felt she would be isolated because she did not think that they could have close contact with the local people for a long time. Whatever she had heard so far about the personality of the Latin Americans made her fear that close friendships would be difficult to achieve, at least for some time, because she had the impression that they were rather temperamental and unstable. Although she admitted to herself that this impression was based on hearsay and fiction, she somehow could not avoid believing it. She had also heard that there was a great deal of anti-American feelings in the country where they would first live. Furthermore, she wondered whether the sanitary conditions would be dangerous to the health of the children. The company had little experience in Latin America, so it would be likely that they would have to find their own way and learn, probably by hard experience, how to get along in these countries. She realized that what disturbed her more than anything else was probably the fact that Tom was going to have to travel a lot. Then she would probably have to face a great deal of the problems of their adaptation there alone, while up until this time they had always shared whatever problems they had to face and they supported each other in finding solutions. This also meant that Tom would see more places, meet more people; in general, he would enjoy more, and probably get more satisfaction out of, the whole experience than she and the children would. She was distressed to realize that she was already resentful toward him for that and angry because she could sense that, although he was discussing the problem with her, he had already made up his mind.

Jane kept these fears more or less to herself, but she did communicate to Tom her reluctance to go, and gave as one of the main reasons her worry about the effect this move was going to have on the education of their children as well as on their health. One discussion went as follows:

JANE: Will the children lose a year or maybe even more going to inferior schools?
TOM: They will learn a new language—make new friends.
JANE: Who knows what kind of doctors there are. . . .
TOM: Most of their doctors are trained in this country. Don't worry about it.
JANE: It will be all so new, so strange.
TOM: The children will adapt after awhile, and the experience will be good for them.
JANE: You'll be traveling quite a bit and I . . .
TOM: We'll both find this enriching, rewarding—not that I underestimate the difficulties involved, but we can overcome them and enjoy all the advantages of life abroad.
JANE [*sighs*]: If you say so.

Inwardly Tom was disappointed with Jane's negative reactions and the difficulties she seemed to be having. He had always believed her to be a woman of courage, endowed with curiosity and interest for the world outside. In times of crisis previously in their life, she had always proved to be strong and supportive, and she had always shown a spirit of adventure and willingness to go ahead. It was a painful surprise for him to realize that this spirit would operate only in the security of the familiar environment, while a more profound change seemed to appear to Jane as a great threat to herself and her family. He had hoped that she would back him in this decision, which was so important to his career. Nevertheless, he maintained his confidence in her, and he believed that she would change her mind in time. He called a Berlitz school nearby and made plans for both of them to take Spanish lessons.

When Jane's parents came to visit during this period of time, Jane told them of the company's offer to Tom. Her father, who had been ailing for some time, was visibly depressed by the news. Her mother said that this was going to be a great experience for them, "a chance of a lifetime," as she put it. Jane knew that her mother had always regretted not being able to travel abroad. Now she was thrilled that the children were given this opportunity, and she promised to come and visit them in Latin America if Tom accepted the job. With her father ill, Jane doubted this very much.

DINNER WITH MR. ABBOTT

A few days later Tom's boss, Mr. Abbott, invited Tom and Jane for dinner, saying that he always talked over a new job abroad with both husband and wife, because he felt that it was very important to take into consideration how the wife felt. Jane had many fears about this dinner. First, she resented being "looked over" by Mr. Abbott, who until now had not really spent much time with them socially. Second, she did not want to reveal her doubts to Tom's boss, who had a reputation for making quick judgments about people, often not very favorable.

The dinner turned out to be a very pleasant one. Mrs. Abbott helped to put everyone at ease throughout the dinner, talking about her pleasant experiences abroad when Mr. Abbott was managing director of a subsidiary branch in Europe. Mrs. Abbott had enjoyed Paris and Rome, but she admitted that she knew little about life in cities like Buenos Aires or Rio.

Mr. Abbott finally turned to Jane and said: "Well, Jane, and what do you think of Tom's new assignment?"

Jane: Oh—I don't know . . . I . . .
Mr. Abbott: I know you realize what a great opportunity this job will be for him. It's a greater challenge than anything he could get here, you know.
Jane: Well, you see, I . . .
Tom: Jane is really a born traveler. I know that she is looking forward to this. She has already found out how she can take lessons in Spanish.
[*Mr. Abbott looked pleased.*]
Mr. Abbott: That's really fine. You know, Tom, that ours is becoming an international company. There will be few opportunities for executives at headquarters whose overseas experience is limited. Our policy is to create a management team that could base its decisions on actual experience abroad. Of course, having the kind of wife who is willing to take the risk of going off to the jungle is quite an asset. You're a lucky man, Tom.

While Jane joined in the laughter, she was inwardly very angry. That night she and Tom had a quarrel:

Tom: Oh, boy, that evening really went beautifully!
Jane: Oh yeah? For whom?
Tom [*surprised*]: Why, for both of us, of course. Don't you think so?
Jane [*angry*]: Do you realize, Mr. Tom Carpenter, that you and Mr. Abbott talked as if you had already accepted the job? That every time I opened my mouth you cut me right off?
Tom: I knew what you would do—ask questions, look hesitant, unsure. Mr. Abbott is not the kind of man you can level with. You have to sound enthusiastic, especially about company decisions.
Jane: And to whom, please, can I show my lack of enthusiasm about the "company's" decision to send me and my children to some godforsaken place?
Tom: For heaven's sake, Jane. What's the matter with you?
Jane [*turning away, crying*]: I'm not going.
Tom: What? And ruin my career, a chance of a lifetime—for both of us? How will this make me look?
Jane: I'm just not ready to go.
Tom: You can just bet this opportunity will never be offered to me again.

Discussing the problem the next day with the children confused Tom and Jane more, because the children's reaction was not clear. Mary was unwilling to go, Jerry was frightened and Ann seemed excited. By now Jane was finding it difficult to sleep, and Tom said that a formal decision was required by next Monday.

They had a long weekend to think over the decision and give a final answer to Mr. Abbott on Monday.

▶ The Case of the Changing Cage

NOTE: *DO NOT READ* this case until directed to do so by your instructor. It has been set up as a Prediction Case so that you can test your analysis by answering questions before reading the entire case.

PART I

The voucher-check filing unit was a work unit in the home office of the Atlantic Insurance Company. The assigned task of the unit was to file checks and vouchers written by the company as they were cashed and returned. This filing was the necessary foundation for the main function of the unit: locating any particular check for examination upon demand. There were usually 8–10 requests for specific checks from as many different departments during the day. One of the most frequent reasons checks were requested from the unit was to determine whether checks in payment of claims against the company had been cashed. Thus efficiency in the unit directly affected customer satisfaction with the company. Complaints or inquiries about payments could not be answered with the accuracy and speed conducive to client satisfaction unless the unit could supply the necessary documents immediately.

Toward the end of 1952, nine workers manned this unit. There was an assistant (a position equivalent to a foreman in a factory) named Miss Dunn, five other full-time employees, and three part-time workers.

The work area of the unit was well defined. Walls bounded the unit

Data for the following case were taken from "Topography and Culture: The Case of the Changing Cage," by Cara E. Richards and Henry F. Dobyns. Reproduced by permission of The Society for Applied Anthropology from *Human Organization*, Vol. 16(1), 1957, pp. 16–20.

on three sides. The one exterior wall was pierced by light-admitting north windows. The west interior partition was blank. A door opening into a corridor pierced the south interior partition. The east side of the work area was enclosed by steel mesh reaching from wall to wall and floor to ceiling. This open metal barrier gave rise to the customary name of the unit—"the voucher cage." A sliding door through this mesh gave access from the unit's territory to the work area of the rest of the company's agency audit division, of which it was a part, located on the same floor.

The unit's territory was kept inviolate by locks on both doors, fastened at all times. No one not working within the cage was permitted inside unless his name appeared on a special list in the custody of Miss Dunn. The door through the steel mesh was used generally for departmental business. Messengers and runners from other departments usually came to the corridor door and pressed a buzzer for service.

The steel mesh front was reinforced by a rank of metal filing cases where checks were filed. Lined up just inside the barrier, they hid the unit's workers from the view of workers outside their territory, including the section head responsible for overall supervision of this unit according to the company's formal plan of operation.

Prediction Questions

1. Identify background factors important in influencing the emergent behavior of this group.
2. Predict the emergent system of the group; that is, its norms, activities, cohesiveness, and so forth.
3. What would you predict is the level of group productivity and satisfaction? Why?

PART II

On top of the cabinets which were backed against the steel mesh, one of the male employees in the unit neatly stacked pasteboard boxes in which checks were transported to the cage. They were later reused to hold older checks sent into storage. His intention was less getting these boxes out of the way than increasing the effective height of the sight barrier so the section head could not see into the cage "even when he stood up."

The girls stood at the door of the cage, which led into the corridor, and talked to the messenger boys. Out this door also the workers slipped unnoticed to bring in their customary afternoon snack. Inside the cage the workers sometimes engaged in a good-natured game of rubberband "sniping."

Workers in the cage possessed good capacity to work together consistently, and workers outside the cage often expressed envy of those in it because of the "nice people" and friendly atmosphere there. The unit had no apparent difficulty keeping up with its workload.

Discussion Question

Wherein were your predictions right and wrong? Analyze why.

PART III

For some time prior to 1952, the controller's department of the company had not been able to meet its own standards of efficient service to clients. Company officials felt the primary cause to be spatial. Various divisions of the controller's department were scattered over the entire 22-story company building. Communication between them required phone calls, messengers, or personal visits, all costing time. The spatial separation had not seemed very important when the company's business volume was smaller prior to World War II. But business had grown tremendously since then, and spatial separation appeared increasingly inefficient.

Finally, in November 1952 company officials began to consolidate the controller's department by relocating two divisions together on one floor. One was the agency audit division, which included the voucher-check filing unit. As soon as the decision to move was made, lower-level supervisors were called in to help with planning. Line workers were not consulted but were kept informed by the assistants of planning progress. Company officials were concerned about the problem of transporting many tons of equipment and some 200 workers from two locations to another single location without disrupting work flow. So the move was planned to occur over a single weekend, using the most efficient resources available. Assistants were kept busy planning positions for files and desks in the new location.

Desks, files, chairs, and even wastebaskets were numbered prior to the move and relocated according to a master chart checked on the spot by the assistant. Employees were briefed as to where the new location was and which elevators they should take to reach it. The company successfully transported the paraphernalia of the voucher-check filing unit from one floor to another over one weekend. Workers in the cage quit Friday afternoon at the old stand, reported back Monday at the new.

The exterior boundaries of the new cage were still three building walls and the steel mesh, but the new cage possessed only one door—the sliding door through the steel mesh into the work area of the rest of the agency audit division. The territory of the cage had also been reduced in size. An entire bank of filing cabinets had to be left behind in the old location to be taken over by the unit moving there. The new cage was arranged so that there was no longer a row of metal filing cabinets lined up inside the steel mesh obstructing the view into the cage.

Prediction Questions

1. How will the change affect the required and emergent systems?
2. What will be the consequences for productivity and satisfaction?

PART IV

When the workers in the cage inquired about the removal of the filing cabinets from along the steel mesh fencing, they found that Mr. Burke had insisted that these cabinets be rearranged so his view into the cage would not be obstructed by them. Miss Dunn had tried to retain the cabinets in their prior position, but her efforts had been overridden.

Burke disapproved of conversation. Since he could see workers conversing in the new cage, he "requested" Miss Dunn to put a stop to all unnecessary talk. Attempts by female clerks to talk to messenger boys brought the wrath of her superior down on Miss Dunn, who was then forced to reprimand the girls.

Burke also disapproved of an untidy working area, and any boxes or papers which were in sight were a source of annoyance to him. He did not exert supervision directly but would "request" Miss Dunn to "do something about those boxes." In the new cage, desks had to be completely cleared at the end of the day, in contrast to the work-in-progress piles left out in the old cage. Boxes could not accumulate on top of filing cases.

The custom of afternoon snacking also ran into trouble. Lacking a corridor door, the food bringers had to venture forth and pack back their snack trays through the work area of the rest of their section, bringing this hitherto unique custom to the attention of workers outside the cage. The latter promptly recognized the desirability of afternoon snacks and began agitation for the same privilege. This annoyed the section head, who forbade workers in the cage to continue this custom.

Prediction Question

With this additional information, reaffirm or revise your previous predictions.

PART V

Burke later made a rule which permitted one worker to leave the new cage at a set time every afternoon to bring up food for the rest. This rigidity irked cage personnel, accustomed to a snack when the mood struck, or none at all. Having made his concession to the cage force, Burke was unable to prevent workers outside the cage from doing the same thing. What had once been unique to the workers in the cage was now common practice in the section.

Although Miss Dunn never outwardly expressed anything but compliance and approval of superior directives, she exhibited definite signs of anxiety. All the cage workers reacted against Burke's increased domination. When he imposed his decisions upon the voucher-check filing unit, he became "Old Grandma" to its personnel. The cage workers sneered at him and ridiculed him behind his back. Workers who formerly had obeyed company policy as a matter of course began to find reasons for loafing and obstructing work in the new cage. One of the changes that took place in the behavior of the workers had to do with their game of rubberband sniping. All knew Burke would disapprove of this game. It became highly clandestine and fraught with dangers. Yet, shooting rubber bands *increased*.

Newly arrived checks were put out of sight as soon as possible, filed or not. Workers hid unfiled checks, generally stuffing them into desk drawers or unused file drawers. Since boxes were forbidden, there were fewer unused file drawers than there had been in the old cage. So the day's work was sometimes undone when several clerks hastily shoved vouchers and checks indiscriminately into the same file drawer at the end of the day.

Before a worker in the cage filed incoming checks, she measured with her ruler the thickness in inches of each bundle she filed. At the end of each day she totaled her input and reported it to Miss Dunn. All incoming checks were measured upon arrival. Thus, Miss Dunn had a rough estimate of unit intake compared with file input. Theoretically, she was able to tell at any time how much unfiled material she had on hand and how well the unit was keeping up with its task. Despite this running "check," when the annual inventory of "unfiled" checks on hand in the cage was taken at the beginning of the calendar year 1953, a seriously large backlog of unfiled checks was found. To the surprise and dismay of Miss Dunn, the inventory showed the unit to be far behind schedule, filing much more slowly than before the relocation of the cage.

Discussion Questions

1. Explain the emergent behavior and its consequences.
2. If you were Mr. Burke, what would you do now?

The Case of the Disgruntled Nurses

INTRODUCTION

Rachel Nelson was executive director of Oneida Home Health Agency (OHHA), a small medicare-certified home health agency serving 11 communities in rural upstate New York. She approached tonight's board of directors' meeting concerned about how to explain most clearly the complex issues facing the agency to the volunteer board, one third of whom were attending their first working meeting. The heavy agenda called for discussion of strategies for increasing visits, reducing staff, and decreasing the agency's long-term deficit. The federal regulations surrounding staffing and reimbursement were complex, and most board members, including the veterans, were not equipped with the technical skills necessary for making informed policy decisions.

Important policy decisions were needed tonight because the slight year-end surplus reported at the annual meeting two months before was short lived. The agency had operated at a deficit for the past three months, visits were down, staff was underutilized, and short-term loans were required to meet each payroll. Even though Rachel also faced some staff unrest, she had decided to concentrate on the issues relating to financial solvency, for which she needed policy decisions from the board in order to act. To describe the current staff problems would only cloud the picture.

This plan quickly dissolved during the early minutes of the meeting. A new board member handed the board president a letter, which he said he had been requested to deliver. The president opened the letter, read it, and passed it to Rachel, saying, "What do you make of this?" The letter,[1] which was unsigned, read:

> To: Board Members of OHHA
>
> From: Staff Council
>
> Subject: Staff Concerns
>
> For the past six weeks concerned members of the staff have been meeting to establish a staff council. We feel that you as board members should be informed of our existence and of our concerns. Our meetings are open to all employees including management. Enclosed is a copy of the council's policy and statement of concerns (Exhibit 1). In response to the enclosed letter (Exhibit 2) sent to all employees today, "We do *not* believe that as employees we are assured a right to discuss freely with management any matter concerning our own or the agency's welfare; nor receive prompt and fair response or resolution for any question, suggestions, problems, or complaint submitted." At this point we feel that small group discussions, as suggested by management, is not a viable solution to the problem.
>
> We feel further exploration of the problem is indicated.

After recovering from her initial shock and anger over this letter to the board, Rachel recalled the events that had precipitated this action by some of the staff.

THE AGENCY

OHHA was organized in 1947 as the Clinton Visiting Nurse Association. During its first 20 years, a part-time public health nurse visited the town's sick residents in their homes. The agency, governed by a five-member committee appointed by the town, led a hand-to-mouth existence, with most financial support coming from the town. Physicians loved the agency because the nurse visited poor patients at home and saved them the trip, for which they almost never received payment. The town welfare officer loved the agency because the dedicated nurse did much of his work with the poorest and most difficult clients, negotiated with fuel companies and stores to donate the basic necessities. The townspeople loved the agency because it fulfilled

[1] This and all other correspondence from staff are reproduced exactly as written by them.

EXHIBIT 1

As employees of OHHA, we feel the need to develop a cooperative working relationship between administration and staff for the betterment of all employees.

Toward the achievement of this goal, we have established an employee-staff council. We meet weekly on Wednesdays in the conference room, alternating times each week at 4 P.M. and 7 P.M., to accommodate individual schedules.

All employees are urged to attend.

In the course of staff council meetings over the past weeks, the following concerns have been expressed.

1. Because of rapid agency growth and change, we feel a pattern of breakdown in communication and trust between staff and administration has developed. We feel a need for more sharing and feedback between administration and staff. This need is particularly felt in regard to decisions that directly affect staff. Therefore:
2. We feel the need to establish a mechanism whereby employees can be assured a fair airing of their concerns, comments, suggestions, etc. (i.e., a grievance procedure) and feel they have the support and direction, if indicated, from fellow staff (i.e., a grievance committee).
3. We feel concern that management is unable to fairly represent the unique experience of staff at board meetings. Therefore we feel the need for two staff members, elected by staff, to represent staff at board meetings. This delegation could provide input on policy that affects staff and also provide a feedback mechanism between board and staff so that we can better understand the agency.

Other concerns expressed by staff briefly are (not necessarily in order of importance):

1. Parking hassles.
2. Improvement in community relationships.
3. Merit increases.
4. Retirement benefits.
5. Tax shelters.
6. Holidays (work schedules, differentials).
7. Weekends, storm days.
8. Agency pride.

their image of the gentle Florence Nightingale nurse running to the aid of the unfortunate, freeing the town's citizens from any responsibility for helping the ailing poor.

The staff, mostly registered nurses, liked the agency because it was the kind of place where a nurse could fit her work schedule to her private life, even if it meant making visits at odd hours. Also the emphasis was on direct patient care and independent judgment without the paperwork and restrictions of a hospital situation.

With the advent of medicare and medicaid in the late '60s, the situation changed. To qualify for medicare reimbursement, the Clinton VNA joined with the other 11 towns in the county (populations ranging from 550 to 18,000), hired qualified staff, and met certification requirements in order to serve poor and elderly patients residing in its service area. As part of this reorganization, the name OHHA was chosen. Even with this merger OHHA remained small for several years, staffed by the nursing director (Dorothy), three part-time nurses, one nurse's aide, and a part-time physical therapist.

EXHIBIT 2

May 14, 1980

Dear

We invite you to participate in one of a series of:

Employee Speak Up Meetings

"An opportunity to share your ideas and concerns about your work environment."

We believe that as employees you are assured of the right to discuss freely with management any matter concerning your own or the agency's welfare, and to receive prompt and fair response or resolution for any question, suggestion, problem, or complaint submitted.

This small group discussion, with a randomly mixed group of employees, is one of several vehicles we will offer to employees to help ensure effective communication on an ongoing basis between each employee and the management staff.

Sincerely,

Rachel Nelson

Rachel Nelson

Annemarie Paradis

Annemarie Paradis

You are invited to an Employee Speak Up Meeting on:

Date:
Time:
Place:

In 1973 the board of directors hired Chuck, a young man with an MBA and experience as a representative for a pharmaceutical company, to be the first full-time executive director. Dorothy continued as the nursing director, responsible for all nursing and preventive health program staff, which numbered 12 full- and part-time personnel.

The next five years were an era when federally funded health and welfare programs flourished. Chuck sought to get as many of these programs under his roof as possible. He added preventive health programs and other primary services such as physical and occupational therapy. The staff grew to 30, including many who were not nurses, as the agency moved toward a multidisciplinary approach.

Chuck also jumped onto the increasingly popular home health bandwagon, becoming a spokesperson for home health at the state and ultimately the national levels. He set his sights on a position in Washington as a paid lobbyist for home health, and during his last three years at OHHA he was away from the agency more than he was there. As a result, more of the responsibility fell on Dorothy, who knew almost nothing about the financial operations. She simply concentrated on ensuring that her patients received quality care and her faithful nurses got periodic salary increases.

After five years, which Chuck glowingly described in his final annual report as "years of prosperous growth during which outstanding health services have been provided to the community by OHHA's happy family of highly qualified, loyal staff," he left for an out-of-state agency five times OHHA's size. At Chuck's last board meeting, the directors learned that Chuck's legacy was a large deficit, the first in the agency's history. Rachel, who had been hired to replace Chuck, heard this news at the same meeting, to which she had been invited to meet the entire board prior to signing a one-year contract.

EVENTS LEADING TO THE LETTER

Rachel should have been warned by the events of Chuck's final board meeting; but feeling up for a challenge, she signed the contract. During the first week at OHHA she discovered the staff wasn't one big happy family nor was the service of the quality everyone claimed. The financial crisis was greater than reported at the board meeting because five months with virtually no leadership had elapsed between the discovered deficit and Rachel's arrival. Receivables averaged 90 days as nearly 40 percent of the bills were held up for at least 60 days, because the billing office didn't have all the information it needed from the nurses. Chuck's erratic personnel management and extended absences from the agency brought employee after employee to Rachel's door, asking for promised raises, reimbursement for working on snow days four months earlier, promotions, etc.

In those early weeks Rachel developed systems to document productivity, changed the accounting system from a simple cash system to a modified accrual system, wrote funding proposals to raise operating capital, made presentations to town and United Way funding committees, and studied medicare regulations, which were totally new to her. As a novice in the home health field, Rachel relied on Dorothy's long years of experience with medicare to keep the nurses delivering appropriate care and the billing office accurate if not timely.

One month after Rachel's arrival at OHHA, Dorothy submitted her resignation, saying she was exhausted after 12 years with the agency, especially after holding the pieces together over the past three years. Dorothy announced she would leave in two months, giving Rachel "plenty of time" to find a replacement and get on her feet. It was little comfort when Dorothy added that she had wanted to retire for a long time and now felt the agency was in competent hands so she could.

The search for a replacement was not easy. After extensive advertising, only two qualified candidates applied, and at the last minute one of them dropped out. Rachel gratefully hired Annemarie, a nurse with 20 years of nursing administration experience, including 4 years as director of a hospital-based home health agency and 6 years as a middle manager with a large insurance company, where she was responsible for provider and professional relations for the medicare program. Annemarie possessed all the skills and knowledge about the home health field and medicare that Rachel lacked.

Annemarie's enthusiasm for the new position was matched by an enthusiastic reception by the staff, especially the nurses, who had met and lunched with her at her second interview. Her arrival coincided with a move to more spacious quarters. Everyone's morale was high, even though there were underlying concerns about the agency's financial condition.

The "honeymoon" period lasted about two months. Daily, Rachel and Annemarie discovered problems resulting from Chuck's and Dorothy's lax and inconsistent management. They vowed to make changes as slowly as possible, recognizing people's natural reluctance to accept change. They set as priorities those items that were essential to reducing the deficit and introduced a number of immediate systems changes to increase accountability, document productivity, improve the quality and timeliness of billing, and increase the efficiency of scheduling.

These changes were carefully explained to the staff involved, including the rationale and anticipated benefits. Because of time pressures related to the serious financial problems, staff were not involved in the planning and decision-making process.

One major change was in the organizational structure. Because the agency continued to grow and diversify, Rachel and Annemarie felt it was inappropriate and inefficient for the director of nursing to provide patient care or direct supervision of the nurses. It was time to develop working supervisors to spread the management of staff downward. This would allow Rachel and Annemarie more time to work on critical fiscal problems and long-range program development. In all but one case, supervisors were chosen from current staff.

When the new organization chart (Exhibit 3) was discussed with the staff at a meeting, public response was positive. Privately it was far from positive, and the seeds of discontent took root. The staff had been accustomed to going directly to the top with problems and complaints. Dorothy had directly supervised all staff except the secretarial and bookkeeping personnel. When the nurses didn't want an assignment, she took it herself, visiting the patient on her way to the office in the morning. When they completed their care plans incorrectly, she rewrote them so medicare would approve them for payment. Supervision was lax, praise flowed freely, and criticism was nonexistent. If for some reason a staffperson couldn't get what she wanted from Dorothy, it was fairly easy to succeed by making a personal appeal to Chuck.

The new emphasis on organizational structure and line of command never set well with the more senior OHHA employees. They felt the new organizational chart, with its two divisions and supervisors, was too bureaucratic. No longer could they go directly to the director of nursing or executive director and ask for special favors or unscheduled raises. They were redirected to their supervisors.

The first supervisor to be developed was Maureen, Dorothy's nonsupervising nursing supervisor. Under Dorothy, Maureen carried a full caseload like the other nurses. The only task that differentiated her from the others, besides title, was scheduling new patients. Even after Maureen's expanded role was explained to the nursing staff, they would not accept Annemarie as a nonsupervising, nonvisiting director of nursing with more global responsibilities. Since she never left the office with a nursing bag and a list of patients to visit, they wouldn't believe she knew patient care. While they didn't want her to supervise them directly because she was too demanding, they felt slighted because she wasn't their supervisor!

In the old days no one measured productivity. The nurses were trusted, considered highly motivated and dedicated, and were believed when they said they made five visits per day. When systems were introduced to measure productivity and estimate visit costs, it became apparent the nurses were making only three visits per day. In an effort to streamline the billing and reduce the 90 days between visits and payment, Annemarie read every bill and the accompanying care plan before approving them for payment. In so doing she discovered the deficiencies in reporting, which Dorothy had always corrected without comment.

Dorothy hadn't completely ignored this problem. She recognized that allowing nurses and therapists to evaluate patients and develop plans of care independently, with only general guidelines, caused problems. She and the nursing staff had discussed the problem and decided to adopt a new and highly respected recording method, the problem-oriented medical record (POMR). Five months before Annemarie joined the staff, Lisa, the in-service educator, had begun teach-

EXHIBIT 3
Oneida Home Health Agency Organization Chart

Board of Directors
Executive Director (Rachel)
Secretary/Reception (Donna)
Business Manager
Bookkeeper
Billing Clerk
Director of Nursing Services (Annemarie)
Home Care Clerk
Social Work Consultant
Social Worker (Elaine)
Nursing Supervisor (Maureen)
3 RNs — Full-time
3 RNs — Part-time (Gretchen Liz & Marie)
Therapy Supervisor
2 P.T.s Full-time (Norine)
2 P.T.s Part-time
1 O.T. Full-time
1 O.T. Part-time
1 S.T.
H/HHA Supervisor
3 H/HHAs Full-time (Loretta)
2 H/HHAs Part-time
Inservice Educator (Lisa)
Health Screening Supervisor (Harriet)
3 EPSDT Outreach Workers
1 EPSDT Clerk Part-time
Teen Parent Program MCH Nurse
WIC Program Director
2 WIC Nutrition Aides

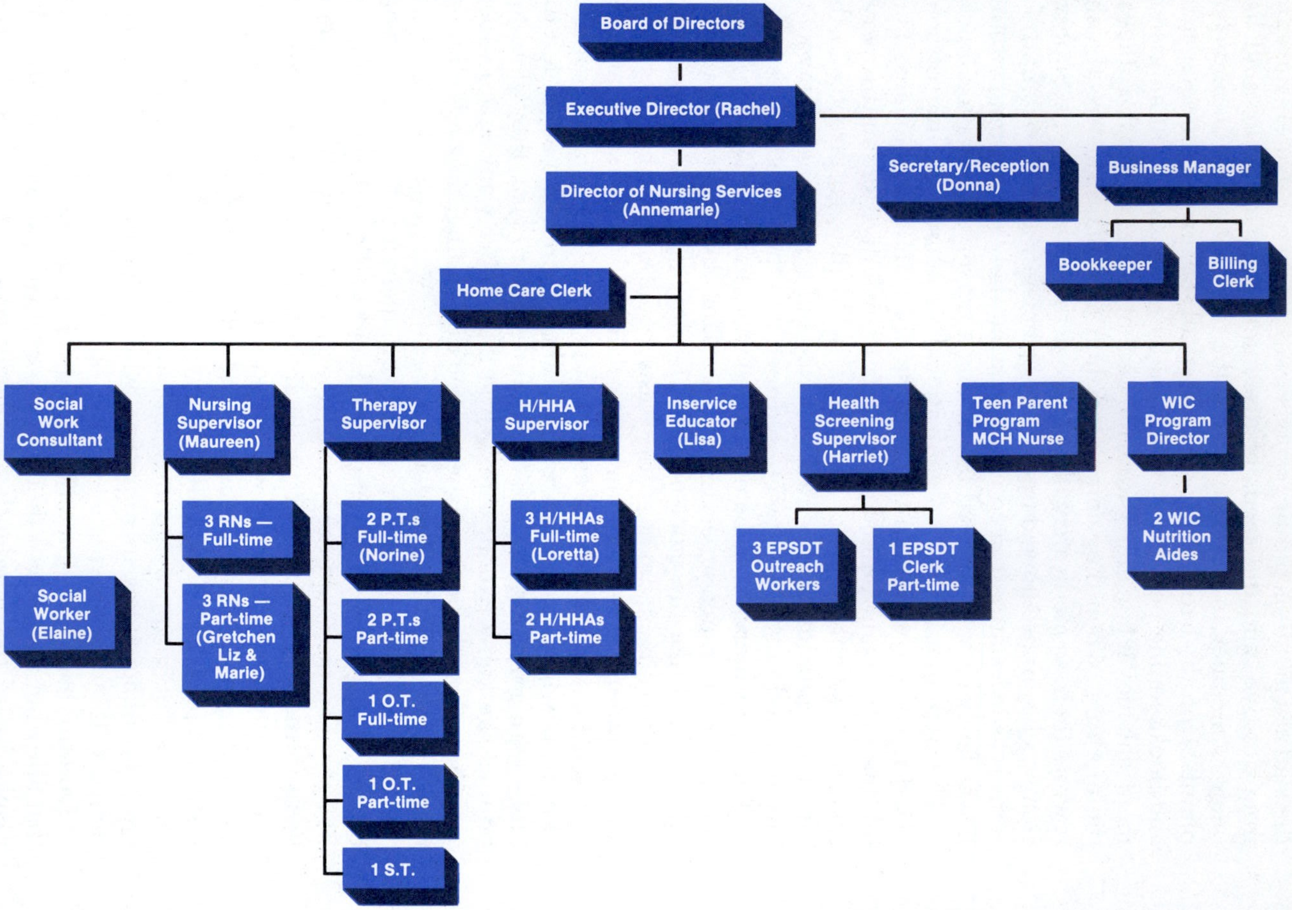

ing the nurses POMR methods. The system was excellent, once mastered, but it was extremely sophisticated. The training was costly in revenue-generating visit time and the results disappointing. The nurses produced reams of paper but were no closer to concise problem statement and analysis. Physicians complained about the volumes of incomprehensible material they were asked to read and approve, and some even stopped opening mail from OHHA. This created serious problems.

In home health, the nurse as primary caregiver may make a single evaluation visit without a physician's order. During that visit she evaluates the patient's situation and draws up a plan of care recommending specific treatment by herself, a nurse's aide, and/or a therapist. Before anyone can begin executing that plan, the patient's physician must approve it. The care plan must be updated and returned to the physician for recertification every 60 days. Without a physician's initial order and subsequent 60-day recertification, additional visits are not reimbursable under medicare or medicaid, and the nurse risks being accused of practicing medicine.

Annemarie took steps to streamline the POMR system to improve quality and reduce volume. With Lisa she developed some shortcut techniques for writing care plans and scheduled an in-service session to explain the new methods. The nurses, who were weary of POMR after months of unsuccessful effort, weren't very receptive even though the methods, if employed, would save time.

At the same time, Annemarie determined that with clerical help the records could be typed. This would improve readability and, combined with her new techniques, reduce volume. She hoped this would encourage the physicians to promptly read and approve the plans of care and recertifications required for nursing and therapy visits to continue. A clerical person could also establish a tickler file for the 60-day recertifications. She could then remind nurses and therapists to write the care plan update and submit it to the physician before the 60-day covered period expired. Rachel wrote a proposal and received CETA[2] support to hire a clerical person. The older staff nurses complained that hiring extra staff meant they would be deprived of raises they deserved, even though the first year's salary was paid by CETA.

Both steps brought positive reactions from new staff members, but the more senior staff nurses didn't like being reminded about their "recerts" or asked to rewrite care plans that didn't meet Annemarie's strict standards. The older nurses were upset as week after week their names remained on the posted "recert" list because their care plan

[2] CETA was the Comprehensive Employment and Training Act, a federal government program designed to pay for employees while they learned new skills.

updates were overdue. They also felt Annemarie's suggestions for improving their patient records were picky. They seemed unable to comprehend the broader financial consequences of improperly written care plans, despite repeated explanations, nor could they relate the importance of clear and concisely written plans to quality of care. The more Annemarie worked with them, the more they resisted, saying, "Annemarie is more concerned about paperwork then she is about patient care. We are good nurses and give excellent care. Just ask our patients." Or, "She hasn't touched a patient in years, so she doesn't know what we do. Besides, with those long fingernails I'd be afraid she would scratch the patients."

Annemarie countered, "If a nurse can't state clearly what the problem is and what steps she is going to take to correct that problem, I doubt that the patient is receiving quality care." Annemarie's doubts were confirmed by fairly frequent calls from physicians complaining about the care plans submitted by some of these older, more resistant nurses.

The accusations flew back and forth. The more Annemarie demanded her high standards be met, the more they resisted. Very soon these older nurses—who had been perceived as highly motivated, dedicated, and trusted by Dorothy and Chuck—were suspected and considered irresponsible by Annemarie. They in turn disliked her intensely. They avoided her, barely speaking when greeted and never initiating conversation. Annemarie responded in like manner after her efforts at friendliness were rebuffed. As the distance widened she stopped meeting with them and began writing notes discussing problems with their record and spelling out what she wanted changed. They felt insulted by receiving "impersonal memos" and avoided Annemarie even more.

Annemarie continued to meet with newer nurses and therapists to discuss problems with their records. Ironically, the older nurses felt Annemarie was showing favoritism through these meetings. Actually, she was often critical and uncompromising, verbally "slapping the hands" of these new staff professionals when they didn't conform to her model and standards. They overlooked this hard side of Annemarie and responded positively to her suggestions, which they considered to be helpful and important to their professional growth. The older nurses, who refused to meet with Annemarie out of fear and dislike, lost an opportunity to know her better, to see her softer side, and to gain skills and insights as professionals.

Before the arrival of Rachel and Annemarie, the formal reward system at OHHA provided no incentive for good performance. Everyone received a 4 percent increase on their anniversary date, and if Chuck had influence with the board they would get a 5–8 percent cost-of-living raise each July. There were no penalties for poor performance;

no one got fired; performance evaluations contained generalized praise for everyone.

With Annemarie, praise had to be earned. Those who met her high standards and accepted her criticisms and suggestions were her favorites and protégés. Eventually, Annemarie held the newer staff members in higher esteem because of this.

Another factor that raised the newer nurses in Annemarie's esteem was the fact that they held higher educational credentials than the older nurses. The newer nurses each held a B.S. in nursing, while the older nurses had graduated from three-year, hospital-based nursing programs. Annemarie had graduated from a three-year program in the late 1950s, but as medicine and nursing became more complex, four-year, college-related nursing programs gained popularity. Annemarie returned to school to get the B.S. degree. When she joined OHHA she indicated she would give priority to a B.S. nurse when hiring. This was seen as implying that the younger B.S. nurse was better than the older diploma nurse, despite the latter's broad experience.

Still another factor that increased the closeness between the newer nursing professionals and Annemarie, while widening the distance with the older nurses, was the former's perceived dedication to nursing as a career. The older nurses described themselves as professionals but didn't consider their job at OHHA as a career. It was a way to gain recognition in the community, contribute to their husbands' earnings, and work part time in a low-key and relaxed atmosphere while maintaining active lives at home and in the community.

Furthermore, they were somewhat conflicted about nursing as a career. In recent years their professional magazines and meetings told them they were partners with physicians with unique contributions to make. In reality they were frequently treated as handmaidens or servants. As a result many were unhappy and disillusioned with career nursing. Furthermore, they felt stuck in their unhappiness. There was no place for them to go at OHHA unless they became supervisors, and most didn't want to assume such responsibilities nor work full time. They didn't want to return to hospital nursing because it was more restrictive than home health. Unlike the younger nurses, who gave nursing a try and left it if it wasn't right for them, the older nurses seemed incapable of taking the necessary action to change careers.

Yet, being home health nurses had given them considerable status in the eyes of the community. Certain patients always asked for them. When they served on committees and volunteer boards, they were given recognition for their helping role and knowledge of the needs of the community's poor and less fortunate residents. In these community groups, a nurse was a nurse; few knew there were differences in education and training.

By contrast, Annemarie was not a resident of any of the communities served by OHHA. She commuted 45 miles to work each day, leaving the office and the community behind her at the end of the day. The status bestowed on the agency nurses by the community meant little to her. More important to her were credentials and willingness to upgrade skills. Diploma nurses who saw no need to return for the B.S. degree had little status in Annemarie's eyes.

Annemarie clearly saw herself as a career nurse and professional nursing administrator. She had few problems relating to physicians, because she expected and demanded treatment as a partner in the care of a patient. She was very clear about the nursing role and how it complemented the physician's role of practicing medicine. Personally she believed in hard work and sacrifice for the sake of her career. She herself had returned to college to earn the B.S. degree in nursing while raising five children as a single parent, caring for her dying mother, and working in a demanding middle-management position in the insurance company. As a result, she had little understanding or respect for nurses who didn't regard nursing as a career to be avidly pursued.

The office layout didn't help matters. All the staff had participated in the decision to move to the new office and had unanimously supported it. Previously, OHHA had occupied three floors of a small house where the employees were very crowded and uncomfortably hot in summer and cold in winter. The nurses shared an 8-by-10 room down the hall and out of sight from Dorothy. There were only two desks, so frequently one or more had to sit on the floor to do their paperwork. If someone was on the phone with a physician or patient (often hard of hearing), the others couldn't concentrate. Even if they had wanted to write better care plans, it was nearly impossible to do so.

The new office was primarily open space divided into sections with filing cabinets and bookcases. The nurses now had their own desks, and phones were shared by only three people. The office shared by Annemarie and Maureen was in an adjacent section, which was approached through an archway. Annemarie's desk was near the door of her office, so when she looked out she could see all the nurses at their desks. Whenever Annemarie turned her chair to speak to Maureen on the other side of the office, she faced the door. The older nurses believed she was spying on them to see if they were working or just talking. In response to this accusation, Annemarie began closing the door when talking with people in her office. This aroused more suspicions. "What is she plotting this time?" the nurses and others asked.

As distrust and suspicion grew, Annemarie felt she was losing control. She responded by establishing more procedures and requiring more accountability. For example, the answering service was instructed to direct all evening calls to Annemarie or Maureen. Rationale: They knew all the patients on service, and the nurses, who had been providing patient care all day, deserved their evenings off. Reality: Annemarie didn't want patients calling their favorite nurse who might make an inappropriate evening visit for which there would be no reimbursement. Annemarie also didn't like the feeling of ownership that nurses had toward "their" patients. She felt it important that all nurses could provide care equally to all patients. Similarly, everyone was required to sign in and out on a large board, listing their patients in order of visit schedule. Rationale: The office needed to know where they were in case there was a change in their schedule or some family member needed to contact them in an emergency. Reality: Annemarie suspected they were using agency time for personal business.

A new procedure that caused the greatest uproar had to do with the scheduling of Thanksgiving and Christmas coverage. It was official agency policy for one nurse and one home health aide to work holidays on a rotation basis, treating those few patients who required seven-day-a-week care. But an unwritten policy, in effect for years, made each nurse responsible for her own patients on these two "family" holidays. It was reasoned that if a nurse had a patient who needed a visit, it wouldn't take much time from the family celebration, and this was preferable to one nurse working the full day. Annemarie overruled the unwritten policy, saying she was uncomfortable knowing all her nurses were having their day ruined when only one would have to sacrifice the holiday once every six years. She refused to hear their arguments for retaining their informal system.

At a meeting of the full staff 18 months after coming to OHHA, Annemarie expressed concerns about the growing divisiveness she observed. Publicly she said she was concerned about a breakdown in communication and a lack of caring for fellow staffpersons when they faced personal crises. Privately she worried that the older, discontented staff nurses were "poisoning" the attitudes of some of the other workers who had been in the agency in the "good old days" before all the new programs and fancy systems. She was also convinced they made life so unpleasant for new staff nurses that they resigned soon after they were trained and had become productive.

At this staff meeting Annemarie suggested that OHHA might form an employee association, and she described some models with which she had experience. After a brief discussion, one of the older nurses volunteered that a "staff council" was just what they needed and when could they organize one? They decided to have an exploratory meeting the next day after work. Annemarie left the staff meeting feeling her suggested vehicle for building communication and trust might actually destroy it.

The next day word spread that management would not be welcome at the meeting. Annemarie and Rachel honored this wish, not wanting to inhibit discussion at this initial meeting. Some of the supervisors did attend but were told, soon after the meeting started, that they were not welcome. About one third of the staff attended that first meeting. A second, unpublicized meeting was held one week later.

At a supervisors' meeting following that second meeting, Annemarie expressed her concern that if this was to be an employee association, all employees of the agency, including supervisors and administration, should be members by virtue of their employment. Harriet, a former staff nurse recently promoted to a supervisory position and the agency's most senior employee, said she felt it was not the intent of the council to exclude supervisors. She did admit, however, that some of the employees did not want supervisors to attend.

The supervisors agreed that since the goals and objectives of the council had not been identified, anyone interested in the formation of such an employee group should attend the meetings. Everyone agreed to tell their subordinates this, and Annemarie asked Harriet to tell the employees organizing the meetings that they should publicize the times and purposes of future meetings so all employees could make a choice about attending.

Further investigation by Rachel and Annemarie revealed that half of the 14 employees who attended the first two staff council meetings felt they were primarily gripe sessions led by older agency employees. The major focus of the complaints was Annemarie. Three more unpublicized meetings were held before or after work on agency

EXHIBIT 4
"Active" Staff Council Members (effective 5/14/80)

Name	*Age*	*Position*	*Education*	*Years at OHHA*	*Full or Part Time*	*Writer of Letter*
Harriet	48	Former staff RN, new supervisor	Diploma	9	Full	
Gretchen	50	Staff RN	Diploma	7	Part	X
Liz	41	Enterostomal therapist, staff RN	B.S.	6	Part	X
Marie	36	Staff RN	Diploma	4	Part	X
Loretta	36	Nurse's aide	1 year college, CNA training	7	Full	
Donna	27	Receptionist, Rachel's secretary	High school	1.5	Full	
Norine*	32	Registered physical therapist	B.S.	1	Full	
Elaine†	49	Social worker	B.S.	1	Full	

* Chosen by therapy department to represent them so they would know what was going on and could offer a different perspective.

† Saw herself as self-appointed staff therapist and liaison between staff and management.

premises and were attended by 8 of OHHA's 40 employees (Exhibit 4). Finally, on May 7, a notice inviting all employees to the next meeting appeared in everyone's mail slot.

During these worrisome weeks, Annemarie became increasingly suspicious, saying the older nurses were organizing a union. She was afraid to attend any of their meetings for fear that it would be considered formal acknowledgment of them as a bargaining unit. Rachel argued they would never encourage communication by pretending the group didn't exist. She urged they take some initiative to gather all employees in small groups and encourage discussion of concerns and solicit suggestions for improving the work environment. As a result, the invitation to attend an "employee speak-up" (which sparked the letter to the board of directors) was written and given to all employees on May 14, the day of the board meeting (Exhibit 2).

THE BOARD RESPONDS

After hearing Rachel's description of the events leading to the letter, the board agreed that it was not their role, at least at this point, to be involved in the day-to-day management of personnel. They did feel they could respond to the staff by asking them to give the board's personnel committee input into the development of a grievance procedure. The committee had already included this task in their work plan for the summer. The board also directed Rachel to solve the problem with expediency so that all major energies could be directed at achieving financial solvency.

Rachel didn't sleep much that night as questions raced through her mind. What factors caused this cry for help from an apparently small but disgruntled group of OHHA employees? Who were they?[3] Did they represent a larger but less vocal segment of the staff? Why did they circumvent the formal lines of communication? Had she become so unapproachable that they felt the only way to be heard was to go directly to the board? Was this a strategy designed to discredit Rachel, or Annemarie, or both? What was it they really wanted? Did they know?

As daylight approached she also wondered how to approach Annemarie, since on the surface it seemed she was at the center of the unrest. Rachel knew Annemarie wasn't perfect, but she had worked hard for OHHA. She believed that Annemarie saw herself as highly organized, caring about getting the job done but balanced with high

[3] The next day Rachel learned that the letter to the board had in fact been written by the three senior nurses, Gretchen, Liz, and Marie. They came to see her and apologized for not going to her, saying that they were just so frustrated they didn't know what to do. They pleaded for the removal of Annemarie from the agency.

care for individuals. She had great compassion for the agency's patients and for the more unfortunate people in the world. But at the office, she was so concerned with accomplishing her goals—her great plan for OHHA—that people who didn't cooperate and conform were criticized and excluded from the inner circle. She asked for input and involvement in planning and decision making when a semblance of participation worked to her advantage, but at times her decisions seemed arbitrary and unilateral. These decisions, such as the change in holiday scheduling, were always made "in the best interests of my people."

Annemarie had high standards, which she spelled out in procedures books, models for record keeping, organization changes, job descriptions, and other "solid management tools." However, her verbal or written communications with staff were often vague, inconsistent, and couched in bureaucratic terms. Often jobs were not done as she thought she had clearly described them because the staffperson didn't receive a clear message. Even the better relationships deteriorated over time as everyone was accused, at one time or other, of not hearing correctly. Annemarie began writing memos with carbon copies to people to prove she had asked something of them; but the memos were often confusing rather than clarifying.

Rachel had to do something, but what?

▶ The Case of the Joint Meeting

It was Tuesday, midway in an experimental course in negotiations and the resolution of conflict, and the class was discussing problems faced by groups in disagreement. The professor, Hugh Spector, suggested that if groups see themselves in competition they will reinforce negative stereotypes of each other. As a number of students recalled situations that seemed to confirm the hypothesis, there was a reference to blacks as generally emotional, short-tempered, vengeful, and prone to using knives in a fight. A student responded with a laugh that this description was ridiculous and left him with an image of frightening-looking blacks slinking around ready to pull out their switchblades at the drop of a hat. At this a white male student exclaimed indignantly, "But they do carry knives," and proceeded to tell a story he had heard about a recent incident. It involved one of his white

This case was prepared by Professors Allan Cohen and Herman Gadon while at the Whittemore School of Business and Economics, University of New Hampshire.

male friends, who was also in the class. The friend was a member of an all-white male fraternity team that had been challenged to a game of touch football by an all-black team of students. The game took place on a Saturday afternoon and had been underway for about 20 minutes when an argument developed between a black and a white player following the completion of a play. As the tension between the two players had mounted, their voices rose and the black player brandished an open switchblade. The student reporting the incident said he thought that the black player was ready to use the knife. There was some jostling, body contact, and shouts, and then players scattered in panic in all directions. As the involved white student listened to his friend retell the story, he became increasingly agitated and finally interrupted to say that he had been plenty scared at the time and was now more frightened of blacks than ever.

Bubba Blair, the only black student in the class of 25, listened intently but quietly as was his custom. When all eyes turned self-consciously to him, he said that he knew the guys they were talking about and he had heard the story differently. Since it was the practice for the class to learn from its own experience whenever possible, Professor Spector made the obvious observation that, "We have under our very noses an example of our hypothesis." Further discussion followed, with disagreement about what had happened on the football field. Blair seemed upset as his reports of his friends' versions were attacked, though as usual he spoke in a soft, diffident way. Members of the class began to take sides.

Time was running out for the class period, and Spector interrupted again to repeat that the class at that very moment had an example of the kind of conflict he had been talking about, presenting an opportunity to test the concepts of the course. He asked if the class were willing to carry on with the issue at the next meeting. There was a general murmur of approval when Bubba said he would be willing to bring some of his friends who had played in the game, and the class ended expecting to continue the discussion two days later.

Hugh Spector was pleased. First, the incident brought to life the learning that he wanted his students to acquire. Second, he was sincerely interested in this particular conflict and hoped to contribute something to its resolution. Third, he had general concerns about black-white relations and saw the coming confrontations as a way to get to issues vital to the campus.

Blacks at North Midwestern State University (NMSU) until recently had been a rarity. Traditionally, 75 percent of the 10,000-member student body was largely undergraduate, white, Protestant, lower-middle to middle class, and rural, coming from within the predominantly white state.

People were generally politically conservative and on racial issues mildly prejudiced, mostly from lack of contact with blacks and other visible minorities. The census count of 1970 showed only 2,500 blacks among the state's 1.5 million residents, mostly concentrated in one urban center. For the most part, students believed that everyone should have a fair chance to make his own place in the world. Many assumed that everyone did have equal chances and thus held blacks responsible for their lower incomes and standings. A substantial "liberal" element was much more sympathetic to minority issues. On the whole, though, attitudes of the student body fairly reflected the attitudes of the majority of the administration, the faculty, and the 4,000 permanent citizens of the residential town of Smithton in which the university was located.

Until 1971 there had been only isolated pockets of student radicalism. When occasional voices of dissent rose, officials in the town and university responded nervously but not in retribution, as nothing more than a noisy rally in front of the administration building had occurred, attended for the most part by the curious rather than the committed. NMSU was relatively quiet during that turbulent time in the lives of universities when there was stormy recognition of social issues, but many there felt socially responsible and anxious to do something to address needs they felt were legitimate. Consequently, like most northern colleges and universities, after prodding from liberal faculty members NMSU had made an effort to bring blacks to its campus in the interest of providing them with new and previously unavailable opportunities for higher education.

By 1971 approximately 100 blacks had been enrolled in the university, mostly recruited from northern urban ghettoes in Chicago and Cleveland, and a few backward rural communities in the South. Bubba had come from a small town in Alabama.

The presence of blacks on the campus and in the town was largely a new experience. Black students had come to Smithton at a time when black self-consciousness was strong and rising in the country. "Black is beautiful" was still fresh and new. There was strong pressure among outnumbered blacks to stick together. Collective strength was seen by many blacks as necessary to cultivate pride and to provide for mutual support in a system in which they still felt that they were treated at best with condescension.

The university and town were populated with many people who saw themselves as having a conscience and being dedicated to the constitutional premise that all men are created equal. They therefore supported recruitment of black students to uphold that belief. Many had been moved by the civil rights struggles of the 1960s.

On the other hand, a substantial number of students, with their beliefs in individualism and lack of contact with minorities, resented the scholarship money and bending of admissions standards required to attract black students.

Both groups were poorly prepared to cope with blacks who seemed to prefer separation to acceptance as integrated members of the community. While university officials were working to integrate them into the ordinary routines of campus life, blacks were segregating themselves. The administration was increasingly facing unexpected dilemmas and crises precipitated by black students, such as a request by them for a special commons building furnished and maintained at university expense and from which whites were excluded. After black threats of picketing and boycotting of classes, a building was provided and student funds were channeled to a black organization. This caused much resentment among some white students who already were financially pressed. Because expected federal funds had not materialized in nearly the quantity necessary to provide sufficient support services to blacks, the administration was constantly struggling to find money.

Hugh Spector believed that much of the stress felt by blacks and whites on campus and the increasing number of unpleasant confrontations were directly traceable to inadequate communications between them. It was his opinion that negative stereotypes were consequently reinforced, increasing the polarization. Spector believed strongly that many of the problems he saw could be resolved if blacks and whites could only talk to each other in the right circumstances in order to test and disconfirm many of their prejudices. He believed that confrontation over real rather than imagined differences would result in increased trust and ultimately lead to solutions that would satisfy everyone.

He had acquired his beliefs through both past experience and study. At one time in the early days of union organization, he had been a consultant to a management team of negotiators and helped achieve a settlement in a very difficult situation. On the campus and in the community, he had become involved in helping individuals to talk more openly and directly with one another. Recently, he had begun advising local groups on how to identify their self-interests, organize on their own behalf to pursue them, and talk constructively with authorities. He had helped to arrange meetings both to improve relations and to negotiate arrangements that better met the needs of the aspiring groups. He felt certain that his human skills were applicable to problems between blacks and whites and was anxious to get those on campus together in a dialogue that would move them toward more understanding and thus contribute to better relations in the larger community. The unexpected opportunity presented by the presence of a scared white student and Bubba, a black student who would talk reasonably openly, pleased him. He hoped to help the coming encounter be a constructive one and was confident that he could handle whatever happened.

Before the next class meeting he reviewed in his own mind what he knew about all the students. Five of the 25 enrolled in the course were graduate students. One of them, Beth, whom he particularly respected, was studying to be a counselor. She was attractive, well liked, sensitive, alert, outspoken, and intelligent. She often picked up things that he had missed in the class, and he felt he could count on her. There were eight women in the class in all, and one black, Bubba Blair. Bubba and the two white male students who had precipitated the confrontation, Doug and Charley, were undergraduate business administration majors as were most of the others. Doug was the one who said that he was threatened with a knife.

Doug, Charley, and Bubba had a direct stake in the affair. Others in the class seemed primarily interested in testing their ability to cope with the conflict, though some had apparently developed allegiances already.

Feelings in the class toward Bubba were difficult to ascertain. He usually spoke softly, seldom, and briefly, except for one instance early in the course when he had talked at some length about his own difficulty in participating in discussions because he felt inadequate and afraid of sounding foolish. His disclosure aroused a lot of sympathy, attracted support, and for awhile seemed to bring other students closer to him. But his customary silence eventually made him a figure of mystery again and kept him relatively isolated. He dressed simply and kept to himself, though he shared a lot privately with Professor Spector. Spector knew, for instance, that Bubba found it difficult to oppose fellow blacks publicly once they had arrived at a formal position, even when he strongly disagreed. Bubba said that he felt bound by loyalty and fear of isolation if he went his own way.

Doug and Charley were seen in the class as jocks, fraternity types, social, light-hearted and light-headed, but harmless. They generally came to class, as did most others, including the women, in conservative slacks, shirts, and loafers. Doug and Charley were often skeptical about the value of the course to themselves as future businessmen, yet remained interested in learning and had invested a lot of themselves in the previous class discussion about the affair on the football field. They seemed as anxious as Spector to have a satisfactory outcome for the coming meeting.

The class met next as usual at 9 A.M. on Thursday. Spector arrived early. Students filed in and settled themselves in their chairs, which were placed as was customary in a large circle to facilitate discussion. The usual chatter preceding the beginning of class filed the room. Spector thought that no one looked particularly keyed up besides himself. Doug and Charley arrived quietly and sat down together next to Professor Spector. Beth came in and sat in a chair across the room directly facing them. The noise subsided in the room and everyone seemed to be present except Bubba and his friends.

At several minutes after nine, the black students appeared in the doorway and moved jauntily to seats next to Beth. Though their eyes swept the room, they faced only each other, joking animatedly, and punctuating their conversation with loud staccato laughter. Bubba came first, dressed inconspicuously as always, followed by a tall, muscular, lean, handsome male with a flashing smile and alert, darting eyes, dressed in a yellow satin shirt open from the throat to mid-chest, tightly fitted hip-hugging jeans, and a black silver-studded belt. He had a short Afro haircut. Alongside him was a pudgy black male at least a head shorter, wearing a vivid purple, floppy wide-brimmed hat pulled down over one eye, a white dashiki, a necklace of animal teeth, red pants and sandals. He was followed by a strikingly beautiful dark female wearing skintight electric-blue jeans, and a white blouse knotted in front, revealing a bare midriff to below the navel. They greeted Beth warmly with, "Hi, Sugar," and sat down.

Professor Spector started class by welcoming the visitors and explaining his hopes for a positive outcome. The blacks smiled at each other, and Bubba identified his friends. His tall friend Steve was the player who was accused of pulling the knife. "Pudge" was a graduate student in the counseling program. He had seen the game. Pudge clowned and mugged constantly while being introduced. Linda was a personal friend who had not been at the game but wanted to come to the class.

Spector suggested that the session begin by Doug and Steve each telling what they thought had happened on the field, urging everyone to listen carefully so that the differences between the two versions were clear. He implored everyone to listen first for understanding and said that arguments should be avoided at least until the real differences had been established. He asked that responses at first be limited to requests for clarification.

Doug began his story. Steve interrupted frequently with sharp questioning, which seemed to fit the ground rules but were in fact a kind of baiting. The early exchange went as follows:

> **Doug:** Steve was going out for a long pass, and I brushed him as he went by to slow him down. I was defending short in the flat.
> **Steve** [*with mock precision and a smile*]: What do you mean "brushed?" Describe a brush to me, will you? You mean you bushwhacked me on the blind side, huh?

Meanwhile, Pudge was singing tauntingly in the background: "A brush in the back is worth two in the hand."

Doug [*defensively*]: I didn't whack you in the back. You're exaggerating.
Steve: I don't want to argue, boy. Just tell me what you mean by "brush." You mean like an elbow in my kidneys?
Doug: I just brushed your shoulder as you went by.
Steve: Where's your shoulder? Mine must be half-way down my back.

Pudge and Linda were laughing and slapping their thighs.

Charley: What did you Negroes come here for anyway?
Steve [*wide-eyed*]: Negroes! Did you hear that? Any NE-GROES here, Pudge?

During this exchange Professor Spector listened and watched with growing apprehension. His own anxiety increased, and he noticed rising tension in the students in the class. Spector also suddenly noted with alarm that Pudge was carrying a large, clear plastic bag, that contained a shredded material that looked suspiciously like marijuana. While Doug and Steve were talking, Pudge was elaborately rolling a cigarette or a joint. Pudge lit up. Spector saw that many of the students had also noticed Pudge's activities and were looking at Spector—waiting, he thought, for a reaction from him. Hugh leaned imperceptibly forward to sniff, and with a sinking feeling, smelled what he was almost sure was "grass."

Pudge was leaning back now with a self-satisfied air after a hard, deep, hissing drag on the cigarette and a long, slow exhalation. He passed the cigarette to Beth, who looked at Spector defiantly he thought, took it and repeated the deep draw and slow, extended exhalation.

Spector remembered that only two days ago 12 students had been busted for possession of marijuana in a raid by town police. There were rumors that a young instructor was involved and would be asked to leave the university. The attitude of the university administration toward punishment for pot smoking was unclear but leaning toward expulsion under pressure from local and state police and public officials. They had been making a tremendous fuss about university toleration of drug use, marijuana in particular, and the administration was under heavy fire.

Spector felt caught in a terrible bind. He had tenure and had been at the university for 10 years. He was married, had a family of three children, and high monthly living expenses. On the one hand, if he challenged the content of the pouch and it wasn't pot, he would make a fool of himself. If it was pot (he was almost certain that it was) and he didn't report it, he would become a conspirator and be vulnerable to being reported by a student. He could then be charged with collusion, presence while marijuana was smoked, or at best "softness," and would then expose both himself and the university to attack or prosecution. If it was pot as he suspected and he did report it, he would be legally clear, but he would expose Pudge and Beth to suspension or expulsion, and the university would face, he was certain, a new crisis with blacks and radical students. He was also worried about what would happen if he insisted that the smoking stop and there was a test of strength. What would he do if he said "stop" and was refused? Should he order Pudge and Beth to leave? What would happen if they wouldn't go? Could he physically force them out of the room? Would Steve pull a knife again? Should he himself leave the room?

The specter of the lost opportunity to bring people together to talk suddenly haunted him. He wondered if a dialogue could be maintained if he said nothing. He felt without being clear about it that this was a very critical test, and he was fearful that if he didn't meet it adequately he would expose himself, the class, and the white community on campus to ridicule. He was sure that within hours after the class was over, the story would be widely known through the grapevine among a large number of students. But if he acknowledged that he noticed the smoking and tried to stop it, the class might explode and destroy the chance for human understanding. While Hugh raced through the alternatives in his head, Doug and Steve continued to spar, Steve taunting Doug, Doug attempting honest answers in indignation, and getting increasingly redder in the face. Spector felt immobilized and terribly uncertain about the correct thing to do; yet he felt that he must do something quickly and that a great deal more than he had bargained for was hanging in the balance.

▶ A Case of Prejudice?

NOTE: *DO NOT READ* this case until directed to do so by your instructor. It has been set up as a Prediction Case so that you can test your analysis by answering questions before reading the entire case.

PART I

Captain Blake, an administration officer, arrived in Vietnam in May 1969 and was assigned to an infantry division. Immediately upon arrival at the division base camp he was interviewed by Colonel Roberts and Major Samuels. Colonel Roberts was in charge of personnel and

This case was prepared by Professors David A. Tansik and Richard B. Chase of the University of Arizona as a basis for classroom discussion and not to illustrate either effective or ineffective handling of an administrative situation. Presented at the Intercollegiate Case Development Workshop, University of Santa Clara, October 18–20, 1973. Used with permission of the authors.

administration, and Major Samuels was his assistant. Colonel Roberts advised Captain Blake that he was to be the personnel management officer. Near the end of the interview, Colonel Roberts made the following remarks to Captain Blake:

Roberts: I am sure you will find your job interesting. As you probably know, the division has approximately 18,000 men. Since this is a one-year tour of duty, personnel turnover is a big problem. Captain Crawley, our last personnel manager, left for home yesterday; but he left you a good crew, so I'll expect good work.

Blake: I'll give it my best.

Roberts: One last thing and I'll let you go. Your office generates quite a few reports and other papers that must go to the "head shed." I expect those papers to be in good order when they hit my desk. I can't let papers go to my boss with errors in them. Crawley never seemed to be able to find a decent typist, so make that your first order of business. My clerk doesn't have time to retype work coming from other offices.

On that note Captain Blake left. Upon arrival at the personnel management office he was greeted by his personnel sergeant, Master Sergeant Brown. Brown introduced him to the men and gave him the normal orientation on what was taking place. This orientation ended with the following conversation between Brown and Blake:

Blake: Who is our typist?

Brown: Right now we don't have one. We just use anyone who is available.

Blake: Colonel Roberts seems to think we need a typist. Do you think you can find one in the next few days?

Brown: No problem, I'll have one in a couple of days.

The next day, Sergeant Brown walked up to Blake's desk with Private Rogers, a tall, slender negro, and announced, "This is your typist, Captain. He will be present for duty in a couple of days. All new troops have to go through two days of Vietnam orientation training before going on the job." Blake welcomed Rogers aboard and chatted briefly before Rogers returned to the replacement training detachment.

The next day Sergeant Brown and five clerks (D'Angelo, Smith, Fenney, Rayes, and Jones) approached Blake's desk, and the following took place.

Brown: Captain, these gentlemen would like to talk to you.

Blake: Oh, what's up?

D'Angelo: It's about the new man.

Blake: You mean Rogers?

D'Angelo: That's right. We have a good group of guys here—we all work well together. In the past, we have been permitted to select the new clerks for this office, and we try to select guys who will fit in with the group. But Sergeant Brown didn't tell us that Rogers was for this office; he just asked us to find a good typist.

Brown: I didn't know that it made any difference where he was to work—a typist is a typist.

Fenney: It does make a difference. In addition to working as a team, everyone in this office also lives in the same building.

D'Angelo: That's right. Right now we have a good group, and that's the main reason we get the job done so well.

Blake: Are you saying that Rogers won't fit in?

D'Angelo: Right. He just won't fit in with this group.

Brown: You mean he isn't your color, don't you?

D'Angelo: No. That has nothing to do with it.

Blake: Don't you think we should at least give him a chance?

D'Angelo: Frankly, no. Vietnam isn't exactly the best place to be, and the guys should at least be happy with the people they live and work with. That's why Captain Crawley always let us select the new men.

Brown: This is nonsense. Why don't you just admit you are prejudiced?

D'Angelo: That's not true.

Blake: I hate to break up the discussion, but we are about to miss dinner. Let's go eat and talk about this again tomorrow.

At this point the men left, and the following conversation between Brown and Blake took place.

Brown: This guy D'Angelo is a pain in the a--. He conned Captain Crawley into that bit about the men selecting new clerks for this office. If he wasn't the best clerk in the office, I would have gotten him transferred a month ago. He heads our assignment team, and that is a big job. (The assignment team interviewed and assigned all new arrivals, which averaged about 75 men per day.)

Blake: Do you think he is prejudiced?

Brown: In this case I think he is, but I haven't noticed any discrimination in the way he assigns new replacements to other units.

Blake: What do you think of the men selecting new clerks for this office?

Brown: I have never seen it done that way before, and I don't really oppose the idea. But in this case with Rogers, I don't think we should back down—I'd just tell them that's the way the ball bounces. Oh well, we had better go eat. Tomorrow is going to be a rough day.

Blake: You're right. I guess we do have a problem, and I'm not sure what the answer is.

Discussion Question

What should Captain Blake do? Why?

PART II

The following day, Blake returned to work, still unsure as to what was taking place. He was concerned about the issue of prejudice, but the opinion of the men that Rogers wouldn't "fit in" was equally interesting. About midmorning, he decided to explore the situation. Blake called each man into his office individually and approached him as follows: "I would like to ask your assistance in a matter that concerns this office. You don't have to participate if you don't want to. But if you are willing, I would like you to take a piece of paper and jot down your response to a few questions. Don't put your name on the paper, and when you have finished, just drop it in the box beside my desk." All 18 clerks volunteered to participate, and each was asked to answer the following five questions. (1) Is Rogers married or single? (2) What is his favorite sport? (3) What is his major hobby? (4) If he is assigned to this office, would you be willing to teach him the essentials of his job? (5) Do you think he would fit in with the rest of the crew?

After the last man had been interviewed, Blake tabulated the results, and found the following responses to each question.

1. Married: 3; Single: 12; Don't know: 3.
2. Basketball: 5; Baseball: 8; Swimming: 3; Track: 2.
3. Don't know: 18.
4. Yes: 12; No: 0; Don't know the job well enough to teach him: 6.
5. Yes: 14; No: 2; Don't know: 2.

Blake then sent for Rogers' personnel records. The records reflected the following:

1. Marital status: Married.
2. Sports interest: Track.
3. Major hobby: Writing poetry.

Shortly before closing time, Blake assembled the entire crew and made the following announcement: "Rogers completes training today, and I find no reason to interfere with his assignment to this office. He is a good typist, and that we need. He is married, likes track, and his hobby is writing poetry. Like most of you, I also missed two out of three of those questions. I don't know if he will fit in or not, but I ask for your cooperation in giving him a chance. With respect to selecting future clerks, the policy established by Captain Crawley will continue as long as it works."

There was no immediate reaction to Blake's announcement. Rogers reported for work the next day, and as time passed, it became obvious that he had indeed fit in with the group. Four months later, D'Angelo was nearing the end of his year in Vietnam. As part of a cross-training effort, Rogers was assigned as his understudy and successor as head of the assignment team. On his final day in the division, D'Angelo dropped by Blake's desk to say farewell. His parting comment was: "Rogers will never be a poet, but he is a darned good personnel clerk!"

Discussion Question

Analyze Blake's handling of the problem and explain the outcome.

A Case of Wasting Assets

Stan Weinstein, a partner in Goldberg, Silverman, Weinstein, Kantor, and Company, Chartered Accountants,[1] was getting ready for a meeting with Paul Abrams. Stan was an extremely competent and amiable professional. He often looked like a professional athlete or a movie star when he was wearing his custom-tailored suits or driving around in his convertible. Recently though, Stan was looking far more harassed and troubled. In fact, he was planning to discuss some of his work problems with Paul Abrams, a CA (chartered accountant) who worked for him. Paul arrived, took one look at Stan, and said, "What the hell is wrong with you?" Stan replied by saying, "I'm absolutely fed up with how things are going here. Our work is way behind. I'm putting in a ridiculous amount of hours here and at home. I don't seem to be getting anywhere. It seems like the only things I ever hear are client complaints—and now my partners are starting to bug me too. Listen, we've done a lot of talking before. I know you're interested in a lot of the managerial and behavioral stuff. You've had good ideas before. You know the guys, and you know the grapevine. I'd like your opinion—what do you think I should do?" Paul said, "Whoa, give me the weekend to think about it." Stan said, "OK, let's have lunch on Monday."

THE FIRM

Goldberg, Silverman, Weinstein, Kantor, and Company, a medium-sized accounting firm, was located on part of the 9th and the entire 10th floor of a large urban building in Ottawa, Ontario, and handled accounts for some 1,000 clients. The company was formed when two smaller firms, Goldberg, Silverman, and Company and Weinstein,

[1] Goldberg, Silverman, Weinstein, Kantor, and Company was a firm that audited the financial statements of its clients. The firm also offered its clients consulting services in the areas of personal and corporate taxation, data processing, systems design, executive search, and general business and financial decision making.

Kantor, and Company, merged in 1965. Goldberg, Silverman was not only the faster growing of the two companies, it was also the younger. Henry Silverman, the youngest of the four senior partners at age 45, was the prime mover, had the greatest influence, and was characterized by an insatiable desire to have the firm grow and become the very best in the business. In fact, when asked about his objectives he would reply, "We want to be as good as the best there is."

Jeff Goldberg and Barney Kantor were in their late 40s and mid-50s, respectively, and Saul Weinstein at age 67 was semiretired from the company. In addition to these 4, there were 11 other partners. Henry Silverman had nine partners who answered directly to him, Goldberg had one, and Saul Weinstein and Barney Kantor loosely supervised Stan Weinstein (Saul's nephew) and the division for which he was responsible.

Although the firm published no formal organization charts, the reporting relationships were approximately as depicted in Exhibits 1 and 2. In addition to the 15 partners, there were approximately 20 chartered accountants, 60 audit staff, and 15 general office staff. Except for the office staff, a great majority of the employees were male. All of the partners and most of the employees in the firm were Jewish. The only exception was the secretarial staff, which was primarily non-Jewish. Some of the partners were leaders in the Jewish community, and all had many contacts in the local business community.

All of the partners and some of the senior nonpartnered CAs were located on the 10th floor. Except for the room where the general secretaries were located, this floor was richly carpeted. The partners' offices were large and expensively decorated to suit the individual part-

EXHIBIT 1
Structure of the Firm

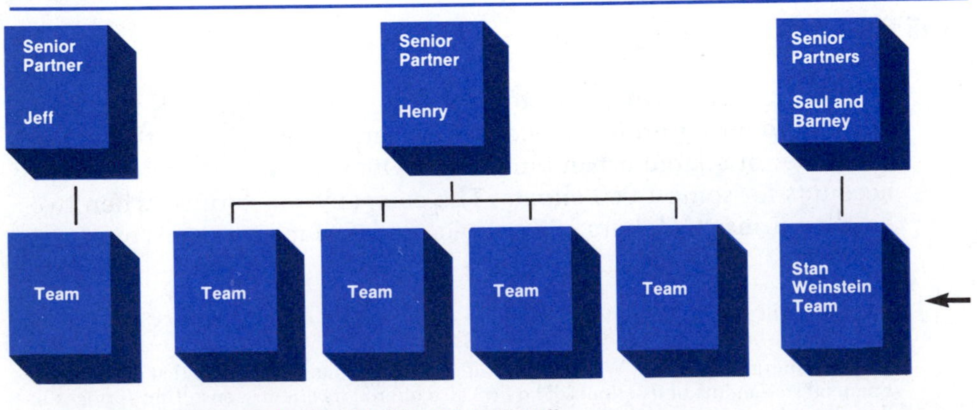

Note: Team is made up of partner(s), CAs, and audit staff.

EXHIBIT 2
Structure of Stan Weinstein's Team

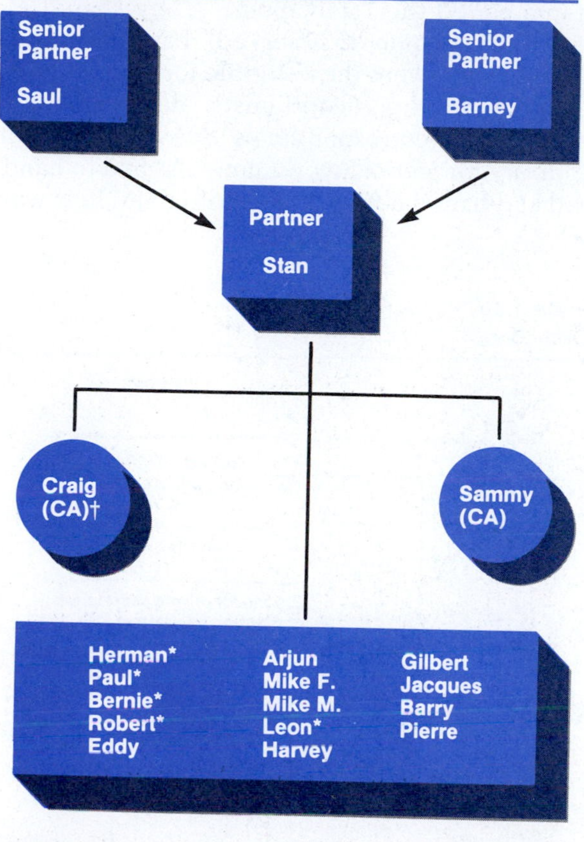

* Project leaders
† Chartered accountant

Project leaders supervised the work done by the staff at a client's office and insured that the two, three, or four people who were working on the job there were properly tieing their work together. The project leaders then reviewed the staff's work and passed it on to either Sammy or Craig. Sammy and Craig would review work submitted to them by the project leaders, pass it on to Stan, and then join Stan in the meetings with clients.

ner's taste. Senior but nonpartnered CAs and partners' private secretaries had inner offices with no windows. The secretaries responsible for typing financial statements and general reports all worked in one tiled room, a room which also housed the client files, supplies, photocopier, and the folding and stamping machine.

The ninth floor housed the less-senior CAs, audit staff, and one secretary who provided clerical services for all on that floor. While each CA occupied a carpeted office, the audit staff were located in one large room called the "staff room." They shared a common pool of desks on a "first come, first served" basis each morning. Only after they became a CA were they eligible for a private office, an individual message slot on the receptionist's desk, printed note pads, and binders for their correspondence. CAs had dictaphones and were given priority for clerical work; non-CAs had to handwrite material to be typed and had to obtain a CA's initial on their work before it could

EXHIBIT 3
Tenth Floor

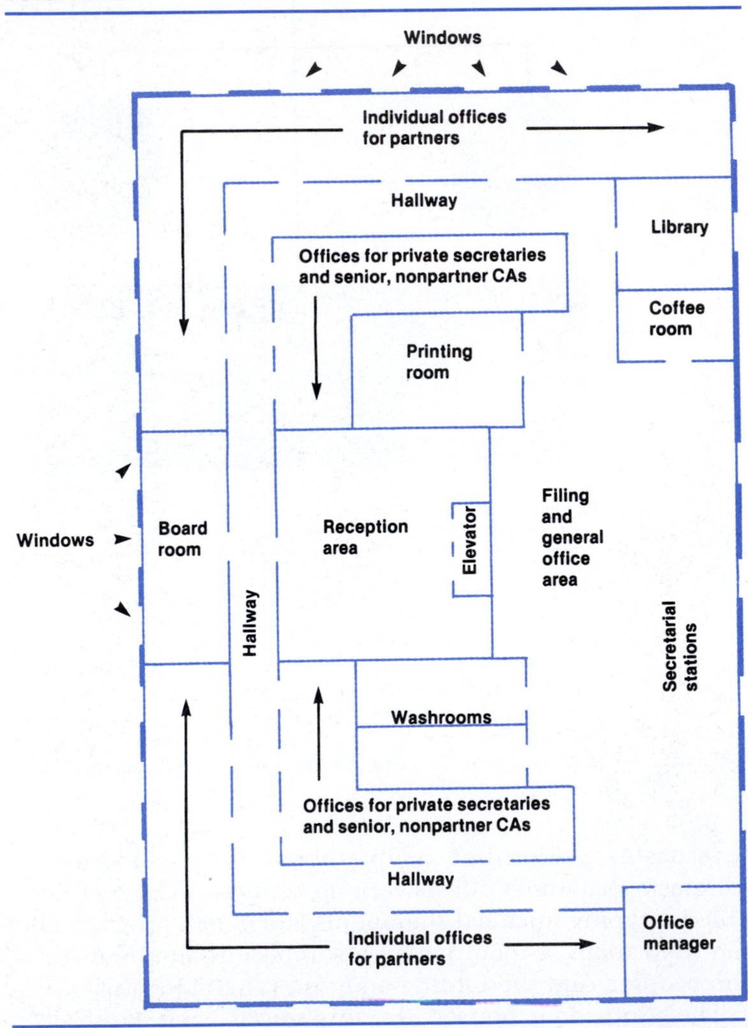

EXHIBIT 4
Ninth Floor

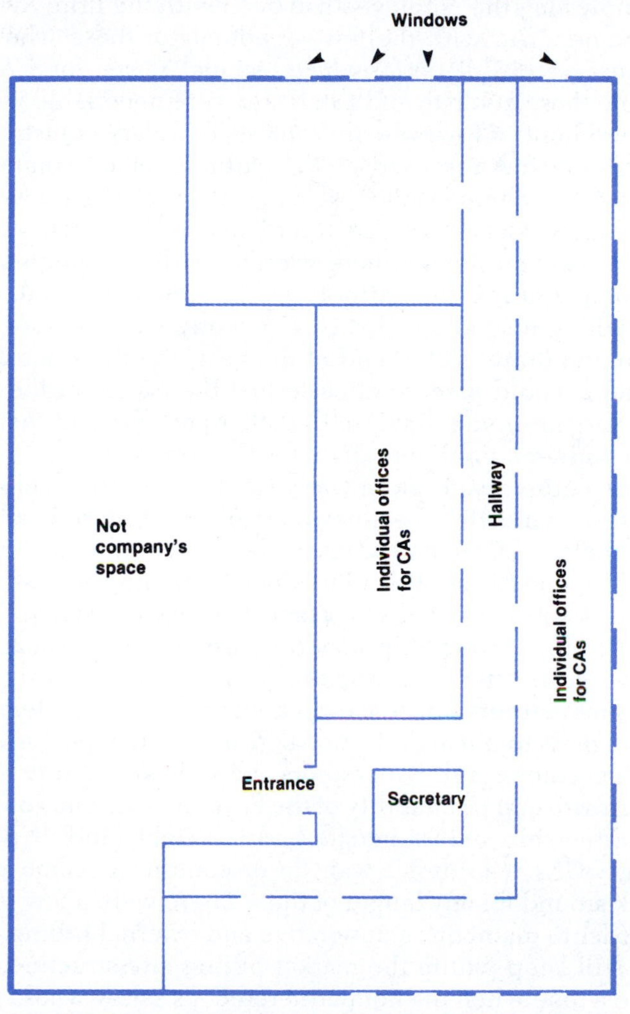

be typed and mailed out. The 9th floor staff had no access to the 10th floor secretarial pool, although 10th floor secretaries occasionally helped the 9th floor secretary in a crisis. Exhibits 3 and 4 show the layouts for the 10th and 9th floors, respectively.

The partners met once a month to discuss various administrative and policy issues. The partners, either together or in subcommittee, designed the compensation schemes and determined the amount of the annual raise that would be given to employees at each level in the organization. Audit staff received a flat, nonnegotiable annual raise of anywhere from $1,200 to $1,800. This could represent a salary increase of 10–20 percent, depending on the actual amount of the raise and how long the employee had been with the firm. All audit staff got the same raise, with the few exceptions of those who received less because of pitiful performance. Annual raises for CAs were about double those given to audit staff and were negotiable within narrowly defined limits. However, all requests for salary adjustments had to be referred to and approved by the partners' salary committee. The design of the compensation scheme made it fairly easy to calculate everyone's salary. Everyone (particularly CAs) was expected to work overtime, even though there wasn't any direct compensation for it.

Compensation for partners was as secretive and mysterious as everything else about them. Apparently each partner had his fixed minimum draw. At the end of the year, the three most active senior partners would meet to allocate first the excess of the annual profits over the minimum draws to the other partners and then to decide on each partner's minimum draw for the coming year.

The entire organization was geared toward the final reward of partnership. Typically, a person would join the firm right after completing a Bachelor of Commerce, majoring in accounting. The staff member would spend his/her first year or two in training and taking courses, all in preparation for the CA exam. CAs were usually considered for admission to partnership sometime around the age of 28, or about four or five years after receiving the professional CA designation. Candidates for partnership were evaluated on their competence, dedication, willingness to put organizational goals ahead of personal desires, ability to get along well with clients and staff, and ability to contribute to the growth and profitability of the firm. Also, no one could be admitted to partnership unless he/she had the right kind of personality and image. CAs who didn't want to or couldn't become partners rarely stuck around for any length of time. There were a few reasons for this. In order to maintain remunerative and external billing differentiation and still keep within the market billing rate structure, there quickly came a time when the nonpartnered CA's salary would virtually reach a ceiling. Also, such CAs were viewed as ones who couldn't "make it." They then had to deal with this and watch their juniors bypass them on the organizational status ladder.

STAN WEINSTEIN'S TEAM

Paul spent most of the weekend mulling over the team's problems, paying particular attention to the personalities involved and the uniqueness of the team. One that struck Paul immediately was that Stan had the largest team in the firm, in terms of audit staff. Overall,

Stan also had the least competent team in the firm. There were a couple of reasons for this. One was that Stan was hurt by employee turnover a few times and had to hire some replacements when competent people were very hard to find. Stan's philosophy was to replace someone who had just left the firm with the most junior person possible while at the same time giving those who remained more responsibility. Stan was the partner in the firm most willing to invest in the training of a totally inexperienced person. This and the fact that Stan seemed to be a low-power partner on the low-power side of the firm virtually guaranteed Stan's not getting the cream of the new college recruits.

Stan, in trying to manage his practice, service his existing clients, and develop new ones, was under tremendous pressure—but he always maintained his smooth and affable manner. He still found time to invite the whole team up to his house for a barbecue and to organize a racquetball tournament and party at his club for the people on his team. Stan was one of the best "raggers" in the tournament and bugged everyone that he, "the old man," was able to finish second. He also played on the firm's intramural and league hockey teams. During the intramural hockey games, Stan was always on the alert because Paul and Bernie, two of his team members, were forever out to catch him with solid bodychecks. Yet all of Stan's fraternizing was done after long days at the office. He would, however, occasionally legitimize Friday afternoon or Saturday morning goofing off with a smirk or comment.

Sammy, Stan's right-hand man, was a very competent professional. In terms of style, though, Stan and Sammy were like night and day. Sammy was on the short side, was slightly pudgy, had short curly hair and a boyish face. Sammy was a complete workaholic, putting in even more time than did Stan. Whereas Stan rarely looked ruffled when he was working hard, Sammy seemed like he was in a constant state of overdrive. Few could read faster, absorb information faster, write faster, or work calculators faster than Sammy; and few could be more picayune when it came to reviewing work done by audit staff. He very badly wanted to be a partner and thought he could attain that status through hard work. Sammy asked his "boys" to work overtime much more than Stan did and often even when the need for it wasn't as urgent as he made it out to be. Sammy didn't come down to the ninth floor as much as Stan did, nor did he lunch with the guys as frequently. One incident that Paul never forgot involved Sammy and Paul lunching together with Sammy returning to the office before Paul had even finished eating. Paul always thought that this incident symbolized Sammy's hardworking, abrasive style.

Craig was another personality altogether. He used to be a partner in the firm of Weinstein, Kantor, and Company, but he didn't maintain that status after the merger. In fact, there was a short time when Henry Silverman was a junior in the firm of Weinstein, Kantor, and Company, reporting to Craig. Craig was moody and finicky. He hated working under pressure, and no one ever knew when his temper would get the better of him. That was one reason why no one really wanted to deal with him. Craig was an old-fashioned auditor—one very different than the new breed. For example, Craig always preferred checking everything in detail to using educated forms of sampling. This was another reason why few wanted to work with him. Craig also serviced a clientele whose owners and managers often had personalities similar to his. That was yet another reason why Craig was everyone's least favorite supervisor. Herman and Craig always worked together. Herman, who had about as much personality as a doorknob, and Craig were seen as "really deserving each other."

Bernie and Paul were probably the two most popular guys on the team. Because Bernie respected few of Stan's partners and their aggressive business attitudes, he doubted whether he even wanted to become a partner in the firm. Even though Bernie liked his teammates, he was becoming increasingly unhappy about being a Catholic French–Canadian in an English-speaking Jewish company. Like Bernie, Paul and Robert were not thrilled about being under as much pressure as they were. Robert and Paul weren't even sure they still wanted to be accountants. Robert didn't really enjoy accounting, but he wasn't clear on what his career interests were. Paul was becoming more and more interested in the behavioral sciences and was, in fact, trying to establish himself as the firm's expert in that area.

Almost everyone else on the team had become a part of a very close-knit group. Those who were working at the same client's office or in the home office always ate lunch together. In fact, 15-minute lunch-planning meetings became a part of the morning ritual. All took part in girl-watching expeditions whenever possible, and some of the married guys socialized after working hours. Lunchtime and even some regular work hours were spent sharing stories about other clients and bitching about how overworked and underpaid everyone was. Yet, with all the bitching, not one member of Stan's team would have accepted a transfer to any other team in the firm. Team members saw Stan as being the nicest and most considerate partner in the firm, having the best and most fun-loving guys in the firm.

Work on Stan's team had been backlogged for a long time. There was the problem of inexperienced staff, but Paul did not think that was all of it. Paul thought that Stan's clientele was very different from other teams' clientele. Although Stan's team serviced the most clients in the firm, it ranked second in total billings. Most of the clients on Stan's team tended to be clients of long standing—ones who had been associated with Saul Weinstein or Barney Kantor for many, many years. These client firms tended to be smaller in size than those serviced by other teams. Smaller clients were less able to hire skilled and educated managers. Consequently, they became fairly dependent on their auditors for the expertise lacking within their organizations. Craig, Sammy, and Stan especially were constantly overloaded with clients' phone calls, many of which probably could have been handled by less senior people. Because of the nature of Stan's clients, the expectations they came to have for good cheap service, his staff, and his own "nice guy" style, Stan was rarely able to charge a client for all the time actually spent on his particular account. As a result, Stan's team had the highest labor/billings ratio in the firm. Paul suspected that the other partners were beginning to get on Stan's back about this.

Sammy handled most of the job scheduling and considered project leaders' requests for staff when allocating team members to jobs. Sammy prepared the following week's schedule every Friday afternoon, frequently involving Stan in the process. However, Sammy or Stan would often change the schedule during the week after hearing from a client who was either in a crisis or just generally irate about the poor service he was getting. Sometimes Stan and Sammy were unaware of changes the other had made. Once the project leaders (Herman, Bernie, Paul, Robert, Leon) were assigned to a job and were going to have considerable autonomy on the job, they began to compete with each other for staff time and for the most competent staff. This competition sometimes resulted in guys being juggled from one client to the next before a job was finished—all in response to the most pressing crisis. Everyone bitched like hell about the juggling. No one liked the time pressure; no one liked losing control over their finished product; no one liked compromising the quality of their work because of the time pressure; and no one, especially Stan, liked the fact that due to inefficiencies the client couldn't be billed for all the time spent.

The most junior guys on the team were really pissed off. They were continually assigned the bulk of the most routine and tedious tasks, and they often complained about the lack of challenge in their work. The juniors wanted to learn and advance, but project leaders were too pressured to afford the time to train them. The juniors were the biggest victims of the client-to-client shuttle, but no one involved appreciated it.

Paul knew Stan's clients were dissatisfied, because he heard cracks about the expensive auditors who gave lousy and untimely service in every office he entered. He also knew clients resented being handled by different CAs and project leaders every year (a violation of the firm's policy); they feared they wouldn't be serviced by the ones having adequate familiarity with their business.

Paul sensed things were coming to a head. Stan seemed more ha-

EXHIBIT 5
Stan Weinstein's Team

Employee	*Position*	*Years with Firm*	*Age*	*Education*	*Current Skill Rating*	*Potential Skill Rating*
Stan Weinstein	Partner	17	34	CA 1963	1	1
Sammy Kraft	CA	9	29	B. Comm., CA 1968	2	1
Craig Gordon	CA	20	47	CA 1958	3	3
Bernie Arsenault	CA	5	26	B. Comm., CA 1972	4	2
Herman Green	CA	5	26	B. Comm., CA 1974	5	4
Paul Abrams*	CA	4	24	B. Comm., CA 1973	4	1
Robert Altman	Staff	5	25	B. Comm.	5	2
Eddy Rosen	Staff	2	25	B. Comm.	5	2
Harvey Stein	Staff	0	22	B. Comm.	10	4
Arjun Jain	Staff	1/2	39	B. Comm.	8	6
Barry Blanshay	Staff	2	27	B. Comm.	7	5
Mike Fried	Staff	0	22	B. Comm.	9	2
Gilbert Tremblay	Staff	0	22	B. Comm.	10	4
Jacques Levy	Staff	0	25	B. Comm.	10	5
Pierre Kahill	Staff	1	25	B. Comm.	7	5
Leon Moses	Staff	6	27	B. Comm. in progress	5	2
Mike Moses	Staff	0	22	B. Comm.	9	2

* Paul was the source of all data for this case; the rating figures represent his personal judgment. 1 is the highest skill rating, 10 the lowest.

rassed than ever before, and clients seemed more dissatisfied than ever before. The guys' tolerance for pressure was at an all-time low and was exaggerated by annual raises that, in their opinion, didn't bring their salaries up to the going market rate. Paul knew Stan was in a real stew, and he wanted to come up with something good to suggest to him. He knew also that his own future was partly dependent on the effectiveness of Stan's team. (See Exhibit 5.)

▶ Chris Cunningham

Elizabeth Stover was the president of Stover Industries, an amalgamation of several small companies in the electrical parts industry. She and her husband had inherited one of the group of companies from her father-in-law. Mrs. Stover, an engineer, elected to run the company while her husband pursued a separate career as a dental sur-

This case was prepared by Professor Todd Jick as an adaptation of an old case titled "Gregory Pellham." The author of that case is unknown.

geon. In addition to the original inheritance, Mrs. Stover had purchased three other companies to make the present Stover Industries. Mrs. Stover was only 31 years old. She was a dynamic individual, full of ideas and drive. In the space of a year she had welded Stover Industries into a profitable organization known for its aggressiveness.

Mrs. Stover integrated the four companies into a unified organization by welding the individual managements into one unit. Some individuals were let go in each organization as it was purchased and became part of Stover Industries. In several other instances, executives of the newly purchased companies resigned because of difficulties in working for such a young and driving boss. The four plants continued as individual manufacturing units of the company and together employed approximately 475 production workers. Some problems arose in integrating the individual sales staffs since the original companies had been competing with each other. Consequently, the salesmen had overlapping territories. This was gradually being worked out; but the salespeople were permitted to keep their own old customers, making it next to impossible to assign exclusive territories to each salesperson.

The sales staff included 17 men and the sales director. The sales director had been with the original Stover Company as sales manager. He knew Elizabeth Stover well and was able to work as her complacent subordinate. Most of his time and energy was devoted to routine direction and coordination of the sales team. Although a trusted lieutenant of Mrs. Stover, the sales director was not much more than titular head of the sales force. Mrs. Stover provided the active leadership.

Mrs. Stover had personally hired Chris Cunningham, a college classmate, as a salesperson for the organization. Chris shared some of Mrs. Stover's drive and enthusiasm and, in a short time, had justified Mrs. Stover's choice with a sensational sales record. In terms of sales performance, Chris Cunningham's record left little to be desired.

Yet Chris represented a thorny problem to Mrs. Stover. The problem, as outlined by Mrs. Stover, appeared to her to shape up in the following fashion:

> I hired Chris because we knew and admired each other in our college days. Chris was always a leader on campus, and we had worked well together in campus affairs. Chris was just the kind of person I wanted in this organization—a lot of drive and originality combined with tremendous loyalty. The way I operate, I need a loyal organization of people who will pitch right in on the projects we develop.
>
> Chris has already been proven a top-notch performer and will probably be our best salesperson in a year or two. Could one ask for anything better than that?
>
> Here is where the rub comes in. Chris is the sort of person who has

absolutely no respect for organization. A hot order will come in, for example, and Chris will go straight to the plant with it and raise hell until that order is delivered. It doesn't make any difference that our production schedule has been knocked to pieces. The order is out, and Chris has a satisfied customer. Of course, that sort of thing gets repeat business and does show well on Chris's sales record. But it has made running our plants a constant headache. It is not only the production people who have felt the impact of Cunningham on the operations. Chris gets mixed up with our engineering department on new designs and has even made the purchasing department furious by needling them to hurry supplies on special orders.

You can just imagine how the rest of the organization feels about all this. The other salespeople are pretty upset that their orders get pushed aside—and are probably a bit jealous too. The production people, the engineers, the purchasing agent, and most of the rest of the staff have constantly complained to me about how Chris gets in their hair. On a personal level, the staff say they like Chris a lot but that they just cannot work with such a troublemaker in the organization.

I have talked with Chris many times about this. I have tried raising hell over the issue, pleading for change, and patient and rational discussion. For maybe a week after one of these sessions, Chris seems like a reformed character, everyone relaxes a bit, and then bang—off we go again in the same old pattern.

I suppose that in many ways Chris is just like me—I must admit I would probably be inclined to act in much the same way. You see, I have a lot of sympathy for Chris's point of view.

I think you can see now what my problem is. Should I fire Chris and lose a star salesperson? That does not make too much sense. In fact, Chris is probably the person who should be our sales director, if not immediately at least in a few years. But without the ability to get along with the organization, to understand the meaning of "channels" and "procedures," Chris is not only a valuable and talented addition to the company, but a liability as well. Should I take a chance on things eventually working out and Chris getting educated to the organization? Should I put on a lot of pressure and force a change? What would that do to Chris's enthusiasm and sales record? If I just let things go, then, there is a real danger to my organization. My executives will think I have given Chris the green light, and they will transfer their antagonism to me. I certainly cannot afford that.

Chris Hammond (A)

She is 26, single, and grew up in Hibbing, Minnesota, "the kind of town where if you dated a boy in high school more than twice you were expected to marry him." A senior market support specialist for a major electronics corporation that has seen tremendous growth in the past 10 years, she currently works in the firm's new office headquarters in southern Vermont and travels frequently. Ultimately she would like to be president of her own company. Right now she is enthused about her present position, the talent of her co-workers, and the matrix organization of the corporation for which she works.

My family has been involved in the mining steel industry back to the 1890s. This heritage of big business is almost second nature to me.

When I look back on it, my dad's career path was very similar to mine, which means that I'm very similar to him, which means that talking about him reveals a lot about myself. He is my role model for how to behave in the business world. My mother is also a role model that I downplay and make fun of, so that some people give me a hard time about not liking my mother. That's not true, but my mother lives vicariously, and I don't. Until last year we were not able to communicate as adults, and she assumed that I was still going through a phase. This year she is beginning to believe in herself as a person and is also treating me like one.

My father is an engineer, and so my brothers and I had a more technical childhood than the average child. I remember a number of things from my early childhood, which may sound unusual but really isn't because I've always been cognizant of my environment and the people in it. Right before my fifth birthday we moved into a huge house. My mother painted and carpeted what I considered to be beautiful wooden floors. Ugh! I was so stubborn that I said, "You aren't going to do anything to my bedroom floor!" She said, "Well then, you'll just have to do it yourself." So I did. I sanded and stained the bedroom floor, at age five! With some help, of course!

What stands out in my childhood? I learned to play the piano before I could read. At age nine I read the story of Helen Keller, which became a source of inspiration for me. That same year my goal was to go eventually to Radcliffe College. I knew Hibbing wasn't the place for me.

This case was prepared by Deborah Downs and Pamela Fuhrer under the direction of Professor Allan R. Cohen for the purpose of classroom discussion. Special thanks is given to Anne Jamar for her assistance.

My two loves in life from age nine on were music and science, especially physics. The physics probably came from reading about Madame Curie—I always enjoyed stories about successful women, and I envisioned myself growing up to be one. I never dreamed of being a mother or being married. I thought playing house was dumb, so I played football and sensible things like that instead (laugh).

Externally I'm a very jovial person, but internally I'm exceedingly serious, which probably explains why I've acquired the story-telling ability I have and why I do some rather cavalier things. When I was young, I was always kidded about my precocious ideas. It was very painful not to be taken seriously. The reason I giggle a lot today is because I used to cry then.

My dad taught us three things to live by, which I do live by today: first, that you had better like what you see in the mirror when you get up in the morning because you're the only person that has to live with yourself all of your life; second, that one should be honest with oneself and with others; and third, that no one is any better than I am, and I'm no better than anyone else in this world. This last one is what I attribute my success in the business world to. In the microcosm of Hibbing it would have been very easy for me to say that I was the best at most everything. But for me it's not that challenging to be a big fish in a small sea.

My mother always told me I was a fat, ugly slob and a stupid klutz, and she pestered me about why I wore ugly clothes and why I didn't date the president of the senior class. I always felt I was a failure to my mother, and to this day I feel that way when I'm around her. My mother's influence was so strong that I always felt that I was hurting her, that I was a failure as her daughter. And when my dad would reinforce that, I always felt like I was really a failure as a human being because my social life was not too great. It's interesting to me that my mother had such a powerful effect on me regarding these things, since they are so important to her but do not really matter much to me.

I graduated from college with a B.A. in math and a low GPA—2.8—after having several majors including piano performance and elementary education. I was very active in school, including student/faculty affairs, racial conflicts, and participation on several committees to improve the teaching of mathematics and social sciences to young people and future teachers. I was also a dorm advisor. In general I had a pretty standard college life, especially considering that I attended college in an era when nearly everyone was going around blowing their brains out on drugs. The incredible thing was that the only two people in the whole wide world who told me that I was a lousy, screwed-up, crazy, hippy freak who was totally unsuccessful and a total disaster were my parents; so at the ripe old age of 19 I said, who needs them? Everyone else in the world has given me fairly positive feedback about my being a nice person, fun to be with, fairly decent looking, pretty smart . . . and I've never really lacked for friends. In fact, I tend to have too many and am often accused of being negligent of them.

One thing I've never had is what I call the "victim mentality." I just assume that no one is going to do anything bad to me, and it usually seems to work out well. People tend to fulfill the dreams that you have for them, to live up to your expectations. If I manipulate people at all, it's along these lines. For example, I'll say to my boss, "You're really terrific . . . you know how to handle women, which is extraordinary. I've worked for seven years, and I've never had a boss who could do that." So he really tried to live up to that expectation. You want him to treat you like a person and not like a sex object or a woman or anybody special. This allows me to say to a manager, "You are really screwing up, I don't like it," and not be afraid of what that's going to do to me. Once a vice president at one company I worked for asked me what I thought was the major problem between the field and headquarters. "You guys are always having meetings," I replied. "Don't you ever even go to the bathroom so you could get your messages? Why don't you put a telephone in the bathroom?" What I was actually saying, of course, was that headquarters was not responsive to the field. Since one of the major requisites in the job is responding to all phone calls in a reasonable amount of time, we were really failing at one of the key dictums. Well, he laughed and jokingly brought the comment to the business management committee. Being able to criticize through humor has served me well, and several people have commented on my ability to make pointed but funny witty remarks.

Why did I choose the minicomputer industry? Because frankly that's where the action is. Minicomputers can do so much for the world. And the future of the industry meshes perfectly with my goals. I want to change the world of education, and it's going to take computers to do it. Audiovisual technology is passé. Someday everyone will have in their home a computer that is going to be tied into their television sets, and they'll be able to get any information they want and are legally authorized to have access to. My role will be to make sure it's good information. I want to do for computers in education what "Sesame Street" has done for television in education.

Computex has a charisma all its own. You have to be a special type to work here. If you need to be told what to do, you leave the company. People don't get fired; they just leave because they can't stand not being told what to do. You can virtually make your own world. It's a company filled with prima donnas and entrepreneurs. You have the opportunity to do your own thing. For example, I decided I wanted to learn more about marketing to government. I could have traveled to any government in North America, but I chose Washington, D.C., instead. Even though it wasn't in my territory, I figured that I couldn't obtain the big picture without it. I presented my ideas to my manager and he said, "Sure, go try it." After my first visit I found five or six projects developed by agencies who are based in Washington. By servicing these agencies, I built up a rapport that now gives me valuable leads. Now I go down on a weekly basis, and it is accepted as part of my job description. I also decided I needed to know COBOL to do my job better. I could register for either a college or an internal course on COBOL, and Computex would pay for it. Every month I write down my goals—people choose what they feel it takes to do their job as defined by them. If they don't determine their goals, they will have nothing to do. The result of this process for me is that I'm buying myself authority by making myself more and more knowledgeable.

Personally, I won't be happy until I'm president of my own company. I truly believe that. I established this goal for myself in college, and what I'm doing now is getting experience. First in finance, then in sales, and now in marketing.

To be successful in business, you have to learn how a company really operates. In my first job out of college, I was so incredibly naive. I had no political awareness, I wasn't cognizant of chauvinism, and I was cocky. I even had a Mickey Mouse hat, ears and all, that I wore when I felt that the work they were giving me was of that level!

When I came to Computex as a sales trainee, I knew what I needed to know and I set up a program to learn it. It's like having an outline for a research paper. The hard part is creating the outline, setting the goal. The easy part is filling in the body between the headings. For example, I knew nothing about computers, sales, marketing, and Computex's organization. I decided to learn how to learn about these things by setting up meetings with the 10 managers in the group and by asking what projects needed to be done that could be done by a trainee but were not being done now because of lack of personnel. The 10 managers each mentioned about a dozen projects. Seven were listed by everyone, and accomplishing those seven would give me experience in sales and marketing situations, answer my questions about computers, and force me to learn Computex' organization by using it to accomplish my objectives. I wrote up the project plan and presented it to my three supervisors; they approved it, and off I went. After completing the projects, I had in fact learned a great deal about the four aspects of the business that I felt I needed to know in order to sell their products successfully. Some people never have any goals and never set forth a program for themselves to follow. Goals can change, by the way, but that's irrelevant. It is important to have goals and a program to achieve them. I do.

I also make decisions. I'm beginning to realize that what made me a leader as a kid was that I made decisions. Most people won't make a decision if they have any way of not making it. If I'm willing to take the heat and think I've done the right thing, my experience is that I'm generally in a good position. So if I decide something, I do so with a series of contingency plans that insure it's going to work out alright. Also I have no problem falling flat on my face and saying, "Hey, that was stupid," and standing up and trying again. I don't expect myself to succeed the first time I try everything, or even the second. I have a longer list of failures than I have successes, but it doesn't matter. If you're doing nothing, then you can't make mistakes. At Computex, the culture is such that you're permitted to fail once at everything you try. You fail once, and the next time you succeed; and then the failure is wiped out completely in everyone's mind. In a fast-growing organization, it's necessary to give people the freedom to make decisions and to try and to learn.

When I was a sales trainee, I knew that if I didn't make the Computex Sales Award, my career at Computex would be ended. Although they wouldn't fire me, I would just be a sales rep, twiddling my thumbs for however long I stayed. You have to make your numbers or nothing happens to you. So there I was, with a manager who had 20 items that he needed to make to achieve his budget by the end of the quarter, and who was trying to make sure that I didn't make the Computex Sales Award. Sales trainees aren't supposed to make the sales award; and if I did, then he should have promoted me to a sales representative. So I asked his secretary what budget numbers he needed. I wasn't being devious; I was really trying to support him. I wanted him to succeed because that was the only way I could succeed. But I had to do it with a power play because he wouldn't treat me seriously.

So I read the numbers and said to myself, "OK, he can't make it in these six areas." As it so happened, I had an account that was going to make the numbers in four of those areas. Then I called up every single lead that we had received in the office over the last four months and on which no one had returned calls, identified the ones that were going to close in a month, and found 15 accounts.

As a sales trainee, that wasn't what I was paid to do; I was paid to learn. But I was tired of being a sales trainee; I was determined to be a sales rep and sell and make the Computex Sales Award—and be the only sales trainee to do it that year.

Another dimension entered into the situation. My manager had a fair-haired boy, a sales rep and the only individual whom he had personally hired; he wanted him to make the sales award. Since I was leaving on July 1, *if* I made the sales award, to take a job at corporate headquarters, my manager reasoned that I should give 50 percent of anything I booked to the sales rep. The motives behind this request were pretty transparent to me. So I told my manager that I didn't think that was fair unless he was willing to give me 50 percent of all the sales rep's bookings, since I had done a considerable amount of work and could document it on two banking orders he had. In effect, however, I was being asked to give the rep a split so that he would make the sales award, and I was getting nothing for it. That was a key link in my strategy, since exposing my manager would not be advantageous for either the manager or the sales rep.

So I went to the district manager and asked whether I would make the sales award if I closed such and such accounts. He said yes. So I said that was not what my manager told me, that he had told me I would have to give 50 percent to the sales representative. The district manager asked why, and when I answered, he looked at me in total disbelief. I explained that I didn't think it was fair that the sales rep should make the award on behalf of my efforts, and if that was the case, the company would not get any of the business I had found. I would leave the company today, take my vacation pay and go. The district manager said to go back and talk to my manager. What none of them knew was that I had already pulled this off, that the bookings were in my drawer and this was not idle conversation. I could make good on any deal I worked with them, and I knew what they needed to make their numbers to look good to their bosses.

So I went in to my manager. There were two weeks left in the quarter, and he was scared now because he wasn't going to make his numbers. I said to him, "I have a problem. I really want to go back to headquarters, and I need your help. I need to make the sales award. You know that, and I know that. I can't go back to corporate as a turkey who hasn't succeeded in making the sales award. I believe I've put forth the sales effort required to do that. I also believe I should go back as a sales rep. I believe I've earned that. Now I think I can make the following budget numbers for you, and I can bring in these two accounts. All that I need from you is the assurance that I will receive the Computex Sales Award if I do it. Otherwise I'm not going to work another day."

He looked at me and finally said, "If you get those orders in, you can make the sales award; and yes, if you bring in that business, then you're more than qualified to be a sales rep." What he was banking on was that I didn't have the orders. I walked into his office with them two days later.

What motivated me for the most part was realizing that they were not taking me seriously and not paying attention to what I was doing, to how many accounts in which I was involved that were closed as a result of my efforts. I also wanted them to know that I was fully aware of their attempt to use me. That kind of approach is a very strong power play and a high-risk strategy, but if you succeed, you are given much more respect and higher levels of managerial credibility.

That's one of the reasons why I don't feel that this kind of power play is self-centered or opportunistic. As an individual you have a choice. You can take what the corporation dishes out to you, or you can choose to modify your own career path within a certain amount of reasonableness. I don't mean that you can walk up to a corporation, your first day on the job, and say "I'm going to be president of this company tomorrow." They'll probably send you to the loony bin. But as long as it's reasonable and you are performing in accordance with or better than the expectations, I think you can succeed and get what you want.

If you don't take risks, I would say that you're not going to go nearly as far as the person who does. For successful individuals, there's an expected behavior that they are risk takers. If someone doesn't have the guts to risk himself, do you really want him risking millions of dollars of the corporation's money?

Most women in management whom I've observed don't seem to have the career direction or goal orientation to say, "OK, if I'm not at such-and-such a point within this time period, I'll have to find out why and do something about it." Most men in management that I know do have a game plan. Several of my business friends, male and female, tell me that I have this kind of direction.

A uniqueness that I think I bring to my job is the ability to deliver constructive criticism to people in frank conversation, without having it come across as an interpersonal conflict. Another point is that I don't appear to any of my management as a female per se. After a short amount of time they forget that I'm a female and treat me as a person.

Concerning my social life, I don't have to strain for one. I had a secure relationship with Jeff for five years in Denver a while back, and I have ample opportunity to go for a drink after work or to blow off steam by playing tennis or racquetball or going sailing or skiing.

I don't make very many sacrifices, because I'm only pursuing what I want to do. However, there are some people who would say that I am giving things up. My mother would claim that I'm forfeiting a social life and a normal life with marriage and children. But I have a very active social life even though no one can get hold of me because of the extensive amount of traveling I do. They generally contact my secretary, and the result is that my calendar is usually full at least a month in advance. I take time for people who are important to me, and I am learning to take more time for myself. I run on my own timetable. For example, I've decided that I will have my first child when I'm 29. It's highly probable that by the time I'm 29 I will be married and pregnant and, of course, working.

I have had an extremely colorful life. I'll try almost anything once; I find all people interesting and enjoy talking to any kind of person. Generally I get a big kick out of life. My outside interests are wide-ranging, and there's hardly anything I'm not interested in. Certainly the love of my life is music . . . it can release all types of emotions. I've managed to maintain a childlike curiosity and honesty and integrity throughout. I can concentrate for 24, 36, 48 hours at a time without any sleep or food. I keep going until something is finished. If I get to the point where I feel I'm making a sacrifice, I'll just quit the task; but that rarely, if ever, happens. On those tests that measure your aptitude in different fields, I always scored high in several categories. The psychologists say that they rarely see a score like that.

From what I have seen in the business world, I have a fairly unique ability to contend with an extremely large amount of pressure. Except when the pressure has negative overtones. I can't cope when people start backbiting or playing "cover your ass" games. The kind of emotional tension that occurs when people are losing their jobs and trying to befriend the ones who aren't really upsets me. I can't survive that; that's where being sensitive can demolish me. I can't put up a shield for those kinds of hassles. All of my good traits go away. I lose my sense of humor; and my interpersonal skills, which are my strongest asset, degenerate. I become autocratic and begin to manifest all those behaviors that are bad if you are male but can kill you if you're a woman. I'm aware of all this, so I have to spend about 40 percent of my time and energy under this kind of pressure making sure that I'm not displaying these behaviors. My credibility and my productivity drop. I tend to call people up and ask, "Why did you do such a horse's-ass job?" and then I have to call them back and apologize and smooth things over.

Men have a very strong belief that they are fair and that their decisions are objective. Only women know that they really aren't. It's a game that men appear to play among themselves, and they all support each other in this belief. Now women come along and shatter their belief on a daily basis, and that's not cool. So if a woman expects to be promoted by a man in a man's world, she has to establish an identity that allows men to measure her with their set of rules. So if you are competing for a promotion with men on a peer group level and none of them have an M.B.A but several have three years, five years, seven years more experience than you, your superiors aren't going to be able to find a reason to justify promoting you even if you're better. They can't do it because they can't explain it to all the other guys, who will all go rushing into their office, and they would be risking perhaps seven people quitting even if your promotion was the right thing to do. You as a female have to set the stage with your peer group, while you are in it, that this is what you want, these are the reasons that you want it, and this is what you're doing to get it. That washes out about 80 percent of them, as about 80 percent of them say, "Yes, I could really work for you," and the other 20 percent are either going to leave or they're the people who emerge as your real competition. The M.B.A degree gives an objective added value. It also shows a dedication to a career, that you're not planning to get married and have children and therefore abandon your work. You have to dispel this image constantly on a daily basis, and even then you never completely succeed in dispelling it.

Things that I'm unsure of in my life? I'm not sure I'm lovable. I'm not sure that I'm loved. I believe one has to give love to receive love, and I have no way to measure that. Love is a gift that other people give to you. You just never can tell. Are you familiar with the song from *Mr. Chips:* "Was I brave and strong and true; did I fill the world with love my whole life through?" This song says a lot about me.

Let me share a theory with you. I see the human being as five entities: an emotional self, a social self, an intellectual self, a physical self, and a spiritual self. My intellectual, spiritual, and physical selves are pretty solid. My emotional self will probably never be totally put together, because I can be jerked around emotionally very easily. If I have a major fault that may hold me back, that is probably it. I recall in my first job that I once came into the conference room filled with people with all my books and papers, slammed them down, and said to my boss, who was also the vice president and treasurer: "If you're so damn smart, why don't you do it yourself." Then I left without waiting for any response. Although I didn't get fired, I didn't get the job I wanted. They let me stay on payroll for three months but without any work to do. I was too stubborn to apologize, and they said I couldn't handle stress.

My social self is the least secure part of me because I don't have any social system. I'm like an infant in that area. I'm totally inept, but you have to know me really well to tell. Certain things get in the way of my developing a social system. I have a value system that says anything you do that is selfish is wrong. Being self-centered is wrong, as is being an opportunist. A lot of this can be traced back to my family life. We are a self-sufficient, self-contained, upstanding, do-it-yourself, all-American, pull-yourself-up-by-the-bootstraps, work-ethic, go-to-church-on-Sunday family. All this led me to feel that needing other people was wrong and showed that you were weak. I know this isn't true, but it's hard to erase all those childhood tapes. I'm going to have to change my value system to improve my social self.

The only real conflict that I and many other people at Computex have is that it's easy to become so involved in your work that you're married to it, so occasionally I'll come home from work and collapse and say to myself, "This is stupid, I'm going to die by the time I'm 30!" But I love my work. . . . It's not work to me; it's fun. As long as I'm aware of what I am doing and what is happening to me and as long as I am happy and having fun at whatever I do, then I know that life is

OK. Whatever happens, happens; and as my grandmother always says in times of trouble, "Everything works out for the best."

Chris Hammond (B)

Computex was a rare breed of company, Chris Hammond was still discovering after three years with the fast-growing, innovative computer firm. Perhaps its most striking characteristic was its matrix management organization, comprising traditional functional departments on the one hand and product lines on the other, which overlapped as circumstances required (see Exhibit 1). This organizational setup agreed with what Chris knew about matrix organizations from her general knowledge of the subject; and she considered the following to be the main features:

People have more than one boss.

Project responsibility becomes unclear.

Open and timely communication is a must, as is a high level of trust.

Good collaboration skills are required.

Tasks come and go—an urgent project today may be tabled indefinitely, so a high degree of flexibility is required.

Competition among teams and groups is more open than in traditional structures and is, in fact, encouraged.

It forces people to think in different ways, in at least *two* dimensions.

Problems occur no less frequently in matrix organizations than in other groups. Computex had only recently encountered problems because of a lack of proper communications and an imbalance between the functional groups and the product lines. For example, the manufacturing department, in an effort to maximize its production, could ignore information from the marketing department, and consequently the mix of the computer products they produced did not always reflect sales trends. This caused inventories to build to an all-time high, and the stock price of the firm plummeted until the president of Computex

This case was prepared by Deborah Downs and Pamela Fuhrer under the direction of Professor Allan R. Cohen as a basis for class discussion. Special thanks is given to Anne Jamar for her assistance.

EXHIBIT 1
Simple Representation of Matrix Organization

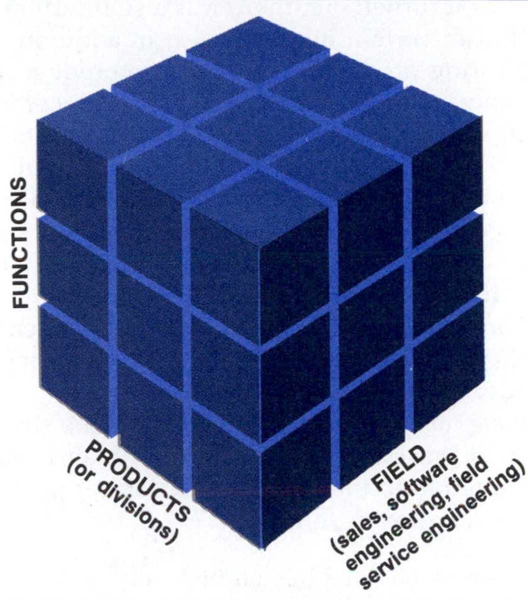

finally intervened. He called a halt to production in order to lower inventories, but the inventories kept building before ultimately dropping off. "He was standing on the bridge of a supertanker shouting '90-degree turn!' and expecting it to respond with the agility of a motorboat!" one outside analyst commented on the event.

A supertanker it was. In the previous year alone, sales had grown by more than 40 percent to nearly $1 billion. R&D expenditures increased by 40 percent over the preceding year to nearly $80 million, and earnings per share also increased handsomely. Nor was that year atypical.

To make this supertanker more manageable and to focus more closely on customer needs, Computex changed half of its matrix structure—the product lines—into four major market, or user, segments. The former product line structure, as its name implied, focused on marketing a specific product to all market segments. Product lines were responsible for the engineering, development, manufacturing, and support for these products. They "managed" the functional departments with respect to their products, and the functional departments were structured in accordance with the product focus. Over time, the product lines began marketing their products to very diverse market segments, each of which required specialized knowledge—for example, medical centers, governmental groups, or schools. Several of the product lines were therefore beginning to focus on a small number of market segments and were using a catch-as-catch-can philosophy for others. As it turned out, there was a significant amount of duplication of effort in certain marketplaces; in addition, several customers were requesting products from multiple product lines. At this point the decision was made to change from a product focus for the marketing organization to a market segment focus and to allow all products needed to service a market segment to be "sold" into that marketplace. Major market segments such as commercial, data communications, and government were organized.

In addition, the market directors were given more influence over the functional departments as a further means of insuring a balanced organization. One result of the change was that customers were now more likely to be called on by just one salesperson rather than the four or five under the previous product line focus.

If the company appeared to have solved the structural problems of the matrix, it was still having some problems with individual employee adaptation to the system. One former personnel manager described the situation as follows:

> My two bosses, one in a line position and the other a staff executive, didn't always share the same priorities. Consequently, I often got caught in the middle. In a matrix or quasi-matrix company like Computex, the pain is felt by the people lower down. . . . What you have—or had until the recent reorganization, which alleviated the problem somewhat—is 30,000 employees around the world, each trying to make his or her own decisions. And the reward system, which compensates people for doing their own thing, compounds the problem.

An outside behavioral consultant commented about Computex and matrix organizations:

> They demand maturity from employees. An immature employee will play one boss off against another. A mature employee will discuss disagreements openly with his boss and, if the boss remains intransigent, respond by acquiescing—but only under the condition that all bosses are apprised of the situation and of the employee's stand on the matter. . . . There are a lot of lost souls at Computex who don't know who their bosses are. The company's response to them has been "Go find out for yourself."

This same consultant had conducted several group sessions among the company's employees regarding norms within the firm. Time and time again, the same norms were revealed. These included:

Be compassionate.

Be a self-starter.

Deal directly with conflicts.

Be responsive.

Treat people informally.

Do your homework—give 120 percent.

Learn to swim fast.

Be yourself.

Be a team player.

Don't mismanage resources.

Don't cover your ass.

Don't listen to your boss if he's wrong.

Spend two years maximum in any one job.

Downplay status.

Work long hours.

This was the Computex that Chris Hammond joined three years ago as a sales trainee. Several things had attracted her to the firm: Sales were growing at such a phenomenal rate that job opportunities not usually found in average-growth firms were being created for those who aspired to them; the company had a reputation for caring about its employees; and it was in an industry that appealed to Chris personally. A math and physics type, she thought that learning about computers would be fun and challenging. Moreover, small computers, for which Computex was renowned, were in her opinion the key to improving education in this country, one of her long-range interests.

Chris progressed to full sales representative within two years at Computex and achieved the respected Computex Sales Award for making her quota. It was well known that this achievement was a prerequisite for continuing upward in the firm.

Her next position was that of marketing representative for government markets, and as such she was responsible for providing support services, developing marketing plans, generating new business opportunities, and arranging trade shows for business in the western half of North America.

As a marketing representative, Chris was brought in to work in Computex' new headquarters, an attractive, two-story, glass-and-concrete structure nestled in the New England woods. The interior was decorated in bright colors, and the offices were a maze of three-sided, shoulder-height module units spread around each floor. Offices had no doors. The only way to recognize a top executive was by the greater amount of floor space inside his module. Quite unlike other firms, where secretaries never occupy prime space, at Computex they were frequently situated so that they had a view of the exterior environment. A further example of the company's egalitarianism was the rule of thumb that transportation on the company helicopter went to employees on a first-come, first-served basis.

The upward job movement had not been as easy for Chris as it appeared on paper. Chris recalled problems because managers had not kept some of their verbal promises and because she had had to resort to power plays in order to extricate herself from situations where individuals were out for the interests of their own department.

Chris was a marketing representative for about 10 months when she began to be disgruntled with the amount of work she was required to do for what she considered a relatively low salary of $17,000. College graduates with no previous work experience were receiving starting salaries of $17,000 as sales trainees. However, before approaching her manager about the matter, she talked to a number of men (there weren't any women at her level or above in her area) to get advice on how to ask most effectively for a raise. She was well prepared when she entered her manager's office.

"You and I have a problem," she began, "which we've both got to solve or else you'll have a problem. And the decision you make will tell me something about us, our relationship, and Computex." She then listed her major accomplishments—assisting in closing one of the biggest pieces of business the company had ever obtained, a multimillion-dollar contract with the government; becoming the first sales trainee ever to receive the Sales Award; receiving three promotions in a little less than three years; and receiving outstanding performance appraisals on several occasions.

Next, she explained her discontent with her low salary. "Though I appreciate pats on the back and commendations for my work, those don't buy groceries. When they do, I'll let you know. I know how much I'm worth on the outside market, and how much other employees in similar jobs are being paid. I'm simply asking the company to put its money where its mouth is."

Reclining in his chair, her manager was pensive for a moment and then said, in an attempt at commiseration, "You're right, but there's really very little we can do right now, especially in view of the hiring freeze and management's limit on salary increases to 8 percent." Chris responded that there were several things he could do, some of them even under current constraints: one, give her 100 shares of stock; two, raise her salary by $5,000 to $22,000; three, give her 6-month rather than annual reviews so that she would receive three over an 18-month period; four, promote her to senior marketing representative; five, enumerate specific reasons why she shouldn't be considered for any of these.

"So that you won't have to worry about setting a precedent, I can give you the names of others at Computex for whom similar things have been done."

After a moment's silence, her boss remarked that she had certainly done her homework.

To emphasize her seriousness, Chris set a time limit. If she didn't receive at least one of the four items within the next three months, she would leave. One month later, the only point that she had not received was the first; she was given a raise, promise of more frequent reviews, and a promotion.

Chris's job changed with her promotion from market support ("answering the telephone" and "holding hands" with the sales force) to project management. She has recently spent most of her time on a special project in which Computex hopes to install minicomputers for use by local police departments. The system will have the capacity to cross-check files, to retrieve data on past criminal records—in short, to cross-reference almost anything in police records in much the same way that library files are cross-indexed. For example, less than 30 seconds will be required to check an auto registration through city, county, state, and federal files. Since a large percentage of crimes are committed by repeat offenders, the information obtained by cross-checking factors involved in crimes may be used to reach quicker solutions to cases and to insure a more consistent sentencing of criminals.

The project is a critical one for several reasons. The first is its size. Several million dollars are involved in this, compared with other sales, which averaged around $100,000. Second, ultimate responsibility for the success of the project lies with Chris. If it fails, she is accountable. Likewise, if it succeeds, she will get much of the credit and her career prospects may benefit accordingly. Third, the vice president of the division knows about the project and expects it to be completed successfully. This involvement of superiors places extra pressure on Chris to perform. Fourth, the project provides an opportunity for Computex to associate its name further with the idea of serving the public good. The public interest nature of the project makes it a potential source of pride for Chris personally and for the company as an organization. Last, if successful, the project will serve as a model for Computex to go out and seek large government contracts instead of sitting back and waiting for business to come to it. This interest in being more aggressive reflects a recent change in the corporation. The president himself has proclaimed a need for the firm to take more aggressive, planned approaches to growth. As Chris sees it:

> This job involves more planning, not a response mode. . . . If we succeed in winning this award, we are proving a prototype for how to go

after a big project. Private industry generally will not write specs like that; they generally don't have to do legal bidding like government contracts.

Early on a particular Friday morning midway into the project, Chris, dressed in a maroon knit suit with a cream-colored blouse, no makeup, scarf at her neck, and gold barrette to keep the hair out of her face, visited the computer terminal room, accompanied by the case-writers. There three software engineers, members of the project team, were ironing out final details for a demonstration (or benchmark, as it is called) in a few weeks, at which time the prospective client will be shown in detail the product and its capabilities. The three software engineers were responsible for preparing a prototype system that would be demonstrated to prove that Computex could indeed design the special systems required and could make them operational. These individuals were on loan, in a sense, to Chris for the duration of the project, although they were to return to Kansas shortly to work on other assignments. Jeffrey had been setting up a sample file to insure that the data could be retrieved accurately, quickly, and easily. Jo-Anne was programming the system in COBOL language, while Carol was testing the screening of data. Chris's expressed reasons for visiting the three in the terminal room were to show concern and to make it clear that she had worked just as hard and long as they had (they had worked until close to midnight the night before). "It's important— it's a motivator. It lets them know you're interested in what they're doing." Her parting words to the group were "See ya."

Chris's major responsibility, as she perceives it, is to put together the right group of people to get the job done. Her team includes 30 individuals in all, drawn from the functional departments (manufacturing, hardware engineering, and so on), the sales and software departments (the field organization), and several marketing groups (see Exhibit 2). However, in order to obtain the best talent for this particular project and to tap the corporation's resources, many of the individuals on the team come from outside the normal liaisons that the matrix structure allows—that is, a three-dimensional working relationship bound together by the appropriate marketing personnel. In addition, the geographical dispersion of the team members required that several very high-level managers had to buy into the support of the project in order to pull resources from one location to the project location.

Such a team makeup "really strained the matrix system," commented Chris, and forced her to invest a great deal of time and effort in developing personal relationships and in using the more familiar hierarchical protocols to obtain resources. "I have to go to the level at which the various branches converge and report to a higher-level manager. I have to get the top person's buy-in and then keep all levels informed of the project's progress."

EXHIBIT 2
Team Players*

Name	*Role*	*Level*	*Organization*	*Location*
John**	Software project coordinator	(4)	Field (software)	St. Louis
Al**	Benchmark expert	(4)	Marketing	Headquarters
JoAnne**	Software engineering expert	(4)	Functional	Headquarters
Tim**	Data center manager	(4)	Functional	Headquarters
Ted	Demo systems coordinator	(1)	Functional	Headquarters
Dick**	Product planning manager	(6)	Marketing	Headquarters
Tom**	Small-systems expert	(5)	Marketing	Headquarters
Carol	Software specialist	(2)	Field (software support services)	Florida
Jeff**	Software consultant	(4)	Field	California
Roger**	Account manager	(3)	Field (sales)	St. Louis
Henry**	Regional manager	(8)	Field (sales)	Chicago
Art	Software engineer	(5)	Functional	Headquarters
Walt	Sales manager	(5)	Field (sales)	Minneapolis
James**	Vice president	(10)	Marketing	Headquarters
Steve**	Marketing manager	(4)	Marketing	Headquarters
Harry**	Technician	(1)	Functional	Headquarters
Fred	Engineering expert	(3)	Functional	Headquarters
Jack	Branch manager	(3)	Field (maintenance)	Omaha
Ken	Supervisor	(2)	Field	Kansas City
Sam	Field service engineer	(1)	Field	Kansas City
Phil**	Corporate marketing	(6)	Functional	Headquarters
Chris**	Project manager	(3)	Marketing	Headquarters
Ed	Software expert	(3)	Field	New Jersey
Kevin**	Regional manager	(8)	Field	New Jersey

* Names and places are fictitious and are used to represent relationships and geographical dispersion.
** Critical team players.
Note: Levels denote a loose hierarchical structure.

Chris had arranged to take several members of the team to lunch on Friday, since they would be returning to Kansas shortly. Following lunch, she had scheduled a meeting to tie up loose ends and check on the status of team members' work. Although the meeting had been planned for 1:30, at 1:45 people were still filtering into the small conference room and seating themselves around a large oblong table with plump comfortable chairs.

John, the software project coordinator from St. Louis, arrived first and settled at one end of the table. Chris arrived, put a pile of papers on the table, and stood by a chair in the middle. "Where's the agenda?" asked John. "It's in my head, John. Would you like to run this meeting?" Silence. Al, a benchmark expert from headquarters whom Chris had previously described as super brilliant and having a short attention span, sauntered in saying, "What time is this meeting supposed to end?" When 6 of the 10 people expected had arrived, Chris opened the meeting amidst laughter and friendly banter. She introduced the casewriter as someone present to see that she did her job, then laughed and explained in a more serious vein. Reluctant to admit that the cases were in fact about her, Chris explained that the casewriter and she were working together on them and that the focus was matrix organization. The casewriter indicated that she would be taking notes. One or two people seemed a little surprised, but no one seemed at all bothered. Chris immediately proceeded with her "agenda." She turned to JoAnne, a software engineering expert seated on her left, and said: "How are you coming along?" As JoAnne reported on the status of her tasks, Chris listened intently and jotted notes on a yellow legal pad in front of her. Later she said to the casewriter:

> I'm a pretty effective team member, and now I'm trying to learn to be a team leader. One of the hard things for me in making the transition is that you can't be a team leader and have opinions. You can't switch those two roles in the same meeting; it doesn't work. Every time I did that I lost the credibility of the group, so what I did in subsequent meetings was to plant all of my ideas with one or two others and then pull those ideas back. That works extremely well.

One of the software specialists, sitting stiffly in her chair, rushed through her report as if she felt that any admission of difficulty would be an admission of inadequacy. Chris listened intently and probed, "What can we do to help you get the time to do this task?"—her efforts to remain patient beginning to show.

> I am very impatient with incompetence, and that's one of my faults that I try to shore up. . . . There were two individuals there who don't belong on the project and don't have the skills required to participate in the project, and in order for the project to succeed we have to work around them. One nice thing about the matrix organization is that you can have team members who are not particularly effective members of the team who can also not hurt the team. All you do is neutralize their ability to hurt the team, which is how we succeeded in overcoming this. By the way, it's not inherent incompetence for those two; they have absolutely no training, background, or information that's relevant—so they are extra baggage, so to speak. And we just do not have excess personnel to allow for two slack resources. Ultimately, we put those people in positions where they are doing very useful work, but if it never gets done, it doesn't matter, and if it does, then we've got fantastic documentation. All the critical tasks are being done by those people trained to do them. It took some finessing for that to occur.

At no time did Chris relax in her chair, though the others were all sitting back in various positions of comfort. Al leaned back so that his head rested against the blackboard behind him and put his hands behind his head. When Chris came to John, the tone of the meeting became a little strained. An unanticipated problem had cropped up, creating a need for John to insure that certain personnel would be at Computex the following Monday. John responded vaguely, suggesting that he would see what he could do but that he couldn't guarantee anything. Chris paused and said, "It's clear that we need to have this person here Monday to keep on schedule, John. What can you do?" In the silence that followed, John mumbled yes, he would call. Chris appeared to be exerting a great deal of self-control simply not to be visibly peeved, and she quietly repeated, "John, quite a few things hinge on his being here Monday." Chris's manager commented later on the overall situation:

> Today Chris walked a very thin line. Since marketing has no authority over sales, Chris has to convince the salesman that he will best meet his quota by selling this group. Her job is as a backup, a resource. At Computex the product line has no access to the customer without the salesman taking you in. John has a very parochial view about who controls the benchmark. He's from Kansas and thinks in terms of "my customer." As the software manager, his responsibility is to insure that all sales made are doable on the system being sold. So Chris has to tread extra finely. She must be acutely aware of his sensitivities. Without him feeling driven by her, she has to get him to do things. If he detects this, he won't cooperate.

Al, visibly bored with the meeting, left as soon as he had given his status report, having referred to several solutions offered by team members to current problems as "tacky, tacky." Chris encouraged his participation, however, as he was clearly adept at problem solving. Her style was very participatory, and leadership seemed to shift from John to Al and back again as both of them assumed the role of skeptics and behaved in a somewhat condescending manner. Chris kept the meeting on track with verbal reminders or questions, kept complete notes of what was said, and clearly appeared to be ticking off agenda items in her head.

At about 2:30, Chris's manager and the corporate contracts negotiator joined the team. A reference was made to another project team's poor communication, and Chris commented: "They make us look as if we have instantaneous communication around here." The other team members laughed, and tension subsided—though John quipped, "They must be really screwed up."

John mentioned that he had a plane to catch and had to leave by three. Chris continued around the table until she was satisfied that everyone was on schedule or had a strategy for getting back on schedule. She did not interrupt; she was more apt to listen until an individual had finished and then push: "What other problems do you have?

Where do you go from here? When would it be reasonable to get that information?" JoAnne also commented that she needed to leave as she had an appointment for an automotive repair, so the meeting ended.

> If you succeed in building a matrix team, then you become the manager of that group, and they look to you for the answers to questions and for direction; and if you don't provide it, then nothing occurs. So eventually you build up the ability to be autocratic because, first of all, they know that you're not going to ask them to do something unreasonable. You can say "I want you to do such and such by Friday," and the decision process goes very fast. The first day on this project was an eight-hour, totally draining, status meeting that I thought wouldn't take very long. Now it's down to half an hour. I say, "Is everything done?" They'll say yes. I say, "I want this and this and this on my desk tomorrow." "Well, those things aren't quite done." "OK, let's negotiate."

The casewriter remained after the meeting to talk with Chris's manager, who said:

> With Chris, you have not chosen the average. . . . She is exceptionally good at matrix management . . . adept at getting people to do things for her. She is very good with people . . . can pick out in a person what motivates them, and she can do this quickly. If you don't have interpersonal relationship skills here, you're not going to move at all. It's a self-driving thing. No one comes to you and says "Can I help you?"
>
> Because Chris is adept at interfacing with other parts of the matrix, she gets exposure at every part of the organization. So she can move in a number of directions; and this is encouraged at Computex. Anything holding her back? The only thing would be lack of experience. That's why I have stayed out of this project. This is something she'll be able to hang her hat on.
>
> Chris is also, however, very impatient and not willing to wait. She gets job offers a lot because she has so many contacts. She tends to poke around outside—not actively—but people tend to recognize her strengths. I encourage her to take advantage of the respect she has built up in this part of the organization because everyone sees her on a daily basis. Openings will occur here eventually. In the meanwhile, it's my job to get her exposure.

Chris pondered her future career plans. "One thing I have learned by this time is that, in a matrix organization, power and recognition flow to those who assume it." The next step, some 12 to 15 months off, is marketing manager, the beginning of top-line management. After that, within a decade's grasp, is a corporate VP post. Or, Chris figured, she could start her own firm by then.

Regarding the more immediate future, the marketing manager job a year away is not a sure thing. Computex rarely promotes anyone from within, let alone a woman, to that position. Part of the reason is that Computex doesn't know how to train people, Chris commented, and few people bother to train themselves. That's where Chris sees herself as different.

She has begun to formulate her strategy. First, she must pull off a marketing coup. A well-conceived, well-implemented project that paid off could prove her marketing prowess. She will also have to convince both her manager and his superior that she is in earnest about her career. If she cannot involve them in her plans, she will, she says, have to seek out someone else to help her along—a mentor. Just the fact that people know that she has kept to the timetable she set for herself five years ago is gaining her respect. In a sense, she is a self-fulfilling prophecy.

Third, Chris says that she will have to gain entry into the "boys club," both on and off the job. The latter will involve learning how to play racquetball and probably golf. She'll have to get the men to call her by her last name and have them be able to swear in her presence without blinking. The "boys club" is, she commented, comprised of aspiring young men of the "in group" who know that they are on a fast track. Being known is terribly important.

In addition, Chris observes that she will have to change her mode of dress, to dress more for success, as the saying goes . . . wear tailored grey suits, navy pleated skirts, and white crepe blouses. And everything she does will have to be done in an honest and open way because that, she says, is her style.

Chuck the Manager

At age 52, Chuck Fielding had spent many years as a successful engineer in various companies. He was well known in the fields of mechanical and aeronautical engineering. Chuck, however, wanted to get more involved in management. Therefore, when one of his old friends at Propwash, Inc., offered him a job as the head of the production engineering department at their Thrust Division, Chuck enthusiastically accepted. Propwash, Inc., was a major aerospace firm. Chuck knew that if he did a good job in their Thrust Division, his future would be most promising.

The first thing Chuck realized was that the Thrust Division was far different from the rest of Propwash. Thrust was strictly in the business

From Robert E. C. Wegner and Leonard Sayles, *Cases in Organizational and Administrative Behavior,* © 1972, pp. 95–101. Reprinted by permission of Prentice-Hall, Inc., Englewood Cliffs, N.J.

of developing and producing missiles and space vehicles. In 1956, Thrust had won the contract for a high-performance ballistic missile. Numerous other contracts for additional space vehicles and missiles had been forthcoming, and Thrust Division had now grown to the point where sales were as large as the rest of Propwash combined.

The division was organized on a project basis normally in line with the governmental agency (Army, Navy, NASA, and so forth) supporting the project. Thrust's general organization chart appears in Exhibit 1.

Primarily the projects were concerned with the design, development, testing, and production of a particular product. They also were concerned with improving the existing product and producing any logical follow-ons. The central and research organizations were concerned with the design, development, testing, and production which was common to all or most projects, or alternatively with projects not yet sufficiently developed to be products. The production engineering department was in central.

EXHIBIT 1
Organization Chart for Propwash, Inc., Thrust Division

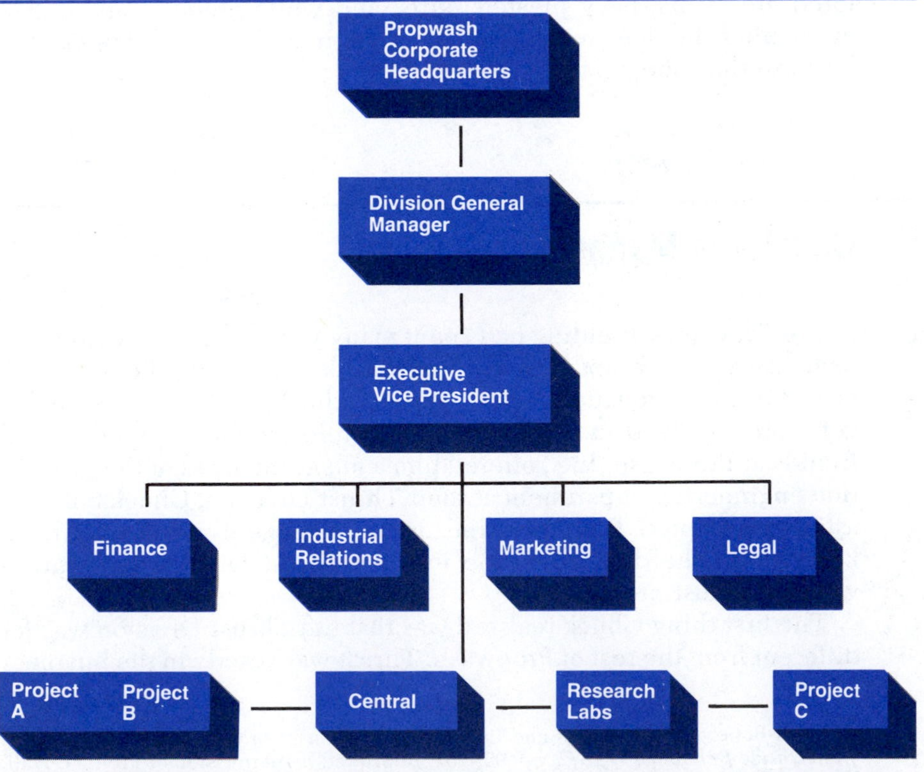

PRODUCTION ENGINEERING

Fielding was amazed by what confronted him. The organization was in complete disunity. The engineers weren't engineering, and the department was the least popular in the company. A combination of events had led to this situation.

First, there was underutilization of manpower. Some of the men had no jobs to do. They were coming in and filling a desk, or inventorying labs, or just sitting about chatting. One of the most popular statements among the few younger engineers who had not as yet left was, "Where else can I be semiretired at the age of 25?" Second, the men showed complete disgust with their technical leadership. Many of the men felt that the company "would buy a project for making gold out of cowdung if you talked fast enough."

Besides this, it appeared that this department was regarded as a joke by the majority of the other departments in the organization. Chuck quickly realized that many sections of the Thrust Division would not give his department any work at all. Soon after he accepted the job, another project manager at his level said, "I'm sorry, Chuck. I can't give you any work. It's not your fault, I know, but I just can't trust the level of work I get from those people who work for you. Why, a year and a half ago one of them sent me a report, and I know some of the data he gave me was phony. Since then, when I've needed development work, I've gone to outside engineering companies."

Others told him that although the work was adequate the time getting this work done was just too long to permit relying on production engineering.

Three years before Chuck took over, Grant Adams had been made manager of the production engineering group. He had received a Ph.D. from the University of California in chemical physics at the age of 23 and had worked for NASA in the Langley Research Center for about 10 years prior to coming to work for Propwash. During this period he had written voluminous research monographs and had become an outstanding voice in the early development on stress corrosion and fatigue in high-strength stainless steel alloys. In hiring Adams, Propwash followed a continuing policy of bringing outstanding minds into the corporation. Such minds presented the basis on which Propwash had built its eminence in the industry, and such names as Adams also helped when they appeared on proposals.

Adams, however, had a tremendous weakness for performing detailed studies. He would often accept jobs for the department and become involved in the specific details of the study rather than in effecting a solution to the entire problem. Because of the tremendous rush to meet schedules in projects, the department frequently was late in issuing reports. The production groups found that they couldn't wait for reports, and therefore either did the work themselves or sent it all the way back down the work flow to research.

Adams found that he was losing work. As he lost work, the supervisors of the groups under him became frustrated and angry. Soon they began going out to drum up business on their own, relying upon their own reputations within Propwash. However, the type of work each supervisor obtained varied considerably. Hence some got jobs which involved fairly basic research. On the other extreme, others were troubleshooting in the shops.

Eventually management became aware that production engineering was a bottleneck, that no work of significance was being accomplished, and Adams was transferred into research in a staff capacity with a small lab and four assistants.

Adams was followed by a succession of three acting managers. Each lasted from two to three months. During this phase, the number of engineers fell from 100 to about 60. About 20 men resigned. The majority of the remainder either voluntarily transferred to other departments or were asked to transfer. During this period the production engineering department sank to its low point. The few budgeted manhours for remaining research went to one or two of the faster-talking engineers who could convince the nontechnical acting managers that they had a good idea. On the other hand, most of the others were running about, troubleshooting in the shops.

This was the situation when Chuck Fielding became manager.

FIELDING'S FIRST STEPS

His first step was to decide on the role of his department. He quickly learned that in the Thrust Division, research was responsible for developing the fundamental concepts which eventually evolved into products. At some time his department would be consulted for input regarding materials, processes, and fabrication techniques. Ultimately the result of these efforts, both separate and joint, would be engineering reports. These would then be forwarded to the project or the central development group to build a prototype.

Although there might come a time when the implementation of the engineering report required that Fielding's department be consulted, he decided that troubleshooting in the shop was *not* desirable in that the individual projects had liaison engineers who were specifically responsible for eliminating causes of trouble in their project. But these liaison engineers resented the fact that the production engineering people were directly contacting the shops for such work. Invariably, if production engineering solved a problem, they claimed the credit. On the other hand, problems and failures were credited to the liaison engineers.

Chuck also found that pure research was outside of the jurisdiction of his department. First, it didn't have the personnel or equipment resources. Second, the people "up on the hill in research" jealously guarded their realm in the company.

The role of his department was from applied research through development. He could characterize the flow of a project as:

Pure research → Applied research and development → Prototype → Product

Fielding's department interfaced with the several research groups on one side and with the manufacturing engineers on the other. In the case of searching out trouble spots, he found it desirable to receive input from the liaison engineers and deal with their problems in a *consultative* manner, with the ultimate decision as the responsibility of the project liaison engineer.

DEALING WITH THE SUPERVISORS

As noted above, each supervisor in the production engineering department was out drumming up business on his own. This resulted in tremendous instability in the relationship with the interfacing departments. Before Chuck had an opportunity to act on this problem, a situation arose that precipitated a change.

Ned Thomas was the supervisor of the metallurgy group. He was loud and vociferous and always ready to get into a fight. Three months after he arrived, Chuck received an angry phone call from a project manager a full level above him who stated that Ned had been in his office that afternoon and attempted to negotiate a job with him. When he refused, Ned slammed a fist on his desk and called him an "s.o.b."

When Ned came back, Chuck called him into his office and asked why Ned had taken it upon himself to interact with someone at that level. Ned told Chuck to "mind his own damn business" and that he didn't intend to let any "damn manager mess up jobs I've spent weeks getting." Ned shouted rather loudly, and most of the people in the area heard him. After Ned stormed out, Chuck made arrangements to have him transferred out of his department.

From his previous jobs Chuck had become friendly with Mel Franks, a division manager at Propwash. Mel had been a driving, energetic technical manager. Two years ago, however, Mel had had a heart attack. After 10 months of illness, he returned to a technical staff position. He was eager to perform in the Propwash environment, but his days of fighting the wars of the ladder of line management were over.

Mel was well liked and knew almost everyone. He had many contacts, and some of these contacts were at a high level. He was easygoing and willing to deal with people in a far more passive manner than the younger and more aggressive supervisors. Chuck made him his staff assistant, ostensibly as an administrator and personnel man.

Chuck then called in the supervisors and made it clear that new business would be cleared on the department level. It was all right for supervisors to meet with other supervisors in order to carry on new business or to discuss the old. It was not all right to go out to drum up new business. Mel had that job, and he would commit the department to new jobs.

DEALING WITH THE ENGINEERS

Mel moved adroitly in gathering new jobs. As this phase progressed, new assignments began to arrive. Chuck attempted to divide the labor so that junior engineers got assignments that would involve following a job from the early stages to the final report. Senior engineers either performed consultative work or led a group of junior engineers. In this way, the young engineers were able to function in their field, gain useful experience, and were kept busy. On the other hand, senior engineers were able to use their experience and gain new experience leading the younger men.

Chuck also added a technical staff man to his personal staff. Recruited from another department at Propwash, Marty Hanson was a capable and intelligent senior staff engineer. He was able to provide Chuck with a strong measure of technical support in evaluating the work of the department.

The engineers were beginning to get work and apparently felt that the work was meaningful. To further help this situation, Chuck attempted to reach an understanding with research as to the approximate lines of jurisdiction. Then he embarked on a program of obtaining contracts from outside agencies such as NASA for projects within his agreed-on jurisdiction, and reached an understanding with research on mutual support arrangements for such projects. By assigning engineers to outside assignments, he gave his men the opportunity to broaden their experience with outside contractors. In addition, they had the opportunity to travel, which was a desirable fringe benefit for the men. At the same time Chuck began to encourage his people to attend more professional societies' meetings and to study toward advanced degrees.

CONCLUSION

As time went on, the production engineering department greatly improved its operations. Chuck found that his control of the department was possible without crossing the natural jurisdictional lines which separated his department from interfacing departments. In turn, he found that these interfacing departments were more willing to deal with him on an equitable basis.

Mel was more capable than he could have expected in carrying on the day-to-day external relationships which were always necessary. Moreover, the supervisors grew to respect Mel's ability in these situations and looked to him for aid.

The supervisors quickly learned that Chuck meant business. They discovered that so long as they carried on their interactions with external departments and with the engineers within the parameters which Chuck had established, they would be permitted a great degree of autonomy in their relationships.

As productivity and morale of the PE department improved, Chuck Fielding's reputation grew. Early this year Chuck moved up to one level below the director of central. The general feeling was that he would continue to move up.

▶ The Consolidated Life Case: Caught Between Corporate Cultures

PART I

It all started so positively. Three days after graduating with his degree in business administration, Mike Wilson started his first day at a prestigious insurance company—Consolidated Life. He worked in the Policy Issue Department. The work of the department was mostly clerical and did not require a high degree of technical knowledge. Given the repetitive and mundane nature of the work, the successful worker had to be consistent and willing to grind out paperwork.

Rick Belkner was the division's vice president, "the man in charge" at the time. Rick was an actuary by training, a technical professional

Reprinted by permission of the publisher from *Journal of Management Case Studies* 1986; 2:238–243, copyright © 1986 by Elsevier Science Publishing Co., Inc. Authors: Joseph Weiss, Mark Wahlstrom, and Edward Marshall.

whose leadership style was laissez-faire. He was described in the division as "the mirror of whomever was the strongest personality around him." It was also common knowledge that Rick made $60,000 a year while he spent his time doing crossword puzzles.

Mike was hired as a management trainee and promised a supervisory assignment within a year. However, because of a management reorganization, it was only six weeks before he was placed in charge of an eight-person unit.

The reorganization was intended to streamline work flow, upgrade and combine the clerical jobs, and make greater use of the computer system. It was a drastic departure from the old way of doing things and created a great deal of animosity and anxiety among the clerical staff.

Management realized that a flexible supervisory style was necessary to pull off the reorganization without immense turnover, so they gave their supervisors a free hand to run their units as they saw fit. Mike used this latitude to implement group meetings and training classes in his unit. In addition, he assured all members raises if they worked hard to attain them. By working long hours, participating in the mundane tasks with his unit, and being flexible in his management style, he was able to increase productivity, reduce errors, and reduce lost time. Things improved so dramatically that he was noticed by upper management and earned a reputation as a "superstar" despite being viewed as free spirited and unorthodox. The feeling was that his loose, people-oriented management style could be tolerated because his results were excellent.

A Chance for Advancement

After a year, Mike received an offer from a different Consolidated Life division located across town. Mike was asked to manage an office in the marketing area. The pay was excellent, and it offered an opportunity to turn around an office in disarray. The reorganization in his present division at Consolidated was almost complete, and most of his mentors and friends in management had moved on to other jobs. Mike decided to accept the offer.

In his exit interview he was assured that if he ever wanted to return, a position would be made for him. It was clear that he was held in high regard by management and staff alike. A huge party was thrown to send him off.

The new job was satisfying for a short time, but it became apparent to Mike that it did not have the long-term potential he was promised. After bringing on a new staff, computerizing the office, and auditing the books, he began looking for a position that would both challenge him and give him the autonomy he needed to be successful.

Eventually word got back to his former vice president, Rick Belkner, at Consolidated Life that Mike was looking for another job. Rick offered Mike a position with the same pay he was now receiving and control over a 14-person unit in his old division. After considering other options, Mike decided to return to his old division, feeling that he would be able to progress steadily over the next several years.

Enter Jack Greely; Return Mike Wilson

Upon his return to Consolidated Life, Mike became aware of several changes that had taken place in the six months since his departure. The most important change was the hiring of a new divisional senior vice president, Jack Greely. Jack had been given total authority to run the division. Rick Belkner now reported to Jack.

Jack's reputation was that he was tough but fair. It was necessary for people in Jack's division to do things his way and "get the work out."

Mike also found himself reporting to one of his former peers, Kathy Miller, who had been promoted to manager during the reorganization. Mike had always "hit it off" with Kathy and foresaw no problems in working with her.

After a week Mike realized the extent of the changes that had occurred. Gone was the loose, casual atmosphere that had marked his first tour in the division. Now, a stricter, task-oriented management doctrine was practiced. Morale of the supervisory staff had decreased to an alarming level. Jack Greely was the major topic of conversation in and around the division. People joked that MBO now meant "management by oppression."

Mike was greeted back with comments like "Welcome to prison" and "Why would you come back here? You must be desperate!" It seemed like everyone was looking for new jobs or transfers. Their lack of desire was reflected in the poor quality of work being done.

Mike's Idea: Supervisor's Forum

Mike felt that a change in the management style of his boss was necessary in order to improve a frustrating situation. Realizing that it would be difficult to affect his style directly, Mike requested permission from Rick Belkner to form a Supervisor's Forum for all the managers on Mike's level in the division. Mike explained that the purpose would be to enhance the existing management training program. The forum would include weekly meetings, guest speakers, and discussions of topics relevant to the division and the industry. Mike thought the forum would show Greely that he was serious about both his job and improving morale in the division. Rick gave the OK for an initial meeting.

The meeting took place, and 10 supervisors who were Mike's peers in the company eagerly took the opportunity to "Blue Sky" it. There was a euphoric attitude about the group as they drafted their statement of intent. It read as follows:

TO: Rick Belkner

FROM: New Issue Services Supervisors

SUBJECT: Supervisors' Forum

On Thursday, June 11, the Supervisors' Forum held its first meeting. The objective of the meeting was to identify common areas of concern among us and to determine topics that we might be interested in pursuing.

The first area addressed was the void that we perceive exists in the management training program. As a result of conditions beyond anyone's control, many of us over the past year have held supervisory duties without the benefit of formal training or proper experience. Therefore, what we propose is that we utilize the Supervisors' Forum as a vehicle with which to enhance the existing management training program. The areas that we hope to affect with this supplemental training are: (*a*) morale/job satisfaction; (*b*) quality of work and service; (*c*) productivity; and (*d*) management expertise as it relates to the life insurance industry. With these objectives in mind, we have outlined below a list of possible activities that we would like to pursue.

1. Further utilization of the existing "in-house" training programs provided for manager trainees and supervisors, i.e., Introduction to Supervision, E.E.O., and Coaching and Counseling.
2. A series of speakers from various sections in the company. This would help expose us to the technical aspects of their departments and their managerial style.
3. Invitations to outside speakers to address the forum on management topics such as managerial development, organizational structure and behavior, business policy, and the insurance industry. Suggested speakers could be area college professors, consultants, and state insurance officials.
4. Outside training and visits to the field. This could include attendance at seminars concerning management theory and development relative to the insurance industry. Attached is a representative sample of a program we would like to have considered in the future.

In conclusion, we hope that this memo clearly illustrates what we are attempting to accomplish with this program. It is our hope that the above outline will be able to give the forum credibility and establish it as an effective tool for all levels of management within New Issue. By supplementing our on-the-job training with a series of speakers and classes, we aim to develop prospective management personnel with a broad perspective of both the life insurance industry and management's role in it. Also, we would like to extend an invitation to the underwriters to attend any programs at which the topic of the speaker might be of interest to them.

cc: J. Greely
Managers

The group felt the memo accurately and diplomatically stated their dissatisfaction with the current situation. However, they pondered what the results of their actions would be and what else they could have done.

PART II

An emergency management meeting was called by Rick Belkner at Jack Greely's request to address the "union" being formed by the supervisors. Four general managers, Rick Belkner, and Jack Greely were at that meeting. During the meeting it was suggested the forum be disbanded to "put them in their place." However, Rick Belkner felt that if "guided" in the proper direction, the forum could die from lack of interest. His stance was adopted but it was common knowledge that Jack Greely was strongly opposed to the group and wanted its founders dealt with. His comment was "It's not a democracy and they're not a union. If they don't like it here, then they can leave." A campaign was directed by the managers to determine who the main authors of the memo were so they could be dealt with.

About this time, Mike's unit had made a mistake on a case, which Jack Greely was embarrassed to admit to his boss. This embarrassment was more than Jack Greely cared to take from Mike Wilson. At the managers' staff meeting that day Jack stormed in and declared that the next supervisor to "screw up" was out the door. He would permit no more embarrassments of his division and repeated his earlier statement about "people leaving if they didn't like it here." It was clear to Mike and everyone else present that Mike Wilson was a marked man.

Mike had always been a loose, amiable supervisor. The major reason his units had been successful was the attention he paid to each individual and how they interacted with the group. He had a reputation for fairness, was seen as an excellent judge of personnel for new positions, and was noted for his ability to turn around people who had been in trouble. He motivated people through a dynamic, personable style and was noted for his general lack of regard for rules. He treated rules as obstacles to management and usually used his own discretion as to what was important. His office had a sign saying "Any fool can manage by rules. It takes an uncommon man to manage without any." It was an approach that flew in the face of company policy, but it had been overlooked in the past because of his results. However, because of Mike's actions with the Supervisors' Forum, he was now regarded as a thorn in the side, not a superstar, and his oddball style only made things worse.

Faced with the fact that he was rumored to be out the door, Mike sat down to appraise the situation.

PART III

Mike decided on the following course of action:

1. Keep the Forum alive but moderate its tone so it didn't step on Jack Greely's toes.
2. Don't panic. Simply outwork and outsmart the rest of the division. This plan included a massive retraining and remotivation of his personnel. He implemented weekly meetings, cross-training with other divisions, and a lot of interpersonal "stroking" to motivate the group.
3. Evoke praise from vendors and customers through excellent service and direct that praise to Jack Greely.

The results after eight months were impressive. Mike's unit improved the speed of processing 60 percent and lowered errors 75%. His staff became the most highly trained in the division. Mike had a file of several letters to Jack Greely that praised the unit's excellent service. In addition, the Supervisors' Forum had grudgingly attained credibility, although the scope of activity was restricted. Mike had even improved to the point of submitting reports on time as a concession to management.

Mike was confident that the results would speak for themselves. However, one month before his scheduled promotion and one month after an excellent merit raise in recognition of his exceptional work record, he was called into his supervisor's, Kathy Miller's, office. She informed him that after long and careful consideration, the decision had been made to deny his promotion because of his lack of attention to detail. This did not mean he was not a good supervisor, just that he needed to follow more instead of taking the lead. Mike was stunned and said so. But, before he said anything else, he asked to see Rick Belkner and Jack Greely the next day.

The Showdown

Sitting face to face with Rick and Jack, Mike asked if they agreed with the appraisal Kathy had discussed with him. They both said they did. When asked if any other supervisor surpassed his ability and results, each stated Mike was one of the best, if not *the* best they had. Then why, Mike asked, would they deny him a promotion when others of less ability were approved? The answer came from Jack: "It's nothing personal, but we just don't like you. We don't like your management style. You're an oddball. We can't run a division with 10 supervisors all doing different things. What kind of a business do you think we're running here? We need people who conform to our style and methods so we can measure their results objectively. There is no room for subjective interpretation. It's our feeling that if you really put your mind to it, you can be an excellent manager. It's just that you now create trouble and rock the boat. We don't need that. It doesn't matter if you're the best now, sooner or later as you go up the ladder, you will be forced to pay more attention to administrative duties and you won't handle them well. If we correct your bad habits now, we think you can go far."

Mike was shocked. He turned to face Rick and blurted out nervously, "You mean it doesn't matter what my results are? All that matters is how I do things?" Rick leaned back in his chair and said in a casual tone, "In so many words, yes."

Mike left the office knowing that his career at Consolidated was over and immediately started looking for a new job. What had gone wrong?

EPILOGUE

After leaving Consolidated Life, Mike Wilson started his own insurance, sales, and consulting firm, which specialized in providing corporate-risk managers with insurance protection and claims-settlement strategies. He works with a staff assistant and one other associate. After three years, sales averaged over $7 million annually, netting approximately $125,000 to $175,000 before taxes to Mike Wilson.

During a return visit to Consolidated Life, three years after his departure, Mike found Rick Belkner and Jack Greely still in charge of the division in which Mike had worked. The division's size had shrunk by 50 percent. All of the members of the old Supervisors' Forum had left. The reason for the decrease in the division's size was that computerization had removed many of the people's tasks.

NOTE: The authors thank Duncan Spelman and Anthony Buono for their helpful comments on this text.

▶ Consumer Materials Enterprises, Inc. (Consummate Corporation)

INTRODUCTION

Paul Rubin, a summer intern at Consumer Materials Enterprises, Inc. (Consummate Corporation), had just spoiled David Gold's day by reporting severe tensions in David's unit. During the late 1970s, Consummate Corporation (a large, highly profitable, and rapidly growing manufacturer of consumer products located in Atlanta) had been running a series of week-long seminars for its management staff designed to accelerate their interest in worker satisfaction. David Gold, 35, manager of Consummate Corporation's refill packaging unit, had recently returned from one of the company's seminars. At that time he had been the manager of the refill packaging unit for about a year and had been feeling good about the progress he had made in solving the department's problems. But now Paul had given him reason to worry.

An engineer by training, David had worked his way up through the company to his present position over a period of 13 years. David was an intelligent, thoughtful person with a dry sense of humor, who managed in a low-key, unaggressive way. He was very accepting of what other people thought, a good listener, and a believer in being supportive of the people who worked for him. When he first started with Consummate Corporation, David had been more aggressive and had tried to cut into the permissive culture of the company. Early in his career in an attempt to shape things up in their units, he and a group of other supervisors had made a 14-point proposal, containing what they thought were not very radical suggestions. For example, they proposed that all employees be required to be present at the beginning and end of the time they were paid for, that work breaks be reasonable in length, that production logs be filled out as per the rules, and so forth.

To his amazement these proposals were rejected, and David and his cosponsors were told at that time that they had to become more understanding of the people who worked for them. Since that time David had made an effort to "soften up" on his employees and had developed a quiet, restrained approach to managing people.

Now he wanted to make a start on improving employee satisfaction in his department and thought he should start with his own immediate subordinates. Satisfied that earlier production problems were under control, he wanted to create the atmosphere of "one big happy family." But suddenly, after the visit from Paul Rubin, a summer intern, he had found that there was more tension among his staff than he had realized, and he was wondering how to proceed.

BACKGROUND OF REFILL PACKAGING UNIT

The product manufactured by Consummate Corporation required many refills. The refill packaging unit performed all of the various packaging operations associated with getting the refills ready for final shipment and sale. An assembly line operation was set up where the previously manufactured refills were slipped into cardboard boxes by machines, grouped together in packages, and then loaded by hand into cardboard cases.

The refill packaging unit was considered to be one of the lowest-status units in Consummate Corporation. The manufacturing of products and refills required a high level of sophistication, but putting the refills into boxes did not. The packaging operation itself did not have a significant impact on profits, though high and growing demand for refills required a high daily volume.

Many of the jobs in the packaging unit were entry-level positions. New employees were typically sent to packaging first and, if they showed promise, were moved out of the unit into the manufacturing units. The same procedure held true for many of the supervisory jobs. Newly hired supervisors would often start in refill packaging and, once they had proven themselves, would be moved into more sophisticated supervisory jobs in the other units of the company.

Because the refill packaging unit was used as an entry-level place for new employees, it experienced a relatively high turnover rate into other positions within the corporation. The people who stayed in the refill packaging unit were seen by others as not holding much future promise and therefore were looked upon as the organization's "losers."

The refill packaging unit was part of a wider organization culture considered to be one of the "softest" human relations programs in all of industry. The company, by long-standing policy, would turn itself inside out for its employees.

The traditional policies and practices elsewhere in the building housing the refill packaging unit were even softer than the rest of the company. For example, it was not uncommon to have people organize their breaks so they could leave a half hour or more before their shift was over. Many breaks were allowed employees during their shifts, and it was not uncommon to "shut down a line" right in the middle of a shift to hold a meeting. Even people caught stealing might not be fired; it was believed by many supervisors to be nearly impossible to get any employee fired regardless of how legitimate the reason.

Because of the need to produce around the clock and some absenteeism, production operators were given the opportunity to work a great deal of overtime; as a result, some took home as much or more money than their supervisors. Many employees, because of the extensive overtime, worked under supervisors from more than one shift and thus were able to see and compare the different supervisory styles that existed across work shifts.

The organizational structure of the refill packaging unit is shown in Exhibit 1.

David Gold had three people reporting directly to him: Jim Whiting, the general supervisor for maintenance (new to the unit); Bill Dane, the general supervisor for production (with whom he was particularly close); and Kevin Flynn, the statistical analyst. The unit operated three shifts around the clock. Members of these shifts did not rotate; in other words, those on the first shift always worked days (7 A.M.–3 P.M.), the second always worked 3–11 P.M., and the third always worked 11 P.M.–7 A.M.

Each shift was required to leave the production lines set up and equipped in order to make it easier for the next shift to get started. Aside from this activity, there was low interdependence among shifts and supervisors.

Each shift had two or three production line supervisors. These supervisors were responsible for several production lines. Each individual production line had a crew chief, who helped the supervisors keep the lines running smoothly and on schedule, and eight operators.

The general supervisors worked mostly when the first shift was present and for about two hours each day of the second shift, but they did not usually have direct daily contact with the third shift.

As a result of this lack of direct face-to-face contact with all three work shifts, a lot of "memos" were passed around to supervisors from the general supervisors and between shift supervisors themselves.

The production supervisors were a mix of college-hired people and experienced, up-through-the-ranks old-timers. The maintenance crew and its supervisor were all skilled tradesmen (mechanics and electricians), and as such, no college graduates were hired for these jobs.

Exhibit 2 shows the backgrounds of the supervisors in the refill packaging unit.

FIRST OFF-SITE MEETING

In the process of assessing the current situation in the refill packaging unit, David Gold reflected back on a two-and-a-half-day, off-site meeting he had held six months ago with the supervisors in his unit.

EXHIBIT 1
Structure of the Refill Packaging Unit

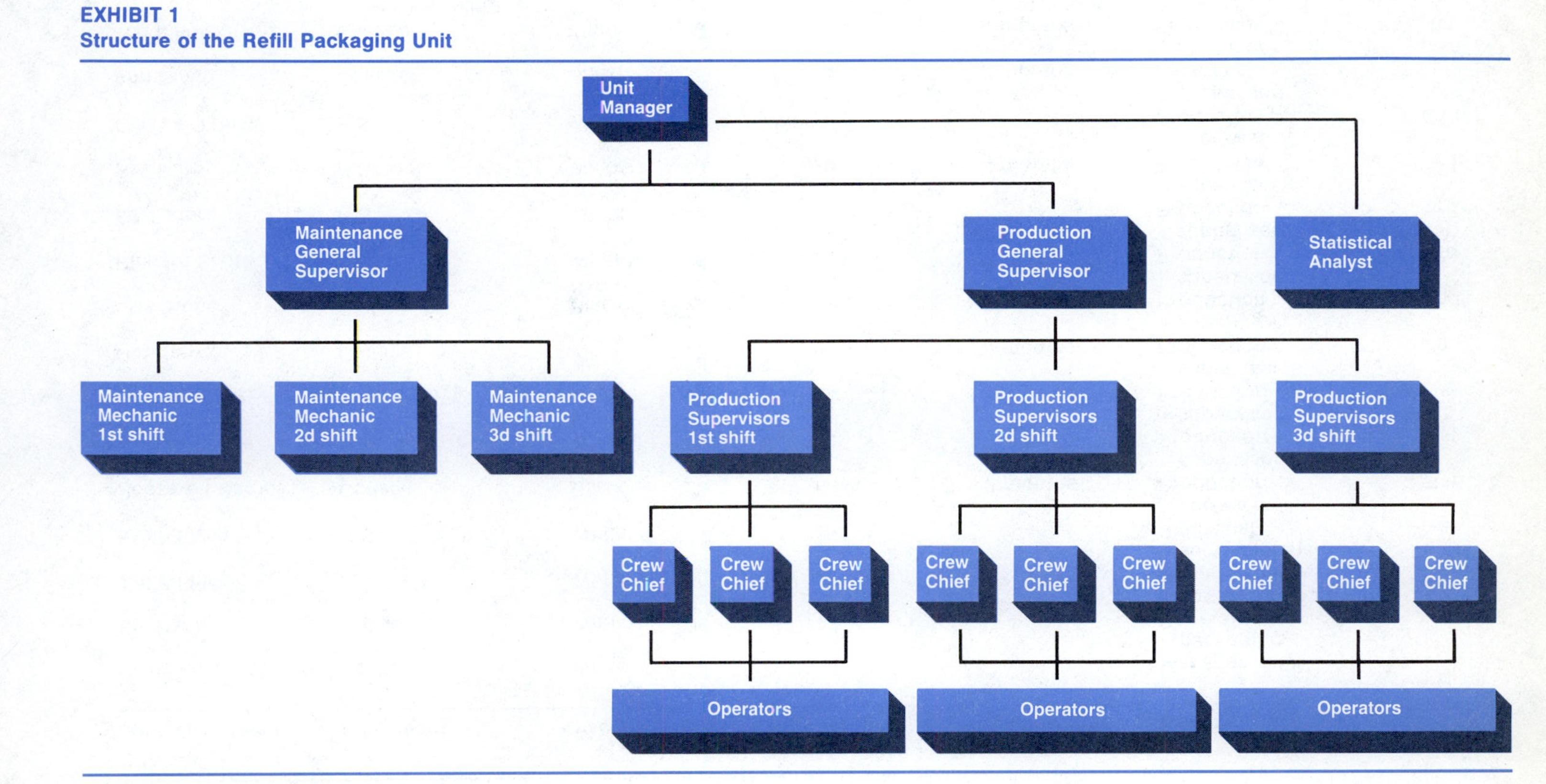

EXHIBIT 2
Background Information on Refill Packaging Unit Supervisory Personnel

Supervisor Name	*Education*	*Race*	*Age*	*Number Years with Company*	*Number Years Packaging Unit*	*Position*	*Work Shift*
David Gold	College	White	35	13	1	Manager, refill packaging	—
Bill Dane	College	White	35	13	3	General supervisor, production	—
Jim Whiting	H.S.	White	40	20	1	General supervisor, maintenance	—
Kevin Flynn	H.S.	White	41	25	4	Statistical analyst	—
Roosevelt Barnes	College	Black	23	new	8 months	Production supervisor	1st
Kathy Flamme	H.S.	White	40	22	5	Production supervisor	1st
Sheldon Levy	H.S.	White	58	14	14	Production supervisor	1st
Dot Stewart	College	White	22	new	5 months	Production supervisor	2nd
Liza Stone	College	Black	22	new	5 months	Production supervisor	2nd
Richard Scott	H.S.	White	55	20+	4	Production supervisor	3rd
Ed Tudor	H.S.	White	42	20	1	Production supervisor	3rd
Ray Burr	H.S.	White	60	20	4 months	Production supervisor	3rd
Charlie O'Reilly	H.S.	White	29	8	2	Production supervisor	2nd
Ann Smith	College	Black	35	5	2 months	Personnel production	—
Ted Marker	College (while working at the company)	White	28	6	4 months	Supervisor trainee	1st
Paul Rubin	College student	White	20	—	2	Summer management trainee	Rotating shifts

He called the meeting because there were many problems in the area he had recently taken over. Production was below target, safety rules weren't enforced, work areas weren't kept clean, and there was too little cooperation across shifts and between production and maintenance supervisors. Several of the long-term supervisors had resisted very strongly going to the first off-site meeting. The person who was most vocal in complaining was Kathy Flamme, 40, married with one child, an experienced supervisor, and known as the "Blonde Bomber" behind her back. Kathy argued that the company should not require anyone to leave home overnight and should not require people to put in extra time or work on the weekends (the meeting had continued through Saturday morning). Kathy clearly demonstrated that she resented the time away, didn't think it was fair, didn't want to invest any extra time and energy in so-called seminars, and in general didn't think there was anything she needed to learn. Although Kathy was the loudest of the long-term supervisors (old-timers), most of the others had voiced similar kinds of complaints as well.

At the meeting, David Gold responded to supervisor complaints about not knowing what he wanted with a clear statement of his goals for packaging. He told the supervisors that this was a new era and the long-term supervisors (the people who had been in the unit for several years) were going to have to be more professional, more effective in involving workers, managing more participatively, and learning new skills ("the old ways will no longer work"). Time was also spent discussing the general sloppiness of the work areas, failure to clean up around the machines, and passing machines along to the next shift with everything out of place and disorganized. In essence, David Gold told his supervisors that they were going to have to become more committed to their jobs.

The supervisors who had been with the packaging unit of the company for several years felt that their job experience wasn't being valued by upper management and that they had never received the recognition they deserved. They worked very hard, their production quotas were almost always met, and they felt they ought to be recognized for their efforts.

It was also discovered at this meeting that it was the supervisors' perception that, in the company, "you're not supposed to make waves" and that they could not really challenge the general supervisors and David Gold. They also perceived that initiative wasn't particularly welcomed in the past, and so they felt they should just stick to their work, do what they were told, and ignore everything and everybody else.

This behavior on the part of the line supervisors had served to confirm David Gold's and the two general supervisors' suspicions about the competence and professionalism of these people. They now saw the supervisors as having tunnel vision. Thus a circular, self-defeating cycle was discovered to be operating, where supervisors behaved as if they were all wearing blinders because they felt that they were ignored and looked down upon, and as a result, Gold's team became even more suspicious of the competence of the supervisors and gave them even less recognition.

In addition, the line supervisors expressed many feelings of powerlessness. They felt constrained by what they perceived to be the company's reluctance to get rid of low-performing employees, by the strength of the Employee Association, by the rapid turnover out of the packaging unit, and by the lack of confidence that supervisors on other shifts and in other parts of their building would support their dealings with employees or management. One story that appeared to confirm the supervisors' belief that they couldn't really fire anybody concerned Kathy. Kathy had once challenged an employee, who she was certain was stealing refills by hiding them in his pants. When stopped, he refused to show her what he had and later claimed it was a dirty book, which he didn't want to show to a female supervisor. Eventually, a vice president excused the employee from the accusation of stealing because there was no proof, and the employee had stayed on.

Part of the consequence of the general attitude of the supervisors was that there were problems with achieving coordination among maintenance and production supervisors on the same shift and across shifts. They were not telling each other what they were doing or had done.

As a result of this lack of communication, very large assumptions were made about what other people were doing, thinking, and feeling on different shifts. At the off-site meeting many instances were revealed. For example, a supervisor would say, "I saw X when I came in on my shift. He was finishing up his shift, and he let people walk out early and never said a word about it. If he's going to take that attitude, well then, to hell with him." Then X would respond, "Wait a second, I didn't let people walk off the shift, so-and-so had a medical thing, so he was going downstairs to the nurse. Why didn't you ask me in the first place?" There were a lot of uncontested assumptions circulating about people on different shifts, and the supervisors would use incidents they observed to confirm their prejudices about one another without doing much testing to see whether what they were observing was really as they perceived it to be.

Out of these discussions at the off-site meeting, a number of commitments were made. As a result of these commitments, production had improved considerably, general housekeeping was much better (machines were being cleaned at the end of each shift), relationships between production supervisors and the maintenance supervisors had improved markedly, there seemed to be more direct communication across shifts, and the supervisors' general understanding of the goals of the packaging unit appeared to be much clearer.

David Gold was pleased with the progress. He knew many felt they were moving in the right direction. Now he felt it was time to move toward real teamwork. He wanted overall commitment to one another and to the unit and wanted to create the feeling of being "one big happy family."

DECISION TO HOLD A SECOND OFF-SITE MEETING

David decided to schedule another off-site meeting of all refill packaging unit supervisors.

About 10 days after he had announced the arrangements for the second off-site meeting, Paul Rubin, a college student who was spending the summer observing the department, arranged for an appointment. Rubin was visibly upset and informed Gold that the problems in the department were alarming. As a "naive student," Rubin had managed to make friends with almost all the supervisors, and they had talked freely with him. He described the situation in the unit as "grim" and told Gold about the tension and hostility between the newly hired college graduates and the older experienced supervisors. Exhibit 3 is a summary of what Rubin had learned and told Gold.

David was rather surprised and had to figure out what to do about the unexpected tension among his staff members.

APPENDIX

Selected comments made to Paul Rubin by the three groups—management, experienced supervisors, and new supervisors at Consummate's refill packaging unit.

Views on Management: Old-Timers

"Why should we have to go away; my family will be upset. . . . What's the point anyway, we don't want to be friends with the people we work with. I don't want to mix my personal life with my work life, so what's the point of it. . . . These meetings management calls are a big waste."

"People who voice opinions have them brought back up to them later. I got penalized for talking at the last meeting. Everything you say around here gets back to the managers. We can't address issues

EXHIBIT 3
Summary of Issues among Subgroups

College Inexperienced See Selves	*College Inexperienced See Experienced Old-Timers*	*Experienced Old-Timers See Selves*	*Experienced Old-Timers See College Inexperienced*	*How Senior Management Sees College Inexperienced*	*How Senior Management See Experienced Old-Timers*
Bright, quick, ambitious, want to learn and grow; like to make own mistakes, yet want guidance from Bill Dane, who isn't available without effort. Become bored when things are running smoothly. Open, willing to deal with problems on job, but eager for session to work things out fully.	Don't want to try anything new. "Did it 6 years ago, and it failed then." Willing to help us but upset when advice not followed. Know many tricks. Have ways of dealing with crew chiefs that work for them but affect the work of our lines. Threatened by us.	Know the ropes. Get production out, reliable. Care about job, dedicated, put in extra time when needed. Know how to keep our mouths shut. Don't need to have everything spelled out. Willing to deal with problems on job—don't feel it necessary to go away in special sessions.	Can't trust them. Crybabies—always running to Bill Dane. Wet behind the ears. Have no respect for us and our ways. Don't really care about job—just want to make a big impression to get ahead.	Ambitious, energetic, creative. Project oriented. More open. Protective, lack of depth, need more detail knowledge. Expectations too high. More promotable.	Valuable. Reliable, dedicated. Knowledgeable. Less mobile, less flexible, more defensive, expectations too low. More people-oriented—more loyal to their "hourlys."

Note: See Appendix for specific comments made by members of each group, as recalled by Paul Rubin.

like working hours, taking breaks, wearing safety glasses, and getting rid of deadweight employees."

"I don't trust anybody. . . . I won't give my comment on things; I've learned to keep my mouth shut about things. . . . What's said at these meetings gets passed on to the 'hourlys'; nothing is kept private. There are only two guys I can trust (old-timers from the same shift)."

"We can't deal with the bad actors . . . . If everyone did their paperwork, there might be a chance that we could get rid of them . . . but at the top someone will give them a second chance, and they'll be back on the floor the next day laughing at you. We'd have a better unit if we had tougher rules. . . . It's not doing us any good to keep bad people on, but we can't take a hard stand as supervisors or we'll get in trouble if we do."

"I haven't seen any changes under the new management. . . . It seems like Gold and the general supervisors are always on a pedestal. They dictate how things are to be done, and we don't have a say at all. There are some hard feelings going around about Dane (general supervisor, production). People say he's a hard-ass and doesn't make it very clear what it is he really wants from us."

"I wish we could get rid of the stiffs (low-performance people). Maybe at this next meeting I'll mention it again."

"If you create waves here, it's all over. . . . The crew chiefs run the show, not Dane or the supervisors. . . . The second shift gets a lot of static from upstairs. Gold is a little Caesar. . . . I don't see the general supervisors or the other supervisors too often; we just communicate through memos, you know. . . ."

Views on Other Experienced Supervisors: Old Timers

"We know the ropes, know how to get the numbers out (make production quotas), and we *care* about our jobs. We're willing to put in extra time where needed, . . . and we don't need everything spelled out for us."

"We're willing to deal with problems on the job as they come up; we don't feel it's necessary to have to go away in a special session to do this."

"We're more dedicated to our jobs than the young ones. . . . We're reliable; you can count on us to get the numbers out on schedule."

"It looks like we're becoming a dying breed around here. I don't like the feeling. . . . Maybe by hiring all these college kids they're trying to tell us something, you know what I mean?"

From Richard Scott (third shift): "That Kathy . . . she's always off someplace having breakfast with her boyfriend when she could come in and find out from me how the night shift has gone."

From Kathy Flamme (first shift): "I know Richard hates me. I hear he's always saying really nasty things about me behind my back. . . . Then he expects me to come in early to meet with him and discuss things—no way!"

Views on College Hires: Old-Timers

"You can't trust them to do what they've agreed to do. . . . They don't want to listen. . . . They can't keep their mouths shut."

"These college kids are a bunch of wise-asses who are still wet behind the ears. They spend all of their time sucking up to Bill Dane (general supervisor, production). While he's too smart to fall for it, they are constantly writing him notes or talking to him, telling him what's going on. Supervisors aren't supposed to do that. . . . You shouldn't go running to the general supervisor every time you have a problem."

"Ted Marker's (supervisor trainee) presence is costing us supervisors overtime pay. Can he or can't he run his own line? They say he has to wait a year, to train first, yet they give him a line when they're short on supervisors. He has a luxury we didn't have. . . . He can step back and watch without having any responsibility to a line or crew."

"You can't trust the college supervisors to keep their mouths shut and to listen. . . . They resent our advice. . . . They're really cocky, and they're not concerned with who's in their way; they're just concerned about climbing the ladder to big success."

"They're always trying to make a big impression on David and the general supervisors. Instead they should pay more attention to getting the numbers out" (meeting production quotas).

"They strike me as being a bunch of crybabies. . . . They're always running to Bill Dane about one thing or another. Bill has probably had it up to here with them and their complaining."

Views on Management: College-Hires, Inexperienced Supervisors

"I'm on the first shift, and we have all the bosses working with us. As a result they tend to make all of our decisions for us. We'd like more responsibility on our shift. The second and third shifts have the luxury of being able to make their own decisions."

"Bill Dane (general supervisor, production) is very arrogant in the way in which he writes notes. . . . He gets his point across very strongly."

"David Gold appears not to care; he acts very casual when being informed about what's going on in his department but gets quite upset if he's not kept informed. He doesn't give support . . . or much of any response. . . . He shows no emotion whatsoever."

"There's very little consistency up there. . . . Some carry out what management tells us to do at a meeting, but others don't."

"Bill Dane writes vicious notes. . . . He seems not to like one-on-one conversations. . . . He spends a lot of time defending the first shift. . . . I'm not really sure what he's thinking most of the time."

"The second shift is blamed for everything. . . . When we're supposed to meet with the first shift they don't show up; they won't stay around to meet with us because it's an intrusion on their time, they say."

"I'm not clear as to what's expected of us—how we are supposed to meet our goals and expectations, how our performance is measured. David needs to tell us what he expects of us. . . . We are always having to ask for meetings. Bill and David should be taking the initiative here, not us."

"You seldom get praised for your work, and when you do there's always a twist added to it—a sort of hidden criticism added in to balance it out."

"Bill's style makes you feel defensive immediately. Bill just says 'wrong,' but doesn't give suggestions for how something should be done."

"I'm not getting the direction I need. . . . I'm told, 'Make your mark,' but I don't know how."

"Bill overreacts; he doesn't think before giving instructions. If you say something to him that he doesn't like, he's on you all the time. . . . Even for petty things . . . he gets charged up. . . . You can't argue with him."

"David delegates to Bill Dane and Jim Whiting. . . . He won't involve himself in the petty stuff, which is reasonable, but it also restricts communications with him."

Views on Fellow College Hires

"I'd like to see us be more honest with each other; everyone gives criticisms so indirectly that you're not really sure what is actually meant by them."

"We work well together, but oftentimes Charlie (old-timer—second shift) gets in our way."

"Four of us were brought in at about the same time, five months ago. I guess in the past they've brought in college supervisors one at a time. Maybe four at the same time is too strong a dose for these old farts around here."

From Roosevelt Barnes (first shift): "Dot (second shift) doesn't trust me—I don't know why. She gets very upset with me at times; in fact, right now we're not even speaking to each other. . . . She thinks she can tell me off whenever she feels like it. . . . I resent that attitude, and I told her off last time."

Views on Old-Timers: College Hires

"Our relationships could be better. I, myself, have had several clashes with Kathy (same shift). We have very different outlooks. She's tough on people; my style is looser. Also I have ideas I'd like to try out. She's opposed to making any changes whatsoever. We've had several disagreements in front of others. . . . I've said what I had to say and walked away from it. I'm very direct, and as a result I've been told by other supervisors to 'bite my tongue.' I've been told several times that Kathy says stuff about me behind my back."

"We have different styles—they're more laid back, don't like to rock the boat; they want to keep things exactly as they are forever. All of us have had run-ins (between the experienced and the inexperienced). The older supers give too much power to the crew chiefs—they let them run the show. As for myself, I don't feel I should have to do somersaults just because the crew chiefs tell me I should."

"Kathy's shift (first shift) leaves at 2:30; our people complain about having to be there from 3–11."

"The experienced supervisors say, 'We just want to share our knowledge with you'; but they get very mad if you don't always follow their advice."

"There are a lot of 'systems' the old-timers have with the crew chiefs, which is OK except it gets in the way of my job. The problem is how do I tell them this without their feeling I'm attacking them. . . . They know ways around things, shortcuts . . . but their shortcuts cause me to have to scramble to cover my behind."

"When you want to try out a new idea, the old-timers say, 'Why bother; they tried that six years ago and it didn't work then.' I get the impression that they feel we don't have any respect for them and their ways of getting things done."

The Devon School Case

Clear River, despite its prosaic name, is a bustling manufacturing and mill community of about 65,000 people. As the only large population center in Tonley County, it also serves as the hub of financial, transportation, and governmental services. On the outskirts of Clear River are smaller population clusters in the manner of suburbs. Devon, known locally as "Nob Hill," is one of them. As its nickname implies, it is the most affluent of these "suburbs" and is the home of many of the area's business and civic leaders.

Devon also attracts professional people, who choose to live in the community because of its beauty, reputation, and higher-quality public services. The town is not all middle and upper-middle class, however; there is a fairly sizable minority of tradesmen, service people, and other "blue-collar" types. Although less well off financially than the rest of the town, this group is able to exert some influence in local politics and community affairs. The township manager and three fourths of the town council are Republican; indeed, registered Republicans outnumber Democrats two to one.

This case was prepared by Mr. James Chambers under the guidance of Professors Allan Cohen and Robin D. Willits.

The following item appeared in the August 15 issue of the Clear River *Examiner:*

NEW SCHOOL OPENS IN SEPTEMBER—DEVON: The recently completed Devon Middle High School will open for classes Tuesday, September 6. The school, under construction for the past 16 months, will represent a radical departure, both architecturally and educationally, from the traditional junior and senior high schools. It is the first of its kind in this area.

Mr. Arthur Magnason of Devon has been appointed principal of the new school. A native of New England with a master's degree in education from the University of Vermont, Magnason has 18 years' experience in teaching and administrative duties in the school systems of Tonley County. He leaves Clear River Central High after four years as its principal.

In discussing the new school, Magnason said, "This is clearly a case where form follows function. The school has been designed and built with the express purpose of using an 'open classroom' concept of teaching and learning. Under this system, small 'learning groups' meet in a large common area and in an environment in which students and teachers are much freer to pursue alternative learning concepts than in traditional programs. The curriculum is also more flexible, and students are sometimes allowed to move from one learning group to another to undertake a new subject of interest to them.

"The upper and middle schools are housed under separate roofs, but a central walkway connects the two both physically and, I think, symbolically."

Enthusiasm for the new school is not confined to its faculty. Mr. Harold Fowles of Devon, president of the Greater Clear River School Committee, said recently, "This new school is a concrete example of the committee's determination to give the young people of this community the most up-to-date and best education possible. The school will embody all of the latest innovations in learning and has been thoroughly equipped to meet the needs of all students whether they plan to go on to college or into a trade after graduation.

"We have brought some excellent teachers to Devon from other schools in the district," Fowles continued, "and have hired only the very best new teachers available."

Designed to serve some 600 students in grades 5–12, the school is indeed an impressive example of a community's dedication to the education of its youth.

Not everyone in the town shared Magnason's and Fowles's enthusiasm, however, due to the unstructured and highly experimental nature of the new school. Some members of the school committee had been outvoted by those members whose views reflected the more active and liberal element in the community. Some parents also had objected to the new school on the grounds that their children might not learn enough to get into top-rated universities, while other parents worried that the new school would encourage permissiveness. The active objections were in the minority, and most people in the area appeared proud of the new facility and its modern educational concepts.

> **MEMO**
>
> To: All Faculty
>
> From: A. Magnason, Principal
>
> Subject: Workshop Orientation
>
> All faculty members are to report to the multipurpose room (a combination auditorium and gym) at 8:30 A.M., Monday, August 23, for the preterm workshop orientation.

Standing almost 6′4″ tall and of solid build, Mr. Magnason at 41 years was an imposing figure as he stood at the rostrum on stage addressing the teachers.

"I would like to take this opportunity to welcome all of you to the Devon Middle High School. We have before us a once-in-a-lifetime opportunity, a chance that most teachers only dream of. We are going to be using the latest innovations in education—open classrooms, flexible schedules and curricula—in buildings designed and equipped for that purpose and with the active support of the community."

Magnason paused for a moment; then moving to the side of the rostrum, he leaned against it and struck a more casual pose. "Now, a lot of this is going to be new for many of us. This is the primary reason that we have hired Paulette Trottier as vice principal."

He nodded to a smallish, trim woman in her early 40s who was seated in a chair beside him on the stage. She returned a brief smile.

"She's done a lot of work with open-classroom systems and possesses outstanding credentials. As you know, she's taught for eight years in similar progressive schools and has, for the past four years, broadened her experience and skills working for the New Jersey Department of Education as an evaluator of programs and policies."

Clearing his throat he, went on, "As I said before, I'm not fully familiar with these new concepts and, like the rest of you, feel that there is much to learn. However, I do feel that, in my 18 years of teaching, I have learned a few things about education and about students." He paused briefly for the polite laughter he knew would follow his mild sarcasm.

"A good school is run efficiently, and I think my record speaks for itself in that regard. Everyone, students and teachers, knows where they're supposed to be and what they're supposed to be doing at all times. When I go into a classroom—oops! I guess I should say into a 'learning group' area, I like to see quiet, attentive students and a teacher in control of the situation. If everything's going well, don't expect to see me. But if things are falling through the crack, you will see me and I'll be asking questions. I think Mrs. Trottier has assembled a great team, and I look forward to the beginning of the term, as I'm sure you do."

Collecting his notes, Magnason turned to Mrs. Trottier. "And now Mrs. Trottier, would you like to say a few words?"

Thanking Magnason as she approached the podium, Mrs. Trottier spoke to the group in a voice whose power belied her size. "I don't have very much to say today, but I do expect to work with all of you more closely in smaller groups over the next week and a half. I think Mr. Magnason made a good point when he said that all of us will be learning a lot over the next school year. I've started and worked successfully with a number of these programs over the years, and each one is different. One thing that I've learned is that we have to be open, flexible, and cooperative with each other. Only by working together and sharing our successes and failures can we make this thing work. Thank you."

Magnason once more approached the podium and suggested they break for coffee and doughnuts, which had been provided in the rear of the room. Then, excusing himself, he left the group to attend to several administrative details concerning the opening of the school.

As the teachers drifted toward the back of the room, three who had sat together during the opening remarks began to talk with each other. They were Katherine Amster, Florence Dix, and Louis Spinella. Assigned to seventh-grade classes, they had all taught previously at Clear River Central and had applied for positions at Devon. Their seniority and their reputations as good teachers with records of successfully applying new educational concepts in their classes won them their new jobs. Although Magnason knew each personally, the actual interviewing had been done by Mrs. Trottier, and the job offer had come from her.

Amster: Well, Lou, what do you think?

Spinnela: He sure spoke well. It doesn't sound like the Magnason I worked for—he would never have admitted having anything to learn.

Dix: Yeah, it kind of surprised me that he even got the job. After all, he's never been exposed to these ideas before, and he's not the most liberally minded administrator in the world. Do you think he can handle it? I think maybe the committee hired him 'cause they didn't want to go all the way.

Spinnela: Maybe he's supposed to keep an eye on Trottier and make sure things don't get out of hand. Anyway, you can be sure of one thing, he'll—how did he used to express it—yeah, he'll "run a tight ship."

Dix: You know what he told me once? I was having some trouble with discipline, and he said that as long as I could "keep the lid on" he would be happy.

Amster: He really stays on top of things, though. I think he's a good administrator. But isn't this place great? Do you still think facilities don't make much difference, Lou?

Spinnela [*smiling ruefully at an old joke*]: You know, Kate, I never felt that a school had to be built to order for an educational concept to be effective. I must admit, though, this place is beautiful. Are there any plans to have the parents in for a "cook's tour"?

Amster: Well, I thought there were some parents who wanted to see where their kids were being transferred to, but I don't know of any plans to have an open house. You know Magnason; he's concentrating on getting things ready to open on time.

As the days went by, the teachers got down to the job of assimilating the new program and making final preparations in their lessons. They also renewed old acquaintances and began to make friends among others.

The teachers who had been newly hired were of a uniformly high caliber. John Langford, for instance, was in his mid-30s and had taught for a number of years at an experimental and exclusive private school in New York City. Alice McNair, though only 25, came to the school from Sacramento, California. She was highly recommended and had experience in a school like Devon. Westley Perron and Emily Geoffrion had both completed master's degrees in June and would be starting their first full-time teaching job when Devon opened the following week. They were assigned to fifth-grade classes.

There were also a number of teachers who, like Amster, Dix, and Spinella, had transferred to Devon from other schools in the district. Paul Addles, a seventh-grade teacher, came from Southside Junior High; and Dave Resca, the physical education coordinator, came from McNelly High in Clear River. Resca, in particular, was ecstatic over Devon's facilities and equipment and exuded enthusiasm as he planned programs for the fall.

Mrs. Trottier worked tirelessly with the teachers in teaching them about the new concepts and how they could be applied to their respective disciplines. Although she was the vice principal and dealt with matters throughout the school, she concentrated her efforts with the middle school faculty. Amster, Dix, and Spinella warmed to her right from the beginning. They were familiar with most of the new ideas she was trying to introduce. At Clear River Central they had used many of them in their classes and had often worked together implementing their ideas.

Mrs. Trottier spent most of her time, however, with the new teachers. She had personally interviewed and hired each of them over the summer and was certain that they were among the best young teachers available in the area.

Paul Greene was one teacher who seemed unaffected by the generally high level of enthusiasm pervading the faculty. He had come to

Devon from Central High like a number of other teachers, but brought with him a reputation as a traditional, procedures-bound teacher. Spinella, a military history buff, called him the "Old Guard." Although his preparation for the coming year evidenced the same quality as that of the other teachers, his lack of participation during meetings and discussion groups led some teachers to doubt the sincerity of his commitment to the new school and its ideas. Once, after such a meeting, Alice McNair mentioned Greene's aloofness to Mrs. Trottier.

"Don't worry about him, Alice," she answered. "He's one of the ones Magnason brought over from Central. We're going to have to put up with him, but if he doesn't get with the program damn quick I'll fire him. That's all there is to it. In the meantime, so long as he stays over in the upper school building, we won't lock horns. If it had been up to me, I never would have hired him, and I think he knows it."

During most of this time, Magnason worked primarily in the administration area dealing with the logistics of getting the school fully ready for opening day. Problems associated with late delivery of a few pieces of equipment kept him busy for most of two days. Then there were the impromptu tours to be conducted for visiting dignitaries. What contact he did have with the middle school teachers was limited to an exchange of pleasantries. Although he didn't participate formally in the preparatory workshop sessions, Magnason did seem to know what was going on generally.

By opening day, Tuesday, September 6, Devon School was ready for classes. All the supplies and equipment had finally arrived, and except for a few minor problems with the air-conditioning, everything was in perfect condition.

The 600 students who assembled in the multipurpose room at 9 A.M. on the 6th for Mr. Magnason's opening address had previously attended junior and senior high schools throughout the Clear River area. A large proportion of the upper school students had been transferred from Clear River Central. All were about to begin a new educational process for the first time, and there was an air of excitement in the room.

Emily Geoffrion was standing at the rear of the room with Kate Amster and Florence Dix when Mr. Magnason entered through a side door and began walking to the stage at the front of the room. As he mounted the stage, muted catcalls of "Tigrrr, Tigrrr" began to rise from the area of the older students.

Kate rolled her eyes to the ceiling and murmured, "Here we go."

EMILY: What do you mean?
FLORENCE: Oh, that's what the kids used to call Mr. Magnason at Central.
EMILY: Tigrrr?
KATE: Yeah, Tigrrr, with the emphasis on the "grrr."
EMILY: Why?

Florence: Oh, he's big, I guess, always stalking around and really making them tow the line. They don't like him very much.

As he approached the podium, it was obvious that Magnason heard the students. And the color rushing to his face made it equally obvious that he knew that it was not a term of endearment. He began with conventional opening and welcoming remarks and then addressed the subject of the new school and curriculum.

"This fine new school has been built for you, the students. Not only is it brand new, it is also the only school of its kind in the whole state. I think that you will learn a lot of important things and that you will have fun doing it. I expect you to accord your teachers with the respect they deserve and to obey the school's rules and regulations."

As he concluded his remarks and began to walk off the stage, whispered calls of "Tigrrr, Tigrrr" once again were heard. They didn't stop until he left the room through the same side door.

The first week or two of school was characterized by the usual administrative confusion and snafus that mark the beginning of any school year. Also, there were a few problems getting used to new equipment. The automatic smoke detector fire alarm set off two false alarms before it was discovered that the detectors in the chemistry lab were too sensitive and would trip the alarm system at the slightest hint of fumes. This was fixed, but the air-conditioning system was still giving some problems. The building was designed for "climate control" and the windows, as a result, were sealed. The fact that the heat of summer lingered through September only made this problem more irritating. But this problem was circumvented by the school's open program which encouraged many teachers to hold classes outdoors.

It was on just such a hot day in mid-September that Magnason walked over to Mrs. Trottier's office in the middle school building and met her in the hallway.

Magnason: Mrs. Trottier, you have a minute?

Trottier: Yes, what can I do for you?

Magnason: I was trying to find McNair's class this morning but couldn't find them anywhere. Do you know where they were?

Trottier: No, not really. She'd probably taken them to a shady spot on the grounds somewhere. The damned air-conditioning was really screwing up this morning.

Magnason [*stiffening noticeably at Mrs. Trottier's choice of words*]: Well, I can't control what's going on when I can't even find out where my teachers have taken their students! Come to think of it, the school seemed half empty this morning. I suppose *all* those students were out roaming the countryside, too? Is this what you mean by open classrooms?

Trottier: Take it easy, Arthur. Giving teachers and students the freedom to make choices is part of the new concept. The teachers have to be able to flow with the direction the class is taking.

Magnason: Well, I'm trying to keep an open mind, but I ought to be able to find out where the teachers of this school are teaching their students if I want to. It used to be that classes followed the direction the teacher was taking.

The presence in the hallway of some students returning from late lunch period ended the conversation.

The next evening Mr. Magnason received a telephone call at home. Calling was Harold Fowles, school committee president.

Fowles: How's it going with your new school, Arthur?

Magnason: Pretty well, Mr. Fowles. Except for that cranky air-conditioner, everything's working beautifully. And you know the way that is; they'll probably get it running perfectly about the time of the first snowfall. Other than that, though, no major problems.

Fowles: You have another one of those false alarms yesterday morning?

Magnason: No, why?

Fowles: Well, I was driving by the school yesterday about 10:30 and there were groups of kids all over the place.

Magnason: Oh that. Well, that's . . . that's part of the concept of open classrooms. Teachers can feel free to take a class outdoors if they want to. And since it's been unusually warm this week and the air-conditioning's not too reliable, more teachers are going outdoors. I'm sure things will settle down in a few weeks.

MEMO

To: All Faculty

From: A. Magnason, Principal

Subject: Guidelines for the conduct of classes out of doors

In an effort to improve control over and the educational value of outdoor class periods, the following guidelines will be observed.

1. Teachers wishing to conduct outdoor classes will submit a written request to their department head no later than one day prior to the day they wish to hold such class.
2. The request will contain, as a minimum, the following information:
   a. Grade level of class.
   b. Number of students.
   c. Location of class on school grounds.
   d. Subject matter to be taught.
   e. Time and duration of class.
3. All classes must be supervised by a teacher and conducted in such a manner that the teacher retains full control over the class. Under no circumstances shall unsupervised groups of students be allowed outside the building.

Fowles: You mean those groups of kids were actually classes?
Magnason: Yes.
Fowles: Well, I don't know. It seemed to me that a lot of them were just running around playing. In fact, I can't remember seeing teachers with some of those groups. They were just off doing what they wanted.
Magnason: It's interesting you should mention that, Mr. Fowles. I just spoke to Paulette Trottier about that very thing yesterday, as a matter of fact. She didn't seem concerned. You get rough spots when you try to put any new program into operation. I do plan to tighten up on that sort of thing, however.
Fowles: Well, this is just the type of permissiveness I was concerned about when this new school was being discussed. But I guess you're right about new programs. We have the same problem at the plant. [Mr. Fowles was president and principal stockholder of Fowles Electronics, Inc., in Clear River. It employed about 400 people in the manufacture of computer and other electronic components.] It sounds as if you're on top of the problem, though. Got to run, good night.
Magnason: Good night, Mr. Fowles.

"Just what is this all about, Arthur?" Mrs. Trottier spoke sharply as she strode into Magnason's office brandishing the memo.

"That, Mrs. Trottier, is an attempt to bring some order and control to these wilderness trails some teachers are taking their classes on," answered Magnason in a measured voice. "We can't allow aimless wandering over the school grounds to continue."

Mrs. Trottier closed the door to his office. "I can read, dammit. What are you trying to do, sabotage the whole program? I told you that the teachers have to be flexible enough to respond to the way their class is going! This 'no later than one day prior' stuff is too rigid. You hired me to implement an open-classroom system at this school."

Magnason clasped his hands on his desk and said, "I am responsible to the school committee to see that their educational objectives for students are met. I am also responsible to the parents of our students to see that they are supervised at all times and not exposed to any danger. And don't forget, not everyone in this town was in favor of this new approach. We're still in the implementation phase. It might be a good idea to proceed with caution."

Standing up, he tried to be conciliatory. "Now, we can still do all of the things you want to do. It's just that I want to make sure we meet all our responsibilities to the school committee and the community."

Mrs. Trottier was about to reply when Magnason's phone rang. As he answered it, she left.

Despite the restrictions on outdoor classes, the implementation of the program seemed to be proceeding smoothly over the next few weeks. Besides, autumn had brought cooler weather so that the air-conditioning was no longer important.

It was during this period that Mrs. Trottier spent more and more time with the middle school and its program while Mr. Magnason concentrated on the upper school. She maintained an "open door" policy with the teachers and always seemed willing to see one of them in her office whether to talk over problems or hash out new ideas.

The Amster-Dix-Spinella triumverate was beginning to work very well. Dedicated teachers all, they worked together as they had at Central High. Pooling ideas and materials, they were imaginative and unstructured in their teaching. They were popular with their students, and it was generally agreed that their students were progressing well. One of the new ideas that they tried was teaching with a minimum of supportive materials. They resorted to textbooks and other such resources only when absolutely necessary. This teaching concept was a particular favorite of Mrs. Trottier's, and their success at it enhanced their prestige as practitioners of the new educational philosophy.

Some of the other teachers were not as successful in using this technique, however. Wes Perron and Emily Geoffrion, in particular, were having problems. They spoke with Mrs. Trottier in her office about their troubles one day.

TROTTIER: I really can't understand the problems you're having. Look at Kate, Florence, and Lou in seventh grade. They're doing very well and enjoying it to boot. Perhaps you have not given it enough of a chance yet.
PERRON: Well, we've talked it over and we feel we need more to work with in class. I just can't teach all day without any books or charts or anything.
GEOFFRION: That's right. Maybe some of these other teachers can do it, but they've been at it a lot longer. When I have as much experience as they do, I'll probably be able to talk all day without a lesson plan too. Right now, it's just too much.
TROTTIER: Look, you're both getting too worried about this. I know it's harder on you because of your lack of experience, but both of you have the makings of excellent teachers. That's why I hired you. Sure, you'll have to work harder but you'll be better teachers for it.
PERRON: It gets pretty rough down there, you know. You ought to take a look for yourself. These kids can be pretty wild.
TROTTIER: Look, I know all about it. But I've put this program across in tougher schools than this. You'll be all right. You just need to work at it a little more.

After leaving Trottier's office, Emily was sullen. "'You just need to work at it a little longer.' Is that the best she can do? Why doesn't she at least come down and sit in on a class or two so she could offer some suggestions?"

"Yeah," agreed Wes, "she won't even take a look at what's going on. All she ever does is sit in her office talking to people and drinking coffee. We're supposed to mark the kids on effort and all we ever get from her is 'try harder.'"

The Wednesday morning before Thanksgiving Mr. Magnason was in the hall outside his office, having just gotten off the phone after trying to placate another upset committee member—this time regarding the curriculum not being as supportive of the vocational arts as had been intended. As he stood musing about the call, he heard shouts and loud laughter from around the corner. Rounding the corner were three seventh-grade boys who were engaging in general horseplay. When they saw him, they immediately fell silent.

"Where are you going?" he demanded.

After a short pause, one said, "Uh, we're going to the library."

"Why?"

The same boy answered, "We want to get a book."

"About what?"

"Animals."

"You know very well that the library isn't in this part of the building," Magnason boomed. "Return to your classes at once."

MEMO

To: All Faculty

From: A. Magnason

Subject: Movement of students throughout building during class time

It is becoming increasingly clear that the unrestricted movement of students within the school building during class time is counterproductive to the educational process.

Therefore, the following means will be used to control student movement:

1. Any student movement will be controlled through the use of passes, which will be issued by a teacher.
2. The pass will be used only for a specific purpose, which will be clearly identified on the pass.
3. Teachers will limit the number of passes issued in any one class period to 10 percent of the number of students present in the class.
4. Students found away from their classes without passes will be considered for disciplinary action.

Passes are being printed now. This policy will become effective upon distribution of passes to each teacher.

"Paulette's going to go through the roof when she sees this one," Kate Amster said as she finished reading the latest memo.

"Progressive school, my foot," snorted Langford. "Why, Magnason doesn't have the slightest idea what we're trying to do here. This place will be just another Central High in a few months. I'm going to call my old school in New York."

During the first few months, it had become a ritual among many of the middle school teachers to meet at the *Silver Pony*, an English-style pub, in Devon every Friday after work. Such a gathering took place in mid-November.

LANGFORD: Today I had the pleasure of the Tigrrr's company in class.
SPINELLA: Hey, John, be careful. The guy's difficult but it's not really right to get down to the kids' level.
LANGFORD: Oh, I know, but he watched my history class today. We were role-playing the Constitutional Convention, and the kids were really getting into it. They were moving around and yelling, but, dammit, they were interested and involved. After the class do you think he said anything about what we had done? Hell no! All he said was that he thought the class was a little unruly and that I should try to control them more.
BETTY SIVILS [*Fiftyish. Though considered one of the "old guard," she was well liked by most of the younger teachers*]: I know how you feel, John, but you must admit that some of these kids are getting out of hand. Open classrooms is one thing, but to have them disrupting things is another. Paulette is undermining discipline. Do you know the kids feel they can go to her and complain about teachers and that she'll listen to them? I don't think that's proper, and I think we can see the damage it's doing to the climate of learning. She doesn't seem to be aware of some of the problems she's creating.
LANGFORD: I still feel that Magnason doesn't care about content as long as our areas are calm and there's no noise coming from them. He's not even trying to understand the new system.
MCNAIR: I agree. He's been an administrator too long. He doesn't care about people, whether they're students or faculty, as long as he can control them. Some of those memos of his. . . .
RESCA: You mean the "Tigrrr Talks?"
MCNAIR [*laughing*]: Yeah, the "Tigrrr Talks." They're very condescending. He treats the faculty like children. And how about our staff meetings? If it's not on the agenda, it doesn't get discussed; and Magnason controls the agenda.
SPINELLA: Changing the subject, but did you know Paulette and Magnason had it out again Tuesday? I don't know the full story, but I guess it was about that latest memo of his.
LANGFORD: You mean the one restricting student movement from class to class.
SPINELLA: Right. Paulette was pretty hot.
MCNAIR: No wonder. That idea's one of the basic premises of the open-classroom concept. If you bog kids down in bureaucracy, exploring new learning experiences will be too much of a hassle.
SPINELLA: You know, this is starting to get pretty serious. Those two are at each other's throats more and more. Things just can't go on like this.

On Sunday evening, December 12, Mr. Fowles made another call to Mr. Magnason's home. After exchanging pleasantries, Fowles brought up the school.

FOWLES: Arthur, I'm starting to feel real concern over what's going on down there in the middle school. We're starting to get an awful lot of adverse reaction from parents. Arthur, it's been over three months since school opened, and I'm beginning to hear complaints from parents that the bugs should be worked out by now.

MAGNASON: But you're going to get that anytime a new school opens. And in our case, we're starting a new curriculum, too.

FOWLES: I know, Arthur, I know. But it's getting to the point where feelings among many parents are running pretty high.

MAGNASON: What are the big complaints?

FOWLES: Well, I guess one of the biggest is that parents never see their kids doing any homework. In fact, they say they never see them with any books at all. Those outside classes in the beginning of the year didn't go over too well, either. Oh yes, another thing. Parents don't feel their kids are learning anything useful. One mother told me her sixth grader spends all day learning about Eskimos. Is that true?

MAGNASON: Oh that. That's the Makos concept, one of Trottier's pet projects. Total immersion learning, where students learn all aspects of a culture and can compare it to their own.

FOWLES: I see. Well, I'm afraid it looks like the committee meeting in January could be stormy. You'd better get your ducks in line because there will be people there who'll be looking for someone's hide. Most of the committee is still not committed totally to the new school, and I think we'll be forced to take a closer look at what's going on from now on.

It started snowing late that night and continued through the next morning, Monday, the 13th. Mr. Magnason had to attend a meeting of school administrators in Clear River and didn't get to Devon School until 1:30 in the afternoon. When he drove up, he saw about 30 students milling around in front of the school chanting unintelligible slogans. Parking his car, he went to the front entrance where he found Mrs. Trottier just inside the doors. She and a few other teachers were watching the students.

"What the hell's going on here, Mrs. Trottier?" he demanded.

"The students are staging a walkout," she said in a matter-of-fact tone of voice.

Magnason started. "A what?"

"I said," she answered in a clipped voice, "the students are staging a walkout."

"Whatever the hell for?"

Sighing audibly, Mrs. Trottier explained, "Some of the eighth graders tried to pull a fast one. One of them called the bus company and said we were closing early because of the snow and to send the buses right over. When the caller didn't give the code word, the bus company got suspicious and called back to confirm. That's how I found out. When the buses didn't show, they started getting restless. When I made an announcement over the PA that the buses would come at the usual time, about 30 of them walked out. They've been out there about a half hour."

"And you've done nothing?"

"Why bother?" she said. "Let them get it out of their system. Besides, they'll get cold pretty soon and come inside."

"And in the meantime," Magnason shouted, "we let everybody know that we're making a bunch of revolutionaries out of their kids!"

"Well, you do something," she snapped. "You're the drillmaster around here."

"What?"

"You're the one who wants them all quietly in their places like good little robots." Mrs. Trottier was shouting now, too. Pointing her finger at Magnason, she went on, "You people are all the same. Who cares if they learn anything as long as they behave themselves long enough for us to ship them to another grade. It makes me sick."

With that she stalked off down the hall.

Livid, Magnason shouted after her, "Mrs. Trottier, come back here!"

Then he became aware of the circle of teachers, some watching him, some looking after Mrs. Trottier.

Dilemma at Devil's Den

My name is Susan, and I'm a business student at Mt. Eagle College. Let me tell you about one of my worst experiences. I had a part-time job in the campus snack bar, The Devil's Den. At the time, I was 21 years old and a junior with a concentration in finance. I originally started working at the Den in order to earn some extra spending money. I had been working there for one semester and became upset with some of the happenings. The Den was managed by contract with an external company, College Food Services (CFS). What bothered me was that many employees were allowing their friends to take free food, and the employees themselves were also taking food in large

This case was prepared by Kim Johnson under the supervision of Professor Allan R. Cohen for classroom discussion.

quantities when leaving their shifts. The policy was that employees could eat whatever they liked free of charge while they were working, but it had become common for employees to leave with food and to not be charged for their snacks while off duty as well.

I felt these problems were occurring for several reasons. For example, employee wages were low, there was easy access to the unlocked storage room door, and inventory was poorly controlled. Also, there was weak supervision by the student managers and no written rules or strict guidelines. It seemed that most of the employees were enjoying "freebies," and it had been going on for so long that it was taken for granted. The problem got so far out of hand that customers who had seen others do it felt free to do it whether they knew the workers or not. The employees who witnessed this never challenged anyone because, in my opinion, they did not care and they feared the loss of friendship or being frowned upon by others. Apparently, speaking up was more costly to the employees than the loss of money to CFS for the unpaid food items. It seemed obvious to me that the employees felt too secure in their jobs and did not feel that their jobs were in jeopardy.

The employees involved were those who worked the night shifts and on the weekends. They were students at the college and were under the supervision of another student who held the position of manager. There were approximately 30 student employees and 6 student managers on the staff. During the day there were no student managers; instead, a full-time manager was employed by CFS to supervise the Den. The employees and student managers were mostly freshman and sophomores, probably because of the low wages, inconvenient hours (late weeknights and weekends), and the duties of the job itself. Employees were hard to come by; the high rate of employee turnover indicated that the job qualifications and the selection process were minimal.

The student managers were previous employees chosen—by other student managers and the full-time CFS day manager—based upon their ability to work and on their length of employment. They received no further formal training or written rules beyond what they had already learned by working there. The student managers were briefed on how to close the snack bar at night but still did not get the job done properly. They received authority and responsibility over events occurring during their shifts as manager, although they were never actually taught how and when to enforce it! Their increase in pay was small, from a starting pay of just over minimum wage to an additional 15 percent for student managers. Regular employees received an additional nickel for each semester of employment.

Although I only worked seven hours per week, I was in the Den often as a customer and saw the problem frequently. I felt the problem was on a large enough scale that action should have been taken, not only to correct any financial loss that the Den might have experienced, but also to help give the student employees a true sense of their responsibilities, the limits of their freedom, respect for rules, and pride in their jobs. The issues at hand bothered my conscience, although I was not directly involved. I felt that the employees and customers were taking advantage of the situation whereby they could "steal" food almost whenever they wanted. I believed that I had been brought up correctly and knew "right" from "wrong," and I felt that the happenings in the Den were wrong. It wasn't fair that CFS paid for others' greediness or urges to show what they could get away with in front of their friends.

I was also bothered by the lack of responsibility of the managers to get the employees to do their work. I had seen the morning employees work very hard trying to do their jobs, in addition to the jobs the closing shift should have done. I assumed the night managers did not care or think about who worked the next day. It bothered me to think that the morning employees were suffering because of careless employees and student managers from the night before.

I had never heard of CFS mentioning any problems or taking any corrective action; therefore, I wasn't sure whether they knew what was going on, or if they were ignoring it. I was speaking to a close friend, Mack, a student manager at the Den, and I mentioned the fact that the frequently unlocked door to the storage room was an easy exit through which I had seen different quantities of unpaid goods taken out. I told him about some specific instances and said that I believed that it happened rather frequently. Nothing was ever said to other employees about this, and the only corrective action was that the door was locked more often, yet the key to the lock was still available upon request to all employees during their shifts.

Another lack of strong corrective action I remembered was when an employee was caught pocketing cash from the register. The student was neither suspended nor threatened with losing his job (nor was the event even mentioned). Instead, he was just told to stay away from the register. I felt that this weak punishment happened not because he was a good worker, but because he worked so many hours and it would be difficult to find someone who would work all those hours and remain working for more than a few months. Although the incident was reported by a customer, I still felt that management should have taken more corrective action.

The attitudes of the student managers seemed to vary. I had noticed that one in particular, Bill, always got the job done. He made a list of each small duty that needed to be done, such as restocking, and he made sure the jobs were divided among the employees and finished before his shift was over. Bill also "stared down" employees who allowed thefts by their friends or who took freebies themselves, yet I had never heard of an employee being challenged verbally, nor had anyone ever been fired for these actions. My friend Mack was concerned about theft, or so I assumed, because he had taken some action about locking the doors, but he didn't really get after employees to work if they were slacking off.

I didn't think the rest of the student managers were good motivators. I noticed that they did little work themselves and did not show much control over the employees. The student managers allowed their friends to take food for free, therefore setting bad examples for the other workers, and allowed the employees to take what they wanted even when they were not working. I thought their attitudes were shared by most of the other employees: not caring about their jobs nor working hard, as long as they got paid and their jobs were not threatened.

I had let the "thefts" continue without mention because I felt that no one else really cared and may even have frowned upon me for trying to take action. Management thus far had not reported significant losses to the employees so as to encourage them to watch for theft and prevent it. Management did not threaten employees with job loss, nor did they provide employees with supervision. I felt it was not my place to report the theft to management, because I was "just an employee" and I would be overstepping the student managers. Also, I was unsure whether management would do anything about it anyway—maybe they did not care. I felt that talking to the student managers or other employees would be useless, because they were either abusing the rules themselves or were clearly aware of what was going on and just ignored it. I felt that others may have frowned upon me and made it uncomfortable for me to continue working there. This would be very difficult for me because I wanted to become a student manager the next semester and did not want to create any waves that might have prevented me from doing so. I recognized the student manager position as a chance to gain some managerial and leadership skills while at the same time adding a great plus to my résumé when I graduated. Besides, as a student manager, I would be in a better position to do something about all the problems at the Den that bothered me so much.

What could I do in the meantime to clear my conscience of the "freebies," favors to friends, and employee snacks? What could I do without ruining my chances of becoming a student manager myself someday? I hated just keeping quiet, but I didn't want to make a fool of myself. I was really stuck.

▶ Dominion Acceptance Company Limited

In May 1973 Mr. B. L. Keast, Atlantic regional manager of operations for Dominion Acceptance Company Limited, faced a number of personnel and operating procedures decisions directly affecting the operations of the Moncton, New Brunswick, branch of DAC. Earlier in the year, changes in the management staffing of the Moncton branch had been made, and after three months the results of these changes were being evaluated in order to make adequate permanent changes in the Moncton operation. As the problems which had led to the changes had been of a particularly serious nature, it was imperative that Mr. Keast thoroughly examine the possible effects of any changes, as well as the causes of the problems arising earlier. In doing so he was compelled to consider the viewpoints of the Moncton branch manager, Mr. Ronald Snell; Snell's current assistant manager, Mr. Alex DeCoste; his previous assistant manager Mr. Jerry MacDonald; and the rest of the Moncton staff. In addition he recognized the importance of keeping the Moncton operation consistent with the other branches in his region as well as with national DAC policy.

BACKGROUND

DAC was one of the largest finance companies in Canada. Its primary business was the acceptance of conditional sales contracts from customers who had purchased customer goods. DAC then paid the retailer while the customer paid DAC in monthly installments. In addition to this retail financing, DAC also made loans to firms either to begin or expand existing businesses. The company was entirely Canadian-owned, and operated on a national basis. Regional offices were located in five major Canadian cities, viz., Halifax, Montreal, Toronto, Winnipeg, and Vancouver. Branch offices were located in most cities and some towns serving as district shopping centres. Atlantic region branch staff sizes varied from 3 to 40 depending on the population of the market being served and the amount of money loaned.

Corporate headquarters were in Toronto and functioned as a central policy-making and administrative centre. Head office established specific policies and procedures regarding loans, branch control, and reporting methods, as well as personnel policies and administrative procedures designed to ensure consistent coast-to-coast operations.

Case material prepared by Mr. William J. MacNeil under the direction of W. H. Cooper, assistant professor of business administration, St. Francis Xavier University, Antigonish, N.S., Canada. Reprinted by permission of Professor Cooper.

To obtain consistency, DAC had in 1968 prepared and distributed to each branch a detailed procedures manual which, in addition to the above policies, prescribed office procedures and provided detailed job descriptions for all branch positions. In the manual the policy of aggressively seeking new profitable accounts was stressed.

The regional managers of operations (RMO) functioned as the intermediary between corporate headquarters and the branches in their respective regions. As with the Halifax RMO, all RMOs had as their primary source of information regarding branch operations the monthly statistics prepared for them by each branch. The format was prescribed by the procedures manual (including the due date of the third of each month covering the previous month's operations) and consisted of statistics on the number and dollar value of accounts, collections made, total branch expenses for the month, and overdue accounts by age. As part of the computer analysis of branch operations, the RMO compiled this data into a regional report comparing all branches in the region and sent copies to each branch as well as to Toronto. Each branch manager could therefore regularly compare his performance against the other individual branches as well as with the region as a whole.

In his evaluation of branch operations and the resulting report, Mr. Keast placed emphasis on the control of payments. The percentage of accounts 30 or more days late was the key evaluation variable, and he expected the collection departments in each branch to give special attention to such deficient accounts. The Atlantic region's average delinquency rate was 3 percent. Branch managers were generally quite sensitive about their office's delinquency rate and how their rate compared with other branches in the region, as shown in the monthly RMO's report.

In addition to the monthly reports, the RMO conducted a yearly visit to each branch (without prior notice being given) to perform several kinds of inspection and audits. The RMO and his staff inspected the accounts and credit records, performed employee evaluations of the manager and assistant manager, and, if time allowed, reviewed the manager's evaluations of the other staff members. As each manager hired his own staff and operated his branch with some autonomy, the results of the monthly and annual evaluations were of particular importance in judging the manager and his staff's ability.

THE FEBRUARY INSPECTION

Mr. Keast's inspection in June 1972 had rated the Moncton branch's overall performance as slightly below average. The July 1972 and subsequent monthly reports began to show a steadily increasing delinquency rate and a decrease in the dollar value as well as in the number of accounts. By January 1973 the delinquency rate stood at 8 percent and the number of customer accounts had fallen from 3,500 in June 1972 to 3,000. This performance decline was significantly poorer than the other branches in southern New Brunswick. After repeated requests for explanations, and unsatisfactory responses, Mr. Keast decided to make his 1973 visit much earlier in the year, and hence on February 14 he arrived in Moncton at 7:15 A.M. Upon entering the airport terminal Mr. Keast and his staff assistant were surprised to find Mr. Snell queuing up for a ticket on the 7:35 A.M. departure for Toronto. An embarrassed Snell explained that he had some personal business in Hamilton, but that it was not urgent and could be delayed, particularly in light of the unexpected annual inspection of the branch which was to be conducted that day.

Traveling to the branch from the airport, Snell explained: "I've been finding it tough to do much to control our late accounts. We've a poor clientele, my assistant isn't qualified, and the girls we've been getting to keep our account records up to date have not worked out. I know it makes the branch look poor, but you know I've tried. I think in a couple of months we'll have the office turned around and be back among the regional leaders where we belong." Keast listened politely and expressed concern that something must be done soon to improve the Moncton operations. "If your staff is not up to the job, maybe we can fix that; but as far as customers go, you've got as good an economic area here as Scott does in Fredericton and Angus in St. John. Anyhow, you certainly have a lot more snow here than we do down in Halifax. Let's see how things are looking in the office." Arriving downtown, Keast and his assistant spent the next few hours going over the account cards and other financial records.

Things did not look good. Over 20 account cards had been found which were over 90 days past due (the January report had shown a total of 12 such accounts), and no note of contact between the office and the customer could be found for most of them for the past 60 days. The office was in disarray, the filing system in chaos, key records and papers took some time to locate, and the customer account clerks seemed unfamiliar with much of the routine office procedure. Keast finished the morning going over the personnel files and noted that the turnover rate for clerical personnel was high, absenteeism a problem, and a key staff member (the accounts supervisor) had been fired a month ago and had not been replaced. Leaving his assistant to tabulate the results of the morning's inspection, Keast took a by now very worried-looking Snell to lunch at Cy's. He intended to utilize lunch to do the performance appraisal and to suggest several courses of action that might be taken to remedy the Moncton problems. He was disturbed and somewhat surprised by what they had uncovered in their morning's work.

The bleak view of the Petitcodiac River at low tide, which was visible from the restaurant window, provided an appropriate backdrop to their luncheon conversation. Keast began: "Look, Ron, you're over $5 million outstanding and $400,000 of that is overdue. We can't find half of what we're looking for in your records, and no one seems to know what they're doing. You admit yourself that things are out of hand." "But Mr. Keast, I've told you that I know we're having problems, but I think it is up to me to solve them. I've been the manager here for eight years, and I promise that within six months we'll have everything back to normal."

Toying with his lobster thermidor, Keast considered what he should and could do. He had certainly given Snell ample notice of dissatisfaction with the branch's operation, and the prospect for improvement seemed dim. On the other hand, Snell had a long record of satisfactory work with only one year of poor operation. He had been manager of the Moncton branch for eight years and had the longest stay of any branch manager in the region, as well as the longest service of any of the current staff at that branch. Keast thought that this visit had impressed on all the Moncton staff the alarm with which their performance was viewed by him. Weighing this, Keast advised Snell that "the inspection this morning has convinced me that changes have to be made. I think you knew this. You have worked well in the past, but it looks to me that you may need some help in bringing the turnaround about." Snell agreed that he needed help. Keast continued: "My assistant worked at the Halifax branch before he became my assistant at regional. You met him this morning. What do you think of him?" Snell responded in a noncommittal fashion, saying, "He certainly seems efficient and gets right to the problem without fooling around. He seems fine. Why?" "Well, Ron, you suggested that Jerry MacDonald isn't doing his job the way you'd like him to. I'll see him this afternoon for his performance appraisal, and I propose to offer him a field salesman position in Prince Edward Island. I would like to replace him temporarily with my assistant, Alex DeCoste." Stunned at this suggestion, Snell could only nod. He had half expected to be fired himself.

Before returning to the office Keast told Snell that this move was only temporary and would last for three months. At the end of that time he would return to Moncton and reinspect the branch. Both expressed the hope that the results would warrant a rerating of the branch from poor to at least satisfactory.

On returning to the office Keast spent half an hour with Jerry MacDonald, explaining the reasons for the changes and his new responsibilities. Jerry was 40 years old and had once been the branch manager in Edmundston, New Brunswick, before coming to Moncton. His performance in Edmundston had resulted in his becoming assistant manager at the Moncton branch. Since then he had not shown much interest in becoming a branch manager again. He accepted the proposed change calmly. Keast then met with Snell and DeCoste, and they discussed the changes that would have to be made in order to eliminate the current operating problems. DeCoste made several suggestions regarding collections, personnel training, and new business, which were greeted with mild interest by Snell. They agreed to explore these ideas more fully when DeCoste returned February 19 to assume his new duties. Keast and DeCoste then left the Moncton branch to catch their return flight to Halifax. On the return flight Keast impressed upon DeCoste the importance of getting the Moncton branch back in shape, not only for the sake of the branch's health, but also because other branch managers in the region were keenly interested in how Keast would handle the situation.

CHANGES

Returning the following Monday, DeCoste and Snell met briefly and exchanged pleasantries. Snell then formally introduced him to the rest of the staff, some of whom DeCoste had met the previous Wednesday. Most of the staff gave DeCoste a warm greeting. The staff consisted of three collection officers, a cashier/cash journal clerk, and three file clerk/typists (a fourth had quit a week earlier). The accounts supervisor position remained unfilled. (See Exhibit 1 for an organizational chart of the Moncton branch.) Snell and DeCoste then returned to discuss the changes that needed to be made.

As with all the DAC branches which had both a manager and an assistant manager, the Moncton manager's job description prescribed his primary duties as that of seeking new customers (both consumer and commercial), promoting sales, and performing all public relations duties. These duties called for significant amounts of field work, and as a result the daily supervision of office work was assigned to the assistant manager. DeCoste would assume all responsibilities for directing and appraising office personnel and acting as liaison between the staff and the manager where necessary. In the Monday meeting, the two men agreed that DeCoste would run the office as his job description indicated, but that any significant changes and decisions that DeCoste might make would be thoroughly discussed with Snell before making them.

On the afternoon of the 19th, DeCoste met with the collections staff and explained the changes to be made in the collection of past due and current accounts. The collection officers were to have all the accounts pulled which were 60 or more days overdue and resolve these accounts according to procedures set forth in the procedures

EXHIBIT 1
Organization Chart: February 19, 1973

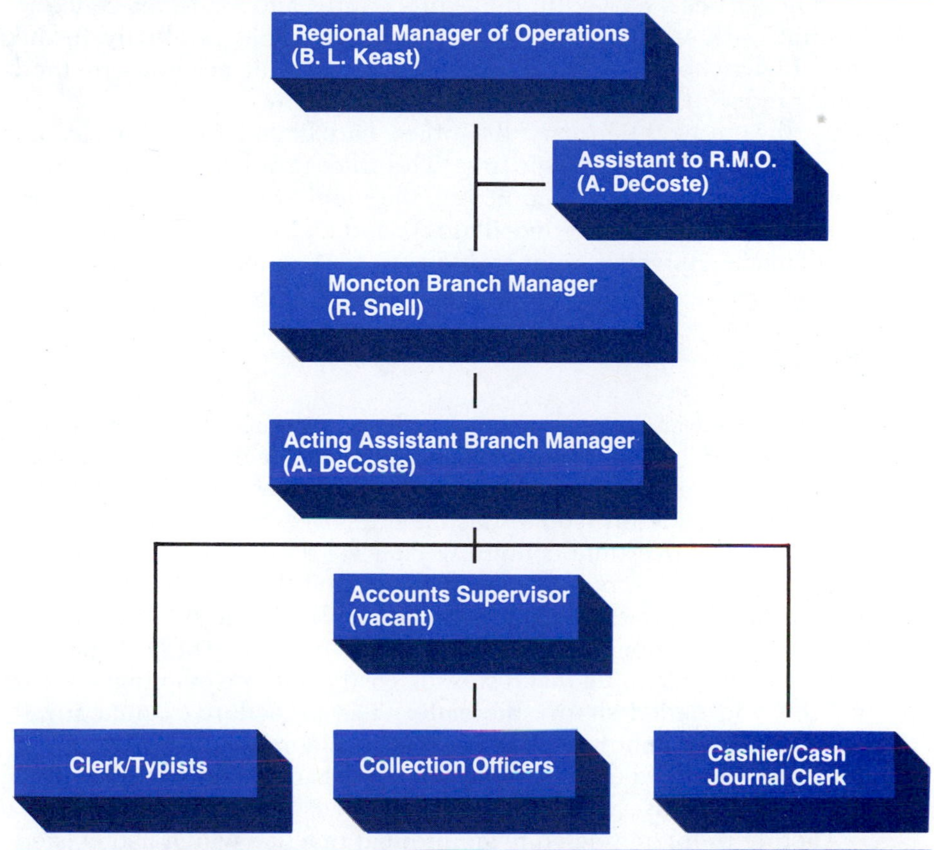

manual. Once these were settled, they would then focus their attention on the next most critical group, the 30 to 60 days overdue accounts. It was agreed that these 250 accounts would be processed in two weeks' time. DeCoste promised that a replacement for the previously fired accounts supervisor would be on the job within two weeks. In the meantime he designated the most senior of the officers as the temporary chief of this concerted effort.

That afternoon DeCoste met with the three clerk/typists and spent the rest of the day reorganizing the filing system and instructing them in the standard procedures for keeping account records current. This procedure consisted of the dating of all payments on the reverse of the customer's account card and the daily pulling of all account cards whose payments were due that day. These cards were then placed at the back of the "accounts payable" file. When accounts were paid, the cashier/journal clerk noted this on the card and placed them in the "to file" box, to be filed by the clerk/typists. Two of the girls claimed to have never been trained in these procedures and made reference to account cards which had been handled somewhat carelessly in the past. It was hoped that this systematic customer accounts method would reduce the number of customer complaints.

By the end of February the office had begun to operate more smoothly than it had for some time. The office now had its full complement of staff, morale had improved, the number of uncollected overdue accounts had been reduced to 100, and DeCoste felt progress was being made. However, new problems were beginning to arise.

MARCH

The first problem arose at the end of the month. The February report was due March 3rd, which meant that the actual completion date would be Thursday, the 1st. It was DeCoste's responsibility to complete the task, and on Wednesday he asked the staff (exclusive of Mr. Snell) to work overtime compiling data for the report. This request met with loud disapproval. The staff claimed that this had not been the practice for some time, and when it had been, the staff had had to buy their own supper. Mr. Snell had ended the policy of DAC paying for the dinner, claiming that it was too costly, and the evening work at month's end ended shortly thereafter. The procedure manual stipulated that agreement to work overtime once a month was a condition of employment and that DAC would pay for any expenses (including meals) incurred as a result.

Another problem related to an informal practice which had existed for some time. Between Keast's inspection visit and DeCoste's arrival as assistant manager, Snell had instructed all the staff that coffee breaks were to be eliminated. Snell continued to take a break twice a day in the coffee shop next door. On two occasions after his arrival, DeCoste accompanied Snell on his coffee break. On both occasions Snell belittled the staff, complaining about their ineptness, criticized his previous assistant manager, and complained that after 18 years of service with the company they had forgotten about him. The staff began to sneak in thermoses of tea and coffee for use during Snell's regular visits to the coffee shop.

A third problem began occurring immediately after DeCoste's arrival. Arguments between staff members began to occur over who was to do what. Snell would hear these disputes, come out of his office, and immediately direct the employees involved to do the tasks in the manner he indicated, all of this before DeCoste could act to resolve the dispute. On these occasions Snell referred to the need to run an efficient office.

An additional problem began during DeCoste's second week at Moncton. One of the collection officers approached him regarding a raise, pointing out that the last raise he had had was 18 months ago and it was for only \$3 per week, raising him to \$118. Alex checked the employee's personnel file and found he had not been appraised since the time of his last raise, despite the fact that it was DAC policy to perform employee reviews annually on the anniversary of their employment. A raise seemed warranted to Alex as the officer was making \$500 below the average for collection officers in the region with similar lengths of service, although there was a considerable range in salaries throughout the region. DeCoste approached Snell but was told that no raises would be granted until the rating of the branch was judged satisfactory by the RMO. He claimed the employee was being overpaid now and referred to the outstanding accounts problem. DeCoste responded, "Look, Mr. Snell, I've examined all the personnel files for all our staff and have found the rates of pay to be well below the DAC rates in the Atlantic region, and our staff knows this. I think we need to catch up on our raises. I know Jerry MacDonald left this to you, but you're too busy as it is and we're way overdue on the annual appraisals. As it is now, none of the staff knows why they have not had raises and that includes Jerry before he left." Snell's response was short and repeated his claim that no raises would be approved until the branch shaped up. DeCoste was sure that Keast had given Snell no directions regarding salary changes. After this conversation of the 27th, Alex informed the employee that he was trying to get a raise of \$10 a week approved and that a strong showing on the outstanding collections would improve his case.

Finally, DeCoste noted that he had inherited a staff who had grown accustomed to going to Snell with any operating problems. This practice had been tacitly approved by Jerry MacDonald, who had become used to having Mr. Snell in the office most of the time and left most matters of consequence for Snell to deal with. MacDonald had not, however, refrained from joining in on the jokes made about Snell on the rare occasions when he was out of the office.

THE MAY INSPECTION

During the February–April period the monthly reports showed the branch's improvement in its accounts collections. The delinquency rate for April 1973 was down to 4 percent and only one clerk/typist had quit. Some of the administrative and operations problems had been resolved, but the problems of raises, office supervision by Snell, and the coffee break prohibitions remained while the number of accounts had continued to fall. Keast had requested a private report from DeCoste regarding the Moncton operations and had received it at the end of April. In it he made observations regarding the various administrative and operating problems and also noted his own frustration in his current position.

Keast was to arrive on May 7 and the Moncton staff anticipated his arrival with varying mixtures of anxiety, hope, and fascination. Keast's own view of the May visit was one of realizing that there was more involved than the health of the Moncton branch. Keast had tried carefully to consider all the factors regarding the Snell case in light of the current control system and the branch manager's job. Keast also had to keep in mind Snell's long service record, his welfare and that of the Moncton staff, as well as the health of the total Moncton operations and its place in the region. On the May 7, 7:30 A.M. flight, he reviewed what he intended to say at that meeting. The weather had improved since his last flight to Moncton, and he hoped the Moncton operation would continue similarly to improve.

▶ The Eager New Lawyer and the Managing Clerk

NOTE: *DO NOT READ* this case until directed to do so by your instructor. It has been set up as a Prediction Case so that you can test your analysis by answering questions before reading the entire case.

PART I

I was a lawyer with Messrs. Allan and Banes for 15 years and watched young lawyers come and go. Ours was a large Australian firm, employing 40 staff people. It was also one of the more prestigious firms, having established over the previous 50 years an enviable reputation for reliability and competency. I think the following case will give you some picture of a newcomer's introduction to our firm and to the profession of law.

Messrs. Allan and Banes had a reputation for conservatism, which reflected the influence of the partners and, to a lesser extent, the nature of the work handled. There were eight partners in the firm: five specialized in corporation work, and the remaining three headed the departments of property, probate (wills and trusts), and common law (court cases such as motor vehicle collisions).

From Robert E. C. Wegner and Leonard Sayles, *Cases in Organizational and Administrative Behavior*, © 1972, pp. 25–29. Case edited slightly and restructured into a prediction case. Reprinted by permission of Prentice-Hall, Inc.

Although the staff (that is, the nonpartners) numbered approximately 40 people, only about 15 actually handled legal work, the balance comprising women of various ages who performed secretarial and receptionist duties. These 15 people fell into two categories: those who were qualified attorneys, and those who were not. Those who were unqualified fell into two subcategories termed *managing clerks* and *articled clerks*. The distinction was important because managing clerks could never advance, whereas articled clerks were generally younger people who had graduated from law school. After graduating, it is necessary to work for a year in an attorney's office for the purpose of supplementing the more theoretical law school with some practical experience. At the conclusion of that year and after satisfying certain further requirements (examinations, character), the articled clerk is admitted to the practice of law and finally becomes qualified as an attorney.

It was into this somewhat rarified atmosphere that Jack Bohnston stepped. He was young, eager, fresh from law school, and bursting with knowledge of the latest trends in law. In short, he knew a lot about what the law is, was, and ought to be. Now he was about to apply it. Nevertheless, Bohnston was not unmindful of the fact that he was fortunate to be doing his articles with Messrs. Allan and Banes and that the attorney to whom he was "articled" was Mr. McLloyd, one of the senior partners of the firm. McLloyd was in the corporation department.

On his first day, Bohnston was advised by McLloyd that over a period of time he would be rotated through each department of the firm. This would enable Bohnston to gain some insight into the main branches of the law so that he would then be in a better position to assess the merits of each department and decide in which field to specialize. The first department was to be the property department; and in view of Mr. McLloyd's busy schedule and the fact that he primarily operated in a different department, Bohnston was advised that he was to be placed under control and direction of Mr. Lawson.

Ned Lawson had been with Messrs. Allan and Banes for about 10 years. He was 63 years of age and due to retire in 2 years. Mr. Lawson was English and had worked for an English firm of attorneys for some 20 years. He decided to leave England, and on his arrival in Australia found employment with Messrs. Allan and Banes. At no time had Lawson become or attempted to become an attorney; he was a managing clerk with considerable experience but no legal qualifications.

The building occupied by the firm was old with large rooms and high ceilings. Lawson had one of the largest offices, and he liked the prestige and the privacy which accompanied it. He also appreciated the fact that he was well regarded in the firm because of his considerable practical experience and that he was assigned a permanent secretary for his sole convenience.

After Jack Bohnston was shown around the offices of the firm by the partner in charge of the property department and introduced to the other partners and staff, he met Lawson. After the usual introductory remarks, the property partner remarked to Bohnston that this was the room where he would work for the immediate future and that in the first instance he was under control of Lawson, then himself, and ultimately Mr. McLloyd.

Discussion Questions

1. What expectations is Lawson likely to have about the role that Bohnston should have? Explain your conclusion by reference to:
   a. Background factors.
   b. Features of the required system.
   c. Lawson's self-concept.
2. What expectations is Bohnston likely to have about his role? Explain your conclusion by reference to:
   a. Background factors.
   b. Features of the required system.
   c. Bohnston's self-concept.
3. What kind of relationship does the task call for?
4. What personal styles of relationships would you conclude that Lawson and Bohnston prefer?
5. What kind of relationship do you predict Lawson and Bohnston will have? What will the consequences be for each in terms of learning and satisfaction?

PART II

On that first day and over the next couple of weeks, a series of events occurred which greatly discouraged Jack Bohnston. These events or incidents were all of a very minor, almost petty, nature.

As mentioned, Lawson's office was spacious, and in the middle of the room stood his large desk. Bohnston's desk, situated in a far corner, was more like a tiny table virtually surrounded by Lawson's filing cabinets. In these first days Bohnston required very little secretarial assistance, but when it was necessary, he was authorized by the property partner to use Lawson's secretary. When he did this, he found that the work was seldom returned to him the same day. Bohnston received few phone calls and held no conferences. Lawson's telephone rang continually, and he held many conferences. During these conferences Lawson occasionally introduced Bohnston to the firm's client with the comment, "This is the new articled clerk. I'm keeping an eye on him." More often, Bohnston was studiously ignored. Lawson handled a heavy volume of work and often requested Bohnston to assist him by performing minor and menial tasks. These requests generally came at a time when Bohnston had other work to complete—work assigned to him not only by the property partners but also by the other partners.

Bohnston did not see any particular significance in these assignments. But although he outwardly remained polite and courteous, the appropriate role for the firm's most recent employee, inwardly he was frustrated and disappointed and anxiously awaited the end of the year when his "penal" servitude would end. He felt he was regarded as an idiot, capable only of running errands; his lengthy and specialized training seemed of little use, and he almost had to beg for his work to be typed. He received virtually no recognition, prestige, or status. The work he was given seemed unimportant, but it often required reference to Lawson, an unqualified person anyway, who gave advice in a grudging and abrupt manner if he gave it at all. And when Lawson did pay attention he wanted to chat about his family.

Each of the partners wanted his work to be done immediately, and thus when Bohnston received several matters on one day, he succeeded in satisfying none of the partners. Bohnston could not help comparing his position with that of a close friend who, on graduating from law school, had decided not to do his articles and had gone straight into a corporation. This friend worked shorter hours, received three times Bohnston's salary, had his own office and secretary, not to mention other corporation fringe benefits.

About a month or so after Bohnston had joined Messrs. Allan and Banes, Bohnston approached Lawson about some matter and again was caught in a family-type conversation during which Lawson remarked that as he was approaching retiring age, Bohnston would be the last articled clerk he trained; indeed he had thought that the previous articled clerk he had trained would be the last.

Discussion Questions

1. What kind of relationship has emerged between Lawson and Bohnston? How do you account for it? In explaining, refer to the respective self-concepts of each, and indicate how they are enhanced or diminished by the relationship.
2. What options are available to Bohnston in order to increase his learning and satisfaction?

PART III

Discussing Lawson's comments that night with a friend, Bohnston got a new insight when his friend asked how he, Bohnston, would feel if at the close of his working years, with age catching up and perhaps his patience and tolerance slowing down, he was asked to train "just one last articled clerk." Bohnston imagined how he would feel! He understood then how he would feel about other matters—such as sharing an office and a secretary.

Along with this new view of Lawson, Bohnston reconsidered his own position. Although there was no question about his legal knowledge and ability, he realized that he was really very ignorant about the procedural aspects of the law. He also realized that this was precisely what Lawson possessed and that McLloyd, in placing him under Lawson, was well aware of Lawson's wealth of experience and hoped that it would be of help to him.

With these new perspectives of Lawson and of himself, Bohnston found everything very different over the next few weeks. He discovered that Lawson usually arrived an hour before the official starting time and that, if he himself also arrived during that hour, Lawson was most affable and quite happy to discuss any current matters and to suggest alternative solutions to problems.

Bohnston now appreciated that during working hours Lawson did not have much time to do this. He still assisted Lawson; but Lawson explained not only what was to be done, but also the background of the matter and why it had to be carried out in a certain manner. Lawson provided Bohnston with technical aid and also gave him personal support. Occasionally a matter of Bohnston's did not develop as it should have, and if Bohnston had previously discussed it with Lawson, then Lawson would also attend the meeting with the property partner and would support Bohnston in the action he took and elaborate on the reasons. When the quantity of work that Bohnston handled increased, Lawson supported Bohnston's application for more secretarial assistance.

Thus Bohnston's attitude toward Lawson and the firm changed completely, but two matters still caused him some concern. The first arose from the fact that he still felt relatively deprived as compared to his friend who was employed by a corporation. The second matter that caused him concern arose from the fact that, notwithstanding the clear chain of command indicated to him at the outset, none of the partners observed this, and he continued to receive work from them all. He really was not sure whose directives were to be followed or in what order.

Discussion Questions and Predictions

1. What kind of relationship has emerged as a consequence of Bohnston's changes in behavior? Why?
2. What are the blind spots of Lawson and Bohnston in the ways in which they perceive each other? How do you explain them?

3. What barriers still remain in the communications between Bohnston and Lawson?
4. What predictions do you now make about the future of the relationship between Bohnston and Lawson and the consequences for each in terms of their self-concepts, development, and satisfaction?

Electronics Unlimited

Mike Craig, an economics major from Laurentian University, was employed by the Department of Agriculture for the last three years at the government offices for this department in the downtown area of Hamilton, Ontario. His work was assessed as above average and his ability to organize and present work efficiently, as noteworthy. His job involved preparing reports and statistics based on current trends and developments in farm management. Mike had a number of colleagues with whom he worked on a cooperative basis, each supplying the others with pertinent data for their studies. The organizational hierarchy under which he worked was a traditional bureaucratic structure; supervisors tended to be formal and impersonal, and there was strict adherence to procedure. It was within this environment that Mike performed his research and administrative activity.

Mike's role was very clearly defined: He was assigned a supervisor to whom he reported directly. His research work was submitted at various intervals, but current progress was frequently examined. While there was cooperative effort among the workers, there was very little enthusiasm for the work. The challenge seemed to be missing from the required task, for seldom were the results of his research implemented into a strategy for action. Instead much of the work was collated with other material for government reports and sent to Ottawa.

Mike had been dissatisfied with his job for about six months. He felt he had nowhere to go in this government position; and since he was still single and without family responsibility, he thought it was time to look for a more challenging job. He therefore watched the newspaper for an interesting position and consulted a Toronto placement agency for opportunities in that capital city. His interests as he described them to an interviewer were in joining a growing and dynamic com-

This case study was prepared by Professor Peter McGrady of Lakehead University as a basis for class discussion rather than to illustrate either effective or ineffective handling of an administrative situation.

pany, possibly a young company looking for people to train as managers in an expanding operation.

Eventually the placement agency in Toronto uncovered an opportunity for Mike in a Willowdale firm called Electronics Unlimited. The company was new and growing in the field of electronic equipment for the home and office. It had a growing sales and distribution network with a production operation to follow in the near future. The product line the company distributed was broad and served both the industrial and commercial markets. There were many new and innovative developments in this field and in this organization. For example, the Willowdale plant was organizing for a more sophisticated warehousing and distribution operation, and plans were forthcoming for a fully integrated marketing department.

Frank Wilson, the personnel manager, interviewed Mike Craig for the opening at Electronics Unlimited. Mike was immediately impressed not only with the organization but by the personal style of Frank Wilson, who as a manager appeared innovative and progressive. He was quite empathetic to Mike's predicament and understood the value of growth opportunities in any company. Also the discussion on money and potential for moving up in the organization seemed very promising. Wilson further discussed the young company's need for energetic managers with ambitious goals for achievement. As he suggested, "We have outlets to develop, contacts to be made, people to recruit, and many more activities that will challenge a young college graduate."

Mike was very excited about his meeting with Frank Wilson and his application with the company. He felt sure that Wilson liked him and would offer him a job with the company. The situation, too, he thought would be a complete change from his current position and a welcome relief from the routine. For the first time in three years Mike was enthusiastic about his life and the prospects it held for him.

The job offer came three weeks later, and he accepted the position with a substantial increase in salary. He was due to begin in early September, and he proceeded to resign from his present position and to find an apartment in Toronto.

The first two months on his new job were a real learning experience as Mike Craig made himself acquainted with the people and the situation. Three other recent college graduates were hired from the area. One of these was John Corrigon, a marketing major from the University of Western Ontario and a very aggressive, outgoing individual. The other two co-workers, Jim Manus and Harry Brown, had degrees from McMaster in engineering and were studying for the M.B.A. degree in the evening. (See Exhibit 1.) The four new employees to the company all seemed to hit it off well at the start.

EXHIBIT 1
Background Information on the New Employees

Name	*Age*	*Marital Status*	*Education*	*Work Experience*	*Personal Interests*	*Career Goals*
Mike Craig	27	Single	B.A. Econ., Laurentian U.	Dept. of Agriculture (3 years).	X-country skiing, bridge.	Management, small mfg. co.
John Corrigon	24	Single	B. Comm. Marketing, U. of Western Ontario.	Sales rep., Proctor & Gamble.	Water skiing, squash.	Marketing manager.
Jim Manus	26	Married, 2 children	Professional engineer (P. Eng.).	Engr. dept., City of Windsor.	Lacrosse, racquet sports, computer games.	Manager, mfg. and/or R&D.
Harry Brown	25	Single	Professional engineer (P. Eng.).	National Electronics (1½ years).	Tennis, golf.	R&D.

At a small convention room in a local motel, the four new staff members got together with the personnel director, Frank Wilson, for an introductory training program. The group met the staff and reviewed general policies and procedures of the company. Actually the procedure manual was quite thin. Slides and promotional material were the extent of the information on the company. The meeting was more a casual get-together that largely addressed the plans of the company for the next few years. Frank Wilson and other staff were heartily enthusiastic about the prospects of making it big in the electronics field. The company was described by them as young and dynamic and one that encouraged and welcomed new ideas. "We are looking for opportunists, staff that will design their own future," he continued. "We encourage open and frank communication and dialogue." He sounded impressive and exciting, and expectations were high when the meeting ended.

Afterward, on their own, the new group convened to a local tavern for informal talks on their prospects with the new company. John Corrigon seemed to lead the group as the conversation began to flow.

"Well, I think the opportunities look good here," said John. "Frank Wilson tells me that 'the sky is the limit for those that can produce.' Their freewheeling structure and interpersonal style seems interesting to me. They don't seem to be hung up on formal channels of communication. Talking to the boss seems like talking to an old friend. I think that sales and marketing could really be exciting. At P&G we got good training, but the opportunity for advancement seemed somewhat limited. I am looking forward to bigger and better things here."

Mike Craig spoke of his experience with the Department of Agriculture and the low level of challenge to the work. "I am looking forward to more opportunities to get involved with decision making at a management level. Frank Wilson has also suggested to me a growth opportunity with Electronics Unlimited. They are really banking on this market developing quickly over the next little while. I am looking forward to meeting customers and being delegated responsibility in the near future. I guess I would like to move cautiously at first though."

Harry Smith had moved here from Quebec where, as he suggested, the political climate was worrisome. National Electronics had also been a growing firm, but when the headquarters moved to Winnipeg he decided to look in the Toronto area for a job. He was a quiet, reserved type who seemed caught up in his world of research and development.

"What about you, Jim," said John Corrigon, "you worked with the City of Windsor. What kind of job was that?"

"Mostly routine work of one sort or another," said Jim. "It was a job at the time when there were very few jobs to be had. I like Toronto and the challenge of this new position. We too were plagued with red tape and bureaucracy."

Corrigon ordered more refreshment, and the conversation continued.

"John Mitchell graduated three years ahead of me at the University of Windsor," continued Jim, "so I know him a little from college days. He is really an ambitious guy. He recruited me when he was in Windsor recently and really sold me on coming to Toronto. He has got big plans for the company and good ideas in the electronics field."

The talk continued and was dominated by Corrigon and Manus who, as it turned out, played college football against each other. A few hours passed and the group broke up with arrangements for another session of this kind.

For the first six months the four young men were expected to get acquainted with the firm's operation and make themselves available to do reports and other tasks required by the managers. Mike Craig and John Corrigon became involved with the distribution and sales side of the organization. Their first task was to generate a report on potential users of electronic equipment in the area on a commercial basis. Their guidelines were to examine demographic trends, store openings, potential volumes, and customer needs. The existing group had made some contacts in this area, but a thorough report and strategy were required. The managers of various departments indicated they would be available for consultation and inquiries. Craig felt very confident about this new assignment. His economics background provided him with all the knowledge to complete a thorough analysis of the area and, though he and Corrigon kept each other informed about their activities, they worked independently in different areas. Their plan was to meet before the date of submission and review their efforts.

Mike followed a steady pattern of work in the next week, confining much of his efforts to written material and research. *Stats Canada, Financial Post* survey of markets, and other books were among his sources of information. He gained confidence as the time passed. Corrigon, on the other hand, to avoid duplication spent much of his time out of the office and in the field. He visited people and talked to them of their needs and requirements. When he was in the office, he frequently visited the executive offices to gather information and to learn about the operation. Mike, for his part, had conversed with the managers only at lunch. He would also take work home with him at night and at weekends. Many of the avenues he was pursuing were of great interest to him, and he wanted to follow them through in what was now becoming a lengthy report.

Craig and Corrigon met at the end of the month just prior to their submission to management. (See Exhibit 2.) It was a brief meeting and involved Corrigon flipping through Craig's typed pages of report material. Then, behind closed doors on the Friday afternoon, two of the managers, Flemming and LeBlanc, discussed the research and activities with the two new employees. The meeting took most of the afternoon, a rather formal atmosphere prevailing throughout the early part of the encounter. Later, however, over coffee the meeting became more relaxed. Jerry Munroe, the president, came in for a moment and exchanged casual comments with the group. It seemed as though Corrigon had gotten to know Jerry, since they were on a first-name basis. Much of the discussion centered around Corrigon's ideas. He quoted names of people in key locations and presented an understanding of the needs and requirements of the area. Corrigon did not hesitate to initiate discussion and, when necessary, to focus the direction of the meeting. Craig, on the other hand, spoke infrequently and made vague references to his written report, his confidence dwindling as the time passed. Mike was continually forced to confirm by figures much of what Corrigon was expressing in his ideas and proposals. At the conclusion of the meeting a short summary was sketched out by Flemming and LeBlanc on a flip chart, summarizing much of what Corrigon had suggested.

Mike Craig left the office that afternoon somewhat dismayed by the results of the meeting. He felt Corrigon had dominated the discussion and not contributed his ideas in their pre-meeting discussion. He thought over the way Corrigon was so much at ease with managers and of the way they responded to him. Ideas and action were clearly becoming the bywords of this company.

In the next few weeks many of the major ideas of the meeting were broken down into smaller areas of focus; both Craig and Corrigon were left alone on their job without too much direction. The managers

EXHIBIT 2
Organizational Chart

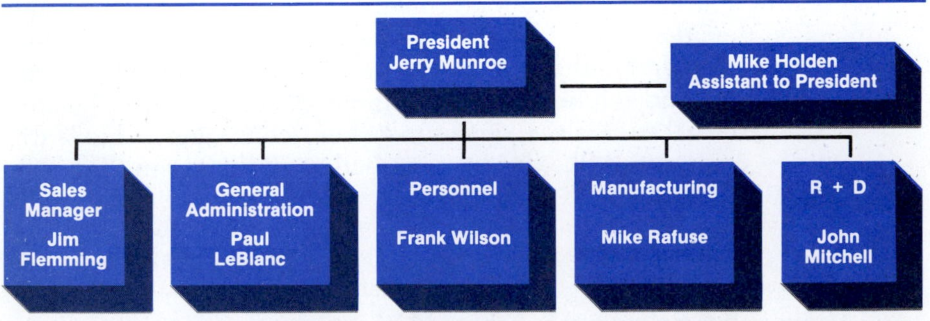

continued to hurry through one task after another. Potential customers were given full details of the company aspirations, and frequently Corrigon was asked to entertain customers and show them the operations. His aggressive and outgoing style seemed most suited to this task. Craig was given small reports to make and was generally left to muddle in the details. He would ask Corrigon for support from time to time on some of the matters, but seldom could he sit him down long enough for a meaningful exchange of ideas or plans. At the bimonthly meetings Corrigon was never short of a comment or an idea for a particular project.

The manufacturing side of Electronics Unlimited was now coming on line for full production. Harry Brown and Jim Manus were working well under Rafuse and Mitchell in their departments. They had settled in their own offices and were very productive in their field, developing changes and ideas for the product line. Both Rafuse and Mitchell were satisfied with the new employees, particularly since they provided current ideas for their work. They had already been invited to Montreal to visit the main plant and production operation.

Flemming and LeBlanc continued to make good use of Corrigon and Craig, who were busy on the marketing side of the operation. However, nothing was clearly defined in this company. John Mitchell, for example, frequently provided data and reports for Paul LeBlanc on distribution networks for the area. The organization was run on a flexible pattern of interactions and responsibilities.

Corrigon continued his aggressive style and developed an excellent rapport with Jim Flemming. They were in the process of hiring salespeople for the field, and Corrigon was given an opportunity to conduct the interviewing and initial screening. Craig, on the other hand, seemed always ready for more reports and analyzing data, largely because he had not been asked to take other responsibilities.

Mitchell and Rafuse had also begun to take advantage of Craig's report writing. By now, however, Craig had had enough and became quite discouraged at these frequent requests. He began to wonder just what he was going to be expected to do on this "dynamic job." This uncertainty bothered him.

At the same time, Corrigon was now beginning to annoy him with his abrasive style. He would ask for information and request of Craig routine jobs a secretary could do. Craig resented these requests but, in the interest of the company, would complete the tasks despite the fact that increased effort at establishing rapport with the sales manager, Flemming, produced no results.

After six months on the job, Craig had still not found it a satisfying experience. He was determined not to give up, however, and proceeded to present lengthy and detailed studies of market trends and other reports that would help the company. All the managers took advantage of his services to the point where Craig was frequently working on weekends.

Corrigon, well on his way to organizing a sales staff, also requested a lengthy analysis of sales potential for the company. Craig had worked himself into a position of complete frustration. He didn't feel he was there just to write reports but rather to become more involved with managing the company. He felt he was receiving little recognition for his contribution, while Corrigon and the other two engineers were progressing much more rapidly.

Craig's frustrations turned to anger as he became more disenchanted with his job at Electronics Unlimited. One day he refused to write a report for Corrigon, which earned him a sharp rebuke from Flemming. This upset him, and he felt he had to redeem himself.

The company had been growing and stabilizing in the months that had passed. The retail outlets had been contacted and connections organized to complete the network of distribution. New products had been developed by the company and were marketed in an effective manner. The administrative staff had been growing to meet the requirements of the production and sales force. An incentive system for the sales force had been designed in the Willowdale office and had received wide recognition throughout the company. Corrigon was instrumental in this effort and was appropriately rewarded for his contribution. A small achievement award was presented to Corrigon for his part in the design of the plan that had been implemented. The award was presented to him at an office get-together.

The event further deflated Craig's self-image in the growing company. What little spirit or camaraderie that had existed between the four original employees who had arrived together had been lost by this time. Mike Craig had retreated into a gloomy silence, anticipating a difficult time in an upcoming evaluation that had been announced.

Notice had come to the desks of the respective employees that they would be evaluated in the next month by the managers. It would be a formal evaluation and one that would take place in their offices over coffee. It would be verbal and based on discussion rather than a written document channeled through personnel.

Craig looked glum as he peered up from his desk after reading the memo, one of the first of its kind. Corrigon, in his usual attitude and cockiness, suggested that he would have to get the boss a bottle of good Scotch but that he really didn't have much to worry about.

Craig had less secure feelings about the whole procedure. He had this terrible feeling that the whole thing was going to be poorly handled. In a brief discussion with Flemming one afternoon he made inquiries about the method of evaluation, pointing out the traditional function of personnel administration. Flemming laughed at this idea, responding that around here they worked to get things done and did not worry too much about who did the evaluation!

The evaluation day arrived and Craig was assigned to Rafuse, the person he felt was least involved with his work. The interview and discussion went smoothly but not very cordially. There were many silent moments during the course of the interview, and he went away feeling that his work was regarded as less than satisfactory. Rafuse had hinted that the company's interest lay in more outgoing individuals. Craig was left with mixed feelings about the company and his future!

Indeed, Craig felt the time had come for a confrontation with the management of the company, and he proceeded to make an appointment with the personnel officer for a lengthy discussion about his future. He felt he might be able to get some straight answers from Frank Wilson, but he knew that he was taking a chance in finding out the worst. Some hard discussions would follow.

Evergreen Willows

Evergreen Willows, a new convalescent home, had been in operation for several months. The large one-story building, which had been specially constructed for its purpose, was divided into two identical wings designated A and B. In the center of the building, separating the wings, was a large living room, a chapel, offices, and a middle wing, which included the kitchen, patients' dining room, and employees' dining room. A and B wings consisted of a nurse's station in the center with a corridor of patients' rooms to each side (see Exhibit 1).

Each nurse's station served the patients for its wing, and each was under the direction of a charge nurse. Other nurses and nurse's aides worked under the charge nurse. From the opening day, each wing had been staffed separately. The director of nurses had assigned the more experienced, older aides to A wing, where she planned to locate sicker patients. She assigned the less experienced aides to B wing, which was to have patients who were more ambulatory. Except on rare occasions, A-wing staff did not work on B wing nor B-wing staff on A wing.

The day shift on B wing consisted of one charge nurse and four nurse's aides. Normally the charge nurse was Jenny, a young registered nurse who had had no previous experience as a charge nurse before working at the home. On her days off, she was replaced by Sue, a licensed practical nurse who worked part time. The nurse's aides

EXHIBIT 1
Evergreen Willows Floor Plan

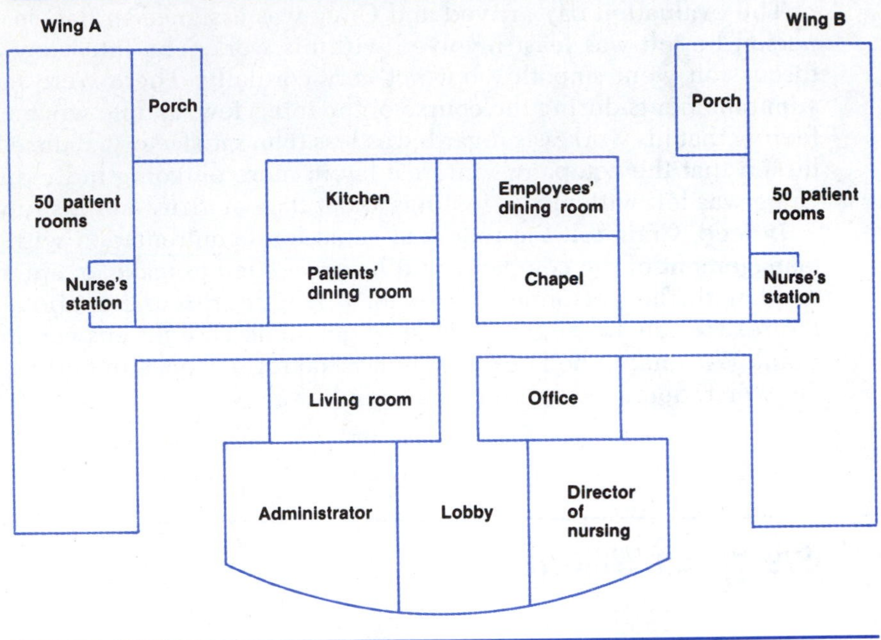

had rotating days off each week so that, except when someone was sick and had to be replaced, the same aides were usually on duty at the same time. The B-wing aides were of similar age and experience, having been hired at the same time. All lived in the local community and tended to see one another socially after hours.

Jenny's duties as charge nurse included dispensing medications, keeping charts and records up to date, and supervising the work of the aides. Actual patient care was the responsibility of the aides. Most of the B-wing patients were at least partially ambulatory. Caring for them involved assisting them in bathing, dressing, walking, and feeding, or what nurses call "activities of daily living." The aides also liked to visit with the lonelier patients whenever time permitted. A number of the patients wandered around during the day, and it was often necessary for the aides to look for them, which consumed a great deal of time considering the size of the building. Jenny, in giving her medications, ranged all over the building in search of patients and was not always to be found on the wing.

From the opening of the home, Jenny had found that there was barely enough time in the day for the work she had to do. She did not give detailed instructions to the aides, and they developed their own routines in caring for the patients. One new aide even said that "it took me weeks before I felt I knew what I was supposed to be doing." Usually they would separate by corridor, each doing the work they saw needing to be done. All helped in passing out breakfast and dinner trays, feeding patients, and in answering lights when a patient called for assistance. All of the B-wing aides kept busy, although sometimes there were complaints by some who felt they were "getting stuck" with the more unpleasant jobs because no one else would do them.

Nonetheless, the atmosphere on the wing was friendly. The aides often spoke of how much they enjoyed the patients. While most of the aides had not sought a job working with older patients, even those who might have preferred a job in a hospital caring for younger patients soon discovered that the "old folks" were interesting people. Consequently, there was much friendly contact between patients and aides as well as among aides and among patients. The patients enjoyed the atmosphere, although sometimes their families worried about the way they were allowed to wander about.

In contrast, A-wing patients were for the most part bedridden and required more actual nursing care. In fact, if a patient on B wing took sick, the home's policy was to transfer that patient to A wing where there was a larger staff/patient ratio. The staff consisted of a charge nurse, Elizabeth, and two or three R.N.s or L.P.N.s and six aides. The charge nurse took care of duties at the nurse's station and drug room, while the other nurses dispensed drugs and did treatments. The nurse's aides did patient care. Many of the patients were unable to walk or stand and helping them up to a chair involved heavy lifting. Fewer patients than on B wing were dressed, most wearing johnnies and bathrobes, and most remained in their rooms. Many of the patients who were confined to their rooms rang for the aides frequently throughout the day, often for only minor requests.

Elizabeth was an older, more experienced nurse than Jenny and supervised the aides working under her in a strict manner. Each morning the aides were paired in teams of two and assigned to 16 specified patients. The assignments were standardized, and the A-wing aides usually worked systematically and on a schedule to complete their work. There was little change from day to day, and patients were generally taken care of at the same time each day and were accustomed to this. Working in teams of two gave each aide someone to assist her when lifting was necessary. Assignments included patients located far apart on the floor, but aides usually cared only for the patients on their assignment sheets. When another patient asked for assistance, they would often answer "Wait until your nurse gets here." Elizabeth kept a close watch on her aides and was very critical of the work they did. Sometimes she could be heard over the intercom saying something like, "Girls, there are five lights on A wing." She insisted that the girls maintain a professional relationship with the patients. While the atmosphere on the wing was far from homey, the sick patient received good technical care and their families felt a good deal of confidence in the quality of care provided on A wing.

The administrator and director of nurses were cheerful and apparently well liked by the nursing staff. They appeared at meetings held approximately every other week for in-service educational training or to update employees on issues of importance. Their response to the work done by the nurses and the aides was favorable. However, they were rarely seen on the wings, and they delegated a great deal of responsibility to the charge nurses.

After several months the director of nurses announced at one of the in-service meetings that aides would now have assignments alternating them between the two wings. While she felt completely satisfied with the performance of both wings, she felt the aides should be more versatile and experienced with all types of patients.

When this new plan went into effect, a series of problems began to develop between the head nurses and aides of the two wings. B-wing aides on A wing found themselves answering lights not belonging to their own patients and falling behind in their own scheduled work. While working on one corridor, an aide would often forget those patients on the other corridor assigned to her, and those patients frequently had their lights on and unanswered for long periods of time. They complained to the head nurse when they had to wait. Thus the B-wing aides were under constant criticism from Elizabeth, but when they tried to talk to her they found she was not listening.

The help Elizabeth had from the other nurses allowed her more free time than Jenny had. She was often seen laughing and talking with the other nurses, but she did not socialize with the aides.

When on their own wing, the B-wing aides now found they had to do even more work than usual. Most of the aides from A wing were lost on B and needed much help in caring for the B-wing patients. Nothing was written down, and Jenny was too busy or not around to help them; so the responsibility of orienting them fell to the B-wing aides.

Stating that there was "nothing to do" on B wing, a few of the A-wing aides took frequent coffee breaks. The regular aides from B wing could not find them when they needed help or did not have the time to go to the employees' dining room to get them. One incident on B wing occurred when an aide was assisting a patient to bed, and the patient slipped to the floor. There was no one nearby, nor did anyone answer the emergency light when the aide called. The aide had to leave the patient to get help. When this situation was reported to Jenny, she reprimanded the A-wing aide who was not on the floor where she was supposed to be and recommended to the director of nurses that she be fired. It was the decision of the director that she "should be entitled to a second chance." The situation did not improve.

A great deal of resentment developed among the nursing staff. Several of the aides, including those considered to be the best workers, quit or began looking for other jobs. The attitude of the administrator and director of nurses was one of little concern. In the words of the director of nursing: "We have many applicants for each vacancy. Anyone can be replaced. Our turnover rate of employees here is better than in most nursing homes."

The Expense Account

Sam Swanson was in a predicament. Last week Sam went down to the branch plant in Baltimore. When he came back, he filled in his expense sheet and was about to hand it in, when Bill Wilson and Jack Martin stopped by. The following conversation took place:

Bill: Come on, wrap it up. It's time for some coffee.
Jack: Sam, we've given you the honor of buying us coffee today.
Sam: Okay, fellows, I accept the honor—but wait until I add that 75 cents to my "swindle sheet" so that I can get paid for it.
Bill: How much are you charging the company for that Baltimore trip?
Sam: Wait, let's see—it comes out to a total of $350.
Jack: $350! My gosh, Sam, you've made some boner. Let's see what you have there.
Sam [*handing sheet to Jack*]: What should it be? I thought I put everything down.
Bill: Seven of us have been going to Baltimore for over three years now, and none of us has ever been lower than $375—and most of the time it's above $400.
Jack: To start off with, Sam, you have only $10 for limousine to the airport. Most of us put down the taxicab rate of $21.50. You don't have any transportation back from the airport—what about that? Those two items alone add up to $31.50. That'll make your total $381.50.
Sam: Betty picked me up at the airport. The regulations on the back say I can't charge for that.
Bill: She had to buy gas, and there's wear and tear on the car.

Professor Rossall J. Johnson, author. From a research project on decision making: "Conflict Avoidance through Acceptable Decision," *Human Relations* 27, no. 1 (1974). Reproduced with the author's permission.

Jack: Didn't you buy someone lunch or dinner while you were there? Your expense account will stand one or two of those.

Sam: Actually, fellows, everyone was buying me lunch or dinner. I didn't get much of a chance to spend money.

Bill: Gosh, Sam, do something with that expense account—don't turn in $350. That'll make the rest of us look pretty bad. Bring it up to $375 anyway, or we'll be in for a rough time.

Jack: I agree; fix it up, Sam. But first let's get that cup of coffee.

While drinking coffee, Jack and Bill explained their philosophy: When away from home on business you are really spending 24 hours a day on the job and only getting paid for 8 hours; therefore the extra expenses are warranted. They also pointed out that there are some hidden costs to the individual—getting clothes cleaned, maintaining luggage, the cost of a baby-sitter so your wife can leave the house while you are away, and other little items that add up.

When Sam came back from coffee, he reexamined his expenses. If he charged $21.50 taxi fare to and from the airport, he would be over the $375 mark. But he really didn't spend this money, so it didn't seem right to put that on the expense sheet.

Sam was new with the company—three months. He was getting along very well with the other men. He also recognized that if they did not like him they could make his work rough—maybe get him into a spot where he couldn't do his job.

Discussion Question

What should Sam do? (Check only one.)

_____ 1. Charge cab fare to and from the airport, so that the total is $381.50.

_____ 2. Charge cab fare from the airport (when his wife picked him up), making a total of $371.50.

_____ 3. Charge limousine fare from the airport to make a total of $360.

_____ 4. Make no change; hand in expense for $350.

_____ 5. Ask his supervisor what he should do.

Explain briefly the reason for your decision.

Fired: "I Just Wasn't Their Kind of Person"

This case is a conversation between the magazine, the AMBA Executive, *and an anonymous MBA who was fired from her first job after graduating from business school. She worked in the computer division of a finance holding company for two and a half years before going to a well-known eastern graduate business school, and joined a western industrial chemical company as a marketing trainee upon completion of her degree. The job lasted six months.*

AMBA: What kind of job did you look for when you were finishing the MBA?

MBA: I became very interested in marketing at school, and I wanted to do product management because it incorporated all aspects from development to promotion to selling. I wanted a traditional company with a set career path. The firm I joined had these and also presented the possibility of going abroad or shifting into one of the diversified acquisitions. It seemed ideal.

AMBA: Who actually hired you?

MBA: I spoke to the divisional vice president in the initial interviews and then to personnel. My main contact while I was there was the vice president—he was "responsible" for me.

AMBA: Let's go back to when you started work.

MBA: I began in their training program. Trainees spend four to six weeks in sales analysis, in an ad agency, in budget, and longer in the field with the sales force. I was very enthusiastic about the program and ready to learn everything about marketing. My first stop was in sales analysis.

AMBA: Can you describe the department?

MBA: There were about 30 people, maybe 20 of whom had college degrees, few MBAs if any. The department head, a woman who had been with the company for 25 years, certainly didn't have an MBA. The rest were clerical employees in their 40s. There were many more women in that division than the others. It was sort of a service bureau for the marketing department.

There could have been cause for resentment because I was a woman coming in at a higher salary than most of them. I was going to be there only a short time and would be promoted faster. Eventually they would work for me.

But that doesn't explain the atmosphere there. The other women were very uptight and quiet, precise. Some of them also seemed

From a copyrighted article in the January 1976 issue of *MBA Executive*, published by the Association of MBA Executives.

rather paranoid—always worried that people were watching them to see if they were working. They did have a point there. The appearance of working was very important; even if there wasn't much to do everyone would flutter around looking very harried and trying to seem busy. The content didn't matter as much.

On the other hand, I'm not exactly loud but more visible than they were. I like people. I work best under pressure when there's a lot to do. There was a definite contrast between those women and me.

On my third day of work they accused me of entertaining men in my office. This was based on one after-lunch visit from a friend who came up to see my new office, stayed for two minutes, and left. On the following day, a trainee from the international division came down and talked to me awhile. My visitors also looked briefly at a sales analysis. On the strength of these two visits and the analysis (which concerned a product discontinued over five years ago), someone complained to personnel. No one in the department said a word to me.

I was called to the personnel office where this guy said, "Well, you've been entertaining all these men in your office, and we've got these complaints." My first reaction was to laugh—it was so preposterous. But then I realized he was serious.

Amba: You probably should have laughed. It would have cleared the air.

Mba: I think I did laugh and then waited for him to. He didn't have any sense of humor, though. He then asked, "How could you get an unauthorized person into the building? The security guards can tell if you don't have the proper badge." I told him that we just went up the elevator, and no one had stopped us or checked anything. He continued, "But they can hear what you say in the halls."

I said, "What do you mean they can hear us." And then he told me that the halls are bugged.

I really didn't believe I was hearing all this. I thought someone had put something in my coffee!

I explained that I was responsible for the first man being there for a total of two minutes. The second man was their own employee. And I asked him to tell me who was complaining and I would straighten it out.

He was very reluctant to tell me; he didn't want to promote bad relations between personnel and sales analysis. But I finally got the name from him. It was the lady in charge of the department.

Amba: Trying to look at the situation from the other side, it sounds as though the personnel man was uncomfortable with the complaint and didn't really know how to handle it. He wasn't sure what was going on and needed you to resolve the problem.

MBA: But he wasn't really interested in what was happening in my office. He was fascinated by telling me the mechanics of the surveillance system, wondering how anyone could get through. He really went off on a tangent.

AMBA: What did you do then?

MBA: I went to the woman who had complained to personnel and tried to talk to her. She said that the studies were classified information, which is as it should be, of course, but I pointed out that this particular one concerned a product discontinued in 1968. She just exploded.

I asked why no one in the department had explained the rules on visitors to me or even asked me who the visitors were. I obviously didn't know the procedures after only three days.

She said, "We don't deal with you except through personnel; you're just a trainee. We don't even sign your vouchers. We just discuss you with personnel, and that's it."

At that point I thought maybe I'd made a real mistake in choosing that company.

She later gave a horrible review of my training period there, even though I'd written a good marketing study based on their data. From then on, I had a terrible time with the company. Interestingly enough, my actual work was never criticized—just my "attitude."

I was automatically under suspicion, and the other departments I went to were warned to watch me thoroughly. I found this out at the next area in the training program. People were almost afraid to say anything good because they would be disagreeing with the consensus, if you see what I mean.

AMBA: There are ways to ask questions that make you an ally and ways that challenge a person's authority. I wonder how the department head interpreted you coming to her to ask about the accusation. The personnel man's reluctance to give you the name indicates that direct confrontation was not the way the company handled such situations. She may have taken your question, "Why didn't anyone tell me the rules?" as a challenge. Her subsequent reaction certainly suggests that she felt threatened.

MBA: But I'd only been there three days! I got there on time, didn't leave early, or take three hours for lunch. I did my work and even bugged people to give me things to do.

There were a couple of outside problems—a paper to finish for school, an illness in the family, and a volunteer project I was managing—which would not normally be the case for most new employees. I may not have looked too happy at my desk, but it didn't affect the work. I don't see what I could have done in so short a time to elicit such a strong reaction.

AMBA: She mentioned a vital point—"We don't even sign your vouchers." It's always a good idea to know whose budget you're part of, who is really responsible for you.

MBA: I was in the divisional budget, not analysis'. But I don't think you can expect the people in your product division to know all the ground rules in the other departments. I see your point, but in this case I don't think it would have made much difference.

AMBA: Was she actually in charge of your training in her department or was there a training program coordinator?

MBA: That was a problem. There wasn't really any direction. Although we were supposed to learn certain things about the company and its functions, nobody ever had time to show us anything. They were reluctant to give us projects because no one knew how long we'd be in a given department. So we sat there twiddling our thumbs, which is boring, and tried to find work.

My vice president had said to ask other people under his jurisdiction for things to work on. So I did, often. And occasionally one of the analysts would spend some time and give me a decent project. Those were interesting and enjoyable.

The company was not using what the MBA was supposed to bring to the job, whether specific skills or a frame of reference or whatever. The main purpose of the training program seemed to be almost military—to make us conform to the company mold. They were very cautious about the trainees and watched us a lot.

The content of the program was minimal. We added up endless columns of figures that a high school grad could have done.

AMBA: What kind of reinforcement did you get from the vice president?

MBA: I talked to him many times. The bad review from the head of analysis made him nervous, though I told him some of the odd incidents, which he also thought were peculiar.

During the second phase of my training, I broke my foot at a party and missed two days of work. He heard about it and was very upset because I hadn't broken it in an auto accident. He was specific about that—you have to have accidents at the right time and place.

AMBA: How was the rest of your training session?

MBA: I went next to one of the ad agencies. The ad agency people were totally flexible; it was like day and night. One of the agency guys called me in and said, "We heard that something happened back at the ranch; this guy has been calling me up and telling me to watch you. I think it's terrible. What's going on?" I told him my version of what had happened and learned a lot about the company's way of doing things from him.

I got a good evaluation from the agency—"She did the work, no problem." But there was the broken foot. That was interpreted as negative by the people back at the company.

Budget was the next area. I worked on a project for them that received very favorable comment. It was a fascinating department, but there was the same rigidity. I picked up a report on the department done in the early 60s which could have been written yesterday. It was an indication of how slowly the company moves—their use of computers was way behind the times.

AMBA: Did the personality tensions ease up at all?

MBA: They became more positive, and I was certainly willing to keep trying. I had invested a certain amount of time and was still very interested in industrial product marketing. I thought that maybe the training period was the worst part and, once through it, everything would be fine.

At one of my talks with the vice president, he said, "You know, things are really working out now. I'm getting all these good reports about your work and a letter commending a project you did."

I was so relieved. Then 10 days later he fired me because he saw me talking on the phone several times and because I had allegedly fallen asleep in a meeting, which was not true.

AMBA: You have described a lot of surface events, your reaction, and your perception of their reaction. But there are things companies fire for and things they don't fire for. It's a very extreme step. The person who fires you must document why, particularly given the pressures on the company for more women in management. As long as you do acceptable work, most large companies will not fire you.

MBA: I asked him that specifically in the final interview. "Are you sure it isn't my work?" He said, "No, they all say that you are very bright and your work is actually quite good. It's just your attitude." He said that a number of times.

I did receive a fair number of personal phone calls, many of which were related to the illness in my family and the volunteer project. Maybe it was that calls indicated I had a life outside the company.

The other reason he mentioned, falling asleep in a meeting, was not valid. This particular meeting began at 8:30 A.M. and continued till after 6. The air-conditioning was turned off at 5, and we were all getting tired and drowsy, but I did not fall asleep.

He said I wasn't serious enough.

AMBA: That's usually code for "You don't consider important what we consider important." Your perception of what was trivial and your accompanying attitude may be why you were fired—what you treated lightly was of major importance to them.

Mba: Well, I guess I didn't consider it important to sit in my cubicle and pretend to be busy when I had nothing to do. I expected to be evaluated on my performance. But how can you be evaluated on your performance if you aren't given anything substantial to work on? The great bulk of what we were assigned *was* sheer make-work.
Amba: What you're talking about is a very common feeling among MBAs when they finish their degree. They want some meaningful work. But for a long time in many companies you're expected to learn how they do things, to get accustomed to their procedures. They don't want to hear from you about being productive until *they* feel you're ready for responsibility.
Mba: You can put up with those preliminaries and suffer through a "training program" provided the people you're dealing with seem reasonable. But some of those I was working with were irrational. If they won't explain the ground rules to you and don't tell you when you're breaking them but go instead to complain to personnel—I just thought it was very peculiar.
Amba: Can you see your experience happening to a man?
Mba: The phone calls would probably be less of a problem, but I can see a male having the same attitude problems very easily. A male acting the way I did—going to people and asking for work—would not have created hostility. They may have expected their men to be more aggressive than their women. If I spoke up at meetings, I was told I was too assertive; if I didn't say anything, I was told that I wasn't being aggressive enough. That sort of harassment wouldn't happen to a man.

Rather than sex, I think the problem is one of adjusting to the company's regimentation.
Amba: What did you learn from this experience?
Mba: To give the company credit—and I may not have stressed that they are very good at what they do—I learned quite a bit about sales analysis techniques, about producing ads, how one company coordinates budgeting and accounting. I also learned that I need a more flexible professional atmosphere in a more aggressive company than that one. I realized that I am more results oriented than image conscious—more interested in what people produce than what they look like and how they act.
Amba: How will you look differently for your next job?
Mba: I'll ask different questions. As an entry-level job seeker, I was very much in awe of everyone doing the things I thought I wanted to do. I kept asking them about their work but neglected to ask about the frustrations, how long they'd been with the company, what previous work experience they'd had, how flexible the company was. A certain line of questions was left out.

Another thing I didn't do before that I'm doing now is conducting exploratory interviews. I've called friends, contacts, other business school alumni and talked to them informally about their companies. I want to find out the strengths and weaknesses of the companies from someone who knows. People are much more open about their work when it's not a "job" interview.

I'm a little more uptight now and more careful. I want to be sure I'd be happy in a place—almost before I talk to them. The atmosphere is almost as important to me as the job content. After one bad judgment, you want to make sure the next job is the right one.

AMBA: When you say you're going to be much more careful, that seems to be the wrong lesson.

MBA: Why?

AMBA: If you get too careful, you won't listen to your own feelings as much. You are trying to get the right thing; you don't want this experience to happen again. But you've got to relax about it. It's dangerous to become too rigid, because you'll close off the emotional feedback about a potential new job. That works against you in making a decision.

MBA: I'm probably more defensive than I should be—I catch myself sometimes and have to remember that it's not that big a deal.

AMBA: How are you explaining your departure to interviewers?

MBA: I say as little as possible and keep away from any negative comments about the company because it sounds like sour grapes. I've told you much more than I'd ever tell a job interviewer.

I checked on my recommendation from the company. They are saying that it was a fit problem, which is fair.

Interestingly, some interviewers have mentioned the company's reputation of being uptight.

AMBA: That's also an interview technique to get you to talk more about what happened. But you don't really have that much to explain or worry about. Your opinion of the company isn't relevant; it's no one else's business. You were part of their training program, but it became apparent that it wasn't the right place for you and you weren't the person for them. It's all you have to say.

The Foster Creek Post Office Case

The U.S. Post Office in Foster Creek, New York, is a small first-class office serving a suburban community of 11,000. Normally, the post office employs 11 people—a postmaster, an assistant postmaster, six carriers (including one parcel-post truck driver), and three clerks.

Each postal employee's job requirements are minutely subdivided and explicitly prescribed by the *Post Office Manual*—a large two-volume publication of the U.S. Post Office Department in Washington, D.C. There is a "suggested" rate per minute and/or day for sorting and delivering letters of which every postal employee is well aware. The work is highly prescribed, routine, and repetitive, with little basis for the development of individual initiative. Although each man contrives a few little tricks (which he may or may not pass along to his fellow workers) for easing his *own* workload, there is little incentive for a postal employee to attempt to improve any part of the mail delivery system *as a whole*. Each man performs pretty much as he is expected to perform (nothing more or less). Roger, the assistant postmaster, clearly verbalized this attitude, "The inspectors can't get us if we go by the book [manual]."

The irregular, unannounced visits by the district postal inspectors arouse a strange fear in *all* employees at the Foster Creek Post Office. Although each of the 11 employees is fairly well acquainted with the inspectors, there is something disturbing about the presence of a man whose recommendations may mean the loss of your job. The security of their position in the post office is highly valued by employees of Foster Creek, some of whom are no longer young and must provide for their families. It is customary, therefore, to see an entire post office staff snap to attention and work harder at the arrival, or possibility of arrival, of a postal inspector.

Larry, the Foster Creek postmaster, had a philosophy regarding the affairs of his office which was: "Keep the patrons and the inspectors happy." Outside of this requirement and an additional one, which made it imperative that each employee punch in and off the time clock at the exact appointed time (this requirement was primarily for the ease of bookkeeping), each man could do his job pretty much as he wished. The clerks reported at 6 A.M. to sort the day's mail into different stacks for the carriers, who arrived at 7 A.M. The carriers then

This case was written under the supervision of Alvar O. Elbing. Names of people and places have been disguised. From *Behavioral Decisions in Organizations* by Alvar O. Elbing.

"cased" (further sorting according to street and number) their letters and usually were "on the road" by 9 A.M. They were required to be back in the office at 3:30 P.M., if possible, for further casing, and at 5 P.M. all the carriers went home.

In the summer months when the mail is relatively light and the weather is clear, each carrier easily finishes his route (including time allowed for a half-hour lunch break) by 1:30 P.M. It is standard procedure for the men to relax at home for two hours before reporting back in at 3:30 P.M. In the winter, on the other hand, with snow piled high in the yards, each carrier can no longer take the shorter route across the yards, and the men often finish long after 3:30 P.M. Larry is well aware of this procedure and says: "It all balances out, and in the hot summer they can use the extra hours to take it easy."

At 3:30 P.M. (or so) the day's big social event takes place at the post office. With the cry of "Flip for Cokes," all the employees except Jane, the one female clerk, match dimes to see who will be the day's loser and provide Cokes for the others. This daily gaming is one of the many examples of the free and frequent sociability which exists among the 10 male employees. Although the office's formal organization is detailed by postal regulations (see Exhibit 1), owing to the similar socioeconomic status and interests of the employees, the post office atmosphere is very relaxed and informal (see Exhibit 2). Many of the men bowl together; they go to the same church; and they often attend high school graduations and funerals affecting the families of their coworkers.

EXHIBIT 1
Foster Creek Post Office Formal Organization

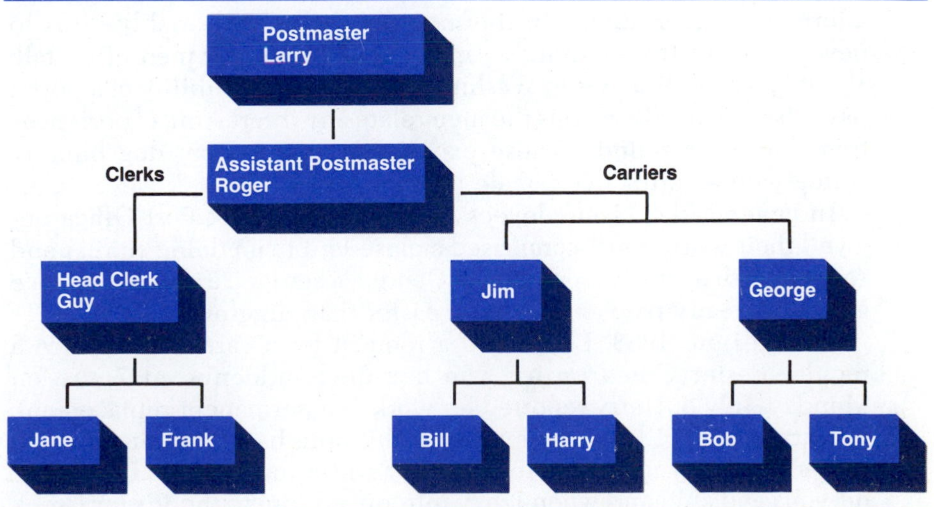

EXHIBIT 2
Foster Creek Post Office Informal Organization

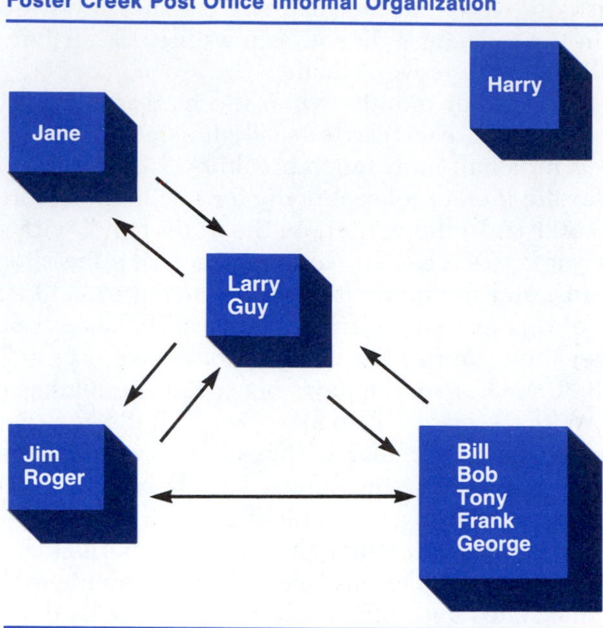

On payday (every Friday) each of the 10 male employees contributes 50 cents of his paycheck to "the fund." This fund is used for coffee and donuts, to provide sick employees with flowers and get-well cards, and to purchase a ham to be shared at work during Christmas time.

Other important parts of each day are the regular morning and afternoon conversations. In the morning the talk invariably turns to news items in the morning's paper. In addition, the men often talk about "those politicians in Washington" and the possibility of a postal pay raise. In the afternoons the men relate any interesting experiences from the day's rounds. These experiences range from dog bites to coffee with an attractive female patron.

In general, the 11 employees of the Foster Creek Post Office enjoyed their work. They comprised a close-knit team doing similar and somewhat distasteful work, but as George, a senior carrier, put it, "We get good steady pay; and it's a lot easier than digging ditches."

In mid-June 1968, Larry filed a request for a carrier to replace a regular Foster Creek carrier who had died suddenly. At 7 A.M. on Monday, July 8, Harry reported for work as a permanent replacement.

Harry was a tall, skinny man with thinning hair, long fingers, and wire-rimmed eyeglasses. He appeared to be in his 50s. He seemed nervous and shy; and when Larry introduced him to the Foster Creek regulars, Harry stared at the floor and said only "Hi!" Initial opinions of this new carrier were mixed. Jim, another senior carrier, probably best expressed the employees' sentiments when he said: "He's not too friendly—yet—he's probably a little nervous here—but, *man*, can he case mail!"

Harry was an excellent caser. For 27 years he had been a clerk in the main post office. The attitudes and work environment in big-city post offices differ markedly from those in smaller offices (as Larry was quick to point out when any of Foster Creek's employees complained). In the city post offices, where competition for the few available positions is extremely keen, a man must not only be very competent but must follow the postal regulations *to the letter*. As Harry said quietly to Roger upon his arrival at Foster Creek, "Things were just too pushy in the city. And besides, my wife and I wanted to move out here in the country to have a house and garden of our own to take care of."

Harry had a well-kept and attractive house and garden. It was apparent that Harry loved to take care of his lawn and garden, because he spent all day Sunday working on it. As a member of the Foster Creek Building and Loan Association, Larry knew that Harry had purchased the property with cash.

On Wednesday, Harry's third day at work, the opinions regarding Harry had become more concrete. As Jim said: "Harry's strange. He thinks he's better than all of us, coming from that city office. He never talks to us or says anything about himself. All he does is stand there and case mail, but, man, is he fast at that!"

The first real problem arose on the fourth day. Harry had learned his route well enough so that he, too, was able to finish by 1:30 P.M. His ability to case and "tie out" (gathering the mail in leather straps) his mail so quickly put him on the road by 8:30 in the morning—ahead of the other four carriers.

On this Thursday afternoon Harry reported back to the post office at 1:15, having finished his entire route. Upon seeing this, Roger's first reaction was to say, "Go home and have some lunch, Harry. Relax at home for a little while."

Harry replied, "I've had my lunch. There are letters on my case. I've got to do them now. I've got to do my job." Having said this, he began to case the several hundred letters which had piled up since the morning. He finished these quickly and then went on and cased all the mail which was lying on the other four carriers' cases. When the four regular carriers returned at 3:30 P.M., they were, to say the least, surprised.

Bill, the youngest and least energetic of the carriers, thanked Harry. However, Jim and George in particular were very angry. They grumbled about having a "newcomer" interfere with his "city tricks" and "fancy casing." They were especially angry that Harry had violated the 3:30 rule. They were determined that he would not be the one who would make them lose their precious privileges, and they complained to Larry about Harry. The postmaster told Harry to case only his own mail and to take it easy when walking his route in the future.

The next day, Friday, was payday. Each man contributed his share to "the fund." Harry refused. "I don't drink coffee," was his only answer. No one pushed the matter further, although discontent over Harry had developed among all the employees.

As the next week passed by, Harry appeared to sink into an even deeper shell. He punched in at 7 A.M. and punched out at 5 P.M. In between, he neither looked at nor spoke to any of the other employees. He continued to report back into the office before 3:30, case all his own mail, and then sit on the stool in front of his case reading magazines. Larry was worried primarily about Harry's exposure to the public as he sat at his case reading, and so on Friday of Harry's second week, Harry's and Bill's cases were switched (see Exhibit 3).

When each of the carriers reported in on Friday afternoon, Bill was told that his case was moved so as to give him more room to handle his quickly growing route (which, in part, was true). Harry said nothing about the switch but went straight to work in his new location.

During Harry's third week at the post office, Larry began to worry even more about his behavior. Although the carrier was hidden from

EXHIBIT 3
Foster Creek Post Office Layout

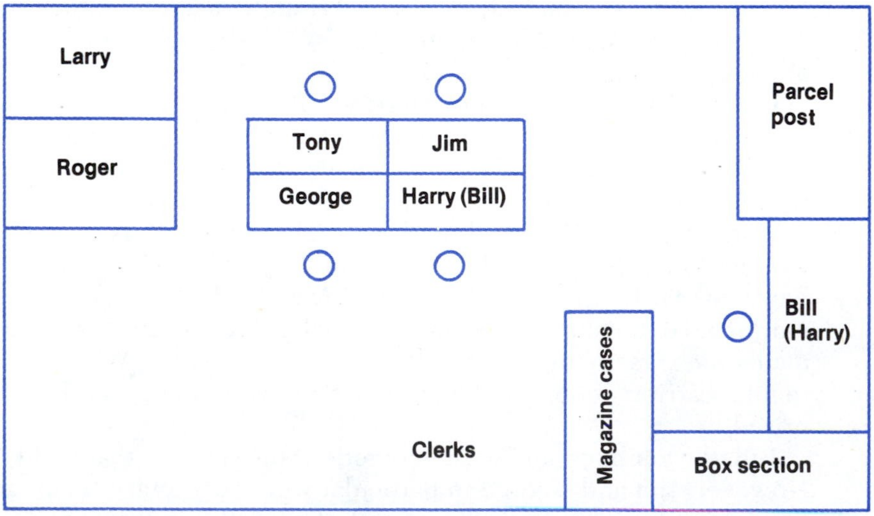

the public now, a postal inspector could catch Harry reading at his case very easily.

On Thursday, July 18, Larry's worst fears were realized. An inspector came to the Foster Creek Post Office. As he walked in, Harry was sitting quietly at his case, reading as usual. The inspector looked at Harry, then at Larry.

Larry explained that Harry had an easier route than the other carriers. Because of this and his ability as a caser, Harry was able to finish his route more easily. Larry pointed out that he did not know what to say to the carrier, for he had finished all his *required* work. The inspector suggested that Larry readjust the routes to give Harry more houses to deliver and more mail to case. This was attempted, but Jim, George, and Tony reacted unfavorably.

▶ From Mosaic to Unit Dosage

NOTE: *DO NOT READ* this case until directed to do so by your instructor. It has been set up as a Prediction Case so that you can test your analysis by answering questions before reading the entire case.

PART I

Jim Simmons was relaxing in his modest downtown apartment, watching the Saturday afternoon baseball game on television. His thoughts often wandered from the game to the great sense of achievement he had obtained from his job as director of the nearby hospital's pharmacy department. Under his supervision the pharmacy had grown and recently contributed a major component in the hospital's efforts to operate efficiently and effectively (provide good health care).

General Hospital's pharmacy was located on the fifth floor of the 600-bed hospital. The department's purpose was to supply all drugs and intravenous devices to the patients in correct quantities and doses. The pharmacy was staffed around the clock. All work was performed in one large self-contained corner room on the fifth floor of the seven-floor building (see Exhibit 1).

Mr. Simmons, age 48, had full control over the department since his recruitment by the hospital five years ago. He was a member of the

EXHIBIT 1
The Pharmacy

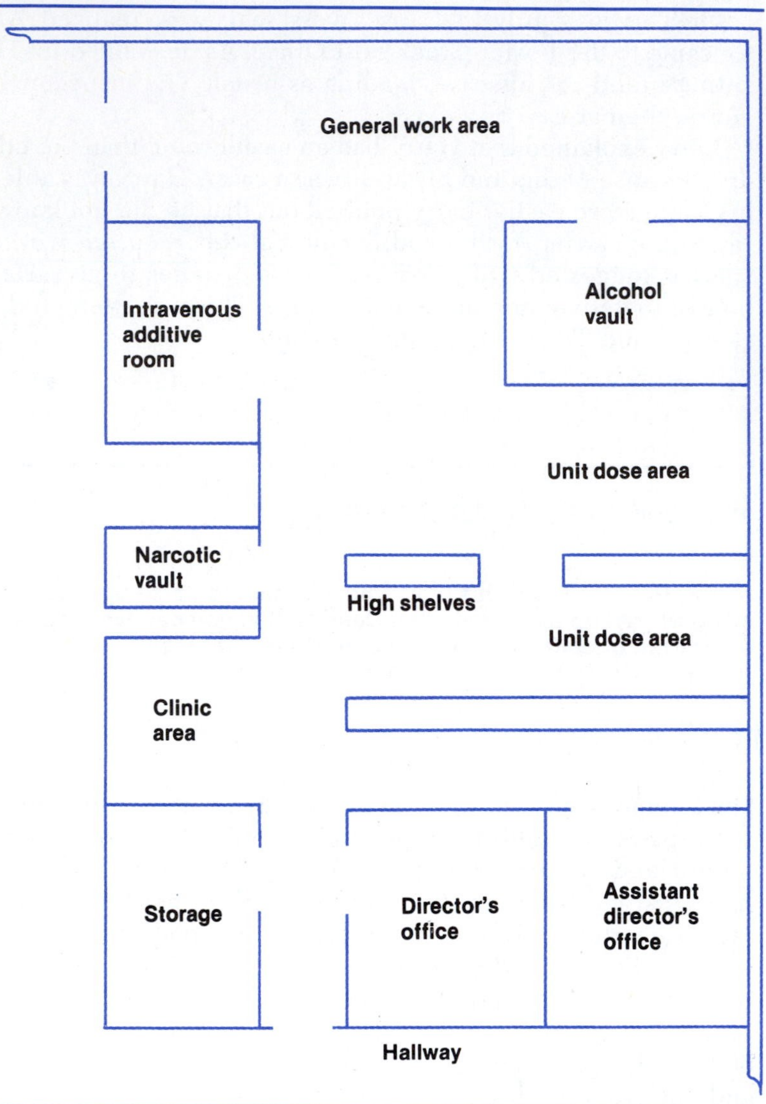

hospital's planning board and concentrated his attention on policy matters, purchasing decisions, and new techniques in the field. When he took over the department, he brought Gary Watson, age 34, with him as assistant director (Gary had worked for him elsewhere). Mr. Watson's main concerns were verifying that schedules were met and resolving any "people problems" within the department. Both Mr.

Simmons and Mr. Watson worked the Monday–Friday day shift and were never present on weekends or at night.

The work force at the pharmacy consisted of 11 pharmacists and 12 technicians. The pharmacists comprised the backbone of the operation, deciding which prescriptions should be worked on first, deciding among themselves who would do which ones, making up the more difficult prescriptions, and seeing that they were administered to the patients in the correct manner. This called for the pharmacists to spend a few hours of the work shift on other floors. The technicians were responsible for arranging the mass of common drugs used so frequently by the patients. A pharmacist would check the technician's work before the drug trays were allowed to be moved to the patients' floors.

Nine of the 11 pharmacists were graduates of highly professional, five-year university programs, while two (both over age 50) were licensed as qualified assistants. All pharmacists were on salaries considered good but not high, although the two qualified assistants earned a little less money. The nine younger pharmacists were quite similar to each other in age and lifestyle. All were in their 20s and early 30s, their ages showing the effect of Mr. Simmons' expansion of programs during the past few years.

The technicians were trained graduates of high school and/or hospital technical schools. Although their jobs were demanding, they were paid rather modest salaries, which were in the range of a skilled secretary. Six of the 12 were around 40 years old, and the other 6 were from 20 to 25 years of age. There were more women (eight) than men (four), reflecting the "between jobs" or "second job" nature of their employment.

There were three basic shifts. The day shift ran from 8 A.M to 4:30 P.M., the evening shift from 3:30 to 11:30 P.M. and the early morning shift from 11 P.M. to 7 A.M. Mr. Watson, the assistant director, made up the work schedules, allowing no individual preference (such as working nights only).

The Monday–Friday day shift consisted of five pharmacists and six technicians, plus Mr. Simmons and Mr. Watson. Mr. Watson often spent one or two days of the week working in his capacity of licensed pharmacist as well as handling his work as assistant director. The evening shift was staffed by two pharmacists and three technicians, and the early morning shift was staffed by one pharmacist and two technicians. All except Mr. Simmons and Mr. Watson were required to work all three shifts and weekends as scheduled throughout the year.

The day shift on weekends consisted of two pharmacists and four technicians. The workload did not subside on Saturdays or Sundays, causing the employees to be harder pressed to get the work out. The load created greater demand on the technicians' concentration and perseverance. The two pharmacists on duty concerned themselves only with essential tasks, eliminating any of the drug-administering feedback sessions with the nurses that occurred during the week. The reason behind the small work force was an established procedure to give as many employees as possible the weekend off; however, during the year, pharmacists tended to get more "off" weekends than technicians.

The pharmacy had earned a reputation as one of the best departments in the hospital in which to work. The atmosphere was pleasant and the work not without challenge and interest. Also, others in the hospital saw the pharmacy staff as having recognizable skills and as being an important factor in patient care. While Mr. Simmons was seen as likable but somewhat aloof due to his frequent absence from the department on matters pertaining to the overall operation of the hospital, the pharmacy's reputation, due in large measure to Gary Watson's efforts, was one of having "good supervision; people who care about people as well as performance."

The usual procedure was to assign one technician to each pharmacist for the work shift. On more difficult assignments, two pharmacists worked together. The rotating shift schedules afforded the opportunity for every member of the department to work with each other at some time over a three-month stretch. The nature of the work permitted conversation in all but the most delicate cases.

There was great harmony among pharmacists and technicians alike. The assistant director, Mr. Watson, was also an active member of the group's doings. Brief periods of foolishness flourished whenever work permitted and Mr. Simmons was away. One of the favorite pastimes of the pharmacists was a hockey-soccer game played with a roll of medical tape. Except for one technician, John, and one pharmacist, Carl, the staff never let these periods of foolishness get out of hand and interfere with work.

The time overlaps between shifts gave the pharmacists the opportunity to leave work "early" on the weekends and on the night shifts. Generally, workloads permitted only one pharmacist to obtain this benefit for each shift overlap. The pharmacist whose turn it was to leave early always asked his replacement if he was "covered" before actually departing. The technicians for the main part did not participate in the "fringe benefit" but were known to leave early on nice weekends by as much as 20 minutes to a half hour. This benefit was never sought by anyone when Mr. Simmons was around during the weekdays, although the assistant director did know of the practice. No one felt particularly guilty about it because they made sure their work was covered before leaving.

The young pharmacists and technicians were close socially outside of the hospital, too. The great majority of them were from outside the local area, and work provided an ideal place to make new friends. Many of the pharmacists played sports together, and family members were invited to summer picnics.

Discussion Questions and Predictions

1. Describe and explain the emergent social system.
2. What are the likely consequences (productivity, satisfaction, and learning)? Why?

PART II

The department had a good reputation for meeting its schedules and maintaining accuracy. The staff was highly satisfied with the job, and all felt they were learning (the technicians from the pharmacists and the pharmacists from the emphasis given by Jim Simmons to new techniques and equipment).

However, for several months the hospital had been instituting new programs aimed at reducing costs. The pharmacy, being a major component of the hospital, had converted under Jim Simmons' direction and guidance to new procedures for dispensing drugs. Mr. Simmons had pushed hard for the new procedure and upon its approval had moved promptly on implementing it.

Prior to the institution of the new procedures, the pharmacy had adhered to the "mosaic system" of drug distribution. Using this system the pharmacy would dispense one container with enough pills or medicine to last each patient one week. This system resulted in a large amount of unused drugs due to patients' hospital stays usually not occurring in one-week blocks and to changes in prescription or dosages. Federal and state laws required that any drugs not used upon patient discharge or prescription change be discarded.

With increased efficiency in mind, the pharmacy had switched to a "unit-dose system." Under this procedure, introduced ward by ward as rapidly as possible over the space of five months, exact dosages were sent bedside at every dosage interval.

A comparison of the two methods readily shows the reduction of drug waste. For example, in the case of a patient prescribed to take a pill every four hours during a three-day hospital stay, the mosaic system would result in one container of 28 pills (4 per day × 7 days) being sent bedside once a week. Under the unit-dosage system, one container of one pill would be sent bedside four times each day for three days, yielding a total of 12 pills dispensed.

The new system was also advantageous to the nurses on the floor. They no longer had to check each patient's prescription to determine dosage and then count it out. They could simply dispense what was sent from the pharmacy.

Mr. Simmons, who was convinced of the unit-dose system's advantages from previous hospital experience, was proud to the point of bragging about the pharmacy's role in overall hospital gains.

The disadvantages of the new system were centered solely in the pharmacy: massive increases in handling and paperwork. This led to the hiring of more staff and the adoption of a formal schedule of work, which Gary Watson updated daily. Overall the pharmacy had a net gain of three new pharmacists (one pharmacist had quit on the spot when he received Mr. Simmons' memo initiating the switch to unit dose) and four additional technicians. Nonetheless, the work tempo in the pharmacy picked up considerably.

Prediction Questions

1. How will the emergent system be affected by the changes? Why?
2. How will productivity, satisfaction, and learning be affected and why?

PART III

The new program stretched the capabilities of both pharmacists and technicians. The end of nearly every shift was characterized by a "scrambling atmosphere" as people rushed to meet Gary's schedule and finish to leave on time. Although the job still allowed for considerable conversation with nearby workers, gone were the hockey-soccer games, the telephone calls to friends, the early departures during shift overlaps, and the time for pharmacists to experiment with new techniques and teach technicians about pharmacology.

Work-related complaints began to surface more frequently; yet Gary, who was seen taking much paperwork home with him in the evenings, didn't seem to be as responsive as previously. Many began to believe that Gary was reluctant to "rock the boat" with his boss by pointing out limitations in the new system. They suspected that Gary was too willing to give in to Mr. Simmons when discussing people problems and no longer willing to go to bat for them.

Before long, Gary stopped coming to picnics and other get-togethers even though invited, and even began to stop playing touch football with the pharmacists.

The pharmacists, who felt that the pressure was likely to result in errors, began to approach Mr. Simmons individually. Ten of the 11 spoke to him expressing their professional concern and personal dissatisfaction with the general work situation. But all reported a common response: Everyone must realize how important the new system was to the hospital and how tight its overall budget. The pharmacists began to wonder if Mr. Simmons was sincere in his concern for their professional judgments and personal well-being.

Finally, as with any group of workers, the department employed a few workers who were less responsible and, in the best of circumstances, were underproducers. The young pharmacist, Carl, and the young technician, John, who were the lowest producers under the old system, consistently failed to complete their share of work under the new programs. Both had worked in General Hospital's pharmacy for several years and were considered experienced. Carl held a full pharmacy degree, but it was rumored that he had struggled through the five-year university program. Both were friendly by nature and had contributed to many of the group's social activities. The technicians who worked with them and the pharmacists who worked near them found themselves finishing Carl's and John's work. Many employees began to show ill feelings toward Carl and John, while other employees simply did the extra work and said nothing except among themselves.

The baseball game Jim Simmons was watching was in the last inning on that Saturday, a Saturday when the weekend pharmacy crew included both Carl and John. Mr. Simmons' phone rang. It was an administrator of the hospital. He wanted to inform Mr. Simmons that the drug tray deliveries to each floor were running an hour and a half behind schedule and had been all day long. Although luckily no great hardships to patients' health had arisen, this was not the first time, only the worst, and such performance was unacceptable and must be corrected!

Discussion Questions

1. Explain what has happened to the pharmacy's social system since the change to the unit-dosage system.
2. What should Mr. Simmons do, if anything, assuming that he has all the facts given above at his disposal? Why?

Fujiyama Trading Co., Ltd.

In December 1976, Mr. R. Nara, executive vice president of Fujiyama American Corporation (hereafter referred to as FAM), was sitting in his office in New York, recalling the day when he decided to hire an American M.B.A. It was in January 1976 when FAM first hired an American M.B.A. as a future manager of the company.

FAM's parent company, Fujiyama Trading Co., Ltd. (hereafter referred to as FTC), is one of the Japanese "sogo-shosha," usually translated as "general trading companies," a distinctly Japanese business enterprise. Unlike specialized trading firms, which limit their activities to specific types of products on a limited geographic basis, the sogo-shosha handles every kind of product and conducts import, export, and offshore transactions worldwide, as well as trade within Japan.

Characteristics of the sogo-shosha are: a great number of items traded; vast sales with small profit margins; worldwide office and information networks; a large number of highly skilled employees of many nationalities; intimate acquaintance with the law, business practices, trading procedures, customs, and languages of many countries; central position in diversified groups of companies and close ties with many other companies; central roles in the Japanese economy; and growing importance in international trade.

As of March 1977, FTC, one of the leading sogo-shosha in Japan, had a total of 8,400 staff members, including 1,400 employed in foreign countries who devoted themselves to customer service through international trade, development, and processing of natural resources overseas, as well as to distribution, financing, and many other areas.

The company transferred staff members on planned rotation through a variety of jobs to help younger staff members develop into well-rounded employees capable of handling all facets of the company's business. These transfers were made not only within FTC's domestic divisions but also to overseas offices and subsidiaries.

FAM is FTC's wholly owned (100 percent shares) subsidiary and contributes a growing percentage (currently over 15 percent) to FTC's overall business. FAM, with 12 offices in the United States, has literally become an American sogo-shosha. At any given moment, FAM's divisions are engaged in the import and export of thousands upon

From S. Fink, S. Jenks, and R. Willits, *Designing and Managing Organizations*, 1983, pages 464–73. Reproduced by permission of Richard D. Irwin, Inc., Homewood, Ill.

thousands of different commodities and products. Simultaneously, they may be working on such diverse ventures as the creation and organization of a consortium of enterprises from different countries to search for and develop new energy or mineral resources. Several may be involved, in unison, in planning and coordinating the construction of ports, plants, or pipelines. Still another division may be guiding an American firm in its first attempt at creating an international market for its products.

FAM's New York head office had 100 Japanese staff members and 200 American staff members. Among the American staff, about 30 were male employees and the remaining were female employees, all of whom were engaged in clerical jobs. In order for the company to meet equal opportunity commitments, some of the top managers of FAM had discussed the hiring of Americans as prospective managers. In other words, in order to avoid trouble and to get government business, it was decided that the company should have a certain percentage of American managers among the total officers of the company.

Mr. Nara, 47, office manager of the New York head office, was in favor of starting and developing this program of hiring prospective American managers. He had spent 25 years with the parent company, including 8 years in the United States as office manager in Los Angeles and 2 years in Argentina. As such, he was interested in management in different cultures and had studied it himself. After one year as an executive vice president, he asked the Personnel Department to find American M.B.A.s suitable as future managers. He commented:

> Through my long experience of working overseas, I have always recognized the differences of managerial cultures. As you are well aware, the American society is based upon individualism, free mobility, and less human-oriented organizations, which has resulted in a very unique and efficient organization. However, it is not necessarily true that this type of organization can function well under any culture and society.
>
> The Japanese organization, of course, is based on the peculiar Japanese value system. In a word, it is often said that America is individual oriented, while Japan is group oriented. In America, personal responsibility is always emphasized, and one's authority and responsibility are clarified. I think that the job description, for example, comes from this idea. The reason why job descriptions have not been developed in Japan as a basis of personnel or organizational administration is because of differences of culture and social value systems.
>
> In Japanese organizations, authority tends to be a vague concept, which makes it somewhat hard for each individual to take clear responsibility. Sometimes responsibility is regarded as an ambiguous concept by the Japanese manager. The process of Japanese decision making is very much like consensus building, which makes it harder to determine who should take final responsibility.

The basic principle of Japanese organization is not an authoritarian command, but *wa* (harmony), which is achieved by mutual consideration. The "group-oriented" tendency of Japanese people is related to such Japanese management practices as lifetime employment and seniority systems. These practices reflect the Japanese concept of household, which holds that the high born and powerful have an obligation and a social responsibility to protect the less fortunate and less powerful.

Under such practices, the future of all employees depends upon the performance of the company as a unit. Therefore in Japan, more than in America, management and employees cooperate in working toward the goal of a successful company. We often say "spirit of belonging" or "love for the company" to express our loyalty, which is the outcome of the above-mentioned atmosphere. In short, for the Japanese people, corporate life does not only mean the profit center, but also the social unit where one achieves emotional satisfaction.

As such, the people we want are those who can demonstrate skill at building good personal relationships and performing so-called team work. When we hire college students, for example, observation of their personality takes priority over their special knowledge such as accounting, economics, marketing, and so forth. Therefore, we usually hire college students as soon as they graduate and train them. After joining a company, the college graduates usually find themselves initially spending some time working and learning in two or three departments in the company. This on-the-job training continues for a couple of years, during which they gain a wide range of experience in all aspects of the company operation.

Because of such differences about the concept of the business community, I don't believe that American managers would work efficiently or happily if we hired them away from other companies. If we really want an American to manage our organization, we have to train him by on-the-job training and keep him with the company for a long time in order for him to feel loyalty.

I do not deny that in any society organizations must be established on the basis of the value system which prevails in that society for the organization to survive and develop in that society. It is easy to say, but hard to do. I can easily imagine that Japanese staff would not be able to work efficiently here, if they have to work in the type of working environment as in the United States. This will result in unfavorable performance of the company, which I, as a manager, have to avoid. Therefore the very crucial thing is, I believe, how to find the meeting point.

Of course, it is necessary for us to be somewhat Americanized, but at the same time, it is also necessary for the Americans to be Japanized, if they want to work for such a company as ours. In other words, we will preserve our basic Japanese system, which is a very good system, but make the proper adaptations to operating in America.

To begin with, Mr. Nara ordered the establishment of Japanese language classes, opened a library with a lot of books about Japan, and offered flower arrangement classes in the company. These programs were offered for the purpose of raising the American staff's sense of belonging to the company and letting them understand various aspects of Japan. Every program was operated at the company's expense. These programs were very well received by the American employees.

Although these programs were offered mainly for the lower-level staff, Mr. Nara thought of having M.B.A.s join them when they were hired, so as to let them understand Japan. Mr. Nara intended, after this, to send M.B.A.s to Japan for several years so that they could learn and experience the Japanese managerial way, business customs, ways of thinking, and so forth; and then to send them back to the United States. By so doing, Mr. Nara believed that M.B.A.s would understand how to bridge the gap between two cultures and function better as international managers.

Upon receiving the order from Mr. Nara, the staff of the Personnel Department, who had just been brought from Japan to establish that department, began to contact several business schools, which were supposed to be interested in Japan, to inform them of the company's desire to hire M.B.A.s. As a result of this, FAM had 15 inquiries, and the personnel staff had an interview with each of them. At that time, the company policy was to hire one or two M.B.A.s on a trial basis. The Personnel Department picked five students who seemed to be interested in working for a Japanese company, and left the final decision to Mr. Nara. Through personal interviews, Mr. Nara decided to hire two prospective M.B.A.s.

Mr. Karl Smith was one of the two hired. He had gone to a small college in Maine that reflected and stressed the traditional "Yankee" values of independence, hard work, and self-reliance. After college he continued his education by studying for an M.A. in international relations at City College of New York. Following this, he took a job with the Savings Bank Life Insurance Company in New York, but continued to study Middle East politics at night. Finally he enrolled full time in the M.B.A. program and joined FAM at the age of 27. At that time, he described himself as follows:

> My personal goal is to become a top manager in a large corporation. Power, status, luxury, and quick decision making . . . that's the life for me. For this purpose, I'll face up to any difficulties and not run away from them. I don't mind if my whole life revolves around business. I am an aggressive type of person and feel bad if someone gets ahead of me.
>
> The M.B.A. program was a great program that emphasized basic principles of management. I found their emphasis, on such ideas as clear job descriptions and individual accountability, as well as on promotions based on merit, compatible with my philosophy that the rewards of life should go to those who perform the best. The program was just the

starting point for my career goals. They gave me some of the skills I will need to be a success!

Mr. Nara made a comment on his decision to hire Karl:

He was more enthusiastic than the others. He personally was interested in Arab countries, and he was a member of a study group about Arab politics with other M.B.A. students at the university. Some of them are actually working over there now.

The passion for one specific thing, which is not necessarily inside the realm of work, is also very important. I remember hiring a guy who was a great college baseball player in Japan, and this led me to feel that he would demonstrate self-discipline, loyalty, and commitment to the company. I have recently seen many young people who don't know what their goals are or even what they would like to do. The person who is vague about these things is useless. If one has devoted himself to a specific thing, it would be possible for him to demonstrate loyalty and commitment to the company for a long time. As a matter of fact, Karl told me that he had a passion for hunting with bow and arrow. I heard that he even makes his own bows and arrows, which is really a specialty.

I also saw another reason for my decision. As you are well aware, Arab countries have a tremendous amount of Eurodollars because of sales of oil, and they are trying to industrialize with their earnings. We have technology and knowledge about how to industrialize. There exists a great possibility for us to win big projects in those countries. In such a situation, if we hired Karl, he will be able to provide us with some valuable information. That is why I have come up with the final decision.

Mr. Nara thought that Ferrous Metal Products Division would be best fitted for Mr. Smith and assigned him to this division as the immediate subordinate of Mr. Y. Kato, who was an assistant manager of the division.

As usual with the Japanese trading company, most college graduates find themselves spending time in two or three departments after joining a company so as to develop their general knowledge. Thereafter they begin to specialize. Since the commodities handled vary tremendously, it is necessary for the company to have a specialist in the particular commodity in order to respond to the customer's needs.

Mr. Nara had been dealing with the exporting of steel products since he joined the company. During the 25 years he had spent in this business, he had brought up many subordinates, a number of whom had become managers of overseas offices themselves. Almost all 120 overseas offices handle steel products. It can be said that Mr. Nara has his subordinates all over the world. One of his subordinates, Mr. Kato, had spent his 15 years with the company in the business of selling steel products. During this period, while he had had several trips overseas, he had never worked in any of the company's overseas offices. At the beginning of January 1976, he was transferred to the FAM New York office as an assistant manager of the Ferrous Metal Products Division. He recalled the first impression he had when he joined the New York office:

> When I was working in Japan, whenever I was not too busy, I used to take subordinates, sometimes including female employees in section, to the bar to have a talk with them over glass of beer. It was very useful to talk to them in an informal place out of office to get to know them. Sometimes they complained about company policy or customers and sometimes they consulted about personal matters. I believe these relationships were very basis of my management style. I don't think I can manage people without knowing them. Interpersonal relationship between subordinates and myself was that of support and dependence instead of dominance and submission. However, when I first came here, I was really shocked with American people's practical and businesslike way of thinking. I couldn't see any warm human relationships. For example, every female employee leaves office exactly at five o'clock. When one female clerk was working most hard the other day, other female clerk sitting next to her never helped at all even though she did not have any work to do because of boss's absence. These kinds of things never happen in Japan. If I ask female employee to work overtime, she willingly did it. When someone was very busy, others gave help. I think this is way it's supposed to be.
>
> However, this does not happen here as in Japan, and in this way. New York office is not comfortable place to work. I am not criticizing company policy about hiring M.B.A.s, because I am loyal and also respect Mr. Nara. But, having American M.B.A. assigned to department is personally unpleasant for me. I've just arrived in this country and I am not good English speaker, so I have hard time dealing with American people. If I cannot communicate well, it's going to be embarrassing to them and me as well.

Mr. Smith joined Mr. Kato's division one month after Mr. Kato was transferred to New York. Mr. Smith quickly learned the steel business through the instruction given him by the other employees and through his inherent aggressiveness and enthusiasm. In the course of teaching the business to him, his peers tried to get him involved in their jobs as well. He had the impression that he was receiving special attention, and he felt pleased that the other managers apparently recognized his knowledge of Arab countries. On the contrary, Mr. Smith's peers were merely trying to make him understand how the Japanese organization works utilizing a group approach.

In October 1976, the company had to send someone to Saudi Arabia for finalizing the business negotiation of exporting steel products to a certain engineering company there. Mr. Kato's boss suggested sending Mr. Smith to Saudi Arabia, because he thought that this opportunity might give Mr. Smith incentive and motivation. However, Mr.

Kato wanted to conclude this business deal without any trouble, and he felt that a Japanese staff member could work more cooperatively with the Japanese staff of Jedda than Mr. Smith could. Furthermore, Mr. Kato thought that Mr. Smith was not yet really ready to represent the company, having observed Mr. Smith's everyday behavior in the office. However, keeping in mind his boss's suggestion, he reluctantly decided to send Mr. Smith, taking into account his abundant knowledge of Arab countries.

At Jedda International Airport, Mr. Smith was welcomed by a staff member of FTC's Jedda office, who had been informed of his arrival beforehand. The staff member spoke to him:

> How do you do, Mr. Smith? How was your trip? If you are not tired, I'd like to have lunch with you and talk about the upcoming business negotiation. Also I can tell you about some of the people you are going to meet, that might be helpful to you. By the way, I used to work as a subordinate of Mr. Nara before and he took very good care of me. How is he doing lately? . . .

Mr. Smith, on the other hand, was surprised with the man's coming to the airport to see him. He thought to himself:

> Gee, I don't understand why he came to the airport to see me, when he must have been very busy with his own job. I could go to my hotel or the company office or luncheon meeting without any help. It is a waste of his time, an unnecessary expense, and surely not a professional way to conduct business when time is short.

Karl spoke courteously with the staff member but kept the conversation on pleasantries and got away from him as soon as he could. This left the staff member feeling very perplexed. He could not understand why Karl asked so few questions of a business nature, nor why he left so abruptly after they reached the Jedda office. He wondered if he had said something that violated American customs, such as mentioning his past association with Mr. Nara (to which Karl had hardly responded). He certainly felt badly that he had been of so little assistance to Mr. Smith.

Besides his original business negotiation, Karl was supposed to meet Mr. Henry Bodwell, his friend from the M.B.A. program, who held an important position in a Saudi Arabian company. When they met, Karl got some confidential information from Mr. Bodwell, which was that Freedman Construction, Inc., of the United States had undertaken a big project for the government of Saudi Arabia. The project was to develop a big outer harbor at Jedda, including construction of berths, highly developed mechanical loaders and unloaders, and many infrastructures. In total, it would amount to about $100 million.

For the steel divisions of FTC and FAM, this type of project was one of the most desirable ones. Since the division earns profit on a commission basis (usually 2.5–3 percent of steel price, which is about $300 per ton) in accordance with the quantity handled, big projects that allow the division to deal with large quantities of steel (15,000–20,000 tons for this project) are always sought by everybody in the division.

Almost all of the people and agencies interested in this project thought that nobody had yet successfully undertaken this project, because the press release was not yet scheduled. Knowing this information, Karl thought there existed the possibility of his selling a large quantity of Japanese steel products to Freedman, Inc., if he approached them before anybody after he got back to New York. On the way back to New York, he was excited about this.

> I'm the one who found out about this project. I can take the initiative and responsibility also. I must finalize this project independently at any cost. This is a damn good opportunity to demonstrate my knowledge about the Arab countries and my confidence in carrying out new business. If I make it, my status in the company will be well established and I will be relied upon by my fellow employees and my bosses as well. The company should appreciate this, and my status will rise. Since I was not familiar with the steel business, I have had to be passive in most cases; however, from now on, I will be able to be more active and assertive.

After getting back to New York, he reported to Mr. Kato about his original business, and quietly started approaching Freedman, Inc.

When he was asked by Mr. Kato or his fellow workers what he was doing, he used to say that it was not important and he never talked much.

> I'm not going to disclose this opportunity to anyone until I've made real progress. If I do, it will be talk, talk, talk, and more talk. Time will be lost, and more than likely someone outside the company will hear about it. If I carry the ball myself, the company will get the jump on other companies, I'll establish my capability and credibility, and everyone will gain an unexpected dividend. As Professor Chandler used to say, the way to get a job done right is to assign it to one man and then hold him responsible for results.

In November, Karl succeeded in making contact with a vice president of engineering for Freedman, Inc. Karl's strategy was to influence the design specifications written by Freedman's Engineering Department. He believed that if he could convince Freedman of the superiority and competitiveness of the quality and price of Japanese steel, then they would write the design specifications in a manner that insured the acceptability, and even favored the use, of Japanese steel. Karl knew that it was important that the specifications not rule out the use of Japanese steel in favor of steel from some other country, and he also knew that in Mr. Kato's experience Japanese steel mills would nominate Fujiyama (FTC) as the exclusive negotiator in appreciation for its efforts in attaining "good" specifications.

Karl's discussions with the Freedman vice president were successful. However, there was one condition; namely, the approval of the specifications by the Saudi government. Time was urgent because Freedman had to send the design drawings containing the specifications to the Saudi government in two weeks.

Karl knew that personal connections were very crucial for doing business in Saudi Arabia, therefore he believed that he had to hold direct negotiations with some suitable person in the Saudi government. Keeping in mind the time element involved to prepare the necessary data, Karl believed that he had to fly to Jedda immediately. He felt sure that he could make an appointment with the "key" men of the Saudi government through the cooperation of Mr. Bodwell; and then through "person-to-person" negotiations have them accept the desired specifications.

Therefore he went to Mr. Kato and told him all about the project and the necessity of getting an approval from the government of Saudi Arabia. He asked Mr. Kato for permission to make the trip to Saudi Arabia at once. Mr. Kato was very surprised with this and said:

> Why have you done this all by yourself so far? As you know, we are not manufacturing steel products, therefore, you are supposed to ask about the possibility of getting such a quantity of steel products from Japan first of all. And you have not gotten any approval from the Tokyo office as to this project. Nor have you ever consulted our two offices in Saudi Arabia. If you keep going with this project without cooperation with offices in Saudi Arabia, they will lose face toward Tokyo office, as will others. You are supposed to know that the overseas offices can get commission as a certain percentage of business transactions around the office area. The more the office is involved in the business, the more commission it can get. . . . This time, I think you had better stay in office and ask the staffs in Saudi Arabia to negotiate with the person in the government. . . .

Mr. Smith was very much disappointed with Mr. Kato's decision and said:

> Maybe you don't know, but personal connections are very important for conducting business over there, and I have that connection. I need no coordinator. This is a project that will be very beneficial to the company; if necessary, I'll ask offices in Saudi Arabia for help myself. I must have permission to go over there.

In order to decide anything, in Japanese business society, people are expected to lay the groundwork and get the consensus of everybody involved before taking any action. Mr. Kato was very dissatisfied with Mr. Smith's taking action on his own and finally told Mr. Smith: "As long as you work for Japanese company, you are supposed to understand the Japanese way."

Very much disappointed with Mr. Kato's words, Mr. Smith went to Mr. Nara's office, told him all about what was going on, and complained:

> I have to leave New York for Jedda at once to get approval from the government of Saudi Arabia. I already have a personal connection, which is a "must" over there for this kind of negotiation. I want to do this even at the risk of losing my job. Since you have influence over the staff of the steel division in Saudi Arabia, you can take care of them. However, I have to go there as soon as possible. Please let me go!

Mr. Nara thought about the impact on everybody and of all the offices that would be affected by his saying yes or no. Whichever his decision, it must be made immediately.

Full Speed Ahead

"Well, if you insist, I can't stop you," Professor McRow concluded, "but I do not think you can get into the M.B.A. program at this time. If you can, it will be all right with me."

McRow peered out from his eyeglasses and looked at the student standing in his office. Max Weber, a first-semester economics student, had informed him that he wished to transfer from the economics department to the university's master of business administration program.

Weber had visited McRow several times before to discuss his misgivings about the economics program. Weber had asserted he felt largely inadequate for the courses. McRow had assured him he was mistaken and that his discomfort was typical of most graduate students. McRow's words had little effect; Weber's impatience and concern grew as each week passed.

He had felt uncertain about graduate work in economics before he had come to the university. He had debated between the M.B.A. and M.A. economics programs and had chosen the latter, but by July of the previous summer he had come to feel he had made a mistake. He had discussed a possible switch with friends to obtain their reactions to such an idea.

"That would be a surprise," remarked Jim Brock. "After all, all I ever see you read is economics."

Another friend registered her opinions more strongly. "Max, that's the most frivolous thing I've ever heard," said Ann Cole. "My god, two weeks into the M.B.A. program and you'll want to switch into the botany department!"

Weber listened to McRow, his friends, and his family; but in the end, he decided to transfer. Rushing about the campus, he completed the necessary paperwork in about a day, and he joined his first M.B.A. class, Professor Taylor's marketing course, on a Thursday afternoon, the fourth week of the semester.

The next few days he spent buying books, picking up syllabi, and beginning the long catch-up process. Weber attended his first statistics and accounting classes on Monday, and on the following day he attended his first session of Professor Probier's class in organizational behavior.

The class was broken up into three discussion groups, and Professor Probier assigned Weber to group B, which consisted of Alex Hamilton, Bill Fast, Mike Graff, Linda Harkness, Ed Kubek, and Henrietta Chase. Weber pulled up a chair, sat down, and decided to himself he would be an active and contributing member to group B. As a "no-nonsense" type of person, he decided to enter the discussion "full speed ahead," quickly trying to solve the problems contained in the case studies selected by the professor.

Ten minutes after he had joined B, however, Weber wanted to ask Professor Probier if he could join another group. He did not like what he saw or heard.

Group B was in the throes of a minor crisis. It had neither a group leader nor a policy for rewarding (grading) individual performance. The group members were discussing among themselves what they should do. Weber was distressed by this situation. The other groups, as far as he could discern, had apparently resolved these issues long ago and were now working on the day's assignment. Weber decided he should try to do something about the situation.

"I kind of think we should work on the case before us," he said. "If none of you really care to see Probier on a regular basis, I'll be willing to do it until you can come up with a final solution." Weber was thinking to himself this would pick him up a few extra grade points, and besides, he wanted to get down to business.

The group continued to talk about the group leader issue—to death, as far as Weber was concerned. "Talk, talk, talk," he thought to himself. "Parkinson was right after all. Work does expand to fill the time allotted." By the end of the class the group had decided Alex Hamilton should continue to serve as spokesperson on a "permanent" basis but subject to change.

When class was over, Weber did not pause to linger with his fellow group members but chose instead to dash out of room 301 as quickly as possible. "Aaagh," he groaned to a fellow dorm resident, "these people are incredible! They can't make up their minds about anything."

"I think they're afraid to offend one another," he continued, "so they end up not accomplishing anything at all. It looks like I'm going to have to do some prodding and pushing of my own if anything is going to be done in that class."

During the next few weeks Weber found himself doing a large amount of "prodding and pushing." "I think we're getting off the track" became a favorite expression with him. He did not hesitate to interrupt and try to change the direction of conversation when he felt it necessary.

He soon sensed his tactics were unpopular, but this did not stop him. He believed Ed Kubek and Bill Fast were especially unfriendly toward him, but Weber told himself he did not care. As far as he could perceive, these two men were not making a sufficient contribution to the group, so their opinions did not matter. He found Linda Harkness agreeing with him many times, and Hamilton often solicited his advice and comments. Weber felt that as long as he had the attention of these two influential members his position was secure.

Yet, certain signals began to crop up that indicated his position of influence in the group was declining. Weber found that members of the group no longer looked at him when they talked to him. Fast would look at Hamilton when answering a question from Weber. Harkness would do the same or look out the window. Graff looked at a wall or at Kubek. Weber found himself talking less. Members of the group would casually remark they did not like his choice of words when he expressed himself. Fast especially disliked the word *thrash*, which Weber used when he wanted to settle a difference of opinion with another member of the group; "I don't think we 'thrash' anything out here," remarked Fast. "We get along pretty well and discuss things without having to 'thrash' them out as you like to say."

Weber recognized his position was on the decline, but he did not know how to arrest that decline. The other group members increasingly ignored him. The group did not respond to any of his feeble efforts to bring the problem into the open. The most he could elicit from the group was a polite "you are more task oriented than the rest of us."

Weber found this kind of reply unsatisfactory. He suggested that if the group wanted to get at the roots of their differences, then they should bring their journals (required by the instructor as a database for a term paper on the group's experiences) to class and read their entries to one another. The response to this proposal was unenthusiastic.

"I don't think that's such a good idea."

"Let's not do that."

"Yeah, let's not."

Weber felt stymied. Fortunately for him, Professor Probier assigned the members of each group to evaluate one another. He also requested each group to list its norms or standards of behavior. Finally, Weber had the opportunity to get a long-smoldering problem out into the open.

The results of the evaluation were largely what he expected. Voted least liked and most threatening, Weber was also voted by the group as being unhelpful, though Hamilton gave him a high rating. There were also a few unpleasant surprises. People whom he thought would have rated him highly in some categories gave him singularly low grades. Harkness, whom Weber had regarded as his greatest ally, viewed him as a threat and put him at the top of her least-liked list.

"Obviously we have some problems here." Weber leaned back in his chair and folded his hands on top of his head. "I've kind of felt there's been something wrong, but I need feedback from you people if I'm going to do anything about it."

The members of the group opened up, and while not harsh in their words, they made it clear to Weber he had not been subscribing to their norms. They told him all members were to be treated alike and with equal respect. Furthermore, they informed him that the individual's self-expression and development came first and the assigned tasks second. Weber had, they felt, tended to dominate the conversation too much. He was prone to cut people off, people who had ideas to express, too.

For Weber this may have been the most fruitful class of the semester. The problem was out in the open, and he could now begin to work on it. He told the group he was unwilling to sacrifice his task-oriented nature but that he would try to maintain a lower profile. Over the next few classes he deliberately talked less and asked more questions. He tried to change his role to that of a coordinator who sometimes plays the devil's advocate.

Weber continued to concentrate on getting the job done in class, and the group came to expect him to fulfill a task role. The group saw him as a prodder, "our old taskmaster" as Bill Fast would phrase it. And Weber had to admit to himself that he felt most comfortable in that role. He considered himself ill-suited to play what he deprecatingly called "touchy-feely." He preferred to deal with the facts or problems devoid of the human equation. Hamilton's open and informal leadership style was more focused on expression of feelings than he would have preferred but allowed him to concentrate on getting the jobs done.

Over the next few weeks, Weber found himself liking the members of the group more than he had in the past. Moreover, he felt the group liked him better and that the group was working more effectively as a unit. This new unity became apparent when it came time to write a group analysis of two cases, "Mr. Haws" and "Chuck, the Manager." Every member participated in the task, especially Mike Graff and Ed Kubek, whom the group had criticized previously for not participating enough. As for Weber, he succeeded in retaining a task-oriented position, but he participated relatively little in the conversation the group had on the project. The group met one night in a conference room to discuss the paper. Weber automatically went to the blackboard and began to write down people's comments. He tried to give the members an outline on the board, and he did not express many opinions of his own. Largely he raised questions, which he hoped would give the discussion a direction and a definite scope.

The meeting went well. An instructor passing by commented that he was impressed, and the group was pleased with his remarks. Weber was tempted to take it as a personal compliment, for he was the one at the blackboard. The group ended the meeting happy with the results. Fast, who had been critical of Weber, praised Weber for the job he had done.

Weber felt he was now at last making progress in gaining both group acceptance and friendship. "I didn't care for you at all at first," Kubek remarked a few days later. "You came on pretty strong. But you've changed, and you aren't so bad after all."

Weber and Harkness wrote the final draft of the Chuck–Haws analysis, and Professor Probier gave the group a 90 percent on the paper. The group decided to give each member an equal share of the grade since all members had participated in the task. Professor Probier, however, found this unacceptable and insisted the group divide the grade on a proportionate basis.

"Why?" asked Hamilton, the group spokesperson. "We all contributed to the output."

"Yes, why can't we divide it up equally?" Weber questioned. "Like Alex said, everyone did something for the paper. I helped to write the final draft, but Alex wrote part of the rough draft, and Henrietta did the typing."

"I think you're avoiding the issue," answered Probier.

"No, we're not," Weber replied a little more emphatically than he would normally. He felt most members had contributed fairly. But he and the group also realized he had spent more time rewriting the paper than the others. He was worried. A discussion on how to divide up the grade might create friction. This was the last thing he wanted. He had worked hard to improve his standing in the group and told himself he was not about to let Professor Probier undo any of the good he had accomplished. In fact, he wrote the defense explaining the group's position, and he was as happy as any other member to see Professor Probier acquiesce to the group's desires.

Weber generally was satisfied with his position in the group. He thought he had overcome the old hurdles. He now had good relations with the other members. Harkness was more cordial to him. Graff suggested Weber and he play paddleball, and Weber developed friendly relations with Kubek and his wife. While not the most influential member of the group, Weber decided he was willing to trade off the opportunity for further influence for more popularity. His main goal became to preserve the status quo.

This "era of good feeling" did not last long for Weber. He began to experience trouble with the group shortly after the completion of the Chuck–Haws analysis. The next assignment was to write a case. The group chose Ed Kubek's proposal, and Kubek wrote a rough draft. A meeting to discuss the paper was held; Kubek provided more information, but the meeting ended with little accomplished. Graff wrote another rough draft, but the group did not feel this second version was adequate.

The task of rewriting and producing a final draft fell into Weber's hands almost by default. Kubek and Graff had written enough, Harkness was ill, Hamilton would be away, and Chase and Fast said they would be unable to help. To Weber it seemed no one wanted to have anything to do with the paper.

Neither did Weber. He had helped to write the previous paper and believed it was someone else's turn. The case write-up promised to take even longer than the previous paper. He had already fallen behind in his other courses, and he had put more than 20 hours into his assistantship that week. This set him back even further. By Friday he found himself tired but faced with a case that the group admitted was far from complete.

That weekend he drove to his parents' home in Lancaster to write the case. Weber also drove to Danford to work on it with Kubek, and by Sunday evening he had finished what he felt would be an acceptable final draft.

On Monday he turned the case over to Hamilton, who had offered to type the paper. Weber asked the members of the group to read the draft before it was turned in to Professor Probier.

For the most part no one seemed interested in the paper. "I'm sure it's all right, Max," commented Henrietta Chase. "The last job you did turned out really well." Fast was also unwilling to read it. "We've worked on that thing long enough; I don't want to start picking things apart now."

Interest in the case, however, mounted when Weber explained how he and Kubek had decided to end it. "I don't think that's the way we should do it," said Hamilton. "I think we should change it so it will help our analysis." Chase and Fast agreed, and with Hamilton and

Weber the four of them went to the student snack bar to discuss the case further.

At the cafeteria the conversation turned to matters unrelated to the case. Weber wished to clear the matter up, so while the other members ate lunch he stepped outside to look for Kubek. Finding Kubek in the social science computer terminal room, Weber brought him back to the snack bar, and in a short time a final change was made that was acceptable to everyone.

Professor Probier returned the case with a grade of 93 percent a week later. The group was pleased with the result, and as was the custom, the grade was divided up equally.

This time Weber held strong misgivings about an equal distribution of the grade. He believed Kubek and he had spent more time on it than the rest and deserved a higher grade.

Yet he did not express this view to Alex Hamilton. "I'm going to leave it up to you and Ed about what to do about the grade," Hamilton said to Weber. Weber turned to Kubek. "I think we should divide it equally," said Kubek. "That's fine with me," Weber answered.

Weber was not pleased with this outcome. He had griped to both Kubek and Hamilton before class that he felt he had been saddled with the paper. He had hoped Hamilton would take the initiative and recommend to the group that Kubek and he receive higher shares of the grade. Instead, Hamilton had passed the decision to Weber. Since Kubek wanted an equal distribution ("It's not worth fighting over," he had told Weber earlier), Weber felt he could not insist on a higher grade. He did not trust how the group would respond and did not want to open the issue for the professor's scrutiny. The matter was closed.

Placed in an awkward position before the group, Weber had chosen to let the matter rest. Weber walked away after class feeling he had been cheated.

"They left me to write the paper," he complained to a fellow M.B.A. student from another group, "but they didn't make any effort to see how it turned out. They just assumed everything would be OK. They forgot it was their paper, too."

"I do not know who was responsible for that paper's success," he concluded, "but I think I do know who would have been held responsible if it had been a failure."

At the time of this incident, new groups were being formed in the class. Weber was assigned to a group that contained some of the members of the old group. Despite his displeasure about the paper's outcome, he was happy to find himself surrounded by familiar faces. But at the first meeting no one displayed any interest in the day's assignment. With Thanksgiving approaching, most members wanted to relax and discuss their plans for the holiday.

With no one eager to begin the task, Weber found himself filling the vacuum of leadership. He asked questions and tried to direct the conversation. He kept notes and delivered a report with which he was dissatisfied to the class. He had found this session especially frustrating, for no one seemed to want to help him to get the job done.

When classes resumed after Thanksgiving, Weber decided he would do as little as possible for his group. "I'm tired of playing secretary and doing everybody else's work. It's not worth it."

He talked less in class. He stopped taking notes. His mind began to wander in class and his notebook filled with doodles. In one class Fast remarked, "Max doesn't seem to be with it at all today."

Fast was right, but Weber was simply grateful the semester was drawing to a close. Exhausted, he hoped he would never have to sit in on another organizational behavior class for the rest of his stay at the university.

▶ Growth at Stein, Bodello, & Associates, Inc.

Changes came hard at Stein, Bodello, & Associates, Inc. (SBA). Following a move to a new location and an upgrading of both the business and project management functions, some unhappiness had developed in the ranks of middle management.

Stein, Bodello, & Associates was a consulting civil engineering firm founded in the mid-1960s by Dan Stein. It was located in the Midwest, employing 100 people in four branch offices. The business had grown rapidly, especially in recent years. In the past three years business volume had grown from $2 million to $5 million annually. As Dan Stein explained, "The firm is committed to growth."

The firm was managed by four principals: the senior partners, Dan Stein and Joe Bodello, and two junior partners, John Lahey and Robert Waters. The senior partners were both in their mid-50s with over 30 years of experience in the field. Dan Stein was the founder of the firm. He had both a B.S. and an M.S. in engineering and had presented more than 20 professional papers over the years. An engineer's engineer, he was oriented to the practical end of the business. He liked to keep abreast technically of the projects in which he was the principal in charge and enjoyed making technical input into solutions; he would rather be an engineer than a manager. As a businessman he was

This case was written for classroom discussion under the supervision of Professor Allan R. Cohen.

conservative and didn't like to take risks. He was sensitive and on several occasions asked what image, such as an older brother or friend, he portrayed to younger employees, most of whom were under 40.

On the other hand, he did not walk around the office to socialize. If he was seen away from his desk, it was because he was on his way out of the building or asking an engineer a technical question about one of his projects. Because principals in the firm were required to have high chargeable ratios for billable work, just as did the staff, they found it hard to find "free time" to socialize with their employees. Likewise they found it hard to find time to be participative leaders or to take on more management responsibility.

Joe Bodello had joined the firm shortly after its founding. He also was a professional engineer but had become more of a businessman and was treasurer of the firm. His management style was quite strict. He spent some time walking around the office, usually visiting engineers twice a day to maintain visibility.

The junior partners had been with the firm for 15 years and had become vice presidents. John Lahey was a professional engineer with 20 years of experience. He was a good practical engineer and managed in a participative, trusting style. He usually mixed with employees at lunch. Robert Waters was not an engineer but had a degree in an engineering-related field. He was an aggressive go-getter. His style was "strictly business," and though he was willing to chat with employees and occasionally would sit and socialize, he was usually too busy to do so. Both vice presidents, however, were regarded as easy-going.

The board of directors, composed of Stein, Bodello, and Lahey, had overall responsibility for management of the firm. However, if an issue didn't meet with Stein's approval it had little chance of being passed. There was also a management committee comprised of the four partners. It functioned as an advisory group to the board of directors to deal with matters of business management, including internal operations, marketing, and profitability. It was a forum for discussion of policy and company goals. In addition, there was a personnel committee comprised of Stein, Bodello, and a senior associate, which functioned as an advisory group to the board of directors on matters of personnel management.

When the firm was young, Stein and Bodello had performed all the functions of the business from field work to engineering to report writing. As the firm grew they gradually had to give up various activities; first the field work and then some of the engineering. However, they continued to want to be involved in the engineering whenever possible. In recent years the senior staff associates and senior-level employees, who were project managers, had the responsibility for seeing projects through to completion. (See Exhibit 1 for an approximate organization chart.) Occasionally, more experienced junior staff would also function as project managers. This included detailed budget tracking, management of personnel assigned to the project, client relationships, approving invoices for billing, and overall projection direction.

Although project managers had a high level of responsibility, they were not provided with all the tools they believed they needed to manage the projects. One issue was whether salary levels or ranges for employees should be made available to the project managers for use in controlling budgets. Dan Stein, as president, was reluctant to make this information available. He explained that he was uncomfortable with allowing staff members to know one another's salaries, because he did not wish to be confronted. Nevertheless, what each employee earned probably was no secret among the project managers and engineers. Other members of the management committee disagreed with Stein and had been trying to persuade him to make the information available.

What budget information was accessible to the project managers was obtained by asking the accounts manager for the data. This usually was provided as a lump-sum figure. Many times the information given to the project manager was late, incomplete, or incorrect. The accounts manager had many other things to do besides developing this type of information. The data was often incorrect due to incorrect recording of labor-hours. This frequently would not be discovered

EXHIBIT 1
Approximate Organization Chart

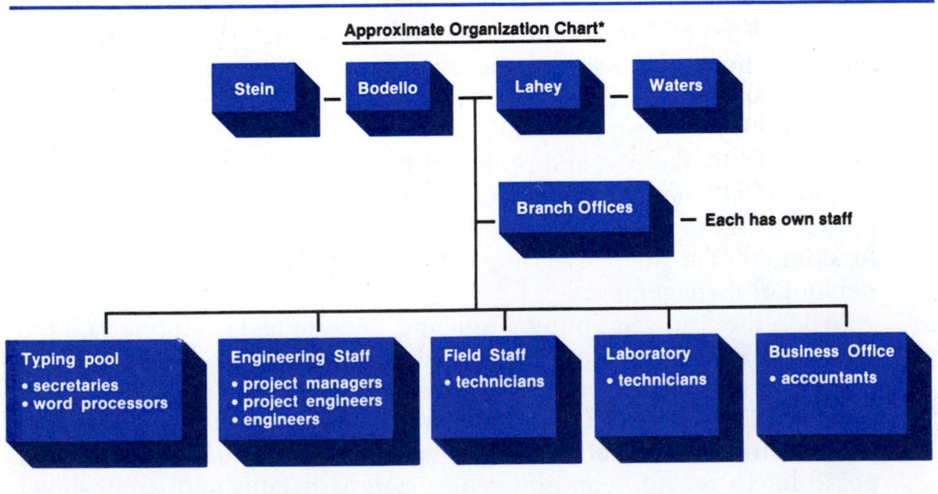

Note: Developed by a junior associate.

until the bills had been made out or until after they had been sent. Engineers were reprimanded when the budgets were significantly overrun, and it reflected poorly on their ability to control budgets. As a result many project managers were frustrated. The issue was often a topic of conversation at lunch or around the office, and the management committee heard rumors about the frustrations and problems with controlling budgets from a few of the more senior employees.

Stein, Bodello, & Associates had formulated a plan whereby partners' stocks would be sold to senior-level employees and associates according to a prearranged formula. The purpose of this was to provide a mechanism for selling the company to employees, provide value to the stock, and provide incentive to younger engineers. Senior staff had recognized this potential and therefore were interested in maintaining SBA as a comfortable place to work as well as maintaining its growth and profitability.

During the past year, an M.B.A. was hired to manage the business office; changes in business and accounting procedures had followed. The computer, purchased two years earlier, was put to use for word processing and financial accounting, which previously had been done manually. Getting the computer system in operation, working out the bugs, and making it useful had been a long, tiring, and frustrating process. Additional staff were hired, procedures formalized, accounts receivable collection tightened, and productivity and profitability stressed by management in the new procedures that were instituted.

Frequent memos announced these changes on short notice. The memos dealt with such issues as time-sheet reporting and charging telephone calls to a project by computerized methods. In some instances, the staff made jokes about the triviality of the requests—for example, charging file clerks' time to the project. One of the real issues, however, was that these memos appeared without any discussion about the reason the changes were being made and without any prior request for suggestions.

Often, only a few weeks after a change had been implemented, the staff reverted to its "old" ways or chose to forget about the new procedure. In many cases, changes were being made by support staff personnel who were responsible for purchasing materials, etc. However, those changes usually had an impact upon the technical staff, who never had an opportunity to provide input.

In one case, several senior associates and staff became quite angered when each employee suddenly was assigned an employee number for accounting purposes. Comments about the loss of the old "homey," informal atmosphere were common. Employees remembered the early years of the firm when it was one big, happy family with direct access to all the principals by all the staff. However, as the firm had grown the senior principals had become more and more removed from the staff. One person commented that instead of insisting on high-quality engineering as in the past, the firm was now satisfied with "adequate" engineering at a profit.

As its growth continued, the firm outgrew its facilities, and a decision was made to move to new, larger quarters. The new building was owned by Stein and Bodello through a realty trust, and the company leased space in the building. Although relocation was rumored for some time, only a few people knew of the actual plans until about two months before the move. Layout of the new facility, office assignments, and space allocations were kept secret. The responsibility for the new office layout belonged to Stein. After all, this was his project. Extensive renovations were required in the building to make it look good, but corners were cut and many things were missed in the new layout. The result was that the new office was less efficient than the old facility in terms of productivity, even though the building was larger.

The old building layout had evolved after many years. There was a common secretarial area centrally located in the middle of the building, and the business office was physically separated from the engineering staff in another part of the building. The principals' offices were adjacent to the common area, and their door opened into the area. Engineering staff, both senior and junior, were located in somewhat larger, two-person offices, each with a door for privacy if needed. Some of the offices were also adjacent to the common area, while the others were clustered along the corridors that led to the common area. Individuals were generally free to decorate and set up their offices as they pleased, and many had worked evenings and weekends doing just that (e.g., painting or building shelves). There was a sense of harmony in the environment, and morale was high. Older employees described it as homey, informal, and a place where you were treated as one of the family.

The new office reflected the "open space" concept. The partners' offices were for the most part isolated in one corner of the building, while senior engineers were given enclosed offices adjacent to a common area where the engineers, secretaries, and accounting personnel were located. The senior staff shared what amounted to good-size, single offices. The accounting staff and secretaries occupied large open areas, but with minimal separation between work areas. They complained that the area was too noisy and distracting. The engineers occupied space in the rear of the common area. The section was divided into four-person work areas by movable partitions that were five feet high. Each engineer had his own 8 by 8 work cubicle with a table providing a separation between engineers. The engineers frequently complained about the noise, distractions, and absence of privacy. (See Exhibit 2 for old and new layouts.)

EXHIBIT 2

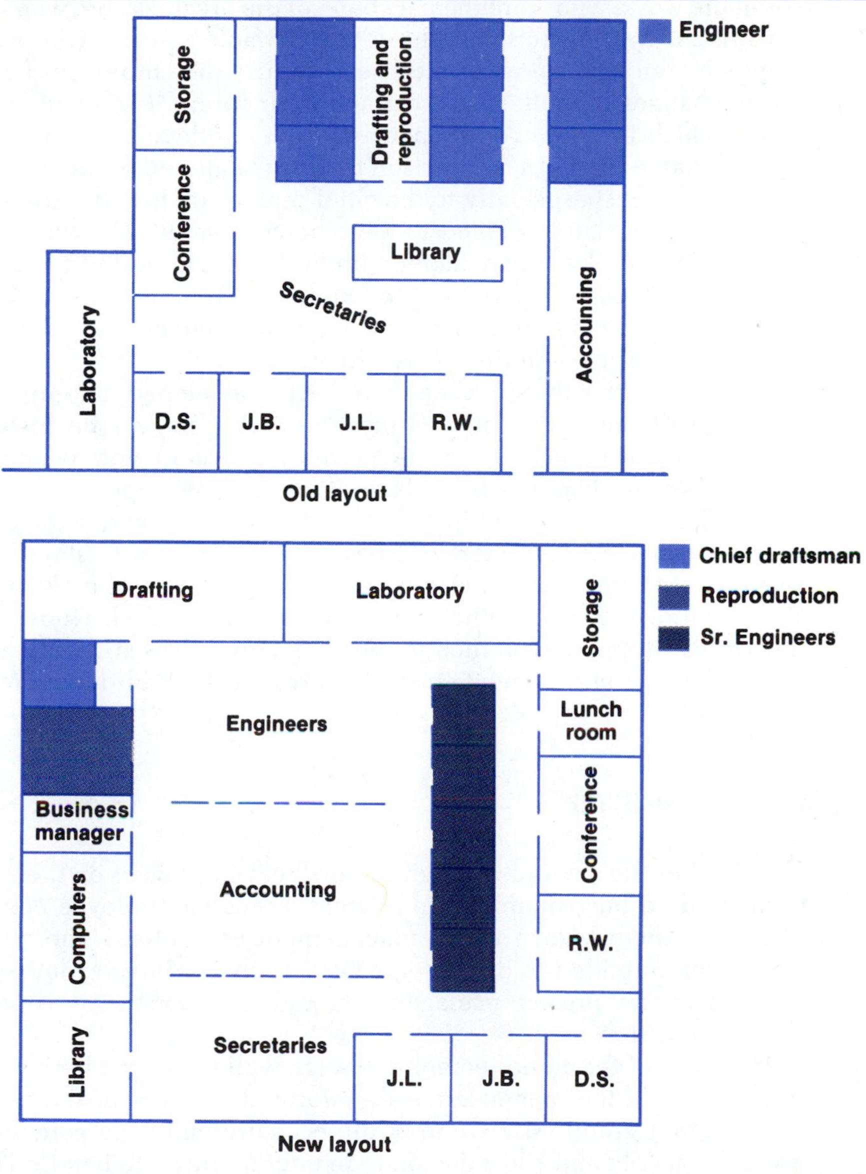

Old layout

New layout

Allocation of space for nontechnical work (on a per-individual basis) was clearly larger; draftsmen, technicians (who were seldom in the office), secretaries, and accounting staff had more space to work in than engineers. The new space for each engineer was smaller than the space he had left in the old building, even though the overall building was larger. One engineer stated that it was clear that, "those who were doing the work, who were the backbone of the organization, who were putting out the projects, got the least desirable space." One senior employee said that he was concerned because the employees had no say in changes that affected them and their future. In this view, his office, which he shared with another senior employee, was too small for productive work. In comparison to the area alloted to the nontechnical employees, especially to the chief draftsman, his allocation was small; and his status seemed to have been lowered. He went on to explain that the draftsman, along with Stein, had allocated the space. When this senior person questioned Stein about the size of the shared office, Stein told him that "if you cleaned out some of your books and shelves, the office wouldn't be so crowded."

When plans for the building were being developed, an employee petition had been circulated requesting that a shower be installed because many employees came in from the field and wanted to shower before changing into office attire. The petition was sent to Stein. The shower was not installed, and no reasons were ever given. This seriously affected morale. Employees who used to stay late to work on a problem began staying only until the end of eight hours. The traditional Friday gatherings after work at the Fish House for a few drinks stopped even though the Fish House was still only a few blocks away. Some isolated attempts to revive the tradition were unsuccessful.

THE AD HOC COMMITTEE

Shortly after the move, a group of senior-level employees on their own formed an ad hoc committee to address issues of employee concern and make them known to the management committee. The ad hoc committee intended to discuss specifics, such as office layout, space allocation, and project management, and to recommend concrete courses of action.

Members of the ad hoc committee were well respected both within and outside of the organization; they formed the core of the project management group. Mike, one of the cochairmen of the committee, was 36 years old and had a doctorate in engineering. He handled both business and engineering matters and had a good rapport with Dan Stein. Bob, the other cochairman, was 34, with a master's degree in engineering. He headed one facet of the engineering section and was on good terms with John Lahey. Both men were associates.

Other members of the committee were all project managers. Larry had been with the firm for five years. He was well respected but was considered a radical. Responsible for the formulation of the ad hoc

EXHIBIT 3

MEMORANDUM

To: Management Committee

From: The Ad Hoc Committee

Subject: Committee Organization

Date: June 17, 1983

Over the past few weeks, the management committee (MC) has been made aware of a certain amount of dissatisfaction on the part of Stein & Bodello employees in general, and senior staff in particular. The initial response of the MC, as transmitted to the senior staff through John Lahey, has been positive and directed toward reducing specific sources of tension (e.g., working-space arrangements).

In an effort to carry forth this encouragement from the MC into productive action, the undersigned have constituted themselves into the ad hoc committee (TAHC). The intent of TAHC is to assist the MC in implementing the administrative policies necessary to maintain Stein & Bodello's profitability in a manner consistent with traditional "family" atmosphere. The means to accomplish this goal will be to develop recommendations to the MC concerning administrative matters and to provide an organization and a cadre of middle-level line managers who will be responsible for implementing procedures authorized by the MC.

We recognize that the growth of our firm has led to some loss of personal contact between principals and staff. Although we may regret this change in the "personality" of our firm, bemoaning this fact will not change it. We believe that middle-management resources can be developed to compensate for the loss of "personal touch" with principals and to take on increased responsibilities within the firm.

TAHC is composed of senior technical staff—i.e., those who deal with clients and have a line responsibility for execution of engineering projects. Staff department heads have not been included, but their experience, opinions, and involvement will be diligently solicited on issues affecting their area of responsibility.

Responding to needs identified by TAHC members and to the request transmitted from the MC through John Lahey, TAHC proposed to address the following matters as the first orders of business: (1) improvement of the work space and (2) accuracy and timeliness of time sheets. TAHC members have agreed to volunteer their time for this effort, meeting after work biweekly or as often as necessary to make progress. Any requests and recommendations developed by TAHC would be set forth in writing for consideration by the MC; further discussions between the MC and TAHC cochairmen might take place at the monthly luncheon meetings held on the day of projection meetings.

The members of TAHC wish to retain the quality of work produced and the quality of working conditions that have always been associated with SBA, and we are prepared to act accordingly. In return we request only that the MC accord us recognition and its full support. TAHC has already begun work on the two priorities listed above.

committee, he was on good terms with Robert Waters. Bruce was also considered a radical. He was very vocal and complained often. Nonetheless, in his six years with the firm, he had become well respected for his engineering ability. He also had a good rapport with Dan Stein. Tony was quiet and easygoing. He had been with the firm for five years and got along well with Dan Stein. Paul was moderate and easygoing. In his three years with the firm, he had developed good relationships with Dan Stein and Joe Bodello.

The committee decided that the way to proceed was through written memos. Face-to-face meetings with Dan Stein were judged to be useless because "he would have no time to waste discussing such matters." The first memo sent to the management committee stated what the ad hoc committee was trying to achieve (see Exhibit 3) and requested that the management committee formally recognize the ad hoc committee. This was never done, although one junior partner told the committee verbally that in his judgment its formulation was a good idea and that he hoped that it would be made use of. Stein's response was that any memos should be sent to him, as president, first. Those issues he agreed with would be given to the proper people for implementation; there was "no need to waste management time on something I've already agreed to." Those issues that he disagreed with would be discussed.

The committee initially sent several memos to the management committee on various issues. Management responded by issuing a memo to staff directing that some of the recommendations be implemented. Nothing was heard regarding other items. Subsequently, the committee decided it was time to address the concerns about office layout and space. To employees, this was a major issue. While it would require some expenditures to redo the job, the ad hoc committee felt that changes in this area would help to restore efficiency, productivity, and morale.

The ad hoc committee did not want to be perceived as a threat to management and to Stein in particular. It wanted to be seen as a valuable resource and to be used to formulate worthwhile recommendations. At the same time, it did not want to waste its time making suggestions if sensitive ones were going to be ignored without discussion. They had to decide how to proceed.

▶ Highland College (Student Affairs Division)

As a case researcher, I visited a friend who had been employed for the past three years as an assistant dean and director of housing at a small western college. I approached her with the intention of getting some leads on case possibilities in that educational institution. After a brief discussion about her work experience, it appeared to me that her employment situation would make a good case study. I stayed with her a few days and had an opportunity to talk further with her and some of her colleagues. The following case evolved as a result of my observations and discussions with the members of the student affairs staff of Highland College, located in Woodstown.

Woodstown is a city of approximately 40,000 people and is surrounded by countryside. Located 20 minutes south of Madison, which is the closest large city, Highland occupies a well-landscaped, 100-acre campus. It exists as a self-contained unit within the residential area of Woodstown.

Highland College is a small, private, liberal arts college with an enrollment of approximately 2,000 students. Founded in the early 1900s as an educational institution for men, it remained that way until it began admitting women five years ago. As a result of the somewhat rigorous admission requirements, the majority of the student body comes from the top 10–20 percent of their respective high school classes. Highland College enjoys a respectable reputation in the academic community due to its well-qualified and accomplished faculty and the high caliber of its students. In this small residential college, the majority of the students live on campus. Consistent with other small colleges of its class, such as Hamilton, Oberlin, Lawrence, Reed, and Swarthmore, comprehensive fees at Highland are quite high. Endowment investments presently total approximately $35 million, largely resulting from strong support by graduates and a well-organized alumni association.

Woodstown is not a city one would typically describe as a "college town." Beyond a few local merchants who offer minimal discounts to students, there is not a close, active relationship between the college and the city. The members of the student affairs staff resided in Woodstown or in one of the rural areas surrounding the city, as did the faculty and other staff members. Much of the nonwork lives of the staff members centered on the college, rather than the city, where they had

From S. Fink, S. Jenks, and R. Willits, *Designing and Managing Organizations*, 1983, pages 498–507. Reproduced by permission of Richard D. Irwin, Inc., Homewood, Ill.

access to the athletic facilities, art facilities, and many cultural events at little or no charge. Staff members were also permitted to take one free course per semester, an opportunity of which many employees took advantage. The college also provided the staff with minimal life insurance coverage and a health insurance and retirement program.

The Student Affairs Division is responsible for all non-academic areas of student life. It reports directly to the Office of the President but also works closely with academic departments. The dean of students is the director of student affairs, and all of the assistant deans and program directors are responsible to him. The dean of students, a Ph.D. in sociology, has been at Highland for the past five years and is also a part-time member of the sociology faculty. He came to Highland from a similar small, liberal arts college where he was the dean of students and a tenured faculty member for 20 years.

Most of the student affairs staff members had been hired by the dean of students following his arrival at Highland. The majority of the program directors and assistant deans were between 25 and 35. Four staff members, the directors of student aid, student activities, health services, and security were over 45 years old and had been in these positions prior to the present dean's employment at Highland.

My friend Dawn was hired as the director of housing upon graduating from a similar college in New England and became an assistant dean at the end of her first year of employment. She had a B.A. in psychology and had not planned on a career in student personnel prior to being hired at Highland. Like the other new staff members, Dawn was enthusiastic about getting this job and thought that working with young people would be interesting and challenging. Having been a student at a similar school, she thought it would be fun to work at a college and also a good opportunity to learn about college administration. She considered this job something that would enable her to develop some skills and learn more about her own ability to deal with responsibility. Kirk Evans and Heidi Johnson (the provost's assistant, not a formal member of student affairs but in close contact with the staff) had master's degrees in student personnel but, like the other younger and newer staff members, had little previous experience in this field and considered their jobs to be good starting points in their careers.

The day that I accompanied Dawn to work we arrived at the office at 10 A.M. and, upon entering, I noticed that all of the other desks and offices were occupied, except Dawn's and the office of the director of admissions, Ted Howard. I questioned her about our late arrival, with which she seemed quite comfortable. She explained that she had an early evening meeting with a group of students and didn't have anything urgent scheduled for the early morning hours. When questioned about Ted Howard's absence, she was equally unconcerned about his whereabouts. As if to calm my worries, she said, "Formal policy *does* say that working hours at Highland College are from 8:30 to 5:00, but members of the student affairs staff usually come and go as we please. Our jobs require us to work closely with many groups of people who oftentimes don't have consistent schedules—so we inevitably end up working strange hours and many weekends." This type of policy seemed to me one that would only invite trouble. Since the offices of all but four staff members were located in different parts of the campus, it was obvious that the dean had no way of knowing when and if someone was putting in enough hours. When I asked Dawn if this wouldn't be an easy system to take advantage of, she said that one staff member had been fired by the dean for not putting enough time in on the job and for other reasons: "Our last affirmative action director had been employed in that position for three years and still wasn't 'doing things right.' He didn't put a lot of time in on the job and wasn't on top of his budget. Eventually, students began complaining that he was never in his office and wasn't following up on their requests. He had frequently been spotted by other staff members on the tennis court for three hours at a time and had earned the reputation of someone who was continually slacking off." The other staff members had earned the trust of the dean and respected and valued the freedom they had been given to set their own hours. It all sounded very interesting to me, but it sure is a lot different than the way I have to work when I'm in my office.

Soon after our arrival, the dean of students, Bruce Powers (age 50) walked by Dawn's office and took time out to greet both of us. I had met him the previous evening at an informal gathering of the staff at his house. To my amazement he was dressed in the same casual manner that he had been the night before. Had I not met him previously I never would have guessed he was the dean of students. I then realized that everyone else was dressed quite informally, the only exception being the director of admissions, who appeared in a sport coat and tie after conducting a tour of the campus for a prospective student and his parents.

When preparing to go to the dean's house the previous evening, Dawn sensed my apprehension since I had never been to my present boss's house, nor had any type of social, informal relationship with him either in the office or outside. Dawn explained that the dean often invited the staff and some of his other colleagues to his house in the evenings. She said that she even felt comfortable just stopping by his house when she needed to talk to him. Expecting to meet a distinguished, easygoing, soft-spoken man, I was surprised to be introduced to someone 6 feet 2 inches tall and very broad-shouldered, with a voice as loud as his size, and who was almost abrasive in his direct and forthright mannerisms. After observing his interactions with his staff members and listening to many conversations about what was going on with specific programs people were working on, I saw another side of the dean. He was very sensitive to the problems people were having and usually could offer helpful advice or insights. He was very direct when giving his opinions, but people seemed to accept his comments as valuable information rather than being hurt by his criticism.

The conversation between staff members at this gathering revolved around specific projects people were working on, problems and experiences they wanted to share. It was obvious that everyone didn't have specific knowledge about the details of each other's jobs, but most people were familiar enough with the general nature of other jobs to be able to discuss them and offer suggestions. The atmosphere was comfortable and friendly, and everyone seemed to get along well. When I later asked Dawn if she felt obligated to attend these get-togethers because they were at the dean's house, she almost looked shocked. She explained that most of the staff members had become relatively good friends and spent much of their free time together. They looked forward to times when they could get together informally, whether at the dean's house or at someone else's apartment or home. Oftentimes they attended campus functions together, such as lectures, plays, and concerts.

Despite being such good friends, Dawn assured me that disagreements did arise occasionally and were dealt with openly and honestly. Curious as to what constituted a "disagreement" in a group of such friendly people, Dawn told me the following story:

> Last spring at a party at the dean's house I had a run-in with Ted Howard. He was in charge of the "Accepted Candidates Day" program, a type of pre-orientation program. Several members of the Women's Caucus, students and staff, wanted to conduct a special program that day for the incoming women students. They thought the development of such a program was particularly important since there were still rather few women faculty members (only five) and few women professional staff members. Ted didn't want to do it at all. He thought it was a bad idea and didn't think we should single out women students; but I disagreed with him. I told him I thought he was wrong and that the women were competent and capable of designing a good program. At this point, David Lawrence (another assistant dean), who had heard the conversation, stepped in and said that he thought we were both ignoring the real issue, which was one of control. He proceeded to point out that Ted seemed opposed to my suggestion because it would mean that he would not have control over that aspect of the program, for which he was responsible. For this reason he was not willing to consider the reasoning behind my argument and was ready to reject the suggestion without further conversation. After a lengthy discussion, we arrived at a procedure for planning and carrying out the program that satisfied Ted's

control needs and allowed the women to develop a program they believed to be important.

At 10:30 Dawn had a meeting with the members of the Student Housing Committee, which I also attended. Over the past two years she and this committee had been working out a new program for room placement and were now in the final stages of planning before implementation for the next year. The old system, which had been in effect for many years, was a "squatter's rights" system where a student could remain in a room for four years if he or she chose to do so. After she became the housing director some students came to her complaining about the unfairness of the present system, so she spent some time talking to students to try and assess their attitudes about the issue. It turned out to be quite a controversial issue and, after analyzing the situation, Dawn decided that a change needed to be made. She discussed the subject with the dean, who offered some suggestions about possible courses of action she could take, but he left the decision up to her. She decided that since this was such a big issue on campus she would need some student input and support and so she proceeded to organize a student committee.

This meeting, which I attended, went smoothly, and the students seemed to exhibit a great deal of respect for Dawn and her ideas, despite the fact that they didn't hesitate to disagree with her on some issues. When the meeting was over, I asked Dawn if it was always that easy to deal with students, thinking that constantly listening to their complaints must get tiring after a while. She replied,

> I love working with students most of the time. I think partly because of my age, I understand their questions and concerns and I have developed a good rapport with them. Generally, students are open-minded and fair, and willing to listen to my point of view as an administrator. Through my dealings with students I think I have made many of them aware of the fact that there is usually more than one side to an issue or problem and that they should at least consider what the people they disagree with are saying. Listening to complaints does get annoying sometimes, but the majority of my interactions with students are stimulating and rewarding.

Then I wondered if she set up student committees for every project she worked on. She said that she used her own discretion in deciding which decisions to make alone and which decisions students should have a part in. She gave the following example:

> After the Student Union was operational I decided that student mailboxes should be moved from the separate dorms to the union. I thought this would be a good way to get many students out of their dorms, where many had a tendency to remain for days if they didn't have any classes to attend. Initially some students complained that they didn't like having

> to walk so far to pick up their mail, but the net result was that students did get out more and it was a much more efficient system.
>
> One great thing about this job is that I can always go to the dean for advice and ideas about problems that arise or programs I am planning, but the final decision is always up to me and my decisions are always supported by the dean and the other staff members.

This fact was soon illustrated to me when an irate parent stormed up to Dawn's desk and demanded to see the dean about a problem with her daughter's room assignment for the following year. It seems that this parent's daughter had one of the better rooms on campus and had mentioned to her mother that she wouldn't be able to keep it for her last two years at Highland. Upon hearing this story, Dawn very politely informed the parent that she was welcome to go in and see the dean but that the dean would probably send her back to speak to Dawn since she was in charge of all housing problems. (In fact, this is exactly what he did.)

Before lunch Dawn had a meeting with the 40 resident advisers, a group she met with regularly to discuss any problems they might be having in the dorms and anything else that was going on. While she was gone she gave me her job description to read. I found out that in addition to meeting with resident advisers and having complete responsibility for student residences and room placement, she was also responsible for planning dorm security programs, for doing a yearly evaluation of the campus food services, and had been involved in planning a large capital budget proposal for housing improvements. Similar to other program directors on the student affairs staff, she was responsible for submitting a yearly budget (all college budgeting was done on a three-year basis) and was required to account for expenses in relation to her budget. I know from previous conversations with her that she was an active member of the President's Commission on the Status of Women and also was working on college budgetary programs with the provost, but those activities were not listed in her job description.

On the way to lunch I asked her about being promoted to assistant dean at the end of her first year of employment and what this promotion involved. She had received a salary increase each year of her employment at Highland based on her job performance as evaluated by the dean of students. Although none of her raises had been very substantial and wages at the college were lower than in area industries, this situation was of little concern to Dawn. The dean was responsible for awarding the "assistant dean of students" title to his staff members, but this promotion didn't automatically include a salary increase. Well, I thought, what is it other than a "title promotion"? When I asked Dawn this question, she explained that assistant deans were given additional responsibilities, such as working on freshman orientation, parents' weekend, and special projects, and that they possessed higher status in the eyes of students, faculty, and other staff members. As a result of taking an increased responsibility and getting involved in additional activities, Dawn felt a sense of growing competence and felt she was learning a great deal, a feeling shared by most of her colleagues.

We had lunch with Laura Clark, the director of career counseling and assistant dean, and the conversation revolved around the recruiters who were scheduled to be on campus during the next few months to interview graduating seniors. Before Laura had been hired, there had been no formal career counseling and placement program at Highland. At the end of her second year in this position, there was a large increase in the number of companies coming to Highland to recruit and a larger percentage of graduates than ever before were being placed in jobs. Laura had been instrumental in getting alumni involved in helping graduates get jobs, and she also had initiated many workshops (interviewing techniques, résumé writing, etc.) and organized many women's programs.

At one point in the conversation Dawn asked what the job prospects were like for this year's graduates. Laura replied, "The jobs are there if the students are willing to put out the effort to find them. Even though it's tough to place liberal arts graduates, I still think the educational experience they get here at Highland is invaluable." Dawn was quick to agree.

After lunch we all went back to Dawn's office since she and Laura had a meeting with the dean at 12:30. While I was waiting in Dawn's spacious, comfortably furnished office, Kirk Evans, the director of the student union, stopped in. He had also been at the dean's house the previous evening, so I recognized him immediately. He had a few things that he needed Dawn's secretary to type for him, so he left Dawn a note with the message on it. I thought to myself, "Her secretary will probably love that, it looks like Dawn gives her enough work to keep three people busy!" Later that afternoon Dawn politely asked her secretary if she would do the typing for Kirk when she had time and, to my surprise, the secretary was more than willing. Evidently, only a few of the staff members have their own secretaries and they are always willing to arrange their work accordingly so that everyone's work gets done.

When Dawn and Laura emerged from their meeting in the dean's office, they were talking excitedly about the ideas they had for a parents' weekend program. The dean had asked them to be co-directors of the program next fall, and they both seemed thrilled with the assignment. After listening to Dawn trying to organize her activities to fit in this new assignment, I was surprised at her eagerness to undertake it. She then explained what effect this project would have on her other duties:

> My workload will not be unique when I start working on this parents' weekend project. Almost everyone on the staff is involved in activities beyond the specific requirements of their individual programs; for example, Laura works voluntarily as the women's field hockey coach, and Ted has started doing some academic counseling beyond what is required in his position. We are encouraged, by Bruce, to get involved in other areas of the college, and partly as a result of this involvement, the student affairs staff has earned a reputation of competence and commitment. Due to this reputation our staff has taken on many new college projects and programs that have previously been done by other departments. If there aren't any qualified people on our staff for a specific project, Bruce will usually hire a new director.

"This must mean that he has unlimited funds at his disposal, is this the case?"

> If a position is transferred to our staff from another department, such as the intramurals program, then additional funds are supplied to student affairs. But Bruce is very capable of using his budget to his advantage and never wastes money. He is able to plan well and has proved himself competent, so when the Planning and Priorities Committee allocates funds, Bruce always gets at least his fair share.

An example of this situation was evident when Dawn told me the story of the creation of the Student Union. Prior to the existence of the union, Highland lacked the "small-college" atmosphere of closeness and familiarity characteristic of other small schools. Students expressed their concern and discontent with this atmosphere and requested the establishment of a place where they could gather. The dean thought this was a good idea and, after speaking with the president and provost, he obtained the necessary funds to convert an old, unused building on campus into the union. He then used the funds he had available in his budget to hire the director and the restaurant/pub manager.

"With such a good reputation, how does your staff avoid taking on projects that really have nothing to do with student affairs?" I asked.

> Occasionally, the president or provost will ask Bruce to undertake a project that is logically not under the jurisdiction of the student affairs staff or that could be done more efficiently by another group or person. In this event he does not hesitate to face up to whomever is making the request and say no. He usually succeeds in pointing out the inappropriateness of his staff undertaking such projects and makes his opinion stick. They respect and trust him.

> On the other hand, there have been times when some staff members have a few projects going at once and are very pressed for time. If this happens to me when we really get involved in organizing parents' weekend, I won't have too much to worry about. I have never been directly involved with the parents' weekend program, but I know that if Laura and I have any problems we can talk to the previous co-chairmen and can get ideas from other staff members. Also, everyone will be aware of the fact that we are working on this project. If we get overwhelmed with work at any point, I am quite confident that any staff member with fewer demands on his or her time will be willing to help us out. Last year when Ted was very busy organizing parents' weekend, I went on some recruiting trips to other colleges and other staff members helped him out by conducting some admissions interviews. Working together in this way happens frequently.

This system was all a little confusing to me. "Wouldn't it be a lot easier if everyone just did their own jobs and stayed out of other people's business?" Dawn was adamant in her reply when she said,

> Well, I suppose things might be a little more orderly around here if we each went our own separate ways and had little interaction with each other. But, I don't think it would be worth the price we'd pay in the long run. Where else could we get an opportunity to learn so much about so many different jobs and to develop such satisfying working and social relationships with our colleagues? Some of our jobs would probably be intolerably routine if we weren't able to do all of the additional things we are doing now.

Our conversation was interrupted when the dean stuck his head in to remind Dawn about the staff meeting and to tell me I was welcome to join them. On our way to the meeting, Dawn quickly explained that attendance at monthly staff meetings was mandatory. Everyone arrived at the conference room promptly at 2:00 and took seats around the table. This was the first time I had seen all of the staff members in the same place since many of them have offices in different parts of the campus. The dean ran this meeting according to an agenda, which began with brief program reports by each director and a discussion of specific problems people were having. It was obvious to me from his questions and comments to each person that he was well aware of the activities of each director and of the status of each project. From what I had observed, in the office and at his house, he had so many informal conversations with staff members and was constantly being sought out for advice, it would be impossible for him not to know what was going on. Dawn later agreed with my observation, adding that Bruce was very accessible and was continually stressing to them the importance of being open, positive, and solution oriented. Because he related to his staff in this way, no one was ever apprehensive about approaching him with a problem, and no one tried to hide things from him.

Following these reports the dean announced that Dawn and Laura would be organizing the next parents' weekend. He also announced that the president had asked him to organize a weekend seminar for student personnel administrators. Bruce was planning to work on this project himself but asked if anyone would like to assist him. David Lawrence eagerly volunteered. He said that the project interested him, he wasn't particularly busy at the present time, and he hadn't worked on any projects for quite awhile. Bruce accepted David's offer, and they set up a later meeting date to further discuss the program.

During the remainder of the meeting the dean talked about other activities on campus and about matters that had come up at the most recent presidential cabinet meeting. Staff members occasionally asked him questions or made comments, but most of the time he talked uninterrupted.

Dawn spent the remainder of the afternoon in her office working on some routine housing matters before her early evening meeting with another group of students. When we returned to her apartment, there was a letter waiting for her from Metropolitan University. The letter contained an invitation to visit Metropolitan about a job.

While at a recent professional conference Dawn had met the vice president for student affairs at Metropolitan and rather casually discussed her job and the nature of student affairs activities at Metropolitan. He had asked her a lot of questions, she realized in retrospect, and must have been checking out her qualifications, because the letter was obviously written to encourage her interest in Metropolitan.

Metropolitan University is located in Culver City (population 300,000) and has a student body of 25,000. The opportunity included a 25 percent salary increase and excellent health insurance and retirement programs. The student affairs function at this school had a reputation of being highly organized and efficiently managed, in addition to being one of the first schools to utilize the computer in housing assignments.

Enclosed in the letter was a lengthy and precise job description, which Dawn read many times before showing it to me. I noted that the very clearly spelled out duties were more limited in number than those Dawn had at Highland, but that they involved responsibility for many more students and authority over the expenditure of many more dollars, as well as a clear potential for moving up. After I had read it she asked me if I thought she should take the job, if it were offered, as she thought likely.

I, Rivethead

I knew in the 10th grade that I would become a shoprat. It was more an understanding of certain truisms found in my hometown than any form of game plan I might have been hatching. In Flint, Michigan, you either balled up your fists and got career motivated the moment the piano quit banging the commencement theme or, more likely, you'd still be left leanin' when the ancestors arrived to pass along your birthright. Here, kid, fetch.

At least up until recently, that's the way it worked. All roads led to General Motors in Flint. Father and son, sister and brother, each of 'em swingin' through the gates to play follow-the-earner.

The pattern began to dissolve with the cutbacks and technological gains of the early 80s. All of a sudden, trying to find an application for work at General Motors was like searching out buried treasure. It's now to a point where Flint youths can no longer entertain "shoprat" as a career option. The evolution of the critter appears at an end, and unless I somehow manage to knock up a GHF spot-welding robot, I rather doubt I'll ever see any of my offspring inside the factory.

I almost didn't make it in myself. After high school, I wasted four prime earning years running around with my tongue stuck out at the smokestacks. I painted apartments. I swept floors. I got married and divorced. As long as I had my birthright stowed in my back pocket, I felt relatively safe in delaying destiny.

During this period, I would oftentimes get drunk and park by one of the factories just to watch the fools pile out at quit time. I hated the looks on their faces. I would sit there with a can of beer in my lap and try to focus in on one alternative career goal. There weren't any. All I ever came back to was the inevitable self-admission that I didn't want to do *anything*. And around these parts, that's just chicken-shit slang for "What time does the line start up on Monday?"

To be accurate, I hired in on a weekend. General Motors was in the midst of one of its boom-boom quota years, so reinforcements were being called in on Saturdays, Sundays, Salad Days—anytime was the right time. It was also the first time I could ever remember being asked out on a Saturday night by a corporation.

Before we were to begin working, the group I was hiring in with was instructed to meet for physical examinations in the plant hospital. We were a sluggish-looking crew. There were about 20 of us altogether—each person chain-smoking and staring at the floor, waiting in

From an article by Ben Hamper published in *Mother Jones*, September 1986, pages 27–32, 55. Reproduced with permission.

silence to be pronounced fit for active drudgery. I had a hunch that there wasn't a marketable skill amongst us.

The urine test was up first. We were each handed a small vial and told to line up at the restroom. The guy in front of me kept looking over his shoulder at me. When it was his turn, he spun around and asked if it would be all right if I donated a little of my urine for his vial. He seemed to be undergoing a mild panic attack. Apparently, the fear was that the company might look down upon any prospective serf who was incapable of bringing forth the pee when it mattered most. No piss, no job, ingrate!

"I just can't go right now," the guy moaned. I didn't care much for the idea of passing my piss around with a total stranger. It didn't seem like a solid career move. Besides, for all either of us knew, I might be holding on to a bad batch. I had a background of hepatitis. My formative years were spent wolfing down a wide variety of menacing chemicals. I drank like a sieve. Heck, I never even wiped off the seat in public bathrooms. Who'd wanna take a crapshoot on the chance that any of that might come floating to the surface of their corporate dossier?

Evidently, this guy. He returned from the john and, true to his word, the vial he held before me was completely empty. "C'mon," he said, "just a squirt. I'll pay you for it."

Christ, that did it. "Gimme the thing," I groaned. It probably wasn't the most noble act of giving one had ever made in behalf of a needy union brother, but somehow it sure seemed like it at the time.

We were almost through with our urine samples when a member of our group, a late arrival, walked into the hospital and began to speak with our overseer. I could sense the guy was in deep trouble. He kept apologizing over and over—something to do with getting messed up in traffic and being detained. Judging by his performance, I doubted that he was lying.

It didn't matter. The man with the clipboard wasn't buying a single word. He stood there shaking his head from one side to the other—just another maggot in a short-sleeve shirt, deputized to protect the status quo. He did his job well.

"You were told to be prompt," he spouted. "There can be *no exceptions.*"

The realization that he'd blown his big audition seemed to overwhelm the late guy. He looked down at the floor, his voice started breaking, and, right there in front of everyone, he began to cry. It all came spillin' out—what was he gonna tell his family, and who would understand? For the sons and daughters of the assembly line, 1977 wasn't the best of years to go fumblin' the family baton.

We stood there clutching our little vials of piss as they escorted him out. We had been on time. We were going to build trucks for Chevrolet. The man with the bow tie and clipboard had written down all of our names. Our friend had been 10 minutes late. He had proven himself undeserving of a hitch on the screw train. There could be no exceptions.

Now and again, I'll find myself still thinking about the late guy. It'll be one of those terribly humid shifts when the parts just aren't going together right and the clock begins to take two steps back for every step forward. Exhausted and desperate, I'll begin to see him over by the pool table in the tavern across the street. He'll have a cold beer in his hand and a grin a mile wide. I imagine myself walking up to him with my safety glasses, my locker key, and my plastic identification badge held out in my hand. "Here, it's all yours, buddy."

Immediately, the jukebox will stop playing. Everyone in the bar turns toward me and begins to laugh. The late guy slips his arm around the waitress, and they both start shaking their heads. "We already started," he'll say. "There can be no exceptions."

I was assigned to the cab shop, an area more commonly known to its inhabitants as "the jungle." Lifers will tell you that on a scale from 1 to 10—with 1 representing midtown Pompeii and 10 being GM Chairman Roger Smith's summer digs—the jungle rates about a −6.

It wasn't difficult to see how they had come up with the name for the place. Ropes, wires, and assorted black rubber cables drooped down and entangled everything. Sparks shot out in all directions—bouncing in the aisles, flying into the rafters, and even ricocheting off the natives' heads. The noise level was deafening. It was like some hideous unrelenting tape-loop of trains having sex. I realized instantly that, as far as new homes go, the jungle left a lot to be desired. Me Tarzan, you fucked.

I had been forewarned. As our group was being dispatched at various drop points throughout the factory, the guy walking beside me kept mumbling about our likely destination. "Cab shop," the prophet would say. "We're headed for cab shop." I somehow wondered if this meant we would be building taxis.

The group would trudge on, leaving a few workers in each new area. We stopped by the trim line. The axle line. The frame line. The fender line. The receding hairline. When we arrived at the motor line, my friend with the bashful bladder hopped off. "Thanks," he said. It was kinda strange. All we had in common was a small, worthless vial of urine. "Have a nice career," I offered.

Soon, all but two rookies had been planted—the prophet and me. We took a freight elevator upstairs, and when the gate opened, my companion moaned loudly: "Goddamn, I knew it. The bastard's lettin' us off in cab shop." By this point, I couldn't have agreed with the guy more. Our overseer was the epitome of bastard. On top of that, he made for one lousy Johnny Appleseed. There could be no exceptions.

"Here you are, boys—the Cab Department. In this area you are advised to wear clothing made from a nonflammable fabric. Also, you will need to purchase a pair of steel-toed work boots, available at fair cost in the shoe store next to the workers' cafeteria. Good luck, boys."

It turned out that the prophet would be working right across from me. His name was Roy, and he'd come to Flint from Oklahoma to live with his brother and find work in the factory. Just your basic "Grapes-of-Wrath-run-aground-in-the-Pizza-Pizza Generation" story line, I suppose.

Our jobs were identical: install splash shields, pencil rods, and assorted nuts and bolts in the rear end of Chevy Blazers. To accomplish this, we worked on a portion of the line where the cabs would rise up on an elevated track. Once the cabs were about five feet off the ground, we'd have to duck inside the rear wheel wells and bust a little ass. Standing across from each other in those cramped wheel wells always reminded me of the two neighbors in the Right Guard commercial who met every morning in their communal medicine cabinet. "Hi, Guy! Care for a scoop of sealer on that pencil rod?"

We adjusted to the heat and grew accustomed to the noise. After awhile, we even got used to the claustrophobia of the wheel wells. The idea that we were being paid handsome wages to mimic a bunch of overachieving simians suited us just dandy. In America there was nothing to accomplish as long as the numbers on your pay stub tumbled out in a sequence that served to justify your daily dread.

The one thing we couldn't escape was the monotony of our new jobs. Every minute, every hour, every truck, and every movement totaled nothing but a plodding replica of the one that had gone before. The monotony especially began to gnaw away at Roy. When the lunch horn sounded, we'd race out to his pickup, and Roy would start pulling these enormous joints from a glove box. His stash was incredible. "Take one," he'd offer. Pot made me nervous, so I would stick to beer or slug a little whiskey.

The numbing process seemed to demand more every night. We'd go out to the truck, and Roy would start burning two joints at once. Now and then, he'd slip down a hit of acid. "I don't know if I'm gonna make my 90 days," he'd tell me. Ninety days was the minimum amount of service required for a worker to apply for sick leave. It was all part of Roy's master plan: reach 90 days' seniority, round up a reliable quack, feign some mysterious injury and with all the paperwork in order, semi-retire to an orbit of disco bars, women and cocktails. The old Ozzie Nelson work ethic festering over and over in the hearts of the young.

Roy never did make his 90. To those who were on hand during his last days of service, it came as no real surprise. We all realized that Roy was cracking up.

First there was the incident involving the sacrificial rodent. Roy had managed to capture this tiny mouse that had been sneaking around under one of the stock bins. He built an elaborate little house for the creature and set it on his workbench. He fed it. He gave it water. He built windows in the house so that his pet could "watch me doin' my job." Any worker who passed through the area was summoned over and given a personal introduction to the mouse. For all the world, it seemed like a glorious love affair.

I could never figure out whether it was because of the dope or the drudgery or some unseen domestic quarrel, but things sure switched around in a hurry after each lunch break. Roy would rush through each job, run back to his workbench, and start screaming at the mouse through the tiny cardboard windows. He insisted that the mouse was mocking the way he performed the job. He ranted and raved. He began shaking the house. Keep in mind that, throughout all of this, we were still somehow managing to build 'em "Chevy Tough!"

Finally, it was over. Roy grabbed the mouse by the tail and stalked up to the welder's platform. He took a brazing torch, gassed up a long blue frame, and, right there in the middle of Jungleland, incinerated his little buddy at arm's length.

It didn't get any better. The day before he quit, Roy approached me with a box-cutter knife in his glove. His request was that I take the blade and give him a slice across the back of his hand. He felt flat sure that this ploy would land him a few days off the job.

I had to refuse. Once again, it didn't seem like a solid career move. Roy went on to the other workers, where he received a couple of charitable offers to cut his throat, but no dice on the hand. He sulked back to his job.

After a half-dozen attempts on his own, Roy finally got himself a gash. He waited until the blood had a chance to spread out a bit and then went dashing off to see the boss. The damage was minimal. A hunk of gauze, an elastic bandage, and a slow, defeated shuffle back to the wheel wells.

After that day, I never saw Roy again. Personnel sent down a young Puerto Rican guy to help me do the Right Guard commercial, and the two of us put in our 90 days without much of a squawk.

The money was right, even if we weren't.

The layoffs grabbed me in 1980. If you have a deep-rooted fear of standing in an unemployment line like I do, I advise that you do everything in your power to hang on to your job. Heap your employer with phony plaudits, offer to baby-sit his kids, gulp amphetamines and perform the workload of 10 servants. If you have to, get down on all fours and smooch his dusty wingtips anew with sheen. In your spare time go to church, pray to Allah, pray to Buddha, plead with Zeus, beg of Jah, implore the graces of whichever deity landed the '69 Mets a pennant, to keep your little butt in the sling and outta the Michigan Employment Security Commission (MESC) logjam of human languish. No, this is not the place to be if you get clammy in a crowd.

First off, the MESC has no windows. Once you pop through the doors, it's like entering a holding tank for sodden sumo wrestlers. You're required to check in at the front desk, where a nice little old lady (who appears to have been a teenager during the Spanish-American War) will put a red check next to your appointment time and ask you if you have any paperwork to turn in. Always answer no or you will be detained for a time approximately the same as was needed to build the pyramids. Paperwork makes these people freeze, reducing them to slow-motion voyagers across the tar pits of eternity. If you have paperwork to hand in, wait until you are absolutely *commanded* to present it—and then give weighty consideration to the benefits of suicide.

After your card has been checked at the front desk, you will be instructed to fall into line. Being a shoprat, the most popular of jobless hacks, I have my choice of line 10, 11, or 12, and without fail I always choose the wrong one. My method is to give a quick glance into the eyes of the prospective claims people and somehow determine just which one is herding them out the fastest. Sometimes I'll choose the stiff old man. Sometimes the pretty young woman. Sometimes the evil lady who looks like Agnes Moorehead ripped from the grave. The strategy never works. Either the pretty young woman gets bogged down with potential Romeos, the old guy has to go shuffling off to the can, or the huffy bat spends a half hour gnawing on some piece of red tape gristle with some dunce who can't remember his age.

A friend of mine insists that the MESC has made a widespread effort to stock its ranks full of people with fetishes for dominance. Though I might hedge a bit on that assertion, it is true that many of its employees seem to delight in having you grovel, squirm, and plead total ignorance to their avalanche of legal brain boggle. They act as though you laid yourself off, that you have no intention of ever lifting another finger, that you're in a frantic rush to get back poolside to your bevy of naked stewardesses, that you hate this country and wanna take their money to buy explosives to lob at the governor's motorcade.

Reading through their standard probes, I'm always tempted to give them a jolt:

Q: Have you received any income during the past two weeks?
A: Yes, I was paid $10,000 to carry out a hit on a U.S. senator.

Q: Are you receiving any benefits from any other state?
A: Yes, I am on a retainer fee from the state of New York as a procurer of male prostitutes.
Q: Have you been able and available for work?
A: No, I haven't. I've been too busy selling cocaine and have been too wasted to hear the phone even if it rang.

One thing about being stranded in the unemployment line that I find preferable to a line at a grocery store or movie is that no one speaks to you. Of course, there is always the exception, like the guy a few weeks ago who must have mistook me for a chaplain, a social worker, or the future biographer of his life's stupid deeds. As we edged closer and closer to the claims desk, at a pace not discernible to the naked eye, I was treated to every fact of this bumpkin's existence—the kids, his taxes, the deep green hue of his lawn, the hunting dog, his asthma, his perceptions of Blanchard, Reagan, Poland, and the "A-Team." What is it that makes people think that I have the slightest interest in what's going on in their lives? I hardly have any interest in mine.

Occasionally, you'll see people get really irked over a development in their claim. The last time I was in for my check, the desk people dropped this big ugly bomb stating that because of blah-blah-blah (read, unlimited technical bullshit), the extended benefits program was being cut and that the majority of these jobless folks had run the old money meter bone dry. Believe me, this message was not received with cheers and beers—as proven by the fact that one enraged cast-off, being of sound strength if not entirely sound mind, saw fit to retreat to the MESC personnel parking lot, pull out a knife, and proceed to play Zorro on the office worker's radials. He was apprehended and stashed in the pokey, where I guess he's pretty much accomplished his objective—the state is still gonna be footing his meal money.

The thing you want to avoid at all costs when visiting the unemployment office is to be detained in the section of seats over by the side wall. That is where they send you if you develop complications in your claim, if you need to file a new claim, if you act unappreciative, or if you go to the bathroom in your pants. If you are instructed to have a seat over in this dreadful limbo, it is advisable that you pack a hefty lunch, bring the complete works of your favorite authors, have your mail delivery halted, and prepare to wait, wait, wait. So far, I've been lucky to avoid taking up a perch in the land that time forgot. What they do with these people is not apparent. Every now and then you see some wire-rimmed weasel in a suitcoat poke his head out from beyond the partition and summon one of the waiting few to follow him.

Never, but never, have I ever seen people reappear once ushered into the boundless back chambers of the MESC. At first I thought that they were merely ducking out a side exit, but casual research into this possible explanation has shown me that *there is no side exit.*

I take it now that this is how it ends. A silent trudge down a narrow hallway, led by a cranky claims executioner with cold eyes and blue lips. Finally having your benefits exhausted, you are a total non-entity. No one misses you. No one can see you. You disappear from the unemployment statistics. You no longer exist.

A miniature Auschwitz has been assembled far behind the clicking of the cashier's keys, far removed from the lazy shuffle of the fresh claimants' feet, off in back where you now only wait for the pellets to drop and the air to get red.

Oh, it could have been worse. You could have been burnt in a house fire. You could have been snagged in a plane prop. You could have been trampled at a Paul Anka concert. You could have had to go find a job.

I was fortunate to be called back to work just one week before my claim was to expire. In a roundabout way, I have only one man to thank for this swell turn of fate—Caspar Weinberger. It was this man's dogged lust for a few billion dollars' worth of military trucks that reopened the doors and pumped new life into my sagging career as a shoprat.

Who could argue? When the call came in askin' if I'd like to come back and help assemble Ronnie's new death wagon, I was quick to respond, "Hell yes, I will go!" Conscientious objection might be a noble path on draft day, but I had to admit to having developed a strong desire to eat food every day, and I didn't think it would be an easy habit to break.

Back on the line I was reincarnated as a rivethead. The placement must have been the right one, because I've been at it now for six years.

The most important thing I've learned during my appointment to the rivet line is a new approach to job monotony. Rather than dreading the tedium that accompanies assembly labor, I've found that one should lie down and wallow in it. Let repetition be its own reward. The key is to grind your job down into a series of empty, vacant gestures. Chew on it until it becomes a flavorless pulp. Keep plowing the same daily rut. Reject change. Reject variety. Aspire to vegetation and dance that trance around.

Once this is accomplished, work on speed. Attempt to shave three seconds per month off your standard performance time. You must always remember that General Motors isn't paying you to think. They've got holes they need screws in, bolts they need nuts on. Goddamn it, give it to 'em! Fast, faster . . . *faster!*

You want an example of perfection? Well, I've mastered dead-head velocity to such an accomplished level that, oftentimes, I must run down the line and examine a prior frame just to make sure that I performed my duties on it. Without fail, the job is always complete. It's proud moments like these when I know I have achieved total zombie nirvana. After all, how can you possibly dread an event that you're not even aware has happened?

Working the rivet line is like being paid to flunk high school the rest of your life: an adolescent time warp that peddles report cards (line audit scores), awards stars (complimentary plastic coffee mugs with corporate logo), causes pimples (carpal tunnel syndrome), and serves up detention (indefinite layoffs). (Carpal tunnel syndrome is bound to affect almost every rivethead sooner or later. The symptoms are easy enough to recognize: you wake up in the morning and your hands feel as though they were underwater. They tingle and feel uncomfortably thick. For an hour or so, it is impossible to write your name or even pick your nose with any semblance of style and grace.)

The parallel could also be stretched to include the fact that I've seen the same number of co-workers (three) sent home after wetting their pants as those sent home after mashing off a finger in a rivet gun. Sing it, Bonehead: "No more pencils, no more books, no more pinkies, we've got hooks!"

We even have our own version of the high school mascot. I wouldn't fib ya, honest. His name is Howie Makem—the "Quality Cat."

GM created Howie six years ago as the messianic embodiment of its new quality drive. A livin', breathin' propaganda vessel hired to spur the troops. Imagine it: "Slogans on free coffee cups just ain't gettin' it, Bill. My suggestion is that we give the men a kitty cat."

Howie stands about five-feet-seven. He has light brown fur, long synthetic whiskers, and a head the size of a Datsun. A very magical cat, he walks everywhere on his hind paws. Sadly, Howie was not entrusted with a dick.

Though it's been six years now, I still get spooked every time Howie appears on one of his rounds. I can never quite prepare myself for the sight of that gigantic corduroy cat's head bouncin' down the aisle, issuing me a quick thumbs-up signal and then disappearing back into the haze.

I will think to myself: *Someone* is in that head. *Someone* whose wife and kids lie sound asleep in another part of town while the stars shine down and the trucks pile up and Daddy haunts the halls in his kitty costume. *Someone* who was forced to go through 12 worthless years of the American education system only to wind up jerry-riggin' the same old acid flashback for the benefit of a bunch of bleary-eyed screw jockeys with 12 o'clock shadow.

There should be exemptions for men who aspire to do nothing more than dress up as house pets in the middle of factories.

Another thought has occurred to me. If Howie Makem is allowed to roam the plant as the spiritual ambassador of the "Quality Concept," why isn't equal time being provided a likewise embodied representative of GM's *foremost* preoccupation—the "Quantity Concept"? For the sake of realism, Howie needs an alter ego. An elusive second self that would lurk amongst the shadows and pounce on any worker who dares cause a stoppage on the line.

I decided I might like the role. Through information passed on by a friend, I learned that Howie had a spare head stowed away somewhere in the audit area. It was my intention to swipe the spare noggin, paint the eyes a violent red, attach giant fangs to its overbite, and carve the word *QUOTA* across its forehead.

With that accomplished, the "Quantity Cat" could set out to terrorize all those responsible for downtime. (How many times had I heard it: "For each minute the line is down, the company loses another $10,000 income.") "Howie Takem" could ambush workers at stoplights. Park next to them in drive-ins. Claw their bedroom windows during the sex act. Growl at them from behind the Beer Nuts rack in Mark's Lounge.

Unfortunately, it didn't work out. I made it as far as locating the very closet where Howie stashed his head, but on each visit, the sucker was padlocked. My source tells me this is because the quality people are taking no chances. Last winter, vandals made off with Howie's legs and torso, and all the quality folks are left with is a couple of disembodied cat heads collecting dust.

This part confuses me. Just because Howie (either version) no longer has a body, what's to stop him from putting on the head and performing his rounds in jeans or coveralls? The way I figure it, as long as you've got a head, you've got a Howie. Right?

It's silly. I make $12.82 an hour. When everything goes right, I have no idea what I'm doing. I retire in the year 2007. I'll believe anything.

It was Dave, Ex-rivethead-turned-door-fit-inspector at the Chevy Truck plant in Flint, who first suggested that we turn to the professional psychiatric world for input and guidance. He was having those nightmares again—the ones in which Roger Smith clutches the end of a limbo stick and plods around the living room on his knees while strange exotic birds hiss, moan, and defecate on stacks of old aluminum.

"Our health insurance will cover the whole shot," reasoned Dave. "It's just as legit as having a busted back. Besides, there may be some time off work in the deal or, at the very least, some get-happy drugs."

Time off work? Get-happy drugs? I didn't see much need for either. As usual, I had no idea of what I wanted, outside of a half tank of gas, some cigarettes, a little pocket change, and a new copy of Alex Chilton's *Like Flies on Sherbet*. I assumed that having a good-paying job that I thoroughly despised verified my position as just another square-jawed carefree American. Dave disagreed: "I believe, more firmly than ever, that you need your head dipped."

We contacted a couple of local analysts—Dave's first-round selections being an eccentric German he summoned up from the Yellow Pages while browsing for "impressive-sounding surnames," and I, in turn, taking potluck from a scroll I had found lying around in the office of my family doctor.

After a couple of visits each, we compared findings. Dave's doctors pronounced him to be a top-notch manic-depressive (hardly a startling revelation considering the fact that if Dave were asked whether a glass of water on the counter was half full or half empty, he would probably reply, "Bone dry and swarming with leeches"). His shrink peeled off a prescription for lithium, suggested that a career move was in order, and pleaded with Dave never to buy a home in his subdivision.

My sessions were somewhat less frantic. According to my shrink, there were two main factors holding me back in life. He felt that I was prone to too much worry, agonizing over things that were beyond my control, and that it was a half-decent hunch that my life was being "controlled by Satan." (The session took on a religious tone once I admitted to being a failed Catholic.) I immediately reasoned that if the latter were true, then the former condition was hardly to be unexpected.

Dave and I aren't seeing psychiatrists anymore. As far as I know, Dave opted for liquor over lithium and is still fondling door jams one floor above me at Chevy Truck.

As for myself, I still worry about everything: hailstorms, dying pets, bad arteries, the Boston Celtics, phone bills, Madonna's marriage, and turning 30. Satan is *not* controlling my life! Bill Cullen is.

It's 11:35 P.M., and I return to the rivet line at GM Truck and Bus. I'm sitting on top of an overturned garbage pail next to my workbench. I have roughly one minute before the next truck frame arrives and I must resume my assembler's duties.

Fifty miles to the south, GM Chairman Roger Smith gnaws at a dish of pears while Johnny Carson unfolds the evening's monologue. Roger's wife is slouching next to him, painting her toenails. I'd guess that neither of them knows I am here pounding rivets.

In an hour and a half, the line'll shut down and I'll be out of here. If I worked in a burger joint or gas station, the boss and I would probably close up and go bowl a few rounds at Eastown Lanes.

But here at GM I've never even seen my boss, Roger Smith, let alone commit tenpins with him. So I think it's time we hit the bowling alley—just Smitty and I. Not my foreman. Not the plant manager. Not even my union honcho, Owen Bieber, who'd probably have some brute with a Made in America tattoo on his biceps bury my face in the ball return.

Nope, it's gotta be Roger, or I ain't gonna dance.

He owes it to me, is the way I got it figured, and I in turn owe it to all my proud ancestors—a dedicated bunch of shoprats if there ever were some. Consider this roll call: my old man worked for the company. My grandpappy worked for the company. My sweet little granny worked for the company. My other grandpappy, God rest his assembler's soul, worked for the company. I'm telling you, damn near everybody who ever leased limb space on the ol' family sap worked for the company, and if you're wondering what happened to my other granny—well, somebody had to stay back home and pack that army a lunch.

Including my nine years of service to GM, we're left staring at something like 126 years devoted to the General Motors Corporation. That's an incredible amount of time to be spent wondering what to do with the 3–10 spare. Seven and a half centuries in dog years and all my clan has got to offer when they drag around the spotlight for show-and-tell is: a few ugly wristwatches, a shoe box fulla pension stubs, lien-free false teeth, and the scar that runs down my dear daddy's back. Excluding having my spine fused back together, I want all those things too! Plus 10 frames of bowling with Rog.

I've approached a number of my co-workers regarding my bowling quest and not one of them has ever laughed at me. They all seemed to handle the subject with a genuine sense of concern. And fascination.

For instance, a recent conversation I had with one of my rivet line pals went like this:

"Wouldn't it be a nice gesture if, on occasion, you went out and had a couple beers with the boss?"

"I'd do it."

"And," I continued, "don't you think that maybe inroads could be made toward tearing down the hostile relationship between labor and management if you and the boss agreed to go bowling once a month?"

"Yeah, that might help," my pal admitted.

"Just you and Roger Smith taking time out and tipping a few Strohs."

"Well, it all depends," the guy hesitated.

"How's that?"

"Who the fuck is Roger Smith?"

It is now 1:30 A.M. and I won't be bowling with Roger Smith tonight. The nights here crawl by indistinguishably from one another, and every Thursday evening Roger sends me a check to show me what a good boy I've been.

Tomorrow I'll punch in and do it all over again. Once every hour an army truck will roll past on the line with its hood latch no doubt pointed at some poor rebel in El Salvador, Lebanon, or maybe Cleveland. I grab my gun and rivet a dual-exhaust tailpipe hanger to its ribs.

The bell rings, the line stops, and I go out, sit in my car, and smoke Newport Menthol Kings until the lot clears. I rub out the last cigarette and go home to drink bourbon from a plastic mug emblazoned with the motto: "We Make Our Own History—50 Years. UAW." This is the best I've felt all day.

If I last that long, I can retire in 21 years.

It's a living. Sorta.

Jim Donovan (A)

Jim Donovan, 37, the new president and chief executive officer of Famous Products, was suddenly in the toughest spot of his life. Having just been selected by Omega Corporation, a huge conglomerate, to take over as president of their latest acquisition, he had been feeling very good about himself. Having grown up on "the wrong side of the tracks," worked his way through engineering college, earned an M.B.A. from Harvard Business School, worked for 10 years as a management consultant and for 2 years as a successful president of a small company, he felt that he had *arrived.* The company he was going to manage was known throughout the world, had a good reputation, and would provide a good opportunity for visibility in the parent company. The pay would be the highest he had ever earned, and while the money itself was not that important (though he'd be able to assure his wife and four children financial security), he enjoyed the indicator of success a high salary provided. And Jim was eager to manage a company with over 1,000 employees; the power to get things done on such a large scale was very attractive to him.

When Omega had selected him, they had told him that Don Bird, the current president of Famous Products, was close to retirement and would be moved upstairs to chairman of the board. Bird had been

This case was prepared by Professors Allan R. Cohen and Michael Merenda, University of New Hampshire, for purposes of classroom discussion.

president of Famous for 22 years and had done reasonably well, building sales steadily and guarding quality. The top management group was highly experienced, closely knit, very loyal to the company, and had been in their jobs for a long time. As long-term employees they all were reported to be good friends of Don Bird. They were almost all in their early 60s and quite proud of the record of their moderate-sized but successful company. Famous had not, however, grown in profits as rapidly as Omega expected of its operating companies, and Omega's president had told Jim that he wanted Jim to "grab ahold of Famous and make it take off."

With this challenge ringing in his ears, Jim flew out to Milwaukee for his first visit to Famous Products. He had talked briefly with Don Bird to say that he'd be arriving Thursday for half a day, then would be back for good after 10 days in New York at Omega. Bird had been cordial but rather distant on the phone, and Jim wondered how Bird was taking Jim's appointment. "I've only got a few hours here," thought Jim. "I wonder how I should play it."

STOP: *DO NOT READ* Part B until requested to do so by your instructor.

Jim Donovan (B)

When Jim pulled up to Famous Product's headquarters in his rented car, he noticed the neat grounds and immaculate landscaping. To his surprise, Don Bird met him at the door. Bird had on a very conservative blue business suit, black tie, black shoes, and white shirt. He peered out at Jim through old-fashioned steel-rimmed glasses and said, "Welcome to our plant. You're just in time for our usual Thursday morning executive meeting; would you like to sit in on that and meet our people?" Jim thought that the meeting would give him a chance to observe the management group in action, and he readily agreed, planning to sit back and watch for as long as he could.

Jim was ushered into the most formal meeting room he could remember ever having seen. The dark-paneled room was dominated by a long, heavy table with 12 high-backed chairs around it. Seven of the chairs were filled with unsmiling executives in dark suits.

Bird led Jim to the front of the room, indicated an empty chair to the left of the seat at the head of the table, then sat down in the place that was obviously his. Turning to the group, he said:

> Gentlemen, I want you to meet Mr. Donovan, but before I turn the meeting over to him, I want you to know that I do not believe he should be here; I do not believe he's qualified, and I will give him no support. Mr. Donovan. . . .

Kingston Company

The Kingston Company, located in Ontario, was a medium-sized manufacturing firm which made a line of machine parts and marketed them to plants in the southeastern section of the province. Harold Kingston, the president and majority shareholder in the company, held a master of business administration degree from an American university and was a vigorous supporter of the usefulness and value of a graduate business education. As a result, he had on his staff a group of four young MBAs to whom he referred as "the think group" or "troubleshooters."

The four members of the group ranged in age from the youngest at 23 to the oldest at 35, with the two intermediate members being 27. They were all from different universities and had different academic backgrounds. Their areas of interest were marketing, organizational behavior, operations research, and finance. All had been hired simultaneously and placed together in the "think group" by Mr. Kingston because, as he put it, "With their diverse knowledge and intelligence, they ought to be able to solve any of this company's problems."

For their first month on the job, the "Big Four," as they became known in the firm, familiarized themselves with the company's operations and employees. They spent a half day every week in conference with Mr. Kingston and his executive committee, discussing the goals and objectives of the company and going over the history of the major policy decisions made by the firm over the years. While the process of familiarization was a continuing one, the group decided after four weeks that it had uncovered some of the firm's problems and that it would begin to set out recommendations for the solution of these problems.

From the beginning, the members of the group had worked long hours and could usually be found in the office, well after the plant had closed, discussing their findings and trading opinions and ideas. The approach to problem solving which they adopted was to attack each problem as a group and to pool their ideas. This seemed to give a number of different slants to the problems and many times helped clear away the bias which inevitably crept into each member's analysis.

Mike Norton, the finance specialist and the youngest member of the group, and Jim Thorne and Dave Knight, the operations research man and the behavioral management man, respectively, spent a lot of time together outside the work environment. They seemed to have similar interests, playing tennis and golf together and generally having a keen interest in sports. They managed to get tickets together to watch the local professional football games, and ice hockey tickets, and so on. The fourth and oldest member of the group, Cy Gittinger, did not share these interests. The only "sports" he played were shuffleboard and croquet; and he didn't join the other three too often after work for a beer in a local bar, since he also abstained from alcohol.

The group, from the beginning, was purposely unstructured. All the members agreed to consider themselves equals. They occupied one large office, each having a desk in an opposite corner, with the middle of the room acting as a "common." Basic decisions were usually made with the four men pacing about in the open area, leaning against the walls and desks, and either squeezing or bouncing "worry balls" of a rubber putty substance, used for cleaning typewriters, off the walls. The atmosphere was completely informal, and the rest of the firm kidded the members of the group about the inordinately large amount of typewriter cleaner used in the room when there were no typewriters to be seen.

While consensus was not required, the group found that they were able to agree on a course of action most of the time. When they were unable to do so, they presented their differing opinions to Mr. Kingston, in whose hands the final decision rested. They acted in a purely staff capacity, and unless requested to help a particular manager and authorized to do so by Mr. Kingston, they confined their reports to the president and his executive committee. Reports were usually presented in written form, with all four members of the group present and contributing verbal support and summation.

The group realized that working in close contact would result in strained relations on occasion, and they agreed to attempt to express their feelings accurately and try to understand issues from the other members' points of view. Jokes about "happiness boys," "junior Baruchs," "peddlers," and "formula babies" were bandied about, and each of the four made a conscious effort to see the biases introduced by his field of interest. Attempts at controlling the discussion and establishing a leadership position were handled by pointing out the behavior to the individual involved.

However, as the months passed, there seemed to be a growing uneasiness in the relationship between Norton, Thorne, and Knight and the fourth member, Gittinger. The three brought their feelings out one day when they were playing golf. At the 19th hole over a drink, Thorne commented on the amount of time Gittinger spent talking to Mr. Kingston in his office. They all spent a great deal of time out of their office talking to managers and workers all through the plant, gathering data on various problems; but Thorne remarked Gittinger seemed to confine his activities to the upper levels of management far more than the others did. The other two had made the same observation but felt that it was really hard to put a finger on anything "wrong" about consulting with the president continually. They agreed that their fact-finding did not generally require as much time at higher levels as Gittinger was devoting, but when the point was brought up in subsequent discussion at the office, Cy explained that in order to get information from Mr. Kingston he found an "indirect" approach, which entailed a certain amount of small talk, was most successful.

After the group had been functioning for 10 months, Kingston called them into a meeting with his executive committee and went through an appraisal of their performance. He was, he said, tremendously pleased that his "think group" had performed so well, and he felt vindicated in his belief in the potency of applying the skills learned in graduate business school. His executives added their words of praise. Then Mr. Kingston brought up a suggestion he said he and Cy Gittinger had been discussing for the past month and a half, to appoint one of the group members as a coordinator. The coordinator's job would be to form a liaison between Kingston and the executive committee on the one hand and the group on the other and also to guide the group, as a result of the closer ties of the coordinator with the management team, in establishing a set of priorities for different problem areas.

When Kingston had finished describing the proposal, which, it seemed, met with his and the committee's approval, Jim Thorne remarked that this procedure seemed to be unnecessary in the light of the previous smooth functioning of the group and began to explain that such a change would upset the structure and goals of the group. He was interrupted by Mr. Kingston, who said he had an important engagement. "We'll leave the working out of all the details to you men," he said. "We don't want to impose anything on you, and we have all agreed that you should be the ones to work out just how this new plan can be implemented." At this point, the meeting ended.

As the group walked back to their office, Gittinger was the only one who talked. He wondered aloud who would be the most suitable man for the coordinator's job and repeated Kingston's words, citing the advantages that would accrue to the company with the creation of such a position. Since it was 4:45 P.M., they all cleared their desks and left the plant together, splitting up outside to go home.

A 6 P.M., Thorne called Norton to ask him what he thought about the developments of the afternoon. The latter expressed surprise, anger, and resentment that the decision had been made without the consultation of the group and remarked that Knight, to whom he had just been talking, felt the same way. The trio made arrangements to meet for dinner at their downtown athletic club at 7 P.M. that evening to discuss the situation.

Larry Ross

The corporation is a jungle. It's exciting. You're thrown in on your own and you're constantly battling to survive. When you learn to survive, the game is to become the conqueror, the leader.

"I've been called a business consultant. Some say I'm a business psychiatrist. You can describe me as an advisor to top management in a corporation." He's been at it since 1968.

I started in the corporate world, oh gosh—'42. After kicking around in the Depression, having all kinds of jobs and no formal education, I wasn't equipped to become an engineer, a lawyer, or a doctor. I gravitated to selling. Now they call it marketing. I grew up in various corporations. I became the executive vice president of a large corporation and then of an even larger one. Before I quit I became president and chief executive officer of another. All nationally known companies.

Sixty-eight, we sold out our corporation. There was enough money in the transaction where I didn't have to go back in business. I decided that I wasn't going to get involved in the corporate battle any more. It lost its excitement, its appeal. People often ask me, "Why weren't you in your own business? You'd probably have made a lot of money." I often ask it myself, I can't explain it, except. . . .

Most corporations I've been in, they were on the New York Stock Exchange with thousands and thousands of stockholders. The last one—whereas I was the president and chief executive, I was always subject to the board of directors, who had pressure from the stockholders. I owned a portion of the business, but I wasn't in control. I don't know of any situation in the corporate world where an executive is completely free and sure of his job from moment to moment.

Corporations always have to be right. That's their face to the public. When things go bad, they have to protect themselves and fire somebody. "We had nothing to do with it. We had an executive that just screwed everything up." He's never really ever been his own boss.

The danger starts as soon as you become a district manager. You have men working for you and you have a boss above. You're caught in a squeeze. The squeeze progresses from station to station. I'll tell you what a squeeze is. You have the guys working for you that are shooting for your job. The guy you're working for is scared stiff you're gonna shove him out of his job. Everybody goes around and says, "The test of the true executive is that you have men working for you that can replace you, so you can move up." That's a lot of baloney. The manager is afraid of the bright young guy coming up.

Fear is always prevalent in the corporate structure. Even if you're a top man, even if you're hard, even if you do your job—by the slight flick of a finger your boss can fire you. There's always the insecurity. You bungle a job. You're fearful of losing a big customer. You're fearful so many things will appear on your record, stand against you. You're always fearful of the big mistake. You've got to be careful when you go to corporate parties. Your wife, your children have to behave properly. You've got to fit in the mold. You've got to be on guard.

When I was president of this big corporation, we lived in a small Ohio town where the main plant was located. The corporation specified who you could socialize with and on what level. (His wife interjects: "Who were the wives you could play bridge with.") The president's wife could do what she wants, as long as it's with dignity and grace. In a small town they didn't have to keep check on you. Everybody knew. There are certain sets of rules.

Not every corporation has that. The older the corporation, the longer it's been in a powerful position, the more rigid, the more conservative they are in their approach. Your swinging corporations are generally the new ones, the upstarts, the *nouveau riche*. But as they get older, like DuPont, General Motors, General Electric, they became more rigid. I'd compare them to the old, old rich—the Rockefellers and the Mellons—that train their children how to handle money, how to conserve their money, and how to grow with their money. That's what happened to the older corporations. It's only when they get in trouble that they'll have a young upstart of a president come in and try to shake things up.

The executive is a lonely animal in the jungle who doesn't have a friend. Business is related to life. I think in our everyday living we're lonely. I have only a wife to talk to, but beyond that. . . . When I talked business to her, I don't know whether she understood me. But that was unimportant. What's important is that I was able to talk out loud and hear myself—which is the function I serve as a consultant.

The executive who calls me usually knows the answer to his problem. He just has to have somebody to talk to and hear his decision out loud. If it sounds good when he speaks it out loud, then it's pretty good. As he's talking, he may suddenly realize his errors and he corrects them out loud. That's a great benefit wives provide for executives. She's listening, and you know she's on your side. She's not gonna hurt you.

Gossip and rumor are always prevalent in a corporation. There are absolutely no secrets. I have always felt every office was wired. You come out of the board meeting and people in the office already know what's happened. I've tried many times to track down a rumor but never could. I think people have been there so many years and have developed an ability to read reactions. From these reactions they make a good educated guess. Gossip actually develops into fact.

It used to be a ploy for many minor executives to gain some information. "I heard that the district manager of California is being transferred to Seattle." He knows there's been talk going on about changing district managers. By using this ploy—"I know something"—he's making it clear to the person he's talking to that he's been in on it all along. So it's all right to tell him. Gossip is another way of building up importance within a person who starts the rumor. He's in, he's part of the inner circle. Again, we're back in the jungle. Every ploy, every trick is used to survive.

When you're gonna merge with a company or acquire another company it's supposed to be top secret. You have to do something to stem the rumors because it might screw up the deal. Talk of the merger, the whole place is in a turmoil. It's like somebody saying there's a bomb in the building and we don't know where it is and when it's going to go off. There've been so many mergers where top executives are laid off, the accounting department is cut by 60 percent, the manufacturing is cut by 20 percent. I have yet to find anybody in a corporation who was so secure to believe honestly it couldn't happen to him.

They put on a front: "Oh, it can't happen to me. I'm too important." But deep down, they're scared stiff. The fear is there. You can smell it. You can see it on their faces. I'm not so sure you couldn't see it on my face many, many times during my climb up.

I always used to say—rough, tough Larry—I always said, "If you do a good job, I'll give you a great reward. You'll keep your job." I'll have a sales contest and the men who make their quota will win a prize—they'll keep their jobs. I'm not saying there aren't executives who instill fear in their people. He's no different than anybody walking down the street. We're all subject to the same damn insecurities and neuroses—at every level. Competitiveness, that's the basis of it.

Why didn't I stay in the corporate structure? As a kid, living through the Depression, you always heard about the tycoons, the men of power, the men of industry. And you kind of dream that. Gee, these are supermen. These are the guys that have no feeling, aren't subject to human emotions, the insecurities that everybody else has. You get in the corporate structure, you find they all button their pants the same way everybody else does. They all got the same fears.

The corporation is made up of many, many people. I call 'em the gray people and the black—or white—people. Black and white are definite colors, solid. Gray isn't. The gray people come there from nine to five, do their job, aren't particularly ambitious. There's no fear there, sure. But they're not subject to great demands. They're only subject to dismissal when business goes bad and they cut off people. They go from corporation to corporation and get jobs. Then you have the black—or white—people. The ambitious people, the leaders, the ones who want to get ahead.

When the individual reaches the vice presidency or he's general manager, you know he's an ambitious, dedicated guy who wants to get to the top. He isn't one of the gray people. He's one of the black-and-white vicious people—the leaders, the ones who stick out in the crowd.

As he struggles in this jungle, every position he's in, he's terribly lonely. He can't confide and talk with the guy working under him. He can't confide and talk to the man he's working for. To give vent to his feelings, his fears, and his insecurities, he'd expose himself. This goes all the way up the line until he gets to be president. The president *really* doesn't have anybody to talk to, because the vice presidents are waiting for him to die or make a mistake and get knocked off so they can get his job.

He can't talk to the board of directors, because to them he has to appear as a tower of strength, knowledge, and wisdom, and have the ability to walk on water. The board of directors, they're cold, they're hard. They don't have any direct-line responsibilities. They sit in a staff capacity, and they really play God. They're interested in profits. They're interested in progress. They're interested in keeping a good face in the community—if it's profitable. You have the tremendous infighting of man against man for survival and clawing to the top. Progress.

We always saw signs of physical afflictions because of the stress and strain. Ulcers, violent headaches. I remember one of the giant corporations I was in, the chief executive officer ate Gelusil by the minute. That's for ulcers. Had a private dining room with his private chef. All he ever ate was well-done steak and well-done hamburgers.

There's one corporation chief I had who worked conservatively 19, 20 hours a day. His whole life was his business. And he demanded the same of his executives. There was nothing sacred in life except the business. Meetings might be called on Christmas Eve or New Year's Eve, Saturdays, Sundays. He was lonesome when he wasn't involved with his business. He was always creating situations where he could be surrounded by his flunkies, regardless of what level they were, presidential, vice presidential. . . . It was his life.

In the corporate structure, the buck keeps passing up until it comes to the chief executive. Then there ain't nobody to pass the buck to. You sit there in your lonely office and finally you have to make a decision. It could involve a million dollars or hundreds of jobs or moving people from Los Angeles, which they love, to Detroit or Winnipeg. So you're sitting at the desk, playing God.

You say, "Money isn't important. You can make some bad decisions about money, that's not important. What is important is the decisions you make about people working for you, their livelihood, their lives." It isn't true.

To the board of directors, the dollars are as important as human lives. There's only yourself sitting there making the decision, and you hope it's right. You're always on guard. Did you ever see a jungle animal that wasn't on guard? You're always looking over your shoulder. You don't know who's following you.

The most stupid phrase anybody can use in business is loyalty. If a person is working for a corporation, he's supposed to be loyal. This corporation is paying him less than he could get somewhere else at a comparable job. It's stupid of him to hang around and say he's loyal. The only loyal people are the people who can't get a job anyplace else. Working in a corporation, in a business, isn't a game. It isn't a collegiate event. It's a question of living or dying. It's a question of eating or not eating. Who is he loyal to? It isn't his country. It isn't his religion. It isn't his political party. He's working for some company that's paying him a salary for what he's doing. The corporation is out to make money. The ambitious guy will say "I'm doing my job. I'm not embarrassed taking my money. I've got to progress and when I won't progress I won't be here." The shnook is the loyal guy, because he can't get a job anyplace else.

Many corporations will hang on to a guy or promote him to a place where he doesn't belong. Suddenly, after the man's been there 25 years, he's outlived his usefulness. And he's too old to start all over again. That's part of the cruelty. You can't only condemn the corporation for that. The man himself should be smart enough and intuitive enough to know he isn't getting anyplace, to get the hell out and start all over. It was much more difficult at first to lay off a guy. But if you live in a jungle, you become hard, unfortunately.

When a top executive is let go, the king is dead, long live the king. Suddenly he's a persona non grata. When it happens, the shock is tremendous. Overnight. He doesn't know what hit him. Suddenly everybody in the organization walks aways and shuns him because they don't want to be associated with him. In corporations, if you back the wrong guy, you're in his corner, and he's fired, you're guilty by association. So what a lot of corporations have done is when they call a guy in—sometimes they'll call him in on a Friday night and say, "Go home now and come in tomorrow morning and clean out your desk and leave. We don't want any farewells or anything. Just get up and get the hell out." It's done in nice language. We say, "Look, why cause any trouble? Why cause any unrest in the organization? It's best that you just fade away." Immediately his Cadillac is taken away from him. His phone extension on the WATS line is taken away from him.[1] All these things are done quietly and—bingo! he's dead. His phone at home stops ringing because the fear of association continues after the severance. The smell of death is there.

We hired a vice president. He came highly recommended. He was with us about six months, and he was completely inadequate. A complete misfit. Called him in the office, told him he was gonna go, gave him a nice severance pay. He broke down and cried. "What did I do wrong? I've done a marvelous job. Please don't do this to me. My daughter's getting married next month. How am I going to face the people?" He cried and cried and cried. But we couldn't keep him around. We just had to let him go.

I was just involved with a gigantic corporation. They had a shake-up two Thursdays ago. It's now known as Black Thursday. Fifteen of 20 guys were let go overnight. The intelligent corporations say, "Clear, leave tonight, even if it's midweek. Come in Saturday morning and clean your desk. That's all. No good-byes or anything." They could be guys that have been there anywhere from 1 year to 30 years. If it's a successful operation, they're very generous. But then again, the human element creeps in. The boss might be vindictive and cut him off without anything. It may depend what the corporation wants to maintain as its image.

And what it does to the ego! A guy in a key position, everybody wants to talk to him. All his subordinates are trying to get an audience

[1] Wide area telecommunications service. A prerogative granted important executives by some corporations: unlimited use of the telephone to make a call anywhere in the world.

with him to build up their own positions. Customers are calling him; everybody is calling him. Now his phone's dead. He's sitting at home, and nobody calls him. He goes out and starts visiting his friends, who are busy with their own business, who haven't got time for him. Suddenly he's a failure. Regardless what the reason was—regardless of the press release that said he resigned—he was fired.

The only time the guy isn't considered a failure is when he resigns and announces his new job. That's the tipoff. "John Smith resigned, future plans unknown" means he was fired. "John Smith resigned to accept the position of president of X Company"—then you know he resigned. This little nuance you recognize immediately when you're in corporate life.

Changes since '42? Today the computer is taking over the world. The computer exposes all. There's no more chance for shenanigans and phoniness. Generally the computer prints out the truth. Not 100 percent, but enough. It's eliminated a great deal of the jungle infighting. There's more facts for the businessman to work from, if the computer gives him the right information. Sometimes it doesn't. They have a saying at IBM: "If you put garbage in the computer, you'll take garbage out." Business is becoming more scientific with regard to marketing, finance, investments. And much more impersonal.

But the warm personal touch *never* existed in corporations. That was just a sham. In the last analysis, you've got to make a profit. There are a lot of family-held corporations that truly felt they were part of a legend. They had responsibilities to their people. They carried on as best they could. And then they went broke. The loyalty to their people, their patriarchy, dragged 'em all down. Whatever few of 'em are left are being forced to sell and are being taken over by the cold hand of the corporation.

My guess is that 20 corporations will control about 40 percent of the consumer goods market. How much room is there left for the small guy? There's the supermarket in the grocery business. In our time, there were little mamma-and-papa stores, thousands and thousands throughout the country. How many are there today? Unless you're National Tea or A&P, there's just no room. The small chains will be taken over by the bigger chains, and they themselves will be taken over. . . . The fish swallows the smaller fish and he's swallowed by a bigger one, until the biggest swallows 'em all. I have a feeling there'll always be room for the small entrepreneur, but he'll be rare. It'll be very difficult for him.

The top man is more of a general manager than he is an entrepreneur. There's less gambling than there was. He won't make as many mistakes as he did before in finance and marketing. It's a cold science. But when it comes to dealing with people, he still has to have that feel and he still has to do his own thinking. The computer can't do that for him.

When I broke in, no man could become an executive until he was 35, 36 years old. During the past 10 years there've been 26, 27. Lately there's been a reversal. These *young* ones climbed to the top when things were good, but during the past couple of years we've had some rough times. Companies have been clobbered and some have gone back to older men. But that's not gonna last.

Business is looking for the highly trained, highly skilled *young* executive who has the knowledge and the education in a highly specialized field. It's happened in all professions, and it's happening in business. You have your comptroller who's highly specialized. You have your treasurer who has to know finance, a heavily involved thing because of the taxation and the SEC. You have the manufacturing area. He has to be highly specialized in warehouse and in shipping—the ability to move merchandise cheaply and quickly. Shipping has become a horrendous problem because costs have become tremendous. You have to know marketing, the studies, the effect of advertising. A world of specialists. The man at the top has to have a general knowledge. And he has to have the knack of finding the right man to head these divisions. That's the difficulty.

You have a nice, plush, lovely office to go to. You have a private secretary. You walk down the corridor and everybody bows and says, "Good morning, Mr. Ross. How are you today?" As you go up the line, the executives will say, "How is Mrs. Ross?" Until you get to the higher executives. They'll say, "How is Nancy?" Here you socialize, you know each other. Everybody plays the game.

A man wants to get to the top of the corporation, not for the money involved. After a certain point, how much more money can you make? In my climb, I'll be honest, money was secondary. Unless you have tremendous demands, yachts, private airplanes—you get to a certain point, money isn't that important. It's the power, the status, the prestige. Frankly, it's delightful to be on top and have everybody calling you Mr. Ross and have a plane at your disposal and a car and a driver at your disposal. When you come to town, there are people to take care of you. When you walk into a board meeting, everybody gets up and says hello. I don't think there's any human being that doesn't love that. It's a nice feeling. But the ultimate power is in the board of directors. I don't know anybody who's free. You read in the paper about stockholders' meetings, the annual report. It all sounds so glowing. But behind the scenes, a jungle.

I work on a yearly retainer with a corporation. I spend, oh, two, three days a month in various corporate structures. The key executives can talk to me and bounce things off me. The president may have a specific problem that I will investigate and come back to him with my ideas. The reason I came into this work is that all my corporate life I was looking for somebody like me, somebody who's been there. Because there's no new problems in business today. There's just a different name for different problems that have been going on for years and years and years. Nobody's come up yet with a problem that isn't familiar. I've been there.

Example. The chief executive isn't happy with the marketing structure. He raises many questions which I may not know specifically. I'll find out and come back with a proposal. He might be thinking of promoting one of his executives. It's narrowed down to two or three. Let's say two young guys who've been moved to a new city. It's a toss-up. I notice one has bought a new house, invested heavily in it. The other rented. I'd recommend the second. He's more realistic.

If he comes before his board of directors, there's always the vise. The poor sonofabitch is caught in the squeeze from the people below and the people above. When he comes to the board, he's got to come with a firm hand. I can help him because I'm completely objective. I'm out of the jungle. I don't have the trauma that I used to have when I had to fire somebody. What is it gonna do to this guy? I can give it to him cold and hard and logical. I'm not involved.

I left that world because suddenly the power and the status were empty. I'd been there, and when I got there it was nothing. Suddenly you have a feeling of little boys playing at business. Suddenly you have a feeling—so what? It started to happen to me, this feeling, oh, in '67, '68. So when the corporation was sold, my share of the sale was such . . . I didn't have to go back into the jungle. I don't have to fight to the top. I've been to the mountaintop. (Laughs.) It isn't worth it.

It was very difficult, the transition of retiring from the status position, where there are people on the phone all day trying to talk to you. Suddenly nobody calls you. This is a psychological . . . (halts, a long pause). I don't want to get into that. Why didn't I retire completely? I really don't know. In the last four, five years people have come to me with tempting offers. Suddenly I realized what I'm doing is much more fun than going into that jungle again. So I turned them down.

I've always wanted to be a teacher. I wanted to give back the knowledge I gained in corporate life. People have always told me I'd always been a great sales manager. In every sales group you always have two or three young men with stars in their eyes. They always sat at the edge of the chair. I knew they were comers. I always felt I could take 'em, develop 'em, and build 'em. A lot of old fogies like me—I can point out this guy, that guy who worked for me, and now he's the head of this, the head of that.

Yeah, I always wanted to teach. But I had no formal education and no university would touch me. I was willing to teach for nothing. But there also, they have their jungle. They don't want a businessman. They only want people in the academic world who have a formalized and, I think, empty training. This is what I'd really like to do. I'd like to get involved with the young people and give my knowledge to them before it's buried with me. Not that what I have is so great, but there's a certain understanding, a certain feeling. . . .

Lisa and the Two Sues

During the past year in which I was a resident assistant in the university dormitory, I encountered a number of situations. One of the most interesting involved three freshmen in a triple room. One was named Lisa. She had a quiet determination about her that became apparent when you talked to her—she had some firm opinions about right and wrong—but she was not a person who stood out in a crowd. She was tall, slender, and soft-spoken; on first meeting she seemed quiet and reserved.

The other two roommates were named Sue—Sue Taylor and Sue Knowles—and were more outgoing. Both had played field hockey while in high school and had been popular socially. In fact, as the semester developed, the two Sues became the driving force behind many a floor party in the dorm.

The two Sues were good friends and had chosen to room together. Lisa, on the other hand, had tried to room with her friend Jane but had been assigned to room with the two Sues in a triple. Lisa clearly had reason to approach the rooming situation less comfortably than did Sue Taylor and Sue Knowles. But let me allow Lisa to tell her own story.

LISA

I did not apply to college until January of my senior year. At first I was reluctant to go. I was tired of school even though I had good grades; it was awfully expensive and I knew Dad was feeling a lot of financial pressure; and finally, my best friend and I had part-time jobs as cashiers. We had talked about working full time after graduation since we knew the people and enjoyed working there together.

But one day I was talking to some of the full-time cashiers, including some friends who had graduated from high school the previous year, and they complained about working eight hours in such dead-end jobs. So when my other friend Jane suggested we both apply to State University and room together, I quickly adopted the idea.

In February we both got our acceptances and sent in our room applications. As I worked the cash register full time that summer, I began to look forward to the day when I could leave the job. Also, the idea of going to college began to sound like fun, as well as study and challenge, as I learned of others from Warrensville who were also planning to go.

In August I received a letter from the housing office and discovered to my horror that I would be rooming with two strangers, both from the same town and both named Susan. The idea of not being able to room with Jane had never entered my mind, and now the fears that I had about going to school became focused on my rooming situation. "What will my roommates be like? Will they be friendly? Or snobbish? Will they let me study? What if they take drugs or want to have guys over for the night? How will they react to my being in their room?"

The tension continued to mount as the summer wore on. The questions running through my mind seemed endless. My mother tried to reassure me by reminding me of the really great roommate our neighbor's daughter had had her freshman year. "That was different," I said. "It was only one person—not two. Besides they became friends—they had the same major. Look—it's only a week before school starts and they haven't called or written me." My mother replied, "Maybe you should call one of them." "Why?" I asked. "They're friends already. They might see me as terribly forward, and besides, I'm the outsider—they should call me. That would only be common courtesy."

On the day that I was supposed to drive to school, my father and I loaded the car while my mother packed all the things I really didn't want (but she thought I needed) into a suitcase—a suitcase which I conveniently forgot when we left. On the drive up I was very quiet. When we got to the campus and found the dorm, I immediately went on ahead to room 92 with one suitcase while my parents unloaded the car. As I approached the door, the "Welcome Lisa" sign the two girls had put on the door eased my tension momentarily. However, as I opened the door all conversation stopped. The echo of silence was awful. I walked in very slowly, trying to be cool and confident but feeling that I was being checked over from head to toe by two pairs of unfriendly eyes. Neither said a word, so I finally blurted out "Hi, which one of you is called Taylor?"—thinking it would be better to use a last name since I didn't know what they called themselves. All I got for an answer was "Me," followed by a muttered comment from the other Susan and giggles and more stares from both.

Just then my parents came up with the rest of my stuff, which we put on the floor. My mother introduced herself to the two Sues and started to tell them all about Warrensville, which she made sound very posh. She sure embarrasses me with that kind of behavior. As soon as I could, I steered my parents out of there and back to the car. After saying good-bye, I returned to room 92 where I knew my silent welcoming committee was still waiting. Once back in the room I tried to unpack, feeling that every move I made was being watched. Susan Knowles said, "Since you're the last one here you get the top bunk and half of each of our closets." I didn't say anything but thought to myself—"How generous." They sat on "their" side of the room talking about their courses and jobs and completely ignoring me. They finally left to go downtown to buy some things for the room, and I had a couple of hours to relax and try to settle in.

The tension returned as soon as they came back with a stack of posters and corkboards. It seemed to me as if they were surprised that I was still there in "their" room. After they sorted through the posters, Sue Taylor said, "Sue, let's go to dinner." I looked up from putting some clothes away and asked directions to the dining hall, expecting them to say "Come with us." Susan K. quickly gave directions and then said, "Come on, Sue. Let's go." I couldn't believe it—they just left me there.

Later that night we managed to talk a little bit. Sue Taylor told me they had applied to room together as had Jane and I. She said, "We were surprised when we found out we'd be living in a triple. We assumed we'd be rooming together, because we're taking the same courses and working on the same work-study job. I still don't understand it, since we're history majors and you're in plant science."

When I asked whom to talk to about work-study jobs, Sue K. told me, but she wasn't very encouraging nor enthusiastic about my applying. After awhile they started talking about hometown friends. Except for once, when Sue T. turned to me and said, "Oh—our boyfriends (who were also good friends) are coming up Saturday around noon for the afternoon and early evening," we didn't talk anymore. I finished unpacking and went to bed.

I left early the next morning (Friday), found Jane, and went to the freshmen orientation program for the day, learning how to find my way around and deciding what courses to take. While I was gone, the two Sues rearranged the room so that all my things were in one corner, and I was totally isolated from them.

Saturday morning the two Sues were up early getting ready for the arrival of their boyfriends. After a curt "good morning" they went back to getting the room ready. I left to have breakfast with Jane. We talked for awhile and then walked around campus and downtown, but she had a meeting that afternoon so I went back to the room after lunch.

I walked in on complete silence—the boyfriends were there, but no one was talking. The two couples were each on a separate bed and nobody introduced me, instead they just stared as I walked to my desk. The silence was too much to bear, so I spoke up and said, "I live here, too." After that somebody introduced me, but then they just all sat there and watched me. I didn't know what to do, so I sat at my desk and read, only to look up after a few minutes to see one couple kissing and the other doing the same thing. I couldn't believe my eyes. I got up and slammed out of the room.

I needed to talk to someone, and I finally found a friend from home. We found Jane and after supper picked up a six-pack of beer and went to my room. The guys were still there, and both couples were sitting on the one bed that was hidden from my corner of the room. My friends and I sat at my desk, talking and drinking the beer. There was no conversation between the two groups—we might have been in two separate rooms. I was really embarrassed, and my friends were amazed. I felt even more isolated than before. After a couple of hours the silence from the other group was too much and we left. When I returned later the guys were gone, the lights were out, and both Sues were asleep. I didn't turn on a light but merely tried to get to bed quietly in the dark.

The next week classes started. Each morning all three alarms went off at the same time. Every morning thereafter, the two Sues hurried off to breakfast before I finished getting my books together. As the week went on, communication between us almost ceased. I spent as little time in the room as possible, and most of that in my bunk. I felt I was "trespassing" if I stepped on "their" side of the room. Jane and I had our meals together, and I found other things to do so I wouldn't have to go back to the room.

I was actually glad that I had to go home at the end of that week to pick up some things—it meant a chance to escape from the cold and oppressive atmosphere. As I walked out of the door, knapsack and coat in hand, I stopped for a minute and looked back into the room. It was empty and uninviting, a reminder of both Sues. I reflected for a few minutes about the past few days and wondered if everything would be the same when I returned.

Low Five

I'm desperate. I've never been so frustrated in all my life. The new basketball coach benched me for the whole game yesterday, just one day after I tried to help her see what her coaching was doing to the team. I had fully promised to support her methods, yet she went ahead and kept me out of the entire game the next day, without saying a word to me. That's the first game I have not started in three years at Burke College. Can't she see how badly she's hurting the whole team? All of us are incredibly upset with her. I'm so frustrated I can hardly keep from bursting into tears. It's not like me to be so emotional.

Let me get hold of myself and tell you what's happened. My name's Paula, and I'm a cocaptain of Burke College's varsity women's basketball team. This year we got a new coach, Shirley Sharpe. She's 23 and was hired by the athletic department this summer to fill a position that never existed at Burke before but was very much needed. Burke's a 1,500-student co-ed liberal arts school, and women's sports are on the upswing. Shirley was appointed as the full-time coach of both women's varsity soccer and women's varsity basketball. She's a lanky six-footer who arrived at Burke in late August from Westbrook State College, where she played on a strong women's soccer team that won a national championship in 1980. She had also been a basketball All-American in high school but surrendered her game to soccer early in her college career. Stepping into a college coaching position, she appeared to be enthusiastic but also skeptical of her new venture. We were also unsure of what we should expect from her.

The soccer season started, and the several new freshmen had respectable soccer backgrounds and skills. On the other hand, many of the veterans and upperclassmen had little, if any, soccer knowledge. This forced Shirley to start with the basics. She showed patience and confidence, using her experiences as a soccer player, to teach valuable lessons and eventually work her way up to teaching more difficult drills and plays.

Throughout the season, the team was impressed and encouraged with her coaching skills and knowledge. The team's final record was not as successful as we had hoped, but we saw a bright future. Shirley expressed that a lot of good things had happened during the season, and she was excited about next year. She often spoke about the high

This case was prepared under the supervision of Professor Allan R. Cohen for classroom discussion.

school games she traveled to and from, talking with prospective soccer players and promising recruits.

Soccer ended, and basketball was about to begin. Having lost no team members to graduation, the nine returning basketball veterans were extremely excited and optimistic about the upcoming season. Although we girls only had a 9–12 record the previous year, we lost most of our games in the first half of the season before Christmas and were powerful and dominant in the latter half. We had favorable attitudes and confidence in our team's play and performance. We had been well conditioned, which allowed us to capitalize on our weaker opponents. We worked hard and had become very effective together. Our team had several strengths, such as pushing the ball down the court to score on a fast break and pressing our opponents to steal the ball. As players, we believed in this strategy and felt our own individual talent was being utilized, which was rewarding to ourselves as well as to our team as a whole. The '82–'83 season concluded on a successful note, with two great team effort victories in back-to-back Friday night and Saturday night games. During the last game, every player on our team made the scorebook, and I was even honored so much as to receive a ball signed by my teammates after scoring my thousandth (1,000) point. In addition, I was selected to the second team All-New England. We all knew I never would have achieved this without our team's cohesiveness and ability to work together. The mood of our team could not have been higher! We were so pleased to end the season in such a positive way, knowing that every game we had ever played was filled with heart and desire. We were psyched for the next year, knowing that we had the talent and ability to win many of those games we had lost. We were upset the season had to come to an end, but we were very cheerful and confident about the year to come.

The next basketball season finally arrived, and the new coach, Shirley, controlled the court. The first few practices were encouraging. They were filled with many conditioning exercises and sprints. Our team wasn't actually fond of sprints, but we realized if we wanted to be good, we had to work hard. After several practices the coach finally introduced the offense she wanted our team to use. It was different in the sense that it was a motion offense rather than an offense with any set plays. A motion offense or free-lance play style of basketball is more conducive to individuality and permissiveness, and it operates without floor balance or objectives other than to get the ball through the basket. A free-lance team learns by doing. Initiative is the byproduct of such an offense, and scrimmage and more scrimmage is the key to this brand of basketball. Furthermore, pattern play requires mechanical conditioning, and the coordination of five players into a team. Each player is mentally and physically conditioned to her individual responsibilities, which coordinate her with other team members.

Floor balance is the foundation of pattern basketball, repetition of drills and more drills is its key, and teamwork is its ultimate goal. In addition, Shirley also set us up into a zone press to use against our opponents. We went through it a few times, but were unhappy when we found Shirley not supplying specific instructions of where to go or how our trap would actually work effectively.

After a couple of weeks, our team found practices to be of less intensity. We weren't forced to do any sprints, and often during practice we saw ourselves doing little, if any, actual running. While trying to work through this new offense, several players commented that it was like a "zoo." Players were running every which way without actually knowing where the ball was or where it should have been. Frustration was developing. The one full-court press we had, compared to the six effective half- and full-court traps we had in the past year, just didn't seem to do the job. Collectively, we began talking outside of practice, expressing our concern. Thinking of the opponents we had to face, we felt we could do things differently, which would be more effective. We saw that the individual skills of our players weren't being used to their maximum, and that a lot of talent was being wasted. One girl, Cheryl, who was small but very fast, had proven time and time again to be an extremely good defensive player, coming up with steal after steal especially on all the trap variations, but Shirley saw none of this. With the one unorganized trap we had now, Cheryl felt useless and unconfident. Others, who were known for having a strong game underneath the boards, felt their ability to get position and score baskets was being overlooked.

Finally, after several weeks, we felt something should be done. As cocaptain, I approached the coach. (The other captain was out due to injury.) I expressed to our coach that we found her new ways to be difficult and thought things were less effective than they should be. Afterwards, the coach briefly told the whole team that we just had to work through it and give it time. She said this type of offense had proven several times to be effective and had won several NCAA championships. Besides, the JV team she once coached had picked it up in two weeks, and her 13- and 14-year-old boys' team developed it with no problem after a short while. We knew it wouldn't necessarily work for us just because it worked for others, but we agreed to give it another try. A couple more weeks went by, and practices never seemed to accomplish much more. We didn't feel coached. Shirley would sit up on the top bleacher while we were playing one-on-one or doing some other drill, and she would constantly be writing in her notebook while observing our performance. One player said she felt "paranoid" by constantly being watched and written about. The coach never came out to criticize or compliment our plays or moves. Oftentimes when Florence, the part-time assistant coach, was there, the two of them got together and spoke quietly as they watched. Our team expressed to each other our uneasiness.

One night we scrimmaged with the faculty. It was a messy game with people running every which way. After the game, one of the staff players, Mr. Swift, approached me and another player and asked, "Were you playing with an offense?" He said that there were lots of open shots, but we never took them. We replied that Shirley wanted the ball to be worked around again and again so that we could waste as much of the 30 seconds that we were allowed before shooting. A few days later, another faculty member who had played asked me what the hell we were doing out there. He also said, "That lady (the coach) doesn't know a thing." He said there were openings after openings to shoot but no one did.

After three games, we had lost two and won one. The first game we lost was a game I felt we definitely should have won, especially since we were up a good 10 points the entire game until the last three minutes, when we didn't score at all. The other team pressed us, and we were helpless in getting around it. Nothing was done, and the coach offered no plays to conquer our difficulty. The other game we lost was played without Shirley ever calling a timeout. She felt there was no need for one even when the other team began to walk away with the victory. This made several players very upset. After this particular game, several of us expressed the need for a team meeting. We had been hesitant right along because we knew we had to give Shirley a fair chance. I and a few others had played for her on the soccer team and thought she had been a great soccer coach. We had grown to like her but now felt we had to do something to preserve our basketball team as well as ourselves. We felt Shirley had been given a fair chance, and now we wanted her to actually know our feelings and possibly suggest to her a few things that were effectively done in the past. Our team couldn't decide on a time everyone could make, so we decided to think about it on the two-hour ride home. Although we had the next day off, I said the sooner the meeting, the better. The coach said she was very busy the next day with soccer recruiting and everything else. Another player also heard her say to the assistant coach that she "didn't want the meeting if it was what she expected."

Once at home, the coach finally decided to hold the meeting two days later, after the next practice.

The next day, on our day off, the injured captain who hadn't gone to the game the night before learned of the situation. She suggested to me that we and a couple of others get together that night and have a beer and talk things over. We talked about the different things that had happened all season and expressed our negative feelings and unhappiness. We were frustrated because our coach objected to even doing certain things we felt capable of and confident with. Although Shirley felt our team's skills were weak, she didn't push us at practice or encourage us to improve. Our team didn't even have shooting practice. Instead, Shirley shied away from these weaker skills, saying she would prefer it if we didn't do them. I felt we had never been given the opportunity to show our ability. The coach disagreed with doing things we had done in the past, thinking they were unnecessary or not effective. Sitting at the pub, I wished we could do the weave and the Celtics drill—two drills that we missed and thought to be beneficial. I was concerned about the meeting because I saw Shirley as taking it personally and likely to become defensive.

The next day while having practice before the team meeting, much to our surprise we found ourselves being told to do the weave and throw baseball passes—which was the main idea of the Celtics drill. I saw no connection with the night before and welcomed the change. Practice this day had gone well. We had a good feeling about it, for the first time in weeks. This improvement in practice made it difficult for us to actually start the meeting, since we had just finished the new drills that we had wanted to suggest to the coach.

Finally, Cheryl began by telling of the success we had last year with several different presses. She expressed that it wasn't right to compare the years, but asked if there was any way our team could possibly have different zone press versions that we knew to be very effective. The coach replied, "No!" She saw no need for several presses and said, "If you can't do one, how can you do six?" Cheryl, the defensive specialist, was shocked and went on to say that she felt "useless out there" and that she was receiving no direction. Shirley once again said we had to give it time and believe in it because it had been proven to be effective. I then tried to express that our team had a real concern about our performance. We knew we were better than we had been performing and wanted to do something about it before it was too late. I said we had trouble seeing the value in the offense, especially since it wasn't proving to be effective for our team. During the games, after a few times down the court, the other teams knew exactly what was happening. They stole the ball while Burke did nothing to change pace or give variety.

Uneasiness was seen growing on Shirley's face, and once again she replied that there was no way our team could do anything else, especially if we couldn't even do this. She said she saw us with less skill than she expected, and now she would have to go back to basics. She said we just didn't understand how it should work and refused to learn.

As captain, I tried to say something else, but Shirley quickly responded with, "Don't analyze everything I say." Shirley was clearly defensive, and I tried to defend myself as well as explain the team's position. As a result, both Shirley and I became more angry with one another, causing the gap between us to grow wider. As the meeting continued, it was obvious that something needed to be done before the conflict got worse. Cheryl added that many girls played basketball for years and were very committed to it. She said that in many cases, the girls who had also played soccer did so to be in shape for basketball. Cheryl went on to say that we were willing to give more than Shirley expected from us. Shirley said she felt we were still trying to play under our previous coach and would not accept change. She said we had to be willing to have faith in her as a coach. It was important for us to have confidence in her ability to do what's best. We agreed, but time and time again things were never done when we thought they should be. Another player, Karen, went on to ask about not calling a timeout during that one particular game. The coach said she had reasons for it. When asked what reasons, she said she wouldn't explain because if she did, it would take over an hour. She did go on to say that she didn't see our team as being "rattled" out on the court and didn't see a timeout as necessary. Karen went on to say "Oh—but they scored 10 points in a row, and we just kept turning the ball over!" It was obvious that Shirley was not enjoying this meeting. She and Florence concluded it by saying that as players, we have to be willing to go along with them. Shirley said the offense had proven itself time and time again, and we had to have faith in her to know what was right.

We left; later, several players said that the meeting was a waste and accomplished nothing. We knew, however, we had to make the best of it because we had a tournament to play in the next two days.

The next day, Friday, was the opening round of the tournament. The coach called and had left a message for me to go to the gym early so she could talk to me. However, I didn't receive the message until later because I had a previously scheduled appointment. When I did arrive at the gym, Shirley said she would talk to me after our game.

Our team lost, and after the game I sat patiently in Shirley's office, waiting for her to come up. When Shirley finally arrived, she also had Florence right at her side. Shirley sat down at her desk, and Florence pulled up a chair. As the two of them faced me, (I was sitting in the corner), Shirley pulled out her notebook, which had everything written down that she wanted to say. Looking down, Shirley began by saying that she was disappointed with me for having the attitude I did as a captain. Shirley was very defensive and said that the team and I started the season great, but now I was the one resisting the change and constantly analyzing everything she did and said. Shirley continued that my influence had a negative effect on everyone else and, as a result, it was affecting my own individual performance as well as the team's. I retaliated by saying that I realized that as a coach, Shirley had her own philosophies and styles, but as a new coach walking into a new situation with a large group of veterans, she herself had to be open to the team's feelings and suggestions. She couldn't take from our team everything we had confidence in, especially since it had worked in the past with the very same people. Shirley further said that it wasn't right for me to analyze her. I saw this as Shirley's resentment of someone questioning her knowledge. I replied that as a player, playing under Shirley in first soccer and now basketball, I saw Shirley to be more relaxed and comfortable with soccer and also more knowledgeable with the game of soccer than with the game of basketball. Shirley immediately objected, saying I had no right to even question or judge her knowledge or capability as a coach. Once again, she stated that she had spent years studying the game. I questioned the difference between studying the game and actually coaching it. Both Shirley and Florence argued that my statement showed how little I knew about the game.

As the conflict escalated, I tried to tell Shirley that in all honesty, the team and I weren't attacking her personally. We were concerned about basketball, something we valued so much. I further said that it had been difficult for the team to approach Shirley because not only was she quiet and low keyed, but we had also grown to like and respect Shirley as a person. We just wanted her to realize that just as much as our team had to be willing to change and adapt to the new situation—she did too, and we were willing to help her. I said it was hard because Shirley wasn't allowing our players to do what we felt we did best, such as run a fast break or press effectively. I also told Shirley that she had to see my view as a captain, too—as one who the players were friends with and one who they were coming to and complaining to. What was I to do? I had to be allowed to express the team's feelings without Shirley thinking they were only mine. I said that there was no communication between Shirley and anyone, and it was definitely needed.

Eventually, Shirley said that she wanted to keep the problem from spreading and that she intended to treat it as though it were cancer, in the sense that it was a problem that could be controlled with radiation, before it got any worse and spread. In addition, I could not understand Florence. Florence was also a new coach this year, and she coached the first-year varsity field hockey team. Throughout the first hockey season I always heard good reports of Florence. She was 27 years old and had been the head field hockey coach at Lincolnsberg University for the past three or four years. Her players found her friendly and personable. I knew Florence had experienced coaching a varsity college team and wished she had been more open to the situation. Florence just seemed to side with Shirley.

Throughout the hour-long conference, I saw that Shirley had become very offended. I also felt that I had been attacked by both Shirley and Florence and that they refused to see anything from my point of view. I knew they wouldn't concede, but I needed to do something, so I promised them that I would make an honest effort to accept what Shirley said and did in games as right and that I would encourage the others to go along with it, too. I admitted that maybe I had been too negative and semihesitant to change but would try to improve the situation now. At the same time, I also said I hoped that they could try and see my position, too. I stressed to them that being the captain, I had the responsibility to go to the coach when players had concerns, whether they were good or bad.

After this meeting I felt as though Shirley had done a good job blaming the team's poor attitude and poor performance on someone. I didn't believe it could be all me, and I still questioned the two coaches' basketball knowledge. Why all the resentment, I asked? For a good 12 years I had played basketball competitively. I had been on one of the top high school teams in Massachusetts and had played with many of the best players in the state. I had been coached by several coaches who had received honors and awards as both players and coaches.

There was also another player on our Burke team, a freshman, who had her high school coach come to the game played earlier that evening. Her coach said that our team should just go out on the court and play our own game. This coach, who had coached with Florence in the past, couldn't believe she was a basketball coach because she knew "nil about the game."

That night, being very upset, I thought about what had to happen next. Possibly, I had been too unwilling to accept all these new philosophies, but I also knew that in 12 years, I had been coached by some of the best; and throughout those 12 years, I had never faced anything so unorthodox. I knew I gave my word to do my best, and I intended to keep it. I wanted my team to do well and to win. However, it wasn't just me who was questioning what was happening. Some of the others were wondering whether they wanted to play the second half of the season. They saw their efforts as useless, and they weren't getting any satisfaction. At this point, I still saw Shirley as very unwilling to change, especially since she insisted she knew more than anyone on the court. Despairingly, I saw that I had to be the one to make the best of it.

The next day was the final day of the tournament. We had lost the night before by 30 points to a team that had beaten us last year by only 3 points. We had to play in the consolation game, and although I believed our team could be more successful with other methods, I was determined to play according to Shirley's wishes. However, to my surprise, I did not start the game nor did I even play in it. Shirley said nothing. It upset me because this was the first time I had not begun a game while playing on this team in three years. It upset me even more to think that my coach did not have the intestinal fortitude to tell me why I didn't play, especially in light of the meeting we had had the night before. I couldn't understand my coach's logic.

I didn't know what to do next. After the game, I didn't go to Shirley because I didn't want to start anything else. Enough was enough. I knew there was no way I could go to the other staff in the department, those above Shirley, because they were not only unaware of the entire situation but because they were viewed by many as unresponsive to students' needs. They received little respect from athletes and deserved none. Furthermore, they were not promoters of women's athletics and didn't even seem concerned with the program. After this last episode, several players expressed to me that they couldn't believe what Shirley did. She was losing more and more respect. The girls said she had no right to bench me, and it wasn't fair to me or the team. They said I was expressing their feelings and not just my own.

Although we felt we would never go to the extreme of quitting—nor did we want to—the thought was still there. We enjoyed the game and loved the team. We wanted to fix things now to save the remaining two thirds of the season.

Our team had to do something, but what? And me? What should I do? Unfortunately, the fun and enjoyment of the sport is gone. Shirley had taken the importance of basketball away. No longer does my heart hold the love I once had for this terrific game.

▶ The Misbranded Goat

In March 1976, I was approached by Fred Wilson, director of engineering of the eastern division of our parent company, about a job assignment that he hoped would interest me. Fred and I had never worked together, but each knew of the other's characteristics and accomplishments. Everyone with whom I spoke knew Fred as brash, impersonal, demanding, and short tempered. During our prejob negotiations, Fred (who had been drafted for this division about one year

This case was prepared under the supervision of David L. Bradford as a basis for class discussion rather than to illustrate either effective or ineffective handling of an administrative situation. Reprinted from *Stanford Business Cases 1983* with permission of Stanford University Graduate School of Business.

ago) confided to me that corporate had given him approval to do whatever was necessary to turn his division into a productive and efficient organization. He also explained that when he delved into the personnel statistics, he found that the group (with a few exceptions) had been formed with lower-quartile people. In order to upgrade the group, he immediately acquired a few key upper-quartile employees. Fred was offering me a new position reporting directly to him. His ultimate goal was to return to the northwest division with me as his replacement in the east.

On my first workday, Fred informed me that there were three "dumb ass" engineering managers working for me that he wanted replaced as soon as possible. Because of my recent arrival, I begged off for 30 days so that I might become familiar with the division. Initially I assumed that Fred was correct in the assessment of the three managers; but as time progressed, one of the three (Ray) appeared to differ from the other two. Ray responded instantly to requests made of him, accepted any task that was put forth, and worked diligently to get good, justifiable solutions. My concerns for the job and the people influenced me to apply more than normal amounts of time observing their work habits and performance. At meetings and in discussions with other organizations it became apparent that Ray had the respect and confidence of everyone on the program with the exception of Fred.

During lunch with Fred one day, I asked him to explain his reasons for wanting to replace the three. His concerns regarding the other two were understandable, but I pursued his opinions on Ray. Fred considered Ray worthless and felt that all of the problems seemed to originate from Ray's area. His releases were usually late and/or incomplete, he lacked the answers to important questions, and he was continually asking for more people even though the manpower curve for the division was in the reducing mode.

After expressing himself very vividly, Fred tensely questioned my concerns about Ray. Listening to my observations, Fred became very upset. He ordered me to quit wasting time with Ray and to speed up the process of his replacement.

My next move was to check on Ray's background. Assessment of Ray's personnel folder revealed no negative statements. Actually it was just the reverse. In his last 14 years of employment in our company he had had a variety of engineering and management assignments. In every case, Ray's capabilities in design, management, and cooperation had been praised. This was later verified when I spoke to his previous supervisors.

Being thoroughly confused at this point, I decided to confront Ray. In the two-hour discussion that followed, Ray stated that Fred had informed him personally, prior to my arrival, that he was going to be fired. I asked Ray to explain his perception of Fred's reasoning. His story concurred with Fred's. His releases were late, even though he was working 40–50 percent overtime. He repeatedly requested additional personnel, and his area was the major origin of problems. He also had difficulty answering some of Fred's questions related to the early parts of the program. But Ray also pointed out that he had been assigned his area of responsibility only six months prior to Fred's arrival. Since the program was over four years old, the design problems had been created by managers that Ray had replaced. However, each time that he had used this reasoning, Fred had become more and more irate. Ray also expressed the feeling that his workload was considerably greater than in other areas. I closed the discussions with the promise that I would continue to work on the problem and that in my opinion the harassment was unjustified. I informed Ray that I appreciated the fine job that he was doing and requested that he continue his good performance.

Next I studied the workload in all areas and found evidence confirming Ray's analysis. I then shuffled available manpower so that the capability was more evenly distributed. I explained to Fred that I had no plans to replace Ray and, in fact, thought that he was doing a creditable job. Fred became furious and made it quite clear that Ray's performance could reflect on me.

In the months that followed, Ray continued to do his tasks well. His group started meeting schedules and eventually eliminated the need for overtime. However, Fred continued his relentless badgering. In meetings and in the group, he continued to try to embarrass Ray, especially when I was present. To my amazement Fred didn't apply the harassment to me. In fact he seemed to give me more and more freedom and responsibility as time went on.

▸ The Montville Hospital Dietary Department

INTRODUCTION

Rene Marcotte briskly walked home from her part-time job with the Montville Hospital Dietary Department. "Mom," she said as she entered the house, "they may have to close down the hospital! The Montville Department of Health has just found the Dietary Depart-

From S. Fink, S. Jenks, and R. Willits, *Designing and Managing Organizations*, 1983, pages 568–75. Reproduced by permission of Richard D. Irwin, Inc., Homewood, Ill.

ment's sanitary conditions to be substandard. Mrs. DeMambro, our chief supervisor, said that we are really going to have to get to work and clean the place or the hospital is in trouble!"

THE HOSPITAL

As Rene continued to tell her mother about this latest event, she thought about her part-time job at the hospital, which she had had now for almost a year. Montville Hospital was a 400-bed community general hospital located in suburban Montville outside of New York City. Montville itself was a racially mixed community of low- and middle-income working families. However, Montville, along with most hospitals, was operating under severe financial pressure and needed to constantly find ways to reduce costs. It offered a range of medical services, but due to the nature of the Montville population, it had an appreciable number of elderly terminal patients. The hospital was well thought of by the community both as a place of treatment and as a source of employment. Through the years it had received strong financial support from the community and had grown as the community had grown. It currently was building a new wing to keep up with expanding demand, and this added to its tight financial situation.

THE DIETARY DEPARTMENT

The Dietary Department, where Rene worked, was located in the wing that had been added during the previous expansion project a little more than 10 years ago. This department employed approximately 100 employees (mostly female) and was under the direction of Mr. Thomas Ellis, food service director. The department employed cooks, dieticians, and "kitchen workers" (of whom Rene was one). The department had two major responsibilities—namely, the planning, preparation, and serving of three meals a day to every patient, and the operation of an employees' cafeteria. Since most of the patients required special diets, such as salt-free diets, the food for each was quite different, although cooked in a common kitchen.

Rene well remembered her initial contact with the department. When applying for a job, she was first "screened" by the hospital personnel office, then sent to be interviewed by Mrs. Kelley, the chief dietary supervisor, and after a second interview by Mrs. Kelley, given a "tour" through the kitchen facilities by one of the supervisors. She never saw Mr. Ellis or Mrs. Johnston, the chief dietician. As she later learned, Mrs. Kelley did all of the hiring and firing, while salary and raises were determined by the payroll department. Rene felt as if Mr.

Ellis were some kind of "god," when she eventually heard of his existence two weeks after starting work.

Upon being hired, Rene was put right to work with no formal instructions in standards or procedures. She, as every other new employee, was expected to learn by watching others and asking her peers. Rene, who undertook the job with a deep sense of responsibility, well remembers one of the older kids saying to her, "Hurry up, you're taking too long; don't bother to clean up those spots of spilled soup."

Along with Rene, the majority of the employees were kitchen workers (diet aides, dishwashers, and porters). Ninety-five percent were female. Twenty-five were full-timers working 40 hours per week, and 50–60 were part-timers, as was Rene.

Ten years ago the Dietary Department was smaller and under the direction of one of the current dieticians. There were no food service director and no chief dietary supervisor positions. While the kitchen was centralized at that time, tray preparation was not. This was done in a kitchenette located on each floor of the hospital. The workers moved from floor to floor, serving food from bulk containers onto individual trays on each floor. The dishroom was also separated physically. When the new wing was built, everything was centralized into one location from which carts of setup trays are sent out to each floor. Now, only the diet aides went to the floors and only for the purpose of distributing and collecting trays from the patients.

The Full-Time Employees

The full-time employees were mostly older women (40–65 years of age) who had been working in the department for a long time; some for 15–20 years. All lived in Montville; most had a high school education; many were married, and most were helping to augment the family income so that their children could be the first in their family to go to college. With few exceptions, they worked a morning shift from either 6:30 A.M. to 3:00 P.M. or 8:00 A.M. to 4:30 P.M.

Most of the women had worked in this organization back in the old days before the hospital expanded and the kitchen was rebuilt. They had many stories to tell about how it used to be and how much easier and less chaotic their jobs had been before the change. One woman, who had recently been reemployed, had worked in the same Dietary Department 20 years ago as a teenager. She was amazed at how different everything was and said how she felt she was in another world from the job she used to know and love 20 years ago. The women, however, took great pride in their work (many had been doing the same job for years). Each woman had her own assigned task, which she did every day, and there was little shifting around of positions.

The dessert- or salad-makers never learned much about the work routine of the tray-coverers, silverware-sorters, or juice-setter-uppers. Every woman was set in a specific routine during a day's work. This routine was heavily controlled by the tight time schedule everyone had to follow. There was no fooling around even though the working atmosphere was very congenial and everyone was on a first-name basis, including the supervisors. There was considerable conversation among the women while they worked, but it did not distract them from doing their jobs—perhaps because management required the workers to completely finish their assigned tasks before leaving for home, even if it meant working overtime, without extra pay.

There was a striking cross section of cultural backgrounds among these full-time employees. There were about equal numbers of whites, blacks, and orientals, and many were immigrants. Many spoke Spanish and very little English. Although a language barrier existed between many of the employees, feelings of mutual respect and friendliness were maintained. Malicious gossip due to racial or ethnic differences was uncommon, and the women helped each other when necessary to finish their jobs on time.

The women often expressed their concern about not getting their jobs done on time, especially when they were working the assembly line. This assembly line consisted of sending a tray down a belt, along which, at certain intervals, each worker put a specific item on the tray as designated by the menu for each patient. After each tray was completed, it was put in an electric cart with each cart containing trays for different floors of the hospital. The carts were then pulled (by men porters) into elevators and transferred to the designated floors. At this time, pairs of diet aides (not working on the line) were sent to the floors to deliver the trays to the patients. Speed and efficiency in delivering trays were very important. If the trays were sent up and then left standing for a long time before delivery to each patient, the food got cold and the Dietary Department received complaints directed at the dieticians. The complaints were relayed to the supervisor, who in turn reprimanded the diet aide(s) responsible for the cold food. This temporarily disrupted the very informal and friendly working relationship between the diet aides and their supervisor, whom they liked and respected, causing uncomfortable guilt feelings for the diet aides. As a result, reprimands were seldom necessary among the full-timers.

At the same time, the diet aides were expected to meet certain established standards governing such matters as size of portion, cleanliness of kitchen facilities, and cleanliness in food handling and preparation. At times, in fact rather often, the standards were overlooked under the pressure of time. For instance, if the line was to be started at exactly 11 A.M. and if by that time the desserts were not wrapped or covered, as required by sanitary regulations, the line might begin anyway, and the desserts went to the patients unwrapped.

The full-time employees received pay raises designated by a set scale based on continuing length of employment. Starting salary was about average for this type of work. They were allowed a certain number of sick days per year as well as paid vacations (the length of which were based on the numbers of years of employment). The uniforms they were required to wear were provided (three per person) by the hospital and could be laundered free of charge at the hospital laundry service. Also the workers paid very little money, if anything at all, for meals eaten at work. Technically they were supposed to pay in full for meals, but seldom did, because of lack of consistent control.

Work performance was evaluated on the basis of group effort. Individual effort usually was not singled out and rewarded in any tangible way. However, supervisors would often compliment an individual on how nice a salad plate looked or how quickly and efficiently a worker delivered the patients' trays. For instance, the woman who prepared fancy salad plates and sandwiches could take pride in the way they looked. Furthermore, the aides recognized that their work could affect a patient's well-being and therefore could be important, and sometimes a patient was a former hospital staff member or neighbor known by the aides. When delivering a tray, a diet aide might chat with a patient and discover particular likes or dislikes, which, when reported to the dietician, sometimes led to a revision in the patient's diet.

Extra care was often taken in arranging food on the tray in an attractive manner to please the patient. Sometimes this dedication produced minor problems such as when a diet aide violated certain rules in order to do something extra for a patient or to promote her own version of efficiency in doing a task. This type of individual initiative (and creativity) was not encouraged. Management set down rigid guidelines for performing all tasks as the only correct way, since they worked out for so many years. Any recommendations for changes in these techniques were approached with caution by management. The equipment also had changed little in the past decade.

The Part-Time Employees

There were 50–60 part-time employees in the Dietary Department whose level of pay was appreciably less than that of the full-timers. They were divided into two teams (team A and team B); each team worked on alternate days of the week and on alternate weekends, a device adopted on the advice of some efficiency experts as a way of avoiding having to pay overtime to anyone. There was no specific supervisor for each team; instead each might have one of two supervisors depending on the day and/or week. Two different shifts exist for the part-timers: 3:30–6:30 and 4:00–8:00 (the kitchen closed at 8 P.M.), but on the average all part-timers including Rene worked a 16-hour week. Their duties were the same as the full-timers, except that part-timers served and cleaned up after dinner instead of after breakfast and lunch. The majority of these workers were young, mostly high school age (16–18 years), working for extra money and because friends were working. Most had not worked in the hospital very long as there was a constant turnover as individuals left to go to college, etc., but other kids were readily available to take their places. There were also several older women, working on a part-time basis, who had been with the organization for many years.

The part-timers' situation exhibited a striking contrast to that of full-timers. There were no permanent task assignments; each night a part-timer did something different, and the kids often asked to do this or that different task. As a group, the night shift was not as unified in spirit or congeniality as the day shift (full-timers). The younger workers tended to form cliques apart from the older women and gossip and poke fun at non–English-speaking workers.

Most of the teenagers also took their work much less seriously than did the older women (the full-timers), doing only what was required at the most minimal level. As was the case with the full-timers, they worked on a tight schedule and their working behavior was heavily controlled by it. However, they seemed more anxious to get their work done as soon as possible. Once they had finished, they were free to leave no matter what time it was at no loss of pay; that is, if everyone was finished at, say, 7:45 P.M., all could leave yet still be paid until 8:00 P.M. It was not uncommon for work areas to become messy, for hands to be left unwashed, and for food to be handled and touched even though it shouldn't be. They also tended to devise their own ways for doing the job, partially to promote efficiency and decrease the time needed for completion. It was not uncommon to hear a more experienced teenage part-timer tell a newcomer, "Oh, come on, we don't have to do it that way. Don't be so eager; relax and enjoy yourself." The supervisor seemed to have little control over the teenagers. They ignored her comments or talked back to her and continued doing things their own way. The working atmosphere was informal and friendly, with everyone on a first-name basis except for the supervisor. At times there was a high pitch of excitement among the kids as everyone kidded one another, sang songs, and generally socialized together. At times this led to mistakes being made, which infuriated the supervisor but didn't bother the kids, as they had little respect for her.

Conflict existed between the supervisor and the teenagers about wearing the required hairnets (especially the boys) and aprons and such procedures as not eating during work. They seldom took reprimands seriously, saying that they "hated their job" but needed the money. In general, however, these young diet aides did complete their required tasks in the time allotted, although the quality was often substandard. There was not a total lack of concern for quality because, if so, they would have lost their jobs, and they knew this; but quality was maintained most strongly only when "it didn't take too long."

There did exist some conflict between the older and younger workers during the night shift. The older women did not approve of the young people's attitudes even though those older women who worked at night did not exhibit as much pride in their work as did their daytime counterparts. They resented the teenagers' new and different ways of doing jobs, as was especially evident when an older woman was assigned to work with a teenager for the evening.

The Management

With regard to the management staff of the Dietary Department, there were several people involved. Mr. Ellis was the man to whom everyone else was ultimately responsible as the food service director. He was an older man, hired by the hospital about five years previously. A flashy dresser, he wore no uniform and spent most of the day in his office. He rarely talked to anyone in the department except the chief dietician and the chief dietary supervisor. He communicated to the rest of the employees by way of memos posted on a bulletin board in the kitchen. His memos usually contained instructions, telling the workers to change or improve some facet of their jobs. He also relayed messages down the ranks via the supervisors to the workers. About once a day he would walk through the kitchen in a very formal manner, apparently observing what was going on. The diet aides (and supervisors) became very conscious of their actions as he walked by, hoping they were doing everything right. When questioned about this man, the workers expressed feelings of curiosity mixed with an element of fear. The only time a diet aide came into direct contact with him was on payday, when she entered his office to receive her check after he signed it. One recently hired employee said that she thought that his main job was signing paychecks. There was obviously much confusion by workers concerning who this man really was. He was the mystery man of management to them.

A second management person was the chief dietician, Mrs. Johnston, a woman in her late 30s. Her job was mainly administrative in nature, acting as a consultant to the dieticians and assisting them when the workload was heavy or someone was out sick. She also helped out in the kitchen once in awhile if the kitchen staff was especially shorthanded. In general, however, she tended to remain relatively formal and distant from the workers, although, when she had suggestions to make, she often went directly to the workers instead of using memos. Her relationship with the four dieticians was informal and friendly, and she was highly respected by them for her technical excellence as a dietician.

The chief dietary supervisor, Mrs. Kelly (about age 44), was in charge of hiring and firing. She was also responsible for making up employee schedules week by week, especially those involving the scheduling of the part-time workers. Workers went to her with gripes and requests for favors and special days off. She was generally sympathetic to employee problems, having been one of them about six years ago before she became the chief supervisor. In general, she was relatively informal with the workers although not on a first-name basis. The employees respected her, and her authority was rarely questioned or challenged by any of the workers. She seemed to be regarded as the real boss, rather than the two people who ranked above her.

These three people constituted the main power structure in the Dietary Department. They tended to keep to themselves socially as well as physically. They never ate with the workers and seldom communicated with them except about their work. If any changes, plans, or decisions were to be made, they were made by these three people, the final say being had by the food service director. The supervisors were then told of any new policy and expected to inform the workers and implement the change. The chief dietary supervisor (CDS) seemed to act as a middleman between the director and the workers. When she (or the director) felt that the workers were "sloughing off," a staff meeting would be called and she would exhort everyone to shape up. For instance, a meeting was called after an unusually large number of complaints were received about patients receiving cold food. The CDS said, "We are here to help these patients get well as best we can—they are sick and deserve the best possible care. They won't eat cold food, and that slows down their recovery. Keeping the food warm is more important than whether or not you want to hurry to get the day's work done."

Other members of the management staff included the supervisors, whose main responsibilities involved the diet aides and other kitchen workers. The supervisors, who in all cases were former diet aides, worked in the kitchen. They assigned jobs, made sure they got done, maintained discipline and order (hopefully), and helped out when needed. In general, they saw that everything ran smoothly. Altogether, there were three supervisors, one of whom was part-time. They took turns covering the weekends and thus had contact with all employees, although they worked with one group most of the time.

The cooks and the dieticians were the other members of the department. The cooks' job was to prepare the food according to standard recipes and to put it on the serving line at meal times. They did their jobs efficiently and effectively. They kept to themselves, eating together and not mingling with the diet aides. The dieticians also kept to themselves both physically and socially. They had their own office and ate together. Little was seen of them by the workers; however, when approached, they seemed quite friendly.

THE CURRENT PROBLEM

The State Board of Health makes periodic, unannounced visits to the Dietary Department to determine whether it meets certain sanitary standards. Although the hospital believes that the Board of Health interprets the regulations too strictly, there is little it can do except make efforts to satisfy any criticisms made by the inspectors.

In the past, the director of the Dietary Department managed to find out when the inspectors were coming and prepared for the visit by a frantic two- to three-day major clean-up campaign. Historically, this has resulted in Montville passing the inspection. However, over the past two to three months, the inspectors have become more successful in making their visits a complete surprise. Frantic efforts to clean up took place the last time during the brief period of time it took the inspectors to get from their car to the kitchen. As a result, the department recently failed the inspection and was given a limited amount of time to correct the situation or else face being shut down. The department did pass a reinspection, but only because of a lot of extra pressure put on workers to do extra cleaning during and after working hours (for overtime pay) for several days. If the organization should fail inspection repeatedly, it will be required to shut down indefinitely. The impact of this would be catastrophic for the hospital as a whole, since it must provide food for both patients and employees! Rene wondered what the hospital would do about the situation and how it might affect her job situation.

▸ Multi-Proaucts, Inc.

"The average young fellow today has no concept of how to beat a competitor and how to squeeze money out of every dollar," Richard B. Haws, president of Multi-Products, Inc., of Los Angeles, California, said in February 1959 to Bertram Stace, an old friend and stockholder. "It's not really their fault—they've just had lousy training over the past 20–30 years, as far as the acceptance of responsibility and of being held accountable for the stewardship of a job is concerned. If we ever begin to have a depression as we did back in 1929–31, God knows how the industries of this country would suffer. Just look at the way they waste money. . . ."

MR. HAWS'S CAREER, 1902–1956

"I was born in 1902, the son of poor parents," Mr. Haws continued. "One day when I was a small boy I was sitting in our hometown drugstore and the wealthy owner of a pottery (his son lost all of it) came in and sat down beside me. He talked to the druggist and then he turned to me and said, 'No use talking to you; you'll never have any money.' I will never forget those words. I don't resent them—they were the greatest driving force in my life. If they've been before my eyes once, they've been before them 5 million times."

Picking up his office copy of *Who's Who*, Mr. Haws showed Mr. Stace that he had attended college for three years, worked as a salesman in a local business for another five, and then moved to New York in 1929 to sell for the Lawton Machinery Company. "We were living in a nice apartment and had all our money in the market when the crash came. I went to our landlord and asked him to let me break the lease, but he pointed out that he needed money more than ever now and refused. I went home to think about it and then returned and pleaded with him to let us move to one of his cheaper apartments. Finally he agreed. He moved us the next day and that night brought up a new lease for me to sign. I looked him in the eye and said, 'Oh no. When you moved us out of that first apartment, you broke the lease. We're moving out of here tomorrow.' That's the sort of sharp thinking—in that case born out of financial necessity—that young fellows don't seem to use today. They certainly don't learn it in business schools."

Mr. Haws thought his Lawton Machine Company days had been an invaluable experience. "Young fellows today are soft—they don't believe me when I tell them that my wife often would wait for my phone call in the late afternoon to see if I'd sold a machine. If so, I'd have enough money for her to buy food for supper! Those were the days when we were ashamed to admit we had lost an order. We were paid straight commission; anyone could ask for a raise but all you got was 'Go out and sell some more machines.' I remember the sales manager used to say, 'Any salesman can come in, push the desk in my lap, and call me a S.O.B. as long as he produces—but he'd better keep on producing.'

"When I was with Lawton, I met a young statistician whose head was full of ideals and up in the clouds, but he was dead broke. I suggested he sell machines until he found another job. I showed him the sales pitch and sent him off with a machine under his arm. The next day he was back saying he couldn't take it. I told him anybody could sell machines, and if he couldn't he had no guts. He stuck with it two months until he got another statistical job. You've got to have guts and imagination to get someplace. A friend of mine who was president of a large company put it this way, 'If I have a guy around me who hasn't been in jail, I have a weak man!'

"It was during my time with Lawton that I realized I wanted a nice house, expensive car, fine clothes—the things that money can buy. I decided then and there I had the ants in my pants to want excitement and to get all or nothing. If you know what you want and what you can afford, it's pretty easy to set up a program for yourself. I've tried to get others to do the same, but they don't. It's pretty difficult for a young man or a student because he's not had the business experience to see what you can get out of life and what money will buy. But then, even older men don't do it. Take my associate, Joel Dennis. He's happy to earn about $15 an hour, save up for a new expensive camera, throw on a $47 suit of clothes that doesn't fit properly, and just lead that sort of life. Maybe he's happy, but he doesn't have the ants in his pants I do. . . ."

Mr. Haws told his friend that he decided he didn't aspire to be a Lawton sales manager but rather wanted a "show of my own" and was willing to pay for the necessary experience. He had left his $18,000 Lawton job to work first for a large company as a $6,000-a-year procedures man and later for a medium-sized company as a financial officer. During his stay with the second company he was given warrants and stock. When he left he had about 27,500 shares, which had cost him some $12,000; by 1959 these shares were worth over $1 million. In

1953 he became president of a small manufacturing company, and four years later he was asked to head Multi-Products, Inc.

MULTI-PRODUCTS, INC., 1946–1956

Mr. Haws's friend, Mr. Stace, was a stockholder in Multi-Products, Inc., and knew something about its early history from published records. The company was founded by Earle M. Cave in January 1946 to make a consumer item. By 1951 the company had lost some $500,000 on five years' sales of $625,000, and Mr. Cave started a new line. During the next two years Multi-Products expanded into two related and one unrelated line through acquiring three small companies. The company's 1954 statements showed a net profit of about $290,000 on $5.7 million sales, a net worth of $3.3 million, and an accumulated deficit of $80,000; however, the auditors "were unable to form an opinion as to the overall results of operation" because management had decided to defer certain expenses totaling $375,000.

The next year, Mr. Stace recalled, the company ran into difficulties. The June 1955 quarterly report showed a six months' profit of about $60,000 on about $2.7 million sales, but when the annual report came out, there were losses of about $3.6 million on $6 million sales.

Early in 1956 the company underwent litigation. Mr. Stace recalled the basic issues were whether the net income for the period ending June 30, 1955, were overstated and both income statement and balance sheet invalid and whether at the time the quarterly report was issued management knew the company was operating at a loss. The testimony showed that four entries, labeled "management adjustments" by the disapproving controller, had turned a $300,000 March-quarter loss into a $60,000 profit before the statement was forwarded to the company's banks. The court ruled that the June profit had been overstated by almost $1 million owing to improper deferment of certain expenses, calculation of the cost of goods sold on the basis of cost formulae rather than by using the cost system, and failure to establish reserves for anticipated losses.

In court Mr. Cave said that accounting, especially details such as divisional operating data or cost entries, was beyond his "purview of operation," interest, or knowledge. He stated that he relied completely on the judgment of Mr. Bangs, vice president of finance, on all accounting matters, and on the auditors on all financial questions pertaining to the company statements. He said that in general "it was not my custom to have any contact whatsoever with the people at the working level, such as Mr. Land or Mr. Heyden (assistant controllers). If I had identified myself at any time with the minutiae between the juniors below any of the vice presidents, then I would have been totally unable to have kept my proper purview of the overall operation of the company and longer-term planning of the company. I stayed expressly away from all matters which fell totally below the vice presidential levels." He said the first time he had "any conception" of the losses was when the new auditors showed him the 1955 financial statements in February 1956 after his return from a vacation. Besides, over $2 million was due to auditors' adjustments.

Both Mr. Cave and the Multi-Products, Inc., counsel stressed that investors bought the company's stock on the basis of its potential long-term growth, not the statements, and so it would not have materially mattered one iota if the six months' statement ending March had shown a profit or a small loss. According to published reports, Mr. Cave never owned over 2 percent of Multi-Products, Inc., stock and did not speculate.

After losing $4 million on $5.9 million sales in 1956, the firm faced financial disaster. Only selling a large block of shares at $2 a share to an investment fund in January 1957 avoided bankruptcy. (Mr. Stace ruefully recalled that the stock back in 1952 had sold for $42 a share.) New directors and a new management, including Mr. Haws, were brought in, and the division making products unrelated to the other lines was sold.

MULTI-PRODUCTS, INC., UNDER MR. HAWS'S MANAGEMENT, 1957–1959

Mr. Haws explained to Mr. Stace that since coming to Multi-Products, Inc., he had concentrated on three areas: organization, acquisitions, and employee motivation and compensation.

Organization

"For about the first month after I joined Multi-Products, Inc., I just watched operations and got the feel of the situation," Mr. Haws said. "Then I went to work on our organization. There were 51 people in the accounting department. I called in the head of the department and told him to move the people into another room. He protested there was only room for 12 there, and I said, 'That's right; by tomorrow you'll only have 12 people in your department.' I also called in the head of the merchandising department and showed him a new room with space for three people and the secretary. He had to reduce his staff from 11. Quality control had seven people and a secretary. I told the superintendent he would have two people including himself to do all the scheduling, the expediting, and control. The department heads said this was impossible. I said, 'All right. I will stay after five o'clock tonight and want you to come in and tell me if you're man enough for the job or else resign.'

"Actually, volume had grown much better than I anticipated, and we still have only 12 people in the accounting department. Goes to show there were a lot of people sitting around on their hands doing nothing. You know, a partially employed person is the most ineffectual person in the business; he is inaccurate, lazy, and—worst of all—keeps other people from working.

"About March I took the department heads to dinner at the hotel. I told them what I was trying to do, put up a sales and profit chart, and said, "We'll start work at 8:15 in the morning and not 8:45 or whenever you seem to feel like wandering in.' The treasurer broke in with, 'Let's take a vote on it.' I said, 'Fine, but if anyone votes against the proposal, I'll accept his resignation.' There was no vote.

"After the meeting the treasurer said, 'You certainly got off easy.' I replied, 'No, I had to listen to you. That's enough anguish for one evening. I don't have enough cash on me, so come in tomorrow morning and you can get your check.' I fired him right there; he was 45 years old but as yet he had not learned that organization conduct was more important than personal convenience."

In reorganizing the company, Mr. Haws said he decided whom to let go almost on a replacement basis. "Who cares about accountants, salesmen, shop supervisors, or treasurers? But purchasing agents, merchandisers, and engineers are rather important to you. You have to know where to start a fight and where not to. You must move slowly because you have not possession of all the facts. . . ."

Acquisitions and New Business

The company needed to generate sufficient new business to utilize the large loss carry-forward generated since December 31, 1955. "The fundamental reason for our being in business is to utilize the tax losses," Mr. Haws explained. During 1957 he revamped the product line, acquired two small companies making similar products, and reduced the size of the loss to about $470,000 on sales of $3.7 million. By June 1958 the company showed earnings $75,000 on sales of about $2 million, but much faster profit generation was needed. Mr. Haws started to diversify.

The first acquisition was the Seward Company, which was obtained through an exchange of stock in July 1958. Shortly before, Seward had invested in a relatively large amount of new fixed assets. By changing the write-off period from 3 years to 10, Multi-Products maximized the immediate profit and thus effectively deferred the tax loss carry-forward beyond its normal expiration date. The extra profit was recorded as deferred income on the statements and was included in income for tax purposes only. By February 1959 Multi-Products had protected almost $1 million of its tax loss.

The other two unrelated businesses were bought in October 1958 and January 1959 on an "incentive" basis. Mr. Haws explained, "The man who owned the first one foresaw estate problems and wanted to sell the business for $1.5 million, its asset value. I said I would offer him $2 million if I could have it my own way with less than 30 percent down. I paid him $500,000 and picked up $400,000 of the company's cash the next day. In order to make up the $1 million balance of his original $1.5 million asking price, he will receive two thirds of the after-tax profit without limit of time. Obviously, if there are never any profits, he will never get any more than the down payment already made. Over the next five years, if his two-thirds share of the profits generate more than the $1.5 million asking price, he gets his excess up to the full $2 million offer. The business is currently producing after-tax profits of $40,000 a month. I was talking to the seller the other day about putting out his fancy profit-sharing ideas, Cadillacs, hotel suites, and other perquisites, and he said he wouldn't work so hard without them. I replied, 'You scare me to death! You've only got $500,000 for your company so far, and that's *all* you get if you don't produce profits.' I paid $25,000 down for the second business, which has $280,000 in cash, and made a similar incentive arrangement for the rest of the sales price.

"In other words, I am giving these men an incentive to continue to produce profits and thus am much more sophisticated than others using similar formulas. Some are good at this sort of thing. They pay an inflated cost above the company's net worth as a *contractual* obligation, which puts ether on the balance sheet as goodwill or some other evasive term, and they have to amortize the ether over a stipulated period on their operating statement, which adversely affects profits and gives their stockholders an untrue picture of earnings. On the other hand, I give the seller the full purchase price above asset value *only* if he earns it.

"I can't understand acquiring a company to add to your losses. Men who contractually overpay must be either awfully young or look too far into the future. Look at this article in today's *Wall Street Journal*[1] about Mr. Zeckendorf's company. Real estate is the safest investment in an inflationary economy, and Webb & Knapp's assets have grown from $7 million in 1945 to $210 million in 1957; yet it lost money last year. The common stockholders have never received a dividend, and the preferred is $60 in arrears. When that happens, something is really wrong! Anytime you increase assets, your return investment should

[1] *The Wall Street Journal*, February 9, 1959, p. 1. Copyright © 1959 by Dow Jones & Company, Inc.

increase proportionately. There's no point in getting big just for bigness' sake. Under my incentive system, we know the management of the purchased company will work hard to show a profit and not allow earnings to show a decreased return on investment."

Employee Motivation and Compensation

"The problem that really concerns me the most is turning young men into cost- and profit-conscious executives who are worried about getting sales, controlling costs, setting profitable prices, and spending the company's money. I put a young man in charge of a division. He'd go out and buy some steel. If it were too brittle, would he tell the purchasing department to send it back? Heavens no! He'd just put it in inventory! Same with capital equipment. He'd buy some machinery, and if it didn't work, he'd put it to one side and forget about it, and not even try to get salvage value out of it. Another division head was losing $120,000 but was very indignant when I called him into the office to hear what he was going to do about it because he thought we could just borrow money from a bank. I said, 'You've got 60 days to turn this situation around. I've got no place in the company for a loser.'

"I've got another fellow who came in and said, 'It has been just 14 months since my last raise.' I said, 'What do you want to talk about?' He replied, 'My raise.' And I said, 'The length of time has no relation as to whether you get a raise or not.' I added that he was reviewed a few months ago, at which time he told me about how many letters he wrote but didn't tell me what business he had brought into the house and the profit that he had earned. He replied, 'I worked hard,' and I said, 'I don't know about that. We've got working rules that you start work at 8:15; you're here at 8:30 or 8:45, and during the baseball season you're at the ball park. Sure, I know that you tell the secretaries that you are calling on a customer, but I just happen to know that you were at the baseball game. You come back tomorrow and tell me how much business you have brought in, and how much profit you have made for the company, and whether you are earning the salary you have.'

"Engineers are far too loyal to what they call their 'professional ethics.' A company may have a contract to do something, but the engineer will see that he could do it just that much better. The customer didn't ask for it, the specifications didn't ask for it, and if we do it, we won't be able to make a profit or deliver on time. But because of this professional idealism, the engineer goes ahead and does it anyway, with the result that we lose money, the customer is mad because we are late, and perhaps it doesn't work any better than it would have anyway.

"All the other professions—doctors, lawyers, teachers—except the engineer have to collect their bills. Ninety-nine percent of the latter are living off somebody else's money. If you ask them what have they contributed to earn their money, they are insulted. And if I suggested I wasn't going to pay them unless they contributed to the company, they'd quit. It's never seemed to dawn on some of them that they have to earn their keep.

"Dr. Collins is an example. I noticed that he had more and more unexcused absences and was coming in at 9 to 10 A.M. and leaving at 3 P.M. so I inquired around and learned he was discussing setting up his own company. I called him in the next day and said, 'Let's let our hair down. I'm not going to have this sloppy behavior.' He said, 'You never said anything about my working Saturdays and Sundays when we set up that new division,' to which I replied, 'No, I didn't say anything about my doing it either, but that's why we pay you a good salary. When are you going to leave?' He asked me when I wanted him to and got the reply, 'Tomorrow.' He said, 'I'd hoped you'd let me stay around until I get my company going. Anyway, my time ought to be my own.' And I said, 'OK, fine. I'll give you a check tomorrow and you'll have all the free time you want.' You know, he's got a wife, two kids, is buying a home, but doesn't recognize the security he owes his family judging by the way he treated his job. His company never got off the ground, and now he's broke and looking for a job. I'd like to help him, but my responsibility ended when he transferred his loyalties.

"Expense accounts and perquisites are another problem. Some fellows never put a limit on their hotel bill, so of course they get the most expensive room in the house. I just stopped three executives from leaving in the company plane at 3 P.M. instead of 5 P.M. They just wanted to get to their destination in time for supper; they hadn't thought that their salaries cost the company \$55 an hour, or \$110. Another young fellow came in here and said the company should give him a country club membership for entertaining customers. I said, 'No. You may be entertaining five customers now, but soon it will be 15 people because in fact the company would be paying for your wife's and kids' weekends at the club.'

"You find this lack of cost consciousness at all levels of the organization. Take those three girls out there who are executive secretaries and assistants and are paid from \$450 to \$550 per month. I told them, 'I have a fetish against coffee breaks, which I think are the doom of American industry. Just get a few people around a coffee machine, and I'll bet three out of five of them will have something to gripe about. You are being paid enough money to know that this really does cost money. I don't want coffee drunk at the desk, but if you want to drink coffee, you can check in and out on a time clock and be paid an ordinary clerical salary.' I also asked them to exert their influence on the other girls to try and stop this coffee break business.

"About a week later I went past the coffee machine and found one of the three girls there talking to another secretary. She asked me if I would like a cup of coffee, and I said I couldn't afford it. She said, 'Oh, I would be glad to spend the 10 cents.' And I said, 'That's not the point. The company can't afford the time.' So I put in an order to cut her salary $50 per month. That brought all three girls into my office saying it was a very unfair thing to do. I said, 'I wasn't unfair. Here's a girl who violated an order that I had given. . . .' I then pointed out that I am not running a charitable organization, but running a business, and I can't allow any individuals to destroy the organization. So she has $50 less a month.

"In short I guess people don't realize—and perhaps I didn't either when I was an employee—that you buy manpower the same way you buy productive machinery. You must get a return for your investment.

"We have constant reviews and checks to be sure we're getting a return. Those with an annual salary of $6,000 or less get a semiannual review, while those over $6,000 get an annual one. If the supervisor doesn't recommend a raise, the man has 90 days to correct the faults found. If he does not correct them, he is out. Of course, when I let a man go the supervisors often come in and really squawk; however, they are more careful the next time when writing their appraisals.

"There are several ways I check on the supervisors' evaluations. I sometimes call in a supervisor and make up fictitious stories about how I never saw so-and-so at work, or how I always see him coming in at 9 o'clock in the morning. Then I ask him if he is afraid to put a complete evaluation on somebody. Then I start in on another man. I make him defend all his recommendations. Sometimes they just plain collapse—the supervisors can't really defend their recommendations. They have to have a really good look at what each man does and not just say the whole department has done well. Also, I'll pick out three or four cards sent to me by the personnel department on people coming up for review, and I'll walk around their departments in the morning and at 4:45 in the evening. You can really get an idea of how hard a person works by doing that a couple of times for three or four days. You pick up enough information to justify your comments, and my objections to the supervisors often hit near enough home."

Future Plans

Mr. Haws's long-term objective for the company was to utilize the tax loss carry-forward through more diversification, but he told Mr. Stace that his personal objective was to leave Multi-Products, Inc., after another year or so. "I've really worked myself out of a job; I don't do a darn thing except read The *Wall Street Journal* and look for new acquisitions." His contract, which he—but not the company—could cancel, was up in 1961. His salary was about $35,000 with a $17,500-a-year consulting fee guarantee for five years after leaving the company, and he had 60,000 of the 113,000 outstanding warrants at $2 a share. The stock was selling for $9 a share in February 1959.

In summing up his career, Mr. Haws felt he had learned to take calculated risks and win, but that young men with whom he worked did not do so. "If I ever had $5,000 in the bank, I'd be mad because it is not earning me a penny. When I am 60 or 65, I don't want to be a total dependent on somebody else, as 9/10 of these people are destined to be. I offered 5,000 shares of the company at $2 apiece to one young man, and he said, 'I'll let you know in awhile. I've got to think it over.' I said, 'I'll give you 10 seconds to decide and those 10 seconds have just passed, and the offer is off.' Heavens, a young man should have jumped at a chance like that!"

Newways Records

Robert Reingold, chief executive officer of Newways Records, Inc., leaned back in his leather chair and stared morosely at the gold and platinum records plastering his wall in commemoration of the many recording hits sold by Newways. Reingold looked modishly elegant in his designer tie and light blue-on-blue patterned shirt. He shook his head in perplexity while trying to sum up his problem for the case-writer seated on the other side of the polished wood desk.

> You know, I guess I shouldn't be surprised at this conflict between George England and Henry White; I knew there would be friction between the Newways veterans in sales and some of the marketing people I've brought in. But these two are grown men. They've been around this business a long time. I really think they should have solved their problems by now. Frankly, I'm of a mind that they shouldn't have had any problems in the first place. They have a job to do, and they should do it.

This case was prepared by William E. Zierden, Associate Professor, as a basis for class discussion rather than to illustrate either effective or ineffective handling of an administrative situation.

Newways Records was the subsidiary of a major international recording company. With home offices in a large city in the southeastern United States, Newways covered some 20 states across the entire southern part of the United States. In the past Newways had marketed, promoted, and sold records produced by the parent company, records featuring internationally known artists and performing groups primarily from England, France, and the United States. In addition to its sales activities, Newways had also manufactured records for regional distribution. Historically, the Newways sales force had relied upon the parent company's national marketing organization to promote new records in selected major cities in or adjacent to the Newways sales area. Once a record began to be widely played on key radio stations in the Newways listening area, the Newways sales force would then promote the record with local radio stations, record jobbers and individual store accounts.

Over the years the parent company had introduced numerous successful records. By following the marketing lead of the parent company in other parts of the United States, Newways had been able to grow at about the same pace as that of the record industry in general. Newways commanded a respectable share of the market in its area, a share which remained relatively stable during the early 1970s, an era of industry growth. In 1975 Newways grossed $60 million in sales and employed 400 people. By October 1976, sales were at an annual rate of about $75 million, which was 15 percent ahead of what had been projected for the year.

Marketing and Selling Records

Newways marketed three basic categories of records:

1. Records of enduring popularity, such as classical recordings and music from "classic" Broadway shows.
2. New popular music by known artists or from the soundtracks of current motion pictures.
3. New songs and albums by artists and groups that are generally not well known.

In general, recordings of classical, semiclassical, and show music that have achieved an enduring popularity are sold to dealers through a record company's catalog and to individuals through mail-order record clubs. Recordings in this category are usually promoted by price—a record company offers various albums from its catalog on special pricing arrangements. Special price deals are frequently offered to all customers on the same recording or group of recordings, or special price deals are negotiated by the sales force with large retailing chains, including discount stores and record store chains. In the case of a special promotion with a retail chain, the record company may agree to provide certain promotional support in return for a guaranteed minimum order. Promotional support can include point-of-purchase displays, promotional contests, and radio and newspaper advertising within specific geographical areas.

It is the normal policy in the record industry to accept unsold records that a dealer elects to return, crediting the returns to the dealer's account. Historically, returns have averaged 17–22 percent for the large record companies. Managing the return rate is considered a part of the sales function.

Recordings in the second and third categories require considerable promotional effort. New releases by unknown artists present the most difficult marketing challenge.

An early, critical step in promoting a new record is to have it played by radio disc jockeys in the targeted market areas. Disc jockeys are generally in search of new hit music and like to be able to play hit records before they are aired by other stations in the listening area. They are responsive to record company representatives who bring new releases to their attention before the records become national or international hits. In turn, the record company representative tries to build good relationships with disc jockeys who enjoy wide audience appeal. Since the "payola" scandals of the 1960s, when record company representatives were found to be paying disc jockeys to play their records, promotional incentives have generally been limited to small favors, such as concert tickets or invitations to meet recording stars.

To decide which records to push with a given disc jockey, a promotional representative must have a feel for the music and for the audience that a given radio station is trying to reach. In the case of unknown artists, the promotional representative relies on his or her own intuitive judgment about the potential appeal of a particular artist and song. People in the business talk about "believing in" an artist or a particular recording, with the idea that to promote untried recordings, sales and marketing people must "believe in" a recording in order to "break" it into the market.

Promoting and selling a record requires coordinating public demand and record availability. Public attention is generated through radio shows, local concerts, or, in the case of movie soundtracks, local theater showings. Attention is reinforced by media advertising and point-of-purchase displays. Many different people can play a role in promoting a record in a given market, including the artist, the artist's own promotion manager, radio disc jockeys, retail outlet owners and employers, newspaper and magazine music critics, as well as the various record company employees involved in bringing the record to market. Successfully "breaking" a record requires coordinating the activities of these people for short but intense periods of time.

Because a record will frequently "take off," generating wide appeal in a matter of weeks or even days, many promotional efforts are launched as opportunities present themselves. For example, although a marketing plan for a recording or album may be prepared six months in advance of its anticipated release, a concert schedule change at the last minute can change the timing of the marketing plan overnight. Thus, record marketing and promotion requires careful planning plus the ability to execute a plan rapidly, even while altering the plan to meet new conditions.

Newways Organization and Management

Newways' organization prior to Reingold's arrival in January 1976 is shown in Exhibit 1. William Rouson, who had been with Newways for 12 years, had been appointed president of Newways in 1971. Rouson, a quiet, low-key, and personable manager, had encouraged his managers to work hard. Under Rouson, Newway's managers had enjoyed an expanding company and a climate of personal informality and professional respect. Although his background was in finance and accounting, Rouson showed an interest in all aspects of the business and often toured the plant and offices in slacks and plain white shirt and tie, with a cardigan sweater as the temperature might dictate.

EXHIBIT 1
Organization prior to January 1976

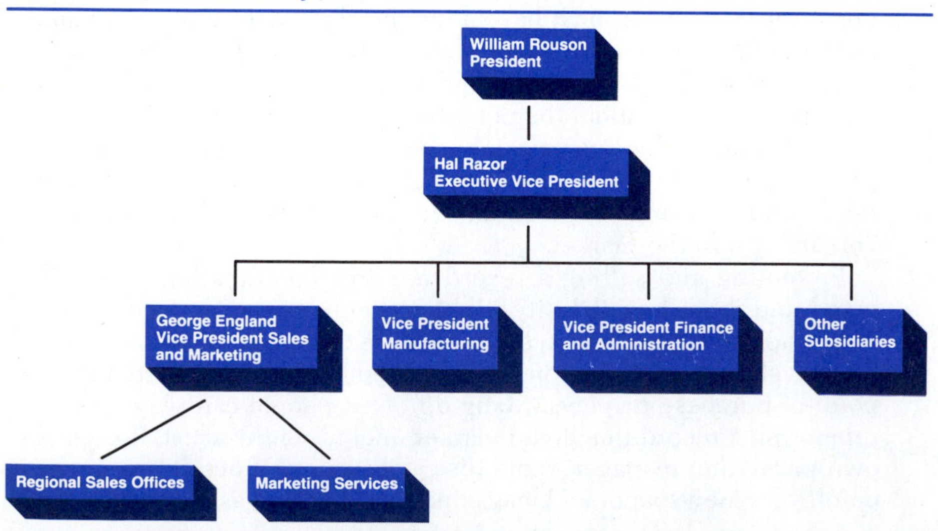

Hal Razor, also a longtime Newways employee, had been promoted to executive vice president under Rouson's administration. He divided his time among several small subsidiaries and special assignments delegated by Rouson. The relationships between Rouson, Razor, and the managers reporting to Rouson were generally free and open, without fixed reporting requirements.

GEORGE ENGLAND AND THE SALES ORGANIZATION

George England had been named vice president of sales and marketing in late 1974, after 17 years with Newways and successful management of two regional sales offices.

A number of the Newways salespeople had developed under England's tutelage, and the sales force gave him their loyalty and respect. Slightly balding, his hair neatly trimmed, England was much like many Newways managers and salespeople in appearance and manner—personable, neat, and conservative in dress and lifestyle. Even so, when England and his sales staff came together for quarterly sales meetings, he promoted one or two good nights on the town, and was alleged to have been the ringleader in a water-balloon-throwing episode when the Newways sales force attended an international gathering of recording executives.

Each year England set challenging but attainable sales objectives for each region, leaving it to the regional managers to decide how to reach these objectives. In particular, regional managers had considerable leeway in developing promotional efforts for their primary markets. Over the years the sales managers had become adept at building a solid base for their yearly sales goals by promoting tried-and-true albums and recordings by known artists.

Many of the Newways salespeople had been with the company for five or more years and in the record industry for even longer. Many were content with their geographic location and had little or no desire to be promoted to the main office staff. In general, the Newways sales force viewed themselves as professionals. Many were in their mid-30s or older and were characterized to the casewriter as "good family men" who, although they conscientiously listened to new releases and enjoyed all types of music, were not part of the rock music generation in temperament or lifestyle.

Under George England the regional sales offices were supported by a small staff of marketing services people who developed promotional materials at the request of the regional sales managers. This promotional support included developing newspaper ad layout for retail chain accounts, creating radio spot advertisements, and inventing and delivering point-of-purchase displays, such as posters, signs, and T-shirts. Display reps, reporting to marketing services, worked out of regional sales offices in large metropolitan markets. Under the direction of regional sales staff, display reps set up point-of-purchase displays. On occasion the salespeople also used display reps to help with other selling tasks, such as taking inventories of records in the stores of large retail accounts.

The marketing services staff also handled promotion of appearances of Newways recording artists in the respective regions, coordinating these appearances with the regional sales staff. Often the sales manager and individual salespeople handled local details associated with concerts, including meetings with the artist, parties, and appearances in retail stores. Newways often sponsored social events for the artist. Such affairs were attended by record jobbers, store owners, disc jockeys, the press, and Newways' own staff. Whenever a big-name star appeared, the request for party invitations far exceeded the number of people who could be invited.

The Arrival of Robert Reingold

During 1975 the senior management of the Newways parent organization had undertaken a strategic review of the record industry and had concluded that although the recording markets in Western Europe and the United States still offered potential for growth, the company should now aggressively stimulate growth in other areas—in particular, Canada and South America. To make best use of its existing marketing capability, the parent company management decided to build the marketing capability within Newways, with the eventual objective of having Newways take the marketing lead in the United States, while shifting the focus of its existing marketing staff toward international markets.

Robert Reingold had been president of a smaller record company, having risen rapidly through the retailing and marketing sides of the record business. By 1975 Reingold had achieved a considerable degree of financial independence as well as a reputation for aggressive and skillful marketing, a reputation well known to those in Newways familiar with the international record industry.

Late in 1975 Reingold was recruited by the staff of the Newways parent company. After discussions between Reingold and parent company management, in which the latter indicated that it would like to retain the present Newways senior managers in recognition of their service to the company, Reingold took office in January 1976, with the title of chief executive officer. The organizational changes initiated by Reingold between January and October 1976 are reflected in the organization chart in Exhibit 2.

In his introductory talk to the Newways managers, Reingold described his primary mission as that of dramatically shifting the empha-

EXHIBIT 2
Organization in October 1976

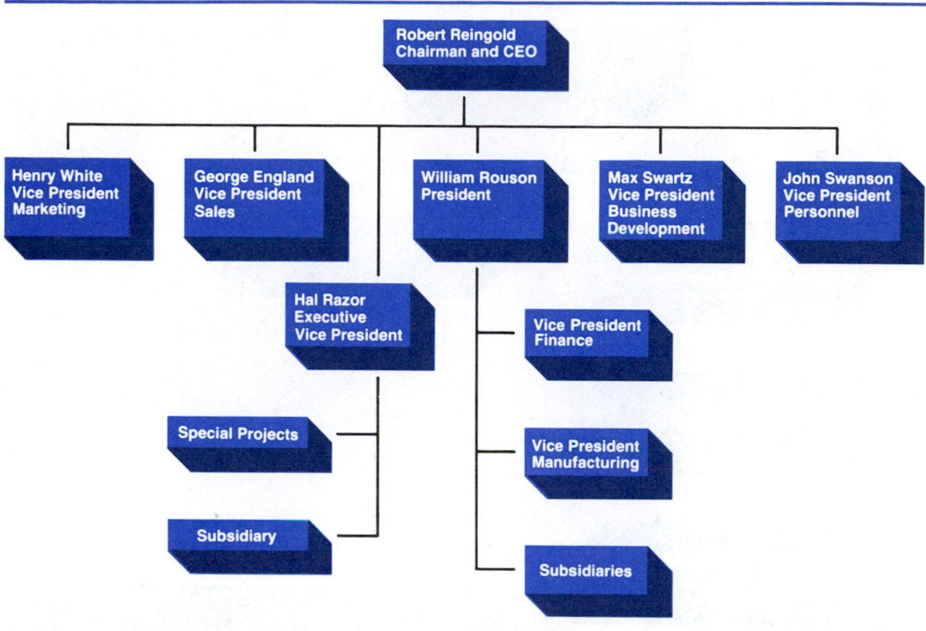

sis in Newways toward aggressive marketing, promotion, and sales. Reingold's remarks were supported by parent company managers, who complimented the Newways managers for their loyal and effective service, saying that Reingold's appointment was an opportunity to acquire a person of significant talent in the industry and was not to be interpreted as an implied criticism of the existing Newways management. Soon after his arrival Reingold visited the regional sales offices where he extensively interviewed sales managers and some salespeople, and he also visited a number of retail outlets with the sales staff.

In late February Reingold created a separate marketing organization. He appointed Henry White, a regional sales manager, as vice president of marketing, reporting directly to Reingold. White and Reingold rapidly recruited staff for the new marketing organization, filling most of the key positions with people having marketing experience in other record companies. Within the new marketing organization, Reingold created five management positions under White. The director of creative services was in charge of design in promotional materials, and the director of artist development was to handle Newways' relations with artists and their promoters. Reingold also appointed two directors of marketing, each responsible for one of the two major record labels that Newways handled: Apricot Records and

EXHIBIT 3
Sales Organization, October 1976

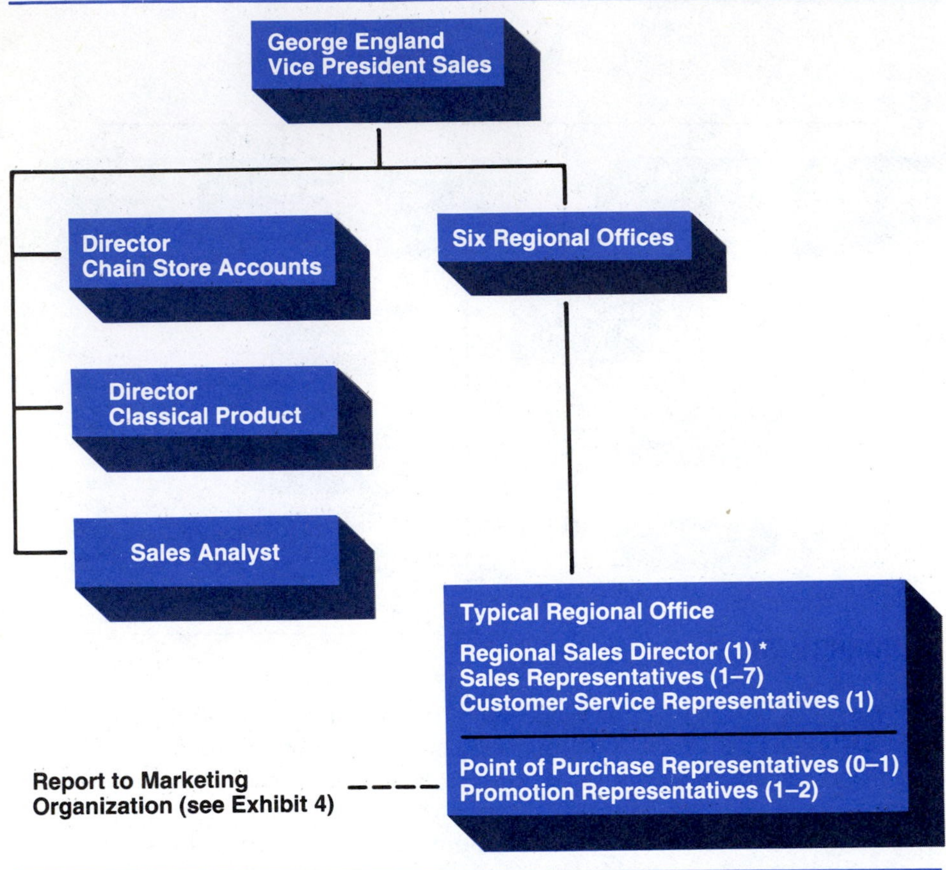

Kumquat Records. Reingold brought both of these directors from his former company. Among other changes, the promotion representatives were assigned to the new marketing organization. Exhibits 3 and 4 show the organization of the new sales and marketing organizations, respectively. Exhibit 5 lists selected examples of the Newways compensation program.

HENRY WHITE AND THE MARKETING ORGANIZATION

Henry White had been very successful in the Florida region both as a salesperson and as regional manager. In his early 30s, White was outgoing, gregarious, and perpetually in motion with nervous energy.

EXHIBIT 4
Marketing Organization, October 1976

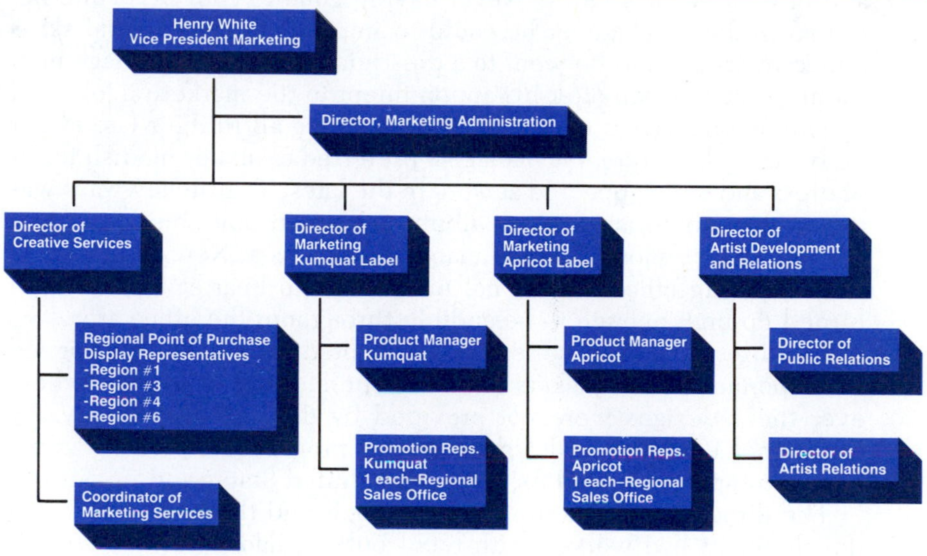

EXHIBIT 5
Compensation Scheme for Selected Newways Personnel

1. Vice presidents of sales and marketing:
   a. ± $35,000 base.
   b. ± $15,000 bonus at discretion of CEO. Bonus from bonus pool for all directors and above based upon Newways annual profits.
2. Directors of marketing, Kumquat and Apricot labels:
   a. ± $25,000 base.
   b. ± $3,500 bonus.
3. Regional sales managers:
   a. ± $22,000 base.
   b. Commission based on meeting regional yearly sales target. 100 percent of target would yield bonus of 50 percent of base salary.
4. Sales reps:
   a. ± $10,000 base (varies with years of service).
   b. Commission based on percentage of dollar sales credited to each salesperson. A good salesperson might earn 100 percent of base, and a super salesperson, 150 percent of base.
5. Promotion reps:
   a. ± $10,000 base.
   b. Bonus based on percentage of sales for the region. A typical bonus might be 50 percent of base salary.

He talked and lived music, often playing electric guitar in impromptu jazz and rock combos. He favored stylish open-collar shirts and jackets and only rarely wore a tie. Never having gone to college, White believed in doing whatever he could to improve his managerial skills and knowledge, and he went to a prestigious two-week management training course soon after his appointment to the marketing job.

The five managers reporting to White were all in their late 20s or early 30s. Like White, his managers preferred casual or modish forms of dress and often appeared at work in the latest T-shirt Newways was using to promote an artist or album. Although one could find hi-fi equipment in almost all of the managers' offices at Newways, around the marketing offices it was not uncommon to hear at least one set turned up high enough to be audible throughout the office area.

The director of creative services, a talented graphic artist, designed all important record jackets and other promotional materials whenever these designs were not provided by the parent company. By October of 1976 he had designed several promotional pieces that the parent company adopted for use in the United States and in Europe.

The directors of marketing for the labels and the director of artist development had worked with retail outlets, had promoted records with radio stations, and had firsthand knowledge of the national youth markets. All three sought out budding musicians and maintained contacts with promoters and independent recording producers. By October 1976 the first artist had been signed for an album that Newways would produce and attempt to "break"—first in its marketing area and later in other U.S. and European markets through the parent company. White expected that this album would be only the beginning of a long-term change that would bring Newways into its own as a recording company.

In addition to the two directors of marketing, White appointed a product manager for each label. The director of marketing was responsible for developing an annual marketing plan for products under the label. The product manager was to implement the marketing plan, product by product. Although individual albums could sometimes be included in a marketing plan a year in advance of their release, the marketing group usually had only 12 to 8 weeks' advance notice of the release dates. Release dates were uncertain, partly because of difficulties encountered in recording the music: stars refused to record, musical groups dissolved and reformed, and concert schedules were changed. Other delays occurred in packaging, manufacturing, and shipping the records. During 1976, for example, many record manufacturing facilities were operating at capacity, and occasionally it was simply not possible to manufacture a record in quantity by a desired date. During 1976 Newways would handle about 400 different albums, 50 of which would be first recordings by new artists.

Each director of marketing hired one promotion representative for each regional sales office. Thus, two promotion representatives worked out of each regional sales office. Each reported to a different director of marketing, although each was expected to support the work of the regional sales manager. The casewriter asked one promotion representative to describe her job. This was her summary:

> Within his or her market area, the promo rep directs all regional radio promotions for products specified by the director of marketing. This job includes managing contests and product giveaways at local radio stations as well as maintaining current information files on programming trends, playing times, and the music preferences and other idiosyncracies of program or music directors and disc jockeys. I also call on wholesalers and retail outlets to set up displays and to check on the sales of Newways' records and those of our competitors. I attend regional sales meetings to present information on sales and on regional music trends. I also get reviews in all regional media, and I service the new product and press kits distributed to reviewers. Finally, I help the director of artist relations to hold press parties and to arrange artists' tours. The job description I was given when I took the job said that I was to use my initiative and travel as necessary.

Most of the promo reps were in their early to mid-20s. Several had been transferred from the sales department, where they had worked for short periods of time as point-of-purchase display representatives. Others were hired from outside Newways. Most were music fans or amateur musicians. Some had worked in retail record stores, several had worked in sales promotion at small record companies, and several had earned money during college by booking on-campus jazz and rock concerts or by managing and promoting budding musicians. More than any other group in Newways, the promo reps closely identified with their youth market, often expressing the sentiment that a person had to "believe" in the music for the artist to be successful in the record business.

COMMENTS BY NEWWAYS' STAFF

Reingold's gloomy summary for the casewriter was interrupted by a lengthy phone call. While waiting to conclude their conversation, the casewriter recalled some of the discussions he had had with other Newways employees during the past few days.

Max Swartz, Vice President of Business Development

Swartz had come to Newways in May 1976, somewhat to the surprise of other Newways managers. Swartz had been the successful president of a small competitor of Newways. Reingold had asked Swartz to become acquainted with all aspects of Newways and to help the vice presidents of sales and marketing as opportunities presented themselves.

"Over the past six months we've been taking control of the streets, seeing to it that Newways records are given the right attention in the stores, pushing the radio stations to play our new releases at the right times. We've been in there belly-to-belly with the guys who can make the records sell.

"Sales and marketing have to work together. Marketing creates demand, and sales gives a push with the wholesalers and retailers. Up until last year England's people essentially did the marketing. I don't think they understand what the marketing department can do for them yet. There's conflict, but I think it is healthy and under control.

"There's a sort of game being played. The sales guys say, 'Why are the marketing people spending all that money on promotional gimmicks? We never had that kind of money to throw around. Then, when we do get people into the store to buy the records, we can't get enough records on time.' The marketing guys say, 'We spent money and got the record moving; the sales guys didn't follow up.'

"There has been a problem in meeting manufacturing schedules. We have every available facility going flat out, and they still can't always meet demand, particularly sudden big demand for an album like [he refers to a movie soundtrack that was an instant hit in the United States and Europe].

"Look, it's a fast, tough game out there; the best a guy or gal can do is run as hard as they can, and every six months or so stick their head up to see how things are going."

Regional Sales Director Number 1

"This marketing push will help us in the long run; I really believe that. But they are going about it the wrong way. Henry [White] brought in all these new people with big egos who have to justify their big budgets by making a name for themselves. Those people are spending money as fast as we bring it in.

"The thing that has changed the most since the new marketing organization was formed is the number of people I have to worry about. The phone rings for me all day—directors of marketing, product managers, promo reps, display reps, George [England], artist relations. Usually they call me to tell me to do something, or they want me to find out something.

"The hardest thing is keeping track of all those people when they are in my territory. The marketing people will fly in and go out and talk to a big customer about a promotion. I may not learn about the trip unless the customer calls to ask me what is going on. Sometimes one of my salespeople will go into a store, and who will be there but a marketing person.

"What they don't understand is that I have to make my numbers [sales target] every month. If I don't, George gets after me. The marketing people don't care about my numbers. They want me to be pushing only one or two new artists so that they can go grab an award for breaking a hit record.

"Of course, the thing that really infuriated me was when [the director of marketing for Kumquat Records] came out here and interviewed people for the promo rep job in my office without letting me know. He hired a kid I've known about for a long time. This kid worked for a local radio station and wasn't somebody I cared to do business with. Now he's assigned to work out of my office."

Regional Sales Director Number 2

"My job is to interpret and implement the marketing plan for my markets. Henry's people do a pretty good job on the plans, except I think they expect things to move too quickly. Also, I don't have any input into the plans when they are prepared. There have been several times when what they wanted us to do to push an album showed that they just did not understand the local market. If they had asked me beforehand, they could have saved us some money and wasted time.

"I've had a chance to meet the marketing people at the last two sales and marketing meetings, and I really like some of those guys. They are in their own world—you know, a lot of hype and hoopla—but I think they've given us a shot in the arm. I just wish they would spend some time out here and get to know this territory like I have.

"I like being able to go to the label heads [directors of marketing] now to ask for money for promotional ideas I have. When I come up with good ideas, they are willing to throw some money at them. That's not the way it was in the old organization. George runs a tight-fisted business.

"One thing I think we need to straighten out is the way the promo reps report. It doesn't make any sense to have them reporting to a central office 1,000 miles away when this is the office they are supposed to help. I need sales support help, but as it is, I don't have any real control over how the promo reps use their time. I think they should be doing one thing, they think they should be doing something else, and when I go to talk to them about it, they claim they are only doing what someone in marketing told them to do. To make things worse, the promo reps have been talking to my customers instead of sticking to the radio stations, which is their job. At least two old customers have called to complain about the promo reps being too pushy.

"George is trying to work with Henry, but I think it's hard for him. He was hurt when Reingold took marketing away, and now having to sit and watch the marketing guys have fun with the kind of budget that George never had is like having salt rubbed in the wound.

"By the way, I heard that marketing was $70,000 over budget in July, and they are now $185,000 over. Either the budget doesn't mean anything or Reingold is waiting until the end of the year to clobber them."

Product Manager for the Apricot Label

"My job is to work out a detailed marketing plan for every piece under my label, old and new. Of course, I spend a lot of time on new products, particularly new artists. I plan ads and point-of-purchase material, and I work with the promo reps on how, when, and where to push a record in their districts. I don't exactly tell the promo reps what to do, but I give them advice and ideas.

"Actually, no one has to tell the promo reps what to do. They are all highly motivated and already working 20 hours a day to push the product. Most of the promo reps have more ideas than any of us can keep going at any one time.

"Also, I meet with the salespeople to go over the label's marketing plan for their districts. We do that every three months, and the promo reps are supposed to participate in district sales meetings every week. I tell the salespeople what we have planned, and I ask them what kind of promotional support they will want.

"The toughest thing I have had to deal with since I've been here has been having some of the salespeople throw a lot of cold water on our promotion plans. They aren't used to spending money yet. I think promotional expenses should be a certain percentage of sales. The salespeople get hypnotized by the annual budget, which was put on paper in September 1975 for 1976. The management here did that because corporate requires that much lead time. I just passed my budget for 1977 up the line. At the rate our sales are growing, that budget is mostly a guess.

"Anyway, I'm spending a percentage of sales for my label's product; the more we sell, the more I spend. Maybe someday I'll have more controls on how I use the company's money. Until that happens, though, it sure is fun while it lasts—and we're making some things happen."

Joe Winslow, Director of Marketing Administration

"I've only been here about six months. Reingold and White recruited me from [another record company] where I was working in marketing while finishing my M.B.A. My job here is to bring marketing and promotion under control. I'm supposed to see all of the expense invoices before they go to accounting, and I'm here to approve all major expense items before the marketing people make actual commitments to spend the money.

"The problem is, things often move so fast that I only see the invoices after the fact. Last week, for example, [he names a well-known rock artist] put on a concert in Dallas with 10 days' notice. A concert had been cancelled somewhere else, there was an open night at the arena, so his promoter booked it and promoted the heck out of the concert. We decided to promote his [the artist's] new album in the Dallas-Fort Worth market at the same time.

"This jumped our marketing plan up three weeks. Most of the promotion material was budgeted, and we spent what we had planned. But this morning a bunch of bills hit my desk for a pre-concert press party—booze, limos, food, T-shirts, embossed drink glasses, the whole works. It looks like we spent 5 or 6 thousand on the party.

"I called [the director of marketing for Apricot Records] and asked him what he thought the party cost, not letting on that I had seen the bills. He said, 'Hey baby, a couple of thou at the most. And what a blast. Two of our biggest customers went in the car to [the artist's hotel] to pick him up and rode in with him. One customer took his 12-year-old daughter and they went backstage. Those guys will never forget us. You watch. Next week they'll push the product from [a competing record company] into the washroom.'

"I'm not sure who is controlling the budgets—which directors, I mean—and I sometimes wonder if most of the marketing people are even aware of what the budget looks like."

Henry White, Vice President of Marketing

"This year has been a combination of excitement and frustration for us. My guys and gals have done a great job of getting this place moving, but a lot of people can't see the point of it yet, and some are resisting because they resent the idea that we aren't doing things their way, the old way.

"What my people get a real high from is breaking a completely unknown artist, and breaking him big. Take [White names a rock group and points to a wall poster], we broke them in Miami before any of the other U.S. radio stations would give them a play. Now they are going to be big in the United States. My people really like to see an artist build recognition, and they feel good when they know they've helped that to happen. They like to make the whole trip—from nowhere to the top.

"Sure, there have been some problems with sales. My people are trying hard to change an old-fashioned image. The sales department has been very conservative—good, solid sales types, but very conservative. They really haven't had a "records" look. Why, Reingold told them all to do something about their cars two weeks after he arrived. He went out for a field visit with George, and the salesman picked them up at the airport in a beat-up Chevy Vega. The radio didn't even work. Reingold was upset when he found out that was the car the salesman had used to drive [he names a rock star] around in before his concert. Now the salespeople are buying nice Cordobas and LTDs with first-class tape decks and speakers. We use a Cadillac limousine whenever an artist is in town now.

"My marketing people are all charged up. They are trying to cooperate with the salespeople in every way they can, but I've told them not to sit and wait just because a salesperson can't fit them into his schedule.

"Maybe there should be one vice president of sales and marketing. But even if George and I reported to one person, we would still have to get along. And it wouldn't change anything at the lower levels. Many of the salespeople have just been resisting what we want to do. A couple of them yell to George that we're wasting money when we spend it in ways that they wouldn't.

"They've caught my guys having themselves picked up at the airport by a limousine a couple of times. If it helps my people to feel good, then so what? They work hard—late nights, hitting nightclubs and concerts. They deserve a limo ride once in a while. The artist has a limo, so why shouldn't the guys and gals who make the artist big have one, too?"

George England, Vice President of Sales

"The salespeople should be operating their own businesses. What turns them on is making their monthly sales target, and seeing an album sell in their districts. They like it when they can take a new album to a big retailer and say, 'Hey, this group is going to go big. If you want to meet them, come to the concert with me three weeks from Monday. You'll see. Now, let's try to push 2,000 in your stores this week, right up front.'

"What makes the salespeople successful over the long haul is good relations with their customers and being able to work from a solid base of a variety of types of music. In the final analysis, it's the store owner who decides whether or not our display goes up front, or if our record becomes the loss leader for the day. So anything that gets between the salesperson and his customers is hurting him. Well, now we never know who's going to show up in a store—the promotion rep (PM), one of the product managers, even somebody from artist relations wanting to photograph an artist in the store.

"Basically, I think the marketing guys have a good idea, but they are going off all over the place, spending money, doing promotions we don't need. They are way over budget, you know. In fact, I expect to be given budget review authority over marketing expenditures until Henry brings it under control.

"Personally, Henry and I get along fine. We always did when he worked for me, and I expect we will in the future."

Reingold's Concluding Thoughts

In Reingold's office, as the casewriter recalled these conflicting testimonies about the sales and marketing problems at Newways, Reingold's voice broke into his thoughts.

> Listen, I haven't told you yet about the latest episode. The last sales and marketing quarterly meeting—two weeks ago—apparently ended in a real blow-up. The marketing people led off by formally airing all their gripes about the sales organization. The salespeople were given time to respond with their views about marketing—but they just said that they didn't have much to say. George was furious. He started shouting at his own sales managers for not having the guts to confront marketing with the complaints that they'd been bringing to him. That pretty well ended the meeting.
>
> Anyway, as soon as I heard about the shouting match, I called George and Henry in here and told them that if they couldn't straighten out their differences, they were going to place me in a position where I would have to choose one or the other of them as the more important. I told them I didn't want to have to do that. I want them to work together.
>
> How much time do you think I should give them to sort themselves out before I make some changes around here?

▶ Nolim (A)

Peter de Jong reread his father's letter as he sat in his New York office. In part the letter read:

> The sudden death of Max makes the situation in the local coal company critical. As you know, Max has been handling most of the day-to-day management even though our partnership has always been 50/50. Each year my businesses have grown increasingly more difficult for me to

This case was prepared by George Taucher under the direction of Professors Herman Gadon and Quinn McKay as the basis for class discussion rather than to illustrate either effective or ineffective handling of an administrative situation.

> handle alone. I think, Peter, that the time is ripe for you to come home and take a part in the business. If I ever needed your help, now is the time. The coal company would be an ideal place to begin. I plan to buy the 50 percent share from Max's wife and that way we would have full control. You could run the business in just the way that Max did, although I would have to spend time with you initially to help teach you the business.

The suddenness of the letter made Peter unsure of how he should reply. It was the first time his father had asked him for help. Until that moment he had not given a thought to returning to Holland. Peter enjoyed living in the United States. The future seemed bright at the International Oil Company, where Peter had spent most of the previous year. Promotions had come rapidly, and at 23 he was clearly ahead of his age group. Peter had done a variety of marketing jobs including running a large training service station on a major turnpike junction. As satisfying as his progress had been, Peter was not sure that he would stay at International over the long term. Already the politics of corporate life was apparent. Some of his colleagues on the international coordination staff "had particularly sharp elbows," Peter noted.

For these and other reasons, Peter was less and less attracted to large corporations and more toward an entrepreneurial situation where "he could be his own man." He already had his eye on a small TBA (tires, batteries, and accessories) distributorship in Philadelphia that was having financial troubles. He felt that what he had learned in petroleum marketing at International would enable him to turn the situation around. Furthermore, recent antitrust rulings in favor of independent distributors in the TBA business had clearly given the distributorship a favorable environment. In short, he saw the possibilities of developing a major growth business. Peter felt that his contacts at International would serve him in good stead. Indeed, John Weber, the International Oil personnel director, was favorable to the idea and had even offered to support him with part of the capital needed. Peter often referred to Weber as his "American father." Weber had hired Peter and had befriended the young Dutchman. Peter was often a guest at the Weber house. One of the things Peter resolved to do before he replied to his father was to talk to John about the letter.

Peter de Jong had a remarkably varied life for his 23 years. A solitary boy and only son, Peter was raised strictly—contrasted even more by the way his three sisters were "spoiled" by their father. At 15, Peter had his first major disagreement with his father. This was to begin a period in which he was away from home, except for short visits, for the next eight years. Peter was doing well in school, and his teacher recommended that he continue on and get his *abitur*.[1] Peter

[1] Preparation for university, e.g., high school, matriculation, A levels.

very much wanted to go to one of the top boarding schools in the Netherlands. Although this would have been socially and financially acceptable, Johann de Jong refused, saying that the local school was adequate and that Peter should continue to live at home. While his father felt that education was important, he also thought it should be highly focused on making Peter a better businessman. After a confrontation that included threats by Peter to leave home, Johann compromised. Peter would take a business apprenticeship program with an old army colleague of Johann. This man was known by Johann to have the same conservative patriarchal view as himself.

Peter spent the next three years away from home learning the shipping supply business, enjoying earning his own way for the first time. Finishing the program at 18, Peter went to England at the recommendation of his father's friend to study at the University of Hull and to perfect his English. However, after a few months, Johann de Jong sent his son a letter telling him he believed that Peter was "wasting his time" in a provincial English university and should gain practical business experience. Peter was to report to the headquarters of the International Oil Company in London "immediately."

This decision had its origin in a business trip to the United States, where Johann was strongly influenced by talks he had with an executive who suggested that his company, International Oil, offered both excellent experience and a scholarship program to American universities. Peter felt that he had to comply since he had no funds of his own, although he felt he was gaining from his work in Hull. The London experience, however, was fortunate from every point of view, and Peter returned home to Friesland within a few months.

Back at home, Peter was able to convince his father that a university degree was important to future business success. Accordingly, Peter enrolled in the three-year commercial university program in Amsterdam—supported financially by his father. Objections on his son's "playboy" lifestyle led Johann to cut off his financial support in the second year. As Johann put it in his confrontation with his son, "I fulfilled my part of the contract by giving you money for your university studies. You failed to live up to your part. Therefore I don't feel that I should continue to support you." Peter returned to his second year and sold newspapers and other door-to-door items to support himself, assisted from time to time by his mother, who was able to send a few guilders. Remarkably, he finished the three-year program in two years. Johann came to the graduation, and there was a moving reconciliation.

After graduation, Peter entered the management trainee program at International Oil in New York through his father's connections. Even there, the going was less than smooth initially. Discovering that his salary as a Dutchman was less than half of that of his American colleagues in the program, Peter quit in disgust and was tending bar in

Baltimore when International decided to rehire him as a regular employee. From there, Peter moved rapidly up the corporate ladder.

Turning over his father's offer in his mind, Peter realized how little he knew about his father's businesses. True to his analytic training in business school, Peter wrote down what little he knew.

Nolim:	An oil distribution company in retail, heating oil, lubes, and agricultural markets. There were 80–100 retail outlets of substantial potential. An exclusive contract with the International Oil Company for all sales in Friesland. Sales were growing rapidly in all areas, corresponding to the rapid growth in Europe in general. Peter knew the Dutch market was growing at well over 10 percent at the time.
The coal company:	A traditional coal distribution company with declining sales, though a move into heating oil was offsetting the decline somewhat. Facilities, including docks, were modern.
The Austin distributorship:	Recently started, Peter knew that this operation was still in the red. Job van Gelden, who had married Peter's sister, was running the distributorship for Johann.
The Mercedes distributorship:	Had been established for a number of years and was doing very well as far as Peter knew.

Peter estimated the sales at about Fl. 15 million for all the companies, guessing that Nolim made up about half of that total. Peter did not have the slightest idea about the profits or financial structure of the companies. He did know, however, that the company had been incorporated two years earlier with the assistance of Paul Van Rijn, his brother-in-law, an Amsterdam lawyer who had married his older sister. He knew that Paul was thinking of taking up legal practice in Friesland so that he could devote more time to the companies.

Peter knew that the most important fact about the family companies was his father. Johann had often said, while sitting around the family dining room table: "I never want these companies to grow so big that I can't handle all of the details myself." Peter knew this to be a guiding force, and few of the employees had much, if any, authority for independent decision making.

Johann de Jong, at 66, was in every sense a self-made man. Having left the family farm after a dispute with his father, he made his own way without much of a formal education. Promotion to officer level in the army led to important connections. An early venture in the hotel business ended in bankruptcy, and it took years to pay off the debts even though there were no legal requirements to do so. A restart as an oil salesman led to many years of hard work and finally the founding of his own oil distributorship. Prior to World War II, growth was very slow and success meager. After the war, however, the recovery changed the climate dramatically, and growth and profits came more easily. Even under prosperous conditions Johann continued to eat, sleep, and live his business.

Peter thought more about the man he might be working with. He had never had much of a personal life with his father. For one thing Johann was seldom able to tear himself away from the business, and when at home, discussions were usually business oriented. Then, too, Johann was already 43 when his son was born. Peter felt close to his mother; the fact that she was 18 years younger than her husband enabled her to relate to Peter more easily than did Johann. Peter's oldest sister was by his father's previous marriage, and Peter always sensed an underlying tension between his mother and half sister. The household was ruled with an iron hand, and Johann never permitted open conflict in the family. Disputes, however small, were swept under the rug.

Johann became an important figure in Friesland and was tempted to go into politics; he decided at the last moment to stick to his business. Johann had come a long way from being a farmer's son to one of the most important businessmen in Friesland. Still he maintained much of the sturdy ethics of Friesland—strong religious conviction, honor, and stolid moderation in his lifestyle.

Peter de Jong put down his father's letter and gazed out of his window across the skyline of New York.

▸ Outsiders in Ootiland

INTRODUCTION

I went to Ootiland as a volunteer worker. I don't think that there was a specific reason for my interest in volunteer work except a strong interest in other people and cultures, and a sense of adventure. My choice of countries was limited to two; the work in Ootiland was more consistent with my background and qualifications so it was the obvious choice.

About 10 months after I had arrived, Mr. Schroeder asked me to write to potential wool suppliers to get wool for one project. I expressed my reluctance to do this, explaining that it was Lily's project and I thought that she would feel that I was interfering. But he still insisted that I go ahead with the letters. When I asked where I was supposed to get information such as the required gauge of wool and the amount needed, he told me to ask Lily. Incidentally, Mr. Schroeder knew about my problem with Lily before he asked me to get involved with the project.

I went to Lily and told her exactly what I was doing and that it was at the request of Mr. Schroeder. She told me that she had done the letters a year ago and had not gotten any replies. I went back to Mr. Schroeder and told him this. While I was there Lily phoned him; I don't know what she said, but after a couple of minutes Lily hung up on him.

He still insisted that I do the letters. I went back to Lily, determined to be aboveboard with everything. Again I asked her for the information. Again she said she did not have it. The only other person who knew what was needed was the supply officer for the army. So I called him, and he gave me what I needed. But evidently he called Lily and wanted to know why she didn't have the information already.

Five minutes before the end of the day, Lily burst into my office and very loudly accused me of trying to steal her project. She literally screamed at me for several minutes. I didn't try to defend myself because I was afraid that she would take whatever I said and repeat it out of context or misquote me and use my words against me at another date. I waited until she stopped, then calmly explained how I happened to get involved with the project in the first place. Then I offered to withdraw completely, but she refused my offer, saying that she did not want any more to do with the project. Then she threw all the information about the project, including the information that I had asked her for, on my lap and stormed out. But before she left she added one last comment, "By the way, Sara, I am not a Boston nigger."

SARA

I am about five feet four inches tall and graduated from college with a major in economics. Before undertaking the volunteer work, I had worked for two years as a manager in a clothing store in Boston. In general I tend to be a bit standoffish when I first meet people, though I make an effort to be friendly. Once I do become friends with a person, I expect them to return the friendship and I trust them not to violate it.

Depending upon my mood, whether I got enough sleep, ate breakfast, and didn't get hit by any cars on my way to work, I almost welcome confrontation. It doesn't distress me as long as I am confronted directly and I'm given the chance to respond to something concrete. But when there is underlying tension and I know that all or some of it has to do with me, then I get very nervous. If possible, I try to bring it to the surface and get the problem settled.

Generally, I like to take control of a situation and organize others. Sometimes I think that I do this just so I won't miss out on anything, because I'm either the catalyst or, if not, then the other people involved must report events to me. Interestingly enough, I would rather confront men with a problem than women. Women in general intimidate me; I'm not sure why, but I don't find women as easygoing in a work situation. Maybe it's because they are a bit unsure of themselves and tend to be too overbearing.

I've found women tend to be more critical, and I really handle criticism badly and generally rebel against authority, especially if they haven't gained the Sara Hoyt seal of approval. (There were a lot of authoritarian folks in the country, generally identified by the safari suit, a black briefcase, and a sign around their necks that says "20 years in Africa—I know everything.")

LILY

Lily had received her bachelor's degree from the University of Indiana and her master's degree in textiles and design from Rhode Island. She was an Angolan and a member of a major tribe. Being close to six feet tall with heels on and very striking looking, Lily was a most imposing woman. At our first meeting, Lily seemed quite friendly and competent, willing to discuss the problems of Ootiland Industries and explain how to get through the incredible bureaucracy. It was a relief to work with someone who had some amount of sophistication.

She was working in Ootiland under a government contract. Lily had arrived about 6 months before me and about 15 months after my predecessor, John. When John left he had alluded to problems with Lily's temper, but since Lily and I had gotten to be quite good friends by then, I attributed this warning to personal friction between them. I did notice that Lily seemed to despise authority, and if anyone tried to tell her what to do she would talk for days about how that person didn't know what they were talking about. In some cases it was obvious that she was wrong, but the more anyone tried to tell her differently, the more she persisted with her opinion. As time went on, I became more and more wary of her; but since our relationship was more on a social basis than a working one, our interaction was hardly affected by such behavior. I was, however, beginning to feel that I should stay on her "good side" as much as possible. I wasn't anxious to have her say about me the things she said about other people. People in headquarters began to refer to Lily as "difficult." Most of them seemed to prefer not to deal with her; in fact, some acted as if they were afraid of her and seemed to avoid her whenever posible.

ABOUT THE COUNTRY AND THE CULTURE

I found Ootiland, which is primarily desert, not very interesting. But the people were very friendly and easygoing and exceptionally westernized in dress and customs. Ootiland had very few of the colorful traditions associated with the rest of Africa. The harsh climate made it harder to "survive" and did not allow time to elaborate on culture. The Ootilanders had traditionally been herdsmen. Cattle, which outnumber people four to one, had been and still were the mainstay of the economy. Cattle were a symbol of wealth and prestige, though only a small percentage of the population owns a large percentage of the cattle. When I was there, the economy was slowly shifting away from cattle to one based on recently discovered mineral resources.

The government was attempting to ensure that this new-found wealth was distributed equitably throughout the population. One of the means that they were using was to promote industries run by Ootiland citizens. Currently most of the businesses were run by expatriates—Indians, South Africans and Europeans. Very few businesses were run by Ootilanders, and those that were, were low-profit retail businesses. Heavy industry and manufacturing companies were run entirely by expatriates. This is understandable when it is realized that Ootiland does not have a tradition in commerce, the vast majority of its people having been subsistence farmers and herdsmen. Also they lacked the education and sophistication to run highly profitable businesses.

The Ootiland pattern of interpersonal relations was amazingly calm and controlled. Confrontation with one another was usually only a last resort. There was a definite hierarchy in Ootiland that was universally recognized and carried over into business, government, and family. At the top was the chief, traditionally an inherited position; but he was advised by the village elders (all male to my knowledge). The elders sanctioned his decisions and often his behavior. There had been one instance of a chief actually being whipped in the village court for being irresponsible. The whipping was according to the demands of his constituents, so there were exceptions to the idea that the chief cannot be challenged or reprimanded. The system was not dissimilar to our own government; it had its checks and balances. The role of chief carried over into government—the president, permanent secretaries, and directors were each looked upon as a "chief." In business it was the director, and in the family it was the eldest man or woman (often there was no male member of the family, but I'll get to that).

Besides mother/son relationships, which I'm not clear about, the ranking was any adult male, then women from eldest to youngest, then children. Women were regarded as property. A man might have more than one wife, which is one reason why often there were no adult males in a family; another more common reason was that women often had children to prove their fertility and thus their desirability as a marriage partner. Though this was still very prevalent in the Ootiland society, the church and the government were trying to change it, each for their own reasons.

Given the hierarchy, confrontation of a man by a woman was very uncommon. In an informal situation a man could provoke a woman to physical violence. If a woman hit a man, she could be arrested and subjected to whatever punishment the chief decided, usually a lashing in the village court, a fine, or imprisonment. Again there were exceptions, and it had happened that the chief would excuse the woman after hearing what happened. But the point is that a woman was chattel and had better think twice before she challenged a man.

If a man were challenged by a woman, his reaction seemed to be disorientation and confusion, not to mention amazement. Later they would treat the woman as if it had never happened; as if she had had a moment of insanity that should be forgotten. I'm sure that this view is slanted a bit because of my experiences as a white foreign woman, whom almost everyone referred to as "my child." I haven't seen too many women challenge men, but the ones that I have seen did elicit the reaction cited above.

Most women there had an awful lot of spunk, especially the older ones. Their life is not at all easy, since they were the ones who ran the family (often extended), did the farming, cooking, cleaning, etc., while the men went to the cattle post and drank and counted their cows (somewhat exaggerated, of course, but not too much).

When confrontation did occur, as a last resort, it was amazingly direct and critical yet very seldom involved constructive criticism. But I *never* saw an Ootilander get excited about anything.

MY ASSIGNMENT

My assignment as a volunteer was to work as a management advisor for an organization called Ootiland Industries (OI). OI was one of the government organizations designed to promote domestic industry by providing subsidized premises and technical and management training to Ootilanders with little or no business experience who were interested in becoming businessmen, or "entrepreneurs" as they were referred to in OI. OI supported several manufacturing and construction industries, including metalworking, garment production, brick making, and woodworking. The industries were divided by their particular line of production and grouped on what are known as estates. For instance, all of the garment producers occupied workshops together, the woodworkers were grouped in a separate area, and so forth. The purpose of this was to facilitate training. On each estate there was an estate manager who administered the other staff and collected rents. Most estates also had a technical advisor who was qualified or skilled in a specific area. There was also a management advisor with training and/or experience in business administration.

OI headquarters contained the central administration as illustrated in Exhibit 1.

The director, Mr. Selole, headed the entire organization and acted as a liaison between the Ministry of Commerce and Industry and OI. The ministry was the ultimate authority and tried to coordinate OI's activities with the other government development agencies.

I was posted to the garment estate as a management advisor. Because of my job in the clothing store, where I had learned a great deal about the marketing of clothes as well as having had to deal with all kinds of management problems, I felt that I would be quite capable of doing a good job at the garment estate.

I soon realized that the 13 companies I was to advise were run by

EXHIBIT 1

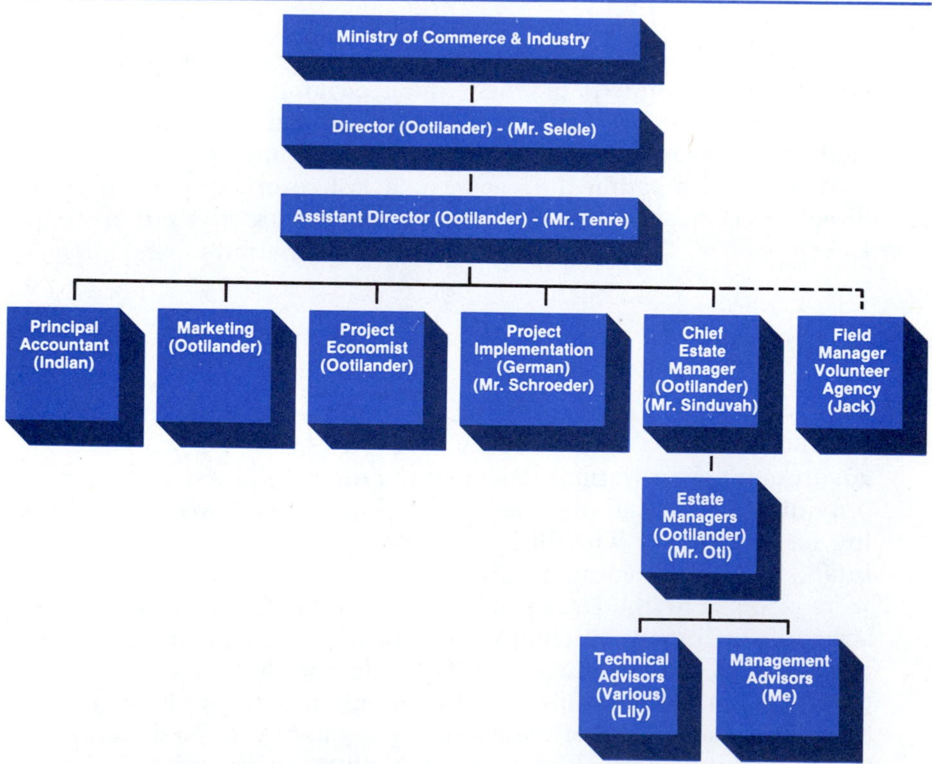

proprietors who had had almost no business training in the four years that they had been with OI and that very few possessed any prior management experience. At best they had worked on assembly lines in clothing factories elsewhere in Africa. A few had been elementary teachers in small rural schools and for the most part had negligible formal education. Most of them ran their businesses as hobbies, not as money-making ventures. Bookkeeping was nonexistent, and employee management was minimal. Several of the women who ran businesses on the estate had husbands in high government positions. They spent much of their time away from the job politicking for their husbands, the party, or themselves as heads of committees. Others usually found excuses not to be in the shop; the excuses had various levels of validity, but they were usually weak (I had to go to hospital because I had a headache, I ran out of thread, etc.). The businesses were seldom money-making propositions. They usually lived off of their husbands' earnings or borrowed from their families. Somehow there was always money somewhere even when theoretically they should have drained all resources.

The companies were a combination of manufacturing and retail, with the bulk of the employees involved in production. Usually only one employee waited on customers and did the bookkeeping, if any existed. Production was usually the construction of school uniforms and simple shirts and dresses. The skill level was low, and there was little supervision or incentive to produce (piecework was illegal in a factory situation). To make matters worse, the employees generally were family or close friends. The work was boring; it was the perfect setup to make work into an eight-hour social gathering. In all of the shops the employees spent more time visiting and standing around than they did working. Marketing and advertising were badly needed, but only small disjointed efforts had been made in this area over a period of five years.

INITIAL ACTIVITIES

It was obvious from the beginning that my work was cut out for me. Unfortunately, much of the work I had to do during the first seven months was work that was supposed to be done by the estate manager, such as workshop rent collection and updating the estate ledgers. The decision that I should do that work was made by OI headquarters. The reason they gave me was "because the estate manager is incompetent."

I protested, and I tried to move the work to him; but headquarters always called on me for the records of rent and loan payments. I found that if I did not keep the records myself, they became hopelessly messed up. It took me two months to unravel one mess that the estate manager created in less than two minutes. Anyway, he was almost never there, so by default I was called upon to do the work.

I was very disappointed that I had so little time to work directly with the entrepreneurs. I felt that since I only had a limited time to work with them, it was a waste to spend time doing clerical work that a national was perfectly capable of doing.

The initial concept of the job was to teach the managers to be managers in all facets of business, but bookkeeping and documentation were stressed simultaneously with personnel management. I wanted to make viable at least those factories with the greatest potential. My aims were very quickly scaled down to teaching basic math skills. By the time I left I would have been happy if each one could at least write an accurate sales receipt for every sale. Often they didn't write a receipt at all; some sales were cash, others credit, but there was no record of the transaction. If you can imagine business violating every business practice that ever existed and still surviving, you'd have an accurate picture of OI-Garment. The only reason it survived was because the government was afraid to see OI fail; Garment was the project that everyone had pinned their hopes on. Therefore the government kept extending credit and loans long after the business should have been liquidated.

During this initial seven months, however, I did set up management classes and basic math classes, and I usually had time to help solve day-to-day problems confronting individual entrepreneurs. But the large problems—such as a cohesive, effective marketing plan or an easily understood bookkeeping system—had to be neglected because of lack of time. In this respect the job was very frustrating.

A NEW ESTATE MANAGER

After my first seven months the estate manager was transferred to another estate in another town. He was replaced by Mr. Oti, who turned out to be quite competent both in recordkeeping procedures and personnel management. I finally had time to work with the entrepreneurs and follow up on some of their problems.

I had known Mr. Oti since I arrived at OI, because he had been the estate manager on a neighboring estate. I wish I had a picture of him; he was a rather rotund man with a huge smile. When he smiled, which was 90 percent of the time, he showed a big gap between his two front teeth. By all appearances no one would give him credit for many smarts. But in reality he wasn't at all stupid. His only problem was that he agreed with everyone and everything.

I think he settled most of the estate personnel problems (quarrels) by agreeing with both parties until they calmed down. Most of the proceedings were carried on in Ootilandish, so I actually never fully understood what was happening. All I know is that he seemed to maintain the status quo.

NEW ACTIVITIES

My first major project was to find a suitable sewing machine mechanic who would be able to maintain the machinery. At that time all machinery had to be repaired in another country at great expense to OI entrepreneurs. The project had been handed over to me by John, but it was to be a joint project with Lily. A mechanic had actually been identified before I started working for OI. All that was left was to write to him to convince him to take the job. Then a contract had to be drawn up and the terms finalized. The entire project was to be overseen by the implementation officer, Mr. Schroeder, whose role was to be a consultant. Though I knew about the project, I didn't do anything about it because I thought that it was Lily's responsibility to keep it going since originally she, along with John, had proposed it. One day Mr. Schroeder called me into his office and told me that Lily had not done anything about the project and to please get the contract drawn up because he had spoken to the mechanic and he was ready to start. From then on Mr. Schroeder excluded Lily from the project. It took about three months to finish the contract, mostly because the mechanic was hard to contact and the agreement involved a lot of negotiations with him.

I could sense that Lily was feeling left out, and I made every effort to keep her informed. If I knew in advance that Mr. Schroeder wanted to speak to me about the mechanic, I tried to get Lily to come with me or I insisted that Mr. Schroeder also ask Lily to come. Unfortunately, I seldom knew in advance when we were going to discuss the mechanic. Usually Mr. Schroeder called me into his office when I was at headquarters on unrelated business.

Communication on this project was further complicated because Mr. Schroeder and the mechanic made agreements about his contract privately, and the only reason that I found out about these agreements was because I had to incorporate them into the written contract.

Finally, one week before I went on a month's leave, everything was set and the mechanic was ready to work. The day I returned from leave the mechanic told me that he had not been paid because no one would sign his payment voucher. I signed it immediately because I felt that OI was obligated to fulfill their part of the agreement, which was to pay the mechanic at the end of each month. I was particularly annoyed because it was Lily's responsibility to see that the mechanic had been paid, since the estate manager was new and did not know anything about him. Further, Lily and I had spent hours working out his terms of payment. In fact, Lily had done most of the work on this part of the contract, but we both had agreed that the terms were fair and met with our satisfaction.

I went back to the estate and asked Lily why the voucher had not been signed. She said that as far as she knew the mechanic had not worked during the month that I was gone. This was contrary to what the mechanic told me.

By this time the director, Mr. Selole, had heard about the problem, and he called a meeting to try to resolve whether or not the mechanic was justified in collecting payment, and also to become fully familiar with the work that OI required of the mechanic. Why he waited until the mechanic already started working to do this, I'll never know, but in so doing he put a lot of pressure on the mechanic to defend his work and even his qualifications for the job.

The meeting lasted over three hours. During the course of the meeting many questions were asked of the mechanic about what his qualifications were, how much work he had done during my absence, how he kept his work records, etc. In short it was as if he was on trial. He and I both felt very embarrassed and confused about the whole process. Unfortunately, Mr. Schroeder was on leave and was not there to help explain how the mechanic was hired. The mechanic and I never got a chance to ask questions or to comment, instead we were only required to answer. It was like an inquisition. Also, the seating arrangement didn't help:

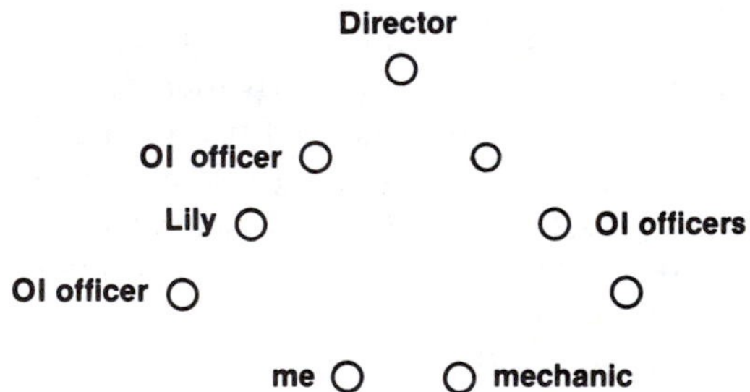

The mechanic and I were the only white people there. We sat in straight-back chairs, which raised us higher than everyone else who was sitting in cushioned arm chairs, and we were directly in front of the director.

Mr. Oti didn't say anything during the entire meeting. Throughout the meeting Lily seemed to be trying everything she could to get the mechanic fired. Over and over again she tried to find something wrong with his work records. She kept saying such things as he could not have fixed a particular machine in only the time recorded on the work record. In each case he was able to defend what he had done. Finally Lily said, "Well, how do I know that you and Sara didn't make up these numbers on his work sheet?" Before I had a chance to reply, the director changed the subject. At this point I was furious with Lily; she seemed determined to undo all the work that I had done getting the mechanic and to discredit me in the process. The only reason I did not return to the subject is because the director never stopped talking once he got going. Even though he would not allow himself to be interrupted, he always interrupted others; so if he wanted to make a point it was futile to try to change the subject, although I suppose I could have manipulated the discussion back to the subject at a later time.

Finally it was decided that the payment was justified. There was an overall consensus that since OI had an agreement with the mechanic, he should be paid at the end of each month, and the agreement would be honored until the end of his contract.

The next day I asked Lily why she got so upset about the mechanic, and she said she felt that she had not been kept informed about the project. I told her she knew as much about the project as I did. Some changes were made by Mr. Schroeder that neither of us knew about before a final decision had been made, but I had done everything I could to keep her informed. This was an uncomfortable situation for both of us and the subject was changed, though I felt that something more was bothering her that she didn't mention.

A few days later I was called to the director's office and shown a letter written by Lily after our meeting. The letter was addressed to the permanent secretary of commerce and industry, with a copy to the director. Though the letter did not mention me by name, the content was clearly in reference to me. In short, it said that a government officer was wasting government funds by hiring a contractor with dubious qualifications—even though I had personally spoken with his references, and they all recommended him highly, and I'd mentioned this several times before we made the final decision to hire the mechanic and also during the course of the meeting.

The director insisted that I write a response to the letter. He seemed to be fed up with Lily and wanted to protect me. Thus he insisted I write a response. The principal accountant offered to help me write a very objective response, once again setting out the reasons why the mechanic was hired and why I approved his payment even though I was not an eyewitness to his work. As far as I knew, that was the end of the matter. I never mentioned the letter to Lily, even though I felt very insulted by it and wanted to know why she wrote it when the same issues that she was questioning were covered thoroughly during the meeting. Mostly I wanted to close the matter once and for all, and I felt that if my reply to her letter didn't accomplish this, then nothing would; and if I told her that I had seen her letter and written a response, I'm sure she would have felt obligated to write a response to my response. After this I did not hear anything about the matter, and I assumed that business would go on as usual whether Lily was satisfied with the arrangement or not.

During the next several months our relationship deteriorated steadily. Often when we passed one another on the estate she would walk right by as if I wasn't there. Her behavior became more and more inconsiderate. Often she would take the estate truck without asking if I needed it or even telling me that she planned to take it. Since that was my only means of transportation, I was often left stranded and forced to change my plans at the last minute. When I said something to her about it, her response was that she told the switchboard operator—the first person I had asked when I wanted to know where the truck was because she kept the keys in her office, but she never knew where the truck was either. I can remember it happening at least three times, twice before I said anything and once after.

Subsequently, Lily began to work harder, or at least she became more active and also more secretive about her work. Often she was involved in work that had nothing to do with the technical aspects of clothing production but was more managerial. I didn't say anything to her even though I felt that much of the work she was doing was work for which I was responsible and, in fact, had already started on. At this point I didn't dare interfere because I didn't want to make things worse than they already were, assuming that I would have to continue working with her.

I became increasingly uncomfortable. It was becoming obvious that she felt she could do all of the work on the estate. I was becoming more intimidated by her and more frustrated because she was taking over more of my work and there was nothing that I could do about it. I had a feeling of helplessness because everyone agreed that Lily was a problem, but no one wanted or dared to do anything about it. I felt that I was not only on my own, but subject to betrayal because several people, in particular Jack and Mr. Schroeder, promised to do something about it but never did.

I went to headquarters and looked up our job descriptions. Hers was comprised of 25 specific duties that she was responsible for. Mine was four pages of rhetoric about the idealistic role of a volunteer. In short it said that the volunteer should do whatever he/she can to aid the entrepreneur, but there wasn't one specific in the whole description.

Hoping that I could get a third party to moderate a discussion between Lily and myself so we could review our differences and attempt to work out a solution, I approached the chief estate manager, Mr. Sinduvah. He said it was just a "woman's problem" and that he wasn't willing to discuss it. I then went to Jack, the field management advisor, who agreed that Lily was a difficult woman, but pointed out that since she was a government officer and OI did not have the means to replace her, there wasn't even a chance of getting rid of her, so just grin and bear it. At one point he almost had me believing that there wasn't actually any serious problem.

Increasingly I received complaints from the support staff that Lily was abusing them by asking them to do unreasonable work or by criticizing the work that they were doing for no reason. I was not in a position to take action on these complaints but had to refer them to the estate manager. One day the switchboard operator, Ruthi, confided in me that Lily was saying a lot of derogatory things about other OI officers. I never passed this information on to anyone because I did not want to get Ruthi into any more trouble with Lily and I felt that if it was passed on to any of my superiors they would think I was paranoid.

At this time I became aware that she was working on a project in conjunction with Mr. Schroeder called the "knitting project." The purpose was to procure the contract for the production of the sweaters worn by the Ootiland Army. If the project succeeded it would be very profitable for the entrepreneur who manufactured knitwear. I purposely did not show any interest in the project, though I was working very closely with this particular entrepreneur. But it was Mr. Schroeder's asking me to write to the potential wool suppliers that led to Lily's outburst in my office and her accusing me of stealing her project.

THE AFTERMATH

A week or two previously, I had discussed the general problem of staff complaints with the estate manager, Mr. Oti. He said that he was aware of the complaints, and he felt that in the future the personnel problems should be referred to me in his absence, especially since I was the assistant estate manager and was responsible for the estate whenever he was gone.

After Lily left my office after screaming at me, I decided that it was time to talk to her about the staff complaints. I'm sure that I did this just to tease her because I knew it would further infuriate her. As she was coming out of her office to go home I stopped her and asked her to please refer the problems she was having with the staff to me, as I was supposed to manage the estate when Mr. Oti was gone. She insisted that I tell her who the employees were and what their complaints were. I did not feel that this was appropriate and refused. At this point she grabbed my coat and told me that I was not the assistant estate manager, she had even checked with Mr. Sinduvah. I told her that as far as I knew, I was, but if it turned out that I was wrong I would apologize.

Lily was practically hysterical. She kept insisting that we have a staff meeting immediately to sort this out. The estate manager showed up and tried to calm her down. He convinced her to wait until the next day to hold a staff meeting.

Lily called the meeting, which she said was to be attended by Mr. Oti, the assistant director, Mr. Tenre, Mr. Sinduvah, Lily, and myself. We waited an hour in my office for the people from headquarters to arrive. While Lily, Mr. Oti, and I waited, Lily said to me, "You know, Sara, I am a professional. I get paid for my work; I am not a volunteer." I answered, "Just because I am a volunteer does not mean that I can be abused."

She went on to say that as a volunteer I was not qualified for my job,[1] and my reasons for becoming a volunteer were purely selfish—I wanted a cheap way to travel.

I told her that I was engaged for volunteer work on the basis of my qualifications, and I did not want to discuss the matter until she had all of her facts. She insisted that she had the facts. She then insinuated that the volunteer agency recruited to fill a specific number of positions and they were not concerned about qualifications. Finally she said that my integrity was not to be trusted; I assumed that that was in reference to my response to her letter where I said that, though the mechanic had reportedly not worked, we had an obligation to pay him his monthly salary and a further obligation to take his word that he had worked until we could prove otherwise. There was nothing said about not trusting Lily's word nor was it intentionally implied. Throughout I tried to sound very matter of fact and unemotional. I didn't want her to think that she "had" me. I never raised my voice above a conversational tone. Incidentally, during this whole conversation Mr. Oti did not say a word. He stayed at his desk engrossed in paperwork.

The meeting was finally held. It was attended by the director, Mr. Selole, instead of Mr. Tenre and Mr. Sinduvah. Mr. Selole persuaded Lily to continue working on the knitting project, but the other issues were not discussed.

I took a detached role during this meeting. It was almost as if I wasn't involved. I was curious to see what Lily wanted to discuss, and I was prepared to answer any questions. It wasn't nearly as long and detailed as I had anticipated and the matter of who was in charge of the estate when the estate manager was gone wasn't addressed. I wanted to bring it up, but Mr. Selole was supposed to be in another

[1] This is the type of logic Lily used continually. This incident was not my first nor my last exposure to it. At times I really wondered if Lily was playing with a full deck.

meeting with the director. It was only coincidental that he appeared just when we wanted to hold a meeting to hash this out; as soon as Lily agreed to take over the knitting project, he excused himself and left.

I decided that things were not ever going to get better between Lily and me so I went to see the volunteer agency area head to ask for a change of assignment. They were sympathetic and actually ready to change me if OI would release me. I went to OI and spoke to Jack about the chances of getting a release. I also told him that if nothing was done about my situation I would go home. There was no way that I would work with Lily for more than another week. Jack said that he would speak to Mr. Selole on my behalf, as he agreed that I should not work with Lily any longer. Jack did not get any results from the director, so I wrote a confidential letter to the estate manager, with a copy to the director and to the volunteer agency, requesting a transfer within OI or a release from the program on the grounds that our working relationship was irreparably damaged and it was not in the best interests of OI for us to continue working together.

In reply, the director asked Mr. Oti to speak to Lily and me separately and find out what our individual complaints were so that they could be acted on. I made it clear to Jack that I didn't think anything could be accomplished by bringing us together to discuss our problems because we were no longer on speaking terms.

As it happened the director's instructions were misunderstood, and Lily and I were brought together by Mr. Oti to discuss our complaints. After some seconds of silence in which everyone was looking at me and I was looking at Mr. Oti to start the meeting, I finally started because I felt that way I could set the tone and direction. I explained that I thought that there was a problem in our working relationship. Lily's reply was that she was not aware of the problem, and wanted me to be specific.

Her response gave me a sense of hopelessness. I knew that she would just deny everything I said or keep asking for specifics and avoid the main issue. Instead of refusing to talk about specifics I decided that maybe we could start the discussion there and move on to discuss how we could both try to work together better. A logical "specific" was when she screamed at me about stealing her project, or any of the other subsequent remarks that she made about my qualifications, etc. But I wasn't ready to talk about these with her, so I picked a legitimate gripe—the times she took the truck without telling me or anyone else. I felt that this was "safe" because she could have responded by saying something like, "I did that unintentionally, and I will try not to do it again," which would give her a graceful way to excuse herself. But instead she flatly denied it. There was no sense in discussing anything further; I felt that I had given my best shot and not gained anything, so I refused to say more. If I had spoken quietly and said "That is not true," I think that she would have just ignored me. I know that it would have become a screaming match if I had accused her of lying.

To my astonishment Mr. Oti gave her a copy of my letter asking for a transfer. Lily felt that the letter was a personal insult in that it damaged her reputation, and she felt obligated to write a response. I explained that my reasons for transfer were because we could not work together, and the reason might be with myself, not necessarily because of her. Mr. Oti asked me to withdraw my request to transfer. I felt entirely defeated and ready to give up, so I agreed. I reconciled myself to dealing with a bad working environment for the final year of my obligation.

A week later I saw the volunteer agency area head in town and he asked me what I was doing about OI. I explained to him that I no longer wanted to pursue a transfer and as far as I was concerned the subject was closed. Without telling me why, he suggested that I keep pushing for a transfer. I told him that I really did not want to, but I agreed to discuss it with him the following day. That same evening I saw Jack, who told me that he heard that Lily was suing me for slander. It was the "last straw." Also I was positive that I could not get action out of the volunteer agency and/or OI. Neither organization wanted to be involved in a court case.

Another meeting was set up with the director, Jack, and myself. For about two hours I was interrogated by the director. I repeated the entire incident when Lily stormed my office. I also told him that I had already brought the problem to headquarters and it was dismissed as a "woman's problem."

The director called in Mr. Oti to verify the conversation that Lily and I had had prior to our first meeting. Mr. Oti said that he was not listening to the conversation as it did not concern him, therefore he did not know what was actually said. Just before this meeting was adjourned the director asked Mr. Oti if he considered this a "woman's problem" that they could work out themselves. Mr. Oti was sure that it was.

Another meeting was held that afternoon with just Mr. Selole and myself. During this meeting he laid out the options that he felt were available. They were various transfers. No mention was made of transferring Lily, probably because management advisors are needed full time at each estate. However, Lily was only needed at the garment estate part time, and occasionally she was needed at one or two other estates. The director reminded me that I was needed very much at the garment estate and by requesting a transfer I was putting OI in a difficult position.

By this time I felt that no one was taking me seriously, with the exception of Jack. I told Mr. Selole that I really no longer cared what happened at OI, and I did not see how he expected me to be concerned with OI when the OI organization did not have any concern for me. I gave him a reasonable deadline to make a decision. I never threatened to quit, but it wasn't necessary; he agreed to the deadline. Within a week and a half, I was moved to another estate.

EPILOGUE

One reason I wanted to write this case was that hopefully many agencies can use it for training workers going abroad. My agency preached cultural sensitivity until you hear it in your sleep. This is all well and good, but it becomes a little unrealistic if it neglects personal sensitivity. I saw a lot of volunteers neglect their own personal feelings because they were afraid of offending a national. One example is whether to lend someone $10 because he says that he's going to the cattle post and needs it badly. Now there is no way you can spend $10 at a cattle post. Roughly translated, the man needs $10 to buy a case of beer to take to the cattle post. There are more extreme examples. My agency was very concerned about not offending. Basically I think that we were supposed to complete our assignment at all costs but keep a low profile and ruffle no one.

Parrish Hospital Pharmacy

I had just completed a year of training as a pharmacy technician and was looking forward to my first full-time work experience. My head was buzzing with questions, and I approached my new job in my new profession with excited anticipation. I had been hired by Jim, the chief pharmacist. In addition to other managerial duties, he was responsible for hiring and firing the members of the work group. Jim was friendly toward me and this made me feel comfortable about the new job, but he did seem busy and rather preoccupied with other matters.

The work group consisted of 14 full-time employees: Jim Jones, chief pharmacist (35 years old, married); six full-time pharmacists, all about 25 years old, male (five married); six full-time technicians, all female, single, and between 19 and 21 years old; one secretary, about

30 years old, married. There were also six pharmacology students. Part-time people were hired for nights and weekend work. They were all young people.

The pay for starting technicians was $2.50 an hour, with a 10-cents-an-hour raise after one year. The one exception to this was Sally, the intravenous medication (IV) technician. This job was for the most senior technician and paid $3.00 an hour. Everyone had the same basic benefits:

1. Two weeks' paid vacation after one year.
2. Paid holidays.
3. 50 cents per week for Blue Cross/Blue Shield and Master Medical.
4. Free life insurance.
5. Prescriptions at cost.

We worked 40 hours a week, 8 to 4:30, and rotated weekends. Everyone worked every third weekend. Scheduling for vacations and days off, as well as promotions and pay raises, was done strictly according to length of employment.

Actual training for the job lasted about two weeks, although it took most technicians nearly two months to familiarize themselves fully with the work area. I later learned that the hospital figured that training a new technician cost about $400, not to mention their lesser productivity during the first two months. Marty, Susan, Sally, and I had all attended one year of school to be trained as medical assistants. Part of our training was actually done in this particular pharmacy. Debora and Nancy, friends from high school, had not attended school for this special training. Debora had been working there longer than anyone except Sally, and Nancy was hired later. During high school and after graduation, Nancy had worked in the Parrish Hospital kitchen. When a position opened in the pharmacy, Debora had quickly informed Nancy. She applied for the job, was hired, and then transferred to the pharmacy. None of the workers looked down on Nancy and Debora because they hadn't gone to school, although from comments Debora made to me, I don't think she ever quite believed that. As a person she was quiet, not very outspoken, but likable and a willing worker before Nancy was hired and when Nancy was absent.

Nancy was a very different personality. She had definite opinions on many subjects and was quick to speak up for what she wanted. When she joined the department, she expressed satisfaction about getting away from the kitchen supervisor who was "a tough old guy who watched what we were doing all the time."

The technician seniority scale looked like the following:

Sally—two years.

Debora—eight months.

Marty—six months.

Me—four months.

Nancy—two months.

Susan—just hired.

The procedure in the pharmacy was routine. The physician wrote the medication order at the nurse's station, and the nurse copied it into her book for the record. A copy of the order was then sent to the pharmacy. Our task as technicians was to write the orders we did in our own individual record books and then fill the medication carts for the respective floors.

Each floor had its own cart, and each patient on that floor had a drawer in the cart. A book was kept in the pharmacy for each patient, and the frequency with which his/her medication was to be delivered was recorded in the book. The carts were sent up to the floors three times a day at 9:30, 2:00, and 7:00, stocked with all the necessary medication for that time interval. In the event that medication was needed immediately, a technician usually hand-carried it to the floor.

Other duties included filing the medication orders after they were written in the books, typing up drawer labels for newly admitted patients, restocking the bins with medications, and other odd jobs. Sally's job as the IV technician was to make up IVs for patients each day. This was done in a separate area in conjunction with two of the pharmacists. She was not required to do any of the secretarial-type tasks, except when she worked weekends.

The pharmacy was located in the basement of the hospital, next to the morgue. The kitchen and a large locker room were also in the basement. The physical layout was such that whenever Mr. Jones was at his desk he was isolated from the work area. Most of the time, he was out of the pharmacy area tending to his many administrative duties.

The first few months were a lot of fun for me. The atmosphere in the pharmacy was one of friendliness yet responsible interest in the work. A cooperative spirit prevailed, and socializing was accepted as long as the tasks were completed as scheduling demanded. Employees were assumed to be trustworthy and were thus given responsibility. There was no one timing, regulating, or watching us.

As time passed, Nancy and Debora were quick to volunteer for more and more trips to hand-carry medications to the floors. Soon, these trips began to take a few minutes longer each time. Since there was no smoking allowed in the pharmacy, Debora and Nancy were taking a "smoke break" every opportunity they could. The breaks were taken in the ladies' locker room that was used by the custodial staff at the hospital. None of the pharmacists smoked cigarettes, and they were opposed to the constant breaks Nancy and Debora took.

The secretary, Frances, smoked as did Marty, but they didn't take breaks very often; although as time went on, they too began to take more and longer breaks.

Soon Debora and Nancy began to be tardy for work in the morning by at least 20 minutes. Some of the other technicians had to travel 60 miles to work, but Nancy and Debora each lived within 1 mile of the hospital. Their coffee breaks began to get longer along with their lunch breaks. Many times one of them would call in sick, and occasionally they both did on the same day. The structure of the job was such that when anyone was missing, the other technicians had to take on an extra share of the workload. The most difficult time of the day was in the early morning. At this time the cart had to be filled and checked by the second technician before going upstairs at 9:30. If the hospital had been busy the night before, there were many new medication orders to be written in the books even before the cart was filled. When Nancy and Debora were late, the other technicians didn't have enough time to finish everything. When this happened, some of the pharmacists had to help fill up the carts. They really disliked filling the carts, both because it was tedious work and they weren't as efficient since they didn't do it routinely. It took them longer so that their assistance really wasn't very beneficial. They would occasionally remark to Nancy and Debora, "Get going; you haven't done anything all day." But this was casually disregarded.

Mr. Jones became aware of the situation when he arrived early one day and saw pharmacists filling carts. He called a meeting with everyone present. After some discussion he suggested that there be a rotating work schedule. With this system, tasks would be assigned to specific technicians to prevent work piling up on any one person. Everyone nodded their heads in agreement with this.

Even with the schedule posted, Nancy and Debora fell behind in filling their assigned carts. The smoke breaks and the fooling around were as prevalent as ever. The other technicians ended up helping them with their carts because the carts *had* to be sent up on time. Debora worked well when Nancy was on a day off but never produced when they were together. When they were both gone, and the tension was reduced, the rest of us actually had a good time. Naturally, Nancy and Debora were talked about. It was evident that they were disliked, and the general attitude toward them was one of "We'd be better off without them; they don't seem to understand that a technician is still a professional whose work affects the well-being of the patient."

Along with the new task schedule, a lunch and coffee break schedule was devised. This too rotated on a weekly basis. Whenever I went to lunch without Nancy and Debora, everyone talked about them and was angered that they "got away with doing nothing." Frances usually sided with whomever she was lunching with and then managed a way to let others know what was said about them. Almost invariably the girls from the pharmacy sat together and the pharmacists sat together at another table. On one occasion when I was scheduled for lunch at the same time as Nancy and Debora, I sat with a friend of mine who worked in a different department of the hospital. The rest of the day, they ignored me and were unfriendly and sarcastic. I later found out from Frances that they felt insulted because I had sat with someone else. They said that I didn't think they were good enough to sit with me.

By the spring, Nancy and Debora were closer than ever and their goofing off worse. Once after both of them had called in sick two days in succession, several of us walked into Happy's, a local bar, and came upon them sitting there, hardly sick from what we could see.

One of the pharmacists finally told Mr. Jones of this incident, and a second meeting was called. He began the meeting by saying, "It has come to my attention that certain people are not doing their share of the work."

Immediately, Nancy spoke up, "I don't see what the big deal is. The work is being done. I think we all do about the same amount of work."

Mr. Jones remained silent, looking for our reaction. As usual, no one said much. The tension level rose, but everyone just looked around at each other. Nothing significant was said. No one ventured to speak their mind or repeat any of the things that were usually said in Nancy and Debora's absence.

The meeting ended without really accomplishing anything. The workers all talked among themselves afterward, but no comments were ever directed toward Nancy and Debora. Their work habits continued in the same way. Dissatisfaction among the rest of us increased.

Shortly thereafter Sally announced that she was leaving in a month. Mr. Jones said that Sally's job would be filled by the next one in line, Debora. Everyone thought this was unfair, but Mr. Jones planned to "stick with the seniority policy." We didn't know what to do.

A Particle of Evidence

Mark King, monorator department manager for Blue Sky Research (BSR), was unable to fall asleep after getting home from work. An accident caused by one of his best operators had contaminated the building. Mark was afraid that the accident had been a result of the operator smoking marijuana on the unsupervised night shift. Although it was the middle of the night, the cleanup crew was still at work. Now Mark was struggling with what he should do the next day.

Blue Sky Research was a medium-sized company in the Southwest that produced chemicals and gases for a variety of industrial and military purposes. Monorators were a special kind of large-scale equipment used to manufacture and alter highly dangerous gases.

Mark King had been with BSR as the monorator department manager for five successful years. Under him in the department were his assistant manager, two chemists, and 14 operators. Mark enjoyed a comfortable, informal relationship with his subordinates and could usually be found joking with the monorator operators in his spare time. He was also very active on the company's tennis team. He took this time from his personal life not only because he loved the sport but also because many of the company's senior management played, and he saw this as a good way to make connections and build relationships with his superiors.

The monorator department's job was to operate the equipment 24 hours a day, six to seven days a week, and to perform necessary repairs. To accomplish this, employees worked three separate shifts. The first was composed of Mark, his assistant manager, the two chemists, and six operators. The second and third shifts consisted of four operators each. Mark gave the operators the responsibility to monitor the control board on the monorator and to correct all minor problems.

In order to repair the monorators, the operators had to enter the outer chamber, thus exposing themselves to the inhalation and/or contact with toxic residues created by the machines. The residue particles were so small and so potent that even with safety outfits and masks a certain amount of absorption was inevitable. In response to the medical hazards of the operator's job, which included the possibility of cancer developing up to 20 years later, the government had set maximum toxic absorption levels that an operator could be exposed to in a year. BSR had taken these restrictions one step further by setting their own maximum level at one half that of the legal limit. If any employee

This case was written by David Rothstein for classroom discussion purposes.

exceeded this limit, he was temporarily assigned to another department where the exposure was minimal. The company monitored this absorption by requiring each employee to wear electronic devices clamped to body hair to measure the amount of residue absorbed internally through inhaling it or from contact with the skin. Urine and blood samples were periodically analyzed as additional safety tests.

Even with these thorough tests and precautions, BSR still felt the best protection for their employees was their own common sense. They believed that the only way their employees could act in a sensible and responsible way was to be educated about the dangers of residues and how to handle them. This philosophy led to the creation of an intensive four-day course, after which the participants had to pass an exam before being allowed to work in the monorator department.

As a result of this program, many employees conducted themselves in a much safer manner. A few were very nervous about the long-term consequences of working with chemicals that could cause cancer, but no one objected to those who were concerned and who avoided going in the chamber. Most were cautious; however, there were still a reckless few that acted as if they thought residue could not hurt them because they could not see, smell, or feel the minute amounts. Such people did not stay very long in the department, as they soon exceeded their exposure limit and were transferred.

The monorator operators ranged in age from 20 to 26. They were all males and high school graduates; women were legally prohibited from working in the department because of the dangers of causing birth defects. Although the 14 operators were separated by shifts, they were able to interact while changing shifts, working overtime, and participating in outside activities, such as BSR's interdepartmental basketball tournament. They all got along very well and frequently went out "on the town" together at night.

Each operator had his own reasons for working in that department. Some were going to college at night and worked there because they could study at work (watching a control board does not take one's constant attention). Others worked there because they didn't have to do much but were well paid. They valued the overtime premiums possible from working late or double shifts. Still, there were a few that wanted to learn about the field and hoped to move up in the company's ranks.

As operators spent more time in the department, they learned more about the monorator. The newer workers were informally introduced to the more technical maintenance problems by the more experienced operators. If they were interested in learning more about the equipment than what was necessary to perform their jobs, the more experienced operators were happy to teach them. This additional learning was not required of the operators but was encouraged by BSR and considered during evaluations for raises and/or promotions.

As a whole, the operators took great pride in their ability to keep the monorator running, and even more pride in their individual output, or "volume/min." average. Every week each operator's volume/min. average was posted, and everyone tried to be on the top of the list.

Recently, when BSR was building an additional monorator, they hired a new operator: 26-year-old Bruce Altman. Bruce had a high school diploma and a natural aptitude for technical and electronic work. His father had owned an air-conditioning store, and in this environment Bruce had been able to develop and exercise his skills. Bruce fit in well with the other operators and the organization. As BSR proceeded to build the new monorator that Bruce was to operate, he watched and learned a great deal about the device and how it worked. Bruce became somewhat attached to this machine since he had helped to build it. He often stopped by BSR in his free time to see if everything was going well. He never asked for extra pay when he stayed to fix the equipment because he enjoyed it.

Bruce was respected by his peers as well as by Mark for his knowledge of the monorators and for his constant number-one ranking in volume/min. averages. He was also admired for his ingenuity in increasing the equipment's production rate. For example, he found that an ordinary screwdriver wedged in the seal at the top of the monorator altered the vacuum pressure and increased its efficiency. The other operators loved it when Bruce got a chance to "beat out" the scientists, whom they thought were nice but strange because the scientists wore long beards, flowered shirts, and love beads—despite being in their 50s. One instance of Bruce's ingenuity was that when he was on vacation, one of the monorators broke down and no one could figure out what was wrong, including the scientists. They ordered a complete overhaul to be conducted. The overhaul itself would only take a week, but they had to first scrub for a week to lower the toxicity level before anyone could spend any length of time inside the chamber to fix it. Bruce came back to work the day the overhaul was to begin on the washed-down chamber. He could not believe the scientists were going to waste a whole week fixing it; he went in the chamber and fixed it in two hours. The scientists were mostly amused by the progress of Bruce and other operators, although occasionally they were a bit embarrassed.

BSR recognized how boring the operators' jobs could be and permitted them to bring reading material and other diversions to pass the time. This reading material consisted of everything from *The Wall Street Journal* to *Playboy*. As long as the monorators were in good working order, producing the expected amount, and safety requirements were being observed, the company was satisfied. Operators were usually left to themselves to do things their way. The managers only worked the first shift and were never there on the weekends. During these unsupervised hours it was not uncommon for the operators to bring in a TV or radio, or occasionally even beer or marijuana. One operator claimed to the others he had seen even Mark drinking a beer in his parked car one lunch hour. The work seemed so easy most of the time that the operators didn't worry about any effects of alcohol or pot.

The managers were not stupid and suspected that the mice did play while the cat was away. However, they had no real evidence of the beer and marijuana and did not really see any point in researching the issue as long as it was kept under control. They did not want to jeopardize their rapport with the operators, nor did they want the operators rebelling against their authority. Both could result from accusing the operators of doing something that the managers were not sure was really going on.

Late one night, Bruce and another operator were putting in some overtime. The two had been smoking pot, listening to the radio, and joking around. Suddenly one of the monorators broke down, and all meters read zero. Bruce put on his safety gear and went into the outer chamber to fix it as he usually did. While working on the equipment, he accidently dropped one of the valves on the floor. This valve connected to the inner tank of the machine and was highly contaminated. Instead of picking it up with the tongs as was always done, he used a piece of equipment not designed for that purpose. He placed the valve in a safety cart to take it to another lab for repair. As he pushed the cart out of the chamber, he ran over the spot where the part had fallen, contaminating the wheels of the cart with toxic residue. As he maneuvered the cart through the halls, the wheels contaminated the entire building, triggering the electronic "sniffer" alarm. It was later discovered that he had spent too much time in the chamber, a careless error, and had breathed in more vapor than his mask could filter. He would have to be temporarily transferred to another department.

When the night security guard heard the alarm, he immediately called Mark King at home. Mark then ordered an emergency cleanup crew to meet him at the plant. When Mark arrived, he went to the control room where Bruce and the other operator were sitting. Mark noticed a partially smoked joint sitting in the ashtray and inconspicuously put it in his pocket. He told the two operators to go to the chemical analysis center for an immediate absorption check. Then he supervised the decontamination of the plant.

Mark finally got home at 3:30 A.M. He tried to fall asleep, but it was futile. The question of what to do about Bruce was bothering him too much. Bruce was one of his best workers and was well liked by most everyone, including Mark. But Mark worried that if anyone ever found out he knew about the smoking, he'd be fired. Mark felt himself to be a fair man, giving his subordinates lots of room in which to work, but now he was caught between a rock and a hard place.

Scott Trucks, Ltd

"Mr. McGowan will see you now, Mr. Sullivan," said the secretary. "Go right in."

Sullivan looked tired and tense as he opened the door and entered McGowan's office. He had prepared himself for a confrontation and was ready to take a firm approach. McGowan listened as Sullivan spoke of the problems and complaints in his department. He spoke of the recent resignation of Tobin and the difficult time he had in attracting and keeping engineers. McGowan questioned Sullivan as to the quality of his supervision and direction, emphasizing the need to monitor the work and control the men.

"You have got to let them know who is boss and keep tabs on them at all times," said McGowan.

"But Mr. McGowan, that is precisely the point; my engineers resent surveillance tactics. They are well-educated, self-motivated people. They don't want to be treated like soldiers at an army camp."

The discussion was beginning to heat up. McGowan's fist hit the table. "Listen Sullivan, I brought you in here as a department manager reporting to me. I don't need your fancy textbook ideas about leading men. I have 10 years as a military officer, and I have run this plant from its inception. If you can't produce the kind of work I want and control your men, then I will find someone who can. I don't have complaints and holdups from my other managers. We have systems and procedures to be followed, and so they shall or I will know the reason they aren't."

"But that is just the point," continued Sullivan, "my men do good work and contribute good ideas and, in the face of job pressures, perform quite well. They don't need constant supervision and direction and least of all the numerous and unnecessary interruptions in their work."

"What do you mean by that?" asked McGowan.

"Well, both Tobin and Michaels have stated openly and candidly that they like their work but find your frequent visits to the department very disconcerting. My engineers need only a minimal amount of control, and our department has these controls already established. We have weekly group meetings to discuss projects and routine work. This provides the kind of feedback that is meaningful to them. They don't need frequent interruptions and abrasive comments about their work and the need to follow procedures."

"This is my plant and I will run it the way I see fit," screamed McGowan. "No department manager or engineer is going to tell me otherwise. Now I suggest, Mr. Sullivan, that you go back to your department, have a meeting with your men, and spell out my expectations."

By this time Sullivan was intimidated and very frustrated. He left the office hastily and visibly upset. McGowan's domineering style had prevailed, and the meeting had been quite futile. No amount of pleading or confrontation would change McGowan's attitude.

Sullivan returned to his department and sat at his desk quite disillusioned with the predicament. His frustration was difficult to control, and he was plagued with self-doubt. He was astonished at McGowan's intractable position and stubbornness.

He posted a notice for a meeting that would be held the next day with his department. He outlined an agenda and included in it mention of resignation. He left the plant early, worrying about the direction he should take.

BACKGROUND

Scott Trucks is housed in an old aircraft hangar in the Debert Industrial Park, near Truro, Nova Scotia. The government of Nova Scotia sold the building for a modest sum as it no longer had use for the hangar after the armed forces had abandoned it. The facility, together with the financial arrangements organized by Mr. McGowan, the president of Scott, made the enterprise feasible.

Inside the building, renovations have provided for an office area, a production operation, and an engineering department. The main offices are located at the front of the building, housing the sales team and the office clerks. The sales manager, Mike McDonald (see Exhibit 1), and two assistants make up the sales team at the Debert location of Scott Trucks. Three or four field representatives work in southern Ontario and the United States.

Mike is considered a good salesman and often assumes a role much broader than sales. Customer complaints, ordering, and replacement parts also fall into his domain. The production manager frequently makes reference to Mike's ability to talk on two phones at the same time!

EXHIBIT 1
Organizational Chart, Scott Trucks

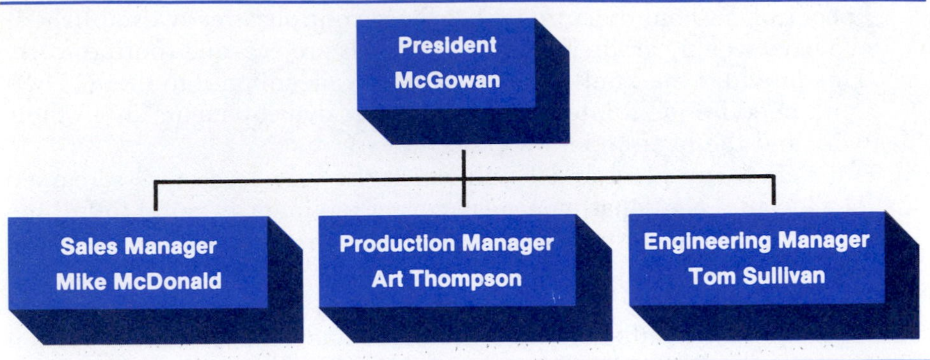

Art Thompson has been production manager at Scott Trucks for eight years. The area he manages is behind the sales office and takes up most of the space in the building. The engineering department, comprising small offices, is located behind the production department, which is divided into two areas by a long, narrow corridor. The shop floor is divided into basic sections of assembly with a paint, a welding, and a cab section as well as other areas used to assemble the large Scott trucks.

Owing to the limited capacity of the plant, only two or three truck units are in production at any one time. Another constraint on capacity is the nature of the system used to produce the trucks. There are no pulleys, belts, or assembly lines used in the system; rather the production takes place in large bays where sections of the truck are individually completed in preparation for the final assembly.

The truck units are used for a variety of functions, particularly where a heavy truck requirement is in demand. Fire trucks, highway maintenance trucks, and long-distance hauling trucks are some of the units produced by Scott. To some extent the trucks are custom made, as each purchaser will request changes on the basic design. The engineers also adapt the trucks to meet the various standards and specifications of the Canadian government and the rigorous Canadian climate.

Tom Sullivan, who is a recent graduate of Nova Scotia Technical Institute with a degree in engineering, is the newest of the managers at Scott. He shows good promise as an engineer but, as with his predecessor, is having adjustment problems as a manager. Tom received an M.B.A. from Dalhousie University and majored in management science and organizational behavior. He completed project work in participative management styles under the direction of a specialist in this area. He tries to practice this approach in his new position and enjoys the ideas and flow of discussion at the department meetings. Tom works in a department with men much his senior and is the youngest of the department managers at Scott Truck. He works hard and is well liked by his subordinates. Personal satisfaction, though infrequent, comes as a direct result of the open and participative management style he uses.

THE ENGINEERS

The composition of the group of engineers at Scott is unusual. One of the group is not an engineer by qualification but had many years of practical experience. He moved from Detroit to Truro, having worked with Ford Trucks for 15 years. Since his recruitment by McGowan he has worked with Scott for eight years. Retirement for this man is not far off, a fact he frequently makes known to the group. His work is good, and he seems to have many answers to difficult problems—a redeeming factor in the absence of an engineering degree. Don Jones, another member of the group, is a good engineer. His workday is solid. However, most evenings are spent at a local tavern. His wife was killed recently, and he does not seem to care any more. The remainder of the group are a combination of senior and junior men who have been with the company for a number of years. Two engineers had just left the group for better jobs and for a "less confining" atmosphere, as they put it. Tom Sullivan's effort to lead the group is proving to be a difficult task.

THE PRODUCTION WORKERS

Work for the men in the production plant is reasonably stable. A good-paying job in production in Truro is difficult to find, a situation of which the men are fully aware; many of them have experienced the monotony of unemployment and job hunting before this opening presented itself.

With the exception of a few French-Canadian welders, the workers are Maritimers whose experience and skills range from those of a skilled tradesman to those of a casual laborer. The local trades school in Truro has provided the organization with a number of good machinists, welders, and painters that the foreman hired and began to develop.

The morale on the plant floor has been very good, particularly since the company has improved its sales position. The once-frequent layoffs that were due to work shortage have ceased in the presence of higher demand for the trucks. The new field sales group contributes significantly to the situation with their efforts in southern Ontario and the northern United States. The pay scale is above average for the area, and there is a good rapport between the production manager and the workers.

ADMINISTRATIVE CONTROL

Administrative control in the plant has been accomplished by two methods; one in terms of the quality of the product and the other in terms of its cost. Attention has been paid to the quality control function through a quality control supervisor whose task it is to examine the end product in a thorough manner using rigorous criteria. The other method of control is that implemented by the accounting office. Through the adoption of a standard cost program, material, labor, and overhead variances are accumulated and presented on data report sheets.

The production manager, Art Thompson, is responsible for collecting cost data and for sending it to the office on a weekly basis. Art is not an easygoing person; he frequently gets upset when problems occur on the shop floor. He is closely watched by Mr. McGowan, the president. Consequently, to Art the monthly meetings of the managers are a real ordeal, since McGowan, as owner, tries to watch the costs very carefully and to make sure the plant is running as efficiently as possible.

McGowan uses three approaches to managing the operation at Scott Trucks. The first is a monthly meeting with the three managers. The second technique is a series of interdepartmental memos that interpret the results of cost figures presented to him throughout the month. The third method is by frequent plant visits and observations.

None of these controls is favorably received by the managers, as they feel they are being watched too carefully. Interdepartmental memos may read as follows:

May 12, 19__

To: Mr. Art Thompson, production manager

From: Mr. McGowan, president, Scott Trucks

Re: Materials quantity variance

I noticed a considerable amount of materials quantity variance in your production reports for last week. The standard cost system has been implemented for six weeks now, and it no longer suffices to say that you are still "working the bugs out of the system." It is time you paid closer attention to the amount of materials going into the production process and to avoiding any spoilage.

Another example of an interdepartmental memo reads as follows:

May 20, 19__

To: Mr. Art Thompson, production manager
From: Mr. McGowan, president, Scott Trucks
Re: Inaccurate recording of time, and use of time cards

I noticed last week on your labor cost submissions that a number of employees have been neglecting to punch time cards. Please see that this system is properly followed.

Art Thompson's reaction to these memos has been one of apprehension and concern. It is the practice of the foreman and himself to try to resolve the problems as quickly as possible, and together they have been able to rectify these difficulties quite rapidly as the men are eager to cooperate.

The plant visits to the production area made by Mr. McGowan are frequent and effective. He has been known to come out in shirtsleeves and literally assume the workman's job for a period of time. This is particularly true of a new worker or a young worker, where he will dig in and instruct the individual on how he should be doing his job. On such occasions he will give specific instructions as to how he wants things done and how things should be done.

It makes McGowan feel right at home when he is involved with the workers. He spent 15 years as a navy commander, and he often used to remark that there was only one way to deal with his subordinates. The reaction of the workers to this approach is mixed. Some of the production people dislike this "peering over the shoulders;" others do not seem to mind and appreciate McGowan's concern for a "job well done." The workers grumble at McGowan's approach but feel most of his criticisms to be constructive.

McGowan's management approach in the monthly meetings is not considerably different from that with the production workers. McGowan assumes a very authoritarian style in dealing with his managers.

The monthly meetings are an integrative effort among engineering, sales, and production, with the purpose of ironing out difficulties both on a personality basis and on a work basis. The workload in the engineering department has been growing for the last six months at a considerable rate. This reflects the increase in production and the need for people in the area of engineering and design to provide a high quality of technical expertise.

The number of engineers currently working at Scott is eight. Relations between the engineering department and other departments have been less than satisfactory, and a good deal of conflict has occurred over a number of issues. For example, the reports from quality control at Scott have been poor from time to time, and increasingly the problem has been traced to unclear engineering specifications. Upset about these conditions, McGowan has expressed strong disapproval in his memos to the department.

Lately the engineers have been bombarded with McGowan's memos, the results of more frequent complaints about the engineering department from the quality control manager and the production manager. Along with other factors, they have provided the ammunition McGowan needed to confront the engineering department. The engineers, however, have resisted, refusing to accept these memos in the same way that the production people have. As a result of these memos, complaints and misunderstandings have arisen. The engineers have responded by suggesting that the production people cannot interpret the blueprints and that they never bother to question them when a change is not understood or clear.

Disturbed by this situation, McGowan has made it a point to visit the engineering section at regular intervals, and his tactics have been much the same as with the production people. Unfortunately, the engineering manager, Tom Sullivan, was feeling the pressure and could not seem to keep his department running smoothly. Being new to the job, he did not know how to handle McGowan. The two engineers had quit recently and left the company, not explaining their discontent but only referring to better jobs elsewhere.

Tom Sullivan had reacted poorly to this situation and had been in a somber mood for about two months. His work and his adjustment had not been successful. The veterans in the department, though understanding his frustration, could not help Sullivan, who felt he was better off trying to accommodate McGowan than resisting him. To make matters worse the two engineers who had recently quit had left a large backlog of work incomplete, and efforts to recruit new engineers had been a strain on Sullivan. The marketplace quickly absorbed all the engineers graduating from Nova Scotia Tech, and Debert, Nova Scotia, had few attractions available to enable it to compete with larger centers.

Tom did get a big break, however, in his recruiting drive when he discovered through a contact in Montreal two engineers who were wishing to return to the Maritimes. Both men were young and had experience and good training in engineering. In their interview they discussed their experiences and their ability to work independently. Moreover, both were looking for a quieter environment. Sullivan liked their credentials and hired the two men.

McGowan had been on vacation at the time and had not met the new engineers until a month after they had been on the job. His first encounter, however, was a cordial meeting with the two engineers and, although the climate in the department was always unpredictable and changing, activities and relations were smooth for a month or two, much to the relief of Sullivan. McGowan maintained his surveillance of the plant, including the engineers. Tim Michaels and Bill Tobin, the new engineers, felt uncomfortable with McGowan around but just proceeded with their work and ignored the long stares and the continued presence of the "boss."

One Friday afternoon McGowan walked into the engineering section with a smug look on his face. It was near the end of the month, just prior to the monthly meeting. Sullivan looked up immediately as McGowan moved towards Tobin's drafting table. McGowan was irate. He began talking to Tobin in a loud voice. Shaking his fist, he threw down a report on a change proposed by Tobin for the interior of the cabs made at Scott.

"What gives you the right to implement such a change without first going to Sullivan, then to me?" screamed McGowan. "You have only been with this company for two and a half months and already you feel you can ignore the 'system.' "

"Well, Mr. McGowan, I thought it was a good idea, and I have seen it work before," responded Tobin, flustered by McGowan's attack.

In the meantime Sullivan came out from his office to see what the problem was about. McGowan turned to him and asked him why he couldn't control his men, adding that the changes were totally unauthorized and unnecessary. Sullivan glanced at the blueprint and was taken by surprise when he examined it more carefully. In the meantime McGowan raved on about Tobin's actions.

"Oh, um, ah, yes, Mr. McGowan, you're right; this should have been cleared between, uh, you and me before production got it; but, ah, I will see that it doesn't happen again."

McGowan stormed out, leaving Tobin and Sullivan standing by the desk. Tobin was upset by "this display of rudeness," as he put it.

"Tom," he went on, "this was a damn good idea and you know it."

Sullivan shook his head, "Yes, you're right. I don't know how to deal with McGowan; he wears me down sometimes. But also, Bill, you have to channel your changes through the system."

Tobin turned back to his table and resumed his afternoon work.

For the next six weeks the plant operated smoothly as production picked up and more people were hired. Work in the engineering department increased correspondingly as people wanted new and better parts on their trucks. New engine and cab designs were arriving and put an increased burden on the engineering department. In fact it fell well behind in its efforts to change and adapt the truck specifications to meet the Canadian environment. The lengthy review process required to implement change also put an added burden on the operation at Scott.

These difficulties were compounded further by the fact that engineers were hard to find, and at Scott they were also hard to keep. Moreover, summer was approaching, which meant decreased manpower owing to the holidays.

McGowan's frequent visits added to the difficult situation in the engineering department. Sullivan had taken to group meetings once a week with the engineers in an attempt to solve engineering problems and personal conflicts. At each meeting Tobin and Michaels discussed their work with the group and showed signs of real progress and development. They were adjusting well and contributing above expectations. At these meetings, however, they both spoke openly and frankly about McGowan's frequent visits and his abrasive style. A month had passed since they first suggested to Sullivan that he talk to McGowan about the problems he presented to the engineers by his visits to the department. At first the rest of the group agreed passively to the idea that Sullivan confront McGowan on this issue, but by the fourth week the group was being very firm with Sullivan on this issue, insisting he talk with McGowan.

Tom Sullivan knew the time had come and that he would have to face McGowan. That very morning he had received a call from a local company about Mr. Tobin and the quality of his work. Presumably Tobin had been looking for work elsewhere. This was the last straw. Sullivan picked up the phone and asked the secretary for an appointment with Mr. McGowan.

He wondered as he hung up the phone how he would deal with the problems he faced in his department and with Mr. McGowan.

Shay's Hardware

Shay's Hardware Store is a family-operated business located in a small New England town. Harold Shay and his wife have run the business for over 30 years and have been able to earn a modest living from it. Harold and his wife are getting old, however, and for about the past 10 years the bulk of the operation has been left in the hands of their son Ray.

Ray Shay has worked in his father's store ever since he was old enough to sweep floors. He has spent most of his life learning the business from the inside, and when he took over, Shay's was left in capable hands. Married and in his early 30s, Ray was ambitious, energetic, and extremely skilled with his hands. He was able to save Shay's from the fate of most small-town stores. Seeing that they would be unable to compete with the prices of larger, more diversified stores in the cities, he concentrated on providing services to go along with the products. Shay's engaged in almost any activity associated with the business: painting, plumbing service, TV repair, antenna installation, landscaping, appliance service, and anything else Ray could do. Everybody in town knew Ray to be reliable and reasonable in price, and most people called Shay's when they needed something fixed before going somewhere else.

During most of the year the jobs he undertook were on a small scale, and he was able to handle them on his own. Harold and Mrs. Shay operated the store while Ray was out on call.

Sam Welch, 18, also worked at the store, part time during the school year and full time during the summer. He had now worked for the Shays for almost three years. During the school year he stayed mostly at the store, taking orders from Harold, doing most of the heavy work, and occasionally helping Ray. Shay's busy season was during the summer when Sam would work with Ray full time and a younger boy would be hired at the store.

For a high school student, working for Shay's was an extremely good summer job, and Sam knew it. While most of his friends spent the summer in a factory or restaurant doing the same things day after day, he would be outdoors doing something different practically every week. Furthermore, Ray was a good-natured boss, and the two got along quite well.

Sam was also quite handy, eager to learn, and Ray enjoyed teaching him. They became good friends. As Sam grew more skillful, Ray would give him more and more responsibility, even to the point where he would be sent on some jobs alone. Ray had even promised him a permanent job after graduation, and Sam was seriously considering taking it.

A recent summer was a particularly busy one at Shay's as a result of Ray's decision to expand the paint department. He was hoping that if he could employ kids of Sam's age at summer wages and train them to paint houses, people would hire Shay's instead of costlier professional painters. The idea worked well. During the spring, he contracted to paint several houses to be done over the summer months. The volume was heavy enough that he could keep two extra helpers employed full time painting houses with Sam, which would leave him free to concentrate on other jobs.

Ray hired two of Sam's classmates, Jeffrey Brown and Jack Meredith, on Sam's recommendation. Both were enrolled in college for the fall semester and were willing to work cheap. They agreed to work for

$2.50 per hour compared to Sam's wage of $3.15. Both had some experience painting houses—in fact, more than Sam did. Sam was excited about their employment. He was really looking forward to spending the summer with two of his best friends while continuing to help Ray.

The first job went quite smoothly. Under Ray's supervision Sam learned quickly, as usual, while Jeff and Jack needed no help at all. Jack was extremely fast and did a good job on clapboards, while Jeff was especially capable on trim and windows. Sam was able to hold his own but was a little slower than the other two. Ray was confident that the three could handle all of the houses he had contracted and that they could be trusted to be left alone for extended periods.

One day early in July, Ray was installing a TV antenna and fell off the roof. Luckily, it was a one-story house, and he landed on his feet. Unfortunately, he suffered a severe back sprain and had to remain in bed for a couple of weeks.

Many of Shay's services had to be temporarily curtailed, but Ray was reluctant to end his profitable house-painting venture. The boys had done well so far under his minimal supervision, and he was confident that Sam could handle the responsibilities. With Harold's approval, he sent word to Sam to take over and keep the job going.

Things went smoothly for the next two weeks as Sam didn't have to exercise any of his authority. Jeff and Jack really didn't have to be told what to do. The procedure had become almost routine. Between the fussy homeowners and the constant supervision of the "sidewalk superintendents," there was little time to goof off. Once in awhile they would have a few beers on a hot afternoon or spray the garden hose on each other. Sam, who took part in these activities, was sure that Ray would not have minded.

During the first week of August they started work on Austin Miller's house. Mr. Miller was president of the local bank and owned one of the largest houses in town. The Millers also had a huge, tempting swimming pool in the back yard. Jack particularly had been looking forward to this job because he had been dating Mr. Miller's daughter Kathy for some time. While Mr. and Mrs. Miller were gone most of the time, Kathy usually had several friends over; and they often spent the whole day sunning themselves by the pool.

Under the circumstances it became increasingly difficult for the three to concentrate on their work (especially when they were in sight of the pool), and to make matters worse, the weather turned unbearably hot. Kathy invited them to spend their lunch breaks by the pool. Sam soon noticed that every day the lunch period seemed to get longer and work periods shorter and less productive. It wasn't long before the work was behind schedule.

At first Sam was a willing participant and took as much time off as the other two, but it soon became apparent to him that they would not be able to finish the house in the allotted three weeks unless they got to work. He also knew that Ray would be out of bed in a few days and would probably be around for inspection. Sam wanted him to be pleased at their progress.

He was reluctant to order his friends around, especially in front of the girls. Most of the time he was able to end the lunch breaks by using gentle persuasion. He would say something like "Hey, I guess it's time to get back to work," and hope that Jack and Jeff would follow him. After awhile this method became less and less effective as the two would work when they chose and paid little attention to Sam. Sam felt more and more anxious and helpless.

One afternoon Sam was finishing a small piece in the front of the house while Jack and Jeff went around to the other side to begin a new section. After he finished his end, he went around to the side to find nothing done, two paint brushes hardened in the sun, and no sign of Jack or Jeff. He soon found them playing volleyball with the girls by the pool.

Sam finally lost his temper and started yelling at them, ordering them to get back to work. The two found this amusing, and Jack replied, "Sure pal, soon as we win two out of three." Seeing that the situation was hopeless, Sam went back to work and they joined him half an hour later.

That Friday Mr. Miller went to the store and complained to Harold that the boys had been working on his house for two weeks and it wasn't even half finished. Harold told him that Ray was coming back to work Monday and would find out what the problem was. When Harold told him of the complaint, Ray decided that a surprise visit would provide him with the best answer.

Ray arrived at the Millers about one o'clock Monday afternoon, just in time to catch Jack and Jeff in one of their extended lunches at the pool while Sam was working alone. When Ray found Jack and Jeff, he nearly fired both of them on the spot, but instead he told them either to get to work or go home. He was also furious at Sam. "I made you the boss here, and it was up to you to get this job done. Is this how you run an operation, by letting your workers loaf all day? If they wouldn't work, you should have told me right away and I would have straightened them out. I thought you were more responsible than this."

▶ The Seacoast Mutual Insurance Co.

PART I

As he stared out of the window of his spacious office, Peter Shea, vice president and manager of the Accounting Department of the Seacoast Mutual Insurance Company, pondered the alternatives of the decision he was about to make.

Ed Maddix, supervisor of the Data Entry Department, had just left and had urged Peter to move the Data Entry Department from its present location beside a large picture window to a larger location set aside from the normal traffic flow. (See Exhibit 1.) Ed had been unsuccessful in getting the women in his department to stop staring out the window and talking to other employees; he felt that the move would increase their productivity and stop the dysfunctional behavior.

The Seacoast Mutual Insurance Company, commonly referred to by its employees as "The Seacoast," was a small, conservative New England company located about 30 miles from Boston. Having been in existence for over 100 years, the company was striving to continue its recent growth rate of 10 percent per year and harbored hopes of even increasing its growth rate in the future.

The Seacoast employed over 150 employees, many of whom were lifelong residents of the area. There was little turnover, and few people were ever fired or laid off. Within the community, the Seacoast had the reputation of being a secure, dependable company and a clean, pleasant place to work.

Because of the ample supply of available workers, salaries at the Seacoast were lower than the regional average. Many of the employees could earn more money by commuting to Boston, but they were reluctant to do so; although many employees complained about the low wages, they preferred to remain at the Seacoast with its security, good fringe benefits, suburban setting, and known type of co-workers, rather than commute into Boston.

Close to three fourths of the employees were women, mainly filling clerical and support positions. Many had lived in the area all their lives and had worked at the Seacoast since graduating from high school. The ages of the women ranged from 18 to 65, with the majority being in their 20s and 30s. Most of the women had families, and their salaries were needed to supplement their husbands' incomes. Many

From S. Fink, R. S. Jenks, and R. Willits, *Designing and Managing Organizations*, 1983, pages 597–602. Reproduced by permission of Richard D. Irwin, Inc., Homewood, Ill.

EXHIBIT 1
Layout of the Third Floor of the Seacoast Mutual Insurance Company

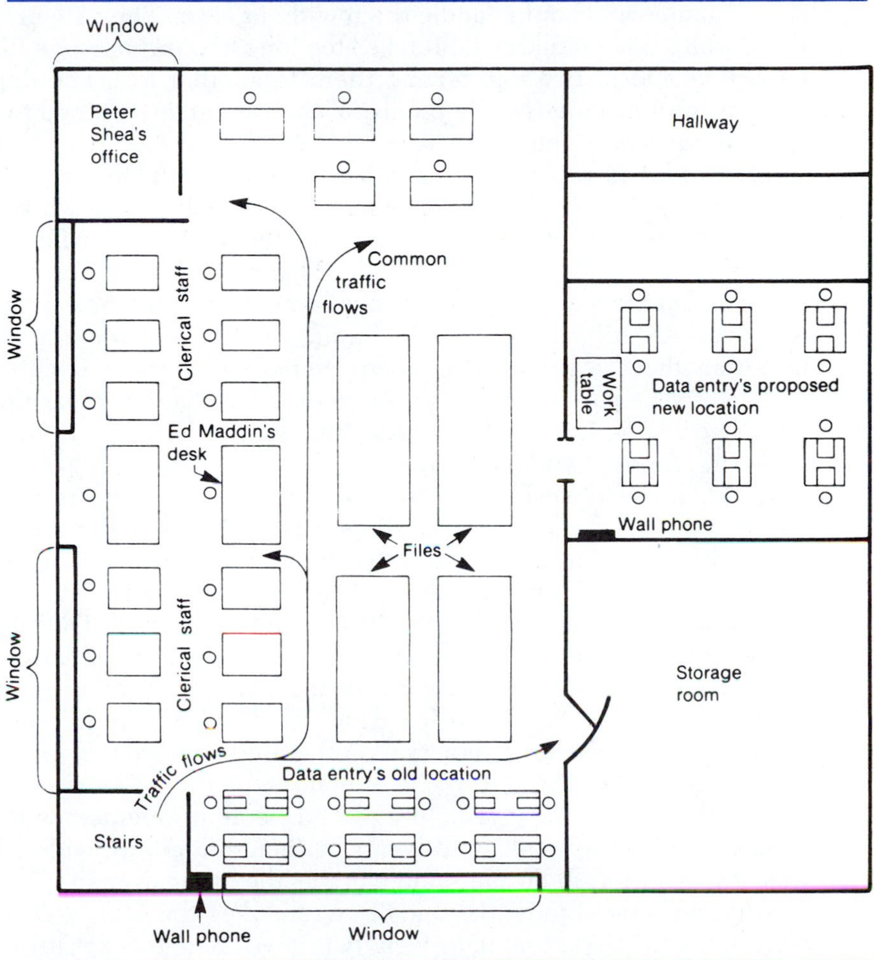

of the women felt that they were fortunate to have a job, especially one so close to home.

The Data Entry Department consisted of 11 keypunch operators. All of the operators had been employed by the company for at least two years, and many had been in the department for five to seven years. Data entry was one of the lower-paying departments, and the women were rarely transferred out of the department or promoted.

The job of data entry operator required keyboard skills and involved the keypunching of account information for input into the computer. New operators learned only one type of account at a time, and after they mastered one type, they moved on to another. The operators agreed that it took nearly one year before they had been exposed to and mastered all of the different policies and accounts that the Seacoast handled and could handle them without error. Their supervisor, Ed Maddix, once remarked, "It takes too long to train someone in this department to justify transferring them to another job. The department is most productive when most of the women are trained to process all types of accounts."

The workload was not constant in the department. Once or twice a day, someone from mail and message would leave new work on a table in the middle of the department, and the operators would go and get the work that they knew how to do. The work tended to be heavier at the end of the week when other departments cleared their desks for the weekend. All accounts were computer run on Saturday, so it was important that the accounts be processed before Saturday. Usually the Data Entry Department was able to work extra hard to clear up the work backlog by Fridays at 4:30 P.M. Oftentimes there was little work to do on Mondays and Tuesdays.

Ed Maddix had worked for the Seacoast for nearly 30 years. Most of the men in management were younger than Ed, who had reached his top position and was waiting for retirement. Ed had other responsibilities in addition to supervising the Data Entry Department, and his desk was located approximately 50 feet away from the Data Entry Department. Although the department was in full view of Ed's desk, he rarely went into the department. Instead, he would call the group's work leader, Jane Smith, to his desk. Ed would relay information through Jane. Because of his actions and attitude toward the operators, Ed was generally disliked by the operators.

Jane Smith was 28 years old and had been an operator with the Data Entry Department for 10 years. Although a group leader, Jane was still required to do the same work as the other women. She was considered "one of the girls" and often remarked that she had trouble controlling the department, especially if it was something that Ed had ordered her to do. As an operator, Jane had shared the department's dislike for Ed, but after being promoted to group leader, she rarely joined in the women's open criticism of him.

The Data Entry Department was located on the third floor and situated beside a very large picture window that overlooked a scenic, tree-lined street. The buildings along the street were colonial and had large well-kept grounds. The window faced south, and the sunlight would shine into the department most of the day, adding light and warmth to the atmosphere. The keypunch machines were situated so that each operator had a window view. The building was old and not well insulated, and the department was often hot in the summer and drafty in the winter. The women often complained about the temperature, saying that the condition was the cause of many colds.

The women would remain in the department for coffee and lunch breaks. Often they would stop working for several minutes to watch something out the window. Other employees, especially those who worked on the third floor, often stopped by to enjoy the view. When this happened, the visitors and operators would engage in casual conversation.

Located near the department was a main stairway. Since the stairs were used frequently, there was a steady stream of people walking by the department and in winter continuous blasts of cold air from the unheated stairwell. Because of the traffic, however, the operators often engaged in conversation with others in the company, and with people always coming and going, the department had a "hustle-bustle" appearance.

The window watching and conversations greatly disturbed Ed Maddix. Maddix felt that conversations while working led to mistakes, lack of efficiency, and an unprofessional tone. From his desk, Ed would often telephone Jane Smith and command her to make the operators stop talking and get back to work. Jane would reluctantly tell the operators to stop. The conversations would stop, but it was not long before the next one would start up again.

Ed had made his feelings known to Peter Shea, his boss. Peter had always let Ed handle the problems of the department, and he felt that it was Ed's job to control his workers. However, Peter had become increasingly concerned about the window watching and the conversations, and he, too, wanted to see the behavior stopped. Peter realized that Ed's methods were not working and soon something would have to be done.

Peter's conversation with Ed this morning went like this:

Ed: Peter, I just can't stand it. These girls just don't want to stop looking out of the window and talking with every single person who wanders by their department.

Peter: I know, Ed. How much has this window watching backlogged the department?

Ed: At the moment, not very much. But if we continue to increase our volume of business, someday we are either going to have to hire more girls and buy more equipment, or be backlogged. Of course, if we could find a way to put an end to the window watching, we could probably handle the increased volume of business with our current number of girls.

Peter: Well, you have spoken to them a number of times, and that doesn't seem to stop them. What do you suggest we do?

Ed: If they are going to ignore me, I think that we should let them know we mean business. I think that we should move the department away from the window and away from the flow of people going past them all day. I think that the old word processing area that we are now using for storage files would be ideal. It's larger than the present location and well lit with fluorescent lights. It has walls on three sides and six-foot partitions in front, screening the room from the rest of the floor. On top of that, it's air-conditioned and carpeted. You know how they complain about the fluctuation in temperature near the windows. They should like it a lot.

PETER: Well, Ed, that's a pretty drastic step.

ED: I know it is, but I think that it's about time we did something drastic around here. People have got to realize that we mean business and that they are here to work, not to talk and have a good time.

PETER: You're right, Ed. Let me think about it, and I'll get back to you.

PART II

The following morning, Ed telephoned Jane and informed her that the department was being moved across the floor to an area now occupied by the storage files. He told Jane that the reason for the move was because of the great amount of talking and socializing that occurred, and that the new location would not provide them with any distractions.

The data entry operators were very upset over the move. Convinced that they had no choice but to comply, they complained among themselves and to friends but did not talk to Peter Shea or Ed Maddix.

The move was accomplished that weekend, and on Monday the women reported to their new location. Without the sun streaming in the window, the new department seemed darker than the previous location. Although both locations had walls that were painted pale gray, the operators, who had never minded the walls before the move, now felt that the walls were dingy and unpleasant. Combined with the dark green partitions, the plainness of the location seemed to stand out. Other employees still stopped by, but the opportunity to do this was greatly reduced. The lack of contact with others in the company further increased their feelings of isolation.

The change had drastic effects on the department. The women no longer remained in the department for breaks and lunch. Since the new location shielded them from Ed's desk, they were able to read paperbacks and magazines at their machines.

The hoped-for increase in productivity did not materialize. Within several months, three operators left the company. Personnel was able to quickly get replacements, but it would be months before they would be as capable as the operators who quit. In addition, there didn't seem to be the drive to complete the workload by the end of the week. Errors increased, and it took additional time to correct and rekeypunch the data.

Now, six months after the move, Peter Shea wondered if he had made the correct decision. Since the new location was larger and more comfortable, he could not understand why the women would not accept their new location. Peter could move the department back to the original location, or he could keep it in the present location and "ride the storm." As he wondered what he should do, he continued to look out of the window.

The Slade Company

Ralph Porter, production manager of the Slade Company, was concerned by reports of dishonesty among some employees in the plating department. From reliable sources he had learned that a few men were punching the time cards of a number of their workmates who had left early. Mr. Porter had only recently joined the Slade organization. He judged from conversations with the previous production manager and other fellow managers that they were, in general, pleased with the overall performance of the plating department.

The Slade Company was a prosperous manufacturer of metal products designed for industrial application. Its manufacturing plant, located in central Michigan, employed nearly 500 workers who were engaged in producing a large variety of clamps, inserts, knobs, and similar items. Orders for these products were usually large and on a recurrent basis. The volume of orders fluctuated in response to business conditions in the primary industries which the company served. At the time of this case, sales volume had been high for over a year. The basis upon which the Slade Company secured orders, in rank of importance, were quality, delivery, and reasonable price.

The organization of manufacturing operations at the Slade plant is shown in Exhibit 1. The departments listed there are, from left to right, approximately in the order in which material flowed through the plant. The diemaking and setup operations required the greatest degree of skill, supplied by highly paid, long-service craftsmen. The finishing departments, divided operationally and geographically between plating and painting, attracted less highly trained but relatively skilled workers, some of whom had been employed by the company for many years. The remaining operations were largely unskilled in nature and were characterized by relatively low pay and high rate of turnover of personnel.

EXHIBIT 1
Manufacturing Organization

President
Production Manager (Ralph Porter)
Receiving and Shipping Department (Foreman)
Production Control (Foreman)
Maintenance Department (Foreman)
Tool and Die Department (Foreman)
Stamping Department (Foreman)
Plating Department (Foreman: O. Schell)
Paint Department (Foreman)
35 Workers
27 Workers
35 Toolmakers
30 Setup Men
8 Sections (8 Assistant Foremen)
38 Workers
28 Workers
In-Process Storage (Assistant Foremen)
Materials Handling (Assistant Foreman)
Scheduling (Assistant Foreman)
200 Workers
18 Workers
32 Workers
10 Clerks
6 Expediters

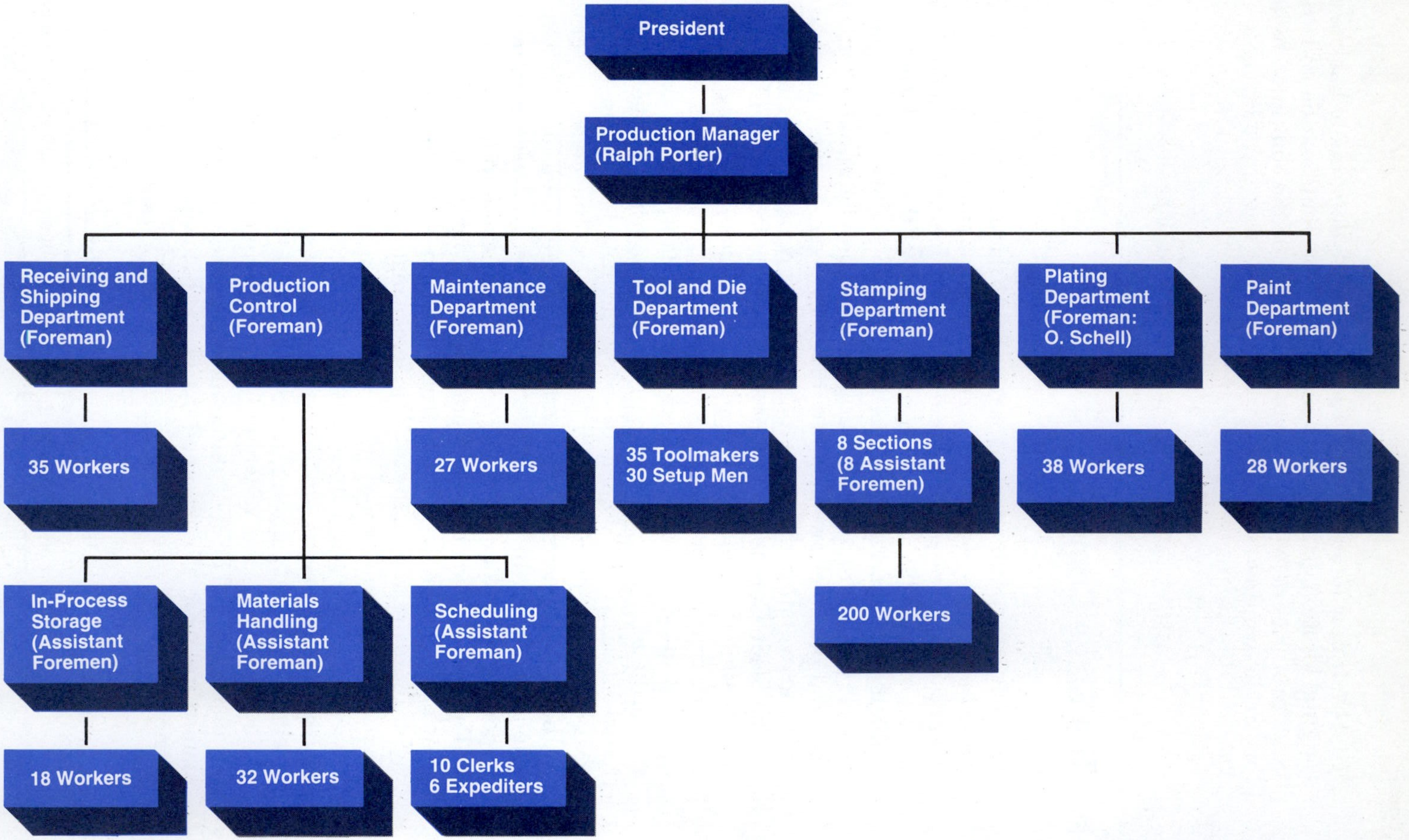

The plating room was the sole occupant of the top floor of the plant. Exhibit 2 shows the floor plan, the disposition of workers, and the flow of work throughout the department. Thirty-eight men and women worked in the department, plating or oxidizing the metal parts or preparing parts for the application of paint at another location in the plant. The department's work occurred in response to orders communicated by production schedules, which were revised daily. Schedule revisions, caused by last-minute order increases or rush requests from

EXHIBIT 2
Plating Room Layout

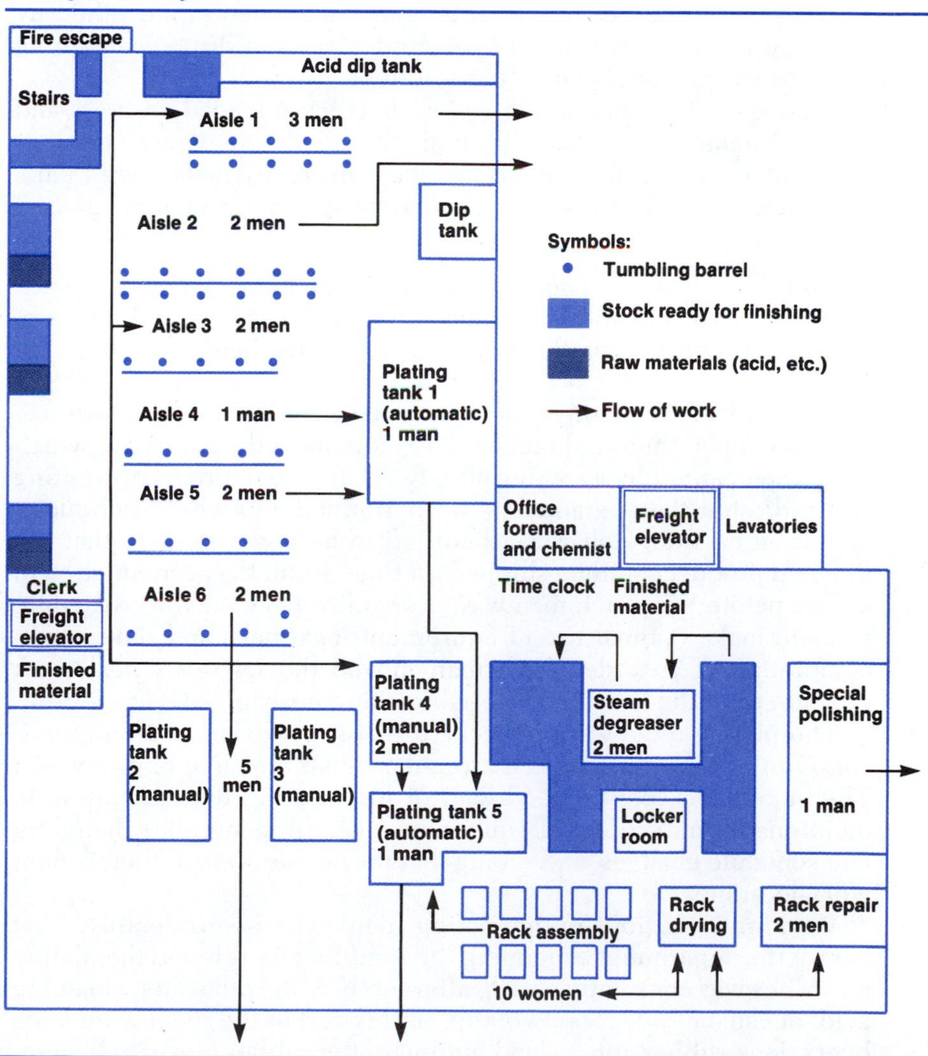

customers, resulted in short-term volume fluctuations, particularly in the plating, painting, and shipping departments. Exhibit 3 outlines the activities of the various jobs, their interrelationships, and the type of work in which each specialized. Exhibit 4 rates the various types of jobs in terms of the technical skill, physical effort, discomfort, and training time associated with their performance.

The activities which took place in the plating room were of three main types:

1. Acid dipping, in which parts were etched by being placed in baskets which were manually immersed and agitated in an acid solution.
2. Barrel tumbling, in which parts were roughened or smoothed by being loaded into machine-powered revolving drums containing abrasive, caustic, or corrosive solutions.
3. Plating—either manual, in which parts were loaded on racks and were immersed by hand through the plating sequence, or automatic, in which racks or baskets were manually loaded with parts which were then carried by a conveyor system through the plating sequence.

Within these main divisions there were a number of variables such as cycle times, chemical formulas, abrasive mixtures, and so forth, which distinguished particular jobs as they have been categorized in Exhibit 3.

The work of the plating room was received in batch lots whose size averaged 1,000 thousand pieces. The clerk moved each batch, which was accompanied by a routing slip, to its first operation. This routing slip indicated the operations to be performed and when each major operation on the batch was scheduled to be completed, so that the finished product could be shipped on time. From the accumulation of orders before him, each man was to organize his own work schedule so as to make optimal use of equipment, materials, and time. Upon completion of an order, each man moved the lot to its next work position or to the finished material location near the freight elevator.

The plating room was under the direct supervision of the supervisor, Otto Schell, who worked a regular 8-to-5 day, five days a week. The supervisor spent a good deal of his working time attending to maintenance and repair of equipment, procuring supplies, handling late schedule changes, and seeing that his people were at their proper work locations.

Working conditions in the plating room varied considerably. That part of the department containing the tumbling barrels and the plating machines was constantly awash, alternately with cold water, steaming acid, or caustic soda. Men working in this part of the room wore knee boots, long rubber aprons, and high-gauntlet rubber gloves. This uni-

EXHIBIT 3
Outline of Work Flow, Plating Room

Aisle 1: Worked closely with Aisle 3 in preparation of parts by barrel tumbling and acid dipping for high-quality* plating in Tanks 4 and 5. Also did a considerable quantity of highly specialized, high-quality acid-etching work not requiring further processing.

Aisle 2: Tumbled items of regular quality* and design in preparation for painting. Less frequently, did oxidation-dipping work of regular quality, but sometimes of special design, not requiring further processing.

Aisle 3: Worked closely with Aisle 1 on high-quality tumbling work for Tanks 4 and 5.

Aisles 4 and 5: Produced regular tumbling work for Tank 1.

Aisle 6: Did high-quality tumbling work for special products plated in Tanks 2 and 3.

Tank 1: Worked on standard automated plating of regular quality not further processed in plating room, and regular work further processed in Tank 5.

Tanks 2 and 3: Produced special high-quality plating work not requiring further processing.

Tank 4: Did special high-quality plating work further plated in Tank 5.

Tank 5: Automated production of high- and regular-quality, special- and regular-design plated parts sent directly to shipping.

Rack assembly: Placed parts to be plated in Tank 5 on ranks.

Rack repair: Performed routine replacement and repair of racks used in Tank 5.

Polishing: Processed, by manual or semimanual methods, odd-lot special orders, which were sent directly to shipping. Also, sorted and reclaimed parts rejected by inspectors in the shipping department.

Degreasing: Took incoming raw stock, processed it through caustic solution, and placed clean stock in storage ready for processing elsewhere in the plating room.

* Definition of terms: *high or regular quality:* The quality of finishes could broadly be distinguished by the thickness of plate and/or care in preparation. *Regular or special work:* The complexity of work depended on the routine or special character of design and finish specifications.

EXHIBIT 4
Skill Indices by Job Group*

Jobs	*Technical Skill Required*	*Physical Effort Required*	*Degree of Discomfort Involved*	*Degree of Training Required*†
Aisle 1	1	1	1	1
Tanks 2–4	3	2	1	2
Aisles 2–6	5	1	1	5
Tank 5	1	5	7	2
Tank 1	8	5	5	7
Degreasing	9	3	7	10
Polishing	6	9	9	7
Rack assembly and repair	10	10	10	10

* Rated on scales of 1 (the greatest) to 10 (the least) in each category.
† Amount of experience required to assume complete responsibility for the job.

form, consistent with the general atmosphere of the "wet" part of the room, was hot in the summer, cold in winter. In contrast, the remainder of the room was dry, relatively odor-free, and provided reasonable, stable temperature and humidity conditions for those who worked there.

The men and women employed in the plating room are listed in Exhibit 5. This table provides certain personal data on each department member, including a productivity-skill rating (based on subjective and objective appraisals of potential performance), as reported by the members of the department.

The pay scale implied by Exhibit 5 was low for the central Michigan area. The average starting wage for factory work in the community was about $1.25. However, working hours for the plating room were long (from 60 hours to a possible and frequently available 76 hours per week). The first 60 hours (the normal five-day week) were paid for on straight-time rates. Saturday work was paid for at time and one half. Sunday pay was calculated on a double-time basis.

As Exhibit 5 indicates, Philip Kirk, a worker in Aisle 2, provided the data for this case. After he had been a member of the department for several months, Kirk noted that certain members of the department tended to seek each other out during free time on and off the job. He then observed that these informal associations were enduring, built upon common activities and shared ideas about what was and what was not legitimate behavior in the department. His estimate of the pattern of these associations is diagrammed in Exhibit 6.

The Sarto group, so named because Tony Sarto was its most respected member and the one who acted as arbiter between the other members, was the largest in the department. The group, except for Louis Patrici, Al Bartolo, and Frank Bonzani (who spelled each other during break periods), invariably ate lunch together on the fire escape near Aisle 1. On those Saturdays and Sundays when overtime work was required, the Sarto group operated as a team, regardless of weekday work assignments, to get overtime work completed as quickly as possible. (Few department members not affiliated with either the Sarto or the Clark groups worked on weekends.) Off the job, Sarto group members often joined in parties or weekend trips. Sarto's summer camp was a frequent rendezvous.

Sarto's group was also the most cohesive one in the department in terms of its organized punch-in and punch-out system. Since the men were regularly scheduled to work from 7 A.M. to 7 P.M. weekdays and since all supervision was removed at 5 P.M., it was possible almost every day to finish a "day's work" by 5:30 and leave the plant. What is more, if one man were to stay until 7 P.M., he could punch the time cards of a number of men and help them gain free time without pay loss. (This system operated on weekends also, at which times members of supervision were present, if at all, only for short periods.) In Sarto's group the duty of staying late rotated, so that no man did so more than once a week. In addition, the group members would punch in a man in the morning if he were unavoidably delayed. However, such a practice never occurred without prior notice from the man who expected to be late and never if the tardiness was expected to last beyond 8 A.M., the start of the day for the supervisor.

Sarto explained the logic behind the system to Kirk:

> You know that our hourly pay rate is quite low compared to other companies. What makes this the best place to work is the feeling of security you get. No one ever gets laid off in this department. With all the hours in the week, all the company ever has to do is shorten the workweek when orders fall off. We have to tighten our belts, but we can all get along. When things are going well, as they are now, the company is only interested in getting out the work. It doesn't help to get it out faster than it's really needed—so we go home a little early whenever we can. Of course, some guys abuse this sort of thing—like Herman—but others work even harder, and it averages out.
>
> Whenever an extra order has to be pushed through, naturally I work until 7. So do a lot of the others. I believe that if I stay until my work is caught up and my equipment is in good shape, that's all the company wants of me. They leave us alone and expect us to produce—and we do.

When Kirk asked Sarto if he would not rather work shorter hours at higher pay in a union shop (Slade employees were not organized), he just laughed and said, "It wouldn't come close to an even trade."

The members of Sarto's group were explicit about what constituted a fair day's work. Customarily, they cited Herman Schell, Kirk's work partner and the supervisor's brother, as a man who consistently produced below that level. Kirk received an informal orientation from Herman during his first days on the job. As Herman put it:

> I've worked at this job for a good many years, and I expect to stay here a good many more. You're just starting out, and you don't know which end is up yet. We spend a lot of time in here; and no matter how hard we work, the pile of work never goes down. There's always more to take its place. And I think you've found out by now that this isn't light work. You can wear yourself out fast if you're not smart. Look at Pearson up in Aisle 4. There's a kid who's just going to burn himself out. He won't last long. If he thinks he's going to get somewhere working like that, he's nuts. They'll give him all the work he can take. He makes it tough on everybody else and on himself, too.

Kirk reported further on his observations of the department:

> As nearly as I could tell, two things seemed to determine whether or not Sarto's group or any others came in for weekend work on Saturday or Sunday. It seemed usually to be caused by rush orders that were re-

EXHIBIT 5
Plating Room Personnel

Location	*Name*	*Age*	*Marital Status*	*Company Seniority (in years)*	*Department Seniority (in years)*	*Pay per Hour*	*Education**	*Familial Relationships*	*Productivity-Skill Rating†*
Aisle 1	Tony Sarto	30	M	13	13	$1.50	HS	Louis Patrici, uncle Pete Facelli, cousin	1
	Pete Facelli	26	M	8	8	1.30	HS	Louis Patrici, uncle Tony Sarto, cousin	2
	Joe Iambi	31	M	5	5	1.20	2 years HS		2
Aisle 2	Herman Schell	48	S	26	26	1.45	GS	Otto Schell, brother	8
	Philip Kirk	23	M	1	1	.90	College		‡
Aisle 3	Dom Pantaleoni	31	M	10	10	1.30	1 year HS		2
	Sal Maletta	32	M	12	12	1.30	3 years HS		3
Aisle 4	Bob Pearson	22	S	4	4	1.15	HS	Father in tool and die dept.	1
Aisle 5	Charlie Malone	44	M	22	8	1.25	GS		7
	John Lacey	41	S	9	5	1.20	1 year HS	Brother in paint dept.	7
Aisle 6	Jim Martin	30	S	7	7	1.25	HS		4
	Bill Mensch	41	M	6	2	1.10	GS		4
Tank 1	Henry LaForte	38	M	14	6	1.25	HS		6

Tanks 2 and 3	Ralph Parker	25	S	7	7	1.20	HS		4
	Ed Harding	27	S	8	8	1.20	HS		4
	George Flood	22	S	5	5	1.15	HS		5
	Harry Clark	29	M	8	8	1.20	HS		3
	Tom Bond	25	S	6	6	1.20	HS		4
Tank 4	Frank Bonzani	27	M	9	9	1.25	HS		2
	Al Bartolo	24	M	6	6	1.25	HS		3
Tank 5	Louis Patrici	47	S	14	14	1.45	2 yrs. college	Tony Sarto, nephew Pete Facelli, nephew	1
Rack assembly	10 women	30–40	9M, 1S	10 (av.)	10 (av.)	1.05	GS (av.)	6 with husbands in company	4 (av.)
Rack maintenance	Will Partridge	57	M	14	2	1.20	GS		7
	Lloyd Swan	62	M	3	3	1.10	GS		7
Degreasing	Dave Susi	45	S	1	1	1.05	HS		5
	Mike Maher	41	M	4	4	1.05	GS		6
Polishing	Russ Perkins	49	M	12	2	1.20	HS		4
Supervisor	Otto Schell	56	M	35	35	na	HS	Herman Schell, brother	3
Clerk	Bill Pierce	32	M	10	4	1.15	HS		4
Chemist	Frank Rutlage	24	S	2	2	na	2 yrs. college		6

* HS = high school; GS = grade school.

† On a potential scale of 1 (top) to 10 (bottom), as evaluated by the men in the department.

‡ Kirk was the source of data for this case and therefore in a biased position to report accurately perceptions about himself.

EXHIBIT 6
Informal Groupings in the Plating Room

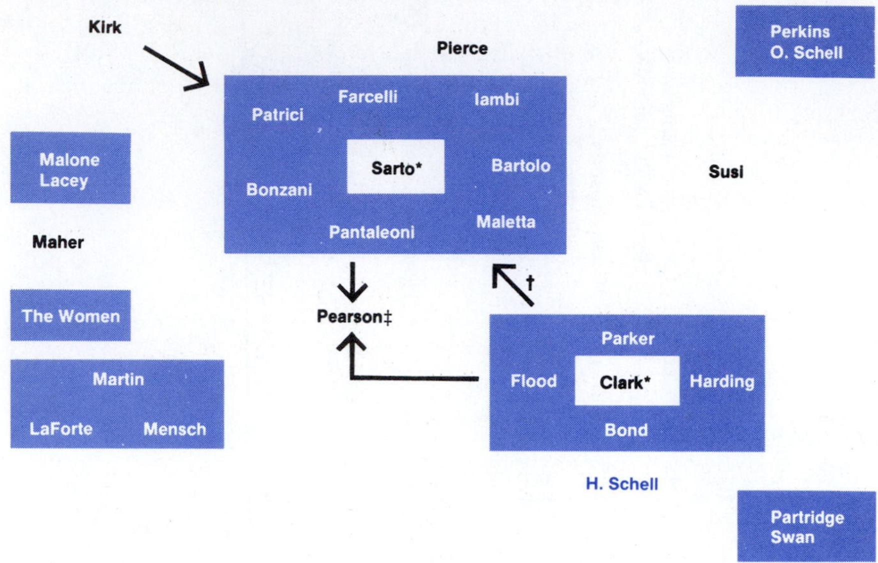

* The white boxes indicate those men who clearly demonstrated leadership behavior (most closely personified the values shared by their groups, were most often sought for help and arbitration, and so forth).

† While the two- and three-man groupings had little informal contact outside their own boundaries, the five-man group did seek to join the largest group in extraplant social affairs. These were relatively infrequent.

‡ Though not an active member of any group, Bob Pearson was regarded with affection by the two large groups.

ceived late in the week, although I suspect it was sometimes caused by the men having spent insufficient time on the job during the previous week.

Tony and his group couldn't understand Herman. While Herman arrived late, Tony was always half an hour early. If there was a push to get out an extra amount of work, almost everyone but Herman would work that much harder. Herman never worked overtime on weekends, while Tony's group and the men on the manual tanks almost always did. When the first exploratory time study of the department was made, no one in the aisles slowed down, except Herman, with the possible exception, to a lesser degree, of Charlie Malone. I did hear that the men in the dry end of the room slowed down so much you could hardly see them move; but we had little to do with them, anyway. While the men I knew best seemed to find a rather full life in their work, Herman never really got involved. No wonder they couldn't understand each other.

There was quite a different feeling about Bobby Pearson. Without the slightest doubt, Bob worked harder than anyone else in the room. Because of the tremendous variety of work produced, it was hard to make output comparisons, but I'm sure I wouldn't be far wrong in saying that Bob put out twice as much as Herman and 50 percent more than almost anyone else in the aisles. No one but Herman and a few old-timers at the dry end ever criticized Bobby for his efforts. Tony and his group seemed to feel a distant affection for Bob, but the only contact they or anyone else had with him consisted of brief greetings.

To the men in Tony's group the most severe penalty that could be inflicted on a man was exclusion. This they did to both Pearson and Herman. Pearson, however, was tolerated; Herman was not. Evidently Herman felt his exclusion keenly, though he answered it with derision and aggression. Herman kept up a steady stream of stories concerning his attempts to gain acceptance outside the company. He wrote popular music, which was always rejected by publishers. He attempted to join several social and athletic clubs, mostly without success. His favorite pastime was fishing. He told me that fishermen were friendly, and he enjoyed meeting new people whenever he went fishing. But he was particularly quick to explain that he preferred to keep his distance from the men in the department.

Tony's group emphasized more than just quantity in judging a man's work. Among them had grown a confidence that they could master and even improve upon any known finishing technique. Tony himself symbolized this skill. Before him, Tony's father had operated Aisle 1 and had trained Tony to take his place. Tony in his turn was training his cousin Pete. When a new finishing problem arose from a change in customer specifications, the supervisor, the department chemist, or any of the men directly involved would come to Tony for help, and Tony would give it willingly. For example, when a part with a special plastic embossing was designed, Tony was the only one who could discover how to treat the metal without damaging the plastic. To a lesser degree the other members of the group were also inventive about the problems which arose in their own sections.

Herman, for his part, talked incessantly about his feats in design and finish creations. As far as I could tell during the year I worked in the department, the objects of these stories were obsolete or of minor importance. What's more, I never saw any department member seek Herman's help.

Willingness to be of help was a trait Sarto's group prized. The most valued help of all was of a personal kind, though work help was also important. The members of Sarto's group were constantly lending and borrowing money, cars, clothing, and tools among themselves and, less frequently, with other members of the department. Their daily lunch bag procedure typified the common property feeling among them. Everyone's lunch was opened and added to a common pile, from which each member of the group chose his meal.

On the other hand, Herman refused to help others in any way. He never left his aisle to aid those near him who were in the midst of a rush of work or a machine failure, though this was customary throughout most of the department. I can distinctly recall the picture of Herman leaning on the hot and cold water faucets, which were located directly above each tumbling barrel. He would stand gazing into the tumbling pieces for hours. To the passing casual visitor, he looked busy; and as he told me, that's just what he wanted. He, of course, expected me to act this same way, and it was this enforced boredom that I found virtually intolerable.

More than this, Herman took no responsibility for breaking in his assigned helpers as they first entered the department or thereafter. He had had four helpers in the space of little more than a year. Each had asked for a transfer to another department—publicly citing the work as cause, privately blaming Herman. Tony was the one who taught me the ropes when I first entered the department.

The men who congregated around Harry Clark tended to talk like and copy the behavior of the Sarto group, though they never approached the degree of inventive skill or the amount of helping activities that Tony's group did. They sought outside social contact with the Sarto group; and several times a year, the two groups went "on the town" together. Clark's group did maintain a high level of performance in the volume of work they turned out.

The remainder of the people in the department stayed pretty much to themselves or associated in pairs or triplets. None of these people was as inventive, as helpful, or as productive as Sarto's or Clark's groups, but most of them gave verbal support to the same values as those groups held.

The distinction between the two organized groups and the rest of the department was clearest in the punching-out routine. The women could not work past 3 P.M., so they were not involved. Malone and Lacey, Partridge and Swan, and Martin, La Forte, and Mensch arranged within their small groups for punch-outs, or they remained beyond 5 and slept or read when they finished their work. Perkins and Pierce went home when the supervisor did. Herman Schell, Susi, and Mather had no punch-out organization to rely upon. Susi and Mather invariably stayed in the department until 7 P.M. Herman was reported to have established an arrangement with Partridge whereby the latter punched Herman out for a fee. Such a practice was unthinkable from the point of view of Sarto's group. It evidently did not occur often because Herman usually went to sleep behind piles of work when his brother left or, particularly during the fishing season, punched himself out early. He constantly railed against the dishonesty of other men in the department, yet urged me to punch him out on several emergency occasions.

Just before I left the Slade Company to return to school after 14 months on the job, I had a casual conversation with Mr. Porter, the production mamager, in which he asked me how I had enjoyed my experience with the organization. During the conversation, I learned that he knew of the punchout system in the plating department. What's more, he told me, he was wondering if he ought to "blow the lid off the whole mess."

▶ Smokestack Village, Inc.

Thomas J. Bronston, chairman of the board of trustees and general manager of Smokestack Village, was worried about the developing problem between his employees and Karl Olson, the man he wished to have replace him as general manager.

Smokestack Village was a tourist attraction located near the Continental Divide in central Colorado. It offered visitors a large railroad museum and daily excursion rides on old railroad lines. The museum had over 40 steam locomotives on display and many other exhibits relating to the days of steam railroading. The excursion rides were operated during the summer and fall months over 26 miles of track winding through a valley high in the Rockies. It had been founded by Miles E. Smith, a semiretired railroad buff, with Mr. Bronston's assistance in arranging financing.

Mr. Smith served as general manager during the early years of slow growth. When he was unexpectedly killed in an automobile accident, Mr. Bronston tried to find someone to take care of the day-to-day operating responsibility. This included short-range planning, ordering supplies, handling the finances, and coping with "nosey federal inspectors." When unsuccessful in finding someone he considered satisfactory, he reluctantly took on the task himself. This meant closing up his own business as an investment counselor and moving from Denver to Grenoble, which was closer but still 45 miles from Smokestack Village.

He had been general manager for the past five years. During that time, the museum had started running the excursion trains, and the many engines that had been sitting around the turntable rusting had been stored under cover during the winter and restored on a regular basis. Attendance had tripled over the five-year period. He now felt that it was time for "new blood" in management, and he was informally looking for a replacement. The long commute was also getting to him.

Assistant manager Jim Harris, 28, was in charge of restoration, painting, lawnmowing, and ticket sales. Working for him were three girls who sold tickets and staffed the exhibit cars. Also under his direction were five high school boys who worked around the locomotive displays, painting, restoring the engines to their original looks, lawnmowing, weeding, sweeping walks, and doing trackwork. Jim spent most of his day making sure the boys were working and not goofing off from what they considered to be "just a summer job in which you put in your 40 hours."

Contact between Harris's crew and a crew that operated the excursion trains was limited because of the physical layout of Smokestack Village (see Exhibit 1) and the jobs they did. The train crew spent the day either in the station or up the line, while the museum crew was working around the display engines a distance away.

Sven Olson was in charge of the train crew and was also the engineer on the train. Sven was a veteran of 50 years' service as an engineer for the Great Western Railroad, and he knew his business. The other employees used to joke that he knew more about railroads than they would ever have time to forget. At 75, he was still capable of working longer and harder than most of the other employees 55 years younger than he.

Ned Bronston, 17, the son of Mr. Bronston, was the fireman. He lived with Sven in the bunk car parked near the enginehouse. It was

EXHIBIT 1

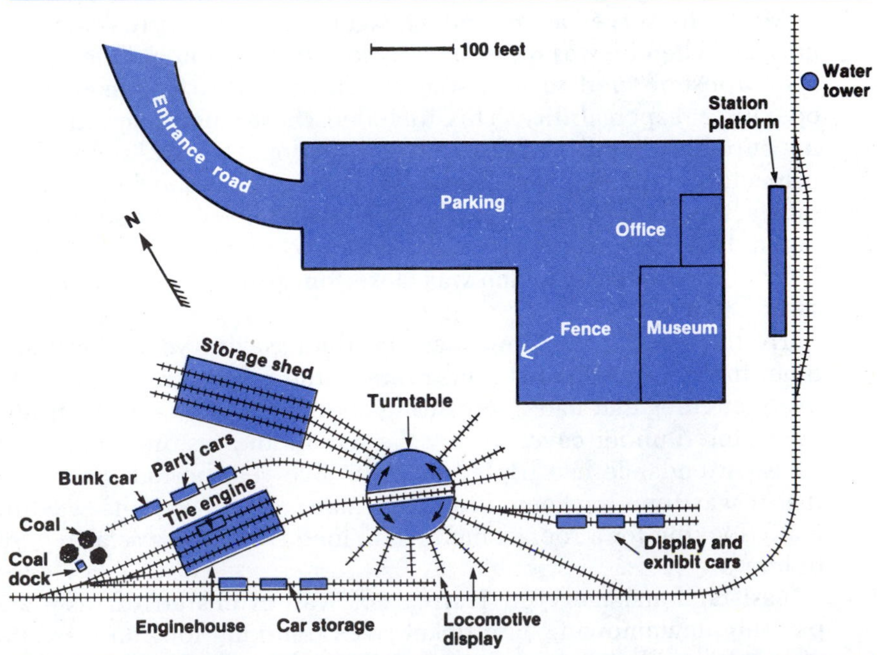

the first summer working at Smokestack Village for both of them, although Ned had spent many days at Smokestack with his father over the years.

Working with them were three other employees who had worked at Smokestack Village in the past. Bob Johnson, 30, had worked for the village for four years as conductor for the passenger train in the summer and in the office in the winter.

The brakemen were Al Stanhope, 18, and Peter Townshend, also 18. They had worked at Smokestack for the past two summers on the museum crew, and it was their first summer on the train.

The five of them became fast friends. They worked well together and enjoyed each other's company both during and after work. It was not unusual for them all to go out to dinner at the end of the day or sit around the bunk car half the night talking about railroads. Al and Peter kept sleeping bags at the bunk car and frequently stayed overnight.

Al, Peter, and Ned, with Sven's consent, traded jobs occasionally; Ned worked as brakeman while Al or Peter fired the engine. Frequently Sven would allow the fireman to run the engine while he fired. Most railroads allowed this, and Mr. Bronston knew that with Sven in the cab, nothing could go wrong. The practice allowed for the training of future engineers. Mr. Bronston only asked that the train leave and arrive in the village on time. How this was to be done was left up to the five of them. They found it best to work as a team; each of them knew the other's job well enough from the practice of switching jobs to know what to expect from the others. Arguments were few and far between.

The day started for Sven and Ned at 8:30 A.M. Being fireman, Ned had many duties to tend to before the engine could be run that day. The fire had to be rebuilt from the day before, lubricators filled, water worked out of the cylinders, and the engine coaled. The coal dock was 75 yards from the enginehouse, and this gave Ned an opportunity to run the engine a bit. If he had time and the engine warranted it, he would polish the engine, wiping oil and cinders from the boiler and wheels.

While Ned was working on the engine, Sven would be preparing a sumptuous breakfast for the two of them. He would also boil a large pot of coffee for Bob, Al, and Peter, who would arrive at 10. Breakfast started at 9:30, and the train crew would join them at 10 for a half hour of railroad talk. The talk usually turned to girls, sports, and movies; the breakfast hour was enjoyed by all.

At 10:30 it was time to take the engine and passenger cars down to the station in preparation for the first run, leaving at 11. Mr. Bronston would be waiting on the platform for the train's arrival. He would climb into the cab to talk with Sven about the engine. He would inquire as to whether the engine was running well, the coal supply was lasting, and any other details related to the operating department. Satisfied that all was going well, he would head back to his office.

Mr. Bronston felt that he had a responsible crew working on the train. There was an unstated understanding between him and the train crew that as long as things went smoothly, he would not interfere in their routine. Sven worked hard with the train crew, drilling them on railroad procedures and safety measures. Running a railroad is serious business, and they all knew it. Fooling around could not be tolerated when 800 people were on the train. There were instances where local kids had tried to derail the train by placing ties and spikes on the track. Al and Ned had managed to catch the culprits, and they were turned over to the state police.

The arrival of the train back in Smokestack Village after the first trip marked the beginning of lunch for both the museum and train crews. Ned would buy lunch for Sven and himself and return to the engine. One of them stayed on the engine at all times. After eating, Sven would climb down off the engine and wander around talking with visitors, while other visitors would climb into the cab for a look around and maybe a chance to blow the whistle.

Two more trips would be made before the end of the day at 6 P.M. It took Ned about an hour to shut down the engine for the night. If the train crew was going out to dinner together, they would all pitch in to get the work done, otherwise Sven would start dinner for Ned and himself while Bob, Al, and Peter would head home for dinner.

There were times when the engine needed major repair due to some malfunction. When this happened, the museum crew would join the train crew in repairing the locomotive. Sometimes the work would take all night—nobody complained. It had to be done if the train was to run the next day. Sven and Ned would work with the crews until midnight and then retire. If they were to function the next day, they needed their sleep. The two of them put in the hardest day of all the employees.

Each morning at 3 A.M. Ned would wake up and go out to the engine to check the water level, steam pressure, and the fire, which was left burning from the day before. The engine had a habit of building up steam pressure when left unattended, and this led to difficulties the next morning, the worst being a boiler explosion.

In doing this, Ned violated federal law, which requires that railroad employees not work more than 16 hours followed by a 10-hour rest period. Ned was well aware of this law but chose to ignore it. Smokestack Village would have had to hire a night hostler to watch the engine, and this was costly. So he did it himself.

Employees turned in their time cards each Wednesday. They were to write down the hours they had worked and what they had done. Average pay for the museum and train crews was $1.60 an hour. Bob earned a higher wage since legally the responsibility of the train and the hundreds of passengers was his, and his higher pay was justified. The train crew only put in for a 44-hour week, although 50 and 60 hours of actual work was not unusual. They never asked for pay for the nights they worked repairing the engine. Working on steam engines was considered a privilege. Al, Peter, and Ned spent many evenings working on one engine in the exhibit area that was their favorite. They had painted the engine and spent many hours hunting through the storage shed and spare parts boxcars looking for gauges, valves, and other parts to replace ones missing from the locomotive. They didn't ask to be paid for this.

The museum crew, for the most part, did the same thing with their time cards. They only asked for overtime when the work was not with the engines. They had a few pet projects that they also worked on after hours; for example, they had been painting the railroad name on the sides of the passenger cars, doing one side of one car an evening.

During the times when the two crews were working in the evenings, Jim Harris and Sven were never around. The evening projects were the idea of the employees involved, and they wished to do it on their own. Mr. Bronston, on his daily inspection tours of the grounds, would only offer suggestions as to what might look better or more realistic. The final decisions were left up to the crews. The two groups stayed to themselves most of the time. The only time the two crews worked together was when the engine that Al, Peter, and Ned were working on had to be lettered. The museum crew stenciled the engine for the three of them to paint. The museum crew had offered to do the job, and the offer was gladly accepted. Once the job was done, the two crews went back to the original format of working by themselves.

The museum crew's attitude of it being "just a summer job" changed during the month of June. Once the lawnmowing and trackwork and other tasks were done, they were permitted to work on the engines, which was much more interesting and enjoyable to the point that they stayed late on their own time.

Sven had one son, Karl, 50, who lived in Wyoming. Karl was a successful mechanical engineer with a long list of patents to his credit. He had been involved in the production of a sound movie projector for a large camera producer, and his expertise had helped send a man to the moon. He had started many engineering consulting firms with clients like NASA, the armed services, the automobile industry suppliers, and railroads. He had sold his businesses over the past few years and was now in semiretirement, taking on consulting work out of his home when he wanted.

During the month of June he made several trips with his wife Henrietta to Smokestack Village and the area to visit his father. He would ride in the cab of the engine, and Ned would sometimes let him sit in the fireman's seat. Karl considered this a privilege and was grateful to Ned. Sven and Karl got along quite well. Karl never interfered with Sven's work, realizing that he was in the presence of one of the best and most well-known engineers in the country.

It was not long before Karl was seen in the office with Mr. Bronston discussing Smokestack Village. Karl had many ideas on how to increase patronage at the museum. He knew some people in the TV advertising business, and he arranged for low-cost TV commercials to be aired in major cities of the area.

Karl started spending more and more time at the museum. Mr. Bronston, realizing that Karl had plenty of spare time that might be put to constructive use at Smokestack Village, asked him if he would be interested in becoming a trustee. Karl accepted the offer, and he and his wife moved into a local motel for an indefinite stay.

Prior to Karl's becoming a trustee, Mr. Bronston had asked Ned what he thought of Karl. Ned couldn't think of anything negative at the time and told his father that he would get the other employee's reactions. The museum crew didn't have much contact with Karl; only Jim knew who he was, and he thought Karl was OK. The train crew had only known Karl for a month at that point and didn't register any complaints about him either. They knew that Mr. Bronston was looking for a replacement, but since Mr. Bronston had left the operating department to them and didn't interfere, they didn't care who was the boss. In the next two weeks they would all have reason to care after all.

Karl, now a trustee, began to make his appearance in the bunk car every morning at 9 to start issuing orders. The train crew started to grumble that they didn't need this intrusion in their morning routine. Karl no longer allowed the morning coffee break. The work that Al, Peter, and Ned did in the evenings was now to be done in the morning starting at 9. Ned, having to work on the engine, couldn't participate. Ned's work in the morning was under constant fire from Karl. As a result, the "extra bit" Ned did polishing the engine was neglected. Karl also ordered that the engine and train be ready in the station at 10:15 each morning. Sven and Ned were incensed at this. It meant getting up earlier and rushing breakfast on what they considered to be their own time. Sven was also told by Karl that when the engine was moved even a foot, he had better be at the throttle or Karl would find a new engineer. Ned was no longer allowed to run the engine to the coal dock, and the firemen were not allowed to run the engine on the mainline. At lunch time Ned could no longer leave the engine to get lunch for Sven and himself from the cafeteria in the station. They were both to stay on the engine at all times during the day. The conductor and brakemen were not subjected to the same restriction, and this caused hard feelings between the engine and train crews.

When Sven had asked Karl how he was to get lunch, Karl told him to bring a sandwich with him in the morning. Sven told the four men he worked with to ignore Karl. Mr. Bronston had given Sven his orders and those were the ones to follow. Karl seemed careful not to give orders when Mr. Bronston was around.

The employees began to look around to see if Karl was watching and, if he was, to do it his way. Nobody dared cross him. But the trips allowed the train crew a chance to get away from Karl and do things their own way. Once the train left the station, they would stop looking over their shoulders to see if Karl was watching. Bob got in the habit of signaling Sven to start when Karl was nowhere in sight, while Al and Peter would walk the length of the train to see if Karl had gotten on while they weren't watching and, if so, tell the engine crew through a prearranged hand signal. If Karl was on the train, the trip would be slower and the whistle wasn't blown as much, which upset Sven because he felt that the people had paid for a train ride and he was going to give them a ride they would never forget.

Mr. Bronston had told the employees that Karl had been made a trustee but had not made any mention of any authority that Karl might have when dealing with employees. The Smokestack Village board had 15 trustees on it. They were all known by the employees, and many of them came to Smokestack on weekends to look around. They frequently asked the employees how projects were coming but never ordered anyone around. For the most part they were fund-raisers for the organization and policy makers. On one trustee's visit, he asked one of the museum crew workers to wear cleaner clothes because the employees were in the limelight. It was the only incident where a trustee other than Karl confronted an employee all summer.

Karl had made it understood that anyone who didn't do as he said would be fired. The way he gave orders, the message was clear: "Do it my way, or you're out."

Morale hit bottom. Employees came to work at nine and left at five. Before, when the engine needed repair, Jim had asked who would like to stay late to help fix the engine and the museum crew would head for the phone to call home to cancel dinner or their girlfriends to cancel dates. This was no longer true. Sven and Jim had to plead with the museum crew to stay, and they would agree only if it were understood that they were free to leave if Karl showed up. Ned and Al and Peter would stay, even if he did show, because they needed the engine. The time cards started to show exactly how many hours each employee worked. Fifty and 60 hours was not unusual, and the payroll was doubled with the overtime.

About two weeks after Karl's appointment as a trustee, Mr. Bronston was made aware of the payroll increase by his secretary, Jean, who handled the payroll accounts. Jean, the employees' "second mother," offered no explanation, although she did know what was happening. Mr. Bronston decided to accept Sven's standing invitation for dinner in the bunk car with Ned and himself. The conversation that night finally turned to Karl. Sven related some of the incidents that made him angry with his son Karl. Ned, at Sven's insistence, let it be known that Karl was ruining a good working environment. Employees were rebelling by "misplacing" valuable locomotive tools and parts, painting and restoration work was slowing down, and little jobs such as picking up trash were not being done. If Mr. Bronston wanted the stenciling and lettering of the passenger cars finished, he would have to order it finished on Smokestack Village's time. Ned also stated that he and most of the other workers felt it difficult to follow two bosses. They were all at a loss as to whose orders to follow: Karl's, as he was always around the grounds, or Mr. Bronston's, who was the boss even when he was working in the office.

Mr. Bronston thanked the two of them for dinner and got in his car for the 45-minute trip home. As he drove, he reflected upon the situation. Karl looked like a man capable of taking his place. He had plenty of spare time, which he was willing to devote to the village, and was a successful businessman with many connections in the railroad industry. Karl would make the village his life, something that Mr. Bronston didn't want to do. Living in Grenoble, a poor mill town, wouldn't bother Karl as he didn't have any children and didn't much care what his wife thought. Ned had overheard Karl tell Sven that his wife had cancer, "so she'll be gone soon."

The present circumstances cast a doubt in Mr. Bronston's mind as to whether he could entrust Karl with the museum. The next trustees' meeting would be in October. He knew he would have to stay on as general manager until then, when Karl might take the job. Now if he could figure out a way to keep peace until then. . . .

ST Industries, Inc.

Stover Industries was an amalgamation of several small companies in the electrical parts industry. Elizabeth Stover and her husband had inherited one of the group of companies from her father-in-law. Mrs. Stover, an engineer, elected to run the company while her husband

This case was written by Professor Robin Willits. It is based on the *Chris Cunningham* case, which was prepared by Professor Todd Jick as an adaptation of an old case titled *Gregory Pellham* (author unknown).

pursued a separate career as a dental surgeon. In addition to the original inheritance, Mrs. Stover had purchased three other companies to create the present Stover Industries. Mrs. Stover, at 31 years of age, was a dynamic individual, full of ideas and drive.

Chris Cunningham had been a salesperson for Stover Industries for about nine months. Chris had joined Stover Industries about three months after Elizabeth Stover, a college classmate, had become president of the company and had offered Chris a job. After talking to Mrs. Stover and hearing about her plans for the company, Chris had jumped at the opportunity to move from a large, reputable, but slow-moving company to Stover Industries, where the prospects from being part of a small, aggressive organization looked great.

After talking to Elizabeth Stover at the time of hiring, Chris knew that Mrs. Stover planned to integrate the four companies into a unified organization by welding the individual managements into one unit. Chris also knew that Mrs. Stover was determined to remake the company from the rather complacent organization it had become into a dynamic, aggressive, and highly profitable business. In Chris's view, Liz Stover had accomplished a lot, although she had not moved as rapidly as Chris had expected her to. Several of the executives of the old companies, who obviously could not keep up with their new, young, and driving boss, had resigned, but others remained. Also, the question of sales territories had not been resolved. Many of the salespeople from the original companies still had their old customers, which meant that their territories often overlapped. Furthermore, the sales director, whom Mrs. Stover had known for a long time as the sales director of the original Stover Company, spent most of his time attending to routine matters. If it weren't for Liz Stover's own input, there would be no real sales leadership at all. Finally, there were the people in production—who, in Chris's view, were far from dynamic.

Chris liked the job and developed a good sales record. More than that, Chris felt that record constituted a significant contribution to the progress the company was making. But there was one cloud in an otherwise satisfying nine months, which Chris expressed as follows:

> Every now and then Liz seems to act like a different person, suddenly treating me as a child. When this happens, Liz usually gets very protective of the weak characters she still has working for her in production and starts telling me to baby them even though it's obvious that the company is going to suffer.
>
> Why, only last week, I had to push the purchasing agent to get some supplies that were needed to fill a special order that one of our best customers needed to complete a prototype. If I hadn't built a little bit of a fire under that guy we would have missed the delivery date I promised and undoubtedly lost out on an order next year that will really benefit Stover. Most of the production people are still so used to the old compla-

cent ways of doing things that the only way to insure that Stover builds good customer relations is to directly insist that they show the kind of aggressiveness this company needs. I don't see how Liz puts up with them. I've tried asking them politely when we need to make a special effort, I've tried logical persuasion, and I've tried begging—but nothing seems to work except a little heat. So when Liz is in one of her protective moods, I back off, but I find that soon I have to begin to prod those people again.

I don't understand this pattern in Liz. She wants to turn the company around, and usually acts in a forceful manner; but she seems to get sentimental about some of those old-timers in production every now and then and lets their feelings come ahead of what's best for Stover Industries—and this has me concerned. I like Liz, I think the company has a lot of potential, but I'm beginning to wonder if Liz has the stuff to make the tough decisions that a president has to make.

Suddenly a Branch Manager

Ganesan sat at the desk of the branch manager looking through the glass partition toward the general office of the Kurunegala branch of the Colombo National Bank. He felt overwhelmed and a bit angry with the latest turn of events in his career. Having come to Kurunegala six weeks ago on a temporary assignment, he had begun to think about returning to the central office in Colombo where he could live at home and see more of his family and friends. But now a letter had arrived appointing him as the branch manager. He had certainly never agreed to come to Kurunegala permanently, and now it seemed he had no choice but to stay. He felt trapped.

When the letter had first come he had complained to the district manager in Anuradhapura, with whom he was on close and friendly terms, but without success. The district manager was helpless; the letter had come from top management in the central office. The district manager didn't even know why the change was being made, since the old branch manager was not in any trouble and was merely being given a lateral transfer (neither promoted or demoted) after two years at Kurunegala. Apparently the old manager was needed elsewhere and the central office had confidence in Ganesan's ability to learn the job and run the Kurunegala branch effectively.

Ganesan had to admit that the appointment spoke well for his reputation, since he had never been manager of a branch before and had only had the past six weeks to observe the workings of a branch serving a predominately industrial market. But Kurunegala? Kurunegala was not his idea of an ideal location.

As Ganesan continued to observe the general office and the staff, he glanced at each employee and began to review what he had observed and heard seated among them during his six weeks on temporary assignment.

COLOMBO NATIONAL BANK

Colombo National Bank was one of the older, middle-sized banks in Sri Lanka with branches in a number of the larger towns on the island as well as throughout the greater Colombo area. The Kurunegala branch was somewhat unique because its market was more industrial than most branches. A large part of its business was providing loans to small- and medium-sized industrial concerns in the Kurunegala area, a community located two and one-half hours north of Colombo on the main rail line to Anuradhapura, which was four and one-half hours from Colombo. The branch came under the jurisdiction of the district manager in Anuradhapura and employed 20 people. Internally the branch was divided into three departments:

Loan department.

Cash department (checking and savings).

Clearing department.

Each department was headed up by an officer of the bank and had four clerks. These three officers and a fourth officer, who handled special assignments, reported to the branch manager, who in turn reported to the district manager in Anuradhapura. The loan department dealt with customers who were seeking financing for their businesses. The cash department handled over-the-counter deposits and withdrawals. The transactions of these two departments in turn were recorded and cleared through the clearing department. Employee salaries in all departments were based strictly on seniority and position, with promotion to higher positions based on merit as well as on seniority.

The branch had been established four years ago and staffed initially with employees already with the bank who were happy to transfer to Kurunegala because it was their home territory. Subsequently, as the branch grew, new and untrained individuals were hired. Most of these were ambitious and had been willing to join the right-oriented union that the bank had established following the election of the UNP government (the free-enterprise–oriented party) in 1977. The branch was viewed by higher management as potentially one of the best earners on the island. The city of Kurunegala was industrial, and the general area was economically well off. While a typical branch could return 22–25 percent on income, Kurunegala was seen as having the potential to reach 30 percent or more and to grow and provide good opportunities for promotion as new supervisory positions were added.

GANESAN'S BACKGROUND

At 30 years of age, Ganesan was one of the younger officers of the Colombo National Bank. He had been hired six years previously, shortly after graduating from the Colombo Campus of the University of Sri Lanka with a major in sociology. His first assignment was to the Hambanota branch for five months of training. At the end of that period he had received a good recommendation and had been assigned to the Polonnaruwa branch. At the time, Ganesan had hoped to get a post in Colombo but had accepted the assignment to Polonnaruwa because he believed that his career would benefit if he accepted an assignment to an area where others were reluctant to go. (In fact, Polonnaruwa was known as a "godforsaken" location because of its arid climate and distance from Colombo.) At Polonnaruwa he was responsible for small agricultural loans and handled the assignment so well that his performance became known to the top management in Colombo. This led to his being transferred to another godforsaken post at Medirigiriya with the challenge of handling the "factoring"[1] of large agricultural produce receipts. Here Ganesan was also effective and topped all other districts in the amount of rupees earned.

At both Polonnaruwa and Medirigiriya, Ganesan came to understand and appreciate the life of the rural people in the arid zones; but he was glad to eventually be transferred to Colombo, where he was assigned to the international division, handling exports. While there, he was promoted to assistant manager. Sometime thereafter he was once again sent outstation to Anuradhapura for a year as assistant to the district manager. This was also a productive experience because initially the district manager was rather weak and Ganesan took on many of the administrative duties normally done by an assistant district manager. Eventually that manager was replaced by a strong manager who continued to utilize Ganesan as if he were the assistant district manager, making him an important member of the transfer committee that handled all transfers of clerks and supervisors (nonofficers) throughout the district.

[1] Farmers, upon delivery of produce to the government purchasing stores, would take the receipt to the bank and exchange it for cash rather than wait the long period that the government took between delivery and payment.

Thereafter Ganesan was assigned to Kurunegala on special assignment, still with the rank of assistant manager. His job was to do field work, visiting customers and gathering data with which the bank could assess its industrial loan policies and procedures. This meant that he was out of the office a lot on site visits, but in the general office at one of the desks a portion of each day, recording his notes. Both he and the district manager considered his assignment as temporary (an estimated two months' duration).

Although Ganesan was Tamil,[2] he was fluent in Sinhala, the language of most of the branch employees. He had a reputation around the bank as a fair-minded and friendly officer, and was able to develop rapport with the employees he sat amongst.

GANESAN'S INITIAL IMPRESSIONS OF THE BRANCH

As Ganesan thought about his situation, he realized that he had developed a number of definite impressions about the Kurunegala branch almost from the day he first sat at a desk in the general office. He remembered an early awareness that people seemed to be going their own way, minding their business, with little interaction. There didn't seem to be much cordiality. It was not an office where people were obviously friendly and sociable. Instead the atmosphere was subdued: neither warm and friendly nor busy and intense. The amount of face-to-face contact between people was clearly less than the physical

[2] Sri Lanka's population is approximately 71 percent Sinhalese, 11 percent Sri Lankan Tamils, 9 percent Indian Tamils, and 7 percent Moors, with Burghers and other small ethnic groups comprising the rest. Sixty-seven percent are Buddhist (largely the Sinhalese), 17 percent Hindus (the Tamils), 8 percent Christians (Burghers, some Sinhalese, and others), and 7 percent Muslim (the Moors).

Sri Lanka (earlier known as Ceylon) was a British colony until 1948. It is now an independent state with a parliamentary form of government headed by an elected president. Since 1948 there have been regular elections and the two major political parties—the United National Party (U.N.P. similar to the British Conservative Party) and Sri Lanka Freedom Party (SLFP similar to the British Labour Party) have alternatively formed governments. Universal suffrage has been practiced since the early 1930s and the society is highly politicised; over 85% of the electorate vote at elections. The free education system has raised the level of literacy over 90%. However, the island is faced with serious problems of unemployment, low income levels (1986 per capita income of $350), low level of industrialization and low productivity. In this environment the political party in power wields much authority and the politicians act as patrons of the people so as to win and maintain electoral power. Managers of the public corporations and even managers of private corporations who cross the will of powerful politicians usually meet with social and economic disaster. The employees who are well aware of this situation avoid confrontation and even switch their allegiance and join unions in favor with the government to maintain security of employment and win tenure prospects. Similarly, managements adapt their policies to changes in the government although many, especially those with a long-range view, seek to maintain some balance between opposing political forces within and without the organization.

layout allowed, and communication between departments was usually by written notes or messenger.

FURTHER OBSERVATIONS AND IMPRESSIONS

As time went on, Ganesan noticed other characteristics of the branch and its people. He soon became aware that the branch manager had control over the operations. Everything passed through his hands. He dictated and signed every letter that left the branch. At any moment, one could see papers and files piled on his desk awaiting his attention. Also, he didn't hesitate to "box" people (i.e., record the lateness of those who were even two minutes late).

It was also apparent that the employees were careful to check with the manager about departures from established procedures. Typical was the situation that sometimes arose when a customer presented a check on which there was a slight misspelling of a long Sinhalese or Tamil name. The clerk would refer it to an officer, and the officer would refer it to the branch manager. If he said it should be cashed, it was; if he said not to, it wasn't.

But Ganesan also recalled that at one time or another he had overheard nearly every employee ridiculing the branch manager's lack of fluency in Sinhala (the branch manager was a Tamil) and that several of the senior clerks often referred to the manager as a "Pandam Kayara"[3] for management. Finally, he remembered several occasions when someone had come out of the manager's office with a flushed face and slammed the files on their desk, muttering, "I still think my idea might work."

Nevertheless, Ganesan noticed that some people, the younger people, had a special relationship with the manager. He would chat with them now and then during the day, and Ganesan often saw him visiting with one or two of them at the end of the workday.

Ganesan had noticed also that there was an uneven flow of work, particularly within each department. A younger clerk would bring something to a more senior person to check, and end up waiting for quite awhile. Sometimes the customer, who was also waiting, would become irritated and criticize the clerk for being slow and would even complain to the manager. This was obviously not a pleasant situation for the young clerk. Similarly, Ganesan had seen instances where one department was delayed by another department. For example, the clearing department had a strict schedule for its operations and would not accept any new work after about 2:30 P.M. Sometimes another

[3] Literally, one who holds a lamp to light the way—hence, a henchman for management.

department, especially the loan department, would start a transaction before 2:30 but could not complete its work before closing because it could not clear the transaction through clearing after 2:30. This caused work to pile up and was resolved only by an appeal to the manager and by him requiring the clearing department to modify its schedule.

Throughout the six weeks, Ganesan had developed rapport with many of the people. They even treated him as something of a confidant about their personal problems. Apparently his reputation as a fair and friendly person from his service on the transfer committee had given them reason to be comfortable with him. During these conversations, Ganesan had also heard complaints that the manager gave preferential treatment when it came to scholarships, leave-time to attend lectures, etc. Some of the remarks he had heard were quite nasty. In the few days between the announcement of the transfer of the old manager and the public announcement of his appointment Ganesan even overheard some people saying to some others, "Just because you're better educated, don't try to pull any of your tricks to get preferred treatment with the new manager."

FOLLOWING HIS APPOINTMENT

When the letter arrived appointing him branch manager, Ganesan was too surprised and angry to think clearly; but after talking to the district manager and realizing that he had little choice, he began to think about how to manage the branch. First, he looked over the personnel records to learn more about the staff that he was now in charge of (see Exhibit 1).

Second, he got a profitability statement (see Exhibit 2) showing income and expenses for salaries, overtime, medical benefits, and overhead. With this he was able to calculate an average net earnings per employee by department. He believed that these data would show him where the branch stood and provide a benchmark against which to assess his own efforts as a manager.

Third, he thought about the quality of the overall employee group. He knew that a number of employees had roots in the Kurunegala area. All of those were individuals of integrity with personal reputations in the community as people of means and status (many were influential church officials and were from more-wealthy families who owned paddy fields, small businesses, etc.). The people of Kurunegala obviously liked dealing with them for their banking needs. While conservative by nature and satisfied with the current banking procedures and state of affairs, all were very loyal to the bank as an institution, but likely to deal with a manager in a straightforward manner without trying to curry favor. Ganesan also knew that a number of

EXHIBIT 1

Name	Union Affiliation	Home Village*	Age	Religion†	Educational Level‡	Years with Bank	Years at Branch	Total Years as Clerk or Officer	Current Position
Mr. R. Senaratne	Left-oriented	KU	37	B	JSC	15	3	5	Officer
Miss Seyamala Fernando	Pro-government	KU	23	C	GCE (A/L)	4	2	4	Clerk
Mr. K. Nandalochana	Left-oriented	O/S	32	C	GCE (O/L)	9	3	9	Clerk
Mrs. Dhammi Borelassa	Pro-government	O/S	29	B	GCE (A/L)	7	2	7	Clerk
Mr. K. Bandara	Left-oriented	KU	30	B	GCE (O/L)	10	4	4	Officer
Mr. Dayananda Silva	Left-oriented	KU	29	B	GCE (O/L)	8	2	8	Clerk
Mrs. Hiacinth Almeida	Pro-government	O/S	27	B	GCE (A/L)	3	2	3	Clerk
Mr. Susantha Siriwardena	Left-oriented	KU	34	C	JSC	14	3	14	Clerk
Miss Vasantha De Soyza	Pro-government	O/S	23	B	1st degree in arts	3	2	3	Clerk
Mr. Reggie Samaraweera	Left-oriented	KU	29	B	GCE (O/L)	9	4	9	Clerk
Mr. Ralph Peiris	Left-oriented	KU	31	B	GCE (O/L)	8	4	8	Clerk
Mr. Raja Siripala	Pro-government	O/S	24	B	GCE (A/L)	3	3	1	Chief clerk
Mr. Karunapala Mendis	Left-oriented	KU	29	B	GCE (O/L)	8	4	8	Chief clerk
Mr. Nimal Ratnasiri	Pro-government	O/S	27	C	Bus. adm. degree	6	1	2	Officer
Miss Asuntha De Mel	Left-oriented	O/S	29	B	GCE (A/L)	9	3	9	Clerk
Mr. Suresh Ramanayake	Left-oriented	KU	32	C	GCE (O/L)	12	2	2	Officer asst.

* KU—Kurunegala; O/S—Outstation area.
† B—Buddhist; C—Christian.
‡ JSC—Junior school certificate; GCE—General certificate of education; O/L—Ordinary level; A/L—Advanced level.

EXHIBIT 2
Profitability Statement (typical month of operation)

		Expenses (in rupees)					
Department	Income Generation*	Salaries	Overtime	Medical Benefit	Overhead	Net Return	Net Income per Employee†
Loan: 4 clerks 1 officer	140,000	8,500	500	1,000	70,000	60,000	10,000
Cash: 4 clerks 1 officer	10,000	9,500	300	1,100	20,000	(21,000)	(4,200)
Clearing: 4 clerks 1 officer	20,000	8,000	200	800	15,000	(4,000)	(800)
General overhead (includes salaries of branch manager and peons, messengers, etc.)	—	3,500	100	500	—	(4,100)	
	170,000	29,500	1,100	3,500	105,000	30,900	

* Major share of income comes from loan department.
† Net income per employee (nonmanagement) on total basis: 30,900 ÷ 15 = 2,060 rupees.

employees were enthusiastic, ambitious, and hardworking individuals whose capabilities appeared good but who were as yet relatively untested. Overall it was not a bad group with which to have to work. There were no cheats or slackers or real troublemakers.

The location was disappointing, but the work situation could be a lot worse. The obvious question was: What should he do? How should he approach his job?

The Surprised Roommates

I want to tell you about a rooming situation that occurred in the freshman dormitory where I was a resident assistant. There were three roommates; Sue Taylor, Sue Knowles, and Lisa. Both Sues were outgoing and energetic. They had played field hockey while in high school together and were popular socially. In fact, as the semester progressed, they became the driving force behind a number of dorm parties.

Lisa was much quieter, at least on first meeting. She was not a person who stood out in a crowd, but nonetheless had a quiet determination about her that became more apparent as you talked with her. She had some firm opinions about right and wrong.

The two Sues were good friends from high school and had chosen to room together, only to find that Lisa, a total stranger, had been assigned to live with them in a triple. As you can imagine, they would have preferred a double. But let them tell you their own story:

Sue T.: Around November of our senior year we both decided to apply to State University. A lot of people from our high school class had applied, and it seemed like the college to apply to. When we got our acceptance letter, we applied to room together. We also applied for work-study jobs and got jobs in the same office. It never occurred to either of us that we wouldn't be rooming together.

Sue K.: Yeah! Imagine how surprised we both were when the letter from the housing office came in August, and we found out we'd be in a triple (room 92)—with someone we didn't even know, and who was taking a totally different major (plant science, not history).

Sue T.: It was a surprise all right—sure we'd still be rooming together, but who was this girl? And why did we get stuck with her? Well, we talked it over and decided we'd try to make the best of it. Sue and I talked about calling Lisa but there just wasn't enough time. We were both busy with our jobs and involved seeing friends before we left for college. Besides, we figured she could always call us if she wanted to.

We had our parents drive us to campus early the day we were supposed to arrive so that we'd have time to settle in and explore the town a bit. Also we wanted to get there before Lisa if we could, so that we could see about organizing the room. We got our things unpacked after our parents left, giving Lisa half of each of our closets as well as the top bunk. I made a "Welcome Lisa" sign and hung it on the door—it seemed like a good way to let her know we were ready to be friendly. While we were talking about how we could arrange the room, one of us remembered that our boyfriends were coming for the day Saturday. "I guess we should let Lisa know they're coming," I said. Sue K. answered, "Yes, I'm sure if we just mention it, she'll understand we want the room to ourselves for the afternoon. I mean, she must know somebody here—so she won't have need to hang around here all day, and surely she'll have the courtesy to let us have the room to ourselves for a while." Before I could say anything else, the door opened and there was Lisa.

Sue K.: Of course, we automatically stopped talking, and she walked in looking kind of aloof and distant. Then she demanded to know which one of us was Taylor. Sue answered while I muttered, "I guess it's better than asking which one of us is Suzie." After that her parents arrived with the rest of her stuff, and her mother gave us an earful about what a wonderful highfalutin' town Lisa was from! When Lisa left to walk to the car with her parents, Sue T. said to me, "I don't know, I had hoped she'd be friendlier. She certainly was aloof and abrupt—things might not work out as well as we thought."

Sue T.: When Lisa returned, Sue suggested that we go into town and look for some posters. As we were walking out of the dorm, I asked Sue what was the big rush to get posters. Sue said, "I thought it might be courteous to leave her alone for a while and let her unpack. Things might be better when we get back."

It was late afternoon by the time we got back, and Lisa was still unpacking when we came in with posters and corkboard. As we were approaching the dorm, I had suggested that we get rid of our stuff and get something to eat. Sue had agreed, so after we sorted through some of the things we had gotten, I said to her, "Let's go to dinner." Lisa asked directions to the dining hall, which Sue gave her, and we went back into town to get a pizza.

Sue K.: We talked to Lisa for awhile that night; she asked about our work-study jobs, but she didn't seem all that interested. I told her who to go see, but I didn't think she would really go through with it. After a while we started talking about friends from home, and I made it a point to say, "Oh—Lisa, our boyfriends will be coming Saturday afternoon." Lisa said nothing, and I really didn't know what else to say so I started talking to Sue again.

The next day Lisa went off to orientation, and we decided to get the posters and corkboard up before our boyfriends arrived. This required moving some furniture. I said, "Look, while we're doing this, why don't we give Lisa her own area and we take the rest of the room? That way she can have her friends in here without bothering us or our friends bothering her." Sue said, "Sounds like a good idea. It will make it seem like she has her own room that way—and she can put up whatever posters she wants." We arranged the room so that she could have more privacy if she wanted to.

The next morning we were up early, getting everything set for Chuck and Bill. Lisa got up and left, saying good morning on her way out the door. I was relieved and said "Good, she apparently understood that we wanted the room today. Hopefully, she will give us all afternoon to be by ourselves with Chuck and Bill.

Sue T.: But were we in for a surprise! A few hours later Lisa walked in on the four of us and sat down at her desk. Suddenly she announced that "I live here, too." We introduced her to the guys and watched to see what she'd do next. When it became obvious that she was going to sit at her desk and read, Chuck whispered to me, "Maybe if she sees me kissing you, she'll leave." A couple of minutes later Lisa slammed out of the room, but none of us felt very certain that she wouldn't pop back in any moment.

That night she brought some friends back; they had some beer and sat at Lisa's desk drinking it. We all sat on Sue K's bed, which was hidden from the desk by a bureau, and talked for awhile. Eventually they left, but it sure was embarrassing for us to have Lisa and her friends there when Chuck and Bill were here! After the guys left, Sue and I both went to bed. Sue said she heard Lisa come in much later.

Sue K.: The next week, classes started. Since Sue and I had the same early morning schedule, we set our alarms to go off at the same time. Sue and I hurried out every morning with just enough time to have coffee before the first class. Lisa was almost never in the room that week—and when she was, she was in her bunk. We were too busy with classes and jobs to say much more than hello and good-bye, but after those first few encounters with her I was just as glad.

At the end of the week, Lisa left a note saying that she'd gone home for the weekend to pick up some things. Were we relieved to have her out of the room for the weekend as our boyfriends were coming to visit! Both Sue and I were worried that things would be just as bad when she returned and wondered what to do about the situation.

The Ultimate Frisbee Team's Dilemma

Harry, Jere, George, and Bob L. were students at Centerville University who enjoyed playing Ultimate Frisbee, a game requiring two teams of seven. Since it was hard to round up 14 players every time they wished to play, they decided to start a regular frisbee team. Their hopes were to get some potentially good frisbee players together and teach them how to play Ultimate. They realized they would need to publicize the team. One of them, Jere, spoke to a reporter from the school newspaper, and a short article appeared about the team (see

Exhibit 1). In the interview Jere stated, "The team is open to all students, especially girls." Any of the four could have spoken to the reporter, but Jere took the initiative. Jere also announced a practice through the newspaper. Eleven people came to that initial practice: Jere, Fred, Roger (Fred's roommate), Jim H., Jean, Bob L., George, Pete C., Pete R., Paul, and Harry. Jere took their names, addresses, and telephone numbers and announced that practices would be held at 4 P.M. on Tuesdays and Thursdays (a time that was convenient for Jere). It wasn't clear why Jere should be the one to decide this, but since he was taking names, he was the one asked by the newcomers.

At the second practice some new people showed up: Chas, Alex, Bert, Gene (all of whom lived together), Bob M., Linda, Sharon, and Jack. However, some people from the first practice didn't come because they had conflicting classes. Jere took these new people's names and toyed with the idea of taking attendance, but nothing came of it because, as he said to his roommate, "I didn't want to turn people off or make them feel they had to come." However, many players made a mental note of who was there and who wasn't. Different people came and went like this at each practice thereafter.

Jere and several others knew how to play Ultimate and spent the first few practices teaching the others. Jere dominated the direction of these early practices, but after a short time the rest of the players were as good and some even better. Everyone had a lot of fun learning and playing. Jack and Chas were two players who stood out at practice. Jack (a grad student) was calm and collected, never became angry, and always played fairly. Chas had been the captain of his high school football team and always organized the team he was on, deciding who should play and who should sit out.

Jere dealt with much of the administrative work, such as announcing to the school radio and newspaper where and when practices would be held. No one asked Jere to do this, but attendance was sporadic and he hoped to get new people to fill the gaps at practice. However, response to the newspaper and radio announcements was minimal; consequently, Jere felt there should be an organizational meeting at night, which hopefully would generate interest and attract more players. At the next practice Jere announced the meeting and explained that it was also to set up officers, dues, and so forth. Jack had 200 flyers printed up, and he and Chas posted them around campus.

Jere came to the meeting late and found that strong opposition had developed against dues and against organization in general. Jere tried to explain that in order to receive funding from the university or to use university vehicles, the team must be organized with officers and a constitution, saying that the sports director for the university had told him this. A vote on dues barely passed, whereupon several members left the meeting vowing they had quit. Jere followed them into the

EXHIBIT 1
The *Centerville News*, March 1, 1974

"ULTIMATE FRISBEE" ARRIVES WITH SPRING
By Janice M. Dupre

Springtime is just around the corner, and for frisbee lovers it's time to warm up the old throwing arm.

This spring a group of frisbee enthusiasts are trying to get together a frisbee team at Centerville University (CU). Originator of the team is Jere Harris.

Many people are familiar with the frisbee as simply a plastic disc used for throwing around on a beach.

But there is an official game played with a frisbee. It's called Ultimate Frisbee, and it's like soccer in many ways.

"In Ultimate Frisbee there are seven players per team on the field. There is a kickoff, but you can't run with the frisbee in your hand," explains Harris. "It's an extremely fast game with two 24-minute halves."

According to Harris, a Middle States Frisbee League is now being formed by a student from Amerion College. Colleges that already have teams and will hopefully be joining the league include: Western Reserve, Ohio Wesleyan, Wayne University, and Clarke. One of the best frisbee teams in the area is the New Hampton College team.

In past years individuals from CU have gotten together to play other schools, but there never has been an official team.

"I've been playing frisbee all my life, but I never heard of Ultimate Frisbee until a friend of mine told me about the game last year. It's really a fast-moving game with lots of collisions because the frisbee is always in the air with everyone diving for it," said Harris, a junior hospital administration major.

Ultimate Frisbee is by no means a gentle game. At this moment Bob LaPointe, future cocaptain of the forming CU team, has a dislocated shoulder from a frisbee game he recently played in.

The friend that introduced the game to Jere Harris last year was a graduate of Columbia High School in New Jersey. It was at Columbia where the first game was played.

"The Columbia High team can beat any team in the nation," said Harris. "They won over 30 games at the national tournament held in Michigan last year. Columbia High School also publishes the Ultimate Frisbee rulebook."

Each year a national frisbee tournament is held at Copperhopper, Michigan. Hundreds of Ultimate Frisbee teams from the United States and Canada come to take part in the tournament. The game of Frisbee is not confined to North America; it's very popular overseas and, according to Harris, is just being introduced to Red China.

So far the CU Frisbee team comprises about 10 members. Harris is hoping to get the team off the ground and start practicing soon. He is planning to announce practices as soon as he can arrange a time in the indoor track and as soon as the weather is nice.

"Frisbee is open to women," stresses Harris. "To play you don't have to be a super frisbee thrower; you just have to be able to throw and catch the frisbee and to run."

Along with all the food, energy, and political crises there is also a frisbee crisis. Frisbees are made with plastics, and since there is a plastic shortage the frisbees are an endangered species. Harris said that the major frisbee companies, such as Whamo, are urging people to buy their frisbees now because soon they will be hard to come by.

But until that time comes, frisbees will continue to fly in the sky on warm spring days at Centerville.

hall pleading with them to be sensible but could overhear two other members saying, "So what, we don't need them anyway." A debate ensued for a few minutes, and Jere called an end to the meeting, putting off a vote on a captain because he feared it would create further division among the team, since either Jere, Jack, or Chas might have made a good captain. Many new people who had shown up to the meeting explained they couldn't make practices as currently scheduled. Jere shrugged and said he'd try to set up alternative practices; however, this was never done.

A new group of players arrived after about 10 practices: Stan, Reggie, Mark, Bill T., and Howie. They always came and left together and often played on the same team. They were good players and talked about the coming games and their anticipated role in them. Reggie asked Jere at his first practice, "Do you think I'll start the first game?" Jere just shrugged.

By this time over 20 people had come out for the team, including 3 girls (see Exhibit 2). The players fell into five friendship groups, as shown in Exhibit 3. As practices continued, they became hard and

EXHIBIT 2

Name	*Attendance†*	*Initial Appearance*	*Ability†*	*Age*	*Class*	*Showed Up for Bus*
Jack	regular	2nd practice	A	23	Grad.	XX
Fred	regular	1st practice	A	19	Fresh.	XX
Jere*	regular	1st practice	B	20	Jr.	XX
Jean	regular	1st practice	C	19	Soph.	XX
Harry*	regular	1st practice	A	21	Sr.	XX
Roger	sporadic	1st practice	B	21	Sr.	XX
Reggie	regular	10th practice	A	18	Fresh.	XX
Mark	regular	10th practice	A	18	Fresh.	XX
Howie	regular	10th practice	A	18	Fresh.	XX
Stan	regular	10th practice	A	19	Fresh.	XX
Paul	sporadic	1st practice	B	19	Soph.	XX
Jim H.	regular	1st practice	A	19	Jr.	XX
Chas	regular	2nd practice	A	20	Soph.	XX
Gene	sporadic	2nd practice	B	20	Soph.	XX
Bert	sporadic	2nd practice	B	19	Soph.	XX
Sharon	regular	2nd practice	C	20	Jr.	XX
Linda	sporadic	2nd practice	C	18	Fresh.	XX
George*	regular	1st practice	A	19	Soph.	XX
Bob L.*	sporadic	1st practice	B	19	Soph.	XX
Bob M.	sporadic	2nd practice	B	20	Jr.	XX
Pete C.	sporadic	1st practice	B	19	Fresh.	XX
Bill T.	regular	10th practice	C	19	Soph.	XX
Alex	sporadic	2nd practice	C	19	Soph.	
Pete R.	sporadic	1st practice	C	18	Fresh.	XX

* Founders of the team.
† Based on Jere's "mental notes."

EXHIBIT 3
Subgroups (with spokesperson listed first)

Group A: Jere, Harry, Bob L., George.
Group B: Chas, Gene, Alex, Bert.
Group C: Jack, Jean, Linda, Sharon, Jim H.
Group D: Stan, Reggie, Mark, Howie, Bill T.
Group E: Fred, Roger, Pete C., Paul.
All the rest are independents, coming under no group.

competitive, and a lot of the fun that had been evident in the beginning seemed to disappear. One day Jere enraged Sharon by taking the frisbee away from her and throwing it himself. She started to walk off the field, but Jere called her back and the two had an argument right out in the middle of the field where everyone could see and hear it. She stayed at practice but was silent the rest of the day.

As the date for the first game drew near, all of the dues money was used to rent a 15-seat bus for the 50-mile trip to the other school. The day before the game about 12 people attended a meeting to discuss travel plans. Jack brought a letter written by Sharon. It was addressed to the team, but started:

> Dear Jack:
>
> The incident at this afternoon's practice was the last straw, but I would like to impress, far from the only one. I'm writing this to you because you are the only one on the team who ever gave me any encouragement or made me feel like a real live person and not a bumbling incompetent.
>
> I joined the frisbee team because I enjoy playing vigorous frisbee in the comradeship of others, and to develop my own skill and confidence; but none of these are achievable under the present conditions.
>
> How can I enjoy and concentrate on the game, when not a minute goes by that I must force myself to ignore and rise above degrading and humiliating sexist treatment? It's often said that a female, be it a filly race horse or me on the frisbee team, must be three times as good as a male in order to be considered equal. Nothing truer has ever been said. Even Jere, who's practiced with me so much and encouraged my progress, turns overtly sexist in the presence of his teammates. Certainly the issues are not completely imagined in my mind—ask the other female players.
>
> I am not against competitiveness as long as the competition element stimulates constant improvement. But when point-making takes priority over the freedom to make mistakes or try new things, then I think something is wrong. Maybe, if anyone cares you could let them in on this. . . .

With this Sharon announced her resignation from the team. The letter was received with much debate by the team, and some players

EXHIBIT 4
Comparative Lists: Should Go to the Game

Jack's List	*Group D's List*
Jere	Reggie
Jack	Mark
Fred	Howie
Jean	Stan
Roger	Paul
Jim H.	Jere
Sharon	Jack
Linda	Fred
Bob L.	Roger
George	Jim H.
Harry	Chas
Paul	Gene
Pete R.	Bert
Chas	George
Gene	Harry

refused to read the letter. Jack sided with the opinions stated in the letter and was joined in this opinion by many of the original members, including the two remaining girls. Jere remained silent, unable to side with one view or the other.

Obviously some choice had to be made as to who would go on the bus. Group D insisted on "Sending down the best 15," in which case all of them would go. Group C said, "Take those who have come to the most practices." Jere felt that this was the fairest solution, but it was hard to implement since no one was sure as to who had attended how many practices.

Jere, Jack, and Stan sat down and wrote up several lists of 15 (see Exhibit 4), but none was acceptable to all of the groups. Jere put off making any decision; several people got quite sore. Jere felt caught in the middle, and it was not something he could shrug off. He tried to act as the moderator of the dispute but kept saying, "Does anyone have any ideas?" Argument continued and people began to leave very upset, with no decision reached. Jere felt that he had been responsible for letting the scene get out of hand.

The day of the game came, and 19 people stood outside near the bus. Everyone wondered what to do. Some expressed the opinion that a captain should be elected to make the decision.

▶ What to Do with Bob and Nancy?

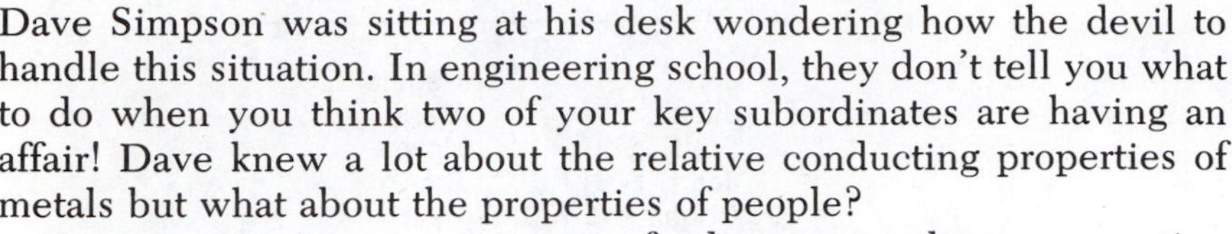

Dave Simpson was sitting at his desk wondering how the devil to handle this situation. In engineering school, they don't tell you what to do when you think two of your key subordinates are having an affair! Dave knew a lot about the relative conducting properties of metals but what about the properties of people?

Dave was engineering manager of a division in a large corporation situated on the East Coast. The division was comprised of 3 engineering supervisors, 5 lead engineers, and approximately 55 engineers (see Exhibit 1). The past two years had seen several reductions in manpower due to a temporary decline in the business base. The remaining men and women in the organization were "cream of the crop," all hard workers with a professional attitude about their jobs; any deadwood was long gone. The division had just won a large contract, which would provide for long-term growth but would also require a heavy workload until new people could be hired and trained.

The work of the organization was highly technical and required considerable sharing of ideas within and between the individual groups. This need for internal cooperation and support had been amplified because the organization was still undermanned and staffing up.

Dave's previous secretary had transferred to an outplant location just before the new contract award, and it had taken a long time to find a suitable replacement. Because of a general shortage within the company, Dave had been forced to hire temporary help from a secretarial service. After several months he found Nancy and felt very fortunate to have located an experienced secretary from within the company. She was in her mid-30s, attractive, had a pleasant disposition, and was very competent.

In the electronic design group was an enthusiastic, highly respected lead engineer named Bob. Bob and Dave had been close friends for several years, having started with the company at the same time. They shared several common interests, which had led to spending a fair amount of time together away from work.

Bob was struggling to get into management, and Dave's more rapid advancement had put a strain on the friendship. Dave had moved up from co-worker to being his boss and finally to being his boss's boss.

This case was prepared under the supervision of David L. Bradford, Lecturer in Organizational Behavior, as the basis of class discussion rather than to illustrate either effective or ineffective handling of an administrative situation. Reprinted from *Stanford Business Cases 1983* with permission of Stanford University Graduate School of Business,

EXHIBIT 1
Table of Organization

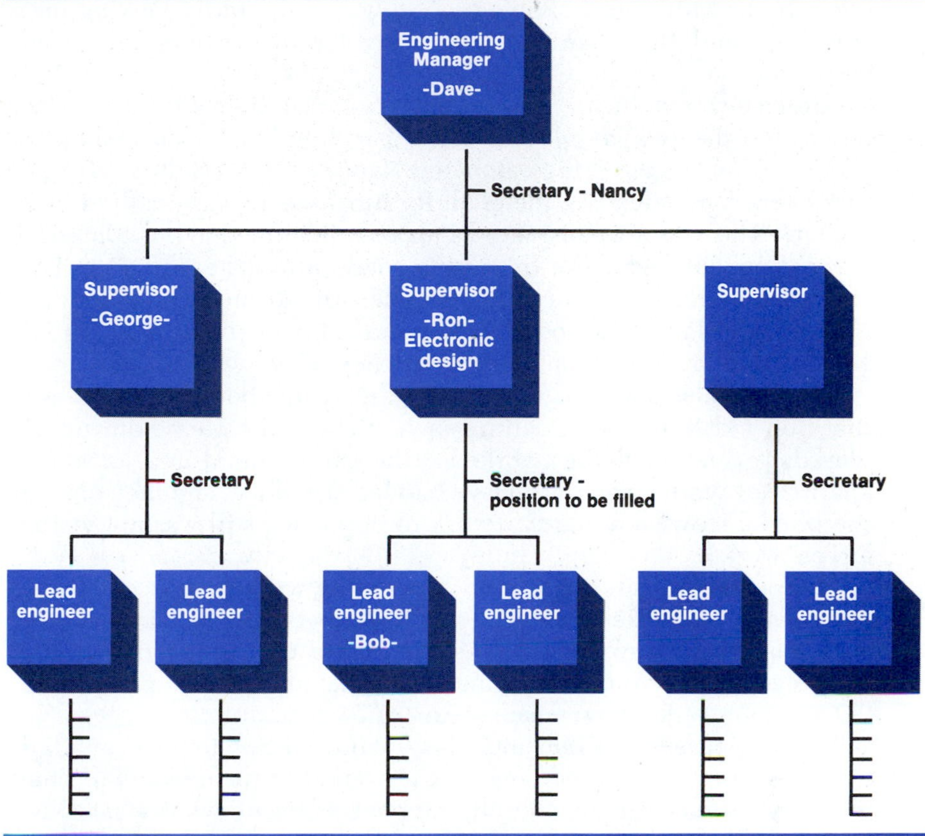

Dave felt they could still be good friends at work, but he could not show Bob any favoritism. Bob understood the situation.

From Nancy's first day on the job, Bob began to hang around her desk. He would go out of his way to start conversations and draw her attention. This was not a surprise, since Nancy was attractive and Bob had gained a reputation over the years as being a bit of a "wolf." He was always the first on the scene when an attractive new female joined the program.

Before long Bob and Nancy began eating lunch together. As time passed, the lunch dates became a regular routine as did their trips together to the coffee machine. Their conversations during the working day also became more frequent. Dave felt slightly concerned about the wasted time, but since the quality and quantity of their work was not suffering in any measurable way, he did not say anything to either person. Furthermore, it was not unreasonable for Bob to be having numerous conversations with her, since she had been instructed to provide typing and clerical support to the engineers whenever she had idle time. (Bob's section was temporarily looking for a secretary, and the engineers were developing several new documents.)

After a few months Bob and Nancy introduced their spouses to each other, and the two couples began to get together for an increasing number of social gatherings. Bob and Nancy continued their frequent lunch dates, now leaving the plant for lunch and occasionally returning late. This was not considered a major rule infraction if the lateness was infrequent and if the time were made up in the long run. This tolerance policy was generally respected by all, including Bob and Nancy. On balance, the company seemed to be receiving at least a full week's work from both of them, since they often worked late.

What was also going on (but Dave didn't learn about until later) was that Bob and Nancy were calling each other on the phone during the workday even though they worked in the same general area, just desks apart. They would wait until Dave had left the office, and then chat on the phone. However, Nancy's work performance still was not visibly affected.

Of course the internal grapevine was at work, and occasionally Dave would be asked about the situation between Bob and Nancy. "Do you know they've been seen having cocktails together in the evening?" "Did you know Nancy was having marital problems?" "Does Bob's wife know what's going on?"

It was apparent that Bob and Nancy were starting to have an affair, but how serious it was and how long it would last wasn't known. They were being very careful around Dave, and almost all of what Dave knew was based upon second- and third-hand information and rumors. At this point, about four months after Nancy had started work, Dave did speak to Ron, Bob's supervisor, about it; but Ron was anxious to downplay the whole thing. He was willing to talk to Bob about the late lunches but unwilling to discuss anything else. This seemed appropriate since, from the company's standpoint, employees' private lives were their own business. Ron was new to the organization, and this factor contributed to his reluctance to discuss a delicate issue.

Dave decided not to confront Bob directly. If their relationship had been as close as it had been in years past, he might have spoken to Bob about the rumors going around, but during this period the friendship had further deteriorated. They were talking on a less personal level, and Bob was spending less off-hours time with old friends. Furthermore, Dave knew from previous discussions that Bob was particularly sensitive about private matters. "He probably wouldn't welcome my advice," thought Dave.

Dave did speak to Nancy about the need to be back in the office at the end of the lunch hour, but he had not made an issue out of it. Even though it was a definite annoyance when she was not there to answer the phone or type a memo, her performance had not declined. Dave certainly did not want to bring up with Nancy the issue of an affair. He imagined what might arise: tears, defensive denial (much of what Dave thought was going on would be difficult to substantiate if Nancy were to challenge his assessment), and even potential legal ramifications if the situation were handled improperly. Bob and Nancy could claim that their reputations or careers had been damaged. (Dave also didn't want to raise this issue with personnel; it might permanently tarnish both of their records.)

During this same time frame there was a dramatic change in Bob's personal appearance. Instead of his usual coat-and-tie attire, he started wearing open-front shirts and a beaded necklace in an attempt to acquire the current "macho" look. Although perhaps acceptable in a Southern California business office, it certainly was out of place in the Northeast with the more conservative environment of the company. As a lead engineer, Bob directed and often presented to management the work of 12 other engineers. The custom was for all engineers and managers to wear a coat and tie, especially since they might be called upon with little notice to meet with a customer or higher management. Even though Bob's attire was considered unprofessional, there was nothing in the company's written dress code requirement to forbid it.

Up to this point there had been no serious violation of company rules by either Bob or Nancy, although rules were being bent and tolerance policies abused.

Then the situation took a turn for the worse while Dave was on a two-week company trip with Ron. Bob and Nancy used the opportunity to go out for a very long lunch. When they returned just before quitting time, George, one of the other supervisors, called Bob into his office and suggested that he "clean up his act." George told Bob that he was being foolish in chasing Nancy and that, among other things, he was jeopardizing his career opportunities with the company. Bob denied being anything more than friends with Nancy and politely told George to stay out of his private affairs.

When Dave returned from his trip and heard of the incident, he told Ron to reprimand Bob and make it clear to him that "his actions are unacceptable and that further long lunch periods will not be tolerated." Bob apologized, said he would make up the time and that it wouldn't happen again.

Dave spoke to Nancy, and she also promised that there would be no more long lunches. But this was not the end of their noontime, outplant lunch dates, and before long, Nancy's husband Ted got involved. Ted was a salesman for the company and worked in the same building. He began to drop by at lunchtime to question the engineers about Nancy's whereabouts. In addition he started calling Dave after work, wanting to know when Nancy had left and expressing concern that she had not yet arrived home. This questioning was an unpleasant experience for everybody.

By now the entire organization was well aware of the irregular relationship, and was growing disrespectful of both Bob and Nancy. This was a difficult situation for the engineers. The attitude of the organization had always been very professional, and the success of each group depended upon teamwork and strong leadership from its lead engineer. Bob had been highly respected for his technical competence and ability to direct. In addition the members of his group knew Bob's family and had always considered him to be a good family man. Now this image had been destroyed. From a technical standpoint, Bob was still an excellent engineer and a vital resource on the new contract. But with the group's declining respect, Bob was becoming less effective as a leader. Bob's own engineers felt very uncomfortable about the situation. They believed that Bob's real interests at work were more with Nancy than with them.

The situation had now deteriorated to the point where total organization effectiveness was being measurably affected. Something had to be done to remedy this situation. But what to do?

▶ Why Play Football?

PART I

Alan Lake and Frank Parker left the locker room together talking enthusiastically about the coming season and discussing their chances of having a good team. They were both seniors and cocaptains of the football team at Woodlawn College. They knew it would be hard to match the 8–1 record of the previous season, especially since so many of their best players had graduated, but nonetheless they looked forward to the challenge.

Woodlawn College is a small, private, liberal arts college with an enrollment of 2,200 students. Located in farming country, it is a small residential college that exists as a self-contained unit in the town of

From S. Fink, S. Jenks, and R. Willits, *Designing and Managing Organizations*, 1983, pages 616–24. Reproduced by permission of Richard D. Irwin, Inc., Homewood, Ill.

Woodlawn. Having gone coed four years ago, the student body consists of both men and women from all 50 states and many foreign countries. The majority of the American students come from the East.

Throughout the years, Woodlawn College has developed the reputation of a prestigious institution known for its academic excellence, and admissions are selective. Combined expenses (tuition and room and board) are quite high, but only 30 percent of the students receive some type of financial aid. The majority of students pay the full expenses on their own; many of them come from upper-income families.

Founded in the early 1800s, Woodlawn had a long football tradition. The college catalog states that the purpose of all athletic programs (physical education, intramurals, and intercollegiate sports) is to contribute to the development of strong minds, bodies, and character. In reference to intercollegiate sports, it goes on to say that the program is "college-level athletics, sports within the framework of a total education." The intercollegiate athletic program is "based on the principle that people play for the enjoyment of competition and the love of the game."

Athletic scholarships are not awarded, but many athletes do receive financial aid in the form of loans and grants. The financial aid officers are aware of the fact that campus jobs would interfere with varsity practices and games, so they refrain from assigning these jobs to members of intercollegiate teams.

Woodlawn is a member of the Small College Athletic Conference, which includes 11 other schools. The purpose of this conference is very similar to that of sports programs at Woodlawn: to insure that intercollegiate athletics remain within the framework of the educational philosophies for which these schools are renowned. Conference schools, by tradition, play several nonconference schools rather than just conference schools during a season, and the conference consciously avoids naming a "conference champion."

Both Alan and Frank, like almost all of their teammates, had played football since their freshman year. Each year, between 20 and 25 freshmen go out for football, and usually not more than 5 to 10 quit the team. The varsity squad is made up of sophomores, juniors, and seniors; it has approximately 50 members each year. Since the school is so small, there aren't enough players for a junior varsity team. Everyone who completes summer camp before the season begins makes the varsity squad; very rarely is anyone cut.

As they left the locker room they talked about their experiences of the past three years and how they wanted to make their last year on the team different.

ALAN: Remember how awful it was on the freshman team? I didn't think I would last.

Frank: Yeah, it's too bad we couldn't just take that year in stride and realize it was something everyone has to go through. I think we really did benefit from sticking it out together as a class.

Alan: That's true, at the end of last season I was talking with the coach about how they originally decided to have freshmen on a team by themselves. He said that they thought it was a good way to get a class identity formed so by the time we are seniors, and on the varsity, we'll really feel like a group, like a real team.

Frank: I'm glad they do it this way. At least when we were freshmen we all got to play a lot, so that it wasn't so bad sitting on the bench a lot during varsity games sophomore year. Can you imagine what it would have been like as a freshman on a freshman/sophomore team?

Alan: Sure, the freshmen would never get to play and their morale would be pretty low. But at a school this size we really need sophomores on the varsity squad. We couldn't make it without them as second-stringers.

Frank: Besides being "dummies" for the varsity to practice with when we were freshmen, the attitude toward football around here was really hard for me to take.

Alan: I know what you mean. I guess we were all so used to being "stars" in high school that it was a rude awakening to come here and be looked down on for being a "jock."

Frank: I couldn't believe the first varsity game I went to when I was a freshman. Hardly anyone was there to watch except a few fraternity members, and I'm sure banners and posters were unheard of. This was the only college I'd ever heard of that didn't have a band.

Alan: And, do you remember the varsity guys telling us which professors would never let you miss their class or leave their class early for away games? I guess those guys all went to school when a prerequisite for being an athlete was being stupid.

Frank: I'm glad that situation is beginning to change. I think one reason it's changing is that the campus unrest of the late '60s, early '70s has died down, and so have a lot of the attitudes that were prevalent then—now it's OK to like sports again. But in a school like this where athletics are always secondary to academic achievement, that attitude will probably always exist to a certain extent, even despite the coaches' efforts to have the team get around campus and mix with people other than our fraternity brothers.

Alan: That's true, but the lack of strong campus interest may be to the team's benefit in the long run. [*Frank looked quizzical so Alan continued to explain.*] I think almost everyone on the varsity team is here because they really like the sport and want to play football. I can remember a few people who have quit the freshman team through the years because they expected team membership to give them high status on campus.

Frank: You're right, we do have a bunch of really dedicated guys. I hope it will be a good team. I've been thinking about what we can do to make it a good team. I think we should try to loosen things up a little and see if we can get some real team spirit going.

Alan: You took the words right out of my mouth! We've won a lot of games these past few years and a lot of records have been set, but I don't think we've worked together very well as a team. For me, it hasn't been much fun being a member of this team. Practices have been a real drag—people were either trying so hard to get a starting position that they didn't care about anyone around them, or so frustrated that they didn't try at all. I even saw some guys deliberately trying to hurt other guys on the field, not to mention some of the things I heard people saying about each other.

Frank: Yeah, the atmosphere has been pretty intense. I guess when you get a bunch of equally talented guys competing for a limited number of positions it gets pretty cut-throat. I've seen a lot more brown-nosing and lack of cooperation around here than I ever expected, despite the coaches' saying that they wanted everyone to get some playing time.

Alan: I think that's one of the problems of a team like this. It's really hard to strike a balance between competition and cooperation, working together as a team. I guess I'm saying that for many of us winning isn't everything if no one enjoys being a team member.

Frank: I wonder who they chose to be the team managers this year. Since we started having women as team managers two years ago, things haven't been the same.

Alan: I heard that the two women who got the job are very good. I do think the president is right that having women managers is a good way to help integrate the women students on campus, and to promote the school's affirmative action goals, but I don't think the coaches will ever get used to it. They're always griping about it.

They continued to discuss how they could facilitate the growth of a more relaxed atmosphere and increase teamwork, but at the same time be as successful as possible. They arrived at a team motto: "fun, fair play, and excellence," which summarized all of their feelings about how the team should function. They thought that by fulfilling this motto as students, athletes, and team members, by trying their hardest and doing their best, yet having some fun, the end result would be a winning team.

The first practice started with the distribution of the playbook, which stated:

> By electing to become a member of this team, you have acknowledged your responsibility to contribute to the maintenance of the tradition of excellence which has become a part of Woodlawn College. This tradition has grown to the degree that winning is accepted and expected of all Woodlawn football teams.

This playbook was distributed exclusively to the coaches and players, and they were instructed (by the head coach) to keep these books in the locker room at all times. He also informed everyone that the playbooks would be collected at the end of the season.

The team members initially started out as in previous years, fiercely competitive for starting positions and showing little intention of cooperating beyond the minimum level necessary to function as a team. But after a few practices, attitudes slowly started changing. Alan and Frank were well liked and respected by the team members, and their behavior and attitudes were soon adopted by the other players. Almost everyone was soon joking around a lot and helping each other out during practice, and they soon became a unified team.

The majority of the varsity football players were members of one of the two biggest fraternities on campus. While they socialized primarily with their fraternity brothers, as a team they got along well and their external social allegiances had no disruptive effect on the team's cohesiveness.

The season progressed smoothly, and almost all of the team members had adopted the "fun, fair play, and excellence" motto. Most of the team members were good friends, and the atmosphere of the team was relaxed. However, during a game against Woodlawn's arch rival, Alan got so caught up in winning that he completely lost sight of the team motto. He was playing opposite the other team's best player, and he had to play extremely well in order for Woodlawn to win. Throughout many practices the coaches got him psyched to play against this guy, and by the third quarter of the game Alan was doing an outstanding job. At this point his emotions got the best of him, and while down on the line he began cussing at his opponent and calling him derogatory racial names. Woodlawn won the game, and Alan was carried off the field on the shoulders of his teammates in recognition of his good performance. In the meantime, his teammates playing next to Alan in the line told the coach about his behavior. His reaction was one of disbelief, since it was so out of character for Alan to behave that way, and "dirty play" was not acceptable to the Woodlawn team or any other teams in the league. In the locker room the coach told Alan to write a letter to the coach and player of the other team and apologize for his behavior. Alan felt surprise and shame at the way he had acted and wrote the letter at once.

By mid-season the team's record was 2–2, and a problem had arisen that neither the coaches nor cocaptains knew how to deal with. One of the most talented players was not a "team member" in the true sense of the word. Unlike the other players, he was boastful and a loudmouth, always "blowing his own horn." He didn't work hard in practice; instead he tried to impress everyone by making fancy moves, which didn't fit in with the plays. On Thursdays and Fridays the team practiced without full uniforms, concentrating on timing and polishing up the plays they had worked out against their upcoming opponent's defensive patterns. It was on these days that Jim would come charging through the line and knock someone over when they least expected it, as if everyone was dressed in full pads and hitting their hardest. He wasn't well liked by other players, and he didn't associate with team members socially.

In the middle of many close games, during which he had been sitting on the bench, the coach would send him in to play. His presence was often the determining factor in the outcome of the game; the team's chances of winning were much better when he was playing. The following is a typical conversation about this player that occurred during staff meetings attended by coaches and cocaptains:

Asst. Coach: I really think we should cut Jim from the team. His attitude is one of the worst I've ever seen—and he has been warned.

Head Coach: Yes, we have discussed this problem with him, and he hasn't made any effort to fit in, but I don't think we should cut him. After all, he is a great athlete, and he has really helped out in the games we've won this season. He knows he's capable of being in a permanent starting position but doesn't seem to want it enough to change his attitude.

Frank: Yeah, even though he's against almost everything the team stands for, he sure has helped us out of some tight situations.

Alan: I know that some players wish he played more to improve our chances of winning while other players would rather take the chance and let another teammate play, leaving Jim on the bench.

Head Coach: Since he doesn't play all of the time it does give the other fullbacks a chance to play, and I do like to get as many guys on the field as possible during a game.

This dilemma was never completely resolved. Jim remained on the team, sometimes starting, sometimes sitting on the bench. The coaches were thankful that he was a senior and were glad that none of the younger team members had adopted Jim's attitude.

The season ended with a 5–4 record, and both Alan and Frank had enjoyed the experience of being captains of this team. The coach told them that they had really accomplished something—that it had been a long time since he had seen the varsity football team work so well together and have such a good time doing it. Nevertheless, Alan felt a sense of incompleteness, which he discussed with Frank after the awards banquet.

Alan: I know we had a good team and a lot of student support by the end of the season, but I still feel like something is missing.

Frank: Well, we didn't win as many games as we did last season, but I think we lived up to our motto as best we could.

Alan: I guess that's it; it was good to hear the coach say he thought we had accomplished something, but if we had had a winning season I'd feel like we accomplished more. I do feel that we accomplished something; we were a real team, people trusted each other, worked hard, and got along well together.

Frank: And I can think of a lot of instances where that was really important. How about the time John and Todd [two senior linemen] were competing for the same position? The team divided into cliques made up of their closest friends for a short time, until the coaches decided to rotate them in the starting position. After that the cliques dissolved and there weren't any hard feelings. If that had happened last year, one of them probably would have quit the team, and the team would have been split in two for the whole season.

Alan: We've had a lot better relationships between the offense and defense this year, too. Remember how each group would always complain about how the other group was playing—and say nasty things behind their backs?

Frank: Sure, but this year the offense and defense were always pulling for each other and helping each other out whenever they could.

Alan: It always helps to have some guys in more than one group.

Frank: You're right; our first-string offense and defense were the only really distinct groups. Some second-stringers went both ways, and our specialty teams were made up of a mixture of first- and second-stringers from the offense and defense.

Alan: Well, we have been successful in a lot of respects, but too bad the record doesn't show it.

PART II

Each year two members of the varsity football team are chosen by the coaches to act as graduate assistants the following year. These assistants are employed as the coaches of the freshman team and are also members of the varsity coaching staff. The freshman team practiced three days per week with the varsity. The majority of this time was spent running the formations of the upcoming opponents against the varsity to give them practice. The other two practice days were spent learning Woodlawn's formations and getting ready for their own games. The duties of the graduate assistants included supervising the freshmen in their practices with the varsity, coaching them as a team by themselves, counseling them if they were having problems, scouting varsity opponents, analyzing films of varsity opponents, and doing some varsity coaching during games.

Frank and Alan were chosen for these positions, and they were both looking forward to the opportunity of getting some coaching experience. They approached the job with an attitude similar to the one they had as captains. Even though their time to practice together as a team was minimal, Alan and Frank wanted them to work together as a team and do their best.

There were weekly meetings of the varsity coaching staff, and Alan and Frank were immediately accepted as members of the group. They had gotten along well with the coaches as players, the coaches respected them and talked candidly in front of them. After one meeting early in the season, Alan and Frank had dinner together and discussed the meeting.

Alan: It sure is different being on the other side of the fence. Could you believe the way they were talking about the players? They sure didn't give a damn about Joe's desire to play in front of his parents, who will be here for the weekend from California, nor about poor, awkward Harold, who never did get into any games. They didn't seem too concerned about how serious Tim's sprained ankle is, as long as they can find someone to take his place who can run as well as he can. They were certainly talking about shuffling personnel around like game pieces. I had no idea that kind of planning went on when we were on the team.

Frank: I think they're under a lot more pressure than we were ever aware of. I heard the coach talking to John [assistant coach] about how the baseball coach got the word from the president: he's out if he doesn't have a winning season this year.

Alan: No wonder it was so hard to decide what to do about Jim last year—our record probably would have been worse if he hadn't played at all.

Frank: I can understand the president's concern; winning teams get more publicity for the school, attract better athletes, and I believe get more alumni support, but I think that our experiences of the past four years showed us that winning isn't everything.

Alan: Another thing that surprised me is the coach's preoccupation with having the best record on campus.

Frank: I know what you mean. It sounds like he and the soccer coach have a running battle going to see who can win the most games.

The conversation then switched to the problems they were having coaching the freshman team.

Alan: That cracked me up when the coach told us that it was our duty to make this experience as good as possible for the freshmen so they won't quit the team. We've only been practicing three weeks, and it seems like morale is already slipping.

Frank: I can really sympathize with them; I think we felt the same way when we were freshmen. It's bad enough going from being a high school "star" to the anonymity of the freshman team, without the added frustration of spending three days a week getting your head bashed in by the varsity.

Alan: I think they are even more discouraged by the fact that it is next to impossible to get a winning team together with so little practice time to ourselves.

Frank: That's true, but you know how much we needed those practices with the freshmen when we were on the varsity team. We would have been lost without them.

Alan: By the way, have you spent much time counseling any of the guys on the freshman team? We are supposed to be helping them out with any problems they're having. I sure haven't had a chance.

Frank: I haven't either; we really should try to make some time for that sooner or later. Right now we have to work on those plays for the next game.

The day before the freshman team's third game, the head coach of the varsity pulled one of the best freshman players to act as a safety replacement in the varsity's next game, two days away. One of the starting varsity players had been injured in practice, and the freshman was needed as a backup player. This incident disrupted the game plans for the freshman team. Alan and Frank tried to reorganize as best they could in the short amount of time available, but they lost the game.

At the next coaches' meeting, Alan made a joking remark about how it would be a lot easier to win if his players weren't being snatched away at the last minute and then only to sit on the bench just in case they were needed. The head coach told him he wasn't fond of doing that, but it was something that couldn't be avoided.

As the season progressed, Alan and Frank did whatever they could to make the experience as tolerable as possible for the freshman team. To break up the monotony of practices with the varsity, they would do things like send in unorthodox plays and formations, which would invariably provide a good laugh and throw off the varsity players. At times Alan and Frank would even run onto the field and play a position, which also added little to the seriousness of practice. On occasion the coach would call one of them over and tell him it was time to "get to work," but most of this behavior was overlooked.

Near the end of the season the freshman players who remained (only four had quit) had adopted an attitude of resigned acceptance of their situation and were glad they would be on the varsity squad next year. After losing three games as a result of players being pulled to serve as varsity replacements, Alan and Frank were more disconcerted than ever.

Alan: You'd think that they aren't even aware of the fact that we'd like to win a few games too.

Frank: Yeah, it's hard to believe that it matters so much to us this year. We did make it as good an experience as possible for the team, but they're the only ones that know that.

Alan: The only thing any of my friends ask is "Did you win?"

During the last varsity game, Alan was giving a varsity player advice before an important play. As the player ran into the huddle, Alan turned to Frank and remarked, "This is crazy; just yesterday I was yelling at that guy for blocking too hard against some of the freshmen, and here I am telling him to go out there and do whatever he has to do to block his man!"

Who's in Charge? (the Jim Davis case)

James Davis began his employment with Hereford National Bank in October, 1981. He had been hired away from an investment firm on the recommendation of Eric Johnson, vice president in charge of marketing. Mr. Johnson had heard through a friend at IDS, the company that Davis was employed by, that Jim was unhappy in his position there and thought of looking for employment elsewhere. Mr. Johnson felt that because of his experience in the investment world and in sales techniques (Davis had been a sales representative for IDS, helping people plan for their financial future and at the same time selling them the company's services), Davis could prove to be a valuable asset to his division. Since Jim was only 23 years old and had been out of school for two years, Johnson felt that he could offer him less of a salary than the job was worth and save some money. Davis was contacted and seemed interested. An initial interview was arranged, and both decided that Jim was suited to the job. He began working the following month.

Because he was not familiar with the bank and its operations, Jim was put through a five-week training session. It was very informal and consisted of exposure and practice in different areas of banking services. On November 2, Jim began in his new position. He was placed in charge of the retirement division. See Exhibit 1 for partial organization chart.

This division was a relatively new area for the bank. It dealt basically with IRA and Keogh retirement accounts. As acting head and sole employee of this division, Jim's job was to sell these services to the public as well as handle the administrative work. He was given a desk on the first floor, which he had to share with the coordinator for the branch managers, Allen Jones.

One of the first tasks to be performed was to transfer balances of certain savings accounts into IRAs (individual retirement accounts). Jim prepared all the calculations and brought them down to the computer operator to be punched in. Two weeks later, calls started coming in from the people whose accounts had been transferred. They had all received notices that their accounts had a zero balance and wanted to know what was going on. Jim answered them that it was a clerical error and that their money was intact. Upon investigating the incident, he found that it was bank policy to issue statements whenever an

This case was prepared by Danny J. Mainolfi under the supervision of Professor Allan R. Cohen for classroom discussion.

EXHIBIT 1
Hereford National Bank Organizational Chart (partial)

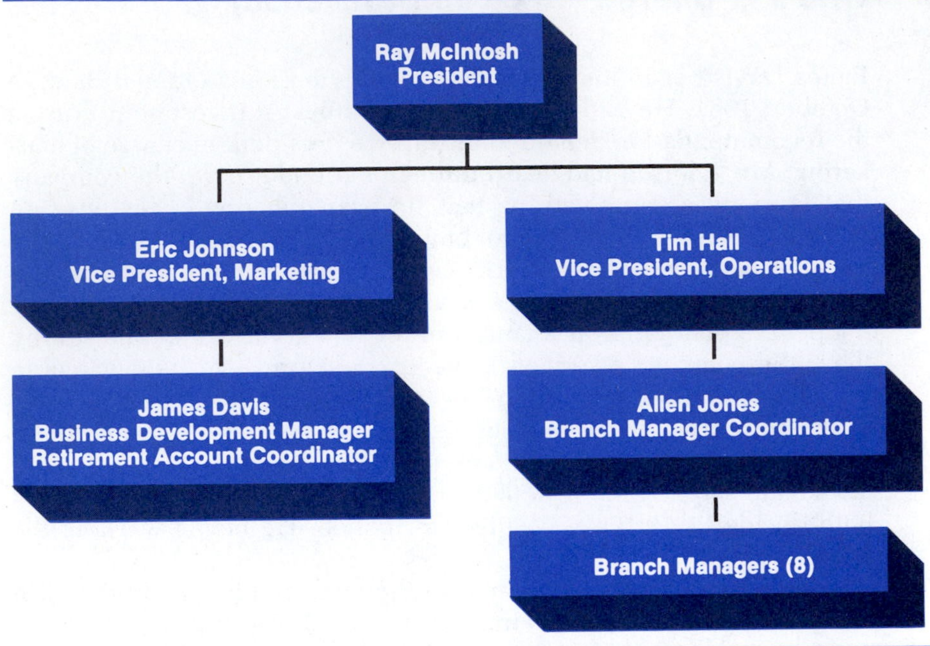

account reached a zero balance. When all the money was transferred from savings to IRA, the savings accounts were left with a balance of zero. Jim tried to find out why this policy had not been explained to him; however, he could not get a straight answer. The problem was not a major one, though, and it had been cured rather easily, so he let it pass. The last thing he wanted was to start any bad relationships.

Over the next two months Davis accomplished a lot. The people he worked with on the first floor seemed to be more than friendly once they got to know him. They were always willing to help and give their advice if needed. Jim and Allen became good friends. They played racquetball twice a week and often had lunch together. Allen, like Jim, had been hired away from another firm. Currently working on his master's degree, Allen had been with the bank for three years as the branch manager coordinator. In this role, all eight branch managers reported directly to him. Through Allen, Jim met the bank's branch managers. Allen frequently talked about the managers and the problems he had with them. It seemed that Allen was having trouble exerting authority over these managers. Jim always listened but never advised. He always made it policy not to discuss business matters with friends. To him it was just not a good idea.

In January 1982, Jim was promoted to business development manager; until that time the bank had no business development department. In order to keep up with the competition, it was decided by the board of directors that one should be established. Business development dealt with the sales of bank services to the general public as well as all types of businesses. Johnson told Davis that he would have to keep up with the retirement division also, since there was not enough money to employ another person just for this role. Jim's salary was increased, and he was given an office on the third floor (with the other bank executives).

Within a week, Davis saw that he had too much work to handle himself and made a request for a part-time secretary. Johnson told him that he would look for someone, but in the meantime Jim could make use of the administrative personnel on the first floor. "All you have to do is call and they will be happy to help out," Johnson said. "After all, that's all they are there for." Jim decided that although he really didn't want to, he would make use of this benefit. The next day he called down to ask two clerks to come up for an hour to classify and file some applications. He was referred to the supervisor, who rather impolitely asked him why he couldn't do it himself. "After all," she said, "it is your job." Infuriated, Jim went directly to Mr. Johnson to ask him what was going on. Mr. Johnson told him not to worry about it; he would have two people for Jim within the hour. No one showed up that afternoon; however, the next morning two clerks were waiting for Jim when he came into the office. A week later he had a part-time secretary.

Davis spent the next three months organizing a handbook on bank policy and sales techniques to be distributed to the branch managers. Johnson had told him that it would be the branch managers' job to carry out the policies handed down from development. Although the managers had never actually involved themselves in the sale of bank services in the past, it was in their job description. Johnson told Jim that it should be no problem and that the branch managers would cooperate in any way they could. Jim decided to play it safe, though, and not jump headfirst into the situation.

He was playing racquetball with Allen the next evening and, although he didn't want to, he decided that he would ask Allen what he thought. After the game, Jim told Allen what was going on and what Mr. Johnson had said. Allen replied that although nothing had been said to him, he had heard something about it. "I don't know, Jim," Allen said slowly as he paused to take a sip of his drink. "You might have a little bit of a problem. You see, these branch managers have been here for a long time—Patty for 25 years. Out of the eight of them, only Ted Yurek has a college education; the rest have only been to high school. None of them have any sales skills, and somehow I don't think that they are going to like having to learn them. God . . . I have a hard time keeping them in line . . . and I'm their boss." Jim told Allen that he thought this could be the case and asked him if he thought a training session would help. Allen replied that he thought it would be a good idea, and if Jim wanted to, they would sit down and analyze each manager individually so that the training session could be tailored to the group. Jim gladly accepted. Each of the branch managers was notified that selling bank services was to become a major portion of their job, and that Jim would keep them up to date on all developments.

The initial training session was scheduled for July 15. On July 1, Jim and Allen held a short, informal meeting for the branch managers. They handed out the handbooks, went over the goals of the program, and asked if there were any questions.

Patty Mathews raised her hand and spoke. "What is the situation with expense accounts . . . like . . . suppose we have to take a client out to dinner?" Jim and Allen looked at each other in surprise. Jim knew that his department did not have the money nor would the bank allow it even if he did. "At this point," Jim responded, "I see no reason to have expense accounts; the people you will be dealing with won't be of that type. If, however, we feel that a dinner is needed to help close a sale, come and see me and we can decide." "Well," said Patty, "I don't see why we can't have expense accounts. All the executives do!" Allen pointed out that the only expense accounts the executives had was for when they were away from the bank on business. All employees are entitled to this privilege, and anyone who had reason could use it. This remark was, however, ignored by Mrs. Mathews. There were no more questions, and the meeting was adjourned.

On July 15, all the managers were scheduled to go through the training session that Jim and Allen had designed. They were all informed that they could use their expense accounts to get to and from the meeting location and that lunch was being provided by the bank. Jim and Allen had decided in advance that if all went well they would take the group out for drinks afterward. The session was scheduled to begin at 9 A.M. By 8:45 A.M. everyone was there with the exception of Patty Mathews. When she had not shown up by 9:30 A.M., Jim called her branch office and was told that she had called in sick. The training session went as planned, and both Allen and Jim were very pleased with the results.

Jim, however, was undecided as to what to do about Patty Mathews. He had a feeling that she was not really sick, but he could not prove it. Even if he could, though, she had been with the bank longer than any other manager. He did not want to get on her bad side, since she carried a lot of weight with the other managers. Still he refused to allow this situation to go by without some form of reprimand. Jim decided to consult both Allen and Mr. Johnson before acting on this situation.

Work Group Ownership of an Improved Tool

Whirlwind Aircraft Corporation was a leader in its field and especially noted for its development of the modern supercharger. Work in connection with the latter mechanism called for special skill and ability. Every detail of the supercharger had to be perfect to satisfy the exacting requirements of the aircraft industry.

In 1941 (before Pearl Harbor), lathe department 15-D was turning out three types of impeller, each contoured to within 0.002 inch and machined to a mirrorlike finish. The impellers were made from an aluminum alloy and finished on a cam-back lathe.

The work was carried on in four shifts, two men on each. The personnel in the finishing section were as follows:

1. *First shift*—7 A.M. to 3 P.M., Sunday and Monday off.
   a. Jean Latour, master mechanic, French-Canadian, 45 years of age. Latour had set up the job and trained the men who worked with him on the first shift.
   b. Pierre DuFresne, master mechanic, French-Canadian, 36 years of age. Both these men had trained the workers needed for the other shifts.
2. *Second shift*—3 P.M. to 11 P.M., Friday and Saturday off.
   a. Albert Durand, master mechanic, French-Canadian, 32 years of age; trained by Latour and using his lathe.
   b. Robert Benet, master mechanic, French-Canadian, 31 years of age; trained by DuFresne and using his lathe.
3. *Third shift*—11 P.M. to 7 A.M., Tuesday and Wednesday off.
   a. Philippe Doret, master mechanic, French-Canadian, 31 years of age; trained by Latour and using his lathe.
   b. Henri Barbet, master mechanic, French-Canadian, 30 years of age; trained by DuFresne and using his lathe.
4. *Stagger shift*—Monday, 7 A.M. to 3 P.M.; Tuesday, 11 P.M. to 7 A.M.; Wednesday, 11 P.M. to 7 A.M.; Thursday off; Friday, 3 P.M. to 11 P.M.; Saturday, 3 P.M. to 11 P.M.; Sunday off.
   a. George MacNair, master mechanic, Scotch, 32 years of age; trained by Latour and using his lathe.

This case was written by Professor Paul Pigors and is reprinted with his permission.

b. William Reader, master mechanic, English, 30 years of age; trained by DuFresne and using his lathe.

Owing to various factors (such as the small number of workers involved, the preponderance of one nationality, and the fact that Latour and DuFresne had trained the other workers), these eight men considered themselves as members of one work group. Such a feeling of solidarity is unusual among workers on different shifts, despite the fact that they use the same machines.

The men received a base rate of $1.03 an hour and worked on incentive. Each man usually turned out 22 units a shift, thus earning an average of $1.19 an hour. Management supplied Rex 95 High-Speed Tool bits, which workers ground to suit themselves. Two tools were used: one square bit with a slight radius for recess cutting, the other bit with a 45-degree angle for chamfering and smooth finish. When used, both tools were set close together, the worker adjusting the lathe from one operation to the other. The difficulty with this setup was that during the rotation of the lathe, the aluminum waste would melt and fuse between the two tool bits. Periodically the lathe had to be stopped so that the tool bits could be freed from the welded aluminum and reground.

At the request of the supervisor of lathe department 15-D, the methods department had been working on this tool problem. Up to the time of this case, no solution had been found. To make a firsthand study of the difficulty, the methods department had recently assigned one of their staff, Mr. MacBride, to investigate the problem in the lathe department itself. Mr. MacBride's working hours covered parts of both the first and second shifts. MacBride was a young man, 26 years of age, and a newcomer to the methods department. For the three months prior to this assignment, he had held the post of "suggestion man," a position which enabled newcomers to the methods department to familiarize themselves with the plant setup. The job consisted of collecting, from boxes in departments throughout the plant, suggestions submitted by employees and making a preliminary evaluation of these ideas. The current assignment of studying the tool situation in lathe department 15-D with a view to cutting costs was his first special task. He devoted himself to this problem with great zeal but did not succeed in winning the confidence of the workers. In pursuance of their usual philosophy—"Keep your mouth shut if you see anyone with a suit on"—they volunteered no information and took the stand that since the methods man had been given this assignment, it was up to him to carry it out.

While MacBride was working on this problem, Pierre DuFresne hit upon a solution. One day he successfully contrived a tool which combined the two bits into one. This eliminated the space between the two tool bits, which in the past had caught the molten aluminum waste and allowed it to become welded to the cutting edges. The new tool bit had two advantages: it eliminated the frequent machine stoppage for cleaning and regrinding the old-type tools, and it enabled the operator to run the lathe at a higher speed. These advantages made it possible for the operator to increase his efficiency 50 percent.

DuFresne tried to make copies of the new tool but was unable to do so. Apparently the new development had been a "lucky accident" during grinding, which he could not duplicate. After several unsuccessful attempts, he took the new tool to his former teacher, Jean Latour. The latter succeeded in making a drawing and turning out duplicate tool bits on a small grinding wheel in the shop. At first the two men decided to keep the new tool to themselves. Later, however, they shared the improvement with their fellow workers on the second shift. Similarly it was passed on to the other shifts. But all these men kept the new development a closely guarded secret as far as "outsiders" were concerned. At the end of the shift, each locked the improved tool bit securely in his toolchest.

Both DuFresne, the originator of the new tool, and Latour, its draftsman and designer, decided not to submit the idea as a suggestion but to keep it as the property of their group. Why was this decision made? The answer lies partly in the suggestion system and partly in the attitude of Latour and DuFresne toward other features of company worklife and toward their group.

According to an informational bulletin issued by the company, the purpose of the suggestion system was to "provide an orderly method of submitting and considering ideas and recommendations of employees to management; to provide a means for recognizing and rewarding individual ingenuity; and to promote cooperation." Awards for accepted suggestions were made in the following manner: "After checking the savings and expense involved in an adopted suggestion [the suggestion committee] determined the amount of the award to be paid, based upon the savings predicted upon a year's use of the suggestion." "It is the intention of the committee . . . to be liberal in the awards, which are expected to compensate adequately for the interest shown in presenting suggestions." In pursuance of this policy, it was customary to grant the suggestor an award equivalent to the savings of an entire month.

As a monetary return, both DuFresne and Latour considered an award based on one month's saving as inadequate. They also argued that such awards were really taken out of the workers' pockets. Their reasoning was as follows: all awards for adopted suggestions were paid out of undistributed profits. Since the company also had a profit-sharing plan, the money was taken from a fund that would be given to the workers anyway, which merely meant robbing Peter to pay Paul.

In any case, the payment was not likely to be large and probably would be less than they could accumulate if increased incentive payments could be maintained over an extended period without discovery. Thus there was little in favor of submitting the new tool as a suggestion.

Latour and DuFresne also felt that there were definite hazards to the group if their secret were disclosed. They feared that once the tool became company property its efficiency might lead to layoff of some members in their group or at least make work less tolerable by leading to an increased quota at a lower price per unit. They also feared that there might be a change in scheduled work assignments. For instance, the lathe department worked on three different types of impeller. One type was a routine job and, aside from the difficulty caused by the old-type tool, presented no problem. For certain technical reasons, the other two types were more difficult to make. Even Latour, an exceptionally skilled craftsman, had sometimes found it hard to make the expected quota before the new tool was developed. Unless the workload was carefully balanced by scheduling easier and more difficult types, some of the operators were unable to make standard time.

The decision to keep the tool for their own group was in keeping with Latour's work philosophy. He had a strong feeling of loyalty to his own group and had demonstrated this in the past by offering for their use several improvements of his own. For example, he made available to all workers in his group a set of special gauge blocks, which were used in aligning work on lathes. To protect himself in case mistakes were traced to these gauges, he wrote on them: "Personnel [*sic*] Property—Do not use. Jean Latour."

Through informal agreement with their fellow workers, Latour and DuFresne "pegged production" at an efficiency rate that in their opinion would not arouse management's suspicion or lead to a restudy of the job with possible cutting of the rate. This enabled them to earn an extra 10 percent incentive earnings. The other 40 percent in additional efficiency was used as follows: the operators established a reputation for a high degree of accuracy and finish; they set a record for no spoilage and were able to apply the time gained on the easier type of impeller to work on the other types, which required greater care and more expert workmanship.

The supervisor of the lathe department learned about the new tool soon after it was put into use but was satisfied to let the men handle the situation in their own way. He reasoned that at little expense he was able to get out production of high quality. There was no defective work, and the men were contented.

Mr. MacBride was left in a very unsatisfactory position. He had not succeeded in working out a solution of his own. Like the supervisor, he got wind of the fact that the men had devised a new tool. He urged them to submit a drawing of it through the suggestion system; but this advice was not taken, and the men made it plain that they did not care to discuss with him the reasons for this position.

Having no success in his direct contact with the workers, Mr. MacBride appealed to the supervisor, asking him to secure a copy of the new tool. The supervisor replied that the men would certainly decline to give him a copy and would resent as an injustice any effort on his part to force them to submit a drawing. Instead he suggested that MacBride should persuade DuFresne to show him the tool. This MacBride attempted to do but met with no success in his efforts to ingratiate himself with DuFresne. When he persisted in his attempts, DuFresne decided to throw him off the track. He left in his lathe a tool bit which was an unsuccessful copy of the original discovery. At shift change, MacBride was delighted to find what he supposed to be the improved tool. He hastily copied it and submitted a drawing to the tool department. When a tool was made up according to these specifications, it naturally failed to do what was expected of it. The workers, when they heard of this through the "grapevine," were delighted. DuFresne did not hesitate to crow over MacBride, pointing out that his underhanded methods had met with their just reward.

The supervisor did not take any official notice of the conflict between DuFresne and MacBride. Then MacBride complained to the supervisor that DuFresne was openly boasting of his trick and ridiculing him before other workers. Thereupon, the supervisor talked to DuFresne, but the latter insisted that his ruse had been justified as a means of self-protection.

When he was rebuffed by DuFresne, the supervisor felt that he had lost control of the situation. He could no longer conceal from himself that he was confronted by a more complex situation than what initially he had defined as a "tool problem." His attention was drawn to the fact that the state of affairs in his department was a tangle of several interrelated problems. Each problem urgently called for a decision that involved understanding and practical judgment. But having for so long failed to see the situation as a whole, he now found himself in a dilemma.

He wished to keep the goodwill of the work group, but he could not countenance the continued friction between DuFresne and MacBride. Certainly he could not openly abet his operators in obstructing the work of a methods man. His superintendent would now certainly hear of it and would be displeased to learn that a supervisor had failed to tell him of such an important technical improvement. Furthermore, he knew that the aircraft industry was expanding at this time and that the demand for impellers had increased to such an extent that management was planning to set up an entire new plant unit devoted to this product.

The Zookeeper

In June 1972, I went to work for the Homestead Bank as a management trainee. As it turned out, another trainee named Steve started on the same day as I, and we became and still are today the best of friends. During the first months, we were each put on a schedule that would give us an opportunity to spend from two to three months in the various departments of the main office to become familiar with their operations. This later proved to be very helpful to me, not only because I learned how these functions operated but also (and probably of equal or greater importance) because I met and came to know the right people to contact to get the correct answers to questions in the shortest amount of time possible.

Each of our schedules was drawn up for an 18-month period, after which time we would be given our first permanent assignments. However, from what we had been told by others, the last six months of a trainee's schedule was usually "flexible," and in most cases assignments actually were made at the end of 12 months. As Steve and I had lunch together often, we had ample opportunity to speculate on where we would go when the time finally came for our assignments. At the time, the bank had approximately 30 branches around the state in addition to a main office and centralized operations center. There was a standing joke among the people at the main office (where training took place) that if they (senior management) did not like you, then you would be issued a heavy coat and assigned to the Mountainville bank. As the last trainee in the program before us had been sent to Mountainville, we felt pretty safe that the odds were in our favor and that we would be saved from exile to the hill country. There were, however, other offices and departments to which we decided we would prefer not to be assigned. I can, for example, remember laughing at the thought of being told I was to be placed in charge of the centralized bookkeeping department, a department often referred to as the "zoo."

THE ASSIGNMENT

Yes, you guessed it. I was assigned to the zoo! The way the assignment was explained to me was that I was to receive extensive in-depth training in the operations aspects of the company. Too many of the recent graduates of the training program were being assigned to branch management or commercial lending, and the operations division felt they were being ignored. I was to spend one year in charge of the bookkeeping department and would divide my time equally, during the second year, between the proof and transit department and the payroll processing section. My specific task assignment, while I was the supervisor of the bookkeeping section, was to "provide new ideas and improve the overall efficiency of the department."

THE DEPARTMENT

The bookkeeping department performed several functions related to check processing for all of the banks in the group. Economies of scale were supposed to be realized by centralizing the entire check processing operation. The tasks performed by the individuals of the department were as follows:

1. *Overdrafts:* An individual in bookkeeping would call a designated person at each bank, tell them which of their customers had overdrawn their checking accounts that day, and in turn be instructed whether or not to pay the checks in question.
2. *Stop-payments:* The person responsible would check the daily work to insure that orders to stop payments on particular checks were carried out. Any new stop-orders called in during the day were given to this person.
3. *Holds:* Whenever a teller cashed a check drawn on one of the banks in the group, they could call the department to verify the balance and to have a hold placed on the account for the amount of the check.
4. *Charge-backs:* These individuals would receive previously deposited checks that had bounced for some reason, and charge them to the account to which they were originally deposited.
5. *Return items:* These individuals would return checks, which had been written by customers, for any one of a number of reasons: overdrawn account, not signed, payment stopped, account closed, etc.
6. *Posting rejects:* These individuals would determine the proper disposition of all the items rejected by the computer because of a problem with the account number: it was missing, invalid, poorly encoded, etc.
7. *File checks and render statements:* During the month, these individuals would file all the paid checks in the "pocket" provided for each customer and, approximately every 30 days, send those items to the customer along with their statement.

In addition to these specific duties, the department received phone calls from customers, customer service representatives, tellers, managers, and officers. Also, the numerous computer-generated reports had to be filed daily so the information could be accessed easily in the future if necessary.

PERSONNEL

There were 30 employees in the bookkeeping department, and the budget would not allow for any additional staff. All were female and, with the exception of three, were between the ages of 18 and 25. Most were not married. All were high school graduates, one had a college degree, and several had taken some introductory banking courses offered by the American Institute of Banking. Approximately two thirds of the staff had been hired within the last 18 months. Those with the most seniority had the job of handling the overdrafts.

THE LAYOUT

Exhibit 1 shows the layout of the department. It was confined to one large room, which was located in the center of the building and therefore had no windows. There were 12 desks, all of which were equipped with typewriters and telephones. Six of the nine check files

EXHIBIT 1

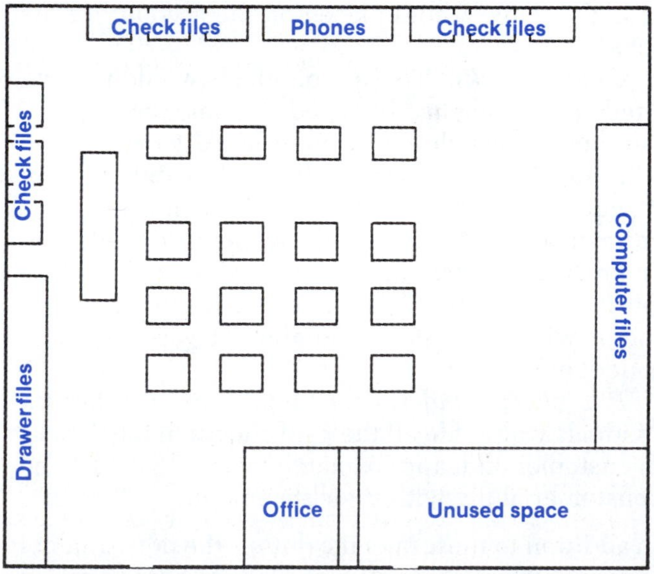

Check files
Phones
Check files
Check files
Computer files
Drawer files
Office
Unused space

were located along the front wall of the department, with the remaining three along the side wall. Two people sat at each check file. The remainder of the side wall space was occupied by storage files. Toward the left side of the room, there was a long table on which the daily work would be placed in the morning for distribution. My office was located in the center at the back of the department and had glass walls on the front and left sides.

The one remaining item of significance was a long shelf-like table that ran along the front wall, separating equally the six check files. Upon this table sat the reason for the former reference to this department as a zoo: 12 telephones, all direct lines from the affiliated banks in the group. Each of the six banks had two phones on the table. They were utilized primarily by employees of the bank; however, many times a customer would be transferred by the switchboard operator at the affiliate to one of these extensions. Unfortunately no one who worked in the department was hired specifically to sit at this table and answer these phones, and they were always quite busy.

THE GROUPS

Generally speaking, there were two types of jobs in bookkeeping. You could have a "desk job," or you could be a check filer. Being a check filer had the reputation of being only a little better than being unemployed. It was looked upon as purely an entry-level position that a person should be promoted out of within six months; if not, they could forget about future advancement. At times it was also utilized as a slot into which to transfer someone from another department who was not able to cut it at their current job. It was the responsibility of those at the check files to answer the telephones on the front wall in addition to filing all the paid checks.

It was understood that those in the department with desk jobs would help out the check filers in two ways. If the phones were ringing and all of the check filers were already on a phone, then they were supposed to help answer phones. Also, if toward the end of the day they completed their own job early, they were to help file checks as well as answer telephones. It was also understood that at the end of every month, when the largest number of statements had to be prepared and mailed, everyone would work late and assist in this process.

As soon as I began my new assignment, several things became evident to me immediately. The first was that the phones rang constantly, and people had to run from one place to another. Second, I started to get calls directly from a variety of people asking me to look up some information for them, which I felt could have been done more appropriately by someone else. When I began to ask why I was being called for this information instead of the call being directed to the tie line, the answer most often given was "because the people that answer those phones don't know what they're talking about!" Another complaint was the fact that they never got to talk to the same person twice.

Third, customers were complaining to bank personnel that their statements were missing checks or that someone else's checks had been included in their statement. They were also upset about the fact that the statements were frequently mailed late.

A factor contributing to the numerous complaints to the bookkeeping department was the fact that the branches were not totally sold on the concept of centralized operations. The company had grown through merger and acquisition of other independent banks (now the branches). Centralization of operations meant that these banks had to give up control of processes that they had had since day one. This fact created the tendency to be especially critical of any mistakes that were made, which added significantly to the difficulties being experienced by everyone within the department.

I also observed that it seemed to be the exception rather than the rule that anyone with a desk job would finish early and assist the check filers. In fact, some complained that they were unable to finish on time because they were spending so much time answering the phones or helping those who did to locate the information. The last week of the month seemed to be the exception, however. If it appeared that the check filers were getting behind, the desk job holders would show up in greater numbers to file in an effort to avoid overtime at the end of the month and into the next month. This created a degree of animosity between the two groups. One group felt it had to do the other's job for them.

Morale in the department was poor and declining steadily. The workers were totally frustrated with a situation they felt was impossible. They felt they were being asked to perform above and beyond the call of duty. Many expressed the sentiment that the department was understaffed. They also realized the department as a whole was being criticized for general shortcomings. Most genuinely felt badly about the situation, since they cared and wanted to have pride in themselves and their department.

As the days and weeks went by, the phones seemed to ring louder and more frequently. The complaints from the affiliate bank personnel came with more regularity. The stacks of checks that wouldn't be filed until the next day grew taller, and the looks on the faces of those at the desks became more and more impatient when they had to answer a phone or file a check. I knew that the day would come when all 12 phones could be disconnected and taken away. New systems were on the drawing boards that would give all bank personnel instant access to the same information for which they now had to call bookkeeping. The problem was the fact that it would be well over a year before any of that would take place, and the status quo would not do until that time.

I knew I had to do something but wasn't sure just what. Was there any way to turn the zoo around?

Photo Credits

2 Management tour, *Alan Carey/The Image Works*

2 Office meeting, *Mike Tappin*

3 Women conversing (silhouette), *Jon Feingersh/Click, Chicago*

38 High-wire walkers, *Cary Wolinsky/Stock, Boston*

38 Elephants, *David Krathwohl/Stock, Boston*

39 Raising a house, *David Powers/Stock, Boston*

64 California Water Project control room, *Peter Menzel/Stock, Boston*

64 Assembling computer fans, *Alan Carey/The Image Works*

65 Aerial view of office, *Joseph Sterling/Click, Chicago*

98 High-school students, *Jean-Claude Lejeune/Stock, Boston*

98 Managers and workers, *Michael Hayman/Stock, Boston*

99 Boat crew, *Fred Bavendam*

114 Parade group, *Alan Carey/The Image Works*

114 Man detached from group, *Jean-Claude Lejeune/Stock, Boston*

115 Business conference, *Jim Pickerell/Click Chicago*

140 High school football team, *Dan Chidester/The Image Works*

140 Business meeting, *Hazel Hankin/Stock, Boston*

141 Football coach Mike Ditka, *John E. Biever/Click, Chicago*

168 Supervisor, *Donald Dietz/Stock, Boston*

168 Guitar maker, *Alan Carey/The Image Works*

169 Sand castle contest, *Elizabeth Crews/Stock, Boston*

198 Man on street, *Charles Gatewood/The Image Works*

198 Man on beam, *Ulrike Welsch/Stock, Boston*

199 Basketball player, *Pam Schuyler/Stock, Boston*

246 Construction workers, *Mark Antman/The Image Works*

246 Glass blowers, *Howard Dratch/The Image Works*

247 Football players, *Paul Fortin/Stock, Boston*

270 Woman construction worker, *Ellis Herwig/Stock, Boston*

270 Machine shop, *Dan Chidester/The Image Works*

271 Highway engineers, *Joe Viesti/Click, Chicago*

306 Violin player, *Mike Tappin*

306 Basketball team, *Alan Carey/The Image Works*

307 Contract negotiation, *Michael Hayman/Stock, Boston*

336 Hospital administrator, *Mike Tappin*

336 Conference meeting, *Gans/The Image Works*

337 Conductor Seiji Ozawa, *Milton Feinberg/Stock, Boston*

376 Technician installing engine, *Cameramann, International, Ltd.*

376 Technician installing electrical components, *Cameramann, International, Ltd.*

376 Technician installing electrical components, *Cameramann, International, Ltd.*

376 Automobile assembly line, *Michael Hayman/Stock, Boston*

377 Automobile assembly line, *Michael Hayman/Click, Chicago*

404 Softball players, *Rick Mansfield/The Image Works*

404 Assembling computer, *Aronson Photographics/Stock, Boston*

405 Man with adding machine, *Carol Lee/Click, Chicago*

Index

G

U–V

W

X–Z